REFUTATION OF ALL HERESIES

WRITINGS FROM THE GRECO-ROMAN WORLD

Number 40
Volume Editor
Joshua L. Langseth

REFUTATION OF ALL HERESIES

Translated with an Introduction and Notes by

M. David Litwa

Atlanta

Library of Congress Cataloging-in-Publication Data

Hippolytus, Antipope, approximately 170–235 or 236.
Refutation of all heresies / [translated] by M. David Litwa.
p. cm. — (Writings from the Greco-Roman World ; number 40)
Includes bibliographical references and indexes.
ISBN 978-0-88414-085-6 (pbk. : alk. paper) – ISBN 978-0-88414-086-3 (electronic book) – ISBN 978-0-88414-087-0 (hardcover : alk. paper)
1. Christian heresies–History–Early church, ca. 30–600. 2. Christian heresies–Early works to 1800. I. Litwa, M. David, translator. II. Hippolytus, Antipope, approximately 170–235 or 236. Refutation of all heresies. III. Hippolytus, Antipope, approximately 170–235 or 236. Refutation of all heresies. English. IV. Title.
BR65.H83R4413 2015
273'.1—dc23 2015025647

Printed on acid-free paper.

For Blaire French and Judith Kovacs,
Lasting Friends

Contents

Preface

This book was motivated by my own need for a useable, scholarly edition and translation of the *Refutation of All Heresies.* Previous (complete) translations are now outdated, and the most recent critical edition is virtually unusable. J. H. MacMahon's translation in the *Ante-Nicene Fathers* is based mainly on the *editio princeps* of the *Refutation* printed in 1851 by Emmanuel Miller. In 1921, F. Legge made a second English translation based on the 1860 edition of Patricius Cruice. MacMahon had a lively style, but his translation is marred by its many faulty readings and outdated vocabulary. Legge's translation is literal to the point of agony and was based on an edition of the Greek text that had been, even in his time, replaced by that of Wendland (1916). The most recent critical edition (Marcovich, 1986—with a preface dated to 1980) has sat idle for almost thirty years with no translator coming forward. After reading the reviews, there is little wonder. Although Marcovich's double apparatus and indices are generous, his *libido emendationis* altered readings on almost every paragraph, making the text a minefield for scholars whose eyes are not constantly trained on the apparatus. Consequently, my initial desire to produce a working translation also necessitated a new edition of the text more faithful to the manuscript tradition. I offer the edition here as a service to the scholarly community.

Sincere thanks go to the editors of Writings from the Greco-Roman World. My friend Blaire French kindly proofread my initial translation of the *Refutation*. Emanuele Castelli offered helpful comments on my introduction. Special appreciation is owed to Joshua Langseth, who meticulously and efficiently checked the translation and notes. Many of his corrections and suggestions are incorporated throughout this edition. Any errors that remain are my responsibility.

My hope is that this edition will spark renewed attention and interest in this bizarre masterpiece. What was meant as the heresiography to end all heresiography is in effect a mine of (in many cases, uniquely preserved)

information on ancient philosophy, early Christology, gnostic thought, ancient magic, astrology, numerology, mystery cults, and a host of other esoterica. A full translation is offered in the hopes that the text will not *merely* be mined, however, but appreciated and studied as a rhetorical and polemical work in its own right. No longer can this author depend on the famous but misty figure of Hippolytos to lend succor to his reputation. Still, the sympathetic reader will discover that this author, whom time and political circumstance have stripped of a name, is well worth reading in his own right.

You, O reader, may not ever break through this "labyrinth of heresies," but the treasures that await you will appear at every turn.

Charlottesville
St. Patrick's Day, 2015

Abbreviations

Primary Sources

1 Apoc. Jas.	(First) Revelation of James
1 Apol.	Justin Martyr, *Apologia i* (*First Apology*)
1 Clem.	1 Clement
1QS	Rule of the Community
2 Bar.	2 Baruch
2 Clem.	2 Clement
2 En.	2 Enoch
11QMelch	Melchizedek
Abr.	Philo, *De Abrahamo* (*On the Life of Abraham*)
Abst.	Porphyry, *De abstinentia* (*On Abstinence*)
Acad.	Cicero, *Academicae quaestiones*
Acts John	Acts of John
Acts Pet.	Acts of Peter
Acts Thom.	Acts of Thomas
Adv. Col.	Plutarch, *Adversus Colotem* (*Against Colotes*)
Adv. Eun.	Basil, *Adversus Eunomium* (*Against Eunomius*)
Adv. nat.	Arnobius, *Adversus nationes* (*Against the Nations*)
Adv. omn. haer.	Pseudo-Tertullian, *Adversus omnes haereses* (*Against All Heresies*)
Aen.	Vergil, *Aeneid*
Aet.	Philo, *De aeternitate mundi* (*On the Eternity of the World*)
Ag. Ap.	Josephus, *Against Apion*
Agr.	Philo, *De agricultura* (*On Agriculture*)
Alcib.	Plato, *Alcibiades major* (*Greater Alcibiades*)
Alex.	Lucian, *Alexander* (*the False Prophet*)
Alim.	Hippokrates, *De alimento* (*On Nutriment*)

All.	Herakleitos, *Allegoriae / Quaestiones homericae* (*Homeric Problems*)
An.	Tertullian, *De anima* (*On the Soul*)
Anab.	Arrian, *Anabasis*
An. procr.	Plutarch, *De animae procreatione in Timaeo*
Ant.	Josephus, *Jewish Antiquities*
Anth.	Vettius Valens, *Anthologia*
Antichr.	Hippolytos, *De antichristo* (*Antichrist*)
Ap. Jas.	Secret Book of James
Ap. John	Secret Book of John
Apoc. Adam	Revelation of Adam
Apoc. Mos.	Apocalypse of Moses
Apoc. Paul	Revelation of Paul
Apoc. Pet.	Revelation of Peter
Apol.	Apuleius, *Apologia*
Arg.	Apollonios of Rhodes, *Argonautika*
Arithm.	Diophantos of Alexandria, *Arithmetica*
Ars	Ovid, *Ars amatoria* (*The Art of Love*)
Ars gramm.	Dionysius Thrax, *Ars grammatica* (*Art of Grammar*)
Ascen. Isa.	Martyrdom and Ascension of Isaiah
Astr.	Lucian, *Astrologia*
Astron.	Manilius, *Astronomica*
Autol.	Theophilos, *Ad Autolycum* (*To Autolycus*)
Ax.	[Plato], *Axiochus*
Barn.	Barnabas
Bell. gall.	Gaius Julius Caesar, *Bellum gallicum* (*Gallic War*)
Bibl.	Photios, *Bibliotheca*
Bibl.	Pseudo-Apollodoros, *Bibliotheca* (*Library*)
Bibl. hist.	Diodoros of Sicily, *Bibliotheca historica* (*Library of History*)
Cael.	Aristotle, *De caelo* (*On the Heavens*)
Cael.	Kleomedes, *Caelestia* (*Heavenly Phenomena*)
Cal.	Suetonius, *Gaius Caligula*
Carn. Chr.	Tertullian, *De carne Christi* (*On the Flesh of Christ*)
Cat.	Aristotle, *Categoriae* (*Categories*)
Cataster.	Pseudo-Eratosthenes, *Catasterismi*
Cels.	Origen, *Contra Celsum* (*Against Celsus*)
Charm.	Plato, *Charmides*
Chron.	[Hippolytos], *Chronicle*

Civ.	Augustine, *De civitate Dei* (*The City of God*)
Clem. Alex.	Clement of Alexandria
Cohort.	Pseudo-Justin, *Cohortatio ad Graecos* (*Exhortation to the Greeks*)
Comm. Dan.	Hippolytos, *Commentarium in Danielem* (*Commentary on Daniel*)
Comm. in Arat.	*Commentariorum in Aratum reliquiae*
Comm. Jo.	Origen, *Commentarii in evangelium Joannis* (*Commentary on John*)
Comm. Matt.	Origen, *Commentarium in evangelium Matthaei* (*Commentary on Matthew*)
Comm. not.	Plutarch, *De communibus notitiis contra stoicos* (*On Common Notions*)
Conf.	Augustine, *Confessionum libri XIII* (*Confessions*)
Conf.	Philo, *De confusione linguarum* (*On the Confusion of Tongues*)
Congr.	Philo, *De congressu eruditionis gratia* (*On the Preliminary Studies*)
Contempl.	Philo, *De vita contemplativa* (*On the Contemplative Life*)
Corp. herm.	Corpus hermeticum
Crass.	Plutarch, *Crassus*
Crat.	Plato, *Cratylus*
Curios.	Plutarch, *De curiositate*
De an.	Aristotle, *De anima* (*On the Soul*)
Decal.	Philo, *De decalogo* (*On the Decalogue*)
Def.	Pseudo-Plato, *Definitiones* (*Definitions*)
Def. orac.	Plutarch, *De defectu oraculorm* (*Obsolescence of Oracles*)
Deipn.	Athenaios, *Deipnosophistae* (*The Learned Banqueters*)
Demetr.	Plutarch, *Demetrius*
De or.	Cicero, *De oratore*
Descr.	Pausanias, *Graeciae descriptio* (*Description of Greece*)
Deus	Philo, *Quod Deus sit immutabilis* (*That God Is Unchangeable*)
Dial.	Justin Martyr, *Dialogus cum Tryphone* (*Dialogue with Trypho*)
Dial. Sav.	Dialogue of the Savior

Diatr.	Epiktetos, *Diatribai* (*Dissertationes*)
Did.	Didache
Did. Jul.	Didius Julianus
Die nat.	Censorinus, *De die natali* (*Birthday Book*)
Diis mund.	Sallustius, *De diis et mundo* (*On the Gods and the World*)
Diogn.	Diognetus
Diog. L.	Diogenes Laertios
Disc. 8–9	Discourse on the Eighth and Ninth
Div.	Cicero, *De divinatione*
Ebr.	Philo, *De ebrietate* (*On Drunkenness*)
Ecl.	Clement of Alexandria, *Eclogae propheticae*
Ecl.	Ioannes Stobaios, *Eclogae*
Ecl.	Vergil, *Eclogae*
E Delph.	Plutarch, *De E apud Delphos*
Elem.	Euclid, *Elementa* (*The Elements*)
Enn.	Plotinos, *Enneades*
Ep.	*Epistulae* (*Letters*)
Ep. Apos.	Epistle of the Apostles
Eph.	Ignatios, *To the Ephesians*
Ep. Hdt.	Epikouros, *Epistula ad Herodotum* (*Letter to Herodotus*)
Epiph.	Epiphanios
Epit.	Alkinoos, *Epitome doctrinae platonicae* (*Handbook of Platonism*)
Epitaph. Adon.	Bion of Smyrna, *Epitaphius Adonis*
Ep. Men.	Epikouros, *Epistula ad Menoeceum* (*Letter to Menoeceus*)
Ep. Pyth.	Epikouros, *Epistula ad Pythoclem* (*Letter to Pythocles*)
Eth. eud.	Aristotle, *Ethica eudemia*
Eth. nic.	Aristotle, *Ethica nicomachea*
Eugnostos	Eugnostos the Blessed
Euth.	Plato, *Euthydemos*
Exc.	Clement of Alexandria, *Excerpta ex Theodoto*
Exeg. Soul	Exegesis of the Soul
Exil.	Plutarch, *De exilio*
Exp. math.	Theon of Smyrna, *Expositio rerum mathematicarum* (*Exposition of Mathematics*)

Fac.	Plutarch, *De facie in orbe lunae* (*The Face in the Moon*)
Faust.	Augustine, *Contra Faustum Manichaeum* (*Against Faustus the Manichaean*)
Fin.	Cicero, *De finibus* (*On Moral Ends*)
Flor.	Apuleius, *Florida*
Flor.	Ptolemy, *Epistula ad Floram*
Flor.	Ioannes Stobaios, *Florilegium*
Fug.	Philo, *De fuga et inventione* (*On Flight and Finding*)
Gen. an.	Aristotle, *De generatione animalium*
Gen. corr.	Aristotle, *De generatione et corruptione*
Generat.	Pseudo-Hippokrates, *On Generation*
Geogr.	Strabo, *Geographica*
Gig.	Philo, *De gigantibus* (*On Giants*)
Gorg.	Plato, *Gorgias*
Gos. Eb.	Gospel of the Ebionites
Gos. Eg.	Gospel of the Egyptians
Gos. Jud.	Gospel of Judas
Gos. Phil.	Gospel of Philip
Gos. Thom.	Gospel of Thomas
Gos. Truth	Gospel of Truth
Haer.	Filastrius, *Diversarum haereseon liber* (*On Diverse Heresies*)
Haer.	Irenaeus, *Adversus haereses* (*Against Heresies*)
Haer. fab.	Theodoret, *Haereticarum fabularum compendium* (*Compendium of Heretical Fables*)
Hal.	Oppian, *Halieutica*
Her.	Philo, *Quis rerum divinarum heres sit* (*Who Is the Heir?*)
Herm.	Tertullian, *Adversus Hermogenem* (*Against Hermogenes*)
Herm. Sim.	Shepherd of Hermas, Similitudes
Hipp.	Hippolytos
Hist.	Herodotos, *Historiae*
Hist.	Tacitus, *Historiae* (*Histories*)
Hist. an.	Aristotle, *Historia animalium* (*History of Animals*)
Hist. eccl.	Eusebios, *Historia ecclesiastica*
Hist. phil.	*Historia philosopha* (*Philosophical History*)
Hist. philos.	Porphyry, *Historia philosophica* (fragments)

Hist. Rom.	Dio Cassius, *Historiae Romanae* (*Roman History*)
Hom. Hymn Apollo	Homeric Hymn to Apollo
Hom. Hymn Merc.	Homeric Hymn to Mercury (Hermes)
Hymn Iov.	Kleanthes, *Hymn to Zeus*
Idol.	Tertullian, *De idololatria* (*On Idolatry*)
Id.	Theokritos, *Idylls*
Il.	Homer, *Iliad*
In ev. Io.	Augustine, *In Iohannis evangelium tractatus CXXIV* (*Tractates of the Gospel of John*)
In Hipp. de humor.	Galen, *Commentary on Hippocrates, Concerning Humors*
In Hippoc. alim.	Galen, *Commentary on Hippocrates, Concerning Nourishment*
In phys.	Simplikios, *In Aristotelis physicorum*
In somn. Sc.	Macrobius, *Commentarii in Somnium Scipionis*
In Tim.	Chalkidios, *Commentarius in Timaeum Platonis*
In Tim.	Proklos, *In Platonis Timaeum commentaria*
Intro.	Porphyry, *Introduction*
Ira	Seneca, *De ira*
Iren.	Irenaeus
Irris.	Hermias, *Irrisio gentilium philosophorum* (*Satire of Pagan Philosophers*)
Is. Os.	Plutarch, *De Iside et Osiride* (*Isis and Osiris*)
Jejun.	Tertullian, *De jejunio adversus psychicos* (*On Fasting, against the Psychics*)
Jov.	Jerome, *Adversus Jovinianum*
Jupp. trag.	Lucian, *Juppiter trageodus*
J.W.	Josephus, *Jewish War*
LAB	Liber antiquitatum biblicarum (Pseudo-Philo)
Leg.	Athenagoras, *Legatio pro Christianis* (*Embassy for the Christians*)
Leg.	Cicero, *De legibus* (*On the Laws*)
Leg.	Philo, *Legum allegoriae* (*Allegorical Interpretation*)
Leg.	Plato, *Leges* (*Laws*)
Legat.	Philo, *Legatio ad Gaium* (*On the Embassy to Gaius*)
Lib. ed.	[Plutarch], *De liberis educandis*
Lib. gen.	*Liber generationis* (Latin Chronicle based on [Hipp.] *Chron.*)
Life	Josephus, *The Life*

Ling.	Varro, *De lingua latina* (*On the Latin Language*)
Mag. mor.	[Aristotle], *Magna moralia*
Magn.	Ignatios, *To the Magnesians*
Marc.	Tertullian, *Adversus Marcionem* (*Against Markion*)
Mart. Pol.	Martyrdom of Polycarp
Math.	Sextus Empiricus, *Adversus mathematicos* (*Against the Professors*)
Max. princ.	Plutarch, *Maxime cum principibus philosophiam esse disserendum* (*A Philosopher Ought to Converse with Rulers*)
Melch.	Melchizedek
Mel. Xen. Gorg.	Pseudo-Aristotle, *De Melisso Xenophane Gorgia*
Mem.	Xenophon, *Memorabilia*
Men.	Lucian, *Menippus* (*Necyomantia*)
Metam.	Apuleius, *Metamorphoses*
Metam.	Ovid, *Metamorphoses*
Metaph.	Aristotle, *Metaphysica* (*Metaphysics*)
Mete.	Aristotle, *Meteorologica* (*Meteorology*)
Migr.	Philo, *De migratione Abrahami* (*On the Migration of Abraham*)
Mor.	Plutarch, *Moralia*
Mos.	Philo, *De vita Mosis* (*On the Life of Moses*)
Mund.	Pseudo-Aristotle, *De mundo*
Mus.	Plutarch, *De musica*
Mut.	Philo, *De mutatione nominum* (*On the Changing of Names*)
Nat.	Pliny the Elder, *Naturalis historia* (*Natural History*)
Nat.	Seneca, *Naturales quaestiones* (*Natural Questions*)
Nat. an.	Aelian, *De natura animalium* (*Nature of Animals*)
Nat. d.	Cicero, *De natura deorum*
Nat. d.	Cornutus, *De natura deorum* (*On the Nature of the Gods*)
Nat. mund. an.	Pseudo-Timaios, *The Nature of the World and the Soul*
Nat. puer.	Pseudo-Hippokrates, *De natura pueri* (*On the Nature of the Child*)
Nat. Rulers	Nature of the Rulers
Noct. att.	Aulus Gellius, *Noctes atticae* (*Attic Nights*)
Noet.	[Hippolytos], *Contra Noetum* (*Against Noetos*)

Oct.	Minucius Felix, *Octavius*
Od.	Homer, *Odyssey*
Odes Sol.	Odes of Solomon
Oed.	Seneca, *Oedipus*
Oet.	[Seneca], *Hercules Oetaeus*
On Bap. A.	On Baptism A
Oneir.	Artemidoros, *Oneirocritica*
Op.	Hesiod, *Opera et dies* (*Works and Days*)
Opif.	Philo, *De opificio mundi* (*On the Creation of the World*)
Or.	*Orationes* (*Orations*)
Or.	Tatian, *Oratio ad Graecos* (*Oration to the Greeks*)
Orac. chald.	De oraculis chaldaicis (Chaldaean Oracles)
Orat. paneg.	Gregory the Wonderworker, *Oratio panegyrica in Origenem* (*Panergyric on Origen*)
Orig. World	On the Origin of the World
Orph. Hymn	Orphic Hymns
P	Parisinus Supplément grec 464 (*Refutation* 4–10)
Paed.	Clement of Alexandria, *Paedagogus* (*Christ the Educator*)
Pan.	Epiphanios, *Panarion* (*Medicine Chest*)
Pap. Genev. inv. 271.	Geneva papyrus 271 (prototype of Palladius, *Vita Brag.*)
Paraph. Shem	Paraphrase of Shem
Parm.	Plato, *Parmenides*
Phaed.	Plato, *Phaedo*
Phaedr.	Plato, *Phaedrus*
Phaen.	Aratos, *Phaenomena*
Phileb.	Plato, *Philebus*
Philops.	Lucian, *Philopseudes*
Phys.	Aristotle, *Physica* (*Physics*)
Phys. op.	Theophrastos, *Physicorum opiniones* (*Opinions of the Natural Philosophers*)
Pist. Soph.	Pistis Sophia
Plac.	Aëtios, *Placita*
Plac. philos.	Pseudo-Plutarch, *De placita philosophorum* (*Opinions of the Philosophers*)
Plant.	Philo, *De plantatione* (*On Planting*)
Plat.	Apuleius, *De Platone* (*On Plato*)

Pol.	Ignatios, *To Polycarp*
Pol.	Plato, *Politicus* (*Stateman*)
Post.	Philo, *De posteritate Caini* (*On the Posterity of Cain*)
Praep. ev.	Eusebios, *Praeparatio evangelica* (*Preparation for the Gospel*)
Praescr.	Tertullian, *De praescriptione haereticorum* (*Prescription against Heretics*)
Prax.	Tertullian, *Adversus Praxean* (*Against Praxeas*)
Prim. frig.	Plutarch, *De primo frigido* (*On the Principle of Cold*)
Princ.	Origen, *De principiis* (*On First Principles*)
Prob.	Philo, *Quod omnis probus liber sit* (*That Every Good Person Is Free*)
Prot.	Plato, *Protagoras*
Protr.	Clement of Alexandria, *Protreptikos*
Protr.	Iamblichos, *Protreptikos*
Ps.-	Pseudo-
Ps.-Apoll.	Pseudo-Apollodoros
Ps.-Clem. Hom.	Pseudo-Clementine, Homilies
Ps.-Clem. Rec.	Pseudo-Clementine, Recognitions
Pss. Sol.	Psalms of Solomon
Ps.-Tert.	Pseudo-Tertullian
Pud.	Tertullian, *De pudicitia* (*On Modesty*)
Pyr.	Sextus Empiricus, *Pyrrhoniae hypotyposes* (*Outlines of Pyrrhonism*)
QG	Philo, *Quaestiones et solutiones in Genesin* (*Questions and Answers on Genesis*)
Quaest. conv.	Plutarch, *Quaestionum convivialum libri IX*
Quaest. plat.	Plutarch, *Quaestiones platonicae*
Quaest. rom.	Plutarch, *Quaestiones romanae et graecae*
Quis div.	Clement of Alexandria, *Quis dives salvetur*
Ran.	Aristophanes, *Ranae* (*Frogs*)
Rat. sent.	Epikouros, *Ratae sententiae* (*Principal Doctrines*)
Ref.	*Refutation of All Heresies*
Rep.	Cicero, *De republica*
Rer. nat.	Lucretius, *De rerum natura* (*On Nature*)
Res.	Athenagoras, *De resurrectione*
Res.	Methodios, *De resurrectione*
Res.	Tertullian, *De resurrectione carnis* (*On the Resurrection [of the Flesh]*)

Resp.	Plato, *Respublica* (*Republic*)
Sacr.	Philo, *De sacrificiis Abelis et Caini* (*On the Sacrifices of Cain and Abel*)
Scholia in Arat.	*Scholia in Aratos*
Sent. Sextus	Sentences of Sextus
Sext. Emp.	Sextus Empiricus
Sib. Or.	Sibylline Oracles
Soll. an.	Plutarch, *De sollertia animalium* (*On the Cleverness of Animals*)
Somn.	Philo, *De somniis* (*On Dreams*)
Spec.	Philo, *De specialibus legibus* (*On the Special Laws*)
Stoic. rep.	Plutarch, *De Stoicorum repugnantiis* (*Stoic Contradictions*)
Strom.	Clement of Alexandria, *Stromata*
Strom.	Pseudo-Plutarch, *Stromata* (*Miscellanies*)
Suav. viv.	Plutarch, *Non posse suaviter vivi secundum Epicurum* (*A Pleasant Life is Impossible for Epicurus*)
Subl.	Longinus, *De sublimitate* (*On the Sublime*)
Suppl.	Euripides, *Supplices* (*Suppliants*)
Symp.	Plato, *Symposium*
Sympath. Antipath.	Pseudo-Demokritos, *On Sympathy and Antipathy*
T. Job	Testament of Job
T. Levi	Testament of Levi
Teach. Silv.	Teachings of Silvanus
Tert.	Tertullian
Testim. Truth	Testimony of Truth
Tetrab.	Claudius Ptolemy, *Tetrabiblos*
Theaet.	Plato, *Theaetetus*
Them.	Plutarch, *Themistocles*
Theog.	Hesiod, *Theogonia*
Theolog. arith.	Nikomachos, *Theologoumena arithmeticae*
Three Forms	Three Forms of First Thought
Thund.	Thunder: Perfect Mind
Tim.	Plato, *Timaeus*
Top.	Aristotle, *Topica*
Tri. Trac.	Tripartite Tractate
Univ.	*De Universo* (*On the Universe*)
Usu part.	Galen, *De usu partium* (*On the Use of Parts*)

Val.	Tertullian, *Adversus Valentinianos* (*Against the Valentinians*)
Var. hist.	Aelian, *Varia historia* (*Historical Miscellany*)
Vera hist.	Lucian, *Vera historia* (*True History*)
Vir. ill.	Jerome, *De viris illustribus* (*On Famous Men*)
Virt. herb.	Thessalos of Tralles, *De Virtutibus Herborum*
Virt. prof.	Plutarch, *Quomodo quis suos in virtute sentiat profectus* (*Progress in Virtue*)
Vit. Apoll.	Philostratos, *Vita Apollonii* (*Life of Apollonius*)
Vit. auct.	Lucian, *Vitarum auctio*
Vit. Hom.	Pseudo-Plutarch, *De vita et poesi Homeri*
Vit. phil.	Diogenes Laertios, *Vitae philosophorum* (*The Lives of Philosophers*)
Vit. Pyth.	Iamblichos, *De vita Pythagorica* (*On the Pythagorean Life*)
Vit. Pyth.	Porphyry, *Vita Pythagorae* (*Life of Pythagoras*)
Vita Brag.	Palladius, *De vita Bragmanorum*
Vita Mos.	Gregory of Nyssa, *Vita Mosis* (*Life of Moses*)

Secondary Sources

ACW	Ancient Christian Writers
AION	*Annali dell'Istituto Orientale di Napoli*
ANF	*Ante-Nicene Fathers*
ANRW	*Aufstieg und Niedergang der römischen Welt: Geschichte und Kultur Roms im Spiegel der neueren Forschung.* Part 2, *Principat.* Edited by Hildegard Temporini and Wolfgang Haase. Berlin: de Gruyter, 1972–.
Aug	*Augustinianum*
BCNH	Bibliothèque copte de Nag Hammadi
BDAG	Danker, Frederick W., Walter Bauer, William F. Arndt, and F. Wilbur Gingrich. *Greek-English Lexicon of the New Testament and Other Early Christian Literature.* 3rd ed. Chicago: University of Chicago Press, 2000.
BDB	Brown, Francis, S. R. Driver, and Charles A. Briggs, eds. *Brown-Driver-Briggs Hebrew and English*

	Lexicon with an Appendix Containing the Biblical Aramaic. Boston: Houghton Mifflin, 1906.
BEHER	Bibliothèque de l'École des hautes études: Sciences religieuses
BG	Berlin Gnostic Papyrus
BHT	Beiträge zur historischen Theologie
BNP	*Brill's New Pauly: Encyclopedia of the Ancient World.* Edited by Manfred Landfester, Hubert Cancik, and Helmuth Schneider. 5 vols. Leiden: Brill, 2006–.
BSGRT	Bibliotheca Scriptorum Graecorum et Romanorum Teubneriana
Budé	Collection des universités de France, publiée sous le patronage de l'Association Guillaume Budé
BZNW	Beihefte zur Zeitschrift für die neutestamentliche Wissenschaft
CBQMS	Catholic Biblical Quarterly Monograph Series
CCSL	Corpus Christianorum: Series Latina. Turnhout: Brepols, 1953–
CCTC	Cambridge Classical Texts and Commentaries
CIL	*Corpus Inscriptionum Latinarum.* Berlin, 1862–
CJ	*Classical Journal*
ClQ	*Classical Quarterly*
Comp	*Compostellanum*
CP	*Classical Philology*
CSEL	Corpus Scriptorum Ecclesiasticorum Latinorum
CSHB	Corpus Scriptorum Historiae Byzantinae
DCB	*Dictionary of Christian Biography.* Edited by William Smith and Henry Wace. 4 vols. London: Murray, 1877–1887.
DGWE	*Dictionary of Gnosis and Western Esotericism.* Edited by Wouter J. Hanegraaff et al. 2 vols. Leiden: Brill, 2005.
DK	Diels, Hermann, and Walther Kranz, eds. *Fragmente der Vorsokratiker, griechisch und deutsch.* 7th ed. 3 vols. Berlin: Weidmann, 1954.
EPRO	Études préliminaires aux religions orientales dans l'empire romain
EstEcl	*Estudios eclesiásticos*

FARG	Forschungen zur Anthropologie und Religionsgeschichte
FGH	*Die Fragmente der griechischen Historiker*. Edited by Felix Jacoby. Leiden: Brill, 1954–1964.
FHSG	Theophrastos of Eresos. *Sources for His Life, Writings, Thought, and Influence.* Edited by William Fortenbaugh, Pamela Huby, R. W. Sharples, and Dimitri Gutas. 2 vols. PhA. Leiden: Brill, 1992.
GCS	Die griechischen christlichen Schriftsteller der ersten [drei] Jahrhunderte
Herm	*Hermathena*
HR	*History of Religions*
HTR	*Harvard Theological Review*
HUCA	*Hebrew Union College Annual*
ICS	*Illinois Classical Studies*
IG	*Inscriptiones Graecae. Editio Minor.* Berlin: de Gruyter, 1924–.
Inwood	Inwood, Brad, ed. *The Poem of Empedocles: A Text and Translation with an Introduction.* 2nd ed. Toronto: University of Toronto, 2001.
JAC	*Jahrbuch für Antike und Christentum*
JBL	*Journal of Biblical Literature*
JECS	*Journal of Early Christian Studies*
JEH	*Journal of Ecclesiastical History*
JQR	*Jewish Quarterly Review*
JSJ	*Journal for the Study of Judaism in the Persian, Hellenistic, and Roman Periods*
JTI	*Journal of Theological Interpretation*
JTS	*Journal of Theological Studies*
KD	*Kerygma und Dogma*
LCL	Loeb Classical Library
LSJ	Liddell, Henry George, Robert Scott, Henry Stuart Jones. *A Greek-English Lexicon.* 9th ed. with revised supplement. Oxford: Clarendon, 1996.
MH	*Museum Helveticum*
Mnemosyne	*Mnemosyne: A Journal of Classical Studies*
Mus	*Muséon: Revue d'études orientales*
NHC	Nag Hammadi Codices
NHS	Nag Hammadi Studies

NHMS	Nag Hammadi and Manichaean Studies
NovT	*Novum Testamentum*
NovTSup	Supplements to Novum Testamentum
NTApoc	*New Testament Apocrypha*. Edited by Wilhelm Schneemelcher. 2 vols. Rev. ed. English trans. ed. Robert McL. Wilson. Cambridge: Clarke; Louisville: Westminster John Knox, 1991.
NTS	*New Testament Studies*
OCP	*Orientalia Christiana Periodica*
OCT	Oxford Classical Texts
OECT	Oxford Early Christian Texts
OF	*Orphic Fragments*. Edited by Alberto Bernabé. *Poetae epici graeci testimonia et fragmenta: Part 2*. 3 vols. Leipzig: K. G. Saur, 2004–2007.
Parab	*Parabola*
PG	Patrologia Graeca. Edited by Jacques-Paul Migne. 162 vols. Paris, 1857–1886.
PGL	*Patristic Greek Lexicon*. Edited by Geoffrey W. H. Lampe. Oxford: Clarendon, 1961.
PGM	*Papyri Graecae Magicae: Die griechischen Zauberpapyri*. Edited by Karl Preisendanz. 2nd ed. Stuttgart: Teubner, 1973–1974.
PhA	Philosophia Antiqua
Phil	*Philologus*
PTS	Patristische Texte und Studien
RAC	*Reallexikon für Antike und Christentum*. Edited by Theodor Klauser et al. Stuttgart: Hiersemann, 1950–.
RE	*Realencyklopädie für protestantische Theologie und Kirche*
REA	*Revue des études ancienne*
RevPhil	*Revue de Philologie*
RevScRel	*Revue des sciences religieuses*
RGRW	Religions in the Graeco-Roman World
Roeper	G. Roeper. "Emendationsversuche zu Hippolyti Philosophumena." *Phil* 7 (1852): 511–53.
RTAM	*Recherches de théologie ancienne et medieval*
RVV	Religionsgeschichtliche Versuche und Vorarbeiten
SAC	Studies in Antiquity and Christianity

SAPERE	Scripta Antiquitatis Posterioris ad Ethicam Religionemque pertinentia
SBLHS	*Society of Biblical Literature Handbook of Style*. 2nd ed. Atlanta: SBL Press, 2014.
SBLSP	Society of Biblical Literature Seminar Papers
SC	Sources chrétiennes
SCO	*Studi classici e orientali*
SEAug	Studia Ephemeridis Augustinianum
SecCent	*Second Century*
SHA	*Scriptores Historiae Augustae*. Edited by David Magie. 3 vols. LCL. London: Heinemann, 1921.
SHR	Studies in the History of Religions (supplements to *Numen*)
SMSR	*Studi e materiali di storia delle religioni*
STAC	Studien und Texte zu Antike und Christentum
StPatr	*Studia Patristica*
SVF	*Stoicorum Veterum Fragmenta*. Hans Friedrich August von Arnim. 4 vols. Leipzig: Teubner, 1903–1924.
SVTQ	*St. Vladimir's Theological Quarterly*
TDNT	*Theological Dictionary of the New Testament*. Edited by Gerhard Kittel and Gerhard Friedrich. Translated by Geoffrey W. Bromiley. 10 vols. Grand Rapids: Eerdmans, 1964–1976.
ThH	Théologie historique
TS	Texts and Studies
TSAJ	Texte und Studien zum antiken Judentum
TU	Texte und Untersuchungen
TUGAL	Texte und Untersuchungen zur Geschichte der altchristlichen Literatur
TZ	*Theologische Zeitschrift*
VC	*Vigiliae Christianae*
VCSup	Supplements to Vigiliae Christianae
WGRW	Writings from the Greco-Roman World
WUNT	Wissenschaftliche Untersuchungen zum Neuen Testament
ZAC	*Zeitschrift für Antikes Christentum*
ZKT	*Zeitschrift für katholische Theologie*

ZNW	*Zeitschrift für die neutestamentliche Wissenschaft und die Kunde der älteren Kirche*
ZPE	*Zeitschrift für Papyrologie und Epigraphik*
ZTK	*Zeitschrift für Theologie und Kirche*

Introduction

The Manuscript Tradition

The *Refutation of All Heresies* is not a well-attested work. There are five manuscripts of book 1, all of which ascribe the work to Origen.[1] Books 2 and 3 are lost. Books 4–10 exist in a single fourteenth-century manuscript found in 1841 at Mount Athos by Constantinus Minoides Mynas.

Mynas was sent east by the University of Paris to collect ancient manuscripts. On February 25, 1842, he reported by letter that he had acquired thirty-five texts. Among them was an anonymous refutation composed in six books. Mynas attributed the work to Origen because the form of argument, he thought, resembled the *Contra Celsum*. The manuscript, labeled Parisinus Supplément grec 464 (hereafter P), was deposited in the Bibliothèque Royale.[2]

The books of the *Refutation* were then recompiled. In 1851, book 1 was combined with books 4–10 in the Oxford edition of Emmanuel Miller.[3] Miller attributed the entire work to Origen. Eight years later, the edition of L. Duncker and F. G. Schneidewin ascribed the work to the misty figure of Hippolytos.[4] The 1860 edition of Patricius Cruice did not record

1. Codex Laurentianus IX 32 (fourteenth century), Ottobonianus 194 (sixteenth–seventeenth century), Barberinianus 496 (sixteenth–seventeenth century), Barberinianus 362 (sixteenth–seventeenth century), and Taurinensis B VI 25 (sixteenth century). For details, see Miroslav Marcovich, ed., *Hippolytus: Refutatio omnium haeresium*, PTS 25 (Berlin: de Gruyter, 1986), 2.

2. The story of Mynas's discovery is variously told. See, e.g., Pierre Nautin, *Hippolyte et Josipe: Contribution à l'histoire de la littérature chrétienne du troisième siècle* (Paris: Cerf, 1947), 20–21.

3. Emmanuel Miller, ed., Ὠριγένους Φιλοσοφούμενα ἤ Κατὰ πασῶν αἱρέσεων ἔλεγχος. *Origenis Philosophumena sive Omnium haeresium refutatio e codice Parisino* (Oxford: Academic, 1851).

4. L. Duncker and F. G. Schneidewin, eds., *S. Hippolyti episcopi et martyris: Refutationis omnium haeresium librorum decem quae supersunt* (Göttingen: Dieterich, 1859).

an author but indicated that the work was ascribed to Origen (*opus Origeni adscriptum*).[5]

Title

Although we lack a title in the manuscripts for the treatise as a whole, the brief tables of contents at the head of each book consistently refer to the work as Ὁ *κατὰ πασῶν αἱρέσεων ἔλεγχος*: *The Refutation of All Heresies.* Yet the word "refutation," from the Latin *refutatio*, has the potential to mislead. The author did indeed aim to refute his opponents. Yet he also, and primarily, intended to *denounce, unmask, and expose* his enemies as plagiarists—with the ultimate goal of showing them "naked and full of shame" (*Ref.* 1, *pref.* §11).[6]

A generation earlier, Irenaeus claimed that to expose the doctrines of the "gnostics" was to refute them (*Haer.* 1.31.3). But his exposé was accompanied by four books of rational, scriptural, and rhetorical arguments attempting to refute his opponents. In the *Refutation*, as Gérard Vallée has pointed out, "we witness … almost a complete disappearance of this type of argumentation."[7] The truth alone so effectively topples error, affirms the author of the *Refutation*, it has only to manifest itself "inexorable and unadorned" (*Ref.* 10.5.1).

For a long time in English, the *Refutation* was also called *Philosophoumena* (or *Philosophumena*). Indeed, F. Legge (following Cruice) gave it this title in the last full English translation (1921).[8] The author of the *Refutation* refers to τὰ φιλοσοφούμενα in 9.8.2: "Now, even though I formerly set out the theory of Herakleitos in τὰ φιλοσοφούμενα…." Miroslav Marcovich believed that τὰ φιλοσοφούμενα referred to book 1.[9] Jaap Mansfeld viewed

5. Patricius Cruice, ed., *Philosophumena sive haeresium omnium confutatio opus Origeni adscriptum e cod. Paris. rec.* (Paris: Imperial, 1860).

6. Daniel A. Bertrand, "La notion d'apocryphe dans l'argumentation de la Réfutation de toutes le hérésies," in *Apocryphité: Histoire d'un concept transversal aux religions du livre en hommage à Pierre Geoltrain*, ed. Simon Claude Mimouni, BEHER 113 (Turnhout: Brepols, 2002), 131–40 (138). Cf. Gérard Vallée, *A Study in Anti-gnostic Polemics: Irenaeus, Hippolytus and Epiphanius* (Waterloo: Wilfred Laurier University Press, 1981), 52.

7. Vallée, *Study*, 51.

8. F. Legge, trans., *Philosophoumena, or the Refutation of All Heresies*, 2 vols. (London: SPCK, 1921).

9. Marcovich, *Refutatio*, 1. He also notes that φιλοσοφούμενα appears as a title at

φιλοσοφούμενα as a title or subtitle for the work as a whole.[10] Against Mansfeld, Clemens Scholten argued that φιλοσοφούμενα refers in *Ref.* 9.8.2 and elsewhere to the philosophical teachings of particular individuals.[11] The author of the *Refutation*, it seems, did not intend to call his entire treatise *Philosophical Teachings*.

Photios, patriarch of Constantinople (858–867, 877–886) noted that "some people" (φάσι) say that Gaius of Rome composed a book called *The Labyrinth* (τὸν λαβύρινθον, *Bibl.* chap. 48). According to Photios, Gaius testified at the end of *The Labyrinth* that he had written a work about the nature of the universe (περὶ τῆς τοῦ παντὸς οὐσίας). At the end of the *Refutation*, the author refers to his treatise περὶ τῆς τοῦ παντὸς οὐσίας (10.32.4)—exactly the same words used by Photios. Emmanuele Castelli uses this passage as evidence that the author of the *Refutation* once called his work *The Labyrinth*, with *The Refutation of All Heresies* serving as a subtitle.[12] Naturally, *The Labyrinth* could also be a title later applied to the work, based on the opening line of book 10: "I have broken through the labyrinth of heresies" (τὸν λαβύρινθον τῶν αἱρέσεων … διαρρήξαντες, 10.5.1). One wonders whether the author would have named his work using a term that refers to the intricate doctrines of his opponents. Given the present state of knowledge, it seems best simply to call our work *The Refutation of All Heresies*.

The Edition of Marcovich

The translator must confront head on the problems of the most recent critical edition of the *Refutation* produced by the accomplished scholar Miroslav Marcovich (1986). Marcovich has been regularly and rightly taken to task for his invasive, unnecessary, and conjectural emendations to our only surviving manuscript of books 4–10. Some scholars have deemed Marcovich's edition "unusable"—apart from its indices—and revert to the older

---

the end of book 4 and the beginning of book 9 (8–9). He concludes that "*Philosophumena* was extended from Book I to the entire work by the *posterior* tradition only" (9).

10. Jaap Mansfeld, *Heresiography in Context: Hippolytus' Elenchos as a Source for Greek Philosophy*, PhA 56 (Leiden: Brill, 1992), 1.

11. Clemens Scholten, "Der Titel von Hippolyts *Refutatio*," *StPatr* 31 (1997): 343–48.

12. Emanuele Castelli, "Saggio introduttivo: L'Elenchos, ovvero una 'biblioteca' contro le eresie," in *'Ippolito': Confutazione di tutte le eresie*, ed. Aldo Magris (Brescia: Morcelliana, 2012), 30. See further idem, *Un falso letterario sotto il nome di Flavio Giuseppe*, JAC Ergänzungsband 7 (Münster: Aschendorff, 2011), 44–51.

edition of Paul Wendland (1916).[13] Wendland, although he suggested many emendations, was less inclined to intervene in the text itself. This tendency led him, on occasion, to print an illogical text.[14]

Marcovich realized that P is an extremely corrupt text. As he puts it: "The codex is plagued with huge textual gaps, countless word omissions, displacement of words and even entire clauses, intrusive marginal glosses, and above all many scribal errors."[15] These corruptions must be taken seriously. By the time of his edition, Marcovich had already spent eighteen years with the *Refutation*. In a series of articles, he literally printed nothing but an army of emendations.[16] The majority of his emendations were cosmetic (the addition of particles, articles, the standardization of spelling, and so on).[17] Many others were necessary to restore sense to the text, especially in poorly transmitted sections and those dealing with arithmetical speculation. Some other emendations, though strictly speaking unnecessary, remain plausible and should be considered valid attempts to restore the text.[18]

Nevertheless, a great many of Marcovich's emendations are too clever by half. They reflect the mind-set of nineteenth-century philologists who proposed emendations as trophies of erudition. Overall, Marcovich has done the work of a translator: he clarified antecedents and transitions by prodigally inserting verbs and connecting particles—in general filling in

13. See the reviews of Marcovich's edition by Manlio Simonetti in *Aug* 27 (1987): 631–34; Dieter Hagedorn in *JAC* 32 (1989): 210–14. Cf. Castelli, *Falso letterario*, 4 n. 6. The most recent Italian translation of *Ref.* (Magris, *Confutazione*) translates Wendland's text.

14. An example of an illogical reading is *Ref.* 4.4.7, where Wendland printed παραφυλάξασθαι τὴν τοῦ γεννηθέντος ὥραν κατ' οὐρανὸν βλεπομένην. This reading indicates that the astrologer observes the hour of the native's birth in the sky. But the *hour* cannot be seen in the sky, only the stars. Cf. Wendland's text at *Ref.* 1.8.4. Marcovich also accused Wendland of misreading P and of omitting Greek words (*Refutatio*, 7).

15. Marcovich, *Refutatio*, 6–7.

16. Marcovich lists his contributions in *Refutatio*, xv.

17. A large amount of his cosmetic emendations produce a smoother, more readable text. Unfortunately, most are unnecessary, and some are based on philological pedantry (e.g., the need to avoid hiatus).

18. Unlike Wendland, Marcovich also makes heavy use of angled brackets (< >), which immediately alert the reader to textual emendations (though Marcovich is not entirely consistent in this practice). Marcovich's apparatus also covers orthographic variants and itacisms not recorded elsewhere. Marcovich's use of parentheses is ambiguous: they contain letters faded or illegible in P as well as letters that Marcovich has added to fill out an abbreviation.

logical gaps that could be inferred from parallel constructions. Occasionally, when one of the more bizarre passages of the *Refutation* (and they are legion) struck him as illogical, he restored the logic but destroyed the sense. At times, he thought that he could insert words based on far-flung "parallels" from both well-known and obscure sources. He "restored" some readings in the "gnostic" material based on what he thought was "standard terminology."[19] Especially confusing for source criticism is his tendency to insert *φησίν*, or change *φησίν* to *φάσι* (and *vice versa*), in the reports. A host of other (no less irksome) emendations can be described as (in the words of Josef Frickel) "right in terms of meaning, but text-critically false" (*sinngemäß zwar richtig, texkritisch jedoch falsch*).[20] In these cases, Marcovich produced a text that made good sense only to replace one that made equally good sense. Marcovich was not the first interventionist editor to lay his hands on the *Refutation*. Nonetheless, he compounded problems by printing some of the daring emendations of his predecessors. A cursory overview of his edition will reveal that he left no paragraph untouched.

Consequently, Marcovich's edition cannot be the basis of a new translation. Yet merely returning to Wendland's text is also methodologically unsound, since it neglects the hard work of judging, one by one, the worth of Marcovich's emendations. A third option is required here, in accord with the biblical counsel: *πάντα δοκιμάζετε, τὸ καλὸν κατέχετε* ("test all things, and retain what is good," 1 Thess 5:21). What is required is a new text, one that retains Marcovich's helpful and plausible emendations while discarding those that are speculative, decorative, and unnecessary. I have attempted to provide such an edition here. In text-critical decisions, there is a general and simple rule followed throughout: where the text of P makes adequate grammatical and logical sense, it stands. Where it does not make sense, the least disruptive and most plausible emendations are sought. Accepted emendations of Marcovich that significantly alter the sense of the text are flagged in the notes.[21]

19. Marcovich, *Refutatio*, 8.

20. Josef Frickel, "Hippolyt von Rom: Refutatio, Buch X," in *Überlieferungsgeschichtliche Untersuchungen*, ed. Franz Paschke (Berlin: Akademie, 1981), 217–44 (220).

21. Here one must add a brief notice about Marcovich's list of parallel texts (housed in his upper apparatus). This apparatus is considerably fuller than Wendland's, causing joy in the hearts of uninitiated readers. One feels a duty to warn them, however, that dozens of these references are in fact false parallels and miscitations that will lead the reader on many a wild goose chase. An attempt is made here to filter out these false parallels, leaving only references of direct relevance to the *Refutation*.

The Question of Authorship[22]

In the recent second edition of the *Society of Biblical Literature Handbook of Style*, the *Refutation* is the only work (to my knowledge) with the honor of being ascribed to two authors. The authors are, to be sure, quite closely related. One is called "Hippolytus" and the other "Hippolytus of Rome."[23] This double attribution in a standard manual highlights the fact that questions about the *Refutation*'s authorship have yet to be settled.

As it stands, P is anonymous. Only in a marginal note in book 10 (immediately before chapter 32) does a scribe write in red: ὡριγένης καὶ ὡριγένους δόξα ("Origen and the Doctrine of Origen"). Manuscripts of book 1, however, clearly attribute the work to Origen. As we have seen, the first editor of the *Refutation* (Miller) attributed the entire ten books to the Alexandrian theologian.

Nevertheless, surging doubts about Origenic authorship in the mid-nineteenth century gave rise to a circus of attributions. As J. H. MacMahon wrote: "Heuman attributed the *Philosophumena* to Didymus [the Blind] of Alexandria, Gale to Aetius [an Arian bishop of the fourth century].… Fessler and Bauer ascribed it to Caius [i.e., Gaius, a Roman apologist in the early third century], but the Abbe Jellabert to Tertullian."[24] In the race to determine the author, Epiphanios and Novatian also came in for honorable

22. For the earliest hypotheses about authorship, see Josef Frickel's summary in *Das Dunkel um Hippolyt von Rom: Ein Lösungsversuch; Die Schriften Elenchos und Contra Noëtum* (Graz: Graz University Press, 1988), 95–99. Recent general treatments of Hippolytos and his works include Ronald E. Heine, "Hippolytus, Ps.-Hippolytus and the Early Canons," in *The Cambridge History of Early Christian Literature*, ed. Frances Young, Lewis Ayres, and Andrew Louth (Cambridge: Cambridge University Press, 2004), 142–51; Claudio Moreschini and Enrico Norelli, *Early Christian Greek and Latin Literature: A Literary History*, trans. Matthew J. O'Connell, 2 vols. (Peabody, MA: Hendrickson, 2005), 1:232–47; Ulrich Volp, "Hippolytus of Rome," in *Early Christian Thinkers: The Lives and Legacies of Twelve Key Figures*, ed. Paul Foster (Downers Grove, IL: IVP Academic, 2010), 141–53. For the author of the *Refutation*, see esp. the essays by Manlio Simonetti, Clemens Scholten, Allen Brent, and Emanuele Castelli published in Gabriella Aragione and Enrico Norelli, eds., *Des évêques, des écoles et des hérétiques: Actes du colloque international sur la "Refutation de toutes les heresies" Genève, 13–14 juin 2008* (Prahins: Éditions du Zèbre, 2011).

23. *SBLHS*, 153–54.

24. J. H. MacMahon, "Introductory Notice to Hippolytus," in *ANF* 5:5.

mention.[25] But when the dust of argument settled, it was Hippolytos who won the prize of authorship.

The success of Hippolytos—whose name amalgamates at least two legendary martyrs in the Roman Catholic Church—was largely due to the work of Catholic historian of Christianity Johann Joseph Ignatius von Döllinger.[26] Döllinger emphasized that the author of the *Refutation* supposed himself to be a bishop—actually a "high priest" (see *Ref.* 1, *pref.* §6)—in apostolic succession over a community that rivaled the self-proclaimed "catholic" church. At the time, the largest Roman church was led by Bishop Kallistos (or Callistus, 217–222 CE) and his successor Urban (222–230 CE).[27] The provenance of the *Refutation* is thus Roman. The combination of Roman provenance and the author's episcopal status, Döllinger believed, eliminated Hippolytos's contenders for authorship. Eusebios in the fourth century called Hippolytos προεστώς ("presider") of an unknown church (*Hist. eccl.* 6.20). Jerome took the word to mean *episcopus*, but he too was strangely ignorant of Hippolytos's provenance (*Vir. ill.* 61). Since the location of Hippolytos's episcopal see was thus "open," so to speak, Döllinger could install him at Rome.

According to Döllinger, Hippolytos set himself up as antipope (*Gegenpapst*) to Kallistos.[28] Two notices in the *Chronography of 354* mention a Roman Hippolytos. The first notice (in the *Liberian Catalogue*) reports that in 235 CE a "presbyter" (*presbiter*) called Hippolytos was exiled to Sardinia with Urban's successor Pontian (230–235 CE). In the second notice (the *Deposition of Martyrs*) it is recorded that a Hippolytos was buried on August 13. The year of his deposition is not specified, but it is the same day that Pontian was laid to rest.[29] Döllinger identified Hippolytos the Roman presbyter and martyr with Hippolytos the bishop and putative writer of the *Refutation*. The fact that Pope Fabian (236–250 CE) buried Pontian and the presbyter Hippolytos on the day celebrating the union of the Latin tribes

---

25. J. J. Ignatius von Döllinger, *Hippolytus und Kallistus: Oder, Die römische Kirche in der ersten Hälfte des dritten Jahrhunderts* (Regensburg: G. J. Manz, 1853), appendix E, 354–55.

26. Below I quote the English translation of Döllinger by Alfred Plummer, *Hippolytus and Callistus: The Church of Rome in the First Half of the Third Century* (Edinburgh: T&T Clark, 1876).

27. *Ref.* 9.7.2–3; 9.9.11–12.

28. Döllinger, *Hippolytus and Callistus*, xiv.

29. Castelli, "Saggio introduttivo," in Magris, *Confutazione*, 37, who cites the most recent edition of the *Chronography*.

(August 13) indicated to Döllinger that a reconciliation had occurred between the author of the *Refutation* and the larger catholic community sometime before the author's death.[30]

Hippolytan authorship of the *Refutation* eventually assumed the status of received scholarly tradition. There were a few protests, notably from Cardinal Newman, who could not believe that Hippolytos, "who has ever been in the brightest light of ecclesiastical approbation," could be "*the author of that malignant libel on his contemporary* Popes" (referring to *Ref.* 9.11–12).[31] At the same time, certain Anglican divines were delighted to have papal authority (recently made infallible) torn to shreds by a respected ancient authority—and competing "pope" no less.[32]

In the mid-twentieth century, Döllinger's theory was battered—but hardly toppled—by the young scholar Pierre Nautin. Nautin proposed that, due to methodological, stylistic, and theological differences, the author of the *Refutation* could not be the same man as the Hippolytos who wrote the extant heresiological work *Contra Noetum* as well as the biblical commentaries ascribed to Hippolytos.[33] There were thus two authors, Nautin argued, with different names. One author was Hippolytos, a church leader located somewhere in the east. The other author composed the *Refutation*. He was a Roman bishop known by the name of Ἰωσήπος (or Josephus)—a name that Nautin plucked from Photios, *Bibliotheca*, chapter 48.

The *name* of Nautin's rival bishop did not stand scrutiny, but his two-author theory eventually secured support among Italian scholars.[34] A

30. Döllinger, *Hippolytus and Callistus*, 72. Allen Brent adds that the compiler of the *Liberian Catalogue* situated his report about Hippolytos in the context of other schisms that were healed ("St Hippolytus, Biblical Exegete, Roman Bishop, and Martyr," *SVTQ* 48 [2004]: 207–31 [220–21]).

31. Newman, as quoted by Plummer in appendix B to Döllinger, *Hippolytus and Callistus*, 342–43, emphasis original. According to Newman, the writer of the *Refutation* "did not scruple in set words to call Pope Zephyrinus a weak and venal dunce, and Pope Callistus a sacrilegious swindler, an infamous convict, and an heresiarch *ex cathedra*" (343).

32. See, e.g., Christopher Wordsworth, *St. Hippolytus and the Church of Rome in the Earlier Part of the Third Century*, 2nd ed. (London: Francis & John Rivington, 1880).

33. See esp. Nautin, *Hippolyte et Josipe* (entire).

34. For a full history of research, see Frickel, *Dunkel*, 99–118; Manlio Simonetti, ed., *Ippolito: Contro Noeto*, Biblioteca Patristica (Bologna: Dehoniane, 2000), 71–139. For scholars opposing Nautin, see the contributions of Josef Frickel ("Ippolito di Roma Scrittore e Martire") and V. Saxer ("La questione di Ippolito romano: A proposito di un

prominent representative, Manlio Simonetti, tentatively proposed that there were *two men* named Hippolytos: one an eastern bishop and the other the author of the *Refutation.*[35] The first Hippolytos authored an exegetical block of works that include *Antichrist*, the *Commentary on Daniel*, *David and Goliath*, *Commentary on the Song of Songs*, *The Blessings of Isaac and Jacob*, and *The Blessings of Moses.* The second Hippolytos composed our *Refutation*, along with two works now commonly called *On the Universe* and *Chronicle* (Συναγωγή Χρονῶν, edited by Bauer and Helm).[36]

According to Vincenzo Loi, the two groups of texts reveal two authors who were both psychologically and culturally distinct. The writer of the *Refutation* was a man of learning, self-conscious, aggressive, and philosophical. Hippolytos the commentator, by contrast, was a homilist with no special interest in philosophy, a pastor of souls who was opposed (or at least indifferent) to Roman rule.[37]

In his 1986 edition of the *Refutation*, Marcovich seems to have been unaware of—or simply ignored—these developments among Italian scholars. He assumes one Hippolytos and calls the circumstantial evidence for Hippolytan authorship of the *Refutation* "overwhelming."[38]

Marcovich bases his claim primarily on book titles. The self-citations in the *Refutation* permit one to ascribe to him three other works. Two were just mentioned: *Chronicle* (*Ref.* 10.30.1, 5) and *On the Universe*

libro recente") in *Nuove ricerche su Ippolito*, SEAug 30 (Rome: Patristic Institute, 1989), 23–42, 43–60, respectively.

35. Manlio Simonetti, "A modo di conclusione: Una ipotesi di lavoro," in *Ricerche su Ippolito*, SEAug 13 (Rome: Patristic Institute, 1977), 151–56; cf. idem, "Aggiornamento su Ippolito" in *Nuove ricerche*, 75–130. Moreschini and Norelli provide a concise summary of Simonetti's position (which they follow) (*Literary History*, 1:236–37).

36. Vincenzo Loi, "La Problematica storico-letteraria su Ippolito di Roma," in *Ricerche su Ippolito*, 9–16. Osvalda Andrei argues that the Συναγωγή Χρονῶν is a work of the eastern Hippolytos ("Dalle *Chronographiai* di Giulio Africano alla *Synagoge* di 'Ippolito': Un dibattito sulla scrittura Cristiana del tempo," in *Julius Africanus und die christliche Weltchronik*, ed. Martin Wallraff [Berlin: de Gruyter, 2006], 113–46 [114–15, 140–41]; idem, "Spazio geografico, etnografia ed evangelizzazione nella *Synagoge* di Ippolito," *ZAC* 11 [2007]: 221–78 [234–45]). He is opposed by Manlio Simonetti, "Per un profile dell'autore dell'*Elenchos*," in Aragione and Norelli, *Des évêques*, 257–76 (257–58 n. 4).

37. Vincenzo Loi, "L'identità letteraria di Ippolito di Roma," in *Ricerche su Ippolito*, 67–88 (87). Loi lists five basic theological and exegetical differences between the two writers on 88–89.

38. Marcovich, *Refutatio*, 10.

(*Ref.* 10.32.4). A third (lost) work, now commonly called *Syntagma*, was a short heresiological treatise by our author that predated the *Refutation*.[39] Linguistic, stylistic, and doctrinal correspondences also indicate that the author of these three works is the same.[40]

Marcovich then turns to a list of works discovered on the plinth of a headless statue found by Pirri Ligorio in 1561. Unfortunately, the damaged state of the female represented (who, as it turns out, became male in Ligorio's "reconstruction") as well as doubts about the place of the statue's discovery do not allow us to identify the author(s) of the works inscribed on the plinth.[41] Nevertheless, two of the titles on the plinth seemed to match works of our author:

1. A *Chronicle* (Χρονικῶν on the statue) ≈ ἕτεραι βίβλοι in *Ref.* 10.30.1, 5.
2. *Against the Greeks and against Plato or On the Universe* (Πρὸς Ἕλληνας καὶ πρὸς Πλάτωνα ἤ καὶ περὶ τοῦ παντός on the statue) ≈ περὶ τῆς τοῦ παντὸς οὐσίας in *Ref.* 10.32.4.[42]

It is somewhat daring to attribute Χρονικῶν to the author of the *Refutation*, since the actual contents of the work named on the statue are unclear, and *Ref.* 10.30.1, 5 do not actually supply a title for the "other books" mentioned (although it is clear that they dealt with the genealogies in Jewish scripture). Slightly more promising is the (not entirely) overlapping title of the second work. Here, however, *Ref.* 10.32.4 seems to *refer* only to the work in question. It does not record its proper title. Nevertheless, the verbal overlap in περὶ τοῦ παντός became the golden link that, Marcovich believed, connected the author of the *Refutation* with the author of the works on the Ligorio statue.

39. *Ref.* 1, *pref.* §1. Pierre Nautin offers a still valuable introduction to the *Syntagma* in *Hippolyte contre les heresies* (Paris: Cerf, 1949).

40. See further Loi, "L'identità letteraria," 67.

41. See further Margherita Guarducci, "La 'Statua di Sant'Ippolito' et la sua provenienza," in *Nuove ricerche*, 61–74; Allen Brent, *Hippolytus and the Roman Church in the Third Century: Communities in Tension before the Emergence of a Monarch-Bishop*, VCSup 31 (Leiden: Brill, 1995), 51–114.

42. Castelli argues that the original title was Πρὸς Ἕλληνας καὶ πρὸς Πλάτωνα ἤ καὶ περὶ τοῦ παντός (*To* [not *Against*] *the Greeks and to Plato, or On the Universe*) (*Falso letterario*, 59).

But to whom do the rest of the works carved on the statue plinth belong? According to Marcovich, five other titles there match works attributed to Hippolytos elsewhere.[43] They include:

1. *On the Pascha* (Ἀπόδειξις χρόνων τοῦ Πάσχα [κ]αὶ τὰ ἐν τῷ πίνακι on the statue) ≈ Περὶ τοῦ Πάσχα in Eusebios, *Hist. eccl.* 6.22.
2. *On the Psalms* ([Εἰς τοὺς ψ]αλμούς on the statue) ≈ *De Psalmis* in Jerome, *Vir. ill.* 61.[44]
3. *On the Sorceress* ([Εἰς ἐγ]γαστρίμυθον on the statue) ≈ *De Saul et pytonissa* in Jerome, *Vir. ill.* 61.
4. *On John's Gospel and Apocalypse* ([Τ]ὰ ὑπὲρ τοῦ κατὰ Ἰωάνην εὐα[γ]γελίου καὶ ἀποκαλύψεως on the statue) ≈ *De Apocalypsi* in Jerome, *Vir. ill.* 61.[45]
5. *On God and the Resurrection of the Flesh* (Περὶ θ[εο]ῦ καὶ σαρκὸς ἀναστάσεως on the statue) ≈ *De resurrectione* in Jerome, *Vir. ill.* 61.[46]

Marcovich reasons that, (1) because these other five works on the Ligorio statue concur in title with works of Hippolytos mentioned in Eusebios and Jerome and (2) one title on the statue (*On the Universe*) agrees (more or less) with a work self-cited by the author of the *Refutation*, then (3) the author of the *Refutation* must be Hippolytos.[47]

---

43. Marcovich, *Refutatio*, 12–13.

44. See the Greek fragment of this work in Pierre Nautin, *Le dossier d'Hippolyte et de Méliton dans les florilèges dogmatiques et chez les historiens modernes* (Paris: Cerf, 1953), 165–83. The Syriac version attributes the text to Hippolytos (127).

45. Cf. the fragments of this work in *Hippolytus: Kleinere exegetische und homiletische Schriften*, ed. Hans Achelis, GCS 1.2 (Leipzig: Hinrichs, 1897), 231–38.

46. Cf. ibid., 251–53. The Hippolytos scholar Marcel Richard was ambivalent about the authenticity of this work ("Les difficultés d'une edition des oeuvres de S. Hippolyte," *StPatr* 12 [1975]: 51–70 [69]).

47. Loi points out additional doctrinal, stylistic, and linguistic correspondences between some of the five works listed above and the author of the *Refutation* ("L'identità letteraria," 71–72). For instance, *On the Resurrection* frag. 8 speaks of Christ as ἐκ τοῦ αὐτοῦ φυράματος as the human race, and as the ἀπαρχή of the resurrection. Similar language occurs in *Ref.* 10.33.16–17: τοῦτον [i.e., the Logos] … τοῦ καθ' ἡμᾶς φυράματος … ἀπαρξάμενος ἐν πᾶσι τούτοις τὸν ἴδιον ἄνθρωπον. Moreover, both the author of *On the Psalms* and the author of the *Refutation* refer to Christ as παῖς before his incarnation ("L'identità letteraria," 74–75; see further 75–77).

But Marcovich does not explain why the author's ten-volume *magnum opus*—the *Refutation*—went without mention on the statue.[48] He also does not clarify why John Damascene, Photios, and John Philoponos never identified *On the Universe* (which they knew) as a work of Hippolytos.

Marcovich's major misstep, however, was his failure to take seriously the two-author theory, which had the potential to undermine his entire argument. He dealt curtly with Nautin, nimbly skirting around his two-author thesis.[49] He then took no account of Loi and Simonetti's proposal about two authors (one eastern, one Roman) who composed two separate groups of works.[50] In the same volume presenting Loi and Simonetti's theory, Margherita Guarducci electrified Hippolytos scholars by proving that the Ligorio statue represented a woman and therefore was not a physical representation of Hippolytos.[51]

After Marcovich's edition, there emerged additional problems about the works inscribed on the statue. In 1995, Allen Brent pointed out that although Eusebios and Jerome separately list works of Hippolytos, their *two* lists overlap with the statue *only* in regard to two works: Περὶ τοῦ

48. Marcovich calls the *Refutation* "*Hippolytus' Magnum Opus*" (*Refutatio*, 32, italics his). Both Eusebios and Jerome ascribe to Hippolytos a work called *Against All Heresies* (Πρὸς ἁπάσας τὰς αἱρέσεις [*Hist. eccl.* 6.22]; *Adversus omnes haereses* [*Vir. ill.* 61]). Marcovich understands this work to refer not to the *Refutation* but to Hippolytos's lost *Syntagma*, a work also referred to by the seventh-century CE *Chronicon paschale* (PG 92:80b) as πρὸς ἁπάσας τὰς αἱρέσεις συντάγματι and by Photios (*Bibl.* chap. 121 [Henry, 2:95–96]). It was this work, not the *Refutation*, that Epiphanios (*Pan.*), Pseudo-Tertullian (*Adv. omn. haer.*), and Filastrius (*Haer.*) used, according to R. A. Lipsius, to construct their own antiheretical works (*Die Quellen der ältesten Ketzergeschichte neu untersucht* [Leipzig: J. A. Barth, 1875], 117–57). But it is not certain that Πρὸς ἁπάσας τὰς αἱρέσεις mentioned by Eusebios is identical to the τὸ σύνταγμα κατὰ αἱρεσέων mentioned by Photios, or that either work is identical with the general (ἁδρομερῶς) refutation referred to by our author in *Ref.* 1, *pref.* §1.

49. Marcovich, *Refutatio*, 14–15. Marcovich merely attacks Nautin's idea that the author of the *Refutation*, *On the Universe*, and the *Chronicle* was called "Josephus."

50. Loi, "Problematica," 9–16; idem, "L'identità letteraria," 67–88; Manlio Simonetti, "Due note su Ippolito: Ippolito interprete di Genesi 49; Ippolito e Tertulliano," in *Ricerche su Ippolito*, 121–36; idem, "A modo di conclusione," 151–56.

51. Margherita Guarducci, "La statua di 'Sant'Ippolito,'" in *Ricerche su Ippolito*, 17–30. Guarducci's mature reflections can be found in *San Pietro e Sant'Ippolito: Storia di statue famose in Vaticano* (Rome: Istituto Poligrafico, 1991), 111–40. For further speculation on the symbolic meaning of the statue in the second and third centuries CE, see the sources in Castelli, "Saggio introduttivo," 44 n. 64.

Πάσχα (*On the Pascha*) and Πρὸς Μαρκίωνα (*Against Markion*).[52] Yet the statue reads, not Πρὸς Μαρκίωνα, but Περὶ τἀγαθοῦ καὶ πόθεν τὸ κακόν (*Concerning the Good and the Source of Evil*)—hardly a strict match. Other works on the statue that overlap with Jerome's list (e.g., *On the Sorceress, On the Psalms*) are "titles for scriptural commentaries in general that are quite frequently shared by multiple authors."[53] Brent concludes that only *On the Pascha* was a secure work of Hippolytos that was also attested on the statue.[54] Recently, however, J. A. Cerrato has pointed out that since Hippolytos's paschal work is lost, we have "no basis by which to identify it with the statue inscriptions."[55]

In the past twenty years, the thread connecting Hippolytos and the *Refutation* has reached its breaking point. In his 1995 study, Brent presents a complex two-author theory. He argues that the Ligorio statue is a community artifact listing works of *multiple* authors.[56] In Brent's reconstruction, the author of the *Refutation* becomes an anonymous early third-century bishop who dies, leaving his community to a member of the same school—in fact the "real" Hippolytos, who reconciles with the successors of Kallistos, is subsequently acknowledged as a presbyter and suffers martyrdom with Pontian in 235 CE. The statue plinth refrains from listing the *Refutation* due to its inflammatory attack on Kallistos.[57]

In his 2002 study, Cerrato further distances Hippolytos and the author of the *Refutation*. Cerrato accepts the theory of an eastern Hippolytos—probably from Asia Minor—who composed the exegetical commentaries. Yet there are no longer two writers called Hippolytos, as Simonetti and Loi proposed. All links are severed between (the eastern) Hippolytos and the anonymous author of the *Refutation*. In fact, there was no prolific writer called "Hippolytos of Rome" at all—at least not the one reconstructed by Döllinger. Cerrato thus feels at liberty to omit discussing the author of the *Refutation*'s identity and biography.

Clearly in the confined space of this introduction the question of authorship cannot be settled. It suffices to face these facts: we know little about the circumstances of the *Refutation*'s publication and the form

52. Brent, *Hippolytus*, 201.

53. Ibid., 202.

54. Ibid., 307–11.

55. J. A. Cerrato, *Hippolytus East and West: The Commentaries and the Provenance of the Corpus* (Oxford: Oxford University Press, 2002), 122.

56. Brent, *Hippolytus*, 3–367.

57. Ibid., 368–535.

in which it was circulated.[58] It is never cited as a work of Hippolytos by ancient or medieval scholars.

Thus in the end, we return to the state of blessed—though not naïve—ignorance that prevailed soon after the *Refutation*'s discovery. We do not know the name of its author. To call him "Pseudo-Hippolytos" would be misleading, since he never claimed to be Hippolytos, and the manuscripts never attribute the work to Hippolytos.[59] To call him "Hippolytos II" (or some such) as opposed to "Hippolytos I" (the exegetical writer) is historically confusing, since we have no secure evidence of two contemporary *writers* called Hippolytos. Indeed, to call him "Hippolytos" at all—even with the recognition that the name is a mere cipher—is methodologically questionable. In later church history, Hippolytos's name came to represent Christian orthodoxy. Our author's views of the Logos and his theology of the Holy Spirit (or lack thereof; see *Ref.* 10.32–33) do not accord with later orthodoxy. For scholars, conventional attributions based on questionable evidence should not have normative status. In the current state of research, we best confront our *horror vacui* and call our anonymous writer "the author of the *Refutation*." For simplicity, I will refer to him here and in the notes as "our author."

The Man

Despite the fact that we do not know our author's name, from the work itself we possess vivid details about his life. The author depicts himself as a learned and hard-working scholar-bishop, a genuine intellectual in stark contrast to the putatively ignoramus bishop Zephyrinos and ex-slave banker Kallistos. Our author strongly opposes Kallistos, who claimed the laurels of leading the "catholic" (i.e., "universal") church in Rome (217–222 CE). The writer of the *Refutation* seems to have exercised episcopal—what he calls "high-priestly"—authority over another Christian community in Rome (which, in his mind, represents the true church). Nonetheless, it is almost certainly wrong to think of our author as an "antipope," since the institution of the monarchial papacy had not yet been consolidated.[60]

58. Some have speculated that the *Refutation* did not receive a final revision before its publication (e.g., E. Prinzivalli, "Eresia ed eretici nel corpus Ippolitiano," *Aug* 25 [1985]: 711–22 [712]).

59. Castelli, "Saggio introduttivo," 46.

60. Brent, *Hippolytus*, 409–15; idem, "The Elenchos and the Identification of

The church that our author led looks much more like a sect in the modern sociological church-sect theory.[61] Our author supports a strict morality and the preservation of social hierarchies. He is painfully conscious of living under the shadow of a dominant ecclesial "other." He takes pride in the fact that he hounds Kallistos for his putative heresy and opposes him in open debate (*Ref.* 9.12.15). If the author was not a "schismatic" (a frankly pejorative term rooted in ecclesiastical politics), he was certainly opposed to the most populous Roman church at the time and vied with its bishop for equal power and influence.[62]

Our writer was alive during and after the time of Bishop Zephyrinos and Kallistos in the early third century. Kallistos's death in 222 CE provides the *terminus post quem* for the *Refutation.* Since our author does not attack Kallistos's successors and speaks of few post-Kallistan developments, the work was most likely published not long after 222 CE.

The author of the *Refutation* lived in Rome, and we have no overwhelming reason to believe that he came from elsewhere. The fact that he wrote in Greek, knew the basics of Greek philosophy, and proffered a version of Logos theology does not reliably establish his eastern origin.[63]

The author of the *Refutation* was the last major theologian in Rome to write in Greek. He wrote apologetic and heresiological works. Due possibly to his sectarian tendencies, his works were either circulated anonymously or were—rather swiftly—attributed to other authors.[64] Parts of the *Refutation* (namely, books 1 and 10) were assigned to Origen. *On the Universe*

Christian Communities in Second–Early Third Century Rome," in Aragione and Norelli, *Des évêques*, 275–314.

61. According to Rodney Stark and William Sims Bainbridge, sects are subcultures characterized by "*difference* from the standards set by the majority or by powerful members of society, *antagonism* between the sect and society manifested in mutual rejection, and *separation* in social relations leading to the relative encapsulation of the sect" (*The Future of Religion: Secularization, Revival and Cult Formation* [Berkeley: University of California Press, 1985], 67, emphasis theirs. See further 24–26, 48–65, 99–125).

62. See further Brent, *Hippolytus*, 415–17. The theological context and beliefs of our author are discussed in my notes on the *Refutation*. For a summary, see Castelli, "Saggio introduttivo," 46–51.

63. Justin Martyr in Rome and Tertullian in Africa also vouched for a Logos theology.

64. Emanuele Castelli, "The Author of the *Refutatio omnium haeresium* and the Attribution of the *De universo* to Flavius Josephus," in Aragione and Norelli, *Des évêques*, 219–31 (230–31).

was attributed to Josephus. If our author wrote the Συναγωγή Χρονῶν, it was circulated anonymously.[65]

Our author died under unknown circumstances. He cannot be confidently identified with the presbyter and martyr Hippolytos mentioned in the *Chronography of 354*.[66] The author's works were not associated with the name "Hippolytos," and he would not likely have accepted a demotion from bishop to presbyter. Thus there is little reason to believe that he died as a martyr or was ever reconciled to the majority "school" of self-identifying catholics in Rome (*Ref.* 9.12.21). Indeed, given Brent's reconstruction—and our author's uncompromising attitude—he was likely never integrated into the "catholic" fold and would have viewed such integration as capitulation to heresy.

The Thesis of the *Refutation*

A major task of ancient literary criticism was to discover the overall thesis (σκόπος, ὑπόθεσις) of a work. Our author's general thesis is well known and can be summed up in a single word that still strikes terror in the hearts of academics: plagiarism.[67] As he programmatically states in his preface (*Ref.* 1, *pref.* §8):

> I intend (1) to expose these heretics as godless in opinion, character, and deed; (2) to expose the source of their arguments; and (3) to show that what they schemed they hardly took from the holy scriptures or arrived

65. The (*Syntagma*) *against All Heresies* is lost but summarized in Photios, *Bibl.* chap. 121 (Henry).

66. Castelli points out that the *Liberian Catalogue* does not say that the presbyter Hippolytos actually died in Sardinia, nor does the *Deposition of Martyrs* provide the year of his death. Possibly, then, this Hippolytos returned from Sardinia only to be martyred later around 250 CE, as testified in an epigram of Pope Damasus ("Saggio introduttivo," 38–39).

67. Clement also accused the philosophers of plagiarism (using a form of σκευωρέομαι, "ransack") (*Strom.* 2.1.1.1; cf. Diog. L., *Vit. phil.* 2.61). Porphyry calls plagiarism κλοπή ("theft") and views it as both morally reprehensible (μέμφομαι) and degrading (διαφθείρων) (frag. 408; cf. 409–10 [Smith]). Our author possibly coins a new term for plagiarism, κλεψιλογέω, and he refers to his enemies as κλεψίλογοι (*Ref.* 1, *pref.* §11). Marcovich argues that our author was a "*reckless plagiarist*" himself (*Refutatio*, 36, emphasis his). See further Miroslav Marcovich, "Hippolytus Plagiarizes the Gnostics," in *Athlon: Satura Grammatica in honorem Francisci R. Adrados*, ed. P. Bádenas de la Peña, 2 vols. (Madrid: Editorial Gredos, 1987), 2:587–92.

> at by preserving the teaching handed on by any holy person. Rather, I intend to prove that they took the starting point of their doctrines from Greek wisdom [ἐκ τῆς Ἑλλήνων σοφίας], from the dogmas of the philosophers [ἐκ δογμάτων φιλοσοφουμένων], from manufactured mysteries [μυστηρίων ἐπικεχειρημένων], and from wandering astrologers [καὶ ἀστρολόγων ῥεμβομένων].

In short: our author's thesis is that his opponents stole material from Greek philosophy, astrology, and the mystery cults. The accusation of plagiarism, especially among the philosophical schools, had a long history prior to our author. Among poets and philosophers, plagiarism was widely considered to be a form of stealing (κλοπή, *furtum*) and thus morally reprehensible.[68] By attacking the character of his putatively larcenous opponents, our author attempts to undermine the validity and credibility of their doctrines. At the same time, the writer of the *Refutation* seeks to validate himself. He poses as a kind of philological expert, working with the tools of linguistic comparison to prove that he is more skilled and more knowledgeable than his competitors. Unlike the theology of all others, his own theology does not, supposedly, derive any material from human learning.

In his focus on plagiarism, our author goes beyond earlier Christian apologists. Clement of Alexandria, for instance, repeatedly tried to show that the philosophers stole from the Hebrew scriptures (which contain the Hebrew philosophy).[69] In this scheme, philosophers are the plagiarists (even if they were guided by providence), while ancient Jews and Christians become the true philosophers.

---

68. For plagiarism in antiquity, see Katharina Schickert, *Der Schutz literarischer Urheberschaft im Rom der klassischen Antike* (Tübingen: Mohr Siebeck, 2005), 66–79; Gabriella Aragione, "Aspetti ideologici della nozione di plagio nell'antichità classica e Cristiana," in *Cristianesimi nell'antichità: Fonti, istituzioni, ideologie a confronto* (Hildesheim: Olms, 2007), 1–15; Bart Ehrman, *Forgery and Counterforgery: The Use of Literary Deceit in Early Christian Polemics* (Oxford: Oxford University Press, 2013), 52–55. For plagiarism and our author, see Adolf Hamel, *Kirche bei Hippolyt von Rom* (Gütersloh: Bertelsmann, 1951), 83–93; Bernard Pouderon, "Hippolyte, un regard sur l'hérésie entre tradition et invention," in Aragione and Norelli, *Des évêques*, 43–71 (61–69); Onofrio Vox, "Das Plagiat als polemisches Motiv und die 'Refutatio omnium haeresium,'" in *Lessio, argomentazioni e strutture retoriche nella polemica di età Cristiana (III–V sec.)*, ed. Alessandro Capone, Recherches sur les Rhétoriques Religieuses 16 (Turnhout: Brepols, 2012), 175–87.

69. Clem. Alex., *Strom.* 6.2.4.3 (κλοπή, "theft"). In 6.2.4–27, partially copied in Eusebios, *Praep. ev.* 10.2, Clement presents a long treatment of how Greek writers putatively copied each other.

The author of the *Refutation* also believes that philosophers took their teachings from non-Greeks (he mentions Egyptians, Persians, and Babylonians), but he shows little interest in depicting the Jews as the fountainhead of philosophy. The Jews come from the race of "God-fearers" (*Ref.* 10.30.8) who predate the philosophers. Yet what the philosophers took from the Jews, if anything, is left unexplained. In his discussion of the Jews in 9.18–29, our author focuses on Jewish customs and practices; he only briefly touches on Jewish thought (9.30). In 10.30–31, he gives a snapshot of Jewish history but again seems to avoid their theology. Our author does not draw a firm connection between Judaism and philosophy, because, it seems, he does not want his opponents to share even a spark of truth. They plagiarized philosophical systems that were, in effect, already wholly Hellenic and cut off from truth. "Heretical" systems that are entirely dependent on "pagan" falsehood (i.e., philosophy) are thus rhetorically de-Christianized and delegitimated.

Organization

The overall organization of the *Refutation* is tripartite. In books 1 and 4, our author presents the sources that are putatively plagiarized by his opponents (namely, Greek philosophy, the mystery cults, astrology, and magic). Second, in books 5–9 he deals with his (mostly Christian) opponents in what he believes to be roughly chronological order. He conceives of them as belonging to a kind of "succession."[70] Initially, there are the servants of the "snake" (Naassenes, Sethians, Peratai), then the two fountainheads of gnosis (Simon and Valentinus). Following them are more recent offshoots (Tatian, Hermogenes, Apelles, and so on). Finally, there are contemporary "heresies" (Noetians, Kallistians, and Elchasaites). Third, after a somewhat uneven summary in book 10, our author presents his own "True Doctrine" (ὁ τῆς ἀληθείας λόγος, 10.4). This doctrine, he believes, possesses no derivation except God alone.

In many ways, our author attempts to compose a work that—despite its size—is relatively "user-friendly." Apparently, our author himself adds the tables of contents that begin each book. He often provides summaries of material dealt with before when he thinks that they facilitate his comparison. In book 10, he offers a fairly generous, if selective, summary of all his

70. On succession, see further Allen Brent, "Diogenes Laertius and His Apostolic Succession," *JEH* 44 (1993): 367–89.

opponents' teachings. He does so in order to more readily compare these teachings with his own "true doctrine."[71]

Genealogy

The author's primary heresiographical procedure can be summed up in a single line: he exposes (or rather imposes) a genealogical connection between Hellenes and "heretics." He announces this procedure, once again, in his preface:

> In order to prove these facts, it seems right first of all to exhibit plainly the doctrines of the Greek philosophers to my readers, since these opinions are older than the heresies and more reverent toward the divine. Second, I will compare each heresy with each philosopher since the founder of the heresy, after applying himself to these arguments, stole them by adopting their basic rudiments and from them—rushing headlong to worse teachings—established his dogma. (*Ref.* 1, *pref.* §§8–9)

Once our writer has established a genealogical link between his Christian opponents and Hellenic learning, he constructs a succession between the "heretics" themselves. The first "gnostics" were the Naassenes, and from them derived every later heresy (*Ref.* 5.6.4). Gnostic, it seems, is not a technical self-designation of these groups but a diffuse, global category that our author uses to connect his opponents.[72] The gnostic groups are not limited to book 5 but include others in later books (*Ref.* 7.36.2).

In *Ref.* 5.11.1, the author likens the Naassenes to the first head of the hydra, from which all other heads emerged. Thus, if he initially strikes the Naassenes (the archetypal heresy), he believes that he can "kill the whole beast."[73] This is because, as he claims, "neither do the other heresies declare a doctrine significantly different from this [Naassene teaching] (coiled together as they are by a single spirit of deceit!).… It is only by the exchange of words and names that they want the heads of the snake to multiply!" In 5.23.3, he repeats his thesis that "all" (πάντες) heretical groups are "driven

---

71. On *Refutation*'s organization, see further Castelli, "Saggio introduttivo," 23–29.

72. On those who used γνώστικος as a self-designation, see David Brakke, *The Gnostics: Myth, Ritual, and Diversity in Early Christianity* (Cambridge: Harvard University Press, 2010), 30–40.

73. Irenaeus had already compared the Valentinian school to the hydra (*Haer.* 1.30.15). On heresies as introducing and multiplying difference, see Pouderon, "Hippolyte, un regard," 49–52.

by one spirit … as they variously narrate and relate the same doctrines in different ways." This statement indicates that the writer saw an inner (putatively spiritual) connection shared among the heresies. This inner relation, he infers, constitutes a genealogical link.

To demonstrate how thin lines of doctrinal similitude can turn into genealogical succession, we turn to book 9. Here our author connects seriatim thinkers as diverse as Herakleitos, Noetos, Epigonos, Kleomedes, Zephyrinos, and Kallistos—boasting that he has revealed the "succession of their genealogy" (γενεαλογίας αὐτῶν τὴν διαδοχήν) (*Ref.* 9.8.1). The basis of his claim is a tendentious exposition of Herakleitos that attempts (in simple terms) to derive Christian Monarchianism from this Presocratic philosopher (*Ref.* 9.8–10.8).[74]

The author of the *Refutation* has been roundly (and rightly) criticized for making strained comparisons between his enemies and Greek philosophers.[75] But despite the invented genealogical links that he constructs, his comparisons are often creative, occasionally illuminating, and always thought-provoking.[76]

Precursors

Our author had at least two immediate precursors for genealogically tracing "heretics" to philosophers: Irenaeus of Lyons and Clement of Alexandria.

For the bishop of Lyons, gnostic number speculation was perverted Pythagoreanism (*Haer.* 1.1.1), the Basilideans borrowed their principles from astrologers (*Haer.* 1.24.7), and the followers of Ptolemy the Valentinian took their theology from Homer (*Haer.* 1.12.1). Irenaeus likened the

---

74. On our author's heresiographical techniques, see further Hervé Inglebert, *Interpretatio Christiana: Les mutations des saviors* (Paris: Institut d'Études Augustiniennes, 2001), 434–37; Winrich Löhr, "The Continuing Construction of Heresy: Hippolyt's Refutatio in Context," in Aragione and Norelli, *Des évêques*, 25–42; Kendra Eshleman, *The Social World of Intellectuals in the Roman Empire: Sophists, Philosophers, and Christians*, Greek Culture in the Roman World (Cambridge: Cambridge University Press, 2012), 228–35.

75. Vallée, *Study*, 50; Klaus Koschorke, *Hippolyt's Ketzerbekämpfung und Polemik gegen die Gnostiker: Eine tendenzkritische Untersuchung seiner "Refutatio omnium haeresium"* (Wiesbaden: Harrassowitz, 1975), 100. Note also Bertrand, "Notion."

76. For a reasonable defense of our author's comparative endeavors, see Catherine Osborne, *Rethinking Early Greek Philosophy: Hippolytus of Rome and the Presocratics* (London: Duckworth, 1987), 35–182.

birth of the Savior, fruit of the Fullness, to the making of Pandora in the poetry of Hesiod (*Haer.* 2.14.4; cf. 2.21.2; 2.30.4).

Especially significant is *Haer.* 2.14.2–6, where Irenaeus—his pen dripping with irony and disdain—lists the "real" sources of Valentinian thought as Thales, Homer, Anaximandros, Anaxagoras, Demokritos, Epikouros, Plato, Empedokles, the Stoics, Hesiod, the Cynics, Aristotle, and the Pythagoreans (2.14.2–6).[77] All the figures in this list reappear in the *Refutation*.

In his *Protreptikos*, Clement of Alexandria asserts that all philosophers conceptualized material elements as the first principles of the universe. Thales "praised" water, Anaximenes air; Parmenides introduced fire and earth as gods, while Hippasos and Herakleitos deified fire. Empedokles reckoned Strife and Love (although not material forces) with the four elements. Thus all these philosophers, Clement charged (in a patently polemical inference), worshiped earth as the mother of material elements.[78]

Although they are less obviously materialist, Clement goes on to mention Anaximandros, Anaxagoras, Archelaos, Leukippos, Metrodoros, and Demokritos as those who believed in immanent first principles. He likewise censures the Stoics, "who say that the divine passes through all matter." Aristotle is no better, since his high God is thought to be "the soul of the universe," and the universe itself. Clement consequently cries out:

> For why, O Philosophy?… Why do you infect my life with idols, imagining both wind and air or fire or water or dirt or stones or wood or iron, *this world here*, to be "gods," speaking sublimely (and yet childishly) of the stars and planets as gods to those human beings who are truly wandering through this much-touted astrology (not astronomy)? I yearn for the Lord of the winds, the Lord of the fire, the creator of the universe, the one who leads out the light of the sun. I seek *God*, not the works of God! (*Protr.* 67; cf. *Strom.* 2.4.14.2)[79]

---

77. See further Alain Le Boulluec, *La notion d'hérésie dans la literature grecque, IIe-IIIe siècles*, 2 vols. (Paris: Études augustiniennes, 1985), 1:123–24.

78. Clem. Alex., *Protr.* 64; cf. *Strom.* 1.11.52.4; 6.6.53.2–5.

79. Tertullian, our author's contemporary, also tried to root heresy in philosophy. He called Valentinus *Platonicus* and claimed that whenever the heretics mention a "fiery god" they depend on Herakleitos (*Praesc.* 7). Markion, Tertullian charged, was a zealous student of Stoicism (*Praescr.* 30). In general, philosophers are the "patriarchs of the heretics" (*haereticorum patriarchae*) (*Herm.* 8.3; cf. *An.* 3.1).

Clement is here voicing a widespread philosophical sentiment. Materialism and immanent conceptions of God, so popular in the Hellenistic period, were considered less and less compelling as one moves into Late Antiquity. Second- and third-century patristic writers depended on what might be called "the transcendental (or Platonic) turn" in philosophy, a turn that located ultimate deity in an extracosmic, incorporeal God, untouched by matter and passions. Jews and Christians seized upon this theology as a means to express the transcendence of the biblical God and his rational mediator, the Logos.

Deeply affected by these philosophical trends, the author of the *Refutation* is both more thoroughgoing in his comparisons than Irenaeus and more detailed than Clement. In nine books and most of a tenth, he delays his own teachings to expound, by long excerpts, the doctrines of philosophers and their "heretical" heirs. He devotes an entire book to philosophy (book 1) and offers long summaries of philosophical teachings at key points.

The author of the *Refutation* repeatedly resists seeing any reliable truth in philosophy or Greek wisdom. Clement had tried to claim "truth-loving" Plato and Pythagoreanism for Christianity and repeatedly quoted the "noble" (*γενναῖον*) Herakleitos with respect.[80] Our author, although he faithfully records philosophical ideas, does not see them as sources of truth. Clement cites the poets Homer, Hesiod, Aratos, and Orpheus as poetic witnesses to truth.[81] Our writer—ranking them with the philosophers—views their poems as springboards for heresies. True, the philosophers are "more reverent toward the divine" (*Ref.* 1, *pref.* §8), but they were all wrong in deifying creation (1.26.3).

Unlike most second-century apologists, our author feels no need to make compromises or draw analogies with Greek culture (cf., e.g., Justin, *1 Apol.* 21.1–6). He rhetorically poses as an enemy to all things Greek—apparently viewing most of Greek science as wasted labor (e.g., *Ref.* 4.12.1–2). At the same time, his regular use of Greek tropes and intellectual culture ironically makes him more Hellenic than his predecessors. Our author regularly displays his learning of Greek myths and exegetical techniques, making his own allegories of the hydra (*Ref.* 5.11.1), the stables of Auge-

80. Clem. Alex., *Strom.* 5.10.66.3 (truth-loving Plato); 2.2.8.1 (the noble Herakleitos); cf. *Protr.* 69–72; *Strom.* 1.16.80.5–17.87.7; 1.20.99.1; 4.3.9.1. For Clement's view of philosophy, see *Strom.* 1.1.17–1.2.21; 1.5.28–1.7.38; 5.1.10; 5.5.29.3–6.

81. Clem. Alex., *Protr.* 73–74, 76.

ias (5.27.6), the voyage of Odysseus (7.13.1–2), and the Cretan labyrinth (10.5.1). He writes an entire book against Plato (*On the Universe*) and continues to criticize this famous philosopher in the *Refutation* (1.19). Despite these attacks, our author supports a theology deeply imbued with Platonic thought and categories (*Ref.* 10.32–33).

Comparison and Chronology

There are two primary heresiological methods that our author uses to establish a genealogical connection between Hellenes and "heretics." The first is comparison. Our author believes that by directly comparing his opponents with the teachings of philosophers, their plagiarism becomes obvious. His major term for "comparison" is ἀντιπαράθεσις, paired with the companion verb ἀντιπαρατίθημι.[82]

His comparative method can be described in large part as "juxtaposition plus intuition." That is to say, our author characteristically juxtaposes two sets of ideas, often overloading the reader with information. He then (sometimes much later) makes a genealogical conclusion (x derives from z), inviting his readers to accept as self-evident what in fact requires an imaginative leap.

On four occasions (treating Pythagoras-Valentinus, Aristotle-Basileides, Empedokles-Markion, Herakleitos-Noetos), our author makes direct and relatively focused comparisons, wherein his "parallelomania" reaches epic proportions.[83] But even here his method of juxtaposition plus intuition predominates. His rhetorical strategy is in fact to dazzle the reader with a show of knowledge, leaving much up to their expected sympathy and imagination.[84]

In *Ref.* 10.30–31, we see a second major strategy at work: chronological priority. Here the Jews become useful to our author—but only when reinterpreted as descendants of the "race of God-fearers." This antediluvian "race" was earlier than Greek and non-Greek "races" and was the conduit of every good idea about God. It was from this God-fearing race that

---

82. *Ref.* 5.13.13; 7.29.3. Cf. the antithetical method of Markion in *Ref.* 7.30.1–2; 7.37.2. Our author can also use παράθεσις and σύγκρισις, e.g., in 6.21.2–3 (διὰ τῆς ἐγγίονος παραθέσεως ὁμοῦ καὶ συγκρίσεως).

83. Samuel Sandmel, "Parallelomania," *JBL* 81 (1962): 1–13.

84. Cf. Ian Mueller, "Hippolytus *Retractatus*: A Discussion of Catherine Osborne, *Rethinking Early Greek Philosophy*," *Oxford Studies in Ancient Philosophy* 7 (1989): 233–51 (236).

Babylonians and Egyptians borrowed; the Greeks subsequently took from them; and from them, in turn, the "heretics" derived the rudiments of their teachings in a spiral of degradation. That is to say, as the truths were passed on, they progressively devolved into lies, with the end result that, as Paul wrote, people worshiped the creation rather than the creator (Rom 1:25; cf. *Ref.* 1.26.3; 4.43.1–2; 10.32.5).

The surprisingly late and brief appearance of our author's "true doctrine" (*Ref.* 10.32–33) does not undermine its importance. By offering his own exposition of truth for a final comparison, our author believes that he can decisively unmask and debunk the whole ten books of lies that precede it.[85] It is this "rod of truth" that he uses to beat down the gnostic hydra (5.11.1); it is the wax he uses to drown out the Siren song of his opponents (7.13.1–2); it is, finally, the hammer that he employs to break through the "labyrinth of heresies" (10.5.1).

Audience

Our author boldly addresses his audience in the final book of the *Refutation*: "So master this logic, you Greeks, Egyptians, Chaldeans, and every nation of human beings! And learn from me, the friend of God, the nature of the divine and the nature of his well-ordered craftsmanship" (10.31.6). In his final peroration, he cries out: "Such is the true doctrine of the divine, O mortal Greeks and Barbarians, Chaldeans and Assyrians, Egyptians and Libyans, Indians and Ethiopians, Kelts and Latins who lead in war—all you dwelling in Europe, Asia, and Libya!" (10.34.1). Our author's address to the nations is not a shift from a Christian to a non-Christian audience. Throughout the *Refutation*, the author appeals to a broad readership of Christian and non-Christian φιλομαθεῖς ("diligent students") (e.g., 4.45.2; cf. 5.6.1). In essence, he addresses *every* cultured reader. Keeping in mind this audience is important for understanding our author's larger project: to make Christianity appear intellectually respectable to the cultured elite.

In particular, our author addresses himself to the young, impressionable intellectual whom he seeks to steer into the harbor of salvation. After his exposé of magic, for instance, our author explains: "Nevertheless, my present concern—that many young people have the chance to be saved—has convinced me to instruct and proclaim these things as a safeguard"

85. Mansfeld, *Heresiography*, 59.

(*Ref.* 4.34.4). After relaying "all" of Greek and non-Greek philosophy, our author believes that he leaves "behind to all people [πᾶσι τε ἀνθρώποις] no small provision for life" (9.31.2). His conclusion to his philosophical section is especially noteworthy:

> I observe that my careful attention to these [philosophical] matters has hardly been useless. I observe that my account has become useful not only for a refutation of the heresies but also for the very people who venerate these teachings. If they read the product of my abundant care, they will marvel at my diligent study! They will not despise my scholarly diligence, nor declare that Christians are idiots, when they look into what *they* so idiotically believe! Still more: my account will teach those eager students devoted to truth and will make them more intellectually prepared to easily overturn those who dare to deceive them, since they will have learned not only the principles of the heresies but also the so-called philosophical theories [that back them]. (*Ref.* 4.45.1–2)

In short, the great learning of our author is intended to overturn the lingering suspicion that Christianity appeals to uneducated "idiots" (cf., e.g., Kelsos in Origen, *Cels.* 1.9).

The "Gnostic" Sondergut

George Salmon noted long ago what a valuable addition the *Refutation* made "to our previous knowledge of the Gnostic sects." Groups "which formerly had scarcely been known to us except through the refutations of their opponents, and some whose very names had been unheard of, were now presented to us as described in the very words of those who maintained them."[86]

Some of the excitement wore off, however, when Salmon and later Hans Staehelin argued for an earlier composer of this special material—in fact, a forger who bamboozled our hapless "high priest" and hunter of heresies.[87] The argument was based on certain strangely similar concepts, phrases, and quotes in what became known as the "gnostic Sondergut"

86. George Salmon, "The Cross-References in the 'Philosophumena,'" *Herm* 5 (1885): 389–402 (390).

87. Hans Staehelin, *Die Gnostischen Quellen Hippolyts in seiner Hauptschrift gegen die Häretiker* (Leipzig: August Pries, 1890), 105–6.

(namely, the unique reports on the Naassenes, Peratai, Sethians, Justin, Simon, Basileides, the Doketai, and Monoïmos).[88]

The forger hypothesis was assailed from multiple quarters and collapsed.[89] But out of the rubble there remained the theory of a Sondergut redactor who introduced the verbal and conceptual similarities before our author discovered the Sondergut reports. Nevertheless, no consensus on the identity of this supposed Sondergut redactor has emerged, and no solid proof that our author received the Sondergut as a redacted collection has been adduced.

A perusal of the similarities shows, I believe, that they can be explained (1) by independent use of biblical images and motifs and (2) by the interpolating tendency of our author himself. Our author's interpolations were governed by his threefold aim: (1) to genetically link the "heretics" to each other, (2) to genetically link the "heretics" to "pagan" philosophy and/or religion, and (3) to display his learning to his ideal, cultured readers.[90]

What can one conclude about the Sondergut? In spite of many attacks on its reliability, it remains a great treasure for gnostic studies. Overall, our author felt no need to totally rewrite his sources, since he believed that the very words of his opponents would show their connection to Greek philosophy. Our author did indeed interpolate phrases and quotes in line with his own heresiographical aims—but nothing he adds destroys the basic reliability of the reports. Granted, one must identify his interpolations and distinguish them from his sources, but this is a skill critical scholars already possess. The hazards of interpretation need not hinder us from studying this treasure trove of early (mostly second-century) gnostic writings. Through a gossamer line of transmission—a single manuscript—our author delivered to us eight significantly different writings of (primarily) Christian gnosis in

88. A chart summarizing key similarities in the Sondergut can be found in Marcovich, *Refutatio*, 46–47.

89. See the history of research in Josef Frickel, *Die "Apophasis Megale" in Hippolyt's Refutatio (VI 9–18): Eine Paraphrase zur Apophasis Simons* (Rome: Pontifical Institute of Oriental Studies, 1968), 17–25.

90. On the intellectual culture during our author's time, see G. R. Boys-Stones, *Post-Hellenistic Philosophy: A Study of Its Development from the Stoics to Origen* (Oxford: Oxford University Press, 2001), 151–75; Michael Trapp, "Philosophy, Scholarship, and the World of Learning in the Severan Period," in *Severan Culture*, ed. Simon Swain, Stephen Harrison, and Jaś Elsner (Cambridge: Cambridge University Press, 2007), 470–88; Clemens Scholten, "Autor, Anliegen und Publikum der Refutatio," in Aragione and Norelli, *Des évêques*, 135–66.

their original tongue—treasures that, whatever the faults of the transmitter, we are grateful that he preserved.[91]

A Note on this Translation

The *Refutation of All Heresies* is a difficult text to translate due as much to its transmission history as to the author's consistent method of "cut, paste, tweak, and gloss." Since this translation is primarily meant for scholars, I have endeavored to adhere closely to the Greek. Where possible, I attempt to preserve something of the author's strung-out periods (prominent in his prefaces), daring use of puns, and penchant for rhetorical flourish. To maximize comprehension, however, I have occasionally added words or phrases that fill out clipped summary statements (especially in book 10). Spellings of Greek names are for the most part not Latinized. Due to scholarly convention, however, I have preserved certain forms (e.g., Irenaeus, not Eirenaios; Clement, not Klemens; Aristotle, not Aristoteles). Some names I have enclosed in quotation marks in my notes (e.g., "Valentinus" and "Simon"). This convention is simply to acknowledge that these figures, whom our author purports to expose, are not the actual (historical) subjects of his reports. For some groups (e.g., the "Sethians"), our author seems to have chosen a name that the group (or writer) in question may not have chosen for themselves. Finally, the names of the editors that appear in the notes (i.e., Miller, Duncker and Schneidewin, Wendland, and Marcovich) refer to their respective editions of the *Refutation* (for which see the Bibliography, under Critical Editions).

---

91. See further Aldo Magris, "Gli 'altri gnosticismi' di Ippolito," in Magris, *Confutazione*, 359–80.

Sigla for the Greek Text

- Words in < > are added to reestablish the text.
- Words in [ ] are suspect and not represented in the translation.
- Words in ( ) are faded in the manuscript(s) or fill out intentional scribal abbreviations.
- An ellipsis (…) indicates a lacuna in the text.
- An ellipsis in angled brackets (<…>) indicates a suspected lacuna.

Outline of the Work

1. The numbers in parentheses are page numbers in this volume.

Ὁ κατὰ πασῶν αἱρέσεων ἔλεγχος

<ΤΟΥ ΚΑΤΑ ΠΑΣΩΝ ΑΙΡΕΣΕΩΝ ΕΛΕΓΧΟΥ Α>

1. Τάδε ἔνεστιν ἐν τῇ πρώτῃ τοῦ κατὰ πασῶν αἱρέσεων ἐλέγχου·

2. Τίνα τὰ δόξαντα τοῖς φυσικοῖς φιλοσόφοις καὶ τίνες οὗτοι· καὶ τίνα τὰ τοῖς ἠθικοῖς καὶ τίνες οὗτοι· καὶ τίνα τὰ τοῖς διαλεκτικοῖς καὶ τίνες οἱ διαλεκτικοί.

3. Φυσικοὶ μὲν οὖν Θαλῆς, Πυθαγόρας, Ἐμπεδοκλῆς, Ἡράκλειτος, Ἀναξίμανδρος, Ἀναξιμένης, Ἀναξαγόρας, Ἀρχέλαος, Παρμενίδης, Λεύκιππος, Δημόκριτος, Ξενοφάνης, Ἔκφαντος, Ἵππων.

4. Ἠθικοὶ Σωκράτης Ἀρχελάου μαθητὴς τοῦ φυσικοῦ, Πλάτων Σωκράτους μαθητής· οὗτος τὰς τρεῖς φιλοσοφίας ἔμιξεν.

5. Διαλεκτικοὶ Ἀριστοτέλης Πλάτωνος μαθητής· οὗτος τὴν διαλεκτικὴν συνεστήσατο. Στωϊκοὶ δὲ Χρύσιππος, Ζήνων.

6. Ἐπίκουρος δὲ σχεδὸν ἐναντίαν δόξαν πᾶσιν ἐπεχείρησεν. Πύρρων ὁ Ἀκαδήμιος· οὗτος ἀκαταληψίαν τῶν πάντων λέγει.

Βραχμᾶνες οἱ ἐν Ἰνδοῖς, Δρυΐδαι οἱ ἐν Κελτοῖς, καὶ Ἡσίοδος.

1. Οὐδένα μῦθον τῶν παρ' Ἕλλησιν ὠνομασμένων παραιτητέον· πιστὰ γὰρ καὶ τὰ ἀσύστατα αὐτῶν δόγματα ἡγητέον διὰ τὴν ὑπερβάλλουσαν τῶν

BOOK 1

[TABLE OF CONTENTS]

1. The following is contained in the first book of the *Refutation of All Heresies*.

2. The doctrines and identities of the natural, ethical, and dialectical philosophers.

3. The natural philosophers include Thales, Pythagoras, Empedokles, Herakleitos, Anaximandros, Anaximenes, Anaxagoras, Archelaos, Parmenides, Leukippos, Demokritos, Xenophanes, Ekphantos, and Hippon.

4. The ethical philosophers include Sokrates, a student of Archelaos the natural philosopher, and Plato, student of Sokrates. Plato mixed the three types of philosophy.

5. The dialectical philosophers include Aristotle, student of Plato. Aristotle established the art of dialectic. Also included are the Stoics Chrysippos and Zenon.

6. Epikouros argued a doctrine virtually opposite to all. Pyrrhon the Academic declares the incomprehensibility of all things.

The Brahmans among the Indians, the Druids among the Kelts, and Hesiod.

PREFACE

INTRODUCTION. 1. We must reject no myth touted by the Greeks.[1] Their inconsistent doctrines must be considered trustworthy on account of the

1. On this (ironic) first line, see Enrico Norelli, "Construire l'opposition entre orthodoxie et hérésie à Rome, au IIIe siècle," in Aragione and Norelli, *Des évêques*, 233–55 (252); Gabriella Aragione, "Guerre-éclaire contre les hermétiques, guerre de position contre les philosophes: L'Elenchos et ses protagonistes," in Aragione and Norelli, *Des évêques*, 73–101. On μῦθος used by Christian authors, see Heinz-Günther Nesselrath, "Zur Verwendung des Begriffes μῦθος bei Sokrates von Konstantinopel

αἱρετικῶν μανίαν, οἳ διὰ τὸ σιωπᾶν ἀποκρύπτειν τε τὰ ἄρρητα ἑαυτῶν μυστήρια ἐνομίσθησαν πολλοῖς θεὸν σέβειν. ὧν καὶ πάλαι μετρίως τὰ δόγματα ἐξεθέμεθα, οὐ κατὰ λεπτὸν ἐπιδείξαντες, ἀλλὰ ἁδρομερῶς ἐλέγξαντες—μὴ [ἂν] ἄξιον ἡγησάμενοι τὰ ἄρρητα αὐτῶν εἰς φῶς ἄγειν—, ὅπως, δι' αἰνιγμάτων ἡμῶν ἐκθεμένων τὰ δόξαντα αὐτοῖς, αἰσχυνθέντες μήποτε καὶ τὰ ἄρρητα ἐξειπόντες ἀθέους ἐπιδείξωμεν, παύσωνταί τι τῆς ἀλογίστου γνώμης καὶ ἀθεμίτου ἐπιχειρήσεως.

2. ἀλλ' ἐπεὶ ὁρῶ μὴ δυσωπουμένους αὐτοὺς τὴν ἡμετέραν ἐπιείκειαν μηδὲ λογιζομένους ὡς θεὸς μακροθυμεῖ ὑπ' αὐτῶν βλασφημούμενος, ὅπως ἢ αἰδεσθέντες μετανοήσωσιν ἢ ἐπιμείναντες δικαίως κριθῶσι, βιασθεὶς πρόειμι δείξων αὐτῶν τὰ ἀπόρρητα μυστήρια.

Ἃ τοῖς μυουμένοις μετὰ μεγάλης ἀξιοπιστίας παραδιδόασιν, οὐ πρότερον ὁμολογήσαντες εἰ μὴ τὸν τοιοῦτον δουλώσωνται, χρόνῳ ἀνακρεμάσαντες καὶ βλάσφημον πρὸς τὸν ὄντως θεὸν κατασκευάσαντες, καὶ περιεργίᾳ γλιχόμενον τῆς ἐπαγγελίας ἴδωσι. 3. καὶ τότε, δοκιμάσαντες δέσμιον εἶναι τῆς ἁμαρτίας, μυοῦσι τὸ τέλειον τῶν κακῶν παραδιδόντες, ὅρκοις δήσαντες μήτε ἐξειπεῖν μήτε τῷ τυχόντι μεταδοῦναι εἰ μὴ ὁμοίως δουλωθείη. οὗ μόνον παραδοθέντος οὐκέτι ὅρκος ἀναγκαῖος ἦν· ὁ γὰρ ὑπομείνας παθεῖν καὶ παραλαβεῖν τὰ τέλεια αὐτῶν μυστήρια ἱκανῶς αὐτῷ τῷ ἔργῳ πρός τε τὴν ἰδίαν συνείδησιν καὶ πρὸς τὸ ἑτέροις, μὴ ἐξειπεῖν ἔσται δεδεμένος. 4. εἰ γὰρ ἐξείποι τινὶ ἀνθρώπων τὸ τοιοῦτον ἀνόμημα, οὔτε ἐν ἀνθρώποις λογισθήσεται, οὔτε τὸ φῶς ὁρᾶν ἄξιος ἡγηθήσεται. <...> ἃ καὶ ἄλογα ὄντα. τοιοῦτον ἀνόμημα οὐκ ἐπιχειρεῖ, καθὼς ἐν τοῖς τόποις γενόμενοι ἐροῦμεν.

5. Ἀλλ' ἐπεὶ ἀναγκάζει ἡμᾶς ὁ λόγος εἰς μέγαν βυθὸν διηγήσεως ἐπιβῆναι, οὐχ ἡγούμεθα σιγᾶν, ἀλλὰ τὰ πάντων δόγματα κατὰ λεπτὸν ἐκθέμενοι οὐδὲν

excessive insanity of the heretics. Most people suppose that these heretics worship God due to their silence and the concealed nature of their secret mysteries. A long time ago, I presented their doctrines in a limited fashion, not exposing them in detail, but refuting them in a general way. I did not think it proper to bring their unspeakable mysteries into the light, so that, when I presented their opinions in enigmas (ashamed as I was to declare what is secret and expose them as godless), they might cease somehow from their irrational mind-set and unlawful endeavor.[2]

2. But since I see that they have not blushed before my leniency, nor taken into account the patience of God (though blasphemed by them) that they might repent out of shame or, by remaining intransigent, be judged in righteousness, I will proceed—forced as I am—to reveal their secret mysteries!

These mysteries they hand on to initiates whose loyalty is securely confirmed. They do not profess them beforehand unless they have enslaved their devotee. They dangle him in suspense by the length of time and make him a blasphemer against the true God until they see him inquisitively clinging to their promise with excessive curiosity. 3. Then, having approved him as a prisoner of sin, they initiate him, handing on the perfect rite of their vices,[3] binding him with oaths neither to declare nor to deliver their mysteries to anyone they meet—except one similarly enslaved. Upon simple delivery of the mysteries, an oath is no longer necessary. For the one who waited to experience and receive their perfect mysteries will be, by the deed itself, sufficiently bound in his own conscience and in his duty to others not to reveal them. 4. If he declares to any person so great a crime, he is not recognized among human beings, nor considered worthy to see the light. (These practices are irrational.) He does not dare perform such a crime, as I will explain when I come to the proper passages.[4]

5. But since the treatise forces me to embark on a great abyss of exposition, I do not consider it right to keep secrets. To the contrary: by presenting

und anderen christlichen Autoren der Spätantike," in *Alvarium: Festschift für Christian Gnilka*, ed. W. Blümer, R. Heke, and M. Mülke (Münster: Aschendorff, 2002), 293–301.

2. For speaking in enigmas, see *Ref.* 6.37.2 (a citation of Plato). On the topic of secrecy, see Albert de Jong, "Secrecy I: Antiquity," *DGWE* 1050–54; Bertrand, "Notion," 137; Vallée, *Study*, 53; Christian H. Bull, Liv Ingebord Lied, and J. D. Turner, eds., *Mystery and Secrecy in the Nag Hammadi Collection and Other Ancient Literature: Ideas and Practices; Studies for Einar Thomassen at Sixty*, NHMS 76 (Leiden: Brill, 2012).

3. Τὸ τέλειον τῶν κακῶν, punning on τελετή, "rite," or "initiation."

4. See *Ref.* 5.23.1–2; 5.24.1–2 (Justin); 9.23.4 (Essenes).

σιωπήσομεν. δοκεῖ δέ, εἰ καὶ μακρότερος ἔσται ὁ λόγος, μὴ καμεῖν· οὐδὲ γὰρ μικράν τινα βοήθειαν τῷ τῶν ἀνθρώπων βίῳ καταλείψομεν πρὸς τὸ μηκέτι πλανᾶσθαι, φανερῶς πάντων ὁρώντων τὰ κρύφια αὐτῶν καὶ ἄρρητα ὄργια, ἃ ταμιευόμενοι μόνοις τοῖς μύσταις παραδιδόασιν.

6. Ταῦτα δὲ ἕτερος οὐκ ἐλέγξει ἢ τὸ ἐν ἐκκλησίᾳ παραδοθὲν ἅγιον πνεῦμα, οὗ τυχόντες πρότεροι οἱ ἀπόστολοι μετέδοσαν τοῖς ὀρθῶς πεπιστευκόσιν. ὧν ἡμεῖς διάδοχοι τυγχάνοντες, τῆς τε αὐτῆς χάριτος μετέχοντες ἀρχιερατείας τε καὶ διδασκαλίας, καὶ φρουροὶ τῆς ἐκκλησίας λελογισμένοι, οὐκ ὀφθαλμῷ νυστάζομεν οὐδὲ λόγον ὀρθὸν σιωπῶμεν, ἀλλ᾽ οὐδὲ πάσῃ ψυχῇ καὶ σώματι ἐργαζόμενοι κάμνομεν ἄξια ἀξίως θεῷ τῷ εὐεργέτῃ ἀνταποδιδόναι πειρώμενοι· καὶ οὐδὲ οὕτως κατ᾽ ἀξίαν ἀμειβόμενοι, πλὴν ἐν οἷς πεπιστεύμεθα μὴ ἀτονοῦντες, ἀλλὰ τοῦ ἰδίου καιροῦ τὰ μέτρα ἐπιτελοῦντες καὶ ὅσα παρέχει τὸ ἅγιον πνεῦμα πᾶσιν ἀφθόνως κοινωνοῦντες. 7. οὐ μόνον ἀλλότρια δι᾽ ἐλέγχου εἰς φανερὸν ἄγοντες, ἀλλὰ καὶ ὅσα ἡ ἀλήθεια ὑπὸ τῆς τοῦ πατρὸς χάριτος παραλαβοῦσα ἀνθρώποις διηκόνησε, ταῦτα καὶ διὰ λόγου σημειούμενοι καὶ διὰ γραμμάτων ἐμμάρτυρα ποιούμενοι ἀνεπαισχύντως κηρύσσομεν.

8. Ἵνα οὖν, καθὼς φθάσαντες εἴπομεν, ἀθέους αὐτοὺς ἐπιδείξωμεν καὶ κατὰ γνώμην καὶ κατὰ τρόπον καὶ κατὰ ἔργον, ὅθεν τε τὰ ἐπιχειρήματα αὐτοῖς γεγένηται, καὶ ὅτι μηθὲν ἐξ ἁγίων γραφῶν λαβόντες ταῦτα ἐπεχείρησαν, ἤ τινος ἁγίου διαδοχὴν φυλάξαντες ἐπὶ ταῦτα ὥρμησαν, ἀλλ᾽ ἔστιν αὐτοῖς τὰ δοξαζόμενα <τὴν> ἀρχὴν μὲν ἐκ τῆς Ἑλλήνων σοφίας λαβόντα, ἐκ

the teachings of all in detail, I will keep no secrets. It seems right, even if my account will be quite long, not to grow faint. For I will leave behind no small aid to the life of human beings to prevent future error, when everyone clearly sees all their hidden and secret rites, which they, holding in reserve, hand on only to their initiates.

6. Yet no other will refute these teachings except the Holy Spirit handed on in the church.[5] The apostles obtained this Spirit beforehand and shared it with orthodox believers. I, their successor, participate in the same grace of high priesthood and teaching.[6] Accounted as a guardian of the church, my eyes do not sleep, nor do I keep secret the orthodox doctrine.[7] Nevertheless, not even as I labor with my whole soul and body do I grow faint as I endeavor worthily to make worthy repayment to God my benefactor. Not even by such labor do I make a fair exchange! Still, I am not slack in those matters with which I have been entrusted. I fulfill the due measures of my time and generously share with all whatever the Holy Spirit provides. 7. I preach without shame, bringing out into the open not only alien and dangerous material through an exposé but also whatever the Truth has received by the Father's grace and administered to human beings—these things I both record from conversation and bring as testimony from written reports.[8]

THESIS. 8. Therefore, as I began to say, I intend (1) to expose these heretics as godless in opinion, character, and deed; (2) to expose the source of their arguments; and (3) to show that what they schemed they hardly took from the holy scriptures or arrived at by preserving the teaching handed on by any holy person. Rather, I intend to prove that they took the starting point of their doctrines from Greek wisdom, from the dogmas

---

5. For the Spirit handed on (*παραδοθέν*) in the church, see Pouderon, "Hippolyte, un regard," 43–49.

6. Concerning the author's high priesthood (*ἀρχιερατείας*), see Hamel, *Kirche bei Hippolyt*, 163–72; Brent, *Hippolytus*, 475–81, 511–12. On the teaching (*διδασκαλία*) of the bishop, see Mart. Pol. 16.2 (where Polycarp is called "an apostolic and prophetic teacher" [*διδάσκαλος ἀποστολικὸς καὶ προφητικός*]). Further texts in *PGL*, s.v. *ἐπίσκοπος* B.3.h.

7. Ὀρθὸς λόγος ("orthodox doctrine") is a widely used philosophical phrase adopted by church writers (e.g., Justin, *Dial.* 3.3: *ἄνευ δὲ φιλοσοφίας καὶ ὀρθοῦ λόγου* ["without philosophy and right reason"]; Clem. Alex., *Paed.* 1.101.1: *πᾶν τὸ παρὰ τὸν λόγον τὸν ὀρθὸν τοῦτο ἁμάρτημά ἐστιν* ["everything against right reason is sin"]).

8. For preaching without shame, see Rom 1:16 (Οὐ *γὰρ ἐπαισχύνομαι τὸ εὐαγγέλιον* ["for I am not ashamed of the gospel"]).

δογμάτων φιλοσοφουμένων καὶ μυστηρίων ἐπικεχειρημένων καὶ ἀστρολόγων ῥεμβομένων· δοκεῖ οὖν πρότερον ἐκθεμένους τὰ δόξαντα τοῖς τῶν Ἑλλήνων φιλοσόφοις ἐπιδεῖξαι τοῖς ἐντυγχάνουσιν ὄντα τούτων παλαιότερα καὶ πρὸς τὸ θεῖον σεμνότερα, 9. ἔπειτα συμβαλεῖν ἑκάστην αἵρεσιν ἑκάστῳ, ὡς τούτοις τοῖς ἐπιχειρήμασιν ἐπιβαλόμενος ὁ πρωτοστατήσας τῆς αἱρέσεως ἐπλεονέκτησε λαβόμενος τὰς ἀρχὰς καὶ ἐκ τούτων ἐπὶ τὰ χείρονα ὁρμηθεὶς τὸ δόγμα συνεστήσατο.

10. Ἔστι μὲν οὖν πόνου μεστὸν τὸ ἐπιχειρούμενον καὶ πολλῆς δεόμενον ἱστορίας, ἀλλ' οὐκ ἐνδεήσομεν· ὕστερον γὰρ εὐφρανεῖ, ὡς ἀθλητὴν μετὰ πολὺν πόνον στεφάνου τυχόντα ἢ ἔμπορον μετὰ μέγαν θαλάσσης σάλον κερδάναντα ἢ γεωργὸν μετὰ ἱδρῶτα προσώπου καρπῶν ἀπολαύσαντα ἢ προφήτην μετὰ ὀνειδισμοὺς καὶ ὕβρεις ὁρῶντα τὰ λαληθέντα ἀποβαίνοντα.

11. ἀρξάμενοι τοίνυν ἐροῦμεν, τίνες οἱ παρ' Ἕλλησι πρῶτοι φιλοσοφίαν φυσικὴν ἐπιδείξαντες—τούτων γὰρ μάλιστα γεγένηνται κλεψίλογοι οἱ τῶν αἱρέσεων πρωτοστατήσαντες, ὡς μετέπειτα ἐν τῇ πρὸς ἀλλήλους συμβολῇ ἐπιδείξομεν—, ἑκάστῳ τε τῶν προαρξαμένων τὰ ἴδια ἀποδιδόντες γυμνοὺς καὶ ἀσχήμονας τοὺς αἱρεσιάρχας παραστήσομεν.

of the philosophers, from manufactured mysteries, and from wandering astrologers. In order to prove these facts, it seems right first of all to exhibit plainly the doctrines of the Greek philosophers to my readers, since these opinions are older than the heresies and more reverent toward the divine. 9. Second, I will compare each heresy with each philosopher since the founder of the heresy, after applying himself to these arguments, stole them by adopting their basic rudiments and from them—rushing headlong to worse teachings—established his dogma.[9]

10. Now, my project is full of toil and requires much research, but I will not be without resources. In time to come these labors will make me glad, as in the case of an athlete who—after much toil—obtains a crown, or a merchant who—after a great surging of the sea—makes a profit, or a farmer who—after much sweat from his face—enjoys his harvest, or a prophet who—after rebukes and acts of violence—sees what he has spoken come to pass.[10]

11. To begin, then, I will pronounce who among the Greeks were the first to profess natural philosophy—for of these especially those who founded heresies have become plagiarizers (as I will show later when comparing them).[11] Then, when I restore to these authors their own teachings, I will present the leading heretics naked and full of shame.[12]

---

9. On the understanding of ἑκάστῳ as ἑκάστῳ φιλοσόφῳ ("with each philosopher"), see Koschorke, *Ketzerbekämpfung*, 9.

10. For sweat on the face, see Gen 3:19. For the other images of toil and victory, see, e.g., 1 Cor 9:24–27; Jas 5:7; Ignatios, *Pol.* 2.3; 3.1; 2 Clem. 7.3.

11. "Plagiarizers" here translates κλεψίλογοι, possibly our author's own coinage. Jan Bergman shows how this word appears at key points in the *Refutation* ("Kleine Beiträge zum Naassenertraktat," in *Proceedings of the International Colloquium on Gnosticism: Stockholm, August 20—25, 1973*, ed. Geo Widengren [Stockholm: Almqvist & Wiksell, 1977], 74–100 [76–77]).

12. Like Adam, who sinned (Gen 3:10–11). In organizing the philosophers that follow, our author identifies the putative founder of a particular school and then treats the later philosophical members of that school. He begins with Thales, head of the Ionian school. He proceeds immediately to Pythagoras, founder of the Italian school, and its philosophical members, namely, Empedokles and Herakleitos. Beginning in chap. 5, he realizes that he must attend to the members of the Ionian school, which he does in chaps. 6–9. He subsequently turns to the Eleatics in chaps. 11–16. In chap. 18 he treats Sokrates as continuing the Ionian succession, but also starting a new branch of ethical philosophy. A long chapter on Plato (19), treats him as a catch-all figure who combined the various philosophies. Aristotle is connected to Plato but starts his own dialectical branch of philosophy. Then come the Hellenistic (Stoic, Epicurean, Skeptic) and foreign (Brahman, Druid) philosophers, with Hesiod as an appendix. Cf.

1. 1. Λέγεται Θαλῆν τὸν Μιλήσιον, ἕνα τῶν ἑπτὰ σοφῶν, πρῶτον ἐπικεχειρηκέναι φιλοσοφίαν φυσικήν. 2. οὗτος ἔφη ἀρχὴν τοῦ παντὸς εἶναι καὶ τέλος τὸ ὕδωρ· ἐκ γὰρ αὐτοῦ τὰ πάντα συνίστασθαι πηγνυμένου καὶ πάλιν διανιεμένου, ἐπιφέρεσθαί τε αὐτῷ τὰ πάντα. 3. ἀφ' οὗ καὶ σεισμοὺς καὶ πνευμάτων συστροφὰς καὶ <ἄστρων> κινήσεις γίνεσθαι. καὶ τὰ πάντα φέρεσθαί τε καὶ ῥεῖν, τῇ τοῦ πρώτου ἀρχηγοῦ τῆς γενέσεως αὐτῶν φύσει συμφερόμενα. θεὸν δὲ τοῦτ' εἶναι, τὸ μήτε ἀρχὴν μήτε τελευτὴν ἔχον.

4. οὗτος περὶ τὸν τῶν ἄστρων λόγον καὶ τὴν ζήτησιν ἀσχοληθεὶς Ἕλλησι ταύτης τῆς μαθήσεως αἴτιος πρῶτος γίνεται. ὃς ἀποβλέπων πρὸς τὸν οὐρανὸν καὶ τὰ ἄνω ἐπιμελῶς κατανοεῖν λέγων, εἰς φρέαρ ἐνέπεσεν· ὃν ἐγγελῶσά τις θεραπαινὶς Θρᾷττα τοὔνομα ἔφη· τὰ ἐν οὐρανῷ προθυμούμενος εἰδέναι, τὰ ἐν ποσὶν οὐκ εἶδεν.

ἐγένετο δὲ κατὰ Κροῖσον.

THE IONIAN SUCCESSION

THALES. 1. 1. It is said that Thales the Milesian, one of the Seven Sages, was the first to pursue natural philosophy.[13] 2. He affirmed that water was the beginning and end of the universe.[14] From it all things are composed when water is successively condensed and dissolved, and all things float on top of it. 3. From water also come earthquakes, whirlwinds, and the movements of heavenly bodies.[15] In addition, all things are borne along in flux, naturally agreeing with the author of their generation.[16] Water is God, since it has neither beginning nor end.[17]

4. This fellow, busying himself with an account and investigation of the heavenly bodies, became the first cause of this learning among the Greeks. He it was who, gazing at the sky and saying that he carefully understood the things above, fell into a well. Laughing at him, a serving girl (whose name was Thratta) said: "Eager to know what is in the sky, he did not see what was at his feet!"[18]

He was alive in the time of Kroisos.

---

the pattern of succession in Clem. Alex., *Strom.* 1.14.62–64. See further Robert M. Grant, *After the New Testament* (Philadelphia: Fortress, 1967), 85–112; David Runia, "What Is Doxography?" in *Ancient Histories of Medicine: Essays in Medical Doxography and Historiography in Classical Antiquity*, ed. Philip J. van der Eijk, Studies in Ancient Medicine 20 (Leiden: Brill, 1999), 33–55.

13. The most comprehensive collection of Thales fragments is Georg Wöhrle and Richard McKirahan, *The Milesians: Thales*, Traditio Praesocratica 1 (Berlin: de Gruyter, 2014). For the current passage, with parallels, see ibid., 184. Diogenes Laertios also presents an account of Thales roughly contemporary to our author (*Vit. phil.* 1.22–44).

14. Cf. Iren., *Haer.* 2.14.2.

15. The "heavenly bodies" (ἄστρων) is an emendation for P's "airs" (ἀέρων). Cf. Apuleius, *Flor.* 18.30–35, who mentions both the blowing of winds and the movements of heavenly bodies. Water as the cause of earthquakes is also attributed to Thales in Ps.-Plutarch, *Plac. philos.* 3.15, 896c; Seneca, *Nat.* 3.14.1.

16. Universal flux is reminiscent of Herakleitos.

17. In response to the question "What is the divine?" Thales reportedly answered: "What has neither beginning nor end" (τὸ μήτε ἀρχὴν μήτε τελευτὴν ἔχον) (Clem. Alex., *Strom.* 5.14.96.4; Diog. L., *Vit. phil.* 1.36). That water *is* God may be a deduction of our author.

18. This story is told in Plato, *Theaet.* 174a; Diog. L., *Vit. phil.* 1.34. It serves a polemical function here. See further H. Blumenberg, "Der Sturz des Protophilosophen: Zur Komik der reinen Theorie anhand einer Rezeptionsgeschichte der Thales Anekdote," in *Das Komische*, ed. Wolfgang Preisendanz and Rainer Warning, Poetik und Hermeneutik 7 (Munich: W. Fink, 1976), 11–64.

2. 1. Ἔστι δὲ καὶ ἑτέρα φιλοσοφία οὐ μακρὰν τῶν αὐτῶν χρόνων, ἧς ἦρξε Πυθαγόρας, ὃν Σάμιόν τινες λέγουσιν. ἣν Ἰταλικὴν προσηγόρευσαν διὰ τὸ τὸν Πυθαγόραν φεύγοντα Πολυκράτην τὸν Σαμίων τύραννον οἰκῆσαι πόλιν τῆς Ἰταλίας κἀκεῖ τὸν βίον πληρῶσαι. οὗ τὴν αἵρεσιν οἱ διαδεξάμενοι οὐ πολὺ διήνεγκαν τοῦ αὐτοῦ φρονήματος.

2. καὶ αὐτὸς δὲ περὶ φυσικῶν ζητήσας ἔμιξεν ἀστρονομίαν καὶ γεωμετρίαν καὶ μουσικήν· καὶ οὕτως μονάδα μὲν εἶναι ἀπεφήνατο τὸν θεόν, ἀριθμοῦ δὲ φύσιν περιέργως καταμαθὼν μελῳδεῖν ἔφη τὸν κόσμον καὶ ἁρμονίᾳ συγκεῖσθαι, καὶ τῶν ἑπτὰ ἄστρων πρῶτος τὴν κίνησιν εἰς ῥυθμὸν καὶ μέλος ἤγαγεν.

3. θαυμάσας δὲ τὴν διοίκησιν τῶν ὅλων ἠξίωσε τὰ πρῶτα σιγᾶν τοὺς μαθητάς, οἱονεὶ μύστας τοῦ παντὸς εἰς τὸν κόσμον ἥκοντας· εἶτα ἐπειδὰν αὐτοῖς

THE ITALIAN SUCCESSION

PYTHAGORAS. **2.** 1. There is another nearly contemporary philosophy that Pythagoras, whom some call a Samian, initiated.[19] It was a philosophy they called "Italian," since Pythagoras, after he fled the Samian tyrant Polykrates, made his home in a city of Italy and there completed his life. The successors of his sect did not differ much from Pythagoras's way of thinking.

2. He also inquired about the things of nature and mixed together the sciences of astronomy, geometry, and music.[20] In accordance with these sciences, he declared that God was a monad.[21] Secondly, after his intensive study of the nature of number, he said that the cosmos plays a tune and is harmonically arranged.[22] He was the first to conduct the movement of the seven planets into rhythm and melody.[23]

TEACHING METHOD. 3. Astounded at the arrangement of the universe, he bid his students keep the preliminary matters secret, as if, when approaching the cosmos, they were initiates of the universe. Then, when he determined that they were capable of instruction in the doctrines, he

---

19. Mansfeld points out the parallels between Ps.-Plutarch, *Plac. philos.* 1.3, and our author's account of Pythagoras, concluding that they depend on the same tradition (*Heresiography*, 22–25).

20. For Pythagorean science, see Walter Burkert, *Lore and Science in Ancient Pythagoreanism*, trans. Edwin L. Minar (Cambridge: Harvard University Press, 1972), 299–482; Robert Tubbs, *What Is a Number? Mathematical Concepts and Their Origins* (Baltimore: Johns Hopkins University Press, 2009), 1–22.

21. Ps.-Plutarch, *Plac. philos.* 1.7, 881e, and Stobaios, *Ecl.* 1.1.29^{b} (Wachsmuth and Hense, 1:34), inform us that God is the monad, the Good, and mind itself. For the distinction between the monad (μόνας) and the number one (ἕν), see Theon of Smyrna, *Exp. math.* (Hiller, 19,7–21,14); [Iamblichos], *Theolog. arith.* 1–7 (de Falco); Philo, *QG* 4.110; Clem. Alex., *Paed.* 1.8.71.2. See further Joel Kalvesmaki, *The Theology of Arithmetic: Number Symbolism in Platonism and Early Christianity*, Hellenic Studies 59 (Washington, DC: Center for Hellenic Studies, 2013), 126, 175–82.

22. Harmonic arrangement is also affirmed below in *Ref.* 1.2.13. A similar idea is attributed to Plato in *Ref.* 4.10.5. Cf. Aristotle, *Metaph.* 1.5, 986a3–4 (τὸν ὅλον οὐρανὸν ἁρμονίαν εἶναι καὶ ἀριθμόν); Plutarch, *Mus.* 1147a (πάντα γὰρ καθ' ἁρμονίαν); Sext. Emp., *Math.* 4.6 (τὸν ὅλον κόσμον κατὰ ἁρμονίαν); Diog. L., *Vit. phil.* 8.33 (καθ' ἁρμονίαν συνεστάναι τὰ ὅλα). See further Arnold Hermann, *To Think Like God: Pythagoras and Parmenides* (Las Vegas: Parmenides, 2004), 93–98.

23. Cf. Plato, *Tim.* 35a–37a. This theory is explained and criticized by Aristotle, *Cael.* 2.9, 290b12–291a27. See further Burkert, *Lore and Science*, 350–57; Hermann, *To Think Like God*, 99–106.

ἱκανῶς παιδείας τῆς τῶν λόγων δόξῃ μετεῖναι καὶ δυνατῶς περὶ ἄστρων καὶ φύσεως φιλοσοφήσωσι, καθαροὺς κρίνας τότε κελεύει φθέγγεσθαι. 4. οὗτος τοὺς μαθητὰς διεῖλε καὶ τοὺς μὲν ἐσωτερικούς, τοὺς δὲ ἐξωτερικοὺς ἐκάλεσεν· τοῖς μὲν γὰρ τὰ τελεώτερα μαθήματα ἐπίστευε, τοῖς δὲ τὰ μετριώτερα.

5. ἐφήψατο δὲ καὶ μαγικῆς, ὥς φασι, καὶ φυσιογνωμονικὴν αὐτὸς ἐξεῦρεν.

Ἀριθμούς τινας καὶ μέτρα ὑποθέμενος λέγει τὴν ἀρχὴν τῆς ἀριθμητικῆς φιλοσοφίαν κατὰ σύνθεσιν περιέχειν τόνδε τὸν τρόπον. 6. ἀριθμὸς γέγονε πρῶτος ἀρχή—ὅπερ ἐστὶν ἕν, ἀόριστον, ἀκατάληπτον—, ἔχων ἐν ἑαυτῷ πάντας τοὺς ἐπ᾽ ἄπειρον δυναμένους ἐλθεῖν ἀριθμοὺς κατὰ τὸ πλῆθος. τῶν δὲ ἀριθμῶν ἀρχὴ γέγονε καθ᾽ ὑπόστασιν ἡ πρώτη μονάς, ἥτις ἐστὶ μονὰς ἄρσην, γεννῶσα πατρικῶς πάντας τοὺς ἄλλους ἀριθμούς.

δεύτερον ἡ δυάς, θῆλυς ἀριθμός, ὁ δὲ αὐτὸς καὶ ἄρτιος ὑπὸ τῶν ἀριθμητικῶν καλεῖται.

τρίτον ἡ τριάς, ἀριθμὸς ἄρσην· 7. οὗτος καὶ περισσὸς ὑπὸ τῶν ἀριθμητικῶν νενομοθέτηται καλεῖσθαι.

ἐπὶ πᾶσι δὲ τούτοις ἡ τετράς, θῆλυς ἀριθμός, ὁ δὲ αὐτὸς καὶ ἄρτιος καλεῖται, ὅτι θῆλύς ἐστιν.

8. γεγόνασιν οὖν οἱ πάντες ἀριθμοὶ ληφθέντες ἀπὸ γένους τέσσαρες—ἀριθμὸς δ᾽ ἦν τὸ γένος ἀόριστος—, ἀφ᾽ ὧν ὁ τέλειος αὐτοῖς συνέστηκεν ἀριθμός, ἡ δεκάς· τὸ γὰρ ἕν, δύο, τρία, τέσσαρα γίνεται δέκα, ἐὰν ἑκάστῳ τῶν ἀριθμῶν φυλάσσηται κατ᾽ οὐσίαν τὸ οἰκεῖον ὄνομα. 9. ταύτην ὁ Πυθαγόρας ἔφη ἱερὰν τετρακτύν,

imparted them. If they philosophized ably about the heavenly bodies and nature, he judged them pure, and afterward allowed them to speak.[24] 4. He divided his students, calling some "the inner circle" and others "the outer circle." To the first group he entrusted his more perfect lessons, while to the latter the more limited.[25]

5. He applied himself to magic too, as they say, and himself invented the art of physiognomy.[26]

THEORY OF NUMBER. Proposing certain numbers and measures, he teaches that the first principle of arithmetic contains philosophy according to a process of calculation.[27] 6. The first principle is the first number: the number one. The number one is unlimited, incomprehensible, and holds in itself all the numbers capable of reaching infinity by multiplication. As a base, the primal monad is the first principle of numbers. The monad is male, generating all the other numbers like a father.

The second number is the dyad, a female number, called "even" by the arithmeticians.[28]

The third is the triad, a male number. 7. This one is as a rule called "odd" by the arithmeticians.

Over all these is the tetrad, a female number, called "even," since it is female.

8. So all the numbers arose, stemming from four classes (number itself being an undefined class). From these classes, the perfect number was composed: the decad. For one plus two plus three plus four equals ten, if we preserve for each of the numbers their essential and appropriate name.[29] 9. Pythagoras called the decad "the holy Tetraktys":

24. See below *Ref.* 1.2.16–18; cf. Iamblichos, *Vit. Pyth.* 72–74.

25. See further Burkert, *Lore and Science*, 192–208.

26. Physiognomy is the study of the features of the face or the form of the body to judge character. It is reported that Pythagoras would judge someone's character from their physical features before admitting them to discipleship (Porphyry, *Vit. Pyth.* 13, 54; Iamblichos, *Vit. Pyth.* 71, 74).

27. This section on number theory is largely reproduced in *Ref.* 4.51.4–8; cf. 6.23.1–5.

28. For the monad and dyad, see Diog. L., *Vit. phil.* 8.25, with the commentary of A. Delatte, *La vie de Pythagore de Diogène Laërce* (Brussels: Académie royale de Belgique, 1922), 198–200; Ps.-Plutarch, *Plac. philos.* 1.3, 876e; Sext. Emp., *Math.* 10.261–262, 276–277; Iren., *Haer.* 2.14.6; Burkert, *Lore and Science*, 53–59.

29. On the decad, see Theophrastos, frag. 227a (FHSG 1:412–13): "The Pythago-

πηγὴν ἀενάου φύσεως [ὡς] ῥιζώματ᾽ ἔχουσαν

ἐν ἑαυτῇ, καὶ ἐκ τούτου τοῦ ἀριθμοῦ πάντας ἔχειν τοὺς ἀριθμοὺς τὴν ἀρχήν· ὁ γὰρ ἕνδεκα καὶ ὁ δώδεκα καὶ οἱ λοιποὶ τὴν ἀρχὴν τοῦ εἶναι ἐκ τοῦ δέκα μετέχουσιν.

ταύτης τῆς δεκάδος, τοῦ τελείου ἀριθμοῦ, τὰ τέσσαρα καλεῖται μέρη·

1. ἀριθμός,
2. μονάς,
3. δύναμις,
4. κύβος.

10. ὧν καὶ ἐπιπλοκαὶ καὶ μίξεις πρὸς γένεσιν αὐξήσεως γίνονται, κατὰ φύσιν τὸν γόνιμον ἀριθμὸν ἀποτελοῦσαι· ὅταν γὰρ δύναμις αὐτὴ ἐφ᾽ ἑαυτὴν κυβισθῇ, γέγονε δυναμοδύναμις· ὅταν δὲ δύναμις ἐπὶ κύβον, <γέγονε δυναμόκυβος· ὅταν δὲ κύβος ἐπὶ κύβον,> γέγονε κυβόκυβος· ὡς γίνεσθαι τοὺς πάντας ἀριθμούς, ἐξ ὧν ἡ τῶν γινομένων γένεσις γίνεται, ἑπτά·

1. ἀριθμόν,
2. μονάδα,
3. δύναμιν,
4. κύβον,
5. δυναμοδύναμιν,
6. δυναμόκυβον,
7. κυβόκυβον.

A fount possessing the roots of ever-flowing nature

in itself.[30] From this number all numbers have their first principle. For eleven, twelve, and the remaining numbers share their source of being from ten.

There are what are called "four components" of the decad, or perfect number:

1. a number,
2. a single number (x),
3. a squared number (x^2), and
4. a cubed number (x^3).[31]

10. From these components there arise further multiplications and combinations for the origin of growth, bringing to natural completion the productive number. For x^2 times x^2 is a square squared (x^4).[32] When x^2 is multiplied by x^3, it becomes a cube squared (x^5). When x^3 is multiplied by x^3, it becomes a cube cubed (x^6). Accordingly, all the numbers from which come the origin of all generated beings are seven:

1. number,
2. a single number,
3. the squared number,
4. the cubed number,
5. the square squared,
6. the cube squared, and
7. the cube cubed.[33]

---

reans said that the numbers from the monad to the decad were the principles of all things [ἀρχὰς ἔλεγον τῶν ἁπάντων]."

30. This verse is variously quoted in *Ref.* 4.51.7; 6.23.4; 6.34.1 ("Valentinus"). Cf. [Iamblichos], *Theolog. arith.* 22–23 (de Falco). See further A. Delatte, *Études sur la littérature pythagoricienne* (Paris: Librairie Ancienne, 1915), 249–68; Paul Kucharski, *Étude sur la doctrine pythagoricienne de la Tétrade* (Paris: Belles Lettres, 1952); Burkert, *Lore and Science*, 72–73, 186–90; R. Apatow, "The Tetraktys: The Cosmic Paradigm of the Ancient Pythagoreans," *Parab* 24.3 (1999): 38–43; Kalvesmaki, *Theology*, 183–86.

31. For the four parts of number, see Kalvesmaki, *Theology*, 181–82.

32. Early it was recognized that κυβισθῇ must have the sense of πολυπλασιάζειν ("multiply") (G. Roeper, "Emendationsversuche zu Hippolyti Philosophumena," *Phil* 7 [1852]: 511–53 [532]).

33. Cf. Diophantos, *Arithm.* 1 (Tannery).

11. Οὗτος καὶ ψυχὴν ἀθάνατον εἶπε καὶ μετενσωμάτωσιν· διὸ ἔλεγεν ἑαυτὸν πρὸ μὲν τῶν Τρωϊκῶν Αἰθαλίδην γεγονέναι, ἐν δὲ τοῖς Τρωϊκοῖς Εὔφορβον, μετὰ δὲ ταῦτα Ἑρμότιμον Σάμιον, μεθ᾽ ὃν Πύρρον Δήλιον, πέμπτον Πυθαγόραν.

12. Διόδωρος δὲ ὁ Ἐρετριεὺς καὶ Ἀριστόξενος ὁ μουσικός φασι πρὸς Ζαράταν τὸν Χαλδαῖον ἐληλυθέναι Πυθαγόραν. τὸν δὲ ἐκθέσθαι αὐτῷ δύο εἶναι ἀπ᾽ ἀρχῆς τοῖς οὖσιν αἴτια, πατέρα καὶ μητέρα· καὶ πατέρα μὲν φῶς, μητέρα δὲ σκότος· τοῦ δὲ φωτὸς μέρη θερμόν, ξηρόν, κοῦφον, ταχύ· τοῦ δὲ σκότους ψυχρόν, ὑγρόν, βαρύ, βραδύ· ἐκ δὲ τούτων πάντα τὸν κόσμον συνεστάναι, ἐκ θηλείας καὶ ἄρρενος.

TRANSMIGRATION. 11. This Pythagoras also asserted that the soul is immortal and that there is a transfer from one body to another. Thus he used to say that he himself was Aithalides before the Trojan War, Euphorbos in the Trojan War, then after the war Hermotimos the Samian, subsequently Pyrrhos the Delian, and as fifth in line, Pythagoras.[34]

RELATION TO ZARATAS. 12. Diodoros of Eretria and Aristoxenos the musician say that Pythagoras traveled to Zaratas the Chaldean.[35] He expounded to Pythagoras that, at the beginning, there were two causes of existing things: Father and Mother.[36] Now the Father is light, and the Mother is darkness. The constituents of light are heat, dryness, lightness, and quickness; those of darkness are cold, moisture, heaviness, and slowness. From these, the entire cosmos came together, namely, from female and male principles.

---

34. This tradition is ascribed to Herakleides Pontikos in Diog. L., *Vit. phil.* 8.4—5, and to Pherekydes in *Scholia in Apollonium Rhodium* 1.643 (Wendel). Cf. Diodoros, *Bibl. hist.* 10.6.2; Porphyry, *Vit. Pyth.* 27, 45; Iamblichos, *Vit. Pyth.* 63; Tert., *An.* 28.3–4; *Scholia in Sophoclis Electram* 62 (Xenis). See further Burkert, *Lore and Science*, 138–41.

35. Diodoros of Eretria is an otherwise unknown early Pythagorean. See further *FGH* 1103 (4A: 400–403). Aristoxenos was a Pythagorean writer on music (frags. in Fritz Wehrli, *Die Schule des Aristoteles*, vol. 2 [Basel: B. Schwabe, 1945]). On Zaratas, see *Ref.* 1.2.13; 6.23.2. Pliny distinguished Zoroaster the Persian from Zaratus the Mede (*Nat.* 30.3, 5). Clement of Alexandria says that Pythagoras was student of both Ζωροάστρης the Magos and Ζαράτος the Assyrian (*Strom.* 1.15.69.6–70.1 [the latter tradition from Alexander Polyhistor]). The Peratai use the form Ζωρόαστρις (*Ref.* 5.14.8). For Zaratas/Zarathustra as teacher of Pythagoras, see the texts in Heinrich Dörrie and Matthias Baltes, *Der Platonismus in der Antike: Grundlagen-System-Entwicklung*, 7 vols. (Stuttgart: Bad Cannstatt, 1993), 2:178–85. See further J. Bidez and F. Cumont, *Les mages hellénisés: Zoroastre, Ostanès et Hystaspe d'après la tradition grecque*, 2 vols. (Paris: Belles Lettres, 1938), 1:34 n. 2, 96, 114; Walter Spoerri, "A propos d'un texte d'Hippolyte," *REA* 57 (1955): 267–90; Roger Beck, "Thus Spake Not Zarathuštra: Zoroastrian Pseudepigrapha of the Greco-Roman World," in *A History of Zoroastrianism under Macedonian and Roman Rule*, ed. Mary Boyce and Frantz Grenet, 3 vols. (Leiden: Brill, 1991), 3:491–565, esp. 521–39, 553–64; Albert de Jong, *Traditions of the Magi: Zoroastrianism in Greek and Latin Literature*, RGRW 133 (Leiden: Brill, 1997), 317–20; Guillaume Ducoeur, "Les hérésiarques chrétiens à l'École des sages d'Orient?" in Aragione and Norelli, *Des évêques*, 167–88 (175–76).

36. According to Plutarch, Zarathustra called the number one (τὸ ἕν) "Father" and the dyad (δυάδα) "Mother" (*An. procr.* 2, 1012e).

13. εἶναι δὲ τὸν κόσμον <κατὰ φύσιν> μουσικὴν ἁρμονίαν· διὸ καὶ τὸν ἥλιον ποιεῖσθαι τὴν περίοδον ἐναρμόνιον.

περὶ δὲ τῶν ἐκ γῆς καὶ κόσμου γινομένων τάδε φασὶ λέγειν τὸν Ζαράταν· δύο δαίμονας εἶναι, τὸν μὲν οὐράνιον, τὸν δὲ χθόνιον· καὶ τὸν μὲν χθόνιον ἀνιέναι τὴν γένεσιν ἐκ τῆς γῆς—εἶναι γὰρ ὕδωρ—, τὸν δὲ οὐράνιον <ἐκ τοῦ κόσμου—εἶναι γὰρ> πῦρ μετέχον τοῦ ἀέρος—· θερμὸν καὶ ψυχρόν. διὸ καὶ τούτων οὐδὲν ἀναιρεῖν οὐδὲ μιαίνειν φησὶ τὴν ψυχήν· ἔστι γὰρ ταῦτα οὐσία τῶν πάντων.

14. Κυάμους δὲ λέγεται παραγγέλλειν μὴ ἐσθίειν αἰτίᾳ τοῦ τὸν Ζαράταν εἰρηκέναι κατὰ τὴν ἀρχὴν καὶ σύγκρισιν τῶν πάντων, συνισταμένης τῆς γῆς ἔτι καὶ συνσεσημμένης, γενέσθαι <τὸν ἄνθρωπον καὶ> τὸν κύαμον. τούτου δὲ τεκμήριόν φησιν, εἴ τις καταμασησάμενος λεῖον τὸν κύαμον καταθείη πρὸς ἥλιον χρόνον τινά—τοῦτο<ν> γὰρ εὐθέως ἀντιλήψεσθα—, προσφέρειν ἀνθρωπίνου γόνου ὀσμήν. 15. σαφέστερον δὲ εἶναι καὶ ἕτερον παράδειγμα λέγει· εἰ ἀνθοῦντος τοῦ κυάμου λαβόντες τὸν κύαμον καὶ τὸ ἄνθος αὐτοῦ καὶ καταθέντες εἰς χύτραν ταύτην τε καταχρίσαντες εἰς γῆν κατορύξαιμεν καὶ μετ᾽ ὀλίγας ἡμέρας ἀνακαλύψαιμεν, ἴδοιμεν αὐτὸ εἶδος ἔχον τὸ μὲν πρῶτον ὡς αἰσχύνην γυναικός, μετὰ δὲ ταῦτα κατανοούμενον παιδίου κεφαλὴν συμπεφυκυῖαν.

16. Οὗτος ἐν Κρότωνι τῆς Ἰταλίας ἅμα τοῖς μαθηταῖς ἐμπυρισθεὶς διεφθάρη.

ἔθος δὲ τοῦτο ἦν παρ᾽ αὐτῷ, ἐπειδὰν προσίῃ τις μαθητευθησόμενος, πιπράσκειν τὰ ὑπάρχοντα καὶ τὸ ἀργύριον κατατιθέναι ἐσφραγισμένον παρὰ τῷ Πυθαγόρᾳ. καὶ ὑπέμενε σιωπῶν ὁτὲ μὲν ἔτη τρία, ὁτὲ δὲ πέντε καὶ μανθάνων· αὖθις δὲ λυθεὶς ἐμίσγετο τοῖς ἑτέροις καὶ παρέμενε μαθητὴς καὶ συνειστιᾶτο ἅμα· εἰ δ᾽ οὔ, ἀπελάμβανε τὸ ἴδιον καὶ ἀπεβάλλετο.

13. The cosmos is by nature a musical harmony.[37] Therefore the sun makes a harmonic revolution.

Concerning the beings that arise from earth and the cosmos, they report that Zaratas spoke as follows. There are two divine beings: the one celestial, and the other earthly. Now, the earthly one brings up generation from the earth—for he is water—whereas the celestial one brings up generation from the cosmos—for he is fire participating in air (thus hot and cold).[38] And so none of these elements, he says, kills or defiles the soul, as they are the substance of all things.

14. It is reported that Pythagoras forbade the eating of beans because Zaratas had said that in the beginning there was a mixture of all things, and when the earth was coming together and fermenting, there arose humanity and the bean.[39] The proof, he says, is this: if anyone chews the bean up into a fine pulp and lays it in the sun for some time (for this will immediately aid the process of putrefaction), it produces the smell of human semen. 15. But there is another clearer proof, he says. If we were to take from a bean plant in flower the bean itself and its flower, set them down in an earthen pot, smear it [with oil], bury it in earth, and after a few days uncover it, we would see it first having an appearance like female genitals, and later—when closely examined—the head of a small child sprouted from it.[40]

16. This fellow, together with his disciples, perished when set on fire in Kroton, Italy.[41]

INITIATING NEW MEMBERS. Pythagoras had a custom that whenever someone came to him to be a student, the student sold his belongings and deposited his money, kept sealed, with Pythagoras. Then the student would remain in silence sometimes for three, sometimes for five years while learning. When permitted again to speak, he would mix with the others, remain as a student, and have a share at table. But if not, he would receive back his property and be expelled.[42]

---

37. "By nature" (κατὰ φύσιν) is Marcovich's emendation for P's φύσιν καί.

38. Marcovich supplies ἐκ τοῦ κόσμου—εἶναι γὰρ (here: "from the cosmos—for he is …").

39. Marcovich supplies τὸν ἄνθρωπον καὶ (here: "humanity and …").

40. Cf. Porphyry, *Vit. Pyth.* 44; Clem. Alex., *Strom.* 3.3.24.2. See further Miroslav Marcovich, "Pythagorica," *Phil* 108 (1964): 29–44 (29–39).

41. Traditions about Pythagoras's death varied. For the burning in Kroton, cf. Diog. L., *Vit. phil.* 8.39; Porphyry, *Vit. Pyth.* 55; Iamblichos, *Vit. Pyth.* 249.

42. Cf. Plutarch, *Curios.* 519c (five-year silence); Gellius, *Noct. att.* 1.9.3–4, 12

17. οἱ μὲν οὖν ἐσωτερικοὶ ἐκαλοῦντο Πυθαγόρειοι, οἱ δὲ ἕτεροι Πυθαγορισταί. τῶν δὲ μαθητῶν αὐτοῦ οἱ διαφυγόντες τὸν ἐμπρησμὸν Λῦσις ἦν καὶ Ἄρχιππος καὶ ὁ τοῦ Πυθαγόρου οἰκέτης Ζάμολξις, ὃς καὶ τοὺς παρὰ Κελτοῖς Δρυΐδας λέγεται διδάξαι φιλοσοφεῖν τὴν Πυθαγόρειον φιλοσοφίαν.

18. τοὺς δὲ ἀριθμοὺς καὶ τὰ μέτρα παρ' Αἰγυπτίων φασὶ τὸν Πυθαγόραν μαθεῖν· ὃς καταπλαγεὶς τῇ τῶν ἱερέων ἀξιοπίστῳ καὶ φαντασιώδει καὶ δυσχερῶς ἐξαγορευομένῃ σοφίᾳ, μιμησάμενος ὁμοίως καὶ αὐτὸς σιγᾶν προσέταττεν καὶ ἐν ἀδύτοις καταγείοις ἠρεμεῖν ἐποίει τὸν μανθάνοντα.

3. 1. Ἐμπεδοκλῆς δὲ μετὰ τούτους γενόμενος καὶ περὶ δαιμόνων φύσεως εἶπε πολλά, καὶ ὡς ἀναστρέφονται διοικοῦντες τὰ κατὰ τὴν γῆν, ὄντες πλεῖστοι. οὗτος τὴν τοῦ παντὸς ἀρχὴν νεῖκος καὶ φιλίαν ἔφη, καὶ τὸ τῆς μονάδος νοερὸν πῦρ τὸν θεόν, καὶ συνεστάναι ἐκ πυρὸς τὰ πάντα καὶ εἰς πῦρ ἀναλυθήσεσθαι·

PYTHAGORAS'S STUDENTS. 17. Now those of the inner circle were called "Pythagoreans," but the others "Pythagorists."[43]

Those of his students who escaped the fire were Lysis, Archippos, and Zalmoxis, Pythagoras's household slave. It is reported that Zalmoxis taught the Druids among the Kelts to live in accordance with the Pythagorean philosophy.[44]

RELATION TO EGYPT. 18. They say that Pythagoras learned numbers and measurements among the Egyptians. After he was impressed with the wisdom of the priests—a fantastical wisdom, hard to declare, and given only to those trustworthy—he imitated them closely. He ordained silence and made his students lead a quiet life in underground shrines.[45]

EMPEDOKLES. 3. 1. Empedokles arose after these men and spoke many things about the nature of divine beings, and how they in all their host spend time administering the affairs of earth.[46] He said that the first principle of all is Strife and Love, that God is the intelligible fire of the monad, and that all things are composed from fire and will be dissolved into fire.[47] Generally speaking, the Stoics agree with him in doctrine, since they

---

(silence and shared property); Diog. L., *Vit. phil.* 8.10 (shared property); Iamblichos, *Vit. Pyth.* 30, 72–74, 90, 168 (silence, shared property, expulsion).

43. On the "inner circle," cf. Iamblichos, *Vit. Pyth.* 72.

44. On Zalmoxis, see *Ref.* 1.25.1 below; cf. Herodotos, *Hist.* 4.95–46; Porphyry, *Vit. Pyth.* 14; Iamblichos, *Vit. Pyth.* 173.

45. According to Diodoros, Pythagoras learned from the Egyptians theology, geometry, number theory, and transmigration (*Bibl. hist.* 1.98.2). Porphyry has Pythagoras learn divination, hieroglyphics, and theology from the Egyptians (*Vit. Pyth.* 7–9, 11–12). Iamblichos says that Pythagoras spent twenty-two years in Egypt studying astronomy, geometry, and mystic rites (*Vit. Pyth.* 18–19). For spending time underground, see Porphyry, *Vit. Pyth.* 9, 34; Iamblichos, *Vit. Pyth.* 27.

46. Concerning *Ref.* 1.3, see J. P. Hershbell, "Hippolytus' *Elenchos* as a Source for Empedocles Re-examined, I," *Phronesis* 18 (1973): 97–114 (101–4); Osborne, *Rethinking*, 87–88. Empedokles is more fully treated in *Ref.* 7.29.2–26. On daimones in Empedokles, see DK 31 B115.5, 122 (= Inwood 11.5, 120).

47. On God as monad, see *Ref.* 1.2.2 (Pythagoras). On intelligible fire (an originally Stoic concept), see *Ref.* 1.4.2 (Herakleitos); 9.10.7 (Empedokles); *SVF* 1.120 (on the nature of intelligible fire); *SVF* 2.1031 (God is intelligible fire); and G. S. Kirk, *Heraclitus: The Cosmic Fragments* (Cambridge: Cambridge University Press, 1954), 352–57. Clement of Alexandria also presents Empedokles as teaching the conversion of all things to fire (*Strom.* 5.14.103.6).

ᾧ σχεδὸν καὶ οἱ Στωϊκοὶ συντίθενται δόγματι, ἐκπύρωσιν προσδοκῶντες. 2. μάλιστα δὲ πάντων συγκατατίθεται τῇ μετενσωματώσει, οὕτως εἰπών·

ἤτοι μὲν γὰρ ἐγὼ γενόμην κοῦρός τε κόρη τε
θάμνος τ' οἰωνός τε καὶ ἐξ ἁλὸς ἔμπορος ἰχθύς.

3. οὗτος πάσας εἰς πάντα τὰ ζῷα μεταλλάττειν εἶπε τὰς ψυχάς. καὶ γὰρ ὁ τούτων διδάσκαλος Πυθαγόρας ἔφη ἑαυτὸν Εὔφορβον γεγονέναι τὸν ἐπὶ Ἴλιον στρατεύσαντα, φάσκων ἐπιγινώσκειν τὴν ἀσπίδα.

ταῦτα μὲν οὖν ὁ Ἐμπεδοκλῆς.

4. 1. Ἡράκλειτος δὲ φυσικὸς φιλόσοφος ὁ Ἐφέσιος τὰ πάντα ἔκλαιεν, ἄγνοιαν τοῦ παντὸς βίου καταγινώσκων καὶ πάντων ἀνθρώπων, ἐλεῶν τε τὸν τῶν θνητῶν βίον· αὐτὸν μὲν γὰρ ἔφασκεν τὰ πάντα εἰδέναι, τοὺς δὲ ἄλλους ἀνθρώπους οὐδέν. 2. καὶ αὐτὸς δὲ σχεδὸν σύμφωνα τῷ Ἐμπεδοκλεῖ ἐφθέγξατο,

expect a conflagration. 2. But more than everything, Empedokles affirms transmigration, saying as follows:

> In very truth I was a boy and a maiden,
> A bush and a bird and a fish conveyed from brine.[48]

3. He says that all souls transfer into all animals. Indeed the teacher of these men, Pythagoras, said that he had been Euphorbos, who campaigned at Ilion, claiming that he recognized his shield.[49]

These are the doctrines of Empedokles.

HERAKLEITOS. **4.** 1. Herakleitos the Ephesian natural philosopher wept about all things, since he recognized the ignorance of all life and of all people and pitied the life of mortals.[50] He claimed that he himself knew all things but that other people knew nothing.[51] 2. He pronounced a teaching

---

48. Empedokles, DK 31 B117 (= Inwood 111). "Conveyed," translating ἔμπορος, appears in the manuscripts of *Ref.* 1. In contrast, Diogenes Laertios gives "fiery" (ἔμπυρος) (*Vit. phil.* 8.6; cf. 8.77), Clement of Alexandria offers "mute/scaly" (ἔλλοπος) (*Strom.* 6.2.24.3), and Athenaios "from the sea" (ἔξαλος) (*Deipn.* 8.365e). See further N. van der Ben, *The Proem of Empedocles' "Peri Physios": Towards a New Edition of All the Fragments* (Amsterdam: B. R. Grüner, 1975), 217–21.

49. That is, Pythagoras (or Hermotimos, his previous incarnation) recognized the shield he carried when incarnated as the Trojan soldier Euphorbos. See the note in *Ref.* 1.2.11. Other ancient authors (including Empedokles himself) indicate that Empedokles was a disciple of Pythagoras (DK 31 B129; Diog. L., *Vit. phil.* 8.54–56; Iamblichos, *Vit. Pyth.* 104, 135, 267). See further Burkert, *Lore and Science*, 289 n. 59; Mansfeld, *Heresiography*, 40.

50. Cf. Seneca, *Ira* 2.10.5 (*Heraclitus ... flebat, miserebatur omnium* ["Heraclitus constantly wept and pitied all"]); Lucian, *Vit. auct.* 14 (σφέας καὶ ὀδύρομαι ["these (people) I (Herakleitos) bewail"]). The portrait of Herakleitos the weeping philosopher, originating in the first century CE, is derived from a (mis)understanding of the term μελαγχολία (cf. Theophrastos at Diog. L., *Vit. phil.* 9.6). To be "melancholic" is to be affected by hot black bile (μέλαινα χολή), which makes one easily excitable and prone to strong feelings (Aristotle, *Eth. nic.* 7.7, 1150b25). Later it came, as in the English derivative "melancholic," to mean "sad" or "gloomy." The portrait of the gloomy Herakleitos is also rooted in his pessimism and social-ethical criticisms. See further Cora Lutz, "Democritus and Heraclitus," *CJ* 49 (1953–1954): 309–14.

51. Cf. *Ref.* 9.9.3 = DK 22 B1 (= Miroslav Marcovich, *Heraclitus: Greek Text with a Short Commentary* [Mérida: Los Andes University Press, 1967], §1). See also DK 22 B101 (= Marcovich, *Heraclitus*, §15).

στάσιν καὶ φιλίαν φήσας τὴν τῶν ἁπάντων ἀρχὴν εἶναι, καὶ πῦρ νοερὸν τὸν θεόν, συμφέρεσθαί τε τὰ πάντα ἀλλήλοις καὶ οὐχ ἑστάναι. 3. καὶ ὥσπερ ὁ Ἐμπεδοκλῆς πάντα τὸν καθ' ἡμᾶς τόπον ἔφη κακῶν μεστὸν εἶναι καὶ μέχρι μὲν σελήνης τὰ κακὰ φθάνειν ἐκ τοῦ περὶ γῆν τόπου ταθέντα, περαιτέρω δὲ μὴ χωρεῖν, ἅτε καθαρωτέρου τοῦ ὑπὲρ τὴν σελήνην παντὸς ὄντος τόπου, οὕτω καὶ τῷ Ἡρακλείτῳ ἔδοξεν.

5. 1. Μετὰ τούτους ἐγένοντο καὶ ἕτεροι φυσικοί, ὧν οὐκ ἀναγκαῖον ἡγησάμεθα τὰς δόξας εἰπεῖν, μηδὲν τῶν προειρημένων ἀπεμφαινούσας. ἀλλ' ἐπεὶ καθόλου οὐ μικρὰ γεγένηται ἡ σχολὴ πολλοί τε οἱ μετέπειτα φυσικοὶ ἐξ αὐτῆς γεγένηνται, ἄλλοι ἄλλως περὶ φύσεως τοῦ παντὸς διηγούμενοι, δοκεῖ ἡμῖν τὴν ἀπὸ Πυθαγόρου ἐκθεμένους φιλοσοφίαν κατὰ διαδοχὴν ἀναδραμεῖν ἐπὶ τὰ δόξαντα τοῖς μετὰ Θαλῆν, καὶ ταῦτα ἐξειπόντας ἐλθεῖν ἐπί τε τὴν

almost entirely in agreement with Empedokles, since he declared that Discord and Love are the origin of all things,[52] that God is an intelligible fire,[53] that all things are in harmony with each other,[54] and that nothing stands still.[55] 3. Herakleitos taught just like Empedokles that our entire realm is full of evils and that evils reach as far as the moon, spread out from the region around the earth. Yet beyond the moon evils do not advance, since the entire region above the moon is purer.[56]

RETURN TO THE IONIAN SUCCESSION

5. 1. After these men there came to be other natural philosophers, whose doctrines I have not considered it necessary to relate, since they are not at all different from what was previously reported.[57] But since in general the school came to be rather large, and since many of the natural philosophers later came from this school—some relating one thing, and some another about the nature of the universe—in my opinion it seems good, now that I have presented Pythagorean philosophy in succession, to backtrack to the doctrines that came after Thales.[58] After I have pronounced on

---

52. Cf. Herakleitos, DK 22 B80, 51 (= Marcovich, *Heraclitus*, §§28 and 27). See further Kirk, *Cosmic*, 25.

53. Cf. Herakleitos, DK 22 B64 (= Marcovich, *Heraclitus*, §79). Cf. *Ref.* 9.10.7. Virtually the same teaching is attributed to Empedokles in the previous section (*Ref.* 1.3.1).

54. Cf. Herakleitos, DK 22 B51 (ἁρμονίη), 10 (συμφερόμενον) (= Marcovich, *Heraclitus*, §§27, 25).

55. Cf. the river saying in DK 22 B12, 49a, 91 (= Marcovich, *Heraclitus*, §40*a*, *c2*, *c3*). For "nothing stands still," see Plato, *Crat.* 401d, 402a; Aristotle, *Metaph.* 3.5, 1010a13–15. Further references in Kirk, *Cosmic*, 14, 17–18.

56. Similar ideas are attributed to Aristotle later in *Ref.* 1.20.6; cf. 7.19.2. Cf. Diog. L., *Vit. phil.* 9.10 (for Herakleitos the moon is earthlike since it is not in a pure location). See further *Ref.* 9.8–10.

57. For these other natural philosophers, see Mansfeld, *Heresiography*, 27.

58. For ἀναδραμεῖν (here: "backtrack"), see ibid., 14–18. The phrase "in succession" (κατὰ διαδοχήν) could refer to the previous succession (Pythagoras to Herakleitos) or to the forthcoming (Ionian) succession. The Greek (I believe) supports the former view, but our author thinks of both the Italian and Ionian schools as successions. On the organization of this material, Hermann Diels proposes that our author used two different sources: a low-quality biographical succession source for chaps. 1–4, 18–25, and a superior doxography, ultimately dependent on Theophrastos for chaps. 6–16 (*Doxographi graeci* [Berlin: Reimer, 1879], 145–49, 153–54). Jørgen Mejer prefers to see two doxographical texts of varying quality (chaps. 1–4 poor; chaps.

ἠθικὴν καὶ λογικὴν φιλοσοφίαν, ὧν ἦρξαν Σωκράτης μὲν ἠθικῆς, Ἀριστοτέλης δὲ διαλεκτικῆς.

6. 1. Θαλοῦ τοίνυν Ἀναξίμανδρος γίνεται ἀκροατής· Ἀναξίμανδρος Πραξιάδου Μιλήσιος. οὗτος ἀρχὴν ἔφη τῶν ὄντων φύσιν τινὰ τοῦ ἀπείρου, ἐξ ἧς γίνεσθαι τοὺς οὐρανοὺς καὶ τοὺς ἐν αὐτοῖς κόσμους. ταύτην δὲ ἀίδιον εἶναι καὶ ἀγήρω, ἣν καὶ πάντας περιέχειν τοὺς κόσμους. λέγει δὲ καὶ χρόνον, ὡς ὡρισμένης καὶ τῆς γενέσεως τοῖς οὖσι καὶ τῆς φθορᾶς.

these, I will come to both ethical and logical philosophy. Sokrates initiated ethical philosophy, and Aristotle initiated dialectical philosophy.

ANAXIMANDROS. 6. 1. Anaximandros became the pupil of Thales.[59] Anaximandros son of Praxiades was a Milesian. He said that the first principle of existing things is a certain nature of the Boundless, from which originates the heavens and the worlds in them.[60] This Boundless nature is eternal and ageless and also encompasses all the worlds.[61] He also speaks of time as the period when generation and corruption are fixed for existing beings.[62]

6–16 good), probably mediated through a Skeptical source (*Diogenes Laertius and His Hellenistic Background* [Wiesbaden: Franz Steiner, 1978], 83–85). Osborne argued for three main divisions of the material based on style and subject: chaps. 1–4, 6–9, and 11–16. Chapters 6–9 are the most systematic and discuss only physical theories. These chapters, she believed, come from a separate Theophrastean source here copied nearly verbatim. For chaps. 1–4 and 11–16, which do not significantly differ in character, our author selectively used a full and varied doxographical source (*Rethinking*, 187–211). Mansfeld preferred a division into five sections: chap. 1, chaps. 2–4, chaps. 6–9, chaps. 11–15, and chap. 16. Chapter 1 on Thales is not qualitatively different from the Ionic succession in chaps. 6–9. The Ionian succession runs from Thales to Archelaos (chaps. 1, 6–9). Thus the Pythagorean succession (chaps. 2–4) is a kind of tangent and represents a separate source (*Heresiography*, 7–42, summary chart on 43).

59. Anaximandros was elsewhere portrayed as the pupil of Thales. See the testimony of Theophrastos, frag. 226a (FHSG 1:408–9). Cf. Diog. L., *Vit. phil.* 1.13; Iren., *Haer.* 2.14.2–6; Clem. Alex., *Protr.* 66.1; *Strom.* 1.14.63.2. See further Ian Mueller, "Heterodoxy and Doxography in Hippolytus' 'Refutation of All Heresies,'" *ANRW* 36.6:4309–74 (4360–61).

60. The wording in Theophrastos, frag. 226a (FHSG 1:408–9), is similar and suggests a common Theophrastean tradition. On the Boundless as "first principle" (ἀρχή), see Ps.-Plutarch, *Plac. philos.* 1.3; Stobaios, *Ecl.* 1.10.12 (Wachsmuth and Hense, 1:122). On the "Boundless" (ἄπειρον), see Charles H. Kahn, *Anaximander and the Origins of Greek Cosmology* (New York: Columbia University Press, 1960), 231–39; Dirk L. Couprie, Robert Hahn, and Gerard Naddaf, eds., *Anaximander in Context: New Studies in the Origins of Greek Philosophy* (Albany: SUNY Press, 2003), 167, 237. The plural "heavens" (οὐρανούς) may refer to the rings of the heavenly bodies. For the sense of κόσμοι (here: "worlds"), see ibid., 33–34, 43–44, 188–93, 219–30.

61. "Eternal and ageless" (ἀΐδιον … καὶ ἀγήρω) are stock properties of the gods. Aristotle notes that the Boundless is "the divine [τὸ θεῖον]; for it is immortal and indestructible [ἀθάνατον … καὶ ἀνώλεθρον], as Anaximandros says" (*Phys.* 3.4, 203b10–15).

62. Cf. Anaximandros, DK 12 B1; Ps.-Plutarch, *Strom.* 2 (Diels, *Doxographi*, 579).

2. οὗτος μὲν οὖν ἀρχὴν καὶ στοιχεῖον εἴρηκεν τῶν ὄντων τὸ ἄπειρον, πρῶτος τοὔνομα καλέσας τῆς ἀρχῆς. πρὸς δὲ τούτῳ κίνησιν ἀίδιον εἶναι, ἐν ᾗ συμβαίνειν γίνεσθαι τοὺς οὐρανούς. 3. τὴν δὲ γῆν εἶναι μετέωρον, ὑπὸ μηδενὸς κρατουμένην, μένουσαν δὲ διὰ τὴν ὁμοίαν πάντων ἀπόστασιν. τὸ δὲ σχῆμα αὐτῆς γυρόν, στρογγύλον, κίονι λίθῳ παραπλήσιον· τῶν δὲ ἐπιπέδων ᾧ μὲν ἐπιβεβήκαμεν, ὃ δὲ ἀντίθετον ὑπάρχει.

4. Τὰ δὲ ἄστρα γίνεσθαι κύκλον πυρός, ἀποκριθέντα ἐκ τοῦ κατὰ τὸν κόσμον πυρός, περιληφθέντα δ' ὑπὸ ἀέρος. ἐκπνοὰς δ' ὑπάρξαι, πόρους τινὰς αὐλώδεις, καθ' οὓς φαίνεσθαι τὰ ἄστρα· διὸ καὶ ἐπιφρασσομένων τῶν ἐκπνοῶν τὰς ἐκλείψεις γίνεσθαι. 5. τὴν δὲ σελήνην ποτὲ μὲν πληρουμένην φαίνεσθαι, ποτὲ δὲ μειουμένην κατὰ τὴν τῶν πόρων ἐπίφραξιν ἢ ἄνοιξιν. εἶναι δὲ τὸν κύκλον τοῦ ἡλίου ἑπτακαιεικοσαπλασίονα <τῆς γῆς>, <…> τῆς σελήνης, καὶ ἀνωτάτω μὲν εἶναι τὸν ἥλιον· κατωτάτω δὲ τοὺς τῶν ἀπλανῶν <καὶ πλανήτων> ἀστέρων κύκλους.

6. Τὰ δὲ ζῷα γίνεσθαι <ἐξ ὑγροῦ>, ἐξατμιζομένου ὑπὸ τοῦ ἡλίου. τὸν δὲ ἄνθρωπον ἑτέρῳ ζῴῳ γεγονέναι—τουτέστιν ἰχθύι—παραπλήσιον κατ' ἀρχάς.

2. So then, this Anaximandros declared that the first principle and element of existing things is the Boundless. He was the first to use the terminology "first principle."[63] In addition, motion is eternal. By this motion the generation of the heavens occurs.[64] 3. The earth is hanging in the air, held by nothing, but remaining still on account of being equidistant from all things.[65] Its shape is circular, round—very much like a stone column.[66] We walk on one of the surfaces, yet there exists an opposite side.[67]

4. The heavenly bodies arise as a circle of fire, separated off from the cosmic fire and enveloped by air.[68] There exist vents, tube-like passages through which the heavenly bodies appear. Consequently, when the vents are blocked, eclipses occur. 5. The moon sometimes appears waxing, and sometimes waning, according to the obstruction or opening of the passages. The circle of the sun is twenty-seven times that of the earth … of the moon.[69] The sun is the highest circle. Lowest are the circles of the fixed stars and planets.[70]

6. Animals arise from moisture evaporated by the sun.[71] In the beginning, humankind was born quite similar to a different animal, namely, the fish.[72]

---

63. On the translation of this phrase, see Kahn, *Anaximander*, 30–31.

64. Cf. Hermias, *Irris.* 10. See further Kahn, *Anaximander*, 39–42.

65. Cf. Aristotle, *Cael.* 2.13, 295b10–16; Diog. L., *Vit. phil.* 2.1. See further Kahn, *Anaximander*, 54, 80; Couprie, Hahn, and Naddaf, *Anaximander*, 202–8.

66. Cf. Ps.-Plutarch, *Plac. philos.* 3.10.2, 895d (λίθῳ κίονι); Ps.-Plutarch, *Strom.* 2 (κυλινδροειδῆ).

67. See further Kahn, *Anaximander*, 84–85.

68. This theory is more fully explained in Ps.-Plutarch, *Strom.* 2; cf. Ps.-Plutarch, *Plac. philos.* 2.13, 888d. See further Kahn, *Anaximander*, 86–87.

69. Marcovich adds τῆς γῆς ("of the earth"). If accepted, one must assume that something has dropped out before the phrase "of the moon."

70. Marcovich adds καὶ πλανήτων ("and planets") by comparison with Diels's reconstruction of Aëtios, *Plac.* 2.15.6. On the moon and the circles of the heavenly bodies, see Ps.-Plutarch, *Strom.* 2; Ps.-Plutarch, *Plac. philos.* 2.15, 889b; 2.16, 889c; 2.20, 889f; 2.21, 890c; 2.24, 890f; 2.25, 891b; 2.29, 891e. For commentary, see Kahn, *Anaximander*, 58–63, 87–98.

71. Marcovich, following Diels, adds ἐξ ὑγροῦ ("from moisture") from Censorinus, *Die nat.* 4.7 (*ex aqua*). Cf. Diog. L., *Vit. phil.* 2.9 (ζῷα γίνεσθαι ἐξ ὑγροῦ καὶ θερμοῦ καὶ γεώδους ["animals come from moisture, heat, and earth"]); Ps.-Plutarch, *Plac. philos.* 5.19, 908d (ἐν ὑγρῷ γεννηθῆναι τὰ πρῶτα ζῷα ["the first animals were born in moisture"]).

72. Censorinus, *Die nat.* 4.7: *sive pisces seu piscibus simillima animalia; in his homines concrevisse fetusque ad pubertatem intus retentos, tunc demum ruptis illis viros*

7. ἀνέμους δὲ γίνεσθαι τῶν λεπτοτάτων ἀτμῶν ἐκ τοῦ ἀέρος ἀποκρινομένων καὶ ὅταν ἀθροισθῶσι κινουμένων· ὑετοὺς δὲ ἐκ τῆς ἀτμίδος τῆς ἐκ γῆς ὑφ' ἥλιον ἀναδιδομένης· ἀστραπὰς δέ, ὅταν ἄνεμος ἐκπίπτων διιστᾷ τὰς νεφέλας.

οὗτος ἐγένετο κατὰ ἔτος τρίτον τῆς τεσσαρακοστῆς δευτέρας ὀλυμπιάδος.

7. 1. Ἀναξιμένης δέ, καὶ αὐτὸς ὢν Μιλήσιος, υἱὸς δὲ Εὐρυστράτου, ἀέρα ἄπειρον ἔφη τὴν ἀρχὴν εἶναι, ἐξ οὗ [τὰ γινόμενα τὰ γεγονότα καὶ τὰ ἐσόμενα καὶ] θεοὺς καὶ θεῖα γίνεσθαι, τὰ δὲ λοιπὰ ἐκ τῶν τούτου ἀπογόνων. 2. τὸ δὲ εἶδος τοῦ ἀέρος τοιοῦτον· ὅταν μὲν ὁμαλώτατος ᾖ, ὄψει ἄδηλον, δηλοῦσθαι δὲ τῷ ψυχρῷ καὶ τῷ θερμῷ καὶ τῷ νοτερῷ καὶ τῷ κινουμένῳ. κινεῖσθαι δὲ ἀεί· οὐ γὰρ ἂν μεταβάλλειν ὅσα μεταβάλλει, εἰ μὴ κινοῖτο. 3. πυκνούμενον δὲ καὶ ἀραιούμενον διάφορον φαίνεσθαι· ὅταν γὰρ εἰς τὸ ἀραιότερον διαχυθῇ, πῦρ γίνεσθαι· <ἄνεμον> δὲ πάλιν εἶναι ἀέρα μέσως πυκνούμενον· ἐξ ἀέρος δὲ νέφος ἀποτελεῖσθαι κατὰ τὴν πίλησιν· ἔτι δὲ μᾶλλον ὕδωρ, ἐπὶ πλεῖον δὲ πυκνωθέντα γῆν καὶ εἰς τὸ μάλιστα πυκνότατον λίθους. ὥστε τὰ κυριώτατα τῆς γενέσεως ἐναντία εἶναι, θερμόν τε καὶ ψυχρόν.

7. Winds arise from the finest vapors separated from the air, propelled when massed together.[73] Rains arise from the vapor rising from the earth exuded underneath the sun. Bolts of lightning arise when wind, colliding with the clouds, rips them apart.[74]

This Anaximandros was born about the third year of the forty-second Olympiad.[75]

ANAXIMENES. 7. 1. Anaximenes, also a Milesian, was the son of Eurystratos.[76] He said that the first principle is boundless air, from which gods and divine beings arise, while the rest comes to be from air's offspring.[77] 2. The appearance of air has the following quality: when it is uniform it is invisible to sight, but it becomes visible (a) under cold conditions, (b) under warm conditions, (c) under damp conditions, and (d) under windy conditions. It is always in motion, for what changes cannot change unless it is moved. 3. It appears different in its condensed and rarified states. When diffused in its rarified state, it becomes fire. In turn, it becomes wind when the air is moderately condensed.[78] From air, a cloud is produced according to the degree of compression. With still more compression, it becomes water; when condensed to a greater degree, it becomes earth; and when most condensed, it is changed into stones. As a result, the chief causes of generation are opposites: heat and cold.[79]

---

mulieresque, qui iam se alere possent, processisse ("in fish, or animals nearly identical to fish, humans coalesced, kept inside as embryos until puberty. Then at last, when their pods were broken through, they emerged as men and women who could feed themselves"). See further Kahn, *Anaximander*, 109–13; Couprie, Hahn, and Naddaf, *Anaximander*, 13–17.

73. Cf. Ps.-Plutarch, *Plac. philos.* 3.7, 895a.

74. Cf. Ps.-Plutarch, *Plac. philos.* 3.3, 893d; 3.7, 895a; Seneca, *Nat.* 2.18. For Anaximandros's meteorology, see Kahn, *Anaximander*, 100–102.

75. That is, in 610/609 BCE. Cf. Diog. L., *Vit. phil.* 2.2.

76. On our author's treatment of Anaximenes, see Mueller, "Heterodoxy," 4361.

77. Before θεούς Marcovich deletes the phrase τὰ γινόμενα τὰ γεγονότα καὶ τὰ ἐσόμενα ("present, past, and future things"), which seems to be identical with τὰ δὲ λοιπά later in the sentence. Cf. Augustine, *Civ.* 8.2. Air's offspring are the three other elements: earth, water, and fire (see *Ref.* 1.7.3; cf. Cicero, *Acad.* 2.118).

78. Marcovich adds ἄνεμον ("wind") from Theophrastos, frag. 226b (FHSG 1:410–11).

79. For the process of condensation-rarefaction, see Theophrastos, frag. 226a–b (FHSG 1:408–11); Ps.-Plutarch, *Strom.* 3 (Diels, *Doxographi*, 579–80); Plutarch, *Prim. frig.* 947e–948a. See further Joachim Klowski, "Ist der Aer des Anaximenes als ein Substanz konkipiert?" *Hermes* 100 (1972): 131–42 (133–40).

4. Τὴν δὲ γῆν πλατεῖαν εἶναι, ἐπ’ ἀέρος ὀχουμένην· ὁμοίως δὲ καὶ ἥλιον καὶ σελήνην καὶ τὰ ἄλλα ἄστρα πάντα πύρινα ὄντα ἐποχεῖσθαι τῷ ἀέρι διὰ πλάτος. 5. γεγονέναι δὲ τὰ ἄστρα ἐκ γῆς διὰ τὸ τὴν ἰκμάδα ἐκ ταύτης ἀνίστασθαι· ἧς ἀραιουμένης τὸ πῦρ γίνεσθαι, ἐκ δὲ τοῦ πυρὸς μετεωριζομένου τοὺς ἀστέρας συνίστασθαι. εἶναι δὲ καὶ γεώδεις φύσεις ἐν τῷ τόπῳ τῶν ἀστέρων συμπεριφερομένας ἐκείνοις. 6. οὐ κινεῖσθαι δὲ ὑπὸ γῆν τὰ ἄστρα λέγει, καθὼς ἕτεροι ὑπειλήφασιν, ἀλλὰ περὶ γῆν, ὡσπερεὶ περὶ τὴν ἡμετέραν κεφαλὴν στρέφεται τὸ πιλίον. κρύπτεσθαι δὲ τὸν ἥλιον οὐχ ὑπὸ γῆν φερόμενον, ἀλλ’ ὑπὸ τῶν τῆς γῆς ὑψηλοτέρων μερῶν σκεπόμενον, καὶ διὰ τὴν πλείονα ἡμῶν αὐτοῦ γενομένην ἀπόστασιν. τὰ δὲ ἄστρα μὴ θερμαίνειν διὰ τὸ μῆκος τῆς ἀποστάσεως.

7. Ἀνέμους δὲ γεννᾶσθαι, ὅταν ἐκ <μέρους> πεπυκνωμένος ὁ ἀὴρ ἀρθεὶς φέρηται· συνελθόντα δὲ καὶ ἐπὶ πλεῖον παχυνθέντα νέφη γεννᾶσθαι, καὶ οὕτως εἰς ὕδωρ μεταβάλλειν. χάλαζαν δὲ γίνεσθαι, ὅταν ἀπὸ τῶν νεφῶν τὸ ὕδωρ καταφερόμενον παγῇ· χιόνα δέ, ὅταν αὐτὰ ταῦτα ἐνυγρότερα ὄντα πῆξιν λάβῃ· 8. ἀστραπὴν δ’, ὅταν τὰ νέφη διϊστῆται βίᾳ πνευμάτων· τούτων γὰρ διϊσταμένων λαμπρὰν καὶ πυρώδη γίνεσθαι τὴν αὐγήν. ἶριν δὲ γεννᾶσθαι τῶν ἡλιακῶν αὐγῶν εἰς ἀέρα συνεστῶτα πιπτουσῶν· σεισμὸν δὲ τῆς γῆς ἐπὶ πλεῖον ἀλλοιουμένης ὑπὸ θερμασίας καὶ ψύξεως.

ταῦτα μὲν οὖν Ἀναξιμένης. οὗτος ἤκμασεν περὶ ἔτος πρῶτον τῆς πεντηκοστῆς ὀγδόης ὀλυμπιάδος.

4. The earth is flat and rides on air. Similarly, sun, moon, and the other heavenly bodies are all fiery and float upon the air since they are broad disks.[80] 5. The stars arose from earth on account of the moisture rising from it that—when rarefied—becomes fire. From the fire that is brought high into the air, the heavenly bodies were composed. There are earthly natures in the realm of the heavenly bodies that are carried round with them.[81] 6. He says that the heavenly bodies do not move beneath the earth, as others supposed, but *around* the earth—just as a felt cap turns around our head. The sun is hidden not when traveling below the earth, but when covered by the parts higher than the earth, and because of its increased distance from us on earth.[82] The heavenly bodies are not hot to our senses due to the extent of their distance from us.

7. Winds arise whenever the air, partially condensed and lifted up, is whipped along.[83] When it comes together and is more and more condensed, clouds are born, and in this way [air] changes into water. Hail arises whenever the water, brought down from the clouds, solidifies. Snow arises whenever these same clouds, more moistened, freeze. 8. Lightning arises whenever the clouds are ripped apart by the force of winds—for when these are ripped apart, the flash is bright and fiery. A rainbow is produced from solar rays falling into condensed air. An earthquake occurs when the earth greatly shifts by the forces of heat and cold.[84]

These are the doctrines of Anaximenes. He reached his height around the first year of the fifty-eighth Olympiad.[85]

---

80. Cf. Aristotle, *Cael.* 2.13, 294b13–21; Ps.-Plutarch, *Plac. philos.* 3.15, 896d.

81. Cf. the doctrine of Anaxagoras in *Ref.* 1.8.6. See also Ps.-Plutarch, *Plac. philos.* 2.13, 888d.

82. The parts higher than the earth are the heights in the north (Aristotle, *Mete.* 2.1, 354a28–32). See also Ps.-Plutarch, *Plac. philos.* 2.16, 889c; Diog. L., *Vit. phil.* 2.3.

83. Marcovich prints ἐκ μέρους πεπυκνωμένος. Most manuscripts of *Ref.* 1 read ἐκπεπυκνωμένος. According to Galen, Anaximenes said that winds come from water and air violently whipped up by an unknown rush extremely fast like the flapping of wings (*In Hipp. de humor.* 3.13 [Kühn, 16:395–96]).

84. On earthquakes, see further Aristotle, *Mete.* 2.7, 365b6–12; Ps.-Plutarch, *Plac. philos.* 3.15, 896c; Seneca, *Nat.* 6.13.2–6 (the opinion of Straton). On lightning, see Ps.-Plutarch, *Plac. philos.* 3.3, 893d. On clouds, snow, and hail, see *Plac. philos.* 3.4, 894a. On rainbows, see *Plac. philos.* 3.5, 894e.

85. That is, 550/549 BCE. Diogenes Laertios puts Anaximenes somewhat later, in the Sixty-Third Olympiad (*Vit. phil.* 2.1).

8. 1. Μετὰ τοῦτον γίνεται Ἀναξαγόρας Ἡγησιβούλου ὁ Κλαζομένιος. οὗτος ἔφη τὴν τοῦ παντὸς ἀρχὴν νοῦν καὶ ὕλην· τὸν μὲν νοῦν ποιοῦντα, τὴν δὲ ὕλην γινομένην· ὄντων γὰρ πάντων ὁμοῦ, νοῦς ἐπελθὼν διεκόσμησεν. τὰς δὲ ὑλικὰς ἀρχὰς ἀπείρους ὑπάρχειν καὶ τὰς σμικροτάτας αὐτῶν ἄπειρα λέγει. 2. κινήσεως δὲ μετέχειν τὰ πάντα ὑπὸ τοῦ νοῦ κινούμενα συνελθεῖν τε τὰ ὅμοια. καὶ τὰ μὲν κατὰ τὸν οὐρανὸν κεκοσμῆσθαι ὑπὸ τῆς ἐγκυκλίου κινήσεως· τὸ μὲν οὖν πυκνὸν καὶ τὸ ὑγρὸν καὶ τὸ σκοτεινὸν καὶ τὸ ψυχρὸν καὶ πάντα τὰ βαρέα συνελθεῖν ἐπὶ τὸ μέσον, ἐξ ὧν παγέντων τὴν γῆν ὑποστῆναι· τὰ δ᾽ ἀντικείμενα τούτοις, τὸ θερμὸν καὶ τὸ λαμπρὸν καὶ τὸ ξηρὸν καὶ τὸ κοῦφον, εἰς τὸ πρόσω τοῦ αἰθέρος ὁρμῆσαι.

3. Τὴν δὲ γῆν τῷ σχήματι πλατεῖαν εἶναι καὶ μένειν μετέωρον διὰ τὸ μέγεθος καὶ διὰ τὸ μηδὲν εἶναι κενὸν καὶ διὰ τὸ τὸν ἀέρα ἰσχυρότατον ὄντα φέρειν ἐποχουμένην τὴν γῆν. 4. τῶν δὲ ἐπὶ γῆς ὑγρῶν τὴν μὲν θάλασσαν ὑπάρξαι τε τῶν ἐν αὐτῇ ὑδάτων, <ὧν> ἐξατμισθέν<των> τὰ ὑποστάντα οὕτως γεγονέναι, καὶ ἀπὸ τῶν καταρρευσάντων ποταμῶν. 5. τοὺς δὲ ποταμοὺς καὶ ἀπὸ τῶν ὄμβρων λαμβάνειν τὴν ὑπόστασιν καὶ ἐξ ὑδάτων τῶν ἐν τῇ γῇ· εἶναι γὰρ αὐτὴν κοίλην καὶ ἔχειν ὕδωρ ἐν τοῖς κοιλώμασιν. τὸν δὲ Νεῖλον αὔξεσθαι κατὰ τὸ θέρος καταφερομένων εἰς αὐτὸν ὑδάτων ἀπὸ τῶν ἐν τοῖς <ἀντ>αρκτ<ικ>οῖς χιόνων.

6. ἥλιον δὲ καὶ σελήνην καὶ πάντα τὰ ἄστρα λίθους εἶναι ἐμπύρους, συμπεριληφθέντας ὑπὸ τῆς τοῦ αἰθέρος περιφορᾶς. εἶναι δ᾽ ὑποκάτω τῶν ἄστρων ἡλίῳ καὶ σελήνῃ σώματά τινα συμπεριφερόμενα, ἡμῖν ἀόρατα. 7. τῆς

ANAXAGORAS. 8. 1. After him arose Anaxagoras son of Hegesiboulos the Klazomenian.[86] He said that the first principle of all is Mind and matter. Mind acts, and matter arises. For when all things were together, Mind arrived and put the cosmos in order. There are boundless material principles, and he calls even the smallest of them "boundless." 2. All things participate in motion, moved by Mind, and homogenous entities come together.[87] Heavenly things are put in order by a circular motion.[88] The dense, the moist, the dark, the cold, and all heavy elements come together in the middle. From them, when they are solidified, the earth is established. Conversely, their opposites—the hot, the bright, the dry, and the light—rush upward toward the aether.[89]

3. The earth is flat in shape and remains floating in the air due to its magnitude. This is because there is no void, and because the air has immense power to bear the earth as it rides upon it. 4. The sea exists from (a) the reserves of moisture on the earth, (b) the waters in the earth (which, when drawn off like vapor, became standing pools), and (c) rivers as they flow down.[90] 5. The rivers receive their contents from the rains and from the waters in the earth (for the earth is hollow and has water in its hollow portions). The Nile River grows in summer when waters are brought down into it from the snows in the Antarctic regions.[91]

6. The sun and moon and all the stars are fiery stones, spun round by the revolution of the aether.[92] There are below the stars certain bodies, invisible to us, whirled round with sun and moon.[93] 7. The heat of the stars

---

86. For our author's treatment of Anaxagoras, see Mueller, "Heterodoxy," 4362–63.

87. Anaxagoras, DK 59 B1, 3, 4, 6; Theophrastos, frag. 228a (FHSG 1:416–19); Diog. L., *Vit. phil.* 2.6, 8; Ps.-Plutarch, *Plac. philos.* 1.3, 876b–c.

88. Anaxagoras, DK 59 B12.

89. Anaxagoras, DK 59 B15; Ps.-Plutarch, *Plac. philos.* 1.4, 878e–f; Diog. L., *Vit. phil.* 2.8.

90. In the manuscripts we read: *τά τε ἐν αὐτῇ ὕδατα ἐξατμισθέντα ὑποστάντα κτλ.*, which Wendland printed after changing *αὐτῇ* to *αὐτῇ*. Printed here is Diels's reconstruction. On the formation of the sea, see Aristotle, *Mete.* 2.1, 353b6–8; Ps.-Plutarch, *Plac. philos.* 3.16, 896f–897a; Diog. L., *Vit. phil.* 2.8.

91. I emend *ἀρκτοῖς* to *ἀνταρκτικοῖς* ("Antarctic") following Mueller, "Heterodoxy," 4362. For speculations on why the Nile rose in summer, see Ps.-Plutarch, *Plac. philos.* 4.1, 897f–898b; Diodoros, *Bibl. hist.* 1.38.4; Seneca, *Nat.* 4a.2.17; *Scholia in Apollonium Rhodium* on *Arg.* 4.269 (Wendel).

92. Cf. Ps.-Plutarch, *Plac. philos.* 2.20, 890a; 2.13, 888d; Diog. L., *Vit. phil.* 2.9.

93. See the teaching ascribed to Anaximenes in *Ref.* 1.7.5. Cf. Aristotle, *Cael.* 2.13, 293b21–33 (attributed to "some people").

δὲ θερμότητος μὴ αἰσθάνεσθαι τῶν ἄστρων διὰ τὸ μακρὰν εἶναι τὴν ἀπόστασιν τῆς γῆς· ἔτι δὲ οὐχ ὁμοίως θερμὰ τῷ ἡλίῳ διὰ τὸ χώραν ἔχειν ψυχροτέραν. εἶναι δὲ τὴν σελήνην κατωτέρω τοῦ ἡλίου, πλησιώτερον ἡμῶν. 8. ὑπερέχειν δὲ τὸν ἥλιον μεγέθει τὴν Πελοπόννησον. τὸ δὲ φῶς τὴν σελήνην μὴ ἴδιον ἔχειν, ἀλλὰ ἀπὸ τοῦ ἡλίου. 9. τὴν δὲ τῶν ἄστρων περιφορὰν ὑπὸ γῆν γίνεσθαι. ἐκλείπειν δὲ τὴν σελήνην γῆς ἀντιφραττούσης, ἐνίοτε δὲ καὶ τῶν ὑποκάτω τῆς σελήνης, τὸν δὲ ἥλιον ταῖς νουμηνίαις σελήνης ἀντιφραττούσης. τροπὰς δὲ ποιεῖσθαι καὶ ἥλιον καὶ σελήνην ἀπωθουμένους ὑπὸ τοῦ ἀέρος. σελήνην δὲ πολλάκις τρέπεσθαι διὰ τὸ μὴ δύνασθαι κρατεῖν τοῦ ψυχροῦ.

10. οὗτος ἀφώρισε πρῶτος τὰ περὶ τὰς ἐκλείψεις καὶ φωτισμούς. ἔφη δὲ γηίνην εἶναι τὴν σελήνην ἔχειν τε ἐν αὐτῇ πεδία καὶ φάραγγας. τὸν δὲ γαλαξίαν ἀνάκλασιν εἶναι τοῦ φωτὸς τῶν ἄστρων, τῶν μὴ καταλαμπομένων ὑπὸ τοῦ ἡλίου. τοὺς δὲ μεταβαίνοντας ἀστέρας ὡσεὶ σπινθῆρας ἀφαλλομένους γίνεσθαι ἐκ τῆς κινήσεως τοῦ πόλου.

11. Ἀνέμους δὲ γίνεσθαι λεπτυνομένου τοῦ ἀέρος ὑπὸ τοῦ ἡλίου καὶ τῶν ἐκκαιομένων πρὸς τὸν πόλον ὑποχωρούντων καὶ ἀποφερομένων. Βροντὰς δὲ καὶ ἀστραπὰς ἀπὸ τοῦ θερμοῦ γίνεσθαι, ἐμπίπτοντος εἰς τὰ νέφη. 12. σεισμοὺς δὲ γίνεσθαι τοῦ ἄνωθεν ἀέρος εἰς τὸν ὑπὸ γῆν ἐμπίπτοντος· τούτου γὰρ κινουμένου καὶ τὴν ὀχουμένην γῆν ὑπ' αὐτοῦ σαλεύεσθαι.

ζῷα δὲ τὴν μὲν ἀρχὴν ἐν ὑγρῷ γενέσθαι, μετὰ ταῦτα δὲ ἐξ ἀλλήλων· καὶ ἄρρενας μὲν γίνεσθαι, ὅταν ἀπὸ τῶν δεξιῶν μερῶν ἀποκριθὲν τὸ σπέρμα τοῖς δεξιοῖς μέρεσι τῆς μήτρας κολληθῇ, τὰ δὲ θήλεα κατὰ τοὐναντίον.

13. οὗτος ἤκμασεν ἔτους πρώτου τῆς ὀγδοηκοστῆς ὀγδόης ὀλυμπιάδος, καθ' ὃν καιρὸν καὶ Πλάτωνα λέγουσι γεγενῆσθαι. τοῦτον λέγουσι καὶ προγνωστικὸν γεγονέναι.

is not felt on account of their great distance from the earth. Moreover, they do not have equal heat to the sun, because they occupy a colder region. The moon is lower than the sun and closer to us. 8. The sun exceeds the Peloponnese in size.[94] The moon has not its own light but that from the sun.[95] 9. The stars revolve under the earth. The moon is eclipsed when the earth blocks it, but sometimes it is also blocked by the objects below the moon. The sun is eclipsed during new moons when the moon blocks it.[96] Both sun and moon are made to turn round when pushed back by the air.[97] The moon is often turned because it cannot dominate the cold.

10. Anaxagoras was the first to define the nature of eclipses and the refulgence of heavenly bodies. He said that the moon has the soil of earth and has on it plains and valleys.[98] The Milky Way is the reflection of the light from the stars that are not illumined by the sun. Shooting stars leaping away like sparks come from the motion of the cosmic axis.[99]

11. Winds arise when the air is thinned out by the sun. When the winds become burning hot, they withdraw and are wafted back to the pole. Thunder and lightning arise from the heat that collides with the clouds.[100] 12. Earthquakes arise from the upper air colliding with the air that exists below the earth. When this subterranean air is agitated, the earth, borne upon it, is shaken by it.[101]

Animals originate in moisture and afterward from each other. Males are born when the seed is separated from the parts on the right side and sticks to the right-sided parts of the womb (and *vice versa* for females).[102]

13. This Anaxagoras reached his height on the first year of the eighty-eighth Olympiad in the time that they say Plato was born.[103] They also say that he could foretell the future.

---

94. Cf. Ps.-Plutarch, *Plac. philos.* 2.21, 890c; Diog. L., *Vit. phil.* 2.8.

95. Cf. Plato, *Crat.* 409a; Ps.-Plutarch, *Plac. philos.* 2.28, 891d.

96. Cf. Ps.-Plutarch, *Plac. philos.* 2.29, 891e.

97. Cf. Ps.-Plutarch, *Plac. philos.* 2.23, 890d.

98. Cf. Ps.-Plutarch, *Plac. philos.* 2.25, 891c; 2.30, 892a; Diog. L., *Vit. phil.* 2.8.

99. Cf. Diog. L., *Vit. phil.* 2.9.

100. Cf. Ps.-Plutarch, *Plac. philos.* 3.3, 893e–f; Diog. L., *Vit. phil.* 2.9.

101. Cf. Ps.-Plutarch, *Plac. philos.* 3.15, 896c; Diog. L., *Vit. phil.* 2.9.

102. Cf. Aristotle, *Gen. an.* 4.1, 763b32–34; Ps.-Plutarch, *Plac. philos.* 5.7, 905e; Diog. L., *Vit. phil.* 2.9. The theory resembles that of Parmenides, DK 28 B17; cf. Ps.-Plutarch, *Plac. philos.* 5.11, 906d.

103. That is, in 428/427 BCE; cf. Diog. L., *Vit. phil.* 2.7; 3.2.

9. 1. Ἀρχέλαος τὸ μὲν γένος Ἀθηναῖος, υἱὸς δὲ Ἀπολλοδώρου. οὗτος ἔφη τὴν μίξιν τῆς ὕλης ὁμοίως Ἀναξαγόρᾳ, τάς τε ἀρχὰς ὡσαύτως, αὐτὸς δὲ <τοῦ νοῦ> ἐνυπάρχειν τι εὐθέως <τῷ> μίγμα<τι>. 2. εἶναι δὲ ἀρχὴν τῆς κινήσεως τὸ ἀποκρίνεσθαι ἀπ᾽ ἀλλήλων τὸ θερμὸν καὶ τὸ ψυχρόν, καὶ τὸ μὲν θερμὸν κινεῖσθαι, τὸ δὲ ψυχρὸν ἠρεμεῖν. τηκόμενον δὲ τὸ ὕδωρ εἰς μέσον ῥεῖν, ἐν ᾧ [καὶ] κατακαιόμενον ἀέρα γίνεσθαι καὶ γῆν· ὧν τὸ μὲν ἄνω φέρεσθαι, τὸ δὲ ὑφίστασθαι κάτω. 3. τὴν μὲν οὖν γῆν ἠρεμεῖν καὶ <ψυχρὰν> γενέσθαι διὰ ταῦτα· κεῖσθαι δὲ ἐν μέσῳ, οὐδὲν μέρος οὖσαν, ὡς εἰπεῖν, τοῦ παντός· <τὸν δὲ ἀέρα> ἐκδεδομένον ἐκ τῆς πυρώσεως. ἀφ᾽ οὗ πρῶτον ἀποκαιομένου τὴν τῶν ἀστέρων εἶναι φύσιν, ὧν μέγιστον μὲν ἥλιον, δεύτερον δὲ σελήνην, τῶν δὲ ἄλλων τὰ μὲν ἐλάττω, τὰ δὲ μείζω.

4. Ἐπικλιθῆναι δὲ τὸν οὐρανόν φησι καὶ οὕτως τὸν ἥλιον ἐπὶ τῆς γῆς ποιῆσαι φῶς, καὶ τόν τε ἀέρα ποιῆσαι διαφανῆ καὶ τὴν γῆν ξηράν. λίμνην γὰρ εἶναι τὸ πρῶτον, ἅτε κύκλῳ μὲν οὖσαν ὑψηλήν, μέσον δὲ κοίλην· σημεῖον δὲ φέρει τῆς κοιλότητος, ὅτι ὁ ἥλιος οὐχ ἅμα ἀνατέλλει τε καὶ δύεται πᾶσιν, ὅπερ ἔδει συμβαίνειν εἴπερ ἦν ὁμαλή.

5. περὶ δὲ ζῴων φησὶν ὅτι θερμαινομένης τῆς γῆς τὸ πρῶτον ἐν τῷ κάτω μέρει, ὅπου τὸ θερμὸν καὶ τὸ ψυχρὸν ἐμίσγετο, ἀνεφαίνετο τά τε ἄλλα ζῷα πολλὰ καὶ οἱ ἄνθρωποι, ἅπαντα τὴν αὐτὴν δίαιταν ἔχοντα, ἐκ τῆς ἰλύος τρεφόμενα—ἦν δὲ ὀλιγοχρόνια—· ὕστερον δὲ αὐτοῖς ἡ ἐξ ἀλλήλων γένεσις συνέστη. 6. καὶ διεκρίθησαν ἄνθρωποι ἀπὸ τῶν ἄλλων καὶ ἡγεμόνας καὶ νόμους καὶ τέχνας καὶ πόλεις καὶ τὰ ἄλλα συνέστησαν. νοῦν δὲ λέγει πᾶσιν ἐμφύεσθαι

ARCHELAOS. 9. 1. Archelaos, son of Apollodoros, was from an Athenian family.[104] He spoke of the mixture of matter as did Anaxagoras and said the same about first principles.[105] He himself affirmed that something of Mind exists directly in the mixture.[106] 2. The beginning of movement is the separation of heat and cold from each other. The heat is moved, whereas the cold stays still. In its fluid state, water flows into a central area in which, when the water is fully boiled, arise air and earth. Air is carried upward, while earth settles below. 3. Now the earth stays still and becomes cold for this reason: it lies in the middle, making up no part, so to speak, of the universe.[107] The air is released from the conflagration.[108] At first, it was from this air, when burned off, that the nature of the heavenly bodies came into existence. The largest heavenly body is the sun, and the second largest is the moon. As for the other heavenly bodies, some are smaller, and some larger.

4. The sky is inclined at an angle, he says, and in this way the sun illumines the earth and makes the air clear and the earth dry. For at first the earth was a basin, inasmuch as it was high at the periphery and hollow in the middle. He indicates its concavity by the fact that the sun does not rise and set on all people at the same time, which would necessarily occur if the earth were level.

5. Concerning animals, he says that the earth first grew hot in the lower part, where the hot and the cold were mixed, and there appeared many other animals, as well as human beings. Everything had the same mode of life, nourished from the mud—but this was only for a short time. Later, there arose sexual reproduction. 6. Humans were then distinguished from the other animals and established leaders, laws, arts, cities, and the

---

104. For our author's treatment of Archelaos, see Mueller, "Heterodoxy," 4363–64.

105. Cf. Theophrastos, frag. 228a (FHSG 1:418–19).

106. Marcovich changes τῶ νόῶ of the manuscripts to τοῦ νοῦ after comparison with Augustine, *Civ.* 8.2 (*ut inesse* [i.e., *particulis*] *etiam mentem diceret* ["he says that Mind too exists in (the separate bits)"]), and Anaxagoras, DK 59 B12—which actually says that νοῦς is mixed with nothing (μέμειχται οὐδενὶ χρήματι). Marcovich also emends the μίγμα of the manuscripts to τῷ μίγματι ("in the mixture").

107. Marcovich adds ψυχράν ("cold") from Plutarch, *Prim. frig.* 954f: ἧς [i.e., τῆς γῆς] ἡ ψυχρότης δεσμός ἐστιν, ὡς Ἀρχέλαος ὁ φυσικὸς εἶπεν ("Cold is the binding element of it [earth], as Archelaos the natural philosopher affirms").

108. Marcovich adds τὸν δὲ ἀέρα ("The air"). Most editors would venture a more fulsome emendation. Wendland, following Diels, prints: τὸν δ' ἀέρα κρατεῖν τοῦ παντός ("the air dominates the universe").

ζῴοις ὁμοίως· χρῆσθαι γὰρ ἕκαστον <τῷ νῷ, ὥσπερ> καὶ τῷ σώματι [ὅσῳ], τὸ μὲν βραδυτέρως, τὸ δὲ ταχυτέρως.

10. 1. Ἡ μὲν οὖν φυσικὴ φιλοσοφία ἀπὸ Θάλητος ἕως Ἀρχελάου διέμεινε· τούτου γίνεται Σωκράτης ἀκροατής. εἰσὶ δὲ καὶ ἕτεροι πλεῖστοι διαφόρους δόξας προενεγκάμενοι περί τε τοῦ θείου καὶ τῆς τοῦ παντὸς φύσεως· ὧν εἰ πάσας τὰς δόξας ἐβουλόμεθα παραθεῖναι, πολλὴν ἂν ὕλην βιβλίων ἔδει κατασκευάζειν. 2. ὧν δὲ ἔδει, μάλιστα ἐπ' ὀνόματος ὄντων καί, ὡς εἰπεῖν, κορυφαίων γενομένων, πᾶσι τοῖς μετέπειτα φιλοσοφήσασιν ἀφορμὰς δεδωκότων πρὸς τὰ ἐπιχειρούμενα, ὑπομνησθέντες ἐπὶ τὰ ἑξῆς ὁρμήσομεν.

11. 1. Καὶ γὰρ καὶ Παρμενίδης ἓν μὲν τὸ πᾶν ὑποτίθεται ἀίδιόν τε καὶ ἀγένητον καὶ σφαιροειδές, οὐδ' αὐτὸς δὲ ἐκφυγὼν τὴν τῶν πολλῶν δόξαν πῦρ λέγει καὶ γῆν τὰς τοῦ παντὸς ἀρχάς, τὴν μὲν γῆν ὡς ὕλην, τὸ δὲ πῦρ ὡς αἴτιον καὶ ποιοῦν. τὸν δὲ κόσμον ἔφη φθείρεσθαι, ᾧ δὲ τρόπῳ, οὐκ εἶπεν. 2. ὁ αὐτὸς δὲ

other aspects of culture. Mind, he says, is equally inborn in all animals. Each one uses the Mind, just as they do the body—some more sluggishly, and others more swiftly.[109]

10. 1. Natural philosophy lasted from Thales to Archelaos (whose pupil was Sokrates). There are a host of others that have proposed different doctrines about the divine and about the nature of the universe. If it was my plan to present all these doctrines, it would be necessary to prepare a great forest of books. 2. But after noting those who are necessary, particularly noteworthy, and who became, so to speak, the heads for all future philosophers (as they provided the starting points for argumentation), I will proceed to what follows.[110]

THE ELEATIC SUCCESSION

PARMENIDES. 11. 1. Moreover, Parmenides supposed that everything is one, eternal, unborn, and spherical.[111] But not even he escaped the opinion of the majority, since he affirms that fire and earth are first principles of the universe—the earth serving as matter, and fire as cause and maker.[112] He said that the cosmos is destroyed, but how it is destroyed he did not relate.

---

109. Marcovich supplies τῷ νῷ, ὥσπερ ("the Mind, just as"). Cf. Diog. L., *Vit. phil.* 2.16–17.

110. The "heads" (or "leaders") (κορυφαίων), Mansfeld notes, is a technical term (Diog. L., *Vit. phil.* 2.47). It refers to the main successors of Sokrates (*Heresiography*, 28 n. 2). Cf. Plato, *Theaet.* 173c7. Mansfeld argues that the following chapters (11–14; Parmenides to Xenophanes) represent the Eleatic succession, which is compressed by our author (*Heresiography*, 30–32, 34). Usually Xenophanes precedes Parmenides and is depicted as his teacher (Aristotle, *Metaph.* 1.5, 986b22; Theophrastos, frag. 227c [FHSG 1:415]; Diog. L., *Vit. phil.* 9.21).

111. A remnant of our author's rearrangement appears in the opening Καὶ γὰρ καί (here: "Moreover"). The phrase indicates that other material in the source preceded the account of Parmenides.

112. Our author has confused two separate theories of Parmenides (called the "Way of Truth" and the "Way of Opinion") in an apparent attempt to assert a contradiction. In the Way of Truth, there is no genesis of the cosmos; in the Way of Opinion the world begins from fire and earth. Cf. Parmenides, DK 28 B 8.55–61; Aristotle, *Metaph.* 1.5, 986b27–987a2; Theophrastos, frag. 227c–d (FHSG 1:414–17); Plutarch, *Adv. Col.* 1114d; Clem. Alex., *Strom.* 5.9.59.6; Diog. L., *Vit. phil.* 9.21. See further David Gallop, ed. and trans., *Parmenides of Elea: Fragments* (Toronto: University of Toronto Press, 1984), 7–23; Mueller, "Heterodoxy," 4367–68.

εἶπεν ἀίδιον εἶναι τὸ πᾶν καὶ οὐ γενόμενον καὶ σφαιροειδὲς καὶ ὅμοιον, οὐκ ἔχον δὲ τόπον ἐν ἑαυτῷ, καὶ ἀκίνητον καὶ πεπερασμένον.

12. 1. Λεύκιππος δὲ Ζήνωνος ἑταῖρος οὐ τὴν αὐτὴν δόξαν διετήρησεν, ἀλλά φησιν ἄπειρα <τὰ ὄντα> εἶναι καὶ ἀεὶ κινούμενα, καὶ γένεσιν καὶ μεταβολὴν συνεχῶς οὖσαν. στοιχεῖα δὲ λέγει τὸ πλῆρες καὶ τὸ κενόν. 2. κόσμους δὲ <ὧδε> γίνεσθαι λέγει· ὅταν εἰς μέγα κενὸν ἐκ τοῦ περιέχοντος ἀθροισθῇ πολλὰ σώματα καὶ συρρυῇ, προσκρούοντα ἀλλήλοις συμπλέκεσθαι τὰ ὁμοιοσχήμονα καὶ παραπλήσια τὰς μορφάς, καὶ περιπλεχθέντων ἄστρα γίνεσθαι· αὔξειν δὲ καὶ φθίνειν διὰ τὴν ἀνάγκην· τίς δ᾽ ἂν εἴη ἡ ἀνάγκη, οὐ διώρισεν.

13. 1. Δημόκριτος δὲ Λευκίππου γίνεται γνώριμος· Δημόκριτος Δαμασίππου Ἀβδηρίτης, πολλοῖς συμβαλών, γυμνοσοφισταῖς ἐν Ἰνδοῖς καὶ ἱερεῦσιν ἐν Αἰγύπτῳ καὶ ἀστρολόγοις καὶ μάγοις ἐν Βαβυλῶνι. 2. λέγει δὲ ὁμοίως Λευκίππῳ περὶ στοιχείων, πλήρους καὶ κενοῦ, τὸ μὲν πλῆρες λέγων ὄν, τὸ δὲ κενὸν οὐκ ὄν· ἔλεγε δὲ ὡς ἀεὶ κινουμένων τῶν ὄντων ἐν τῷ κενῷ.

2. The same man said that the universe is eternal, unborn, spherical, uniform, not having space in itself, unmoved, and finite.[113]

LEUKIPPOS. 12. 1. Leukippos, an associate of Zenon, did not preserve the same doctrine.[114] He says that existing things are boundless and always moving, with both generation and change constantly occurring.[115] He says that the elements are the "full" and the "void."[116] 2. He says that worlds arise in this way: when many bodies from the periphery are heaped up and flow together into a great void, they hit against each other, and those of like shape and similar form are entangled together.[117] Then, when they are entangled together, they become heavenly bodies. These heavenly bodies grow and perish by necessity. What necessity is, he did not define.[118]

DEMOKRITOS. 13. 1. Demokritos became a pupil of Leukippos. Demokritos son of Damasippos, an Abderite, met with many instructors: naked sages in India, priests in Egypt, as well as astrologers and magi in Babylon.[119] 2. He declares the same doctrines as Leukippos about the elements, as well as about fullness and void, saying that the full "exists" whereas the void "is nonexistent." He reiterates that existing things are always in motion in the void.[120]

---

113. Cf. Parmenides, DK 28 B8.3–4, 6, 22, 25–26, 42–43, 49; 19.2. Most of these attributes of the cosmos belong to the Way of Truth. By successively reporting that Parmenides believed in both the world's destruction and eternality, our author attempts to generate a contradiction. His loose and selective reporting here is more polemical than clumsy.

114. On our author's treatment of Leukippos and Demokritos, see Mueller, "Heterodoxy," 4368–69. Zenon is Zenon of Elea, disciple of Parmenides (thus our author maintains the chain of succession). In Theophrastos, frag. 229 (FHSG 1:420–21), Leukippos is the direct associate of Parmenides. In Diog. L., *Vit. phil.* 9.30–33, Leukippos follows Zenon.

115. Marcovich adds τὰ ὄντα ("existing things") by comparison with *Ref.* 1.13.2 and Aristotle, *Gen. corr.* 1.8, 325a25.

116. Cf. Aristotle, *Metaph.* 1.4, 985b5–8; Theophrastos, frag. 229 (FHSG 1:420–21); Ps.-Plutarch, *Plac. philos.* 1.3, 877d–f; Diog. L., *Vit. phil.* 9.30–33.

117. Marcovich, following Usener, adds ὧδε ("in this way"). For the teachings here, cf. Ps.-Plutarch, *Plac. philos.* 1.4, 878c–f; Diog. L., *Vit. phil.* 9.30–32; Dionysios of Alexandria in Eusebios, *Praep. ev.* 14.23.2–3, 773a–b.

118. For necessity, see Leukippos, DK 67 B2; Diog. L., *Vit. phil.* 9.33.

119. Cf. Clem. Alex., *Strom.* 1.15.69.6; Diog. L., *Vit. phil.* 9.34–35. For the magi, see de Jong, *Traditions*, 387–403.

120. Cf. Theophrastos, frag. 229 (FHSG 1:420–21).

ἀπείρους δὲ εἶναι κόσμους καὶ μεγέθει διαφέροντας· ἔν τισι δὲ μὴ εἶναι ἥλιον μηδὲ σελήνην, ἔν τισι δὲ μείζω τῶν παρ' ἡμῖν καὶ ἔν τισι πλείω. 3. εἶναι δὲ τῶν κόσμων ἄνισα τὰ διαστήματα, καὶ τῇ μὲν πλείους, τῇ δὲ ἐλάττους, καὶ τοὺς μὲν αὔξεσθαι, τοὺς δὲ ἀκμάζειν, τοὺς δὲ φθίνειν, καὶ τῇ μὲν γίνεσθαι, τῇ δὲ λείπειν· φθείρεσθαι δὲ αὐτοὺς ὑπ' ἀλλήλων προσπίπτοντας. εἶναι δὲ ἐνίους κόσμους ἐρήμους ζῴων καὶ φυτῶν καὶ παντὸς ὑγροῦ. 4. τοῦ δὲ παρ' ἡμῖν κόσμου πρότερον τὴν γῆν τῶν ἄστρων γενέσθαι. εἶναι δὲ τὴν μὲν σελήνην κάτω, ἔπειτα τὸν ἥλιον, εἶτα τοὺς ἀπλανεῖς ἀστέρας· τοὺς δὲ πλάνητας οὐδ' αὐτοὺς ἔχειν ἴσον ὕψος. ἀκμάζειν δὲ κόσμον ἕως ἂν μηκέτι δύνηται ἔξωθέν τι προσλαμβάνειν.

οὗτος ἐγέλα πάντα, ὡς γέλωτος ἀξίων πάντων τῶν ἐν ἀνθρώποις.

14. 1. Ξενοφάνης δὲ ὁ Κολοφώνιος Ὀρθομένους υἱός· οὗτος ἕως Κύρου διέμεινεν. οὗτος ἔφη πρῶτος ἀκαταληψίαν εἶναι πάντων, εἰπὼν οὕτως·

εἰ γὰρ καὶ τὰ μάλιστα τύχῃ τετελεσμένον εἰπών,
αὐτὸς ὅμως οὐκ οἶδε· δόκος δ' ἐπὶ πᾶσι τέτυκται.

There are infinite worlds that differ from each other in size.[121] In some there is neither sun nor moon, in others these heavenly bodies are bigger than in ours, and in some there are additional suns and moons. 3. Worlds exist for unequal lengths of time, in some cases more, and in others less. Some worlds grow, others reach their height, while others perish. At one time they arise, at another time they pass away. They are destroyed by colliding with each other. There are some worlds barren of animals and plants and of all moisture. 4. In our world, the earth arose before the heavenly bodies. The moon arose below the earth, then the sun, and then the fixed stars.[122] The planets, for their part, do not have equal height. The cosmos thrives until it is no longer able to receive anything from the outside.

This man was accustomed to laugh at everything, since he deemed all human affairs ridiculous.[123]

XENOPHANES. 14. 1. Xenophanes from Kolophon was the son of Orthomenes.[124] He remained until the time of Cyrus.[125] He was the first to affirm the incomprehensibility of all things,[126] speaking as follows:

> Even if, with optimal luck, one speak what perfectly befalls,
> One would still not know. Opinion is allotted to all.[127]

---

121. Cf. Diog. L., *Vit. phil.* 9.44.

122. Cf. Ps.-Plutarch, *Plac. philos.* 2.15, 889b; Lucretius, *Rer. nat.* 5.627–644.

123. Cf. Ps.-Hippokrates, *Ep.* 17.4–9; Sotion in Stobaios, *Flor.* 3.20.53 (Wachsmuth and Hense, 3:550); Cicero, *De or.* 2.235; Seneca, *Ira* 2.10.5; Lucian, *Vit. auct.* 13.

124. Xenophanes is oddly placed. Chronologically we would expect him before Parmenides. Clement of Alexandria makes Xenophanes the head of the Eleatic school (*Strom.* 1.14.64.2). Mansfeld believes that our author placed the proto-Skeptic Xenophanes after Demokritos in place of another lesser known proto-Skeptic who was the real successor of Demokritos: Metrodoros of Chios (briefly mentioned in *Ref.* 1.14.4) (*Heresiography*, 32–34). As it stands, Xenophanes the proto-Skeptic serves as a transition to the Skeptic Ekphantos (*Ref.* 1.15). See further Mueller, "Heterodoxy," 4365–67.

125. Cf. Apollodoros in Clem. Alex., *Strom.*1.14.64.2. On the dating, see Mansfeld, *Heresiography*, 38–39.

126. This accolade is given to Pyrrhon in *Ref.* 1.23.1, as well as in *Ref.* 1, table of contents §6. According to Diogenes Laertios, Sotion had Xenophanes introduce incomprehensibility (*Vit. phil.* 9.1). See further Diels, *Doxographi*, 148.

127. Xenophanes, DK 21 B34.3–4. For commentary, see *Xenophanes of Colophon, Fragments: A Text and Translation with a Commentary*, ed. J. H. Lesher (Toronto: University of Toronto Press, 1992), 158–69.

2. λέγει δὲ ὅτι οὐδὲν γίνεται οὐδὲ φθείρεται οὐδὲ κινεῖται καὶ ὅτι ἓν τὸ πᾶν ἐστιν ἔξω μεταβολῆς. φησὶ δὲ καὶ τὸν θεὸν εἶναι ἀίδιον καὶ ἕνα καὶ ὅμοιον πάντῃ καὶ πεπερασμένον καὶ σφαιροειδῆ καὶ πᾶσι τοῖς μορίοις αἰσθητικόν. 3. τὸν δὲ ἥλιον ἐκ μικρῶν πυριδίων ἀθροιζομένων γίνεσθαι καθ' ἑκάστην ἡμέραν· τὴν δὲ γῆν ἄπειρον εἶναι καὶ μήτε ὑπ' ἀέρος μήτε ὑπὸ τοῦ οὐρανοῦ περιέχεσθαι. καὶ ἀπείρους ἡλίους εἶναι καὶ σελήνας, τὰ δὲ πάντα εἶναι ἐκ γῆς. 4. οὗτος τὴν θάλασσαν ἁλμυρὰν ἔφη διὰ τὸ πολλὰ μίγματα συρρέειν ἐν αὐτῇ· ὁ δὲ Μητρόδωρος διὰ τὸ ἐν τῇ γῇ διηθεῖσθαι, τούτου χάριν γίνεσθαι ἁλμυράν.

5. Ὁ δὲ Ξενοφάνης μίξιν τῆς γῆς πρὸς τὴν θάλασσαν γίνεσθαι δοκεῖ καὶ τῷ χρόνῳ ὑπὸ τοῦ ὑγροῦ λύεσθαι, φάσκων τοιαύτας ἔχειν ἀποδείξεις, ὅτι ἐν μέσῃ γῇ καὶ ὄρεσιν εὑρίσκονται κόγχαι· καὶ ἐν Συρακούσαις δὲ ἐν ταῖς λατομίαις λέγει εὑρῆσθαι τύπον ἰχθύος καὶ φωκῶν, ἐν δὲ Πάρῳ τύπον ἀφύης ἐν τῷ βάθει τοῦ λίθου, ἐν δὲ Μελίτῃ πλάκας συμπάντων τῶν θαλασσίων. 6. ταῦτα δέ φησι γενέσθαι ὅτε πάντα ἐπηλώθησαν πάλαι, τὸν δὲ τύπον ἐν τῷ πηλῷ ξηρανθῆναι. ἀναιρεῖσθαι δὲ τοὺς ἀνθρώπους πάντας, ὅταν ἡ γῆ κατενεχθεῖσα εἰς τὴν θάλασσαν πηλὸς γένηται· εἶτα πάλιν ἄρχεσθαι τῆς γενέσεως, καὶ ταύτην πᾶσι τοῖς κόσμοις γίνεσθαι καταβολήν.

15. 1. Ἔκφαντός τις Συρακούσιος ἔφη μὴ εἶναι ἀληθινὴν τῶν ὄντων λαβεῖν γνῶσιν, ὁρίζει<ν> δὲ <ἕκαστον> ὡς νομίζει<ν>. τὰ μὲν πρῶτα ἀδιαίρετα εἶναι

2. He says that nothing comes to be nor perishes nor is moved, and that the universe is one and beyond change.[128] He also states that God is eternal and one and similar to all, finite, spherical, and perceptive in every part.[129] 3. The sun comes to be from small fiery particles amassed every day.[130] The earth is infinite and is encompassed neither by air nor by sky.[131] Moreover, there are infinite suns and moons, yet everything is from earth.[132] 4. He said that the sea is salty on account of the many compounds flowing together into it. But Metrodoros says that it becomes salty on account of being strained in the soil.[133]

5. Xenophanes believes that a blending of earth and sea arises and that in time the earth is dissolved by moisture. He offers proofs of this sort: seashells are found inland and on mountains.[134] Further, in the stone quarries of Syracuse, he says that the imprint of a fish and of seals were found. In the quarries on Paros, there was found the imprint of a small fish deep down in the rock. And on Malta slabs with the imprints of all kinds of sea creatures were found. 6. These things came to be, he says, when long ago all things were covered in mud, and the imprint dried in the mud. All human beings are killed when the earth sinks into the sea and becomes mud. Then the process of generation begins again, and this is the beginning of all worlds.[135]

EKPHANTOS. 15. 1. A certain Ekphantos from Syracuse said that no one grasps true knowledge of existing things, but that each person defines them as he supposes them to be.[136] The primary principles (from which

128. Cf. Ps.-Plutarch, *Strom.* 4; Ps.-Plutarch, *Plac. philos.* 2.4, 886e.

129. Cf. Xenophanes, DK 21 B23–24. A similar report is given in Ps.-Aristotle, *Mel. Xen. Gorg.* 977a36–b3; cf. Theophrastos, frag. 227c (FHSG 1:414–15). It is likely that the theology here (*Ref.* 1.14.2) has been detached from the report on Parmenides (due to our author's rearrangement).

130. Cf. Ps.-Plutarch, *Strom.* 4; Theophrastos, frag. 232 (FHSG 1:424–25).

131. Cf. Xenophanes, DK 21 B28; Aristotle, *Cael.* 2.13, 294a23–24; Ps.-Plutarch, *Strom.* 4; Ps.-Plutarch, *Plac. philos.* 3.9, 895d.

132. Cf. Xenophanes, DK 21 B27; Ps.-Plutarch, *Plac. philos.* 2.24, 890f–891a; Ps.-Plutarch, *Strom.* 4.

133. Cf. Aristotle, *Mete.* 2.3, 357a15–19; Theophrastos, *Phys. op.* frag. 23; Ps.-Plutarch, *Plac. philos.* 3.16, 897a.

134. Cf. Herodotos, *Hist.* 2.12; Strabo, *Geogr.* 1.3.4, 49c (Eratosthenes).

135. Cf. Ps.-Plutarch, *Strom.* 4.

136. Pseudo-Plutarch called Ekphantos a "Pythagorean" (e.g., *Plac. philos.* 3.13, 896a). On his placement here, see Mansfeld, *Heresiography*, 34–36. The summary in

σώματα καὶ παραλλαγὰς αὐτῶν τρεῖς ὑπάρχειν, μέγεθος σχῆμα δύναμιν, ἐξ ὧν τὰ αἰσθητὰ γίνεσθαι· 2. εἶναι δὲ τὸ πλῆθος αὐτῶν, ὡρισμένων κατὰ τοῦτο, ἄπειρον. κινεῖσθαι δὲ τὰ σώματα μήτε ὑπὸ βάρους μήτε πληγῆς, ἀλλ' ὑπὸ θείας δυνάμεως, ἣν νοῦν καὶ ψυχὴν προσαγορεύει. τού μὲν οὖν τὸν κόσμον εἶναι ἰδέαν, δι' ὃ καὶ σφαιροειδῆ ὑπὸ θείας δυνάμεως γεγονέναι. τὴν δὲ γῆν μέσον κόσμου κινεῖσθαι περὶ τὸ αὑτῆς κέντρον ὡς πρὸς ἀνατολήν.

16. 1. Ἵππων δὲ Ῥηγῖνος ἀρχὰς ἔφη ψυχρὸν τὸ ὕδωρ καὶ θερμὸν τὸ πῦρ. γεννώμενον δὲ τὸ πῦρ ὑπὸ ὕδατος κατανικῆσαι τὴν τοῦ γεννήσαντος δύναμιν συστῆσαί τε τὸν κόσμον. 2. τὴν δὲ ψυχὴν ποτὲ μὲν ἐγκέφαλον λέγει, ποτὲ δὲ ὕδωρ· καὶ γὰρ τὸ σπέρμα εἶναι τὸ φαινόμενον ἡμῖν ἐξ ὑγροῦ, ἐξ οὗ φησι ψυχὴν γίνεσθαι.

17. 1. Ταῦτα μὲν οὖν ἱκανῶς δοκοῦμεν παρατεθεικέναι· διὸ δοκεῖ λοιπὸν αὐτάρκως διαδραμόντων ἡμῶν τὰ τοῖς φυσικοῖς δόξαντα ἀναδραμεῖν ἐπὶ Σωκράτην καὶ Πλάτωνα, οἳ τὸ ἠθικὸν μάλιστα προετίμησαν.

perceptible things arise) are indivisible and have three alterations—with respect to size, shape, and quality. 2. Their number, when they are defined in this way, is infinite. Bodies are moved neither by weight nor by impact but by a divine power, which he calls "Mind" and "Soul." The cosmos is a semblance of this Mind, since it too becomes spherical by divine power. The earth, the midpoint of the cosmos, moves round its own center in an easterly direction.[137]

HIPPON. 16. 1. Hippon of Rhegion said that the first principles are what is cold (namely, water), and what is hot (namely, fire).[138] Fire born by the power of water conquers the power of its parent and composes the world.[139] 2. Sometimes he speaks of the soul as the brain, and other times as water.[140] Indeed, the semen visible to us is composed of moisture—and from semen, he says, arises soul.[141]

17. 1. These doctrines I consider adequately presented. Consequently, as I have sufficiently run through the opinions of the natural philosophers, it seems fitting now to backtrack to Sokrates and Plato, who valued above all the ethical type of philosophy.[142]

Mueller ("Heterodoxy," 4369–70) tells us almost all we know of him. Marcovich, following Wolf, adds ἕκαστον (here: "each person") to this sentence and changes the verbs to infinitives (indirect discourse).

137. Cf. Ps.-Plutarch, *Plac. philos.* 3.13, 896a.

138. Our author started his account of the natural philosophers with Thales (chap. 1). Hippon was known as a late follower of Thales. The report on Hippon may thus form an *inclusio* binding up the natural philosophers (chaps. 1–16) (Mansfeld, *Heresiography*, 36). See further Mueller, "Heterodoxy," 4370–71.

139. For Hippon's basic principles, see Ps.-Galen, *Hist. phil.* 18 (Diels, *Doxographi*, 610).

140. Cf. Ps.-Plutarch, *Plac. philos.* 4.3, 898d (soul is from water). Censorinus reports that for Hippon the head contains the "ruling part of the mind" (*animi principale*) (*Die nat.* 6.1).

141. Cf. Aristotle, *De an.* 1.2, 405b1–6 (soul is water, seed is primary soul); Theophrastos, frag. 225 (FHSG 1:406–7).

142. Our author already noted that Sokrates was a pupil of Archelaos in *Ref.* 1.10.1 (repeated in 1.18.1). He thus backtracks to that point in the succession. See further Mansfeld, *Heresiography*, 17–18.

18. 1. Ὁ μὲν οὖν Σωκράτης γίνεται Ἀρχελάου τοῦ φυσικοῦ ἀκροατής· ὃς τὸ «γνῶθι σαυτὸν» προτιμήσας καὶ μεγάλην σχολὴν συστήσας ἔσχε πάντων τῶν μαθητῶν ἱκανώτατον τὸν Πλάτωνα, αὐτὸς μὲν μηδὲ<ν> σύγγραμμα καταλιπών· 2. ὁ δὲ Πλάτων τὴν πᾶσαν αὐτοῦ σοφίαν ἀπομαξάμενος συνέστησε τὸ διδασκαλεῖον μίξας ὁμοῦ φυσικὴν ἠθικὴν διαλεκτικήν. ἃ δὲ ὁ Πλάτων ὁρίζει, ἐστὶ ταῦτα.

19. 1. [Πλάτων] Ἀρχὰς εἶναι τοῦ παντὸς θεὸν καὶ ὕλην καὶ παράδειγμα· θεὸν μὲν τὸν ποιητὴν καὶ διακοσμήσαντα τόδε τὸ πᾶν καὶ προνοούμενον αὐτοῦ· ὕλην δὲ τὴν πᾶσιν ὑποκειμένην, ἣν καὶ δεξαμενὴν καὶ τιθήνην καλεῖ. ἐξ ἧς διακοσμηθείσης γενέσθαι τὰ τέσσαρα στοιχεῖα, ἐξ ὧν συνέστηκεν ὁ κόσμος, πυρὸς ἀέρος γῆς ὕδατος, ἐξ ὧν καὶ τὰ ἄλλα πάντα συγκρίματα καλούμενα, ζῷά τε καὶ φυτά, συνεστηκέναι. 2. τὸ δὲ παράδειγμα τὴν διάνοιαν τοῦ θεοῦ εἶναι·

THE "ETHICAL" PHILOSOPHERS

SOKRATES. 18. 1. Sokrates became the pupil of Archelaos the natural philosopher.[143] He valued above all the maxim "know thyself."[144] When he formed a sizeable school, he had Plato as the most gifted of all his students. He himself left behind no treatise. 2. Yet Plato, after swiping all his wisdom, established his school by mixing together natural, ethical, and dialectical philosophy.[145] What Plato ordains is as follows.[146]

PLATO. 19. 1. The first principles of the universe are God, matter, and the model.[147] God is the maker and orderer of this universe and takes providential care of it. Matter, which he also calls "receptacle" and "nurse," underlies all things.[148] From this matter, when it is ordered, arise the four elements. From them—fire, air, earth, and water—the cosmos is composed. From them also all other compounds are composed, both animals and plants. 2. The model is the thought of God.[149] He also calls it "Idea," an

143. Cf. Diog. L., *Vit. phil.* 1.14; 2.16, 19; Porphyry, *Hist. philos.* frag. 215f.22–28 (Smith).

144. Cf. Plato, *Alcib.* 1.130e; 133c; *Phaedr.* 229–230a; *Phileb.* 48d–49a; the Seven Sages in DK 10 §2 (62.8); Χίλων §1 (63.25); Θαλῆς §9 (64.6–7); Herakleitos, DK 22 B116 (= Marcovich, *Heraclitus*, §23); Plutarch, *Adv. Col.* 1118c; Iamblichos, *Vit. Pyth.* 83. For our author's own interpretation of "know thyself," see *Ref.* 10.34.4.

145. For these divisions of philosophy, see Aristotle, *Top.* 1.14, 105b19–26 (ἠθικαί, φυσικαί, λογικαί); cf. Diog. L., *Vit. phil.* 3.56.

146. On our author's sources for Plato (*Ref.* 1.19), see Claudio Moreschini, "La *Doxa* di Platone nella *Refutatio* di Ippolito (I 19)," *SCO* 21 (1972): 254–60. Karin Alt studies our author's treatment of Plato, observing how he fails to mention key Platonic doctrines and occasionally misunderstands his sources ("Hippolytos als Referent platonischer Lehren," *JAC* 40 [1997]: 78–105).

147. For the three principles, see Theophrastos, frag. 230 (FHSG 1:422–23); Ps.-Plutarch, *Plac. philos.* 1.3.21, 878b; Stobaios, *Ecl.* 1.10.16[a] (Wachsmuth and Hense, 1:127–28); Apuleius, *Plat.* 1.5; Alkinoos, *Epit.* 9; Ps.-Justin, *Cohort.* 6.1; 7.1 (Pouderon); Iren., *Haer.* 2.14.3; Hermias, *Irris.* 11. See further Robert W. Sharples, "Counting Plato's Principles," in *The Passionate Intellect: Essays on the Transformation of Classical Traditions Presented to Professor I. G. Kidd*, ed. Lewis Ayres (New Brunswick, NJ: Transaction, 1995), 67–82 (73–82).

148. For the receptacle, see Plato, *Tim.* 49a6; 51a5; 52d5; 88d6. Plato never precisely defined the receptacle as matter, but Middle Platonists did (e.g., Ps.-Plutarch, *Plac. philos.* 1.9, 882c; 1.19, 884a; Alkinoos, *Epit.* 8.1–3; Apuleius, *Plat.* 1.5).

149. On the model (παράδειγμα), see Plato, *Tim.* 28a6–b1; Alkinoos, *Epit.* 9.1–3;

ὃ καὶ ἰδέαν καλεῖ, οἷον εἰκόνισμά τι, ᾧ προσέχων ἐν τῇ ψυχῇ ὁ θεὸς τὰ πάντα ἐδημιούργει.

3. τὸν μὲν θεόν φησιν ἀσώματόν τε καὶ ἀνείδεον καὶ μόνοις σοφοῖς ἀνδράσι καταληπτὸν εἶναι· τὴν δὲ ὕλην δυνάμει μὲν σῶμα, ἐνεργείᾳ δὲ οὐδέπω· ἀσχημάτιστον γὰρ αὐτὴν οὖσαν καὶ ἄποιον, προσλαβοῦσαν σχήματα καὶ ποιότητας γενέσθαι σῶμα. 4. τὴν μὲν οὖν ὕλην ἀρχὴν εἶναι καὶ σύγχρονον τῷ θεῷ. ταύτῃ καὶ ἀγένητον τὸν κόσμον· ἐκ γὰρ αὐτῆς συνεστάναι φησὶν αὐτόν, τῷ δὲ ἀγενήτῳ ἀκολουθεῖν πάντως καὶ τὸ ἄφθαρτον. ᾗ δὲ σῶμά τε καὶ ἐκ πολλῶν ποιοτήτων καὶ ἰδεῶν συγκείμενον ὑποτίθεται, ταύτῃ καὶ γενητὸν καὶ φθαρτόν.

5. Τινὲς δὲ τῶν Πλατωνικῶν ἀμφότερα ἔμιξαν, χρησάμενοι παραδείγματι τοιούτῳ· ὅτι ὥσπερ ἅμαξα δύναται ἀεὶ διαμένειν ἄφθαρτος κατὰ μέρος ἐπισκευαζομένη—κἂν τὰ μέρη φθείρηται ἑκάστοτε, αὐτὴ δὲ ὁλόκληρος ἀεὶ μένει—, τοῦτον τὸν τρόπον καὶ ὁ κόσμος κατὰ μέρη μὲν εἰ καὶ φθείρεται, ἐπισκευαζομένων καὶ ἀντανισουμένων τῶν ἀφαιρουμένων ἀΐδιος μένει.

6. Τὸν δὲ θεὸν οἱ μὲν ἕνα φασὶν αὐτὸν εἰπεῖν, ἀγένητον καὶ ἄφθαρτον, ὡς λέγει ἐν τοῖς Νόμοις· «ὁ μὲν δὴ θεός, ὥσπερ καὶ ὁ παλαιὸς λόγος, ἀρχήν τε καὶ τελευτὴν καὶ μέσα τῶν ὄντων ἁπάντων ἔχων»—οὕτως ἕνα αὐτὸν τὸν διὰ πάντων κεχωρηκότα ἀποφαίνεσθαι.

7. οἱ δὲ καὶ πολλοὺς ἀορίστους, ὅταν λέγῃ· «θεοὶ θεῶν, <ὧν> ἐγὼ δημιουργός τε καὶ πατήρ»· 8. οἱ δὲ καὶ ὡρισμένους, ὅταν λέγῃ· «ὁ μὲν δὴ μέγας

image, as it were, in the soul on which God concentrated as he fashioned all things.[150]

3. Plato says that God is incorporeal and formless and comprehensible only to sages.[151] Matter is body in potentiality not yet in actuality. For it is entirely shapeless and without quality. As it receives shapes and qualities it becomes a body.[152] 4. So Matter is a first principle and coeval with God.[153] In this respect, the world also is unborn—for the world, he says, is composed from matter. (And the fact that it is imperishable self-evidently follows from the fact that it is unborn.)[154] But insofar as he supposes matter to be body and the underlying factor of many qualities and forms, the world is both born and perishable.

5. Some of the Platonic philosophers mixed together both ideas [namely, that the world is born and unborn]. They use this sort of example: just as a wagon can always remain imperishable if repaired part by part—even if each of the parts perishes, the wagon itself always remains whole. In this way also, the world—even though it perishes part by part—remains eternal, since what is taken away is repaired and compensated.[155]

THEOLOGY. 6. Some say that Plato proclaimed God as one, unborn, and imperishable, as he says in the *Laws*: "God—as also the old saying goes—holds beginning, end, and middle of all reality."[156] In this way, he declares that the God who pervades all is one.

7. But others say that Plato affirms the existence of many and limitless gods when he says, "Gods of gods, of whom I am both Fashioner and

---

Apuleius, *Plat.* 1.6. On the model as God's thoughts, see Ps.-Plutarch, *Plac. philos.* 1.3, 878b; Alkinoos, *Epit.* 10.3.

150. Cf. Alkinoos, *Epit.* 2.1–2; Apuleius, *Plat.* 1.7. See further Dörrie and Baltes, *Platonismus*, 374–78.

151. For God as incorporeal, see Cicero, *Nat. d.* 1.30; Alkinoos, *Epit.* 10.3–4, 7–8; Apuleius, *Plat.* 1.5; Diog. L., *Vit. phil.* 3.77.

152. Cf. Plato, *Tim.* 50d–51b; Aristotle, *Gen. corr.* 2.1, 329a32–b3; Alkinoos, *Epit.* 8.2–3; Apuleius, *Plat.* 1.5; Tert., *Herm.* 35.2.

153. Our author will oppose the idea of matter as coeval with God in his attack on Hermogenes (*Ref.* 8.17.1; cf. 9.30.2 [the doctrine of the Jews]; 10.32.1 [our author's own doctrine]).

154. Cf. Philo, *Aet.* 27.

155. Cf. Philo, *Aet.* 143–44.

156. Plato, *Leg.* 715e7–8; also quoted in Alkinoos, *Epit.* 28.3. Cf. Ps.-Aristotle, *Mund.* 7, 401a28 (Ζεὺς κεφαλή, Ζεὺς μέσσα, Διὸς δ' ἐκ πάντα τέτυκται ["Zeus the head, Zeus the middle, all things arise from Zeus"]).

ἐν οὐρανῷ Ζεύς, πτηνὸν ἅρμα ἐλαύνων» καὶ ὅταν γενεαλογῇ τοὺς Οὐρανοῦ παῖδας καὶ Γῆς. οἱ δὲ συστήσασθαι μὲν αὐτὸν θεοὺς γενητούς, καὶ διὰ μὲν τὸ γεγενῆσθαι πάντως αὐτοὺς φθαρῆναι ἀνάγκην ἔχειν, διὰ δὲ τὴν βούλησιν τοῦ θεοῦ ἀθανάτους εἶναι, ἐν ᾧ προσθεὶς λέγει· «θεοὶ θεῶν, ὧν ἐγὼ δημιουργός τε καὶ πατήρ, ἄλυτα ἐμοῦ γε θέλοντος», ὡς ἂν εἰ λυθῆναι αὐτὰ θέλει, ῥᾳδίως λυθησόμενα. 9. δαιμόνων δὲ φύσεις ἀποδέχεται, καὶ τοὺς μὲν ἀγαθοὺς εἶναί φησιν αὐτῶν, τοὺς δὲ φαύλους.

10. Καὶ τὴν ψυχὴν οἱ μέν φασιν αὐτὸν ἀγένητον λέγειν καὶ ἄφθαρτον, ὅταν λέγῃ· «ψυχὴ πᾶσα ἀθάνατος· τὸ γὰρ ἀεικίνητον ἀθάνατον» καὶ ὅταν αὐτοκίνητον αὐτὴν ἀποδεικνύῃ καὶ ἀρχὴν κινήσεως· οἱ δὲ γενητὴν μέν, ἄφθαρτον δὲ διὰ τὴν τοῦ θεοῦ βούλησιν. οἱ δὲ σύνθετον καὶ γενητὴν καὶ φθαρτήν· καὶ γὰρ κρατῆρα αὐτῆς ὑποτίθεσθαι, καὶ σῶμα αὐτὴν ἔχειν αὐγοειδές, τὸ δὲ γενόμενον πᾶν ἀνάγκην ἔχειν φθαρῆναι.

11. οἱ δὲ ἀθάνατον αὐτὴν εἶναι λέγοντες μάλιστα ἐκείνοις ἰσχυρίζονται, <ἐν> ὅσοις καὶ κρίσεις φησὶν εἶναι μετὰ τελευτὴν καὶ ἐν Ἅιδου δικαστήρια, καὶ τὰς μὲν ἀγαθὰς ἀγαθοῦ μισθοῦ τυγχάνειν, τὰς δὲ πονηρὰς ἀκολούθων δικῶν.

12. τινὲς μὲν οὖν φασιν καὶ μετενσωμάτωσιν αὐτὸν ὁμολογεῖν καὶ μεταβαίνειν τὰς ψυχὰς ὡρισμένας οὔσας ἄλλας εἰς ἄλλα σώματα κατ᾽ ἀξίαν ἑκάστην, καὶ κατά τινας περιόδους ὡρισμένας ἀναπέμπεσθαι εἰς τοῦτον τὸν

Father."[157] 8. Still others think that Plato believes in a limited number of gods when he says, "Great Zeus in heaven, driving a winged chariot,"[158] and when he gives the genealogy of the children of Heaven and Earth.[159] Others say that he contrived born gods, and on account of their being born, they must surely perish by necessity. Nevertheless, they are immortal by virtue of God's will in view of the passage in which he adds: "Gods of gods, of whom I am the Fashioner and the Father, indissoluble *because I so will*."[160] (Since if he willed them to be dissolved, they would easily be dissolved.) 9. He accepts that there is a class of lesser divine beings, saying that some of them are good, while others are evil.[161]

THE SOUL. 10. Some say that Plato calls the soul unborn and imperishable when he says, "Every soul is immortal, for what moves forever is immortal," and when he demonstrates that the soul is forever moving and a principle of movement.[162] But others say that Plato calls the soul born yet imperishable, since it depends on God's will.[163] Others say that it is a compound, both born and perishable.[164] In fact, he imagines it in a mixing bowl with a gleaming body, and there is the principle that everything born must perish by necessity.[165]

11. Others, saying that the soul is immortal, are especially corroborated by the many passages in which Plato says that there are judgments after death and courtrooms in Hades, and that good souls meet a good reward, whereas evil souls meet fitting penalties.[166]

12. Some say that Plato acknowledged transmigration, and that souls, when they have been assigned, are transferred to various bodies as each deserves. Moreover, at certain fixed cycles, they are sent into this world again

157. Plato, *Tim.* 41a7; cf. Alkinoos, *Epit.* 15.2.

158. Plato, *Phaedr.* 246e4.

159. Plato, *Tim.* 40e5–41a6.

160. Plato, *Tim.* 41a7–8.

161. Ps.-Plutarch, *Plac. philos.* 1.8, 882b.

162. Plato, *Phaedr.* 245c–e; *Leg.* 891e; 896a–b; cf. Alkinoos, *Epit.* 25.4.

163. According to Alt, only Christian authors (e.g., Justin, *Dial.* 5.2–4) make this affirmation ("Hippolytos," 86–87).

164. For the compound nature of the human body, see Plato, *Tim.* 44d–46c. For the compound of body and soul, see *Tim.* 69c5–7.

165. For the image of the mixing bowl, see Plato, *Tim.* 41d4–7. For the soul subsisting in a luminous body, see Origen, *Cels.* 2.60. See further Alt, "Hippolytos," 87.

166. Plato, *Phaed.* 113d–114b; *Gorg.* 523c–524a; 526c; *Resp.* 614c–616a; *Phaedr.* 249a.

κόσμον πάλιν πεῖραν παρεξομένας τῆς ἑαυτῶν προαιρέσεως. 13. οἱ δὲ οὔ, ἀλλὰ τόπον λαγχάνειν κατ' ἀξίαν ἑκάστην, καὶ χρῶνται μαρτυρίῳ, ὅτι φησὶ μετὰ Διός τινας εἶναι, ἄλλους δὲ μετὰ ἄλλων θεῶν συμπεριπολοῦντας τῶν ἀγαθῶν ἀνδρῶν, τοὺς δὲ ἐν κολάσεσιν ὑπάρχειν αἰωνίαις, ὅσοι πονηρὰ καὶ ἄδικα παρὰ τοῦτον τὸν βίον εἰσὶν ἐξειργασμένοι.

14. Φασὶ δὲ αὐτὸν τὰ μὲν ἄμεσα λέγειν, τὰ δὲ ἔμμεσα, τὰ δὲ μέσα τῶν πραγμάτων· ἐγρήγορσιν μὲν καὶ ὕπνον ἄμεσα, καὶ ὅσα τοιαῦτα· ἔμμεσα δὲ οἷον ἀγαθὰ καὶ κακά· καὶ μέσα οἷον τοῦ λευκοῦ καὶ μέλανος τὸ φαιὸν ἤ τι ἄλλο χρῶμα. 15. ἀγαθὰ δὲ μόνα κυρίως λέγειν φασὶν αὐτὸν τὰ περὶ ψυχήν, τὰ δὲ περὶ σῶμα καὶ τὰ ἐκτὸς οὐκέτι κυρίως ἀγαθά, ἀλλὰ λεγόμενα ἀγαθά, πολλαχοῦ δὲ καὶ μέσα ὠνομακέναι αὐτά· εἶναι γὰρ αὐτοῖς καὶ καλῶς καὶ κακῶς χρῆσθαι.

16. Τὰς μὲν οὖν ἀρετὰς κατὰ τιμὴν ἀκρότητας εἶναί φησιν—τιμιώτερον [μὲν] γὰρ οὐδὲν ἀρετῆς—, κατὰ δὲ οὐσίαν μεσότητας· τὸ γὰρ ὑπερβάλλον αὐτῶν ἢ ἐνδέον εἰς κακίαν τελευτᾶν. οἷον τέσσαράς φησιν εἶναι ἀρετάς, φρόνησιν σωφροσύνην δικαιοσύνην ἀνδρείαν· τούτων ἑκάστῃ παρακολουθεῖν δύο κακίας καθ' ὑπερβολὴν καὶ μείωσιν. οἷον τῇ μὲν φρονήσει ἀφροσύνην κατὰ μείωσιν, πανουργίαν δὲ καθ' ὑπερβολήν, τῇ δὲ σωφροσύνῃ σκαιότητα κατὰ μείωσιν, ἀκολασίαν καθ' ὑπερβολήν, τῇ δὲ δικαιοσύνῃ μειονεξίαν κατὰ μείωσιν,

of their own free will to undergo testing.[167] 13. Others say that there is no transmigration. Rather, each soul obtains the place it deserves. They use as testimony the fact that Plato says that some good men are with Zeus, while others circle round with other gods. Still other souls—as many as have accomplished evil and unjust deeds in this life—exist in eternal punishments.[168]

ETHICS. 14. They say that Plato speaks of some things as without intermediates, others as with intermediates, and others as intermediates. Wakefulness and sleep—and everything of this type—are without intermediates. Things with intermediates are, for example, goods and evils. Finally, an intermediate between white and black is, for instance, gray or some other color. 15. They say that he only properly speaks of goods as matters of the soul. Bodily and external matters are no longer properly speaking "goods" but so-called goods that he often called "intermediates" (for they can be used well or poorly).[169]

16. Now the virtues, Plato says, are extremes in value (for nothing is more valuable than virtue), but according to substance they are intermediates. This is because what excels them or falls short of them ends in vice.[170] For instance, he says that there are four virtues: wisdom, moderation, justice, and courage.[171] Two vices accompany each virtue by excess or deficiency.[172] For example, stupidity follows wisdom by deficiency, cunning by excess; insensitiveness follows moderation by deficiency, licentiousness by excess;[173] claiming less than one's due follows justice by

---

167. Plato, *Phaed.* 81d–82b; *Resp.* 617d–621b; *Phaedr.* 248d–249c; *Tim.* 42a–d; *Leg.* 872e; 903d.

168. Plato, *Phaedr.* 250b–c. For further material on Plato's psychology, see Dörrie and Baltes, *Platonismus*, 3:78–84. Alt believes that our author has mixed a variety of Platonic sources to reconstruct the Platonic afterlife ("Hippolytos," 87–88). The teachings are not consistent—which would seem to be the point.

169. Plato, *Leg.* 697b2; cf. Diog. L., *Vit. phil.* 3.80–81; Stobaios, *Ecl.* 2.7 (Wachsmuth and Hense, 2:55,11–13). See alo *Ref.* 1.20.3 (Aristotle).

170. Aristotle, *Eth. nic.* 2.6, 1106b36–1107a8; Alkinoos, *Epit.* 30.4; Apuleius, *Plat.* 2.5.

171. On the four cardinal virtues, see Plato, *Phaed.* 69a–b; *Resp.* 433b7, 442b–443c, 504a5; *Leg.* 964b5, 965d2; Diog. L., *Vit. phil.* 3.90–91.

172. Cf. Aristotle, *Eth. nic.* 2.2, 1104a12–13 (ὑπὸ ἐνδείας καὶ ὑπερβολῆς φθείρεσθαι ["they (virtues) are vitiated by deficiency and excess"]); [Aristotle], *Mag. mor.* 1.5, 1185b14–33.

173. Cf. Aristotle, *Eth. eud.* 2.3, 1221a2, 12; *Eth. nic.* 2.2, 1104a22–24 (ἀκόλαστος, ἀναίσθητος).

πλεονεξίαν καθ' ὑπερβολήν, τῇ δὲ ἀνδρείᾳ δειλίαν κατὰ μείωσιν, θρασύτητα καθ' ὑπερβολήν. Ταύτας δὲ ἐγγενομένας τὰς ἀρετὰς ἀνθρώπῳ ἀπεργάζεσθαι αὐτὸν τέλειον καὶ παρέχειν αὐτῷ εὐδαιμονίαν.

17. τὴν δὲ εὐδαιμονίαν εἶναί φησιν ὁμοίωσιν θεῷ κατὰ τὸ δυνατόν· τὴν δὲ ὁμοίωσιν τῷ θεῷ, ὅταν τις ὅσιός τε καὶ δίκαιος γένηται μετὰ φρονήσεως· τέλος γὰρ τοῦτο τῆς ἄκρας σοφίας καὶ ἀρετῆς ὑποτίθεται. 18. λέγει δὲ ἀντακολουθεῖν τὰς ἀρετὰς ἀλλήλαις καὶ μονοειδεῖς εἶναι καὶ μηδέποτε ἐναντιοῦσθαι ἀλλήλαις· τὰς δὲ κακίας πολυτρόπους τε εἶναι καὶ ποτὲ μὲν ἀντακολουθεῖν, ποτὲ δὲ ἐναντιοῦσθαι ἀλλήλαις.

19. εἱμαρμένην φησιν εἶναι, οὐ μὴν πάντα καθ' εἱμαρμένην γίνεσθαι, ἀλλ' εἶναί τι καὶ ἐφ' ἡμῖν, ἐν οἷς φησιν· «αἰτία ἑλομένου, θεὸς ἀναίτιος» καὶ «θεσμός τε Ἀδραστείας ὅδε»· οὕτω τὸ καθ' εἱμαρμένην οἶδε καὶ τὸ ἐφ' ἡμῖν.

20. Ἀκούσια δέ φησιν εἶναι τὰ ἁμαρτήματα· εἰς γὰρ τὸ κάλλιστον τῶν ἐν ἡμῖν, ὅπερ ἐστὶν ἡ ψυχή, οὐκ ἄν τινα τὸ κακὸν παραδέξασθαι, τουτέστι τὴν ἀδικίαν· κατὰ ἄγνοιαν δέ <τινας> καὶ σφάλμα τοῦ ἀγαθοῦ, οἰομένους καλόν τι ποιεῖν, ἐπὶ τὸ κακὸν ἔρχεσθαι. 21. καὶ λέξις τούτου ἐμφανεστάτη ἐστὶν ἐν τῇ

deficiency, claiming more than one's due by excess;[174] and finally, cowardice follows courage by deficiency, and rashness by excess.[175] When these virtues are instilled, they produce perfection in the human being and provide human happiness.

17. Now happiness, Plato says, is assimilation to God as far as possible, and assimilation to God occurs when one becomes holy and just with wisdom.[176] He supposes that this assimilation is the height of wisdom and virtue. 18. He says that the virtues are reciprocal and uniform and never oppose one another.[177] The vices, however, are variable, sometimes reciprocal, sometimes opposing each other.[178]

FATE. 19. Plato says that there is fate, but not everything comes to be by fate.[179] Rather, there is also some personal responsibility, as he says in these passages: "the blame is due to the one who chooses; God is not to be blamed,"[180] and "the institution of Necessity is this."[181] Thus he acknowledges both fate and responsibility.

THE ORIGIN OF EVIL. 20. Errors, Plato says, are not willed; for no one would admit evil (that is, injustice) into the most beautiful thing we have within us, namely, the soul. In ignorance, some people—falling short of the good while supposing they do something noble—arrive at evil.[182] 21. The clear-

---

174. Cf. Hierakos, Περὶ δικαιοσύνης in Stobaios, *Flor.* 3.9.54 (Wachsmuth and Hense, 3:365–68); [Aristotle], *Mag. mor.* 1.33, 1193b25–1196b4.

175. Cf. Aristotle, *Eth. nic.* 2.2, 1104a20–22 (δειλός, θρασύς); [Aristotle], *Mag. mor.* 1.5, 1185b23–6; Apuleius, *Plat.* 2.5; Stobaios, *Ecl.* 2.7.20 (Wachsmuth and Hense, 2:140,18–142,5).

176. Plato, *Theaet.* 176b1–3; *Resp.* 613a7; *Tim.* 90d4; Alkinoos, *Epit.* 28.1; Stobaios, *Ecl.* 2.7.3[f] (Wachsmuth and Hense, 2:49); Diog. L., *Vit. phil.* 3.78.

177. Cf. Apuleius, *Plat.* 2.6; Alkinoos, *Epit.* 29.4. The idea that virtues correspond to each other can be traced to Stoic thought. Cf. Diog. L., *Vit. phil.* 7.125 (Zenon) (= *SVF* 3.295); Plutarch, *Stoic. rep.* 1046e (= *SVF* 3.299); cf. *SVF* 3.302; Sext. Emp., *Pyr.* 1.68. On virtues as singular (μονοειδεῖς), cf. [Aristotle], *Mag. mor.* 1.25, 1192a12–14; Philo, *Sacr.* 84; Apuleius, *Plat.* 2.5 (*unimodam*).

178. Cf. Alkinoos, *Epit.* 30.1; see also Apuleius, *Plat.* 1.6; Aristotle, *Eth. eud.* 8.5, 1239b11–12.

179. Cf. Ps.-Plutarch, *Plac. philos.* 1.27, 884f–885a; Alkinoos, *Epit.* 26.1.

180. Plato, *Resp.* 617e4.

181. Plato, *Phaedr.* 248c2.

182. Plato, *Prot.* 345d9; 358c6–7; *Leg.* 731c–d; *Tim.* 86d–e; Alkinoos, *Epit.* 31.1–2; Apuleius, *Plat.* 2.11.

Πολιτείᾳ, ἐν ᾗ φησιν· «πάλιν δ᾽ αὖ τολμᾶτε λέγειν ὡς αἰσχρὸν καὶ θεομισὲς ἡ ἀδικία· πῶς οὖν δή τις τό τοιοῦτον κακὸν αἱροῖτ᾽ ἄν; ἥττων ὃς ἂν ᾖ, φατέ, τῶν ἡδονῶν. οὐκοῦν καὶ τοῦτο ἀκούσιον, εἴπερ τὸ νικᾶν ἑκούσιον; ὥστε ἐκ παντὸς τρόπου τό γε ἀδικεῖν ἀκούσιον λόγος αἱρεῖ». 22. ἀντιτίθεται δέ τις αὐτῷ πρὸς τοῦτο· διὰ τί οὖν κολάζονται, εἰ ἀκουσίως ἁμαρτάνουσιν; ὁ δὲ λέγει· ἵνα τε αὐτὸς ὅτι τάχιστα ἀπαλλαγῇ κακίας καὶ κόλασιν ὑπόσχῃ—τὸ γὰρ κόλασιν ὑποσχεῖν οὐ κακὸν εἶναι ἀλλ᾽ ἀγαθόν, εἴπερ μέλλει κάθαρσις τῶν κακῶν γίνεσθαι—καὶ ἵνα μηδὲ ἁμαρτάνωσιν οἱ λοιποὶ ἀκούοντες ἄνθρωποι, ἀλλὰ φυλάσσωνται τὴν τοιαύτην πλάνην.

23. κακοῦ δὲ φύσιν οὔτε ὑπὸ θεοῦ γενέσθαι οὔτε καθ᾽ αὑτὴν ὑπόστασιν ἔχειν, ἀλλὰ κατ᾽ ἐναντίωσιν καὶ παρακολούθησιν τοῦ ἀγαθοῦ γενέσθαι ἢ καθ᾽ ὑπερβολὴν ἢ κατὰ μείωσιν, ὡς περὶ τῶν ἀρετῶν προείπομεν.

ὁ μὲν οὖν Πλάτων, καθὼς προείπομεν, συναγαγὼν τὰ τρία μέρη τῆς κατὰ πάντα φιλοσοφίας οὕτως ἐφιλοσόφησεν.

20. 1. Ἀριστοτέλης τούτου γενόμενος ἀκροατὴς εἰς τέχνην τὴν φιλοσοφίαν ἤγαγεν καὶ λογικώτερος ἐγένετο.

τὰ μὲν στοιχεῖα τῶν πάντων ὑποθέμενος οὐσίαν καὶ συμβεβηκός· τὴν μὲν οὐσίαν μίαν τὴν πᾶσιν ὑποκειμένην, τὰ δὲ συμβεβηκότα ἐννέα· ποσὸν ποιὸν πρός τι ποῦ πότε ἔχειν κεῖσθαι ποιεῖν πάσχειν. 2. τὴν μὲν οὖν οὐσίαν τοιαύτην εἶναι

est description of this is in the *Republic*, where he says: "Once again you dare to say that injustice is shameful and hated by God. How then does someone choose such an evil? He chooses it, you say, as one conquered by pleasures. Therefore is not this too involuntary if (to be sure) the act of conquering is voluntary? Thus in every way the argument proves injustice to be involuntary."[183] 22. But someone counters him with this remark: then why are they punished if they err unwillingly? He replies: so that (a) one can turn from vice as quickly as possible and endure punishment (for enduring punishment is not something bad but something good, since it will purify from vices),[184] and (b) so that other people who hear about it might not go astray but rather guard against such error.[185]

23. The nature of evil neither came about by the power of God nor has substance in itself. Rather, it arose by opposing the good as something that follows. It arises through either excess or deficiency (as we already said concerning the virtues).[186]

In this way, as I already mentioned, Plato philosophized by bringing together the three parts of a comprehensive philosophy.

ARISTOTLE. 20. 1. Aristotle, Plato's pupil, made philosophy a discipline and became more rationally precise.

THE CATEGORIES. Aristotle supposed that the elements of all things are substance and incidental properties.[187] The underlying substance is one for all things, whereas the incidental properties are nine: quantity, quality, relation, location, time, possession, position, activity, and passivity.[188] 2. Now

---

183. This passage comes not from the *Republic* but from the Platonic dialogue *Klitophon* 407d.

184. Plato, *Gorg.* 477a, 478e, 479a. On κάθαρσις, see Ps.-Plato, *Def.* 416a33; Alkinoos, *Epit.* 31.3.

185. Plato, *Prot.* 324b–c; *Leg.* 934b2.

186. Plato, *Tim.* 86d–e. For the phrase κατὰ παρακολούθησιν, see the teaching of Chrysippos in Gellius, *Noct. att.* 7.1.7.

187. On the "elements" (στοιχεῖα), see Mansfeld, *Heresiography*, 62–68.

188. For a sense of how Aristotle's *Categories* were interpreted close to the time of our author, see Robert W. Sharples, *Peripatetic Philosophy 200 BC to AD 200: An Introduction and Collection of Sources in Translation* (Cambridge: Cambridge University Press, 2010), 47–69. Additional sources (mostly later than our author) are collected by Richard Sorabji, *The Philosophy of the Commentators, 200–600 AD: A Sourcebook*, 3 vols. (London: Duckworth, 2004), 3:56–125. On the categories and their bipartite division, see Mansfeld, *Heresiography*, 59–62.

οἷον θεόν, ἄνθρωπον καὶ ἕκαστον τῶν τῷ ὁμοίῳ λόγῳ ὑποπεσεῖν δυναμένων· περὶ δὲ τὰ συμβεβηκότα θεωρεῖται τὸ μὲν ποιὸν οἷον λευκόν, μέλαν, τὸ δὲ ποσὸν οἷον δίπηχυ, τρίπηχυ, τὸ δὲ πρός τι οἷον πατήρ, υἱός, τὸ δὲ ποῦ οἷον Ἀθήνησι, Μεγαροῖ, τὸ δὲ πότε οἷον ἐπὶ τῆς δεκάτης ὀλυμπιάδος, τὸ δὲ ἔχειν οἷον κεκτῆσθαι, τὸ δὲ κεῖσθαι οἷον κατακεῖσθαι, τὸ δὲ ποιεῖν οἷον γράφειν καὶ ὅλως ἐνεργεῖν τι, τὸ δὲ πάσχειν οἷον τύπτεσθαι.

3. Ὑποτίθεται καὶ αὐτὸς τὰ μὲν μεσότητα ἔχειν, τὰ δὲ ἄμεσα εἶναι, ὡς εἴπομεν καὶ περὶ τοῦ Πλάτωνος. καὶ σχεδὸν τὰ πλεῖστα τῷ Πλάτωνι.

4. σύμφωνός ἐστιν πλὴν τοῦ περὶ ψυχῆς δόγματος· ὁ μὲν γὰρ Πλάτων ἀθάνατον, ὁ δὲ Ἀριστοτέλης ἐπιδιαμένειν καὶ μετὰ ταῦτα καὶ ταύτην ἐναφανίζεσθαι τῷ πέμπτῳ σώματι, ὃ ὑποτίθεται εἶναι [μετὰ] τῶν ἄλλων τεσσάρων—τοῦ τε πυρὸς καὶ τῆς γῆς καὶ τοῦ ὕδατος καὶ τοῦ ἀέρος—λεπτότερον, οἷον πνεῦμα.

5. Ὁ μὲν οὖν Πλάτων μόνα ἀγαθὰ ὄντως τὰ περὶ ψυχὴν εἶναί φησιν καὶ ἀρκεῖν πρὸς τὴν εὐδαιμονίαν· ὁ δὲ Ἀριστοτέλης τριγένειαν τῶν ἀγαθῶν εἰσάγει

substance is a thing like god, a human being, and each entity that can fall into the same definition.[189] Concerning incidental properties, he has in view, for example, white or black for quality, two or three feet for quantity, father and son for relation, in Athens or in Megara for location, on the tenth Olympiad for time, the state of owning something for possession, lying down for position, writing—and in general working on something—for activity, and being hit for passivity.[190]

3. Aristotle also supposes that some things have intermediates, while others have no intermediates (as I said about Plato as well).[191] In almost everything he is at one with Plato.

SOUL. 4. Aristotle is in agreement with Plato except with regard to his doctrine of soul. For Plato said that the soul is immortal, whereas Aristotle said that it continues to exist for some time, and afterward it too disappears into the fifth body.[192] He supposes that the fifth body is beyond the other four elements—fire, earth, water, and air. It is more refined, like a fiery breath.[193]

ETHICS. 5. Now Plato says that matters of soul are the only true goods and that these suffice for happiness. Aristotle, however, introduces a threefold

---

189. For "god" (θεός) as a substance, see Mansfeld, *Heresiography*, 69–70.

190. For this list of incidental properties ("accidents"), see Aristotle, *Cat.* 4, 1b25–2a4; *Top.* 1.9, 103b22–104a2. See further Porphyry, *Intro.* 12–13 (§5); Mansfeld, *Heresiography*, 68–72. On substance, see Aristotle, *Metaph.* 7.2, 1028b36. Our author will attribute substance and incidental properties to Pythagoras in *Ref.* 6.24.2. See further Ross Hamilton, *Accident: A Philosophical and Literary History* (Chicago: University of Chicago Press, 2007), 11–25.

191. *Ref.* 1.19.14. See further Mansfeld, *Heresiography*, 72–75.

192. On the fifth body, or aether, see Aristotle, *Cael.* 1.3, 270b20–24; *Mete.* 1:339b16–30; Ps.-Aristotle, *Mund.* 2, 392a5–9; *Ref.* 10.7.4 (Okellos). See further David Hahm, "The Fifth Element in Aristotle's *De Philosophia*," in *Essays in Ancient Greek Philosophy*, ed. John P. Anton and Anthony Preus, 6 vols. (Albany: SUNY Press, 1983), 2:404–30.

193. Stoics described pneuma as a mixture of air and fire and identified it with the substance of aether (αἰθήρ), or the fiery air that exists in the upper reaches of the universe. It is also Stoic teaching that the souls of good people rejoin the aether after the death of the body (Posidonius in *SVF* 2.812 [= Sext. Emp., *Math.* 9.72–74]; Arios Didymos, frag. 39.4–6 in Diels, *Doxographi*, 471 [= *SVF* 2.821, 809]). By the time of our author, however, the teaching was widespread and had been adapted by Platonists (reported by Tert., *An.* 54.2; 55.4), Jews (Josephus, *J.W.* 2.154–155; 6.47), and Christians (1 Cor 15:39–49).

καὶ λέγει μὴ εἶναι τέλειον τὸν σοφόν, ἐὰν μὴ παρῇ αὐτῷ καὶ τὰ τοῦ σώματος ἀγαθὰ καὶ τὰ ἐκτός. ἅ ἐστι κάλλος ἰσχὺς εὐαισθησία ἀρτιότης· τὰ δὲ ἐκτός, πλοῦτος εὐγένεια δόξα δύναμις εἰρήνη φιλία. τὰ δὲ ἐντὸς περὶ ψυχήν, καθὼς καὶ Πλάτωνι ἔδοξεν, φρόνησιν σωφροσύνην δικαιοσύνην ἀνδρείαν. 6. τὰ δὲ κακά φησι καὶ οὗτος κατ' ἐναντίωσιν τῶν ἀγαθῶν γενέσθαι, καὶ εἶναι ὑπὸ τὸν περὶ σελήνην τόπον, ὑπὲρ δὲ σελήνην μηκέτι.

τὴν δὲ ψυχὴν τὴν μὲν ὅλου τοῦ κόσμου ἀθάνατον εἶναι, καὶ αὐτὸν τὸν κόσμον ἀΐδιον, τὴν δὲ καθ' ἕκαστον, ὡς προείπομεν, ἀφανίζεσθαι.

7. Οὗτος μὲν οὖν ἐν τῷ Λυκείῳ ποιούμενος τὰς διατριβὰς ἐφιλοσόφει, ὁ δὲ Ζήνων ἐν τῇ Ποικίλῃ στοᾷ. ἐκτήσαντο δὲ οἱ μὲν ἀπὸ τοῦ Ζήνωνος ἀπὸ τοῦ τόπου τὸ ὄνομα, τουτέστιν ἀπὸ τῆς στοᾶς, Στωϊκοὶ κληθέντες, οἱ δὲ ἀπὸ τοῦ Ἀριστοτέλους ἀπὸ τοῦ ἔργου· ἐπειδὴ γὰρ περιπατοῦντες ἐν τῷ Λυκείῳ ἐζήτουν, διὰ τοῦτο Περιπατητικοὶ ἐκλήθησαν.

ταῦτα μὲν οὖν καὶ ὁ Ἀριστοτέλης.

21. 1. Στωϊκοὶ καὶ αὐτοὶ μὲν ἐπὶ τὸ συλλογιστικώτερον τὴν φιλοσοφίαν ηὔξησαν καὶ σχεδὸν ὅροις περιέλαβον, ὁμόδοξοι γενόμενοι ὅ τε Χρύσιππος

class of goods and declares that the sage is not perfect if he lacks both bodily and external goods.[194] Bodily goods include beauty, strength, perceptiveness, and soundness. External goods include wealth, noble birth, reputation, power, peace, and friendship. The inner virtues of the soul, as also Plato believed, are wisdom, moderation, justice, and courage.[195] 6. Aristotle also agrees that the vices arise in opposition to goods. They exist below the region of the moon, and not above the moon.[196]

The soul of the whole world is immortal, and the world itself is eternal (whereas the soul of each individual, as I said, disappears).[197]

ORIGIN OF THE NAME "PERIPATETIC." 7. Aristotle practiced philosophy in the Lyceum by making disputations, whereas Zenon did so in the Painted Stoa. The followers of Zenon obtained their name from this place (that is, the Stoa), since they are called "Stoics," but the followers of Aristotle gained their name from their practice. For since they engaged in their inquiries while walking about in the Lyceum, they were for this reason called "Roving Philosophers," or "Peripatetics."[198]

These are the doctrines of Aristotle.

STOICS. 21. 1. The Stoics for their part expanded philosophy with the use of syllogistic argumentation—and defined just about everything. Chrysippos and Zenon were united in their opinions. For their part, they also

---

194. Aristotle, *Eth. nic.* 1.8, 1098b12–19 (threefold class of goods); *Eth. eud.* 2.1, 1218b32–37; [Aristotle], *Mag. mor.* 1.3, 1184b1–6; Diog. L., *Vit. phil.* 5.30; Stobaios, *Ecl.* 2.7.14 (Wachsmuth and Hense, 2:124–28). Later sources in Sharples, *Peripatetic Philosophy*, 155–68. See further idem, "Peripatetics on Happiness," in *Greek and Roman Philosophy 100 BC–200 AD*, ed. Robert W. Sharples and Richard Sorabji, 2 vols. (London: Institute of Classical Studies, 2007), 2:627–38.

195. Cf. *Ref.* 1.19.16. On Aristotelian ethics, see Mansfeld, *Heresiography*, 147–49.

196. Cf. *Ref.* 1.4.3 (Herakleitos and Empedokles); see also Diog. L., *Vit. phil.* 9.10. Aristotle's teaching is more fully explained in *Ref.* 7.19.2. See Plutarch, *Fac.* 928d; 943c–e.

197. *Ref.* 1.20.4. On the eternality of νοῦς as opposed to soul, see Aristotle, *An* 1.4, 408b18–20, 29; 2.2, 413b24–27; 3.5, 430a17–25. Eternality is similarly predicated of "the primal body" in Aristotle, *Cael.* 1.3, 270a13. Later sources in Sharples, *Peripatetic Philosophy*, 174–79.

198. See the texts in Ingemar Düring, *Aristotle in the Ancient Biographical Tradition* (Göteborg: Almqvist & Wiksell, Stockholm, 1957), 404–11.

καὶ Ζήνων. οἳ ὑπέθεντο καὶ αὐτοὶ ἀρχὴν μὲν τῶν πάντων θεόν, σῶμα ὄντα τὸ καθαρώτατον, διὰ πάντων δὲ διήκειν τὴν πρόνοιαν αὐτοῦ.

2. καὶ αὐτοὶ δὲ τὸ καθ' εἱμαρμένην εἶναι πάντα διεβεβαιώσαντο, παραδείγματι χρησάμενοι τοιούτῳ· ὅτι ὥσπερ ὀχήματος ἐὰν ᾖ ἐξηρτημένος κύων, ἐὰν μὲν βούληται ἕπεσθαι, καὶ ἕλκεται καὶ ἕπεται, ποιῶν καὶ τὸ αὐτεξούσιον μετὰ τῆς ἀνάγκης [οἷον τῆς εἱμαρμένης]· ἐὰν δὲ μὴ βούληται ἕπεσθαι, πάντως ἀναγκασθήσεται. τὸ αὐτὸ δήπου καὶ ἐπὶ τῶν ἀνθρώπων· καὶ μὴ βουλόμενοι γὰρ ἀκολουθεῖν ἀναγκασθήσονται πάντως εἰς τὸ πεπρωμένον εἰσελθεῖν.

3. Τὴν δὲ ψυχὴν λέγουσι μὲν ἀθάνατον, εἶναι δὲ σῶμα καὶ γενέσθαι ἐκ τῆς περιψύξεως τοῦ ἀέρος τοῦ περιέχοντος· διὸ καὶ καλεῖσθαι ψυχήν. ὁμολογοῦσι δὲ καὶ μετενσωμάτωσιν γίνεσθαι, ὡρισμένων οὐσῶν τῶν ψυχῶν.

4. προσδέχονται δὲ ἐκπύρωσιν ἔσεσθαι καὶ κάθαρσιν τοῦ κόσμου τούτου, οἱ μὲν παντός, οἱ δὲ μέρους· καὶ κατὰ μέρος γὰρ αὐτὸν καθαίρεσθαι λέγουσιν. καὶ σχεδὸν τὴν φθορὰν καὶ τὴν ἑτέρου ἐξ αὐτῆς γένεσιν κάθαρσιν ὀνομάζουσιν.

supposed that the first principle of all things is God, who is the purest body, and that his providence pervades all things.[199]

FATE. 2. The Stoics strongly affirmed that all things exist by fate, using the following example. A dog bound to a cart, if it wants to follow, is both dragged and follows (acting out both its own free will along with necessity); but if it does not want to follow, it will be entirely forced by necessity. The same situation occurs among human beings as well: for even if they do not want to follow, they are entirely forced by necessity to meet their fate.[200]

THE SOUL. 3. They say that the soul is immortal and corporeal and that it arises from the cooling [περιψύξεως] of the surrounding air (thus it is called soul [ψυχήν]).[201] They agree that transmigration occurs since there is a limited number of souls.[202]

CONFLAGRATION. 4. The Stoics accept the idea that there will be a conflagration, and a purification of this cosmos, some declaring a purification of it all, while others a part of it. In fact, they say that it is purified gradually. And in general, they call the destruction of the cosmos and the birth of another cosmos from destruction "purification."[203]

---

199. Cf. *SVF* 2.310, 1028, 1030, 1051–54. Other sources in A. A. Long and D. N. Sedley, *The Hellenistic Philosophers*, 2 vols. (Cambridge: Cambridge University Press, 1987), 2:271–77, 321–32.

200. Cf. *SVF* 1.527 (Kleanthes); Seneca, *Ep.* 107. See further Long and Sedley, *Hellenistic Philosophers*, 2:382–89.

201. To be precise, Stoic teaching typically allows only the souls of the good to endure, and only until the conflagration. Cf. *SVF* 1.146; 2.810–11, 814, 817, 822; Plutarch, *Suav. viv.* 1107b; Diog. L., *Vit. phil.* 7.156–157. Further sources in Long and Sedley, *Hellenistic Philosophers*, 2:310–21. On the soul as cooled air, see in particular Diogenes of Apollonia, DK 64 A28; Aristotle, *De an.* 1.2, 405b28–29; *SVF* 2.804–8. See also *Ref.* 8.10.1 (Doketai).

202. Cf. Epiph., *Pan.* 1.7.2; Ps.-Galen, *Hist. phil.* 24 (Diels, *Doxographi*, 614.10–16).

203. For the conflagration, see Long and Sedley, *Hellenistic Philosophers*, 2:271–77. See further A. A. Long, "The Stoics on World-Conflagration and Everlasting Recurrence," in *From Epicurus to Epictetus: Studies in Hellenistic and Roman Philosophy*, ed. A. A. Long (Oxford: Clarendon, 2006), 256–82; Pieter W. van der Horst, "'The Elements Will Be Dissolved with Fire': The Idea of Cosmic Conflagration in Hellenism, Ancient Judaism and Early Christianity," in *Hellenism-Judaism-Christianity: Essays on Their Interaction* (Kampen: Kok Pharos, 1994), 227–51. For partial purification, see Dio Chrysostom, *Or.* 36.47–49, 58–59. Conflagration as purification is a Christian idea

5. σώματα δὲ πάντα ὑπέθεντο καὶ σῶμα διὰ σώματος μὲν χωρεῖν, ἀλλὰ ἀνάστασιν εἶναι καὶ πεπληρῶσθαι πάντα καὶ μηδὲν εἶναι κενόν.

ταῦτα καὶ οἱ Στωϊκοί.

22. 1. Ἐπίκουρος δὲ σχεδὸν ἐναντίαν πᾶσι δόξαν ἔθετο.

ἀρχὰς μὲν τῶν ὅλων ὑπέθετο ἀτόμους καὶ κενόν—κενὸν μὲν οἷον τόπον τῶν ἐσομένων, ἀτόμους δὲ τὴν ὕλην, ἐξ ἧς τὰ πάντα—2. ἐκ δὲ τῶν ἀτόμων συνελθουσῶν γενέσθαι καὶ τὸν θεόν, καὶ τὰ στοιχεῖα [πάντα], καὶ <τοὺς κόσμους, καὶ> τὰ ἐν αὐτοῖς πάντα, καὶ ζῷα καὶ ἄλλα, ὡς μηδὲν γίνεσθαι μήτε συνεστάναι, εἰ μὴ ἐκ τῶν ἀτόμων εἴη. τὰς δὲ ἀτόμους τὸ λεπτομερέστατον καὶ καθ᾽ οὗ οὐκ ἂν γένοιτο κέντρον οὐδὲ σημεῖον οὐδέν, οὐδὲ διαίρεσις οὐδεμία, ἔφη εἶναι· διὸ καὶ ἀτόμους αὐτὰς ὠνόμασεν.

3. Τὸν δὲ θεὸν ὁμολογῶν εἶναι ἀίδιον καὶ ἄφθαρτόν φησι μηδενὸς προνοεῖν, καὶ ὅλως πρόνοιαν μὴ εἶναι μηδὲ εἱμαρμένην, ἀλλὰ πάντα κατὰ αὐτοματισμὸν γίνεσθαι. καθῆσθαι γὰρ τὸν θεὸν ἐν τοῖς μετακοσμίοις οὕτω καλουμένοις ὑπ᾽ αὐτοῦ—ἔξω γάρ τι τοῦ κόσμου οἰκητήριον τοῦ θεοῦ ἔθετο εἶναι, λεγόμενον τὰ μετακόσμια—, ἥδεσθαί τε καὶ ἡσυχάζειν ἐν τῇ ἀκροτάτῃ εὐφροσύνῃ, καὶ οὔτε αὐτὸν πράγματα ἔχειν οὔτε ἄλλῳ παρέχειν.

5. The Stoics suppose that all things are bodies and that a body travels through a body. Nevertheless, there is a resurrection. The universe is a fullness, and there is no void at all.[204]

These are the doctrines of the Stoics.

EPIKOUROS. 22. 1. Epikouros proposed a doctrine virtually opposite to all.[205]

ATOMS. He supposed that the first principles of the universe were atoms and void—"void" being as it were a place of things that will exist, and "atoms" being as it were the matter from which all things come. 2. Even God arises from converging atoms, along with the elements and the worlds and all the things in them, both animals and other beings.[206] Consequently, nothing arises or is constituted except from atoms. Atoms are the most subtle bodies; in them there can be no center or point at all; nor, he adds, can they be divided. Thus he called them "atoms" or "indivisibles."[207]

THEOLOGY. 3. Agreeing that God is eternal and imperishable, Epikouros says that God takes no thought for anyone. There is no providence or fate at all. Rather, all things happen at random.[208] God sits in the "metacosmic spaces" (as he calls them). For outside of the cosmos somewhere, he proposes, there is a dwelling place of God, the so-called "metacosmic spaces."[209] He says that God takes his pleasure and rest in the highest delight. Neither is he troubled, nor does he trouble others.[210]

(1 Cor 3:13) and developed by Christian authors. See, e.g., Methodios, *Res.* 1.47.3; Clem. Alex., *Strom.* 5.1.9.4.

204. On Stoic materialism, see Long and Sedley, *Hellenistic Philosophers*, 2:269–71. Mansfeld believes that a doctrine of Stoic resurrection is a Christian interpolation to prove that Greeks took their doctrines from the Jews ("Resurrection Added: The *Interpretatio christiana* of a Stoic Doctrine," *VC* 37 [1983]: 218–33 [222–23]). Our author will later attribute a doctrine of resurrection to Herakleitos (*Ref.* 9.10.6) and the Essenes (9.27.1). For the lack of void, see *SVF* 2.463–81, esp. 479–80.

205. On our author's treatment of Epikouros, see Mueller, "Heterodoxy," 4371–72.

206. Roeper adds τοὺς κόσμους, καί (here: "the worlds and").

207. Cf. Epikouros, *Ep. Hdt.* 43–44, 54–59; Ps.-Plutarch, *Plac. philos.* 1.3, 877f. Other sources in Long and Sedley, *Hellenistic Philosophers*, 2:30–38.

208. Cf. Theophilos, *Autol.* 2.4; Epiph., *Pan.* 8.1.1. Other sources in Long and Sedley, *Hellenistic Philosophers*, 2:143–54.

209. Epikouros, *Ep. Pyth.* 89; Lucretius, *Rer. nat.* 3.18–24; 5.146–155; Cicero, *Nat. d.* 1.18; Diog. L., *Vit. phil.* 10.89.

210. Epikouros, *Rat. sent.* 1: Τὸ μακάριον καὶ ἄφθαρτον οὔτε αὐτὸ πράγματα ἔχει

4. ᾧ ἀκόλουθον καὶ τὸν περὶ τῶν σοφῶν ἀνδρῶν πεποίηται λόγον, λέγων τὸ τέλος τῆς σοφίας εἶναι ἡδονήν. ἄλλοι δὲ ἄλλως τὸ ὄνομα τῆς ἡδονῆς ἐξέλαβον· οἱ μὲν γὰρ <τὴν> κατὰ <τὰς> θνητὰς ἐπιθυμίας, οἱ δὲ τὴν ἐπὶ τῇ ἀρετῇ ἡδονήν. 5. Τὰς δὲ ψυχὰς τῶν ἀνθρώπων λύεσθαι ἅμα τοῖς σώμασιν, ὥσπερ καὶ συγγεννᾶσθαι αὐτοῖς τίθεται· αἷμα γὰρ αὐτὰς εἶναι, οὗ ἐξελθόντος ἢ τραπέντος ἀπόλλυσθαι ὅλον τὸν ἄνθρωπον. ᾧ ἀκολουθεῖ μήτε κρίσεις εἶναι ἐν Ἅιδου μήτε δικαστήρια, ὡς ὅ τι ἂν δράσῃ τις ἐν τῷ βίῳ τούτῳ καὶ διαλάθῃ, ἀνεύθυνον εἶναι παντελῶς.

οὕτως οὖν καὶ ὁ Ἐπίκουρος.

23. 1. Ἄλλη δὲ αἵρεσις φιλοσόφων ἐκλήθη Ἀκαδημαϊκὴ διὰ τὸ ἐν τῇ Ἀκαδημίᾳ τὰς διατριβὰς αὐτοὺς ποιεῖσθαι. ὧν ἄρξας ὁ Πύρρων, ἀφ' οὗ Πυρρώνειοι ἐκλήθησαν φιλόσοφοι, τὴν ἀκαταληψίαν ἁπάντων πρῶτος εἰσήγαγεν, ὡς ἐπιχειρεῖν μὲν εἰς ἑκάτερα, μὴ μέντοι ἀποφαίνεσθαι μηδέν. 2. οὐδὲν γὰρ εἶναι οὔτε τῶν νοητῶν οὔτε τῶν αἰσθητῶν ἀληθές, ἀλλὰ δοκεῖν τοῖς ἀνθρώποις οὕτως ἔχειν· ῥευστὴν γὰρ εἶναι τὴν οὐσίαν πᾶσαν καὶ μεταβλητὴν καὶ μηδέποτε ἐν τῷ αὐτῷ μένειν.

ETHICS. 4. In line with this theology, Epikouros developed his theory about sages, stating that the goal of wisdom is pleasure. Different people understand the term "pleasure" in different ways: some according to mortal lusts, and others with reference to the pleasure that comes with virtue.[211]

SOUL. 5. The souls of human beings are dissolved together with their bodies, just as, he supposes, soul and body were born together.[212] Souls are blood; when it leaves or is altered, the whole human being perishes.[213] From this teaching, it follows that there are neither judgments in Hades nor places of judgment. Consequently, whatever one does in this life and gets away with remains entirely free from censure.[214]

Thus Epikouros.

ACADEMICS (SKEPTICS). 23. 1. Another sect of philosophers was called "Academic" because they debated in the Academy.[215] Pyrrhon initiated these debates; hence these philosophers were called "Pyrrhonists."[216] He was the first to introduce the incomprehensibility of all things, with the result that he argued both sides of a debate, without asserting anything.[217] 2. For nothing is true, either of intelligible or perceptible reality, but reality is what *appears* to human beings. All reality is in flux and is variable and never remains in the same state.[218]

οὔτε ἄλλῳ παρέχει ("The blessed and immortal is itself free from trouble, nor does it afford trouble to anyone else").

211. Epikouros, *Ep. Men.* 129–135. Other sources in Long and Sedley, *Hellenistic Philosophers*, 2:114–29.

212. Cf. Ps.-Plutarch, *Plac. philos.* 4.7, 899c; Sext. Emp., *Math.* 3.72; Diog. L., *Vit. phil.* 10.65–67, 125, 139.

213. The antecedent of "it" (οὗ) is not clear. Cf. Empedokles, DK 31 B105; Lucretius, *Rer. nat.* 3.43; Lev 17:11 LXX (ἡ γὰρ ψυχὴ πάσης σαρκὸς αἷμα). Other sources in Long and Sedley, *Hellenistic Philosophers*, 2:64–75, 154–59.

214. Cf. the doctrine of the Sadducees in *Ref.* 9.29.3. Such ideas are in contrast to Plato (*Ref.* 1.19.11).

215. On our author's treatment of the Academics, see Mueller, "Heterodoxy," 4372–73.

216. The conflation of Pyrrhonists and Academics was strongly opposed by our author's likely contemporary, Sextus Empiricus (*Pyr.* 1.220–235).

217. Diogenes Laertios quotes Askanios of Abdera to the effect that Pyrrhon introduced incomprehensibility (*Vit. phil.* 9.61). Earlier our author gave Xenophanes this accolade (*Ref.* 1.14.1).

218. Cf. Philo, *Post.* 163; *Spec.* 1.27; Sext. Emp., *Pyr.* 3.115–117; *Math.* 8.7; Plu-

3. Οἱ μὲν οὖν τῶν Ἀκαδημαϊκῶν λέγουσι μὴ δεῖν τὴν ἀρχὴν περὶ μηδενὸς ἀποφαίνεσθαι, ἀλλ' ἁπλῶς ἐπιχειρήσαντας ἐᾶν· οἱ δὲ τὸ <οὐ> μᾶλλον προσέθεσαν, λέγοντες οὐ μᾶλλον τὸ πῦρ <πῦρ> εἶναι ἢ ἄλλο τι· οὐ μέντοι ἀπεφήναντο αὐτὸ <τὸ> τί ἐστιν, ἀλλὰ τὸ τοιόνδε.

24. 1. Ἔστι δὲ καὶ παρὰ Ἰνδοῖς αἵρεσις φιλοσοφουμένων ἐν τοῖς Βραχμάναις. οἳ βίον μὲν αὐτάρκη προβάλλονται, ἐμψύχων δὲ καὶ τῶν διὰ πυρὸς βρωμάτων πάντων ἀπέχονται, ἀκροδρύοις ἀρκούμενοι—μηδὲ αὐτὰ ταῦτα τρυγῶντες, ἀλλὰ τὰ πίπτοντα εἰς τὴν γῆν βαστάζοντες ζῶσιν—, ὕδωρ <τε> ποταμοῦ Ταγαβενὰ πίνοντες. 2. διαβιοῦσι δὲ γυμνοί, τὸ σῶμα ἔνδυμα τῇ ψυχῇ ὑπὸ τοῦ θεοῦ γεγονέναι λέγοντες.

3. Consequently, some of the Academics say that it is not necessary to declare a first principle about anything. Rather, after simply making an argument, they jettison [first principles]. But others added the "no more" rule, saying that fire is no more fire than anything else. They declare, to be sure, not its essence but its quality.[219]

NON-GREEK PHILOSOPHY

BRAHMANS. 24. 1. There is in India a sect of philosophers among the Brahmans.[220] They propose a self-sufficient life and abstain from all food of ensouled creatures and that which is cooked by fire. They are content with fruit from trees (they do not even harvest them but live by picking up the fruits that fall on the ground) and drink water from the river Tagabena.[221] 2. They live their whole lives naked, saying that the body is made by God as a covering for the soul.[222]

---

tarch, *E Delph.* 392a–e; *Comm. not.* 1083b. Further sources in Long and Sedley, *Hellenistic Philosophers*, 2:1–9.

219. For the sources of Academic skepticism, see Long and Sedley, *Hellenistic Philosophers*, 2:432–75. On the "no more" rule, see Sext. Emp., *Pyr.* 1.188–191; Diog. L., *Vit. phil.* 9.75. See further Phillip DeLacy, "Οὐ μᾶλλον and the Antecedents of Ancient Scepticism," *Phronesis* 3 (1958): 59–71.

220. On the Brahmans in Greco-Roman culture, see Richard Stoneman, *Alexander the Great: A Life in Legend* (New Haven: Yale University Press, 2008), 91–103. On our author's treatment of the Brahmans, see Rosalia C. Vofchuk, "San Hipólito de Roma: Primer expositor de las doctrinas brahmánicas en Occidente," *EstEcl* 68 (1993): 49–68; Mueller, "Heterodoxy," 4373–74; and esp. Guillaume Ducoeur, *Brahmanisme et encratisme à Rome au IIIe siècle ap. J.C.* (Paris: L'Harmattan, 2001). Our author earlier made Demokritos a disciple of the Indian gymnosophists (*Ref.* 1.13.1). He will later attribute Enkratite doctrine to the Brahmans (8.7) but fails to develop this point in his treatment of the Enkratites (8.20).

221. For the diet of the Brahmans, see Megasthenes in Strabo, *Geogr.* 15.1.59–60; Clem. Alex., *Strom.* 1.15.71.5; 3.7.60.2; Bardesanes in Porphyry, *Abst.* 4.17; Hierokles in Stephanus of Byzantium, *Ethnica*, s.v. Βραχμᾶνες; Palladius, *Vita Brag.* 1.11–12; 2.10, 24, 45 (Derrett). A second-century papyrus, Pap. Genev. inv. 271 (V. Martin), serves as a partial prototype of Palladius (note esp. cols. 1.19–26; 3.51–4.1; 5.6–7). See further Jean W. Sedlar, *India and the Greek World: A Study in the Transmission of Culture* (Totowa, NJ: Rowman & Littlefield, 1980), 33–41; Ducoeur, *Brahmanisme*, 79–82. For the name of the river, see ibid., 66, 72–76, 153–57; Vofchuk, "Doctrinas brahmánicas," 56–57.

222. For the nakedness of the Brahmans (often called "gymnosophists" = naked philosophers), see Strabo, *Geogr.* 15.1.60; Palladius, *Vita Brag.* 1.11; 2.7; Clem. Alex., *Strom.* 3.7.60.3–4; Ducoeur, *Brahmanisme*, 82–84. The body as a covering for the

Οὗτοι τὸν θεὸν φῶς εἶναι λέγουσιν, οὐχ ὁποῖόν τις ὁρᾷ οὐδ' οἷον ἥλιος ἢ πῦρ, ἀλλ' ἔστιν αὐτοῖς ὁ θεὸς λόγος, οὐχ ὁ ἔναρθρος, ἀλλ' ὁ τῆς γνώσεως, δι' οὗ τὰ κρυπτὰ τῆς φύσεως μυστήρια ὁρᾶται σοφοῖς. τοῦτο δὲ τὸ φῶς, ὅ φασι λόγον καὶ θεόν, αὐτοὺς μόνους εἰδέναι Βραχμᾶνες λέγουσιν διὰ τὸ ἀπορρῖψαι μόνους τὴν κενοδοξίαν, ὅ<ς> ἐστι χιτὼν τῆς ψυχῆς ἔσχατος. 3. οὗτοι θανάτου καταφρονοῦσιν, ἀεὶ δὲ ἰδίᾳ φωνῇ <φῶς τὸν> θεὸν ὀνομάζουσιν, καθὼς προείπομεν, ὕμνους τε ἀναπέμπουσιν. οὔτε δὲ γυναῖκες παρ' αὐτοῖς οὔτε τεκνοῦσιν.

4. Οἱ δὲ τοῦ ὁμοίου αὐτοῖς βίου ὀρεχθέντες, ἐκ τῆς ἀντιπέραν χώρας τοῦ ποταμοῦ διαπεράσαντες ἐκεῖσε ἐναπομένουσιν, ἀναστρέφοντες μηκέτι. καὶ

THEOLOGY. The Brahmans say that God is light.[223] He is not the sort of light that one sees nor light like the sun or fire. Rather God is for them the Word, not articulated, but the Word of knowledge through which the hidden mysteries of nature are seen by sages.[224] This light, which they call "Word" and "God," the Brahmans say that they alone know because they alone have thrown aside empty opinion, which is the last garment of the soul.[225] 3. They disregard death.[226] They always call God "light" in their own language, as I said, and offer up hymns.[227] They have no wives and do not father children.[228]

4. Those who aspire to their form of life cross from the regions on the other side of the river and remain in that place, never to return. They

---

soul is a stock philosophical phrase. See Empedokles, DK 31 B126; Plato, *Crat.* 403b; Plutarch, *Def. orac.* 415c; Philo, *Leg.* 2.55–59; Origen, *Cels.* 7.32; Sent. Sextus 449 (Wilson); Palladius, *Vita Brag.* 2.17. See further Vofchuk, "Doctrinas brahmánicas," 57–59; Ducoeur, *Brahmanisme*, 124–31.

223. No previous Greco-Roman writer, it seems, expounds the theology of the Brahmans. Palladius, writing in the fourth century CE, represents Dandamis as saying: "God, the great king, is the source of no violence, but of light, peace, life, water, and of the human body and soul; and he receives the souls that have not been conquered by desire" (*Vita Brag.* 2.15; cf. 2.27). Vofchuk suggests that our author may have had access to oral traditions conveying the principal teachings of the Upanishads ("Doctrinas brahmánicas," 67–68). Ducoeur believes that he used a source of gnostic inspiration probably composed in Alexandria (*Brahmanisme*, 175).

224. Cf. the teaching of the Persians in *Ref.* 4.43.3 (God as light); Philo, *Opif.* 31–32; and our author's own Logos theology in *Ref.* 10.33.1. See further Vofchuk, "Doctrinas brahmánicas," 59–62. Ducoeur views Hermetic thought as the best parallel (*Brahmanisme*, 113–23).

225. On the esoteric knowledge of the Brahmans, see Vofchuk, "Doctrinas brahmánicas," 62–63. Throwing off vainglory as the final garment was a stock phrase (Tacitus, *Hist.* 4.6.1; Athenaios, *Deipn.* 11.507d; Palladius, *Vita Brag.* 2.42). See further Dörrie and Baltes, *Platonismus*, 2:52–57; Marcello Gigante, *L'ultima Tunica*, 2nd ed. (Naples: Giannini, 1988), 21–33.

226. Cf. Clem. Alex., *Strom.* 3.7.60.2; Porphyry, *Abst.* 4.18.1; Strabo, *Geogr.* 15.1.59; Palladius, *Vita Brag.* 2.18, 20. See further Vofchuk, "Doctrinas brahmánicas," 65.

227. Marcovich supplies φῶς ("light"), and Roeper τόν. For the hymns, see Porphyry, *Abst.* 4.17.6; Palladius, *Vita Brag.* 1.11; 2.7, 39. See further Vofchuk, "Doctrinas brahmánicas," 65–66; Ducoeur, *Brahmanisme*, 133–34.

228. Cf. Clem. Alex., *Strom.* 1.15.71.5 (Sarmans do not recognize marriage); 3.7.60.4 (Gymnosophists have no wives); Strabo, *Geogr.* 15.1.59 (Brahmans have many wives); Palladius, *Vita Brag.* 1.13 (Brahmans have periodic intercourse with women). On the discrepancies, see Vofchuk, "Doctrinas brahmánicas," 56. Ducoeur believes that our author describes Brahmans at the fourth stage of life (*Brahmanisme*, 85–86).

αὐτοὶ δὲ Βραχμᾶνες καλοῦνται, βίον δὲ οὐχ ὁμοίως διάγουσιν· εἰσὶ γὰρ καὶ γυναῖκες ἐν τῇ χώρᾳ, ἐξ ὧνπερ οἱ ἐκεῖ κατοικοῦντες γεννῶνται καὶ γεννῶσιν.

5. Τοῦτον δὲ τὸν λόγον, ὃν θεὸν ὀνομάζουσιν, σωματικὸν εἶναι περικείμενόν τε σῶμα ἔξωθεν ἑαυτοῦ—καθάπερ εἴ τις τὸ ἐκ προβάτων ἔνδυμα—φορεῖ· ἀπεκδυσάμενον δὲ τὸ σῶμα, ὃ περίκειται, ὀφθαλμοφανῶς φαίνεσθαι.

Πόλεμον δὲ εἶναι ἐν τῷ περικειμένῳ αὐτῶν σώματι οἱ Βραχμᾶνες λέγουσι καὶ πλῆρες εἶναι πολεμ<ί>ων αὐτοῖς τὸ σῶμα νενομίκασιν, πρὸς ὃ ὡς πρὸς πολεμίους παρατεταγμένοι μάχονται, καθὼς προδεδηλώκαμεν. 6. πάντας δὲ ἀνθρώπους λέγουσιν αἰχμαλώτους εἶναι τῶν ἰδίων συγγενῶν πολεμίων, γαστρὸς καὶ αἰδοίων, λαιμοῦ, ὀργῆς, χαρᾶς, λύπης, ἐπιθυμίας καὶ τῶν ὁμοίων· μόνος δὲ πρὸς τὸν θεὸν χωρεῖ ὁ κατὰ τούτων ἐγείρας τρόπαιον.

7. διὸ Δάνδαμιν μέν, πρὸς ὃν Ἀλέξανδρος ὁ Μακεδὼν εἰσῆλθεν, ὡς νενικηκότα τὸν πόλεμον τὸν ἐν τῷ σώματι Βραχμᾶνες θεολογοῦσιν, Καλάνου δὲ καταφέρονται ὡς ἀσεβῶς ἀποστατήσαντος τῆς κατ' αὐτοὺς φιλοσοφίας.

ἀποθέμενοι δὲ Βραχμᾶνες τὸ σῶμα, ὥσπερ ἐξ ὕδατος ἰχθύες ἀνακύψαντες εἰς ἀέρα καθαρὸν ὁρῶσι τὸν ἥλιον.

too are called "Brahmans" but do not live the same form of life. For their wives reside in that place as well. From them, the inhabitants are born and beget children.[229]

5. Now this Word, whom they call "God," is embodied and is robed with a body external to himself. He wears it just as one wears a sheepskin. When he takes off the body that he wore, he shines visibly to the eye.[230]

ETHICS. The Brahmans say that there is a war in their surrounding body. They suppose that the body is full of enemies opposed to them. They array themselves against the body and fight against it as though against enemies (as I have already showed). 6. They say that all human beings are captives of their own inborn enemies, namely, the stomach, the genitals, the gullet, as well as wrath, joy, sadness, desire, and the like. Only he who has raised a trophy over these goes to God.[231]

7. Thus the Brahmans speak of Dandamis as a god, since he won the battle in the body. He it was whom Alexander of Macedon consulted.[232] But they accuse Kalanos of impiously apostatizing from their philosophy.[233]

Brahmans leave behind the body just as fish popping their heads up out of water into the air see the sun in its purity.[234]

---

229. Cf. Palladius, *Vita Brag.* 1.13. See further Ducoeur, *Brahmanisme*, 86–92.

230. Ducoeur calls the so-called Indian theology of the Logos, elsewhere unattested, *pure construction savante* ("Hérésiarques chrétiens," 174). The parallelism between humans who wear the body as a tunic and the Word who wears a body as a sheepskin is striking. When the garment is removed, presumably, the true nature of both is revealed. See further Vofchuk, "Doctrinas brahmánicas," 63–65; Ducoeur, *Brahmanisme*, 131–33.

231. Here Cynic self-understandings are mixed in with the Indian material. Cf. Palladius, *Vita Brag.* 2.6–7, 21, 23. See further Vofchuk, "Doctrinas brahmánicas," 66–67; Ducoeur, *Brahmanisme*, 134–37.

232. On Dandamis, see Arrian, *Anab.* 7.2.3–4; Palladius, *Vita Brag.* 2.19–40. Palladius has Alexander report to Dandamis: "They say that you are like a god" (2.20). Dandamis claims that god is alive within him (2.24; cf. 2.32). Alexander later gives Dandamis gifts "worthy of a god" (2.35). See further Sedlar, *India*, 68–74; Ducoeur, *Brahmanisme*, 142–43; Richard Stoneman, *The Legends of Alexander the Great*, rev. ed. (London: I. B. Tauris, 2012), 43–47; Beverly Berg, "Dandamis: An Early Christian Portrait of Indian Asceticism," *Classica et Mediaevalia* 31 (1970): 269–305.

233. On Kalanos, see Megasthenes in Strabo, *Geogr.* 15.1.68; Pap. Genev. inv. 271, col. 4.19–25 (V. Martin); Arrian, *Anab.* 7.2.4–3.6; Palladius, *Vita Brag.* 2.4, 11, 41. For a different view of Kalanos, note Philo, *Prob.* 96.

234. Cf. Philostratos, *Vit. Apoll.* 1.23.

25. 1. Δρυΐδαι οἱ ἐν Κελτοῖς τῇ Πυθαγορείῳ φιλοσοφίᾳ κατ' ἄκρον ἐγκύψαντες, αἰτίου αὐτοῖς γενομένου ταύτης τῆς ἀσκήσεως Ζαμόλξιδος δούλου Πυθαγόρου, γένει Θρᾳκίου· ὃς μετὰ τὴν Πυθαγόρου τελευτὴν ἐκεῖ χωρήσας αἴτιος τούτοις ταύτης τῆς φιλοσοφίας ἐγένετο. 2. τούτους Κελτοὶ ὡς προφήτας καὶ προγνωστικοὺς δοξάζουσιν διὰ τὸ ἐκ ψήφων καὶ ἀριθμῶν Πυθαγορικῇ τέχνῃ προαγορεύειν αὐτοῖς τινα, ἧς καὶ αὐτῆς τέχνης τὰς ἐφόδους οὐ σιωπήσομεν, ἐπεὶ καὶ ἐκ τούτων τινὲς αἱρέσεις παρεισάγειν ἐτόλμησαν. χρῶνται δὲ Δρυΐδαι καὶ μαγείαις.

26. 1. Ἡσίοδος δὲ ὁ ποιητὴς καὶ αὐτὸς περὶ φύσεως οὕτω λέγει ἀκηκοέναι παρὰ Μουσῶν. Διὸς δὲ εἶναι τὰς Μούσας θυγατέρας· ἐννέα γὰρ νύκτας ὁμοῦ

DRUIDS. 25. 1. The Druids among the Kelts peered into the inmost depths of Pythagorean philosophy.[235] Zalmoxis the slave of Pythagoras, a Thracian by race, was the founder of their mode of life. He, after the death of Pythagoras, moved there and became for them the founder of this philosophy.[236] 2. The Kelts glorify the Druids as prophets and knowers of the future because they foretell events by the Pythagorean art from symbols and numbers.[237] The methods of this particular art I will not keep secret, since some dared to introduce from these practices certain heresies.[238] The Druids also perform acts of magic.[239]

HESIOD

26. 1. Hesiod the poet[240] testifies about himself that he heard about nature from the Muses.[242] (Now the Muses are the daughters of Zeus. For

---

235. Strabo presents the Druids as students of nature and moral philosophy (*Geogr.* 4.4.4; cf. Diodoros, *Bibl. hist.* 5.31.3). According to Caesar, the Druids taught young disciples about the "stars and their motion," the measurement of the earth, nature, and the power and majesty of the immortal gods (*Bell. gall.* 6.14). Our author is keen on tracing the learning of the Druids to Pythagoras (Clement of Alexandria teaches the reverse, *Strom.* 1.1.15.71). Other authors associate Druids and Pythagoreans (e.g., Timagenes in Ammianus Marcellinus 15.9.8). Our author oddly fails to mention the Druid belief in the soul's immortality, a point emphasized by others (Strabo, *Geogr.* 4.4; Caesar, *Bell. gall.* 6.14). For how classical authors received their knowledge of the Druids, see Barry Cunliffe, *Druids: A Very Short Introduction* (Oxford: Oxford University Press, 2010), 50–61. On the Druids as philosophers, see Peter Berresford Ellis, *The Druids* (London: Constable, 1994), 167–89.

236. For Zalmoxis, see *Ref.* 1.2.17; Clem. Alex., *Strom.* 4.8.57.2. Zalmoxis moved "there" (ἐκεῖ)—but where exactly? Herodotos (from whom accounts of Zalmoxis generally derive) puts Zalmoxis in Thrace, not the land of the Kelts.

237. Strabo and Diodoros distinguish three classes of Kelts: the Bards, the Vates/Seers, and the Druids. The Vates foretell the future from sacrifices, and the Druids study nature and ethics (Cunliffe, *Druids*, 68–69). Nonetheless, the distinction between Druids and Vates was blurred by the time of our author (ibid., 74, 76, 92). See Cicero, *Div.* 1.90; Tacitus, *Hist.* 4.54.2; Dio Chrysostom, *Or.* 49.8. On "symbols" (translating ψήφων), see Burkert, *Lore and Science*, 427.

238. See below, *Ref.* 4.51.

239. For the Druids and magic, see Pliny, *Nat.* 16.249; 24.103–104; 29.52–54.

240. Hippias of Elis's compendium of earlier wisdom (late fifth century BCE) included Hesiod (Clem. Alex., *Strom.* 6.2.15.1–2). Aristotle treats Hesiod as one who philosophized (*Metaph.* 1.4, 984b23–31). Mueller notes that in Diog. L., *Vit. phil.* 1.1–11, Brahmans and Druids are treated as forerunners of the Greek philosophers

καὶ ἡμέρας δι' ὑπερβολὴν ἐπιθυμίας ἀδιαλείπτως συνευνηθέντος τῇ Μνημοσύνῃ τοῦ Διός, ἐννέα ταύτας τὴν Μνημοσύνην συλλαβεῖν ἐν μιᾷ γαστρί, ἐφ' ἑκάστης νυκτὸς ὑποδεξαμένην μίαν. 2. καλέσας οὖν τὰς ἐννέα Μούσας ἀπὸ τῆς Πιερίας, τουτέστιν ἀπὸ τοῦ Ὀλύμπου, διδαχθῆναι παρεκάλει

ὡς τὰ πρῶτα θεοὶ καὶ γαῖα γένοντο
καὶ ποταμοὶ καὶ πόντος ἀπείριτος οἶδμά τε πόντου
ἄστρα τε λ<αμ>πετόωντα καὶ οὐρανὸς εὐρὺς ὕπερθεν·
ὥς τ' ἄφενον δάσ<σ>αντο καὶ ὡς τιμὰς διέλοντο,
ἠδὲ καὶ ὡς τὰ πρῶτα πολύπτυχον ἔσχον Ὄλυμπον.

ταῦτά μοι Μοῦσαι, φησίν, ἔσπετ'

ἐξ ἀρχῆς, καὶ ἔπειθ' ὅ τι περ πρῶτον γένετ' αὐτῶν.
Ἤτοι μὲν [γὰρ] πρώτιστα Χάος γένετ'· αὐτὰρ ἔπειτα
Γαῖ' εὐρύστερνος, πάντων ἕδος ἀσφαλὲς αἰεὶ
ἀθανάτων, οἳ ἔχουσι κάρην νιφόεντος Ὀλύμπου,
Τάρταρά τ' ἠνεμόεντα μυχῷ χθονὸς εὐρ<υ>οδείης,
ἠδ' Ἔρος, ὃς κάλλιστος ἐν ἀθανάτοισι θεοῖσιν,
λυσιμελής, πάντων τε θεῶν πάντων τ' ἀνθρώπων
δάμναται ἐν στήθεσφι νόον καὶ ἐπίφρονα βουλήν.
Ἐκ Χάεος δ' Ἔρεβός τε μέλαινά τε Νὺξ ἐγένο<ν>το·

a total of nine nights and days—due to his excessive lust—Zeus ceaselessly shared the bed of Memory, and Memory conceived these nine Muses in one womb, conceiving one each night.)[243] 2. Having called them nine Muses from Pieria (that is, from Olympus), Hesiod asked to be taught:

> How at first Gods and Earth came to be
> And Rivers and boundless Sea with the swelling of Sea,
> And gleaming stars and broad Heaven above,
> How they divided up wealth and distributed honors,
> As well as how at first they took possession of Olympus with its many clefts.[243]

"Tell me these things," he says, "O Muses,"[244]

> From the beginning, and then who it was that of them first came to be:
> Truly Chaos came about first of all, then
> Broad-breasted Earth, firm and everlasting foundation of all
> Immortals, those who hold the crest of snowy Olympus,
> And misty Tartaros, in the pit of Earth with her broad paths,
> And Eros, who is most beautiful among the immortal gods,
> Who relaxes the limbs of all the gods and all human beings;
> He tames the mind in the breast with its shrewd deliberation.
> From Chaos were born both Erebos and black Night;

("Heterodoxy," 4374). Our author is, typically, interested in Hesiod's "first principles" and cosmogony, and he focuses on the passages that declare that primeval deities were generated. These deities thus belong to the world of birth, which our author equates with created reality (*Ref.* 1.26.3). From the standpoint of our author, then, Hesiod is another example of a thinker who makes generated beings his first principles, not the ungenerated God. For citations of Hesiod from second-century apologists, see Theophilos, *Autol.* 2.5–6 (who cites Hesiod, *Theog.* 73–74, 104–115); Athenagoras, *Leg.* 24.5; Clem. Alex., *Protr.* 14.2 (who makes allusions to *Theog.* 196–200); and the general discussion in Nicole Zeegers-Vander Vorst, *Les citations des poètes grecs chez les apologists chrétiens du IIe siècle* (Leuven: Leuven University Press, 1972), 38–39, 111–15.

242. Hesiod, *Theog.* 22–25.

242. Hesiod, *Theog.* 52–60. See further E. E. Pender, "Chaos Corrected: Hesiod in Plato's Creation Myth," in *Plato and Hesiod*, ed. G. R. Boys-Stones and J. H. Haubold (Oxford: Oxford University Press, 2010), 219–45 (242–44).

243. Hesiod, *Theog.* 108–13.

244. Hesiod, *Theog.* 114.

Νυκτὸς δ' αὖτ' Αἰθήρ τε καὶ Ἡμέρη ἐξεγένοντο.
Γαῖα δέ τοι πρῶτον μὲν ἐγείνατο ἶσον ἑαυτῇ
Οὐρανὸν ἀστερόενθ', ἵνα μιν περὶ πάντα καλύπτοι,
ὄφρ' ε<ἴ>η μακάρεσσι θεοῖς ἕδος ἀσφαλὲς αἰεί,
γείνατο δ' Οὔρεα μακρά, θεᾶ<ν> χαρίεντας ἐναύλους
Νυμφέων, αἳ ναίουσι κατ' οὔρεα βησ<σ>ήεντα,
ἠδὲ καὶ ἀτρύγετον πέλαγος τέκεν οἴδματι θυ<ῖ>ον,
Πόντον, ἄτερ φιλότητος ἐφιμέρου· αὐτὰρ ἔπειτα
Οὐρανῷ εὐνηθεῖσα τέκ' Ὠκεανὸν βαθυδίνην
Κοῖόν τε Κρεῖόν θ' Ὑπερίονά τ' Ἰαπετόν τε
Θεία<ν> τε Ῥείαν τε Θέμιν τε Μνημοσύνην τε
Φοίβην <τε> χρυσοστέφανον Τηθύν τ' ἐρατεινήν.
τοὺς δὲ μέτ' ἀκρότατος γένετο Κρόνος ἀγκυλομήτης,
δεινότατος παίδων, θαλερὸν δ' ἤχθηρε τοκῆα.
Γείνατο δ' αὖ Κύκλωπας ὑπέρβιον ἦτορ ἔχοντας,

καὶ τοὺς ἄλλους πάντας ἀπὸ τοῦ Κρόνου καταριθμεῖ Γίγαντας· ὕστερον δέ που ἐκ τῆς Ῥέας γεγονέναι τὸν Δία.

3. Οὗτοι μὲν οὖν πάντες περὶ τῆς τοῦ παντὸς φύσεώς τε καὶ γενέσεως ταῦτα, καθὼς ἐξεθέμεθα, τῇ αὐτῶν δόξῃ ἐξεῖπον. οἳ δὲ πάντες κάτω τοῦ θείου χωρήσαντες περὶ τὴν τῶν γενομένων οὐσίαν ἠσχολήθησαν, τὰ μεγέθη τῆς κτίσεως καταπλαγέντες καὶ αὐτὰ τὸ θεῖον εἶναι νομίσαντες, ἕτερος ἕτερον μέρος τῆς κτίσεως προκρίναντες, τὸν δὲ θεὸν τούτων καὶ δημιουργὸν μὴ ἐπιγνόντες.

From Night, in turn, Aether and Day were begotten.
But Earth first bore one equal to herself:
Starry Heaven, so as to cover her every part,
So that he could be the firm everlasting foundation for blessed gods.
She produced vast mountains, wild haunts beloved by the divine,
Nymphs who dwell in wooded mountains.
She also bore Sea, the barren expanse of water, seething in his swell,
Without an act of sweet lovemaking. Then,
Bedding with Heaven, she bore Ocean of the deep whirl,
Koios, Kreios, Hyperion, and Iapetos,
Theia, Rhea, Themis, and Memory,
Phoebe crowned with gold, and charming Tethys.
After them was born the youngest: Kronos of twisted counsel,
The most terrible of her children, who hated his lusty father.
She bore also the Kyklopes, whose hearts are arrogant and immensely strong.[245]

He lists all the other giants after Kronos.[246] Sometime later, Zeus was born from Rhea.[247]

CONCLUSION

3. All these men declared these doctrines, as I presented them, according to their opinion about the nature and origin of the universe. They all, advancing to a point below the divine, busied themselves about the substance of generated reality. Each one, struck by the magnitudes of creation, supposing them to be divine, and preferring different parts of creation, did not acknowledge the God and Artificer of these things.[248]

---

245. Hesiod, *Theog.* 115–139. Discussion of this text in Hesiod (specifically, lines 116–134) can be found in G. S. Kirk, J. E. Raven, and M. Schofield, *The Presocratic Philosophers: A Critical History with a Selection of Texts*, 2nd ed. (Cambridge: Cambridge University Press, 1983), 35–41, 73; Hesiod, *Theogony*, ed. M. L. West (Oxford: Clarendon, 1966), 192–203. Theophilos also quotes Hesiod, *Theog.* 116–123, 126–133—with significantly more criticism (*Autol.* 2.5–6).

246. Cf. Hesiod, *Theog.* 50, with the comments of West, *Theogony*, 173.

247. Hesiod, *Theog.* 453–506.

248. Cf. Rom 1:25; *Ref.* 4.43.2; 10.32.5; *Univ.* frag. 1 (in Emanuele Castelli, "Il prologo del Peri Pantos," *Vetera Christianorum* 42 [2005]: 37–57 [46–47]).

4. Τὰς μὲν οὖν τῶν καθ' Ἕλληνας φιλοσοφεῖν ἐπικεχειρηκότων δόξας ἱκανῶς ἐκτεθεῖσθαι νομίζω, παρ' ὧν τὰς ἀφορμὰς λαβόντες οἱ αἱρετικοὶ τὰ μετ' οὐ πολὺ ῥηθησόμενα ἐπεχείρησαν. δοκεῖ δὲ πρότερον ἐκθεμένους τὰ μυστικὰ καὶ ὅσα περιέργως περὶ ἄστρα τινὲς ἢ μεγέθη ἐφαντάσθησαν εἰπεῖν—καὶ γὰρ ἐξ αὐτῶν λαβόντες ἀφορμὰς τερατολογεῖν νομίζονται πολλοῖς—, ἔπειτα ἀκολούθως τὰ [ὑπ'] αὐτῶν ἀδρανῆ δόγματα φανερώσομεν.

4. I believe that the doctrines of those who undertook Greek philosophy have been sufficiently presented. From these doctrines, the heretics took their starting points and argued what will soon be related. It seems fitting first of all to present their secret mysteries and whatever some people have meddlesomely dreamed up to speak about heavenly bodies and magnitudes (for in fact, although they take their starting points from philosophers, they are widely thought to speak wonders). Afterwards, I will proceed sequentially to expose their impotent doctrines in detail.

BOOKS 2–3

Note: Books 2–3 are lost. They apparently dealt with the "secret mysteries" mentioned at the conclusion of book 1 (26.4). The mention of Egyptian, Chaldean, and Babylonian teachings in 10.5.1 may also allude to material dealt with in the missing books. In addition, parts of books 2–3 may be summarized in our author's brief account of Persian and Babylonian theology together with his longer description of Egyptian theology and numerology in *Ref.* 4.43–44.

<ΤΟΥ ΚΑΤΑ ΠΑΣΩΝ ΑΙΡΕΣΕΩΝ ΕΛΕΓΧΟΥ Δ>

1. 1. ... <ὅρια δὲ ἀστέρων προσαγορεύουσιν ἐν ἑκάστῳ ζῳδίῳ, ἐν οἷς ἕκαστος τῶν ἀστέρων ἀπὸ ποστῆς> (μ)οί(ρ)ας ἐπ(ὶ) π(οστὴν μοῖρ)αν π(λεῖστον) δύν(αται· περὶ ὧ)ν (οὐχ ἡ) τ(υχοῦσα) παρ' αὐτ(οῖς ἐ)στι κατὰ (τοὺς πίνακας)

BOOK 4

Note: The table of contents and first part of book 4 are lost. Its surviving contents can be outlined as follows:

DESCRIPTION OF ASTROLOGY

1. 1. … [2] They declare that there are "terms" of planets in each zodiacal sign.[3] In these terms, each of the planets from one particular degree to the next has more influence. Concerning these terms they have no incidental

1. In book 1, our author already expressed his opinion that his opponents take their lead from "wandering astrologers" (*Pref.* 8). Later he will explicitly connect astrology to the Peratai (*Ref.* 5.12–18) and the Elchasaites (9.16.2–4). For the gnostic use of astrology, see Kocku von Stuckrad, *Das Ringen um die Astrologie: Jüdische und christliche Beiträge zum antiken Zeitverständnis*, RVV (Berlin: de Gruyter, 2000), 624–95.

2. Most likely our author began book 4 with his own introduction and then proceeded to adapt Sext. Emp., *Math.* 5.1–36. The text of P picks up with a nearly verbatim rendition of *Math.* 5.37. Karel Janáček argued that our author and Sextus Empiricus depended on a third source ("Hippolytus and Sextus Empiricus," *Listy Filologické* 82 [1959]: 19–21; idem, "Eine anonyme skeptische Schrift gegen die Astrologen," *Helikon* 4 [1964]: 290–96; supported by Alan Bailey, *Sextus Empiricus and Pyrrhonean Scepticism*

διαφ(ωνία. δο)ρυφ(ορεῖσθαι δ') ἀστέρας λέγουσιν, ὅτ(αν μέ)σο(ι) ὦσι(ν) ἄλ(λων) ἀ(στέρων ἐν συνεχείᾳ) ζῳδίων· οἷον <ἐ>ὰν [τι] τοῦ αὐτοῦ (ζῳ)δί(ου ὁ μέν τις ἀ)στὴρ τὰ(ς π)ρώτα(ς ἐ)πέ(χῃ μ)οίρας, ὁ δὲ <τὰς τελευταίας, ὁ δὲ> τὰς ἐν μέ(σῳ, δο)ρυφορεῖ(σθαι λέγεται ὁ ἐν) μέσῳ (ὑπὸ) τῶν τὰς ἐπ' ἄκροις ἐπεχό(ντω)ν μοίρας.

2. (ἐπιβλέπειν δὲ) λέγοντ(α)ι ἀλλή(λους) καὶ συμφωνεῖν ἀλλήλοι(ς ὡς οἱ) <κατὰ τρίγωνον ἢ τετράγωνον> (φ)α(ινόμενοι.) <κατὰ τρίγωνον μὲν οὖν> συσχηματίζονται <καὶ> ἐπιθεωροῦσι<ν> [δὲ] ἀ(λλήλους) <ἀστέρες> (ἐ)πὶ τ(ριῶν) ζῳδίων ἔχοντες τὸ μεταξὺ διάλειμμα, (κατὰ τετράγωνον δὲ) δυεῖν.

disagreement in their tables.[4] They say that planets are "attended" when they come between other planets in a zodiacal constellation. For example: if a planet within the same zodiacal sign extends over the first degrees of the sign, and another extends over the final degrees, and a third the middle degrees, the one in the middle is said to be "attended" by those extending over the degrees at each end.

2. The planets are said to "look upon" each other and "agree" with each other when they appear in trine and quartile relationships. Now when configured in trine, the planets indeed "look upon" each other at an interval of three zodiacal signs between them; they "look upon" each other in quartile at an interval of two zodiacal signs.[5]

[Oxford: Clarendon, 2002], 113), but the weight of evidence opposes this theory (Mansfeld, *Heresiography*, 325). For a table of comparison showing what sections our author adapts from Sextus Empiricus, see David Amand, *Fatalisme et liberté dans l'antiquité grecque* (Leuven: Desclée de Brouwer, 1945), 226–27. For Sextus Empiricus on astrology, see Germaine Aujac, "Sextus Empiricus et l'astrologie," in *Homo Mathematicus: Actas del Congreso Internacional sobre Astrólogos Griegos y Romanos (Benalmádena, 8–10 de Octubre de 2001)*, ed. Aurelio Pérez Jiménez and Raúl Caballero (Málaga: Charta Antiqua, 2002), 207–26; Emidio Spinelli, "Sesto Empirico e l'astrologia," in *Traditions of Theology: Studies in Hellenistic Theology, Its Background and Aftermath*, ed. Dorothea Frede and André Laks (Leiden: Brill, 2002), 239–79.

3. Marcovich adds the first line (ὅρια … ποστῆς) from Sext. Emp., *Math.* 5.37. "Terms" (ὅρια, Latin *termini*) is a technical astrological term referring to the degrees of a sign "ruled by" (i.e., assigned to) the individual planets. The degrees are the thirty degrees in each zodiacal sign (Sext. Emp., *Math.* 5.5). Cf. Ptolemy, *Tetrab.* 1.20–21. See further A. Bouché-Leclercq, *L'astrologie grecque* (Paris: Leroux, 1899), 206–15; Tamsyn Barton, *Ancient Astrology* (London: Routledge, 1994), 97.

4. The "tables" (πίνακας) refer to astrological tables or "ephemerides," which astrologers used to determine the position of the planets at a certain day and hour without actual observation.

5. See fig. 1. The technical term for "looking upon" each other is "to be in aspect," from the Latin *aspectere* ("to look upon"). The theory of aspects is dealt with more fully by Geminos, *Eisagoge* 2.1–26; Ptolemy, *Tetrab.* 1.13; Censorinus, *Die nat.* 8.3–13. There are four basic aspects: "opposition" (signs diametrically opposed on the circle of the zodiac), "quartile" (signs separated by two other signs), "trine" (signs separated by three signs), and "sextile" (signs separated by one sign). Generally, to be in opposition or in quartile relation is an unfavorable aspect. To be in a trine or sextile relationship is favorable. See further *Sesto Empirico: Contro gli astrologi*, ed. Emidio Spinelli (Naples: Bibliopolis, 2000), 128.

κεφαλῇ τὰ ὑποκείμενα μέρη συμπά(σχ)ει καὶ τ(οῖς ὑποκει)μένοις ἡ κεφαλή, οὕτω καὶ τοῖς ὑπερσεληναίοις τὰ ἐπίγεια. ἀ(λ)λ(ά) τίς ἐστιν τούτων διαφορὰ καὶ <ἀ>συμπάθεια, ὡς ἂν μὴ μίαν καὶ τὴν αὐτὴν ἐχόντων ἕνωσιν.

2. 1. Τούτοις χρησάμενοι Εὐφράτης ὁ Περατ(ικὸς) καὶ Ἀκεμβὴς ὁ Καρύστιος καὶ ὁ λοιπὸς τούτων χορός, τῷ λό(γ)ῳ τ(ῷ) τῆς ἀληθείας ἐπονομάσαντες, αἰώνων στάσιν καὶ ἀποστασίας ἀγαθ(ῶν) δυνάμεων εἰς κακὰ καὶ συμφωνίας ἀγαθῶν μετὰ πονηρῶν προσαγορεύουσι, καλοῦντες τοπάρχας καὶ προαστείους καὶ ἄλλα πλεῖστα ὀνόματα· ὧν πᾶσαν τὴν ἐπικεχειρημένην αἵρεσιν ἐκθήσομαι καὶ διελέγξω, ἐπὰν εἰς τὸν περὶ τούτων λόγον φθάσωμεν.

2. νυνὶ δέ, μή ποτέ τις νομίσῃ πιστὰ εἶναι καὶ ἀσφαλῆ τ(ὰ) τοῖς Χαλδαίοις νενομισμένα περὶ τὴν ἀστρολογικὴν (μ)άθη(σιν), οὐκ ὀκνήσομεν τὸν πρὸς τούτους ἔλεγχον δι’ ὀλίγων παραθεῖναι, ἐπιδεικνύντες ματαίαν τὴν τέχνην καὶ πλανᾶν μᾶλλον καὶ ἐξ(α)φανίζειν ψυχὴν δυναμένην ἐλπίζουσαν μάταια ἢ ὠφελεῖν.

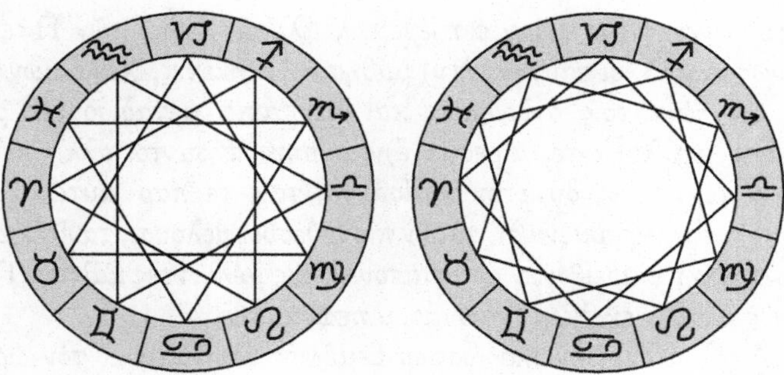

Just as the lower parts of the body are in sympathy with the head (and vice versa), so also things on earth are in sympathy with things above the moon. Still, there is a difference and lack of sympathy such that they are not one and the same.[6]

PREVIEW OF THE PERATICS. 2. 1. Making use of these teachings, Euphrates the Peratic and Akembes the Karystian and the rest of their chorus, after sacralizing it with the name "the true doctrine," speak about a revolution of aeons, the defections of good powers resulting in evils, and the collusions of good with evil powers. They call these powers "lords of the ascendant," "outlying officials," and a host of other names. Their entire manufactured heresy I will present and refute when I reach the account concerning them.[7]

OVERTHROW OF ASTROLOGY

2. But now—so that no one ever supposes that the Chaldean rules of astrological science are reliable and certain—I will not hesitate to present for comparison the exposé against them in summary form.[8] I will unveil the futility of their art by showing that it deceives rather than benefits and can even destroy the soul that fixes its hope on its futile calculations. I do

6. Miller added the alpha privative in <ἀ>συμπάθεια from Sext. Emp., *Math.* 5.44. In Sextus Empiricus, the passage is formulated as an initial, "rather crude" (ἀγροικότερον) critique of astrology offered by "some people" (ἔνιοι).

7. *Ref.* 5.12–18 (esp. 5.13.12).

8. By the early third century, "Chaldean" was a stock name for astrologers of any ethnicity. The astrologers themselves preferred to be called μαθηματικοί (roughly: "professors"), a name originally used in the Pythagorean schools (Bouché-Leclercq, *L'astrologie*, 545–46). See further W. J. W. Koster, "Chaldäer," *RAC* 2:1006–21.

οἷς οὐ κατὰ τέχνης ἐμπειρίαν ἐ(π)έχομεν, ἀλλ' ἐκ (τῆς) τῶν Π<ε>ρατικῶν λόγω(ν γνώσ)εως· 3. οἳ ταύτην τὴ(ν) μάθησιν ἠσκηκότες, Χαλδαίων γενόμενοι ὁμιληταί, ὡς ξένα τοῖς ἀνθρώποις καὶ θαυμάσια μεταδιδόντες μυστήρια, τοῖς ὀνόμασιν ἐναλλάξαντες αἵρεσι(ν ἔ)νθεν συνεστήσαντο. ἀλλ' ἐπεὶ τὴν τῶν ἀστρολόγων τέχνην ὡς δυνατὴν νομίσαντες ταῖς τε παρ' αὐτῶν μαρτυρίαις χρώμενο(ι τ)ὰ ἐπιχειρούμενα δι' αὐτῶν πιστεύεσθαι θέλουσι, τανῦν καθὼς ἔδοξε τὴν ἀστρολογικὴν ἐπιδείξομεν ἀσύστατον, αὖθις μέλλοντες καὶ τὴν Περατικὴν ἀκυροῦν, ὡς κλάδον ἐκ ῥίζης ἀσυστάτου πεφυκυῖαν.

3. 1. Ἀρχὴ μ(ὲν) οὖν καὶ ὥσπερ θεμέλιος ἐστι στῆναι τὸν ὡροσκόπον· ἀπὸ τούτου γὰρ τὰ λοιπὰ τῶν κέντρων λαμβάνεται, τά τε ἀποκλίματα καὶ αἱ ἐπαναφοραὶ τά τε τρίγωνα καὶ <τὰ> τετράγωνα καὶ οἱ κατ' αὐτὰ σχηματισμοὶ τῶν ἀστέρων, ἀπὸ δὲ πάντων τούτων αἱ προαγορεύσεις. 2. ὅθεν ἀναιρεθέντος τοῦ ὡροσκόπου κατ' ἀνάγκην οὐδὲ τὸ μεσουρανοῦν <ἢ δῦνον ἢ ἀντιμεσουρανοῦν> ἐστι γνώριμον, ἀκαταληπτουμένων δὲ τούτων συναφανίζεται πᾶσα Χαλδαϊκὴ μέθοδος.

not provide firsthand experience against their art but offer my report from my knowledge of Peratic documents.[9] 3. They, having long practiced this science as companions of astrologers, construct their heresy from it, altering the terminology and transmitting the mysteries to human beings as if they were strange and wondrous. But since they suppose the astrological art to be effective and want their own arguments to be believed by appealing to the testimonies of astrologers, so now, as determined beforehand, I will prove that astrology is unreliable. Later, I will proceed to invalidate the Peratic heresy like a branch grown from an unreliable root.[10]

3. 1. The beginning and foundation, as it were, of astrology is to establish the ascendant sign. From this sign the rest of the "centers" are taken, as well as the descending signs, those next to rise, the trine relationships, the quartile relationships, and the corresponding configurations of the planets—and from all these the predictions. 2. Therefore, when the ascendant sign is removed, necessarily neither the midheaven nor the descendant nor the anti-midheaven can serve as an indicator. And when all these are indecipherable, the entire astrological procedure is altogether destroyed.[11]

---

9. "Peratic" (Περατικῶν) is Marcovich's emendation from P's πρακτικῶν. If we retain πρακτικῶν λόγων, it would mean something like "practical manuals." The emendation is accepted here since it fits smoothly with the next sentence, in which the Peratai seem to be the subject of συνεστήσαντο.

10. In the following section (*Ref.* 4.3.1–11), our author copies a more or less continuous section of Sext. Emp., *Math.* 5.50–61. For commentary, see Spinelli, *Contro gli astrologi*, 139–48.

11. The difficulty noted here was recognized by astrologers (cf. Manilius, *Astron.* 3.203–218). The technical terms in this passage are discussed in Sext. Emp., *Math.* 5.12–14. To explain briefly: the astrologer draws a "birth theme" (διάθεμα τῆς γενέσεως) by determining four "centers." The first center is the "ascendant" (ὁροσκόπος) or indicator of the zodiacal degree rising at the eastern horizon at the moment of the subject's birth. After the ascendant comes the midheaven (μεσουρανήμα) in the center of the sky, the anti-midheaven (ἀντιμεσουράνημα) below the earth, and the descendant (δύσις) in the western horizon. To each sign of the zodiac are assigned constant psychological and physical features. The planets and the signs that appear at these "centers" especially reveal the client's personality. Superimposed on the signs of the zodiac is a second circle of "places" (τόποι), later called "houses" (οἶκοι, as already in Sext. Emp., *Math.* 5.34). In most systems, there are twelve houses, each of which is assigned a particular area, namely, life (*vita*), wealth (*lucrum*), siblings (*fratres*), parents (*parentes*), children (*filii*), health (*valetudo*), marriage (*nuptiae*), death (*mors*), travels (*peregrinationes*), honors (*honores*), friends (*amici*), and enemies (*inimici*). The revolution of the zodiac within these stationary houses makes possible significant combinations. In addition to the houses, each planet has an "exaltation" at a special place in one sign, and a "depres-

ὅτι δὲ ἀνεύρετον αὐτοῖς ἐστι τὸ ὡροσκοποῦν ζῴδιον, ποικίλως ἔστι διδ(ά)σκειν. 3. ἵνα γὰρ τοῦτο καταληφθῇ, δεῖ πρῶτον μὲν τὴν γένεσιν τοῦ πίπτοντος ἐπὶ τὴν ἐπίσκεψιν βεβαίως κατειλῆφθαι, δεύτερον τὸ διασημαῖνον ταύτην ὡροσκόπιον <ἀπλανὲς> ὑπάρχειν, τρίτον δὲ τὴν ἀναφορὰν τοῦ ζῳδίου πρὸς ἀκρίβειαν συνῶφθαι. 4. ἐπὶ μὲν γὰρ τῆς ἀποτέξεως ἡ ἀ(ν)αφορὰ τοῦ κατ' οὐρανὸν ἀνίσχοντος ζῳδίου τετηρήσθω, ἐπεὶ <ταύτῃ χρῶνται> τὸν ὡροσκόπον ὁρισόμενοι οἱ Χαλδαῖοι· ἐπὶ τῇ ἀναφορᾷ τὸν σχηματισμὸν τῶν ἄστρων ποιοῦνται, ὅπερ διάθεμα καλοῦσιν, ἐφ' ᾧ τὰς προαγορεύσεις δογματίζουσιν.

a. οὔτε δὲ τὴν γένεσιν τῶν ὑπὸ τὴν ἐπίσκεψιν πιπτόντων λαμβάνειν δυνατόν ἐστιν, ὡς παραστήσω, οὔτε
b. τὸ ὡροσκόπιον ἀπλανὲς καθέστηκεν, οὔτε
c. τὸ ἀνίσχον ζῴδιον πρὸς ἀκρίβειαν καταλαμβάνεται.

5. Πῶς οὖν ἄστατος ἡ τῶν Χαλδαίων μέθοδος, νῦν λέγωμεν. τὴν δὴ γένεσιν τῶν ὑπὸ τὴν ἐπίσκεψιν πεσουμένων πρότερον ὁρίσαντες ἐπιζητεῖν ἤτοι ἀπὸ τῆς τοῦ σπέρματος καταβολῆς καὶ συλλήψεως λαμβάνουσιν ἢ ἀπὸ τῆς ἐκτέξεως. 6. καὶ εἰ μὲν ἀπὸ τῆς συλλήψεως λαμβάνειν ἐπιχειρήσει τις, ἄληπτος ἔσται ὁ ἀκριβὴς περὶ τούτου λόγος, ταχὺς ὑπάρχων χρόνος. καὶ εἰκότως· οὐ γὰρ ἔχομεν λέγειν εἴτε ἅμα τῇ καταθέσει τοῦ σπέρματος γέγονεν ἡ σύλληψις εἴτε καὶ μή. 7. δύναται μὲν γὰρ καὶ ἅμα νοήματι τοῦτο συμβαίνειν, ὥσπερ καὶ τὸ προσαχθὲν τοῖς διαπύροις τῶν κλιβάνων στέαρ εὐθὺς κολλᾶται, δύναται δὲ καὶ μετὰ χρόνον. διαστήματος γὰρ ὄντος ἀπὸ τοῦ στόματος τῆς μήτρας μέχρι τοῦ πυθμένος, ἔνθα καὶ τὰς συλλήψεις λέγουσι γίνεσθαι ἰατροί, πάντως ἐν χρόνῳ τινὶ τὸ διάστημα τοῦτο ἀνύειν πέφυκε ἡ καταβαλλομένη τοῦ σπέρμα<τος> φύσις.

8. ἀγνοοῦντες οὖν τὴν ποσότητα τοῦ χρόνου κατὰ τὸ ἀκριβὲς οἱ Χαλδαῖοι οὐδέποτε τὴν σύλληψιν καταλήψονται. τοῦ σπέρματος ὁτὲ μὲν εὐθυβολουμένου καὶ αὐτοῖς προσπίπ<τον>τος ὑφ' ἓν τοῖς εὐφυῶς ἔχουσι πρὸς σύλληψιν τῆς μήτρας <τόποις, ὁτὲ δὲ πολυσπόρως ἐμπίπτοντος, ὑπ' αὐτῆς δὲ τῆς ἐν τῇ

Now the fact that their ascendant sign is undiscoverable can be taught in various ways. 3. For this sign to be deciphered, it is necessary for the inquiry, first of all, that the nativity of the native be deciphered beyond doubt.[12] Second, the signifying ascendant sign must be unvarying. Third, the ascent of the zodiacal sign must be observed with precision. 4. In addition to closely watching the act of parturition, one must observe in the sky the ascent of the rising zodiacal sign, since, by noting this, astrologers determine the ascendant sign.[13] It is from the ascent of the sign that they observe the configuration of the planets. They call this a "birth theme," and on the basis of this theme they decree their predictions. Nevertheless,

a. it is not possible to decipher the [exact] origin of the natives under investigation, as I will substantiate, nor
b. has one set up an invariable instrument for telling time, nor
c. can the rising zodiacal sign be deciphered with precision.

A. The Nativity Cannot Be Deciphered. 5. How unreliable the astrological method is let me now say. First, having determined to investigate the nativity of the natives, they take [that nativity to occur] either from the time of sperm deposition and conception or from parturition. 6. Now if one endeavors to take it from conception, its timeframe cannot be accurately deciphered, since the period is so brief. And naturally: for we cannot say whether conception occurred at the same time as the sperm was deposited or not. 7. This process can occur as swift as a thought, just as dough inserted into red-hot pots immediately sticks. Nevertheless, it can also stick after some time. Since there is a distance from the opening of the womb to the upper part of the uterus (where doctors say that conceptions occur), it is natural that nature, which deposits the seed, completes this distance in a certain amount of time.

8. Thus the astrologers, who do not know the exact amount of time, never decipher the time of conception. Sometimes the sperm is shot in directly and falls into one of those places of the womb naturally fit for conception, but other times it is dispersed in many directions, able to be col-

---

sion" (or "exile") in another (Sext. Emp., *Math.* 5.35). See further Roger Beck, *A Brief History of Ancient Astrology* (Malden: Blackwell, 2007).

12. The "native" (modern astrological parlance) translates τοῦ πίπτοντος. Literally, it is the child "falling [under that zodiacal sign]."

13. Marcovich adds ταύτῃ χρῶνται (here: "noting this").

μήτρᾳ> δυνάμεως <εἰς ἕνα τόπον συνάγεσθαι δυναμένου, τῶν> ἀγνώστων δὲ ὄντων πότε γίνεται τὸ πρῶτον καὶ πότε τὸ δεύτερον, πόσος τε ὁ εἰς ἐκείνην τὴν σύλληψιν ἀναλισκόμενος χρόνος καὶ πόσος <ὁ> εἰς ταύτην· ἀγνοουμένων δὲ τούτων ἦρται καὶ ἡ πρὸς ἀκρίβειαν τῆς συλλήψεως κατάληψις.

9. εἴπερ τε, ὥς τινες τῶν φυσικῶν εἰρήκασιν, ἑψόμενον πρῶτον καὶ προμεταβαλλόμενον ἐν μήτρᾳ τὸ σπέρμα τότε προσέρχεται τοῖς ἀναστομωθεῖσιν αὐτῆς ἀγγείοις—καθάπερ τῇ γῇ τὰ τῆς γῆς σπέρματα—, <αὐτ>όθεν οἱ μὴ εἰδότες τὴν ποσότητα τοῦ τῆς μεταβολῆς χρόνου οὐκ εἴσονται οὐδὲ τὸν τῆς συλλήψεως καιρόν.

10. ἔτι δὲ καὶ ὡς κατὰ τὰ λοιπὰ μέρη τοῦ σώματος διαφέρουσιν ἀλλήλων αἱ γυναῖκες κατὰ ἐνέργειάν τε καὶ τὰς λοιπὰς αἰτίας, οὕτως καὶ κατὰ τὴν τῆς μήτρας ἐνέργειαν, τὰς μὲν θᾶττον συλλαμβανούσας, τὰς δὲ βράδιον. καὶ οὐ παράδοξον, ὅπου καὶ αὐταὶ αὑταῖς συγκρινόμεναι νυνὶ μὲν εὐσύλληπτοι θεωροῦνται, νυνὶ δὲ οὐδαμῶς.

11. τούτου δ' οὕτως ἔχοντος ἀδυνάτων ἐστὶ λέγειν πρὸς ἀκρίβειαν πότε συνέχεται τὸ καταβληθὲν σπέρμα, ἵνα ἀπὸ τούτου τοῦ χρόνου στήσωσιν οἱ Χαλδαῖοι τῆς γενέσεως τὸν ὡροσκόπον.

4. 1. Τούτῳ τῷ λόγῳ ἀδύνατόν ἐστιν ἐκ τῆς συλλήψεως στῆσαι τὸν ὡροσκόπον. ἀλλ' οὐδ' ἐξ ἀποτέξεως. πρῶτον μὲν γὰρ ἄπορόν ἐστ(ι) τὸ πότε ῥηθήσεται ἀπότεξι(ν) εἶναι· ἆρά γε ὅταν ἄρξηται προκύπτειν εἰς τὸν θυραῖον, ἢ ὅτα(ν) ὅλον ἐξίσχῃ, ἢ ὅταν εἰς τὴν γῆν <κατ>ενεχθῇ. οὐδ' ἐν ἑκάστῳ τούτων δυνατόν ἐστι τὸν ἀκριβῆ τῆς ἀποτέξεως [καταλαβέσθαι ἢ] χρόνον ὁρίζειν. 2. καὶ γὰρ διὰ παράστημα ψυχῆς καὶ δι' ἐπιτηδειότητα σώματος καὶ διὰ προαίρεσιν τῶν τόπων καὶ δι' ἐμπειρίαν μα<ίας> καὶ ἄλλας ἀπείρους προφάσεις οὐχ ὁ αὐτός ἐστι χρόνος καθ' ὃν προκύπτει τὸ τικτόμενον ῥαγέντων τῶν ὑμένων ἢ ἐκτὸς ὅλον γίνεται ἢ εἰς τὴν γῆν καταφέρεται, ἀλλ' ἄλλος ἐπ' ἄλλῳ. 3. ὃν πάλιν μὴ δυνάμενοι ὡρισμένως καὶ ἀκριβῶς σταθμήσασθαι οἱ Χαλδαῖοι ἐκπεσοῦνται τοῦ δεόντως τὴν τῆς ἀποτέξεως ὥραν ὁρίζειν.

lected into one place by the very power in the womb.[14] They do not know when the first kind of conception occurs, and when the second, and how much time a delayed or immediate conception takes. Since they are ignorant of these data, the accurate determination of conception is out of reach.

9. And if, as some of the natural philosophers have said, when the seed first fizzles and is transformed in the womb, it then goes to her dilated cavities (just as the seeds of earth go into the earth), obviously those who do not know the amount of time over which the change takes place will not know the exact time of conception.

10. Moreover, as women's bodies differ from each other in their operations and other conditions,[15] so also with regard to the activity of the womb: some conceive quickly, while others more slowly. And no wonder: since they also judge and observe themselves to be able to conceive more easily at one time, while at another they do not conceive at all.

11. Given these facts, the astrologers cannot accurately say when the deposited seed is consolidated so that from that point in time they can establish the ascendant sign of birth.[16]

4. 1. According to this reasoning, it is impossible to establish the ascendant sign from the time of conception. Neither can it be established from the time of parturition. First of all, one is at a loss to say when parturition occurs. Is it when the baby is crowning, or emerges entirely, or when it is brought down to the ground? Not even in any of these cases is it possible to determine the exact time of parturition. 2. For on account of the excited state of [the mother's] mind, the fitness of her body, the choice of place, the experience of the midwife, and innumerable other factors, the time when the child emerges is not always the same—either by breaking through its membranes, or emerging entirely, or being carried down to the ground—but each one of these events occurs at different times. 3. Again, since the astrologers are unable to measure this point in time definitely and accurately, they fail to suitably determine the moment of parturition.[17]

---

14. Duncker and Schneidewin added clauses from Sext. Emp., *Math.* 5.58, to fill out this sentence.

15. "Conditions" translates *αἰτίας*. Αἰτία can refer to a state or circumstance (see BDAG, s.v. *αἰτία* 2). One suspects a Latinism, since *causa* can refer to a state or condition.

16. In the following section (*Ref.* 4.4.1–7), our author adapts Sext. Emp., *Math.* 5.64–70. For commentary, see Spinelli, *Contro gli astrologi*, 151–56.

17. The philosopher Favorinus also wondered how a birth theme could be deciphered if the configuration of stars at conception differed from those at birth (at Gell-

Ὅτι μὲν οὖν ἐπαγγέλλονται ἐπὶ τοῖς τῆς ἀποτέξεως χρόνοις οἱ Χαλδ(αῖοι) τὸν ὡροσκόπον γινώσκειν, οὐκ ἴσασι δέ, ἐκ τούτων συμφανές· ὅτι δὲ οὐδὲ τὸ ὡροσκόπιον ἀπλανὲς αὐτοῖς ἐστι, πάρεστιν ἐπιλογίζεσθαι.

4. ὅταν γὰρ λέγωσιν ὅτι ὁ παρεδρεύων τῇ ὠδινούσῃ ἅμα τῇ ἀποτέξει δίσκῳ σημαίνει τῷ ἐπὶ τῆς ἀκρωρείας ἀστεροσκοποῦντι Χαλδαίῳ, κἀκεῖνος εἰς οὐρανὸν ἀποβλέπων παρασημειοῦται τὸ ἀνίσχον ζῴδιον, τὸ μὲν πρῶτον ἐπιδείξομεν αὐτοῖς ὅτι τῆς ἀποτέξεως ἀορίστου τυγχανούσης, καθὼς μικρῷ πρότερον παρεστήσαμεν, οὐδὲ τῷ δίσκῳ ταύτην διασημαίνειν εὔκολον.

5. εἶτ' ἔστω καταληπτὴν ὑπάρχειν τὴν ἀπότεξιν, ἀλλ' οὔτοι γε πρὸς ἀκριβῆ χρόνον σημειοῦσθαι ταύτην δυνατόν ἐστι· τὸν γὰρ τοῦ δίσκου ψόφον <ἐν> πλείονι χρόνῳ καὶ ἐν συχνῷ πρὸς αἴσθησιν δυναμένῳ μερίζεσθαι [καὶ] κινεῖσθαι συνέβη ἐπὶ τὴν ἀκρώρειαν. 6. τεκμήριον δὲ ἐπὶ τῶν πόρρω δενδροτομούντων θεω(ρ)ούμενον· μετὰ γὰρ ἱκανὴν ὥραν τοῦ κατενεχθῆναι τὸν πέλεκυν ἐξακούεται ἡ φωνὴ τῆς πληγῆς, ὡς ἂν ἐν χρόνῳ πλείονι φθάνουσα ἐπὶ τὸν ἀκούοντα. καὶ διὰ τοῦτο τοίνυν οὐκ ἔστιν ἀκριβῶς τοῖς Χαλδαίοις τὸν χρόνον τοῦ ἀνίσχοντος ζῳδίου καὶ κατ' ἀλήθειαν ὡροσκοποῦντος λαμβάνειν.

7. καὶ μὴν οὐ μόνον φανεῖται πλείων διελθὼν χρόνος, μετὰ τὴν ἀπότεξιν τοῦ παρεδρεύοντος τῇ ὠδινούσῃ κρούσαντος τῷ δίσκῳ, εἶτα μετὰ τὸ κροῦσαι ἀκούσαντος τοῦ ἐπὶ τῆς ἀκρωρείας, <ἀλλὰ> καὶ περισκοποῦντος καὶ βλέποντος ἐν τίνι τῶν ζῳδίων ἐστὶ σελήνη καὶ τῶν λοιπῶν ἀστέρων ἐν τίνι ἕκαστος, φαίνεται ἀναγκαῖον ἀλλοιότερον γενέσθαι τὸ περὶ τοὺς ἀστέρας διάθεμα, τῆς τοῦ πόλου κινήσεως ἀλέκ<τῳ> τάχει φερομένης πρὶν τηρητικῶς <παραπλάσασθαι τῇ> τοῦ γεννηθέντος <ὥρᾳ> κατ' οὐρανὸν <βλεπόμενα>.

Now the fact that the astrologers *profess* to know the ascendant sign at the time of delivery, but do *not* know it, is clear from these observations. It remains to consider that not even their time-measuring device is invariable.

B. The Time Signaled Is Variable. 4. Now they say that the one who attends the woman in labor indicates the time to the astrologer with a gong. The astrologer, examining the stars on a mountain ridge, gazes into heaven and notes the rising zodiacal sign.[18] I first demonstrated to them that the time of parturition is indeterminable. [Here I will demonstrate that] it cannot be easily signified by a gong.

5. Let us assume that the time of delivery can be deciphered; it is still not possible to indicate its exact time. The sound of the gong can be delayed for a rather long time and shifted over a potentially long period in the hearing of the astrologer on the ridge. 6. Proof of this is observed in the case of those cutting trees at a great distance. In this case, the sound of the blow is heard a long time after the axe strikes, appearing to reach the hearer with a significant delay. For this reason, then, it is not possible for the astrologers to accurately grasp the time of the rising zodiacal sign and record it truthfully.

7. Indeed, a significant amount of time passes after the delivery not only because the attendant must hit the gong and [wait for] the sound to travel to the listener on the ridge but also because [the astrologer who hears the gong] must [take time to] look around and observe what sign the moon and each of the other planets are in. Since the movement of the celestial vault continues with unspeakable speed, it appears that the birth theme determined by the positions of the planets must be significantly changed before the objects seen in the sky are carefully correlated with the moment of the child's birth.[19]

---

ius, *Noct. att.* 14.1.19). Ptolemy assumed that "nature" provided for a similar configuration of stars at the moment of conception and parturition (*Tetrab.* 3.1).

18. Cf. Sext. Emp., *Math.* 5.27–28. Here Sextus refers to a method by which astrologers attempted to precisely determine the ascendant. An astrologer sat on a ridge observing the position of the planets while an assistant below marked the exact time of birth by striking a gong. See further Tim Hegedus, *Early Christianity and Ancient Astrology*, Patristic Studies 6 (New York: Lang, 2007), 29–41.

19. Marcovich emends the last clause from Sext. Emp., *Math.* 5.70, since P appears nonsensical: *παραφυλάξασθαι τὴν τοῦ γεννηθέντος ὥραν κατ' οὐρανὸν βλεπομένην* (but the hour of the native's birth cannot be seen in heaven). In the next paragraph (*Ref.*

5. 1. Οὕτως ἀσύστατος <ἐ>δείχθη εἶναι ἡ κατὰ Χαλδαίους τέχνη. εἰ δὲ ἐξ ἐπερωτήσεων φάσκοι τις τοῦ πυνθανομένου σκοπεῖσθαι τὴν γένεσιν [ἢ] περὶ οὗ ἐπερωτᾶται, μηδὲ κατὰ τοῦτον τὸν τρόπον δύνασθαι ἐφικνεῖσθαι ἐπὶ τὸ ἀκριβές. εἰ γὰρ τοσαύτη τις ἐπιμέλεια ἱστόρηται κατ᾽ αὐτοὺς περὶ τὴν τέχνην καὶ μηδ᾽ αὐτοὶ ἐφικνοῦνται ἐπὶ τὸ ἀκριβές, καθὼς ἐπεδείξαμεν, πῶς ὁ ἰδιώτης κατείληφε τῆς ἀποτέξεως τὸν χρόνον ἀκριβῶς, ἵνα παρὰ τούτου μαθὼν ὁ Χαλδαῖος στήσῃ τὸν ὡροσκόπον ἀληθῶς;

2. ἀλλ᾽ οὐδὲ κατὰ τὴν τοῦ ὁρίζοντος ὄψιν πάντῃ ὁ αὐτὸς φανήσεται ἀνίσχων ἀστήρ, ἀλλ᾽ ὅπου μὲν ὡροσκόπος νομισθήσεται τὸ ἀπόκλιμα, ὅπου δὲ ὡροσκόπος ἡ ἐπαναφορά, παρὰ τὴν τῶν τόπων ἐπιφάνειαν, ὄντων ἢ ταπεινοτέρων ἢ ὑψηλοτέρων· ὥστε καὶ κατὰ τοῦτο τὸ μέρος οὐκ ἀκριβὴς φανήσεται ἡ προαγόρευσις, πολλῶν κατὰ πάντα τὸν κόσμον τῇ αὐτῇ ὥρᾳ γεννωμένων, ἄλλου ἄλλως τὰ ἄστρα θεωροῦντος.

3. ματαία δὲ καὶ ἡ διὰ τῶν ὑ<δρι>ῶν νομιζομένη κατάληψις· οὐ γὰρ ὁμοίως ἀμφορεὺς τὸ <κάτω τρη>θεὶς ῥυήσεται πλήρης ὢν ὡς ἀπόκενος, αὐτοῦ τοῦ πόλου κατὰ ἐκείνων λόγον ἑνὶ ὁρμήματι ἰσοταχῶς φερομένου.

4. Εἰ δὲ ἀναστρέψαντες λέγοιεν μὴ τὸν ἀκριβῆ χρόνον λαμβάνειν ἀλλ᾽ ὡς ἔτυχεν ἐν πλάτει, σχεδὸν ὑπ᾽ αὐτῶν ἐλεγχθήσονται τῶν ἀποτελεσμάτων· οἱ

5. 1. So the art of astrology is proved unreliable. If, moreover, someone claims to investigate a native's nativity by asking him questions, not even by this method can one be accurate. For if they undertake so much careful investigation in their art, and still are not themselves accurate, as I showed, how did the average person accurately decipher the time of parturition? And how can the astrologer learn it from the average person in order to genuinely determine his ascendant sign?

C. THE RISING ZODIACAL SIGN CANNOT BE DECIPHERED. 2. Nor will the ascending planet always be the same by examination of the horizon. But wherever the ascendant is, from that point the descending sign will be determined and the signs next to rise, along with the manifestation of the "places," whether they be low or exalted. Consequently, from this perspective too the prediction will not appear accurate, since many people throughout all the world are born at the same moment, and everyone sees a different configuration of planets.[20]

3. Futile, too, is the supposed decipherment through water-clocks, since the jar punctured below will, when full, not flow like one less full. But according to their theory, the celestial vault itself is brought round swiftly at an equal rate of speed.[21]

CONTEMPORANEOUS BIRTHS DO NOT RESULT IN EQUAL FORTUNES. 4. But if, after I have overthrown them, they say that they do not take the accurate

---

4.5.1), our author adapts Sext. Emp., *Math.* 5.86–87. For commentary, see Spinelli, *Contro gli astrologi*, 162.

20. In this paragraph (*Ref.* 4.5.2) our author (drastically) summarizes Sext. Emp., *Math.* 5.82–85. The criticism he notes is at least as old as Panaitios (at Cicero, *Div.* 2.92–93; cf. Favorinus in Gellius, *Noct. att.* 14.1.8–10). Interestingly, our author changes the argument so that it is no longer the fact that one cannot decipher the rising *sign* (ζώδιον, as in Sextus), but one cannot decipher the rising *planet* (ἀστήρ). Astrologers recognized that at different latitudes there were different configurations of stars. In antiquity, tables were typically made for seven climates or latitudes. See further A. A. Long, "Astrology: Arguments pro and contra," in *Science and Speculation: Studies in Hellenistic Theory and Practice*, ed. Jonathan Barnes et al. (Cambridge: Cambridge University Press, 1982), 165–92 (174–75).

21. Our author backtracks to summarize Sext. Emp., *Math.* 5.75, 77. Sextus discusses time measurements through water-clocks in *Math.* 5.23–26. Ptolemy admits that measuring the degree of the ascendant by water-clocks is often inaccurate (*Tetrab.* 3.2). In *Ref.* 4.5.4–6.3 below, our author leaps forward to summarize Sext. Emp., *Math.* 5.88–89. For commentary, see Spinelli, *Contro gli astrologi*, 162–64.

γὰρ ἐν τῷ αὐτῷ χρόνῳ γεννηθέντες οὐ τὸν αὐτὸν ἔζησαν βίον, ἀλλ᾽ οἱ μὲν λόγου χάριν ἐβασίλευσαν, οἱ δὲ ἐν πέδαις κατεγήρασαν. 5. οὐθεὶς γοῦν Ἀλεξάνδρῳ τῷ Μακεδόνι γέγονεν ἴσος, πολλῶν κατὰ τὴν οἰκουμένην ὁμοίως ἀποτεχθέντων αὐτῷ, οὐθεὶς Πλάτωνι τῷ φιλοσόφῳ. ὥστε τὸν ἐν πλάτει τῆς γενέσεως χρόνον <σκοπῶν> ὁ Χαλδαῖος ἀκριβῶς οὐ δυνήσεται λέγειν εἰ <ὁ> κατὰ τοῦτον τὸν χρόνον γεννηθεὶς εὐτυχήσει· 6. πολλοὶ γὰρ κατὰ τὸν αὐτὸν χρόνον γεννηθέντες ἐδυστύχησαν. ὥστε ματαία καὶ ἡ κατὰ τὰ διαθέματα ὁμοιότης.

διαφόρως οὖν καὶ πολυτρόπως τὴν ματαιόπονον σκέψιν τῶν Χαλδαίων διελέγξαντες, οὐδὲ τοῦτο παραλείψομεν ὡς εἰς ἄπορον χωρήσουσιν αἱ προρρήσεις αὐτοῖς. 7. εἰ γὰρ τὸν ἐν τῇ ἀκίδι τοῦ Τοξ<ότ>ου γεννηθέντα, ὡς οἱ μαθηματικοὶ λέγουσιν, ἀνάγκη σφαγήσεσθαι, πῶς αἱ τοσαῦται τῶν βαρβάρων μυριάδες ἀγωνιζόμεναι πρὸς τοὺς Ἕλληνας ἐν Μαραθῶνι ἢ Σαλαμῖνι ὑφ᾽ ἓν κατεσφάγησαν; οὐ γὰρ δή γε ἐπὶ πάντων <ὁ> αὐτὸς ἦν ὡροσκόπος. 8. καὶ πάλιν <εἰ> τὸν ἐν τῇ κάλπῃ τοῦ Ὑδροχόου γεννηθέντα ναυαγήσειν, πῶς οἱ ἀπὸ Τροίας ἀναγόμενοι τῶν Ἑλλήνων περὶ τὰ κοῖλα τῆς Εὐβοίας συγκατεποντίσθησαν; ἀπίθανον γὰρ πάντας μακρῷ χρόνῳ διαφέροντας ἀλλήλων ἐν τῇ κάλπῃ τοῦ Ὑδροχόου γεγεννῆσθαι. 9. οὐ γὰρ ἔστι λέγειν ὅτι δι᾽ ἕνα πολλάκις, ᾧ εἵμαρται κατὰ πέλαγος φθαρῆναι, πάντες οἱ ἐν τῇ νηῒ συναπολοῦνται· διὰ τί γὰρ ἡ τούτου εἱμαρμένη τὰς πάντων νικᾷ, ἀλλ᾽ οὐχὶ διὰ τὸν <ἕνα> ᾧ εἵμαρται ἐπὶ γῆς τελευτᾶν πάντες περισῴζονται;

6. 1. Ἀλλ᾽ ἐπεὶ καὶ περὶ τῆς τῶν ζῳδίων ἐνεργείας λόγον ποιοῦνται, οἷς φασι προσομοιοῦσθαι τὰ ἀποτικτόμενα, οὐδὲ τοῦτον παραλείψομεν· οἷον τὸν ἐν

time but as it happens to be *perceived* and in a *rough estimation*, they are virtually refuted by the very outcomes of people's lives.[22] Those born at the same time do not live the same kind of life. Rather some, for example, ruled as kings, while others grew old in chains. 5. No one, surely, was the equal of Alexander of Macedon or the philosopher Plato, although many throughout the inhabited world were born at the same time. Consequently, the astrologer observing the time of origin in rough estimation will not be able to say accurately whether the one born at this time will possess good fortune.[23] 6. This is because many people born at the same time have met misfortune. As a result, a similar birth theme is worthless.[24]

SIMILAR FORTUNES DO NOT CORRESPOND TO SIMILAR BIRTH THEMES. Now since I have in many and manifold ways refuted the futilely belabored investigation of the astrologers, I will not neglect this: that their predictions lead to hopeless perplexity.[25] 7. If, as the astrologers say, the one born on the arrow point of Sagittarius must be killed, how could so many tens of thousands of non-Greek peoples striving against the Greeks at Marathon or at Salamis be slaughtered at once? Surely all did not have the same ascendant sign![26] 8. And again, if the one born in the pitcher of Aquarius will suffer shipwreck, how was it that the Greeks who sailed from Troy around the coves of Euboia were drowned in the sea? It is unlikely that all who differed so much in age were born in the pitcher of Aquarius! 9. We cannot say in general that, since one man is fated to die at sea, everyone in the boat is destroyed. For why must his fate trump the fates of all? Why not rather should all be saved on account of the one fated to die on land?[27]

DISSONANCE BETWEEN SIGN AND CHARACTER. 6. 1. But since they also ascribe much to the powers of the zodiacal signs, to whom they say off-

22. For ἀποτελέσματα ("outcomes"), see Bouché-Leclercq, *L'astrologie*, 328 n. 1.

23. Marcovich, following Miller, adds σκοπῶν (here: "observing").

24. Cf. Cicero, *Div*. 2.95; Pliny, *Nat*. 7.165. The impossibility of a second Plato arising is mentioned also by Favorinus in Gellius, *Noct. att.* 14.1.29. See further Hegedus, *Early Christianity*, 43–84.

25. In this section (*Ref.* 4.5.6–9), our author summarizes and adapts Sext. Emp., *Math*. 5.92–93. For commentary, see Spinelli, *Contro gli astrologi*, 164–66.

26. Cf. Cicero, *Div*. 2.97.

27. Cf. Favorinus at Gellius, *Noct. att.* 14.1.27. See further Hegedus, *Early Christianity*, 85–89.

Λέοντι γεννηθέντα ἀνδρεῖον ἔσεσθαι, ὁ δὲ ἐν Παρθένῳ τετανόθριξ, λευκόχρως, ἄπαις, αἰδήμων. 2. ταῦτα γὰρ καὶ τὰ τούτοις ὅμοια γέλωτός ἐστι μᾶλλον ἄξια, καὶ οὐ σπουδῆς. ἔστι γὰρ κατ' αὐτοὺς μηδένα Αἰθίοπα ἐν Παρθένῳ γεννᾶσθαι, εἰ δ' οὔ, δώσ<ουσιν> εἶ<ναι> τὸν τοιοῦτον λευκόν, τετανότριχα καὶ τὰ ἕτερα.

3. οἶμαι δὲ μᾶλλον τοὺς ἀρχαίους <τὰ> ὀνόματα τῶν κειμένων ζῴων ἐπίκλη<σιν> τοῖς ἄστροις προστεθεικέναι οἰκειώσεως χάριν, οὐχ ὁμοιοτρόπου φύσεως· τί γὰρ ἔχουσιν ὅμοιον ἄρκτῳ ἑπτὰ ἀστέρες διεστῶτες ἀπ' ἀλλήλων; ἢ δράκοντος κεφαλῇ, ὥς φησιν ὁ Ἄρατος, πέντε·

ἀλλὰ δύο κροτάφοις, δύο δ' ὄμμασιν, εἷς δ' ὑπένερθεν
ἐσχατιὴν ἐπέχει γένυος δεινοῖο πελώρου;

7. 1. Οὕτως καὶ ταῦτα οὐκ ἄξια τοσούτου πόνου δείκνυται τοῖς εὖ φρονεῖν προῃρημένοις καὶ μὴ προσέχουσι τῇ τῶν Χαλδαίων ἐμφυσιώσει, οἳ καὶ βασιλεῖς ἐξαφανίζουσι δειλίαν καταρτίζοντες καὶ ἰδιώτας παραθαρρύνουσι μεγάλα τολμᾶν· 2. εἰ δὲ ἀποτύχοι αὐτῶν <τις> κακῷ περιπαρείς, οὐ πᾶσι γίνεται δ(ι)δάσκαλος ὁ βλαβείς.

οὓς φρεναπατᾶν βουλόμενοι ἐν τοῖς ἀποτεύγμασιν, εἰς ἄπειρον τὸν νοῦν αὐτῶν συνωθοῦντες, λέγουσιν (οὐκ ἄλλ)ως ἐπὶ τὸ αὐτὸ δύνασθαι τὸν σχηματισμὸν τῶν αὐτῶν ἀστέρων γίνεσθαι ἢ διὰ τῆς ἀποκαταστάσεως τοῦ

spring are likened, I will not neglect this either.[28] For instance, the one born in Leo will be brave, and the one born in Virgo will have straight hair, white skin, no children, and a shy disposition.[29] 2. These and similar predictions are worthy of laughter rather than serious consideration. For according to them, no Ethiopian can be born in Virgo. And if this is not the case, they will proffer that one so born is white with straight hair, along with the other traits of Virgo![30]

3. I think, rather, that the ancients gave the names of base animals to the stars because this is what they look like, not because they have the same nature. For what do the seven stars [of the Bear constellations] have in common with a bear when they stand alone? Or the five [stars of the constellation Draco] with the head of a snake, as Aratos says:

> But two [stars] as temples, two as eyes, and one underneath
> Display the edge of a jaw of a terrible monster![31]

7. 1. In this way also these investigations are proved unworthy of so much toil to people who choose to be of sound mind and pay no attention to the inflated pretension of the astrologers. These people destroy even kings by fostering cowardice and embolden common people to start revolutions.[32] 2. But if one of them suffers misfortune, none of them learns from the one injured.

Astrologers, wanting to deceive the minds of those who have experienced failed predictions, forcefully redirect their thoughts into an endless space of time. They claim that a configuration of the same stars cannot

28. In this section (*Ref.* 4.6.1–3), our author adapts Sext. Emp., *Math.* 5.95–98. For commentary, see Spinelli, *Contro gli astrologi*, 167–70.

29. Astrology handbooks differ on what characteristics correspond to which signs. The only commonality between Virgo here and Virgo in the manual of Vettius Valens, for instance, is that the subject will be bashful (αἰδήμων) (*Anth.* 2.50).

30. Ptolemy (and in general all serious astrologers) took account of the differences of longitude and climate on human nature. The major principle was that considerations of country and birth overrode the influences of the stars. Without this principle, one might mistakenly call "the Ethiopian white or straight-haired" (*Tetrab.* 4.10; cf. 2.2; Manilius, *Astron.* 3.301–384). See further Long, "Astrology," 182; Hegedus, *Early Christianity*, 91–107.

31. Aratos, *Phaen.* 56–57. Cf. Sext. Emp., *Math.* 5.97–98.

32. There was a famous story that Chaldeans predicted Alexander's death when he entered Babylon (Diodoros, *Bibl. hist.* 17.112.2). For revolutions, see Tacitus, *Hist.* 1.22 (regarding the emperor Otho).

μεγάλου ἐνιαυτοῦ δι’ ἑπτακισχιλίων ἐτῶν καὶ ἑπτακοσίων ἑβδομήκοντα καὶ ἑπτά. πῶς οὖν φθάσει ἀνθρωπίνη παρατήρησις τοῖς τοσούτοις αἰῶσι συνδραμεῖν ἐπὶ μιᾶς γενέσεως, καὶ ταῦτα οὐχ ἅπαξ ἀλλὰ πολλάκις ... [οἶμαι παρέλιπε.]

3. διὰ πλειόνων ἐληλέγχθαι τὴν Χαλδαϊκὴν τέχνην ἔδει, καίτοι δι’ ἕτερα αὐτῆς ἡμῶν μνησθέντων, οὐχὶ ἰδίως δι’ αὐτήν.

4. ἀλλ’ ἐπεὶ προῃρήμεθα μηδὲν τῶν παρ’ ἔθνεσι δογμάτων καταλιπεῖν διὰ τὴν πολύφωνον τῶν αἱρετικῶν πανουργίαν, ἴδωμεν τί λέγουσι καὶ οἱ περὶ μεγεθῶν τετολμηκότες. οἳ κατιδόντες τὴν τῶν πλειόνων ματαιοπονίαν, ἄλλου ἄλλως διαψευσαμένου καὶ εὐδοκιμήσαντος, μεῖζόν τι ἐτόλμησαν εἰπεῖν, ὅπως ὑπὸ τῶν τὰ μικρὰ ψεύσματα μεγάλως δοξασάντων μειζόνως δοξασθῶσιν. 5. οὗτοι κύκλους καὶ μέτρα τρίγωνά τε καὶ τετράγωνα διπλάσιά τε καὶ τριπλάσια ὑποτίθενται· πολὺς δὲ ὁ περὶ τούτου λόγος, ἀλλ’ οὐ πρὸς τὸ προκείμενον ἀναγκαῖος.

8. 1. Ἱκανὸν οὖν λογίζομαι ἐξειπεῖν τὰ ὑπ’ αὐτῶν τερατολογούμενα· διὸ τοῖς ἐπιτόμοις χρησάμενος ὧν αὐτοὶ λέγουσιν, ἐπὶ τὰ ἕτερα τραπήσομαι. λέγουσι δὲ ταῦτα·

come about in the same places except in the restoration of the Great Year—a period of 7,777 years! Now how can human observation anticipate by backtracking so many centuries with respect to one nativity? And these not once but many times!...[33]

3. It was necessary to expose the art of astrology by many arguments. To be sure, I related them on account of other concerns, not specifically because of the art itself.

ASTRONOMICAL MAGNITUDES

4. But since I decided beforehand to neglect none of the pagan teachings on account of the cacophonous cunning of the heretics, let us also see what those who venture to pronounce on magnitudes declare.[34] These people, after observing the futile labor of most (each one variously deceiving, yet held in honor), dared to say something greater so that they might be more greatly praised by those lauded for their petty deceits. 5. They postulate that there are circles and measures, triangles, rectangles, and multiplications by two and three. The account of this is extensive but not necessary for my purpose.

8. 1. It is sufficient, I think, to pronounce on the fantastic tales they tell. So—using the epitomes of the works that they themselves speak of—I will turn to the other topics.[35] They speak as follows:

---

33. See the fuller sentence in Sext. Emp., *Math.* 5.105: "Human observation will not succeed in backtracking so many centuries even in the case of one nativity, especially when it is interrupted not once but many times, either by the destruction of the universe ... or certainly by a partial upheaval that wholly does away with the continuity of historical tradition." For the Great Year, Sextus gives the figure of 9,977 years. Censorinus (*Die nat.* 18.11) reports ancient hypotheses on the length of the Great Year ranging from 2,434 years (Aristarchos) to infinity. See further Godefroid de Callataÿ, *Annus Platonicus: A Study of World Cycles in Greek, Latin and Arabic Sources* (Leuven: Institut Orientaliste, 1996), 68–72; idem, "Platón astrólogo: La teoría del Gran Año y sus primeras deformaciones," in Pérez Jiménez and Caballero, *Homo Mathematicus*, 317–24.

34. On magnitudes (specifically, *Ref.* 4.8–13), see Mueller, "Heterodoxy," 4317. Geminos, probably Cicero's contemporary, also spoke of the earth's distance from certain heavenly bodies (*Eisagoge* 16.6–12).

35. The phrase "using the[ir] epitomes" offers a rare window into what sort of documents our author was using. He was not inclined, it seems, to turn to primary sources.

κράτος ἔδωκεν ὁ δημιουργήσας τῇ ταὐτοῦ καὶ ὁμοίου περιφορᾷ· μίαν γὰρ αὐτὴν ἄσχιστον εἴασε, τὴν δὲ ἐντὸς σχίσας ἑξαχῇ ἑπτὰ κύκλους ἀνίσους κατὰ τὴν τοῦ διπλασίου <καὶ τριπλασίου> διάστασιν ἑκάστην, οὐσῶν ἑκατέρων τριῶν, κατὰ τὰ ἐναντία μὲν ἀλλήλοις προσέταξεν ἰέναι τοὺς κύκλους, τάχει δὲ τρεῖς μὲν ὁμοίως, τοὺς δὲ τέσσαρας ἀλλήλοις τε καὶ τοῖς τρισὶν ἀνομοίως, ἐν λόγῳ δὲ φερομένους.

2. κράτος μὲν δεδόσθαι τῇ ταὐτοῦ φορᾷ φησιν, οὐ μόνον ἐπειδὴ περιέχει τὴν θατέρου φοράν—τουτέστι τοὺς πλανωμένους—, ἀλλ' ὅτι καὶ τοσοῦτον ἔχει κράτος—τουτέστι τοσαύτην δύναμιν—, ὥστε καὶ τοὺς ἐπὶ τἀναντία [τοὺς πλανωμένους] ἀπὸ δύσεως ἐπ' ἀνατολὴν φερομένους αὐτοὺς τῇ οἰκείᾳ ἰσχύϊ ὁμοίως καὶ ἀπὸ ἀνατολῆς ἐπὶ δύσιν ἑαυτῷ συμπεριάγει. 3. μίαν δὲ καὶ ἄσχιστον εἰᾶσθαί φησι ταύτην φοράν, πρῶτον μὲν ἐπειδὴ πάντων τῶν ἀπλανῶν ἰσόχρονοι αἱ περιφοραὶ καὶ οὐ διῃρημέναι κατὰ πλείους καὶ ἐλάττους χρόνους, ἔπειτα ὅτι μίαν πάντες ἔχουσιν ἐπιφάνειαν τὴν τῆς ἐξωτάτω φορᾶς, οἱ δὲ πλανώμενοι καὶ εἰς χρόνους πλείονας καὶ διαφόρους τῶν κινήσεων καὶ εἰς ἀποστάσεις ἀπὸ γῆς ἀνίσους διῄρηνται.

4. τὴν δὲ θατέρου φησὶν ἑξαχῇ εἰς ἑπτὰ κύκλους ἐσχίσθαι, εἰκότως· ὁπόσαι γὰρ ἂν ὦσιν ἑκάστου αἱ τομαί, μονάδι πλείω τῶν τομῶν γίνεται τὰ τμήματα. οἷον ἐὰν μιᾷ τομῇ <τι> διαιρεθῇ, δύο ἔσται τμήματα, ἂν δυσί, τρία τμήματα· οὕτω δὴ κἂν ἑξαχῇ τι τμηθῇ, ἑπτὰ ἔσται τὰ τμήματα. 5. τὰς δὲ ἀποστάσεις αὐτῶν κατὰ διπλάσια καὶ τριπλάσια ἐναλλὰξ τετάχθαι φησίν, οὐσῶν ἑκατέρων τριῶν, ὅπερ καὶ ἐπὶ τῆς συστάσεως τῆς ψυχῆς ἐπὶ τῶν ἑπτὰ ἀριθμῶν ἔδειξε.

> The Artificer gave dominance to the circle of the Same and the Uniform. For he allowed the [outer] one alone to be indivisible, but the inner revolution he split in six ways, [making] seven unequal circles, each distant by a factor of two or three, with three of each. He ordered the circles to proceed in opposite ways to each other: with three [circles proceeding at a] similar speed, the other four differing in speed from one another and from the [previous] three, [all] revolving in ratio.[36]

2. Dominance was given to the motion of the Same, he says, not only since it encompasses the motion of the Different (that is, the planets) but because it has so much dominance (that is, so much power) that those revolving in the opposite direction from west to east might also revolve with it from east to west by its own native power. 3. He says that he allows one orbit [the circle of the Same] to be indivisible. This is because, first of all, the revolutions of all the fixed stars are simultaneous and not divided according to greater or lesser periods of time, and also since all are on one surface: the outermost orbit. In contrast, the [inner orbits, or planets,] wander and are divided into very many periods and differences of movement and into unequal distances from the earth.[37]

4. The circle of the Different, he says, is divided six ways into seven circles, and reasonably: for however many slices there are of each, the sections created become more than the slices by one. For example, if something is divided by one slice, there will be two sections, if by two, three sections. And so if something is sliced six ways, there will be seven sections. 5. He says that their distances are extended alternately according to multiples of two and three, there being three of each. This he also demonstrated concerning the composition of the soul in regard to the seven numbers. 6. Here is what I mean: counting from the number one, there are three

---

36. The quotation ultimately derives from Plato, *Tim.* 36c–d. The circle of the Same and Uniform is the outermost circle of the fixed stars. The seven inner circles (made from six divisions) are those of the planets (moon, sun, Venus, Mercury, Mars, Jupiter, Saturn) revolving in the opposite direction of the outer circle in harmonic intervals. See further A. E. Taylor, *A Commentary on Plato's Timaeus* (Oxford: Clarendon, 1928), 152–74; Francis Cornford, *Plato's Cosmology: The "Timaeus" of Plato Translated with a Running Commentary* (New York: Liberal Arts, 1957), 74–93.

37. Cf. Plato, *Tim.* 40a–b.

6. τρεῖς μὲν γάρ εἰσιν ἐν αὐτοῖς διπλάσιοι ἀπὸ μονάδος· β′ δ′ η′, τρεῖς δὲ <τριπλάσιοι· γ′ θ′ κζ′> <…>

<διάμετρος μὲν γῆς> μ(υριάδας) η′ καὶ ρη′ σταδίων, περίμετρος δὲ γῆς σταδίων μυ(ριάδας) <κε′> καὶ φμγ′. καὶ ἀπόστημα δὲ ἀπὸ τῆς ἐπιφανείας τῆς γῆς ἐπὶ τὸν σεληνιακὸν κύκλον ὁ μὲν Σάμιος Ἀρίσταρχος ἀναγράφει σταδίων μ(υριάδας) ρξη′, ὁ δὲ Ἀπολλώνιος μυρι(ά)δ(ας) φ′,

7. ὁ δὲ Ἀρχιμήδης μυρι(ά)δ(ας) φνδ′ καὶ μονάδας ͵δρλ′· ἀπὸ δὲ τοῦ σεληνιακοῦ ἐπὶ τὸν τοῦ ἡλίου κύκλον σταδίων μυρι(ά)δ(ας) ͵εκς′ καὶ μονάδ(ας) ͵βξε′· ἀπὸ τού<του> δὲ ἐπὶ τὸν τῆς Ἀφροδίτης κύκλον σταδίων μυρι(ά)δ(ας) ͵βκζ′ καὶ μονάδας ͵βξε′· ἀπὸ τού<του> δὲ ἐπὶ τὸν τοῦ Ἑρμοῦ κύκλον σταδίων μυρι(ά)δ(ας) ͵επα′, μονάδ(ας) ͵ζρξε′· ἀπὸ τούτου δὲ ἐπὶ τὸν τοῦ Πυρόεντος κύκλον σταδίων μυρι(ά)δ(ας) ͵δνδ′, μονάδ(ας) ͵αρη′· ἀπὸ τούτου δὲ ἐπὶ τὸν τοῦ Διὸς κύκλον σταδίων μυρι(ά)δ(ας) ͵βκζ′, μονάδ(ας) ͵εξε′· ἀπὸ τούτου δὲ ἐπὶ τὸν τοῦ Κρόνου κύκλον σταδίων μυρι(ά)δ(ας) ͵δλζ′, μονάδ(ας) ͵βξε′· ἀπὸ τούτου δὲ ἐπὶ τὸν ζῳδιακὸν καὶ τὴν ἐσχάτην περιφέρειαν σταδίων μυρι(ά)δ(ας) ͵βη′, μονάδ(ας) ͵βε′.

9. 1. Τὰ μὲν ἀπ’ ἀλλήλων διαστήματα τῶν κύκλων καὶ τῶν σφαιρῶν βάθη <ἑ>τέ<ρως> ὑπὸ τ(οῦ) Ἀρχιμήδους ἀποδίδοται. τοῦ γὰρ ζῳδιακοῦ τὴν περίμετρον λαμβάνει σταδίων δευτέρων ἀριθμῶν δ′ καὶ μυρι(ά)δ(ας) ͵δψλα′· ὥστε συμβαίνειν τὴν ἐκ τοῦ κέντρου εὐθεῖαν ἄχρι τῆς ἐπιφανείας τῆς ἐσχάτης [γῆς] τὸ ἕκτον εἶναι τοῦ λεχθέντος ἀριθμοῦ· τὴν δὲ ἀπὸ τῆς ἐπιφανείας τῆς γῆς ἐφ’ ἧς βεβήκαμεν ἄχρι τοῦ ζῳδιακοῦ ἄρτι ῥηθέντος ἕκτον τοῦ ἀριθμοῦ λεῖπον τέτρασι μυριάσι σταδίων, ὅ ἐκ τοῦ κέντρου τῆς γῆς μέχρι τῆς ἐπιφανείας αὐτῆς. 2. ἀπὸ τοῦ δὲ Κρόνου κύκλου ἐπὶ τὴν γῆν φησι τὸ διάστημα σταδίων δευτέρων ἀριθμῶν εἶναι μον(άδ)ας δύο καὶ μυρι(ά)δ(ας) ͵βσξθ′ καὶ μον(άδ)ας ͵βψια′· ἀπὸ τοῦ δὲ τοῦ Διὸς κύκλου ἐπὶ γῆν σταδίων δευτέρων ἀριθμῶν μον(άδ)ας δύο καὶ μυρι(ά)δ(ας) σοβ′ καὶ μονάδας χμς′· ἀπὸ δὲ τοῦ Πυρόεντος κύκλου ἐπὶ γῆν δευτέρων ἀριθμῶν μονάδ(α) μίαν καὶ μυρι(ά)δ(ας) ͵γσμα′ καὶ μονάδ(ας) ͵ηφπα′· ἀφ’ ἡλίου ἐπὶ γῆν δευτέρων ἀριθμῶν μονάδ(α) μίαν καὶ μυρι(ά)δ(ας) ͵βρξ′ καὶ μονάδας ͵δυνδ′· ἀπὸ δὲ τοῦ Στίλβοντος ἐπὶ τὴν γῆν μυρι(ά)

multiples of two (namely, two, four, and eight), and three multiples of three (three, nine, and twenty-seven) ...[38]

The diameter of the earth is 80,108 stadia, and the circumference of the earth 250,543 stadia.[39] Moreover, Aristarchos of Samos calculated the distance from the surface of the earth to the moon's circle to be 1,680,000 stadia. Apollonius calculated it to be 5,000,000 stadia.[40]

7. Archimedes calculated the distance from the earth to the moon's circle to be 5,544,130 stadia. He calculated the distance from the moon's to the sun's circle to be 50,262,065 stadia, from this circle to the circle of Venus to be 20,272,065 stadia, from this circle to the circle of Mercury to be 50,817,165 stadia, and from this circle to the circle of Mars to be 40,541,108 stadia, and from this circle to the circle of Jupiter to be 20,375,065 stadia, and from this circle to the circle of Saturn to be 40,372,065 stadia, and from this circle to the circle of the zodiac and the outermost orbit to be 20,082,005 stadia.

9. 1. The distances of the circles from each other and the heights of the spheres are given differently by Archimedes.[41] He understands the circumference of the zodiacal circle to be 447,310,000 stadia. Consequently, a radius drawn from the center to the outer surface is a sixth of the above-mentioned number [namely, 74,551,666.6]. Moreover, a straight line from the surface of the earth on which we walk as far as the zodiacal circle is the just mentioned sixth of the total, minus 40,000 stadia (the distance from the center of the earth to its surface). 2. Yet he says that the distance from the circle of Saturn to the earth is 222,692,711 stadia, and from the circle of Jupiter to the earth 202,720,646 stadia, and from the circle of Mars to the earth 132,418,581 stadia, and from the sun to the earth 121,604,454 stadia, and from the circle of Mercury to the earth 52,688,259 stadia, and from the

38. A lacuna is likely here. Cf. Plato, *Tim.* 35b. Theon of Smyrna, while speaking of the Tetraktys, refers to these same proportions and cites Plato's *Timaios* (*Exp. math.* [Hiller, 94–96]).

39. Marcovich, following previous editors, supplies διάμετρος μὲν γῆς (here: "The diameter of the earth"). Kleomedes calculated the earth's circumference to be 250,000 stadia (*Cael.* 1.7 [Todd]). Eratosthenes of Cyrene (ca. 276–195 BCE) posited 252,000 stadia (cited in Pliny, *Nat.* 2.247–8; Censorinus, *Die nat.* 13). The length of a Greek stadion varied. The Olympic stadion was approximately 176 meters. The Attic/Italic stadion was approximately 185 meters.

40. Cf. Kleomedes, *Cael.* 2.1 (Todd).

41. "Differently" (ἑτέρως) is an emendation of Marcovich (from P's τε).

δ(ας) ͵εσξη', μονάδας ͵ησνθ'· ἀπὸ δὲ Ἀφροδίτης ἐπὶ γῆν μυρι(ά)δ(ας) ͵επα', μονάδ(ας) ͵ερξ'· περὶ σελήνης δὲ ἐλέχθη τὸ πρότερον.

10. 1. Τὰ μὲν οὖν ἀποστήματα καὶ βάθη τῶν σφαιρῶν οὕτως Ἀρχιμήδης ἀποδίδωσιν, ἑτέρως δὲ ὑπὲρ αὐτῶν Ἱππάρχῳ εἴρηται καὶ ἑτέρως Ἀπολλωνίῳ τῷ μαθηματικῷ. ἡμῖν δὲ ἐξαρ(κ)εῖ τῇ Πλατωνικῇ δόξῃ ἑπομένοις διπλάσια μέν<τοι> καὶ τριπλάσια οἴεσθαι τῶν πλανωμένων τὰ ἀπ' ἀλλήλων διαστήματα· σῴζεται γὰρ οὕτως ὁ λόγος τοῦ καθ' ἁρμονίαν συγκεῖσθαι τὸ πᾶν ἐν λόγοις συμφώνοις κατὰ ταῦτα τὰ ἀποστήματα.

2. οἱ δ' ἐκτεθέντες ὑπὸ Ἀρχιμήδους ἀριθμοὶ καὶ <οἱ> ὑπὸ τῶν ἄλλων περὶ τῶν ἀποστημάτων λεγόμενοι λόγοι εἰ μὴ ἐν συμφώνοις εἶεν λόγοις—τουτέστι τοῖς ὑπὸ Πλάτωνος εἰρημένοις διπλασίοις καὶ τριπλασίοις—, ἔξω δὲ συμφώνων εὑρισκόμενοι, οὐκ ἂν σῴζοιεν τὸ καθ' ἁρμονίαν κατεσκευάσθαι τὸ πᾶν. 3. οὐ γὰρ πιθανὸν οὐδὲ δυνατὸν ἄλογά τε καὶ ἔξω συμφώνων καὶ ἐναρμονίων λόγων εἶναι αὐτῶν τὰ ἀποστήματα, πλὴν ἴσως σελήνης μόνης, ἐκ τῶν λείψεων καὶ τῆς σκιᾶς τῆς γῆς· περὶ ἣν μόνην καὶ πιστεῦσαι τις ἂν Ἀρχιμήδῃ <περὶ τῆς> ἀποστάσεως, τουτέστι τῆς σεληνιακῆς ἀπὸ γῆς. ταύτην δὲ λαβοῦσι ῥᾴδιον ἔσται κατὰ τὸ Πλατωνικὸν αὔξοντας κατὰ τὸ διπλάσιον καὶ τριπλάσιον [ὡς ἀξιοῖ Πλάτων] καὶ τὰ λοιπὰ ἀποστήματα ἀριθμῷ περιλαβεῖν.

4. εἰ δὴ κατὰ τὸν Ἀρχιμήδην ἀπὸ τῆς ἐπιφανείας τῆς γῆς ἡ σελήνη ἀφέστηκε σταδίων μυρι(ά)δ(ας) φνδ', σταδίους ͵δρλ', ῥᾴδιον τούτους τοὺς ἀριθμοὺς αὔξοντας κατὰ τὸ διπλάσιον καὶ τριπλάσιον, καὶ τὰ τῶν λοιπῶν εὑρεῖν διαστήματα, ὡς μιᾶς μοίρας λαμβανομένης τοῦ τῶν σταδίων ἀριθμοῦ οὓς ἡ σελήνη τῆς γῆς ἀφέστηκεν.

5. Ὅτι δὲ οἱ λοιποὶ ἀριθμοὶ οἱ ὑπ' Ἀρχιμήδους περὶ τῆς ἀποστάσεως τῶν πλανωμένων λεγόμενοι οὐκ ἐν συμφώνοις <εἰσὶ> λόγοις, ῥᾴδιον γνῶναι <τοὺς> πῶς ἔχουσι πρὸς ἀλλήλους καὶ ἐν τίσι λόγοις εἰσὶ κατανοήσαντας· μὴ εἶναι δὲ

circle of Venus to the earth 50,815,160 stadia. The distance of the moon [to the earth] was given before [namely, 5,544,130].[42]

10. 1. Thus Archimedes gives the distances and heights of the spheres, which are different from those given by Hipparchos and Apollonios the astrologer. It suffices for my purpose to follow the Platonic view and suppose that the distances of the planets from each other are in fact two or three times apart. In this way, the theory is preserved that the universe is structured harmoniously in consonant proportions at regular intervals.[43]

2. Archimedes's calculations and the ratios of the distances calculated by the others, if their numbers are not in harmonious proportions—that is, in Plato's multiples of two and three—are disproportionate and do not preserve the idea that the universe was harmoniously structured.[44] 3. It is neither persuasive nor possible that the distances between the planets are arbitrary, disproportionate, and inharmonious. The only exception, perhaps, is the moon, due to its eclipses and the shadow of the earth. About this alone someone might still believe Archimedes about the distance, that is, the moon's distance from the earth. It will be quite easy for those who assume that this distance is correct, also to calculate the remaining distances according to the Platonic multiples of two and three.

4. If indeed according to Archimedes's theory the moon is distant from the surface of the earth by 5,544,130 stadia, it is quite easy for them to multiply the numbers by two and three, and to find the distances of the rest of the planets, since [each] receives a single multiple of the number of stadia by which the moon is distant from the earth.

5. As to the fact that the remaining numbers calculated by Archimedes about the distance of the planets are not proportional, upon reflection it is simple to find how they are related to each other, as well as to understand

---

42. Our author points out the contradiction that the distances from the outer planets to the earth are much larger than the distance from the earth to the outer surface of the zodiac (the outermost circle). Strangely, in the present list, the sun lies between Mercury and Mars, whereas in the previous list (*Ref.* 4.8.7) it is between the moon and Venus. This different order may indicate that our author has combined two reports. This confusion would contribute something to the "discrepancy" he points out.

43. The Platonic view is also the Pythagorean view, as discussed by Censorinus, *Die nat.* 13.2–5 (the distances between the planets correspond to musical intervals).

44. Macrobius similarly explains that Archimedes calculated in stadia the distances between the planets, but his "figures were rejected by the Platonists for not keeping the intervals in the progression of the numbers two and three" (*In somn. Sc.* 2.3.13–14).

ἐν ἁρμονίᾳ καὶ συμφωνίᾳ ταῦτα, τ(οῦ) καθ' ἁρμονίαν συνεστῶτος κόσμου ὄντα μέρη, ἀδύνατον.

τοῦ μὲν δὴ πρώτου ἀριθμοῦ, ὃν ἀφέστηκεν ἡ σελήνη τῆς γῆς, ὄντος μυρι(ά)δ(ων) φνδ', μονάδων ,δρλ', ὁ δεύτερος ἀριθμός, ὃν ἀφέστηκεν ἥλιος τῆς σελήνης, ὢν μυρι(ά)δ(ων) ,εκζ', μονάδ(ων) ,βξε', ἐν λόγῳ ἐ(στὶ πλ)είον<ι> ἢ ἐ<ννεαπ>λασίῳ· πρὸς δὲ τοῦτον ὁ ἀνωτέρω ἀριθμός, ὢν μυρι(ά)δ(ων) ,βκζ', μονάδ(ων), ,βξε', ἐν λόγῳ ἐστὶ <ἐλάττονι ἢ ἡμίσει· 6. πρὸς δὲ τοῦτον ὁ ἀνωτέρω ἀριθμός, ὢν μυρι(ά)δ(ων) ,επα', μονάδ(ων) ,ζρξε', ἐν λόγῳ ἐστὶ> πλείονι ἢ διπλασίῳ· πρὸς δὲ τοῦτο<ν> ὁ ἀνωτέρω ἀριθμός, ὢν μυρι(ά)δ(ων) ,δνδ', μονάδ(ων) ,αρη', ἐν λόγῳ ἐστὶν ἐλάττονι ἢ ἐπιτετάρτῳ· πρὸς δὲ τοῦτον ὁ ἀνωτέρω ἀριθμός, ὢν μυρι(ά)δ(ων) ,βκζ', μονάδων ,εξε', ἐν λόγῳ ἐστὶ πλείονι ἢ ἡμίσει· πρὸς δὲ τοῦτον ὁ ἀνωτάτω ἀριθμός, ὢν μυρι(ά)δ(ων) ,δλζ', μονάδων ,βξε', ἐν λόγῳ ἐστὶ ἐλάττονι ἢ διπλασίῳ.

11. 1. Οὗτοι δὴ οἱ λόγοι ὅ τε πλείω<ν> ἢ <ἐννεαπλάσιος καὶ> ἐλάττων ἢ ἥμισυς καὶ πλείων ἢ διπλάσιος καὶ ἐλάττων ἢ ἐπιτέταρτος καὶ πλείων ἢ ἥμισυς καὶ ἐλάττων ἢ διπλάσιος ἔξω πασῶν εἰ<σι> συμφωνιῶν· ἐξ ὧν οὐκ <ἂν> ἐναρμόνιόν τι καὶ σύμφωνον σύστημα γένοιτο, ὁ δ' ἅπας κόσμος καὶ τὰ τούτου μέρη κατὰ πάντα ὁμοίως ἐναρμονίως καὶ συμφώνως σύγκειται. 2. οἱ δὲ ἐναρμόνιοι καὶ σύμφωνοι λόγοι σῴζονται, καθάπερ προειρήκαμεν, τοῖς διπλασίοις καὶ τριπλασίοις διαστήμασιν.

εἰ δὴ πιστὸν τὸν Ἀρχιμήδην ἡγησάμεθα ἐν μόνῳ τῷ πρώτῳ ἀποστήματι τῷ ἀπὸ σελήνης μέχρι γῆς, ῥᾴδιον καὶ τὰ λοιπὰ κατὰ τὸ διπλάσιον καὶ τριπλάσιον αὔξοντα<ς> εὑρεῖν. 3. ἔστω δὴ κατὰ τὸν Ἀρχιμήδην τὸ ἀπὸ γῆς μέχρι σελήνης ἀπόστημα σταδίων μυρι(ά)δ(ας) φνδ', μονάδ(ας) ,δρλ'· ἔσται μὲν δὴ τούτου διπλάσιος ἀριθμός, ὃν ἀφέστηκεν ὁ ἥλιος τῆς σελήνης, σταδίων μυρι(ά)δ(ας) ,αρη' καὶ <σταδίους> ,ησξ'· ἀπὸ δὲ τῆς γῆς ἀφέστηκεν ὁ ἥλιος σταδίων <μυριάδας> ,αχξγ' καὶ <σταδίους> ,βτϙ'· καὶ Ἀφροδίτη δὲ ἀφέστηκεν ἀπὸ μὲν ἡλίου σταδίων μυρι(ά)δ(ας) ,αχξγ' καὶ σταδίους ,βτϙ', ἀπὸ δὲ γῆς μυρι(ά)δ(ας) ,γτκς', σταδίους ,δψπ'· 4. Ἑρμῆς δὲ Ἀφροδίτης μὲν ἀφέστηκε σταδίων μυριάδας ,βσιζ', σταδίους ,ϛφκ', ἀπὸ δὲ γῆς μυρι(ά)δ(ας) ,εφμδ', σταδίους ,ατ'· Ἄρης δὲ Ἑρμοῦ μὲν ἀφέστηκε σταδίων μυρι(ά)δ(ας) ,δϡπθ', σταδίους ,ζρο', ἀπὸ δὲ γῆς μυρίας μυριάδας καὶ φλγ', σταδίους ,ηυο'· 5. Ζεὺς δὲ Ἄρεως μὲν ἀφέστηκε <σταδίων> μυρι(ά)δ(ας) ,δυλε', σταδίους ,γμ', ἀπὸ δὲ γῆς <μυρίας> μυρι(ά)δ(ας) καὶ ,δϡξθ', σταδίους ,αφι'· Κρόνος <δὲ> ἀπὸ μὲν Διὸς ἀφέστηκε σταδίων μυρίας μυριάδας καὶ ,δϡξθ', σταδίους ,αφι', ἀπὸ δὲ γῆς μυρίας μυριάδας <β'> καὶ ,θϡλη', σταδίους ,γκ'.

their proportions. It is impossible that these distances not be in harmony and concord, since they are parts of the harmoniously constructed universe.

Now Archimedes's first number—the distance between the moon and earth—is 5,544,130 stadia. His second number—the distance between the sun and moon—is 50,272,065 stadia—more than a 9:1 ratio. The next highest number, 20,272,065 stadia, is less than 1:2 of the previous number. 6. The next highest number, 50,817,165, is more than 2:1 of the previous number.[45] The next highest number, 40,541,108, is less than a ratio of 4:3. The next highest number, 20,275,065, is more than a 1:2 ratio of the previous number. The next highest number, 40,372,065, is less than a 2:1 ratio of the previous number.

11. 1. Now these proportions—more than 9:1, less than 1:2, more than 2:1, less than 4:5, more than a 1:2, and less than 2:1—are out of all harmony![46] From them no harmonious and concordant system would arise, whereas the entire cosmos and its parts in every respect are alike situated harmoniously and concordantly. 2. The harmonious and concordant proportions are preserved, as I said, by means of intervals that are multiples of two and three.

Now suppose we consider Archimedes reliable in only the first distance from the moon to the earth. [From this datum] it is easy to find the others through multiplying by two or three. 3. So, let Archimedes's distance from the earth to the moon (namely, 5,544,130 stadia) be correct. Multiplied by two, the distance between the sun and moon will be 11,088,260 stadia. And from the earth to the sun there will be a distance of 16,632,390 stadia. Moreover, the distance between Venus and the sun will be 16,632,390 stadia, and from the earth 33,264,780 stadia. 4. The distance from Mercury to Venus will be 22,176,520 stadia, and to the earth 55,441,300 stadia. Mars will be distant from Mercury 49,897,170 stadia, and from the earth 105,338,470 stadia. 5. From Jupiter to Mars there will be 44,353,040 stadia, and from the earth 149,691,510 stadia. Saturn will be distant from Jupiter 149,691,510 stadia, and from the earth 299,383,020 stadia.[47]

---

45. Stern, cited by Duncker and Schneidewin, added the material from ἐλάττονι to ἐστί.

46. Duncker and Schneidewin supplied ἐννεαπλάσιος καί.

47. If we take the figures for the intervals between the earth and the seven planets, taking the earth-to-moon distance as a unit, we have: Earth → Moon: x; Moon → Sun: 2x; Sun → Venus: 3x; Venus → Mercury: 4x (2^2); Mercury → Mars: 9x (3^2); Mars → Jupiter: 8x (2^3); Jupiter → Saturn: 27x (3^3). These calculations provide a rubric sup-

12. 1. Τίς οὐ θαυμάσει τὴν τοσαύτην φροντίδα μετὰ τοσούτου πόνου γεγενημένην; οὐκ ἀχρεῖος δέ μοι οὑτοσὶ ὁ Πτολεμαῖος ὁ τούτων μεριμνητὴς δοκεῖ, τοῦτο δὲ μόνον λυπεῖ, ὡς πρόσφατος γενηθεὶς οὐκ εὔχρηστος γεγένηται γιγάντων πα<ι>σίν, οἳ τὰ μέτρα ταῦτα ἠγνοηκότες, ἐγγὺς νομίζοντες εἶναι ὕψη οὐρανοῦ, πύργον μάτην ἐπεχείρησαν ποιεῖν. οἷς οὗ<το>ς εἰ κατ' ἐκεῖνο παρὼν τὰ μέτρα διηγήσατο, οὐκ ἂν μάτην τετολμήκεισαν. 2. εἰ δέ τις τούτῳ φάσκει ἀπιστεῖν, μετρήσας πειθέσθω· ταύτης γὰρ φανερωτέραν ἀπόδειξιν οὐκ ἔχει πρὸς τοὺς ἀπίστους. ὢ ματαιοπόνου [καὶ] ψυχῆς φυσιώσεως καὶ πίστεως ἀπίστου, ἵνα πάντως Πτολεμαῖος σοφὸς νομίζηται παρὰ τοῖς τὴν ὁμοίαν σοφίαν ἠσκηκόσι.

13. 1. Τούτοις ἐν μέρει ἐπισχόντες τινές, ὡς μεγάλα κρίναντες καὶ λόγου ἄξια νομίσαντες, αἱρέσεις ἀμέτρους καὶ ἀπείρους συνεστήσαντο· ὧν εἷς μὲν Κολάρβασος, ὃς διὰ μέτρων καὶ ἀριθμῶν ἐκτίθεσθαι θεοσέβειαν ἐπι<χει>ρεῖ, καὶ ἕτεροι δὲ ὁμοίως, οὓς ἐπιδείξομεν, ἐπὰν τὰ περὶ αὐτῶν ἀρξώμεθα λέγειν. οἳ Πυθαγορείῳ ψήφῳ ὡς δυνατῇ προσέχουσι καὶ τὴν ἀσφαλῆ φιλοσοφίαν δι' ἀριθμῶν καὶ στοιχείων σχεδιάζουσι, μαντευόμενοι μάταια.

2. ὧν ὁμοίως λόγους ἐρανισάμενοί τινες ἀποπλανῶσιν ἰδιώτας, προγνωστικοὺς ἑαυτοὺς φάσκοντες, ἔσθ' ὅτε διὰ τὸ πολλὰ μαντεύεσθαι ἓν ἐπιτυγχάνοντες, καὶ ἐπὶ μὲν τοῖς πολλοῖς ἀποτεύγμασι μὴ αἰδούμενοι, ἐπὶ δὲ τῷ ἑνὶ ἐγκομπάζοντες. οὐδὲ τούτων τὴν ἄσοφον σοφίαν παραπέμψομαι, ἀλλ' ἐκθέμενος τοὺς ἐκ τούτων ἐπιχειροῦντας θεοσέβειαν συνιστᾶν ἐλέγξω ῥίζης ἀσυστάτου καὶ <πα>νουργίας ἀνάπλε<ω> ὄντας μαθητάς.

14. 1. Οἱ μὲν οὖν διὰ ψήφων τε καὶ ἀριθμῶν, στοιχείων τε καὶ ὀνομάτων μαντεύεσθαι νομίζοντες ταύτην ἀρχὴν ἐπιχειρήσεως τοῦ κατ' αὐτοὺς λόγου ποιοῦνται, φάσκοντες πυθμένα εἶναι ἑκάστου τῶν ἀριθμῶν ἐπὶ μὲν τῶν χιλιάδων τοσαύτας μονάδας, ὅσαι ἂν ὦσι χιλιάδες· οἷον τῶν ἑξακισχιλίων ὁ πυθμὴν

CRITIQUE OF ASTROLOGICAL MAGNITUDES. 12. 1. Who will not be amazed at such excogitation wrought by so great a labor? Ptolemy, who is satisfied to agonize over these figures, is not useless to me. This alone I lament: that as one so recently born, he could not be useful to the children of the giants. They, ignorant of these measurements, thought that they were near the heights of heaven and undertook to build a tower for no purpose.[48] If this man had existed at their time and related the measurements, the giants' offspring would not have been vainly reckless. 2. But if anyone claims to disbelieve this Ptolemy, let him take the measurements and be convinced (for there is no clearer proof for the incredulous than this). O futile labor of a puffed-up soul and incredible credulousness, that Ptolemy be considered an all-around expert by those who practice the same science!

13. 1. Some people, in turn, hankered after these calculations. They judged them magnificent, considered them reputable, and concocted measureless and boundless heresies. One of these is Kolarbasos, who endeavors to reckon godliness through measurements and numbers. There are others who do likewise—whom I will expose when I begin to relate their teachings. They devote themselves to Pythagorean number speculation as if it were compelling and improvise their unfailing philosophy through numbers and elements by divining futilities.[49]

2. Some people appropriate these teachings in a similar way and mislead the uneducated, claiming that they are "prognosticators." Sometimes, because they divine so frequently, they chance to get one thing right and—unashamed of their many failures—boast about their one success. I will not omit even their unwise wisdom. Rather I will present a sample of them who endeavor to engineer godliness, and expose them as disciples of a root unstable and suffused with cunning.

NUMBER DIVINATION

14. 1. Now some people suppose that they can divine through calculations and numbers, as well as letters and names. They construct the following as the starting point of their endeavor. They claim that each number

---

plying the distances of the planets from earth: Moon, 1; Sun, 2; Venus, 3; Mercury, 4; Mars, 8; Jupiter, 9; Saturn, 27. We meet this series of numbers in *Tim*. 35b–c (Legge, *Philosophoumena*, 1:81–82 n. 1).

48. A reference to the tower of Babel (Gen 6:4; 11).

49. Our author would seem to have the Valentinians, in particular Markos, in mind (see *Ref.* 6.39–54).

μονάδες ἕξ, τῶν ἑπτακισχιλίων μονάδες ἑπτά, τῶν ὀκτακισχιλίων μονάδες ὀκτώ, καὶ ἐπὶ τῶν λοιπῶν ὁμοίως κατὰ τὰ αὐτά. 2. καὶ ἐπὶ τῶν ἑκατοντάδων ὅσαι ἂν ὦσιν αἱ ἑκατοντάδες, τοσαῦται μονάδες ὁ πυθμήν ἐστιν αὐτῶν· οἷον τῶν ἑπτακοσίων ἑπτά εἰσιν ἑκατοντάδες, ὁ πυθμὴν αὐτῶν ἑπτὰ μονάδες· τῶν ἑξακοσίων ἓξ ἑκ<ατ>οντάδες, ὁ πυθμὴν αὐτῶν <ἓξ μονάδες· τῶν τριακοσίων τρεῖς ἑκατοντάδες, ὁ πυθμὴν αὐτῶν> τρεῖς μονάδες. τὸ ὅμοιον καὶ ἐπὶ τῶν δεκάδων· τῶν μὲν ὀγδοήκοντα <ὁ πυθμὴν> μονάδες ὀκτώ, τῶν δὲ ἑξήκοντα μονάδες ἕξ, τῶν τεσσαράκοντα μονάδες τέσσαρες, τῶν δέκα μονὰς μία. 3. ἐπὶ δὲ τῶν μονάδων πυθμὴν αὐταί εἰσιν αἱ μονάδες· οἷον τοῦ ἐννέα ὁ ἐννέα, τοῦ ὀκτὼ ὁ ὀκτώ, τοῦ ἑπτὰ ὁ ἑπτά. οὕτως οὖν καὶ ἐπὶ τῶν στοιχείων ποιεῖν δεῖ· ἕκαστον γὰρ στοιχεῖον κατά τινα τέτακται ἀριθμόν· οἷον τὸ <ν> <πεντή>κοντα μονάδ(ων) <ἐστί>ν, τῶν πεντήκοντα μονάδων πυθμήν ἐστιν ὁ πέντε, καὶ τοῦ <ν> στοιχείου πυθμὴν ἔσται ὁ πέντε.

4. Ἔστω ἔκ του ὀνόματος τοὺς τούτου πυθμένας λαβεῖν· οἷον τοῦ Ἀγαμέμνων ὀνόματος γίνεται τοῦ μὲν <α> <πυθμὴν> μονὰς μία, τοῦ δὲ <γ> μονάδες τρεῖς, τοῦ ἄλλου <α> μονὰς μία, τοῦ <μ> μονάδες δʹ, τοῦ <ε> μονάδες εʹ, τοῦ <μ> μονάδες δʹ, τοῦ <ν> μονάδες πέντε, τοῦ <ω> μονάδες ηʹ, τοῦ <ν> μονάδες εʹ· ὁμοῦ ἐπὶ τὸ αὐτὸ ἔσονται αʹ γʹ αʹ δʹ εʹ δʹ <εʹ> ηʹ εʹ· ταῦτα συντεθέντα ποιεῖ μονάδας λςʹ. 5. πάλιν τούτων πυθμένας λαμβάνουσι, καὶ γίνονται τῶν μὲν λʹ τρεῖς, τῶν δὲ ἓξ αὐτὰ τὰ ἕξ· συντεθέντα οὖν τὰ τρία καὶ τὰ ἓξ ποιεῖ ἐννέα, τῶν δὲ ἐννέα πυθμὴν ὁ ἐννέα. κατέληξεν οὖν τὸ Ἀγαμέμνων ὄνομα εἰς τὸν ἐννέα πυθμένα.

6. ἔστω τὸ αὐτὸ καὶ ἐπὶ ἄλλου ὀνόματος ποιῆσαι, τοῦ Ἕκτωρ. τὸ Ἕκτωρ ὄνομα ἔχει στοιχεῖα <ε> καὶ κάππα καὶ ταῦ καὶ <ω> καὶ <ρ>· τούτων πυθμένες εʹ βʹ γʹ ηʹ αʹ· ταῦτα συντεθέντα ποιεῖ μονάδας ιθʹ. πάλιν τῶν δέκα πυθμὴν εἷς, τῶν ἐννέα ἐννέα, ἃ συντεθέντα ποιεῖ δέκα· τοῦ <δὲ> δέκα γίνεται πυθμὴν μονάς. ψηφισθὲν οὖν τὸ Ἕκτωρ ὄνομα ἐποίησε πυθμένα μονάδα.

7. εὐκολώτερον δέ ἐστι τὸ <αὐτὸ> οὕτως ποιεῖν· τοὺς εὑρεθέντας ἐκ τῶν στοιχείων πυθμένας, ὡς νῦν ἐπὶ τοῦ Ἕκτωρ ὀνόματος εὕρομεν μονάδας ιθʹ, εἰς ἐννέα μέριζε καὶ τὸ περιλειπόμενον πυθμένα λέγε· οἷον τὰ ιθʹ ἐὰν εἰς ἐννέα μερίζω, περιλείπεται μονάς—ἐννάκις γὰρ δύο ιηʹ καὶ λοιπὴ μονάς· ἐὰν γὰρ ὑφέλω τῶν ιθʹ τὰ δεκαοκτώ, λοιπὴ μονάς—· ὥστε τοῦ Ἕκτωρ ὀνόματος πυθμὴν ἔσται μονάς.

has a "base": in the case of thousands, each thousand counts as a unit. For example, the base of 6,000 is six units, of 7,000 seven units, of 8,000 eight units, and so forth with the rest in the same way. 2. Moreover, for the hundreds, their base is a unit for each hundred. For example: there are seven hundreds in 700, so their base is seven units; in 600 there are six hundreds with a base of six units; in 300 there are three hundreds, with a base of three units. Similarly with the tens: for eighty, the base is eight units, for sixty the base is six units, for forty the base is four units, and for ten the base is one unit. 3. The base of the single digits are the single digits themselves. For example: the base of nine is nine, the base of eight is eight, and the base of seven is seven. So one must do with the letters as well, for each [Greek] letter counts as a number. For example, the letter nu [ν] counts as fifty units, and the base of the fifty units is five, so the base of nu is five.[50]

4. Suppose that we take from someone's name his base numbers. For instance, the name Agamemnon [Αγαμέμνων] has from the alpha a base of one unit, from the gamma three units, from the other alpha one unit, from the mu four units, from the epsilon five units, from the mu four units, from the nu five units, from the omega eight units, and from the nu five units (all together: 1, 3, 1, 4, 5, 4, 5, 8, and 5). Added together, they equal thirty-six units. 5. Then they take the bases of the resulting numbers: [in this case, the base of] of thirty is three, and of six, six itself. Added together, the three and the six make nine, and the base of nine is nine. Thus the name Agamemnon results in a base of nine.

6. Let us do the same with another name, Hektor. The name Hektor [Ἕκτωρ] has the letters epsilon, kappa, tau, omega, and rho. Their bases are five, two, three, eight, and one. Added together, they make nineteen units. Again, the base of ten is one, of nine, nine. Together, they make ten. Ten has a base of one. Thus calculated, Hektor's name makes a base of one.

7. The same calculation can be done more easily if, when the bases of the letters are found (as in this case with Hektor we find nineteen units), one divides by nine and takes the remainder as the base. For example, if I divide nineteen by nine, there is a remainder of one (for it is [9 x 2] + 1; and 19 – 18 = 1), leaving a base of one for Hektor's name.

50. For base numbers and calculations, see the Pythagorean letter fragments printed by M. Paul Tannery, "Notice sur des fragments d'onomatomancie arithmétique," *Notices et extraits des manuscrits de la Bibliothèque Nationale* 31 (1886): 231–60; and A. M. Desrousseaux, "Sur quelques manuscrits d'Italie," *Mélanges d'archéologie et d'histoire* 6 (1886): 483–553 (534–44). Note also Franz Dornseiff, *Das Alphabet in Mystik und Magie* (Leipzig: Teubner, 1922), 117–18.

8. πάλιν τοῦ Πάτροκλος ὀνόματος πυθμένες εἰσὶν ἀριθμοὶ οὗτοι· η′ α′ γ′ α′ ζ′ β′ γ′ ζ′ β′, συντεθέντες ποιοῦσι μονάδας λδ′. τούτων τὸ ἐκλεῖπον μονάδες ἑπτά· τῶν λ′ τρεῖς, καὶ τῶν δ′ αὐταὶ αἱ δ′· πυθμὴν οὖν εἰσι τοῦ Πάτροκλος ὀνόματος μονάδες ζ′.

9. Οἱ μὲν οὖν κατὰ τὸν ἐννεαδικὸν κανόνα ψηφίζοντες ἔννατον λαμβάνουσι τοῦ ἀθροισθέντος ἐκ τῶν πυθμένων ἀριθμοῦ καὶ τὸ περιλειφθὲν πλῆθος τὸν πυθμένα ὁρίζονται, οἱ δὲ κατὰ τὸν ἑβδοματικὸν τὸ ἕβδομον. οἷον εὑρέθη ἐπὶ τοῦ Πάτροκλος ὀνόματος τὸ ἐκ τῶν πυθμένων ἄθροισμα μονάδες λδ′· τοῦτο μερισθὲν εἰς ἑβδομάδας ποιεῖ δ′, ὅ ἐστιν κη′, λοιπαὶ μονάδες ἕξ· λέγουσιν ὅτι ὁ πυθμὴν τοῦ Πάτροκλος ὀνόματός εἰσιν ἓξ κατὰ τὸν ἑβδοματικόν. 10. εἰ δὲ ἔσται μγ′, τὸ ἕβδομον ποιεῖ μβ′—ἑπτάκις γὰρ ἓξ μβ′—καὶ λοιπὸν ἕν· μονὰς οὖν γίνεται ὁ πυθμὴν ὁ ἀπὸ τῶν μγ′ κατὰ τὸν ἑβδοματικόν.

δεῖ δὲ προσέχειν ἐὰν ὁ ληφθεὶς ἀριθμὸς μεριζόμενος ἀπαρτίσῃ· οἷον ἐὰν ἔκ τινος ὀνόματος συντιθεὶς τοὺς πυθμένας εὕρω λόγου χάριν μονάδας λϛ′· ὁ δὲ λϛ′ μεριζόμενος εἰς τὸν ἐννέα δ′ ἀπαρτίζει ἐννεάδας—ἐννάκις γὰρ δ′ λϛ′ καὶ οὐδὲν περιλείπεται—· τὸν πυθμένα οὖν αὐτὸν τὸν θ′ δῆλον εἶναι.

11. καὶ πάλιν <ἐὰν> τὸν τεσσαράκοντα πέντε ἀριθμὸν μερίζοντες εὕρωμεν ἀπαρτίζοντα ἐννέα—καὶ γὰρ ἐννάκις πέντε με′ καὶ λείπεται οὐδέν—ἐπὶ τῶν τοιούτων αὐτὸν τὸν ἐννέα λέγουσι πυθμένα.

καὶ ἐπὶ τοῦ ἑβδοματικοῦ ὁμοίως· ἐὰν λόγου χάριν τὸν κη′ εἰς τὸν ἑπτὰ μερίζοντες ἀπαρτίσωμεν—ἑπτάκις γὰρ δ′ κη′ καὶ περιλείπεται οὐδέν—, <αὐτὸν> τὸν ἑπτὰ λέγουσι πυθμένα.

12. Ὅταν μέντοι <τις> ψηφίζῃ τὰ ὀνόματα καὶ εὑρίσκῃ δὶς τὸ αὐτὸ <φωνῆεν> γράμμα, ἅπαξ αὐτὸ ψηφίζει. οἷον τὸ Πατρόκ<α>λος ὄνομα καὶ τὸ [π] α δὶς ἔχει καὶ τὸ ο δίς· ἅπαξ οὖν τὸ α ψηφίζουσι καὶ ἅπαξ τὸ ο. κατὰ τοῦτο οὖν πυθμένες ἔσονται η′ α′ γ′ α′ ζ′ β′ γ′ β′, καὶ συντεθέντες ποιοῦσι μονάδας κζ′, καὶ ἔσται πυθμὴν τοῦ ὀνόματος κατὰ μὲν τὸν ἐννεαδικὸν αὐτὸς ὁ ἐννέα, κατὰ δὲ τὸν ἑβδοματικὸν ἕξ.

13. ὁμ(οίως) Σαρπηδὼν ψηφισθεὶς ποιεῖ μονάδας κατὰ τὸν ἐννεαδικὸν δύο [πυθμένα], Πάτροκλος δὲ ποιεῖ μονάδας θ′· νικᾷ Πάτροκλος. ὅταν γὰρ ᾖ ὁ μὲν εἷς περισσός, ὁ δὲ ἕτερος ἄρτιος, ὁ περισσὸς νικᾷ ἐὰν μείζων ᾖ.

8. Again, the bases of the name Patroklos [Πάτροκλος] are the numbers eight, one, three, one, seven, two, three, seven, and two. Added together, they make thirty-four. The remainder [when we divide by nine] is seven. [Alternatively, we can take a base of] three from thirty and the identical [base of] four from four to make, when added, the base of Patroklos's name: seven.

9. Now some calculate according to the rule of the ennead. They take a ninth part of the sum of the bases and determine the remainder as the base. Others calculate the seventh part according to rule of the hebdomad. For example: we found the sum of the bases from Patroklos to be thirty-four units. If we divide it into hebdomads, we get four (for 7 x 4 = 28) with a remainder of six. Thus they say that the base of Patroklos's name is "six according to the hebdomad." 10. And if we take forty-three, the seventh part makes forty-two (for 7 x 6 = 42) with a remainder of one. So the base from forty-three according to the rule of the hebdomad is one.

One must note after division if the remainder is even. For example, if from a certain name I find the sum of the bases (for the sake of argument) to be thirty-six, thirty-six divided by nine makes four sets of nine (for 9 x 4 = 36, with no remainder), clearly giving us a base of nine.

11. Again, if dividing forty-five we find nine even (for 9 x 5 = 45, with no remainder), they say that for such numbers there is a base of nine.

Likewise with regard to the rule of the hebdomad: if (for the sake of argument) we divide twenty-eight evenly by seven (for 7 x 4 = 28, with no remainder), they say that seven itself is the base.

12. When, however, someone calculates the names and finds the same vowel letter twice, he counts it once.[51] For instance, in Patroklos's name there are two alphas and two omicrons which are counted once.[52] By this rule, the bases will be eight, one, three, one, seven, two, three, and two, added together to make twenty-seven. Twenty-seven has a base of nine according to the rule of the ennead, and six according to the rule of the hebdomad.

13. Likewise, Sarpedon, when calculated, makes two according to the rule of the ennead, and Patroklos makes nine. Thus Patroklos wins. For when one number is odd and the other even, the odd wins if it is larger.[53]

---

51. Marcovich adds φωνῆεν ("vowel letter") to make the computations work.

52. There are not in fact two alphas in Patroklos's name, although Marcovich conjectures the spelling Πατρόκαλος.

53. For Patroklos's defeat of Sarpedon, see Homer, *Il.* 16.462–507. Terentianus

πάλιν δὲ ἐὰν ᾖ ὀκτὼ ἄρτιος καὶ πέντε περισσός, ὁ ὀκτὼ νικᾷ· μείζων γάρ ἐστιν. εἰ δέ εἰσιν ἀριθμοὶ [δύο οἷον] ἀμφότεροι ἄρτιοι ἢ ἀμφότεροι περισσοί, ὁ ἐλάσσων νικᾷ. 14. πῶς δὲ ὁ Σαρπηδὼν κατὰ τὸν ἐννεαδικὸν ποιεῖ μονάδας δύο; παραλείπεται γὰρ τὸ ω στοιχεῖον. ὅταν γὰρ ᾖ ἐν ὀνόματί <τινι> στοιχεῖα ω καὶ η, παραλιμπάνουσι τὸ ω ἑνὶ στοιχείῳ χρώμενοι· ἰσοδυναμεῖν γὰρ λέγουσι τὰ ἀμφότερα, δὶς δὲ τὸ αὐτὸ οὐ ψηφίζεται, ὡς ἄνωθεν εἴρηται.

15. πάλιν Αἴας <κατὰ τὸν ἐννεαδικὸν> ποιεῖ μονάδας δ′, Ἕκτωρ δὲ [κατὰ τὸν ἐννεαδικὸν] ποιεῖ μονάδα μίαν· καὶ ἔστιν ἡ μὲν τετρὰς ἄρτιος, ἡ δὲ μονὰς περισσή, ἐπὶ δὲ τῶν τοιούτων τὸν μείζονα ἐλέγομεν νικᾶν· νικᾷ ὁ Αἴας.

16. πάλιν Ἀλέξανδρος καὶ Μενέλαος· Ἀλέξανδρος κύριον ἔχει ὄνομα <Πάρις·> Πάρις δὲ ποιεῖ μονάδας κατὰ τὸ<ν> ἐννεαδικὸν δ′, Μενέλαος δὲ κατὰ τὸν ἐννεαδικὸν μονάδας θ′. νικῶσι δὴ αἱ ἐννέα τὰς τέσσαρας. εἴρηται γάρ, ὁπόταν ὁ μὲν περισσὸς ᾖ, ὁ δὲ ἄρτιος, ὁ μείζων νικᾷ, ὅταν δὲ ἀμφότεροι ἄρτιοι ἢ ἀμφότεροι περισσοί, ὁ ἐλάσσων.

17. πάλιν Ἄμυκος καὶ Πολυδεύκης· Ἄμυκος μὲν ποιεῖ μονάδας δύο κατὰ τὸν ἐννεαδικόν, [καὶ] Πολυδεύκης δὲ ἑπτά· νικᾷ Πολυδεύκης.

Αἴας καὶ Ὀδυσσεὺς ἐπάλαισαν ἐν τῷ ἐπιταφίῳ· Αἴας ποιεῖ κατὰ τὸν ἐννεαδικὸν μονάδας δ′, Ὀδυσσεὺς ὀκτὼ κατὰ τὸν ἐννεαδικόν· ἆρ᾽ οὖν μήτι τὸ Ὀδυσσέως ἐπίθετον καὶ οὐ κύριόν ἐστιν; ἐνίκησε γάρ· κατὰ μὲν τοὺς ἀριθμοὺς νικᾷ Αἴας, ἡ δ᾽ ἱστορία Ὀδυσσέα παραδίδωσιν.

18. Ἀχιλεὺς καὶ Ἕκτωρ· Ἀχιλεὺς κατὰ τὸν ἐννεαδικὸν ποιεῖ <μονάδας> τέσσαρας, Ἕκτωρ μίαν· νικᾷ Ἀχιλεύς.

πάλιν Ἀχιλεὺς καὶ Ἀστεροπαῖος· Ἀχιλεὺς ποιεῖ <μονάδας> τέσσαρας, Ἀστεροπαῖος τρεῖς· νικᾷ Ἀχιλεύς.

Again if there is eight (even) and five (odd), the eight wins, since it is larger. If both numbers are even or both odd, the smaller number wins. 14. But how does Sarpedon [Σαρπηδών] make two according to the rule of the ennead? For the letter omega is left out. Answer: when the letters omega and eta are in a name, they leave out the omega, using only one letter. This is because both, they say, are equal in value; thus the same is not counted twice, as was said above.

15. In turn Aias, according to the rule of the ennead, makes four, and Hektor makes one. The number four is even, and one is odd. In this case, we said that the larger wins. 16. Thus Aias wins.[54]

16. In turn, there is Alexandros and Menelaos. The proper name of Alexandros is Paris. Paris makes four according to the rule of the ennead, and Menelaos nine. Nine beats four (for it was said, whenever there is an odd and even number, the larger wins; but when both are even or odd, the smaller number wins).[55]

17. In turn, there is Amykos and Polydeukes. Amykos makes two according to the rule of the ennead, and Polydeukes seven; thus Polydeukes wins.[56]

Aias and Odysseus wrestled at the funeral games. Aias makes four according to the rule of the ennead, and Odysseus eight. But does that not mean that "Odysseus" is an epithet and not a proper name? After all, Odysseus won. According to numbers Aias wins, but history records Odysseus as victor.[57]

18. Let's take Achileus and Hektor: Achileus according to the rule of the ennead makes four, and Hektor one. Achileus wins.[58]

In turn, let's take Achileus and Asteropaios: Achileus makes four, Asteropaios three. Achileus wins.[59]

Maurus indicates that the greater sum of the letters in a hero's name signifies his victory (*De litteris* 265–273).

54. Cf. Homer, *Il.* 7.187–312, where Hektor and the greater Aias duel. The latter does not kill his opponent but draws first blood.

55. Cf. Homer, *Il.* 3.325–380, where Menelaos nearly kills Paris.

56. The reference is to Polydeukes's boxing match with Amykos during the voyage of the Argonauts. See Apollonios, *Arg.* 2.1–97; cf. Ps.-Apoll., *Bibl.* 1.9.20.

57. For the fight of Aias and Odysseus, see Homer, *Il.* 23.708–778.

58. This result accords with Homer, *Il.* 22 (the book in which Achileus [= Achilles] defeats Hektor).

59. Homer, *Il.* 21.140–185.

πάλιν Μενέλαος καὶ Εὔφορβος· Μενέλαος ἔχει μονάδας ἐννέα, Εὔφορβος ὀκτώ· νικᾷ Μενέλαος.

19. Τινὲς δὲ κατὰ τὸν ἑβδοματικὸν μόνοις τοῖς φωνήεσι χρῶνται, ἄλλοι δὲ διαστέλλουσιν ἰδίᾳ μὲν τὰ φωνήεντα, ἰδίᾳ δὲ τὰ ἡμίφωνα, ἰδίᾳ δὲ τὰ ἄφωνα, καὶ τρεῖς τάξεις ποιήσαντες λαμβάνουσι τοὺς πυθμένας ἰδίᾳ μὲν τῶν φωνηέντων, ἰδίᾳ δὲ τῶν ἡμιφώνων, ἰδίᾳ τῶν ἀφώνων, καὶ συγκρίνουσι χωρὶς ἕκαστον.

20. ἄλλοι δὲ οὐδὲ τούτοις τοῖς νενομισμένοις ἀριθμοῖς χρῶνται, ἀλλ' ἄλλοις· οἷον ὑποδείγματος ἕνεκα τὸ π <στοιχεῖον> οὐ θέλουσι πυθμένα ἔχειν η', ἀλλὰ ε', καὶ τὸ ξ στοιχεῖον πυθμένα μονάδας δ', καὶ παντοίως στρεφόμενοι οὐδὲν ὑγιὲς εὑρίσκουσιν. ὅταν μέντοι δεύτερόν τινες ἀγωνίζωνται, ἀφ' ἑκατέρου τῶν ὀνομάτων τὸ πρῶτον στοιχεῖον ἀφαιροῦσιν, ὅταν δὲ τρίτον, τὰ δύο ἑκατέρωθεν, καὶ τὰ λοιπὰ ψηφίσαντες συγκρίνουσιν.

15. 1. Οἶμαι δὲ ἐκδήλως ἐκτεθεῖσθαι καὶ τὴν τῶν ἀριθμητικῶν ἐπίνοιαν, δι' ἀριθμῶν καὶ ὀνομάτων τὸ ζῆν διακρίνειν νομιζόντων. τούτους δὲ κατανοῶ σχολὴν ἄγοντας καὶ ψήφῳ γεγυμνασμένους τεθεληκέναι διὰ τῆς παραδοθείσης αὐτοῖς ἐκ παίδων τέχνης [θέλειν] εὐδοκιμοῦντας μάντεις προ<σ>αγορεύεσθαι. 2. οἳ ἄνω κάτω τὰ στοιχεῖα καταμετροῦντες εἰς λῆρον ἐχώρησαν· ἐπὰν γὰρ ἀποτύχωσι, τὸ ἄπορον προβάλ<λ>οντες λέγουσι, μήτι τοῦτο <τὸ> ὄνομα γενικὸν οὐκ ἐγένετο, ἀλλ' ἐπίθετον, ὡς καὶ ἐπὶ τοῦ Ὀδυσσέως καὶ Αἴαντος ἐκπεσόντες <τοῦτ'> ἐνεκάλουν.

τίς ἐκ ταύτης τῆς θαυμαστῆς φιλοσοφίας ἀφορμὰς λαβὼν καὶ θελήσας αἱρεσιάρχης καλεῖσθαι οὐ δοξασθήσεται;

3. Ἀλλ' ἐπεὶ καὶ ἑτέρα τις τέχνη βαθυτέρα ἐστὶ παρὰ τοῖς πανσόφοις Ἑλλήνων μεριμνηταῖς, οἷς εὔχονται μαθητεύειν οἱ αἱρετικοὶ διὰ τὸ ταῖς αὐτῶν δόξα<ι>ς χρῆσθαι πρὸς τὰ ὑφ' αὐτῶν ἐπιχειρούμενα, καθὼς ὑποδειχθήσεται μετ' οὐ πολύ—αὕτη δέ ἐστι<ν ἡ> μετωποσκοπικὴ μαντεία, μᾶλλον δὲ μανία—, οὐδὲ ταύτην σιωπήσομεν.

In turn, there is Menelaos and Euphorbos. Menelaos has nine, and Euphorbos eight; Menelaos wins.[60]

OTHER METHODS. 19. Some use only vowels according to the rule of the hebdomad; others distinguish vowels, semivowels, and consonants separately, then align them in separate columns and compare them individually.

20. Still others use not these customary numbers but others. For example, they do not want the letter pi [π] to have eight as the base but rather five; and they want the letter xi (ξ) to have four units. And so, spinning every which way, they discover nothing sound. When, moreover, some fighters compete a second time, they remove the first letter from each of the names. When they compete a third time, they remove the first two letters from each of their names, and after counting the rest, compare them.

15. 1. I believe that I have presented the conceit of the numerologists in detail. They suppose that they can analyze life through numbers and names. I have observed these people spending their leisure in arithmetical gymnastics. They take pleasure in being addressed as honored diviners because of the art passed down to them from the time that they were children. 2. These men, precisely measuring the letters this way and that way, have progressed to worthless nonsense. When they fail, they assert that the difficulty lies in the fact that the name in question is not a birth name but an epithet. This, they repeatedly object, is the reason why they were mistaken in the case of Odysseus and Aias.

Who will not be magnificently extolled if he takes his starting points from this wondrous wisdom, wanting to be called leader of a heresy?

ASTROLOGY: SIGNS AND CHARACTER TRAITS

3. Now there is another, deeper art among the all-wise worriers of the Greeks, from whom the heretics boast that they learn because they use their theories for their own designs (as will soon be shown). I refer to the art of metoposcopy, that is, divination (or rather, delirium) from the forehead. I will not keep this secret either.[61]

60. Homer, *Il.* 17.59–60.

61. Metoposcopy is not mentioned again, and its relation to astrological divination is not clarified.

4. εἰσὶν οἳ τοῖς ἄστροις ἀναφέρουσι τὰς μορφὰς τύπων τε ἰδέας καὶ τὰς φύσεις τῶν ἀνθρώπων, ἐπὶ ταῖς ἀστέρων κατὰ γενέσεις <σχέσεσιν> ἀναλογιζόμενοι. οὕτως λέγουσι·

Οἱ <ἐν> Κριῷ γεννώμενοι τοι<οῦτ>οι ἔσονται· κεφαλῇ ἐπιμήκει, τριχὶ πυρρᾷ, ὀφρύσι συνεζευγμέναις, μετώπῳ ὀξεῖ, ὀφθαλμοῖς ὑπογλαύκοις <κ>αλοῖς, μήλοις καθειλκυσμένοις, ἐπίρρινοι, μυκτῆρσιν ἠνεωγμένοις, χείλεσι λεπτοῖς, γενείῳ ὀξεῖ, στόματι ἐπιμήκει. 5. οὗτοι, φησί, μεθέξουσι φύσεως τοιαύτης· προνοητικοί, ποικίλοι, δειλοί, φρόνιμοι, προσχαριώδεις, ἥσυχοι, περίεργοι, βουλαῖς ἀποκρύφοις, παντὶ πράγματι κατηρτισμένοι, πλεῖον φρονήσει ἢ ἰσχύι κρατοῦντες, τὸ παρὸν καταγελασταί, γεγραμματισμένοι, <ἄ>πιστοι, φιλόνεικοι, ἐν μάχῃ ἐρεθισταί, ἐπιθυμηταί, παιδερασταί, νοοῦντες, ἀπεστραμμένοι ἀπὸ τῶν ἰδίων οἴκων, ἀπαρέσκοντες ἅπαντα, κατήγοροι, ἐν οἴνῳ μανιώδεις, ἐξουθενηταί, κατ' ἔτος τι ἀποβάλλοντες, εἰς φιλίαν εὔχρηστοι διὰ τὴν ἀγαθωσύνην· πλειστάκις ἐν ἀλλοτρίᾳ γῇ ἀποθνήσκουσιν.

16. 1. Οἱ δὲ ἐν Ταύρῳ τύπῳ ἔσονται τῷδε· κεφαλῇ στρογγύλῃ, τριχὶ παχείᾳ, μετώπῳ πλατεῖ τετραγώνῳ, ὀφθαλμοῖς μέλασι καὶ ὀφρύσι μεγάλαις, ἐν τῷ λευκῷ φλέβες λεπταὶ αἱματώδεις, βλεφάροις μακροῖς, ὠτίοις παχέσι μεγάλοις, στόματι στρογγύλῳ, ῥώθωνι παχεῖ, μυκτῆρσι στρογγύλοις, χείλεσι παχέσι, <σώματι βραχεῖ,> τοῖς ὑπεράνω μέρεσιν ἰσχύουσι, νωθροὶ γεγενημένοι ἀπὸ σκελῶν. 2. οἱ αὐτοὶ δὲ φύσεως· ἀρέσκοντες, νοοῦντες, εὐφυεῖς, εὐσεβεῖς, δίκαιοι, ἄγροικοι, προσχαρεῖς, κοπιαταὶ ἀπὸ ἐτῶν ιβʹ, ἐρεθισταί, νωθροί· τούτων ὁ στόμαχος μικρός ἐστι, πληροῦνται τάχα, πολλὰ βουλευόμενοι, φρόνιμοι,

4. There are those who refer the body type, shape, and characteristics of persons to the stars, correlating them to the positions of the stars by nativities.[62] They pronounce as follows.[63]

ARIES. Those born in the sign of Aries will be like this: oblong in head, red-haired, with a unibrow, a pointed forehead, lovely bluish eyes, drooping cheeks, a long nose, open nostrils, thin lips, a pointed chin, and a drawn-out mouth. 5. These people, he says, will partake of this character type: they will be cautious, shifty, fearful, prudent, cheerful, peaceful, meddlesome, forging hidden plans, prepared for any task, taking control more by intelligence than by strength, laughing at the present, educated, unreliable,[64] quarrelsome, easily provoked in a fight, lustful, loving boys, intelligent, abandoning their own homes, dissatisfied with everything, ready to blame, crazy when drunk, scornful, throwing out something each year, and helpful in friendship due to kindness. They often die in a foreign land.

TAURUS. 16. 1. Those born in the sign of Taurus will be like this: round-headed, thick-haired, with a broad rectangular forehead, they will be black-eyed with big eyebrows, showing varicose veins on white skin, they will have large eyelashes, big corpulent ears, a round mouth, a thick nose, rounded nostrils, thick lips, and a short body;[65] they are strong in their upper body, though sluggish in their legs. 2. As to their character, they are pleasing, intelligent, naturally clever, pious, just, rustic, pleasant, toilers from the age of twelve, easily provoked, and sluggish. Their appetite is small, and they become full quickly; they plan much, are prudent, sparing with themselves, generous with others, doing good, occasionally prone to

62. Marcovich adds σχέσεσιν ("positions") from Sext. Emp., *Math.* 5.103.

63. In what follows, the source that our author uses typifies people by physical appearance, psychological characteristics, and personality according to the twelve astrological signs (listed in their typical order starting with the sign of the spring equinox). Compare the characteristics supplied in Teukros the Babylonian (first century BCE, printed in Wilhelm Kroll and Alexander Olivieri, eds., *Catalogus codicum astrologorum Graecorum*, 12 vols. [Brussels: Lamertin, 1898–1936], 7:194–213; cf. 8.2:58–59) and Vettius Valens, *Anth.* 1.2.2–78. Manilius offers a catalogue focused not on physical characteristics but on occupation and disposition (*Astron.* 4.122–293); Ptolemy, *Tetrab.* 3.12, 14.

64. Here P reads πιστοί, but Marcovich emends to ἄπιστοι ("unreliable") from the context.

65. Marcovich transposes σώματι βραχεῖ, which appears further down in P, to this location.

φειδωλοὶ εἰς ἑαυτούς, εἰς ἄλλους δαψιλεῖς, ἀγαθοποιοί· [σώματι βραχεῖ] ἐν μέρει εἰσὶ λυπηροί, ἀμελεῖς, εἰς φιλίαν ὠφέλιμοι διὰ τὸν νοῦν, κακοπαθεῖς.

17. 1. Ἐν Διδύμοις τύπος· προσώπῳ κοκκίνῳ, μεγέθει οὐ λίαν μεγάλῳ, μέρεσιν ἴσοις, ὀφθαλμοῖς μέλασιν ὡς ἠλειμμένοις, μήλοις καλοῖς γεγενημένοι, στόματι παχεῖ, ὀφρύσι συντεθειμέναις· συγκρατοῦσι πάντα, <πάντα> ἔχουσιν, ἔσχατα πλούσιοι, σκνιφοί, φειδωλοὶ ἐκ τοῦ ἰδίου, <ἐκ τοῦ ἀλλοτρίου> δαψιλεῖς, πραγμάτων ἀφροδισιακῶν ἐπιεικεῖς, μουσικοί, [πρὸς τὰ ἀφροδισιακὰ] ψεῦσται. 2. οἱ αὐτοὶ δὲ φύσεως· δεδιδαγμένοι, νοοῦντες, περίεργοι, ἰδίᾳ ἀποφάσει, ἐπιθυμητικοί, [φειδωλοὶ ἐκ τοῦ ἰδίου, δαψιλεῖς] ἥσυχοι, φρόνιμοι, δόλιοι, πολλὰ βουλεύονται, ψηφισταί, κατήγοροι, καίριμοι, οὐκ εὐτυχεῖς, ἀπὸ γυναικῶν φιλοῦνται, ἔμποροι, εἰς φιλίαν οὐκ ἐπὶ πολὺ ὠφέλιμοι.

18. 1. Ἐν Καρκίνῳ τύπος· μεγέθει οὐ μεγάλῳ, τριχὶ ὥσπερ κυνείᾳ, χρώματι ὑποπύρρῳ, στόματι ὀλίγῳ, κεφαλῇ στρογγύλῃ, μετώπῳ ὀξεῖ, ὀφθαλμοῖς ὑπογλαύκοις, ἱκανῶς καλοῖς, μέλεσιν ὑποποικίλοις. 2. οἱ αὐτοὶ φύσεως· κακοί, δόλιοι, βουλαῖς κατηρτισμένοι, ἄπληστοι, φειδωλοί, ἀχάριστοι, ἀνελεύθεροι, ἀνωφελεῖς, ἀμνήμονες, οὔτε ἀποδιδόασιν ἀλλότριον οὔτε ἀπαιτοῦσιν ἴδιον, εἰς φιλίαν <οὐκ> ὠφέλιμοι.

19. 1. Ἐν Λέοντι τύπος· κεφαλῇ στρογγύλῃ, τριχὶ ὑποπύρρῳ, μετώπῳ μεγάλῳ ῥυσῷ, ὠτίοις παχέσι, τραχηλιώδεις, ἐν μέρει ὑποφάλακροι, πυρροί, ὀφθαλμοῖς γλαυκοῖς, μεγάλαις γνάθοις, στόματι παχεῖ, τοῖς ἐπάνω μέρεσι παχεῖς, στήθει μεγάλῳ, τοῖς ὑποκάτω μέρεσι λεπτοί. 2. οἱ αὐτοὶ φύσεως· ἰδίας ἀποφάσεως, ἀσυγκέραστοι, ἀρέσκοντες ἑαυτοῖς, ὀργίλοι, θυμώδεις, καταφρονηταί, αὐθάδεις, μηδὲν βουλ<ευ>όμενοι, ἀν<ώμ>αλοι, κακόσχολοι, <ἀ>συνήθεις, εἰς πράγματα ἀφροδισιακὰ ἐκκεχυμένοι, μοιχοί, ἀναιδεῖς, πίστει ἀναλήθεις, αἰτηταί, τολμηροί, σκνιφοί, ἅρπαγες, ἀξιόλογοι, εἰς κοινωνίαν ὠφέλιμοι, εἰς φιλίαν ἀνωφελεῖς.

20. 1. Ἐν Παρθένῳ τύπος· ὁράσει καλῇ, ὀφθαλμοῖς οὐ μεγάλοις, ἐπαφροδίτοις, μέλασιν, ὀρθοῖς, συντεθειμένοις, ἱλαροῖς, κολυμβῶσιν· εἰσὶ δὲ λεπτοὶ σώματ<ος ὑποκάτω>, ὄψει καλῇ, τριχὶ καλῶ<ς> συντεθειμένῃ, μετώπῳ μεγάλῳ, ῥώθωνι προαλεῖ. 2. οἱ αὐτοὶ φύσεως· εὐμαθεῖς, μέτριοι, ἐπινοηταί, παιγνιώδεις, λόγιοι, βραδὺ λαλοῦντες, πολλὰ βουλευόμενοι,

sadness, careless, beneficial as friends on account of their intelligence, and persevering.

GEMINI. 17. 1. Those born in the sign of Gemini will be red-faced, of average stature, with proportionate limbs, eyes black as if polished, lovely cheeks, a large mouth, and joining eyebrows. They dominate everything, have everything, are rich to the hilt, stingy, sparing with their own goods, lavish with others' property,[66] adept at romantic affairs; they are musical, and liars. 2. As to character, they are educated, intelligent, inquisitive, independently minded, covetous, quiet, prudent, cheaters, intense planners, calculators, litigious, timely, unlucky, loved by women, merchants, and not overly helpful as friends.

CANCER. 18. 1. Those born in the sign of Cancer are not large in stature. They will have hair like a dog's, reddish skin, a small mouth, a round head, a pointed forehead, grayish eyes; they will be well endowed with good looks and have limbs subtly different in size. 2. As to character, they are perverse, cheaters, prepared with plans, insatiable, stingy, unfriendly, illiberal, unhelpful, forgetful; they neither give back what is another's nor demand back what is their own, and they are not helpful as friends.[67]

LEO. 19. 1. Those born in the sign of Leo are round-headed, with reddish hair, a large wrinkled forehead, and corpulent ears; they are stiff-necked, partially bald, flushed, with light blue eyes, large cheeks, a big mouth; they are stout in the upper body, with a large chest, yet slender in the lower body. 2. As to character, they are independently minded, intemperate, self-indulgent, wrathful, hot-tempered, scornful, self-willed, planning nothing in advance, inconsistent, mischievous, inexperienced, submerged in erotic affairs, adulterers, shameless, false in loyalty, solicitous, bold, stingy, rapacious, reputable, helpful in partnership, and unhelpful as friends.

VIRGO. 20. 1. Those born in the sign of Virgo are lovely in appearance, with small, lovely, dark, focused, compact, cheerful, and swimming eyes. They are slender in their lower body, with a beautiful face, finely smoothed hair, broad foreheads, and sloping noses. 2. As to their character, they are quick-learning, moderate, inventive, playful, eloquent, speaking slowly,

---

66. Marcovich adds ἐκ τοῦ ἀλλοτρίου (here: "with others").

67. Marcovich supplies οὐκ ("not").

προσχαρεῖς ὡς οἱ παρατηρηταί, ἡδέως πάντα παρατηροῦντες καὶ μαθηταὶ εὐφυεῖς, ἃ ἔμαθον κρατοῦσι, [μέτριοι,] ἐξουθενηταί, παιδερασταί, συνήθεις, ψυχῇ μεγάλῃ, καταφρονηταί, πραγμάτων ἀμελεῖς, διδαχῇ προσέχοντες, καλλίονες <οἰκονόμοι> ἐν ἀλλ<οτρί>οις ἢ τοῖς ἰδίοις, πρὸς φιλίαν ὠφέλιμοι.

21. 1. Ἐν Ζυγῷ τύπος· τριχὶ λεπτῇ, προαλεῖ, ὑποπύρρῳ, ὑπομήκει, μετώπῳ ὀξεῖ, ῥυσῷ, ὀφρύσι καλαῖς, συντεθειμέναις, ὀφθαλμοῖς καλοῖς, κόραις μέλασιν, ὠτίοις μακροῖς, λεπτοῖς, κεφαλῇ ἐπικεκλιμένῃ, στόματι μακρῷ. 2. οἱ αὐτοὶ φύσεως· νοοῦντες, θεοὺς τιμῶντες, ἀλλήλους καταλαλοῦντες, ἔμποροι, κοπιαταί, πορισμὸν μὴ κατέχοντες, ψεῦσται, μὴ φιλοῦντες ἐν πράγμασι<ν ἐπι>νοῆσαι, ἀληθεῖς, ἐλευθερόγλωσσοι, ἀγαθοποιοί, ἀμαθεῖς, [ψεῦσται,] συνήθεις, ἀμελεῖς· τούτοις οὐκ ἐμποιεῖ ἀδίκως ποιῆσαι μέρος. εἰσὶ καταφρονηταί, καταγελασταί, ὀξεῖς, ἔνδοξοι, ἀκουσταί, καὶ τούτοις οὐδὲν προχωρεῖ· πρὸς φιλίαν ὠφέλιμοι.

22. 1. Ἐν Σκορπίῳ τύπος· προσώπῳ παρθενικῷ, εὐμόρφῳ, <παλλεύκῳ>, τριχὶ ὑπομέλανι, ὀφθαλμοῖς εὐμόρφοις, μετώπῳ οὐ πλατεῖ καὶ ῥώθωνι ὀξεῖ, ὠτίοις συντεθειμένοις, μικροῖς, μετώπῳ ῥυσῷ, ὀφρύσι στεναῖς, μήλοις καθε<ι>λκυσμένοις. 2. οἱ αὐτοὶ φύσεως· δόλιοι, κατεστραμμένοι, ψεῦσται, ἴδια βουλεύματα μηδενὶ ἀνατιθέμενοι, διπλῇ ψυχῇ, κακοποιοί, ἐξουθενηταί, μοιχείας ἔνοχοι, εὐφυεῖς, εὐμαθεῖς, εἰς φιλίαν ἄχρηστοι.

23. 1. Ἐν Τοξότῃ τύπος· μήκει μεγάλῳ, μετώπῳ τετραγώνῳ, ὀφρύσι μεσταῖς, συγκρατουμέναις, τριχ<ὶ> συντεθειμένῃ, προαλεῖ, ὑποπύρρῳ. 2. οἱ αὐτοὶ φύσεως· προσχαρεῖς ὡς οἱ πεπαιδευμένοι, ἁπλοῖ, ἀγαθοποιοί, παιδερασταί, συνήθεις, κοπιαταί, φιληταί, φιλούμενοι, ἐν οἴνῳ ἱλαροί, καθάριοι, ὀργίλοι, ἀμελεῖς, κακοί, καταφρονηταί, ψυχαῖς μεγάλαις, ὑβριστικοί, ὑπόδουλοι, εἰς φιλίαν ἄχρηστοι, εἰς κοινωνίαν εὔχρηστοι.

24. 1. Ἐν Αἰγοκέρῳ τύπος· σώματι ὑποπύρρῳ, τριχὶ ὑποπολίῳ, προαλεῖ στόματι στρογγύλῳ, ὀφθαλμοῖς ὡς ἀετοῦ, ὀφρύσι συντεθειμέναις, μετώπῳ

planning often, rejoicing as careful observers, gladly observing all things, natural learners, and they retain what they learn.[68] They are contemptuous, lovers of boys, sociable, noble in soul, despisers, careless in their affairs, attentive to teaching, better stewards of others' property than of their own, and helpful as friends.[69]

LIBRA. 21. 1. Those born in the sign of Libra have thin, straight, reddish, and somewhat long hair. They have a pointed, wrinkled forehead, lovely eyebrows almost touching, lovely eyes, black pupils, long, slender ears, an inclined head, and a large mouth. 2. As to their character, they are perceptive, honoring the gods, slandering each other, merchants, industrious, not holding down a livelihood, liars, not inclined to think over their affairs, reliable, speaking with freedom, doing good, unlearned, sociable, and careless. With these people one cannot double deal. They are scorners, scoffers, passionate, conceited, hearing well, unsuccessful, and helpful as friends.

SCORPIO. 22. 1. Those born in the sign of Scorpio have a girlish, lovely, entirely white face, darkish hair, lovely eyes, a narrow forehead, a pointed nose, small ears close to the head, a wrinkled forehead, narrow eyebrows, and drooping cheeks.[70] 2. As to their character, they are cheaters, perverts, liars, entrusting their plans to no one, two-faced, doing harm, scoffers, guilty of adultery, clever, natural learners, and useless as friends.

SAGITTARIUS. 23. 1. Those born in the sign of Sagittarius are tall, with square foreheads, bushy, touching eyebrows, and smooth, straight, reddish hair. 2. As to their character, they are genteel as people well-cultured, naive, doing good, lovers of boys, sociable, industrious, lovers, loved, cheerful when drunk, clean, irascible, careless, perverse, scornful, magnanimous, arrogant, subservient, useless for friendship, but useful for partnership.

CAPRICORN. 24. 1. Those born in the sign of Capricorn have reddish skin, grayish hair, a sloping, round mouth, eyes like an eagle, eyebrows closely

---

68. The meaning of *προσχαρεῖς ὡς οἱ παρατηρηταί* is obscure. The following quality (*ἡδέως πάντα παρατηροῦντες*) may be an explanatory gloss.

69. Marcovich adds *οἰκονόμοι* ("stewards"), then, with Miller, emends *ἄλλοις* to *ἀλλοτρίοις* ("others' [property]").

70. Marcovich emends P's *ἀλυκω* (nonsensical) to *παλλεύκῳ* ("entirely white").

ἠνοιγμένῳ, ὑποφάλακροι, τὰ ὑποκάτω μέρη τοῦ σώματος ἰσχυρότεροι. 2. οἱ αὐτοὶ φύσεως· φιλόσοφοι, καταφρονηταὶ καὶ τὸ παρὸν καταγελασταί, [ὀργίλοι,] συγχωρηταί, καλοί, ἀγαθοποιοί, πράγματος μουσικοῦ φιληταί, ἐν οἴνῳ ὀργίλοι, γελοῖοι, συνήθεις, λάλοι, παιδερασταί, ἱλαροί, προσφιλεῖς, φιληταί, ἐρεθίζοντες, εἰς κοινωνίαν εὔχρηστοι.

25. 1. Ἐν Ὑδροχόῳ τύπος· μεγέθει <οὐ μεγάλῳ, μετώπῳ> τετραγώνῳ, στόματι ὀλίγῳ, ὀφθαλμοῖς ὀξέσι, λεπτοῖς, γοργοῖς, <ὀφρύσι μεγάλαις.> ἐπιτάκτης, ἀχάριστος, ὀξύς, εὐχερῶς εὑρίσκων, πρὸς φιλίαν εὔχρηστος καὶ πρὸς κοινωνίαν. ἔτι (ἐ)ξ ὑγρῶν πραγμάτων πορίζουσι καὶ τοὺς πορισμοὺς ἀπολλ<ύ>ουσιν. 2. οἱ αὐτοὶ φύσεως· σιγηροί, αἰσχυντηροί, συνήθεις, μοιχοί, σκνιφοί, πράγμασι <πονούμενοι>, θορυβασταί, καθάριοι, εὐφυεῖς, καλοί. [ὀφρύσι μεγάλαις] πολλάκις ἐν λεπτοῖς πράγμασι γεννῶνται, καὶ δίφρων πραγματείαν γυμνάζουσι· <ὧ>τινι ἂν καλῶς ποιήσωσιν, οὐδεὶς αὐτοῖς χάριτας ἀποδιδοῖ.

26. 1. Ἐν Ἰχθύσι τύπος· μήκει μέσῳ, ὡς ἰχθύες μετώπῳ ὀξεῖ, τριχὶ δασείᾳ, πολλάκις πολιοὶ ταχέως γίνονται. οἱ αὐτοὶ φύσεως· ψυχῇ μεγάλῃ, ἁπλοῖ, ὀργίλοι, φειδωλοί, λάλοι, <τῇ> πρώτῃ ἡλικίᾳ ἔσονται ὑπνωτικοί, δι᾽ ἑαυτῶν πραγματείαν πρᾶξαι θέλουσιν, ἔνδοξοι, τολμηροί, ζηλωτικοί, κατήγοροι, τόπον ἀλλάσσοντες, φιληταί, ὀρχησταί, εἰς φιλίαν ὠφέλιμοι.

27. 1. Ἐπεὶ καὶ τούτων τὴν θαυμαστὴν σοφίαν ἐξεθέμεθα τήν τε πολυμέριμνον αὐτῶν δι᾽ ἐπινοίας μαντικὴν οὐκ ἀπεκρύψαμεν, οὐδ᾽ ἐν οἷς σφαλλόμενοι ματαιάζουσι σιωπήσομεν· ἄστρων γὰρ ὀνόμασιν εἴδη καὶ φύσεις ἀνθρώπων παραβάλλοντες πῶς <οὐκ> ἠσθένησαν; 2. τὰ μὲν γὰρ ἄστρα ἴσμεν τοὺς ἀπ᾽ ἀρχῆς, νομίσαντας <εἰδῶν σχήματα> κατανοεῖν, ὀνόμασι κεκληκέναι πρὸς τὸ εὔσημα καὶ εὐεπίγνωστα τυγχάνειν· τίς γὰρ τούτων ὁμοιότης πρὸς τὴν τῶν ζῳδίων εἰκόνα ἢ τίς ὁμοία φύσις πράξεώς τε καὶ ἐνεργείας, ἵνα τις <τὸν>

joined, and a large forehead; they are balding, and stronger in their lower body. 2. As to their character, they are philosophical, despisers and ridiculers of the present, accommodating, good-looking, doing good, lovers of music, angry when drunk, joking, sociable, talkative, lovers of boys, cheerful, affectionate, lovers, quarrelsome, and useful in partnership.

AQUARIUS. 25. 1. Those born in the sign of Aquarius are not large in size, with a square forehead, a small mouth, sharp, small, fierce eyes, and large eyebrows.[71] They are imperious, unpleasant, passionate, devising easily, helpful in friendship and partnership. Still more, they make a living from the sea and lose their livelihoods. 2. As to character, they are taciturn, bashful, sociable, adulterous, stingy, laboring in their tasks,[72] disruptive, clean, clever, and good-looking. Many times they are born in disadvantaged circumstances and train for chariot races. Those they benefit do not return the favor.

PISCES. 26. 1. Those born in the sign of Pisces are of average height, have pointed foreheads like fish, and have thick hair that often grays quickly. As to their character, they are magnanimous, simple, irascible, stingy, talkative, and lethargic in their first stage of life. They want to do business by their own means. They are conceited, bold, competitive, litigious, moving often, lovers, dancers, and beneficial as friends.

27. 1. Since I have now presented their wondrous wisdom and did not hide their niggling and invented divination, I will not keep secret the mistakes they make in their foolishness. How they have failed when they compared the names of constellations with human features and characters! 2. We know that the ancients named the constellations when they thought that they recognized the shapes of images.[73] They did so to make the stars easy to distinguish and recognize. But what similarity is there between these names and the zodiacal signs?[74] And what similar character and activity is there, with the result that one can claim the man born in

71. Marcovich adds *οὐ μεγάλῳ, μετώπῳ* (here: "not large in size, with … forehead") and changes *τετράγωνος* ("square") in P to *τετραγώνῳ* in order to agree with *μετώπῳ*.

72. "Laboring," representing *πονούμενοι*, is Marcovich's emendation of P's *ποιούμενοι* ("making").

73. Marcovich emends P's *ἴδον* to *εἰδώλων σχήματα* ("shapes of idols"). Preferable, however, is *εἰδῶν σχήματα* ("shapes of images"), printed here.

74. Cf. *Ref.* 4.6.3; 4.50.2; Sext. Emp., *Math.* 5.97–98.

ἐν Λέοντι φάσκῃ θυμικόν, τὸν δὲ ἐν Παρθένῳ μέτριον, ἢ <τὸν> ἐν Καρκίνῳ κακόν, τὸν δὲ ἐν ...

28. 1. ... λαβὼν καταγράψαι τὸν πυνθανόμενον ἀξιοῖ <ὅ> τι ἂν πυθέσθαι τῶν δαιμόνων θέλῃ ... μόνον. εἶτα συμψήσας τὸν χάρτην, τῷ παιδὶ δοὺς ἀποπέμπει καυθησόμενον, ἵν' οἴχ(η)ται φέρων ὁ καπνὸς τοῖς δαίμοσι τὰ γράμματα. 2. τοῦ δὲ τὸ κελευσθὲν πράξοντος πρῶτα μὲν ἀφαιρεῖ του χάρτου

Leo is hot-tempered, while the man born in Virgo is temperate, the man in Cancer perverse, and the man in …[75]

AN EXPOSÉ OF MAGIC

A REQUEST FOR AN ORACLE IN WRITING. 28. 1. Taking up [a pen, the practitioner of magic] orders the inquirer to write down whatever he wants to inquire of the demons [secretly and] alone.[76] Then the inquirer erases the slip of papyrus, gives it to the boy, and sends it to be burned so that the smoke can carry the letter to the demons.[77] 2. But when the boy is

75. A lacuna in the text here extends to the opening words of the next chapter (an exposé of magic). Our author was not the first to connect astrology and magic (Hegedus, *Early Christianity*, 139–55; Richard Gordon, "Cosmology, Astrology, and Magic: Discourse, Schemes, Power, and Literacy," in *Panthée: Religious Transformations in the Graeco-Roman Empire*, ed. Laurent Bricault and Corinne Bonnet, RGRW 177 [Leiden: Brill, 2013], 85–111 [85, 103–11]). Magic is a key theme throughout the *Refutation*. In book 1, our author accused Pythagoras and the Druids of using magic (*Ref.* 1.2.5; 1.25.2). In later books he accuses five others: the Elchasaites, Markos the Valentinian, Simon, Karpokrates, and Kallistos. See the summary of Francis C. R. Thee, *Julius Africanus and the Early Christian View of Magic* (Tübingen: Mohr Siebeck, 1984), 394–401. For the present exposé (*Ref.* 4.28–42), see the still useful commentary of Richard Ganschinietz, *Hippolytos' Capitel gegen die Magier: Refut. Haer. IV 28–42*, TU 39.2 (Leipzig: Hinrichs, 1913); as well as Daniel Ogden, "Magic in the Severan Period," in Swain, Harrison, and Elsner, *Severan Culture*, 458–69. James A. Kelhoffer examines *Ref.* 4.28–42 in light of *PGM* ("'Hippolytus' and Magic: An Examination of *Elenchos* IV 28–42 and Related Passages in Light of the Papyri Graecae Magicae," *ZAC* 11 [2008]: 517–48). The "high degree of correspondence" (547) that he claims to exist between *Ref.* 4.28–42 and *PGM* is somewhat overstated. There is at least one fundamental difference between *Ref.* 4.28–42 and *PGM*. The former is a list of tricks, or rather a debunker's manual for how tricks are performed, like that written by Kelsos (κατὰ μάγων, Lucian, *Alex.* 21). In contrast, *PGM* is an insider text—an actual collection of spells (or rather a modern collection of ancient collections). The spell writers in *PGM* assume the reality of divine intervention and that their magic is not simply prestidigitation. Although Kelhoffer is right to conclude that our author "faithfully reproduces copious details from his magical source" (547), one should question the hypothesis that he "had access to an actual collection of magical spells" (547). What our author possessed was likely a debunking manual.

76. The first sentence, with several faded letters, must be reconstructed. My additions (in square brackets) follow the lead of Marcovich.

77. For the boy medium, cf. *SHA* Did. Jul. 7.10 (blindfolded boys proclaim the future of the emperor); Origen, *Princ.* 3.3.3; and *PGM* I. 86–87; II. 56; III. 710; IV. 89; V. 1, 40, 376; VII. 544; LXII. 32–33, 46. See further T. Hopfner, "Die Kindermedien in den griechisch-ägyptischen Zauberpapyri," in *Recueil d'études dédiées à la mémoire de N. P. Kondakov* (Prague: Seminarium Kondakovianum, 1926), 65–74 (74); Apuleius,

μοίρας ἴσας πλείονάς τέ τινας σκήπτεται ἐγγράφειν Ἑβραϊκοῖς γράμμασι δαίμονας· εἶτα μάγων Αἰγυπτίων καταθύσας τὸ καλούμενον κῦφι θυμίαμα, ταύτα<ς> μὲν ἐπαιωρήσας κατὰ τοῦ θυμιάματος φέρει, ὃ δ' ἔτυχε γράψας ὁ πυνθανόμενος θεὶς κατὰ τῶν ἀνθράκων ἔκαυσεν. 3. εἶτα θεοφορεῖσθαι δοκῶν <ὁ παῖς,> εἰσπεσὼν τῷ μυχῷ μέγα καὶ ἀπηχὲς κέκραγε καὶ πᾶσιν ἀσύνετον ...

(π)ολὺ δὲ <...> <εἴσω παρελθεῖν κελεύει> πάντ(ας) τοὺς παρόντας. καὶ τὸν Φρῆ τινα ἢ ἕτερον ἐπικαλοῦντες δαίμονα, ἐπειδὰν εἰσελθόντες παραστῶσιν οἱ παρόντες, ἐπὶ στ<ιβ>ά<δο>ς βαλὼν τὸν παῖδ(α) πολλὰ ἐπιλέγει αὐτῷ—τοῦτο μὲν Ἑλλάδι φωνῇ, τοῦτο δὲ ὡς Ἑβραΐδι—τὰς συνήθεις τοῖς μάγοις ἐπαοιδάς, ὁ δὲ ἐνάρχεται προσπεισόμενος.

4. <Ὃς> δὲ ἔνδον <ὤν,> φιάλῃ ὕδατος πλήρει ἐμβαλὼν χάλκανθον καὶ τήξας τὸ φάρμακον, τὸ δῆθεν ἐξαλειφθὲν χαρτίον δι' αὐτοῦ καταρράνας, τὰ φωλεύοντα καὶ κεκρυμμένα γράμματα πάλιν εἰς φῶς ἐλθεῖν ἀναγκάζει, δι' ὧν μανθάνει ἅπερ ὁ πυθόμενος ἔγραψε.

καὶ διὰ τοῦ χαλκάνθου δέ τις εἰ γράψειε καὶ τῇ κηκῖδι ὑποθυμιάσειε λελειωμένῃ, φανερὰ γένοιτ' ἂν τὰ κεκρυμμένα γράμματα. 5. καὶ γάλακτι δὲ εἰ γράψειέ τις, εἶτα χάρτην <τινὰ> καύσας καὶ λειώσας <καὶ> ἐπιπάσας τρίψει<εν> ἐπὶ τοῖς τῷ γάλακτι γεγραμμένοις γράμμασιν, ἔσται πρόδηλα. καὶ

about to do what was ordered, the magician first tears off from the papyrus equal portions and pretends to list some further names of demons in Hebrew letters.[78] Then he burns the incense of the Egyptian magicians, called kyphi. After waving the papyri slips, he brings them down into the smoke and chars what the inquirer wrote by placing them over the coals.[79] 3. Then the boy, putatively possessed by a god, rushes into the inner room crying out loudly and discordantly things incomprehensible to all ...[80]

[Not] long [afterward] ... the magician bids all those present to come inside.[81] When they come in and stand to one side, he invokes a certain Re or some other demon.[82] He thrusts the boy on a mattress and mumbles many things over him—one phrase in Greek, another supposedly in Hebrew (the familiar enchantments of magicians)—and the demon begins to obey.[83]

4. The magician, while inside, puts blue vitriol in a vessel full of water and, after he dissolves the chemical, sprinkles the bit of papyrus that he has supposedly erased. By this means he forces the concealed and hidden words to come again into the light and learns what the inquirer wrote.

Also, if someone writes with blue vitriol and fumigates it with powdered oak gall, the hidden words become plain. 5. And if someone writes on papyrus with milk, scorches the papyrus sheet, then makes and sprinkles a powder on it, the letters written with milk become plain when the powder is rubbed in. Moreover, urine, fish sauce, spurge juice, and fig juice

---

Apol. 42–44, with the commentary of Adam Abt, *Die Apologie des Apuleius von Madaura und die antike Zauberei*, RVV 4.2 (Giessen: Töpelmann, 1908), 158–90; Kelhoffer, "Hippolytus," 523.

78. Cf. Lucian, *Alex.* 13. On the use of Hebrew, see Ganschinietz, *Capitel*, 33–34.

79. For kyphi incense, see *PGM* IV. 1313–14, 2971. Plutarch gives its composition in *Is. Os.* 80 (*Mor.* 383e–384c). There he notes that it "polishes and purifies like a mirror the faculty which is imaginative and receptive to dreams."

80. Marcovich adds ὁ παῖς ("the boy").

81. After πολὺ δέ Marcovich suspects a lacuna. He inserts εἴσω παρελθεῖν κελεύει ("he bids ... to come inside"). On shouting to invoke spirits, see Lucian, *Men.* 9.

82. "Re" represents Φρῆ, the Greek transliteration of the Coptic ⲠⲢⲎ, the Egyptian sun god. See further Ganschinietz, *Capitel*, 36–37.

83. On the Hebrew phrases, cf. Lucian, *Alex.* 13 (φωνάς τινας ἀσήμους φθεγγόμενος, οἷαι γένοιντο ἂν Ἑβραίων). In *PGM* IV. 88–93, a boy is stripped and laid on linen. A magician claps over him, makes a ringing noise, and pronounces behind him foreign-sounding words in Old Coptic. See further *PGM* VII. 348–58. The spell in *PGM* VII. 540–78 indicates that the boy is supposed to enter a trance state and see a vision of deities (Kelhoffer, "Hippolytus," 524).

οὖρον δὲ καὶ γάρον καὶ τιθυμάλου ὀπὸς καὶ συκῆς ποιεῖ τὸ ὅμοιον. ἐπειδὴ ἔμαθε τὴν ἐρώτησιν οὕτως, τίνα χρὴ τρόπον ἀποκρίνεσθαι προὐνόησε.

6. Καὶ λοιπὸν εἴσω παρελθεῖν κελεύει τοὺς παρόντας, δάφνας ἔχοντας καὶ σείοντας καὶ κεκραγότας καὶ τὸν Φρῆν ἐπικαλοῦντας δαίμονα.—καὶ γὰρ ἐπικαλεῖν τούτοις πρέπει, καὶ τοῦτο αἰτεῖν παρὰ δαιμόνων ἄξιον, ὃ δι' αὑτῶν παρέχειν οὐ θέλουσιν, ἀπολέσαντες τὰς φρένας.—τὸ δὲ ἄκοσμον τῆς βοῆς καὶ ὁ ψόφος οἷς ἐν ἀπορρήτῳ πεποιηκέναι ἐνομίζε<το> παρακολουθεῖν ἐκώλυε. 7. τίνα δὲ ταῦτά ἐστι, καιρὸς λοιπὸν λέγειν.

πολὺ μὲν οὖν τυγχάνει τὸ σκότος· λέγει γὰρ ἀδύνατον τὰ θεῖα ὁρᾶν θνητὴν φύσιν, ἱκανὸν δὲ τὸ ὁμιλεῖν. κατακλίνας δὲ τὸν παῖδα πρηνῆ καὶ δύο τῶν γραμματιδίων ἐκείνων, ἅπερ ἦν ἐγγεγραμμένα Ἑβραϊκοῖς δῆθεν γράμμασιν ὡς δαιμόνων ὀνόματα, πλευρᾷ παραθεὶς ἑκατέρᾳ, τὰ λοιπὰ τοῖς ὠσὶν ἐνθήσειν λέγει. 8. ἔστι δὲ τοῦτ' αὐτ(ὸ) ἀναγκαῖον, ἵνα τι παραθῇ τοῖς ὠσὶ τοῦ παιδὸς ὄργανον, δι' οὗ πᾶν ἔσται σημᾶναι <ὧν> θέλει. <κατ>ηχ<εῖ> οὖν τὸ πρῶτον, ἵνα φοβηθῇ ὁ παῖς, καὶ <τὸ> δεύτερον <ἐ>πιβομβεῖ, ἔπειτα τὸ τρίτον λαλεῖ διὰ τοῦ ὀργάνου ἃ λέγειν τὸν παῖδα βούλεται καὶ τὴν ἔκβασιν τοῦ πράγματος ὡς δοκεῖ. εἶτα τοὺς μὲν παρόντας ἡσυχάζειν ποιεῖ, τὸν δὲ ἃ παρὰ τῶν δαιμόνων ἤκουσε σημαίνειν ἀξιοῖ.

9. Τὸ δὲ τοῖς ὠσὶ παρατεθὲν ὄργανόν ἐστι φυσικὸν ὄργανον, τῶν μακροτραχήλων γεράνων ἢ πελαργῶν ἢ κύκνων ἀρτηρία. ὧν εἰ μηδέτερον παρ<ῇ,> ἔστι καὶ ἕτερα τέχνης ὄργανα· αὐλίσκοι γάρ τινες χάλκεοι τὸν ἀριθμὸν δέκα εἰς ἀλλήλους χωροῦντες, εἰς στενὸν ἀπολήγοντες εὐάρμοστοι γίνονται· δι' ὧν πρὸς τὸ οὖς ὅσα θέλει φθέγγεται. καὶ ταῦτα ὁ παῖς κατακούων, ἐμφόβως ὡς ὑπὸ δαιμόνων λαλούμενα κελευσθεὶς ἀποφθέγγεται.

10. εἰ δὲ καὶ σκῦτός τις ῥάβδῳ περιθεὶς ὑγρόν, ξηράνας καὶ συναγαγὼν προσαρμόσῃ <καὶ> ἀποσπάσας τὴν ῥάβδον αὐλίσκου δίκην τὸ σκῦτος ἐργάσηται, τὸ ὅμοιον ποιεῖ. εἰ δέ τι τούτων μὴ παρῇ, βίβλον λαβὼν <καὶ> ἐπισπασάμενος ἔνδοθεν ὅσον χρήζει ἐπὶ μῆκος ἐκτείνας τὰ ὅμοια ἐνεργεῖ.

11. Εἰ δὲ προειδείη ὅ<σ>τι<ς> πάρεστι πευσόμενος, ἑτοιμότερος πρὸς πάντα γίνεται. εἰ δὲ καὶ τὴν πεῦσιν προμάθοι, γράφει τῷ φαρμάκῳ, καὶ ὡς ἐμπαράσκευος ἱκανώτερος νομίζεται, σαφῶς γράψας <τὴν ἀπόκρισιν πρὸς> τὸ

create the same effect. When the magician has learned the question in this way, he foreknows what kind of response is required.[84]

6. Finally, the magician bids those present to come in. They carry laurel branches, wave them, cry out, and invoke Re. And indeed, to so invoke Re suits them—since they have lost their *re*ason! It is only right for them to ask the demons for what they cannot provide on their own. The confusion of the shouting prevents them from following what the magician is accustomed to do in secret. 7. What he does—it is finally time to tell.

Now it is very dark, for the magician claims that it is impossible for mortal nature to see divine realities; it suffices to commune with them. He makes the boy lie face down and lays on each side of him two of those small bits of papyri inscribed with names of demons in supposedly Hebrew letters. The remaining bits, he says, he will place in the ears. 8. This act is necessary, since it allows him to place some device in the boy's ears, through which he will indicate everything that he wants. Now, first of all, he sends down [through the instrument] a ringing sound, so that the boy takes fright. Second, he makes a deep humming noise. The third time, he speaks through the instrument what he wants the boy to say and relates the outcome of the matter as he sees fit. Then he makes the bystanders be quiet and asks the boy to indicate what he heard from the demons.

9. Now the device placed in the boy's ears is a natural instrument, for instance, the windpipe of long-necked cranes, storks, or swans.[85] If none of these is available, there is an artificial instrument. Ten bronze pipes, nested inside each other and ending in a narrow tube, are well fitted for the task. Through these instruments, the magician utters what he wants in the boy's ear. When the boy hears these things, he, trembling, utters upon command the supposed dispatch of demons.

10. Another method: if someone wraps rawhide still moist around a rod, fits it on by drawing it together and drying it, then pulls out the rod, he can manufacture a flutelike instrument and produce the same effect. If none of these materials is available, the magician takes a rolled scroll, pulls out the spirals from within, extends it to the desired length, and produces the same effect.

11. If the magician knows beforehand who will ask a question, he is better prepared for any circumstance. If he also learns the request beforehand, he writes it with the chemical and is considered to be more fully

84. For the milk, cf. Ovid, *Ars* 3.627–628; Pliny, *Nat.* 26.62.

85. Cf. Lucian, *Alex.* 26.

ἐρωτώμενον. εἰ δὲ ἀγνοεῖ, ὑποτοπάζει καὶ ἀμφίβολον καὶ ποικίλην ἀποφαίνεταί τι δεχόμενον μετάφρασιν, ἵνα τὴν μὲν ἀρχὴν ἄσημος οὖσα ἡ χρησμοδοσία εἰς πολλὰ ἔσται, ἐπὶ δὲ τῇ ἐκβάσει τῶν συμβησομένων πρὸς τὸ συμβὰν πρόρρησις νομίζηται.

12. εἶτα λεκάνην πληρώσας ὕδατος <ὡς> ἄγραφον <τὸν> χάρτην καθίησι, συνεμβαλὼν χάλκανθον· οὕτως γὰρ ἀναπλεῖ τὴν ἀπόκρισιν φέρων ὁ γραφεὶς χάρτης.

Τῷ μὲν δὴ παιδίῳ καὶ φαντασίαι φοβεραὶ γίνονται πολλάκις. καὶ γὰρ πληγὰς ἐμβάλλει εὐπόρως ἐκφοβῶν· λίβανον γὰρ εἰς πῦρ ἐμβαλὼν πάλιν ποιεῖ τοῦτον τὸν τρόπον. βῶλον τῶν λεγομένων ὀρυκτῶν ἁλῶν κηρῷ Τυρρηνικῷ περισκεπάσας καὶ αὐτὸν δὲ <τὸν> λιβάνου βῶλον διχοτομήσας ἐντίθησι τοῦ ἅλατος χόνδρον καὶ πάλιν συγκολλήσας ἐπὶ ἀνθράκων καιομένων τιθεὶς ἐᾷ· τοῦ δὲ συγκαέντος οἱ ἅλες ἀναπηδῶντες φαντασίαν ἀπεργάζονται ὥσπερ ξένου θεάματος γινομένου.

13. αἱματώδη δὲ φλόγα ποιεῖ τὸ Ἰνδικὸν μέλαν ἐνθεὶς τῷ λιβανωτῷ, καθὼς προείπαμεν. αἱματώδη δὲ ὑγρασίαν ποιεῖ κηρὸν ἀγχούσῃ ἀναμίξας καὶ ὡς ἔφην τῷ λιβανωτῷ <τὸν> κηρὸν ἐνθέμενος. ἄνθρακας δὲ κινεῖσθαι ποιεῖ σχιστὴν ὑποθεὶς στυπτηρίαν· ἧς λυομένης καὶ δίκην πομφολύγων διοιδούσης κινοῦνται οἱ ἄνθρακες.

29. 1. Ὠὰ δὲ διάφορα ἐπιδείκνυνται τὸν τρόπον τόνδε· κορυφὴν τρυπήσας ἐξ ἑκατέρων καὶ τὸ λευκὸν ὑπεξαγαγών, αὖθις βάψας ἔμβαλε τῷ μὲν τῆς Σινωπίδος, τῷ δὲ τοῦ γραφικοῦ μέλανος· ἀπόφρασσε δὲ τὰς τρυμαλιὰς ξέσματι τῶν ὠῶν λείῳ, μετ' ὀποῦ συκῆς ἐμπλάσας.

30. 1. Τοῖς δὲ ἀμνοὺς ἀποτέμνεσθαι τὰς κεφαλὰς ἑαυτῶν ποιοῦσιν οὗτος ὁ τρόπος. κρύβδην καυστικῷ φαρμάκῳ χρίσας τὸν φάρυγγα ἐᾷ παρατιθεὶς τὸ ξίφος· ὁ δὲ κνήθεσθαι (θέ)λων, προσπεσὼν τῇ μαχαίρᾳ θλίβων σφάζεται καὶ μικροῦ δεῖν ἀποτέμνεσθαι τὴν κεφαλήν. ἔστι δὲ τὸ φάρμακον βρυωνία καὶ

prepared, since he has clearly written the answer to the question.[86] If the magician does not know, he makes his surmise and declares some ambiguous and intricate turn of phrase, so that the oracle, although meaningless, can be variously adapted and, after the outcome of events, be thought to foretell what happened.[87]

12. Then the magician fills a bowl with water and sinks the slip of supposedly uninscribed papyrus, simultaneously dropping in the blue vitriol. In this way, the inscribed papyrus floats up, bearing a response.

The boy often experiences terrifying visions. Terrified out of his mind, he even inflicts blows. By putting frankincense into the fire, the magician produces this response again. Here is how he does it: the magician covers a lump of so-called rock salt with Tyrrhenian wax. He then divides the lump of frankincense in two and inserts the lump of salt. After again closing the ball of frankincense, he places it over the burning coals and lets it alone. When the lump of frankincense is burned up, the salts leap out and produce an illusion as if some bizarre wonder were happening.[88]

13. By placing indigo within frankincense, he makes a blood-red flame (as I said before). He can make a blood-red liquid by mixing wax with alkanet dye, and then—as I said—by placing the wax in the frankincense.[89] The magician makes the coals move by dropping into the fire sliced alum. As it dissolves and swells up like bubbles, the coals move.

THE EGG TRICK. 29. 1. Different eggs are exhibited this way: the magician pokes through both ends, drains the white, and subsequently dyes them by dipping one egg into Sinopean red clay and the other into writing ink. He then blocks up the holes with smooth egg shell shavings glued on with fig juice.[90]

SHEEP SELF-DECAPITATION. 30. 1. This is the way magicians make sheep cut off their own heads. Secretly a magician anoints a sheep's throat with a corrosive chemical, straps a dagger to the neck, and leaves it there. The sheep, wanting to scratch, rubs hard, scraping against the dagger, killing and almost decapitating itself. (The chemical is bryony, marsh salts, and

86. Marcovich adds τὴν ἀπόκρισιν πρός (here: "the answer to"). The chemical mentioned here, according to Ganschinietz (*Capitel*, 43) is oak gall (*Galläpfellösung*).

87. Cf. Lucian, *Alex.* 22.

88. For incense and rock salt (ἁλὸς ἀμμωνιακοῦ), see *PGM* V. 394–97.

89. Alkanet root was commonly used for rouge in antiquity (see Pliny, *Nat.* 37.48).

90. Cf. Lucian, *Alex.* 14 (Alexander blocks up an egg with wax and white lead).

ἀδάρκη καὶ σκίλλα κατ᾽ ἴσον μεμιγμένα<ι>. 2. ἵνα δὲ λάθῃ φέρων τὸ φάρμακον, φέρει πυξίδα διπλῆν κερατίνην, ἧς τὸ φανερὸν μέρος ἔχει λιβανωτόν, τὸ δὲ ἀφανὲς φάρμακον.

ἀλλὰ καὶ τοῖς ὠσὶ τοῦ τεθνηξομένου ἐμβάλλει ὑδ<ρ>άργυρον· ἔστι γὰρ θανατηφόρον φάρμακον. **31.** 1. Αἰγῶν δὲ κἂν ἐπιπ<λ>άσῃ τις κηρωτῇ τὰς ἀκοάς, φασὶ θνήσκειν μετ᾽ ὀλίγον, ἀναπνεῖν κωλυομένας· ὁδὸν γὰρ αὐταῖς ταύτην εἶναι λέγουσι τοῦ δι᾽ ἀναπνοῆς ἑλκομένου πνεύματος. κριὸν δὲ θνήσκειν φασὶν εἰ κατ᾽ ἀντικρύ τις ἀνακλάσειεν ἡλίου <φῶς>.

Οἶκον δὲ ποιοῦσι καίεσθαι τῶν θαλαττίων τινὸς ἰχῶρι χριόμενον τοῦ καλουμένου δακτύλου. 2. καὶ τὸ διὰ τῆς ἅλμης δὲ πάνυ χρήσιμον· ἔστι δὲ ἀφρὸς θαλάσσης, ἐν ὀστρακίνῳ στάμνῳ μετὰ γλυκέος ἡψημένος· ᾧ ζέσαντι λύχνον ἐὰν προσάγῃς καιόμενον, ἁρπάσαν τὸ πῦρ ἐξάπτεται· καὶ καταχυθὲν τῆς κεφαλῆς οὐ καίει τὸ σύνολον. εἰ δὲ καὶ μάννη<ν> ἐπιπάσσεις ζέοντι, πολλῷ μᾶλλον ἐξάπτεται· βέλτιον δὲ δρᾷ εἰ καὶ θείου τι προσλάβοι.

32. 1. Βροντὴ γίνεται τρόποις πλείοσι· λίθοι τε γὰρ πλείονες καὶ μείζονες κατὰ κρημνῶν φερόμενοι <πεποιημένων> διὰ σανίδων ἐπικαταπίπτουσι χαλκοῖς ἐλάσμασι καὶ βροντῇ παραπλήσιον <ἀπο>τελοῦσι ψόφον. καὶ σανίδα δὲ λεπτήν, ᾗπερ οἱ γναφεῖς τὴν ἐσθῆτα πιέζουσι, σχοινίῳ λεπτῷ περιειλήσαντες, εἶτα ῥοίζῳ τὴν σχοῖνον ἐπισπώμενοι ῥομβοῦσι τὴν σανίδα, ἡ δὲ δονουμένη ἦχον βροντῆς ἀπεργάζεται.

2. Ταῦτα μὲν οὕτως παίζεται· ἕτερα δέ, ἃ καὶ [οἱ] αὐτὰ οἱ παιζόμενοι ὡς μεγάλα νομίζουσιν, ἐκθήσομαι.

squill mixed in equal proportions.[91]) 2. To carry the chemical unnoticed, the magician carries a box made out of ivory with two compartments. In the visible compartment is frankincense, and in the hidden compartment is the chemical.

In addition, one can place mercury—a lethal chemical—into the ears of sheep who will then die.[92] **31.** 1. And if someone plasters the ears of goats with a wax salve, they say that the goats soon die, since they are prevented from breathing. They claim that this is their airway through which they breathe.[93] They add that a ram dies if someone reflects the light of the sun directly at it.

SPONTANEOUS COMBUSTION. They make a house catch fire when it is anointed with the serum of a certain sea creature called the "finger fish."[94] 2. A very useful chemical is one made from salt water, namely, sea foam boiled with grape syrup in a clay jar. If you bring a burning lamp to it when it comes to a boil, it catches fire and lights up. But if it is poured on the head, it does not burn at all. Moreover, if you sprinkle it with frankincense granules as it boils, it lights up much more. It works better if one also adds a pinch of sulfur.[95]

THUNDER. 32. 1. Thunder is produced in a great number of ways. A multitude of large rocks rolled down wooden ramps that then fall on bronze plates makes a sound much like thunder. Alternatively, magicians wind a thin board (the kind with which launderers press cloth) with a thin cord and jerk the cord to make the board rumble. The board, driven about, produces the sound of thunder.[96]

2. This is how they play games. I will present still other games that those who are toyed with find grand!

---

91. On squill, see Pliny, *Nat.* 19.93.

92. Cf. Ps.-Demokritos, *Sympath. Antipath.* 31 (Gemoll): A bull dies if mercury is blown into its ear (θνήσκει δὲ παρ' αὐτὰ ὑδραργύρου εἰς τὸ οὖς αὐτοῦ ἐμφυσηθέντος).

93. For goats breathing through their ears, see Aristotle, *Hist. an.* 1.11, 492a14; Pliny, *Nat.* 8.202; Aelian, *Nat. an.* 1.53.

94. Cf. the shining "finger-mussel" in Pliny, *Nat.* 9.184.

95. Frankincense was often burned on altars, and sulfur was known as the most flammable of substances (see Pliny, *Nat.* 35.177).

96. Thunder was considered a manifestation of the divine (Lucian, *Philops.* 22; Plutarch, *Crass.* 23).

πίσσης λέβητα μεστὸν ἐπ’ ἀνθράκων καιομένων τιθέντες, ἐπὰν βράσῃ, καθιέντες τὰς χεῖρας οὐ καίονται. ἀλλὰ καὶ ἐπὶ ἀνθράκων πυρὸς περιπατοῦντες γυμνοῖς ποσὶν οὐ καίονται. ἀλλὰ καὶ πυραμίδα λιθίνην θεὶς ἐπὶ πυρὰν καίεσθαι ποιεῖ, ἔκ τε τοῦ στόματος πολὺν καπνὸν προφέρει καὶ πυρώδη· εἶτα καὶ σινδόνα ἐπιθεὶς ἐπὶ λεκάνῃ ὕδατος, πολλοὺς ἐπιβαλὼν ἄνθρακας καιομένους, ἄκαυστον φυλάττει τὴν σινδόνα. 3. σκότος δὲ ἐν οἴκῳ ποιήσας, ἐπεισάξειν φάσκει θεοὺς ἢ δαίμονας· καὶ <εἰ φέρε> εἰπεῖν ἀπαιτεῖ <τι>ς Ἀσκληπιὸν δεικνύναι, ἐπικαλεῖται οὕτως λέγων·

Ζῆνα, πάλαι φθίμενον πάϊν ἄμβροτον Ἀπόλλωνος,
κικλήσκ<ω λ>οιβαῖσι μολεῖν ἐπίκουρον ἐμαῖσιν·
ὅς ποτε καὶ νεκύων ἀμενηνῶν μυρία φῦλα,
Ταρτάρου εὐρώεντος ἀεικλαύστοισι μελάθροις
δύσνοστον πλώοντα ῥόον κελάδοντ’ <ἀ>διαύλου
<Κωκυτοῦ, πρὸς> ἅπασιν ἴσον τέλος ἀνδράσι θνητοῖς,
λίμνῃ πὰρ γοόωντα καὶ ἄλλιτα κωκύοντα,
αὐτὸς ἀμειδήτοιο ἐρύσαο Φερσεφονείης·
εἴτ’ ἐφέπεις Τρίκ<κ>ης ἱερῆς ἕδος, εἴτ’ ἐρατεινὴν
Πέργαμον, εἴτ’ ἐπὶ τοῖσιν <Ἰ>αονίαν Ἐπίδαυρον,
δεῦρο, μάκαρ, καλέει σε μάγων <πρόμος> ὧδε <παρεῖναι>.

33. 1. Ἐπὰν δὲ χλευάζων λήξῃ, φαίνεται κατὰ τοῦ ἐδάφους πυρώδης Ἀσκληπιός.

εἶτα θεὶς ἐν μέσῳ λεκάνην πλήρη ὕδατος, πάντας καλεῖ τοὺς θεοὺς καὶ παραγίνονται· ἐγκύψας γὰρ ὁ παρών, ἐν τῇ λεκάνῃ ὄψεται πάντας καὶ τὴν Ἄρτεμιν ἅμα σκύλακας ὑλακτοῦντας ἄγουσαν.

Οὐκ ὀκνήσομεν δὲ καὶ τούτων τὴν ἱστορίαν ὡς ἐπιχειροῦσι διηγήσασθαι.

FIREPROOFING AND OTHER TRICKS. They put a cauldron full of tar on burning coals. When it boils, they put their hands in it but are not burned. Moreover, they walk with bare feet over fiery coals and are not burned. Still more: they put a stone pyramid on a burning altar and make it burn, and they produce thick and fiery smoke from its mouth. Subsequently they put a linen cloth on a bowl of water, lay on it a heap of burning coals, and preserve the cloth unburned. 3. When a magician makes the inside of a house dark, he claims that he will usher in gods or demons. And if, let's say, someone demands that he display Asklepios, the magician makes this invocation:

Zeus, thou immortal though long-perished child of Apollo![97]
I invoke you to approach my drink offerings as my ally;
You who once saved ten thousand tribes of strengthless dead
In the ever-weeping halls of vast Tartaros
As they sailed the roaring, unreturning stream of irreversible
Kokytos to an end equal for all mortal men,
Wailing by the swamp and shrieking unanswered prayers.
It is you who saved them from unsmiling Persephone!
Whether you are visiting the foundation of holy Trikka, or beloved
Pergamon,
Or, along with these, Ionian Epidauros,
Come, Blessed One! The chief magos calls you here to be present![98]

33. 1. When he ceases his jest, a fiery Asklepios appears from the floor.[99]

Then, having placed the bowl full of water in the middle of the room, the magician calls upon all the gods, and they draw near. The one nearby peers into the bowl and will see all the gods, even Artemis at the head of her barking puppies.[100]

I will not hesitate to relate my research into how they contrive these tricks as well.

---

97. The one invoked is Zeus Asklepios. Aristides refers to the temple of Zeus Asklepios (*Or.* 42.4; 47.45, 78). Hans Schwabl collects the epigraphic evidence for him in "Zeus I: Epiklesen," *RE* 10.1: 253–376 (280,48–281,8).

98. On the hymn, see Ganschinietz, *Capitel*, 54–60.

99. Cf. Thessalos of Tralles, *Virt. herb.* 1.22–24 (Friedrich).

100. For lecanomancy, see Apuleius, *Apol.* 42. Artemis here = Hekate. On the barking dogs, see Vergil, *Aen.* 6.257–258 (*canes ululare per umbram / adventante dea*); Seneca, *Oed.* 569 (*latravit Hecates turba*).

2. τῷ γὰρ λέβητι τῆς πίσσης ὡς ἐμβράσσοντι καθίησι τὰς χεῖρας· ὄξος καὶ νίτρον ἐμβαλὼν καὶ πίσσαν ὑγράν, ὑποκαίει τὸν λέβητα· τὸ δὲ ὄξος ἅμα τῷ νίτρῳ μιγέν, ἀντιλαμβανόμενον θέρμης μικρᾶς κινεῖ τὴν πίσσαν, ὡς μέχρι τῆς ἐπιφανείας κινεῖν πομφόλυγας καὶ φαντασίαν μόνην παρέχειν ζέοντος. φθάνει δὲ καὶ τὰς χεῖρας πολλάκις ἅλμῃ νιψάμενος, δι᾽ ὃ οὐ πάνυ τι καίει, κἂν ἀληθῶς ζέῃ. εἰ δὲ μυρσίνῃ καὶ νίτρῳ καὶ σμύρνῃ, μετ᾽ ὄξους μίξας, ἐπιχρίσας ἀπονίψει<ε> τὰς χεῖρας ἅλμῃ πλειστάκις, οὐ καίεται. τοὺς δὲ πόδας οὐ καίεται ἰχθυοκόλλᾳ καὶ σαλαμάνδρᾳ χρισάμενος.

3. τοῦ δὲ τὴν πυραμίδα καίεσθαι δᾳδίου δίκην, οὖσαν λίθον, αὕτη <ἡ> αἰτία· γῆ μέν ἐστι Κρητική, τὸ μὲν σχῆμα πεπλασμένη πυραμίς, τὸ δὲ χρῶμα ὡς λίθος γαλακτικός, κατασκευάζεται δὲ τοῦτον τὸν τρόπον. βρέξας ἐλαίῳ πλείονι τὴν βῶλον, θεὶς ἐπ᾽ ἀνθράκων ὀπτήσας, καὶ πάλιν βρέξας καὶ καύσας δεύτερον καὶ τρίτον καὶ πολλάκις, καίεσθαι δύνασθαι παρασκευάζει, κἂν ὕδατι βραχῇ· ἔχει γὰρ ἐν ἑαυτῷ πολὺ τὸ ἔλαιον. ἀνάπτεται δὲ δι᾽ αὐτῆς, τοῦ μάγου σπένδοντος, ἡ πυρά, τίτανον ὑποκαιομένην ἔχουσα ἀντὶ σποδιᾶς, καὶ λιβανωτὸν λεπτὸν [καὶ] πολύν, καὶ δᾳδίων <ῥητίνῃ> κεχρισμένων αὐτορρύτῳ <φορυτὸν> κηκίδων τε κενῶν, ἔνδον πῦρ ἐχουσῶν. 4. καπνὸν δὲ ἐκ τοῦ στόματος ἀνίει ἐγχρονίσας καὶ πῦρ κηκῖδι ἐμβαλὼν καὶ τῷ στυπείῳ συμπεριβαλὼν καὶ φυσῶν ἐν τῷ στόματι.

τό γε μὴν περικείμενον τῇ λεκάνῃ σινδόνιον, ἐφ᾽ ὃ τίθησι τοὺς ἄνθρακας, διὰ τὴν ὑποκειμένην ἅλμην οὐκ ἐκαίετο· καὶ αὐτὸ δὲ ἦν ἅλμῃ προβεβρεγμένον, εἶτα κεχρισμένον ᾠοῦ τῷ λευκῷ μεθ᾽ ὑγρᾶς στυπτηρίας. εἰ δὲ καὶ χυλὸν ἀειζώου τις τούτοις μετ᾽ ὄξους ἐπιμίξειεν καὶ πρὸ πολλοῦ σφόδρα καταχρίσαι χρόνου, βαφὲν τῷ φαρμάκῳ μένει παντελῶς ἄκαυστον.

2. The magician plunges his hands down into the cauldron of tar when it appears to boil. He heats the cauldron, putting in vinegar, natron, and liquid tar.[101] Now the vinegar mixed with natron, aided by a little heat, causes the tar to stir so that bubbles even burst on the surface—giving only the appearance of boiling. Beforehand, furthermore, the magician repeatedly washes his hands with salt water. Due to this, the tar does not burn [the magician's hands] very much, even if it actually boils. If, in addition, the magician smears his hands with myrtle, natron, and myrrh mixed with vinegar, then repeatedly washes it off with salt water, they are not burned. And his feet do not burn when smeared with isinglass and salamander.[102]

3. This is the reason the pyramid, though [appearing to be] stone, burns like a torch. It is made of Cretan soil colored like milk stone and formed in the shape of a pyramid. It is fashioned as follows: the magician generously soaks the clay with oil, puts it on coals, and fires it. Again he soaks and fires it a second time, then a third, then repeatedly, in order to make it flammable even if he sprays it with water. Since it contains a rich store of oil, it can be ignited on its own when the magician pours a libation. The altar, containing slowly burning lime instead of ashes, also contains a generous supply of fine frankincense, wood chips from torches with fine pine resin, and empty nutshells that have fire inside.[103] 4. In time, the smoke rises from the mouth [of the pyramid], since the magician has placed fire in oak gall and wrapped it with hemp. He also blows into the mouth of the pyramid.

As for the linen cloth heaped with coals covering the bowl, it is not burned due to the salt water below. The cloth is itself soaked with salt water beforehand, then smeared with the white of an egg along with a liquid astringent. And if someone mixes leek juice and vinegar with them and profusely smears it a long time beforehand, the cloth dipped into this chemical remains entirely fireproof.

---

101. Natron is a natural compound of sodium carbonate and sodium bicarbonate and was the primary mineral used for purification in Egypt. Cf. Pliny, *Nat.* 31.115. See further J. R. Harris, *Lexicographical Studies in Ancient Egyptian Minerals* (Berlin: Akademie, 1961), 193–94.

102. For vinegar as a coolant, see Gellius, *Noct. att.* 17.8.14; Pliny, *Nat.* 23.54. The salamander, Legge says, "was no doubt calcined and used in powder" (*Philosophoumena*, 1:98 n. 2). Antigonos of Karystos relates that the salamander extinguishes fire (*Historiae mirabiles* 84 [Westermann]). Pliny says that the salamander "is so chilly that it puts out fire by its contact" (*Nat.* 10.188). Cf. Testim. Truth (NHC IX,3) 71.26–29.

103. Marcovich adds ῥητίνῃ (here: "with pine resin") and φορυτόν ("wood chips").

34. 1. Ἐπεὶ μὲν οὖν [παρὰ] τῶν παρ' αὐτοῖς ἀπορρήτων μαθημάτων συντόμως τὰς δυνάμεις ἐξεθέμεθα εὔκολόν τε τὴν <τῶν> κατ' αὐτοὺς κατάγνωσιν ἐδείξαμεν, οὐδὲ τοῦτο σιωπᾶν βουλόμεθα, ὃν ἀναγκαῖον, ὡς σφραγῖδας λύοντες ἐσφραγισμένα τὰ γράμματα αὐταῖς ταῖς σφραγῖσιν ἀποδιδόασι.

πίσσαν καὶ ῥητίνην καὶ θεῖον, ἔτι δὲ ἄσφαλτον ἴσα τήξαντες, κολλυρίων σχήματι πλάσαντες φυλάττουσι· καιρὸς δὲ ὅταν ᾖ λύειν γραμματίδιον, τὴ(ν) γλῶσσαν ἐλαίῳ δεύσαντες, εἶτα ἐξ αὐτῆς τὴν σφραγῖδα χρίσαντες, πυρὶ συμμέτρῳ τὸ φάρμακον θερμάναντες ἐπιφέρουσι τῇ σφραγῖδι καὶ μέχρι ἂν παγῇ παντελῶς ἐῶσι· καὶ τούτῳ δίκην σημάντρου χρῶνται. 2. φασὶ δὲ καὶ αὐτὸν <τὸν> κηρὸν μετὰ πευκίνης ῥητίνης τὸ παραπλήσιον ποιεῖν, καὶ μαστίχης μέρη δύο μετὰ ξηρᾶς ἀσφάλτου μέρους. καὶ θεῖον δὲ μόνον ἐπιεικῶς ποιεῖ, καὶ γύψου δὲ ἄνθος μεθ' ὕδατος διειμένον καὶ κόμμεως· [ὡς] τοῦτο μὲν δὴ καὶ πρὸς τὸ σφραγίσαι μόλιβδον τετηκότα ποιεῖ κάλλιστα. 3. καὶ <τὸ> διὰ τοῦ Τυρρηνικοῦ δὲ κηροῦ καὶ ῥητίνης φρυκτῆς καὶ πίσσης καὶ ἀσφάλτου <καὶ> μαστίχης καὶ λείας μαρμάρου, ἴσων ἁπάντων ἑψομένων, τῶν μὲν ἄλλων ὧν ἔφην ἐ(στὶ) [μὲν] βέλτιον, τοῦ δὲ διὰ τῆς γύψου οὐκ ἔλαττον. οὕτως μὲν οὖν καὶ τὰς σφραγῖδας λύειν ἐπιχειροῦσι, τὰ ἔνδον γεγραμμένα μανθάνειν πειρώμενοι.

ταύτας δὲ ὤκνουν τὰς μηχανὰς κατ(α)τάξα(ι) ἐν τῇ βίβλῳ, ἐννοῶν μήποτέ τις κακοῦργος ἀφορμὰς λαβὼν ἐπιχειρήσει· 4. νῦν δὲ ἡ πολλῶν δυναμένων σωθῆναι νέων φροντὶς ἔπεισε διδάξαι καὶ προειπεῖν φυλακῆς ἕνεκεν· ὡς γὰρ χρήσεταί τις αὐταῖς πρὸς κακοῦ μάθησιν, οὕτως τις ἕτερος μαθὼν φυλάξεται. καὶ αὐτοὶ δὲ οἱ τοῦ βίου λυμεῶνες μάγοι αἰσχυνθήσονται τῇ τέχνῃ χρώμενοι· μαθόντες γὰρ ἀφ' ἡμῶν ταῦτα προ ... ἐμποδισθήσονται τυχὸν τῆς ἀπονοίας.

ἵνα δὲ μὴ λύηται ταύτῃ ἡ σφραγίς, στέαρ ὕειον καὶ τρίχας τῷ κηρῷ τις μίξας σφραγιζέτω.

35. 1. Ἀλλ' οὐδὲ τὴν λεκανομαντείαν αὐτῶν οὖσαν πανούργημα σιωπήσομαι. οἴκημα γάρ τι κεκλεισμένον σκευάσαντες καὶ κυάνῳ τὸν ὄροφον χρίσαντες, εἰς δὴ τὸ παρὸν ἐπάγονται σκεύη τινὰ κυάνεα καὶ ἀνατείνουσι· μέση δὲ λεκάνη κατὰ τῆς γῆς ὕδατος μεστὴ τίθεται, ἣ τὴν ἀντανάκλασιν τῆς κυάνου

SEALING AND RESEALING LETTERS. 34. 1. Since, then, I have briefly presented the miracles of their secret teachings and exposed the condemnation of their tricks as something easy to understand, I will, as is necessary, not keep secret the following subject as well, namely, how they break seals and deliver letters with the very same seals.

They melt tar, pine resin, sulfur, and bitumen in equal amounts, molding it to preserve the shape of little pellets. When it is time to unseal a letter, they coat their tongues with oil, then use their tongue to smear the seal with oil. Meanwhile, they heat a solution at a low temperature, apply it to the seal, and let it alone until it completely congeals. They then use this as a seal. 2. They also say that wax with pine resin has a similar effect, as well as a solution of two parts mastic, one part dry bitumen. But sulfur alone is reasonably effective, as well as gypsum powder soaked with water and resin. This especially works wonderfully for sealing molten lead. 3. Moreover, a mixture of Tyrrhenian wax, resin, pitch, bitumen along with mastic and smooth marble—all boiled in equal quantities—is better than those recipes that I mentioned; but the gypsum formula is not far inferior. In this way, then, they undertake to dissolve seals, trying to learn the contents of letters.[104]

I hesitated to list these tricks in my book, since I suspected that at some point some conman would use this material as a resource for his schemes. 4. Nevertheless, my present concern—that many young people have the chance to be saved—has convinced me to instruct and proclaim these things as a safeguard. Just as one will use these instructions for education in vice, so another will learn them and be on guard. Moreover, the very magicians who corrupt human life will be ashamed to use this art. For having learned these things from us beforehand … [105] there is a chance that they will be hindered from their insanity.

But, so that your seal might not be broken, mix pig fat and hair with the wax and seal your letters with this.

LECANOMANCY. 35. 1. I will not keep secret their bowl-divination trick either.[106] They prepare a room when it is locked, smear its ceiling with dark blue paint, bring into it vessels smeared with the same paint, and spread them around. Now, in the middle of the room there is a bowl filled with water set in the floor that shows the image of the sky (since it reflects

104. On unsealing and resealing letters, see Lucian, *Alex.* 19–21.

105. Here there is a lacuna in P (a space of about seven letters).

106. For lecanomancy, cf. *Ref.* 4.28.12 above.

προσπεσοῦσαν δίκην οὐρανοῦ ἐνδείκνυσιν. 2. ἔχει δὲ καὶ στόμιόν τι τὸ ἔδαφος λεληθός, ᾧ ἐπικειμένη ἡ λεκάνη τὸν μὲν πυθμένα ἔχει ὑαλοῦ<ν>, αὐτὴ δέ ἐστι πετρίνη. ὕπεστι δὲ οἶκος λεληθώς, εἰς ὃν συμπορευόμενοι οἱ συμπαῖκται σχήματα ὧν ἂν βούληται δεικνύναι ὁ μάγος θεῶν καὶ δαιμόνων ἐνδυσάμενοι ἐμφαίνουσιν. οὓς καθορῶν ὁ πλανώμενος, τὸ πανούργημα καταπέπληγε τοῦ μάγου καὶ λοιπὸν πάντα πιστεύει τὰ ὑπ᾽ αὐτοῦ ῥηθησόμενα.

3. Δαίμονα δὲ ποιεῖ καίεσθαι, ἐν τοίχῳ διατυπώσας σχῆμα ὃ βούλεται· εἶτα λαθραίως ἐπιχρίει φαρμάκῳ μεμιγμένῳ τῷδε τῷ τρόπῳ· ... Λακωνικῷ καὶ ἀσφάλτῳ Ζακυνθίᾳ· εἶτα ὡς ἀποφοιβάζων τὴν λαμπάδα προσφέρει τῷ τοίχῳ, τὸ δὲ φάρμακον ἐκλάμψαν καίεται.

4. Ἑκάτην δὲ δοκεῖν ἔμπυρον διατρέχειν ἐν ἀέρι οὕτω τεχνάζεται· συμπαίκτην τινὰ κρύψας ἐν τόπῳ ᾧ βούλεται, παραλαβὼν τοὺς πλανωμένους πείθει λέγων δείξειν διϊππεύουσαν δι᾽ ἀέρος ἔμπυρον τὴν δαίμονα. οἷς παραγγέλλει τὰς ὄψεις ταχὺ φυλάσσεσθαι ἡνίκα ἴδωσιν ἐν ἀέρι τὴν φλόγα, καλυψαμένους τε ἐπὶ πρόσωπον πίπτειν, ἕως αὐτὸς καλῇ. καὶ ταῦτα διδάξας, ἐν ἀσελήνῳ νυκτὶ δι᾽ ἐπῶν οὕτως φθέγγεται·

5. Νερτερίη, χθονίη τε καὶ οὐρανίη μολὲ Βομβώ·
εἰνοδίη, τριοδῖτι, φαεσφόρε, νυκτεροφοῖτι,
ἐχθρὴ μὲν φωτός, νυκτὸς δὲ φίλη καὶ ἑταίρη,
χαίρουσα σκυλάκων ὑλακῇ τε καὶ αἵματι φοινῷ,
ἂν νέκυας στείχουσα κατ᾽ ἠρία τεθνηώτων,
αἵματος ἱμείρουσα, φόβον θνητοῖσι φέρουσα,
Γοργὼ καὶ Μορμὼ καὶ Μήνη καὶ Πολύμορφε·
ἔλθοις εὐάντητος ἐφ᾽ ἡμετέρῃσι θυηλαῖς.

the blue paint). 2. There is a hidden compartment in the floor in which the bowl is set. The bowl, although made of stone, has a glass bottom. Beneath the floor is a hidden room into which the magician's fellow jesters process, dressed up as the gods and demons that the magician wants to display.[107] Seeing these people, the dupe is stupefied by the magician's trick and believes everything else the magician has to say.[108]

FALSE EPIPHANIES. 3. The magician causes a demon to catch fire by forming the desired image on a wall. Then he secretly anoints it with a chemical mixed in the following way: ... with Spartan and Zakynthian bitumen. Then, as one uttering an oracle, he brings his torch near the wall, and the chemical flashes and ignites.[109]

4. A fiery Hekate is made to appear coursing through the air by the following subterfuge. The magician hides his fellow jester in a place where he wishes. Then, taking along his dupes, he coaxes them by saying that he will show them the fiery demon rushing through the air on a chariot. He orders them, when they see the flame in the air, to immediately cover their eyes, veil themselves, and fall on their faces until he calls them. Having given these instructions, he utters these verses on a moonless night:

5. Approach, you of the netherworld, of earth, and of heaven, Growler![110]
You by the wayside, at the crossroads, light-bearer, night-wanderer,
Enemy of light, friend and companion of night,
Rejoicing in the bark of pups and in bright red blood,
Lurking among the corpses and the tombs of the dead,
Lusting for blood, bringing terror to mortals,
Grim one, Ogress, Moon—you of many forms,
May you come gracious to our immolations![111]

---

107. Cf. *Ref.* 4.32.3.

108. See further Daniel Ogden, *Greek and Roman Necromancy* (Princeton: Princeton University Press, 2011), 193.

109. Cf. the recipe for spontaneous combustion in Julius Africanus, *Cesti* D25; Oppian, *Hal.* 5.646–648.

110. Legge (*Philosophoumena*, 1:100 n. 5), following Dilthey and Miller, thinks that "βομβώ" (here: "Growler") should be emended to "Βαυβώ," a night demon. Cf. *OF* 391(iv). See also Ganschinietz, *Capitel*, 67.

111. The hymn consists mostly of Hekate's epithets (names that please the god-

36. 1. Ταῦτ' εἰπόντος αὐτοῦ πῦρ δι' ἀέρος βλέπεται φερόμενον, οἱ δὲ φρίξαντες τὸ παράδοξον τῆς θέας, καλύψαντες τοὺς ὀφθαλμοὺς ἐπὶ γῆς ῥιπτοῦνται ἄναυδοι.

τὸ δὲ τῆς τέχνης μέγεθος τοῦτον ἔχει τὸν τρόπον· ὁ συμπαίκτης, ὃν ἔφην κεκρυμμένον, ἡνίκα ἀκούσῃ παυσαμένης τῆς ἐπαοιδῆς, ἔχων ἰκτῖν' ἢ γῦπα περιειλημ<μ>ένον στυπείῳ, ἀνάψας ἀπολύει. 2. ὁ δὲ ὑπὸ τῆς φλογὸς ταρασσόμενος εἰς ὕψος ἐπαίρεται καὶ ὀξυτέραν τὴν πτῆσιν ποιεῖται· ὃ ἰδόντες οἱ μάταιοι ὥς τι θεῖον ἑωρακότες κρύπτονται. τὸ δὲ πτηνὸν περιδινούμενον ὑπὸ τοῦ πυρός, οὗ ἂν φθάσῃ καταφέρεται, καὶ ποτὲ μὲν οἰκίας καταφλέγει, ποτὲ δὲ καὶ αὐλάς.

τοιαύτη ἡ μάγων πρόγνωσις.

37. 1. Σελήνην δὲ ἐν ὀρόφῳ φαίνεσθαι δεικνύουσι καὶ ἀστέρας τοῦτον τὸν τρόπον· ἐν μέσῳ τῆς ὀροφῆς μέρει προσαρμόσας κάτοπτρον, τιθεὶς λεκάνην ὕδατος μεστὴν ἐν τῷ μέσῳ <κατὰ> τῆς γῆς κατ' ἴσον, λύχνον δὲ μέσον φαίνον<τα> ἀμαυρὸν μετεωρότερον τῆς λεκάνης θείς, οὕτως ἐκ τῆς ἀντανακλάσεως ἀποτελεῖ σελήνην φαίνεσθαι διὰ τοῦ κατόπτρου. 2. ἀλλὰ καὶ τύμπανον πολλάκις ἀφ' ὑψηλοῦ αἰωρηθὲν ὄρθιον περιβαλὼν ἐσθῆτί τινι, σκεπόμενον ὑπὸ τοῦ συμπαίκτου, ἵνα μὴ πρὸ καιροῦ φανῇ, <καὶ> κατόπιν θεὶς λύχνον, ἐπὰν τὸ σύνθημα παράσχῃ τῷ συμπαίκτῃ, <οὗτος> τοσοῦτον ἀφαιρεῖ τοῦ σκεπάσματος, ὅσον ἂν συνεργήσαι πρὸς τὸ μιμήσα<σθαι> κατὰ τὸν καιρὸν τῆς σελήνης τὸ σχῆμα. χρίει δὲ τὰ διαφαίνοντα τοῦ τυμπάνου μέρη κινναβάρ<ει> καὶ κόμμι.

3. καί τις ἑτοιμό<τερος> δὲ ὀλίγης λαγήνου περικόψας τὸν τράχηλον καὶ τὸν πυθμένα, ἐνθεὶς λύχνον καὶ περιθείς τι τῶν ἐπιτηδείων πρὸς τὸ διαυγεῖν <τὸ> σχῆμα. <...> στὰς ἐφ' ὑψηλοῦ κρύβδην ὑπό τινα σκέπην τις τῶν συμπαικτῶν, μετὰ τὸ λαβεῖν τὸ σύνθημα ἐκ μετεώρου κατάγει τὰ μηχανήματα, ὥ<στ>ε δοκεῖν ἐξ οὐρανοῦ κατιέν(αι) τὴν σελήνην.

4. τὸ δὲ ὅμοιον καὶ διὰ χύτρας γίνεται ἐν ὑλώδεσι τόποις· διὰ δὲ τῆς χύτρας καὶ τὰ κατ' οἶκον παίζεται. βωμοῦ γὰρ κειμένου κατόπιν κεῖται ἡ

36. 1. When he says this, fire is seen tearing through the air. The onlookers shiver at the unexpected vision, covering their eyes and collapsing speechless on the ground.[112]

This magnificent trick is accomplished this way: the fellow jester, hidden (as I said), when he hears the incantation come to an end, ignites a kite or vulture wrapped in hemp and lets it go. 2. The bird, shocked by the flame, soars into the height and picks up speed. Seeing this, the fools hide themselves as if they have beheld something divine. When the bird whirls round, compelled by the heat, it dives as it careens along, sometimes igniting houses and courtyards.

This is the magicians' "foreknowledge"!

APPEARANCE OF HEAVENLY BODIES. **37.** 1. They make the moon and stars appear on the ceiling in this way. In the middle of the ceiling they attach a mirror aligned with a bowl of water placed centrally on the floor. Next, they put a central lamp shining dimly above the bowl. In this way, they produce the appearance of the moon from the reflection in the mirror. 2. Moreover, they often suspend an upright drum from the ceiling covered with a cloth.[113] It is covered by one of the fellow jesters so as not to shine out before the right moment. Now, behind it they place a lamp. When the signal is given to the fellow jester, he removes the covering just enough to mimic the moon in its proper phase. He smears the gaps of the drum through which light passes with vermilion and gum resin.

3. A more daring magician breaks the neck and base of a small clay flask, inserts a lamp, and covers it with something designed to produce an image through filtered light. Meanwhile, a fellow jester stands on high hidden under a screen. After receiving the signal, he lowers the contraption from above so that the moon appears to descend from the sky.

4. The same effect is produced in wooded areas by means of a jar; and the trick is also played by means of a jar indoors. In this case, the jar, hold-

dess). For comparable hymns, see *PGM* IV. 2242–358, 2522–67, 2786–870; Lucian, *Philops.* 13–14, 42. See further Ganschinietz, *Capitel*, 65–69.

112. For epiphanies of Hekate (often associated with fire), see *PGM* IV. 2724–28; Eusebios, *Praep. ev.* 4.23 175c–d; and Orac. chald. 146–148, with the comments of Sarah Iles Johnston, *Hekate Soteira: A Study of Hekate's Roles in the Chaldean Oracles and Related Literature* (Atlanta: Scholars Press, 1990), 111–33.

113. Marcovich fails to note in his apparatus that ὄρθιον ("upright") is Miller's conjecture for P's ὄρθριον (Hagedorn, review of *Refutatio* [ed. Marcovich], 213).

χύτρα ἔχουσα λύχνον φαίνοντα <ἀμαυρόν>· ὄντων δὲ πλειόνων λύχνων οὐδὲν τοιοῦτον δείκνυται.

ἐπὰν οὖν ἐπικαλέσηται ὁ ἐπαοιδὸς τὴν σελήνην, πάντας κελεύει τοὺς λύχνους σβέννυσθαι, ἕνα δὲ ἀμαυρὸν καταλιπεῖν. καὶ τότε ἀντανακλᾷ τὸ φῶς τὸ ἐκ τῆς χύτρας εἰς τὸν ὄροφον καὶ παρέχει φαντασίαν σελήνης [καὶ] τοῖς παροῦσιν, ἐπισκεπασθέντος τοῦ στόματος τῆς χύτρας πρὸς ὃ ἀπαιτεῖν ὁ καιρὸς δοκεῖ, ὡς μηνοειδῆ δείκνυσθαι ἐν τῷ ὀρόφῳ τὴν φαντασίαν.

38. Ἀστέρας δὲ εἶναι δοκεῖν ποιοῦσι θρισσῶν <ἢ> ἱππούρου φολίδες, ὕδατι μετὰ κόμ<μ>εως δεδευμέναι καὶ προσπεπλασμέναι τῷ ὀρόφῳ κατὰ διαλείμματα.

39. Σεισμοῦ δὲ φαντασίαν ποιοῦσιν, ὡς δοκεῖν πάντα κινεῖσθαι, <τοῦτον τὸν τρόπον>· κόπρον ἰχνεύμονος ἅμα τῇ σιδηραγωγούσῃ λίθῳ ἐπ' ἀνθράκων πυρουμένην ...

40. 1. Ἧπαρ δὲ δοκ<οῦν> εἶν<αι> ἐγγεγραμμένον δεικνύουσι <τούτῳ τῷ τρόπῳ>· τῇ μὲν ἀριστερᾷ χειρὶ ἐπιγράφει ὃ βούλεται, πρὸς τὴν πύστιν ἁρμοσάμενος· τὰ δὲ γράμματα κηκῖδι καὶ ὄξει δριμεῖ γράφεται. ἔπειτα ἀνελόμενος τὸ ἧπαρ, ἐπαναπαύσας τῇ ἀριστερᾷ ἐγχρονίζει, τὸ δὲ σπᾷ τὸν τύπον καὶ ὡς <ἐγ>γεγράφθαι νομίζεται.

41. 1. Κρανίον δὲ λαλ<εῖν δοκ>οῦν ἐπὶ γῆς θέντες ἐπιτελοῦσι τούτῳ τῷ τρόπῳ· αὐτὸ μὲν πεποίηται ἐπιπλόου βοείου, <ὃ> πεπλασμένον κηρῷ Τυρρηνικῷ καὶ γύψῳ ἀναπεποιημένῃ, περιτεθέντος τοῦ ὑμένος ἔμφασιν κρανίου ἐνδείκνυται. ὃ πᾶσι λαλεῖν δοκεῖ ἐνεργοῦντος τοῦ ὀργάνου, καθ' ὃν τρόπον καὶ ἐπὶ τοῖς παισὶ διηγησάμεθα· 2. γεράνου ἤ τινος τοιούτου μακροτραχήλου ζῴου φάρυγγα σκευάσας, προσθεὶς τῷ κρανίῳ λεληθότως ὁ συμπαίκτης, ἃ θέλει φθέγγεται. ὃ ἐπὰν ἀφανὲς γενέσθαι θέλῃ, ἀνθράκων πλῆθος κύκλῳ περιθείς,

ing a dimly shining lamp, lies behind a stationary altar.[114] Although there are very many lamps present, nothing like this light appears.

When the enchanter invokes the moon, he orders all the lamps to be extinguished, leaving the one dim lamp. Then the light reflects from the jar on the ceiling and offers a simulation of the moon to the onlookers. The opening of the jar is left covered in accordance with the phase of the moon so that the simulation might be projected on the ceiling as a crescent.

38. Moreover, they make the hard scales of anchovies or a dolphinfish appear like stars by soaking them in water and gum resin, then plastering them on the ceiling at intervals.[115]

EARTHQUAKE SIMULATION. **39.** And they simulate an earthquake—so that everything seems to shake—in this way: mongoose dung heated on coals together with a magnet....[116]

DIVINATION FROM THE LIVER. **40.** 1. They exhibit a liver that appears inscribed in this way: on his left hand the magician writes what he wants, adapting it to the question. The letters are written in oak gall and pungent vinegar. Then, when he lifts out the liver, he rests it on his left hand for a time so that the liver absorbs the impression and so is thought to be inscribed.

A TALKING SKULL. **41.** 1. They place a skull on the ground and make it appear to talk in the following way. It is made of an ox's caul that is molded on Tyrrhenian wax and freshly mixed gypsum. When the membrane is spread around it, it has the appearance of a skull. It seems to speak to all when an instrument is operated, the use of which I also related in the case of the boys.[117] 2. Preparing the windpipe of a crane or some other long-necked animal, a fellow jester secretly attaches it to the skull, uttering what he wants. If he wants it to disappear, he surrounds it with a heap of coals

114. Marcovich adds ἀμαυρόν (here: "dimly").

115. Cf. Aristotle, *Hist. an.* 5.10.2.

116. Marcovich adds τοῦτον τὸν τρόπον ("in this way") here and (with slight variation) in 40.1 below. Earthquakes were trademarks of divine epiphany (e.g., Apollonios, *Arg.* 2.679–680; 3.1218; Vergil, *Aen.* 6.256; Lucian, *Philops.* 22). For earthquakes in magic spells, see *PGM* XIII. 871–72.

117. Cf. *Ref.* 4.28.8–9.

ὡς θυμιῶν ἐμφαίνεται· ὧν τῆς θέρμης ὁ κηρὸς ἀντιλαμβανόμενος λύεται, καὶ οὕτως ἀφανὲς τὸ κρανίον γεγονέναι νομίζεται.

42. 1. Ταῦτα μάγων ἔργα καὶ τοιάδε μυρία, ἃ τῇ τῶν ἐπῶν συμμετρίᾳ καὶ τῶν ἀξιοπίστως δρωμένων ἔργων φαντασίᾳ πείθει τοὺς ἄφρονας. ὧν τὴν τέχνην καταπλαγέντες οἱ αἱρεσιάρχαι ἐμιμήσαντο, τὸ μὲν ἐν ἀποκρύφῳ καὶ σκότῳ παραδιδόντες τὰ δοκούμενα, τὸ δὲ καὶ παραφράζοντες ὡς ἴδια.

2. τούτου χάριν, ὑπομνῆσαι θέλοντες τοὺς πολλούς, περιεργότεροι ἐγενήθημεν, πρὸς τὸ μὴ καταλιπεῖν τινα τόπον τοῖς ἐθέλουσι πλανᾶσθαι, ἀπηνέχθημέν τε οὐκ ἀλόγως εἴς τινα τῶν μάγων ἀπόρρητα, ἃ πρὸς μὲν τὸ προκείμενον οὐ πάνυ ἀναγκαῖα ἦν, πρὸς δὲ τὸ φυλάσσεσθαι [καὶ] τὴν τῶν μάγων πανοῦργον καὶ ἀσύστατον τέχνην εὔχρηστα <ἐ>νομίζετο.

3. Ἐπεὶ τοίνυν, ὡς εἰκάσαι ἔστι, τὰς πάντων δόξας ἐξεθέμεθα, πολλὴν φροντίδα ποιήσαντες πρὸς τὸ φανερῶσαι τὰ ὡς ξένα ὑπὸ τῶν αἱρεσιαρχῶν ἐπεισαγόμενα πρὸς θεοσέβειαν ὄντα μάταια καὶ νόθα, οὐδὲ ἐν αὐτοῖς ἴσως ἄξια λόγου τυγχάνοντα, δοκεῖ διὰ συντόμου λόγου ὑπομνησθῆναι κεφαλαιωδῶς τὰ προειρημένα.

43. 1. Πᾶσι τοῖς κατὰ τὴν οἰκουμένην φιλοσόφοις καὶ θεολόγοις ζητήσασιν οὐ συνεφώνησε περὶ τοῦ θεοῦ, τί ἐστιν ἢ ποδαπός· οἱ μὲν γὰρ αὐτὸν λέγουσιν εἶναι πῦρ, οἱ δὲ πνεῦμα, οἱ δὲ ὕδωρ, ἕτεροι δὲ γῆν· ἕκαστον δὲ τῶν στοιχείων ἔλαττόν τι ἔχει καὶ ἕτερον ὑπὸ τοῦ ἑτέρου ἡττᾶται. 2. τοῦτο δὴ συνέβη τοῖς τοῦ κόσμου σοφοῖς—ὅπερ ἐστὶ τοῖς νοῦν ἔχουσι πρόδηλον·—οἳ ἰδόντες τῆς κτίσεως τὰ μεγέθη, ἐπὶ τῇ τῶν ὄντων οὐσίᾳ ἐταράχθησαν, μείζονα ταῦτα νομίσαντες τοῦ ὑφ᾽ ἑτέρου γένεσιν ἐπιδέξασθαι δύνασθαι. καὶ οὐδὲ ὁμοῦ τὸ σύμπαν αὐτὸ εἶναι τὸν θεὸν ἀπεφήναντο, <ἀλλ᾽> αἴτιον πρὸς θεολογίαν <ἕκαστος> ἓν τῶν βλεπομένων <ἐ>νόμισεν, ὅπερ <προ>έκρινε. καὶ οὕτως ἐπὶ τοῖς ὑπὸ θεοῦ γενομένοις καὶ κατὰ τὴν ἐκείνου ὑπερβάλλουσαν μεγαλειότητα ἐλαχίστοις

and appears to offer incense. The wax, absorbing the heat from the coals, melts, and so the skull is thought to disappear.[118]

42. 1. These magic tricks and ten thousand like them—by the elegance of the magician's poetry and the simulation of credible special effects—convince the dim-witted. Struck with wonder at their art, the chief heretics copied it, both by handing on the teachings under cover of darkness and by adapting them as their own.

2. For this reason, since I wanted to admonish common folk, I have been rather overelaborate so as not to leave an opportunity to those who wish to deceive. I have not unreasonably delved into some of the magicians' secrets, which—although not quite necessary for my purpose—are still thought useful for guarding against their crafty and inconsistent art.

3. Since, then, I presented (as far as one can surmise) the views of them all, exercising great care to expose as alien what the leading heretics surreptitiously introduce into religion (though these matters are useless, counterfeit, and unworthy of account perhaps even among *them*), it seems fitting to briefly remind the reader of what I said earlier, hitting the main points.

THE ERRORS OF THE THEOLOGIANS

43. 1. In all the inquiries that philosophers and theologians have made throughout the world, there has been no agreement about God, his nature, or his origin. Some say that he is fire, others a fiery and intelligent air, others water, and others earth. But each of the elements possesses something inferior, and one element is overcome by another.[119] 2. Surely what happened to the sages of this world (a thing obvious to intelligent observers) is this: they saw the magnificent phenomena of creation, were excited by the nature of existent things, and supposed that these things were too great to receive generation from another being. To be sure, they did not declare that the universe as a whole is God. Rather, each supposed that a single visible reality is the cause in their theology—whatever cause the philosopher preferred.[120] And just so: since they peered at things generated by

118. See further Ogden, *Necromancy*, 210–11.

119. Cf. Philo, *Decal.* 52–53.

120. Cruice adds ἀλλ', and Marcovich, following Miller, adds ἕκαστος (here: "Rather, each"). Marcovich also emends ἔκρινε in P ("judged") to προέκρινε ("preferred").

ὑπάρχουσιν ἐνιδόντες, μὴ δυνηθέντες δὲ εἰς τὸ μέγεθος τοῦ ὄντως θεοῦ ἐκτεῖναι τὸν νοῦν, ταῦτα ἐθεολόγησαν.

3. οἱ δὲ ἐνδοτέρω τῆς ἀληθείας νομίσαντες γεγονέναι Πέρσαι ἔφασαν τὸν θεὸν εἶναι φωτεινόν, φῶς ἐν ἀέρι συνεχόμενον. οἱ δὲ Βαβυλώνιοι ἔφασαν τὸν θεὸν σκοτεινὸν εἶναι, ὅπερ καὶ αὐτὸ <τοῦ> ἑτέρου (ἐ)πακολούθημα φαίνεται· νυκτὶ γὰρ ἐπακολουθεῖ ἡμέρα, τῇ δὲ ἡμέρᾳ νύξ.

4. Αἰγύπτιοι δὲ πάντων ἀρχαιότεροι εἶναι νομίζοντες, τὴν τοῦ θεοῦ δύναμιν ψηφίσαντες τά τε διαστήματα τῶν μοιρῶν, ἐξ ἐπινοίας θειοτάτης ἔφασαν τὸν θεὸν εἶναι μονάδα ἀδιαίρετον καὶ αὐτὴν ἑαυτὴν γεννῶσαν, καὶ ἐξ αὐτῆς τὰ πάντα κατεσκευάσθαι. 5. αὕτη γάρ, φασίν, ἀγέννητος οὖσα τοὺς ἑξῆς ἀριθμοὺς γεννᾷ· οἷον ἐφ' ἑαυτὴν ἡ μονὰς ἐπιπροσ<τε>θεῖσα γεννᾷ τὴν δυάδα, καὶ ὁμοίως ἐπιπροστιθεμένη γεννᾷ τὴν τριάδα καὶ <τὴν> τετράδα μέχρι τῆς δεκάδος, ἥτις <ἡ> ἀρχὴ καὶ τὸ τέλος τῶν ἀριθμῶν, ἵνα γένηται πρώτη καὶ δεκάτη ἡ μονάς, διὰ τὸ καὶ τὴν δεκάδα ἰσοδυναμεῖν καὶ ἀριθμεῖσθαι εἰς μονάδα. 6. κἂν αὕτη δεκαπλασιασθεῖσα γένηται ἑκατοντάς, καὶ <αὕτη> πάλιν γίνεται μονάς· κἂν ἡ ἑκατοντὰς δεκαπλασιασθεῖσα ποιήσῃ χιλιάδα, καὶ αὕτη ἔσται μονάς· οὕτως κἂν τὰ χίλια δεκαπλασιασθέντα ἀπαρτίσωσι τὴν μυριάδα, ὁμοίως ἔσται μονάς. τῆς δὲ μονάδος κατὰ τὴν ἀδ(ιαίρε)τον σύγκρισιν συγγενεῖς ἀριθμοὶ παραλαμβάνονται γ' ε' ζ' [θ']. 7. ἔστι δὲ καὶ ἑτέρ(ου) ἀριθμοῦ συγγένεια πρὸς τὴν μονάδα φυσικωτέρα κατὰ τὴν τῆς ἑξακύκλου ἕλικος πραγματείαν, τῆς δυάδος, κατὰ τὴν ἄρτιον θέσιν τῶν ἀριθμῶν καὶ διαίρεσιν· συγγενὴς δὲ [ὁ] ἀριθμός ἐστι τοῦ δ' καὶ <ὁ> η'.

God and realities entirely inferior to his surpassing majesty, they were not able to stretch their minds to the greatness of the true God.[121]

PERSIAN AND BABYLONIAN THEOLOGY. 3. Now the Persians, thinking themselves insiders to truth, claimed that God is luminous—a light suspended in the air. But the Babylonians said that God is darkness, an opinion that itself appears as a consequence of the previous one—for day follows night, and night follows day.

EGYPTIAN THEOLOGY OF NUMBERS. 4. The Egyptians suppose themselves to be more ancient than everybody else.[122] By reckoning up the power of God and the degree intervals, they declared by most divine insight that God is an indivisible, self-generating monad, and that out of the monad the universe is constructed.[123] 5. Being unborn, they say, the monad gives birth to the numbers that follow it. For example, when it is added to itself, the monad gives birth to the dyad. By a like addition, it gives birth to the triad and the tetrad as far as the decad, which is the beginning and end of numbers. Consequently, the monad becomes first and tenth, since the decad is also of equal value to and numbered as a monad.[124] 6. Ten multiplied by ten equals one hundred, and this again is a monad. One hundred multiplied by ten equals one thousand, and this makes a monad. In the same way, one thousand multiplied by ten equals ten thousand—which is likewise a monad. From the monad are produced numbers that are akin to it in their indivisibility: namely, three, five, and seven.[125] 7. The kinship of another number with the monad is quite natural when viewed in light of this business about the six-circled revolution.[126] Kinship with the dyad is based on a number's evenness and divisibility. Four and eight, for example, are akin to the dyad.

---

121. Cf. *Ref.* 1.26.3; 10.32.5.

122. Cf. *Ref.* 5.7.22; Herodotos, *Hist.* 2.2.

123. Cf. *Ref.* 1.2.2 (Pythagoras).

124. Cf. Philo, *Decal.* 20.

125. Marcovich, following Cruice, deletes θʹ ("nine") here, since it is not a prime number.

126. The meaning of this phrase (*κατὰ τὴν τῆς ἑξακύκλου ἕλικος πραγματείαν*) is uncertain. Our author likely refers to the division of the heavens mentioned in *Ref.* 4.8.1 (cf. Plato, *Tim.* 36c–d). If the phrase denotes an astronomical device, the mechanism may have been explained in one of the lost books.

8. ταῦτα δὲ ἐκ τῆς μονάδος ἀρχὴν λαβόντα πρόνοια[ν] <τῆς ἀρχῆς> ἐχώρισε μέχρι τῶν τεσσάρων στοιχείων, λέγω δὴ τοῦ πνεύματος καὶ πυρός, ὕδατός τε καὶ γῆς. καὶ ἐκ τούτων ποιήσας τὸν κόσμον, ἀρρενόθηλυν αὐτὸν κατεσκεύ(α)σε· καὶ δύο μὲν στοιχεῖα εἰς τὸ ἄνω ἡμισφαίριον προσέταξε, τό τε πνεῦμα καὶ τὸ πῦρ, καὶ καλεῖται τοῦτο <τὸ> ἡμισφαίριον, <ὂν> τῆς μονάδος, ἀγαθοποιόν τε καὶ ἀνωφερὲς καὶ ἀρσενικόν—9. λεπτομερὴς γὰρ οὖσα ἡ μονὰς ποτᾶται εἰς τὸ λεπτότατον μέρος καὶ καθαρώτατον τοῦ αἰθέρος·—τὰ δὲ ἄλλα δύο στοιχεῖα, ὄντα παχύτερα, ἀπένειμεν τῇ δυάδι, γῆν τε καὶ ὕδωρ, καὶ καλεῖται τοῦτο τὸ ἡμισφαίριον κατωφερές, θηλυκόν τε καὶ κακοποιόν.

καὶ αὐτὰ δὲ πάλιν τὰ ἄνω δύο στοιχεῖα ἑαυτοῖς συγκρινόμενα ἔχουσιν ἐν ἑαυτοῖς τὸ ἄρρεν καὶ τὸ θῆλυ, πρὸς εὐκαρπίαν καὶ αὔξησιν τῶν ὅλων· 10. καὶ τὸ μὲν πῦρ ἄρρεν ἐστί, τὸ δὲ πνεῦμα θῆλυ· καὶ πάλιν τὸ ὕδωρ ἄρρεν ἐστίν, ἡ δὲ γῆ θῆλυ. καὶ οὕτως ἀπ' ἀρχῆς συνεβίωσε τὸ πῦρ τῷ πνεύματι, τῇ δὲ γῇ τὸ ὕδωρ· ὥσπερ γὰρ δύναμις τοῦ πνεύματός ἐστι τὸ πῦρ, οὕτως καὶ τῆς γῆς τὸ ὕδωρ.

11. Καὶ αὐτὰ δὲ τὰ στοιχεῖα ψηφιζόμενα καὶ ἀναλυόμενα καθ' ὑφαίρεσιν ἐν<ν>άδων λήγει οἰκείως, ἃ μὲν εἰς τὸν ἀρρενικὸν ἀριθμόν, ἃ δὲ εἰς τὸν θηλυ<κόν>. ὑφαιρεῖται δὲ πάλιν ἡ ἐννὰς διὰ ταύτην τὴν αἰτίαν· διὰ τὸ τὰς τριακοσίας ἑξήκοντα τοῦ ὅλου μοίρας ἐξ ἐννεάδων συνίστασθαι, καὶ διὰ τοῦτο τὰ <τ>έτ<τ>αρα πλινθία τοῦ κό(σ)μου <ὑπὸ> ἐνενήκοντα μοιρῶν περιγεγράφθαι τελείων.

12. προσῳκείωται δὲ τῇ μονάδι τὸ φῶς, τῇ δὲ δυάδι τὸ σκότος· καὶ τῷ μὲν φωτὶ κατὰ φύσιν ἡ ζωή, <τῷ δὲ σκότει> ὁ θάνατος· καὶ τῇ μὲν ζωῇ δικαιοσύνη, τῷ δὲ θανάτῳ ἡ ἀδικία. διὸ πᾶν γεννώμενον ἐν τοῖς ἀρσενικοῖς ἀριθμοῖς ἀγαθοποιόν ἐστι, τὸ δὲ ἐν τοῖς θηλυκοῖς κακο(ποι)όν ἐστιν. 13. οἷον ψηφίζουσι· μονάς—ἵνα ἀπ' αὐτῆς ἀρξώμεθα—γίνεται τξα', ἃ λήγει εἰς μονάδα τῆς ἐννεάδος ὑφαιρεθείσης. ὁμοίως ψήφισον· δυὰς γίνεται χε'· ὕφελε τὰς ἐννεάδας, λήγει εἰς δυάδα, καὶ ἀποκαθίσταται ἕκαστον εἰς τὸ ἴδιον.

EGYPTIAN COSMOGONY. 8. Providence, receiving these numbers as a first principle from the monad, divided them from the first principle until it reached the four elements (namely, air, fire, water, and earth).[127] From these elements, Providence made the world, making it androgynous. Further, Providence arranged two elements for the upper hemisphere: air and fire. It is called the "upper hemisphere" since it derives from the monad, produces benefits, belongs to the upper regions, and is male. 9. (The monad, being of refined composition, hovers in the most refined and purest region of the aether.) Providence allotted the other two elements, being coarser, to the dyad. They are earth and water. This hemisphere is called "lower" because it is female and harmful.

To return to the two upper elements: these combine with each other (as they contain male and female aspects) for the fertility and growth of the universe. 10. Fire is male, and air is female. In turn, water is male, and earth is female. In this way, fire coexisted with air from the beginning, and water with earth. Just as fire is the power of air, so water is the power of earth.

11. These very elements, moreover, when counted up and reduced by the subtraction of multiples of nine, naturally end in either a male or female number.[128] Again, a multiple of nine is subtracted because the 360 degrees of the universe are composed of multiples of nine. For this reason, the four quarters of the world are defined by ninety complete degrees.

12. Light is naturally related to the monad, and darkness to the dyad; life is naturally related to light, and death to darkness.[129] In life is justice, and in death is injustice. Thus everything generated among male [i.e., odd] numbers produces benefits, while everything generated among female [i.e., even] numbers produces harm. 13. For example, they count the monad (to start from this) as 361, which ends at the monad when the multiple of nine [= 360] is subtracted. A similar example: calculate the dyad as 605, subtract the multiple of nine [i.e., 603 = 9 x 67], and it ends at two. In this way, each number is restored to its proper determination.[130]

---

127. Marcovich changes P's πρόνοιαν to πρόνοια ("Providence" as subject). He also emends ἀρετῆς in P to ἀρχῆς (here: "first principle").

128. Marcovich fails to note that ἀναλυόμενα (here: "reduced") is Roeper's emendation for P's ἀποδυόμενα (Hagedorn, review of *Refutatio* [ed. Marcovich], 213).

129. Marcovich emends P's τῇ δὲ δυάδι ("[death is related] to the dyad") to τῷ δὲ σκότει ("to darkness").

130. That is, each number is determined to be akin to the monad (male) or akin to the dyad (female).

44. 1. Τῇ οὖν μονάδι ἀγαθοποιῷ οὔσῃ <ὁμοίως τὰ> εἰς τὸν [ἀ]περίζυγον ἀριθμὸν λήγοντα ὀνόματα ἀνωφερῆ <τε καὶ ἀρσενικὰ καὶ> ἀγαθοποιὰ εἶναι παρατηρούμενα λέγουσι, τὰ δὲ εἰς τὸν ἄρτιον ἀριθμὸν λήγοντα κατωφερῆ τε καὶ θηλυκὰ καὶ κακοποιὰ εἶναι νενόμισται. τὴν γὰρ φύσιν ἐξ ἐναντίων συνισταμένην λέγουσιν, ἔκ τε καλοῦ καὶ κακοῦ· ὥσπερ δεξιὸν καὶ ἀριστερόν, φῶς καὶ σκότος, ἡμέρα καὶ νύξ, ζωὴ καὶ θάνατος.

2. ἔτι δὲ καὶ τοῦτο λέγουσιν, ὡς τὸ θεὸς <ὄνομα>, ψηφισθὲν καὶ μ<ερισθ>ὲν εἰς ἐννάδα, εἰς πεντάδα καταντᾷ, ὅ ἐστιν <ἀν>άρτιον· ὃ ἐπιγραφὲν περιάψαντες θεραπεύουσιν. οὑτωσὶ καὶ βοτάνη τις εἰς τοῦτο λήγουσα τοῦ ἀριθμοῦ ὁμοίως περιαφθεῖσα ἐνεργεῖ, διὰ τὴν ὁμοίαν τοῦ ἀριθμοῦ ψῆφον. 3. ἀλλὰ καὶ ἰατρός <τις> ὁμοίᾳ ψήφῳ ἀρρώστους θεραπεύει· εἰ δὲ ἐναντία ἡ ψῆφος, οὐ θεραπεύει ῥᾳδίως. τούτοις τοῖς ἀριθμοῖς προσέχοντες, ὅσα ὅμοια ᾖ λογίζονται κατὰ τόνδε τὸν νοῦν, ο<ἱ> μὲν κατὰ φωνήεντα μόνα, οἱ δὲ κατὰ πάντα τὸν ἀριθμόν.

τοιαύτη καὶ ἡ Αἰγυπτίων σοφία, δι' ἧς τὸ θεῖον δοξάζοντες γινώσκειν νομίζουσιν.

45. 1. Ἱκανῶς οὖν δοκεῖ ἡμῖν καὶ ταῦτα ἐκτεθεῖσθαι. ἀλλ' ἐπεὶ νομίζω μηδεμίαν δόξαν τῆς ἐπιγείου καὶ χαμαιπετοῦς σοφίας παραλελοιπέναι, οὐκ ἄχρηστον δὴ τὴν εἰς αὐτὰ φροντίδα ὁρῶ ἡμῖν γεγενημένην. οὐδὲ γὰρ μόνον πρὸς ἔλεγχον τῶν αἱρέσεων εὔχρηστον ὁρῶμεν γεγονέναι τὸν λόγον, ἀλλὰ καὶ πρὸς αὐτοὺς τοὺς ταῦτα δοξ(ά)ζοντας· οἳ ἐντυχόντες τῇ γεγενημένῃ ἡμῶν πολυμερι(μν)ίᾳ καὶ τὸ σπουδαῖον θαυμάσουσι καὶ τὸ φιλόπονον οὐκ ἐξουθενήσουσι καὶ μωροὺς οὐκ ἀποφανοῦνται Χριστιανοὺς ἐνιδόντες οἷς αὐτοὶ μωρῶς πιστεύουσιν. 2. ἔτι δὲ καὶ τοὺς τῇ ἀληθείᾳ προσέχοντας φιλομαθεῖς

NUMBER THERAPY. 44. 1. They say that names that end in an odd number are assessed as higher, male, and beneficial (just like the beneficial monad), whereas those ending in an even number are considered to be lower, female, and harmful.[131] They say that nature is composed of opposites like good and bad, right and left, light and dark, day and night, life and death.[132]

2. They say also that the name "God," when counted and divided by nine, leaves a remainder of five, which is uneven.[133] They write this number down and use it to heal by attaching it as an amulet. Similarly, a plant whose name ends with this number [i.e., five] works just like the number when attached as an amulet (because of the same number value).[134] 3. Moreover, a doctor heals the sick with a number of like value. If the number is of unlike value, it does not readily heal. They devote themselves to these numbers and calculate whatever is the same value according to this procedure. Some use only the vowels of a particular name, while others use the numerical value of all the letters.

Such is the wisdom of the Egyptians, through which they suppose they know and glorify the divine!

CONCLUSION TO THE PHILOSOPHICAL SECTION

45. 1. I believe that I have sufficiently presented these teachings. Now, since I think that no opinion of earthly and base wisdom has been omitted, I observe that my careful attention to these matters has hardly been useless. I observe that my account has become useful not only for a refutation of the heresies but also for the very people who venerate these teachings. If they read the product of my abundant care, they will marvel at my diligent study! They will not despise my scholarly diligence, nor declare that Christians are idiots, when they look into what *they* so idiotically believe! 2. Still more: my account will teach those eager students devoted to truth and will

---

131. Marcovich adds ὁμοίως (here: "just like"). He also deletes the initial ἀ in ἀπερίζυγον. Following Miller, he adds τε καὶ ἀρσενικὰ καί (here: "male and").

132. Cf. Aristotle, *Metaph.* 1.5, 986a23–27 (where a similar doctrine is called Pythagorean).

133. Cruice supplied ὄνομα ("name") and adds ἀν- to ἄρτιον (thus: "uneven"). The characters in θέος, when added up, make 284 (9 + 5 + 70 + 200), which divided by 9 equals 31 with a remainder of 5.

134. Cf. Servius on Vergil's *Ecl.* 8.75: "[among the Pythagoreans] uneven numbers are used for healing" (*medendi causa ... impares numeros servari*); cf. Pliny, *Nat.* 28.23.

προβιβάσει ὁ λόγος φρονιμωτέρους πρὸς τὸ εὐκόλως ἀνατρέπειν τοὺς πλανᾶν <αὐτοὺς> τετολμηκότας, μὴ μόνον τὰς τῶν αἱρέσεων μαθόντας ἀρχάς, ἀλλὰ καὶ τὰς τῶν σοφῶν λεγομένας δόξας· ὧν οὐκ ἄπειροι γενόμενοι, οὔθ' ὑπ' αὐτῶν ταραχθήσονται ὡς ἀμαθεῖς, οὔθ' ὑπό τινων πλανηθήσονται ὡς δυνάμει τινὶ δρώντων, ἀλλ' ἔτι καὶ τοὺς πλανωμέ(ν)ους ἐπιτηρήσουσιν.

46. 1. Ἱκανῶς οὖν τὰ <τούτοις> δόξαντα ἐκθέμενοι, λοιπὸν ἐπὶ τὴν τοῦ προκειμένου πραγματείαν χωρήσομεν, ὅπως ὃ τετάγμεθα περὶ τῶν αἱρέσεων ἐπιδείξαντες, ἑκάστοις τε τὰ ἴδια ἀποδοῦναι ἀναγκάσαντες γυμνοὺς τοὺς αἱρεσιάρχας φανερώσωμεν καὶ ἀφροσύνην τῶν πειθομένων κατηγορήσαντες πείσωμεν παλινδρομεῖν ἐπὶ τὸν τῆς ἀληθείας εὔδιον λιμένα.

2. ἵνα δὲ σαφέστερα τοῖς ἐντυγχάνουσι τὰ ῥηθησόμενα φανῇ, δοκεῖ καὶ <τὰ> τῷ Ἀράτῳ πεφροντισμένα περὶ τῆς κατὰ τὸν οὐρανὸν ἄστρων διαθέσεως ἐξειπεῖν, ὥς τινες εἰς τὰ ὑπὸ τῶν γραφῶν εἰρημένα ἀπεικονίζοντες αὐτὰ ἀλληγοροῦσι, μετάγειν τὸν νοῦν τῶν προσεχόντων πειρώμενοι, πιθανοῖς λόγοις προ(σ)άγοντες αὐτοὺς πρὸς ἃ βούλονται, ξένον θαῦμα ἐνδεικνύμενοι, ὡσ<ὰν> κατηστερισμένων τῶν ὑπ' αὐτῶν λεγομένων. 3. οἱ τῷ παραξένῳ θαύματι ἐνορῶντες μικροθαύμαστοι ἁλίσκονται δίκην ὀρνέου τοῦ λεγομένου ὤτου, οὗ τὸ παράδειγμα καλὸν ἐξειπεῖν διὰ τὰ μέλλοντα.

ἔστι δὲ τὸ ζῷον οὐ πολὺ ἀπεμφαῖνον ἀετοῦ οὔτε μεγέθει οὔτε μορφῇ, ἁλίσκεται δὲ τοῦτον τὸν τρόπον. 4. ὁ ἀγρευτὴς τῶν ὀρνίθων, ἐπὰν ἴδῃ ἀγέλην που καταπτᾶσαν, πόρρωθεν ἀνακρουόμενος τὰς χεῖρας ὀρχεῖσθαι σκήπτεται καὶ οὕτω πρὸς ὀλίγον ἐγγίζει τοῖς ὄρνισιν· οἱ δὲ τὴν παράξενον θέαν καταπεπληγότες, ἀπερίβλεπτοι πάντων γίνονται· ἕτεροι δὲ τῶν ἐπὶ τὴν ἄγραν παρεσκευασμένων ὄπισθεν ἐπελθόντες τοὺς ὄρνεις εὐκόλως συλλαμβάνονται θεωμένους τὸν ὀρχηστήν.

make them more intellectually prepared to easily overturn those who dare to deceive them, since they will have learned not only the principles of the heresies but also the so-called philosophical theories [that back them]. When they become so informed, they will not be disturbed like people unschooled, nor will they be deceived by anyone supposedly operating with some miraculous power.[135] Rather, they will keep watch over those who have already been deceived.

46. 1. So, having fully presented their theories, I shall proceed to the treatment of the topic at hand so that, having proved what I specified about the heresies, I might force the leading heretics to return what belongs to each source, and expose them as naked. There is another reason: after I have indicted the stupidity of their votaries, I can convince them to return to the serene harbor of truth.[136]

THEOLOGY FROM ARATOS

2. But in order to make my points clearer to the readers, it seems fitting also to declare the speculations of Aratos about the celestial configurations of the stars, since some people allegorize them by conforming them to verses of scripture. They try to seduce the minds of those interested, enticing them to their views with convincing rhetoric, exhibiting a strange wonder—as if those babbled about by them had truly been raised to the stars![137] 3. Their listeners, gazing on the bizarre sight like naïve dupes, are caught like the proverbial horned owl—whose example, on account of what follows, it is useful to relate.

This animal appears not unlike an eagle in size and shape. It is caught by the following method. 4. The bird catcher, when he sees a flock touch down somewhere, claps his hands from far off and pretends to dance. In this way, he gradually approaches the birds. The birds, struck by the extraordinary event, become unaware of their surroundings. Other hunters, lying ready for the catch, come up from behind the birds and easily capture them as they gawk at the dancer.[138]

---

135. Cf. Eph 4:14.

136. Cf. *Ref.* 1, *pref.* §11.

137. Here and elsewhere our author associates allegory with heretical hermeneutics. See further Pouderon, "Hippolyte, un regard," 53–60.

138. Cf. Athenaios, *Deipn.* 390f–391a; Aristotle, *Hist. an.* 9.12, 597b25.

5. διὸ ἀξιῶ μή τις τοῖς ὁμοίοις θαύμασι καταπλαγεὶς <τῶν> ἐξηγουμένων τὸν οὐρανὸν δίκην ὤτου συλληφθῇ· ὄρχησις γὰρ καὶ λῆρος ἡ τῶν τοιούτων πανουργία, καὶ οὐκ ἀλήθ(εια).

6. Φησὶν οὖν ὁ Ἄρατος οὕτως·

Οἱ μὲν ὁμῶς πολέες τε καὶ ἄλ<λ>υδις ἄλλοι ἐόντες
οὐρανῷ ἕλκονται πάντ' ἤματα συνεχὲς αἰεί

—τουτέστιν οἱ πάντες ἀστέρες·—

αὐτὰρ ὅ γ' οὐδ' ὀλίγον μετανίσσεται, ἀλλὰ μάλ' αὔτως
ἄξων αἰὲν ἄρηρεν, ἔχει δ' ἀτάλαντον ἁπάντη
μεσσηγὺς γαῖαν, περὶ δ' οὐρανὸν αὐτὸς ἀγιν(εῖ).

47. 1. Πολέας φησὶν εἶναι τοὺς κατὰ τὸν οὐρανὸν ἀστέρας—τουτέστι στρεπτούς—διὰ τὸ περιέρχεσθαι ἀπὸ ἀνατολῆς εἰς δύσιν καὶ δύσεως εἰς ἀνατολὴν ἀπαύστως, σφαιροειδεῖ σχήματι.

εἰλεῖσθαι δὲ κατὰ τὰς ἄρκτους αὐτὰς λέγει, οἷόν τι ποταμοῦ ῥεῦμα, μέγα θαῦμα Δράκοντος πελώρου. καὶ τοῦτ' εἶναί φησιν ὃ ἐν τῷ Ἰὼβ πρὸς τὸν <θεὸν ὁ> διάβολος ἔφη· «ἐμπερι(π)ατήσας τὴν ὑπ' οὐρανὸν καὶ περιελθών», τουτέστι περιστραφεὶς (κ)αὶ περισκοπήσας τὰ γινόμενα. 2. τετάχθαι γὰρ νομίζουσι

5. Thus I urge that no one, stunned by the like wonders of those who interpret the sky, be captured like the horned owl. The trickery of their ilk is a dance and worthless nonsense, not truth.[139]

6. Aratos speaks as follows:

Together, many spangled here and there
Are hauled across the sky every day continuously for all time.

(He refers to all the stars.)

Meanwhile, not moving a whit, but in the very same place,
The axis is ever fixed and holds equally balanced on every side
The earth in the center as it spins heaven round.[140]

47. 1. He calls the heavenly bodies "many" [πολέας], that is, "turned [on a pole]," because they revolve from east to west and from west to east unceasingly in the figure of a sphere.[141]

THE SERPENT. Coiled round the Bears, like the winding of a river, he says, is the great spectacle of a monstrous serpent (the constellation Draco).[142] Now this, he says, refers to what the devil said to God in the book of Job: "He roved around and encircled the region under heaven" (i.e., he twisted around and observed what occurs from every direction).[143] 2. For they

---

139. The report below (*Ref.* 4.46.6–49.4) presents an allegorical commentary of an early section of Aratos's *Phaenomena.* The commentary partially parallels Peratic teaching but expresses a different attitude toward Greek learning (Josef Frickel, "Unerkannte gnostische Schriften im Hippolyts *Refutatio*," in *Gnosis and Gnosticism: Papers Read at the Seventh International Conference on Patristic Studies*, ed. Martin Krause, NHS 8 [Leiden: Brill, 1977], 119–37 [121–26]) and lacks gnostic traits (Maria Grazia Lancellotti, "Gli gnostici e il cielo: Dottrine astrologiche e reinterpretazioni gnostiche," *SMSR* 66 [2000]: 71–108 [91–101]). See further Hegedus, *Early Christianity*, 279–86; Giulia Sfameni Gasparro, "I rischi dell'Hellenismòs: Astrologia ed eresia nella *Refutatio omnium haeresium*," in Aragione and Norelli, *Des évêques*, 189–218 (207–14).

140. Aratos, *Phaen.* 19–23. The *Phaenomena* was one of the most widely read works in antiquity. The source that our author used evidently assumes that the poem is inspired and filled with hidden symbols of figures in Jewish and Christian mythology.

141. On the poles, see *Ref.* 5.8.34–35 (Naassenes).

142. Cf. Aratos, *Phaen.* 48–57 (the Bears = Ursa Major and Ursa Minor). This passage is appealed to by the Peratai in *Ref.* 5.16.15 (end).

143. A paraphrase of Job 1:7b LXX, with gloss. Wendland supplied θεόν ("God").

κατὰ τὸν ἀρκτικὸν πόλον τὸν Δράκοντα, τὸν ὄφιν, ἀπὸ τοῦ ὑψηλοτάτου πόλου πάντα ἐπιβλέποντα καὶ πάντα ἐφορῶντα, ἵνα μηδὲν τῶν πραττομένων αὐτὸν λάθῃ. 3. πάντων γὰρ δυνόντων τῶν κατὰ τὸν οὐρανὸν ἀστέρων μόνος οὗτος ὁ πόλος οὐδέποτε δύνει, ἀλλ᾽ ἄνω ὑπὲρ τὸν ὁρίζοντα ἐρχόμενος πάντα περισκοπεῖ καὶ ἐπιβλέπει, καὶ λαθεῖν αὐτὸν τῶν πραττομένων, φησί, δύναται οὐδέν.

ᾗχι μάλιστα
μίσγονται δύσιές τε καὶ ἀντολαὶ ἀλλήλῃσι,

4. <τῇδε> τετάχθαι δή φησιν αὐτοῦ τὴν κεφαλήν. κατὰ γὰρ τὴν δύσιν καὶ ἀνατολὴν τῶν δύο ἡμισφαιρίων κεῖται τὸ κεφάλαιον τοῦ Δράκοντος, ἵνα, φησί, μηδὲν αὐτὸν λάθῃ κατὰ τὸ αὐτὸ μήτε τῶν ἐν τῇ δύσει μήτε τῶν ἐν τῇ ἀνατολῇ, ἀλλὰ πάντα γινώσκῃ τὸ θηρίον ὁμοῦ.

ἔστι δὲ κατ᾽ αὐτῆς τῆς κεφαλῆς τοῦ Δράκοντος ἰδέ<α> ἀνθρώπου δι᾽ ἄστρων θεωρουμένη· ὃ καλεῖ «κεκμηκὸς εἴδωλον» ὁ Ἄρατος καὶ «μογέοντι ἐοικός», καλεῖται δὲ ὁ Ἐν γόνασιν. 5. ὁ μὲν οὖν Ἄρατος οὐκ εἰδέναι φησίν, οὗτος τίς ἐστιν ὁ πόνος καὶ τὸ θαῦμα τοῦτο στρεφόμενον ἐν οὐρανῷ· οἱ δὲ αἱρετικοί, διὰ τῆς τῶν ἄστρων ἱστορίας θέλοντες τὰ ἑαυτῶν δόγματα συνιστᾶν, περιεργότερον τούτοις ἐπισχόντες τὸν Ἐν γόνασί φασιν εἶναι τὸν Ἀδάμ, κατὰ

suppose the Serpent [i.e., the devil] to be arrayed around the north pole, the zenith from where the Serpent observes all and oversees all, so that nothing that is done escapes him. 3. For when all the stars in heaven set, this pole does not set at all. Instead, it travels high over the horizon, observing and overseeing all so that nothing done, he says, can escape his notice:[144]

> the very place where all
> Settings and risings mingle with each other.[145]

4. This is the place, he says, where his head is set. For the Serpent's head lies facing both the east and west hemispheres so that, he says, nothing in either west or east escapes his notice. The beast knows everything alike.[146]

THE KNEELER. Immediately facing the head of the Serpent, there is the form of a human being seen in the stars. Aratos calls him "a figure worn out," "like one in pain," and "the Kneeler."[147] 5. Now Aratos says that he does not know what toil and spectacle this is that turns in the heavens.[148] But the heretics, wanting to establish their own teachings through the stories of the stars, and excessively applying themselves to these subjects, say that the Kneeler is Adam. According to the command of God, he says, Adam,

144. Cf. Homer, *Il.* 18.489 (= *Od.* 5.274). See further *Aratus: Phaenomena; Introduction, Translation, and Commentary*, ed. Douglas A. Kidd (Cambridge: Cambridge University Press, 1997), 199–200.

145. Aratos, *Phaen.* 61–62.

146. For Draco, see further André Le Boeuffle, "Autour du Dragon, astronomie et mythologie," in *Les Astres: Actes du Colloque International de Montpellier I–II*, ed. Béatrice Bakhouche, Alain Maurice Moreau, and Jean-Claude Turpin, 2 vols. (Montpellier: Paul Valéry University, 1996), 1:53–68; Bouché-Leclercq, *L'astrologie*, 122–23.

147. Aratos, *Phaen.* 63–67 and 73. See further Franz Boll, *Sphaera: Neue griechische Texte und Untersuchungen zur Geschichte der Sternbilder* (Leipzig: Teubner, 1903), 100–104; Kidd, *Aratus*, 200–201. The constellation is now known as "Hercules." See the figure above.

148. Cf. Manilius, *Astron.* 1.315.

πρόσταγμα, φησί, τοῦ θεοῦ, καθὼς εἶπε Μωσῆς, φυλάσσοντα τὴν κεφαλὴν τοῦ Δράκοντος, καὶ τὸν Δράκοντα τὴν πτέρναν αὐτοῦ· οὕτως γάρ φησιν ὁ Ἄρατος·

δεξιτεροῦ ποδὸς ἴχνος ἔχων σκολιοῖο Δράκοντος.

48. 1. Παρατ(ε)τάχθαι δέ φησιν αὐτῷ ἑκατέρωθεν—λέγω δὴ τῷ Ἐν γόνασι—Λύραν καὶ Στέφανον, αὐτὸν δὲ γόνυ κλίνειν [καὶ] ἐκτετακότα ἀμφοτέρας τὰς χεῖρας, οἱονεὶ περὶ ἁμαρτίας ἐξομολογούμενον.

εἶναι δὲ τὴν Λύραν μουσικὸν ὄργανον, ὑπὸ νηπίου ἔτι παντελῶς κατεσκευασμένον τοῦ Λόγου· 2. Λόγον δὲ εἶναι παρὰ τοῖς Ἕλλησιν ἀκούομεν τὸν Ἑρμῆν. φησὶ γὰρ ὁ Ἄρατος περὶ τῆς κατασκευῆς τῆς Λύρας·

τὴν δ᾽ ἄρ᾽ ἔτι καὶ παρὰ λίκνῳ
Ἑρμείης ἐτόρησε, Λύρην δ᾽ εἶπε καλέεσθαι.

ἑπτάχορδος ἐστι, διὰ τῶν ἑπτὰ χορδῶν τὴν πᾶσαν ἁρμονίαν καὶ κατασκευὴν ἐμμελῶς ἔχουσαν τοῦ κόσμου. ἐν ἓξ ἡμέραις γὰρ ἐγένετο ὁ κόσμος, καὶ τῇ ἑβδόμῃ καταπέπαυται.

3. εἰ οὖν, φησίν, ἐξομολογούμενος ὁ Ἀδὰμ καὶ τὴν κεφαλὴν φυλάσσων τοῦ θηρίου κατὰ τὸ πρόσταγμα τοῦ θεοῦ ἐκμιμήσεται τὴν Λύραν, τουτέστι κατακολουθήσει τοῖς <προστάγμασι> τοῦ θεοῦ [τουτέστι πειθόμενος τῷ νόμῳ], παρακείμενον αὐτῷ τὸν Στέφανον λήψεται· ἐὰν δὲ ἀμελήσῃ, συγκατενεχθήσεται τῷ ὑποκειμένῳ θηρίῳ καὶ τὸ μέρος ἕξει, φησί, μετὰ τοῦ θηρίου.

just as Moses affirms, guards the head of the Serpent, and the Serpent keeps watch over his heel.[149] To quote Aratos:

He has the sole of his right foot on the twisted Snake.[150]

48. 1. There are arrayed, he says, on both sides of him (that is, the Kneeler) the Lyre and the Crown (the constellations Lyra and Corona Borealis).[151] But he bends a knee and stretches out both hands as if confessing his sins.

THE LYRE AND THE CROWN. The Lyre is a musical instrument, invented by the Word when he was still very much an infant.[152] 2. From the Greeks we learn that Hermes is the Word.[153] Aratos says this about the construction of the Lyre:

… for still in his crib
Hermes carved it out and said it was to be called "Lyre."[154]

It has seven strings, and through its seven strings it melodiously maintains the whole harmony and construction of the world.[155] For in six days the world came to be, and on the seventh there was a cessation.[156]

3. If then, he says, Adam confesses and watches the head of the beast according to the ordinance of God, he will imitate the Lyre—that is, he will follow the commands of God and will take the Crown that lies next to him.[157] If he neglects it, Adam will be brought down to the beast crouching below and will have his lot, he says, with the beast.

---

149. Gen 3:15 LXX.

150. Aratos, *Phaen.* 70; also quoted in *Ref.* 5.16.16 (Peratai).

151. Aratos, *Phaen.* 615; 71; 66–68.

152. For Hermes constructing the Lyre, see Hom. Hymn Merc. 25–67. On the constellation Lyra, see Boll, *Sphaera*, 104–6; Kidd, *Aratus*, 281.

153. The identification of Hermes and the Word is common (Plato, *Crat.* 407e–408b; Herakleitos, *All.* 72; Varro at Augustine, *Civ.* 7.14; Philo, *Legat.* 94, 99; Justin, *1 Apol.* 1.22; Cornutus, *Nat. d.* 16; Plutarch, *Is. Os.* 54 [*Mor.* 373b]).

154. Aratos, *Phaen.* 268–269.

155. Cf. Lucian, *Astr.* 10: ἡ δὲ λύρη ἑπτάμιτος ἐοῦσα τὴν τῶν κινεομένων ἀστέρων ἁρμονίην συνεβάλλετο ("the seven-stringed lyre composed the harmony of the moving stars").

156. Gen 2:2 LXX. The seven days are the seven chords. Cf. *Ref.* 6.14.1 ("Simon").

157. I add προστάγμασι ("commands") (following Marcovich). For the crown rep-

4. ἔοικε δὲ ὁ Ἐν γόνασιν ἑκατέρωθεν ἐπιβάλ<λ>ειν τὰς χεῖρας καὶ τοῦτο μὲν τῆς Λύρας, τοῦτο δὲ Στεφάνου ἐφάπτεσθαι [τοῦτο δὲ ἐξομολογεῖσθαι], ὡς ἔστιν ἰδεῖν δι' αὐτοῦ τοῦ σχήματος. ἐπιβουλεύεται δὲ ὁμῶς καὶ ἀποσπᾶται ὁ Στέφανος αὐτοῦ ὑπ' ἄλλου θ(η)ρίου, <τοῦ> μικροτέρου δράκοντος, ὅ ἐστι γέννημα τοῦ φυλασσομένου ὑπὸ τοῦ Ἐν γ(ό)νασι τῷ ποδί.

5. ἄνθρωπος δὲ ἕστηκεν, ἑκατέραις ταῖς χερσὶ (κ)αρτερῶς κατασφίγγων καὶ εἰς τὰ ὀπίσω ἕλκων (ἀπὸ) τοῦ Στεφάνου τὸν Ὄφιν καὶ οὐκ ἐῶ<ν> ἐφάπτεσθαι βιαζόμενον τοῦ Στεφάν(ου) τὸ θηρίον· Ὀφιοῦχον δὲ αὐτὸν ὁ Ἄρατος καλεῖ, ὅτι κατέχει τὴν ὁρμὴν τοῦ Ὄφεως, ἐπὶ τὸν Στέφανον ἐλθεῖν πειρωμένου. 6. Λόγος δέ, φησίν, ἐστὶ<ν οὗτος ὁ ἐν> σχήματι ἀνθρώπου, ὁ κωλύων ἐπὶ τὸν Στέφανον ἐλθεῖν τὸ θηρίον, οἰκτείρων τὸν ἐπιβουλευόμενον ὑπὸ τοῦ Δράκοντος, ὁμοῦ καὶ τοῦ γεννήματος ἐκείνου.

7. Αὗται δὲ αἱ Ἄρκτοι, φησίν, ἑβδομάδες εἰσὶ δύο, ἐξ ἑπτὰ ἀστέρων συγκείμεναι, δισσῶν κτίσεων εἰκόνες· πρώτη γάρ, φησίν, [ἡ] κτίσις ἡ κατὰ τὸν Ἀδὰμ ἐν πόνοις, <ὅ> ὁ Ἐν γόνασιν ὁρώμενος· δευτέρα δὲ κτίσις ἐστὶν ἡ κατὰ Χριστόν, δι' ἧς ἀναγεννώμεθα, ὅ ἐστιν ὁ Ὀφιοῦχος <ὁρώμενος>, ἀνταγωνιζόμενος τῷ θηρίῳ καὶ κωλύων ἐπὶ τὸν Στέφανον ἐλθεῖν, τὸν ἡτοιμασμένον τῷ ἀνθρώπῳ. 8. μεγάλη δέ ἐστιν Ἄρκτος ἡ Ἑλίκη, φησίν, μεγάλης κτίσεως σύμβολον, πρὸς ἣν πλέουσιν Ἕλληνες—τουτέστι πρὸς ἣν παιδεύονται—καὶ <ᾗ> διὰ τῶν τοῦ βίου φερόμενοι κυμάτων ἐπακολουθοῦσιν· ἑλίκην τινὰ οὖσαν τὴν τοιαύτην κτίσιν—ἢ διδασκαλίαν ἢ σοφίαν—εἰς τὰ ὀπίσω ἄγουσαν τοὺς ἑπομένους τῇ τοιαύτῃ κτίσει· στροφὴ γάρ τις <ἡ> τῆς Ἑλίκης προσηγορία, καὶ ἀνακύκλωσις ἐπὶ τὰ αὐτὰ εἶναι δοκεῖ.

9. μικρὰ δέ <ἐσ>τιν ἡ ἑτέρα Ἄρκτος, οἱονεί τις εἰκὼν τῆς δευτέρας κτίσεως, τῆς κατὰ θεὸν κτισθείσης· ὀλίγοι γάρ, φησίν, εἰσὶν οἱ διὰ τῆς στενῆς ὁδοῦ

4. The Kneeler appears to stretch out his hands on both sides, touching both Lyre and Crown, as one can see through his posture. Nevertheless, another beast conspires after his Crown and draws it away. He is the smaller Serpent, who is an offspring of the one kept in check by the Kneeler's foot.[158]

THE SNAKEHOLDER. 5. But a man stands there vigorously choking the Snake with both hands, dragging it back away from the Crown, and not permitting the beast to break free and reach the Crown. Aratos calls him "Snakeholder" (the constellation Ophiuchos), because he restrains the attack of the Snake as it tries to advance on the Crown. 6. This figure is the Word in human form, he says, who prevents the beast from reaching the Crown out of pity for the one against whom the Serpent conspires in cahoots with his spawn.[159]

THE BEARS. 7. The very Bears (Ursa Major and Ursa Minor), he says, are two hebdomads consisting of seven stars.[160] They are images of a double creation. The first creation, he says, is that of Adam, characterized by toils and shown as the Kneeler. The second creation is that of Christ, through which we are reborn. This is shown as the Snakeholder, striving with the beast and preventing it from reaching the Crown that was prepared for humanity. 8. The Great Bear is Helike, he says, a symbol of the great creation by which the Greeks navigate (that is, by which they are educated).[161] This they follow, as they are tossed on the waves of life. Such a creation (or instruction, or wisdom) is helix-shaped, leading those who follow it in a backward direction.[162] This is because the name Helike means "turning" and he considers the turning to mean revolution back to the same position.

9. The other Bear is small, as though an image of the second creation created in the likeness of God. For few, he says, are those who travel on

---

resenting Christian salvation, see 1 Cor 9:25; 1 Pet 5:4. On the constellation Corona, see Kidd, *Aratus*, 204–5.

158. The smaller serpent is the constellation Serpens. See Aratos, *Phaen.* 82–87, with Kidd, *Aratus*, 206.

159. Aratos, *Phaen.* 74–87.

160. Aratos, *Phaen.* 26–30; cf. Clem. Alex., *Strom.* 6.16.143.1 (ἑπτὰ … ἀγγέλων ἄρχοντες … ἑπτάστεροι δὲ αἱ ἄρκτοι ["there are seven rulers of angels … and the Bears constitute seven stars"]).

161. Aratos, *Phaen.* 37–38.

162. Cf. *Scholium in Arat.* 35 (J. Martin).

πορευόμενοι. στενὴ<ν> δὲ <ὁδὸν> λέγουσιν εἶναι τὴν Κυνοσουρίδα, πρὸς ἣν ὁ Ἄρατός φησιν ὅτι οἱ Σιδόνιοι ναυτί(λ)λονται. Σιδονίους δὲ ἀπὸ μέρους εἴρηκεν ὁ Ἄρατος <τοὺς> Φοίνικας, διὰ τὸ εἶναι τὴν Φοινίκων σοφίαν θαυμαστήν, Φοίνικας δὲ εἶναι Ἕλληνες λέγουσι τοὺς ἀπὸ τῆς Ἐρυθρᾶς θαλάσσης μετοικήσαντας εἰς τοῦτον τὸν χῶρον, οὗ καὶ νῦν οἰκοῦσι· τοῦτο γὰρ Ἡροδότῳ δοκεῖ.

10. Κυνόσουρα δέ, φησίν, <ἐστὶν> αὕτη ἡ Ἄρκτος, ἡ κτίσις ἡ δευτέρα, ἡ μικρά, ἡ στενὴ ὁδός, καὶ οὐχὶ ἡ Ἑλίκη· οὐ γὰρ εἰς τὰ ὀπίσω ἄγει, ἀλλ' εἰς τὰ ἔμπροσθεν ἐπ' εὐθείας τοὺς ἑπομένους <αὐτῇ> ὁδηγεῖ, κ<ύων> τις οὖσα. κύων γὰρ ὁ Λόγος, τοῦτο μὲν φρουρῶν καὶ φυλάσσων τὸ ἐπιβουλευόμενον ὑπὸ τῶν λύκων ποίμνιον, τοῦτο δὲ ἀπὸ τῆς κτίσεως τὰ θηρία κυνηγῶν καὶ διαφθείρων, τοῦτο δὲ γεννῶν τὰ πάντα καί, ὡ<ς> δή φασι, κύων, τουτέστι γεννῶν.

11. ἐντεῦθεν, φασίν, ὁ Ἄρατος περὶ τῆς τοῦ Κυνὸς ἀνατολῆς λέγων εἴρηκεν οὕτως· Κυνὸς δὲ ἀνατείλαντος οὐκέτι φυταλιαὶ ἐψεύσαντο. τοῦτο ἐστιν ὃ λέγει· τὰ φυτευόμενα φυτὰ εἰς τὴν γῆν μέχρι τῆς τοῦ Κυνὸς ἀνατολῆς πολλάκις μὴ ῥιζοβολήσαντα ὅμως τέθηλε φύλλοις καὶ ἐνδείκνυται τοῖς βλέπουσιν ὅτι ἔσται τελεσφόρα καὶ φαίνεται ζῶντα, οὐκ ἔχοντα ζωὴν ἀπὸ τῆς ῥίζης ἐν αὐτοῖς· 12. ἐπειδὰν δὲ <ἡ> τοῦ Κυνὸς ἀνατολὴ γένηται, ὑπὸ τοῦ Κυνὸς τὰ ζῶντα ἀπὸ τῶν νεκρῶν διακρίνεται· μαραίνεται γὰρ ὄντως ὅσα οὐκ ἐρ<ρ>ιζοβόλησεν. οὗτος οὖν, φησίν, ὁ Κύων, Λόγος τις ὢν θεῖος, «ζώντων καὶ νεκρῶν κριτὴς» καθέστηκε.

καθάπερ <ἐπὶ> τῶ<ν> φυτῶν ὁ Κύων τὸ ἄστρον ἐπι<στάτης> τῆς κτίσεως θεωρεῖται, οὕτως ἐπὶ τῶν οὐρανίω(ν) φυτῶν, φησί, τῶν ἀνθρώπων, ὁ Λόγος. 13. διὰ τὴν τοιαύτην οὖν αἰτίαν ἡ δευτέρα κτίσις, Κυνόσουρα, λογικῆς κτίσεως (εἰκ)ὼ(ν) ἕστηκεν ἐν οὐρανῷ.

the narrow path.[163] They say that the narrow path is Cynosura. This is the guiding star, as Aratos says, of the Sidonians.[164] Aratos speaks of the Sidonians by synecdoche for the Phoenicians, since the wisdom of the Phoenicians is impressive. The Greeks, however, say that Phoenicians migrated from the Red Sea to the region where they now live. (This is the opinion of Herodotos.)[165]

THE DOG STAR. 10. This Bear, he says, is Cynosura, the "Dog Tail," the second, smaller creation, the narrow path, and not Helike (i.e., "turning"). This is because Cynosura leads not backward but forward, guiding those who follow it on the straight path, since it is a dog [κύων]. For the Word is a dog who guards and keeps the flock, against which wolves conspire. He hunts and destroys the beasts out of creation and generates all things. They actually claim that he conceives [κύων] (that is, "generates") all things.

11. Next, they say, Aratos speaks about the rising of the Dog Star, or Sirius. When the Dog rises, no longer does "herbage" give a false appearance. Aratos explains that plants planted in the soil up until the rising of the Dog Star often do not send out roots even though they sprout leaves and indicate to onlookers that they will bear mature fruit. They appear to be alive but do not have life in themselves from the root.[166] 12. But when the Dog Star rises, it will distinguish the living from the dead—for what did not send out roots truly withers. So this Dog Star, he says, is a divine Word, established as "judge of the living and the dead."[167]

Just as the Dog Star is viewed as the overseer of the plants of creation, so, he says, the Word oversees the heavenly plants (that is, human beings).[168] 13. By this sort of reasoning, the second creation, Cynosura, stands in heaven as an image of rational creation.

---

163. Matt 7:14.

164. Aratos, *Phaen.* 44.

165. Aratos, *Phaen.* 39. Cf. Herodotos, *Hist.* 1.1. See further Kidd, *Aratus*, 189–90.

166. Aratos, *Phaen.* 332–335; cf. Mark 4:17.

167. Cf. Acts 10:42; 2 Tim 4:1 (Christ as judge of living and the dead). The association of the Dog Star and Christ derives in part from Aratos's derivation of the name of the Dog Star from the verb σειριάω ("to be hot/scorching") (*Phaen.* 330–332; cf. Kidd, *Aratus*, 307–8). The heat represents the heat of Christ's judgment (Hegedus, *Early Christianity*, 285).

168. Marcovich emends ἐπί to ἐπιστάτης ("overseer"). For humans as heavenly plants, see Plato, *Tim.* 90a.

μέσος δὲ ὁ Δράκων τῶν δύο κτίσεων ὑπ(ο)τ(είν)εται, τὰ ἀπὸ τῆς μεγάλης κτίσεως κωλύων ἐπὶ τὴν μικρὰν κτίσιν μετελθεῖν, τά τε ἐν τῇ <μεγάλῃ> κτίσει καθεστηκότα—καθάπερ τὸν Ἐν γόνασι—παραφυλάσσων <καὶ> τηρῶν πῶς καὶ τίνα τρόπον ἕκαστον <τῶν> ἐν τῇ μικρᾷ κτίσει καθέστηκε. 14. τηρεῖται δὲ καὶ αὐτὸς κατὰ τὴν κεφαλήν, φησίν, ὑπὸ τοῦ Ὀφιούχου. αὕτη, φησίν, <τῆς κτίσεως> εἰκὼν ἕστηκεν ἐν οὐρανῷ, σοφία τις οὖσα τοῖς ἰδεῖν δυναμένοις. Εἰ δέ ἐστιν ἀσαφὲς κατα<νοήσει> τοῦτο, δι' ἄλλης εἰκόνος, φησίν, ἡ κτίσις διδάσκει φιλοσοφεῖν.

περὶ ἧς ὁ Ἄρατος εἴρηκεν οὕτως·

Οὐδ' ἄρα Κηφῆος μογερὸν γένος εἰς ἀΐδαο.

49. 1. Ὁ Κηφεύς, φησίν, αὐτοῦ ἐστι πλησίον καὶ ἡ Κασ<σ>ιέπεια καὶ <ἡ> Ἀνδρομέδα καὶ ὁ Περσεύς, μεγάλα τῆς κτίσεως γράμματα τοῖς ἰδεῖν δυναμένοις. Κηφέα γάρ φησιν εἶναι τὸν Ἀδάμ, τὴν Κασ<σ>ιέπειαν Εὔαν, τὴν Ἀνδρομέδαν τὴν ἀμφοτέρων τούτων ψυχήν, τὸν Περσέα Λόγον, πτερωτὸν Διὸς ἔγγονον, τὸ Κῆτος τὸ ἐπίβουλον θηρίον. 2. οὐδ' ἐπ' ἄλλον τινα τούτων ἀλλ' ἐπὶ μόνην τὴν Ἀνδρομέδαν ἔρχεται τὸ θηρίον, ὃ ἀποκτείνας [οὗ] καὶ τὴν Ἀνδρομέδαν πρὸς ἑαυτὸν λαβών, ἔκδοτον δεδεμένην τῷ θηρίῳ, ὁ Λόγος, φησίν, ὁ Περσεὺς ῥύεται. Περσεὺς δέ ἐστιν ὁ (ὑ)π(ό)πτερος ἄξων, ὁ περαίνων ἑκατέρους τοὺς πόλους διὰ μέσης τῆς γῆς καὶ στρέφων τὸν κόσμον.

3. ἔστι δὲ παρὰ τὰς Ἄρκτους καὶ τὸ πνεῦμα τὸ ἐν τῷ κόσμῳ, ὁ Ὄρνις, ὁ Κύκνος, (μουσ)ικὸν ζῷον, τοῦ θείου σύμβολον πνεύματος, ὅτι πρὸς αὐτοῖς ἤδη

In the middle of the two creations, the Serpent stretches up from below, preventing the events of the great creation from shifting to the smaller. He protects the things established in the great creation (just like the Kneeler) and watches over the condition established for each of the realities in the smaller creation. 14. All the while, he says, he is guarded by the Snake-holder, who keeps watch above his head. This image of creation, he says, stands fixed in heaven as wisdom to those with eyes to see it. But if this is hard to understand, he says, creation teaches us to seek wisdom through another illustration.[169]

CEPHEUS, CASSIOPEIA, ANDROMEDA, AND PERSEUS. Aratos speaks of the illustration as follows:

> Nor then the wretched family of Cepheus in Hades[170]

49. 1. Near the Serpent, he says, is Cepheus as well as the constellations Cassiopeia, Andromeda, and Perseus—gigantic pictures of creation for those with eyes to see them. He says that Cepheus is Adam, Cassiopeia Eve, and Andromeda the soul of both; Perseus, winged offspring of Zeus, is the Word, and the Sea Monster (the constellation Cetus) is the conspiring beast.[171] 2. The beast comes to none of these except Andromeda alone.[172] The Word, Perseus, kills the beast, he says, takes Andromeda to himself (since she was chained as an offering to the beast), and delivers her.[173] Perseus is the swift-winged axis that extends across both poles through the middle of the earth and causes the cosmos to revolve.

THE SWAN. 3. Located by the Bears there is also "the Spirit in the world," which is the Bird or Swan (the constellation Cygnus).[174] Now the Swan is a

---

169. Marcovich emends *κατά* to *κατανοήσει* (here: "to understand"). Wendland preferred to delete *κατά*.

170. Aratos, *Phaen.* 179 (where the text has Ἰασίδαο not εἰς ἀΐδαο). Cf. *Ref.* 4.50.2 (ἐν Ἅιδου).

171. For Perseus and Christ, see Justin, *1 Apol.* 22.5; *Dial.* 67.2; 70.5.

172. Aratos, *Phaen.* 354.

173. For the story of Perseus saving Andromeda, see Ps.-Apoll., *Bibl.* 2.4.3; Ovid, *Metam.* 4.663–752. On the catasterisms of these figures see Ps.-Eratosthenes, *Cataster.* 15–17 (Olivieri, 19–21); Manilius, *Astron.* 5.540–618.

174. Aratos, *Phaen.* 272–281, with Kidd, *Aratus*, 284–85; *Scholia in Arat.* 275 (J. Martin); Ps.-Eratosthenes, *Cataster.* 25 (Olivieri, 30–32).

τοῖς τέρμασι γενόμενον τοῦ βίου μόνον ᾄδειν πέφυκε, «μετὰ ἀγαθῆς ἐλπίδος» τῆς κτίσεως τῆς πονηρᾶς ἀπαλ<λ>ασσόμενον, ὕμνους ἀναπέμπον τῷ θεῷ.

4. καρκίνοι δὲ καὶ ταῦροι καὶ λέοντες καὶ κριοὶ καὶ αἶγες καὶ ἔριφοι καὶ ὅσα ἄλλα θηρία διὰ τῶν ἄστρων ὀνομάζεται κατὰ τὸν οὐρανὸν εἰκόνες δή, φησίν, εἰσὶ καὶ παραδείγματα, ἀφ' ὧν ἡ μεταβλητὴ κτίσις λαμβάνουσα τὰς ἰδέας τοιούτων ζῴων γίνεται πλήρης.

50. 1. Τούτοις χρώμενοι τοῖς λόγοις ἀπατᾶν νομίζουσι πολλούς, ὅσοι περιεργότερον τοῖς ἀστρολόγοις προσέχουσιν, ἐντεῦθεν τὴν θεοσέβειαν συνιστᾶν πειρώμενοι, μακρὰν ἀπεμφαίνουσαν τῆς τούτων ὑπολήψεως.

διό, ἀγαπητοί, φύγωμεν τὸ μικροθαύμαστον τοῦ ὄρνιθος τοῦ ὤτου· ταῦτα γὰρ καὶ τὰ τοιάδε ὄρχησίς ἐστι, καὶ οὐκ ἀλήθεια. 2. οὐδὲ γὰρ τὰ ἄστρα ταῦτα δηλοῖ, ἀλλὰ ἰδίως οἱ ἄνθρωποι πρὸς ἐπισημείωσίν τινων ἄστρων ὀνόματα <αὐτοῖς> οὕτως ἐπεκάλεσαν, ἵνα αὐτοῖς εὔσημα ᾖ. τί γὰρ ἄρκτου ἢ λέοντος ἢ ἐρίφων ἢ ὑδροχόου ἢ Κηφέως ἢ Ἀνδρομέδας ἢ τῶν ἐν Ἅιδου ὀνομαζομένων εἰδώλων ὅμοιον ἔχουσιν ἀστέρες διεσπαρμένοι κατὰ τὸν οὐρανόν—πολὺ <μέντοι> μετα(γε)νεστέρ(ων) γεγενημένων τούτων τῶν ἀνθρώπων καὶ τῶν ὀνομάτων ἢ τ(ῶ)ν ἄστρων συνέστηκε γένεσις—, ἵνα καὶ οἱ αἱρετικοὶ κ(α)ταπλαγέντες τὸ θαῦμα οὕτως ἐξεργάσωνται, δι(ὰ) <τῶν> τ(οι)ῶ(ν)δε λόγων τὰ ἴδια δόγματα συνιστᾶν <πειρώμενοι>;

51. 1. Ἀλλ' ἐπεὶ σχεδὸν πᾶσα αἵρεσις διὰ τῆς ἀριθμητικῆς τέχνης ἐφεῦρεν ἑβδομάδων μέτρα καὶ αἰώνων τινὰς προβολάς, ἄλλων ἄλλως τὴν τέχνην διασπώντων καὶ τοῖς ὀνόμασι μόνον διαλ<λ>ασσόντων—τούτων δὲ αὐτοῖς διδάσκαλος γίνεται Πυθαγόρας, πρῶτος εἰς Ἕλληνας ἀπ' Αἰγύπτου τοὺς τοιούτους ἀριθμοὺς παραδούς—, δοκεῖ μηδὲ τοῦτο παραλιπεῖν, ἀλλὰ διὰ συντόμου δείξαντας ἐπὶ τὴν τῶν ζητουμένων ἀπόδειξιν χωρῆσαι.

2. γεγόνασιν ἀριθμητι<κοὶ> καὶ γεωμέτραι—οἷς μάλιστα τὰς ἀρχὰς παρεσχηκέναι δοκεῖ πρῶτος Πυθαγόρας—, καὶ οὗτοι τῶν ἀριθμῶν εἰς ἄπειρον ἀεὶ προχωρεῖν δυναμένων τῷ πολυπλασιασμῷ καὶ τοῖς σχήμασι τὰς πρώτας

musical animal, a symbol of the divine Spirit, because only when it comes to the end of its life does it instinctually sing. That is, it sends up hymns to God when it is being released from an evil creation with good hope.

4. But crabs, bulls, lions, rams, goats, kids, and whatever other beast is named in the stars are—we are to believe—heavenly images, he says, and models from which changing creation receives the forms of such animals and becomes full.

50. 1. Using these discourses, the heretics suppose that they can deceive many who devote themselves too inquisitively to astrologers. From these stories, they try to instill reverence toward God—though their reverence is far different from what they suppose.

Therefore, beloved, let us flee the naïve amazement of the horned owl! For these teachings and those like them are a dancing trick and not the truth. 2. Nor in fact do the stars reveal these teachings, but people have idiosyncratically given them names to indicate certain stars so that they are easy to distinguish. What do the stars spread out across the whole heaven have in common with the figures of a bear or a lion or a kid or a water pourer or Cepheus or Andromeda or the famous shades in Hades? These people—and their names—came about a long time after the origin of the stars! So what right do the heretics have who, struck with wonder, concoct this spectacle, trying through such stories to contrive their own teachings?[175]

PYTHAGOREAN MATHEMATICS

51. 1. Almost every heresy has used arithmetic to discover hebdomadal measurements and emanations of aeons, each one variously pulling arithmetic to pieces and only changing the names. In these matters, Pythagoras became their teacher. He was the first to transmit such numbers from Egypt to Greece. Such being the case, it seems fitting not to omit this either. So, after I have presented a summary, I will proceed to my proof of the topics researched.[176]

2. Now arithmeticians and geometers have long been around. Among their number, it was Pythagoras in particular, it seems, who first provided them with their first principles. These men took their first principles from

175. Marcovich adds πειρώμενοι ("trying"). Cf. the argument in *Ref.* 4.6.3; 4.27.2; Sext. Emp., *Math.* 5.97–99. On the shades in Hades, see further Boll, *Sphaera*, 246–51.

176. As *Ref.* 4.51.3, 9, 14 below indicate, our author considered this material (in part a review of *Ref.* 1.2.5–10) as important background and source material for Simonian and Valentinian teaching in book 6.

ἔλαβον ἀρχὰς οἱονεὶ θεωρητὰς μόνῳ τῷ λόγῳ. γεωμετρίας γάρ, ὡς ἔστιν ἐνιδεῖν, σημεῖόν ἐστιν ἀρχή, ἀμερὲς <ὄν>· ἀπ' ἐκείνου δὲ τοῦ σημείου τῇ τέχνῃ ἡ τῶν ἀπείρων σχημάτων [ἀπὸ τοῦ σημείου] γένεσις εὑρίσκεται. 3. ῥυὲν γὰρ τὸ σημεῖον ἐπὶ μῆκος γίνεται γραμμή [μετὰ τὴν ῥύσιν], πέρας ἔχουσα σημεῖον· γραμμὴ δὲ ἐπὶ πλάτος ῥυεῖσα ἐπίπεδον γεννᾷ, πέρατα δὲ τοῦ ἐπιπέδου γραμμαί· ἐπίπεδον δὲ ῥυὲν εἰς βάθος γίνεται σῶμα· στερεοῦ δὲ ὑπάρξαντος οὕτως, ἐξ ἐλαχίστου σημείου παντελῶς ἡ τοῦ μεγάλου σώματος ὑπέστη φύσις. καὶ τοῦτό ἐστιν ὃ λέγει Σίμων οὕτως· τὸ μικρὸν μέγα ἔσται, οἱονεὶ (σ)ημεῖον ὄν, τὸ δὲ μέγα ἀπέραντον, κατακολουθοῦν τῷ γεωμετρουμένῳ σημείῳ.

4. Τῆς δὲ ἀριθμητικῆς κατὰ σύνθεσιν <περι>εχούσης τὴν φιλοσοφίαν ἀριθμὸς γέγονεν <πρῶτος> ἀρχή, ὅπερ ἐστὶν, ἀόριστον, ἀκατάληπτον, ἔχων ἐν ἑαυτῷ πάντας τοὺς ἐπ' ἄπειρον ἐλθεῖν δυναμένους ἀριθμοὺς κατὰ τὸ πλῆθος. τῶν δὲ ἀριθμῶν ἀρχὴ γέγονε καθ' ὑπόστασιν ἡ πρώτη μονάς, ἥτις ἐστὶ μονὰς ἄρσην, γεννῶσα πατρικῶς τοὺς ἄλλους πάντας ἀριθμούς. 5. δεύτερον ἡ δυάς, θῆλυς ἀριθμός, ὁ δὲ αὐτὸς καὶ ἄρτιος ὑπὸ τῶν ἀριθμητικῶν καλεῖται. τρίτον ἡ τριάς, ἀριθμὸς ἄρσην· οὗτος καὶ περισσὸς ὑπὸ τῶν ἀριθμητικῶν νενομοθέτηται καλεῖσθαι. ἐφ' ἅπασι δὲ τούτοις ἡ τετράς, θῆλυς ἀριθμός, ὁ δὲ αὐτὸς [οὗτος] καὶ ἄρτιος καλεῖται, ὅτι θῆλύς ἐστι. 6. γεγόνασιν οὖν οἱ πάντες ἀριθμοὶ ληφθέντες ἀπὸ [τοῦ] γένους τέσσαρες—ἀριθμὸς δὲ ἦν τὸ γένος ἀόριστος—, ἀφ' ὧν ὁ τέλειος αὐτοῖς ἀριθμὸς συνέστηκεν, ἡ δεκάς· τὸ γὰρ ἕν, δύο, τρία, τέσσαρα γίνεται δέκα, ὡς προαποδέδεικται, ἐὰν ἑκάστῳ τῶν ἀριθμῶν φυλάσσηται κατ' οὐσίαν ὄνομα τὸ οἰκεῖον. 7. αὕτη ἐστὶν ἡ κατὰ Πυθαγόραν ἱερὰ τετρακτύς,

<πηγὴ> ἀενάου φύσεως ῥιζώματ' ἔχουσα

ἐν ἑαυτῇ, τουτέστι τοὺς ἄλλους πάντας ἀριθμούς· ὁ γὰρ ἕνδεκα καὶ <ὁ> δώδεκα καὶ οἱ λοιποὶ τὴν ἀρχὴν τῆς γενέσεως ἀπὸ τοῦ δέκα λαμβάνουσι.

numbers that can extend continuously by multiplication to infinity. They took the first principles of geometric figures as those who theorize by logic alone. For one can see that a point, being indivisible, is the first principle of geometry. From that point, the generation of infinite shapes was discovered by the art of geometry. 3. For the point extended in length becomes a line, ending in another point. A line extended in breadth produces a surface, ending in another line. A surface extended in depth becomes a three-dimensional body. This is how a solid body comes into being. So, from the smallest point, there is constituted the entire structure of a massive body.[177] Now this is what Simon means by his saying, "The small will become great." It is as if what is "small" were a point, and what is "great" something infinitely extended, in accordance with the geometrical point.[178]

THE ORIGIN OF NUMBERS. 4. The beginning of arithmetic, which encompasses philosophy according to a process of calculation, is the primal number.[179] It is unlimited and incomprehensible and has in itself all the numbers that are able to approach infinity by multiplication. The primal monad is by nature the first principle of numbers. The monad is male, generating all the other numbers as a father. 5. The second number is the dyad, a female number called "even" by the arithmeticians. The third number is the triad, a male number, as a rule called "odd" by the arithmeticians. Over all these is the tetrad, which is also called "even," since it is female. 6. Thus all the numbers arose, stemming from four classes (number itself being an undefined class). From these classes, the perfect number was composed: the decad. For one plus two plus three plus four equals ten, as shown previously, if we preserve for each of the numbers their essential and appropriate name. 7. This is, according to Pythagoras, "the holy Tetraktys":

> A fount possessing the roots of ever-flowing nature

in itself. That is, it contains all the other numbers. For eleven, twelve, and the rest receive their source of being from ten.

---

177. Cf. Sext Emp., *Math.* 3.19–20; 4.4–5; 7.99–100; 9.380–381; Philo, *Opif.* 49; *Decal.* 24–26; Euclid, *Elem.* I def. 1; 3; 6; XI def. 2 and Schol. V (Heiberg, 78,15).

178. Cf. *Ref.* 5.9.5 (Naassenes); 6.14.6 ("Simon").

179. Marcovich emends ἐχούσης to περιεχούσης ("encompasses") and adds πρῶτος ("primal") from *Ref.* 1.2.5.

ταύτης τῆς δεκάδος, το(ῦ) τε(λεί)ου ἀριθμοῦ, τὰ τέσσαρα καλεῖται μέρη·

1. ἀριθμός,
2. μονάς,
3. δύναμις,
4. κύβος.

8. οἷς ἐπιπλοκαὶ καὶ μίξεις πρὸς γένεσι(ν) (αὐ)ξήσεως γίνονται, κατὰ φύσιν τὸν γόνιμον ἀριθμὸν ἐπιτελοῦσαι· ὅταν γὰρ δύναμις αὐτὴ ἐφ' ἑαυτὴν κυβισθήσεται, γέγονε δυναμοδύναμις· ὅταν δὲ δύναμις ἐπὶ κύβον, γέγονε δυναμόκυβος· ὅταν δὲ κύβος ἐπὶ κύβον, γέγονε κυβόκυβος· ὡς γίνεσθαι τοὺς πάντας ἀριθμοὺς ἑπτά, ἵνα ἡ τῶν γινομένων γένεσις γένηται ἐξ ἑβδομάδος,

ἥτις ἐστίν·

1. ἀριθμός,
2. μονάς,
3. δύναμις,
4. κύβος,
5. δυναμοδύναμις,
6. δυναμόκυβος,
7. κυβόκυβος.

9. Ταύτην τὴν ἑβδομάδα Σίμων καὶ Οὐαλεντῖνος ὀνόμασιν ἐνδιαλλάξαντες ἐτερατολόγησαν, ὑπόθεσιν ἑαυτοῖς ἐντεῦθεν σχεδιάσαντες. ὁ μὲν γὰρ Σίμων <αὐτὴν> οὕτως καλεῖ· νοῦς, ἐπίνοια, ὄνομα, φωνή, λογισμός, ἐνθύμησις, ὁ ἑστὼς στὰς στησόμενος· καὶ Οὐαλεντῖνος· νοῦς, ἀλήθεια, λόγος, ζωή, ἄνθρωπος, ἐκκλησία καὶ ὁ πατὴρ συναριθμούμενος, κατ<ὰ τ>αὐτὰ τοῖς τὴν ἀριθμητικὴν ἠσκηκόσι φιλοσοφίαν· ὡς ἄγνωστον πολλοῖς θαυμάσαντες, κατακολουθήσαντες, τὰς ὑφ' αὐτῶν ἐπινοηθείσας αἱρέσεις συνεστήσαντο.

There are what are called "four components" of the decad, or perfect number:

1. number,
2. a single number (x),
3. a squared number (x^2), and
4. a cubed number (x^3).[180]

8. From these components, there arise further multiplications and combinations for the origin of growth, bringing to natural completion the productive number. For x^2 times x^2 is a square squared (x^4).[181] When x^2 is multiplied by x^3, it becomes a cube squared (x^5). When x^3 is multiplied by x^3, it becomes a cube cubed (x^6). Accordingly, all the numbers from which come the origin of all generated beings are seven:

1. number,
2. a single number,
3. the squared number,
4. the cubed number,
5. the square squared,
6. the cube squared, and
7. the cube cubed.

APPLICATION TO SIMONIAN AND VALENTINIAN THOUGHT. 9. Simon and Valentinus recounted wondrous myths about this hebdomad (changing out the names), to improvise a basic theorem for themselves. Simon calls it "Mind, Thought, Name, Voice, Reasoning, Conception, and the One Who Stood, Stands, and Will Stand."[182] Valentinus calls the hebdomad "Mind, Truth, Word, Life, Human, Church"—and added to them the Father. He did so according to the same principles as those who practice the philosophy of arithmetic.[183] Struck with wonder by this philosophy—as something unknown to the masses—they imitated it and established their own contrived heresies.

---

180. For the four components of number, see Kalvesmaki, *Theology*, 181–82.

181. For κυβισθήσεται (κυβισθῇ in *Ref.* 1.2.10) meaning πολυπλασιάζειν ("multiply"), see Roeper, "Emendationsversuche," 532.

182. Cf. *Ref.* 6.12.2.

183. Cf. *Ref.* 6.29.6–7.

10. Τινὲς μὲν οὖν καὶ ἀπὸ ἰατρικῆς συνιστᾶν τὰς ἑβδομάδας πειρῶνται, ἐκπλαγέντες ἐπὶ τῇ τοῦ ἐγκεφάλου ἀνατομῇ, λέγοντες τὴν τοῦ παντὸς οὐσίαν καὶ δύναμιν καὶ πατρικὴν θειότητα ἀπὸ τῆς τοῦ ἐγκεφάλου διαθέσεως διδάσκεσθαι. 11. ὁ γὰρ ἐγκέφαλος κύριον μέρος ὢν τοῦ παντὸς (σώ)ματ(ο)ς ἐπίκειται ἀτρεμὴς καὶ ἀκίνητος, ἐντὸς ἑαυτοῦ ἔχων τὸ πνεῦμα.

ἔστι μὲν οὖν ἡ τοιαύτη ἱστορία οὐκ ἀπίθανος, μακρὰ(ν) δὲ τῆς τούτων ἐπιχειρήσεως. ὁ μὲν γὰρ ἐγκέφαλος ἀνατμηθεὶς ἔνδον ἔχει τὸ καλούμενον καμάριον, οὗ ἑκατέρωθεν ὑμένες εἰσὶ λεπτοί, οὓς πτερύγια προσαγορεύουσιν, ἠρέμα ὑπὸ τοῦ πνεύματος κινούμενα καὶ πάλιν ἀπελαύνοντα τὸ πνεῦμα ἐπὶ τὴν παρεγκεφαλίδα. 12. ὃ διατρέχον διά τινος ἀγγείου καλάμῳ ἐοικότος ἐπὶ τὸ κωνάριον χωρεῖ, ᾧ πρόσκειται τὸ στόμιον τῆς παρεγκεφαλίδος, ἐκδεχόμενον τὸ διατρέχον πνεῦμα καὶ ἀναδιδὸν ἐπὶ τὸν νωτιαῖον λεγόμενον μυελόν, ὅθεν πᾶν τὸ σῶμα μεταλαμβάνει τὸ πνευματικόν, πασῶν τῶν ἀρτηριῶν δίκην κλάδου ἐκ τούτου τοῦ ἀγγείου ἠρτημένων. οὗ τὸ πέρας ἐπὶ τὰ γεννητικὰ ἀγγεῖα τερματίζεται· ὅθεν καὶ τὰ σπέρματα ἐξ ἐγκεφάλου διὰ τῆς ὀσφύος χωροῦντα ἐκκρίνεται.

13. ἔστι δὲ τὸ σχῆμα τῆς πα(ρ)εγκεφαλίδος ἐοικὸς κεφαλῇ δράκοντος, περὶ οὗ πολ(ὺ)ς ὁ λόγος τοῖς «τῆς ψευδωνύμου γνώσεως» γίνεται, καθὼς ἐπιδείξομεν.

ἕτεραι δὲ ἐκ τοῦ ἐγκεφάλου φύονται ἓξ συζυγίαι, αἳ περὶ τὴν κεφαλὴν διϊκνούμεναι συνέχουσι τὰ <ἄνω τοῦ> σώματος, ἐν αὐτῇ περατούμεναι· ἡ δὲ ἑβδόμη ἐκ τῆς παρεγκεφαλίδος εἰς τὰ κάτω τοῦ λοιποῦ σώματος, καθὼς εἴπομεν.

14. καὶ περὶ τούτου δὲ πολὺς ὁ λόγος, ὅθεν καὶ Σίμων καὶ Οὐαλεντῖνος εὑρεθήσονται καὶ ἐντεῦθεν ἀφορμὰς εἰληφότες, καὶ εἰ μὴ ὁμολογοῖεν, ὄντες πρῶτον ψεῦσται, εἶτ(α) αἱρετικοί.

HEBDOMADS AND BRAIN ANATOMY

10. Now some try to confirm their hebdomads from medical science, since they are struck with wonder by the anatomy of the brain. They say that the substance, power, and paternal divinity of the universe is taught from the structure of the brain. 11. For the brain, being the ruling part of the whole body, sits unshaken and unmoved and contains breath in itself.[184]

Such a report is not unconvincing but miles away from their argument. For the brain when cut into sections has within it what is called the "fornix" surrounded on both sides by thin membranes called "wings" that are gently moved by the breath. These membranes drive back the breath into the cerebellum.[185] 12. The breath blows through a tube-like vessel and goes to the pineal gland, which is connected to the cerebellum via an opening.[186] The pineal gland receives the breath as it rushes in and transmits it to the so-called spinal marrow. From the spinal marrow, the entire body shares in pneumatic substance, since all the arteries are fed like a branch from this main artery, which ends at the reproductive cavities. Here the sperm from the brain is secreted as it circulates through the loins.[187]

13. The shape of the cerebellum resembles the head of a serpent (this is something frequently chattered about, as I shall demonstrate, in the "knowledge falsely so called").[188]

Six other paired vessels grow out of the brain. They circulate all around the head, maintain the upper parts of the body, and terminate in the head.[189] The seventh pair proceeds from the cerebellum into the remaining lower parts of the body, as I said.

14. The account about this is extensive. From it, both Simon and Valentinus will be found to have taken their starting points—even if they deny it—since they are first of all liars, then heretics.

---

184. The anonymous brain simile here anticipates the brain analogy in the Peratic report (*Ref.* 5.17.11–12; cf. the Naassenes in *Ref.* 5.9.15).

185. For καμάριον, see Galen, *Usu part.* 8.11 (Helmreich, 1:484,9–11).

186. For κωνάριον, see Galen, *Usu part.* 8.14 (Helmreich, 1:489,14–26).

187. Cf. Ps.-Hippocrates, *Generat.* (Περὶ Γονῆς) 1 (Joly, 44); Galen, *Usu part.* 9.4 (Helmreich, 2:12,20). See further, Jared Secord, "Medicine and Sophistry in Hippolytus' *Refutatio*," *StPatr* 65 (2013): 217–24 (222–24).

188. "Knowledge falsely so called" (ψευδωνύμου γνώσεως) is taken from 1 Tim 6:20b.

189. Marcovich adds ἄνω τοῦ (here: "upper parts of the").

ἐπεὶ οὖν καὶ ταῦτα δοκεῖ ἱκανῶς ἡμᾶς ἐκ(τε)θεῖσθαι, πάντα τε τὰ δοκοῦντα <ἀληθῆ> εἶναι τῆς ἐπιγείου φιλοσοφίας δόγματα περιείληπται ἐν τέσσαρσι βιβλίοις, δοκεῖ ἐπὶ τοὺς τούτων χωρεῖν μαθητάς, μᾶλλον δὲ κλεψιλό(γους).

CONCLUSION

Since, then, I have fully presented these additional matters, and since all the doctrines of the earthly philosophy supposed to be true are encompassed in four books, it is fitting to proceed to the disciples of the philosophers—or rather, their plagiarizers.[190]

190. Marcovich adds ἀληθῆ (here: "true").

ΤΟΥ ΚΑΤΑ ΠΑΣΩΝ ΑΙΡΕΣΕΩΝ ΕΛΕΓΧΟΥ Ε

1. Τάδε ἔνεστιν ἐν τῇ πέμπτῃ τοῦ κατὰ πασῶν αἱρέσεων ἐλέγχου·

2. Τίνα οἱ Να<α>σσηνοὶ λέγουσιν, οἱ ἑαυτοὺς γνωστικοὺς ἀποκαλοῦντες, καὶ ὅτι ἐκεῖνα δογματίζουσιν ἃ πρότερον οἱ Ἑλλήνων φιλόσοφοι ἐδογμάτισαν καὶ οἱ τὰ μυστικὰ παραδόντες, ἀφ' ὧν τὰς ἀφορμὰς λαβόντες αἱρέσεις συνεστήσαντο.

3. Καὶ τίνα τὰ τοῖς Περάταις δοκοῦντα, καὶ ὅτι μὴ ἀπὸ τῶν ἁγίων γραφῶν τὸ δόγμα αὐτοῖς συνίσταται, ἀλλ' ἀπὸ ἀστρολογικῆς.

4. Τίς ὁ κατὰ τοὺς Σηθιανοὺς λόγος, καὶ ὅτι ἀπὸ τῶν καθ' Ἕλληνας σοφῶν κλεψιλογήσαντες Μουσαίου καὶ Λίνου καὶ Ὀρφέως τὸ δόγμα ἑαυτῶν συνεκάττυσαν.

5. Τίνα τὰ Ἰουστίνῳ δοκοῦντα, καὶ ὅτι μὴ ἀπὸ τῶν ἁγίων γραφῶν τὸ δόγμα αὐτῷ συνίσταται, ἀλλ' ἐκ τῶν Ἡροδότου τοῦ ἱστοριογράφου τερατολογιῶν.

6. 1. Πάνυ νομίζω πεπονημένως <ἡμᾶς> τὰ δόξαντα πᾶσι τοῖς καθ' Ἕλληνάς τε καὶ βαρβάρους <φιλοσόφοις> περί τε τοῦ θείου καὶ τῆς τοῦ κόσμου δημιουργίας ἐκτεθεῖσθαι ἐν ταῖς πρὸ ταύτης τέσσαρσι βίβλοις· ὧν οὐδὲ τὰ περίεργα ἀποκαλύψας, οὐ τὸν τυχόντα πόνον ἀναδέδεγμαι τοῖς ἐντυγχάνουσι, προτρεπόμενος πολλοὺς πρὸς φιλομάθ(ειαν) καὶ ἀσφάλειαν τῆς περὶ τὴν ἀλήθειαν γνώσεως. 2. περιλείπεται τοίνυν ἐπὶ τὸν τῶν αἱρέσεων ἔλεγχον ὁρμᾶν· (τ)ού(του) χάριν καὶ τὰ προειρημένα ἡμῖν ἐκτεθείμεθα· ἀφ' ὧν τὰς ἀφορμὰς μετασχόντες οἱ αἱρεσιάρχαι, δίκην παλαιορράφων (συγκ)αττύσαντες πρὸς τὸν

BOOK 5

[TABLE OF CONTENTS]

1. These are the contents of the fifth book of the *Refutation of All Heresies.*

2. The teaching of the Naassenes, who call themselves "gnostics." The proof that what they pronounce, the philosophers of the Greeks and tradents of the mysteries pronounced beforehand. The Naassenes took their starting points from them and concocted heresies.

3. The teachings of the Peratai, and the proof that they composed their teaching not from the holy scriptures but from astrology.

4. The Sethian report, with proof that they patched together their teaching by plagiarizing from the Greek sages Musaios, Linos, and Orpheus.

5. The teachings of Justin, with proof that he composed his doctrine not from the holy scriptures but from the fantastical tales of the historical writer Herodotos.

INTRODUCTION

6. 1. I believe that, with great toil, I have in the previous four books fully presented the theories of all Greek and foreign philosophers about the divine and the fashioning of the world—whose meddlesome inquiries I have exposed.[1] I have not published any old labor for my readers, since I have exhorted many to diligent study and secure knowledge concerning truth. 2. What remains for the present is to begin the refutation of heresies. It was for this purpose that I presented the foregoing teachings. From them, the chief heretics received their starting points. They, like shoe menders, patched together doctrines to fit their peculiar meaning and pre-

1. Duncker and Schneidewin added φιλοσόφοις ("philosophers").

ἴδιον νοῦν, τὰ τῶν παλαιῶν σφάλματα ὡς καινὰ παρέθεσαν τοῖς πλανᾶσθαι δυναμένοις, ὡς ἐν τοῖς ἀκολούθοις δείξομεν.

3. Τὸ λοιπὸν προκαλεῖται ἡμᾶς ὁ χρόνος ἐπὶ τὴν τῶν προκειμένων πραγματείαν χωρεῖν, ἄρξασθαι δὲ ἀπὸ τῶν τετολμηκότων τὸν αἴτιον τῆς πλάνης γενόμενον ὄφιν ὑμνεῖν διά τινων ἐφηυρημένων κατὰ <τὴν> αὐτοῦ ἐνέργειαν λόγων. οἱ οὖν ἱερεῖς καὶ προστάται τοῦ δόγματος γεγένηνται πρῶτοι ἐπικληθέντες Νaaσσηνοί, τῇ Ἑβραΐδι φωνῇ οὕτως ὠνομασμένοι—νάας γὰρ ὁ ὄφις καλεῖται·—4. μετὰ δὲ ταῦτα ἐπεκάλεσαν ἑαυτοὺς γνωστικούς, φάσκοντες μόνοι τὰ βάθη γινώσκειν. ἐξ ὧν ἀπομερισθέντες πολλοὶ πολυσχιδῆ τὴν αἵρεσιν

sented the errors of the ancients as newfangled teachings to those susceptible to deceit—as I will show in what follows.

NAASSENES

3. For what remains, time bids me to advance to the discussion of those heresies that I have proposed, and to begin with those who have dared to sing hymns to the one who became the cause of deceit—the snake—by means of certain lyrics invented under his influence.[2] Now the priests and leaders of this teaching were first called "Naassenes."[3] They took this name from the Hebrew language (for the snake in Hebrew is called *naas*).[4] 4. Later, they called themselves "gnostics," claiming that they alone know [γινώσκειν] the deep mysteries.[5] From these people, many splintered off

---

2. Our author thematically groups the Naassenes, Peratai, and Sethians together based on snake imagery. In *Ref.* 5.11.1, he compares them to the many heads of the hydra, and in 5.6.6 he asserts that they all derived their starting points from the snake (= Satan). Since, apparently, Justin presents the angel Naas ("Snake") as a main character (5.26.4), he also finds himself among the "snake heresies."

3. Richard Reitzenstein viewed the Naassene report (which he called a "Sermon" [*Predigt*]) as "a pagan text with gnostic-Christian scholia … excerpted by an opponent who did not know this state of affairs, and thus first used by" our author (*Poimandres: Studien zur griechisch-ägyptischen und frühchristlichen Literature* [Leipzig: Teubner, 1904], 82). In a later publication, Reitzenstein conceded influence from Hellenistic Jews because many passages from the Hebrew Bible could not be excised without violence (Reitzenstein and H. H. Schaeder, *Studien zum antiken Synkretismus aus Iran und Griechenland* [Leipzig: Teubner, 1926], 105–6). Josef Frickel also assumed a pagan origin and proposed two gnostic revisions (*Hellenistische Erlösung in christlicher Deutung: Die gnostischen Naassenerschrift; Quellenkritische Studien, Strukturanalyse, Schichtenscheidung, Rekonstruction der Anthropos-Lehrschrift* [Leiden: Brill, 1984], 116–71). More recently, Maria Grazia Lancellotti and Tuomas Rasimus consider the Sermon to be a genuinely Christian attempt to explain Greco-Roman myths from a consistent ideology (Lancellotti, *The Naassenes: A Gnostic Identity among Judaism, Christianity, Classical and Ancient Near Eastern Traditions*, FARG 35 [Münster: Ugarit-Verlag, 2000], 10–29; Rasimus, *Paradise Reconsidered in Gnostic Mythmaking: Rethinking Sethianism in Light of the Ophite Evidence*, NHMS 68 [Leiden: Brill, 2009], 187–88).

4. For the Hebrew נחש, see BDB, 618. Our author will also define *naas* in *Ref.* 5.9.11–12. On the snake imagery among the Naassenes, see Rasimus, *Paradise*, 82–83.

5. Cf. 1 Cor 2:12 (τὰ βάθη τοῦ θεοῦ); Rom 11:33 (Ὦ βάθος πλούτου); Clem Alex., *Strom.* 5.13.88.5 (τὰ τῆς γνώσεως βάθη); *Ref.* 6.30.7 ("Valentinus"); Acts Thom. 143 (Jesus is the "son of Depth," *NTApoc* 2:396). See further Heinrich Schlier, "βάθος," *TDNT* 1:517–18. If the Naassenes called themselves "knowers"/"gnostics" (cf. *Ref.* 5.8.1; 5.11.1; 5.23.3), they were not necessarily part of the "gnostic school" (Iren., *Haer.*

ἐποίησαν <οὖσαν> μίαν, διαφόροις ὀνόμασι τὰ αὐτὰ διηγούμενοι, ὡς διελέγξει προβαίνων ὁ λόγος.

Οὗτοι <πρὸ> τῶν ἄλλων ἁπάντων παρὰ τὸν αὑτῶν λόγον τιμῶσιν ἄνθρωπον καὶ υἱὸν ἀνθρώπου· ἔστι δὲ <ὁ> ἄνθρωπος οὗτος ἀρσενόθηλυς, καλεῖται δὲ Ἀδάμας παρ' αὐτοῖς. 5. ὕμνοι δὲ εἰς αὐτὸν γεγόνασι πολλοὶ καὶ ποικίλοι· οἱ δὲ ὕμνοι, ὡς δι' ὀλίγων εἰπεῖν, λέγονται παρ' αὐτοῖς τοιοῦτόν τινα τρόπον·

ἀπὸ σοῦ πατὴρ καὶ διὰ σὲ μήτηρ,
τὰ δύο ἀθάνατα ὀνόματα, αἰώνων γονεῖς,
πολῖτα οὐρανοῦ,
μεγαλώνυμε ἄνθρωπε.

6. διαιροῦσι δὲ αὐτὸν ὡς Γηρυόνην τριχῇ· ἔστι γὰρ τούτου, φασί, τὸ μὲν νοερόν, τὸ δὲ ψυχικόν, τὸ δὲ χοϊκόν, καὶ νομίζουσιν εἶναι τὴν γνῶσιν αὐτοῦ

and split the heresy into many factions. Although the heresy is essentially one, these schismatics narrated the same teachings with different terminology, as the forthcoming report will prove.

THE GOD "HUMAN" AND HIS THREE ASPECTS. According to their own report, these people honor above all others the "Human" and the "Son of the Human."[6] This Human is androgynous. They call him "Adamas."[7] 5. There have arisen many hymns to him of all sorts. The hymns that they sing, to cite a sample, are of this character:

From you, O you Citizen of heaven,
O Human whose name is great,
Comes father, and because of you there is mother—
The two immortal names, parents of aeons![8]

6. They divide him in three ways like Geryon, for he has, they say, intellectual, animate, and earthly aspects.[9] Moreover, they suppose that knowledge of him is the beginning of the ability to know God. As they say:

1.11.1). See further Luise Abramowski, *Drei christologische Untersuchungen*, BZNW 45 (Berlin: de Gruyter, 1981), 53–54; M. J. Edwards, "Gnostics and Valentinians in the Church Fathers," *JTS* 40 (1989): 26–47 (31–32).

6. Marcovich adds πρό to this sentence. Hans-Martin Schenke argued that both the high God and the mediate deity in Naassene thought are called Human, while only the mediate Human became stuck in a human body (*Der Gott "Mensch" in der Gnosis* [Göttingen: Vandenhoeck & Ruprecht, 1962], 57–58). For Lancellotti, only the Naassene "second God" is the Human, but split into two aspects: one unformed, one trapped in matter (*Naassenes*, 75–77, 80, 82).

7. The name Ἀδάμας relates to the name of the protoplast Ἀδάμ, the adjective ἀδάματος ("unconquered"), and the hardest metal ἀδάμας ("adamant") (*Ref.* 5.7.35). See further Roelof van den Broek, "Naassenes," *DGWE* 820–22. For the Son of the Human in the "gnostic" Sondergut, see Mogens Müller, *The Expression 'Son of Man' and the Development of Christology: A History of Interpretation* (Sheffield: Equinox, 2008), 38–41.

8. The language of this hymn reappears in *Ref.* 8.12.5 (Monoïmos). See further Bergman, "Kleine Beiträge," 83.

9. In our author's epitome (*Ref.* 10.9.1), the one triply divided is apparently the Son of the Human (cf. Monoïmos in *Ref.* 8.13.3–4). As the Logos of God, the Son of the Human contains all the forms of reality. He is the paradigm for noetic, material, and animate beings. In him, all three levels of being are noetic. For Geryon, see *Ref.* 5.8.4 below.

ἀρχὴν τοῦ δύνασθαι γνῶναι τὸν θεόν, λέγοντες οὕτως· «ἀρχὴ τελειώσεως γνῶσις ἀ(νθρώπου, θεοῦ) δὲ γνῶσις ἀπηρτισμένη τελείωσις».

7. ταῦτα δὲ πάντα, φησί, τὰ νοερὰ καὶ ψυχικὰ καὶ χοϊκὰ κατεχώρησε καὶ κατῆλ(θεν εἰ)ς ἕνα ἄνθρωπον ὁμοῦ, Ἰησοῦν τὸν ἐκ τῆς Μαρίας γεγεννημένον, καὶ ἐλάλ(ουν), φησίν, ὁμοῦ κατὰ τὸ αὐτὸ οἱ τρεῖς οὗτοι ἄνθρωποι ἀπὸ τῶν ἰδίων οὐσιῶν τοῖς ἰδίοις ἕκαστος. ἔστι γὰρ τῶν ὅλων τρία γένη κατ' αὐτούς, ἀγγελικόν, ψυχικόν, χοϊκόν· καὶ τρεῖς ἐκκλησίαι, ἀγγελική, ψυχική, χοϊκή· ὀνόματα δὲ αὐταῖς ἐκλεκτή, κλητή, αἰχμάλωτος.

7. 1. Ταῦτά ἐστιν ἀπὸ πολλῶν πάνυ λόγων τὰ κεφάλ(αια), ἅ φησί παραδεδωκέναι Μαριάμμη τὸν Ἰάκωβον, τοῦ κυρίου τὸν ἀδελφόν. Ἵν' οὖν μήτε Μαριάμμη<ς> ἔτι καταψεύδωνται οἱ ἀσεβεῖς, μήτε Ἰακώβου, μήτε τοῦ σωτῆρος αὐτοῦ, ἔλθωμεν ἐπὶ τὰς τελετάς—ὅθεν αὐτοῖς οὗτος ὁ μῦθος—, εἰ δοκεῖ, ἐπὶ τὰς βαρβαρικάς τε καὶ Ἑλληνικάς, καὶ ἴδωμεν ὡς τὰ κρυπτὰ καὶ ἀπόρρητα πάντων ὁμοῦ συναγ<αγ>όντες οὗτοι μυστήρια τῶν ἐθνῶν, καταψευδόμενοι τοῦ Χριστοῦ ἐξαπατῶσι τοὺς ταῦτα οὐκ εἰδότας <ὄν>τα τῶν ἐθνῶν ὄργια.

2. ἐπεὶ γοῦν ὑπόθεσις αὐτοῖς ὁ ἄνθρωπός ἐστιν Ἀδάμας καὶ λέγουσι γεγράφθαι περὶ αὐτοῦ «τὴν γενεὰν αὐτοῦ τίς διηγήσεται», μάθετε πῶς κατὰ μέρος παρὰ τῶν ἐθνῶν τὴν ἀνεξεύρετον καὶ διάφορον τοῦ ἀνθρώπου γενεὰν λαβόντες ἐπιπλάσσουσι τῷ Χριστῷ.

"Knowledge of the Human is the beginning of perfection, but knowledge of God is completed perfection."[10]

7. All three aspects, he says—intellectual, animate, and earthly—came down and came into one person at once: Jesus born from Mary. These three humans were speaking together at the same time, each individually from their own substances to their own people.[11] There are, according to them, three kinds of people in the universe, angelic, animate, and earthly, and three churches, angelic, animate, and earthly.[12] They are called "the elect," "the called," and "the captive."[13]

7. 1. These are the chief points from a host of speeches that, he says, James the Lord's brother delivered to Mariamme.[14] In order that these sacrilegious people might not any longer speak lies about Mariamme or James or the Savior himself, let us proceed to their mystery rites (from which their story derives)—to the rites, if you please, of both foreign peoples and Greeks—and let us observe how they, amassing the hidden and secret mysteries of all the pagans, speak falsely of Christ, and so deceive those who do not know that these are pagan rites.[15]

2. Now since the Human Adamas is their main character, and they claim that the scriptural phrase "who will relate his generation?"[16] was written about him, learn in every detail how they took his "undiscoverable and superior generation" from the pagans and apply this fiction to Christ.

---

10. Repeated in *Ref.* 5.8.38 below. Cf. Iren., *Haer.* 1.6.1 (*homines qui perfectam agnitionem habent de deo* ["people who have perfect knowledge about God"]).

11. Cf. *Ref.* 5.12.4 (τριδύναμον ἄνθρωπον καλούμενον Χριστόν, affirmed by the Peratai), and the three Adams in Orig. World (NHC II,5) 117.28–35; 122.6–9. See further Antonio Orbe, *Cristología Gnóstica: Introducción a la soteriología de los siglos II y III*, 2 vols. (Madrid: La Editorial Catolica, 1976), 1:416–17.

12. Cf. Iren., *Haer.* 1.8.3 (*tria autem genera hominum ostendisse docent eum: hylicum … animale … spiritale* ["they teach that he manifested three types of human being: material … animate … and spiritual"]).

13. For the called and elect, see Matt 22:14; Rev 17:14.

14. Cf. *Ref.* 10.9.3 (Naassene summary). For Μαριάμμη (Mary Magdalene), see Origen, *Cels.* 5.62; 6.30 (Mariamnites). See further Antti Marjanen, *The Woman Jesus Loved*, NHMS 40 (Leiden: Brill, 1996), 63–64; Silke Petersen, *"Zerstört die Werke der Weiblichkeit!" Maria Magdalena, Salome und andere Jüngerinnen Jesu in christlich-gnostischen Schriften*, NHMS 48 (Leiden: Brill, 1999), 94–195, 296–99. On James, note Gal 1:19; Gos. Thom. 12; Lancellotti, *Naassenes*, 58–67. On both figures, see Bergman, "Kleine Beiträge," 78–87.

15. Marcovich changes τά ("who do not know *the* pagan rites") to ὄντα ("who do not know that these *are* pagan rites").

16. Isa 53:8 LXX.

3. Γῆ δή, φασὶν οἱ Ἕλληνες, ἄνθρωπον ἀνέδωκε πρώτη, καλὸν ἐνεγκαμένη γέρας, μὴ φυτῶν ἀναισθήτων μηδὲ θηρίων ἀλόγων, ἀλλὰ ἡμέρου ζῴου καὶ θεοφιλοῦς ἐθέλουσα μήτηρ γενέσθαι. 4. χαλεπὸν δέ, φησίν, ἐξευρεῖν

εἴτε Βοιωτοῖς Ἀλ<αλ>κομενεὺς ὑπὲρ λίμνης Κηφισίδος ἀνέσχε
πρῶτος ἀνθρώπων·
εἴτε Κουρῆτες ἦσαν Ἰδαῖοι, θεῖον γένος, ἢ Φρύγιο(ι)
Κορύβαντες, οὓς πρώτους ἥλιος ἐπεῖδε δενδροφυεῖς ἀναβλαστάνοντας·
εἴτε προσεληναῖον Ἀρκαδία Πελασγόν, ἢ Ῥαρίας οἰκήτορα Δυ<σ>αύλην
Ἐλευσίν, ἢ Λῆμνος καλλίπαιδα Κάβιρον ἀρρήτῳ ἐτέκνωσεν ὀργιασμῷ·
εἴτε Πελλήνη Φλεγραῖον Ἀλκυονέα, πρεσβύτατον Γιγάντων.
5. Λίβ<υ>ες δὲ Ἰάρβαντά φασι πρωτόγονον αὐχμηρῶν ἀναδύντα
πεδίω<ν> γλυκείας ἀπάρξασθαι Διὸς βαλάνου·
Αἰγυπτίαν δὲ Νεῖλος ἰλὺν ἐπιλιπαίνων <καὶ> μέχρι σήμερον ζωογονῶν,
φησίν,
ὑγρᾷ σαρκούμενα θερμότητι ζῷα [καὶ σῶμα] ἀναδίδωσιν·

DIFFERENT TRADITIONS OF THE FIRST HUMAN. 3. It was Earth, the Greeks say, who first produced a human being. She won a noble prize, since she desired to be the mother not of insensate plants, nor of irrational beasts, but of a gentle animal dear to the gods.[17] 4. But it is difficult to discover, he says,

> whether Alalkomeneus emerged as the first of humans beyond lake Kephisos as the Boiotians believe,[18]
> or whether the Idaian Kouretes, a divine race, were first,
> or the Phrygian Korybantes on whom the Sun first looked when they sprouted forth like trees,
> or whether Arcadia produced Pelasgos, who is more ancient than the moon,[19]
> or whether Eleusis bore Dysaules, dwelling on the Rarian field,[20]
> or whether it was Lemnos who mothered the beautiful child Kabiros by an unuttered rite,
> or whether Pellene mothered Alkyoneus of Phlegra, oldest of giants.[21]
> 5. The Libyans say that Iarbas was the firstborn who rose up from the parched fields to offer the first fruits of Jove's sweet acorn.[22]
> The Nile makes rich the Egyptian mud and generates life till the present day,
> and produces animals whose flesh is formed by moisture and heat.[23]

---

17. Cf. Plato, *Tim.* 41e.

18. Cf. Plutarch in Eusebios, *Praep. ev.* 3.1.6 (Alalkomeneus the earth-born man taught Zeus).

19. Cf. Asios in Pausanias, *Descr.* 8.1.4 ("The godlike Pelasgos … black Earth produced"); Clem. Alex., *Protr.* 1.6.4; Diodoros, *Bibl. hist.* 1.9.3; Origen, *Cels.* 4.36.

20. Dysaules was one of the earth-born people born at Eleusis (Clem. Alex., *Protr.* 20.2). In some traditions, he is the father of Triptolemos; in others, Triptolemos is fathered by Raros (Pausanias, *Descr.* 1.14.3), or Raros is his grandfather (*Suda*, s.v. Ραρίας [Adler, 4:285]). The Rarian field is the site of the first agriculture (Pausanias, *Descr.* 1.38.6). See further Hesychios, *Lexicon*, s.v. Κράναου υἱός.

21. For Pellene and Alkyoneus, see Ps.-Apoll., *Bibl.* 1.6.1–2.

22. Iarbas (Ἰάρβαντα) is Schneidewin's correction of P's τάρβαντα. Wendland prints Γαράμαντα, comparing Vergil, *Aen.* 4.198 (*Garamantide nympha*). Cf. Athenaios, *Deipn.* 2, 54d.

23. Cf. Diodoros, *Bibl. hist.* 1.10.1–7; Pausanias, *Descr.* 8.29.4.

6. Ἀσσύριοι δὲ Ὠάννην ἰχθυοφάγον γενέσθαι παρ' αὐτοῖς,
Χαλδαῖοι δὲ τὸν Ἀδάμ.

καὶ τοῦτον εἶναι φάσκουσι τὸν ἄνθρωπον, ὃν ἀνέδωκεν ἡ γῆ, <σῶμα> μόνον· κεῖσθαι δὲ αὐτὸν ἄπνουν, ἀκίνητον, ἀσάλευτον, ὡς ἀνδριάντα, εἰκόνα ὑπάρχοντα ἐκείνου τοῦ ἄνω, τοῦ ὑμνουμένου Ἀδάμαντος ἀνθρώπου, γενόμενον ὑπὸ δυνάμεων [τῶν] πολλῶν, περὶ ὧν ὁ κατὰ μέρος λόγος ἐστὶν πολύς.

7. Ἵν' οὖν τελέως ᾖ κεκρατημένος ὁ μέγας ἄνθρωπος ἄνωθεν—«ἀφ' οὗ», καθὼς λέγουσι, «πᾶσα πατριὰ ὀνομαζομένη ἐπὶ γῆς καὶ ἐν τοῖς οὐρανοῖς» συνέστηκεν—, ἐδόθη αὐτῷ καὶ ψυχή, ἵνα διὰ τῆς ψυχῆς πάσχῃ καὶ κολάζηται καταδουλούμενον τὸ πλάσμα τοῦ μεγάλου καὶ καλλίστου καὶ τελείου ἀνθρώπου—καὶ γὰρ οὕτως αὐτὸν καλοῦσι.

8. ζητοῦσιν οὖν <αὖ> πάλιν τίς ἐστιν ἡ ψυχὴ καὶ πόθεν καὶ ποταπὴ τὴν φύσιν, ἵν' ἐλθοῦσα εἰς τὸν ἄνθρωπον καὶ κινήσασα καταδουλώσῃ καὶ κολάσῃ τὸ

6. The Assyrians say it was Oannes the fish-eater who arose in their country,[24]
But the Chaldeans say it was Adam.[25]

Now this is the human, they claim, whom Earth brought forth as a body only.[26] He lay without breath, without moving, without stirring—like a statue—as an image of that Human above, Adamas, to whom they sing hymns.[27] The earthly human was generated by many powers. The report about them, when given in detail, is extensive.[28]

SOUL ADDED TO THE FIRST HUMAN. 7. Now, in order that the great Human ("from whom," as they say, "every family named on earth and heaven" is composed) might be completely dominated from the beginning, a soul was given to him as well, so that the enslaved bodily formation of the great, most beautiful, and most perfect Human (for so they call him) might suffer and be punished through his soul.[29]

8. In turn, they investigate the nature, source, and character of the soul that enters the human, sets him in motion, enslaves and punishes the

---

24. Oannes, according to Berossos, was a fish-human hybrid who brought culture to human beings (*FGH* 680, frag. 1.4).

25. The "Chaldeans" refer to the Hebrews. D. L. Page presents this hymn in metrical form (*Poetae melici graeci* [Oxford: Clarendon, 1962], no. 985). R. Scott Birdsall points out that the first-human myths come from areas in the eastern Mediterranean "from Greece through Asia Minor into Mesopotamia and thence back to Egypt and Libya" ("The Naassene Sermon and the Allegorical Tradition: Allegorical Interpretation, Syncretism, and Textual Authority" [PhD diss., Claremont Graduate School, 1984], 212, 231).

26. Marcovich, following Reitzenstein, adds σῶμα ("body").

27. Cf. Gen 1:26; 2:7; Tert., *An.* 23. For ἀκίνητον, see *Ref.* 7.28.3 (Satorneilos). See further Lancellotti, *Naassenes*, 92.

28. Our author may have omitted material here on the creation of the earthly Adam in an attempt to "summarize." Later he will reveal that the direct creator of the earthly Adam is Esaldaios (*Ref.* 5.7.30, end). On the creation of Adam in the likeness of the Human above, see Valentinus, frag. 1 (Völker). See further Lancellotti, *Naassenes*, 87–104; Rasimus, *Paradise*, 187–88.

29. The quote comes from Eph 3:15, cited again in *Ref.* 5.7.35 below. Apparently, as in other gnostic texts, the powers created the earthly Adam to control (in vain) the God-Human above. But they can only punish the human made in the image of the God-Human. On the soul, see Frickel, *Naassenerschrift*, 104–8.

πλάσμα τοῦ τ(ε)λ(είου) ἀνθρώπου· ζητοῦσι δὲ οὐκ ἀπὸ τῶν γραφῶν, ἀλλὰ καὶ τοῦτο ἀπὸ τῶν μυστικῶν.

εἶναι δέ φασι τὴν ψυχὴν δυσεύρετον πάνυ καὶ δυσκατανόητον· οὐ γὰρ μένει ἐπὶ σχήματος οὐδὲ μορφῆς τῆς αὐτῆς πάντοτε, οὐδὲ πάθους ἑνός, ἵνα τις αὐτὴν ἢ τύπῳ εἴπῃ ἢ οὐσίᾳ καταλήψεται. 9. τὰς δὲ ἐξαλλαγὰς ταύτας τὰς ποικίλας ἐν τῷ ἐπιγραφομένῳ κατ' Αἰγυπτίους εὐαγγελίῳ κειμένας ἔχουσιν. ἀποροῦσιν οὖν—καθάπερ οἱ ἄλλοι πάντες τῶν ἐθνῶν ἄνθρωποι—πότερόν ποτε ἐκ τοῦ προόντος ἐστὶν <ἢ> ἐκ τοῦ αὐτογενοῦς ἢ ἐκ τοῦ ἐκκεχυμένου χάους.

καὶ πρῶτον ἐπὶ τὰς Ἀσσυρίων καταφεύγουσι τελετάς, τὴν τριχῇ διαίρεσιν τοῦ ἀνθρώπου κατανοοῦντες· πρῶτοι γὰρ Ἀσσύριοι τὴν ψυχὴν τριμερῆ νομίζουσιν εἶναι καὶ μίαν.

10. Ψυχῆ<ς> δέ, φασί, πᾶσα φύσις, ἄλλη δὲ ἄλλως ὀρέγεται. ἔστι γὰρ ψυχὴ πάντων τῶν γινομένων αἰτία· πάντα γὰρ ὅσα τρέφεται, φησί, καὶ αὔξει, ψυχῆς δεῖται—οὐδὲν γὰρ οὔτε τροφῆς, φησίν, οὔτε αὐξήσεως οἷόν <τέ> ἐστιν ἐπιτυχεῖν ψυχῆς μὴ παρούσης.—καὶ δὲ οἱ λίθοι, φησίν, εἰσὶν ἔμψυχοι·

bodily formation of the perfect Human.[30] They make their investigations not from the scriptures, but this doctrine too is taken from the mysteries.

They say that the soul is extremely hard to discover and to understand. This is because it does not always remain in the same shape or form or in a single condition, so that one might understand it schematically or essentially. 9. (They have these manifold alternations contained in the Gospel according to the Egyptians.)[31] Thus they are at a loss to say (just as all the other pagans) whether the soul was once from the Preexistent or from the Self-Born or from sprawling Chaos.[32]

First of all, they resort to the Assyrian mystery rites in order to understand the threefold division of the human. For it was the Assyrians who first considered the soul to be threefold yet one.[33]

COMMENTARY ON A HYMN TO ATTIS (*REF.* 5.9.8). 10. They say that every nature strains for soul in various ways.[34] This is because soul is the cause of all generated reality. Everything nourished and growing, he says, needs a soul. For when a soul is not present, he says, nothing can obtain either nourishment or growth. Even the stones, he says, are ensouled, for they

30. Schneidewin and Duncker replace αὐτόν in P with αὖ. Frickel prefers αὐτοί, emphasizing the subject "they" (*Naassenerschrift*, 56–57). It is odd that the soul is used to enslave the body (it is often the reverse, as in Corp. herm. frag. 23.25 [Nock and Festugière]). The soul is apparently under the control of the (evil) powers.

31. Frickel notes that ἐξαλλαγάς ("alternations") are reminiscent of transmigrations (*Naassenerschrift*, 31; cf. Corp. herm. 10.7: τούτων τοίνυν τῶν ψυχῶν πολλαὶ αἱ μεταβολαί). The Gospel according to the Egyptians mentioned here is not the book of the same title found at Nag Hammadi but apparently the Gospel cited by several patristic writers (*NTApoc* 1:209–15). See further Lancellotti, *Naassenes*, 315–16.

32. Technically, chaos is a cosmological principle, not one of the two theological principles (the Human and Son of Human) mentioned before (*Ref.* 5.6.5). The "Preexistent" is the Human who gives birth to the Son of the Human (cf. *Ref.* 5.9.1 below). The Son of the Human is here apparently called the "Selfborn." The ἤ ("or") separating the Preexistent from the Selfborn is an addition of Marcovich, following Miller. Marcovich, following Bunsen, emends P's αὐτοῦ γένους to αὐτογενοῦς ("Selfborn"). This emendation is criticized by Frickel, who prefers the correction of Abramowski to αὐτοῦ γε νοός ("his Mind") (*Naassenerschrift*, 60-61). For both Mind and sprawling chaos, cf. the initial lines of the Naassene Psalm (*Ref.* 5.10.2).

33. For the tripartite division, see *Ref.* 5.6.6 above.

34. Cf. Plutarch, *Fac.* 944e (ψυχῆς ... πᾶσα φύσις, ἄλλη δὲ ἄλλως ὀρέγεται). For comments, see Birdsall, "Naassene Sermon," 262–65. The phrase reappears below in *Ref.* 5.9.4; 7.22.8 ("Basileides"). The Soul (or World Soul) allegorically represents Attis/Adamas.

ἔχουσι γὰρ τὸ αὐξητικόν· αὔξησις δὲ οὐκ ἄν ποτε γένοιτο χωρὶς τροφῆς—κατὰ προσθήκην γὰρ αὔξει τὰ αὐξανόμενα· ἡ δὲ προσθήκη τροφὴ τοῦ τρεφομένου.

11. πᾶσα οὖν φύσις «ἐπουρανίων», φησί, «καὶ ἐπιγείων καὶ καταχθονίων» ψυχῆς ὀρέγεται. καλοῦσι δὲ Ἀσσύριοι τὸ τοιοῦτον Ἄδωνιν ἢ Ἐνδυμίωνα· καὶ ὅταν μὲν Ἄδωνις καλῆται, Ἀφροδίτη, φησίν, ἐρᾷ καὶ ἐπιθυμεῖ τῆς ψυχῆς, <τουτέστι> τοῦ τοιούτου ὀνόματος—Ἀφροδίτη δὲ ἡ γένεσίς ἐστι κατ᾽ αὐτούς·—12. ὅταν δὲ ἡ Περσεφόνη—ἡ καὶ Κόρη—ἐρᾷ τοῦ Ἀδώνιδος, θνητή, φησί, τὶς τῆς Ἀφροδίτης κεχωρισμένη—<τουτέστι> τῆς γενέσεως—ἐστὶν [ἡ] ψυχή· ἐὰν δὲ ἡ Σελήνη Ἐνδυμίωνος εἰς ἐπιθυμίαν ἔλθῃ καὶ ἔρωτα μορφῆς, ἡ τῶν ὑψηλοτέρων, φησί, κτίσις προσδεῖται καὶ <αὐτὴ> ψυχῆς. 13. ἐὰν δέ, φησίν, ἡ μήτηρ τῶν θεῶν ἀποκόψῃ τὸν Ἄττιν—καὶ αὐτὴ τοῦτον ἔχουσα

have the ability to grow.[35] Growth could never occur without nourishment—for whatever grows, grows by addition. The addition is the nourishment of the one nourished.[36]

A. ASSYRIAN MYSTERIES ABOUT THE HUMAN. 11. Thus every "heavenly and earthly and underworldly" nature, he says, yearns for soul.[37] The Assyrians call this sort of thing "Adonis" or "Endymion."[38] When it is called "Adonis," he says, Aphrodite loves and desires the soul (that is, the soul of this sort of person). For them, Aphrodite represents generation. 12. When Persephone (or Kore) loves Adonis, the soul is separated from Aphrodite (that is, generation) and is subject to death.[39] But whenever Selene desires Endymion and loves his form, the very system of the higher realities stands in need of a soul.[40] 13. But if, he says, the Mother of Gods castrates Attis—though

35. Cf. Demokritos, DK 68 A164.

36. Cf. Aristotle, *De an.* 2.4, 416b10–13 with the comments of Birdsall, "Naassene Sermon," 267–68.

37. The quote derives from Phil 2:10. Similar language reappears below in *Ref.* 5.8.22; 5.16.14 (Peratai).

38. The identity of "this sort of thing" (τὸ τοιοῦτον) is not clear. In *Ref.* 5.7.28 the phrase refers to a phallic object or statue. Adonis appears in the Attis hymn (*Ref.* 5.9.8). For the myth of Adonis, see Ps.-Apoll., *Bibl.* 3.14.3–4; Ovid, *Metam.* 10.469–559, 708–739. For the myth of Endymion, see Ps.-Apollodoros, *Bibl.* 1.7.5; 3.14.4; Plutarch, *Fac.* 945a–b.

39. According to the myth, Aphrodite loved the child Adonis, put him in a chest, and asked Persephone to take care of him. When the latter would not give him back, Zeus judged that Adonis should spend four months with Persephone in the underworld, and the rest of the year with him and Aphrodite. See further Hoda Adra, *Le mythe d'Adonis: Culte et interpretation* (Beirut: Université Libanaise, 1985), 9–70; Hélène Tuzet, *Mort et resurrection d'Adonis: Étude de l'évolution d'un mythe* (Paris: Librairie José Corti, 1987), 11–94.

40. Adonis desired by Aphrodite, Persephone, and Selene is "thrice-desired Adonis" according to the hymn (*Ref.* 5.9.8). For the epithet, see Bion of Smyrna, *Epitaph. Adon.* 58; Theokritos, *Id.* 15.86 (τριφίλητος Ἄδωνις). According to J. Montserrat-Torrents, Adonis is an allegory of the Platonic tripartite soul. Aphrodite is the desiring part, Persephone is the spirited part; when Adonis is replaced by Endymion, Selene comes as the rational part ("La notice d'Hippolyte sur les Naassènes," *StPatr* 17 [1982]: 231–42 [236]). For Birdsall, Adonis is the soul. His dalliance with Aphrodite and Persephone are symbolic of the soul's involvement in procreation and death. "Endymion's affair with Selene points to the need of the higher realms … for soul" ("Naassene Sermon," 213). The three goddesses are related to the three levels of creation in Phil 2:10. The earthly corresponds to Aphrodite; the subterranean corresponds to Persephone; and the heavenly corresponds to Selene (Miroslav Marcovich, *Stud-*

ἐρώμενον—ἡ τῶν ὑπερκοσμίων, φησί, καὶ αἰωνίων ἄνω μακαρία φύσις τὴν ἀρρενικὴν δύναμιν τῆς ψυχῆς ἀνακαλεῖται πρὸς αὑτήν· ἔστι γάρ, φησίν, ἀρσενόθηλυς ὁ ἄνθρωπος.

14. κατὰ τοῦτον οὖν αὐτοῖς τὸν λόγον, πάνυ πονηρὸν καὶ κεκωλυμένον, <οὐ> κατὰ τὴν διδασκαλίαν ἡ γυναικὸς πρὸς ἄνδρα δεδειγμένη καθέστηκεν ὁμιλία. 15. ἀπεκόπη γάρ, φησίν, ὁ Ἄττις—τουτέστιν ἀπὸ τῶν χοϊκῶν τῆς κτίσεως κάτωθεν <ἐχωρίσθη> μερῶν—, καὶ ἐπὶ τὴν αἰωνίαν ἄνω μετελήλυθεν οὐσίαν, ὅπου, φησίν, οὐκ ἔστιν οὔτε θῆλυ οὔτε ἄρσεν, ἀλλὰ «καινὴ κτίσις», «καινὸς ἄνθρωπος», ὅ<ς> ἐστιν ἀρσενόθηλυς. ποῦ δὲ ἄνω λέγουσι, κατὰ τὸν οἰκεῖον ἐλθὼν δείξω τόπον.

16. Μαρτυρεῖν δέ φασιν αὐτῶν τῷ λόγῳ οὐχ ἁπλῶς μόνην τὴν Ῥέαν, ἀλλὰ γάρ, ὡς ἔπος εἰπεῖν, ὅλην τὴν κτίσιν. καὶ τοῦτο εἶναι τὸ λεγόμενον ὑπὸ τοῦ λόγου διασαφοῦσι·

still possessing him as her beloved—the blessed, higher nature of the supercosmic beings and aeons calls up the male power of the soul to itself (for the Human, he says, is androgynous).[41]

14. According to this doctrine of theirs, the intercourse of a woman with a man is exposed and established as an entirely evil and forbidden act, not in accord with their teaching.[42] For Attis is castrated, he says. 15. That is, he is removed from the earthly parts of creation down here and has crossed over to the eternal reality above, where, he says, there is neither female nor male, but a "new creation," a "new human being" who is androgynous.[43] (Where they say "above" is, I will indicate when I come to the proper place.[44])

16. They say that not only Rhea, but indeed, one might say, all creation attests to their teaching.[45] Indeed they make clear that this is what is meant by the scriptural verse:

---

ies in Graeco-Roman Religions and Gnosticism [Leiden: Brill, 1988], 87). For κτίσις as "system/structure," see 1 Pet 2:13.

41. For Attis mythology, see Pausanias, *Descr.* 7.17.10–12; Arnobius, *Adv. nat.* 5.5–7; Ovid, *Fasti* 4.221–244. See further Lynn E. Roller, *In Search of God the Mother: The Cult of Anatolian Cybele* (Berkeley: University of California Press, 1999), 237–59; Philippe Borgeaud, *Mother of the Gods: From Cybele to the Virgin Mary*, trans. Lysa Hochroth (Baltimore: Johns Hopkins, 2005), 102–7; Maria Grazia Lancellotti, *Attis: Between Myth and History; King, Priest and God*, RGRW 149 (Leiden: Brill, 2002), 16–118; Jaime Alvar, *Romanising Oriental Gods: Myth, Salvation and Ethics in the Cults of Cybele, Isis and Mithras*, trans. Richard Gordon (Leiden: Brill, 2008), 63–74. For a history of scholarship on Attis, see John North, "Power and Its Redefinitions: The Vicissitudes of Attis," in Bricault and Bonnet, *Panthée*, 279–93. For Attis's castration allegorized, see Clem. Alex., *Protr.* 19.4; Julian, *Or.* 5.9, 168d–169b; Sallustius, *Diis mund.* 4.7–11. The "male power" of the soul is the soul cut off from generation. See further on Attis *Ref.* 5.8.22–9.6 below.

42. Marcovich adds οὐ ("not").

43. Reitzenstein supplies ἐχωρίσθη. For the language of sexlessness, see Gal 3:28; Mark 12:25 par.; Gos. Thom. 22; Philo, *Opif.* 134; Clem. Alex., *Strom.* 3.13.92.2–93.1; *Paed.* 1.10.3; Corp. herm. frag. 24.8 (Festugière and Nock); Tert., *An.* 36. For the language of "new creation," see 2 Cor 5:17; Gal 6:15; and our own author's teaching in *Ref.* 10.33.15. For the "new human being," see Eph 4:24; *Ref.* 6.35.4 ("Valentinus"); [Hipp.], *Noet.* 17. The denial of sex seems extreme, yet it is deeply rooted in Christian eschatology. See B. Lang, "No Sex in Heaven: The Logic of Procreation, Death, and Eternal Life in the Judaeo-Christian Tradition," in *Mélanges bibliques et orientaux en l'honneur de M. Mathias Delcor*, ed. A. Caquot, S. Légasse, and M. Tardieu (Neukirchen-Vluyn: Neukirchener, 1985), 237–53.

44. Cf. *Ref.* 5.7.38–41 below.

45. The reference to Rhea points forward to the Attis hymn (*Ref.* 5.9.8).

τὰ γὰρ ἀόρατα αὐτοῦ ἀπὸ τῆς κτίσεως τοῦ κόσμου τοῖς ποιήμασιν αὐτοῦ νοούμενα καθορᾶται, ἥ τε ἀΐδιος αὐτοῦ δύναμις καὶ θειότης, πρὸς τὸ εἶναι αὐτοὺς ἀναπολογήτους· διότι γνόντες τὸν θεὸν οὐχ ὡς θεὸν ἐδόξασαν ἢ ηὐχαρίστησαν, ἀλλ' ἐματαιώθη ἡ ἀσύνετος αὐτῶν καρδία. 17. φάσκοντες γὰρ εἶναι σοφοὶ ἐμωράνθησαν, καὶ ἤλλαξαν τὴν δόξαν τοῦ ἀφθάρτου θεοῦ ἐν ὁμοιώμασιν εἰκόνος φθαρτοῦ ἀνθρώπου καὶ πετεινῶν καὶ τετραπόδων καὶ ἑρπετῶν. διὸ καὶ παρέδωκεν αὐτοὺς ὁ θεὸς εἰς πάθη ἀτιμίας· αἵ τε γὰρ θήλειαι αὐτῶν μετήλλαξαν τὴν φυσικὴν χρῆσιν εἰς τὴν παρὰ φύσιν.

—τί δέ ἐστιν ἡ φυσικὴ κατ' αὐτοὺς χρῆσις, ὕστερον ἐροῦμεν.—

18. ὁμοίως τε καὶ οἱ ἄρρενες ἀφέντες τὴν φυσικὴν χρῆσιν τῆς θηλείας ἐξεκαύθησαν ἐν τῇ ὀρέξει αὐτῶν εἰς ἀλλήλους, ἄρρενες ἐν ἄρρεσι τὴν ἀσχημοσύνην κατεργαζόμενοι.

ἀσχημοσύνη δέ ἐστιν ἡ πρώτη καὶ μακαρία κατ' αὐτοὺς ἀσχημάτιστος οὐσία, ἡ πάντων σχημάτων τοῖς σχηματιζομένοις αἰτία.

καὶ τὴν ἀντιμισθίαν ἣν ἔδει τῆς πλάνης αὐτῶν ἐν ἑαυτοῖς ἀπολαμβάνοντες.

19. ἐν γὰρ τούτοις τοῖς λόγοις, οἷς εἴρηκεν ὁ Παῦλος, ὅλον φασὶ συνέχεσθαι τὸ κρύφιον αὐτῶν καὶ ἄρρητον τῆς μακαρίας μυστήριον ἡδονῆς· ἡ γὰρ ἐπαγγελία τοῦ λουτροῦ οὐκ ἄλλη τίς ἐστι κατ' αὐτοὺς ἢ τὸ εἰσαγαγεῖν εἰς

> For from the creation of the world, his invisible workings have been understood and observed by what he has made—namely, his eternal power and Godhead—in order to render them without excuse. Thus, although they knew God, they did not glorify him as God or offer him thanks, but their senseless heart was made foolish. 17. For although they claimed to be sages, they became fools, and exchanged the glory of the incorruptible God into the likeness of an image of corruptible humanity, birds, cattle, and reptiles. And so God handed them over to dishonorable passions. Even their females exchanged the natural use for what is against nature.[46]

(What "the natural use" means to them, I will explain later.)

> 18. Likewise the males, after abandoning the natural use of the female, were fired in their yearning for one another—males with males performed the work of formlessness.[47]

For them, formlessness [ἀσχημοσύνη] means the primal and blessed Being. According to them, he is formless [ἀσχημάτιστος] and the cause of all forms for entities that are formed.[48]

> And they received within themselves the reward due for their deviation.[49]

19. In these words, spoken by Paul, they say that their entire hidden and secret mystery of blessed pleasure is contained. For the promise of the washing is for them nothing else than the introduction into unfading

---

46. Paul's text has been abbreviated (Rom 1:20–27a, minus vv. 24–25).

47. Rom 1:27b. Ἀσχημοσύνη, usually translated "shame" or "disgrace," has here been translated "formlessness" to bring out the etymological play of the Naassene writer.

48. Among the Naassenes, spiritualized sexual activity between spiritual "men" (i.e., those shorn of their female or earthly element) produces something good—not disgrace (ἀσχημοσύνη) but that which is without form (ἀσχημάτιστος). Plato called the world of Forms ἀσχηματίστος (*Phaedr.* 247c6–7; cf. *Parm.* 137d9–10). For the Naassene writer, the Unformed One is the source of spiritual generation (or formation). On this kind of exegetical inversion, see Michael Williams, *Rethinking "Gnosticism": An Argument for Dismantling a Dubious Category* (Princeton: Princeton University Press, 1996), 56–78.

49. Rom 1:27c.

τὴν ἀμάραντον ἡδονὴν τὸν λουόμενον κατ' αὐτοὺς ζῶντι ὕδατι καὶ χριόμενον ἀλ<ά>λῳ χρίσματι.

20. Οὐ μόνον αὐτῶν ἐπιμαρτυρεῖν φασι τῷ λόγῳ τὰ Ἀσσυρίων μυστήρια καὶ Φρυγῶν, <ἀλλὰ καὶ τὰ Αἰγυπτίων> περὶ τὴν τῶν γεγονότων καὶ γινομένων καὶ ἐσομένων ἔτι μακαρίαν κρυβομένην ὁμοῦ καὶ φανερουμένην φύσιν, ἥνπερ φησὶν <τὴν> ἐντὸς ἀνθρώπου βασιλείαν οὐρανῶν ζητουμένην. περὶ ἧς διαρρήδην ἐν τῷ κατὰ Θωμᾶν ἐπιγραφομένῳ εὐαγγελίῳ παραδιδόασι λέγοντες οὕτως· «ἐμὲ ὁ ζητῶν εὑρήσει ἐν παιδίοις ἀπὸ ἐτῶν ἑπτά· ἐκεῖ γὰρ ἐν τῷ τεσσαρεσκαιδεκάτῳ αἰῶνι κρυβόμενος φανεροῦμαι».

21. τοῦτο δὲ οὐκ ἔστιν Χριστοῦ, ἀλλὰ Ἱπποκράτους λέγοντος «ἑπτὰ ἐτῶν παῖς πατρὸς ἥμισυ»· ὅθεν οὗτοι, τὴν ἀρχέγονον φύσιν τῶν ὅλων ἐν ἀρχεγόνῳ τιθέμενοι σπέρματι, τὸ Ἱπποκράτειον ἀκηκοότες ὅτι ἐστὶν ἥμισυ πατρὸς παιδίον

pleasure of one who is washed with their "living" water and anointed with "unspeakable" ointment.[50]

B. EGYPTIAN MYSTERIES ABOUT THE HUMAN. 20. But not only, they say, do the Assyrian and Phrygian mysteries testify to their teaching but also those of the Egyptians concerning the blessed nature—both hidden and revealed—of things that were, that are, and will yet be.[51] He calls this blessed nature the "kingdom of heaven sought from within a human being."[52] Concerning this kingdom, they transmit a direct quote from the Gospel entitled According to Thomas: "The one who seeks me will find me in little children seven years old and up. For there, though hidden in the fourteenth aeon, I am being revealed."[53]

21. But this teaching is not Christ's but that of Hippokrates, who says, "a boy of seven is half a father."[54] Hence these heretics, depositing the primordial nature of the universe in a primordial seed, heard Hippokrates's

50. Baptism and chrism were common Christian sacraments at this time. For living water, see John 4:10. The "unspeakable" (ἀλάλῳ) ointment is an emendation for P's ἄλλω ("other"). Cf. *Ref.* 5.9.22.

51. Reitzenstein and Wendland add ἀλλὰ καὶ τὰ Αἰγυπτίων (here: "but also those of the Egyptians").

52. Cf. Luke 17:21 (ἡ βασιλεία τοῦ θεοῦ ἐντὸς ὑμῶν ἐστιν); *Ref.* 5.8.8; Gos. Thom. 3–4, 103–5. See further Josef Frickel, "Naassener oder Valentinianer?" in *Gnosis and Gnosticism: Papers Read at the Eighth International Conference on Patristic Studies (Oxford, September 3rd–8th 1979)*, ed. Martin Krause, NHS 17 (Leiden: Brill, 1981), 104–12.

53. On children, see Matt 11:25; 18:3–5; 19:14. Steven R. Johnson argues that *Ref.* 5.7.20 presents a conflation of elements from Greek Gos. Thom. 2–5. For being hidden and revealed, see Gos. Thom. 5.1–2; for seeking, see 2.1; for the kingdom within a person, see 3.3; for the one who seeks and finds, see 2.1; and for the little children, see 4.1. The conflation is due to the Naassene writer and not to our author. Johnson leaves open whether or not the Naassene writer had a distinct recension of the Gospel of Thomas ("Hippolytus's *Refutatio* and the Gospel of Thomas," *JECS* 18 [2010]: 305–26 [esp. 314–20]).

54. "According to Greek belief, a boy reaches … puberty with the age of fourteen; that is why the Naassene Jesus reveals himself in the fourteenth Aeon" (Marcovich, *Studies*, 113). Cf. Theon of Smyrna, *Exp. math.* (Hiller, 104,6); Aristotle, *Hist. an.* 5.14, 544b25 (semen is produced at age fourteen); Ps.-Plutarch, *Plac. philos.* 5.23, 909c–d; cf. 4.11, 900c; Philo, *Opif.* 105 (Hippokrates says that a boy of fourteen is capable of emitting seed [γονῆς ἐκφύσιος]); Censorinus, *Die nat.* 14.3 ("Hippocrates the doctor distributed the ages into seven stages. The end of the first period, he thought, was the seventh year, the second ended at fourteen" [Parker]). See further Lancellotti, *Naassenes*, 229.

ἑπτὰ ἐτῶν, ἐν τοῖς τέσσαρσι <καὶ δέκα> φασὶν ἔτεσι, κατὰ τὸν Θωμᾶν, εἶναι φανερούμενον. 22. Οὗτος ἐστιν ὁ ἀπόρρητος αὐτοῖς λόγος καὶ μυστικός.

λέγουσι γοῦν ὅτι Αἰγύπτιοι, πάντων ἀνθρώπων μετὰ τοὺς Φρύγας ἀρχαιότεροι καθεστῶτες καὶ πᾶσι τοῖς ἄλλοις ἀνθρώποις ὁμολογουμένως τελετὰς καὶ ὄργια θεῶν πάντων ὁμοῦ μετ' αὐτοὺς πρῶτον κατηγγελκότες ἰδέας καὶ ἐνεργείας, ἱερὰ καὶ σεβάσμια καὶ ἀνεξαγόρευτα τοῖς μὴ τετελεσμένοις τὰ Ἴσιδος ἔχουσι μυστήρια. 23. τὰ δ' εἰσὶν οὐκ ἄλλο τι ἢ <τὸ> ἡρπασμένον καὶ ζητούμενον ὑπὸ τῆς ἑπταστόλου καὶ μελανείμονος—αἰσχύνη Ὀσίριδος.

Ὄσιριν δὲ λέγουσιν ὕδωρ· ἡ δὲ Ἶσις ἑπτάστολος, περὶ αὐτὴν ἔχουσα καὶ ἐστολισμένη ἑπτὰ στολὰς αἰθ<ε>ρίους—τοὺς πλάνητας γὰρ ἀστέρας οὕτω προσαγορεύουσιν ἀλληγοροῦντες καὶ <διὰ τοῦτο> αἰθ<ε>ρίους καλοῦντες, καθὼς <...> ἡ μεταβλητὴ γένεσίς <ἐστιν, ἣ> ὑπὸ τοῦ ἀρρήτου καὶ ἀνεξεικονίστου καὶ ἀνεννοήτου καὶ ἀμόρφου μεταμορφουμένη κτίσις ἀναδείκνυται. 24. καὶ τοῦτ' ἔστι τὸ εἰρημένον, φησίν, ἐν τῇ γραφῇ· «ἑπτάκις πεσεῖται ὁ δίκαιος καὶ ἀναστήσεται»· αὗται γὰρ αἱ πτώσεις, φησίν, αἱ τῶν ἄστρων μεταβολαί, ὑπὸ τοῦ πάντα κινοῦντος κινούμεναι.

maxim that a child of seven is half a father and say that, according to Thomas, it is revealed in fourteen years. 22. This is their secret and mystic doctrine!

Now they say that Egyptians arose (together with the Phrygians) as the most ancient of all peoples, and, by common consent, they first proclaimed to all other peoples after them rites and initiations of all the gods together with their forms and activities. They possess the mysteries of Isis as holy, revered, and undisclosed to the uninitiated. 23. But these mysteries are nothing other than what was stolen and sought for by the seven-stoled, sable-clad goddess—the genitals of Osiris.[55]

Osiris, they say, represents water.[56] Seven-stoled Isis is wrapped and robed with seven aetherial robes.[57] These robes are called "aetherial" because they allegorically refer them to the planets, just as …[58] Changeable generation is revealed as creation transformed by the Unspeakable, Unimaginable, Unconceived, and Unformed One.[59] 24. This is what the scriptural verse means: "the just person falls seven times yet will rise."[60] These "falls," he explains, are the changing positions of the planets, moved by the one who moves everything.

---

55. On the myth of Isis and Osiris, see Alvar, *Romanising*, 39–52; Marcovich, *Studies*, 52–54. For the black garment, see Plutarch, *Is. Os.* 52 (*Mor.* 372d) (with a cosmological interpretation); Apuleius, *Metam.* 11.3. She is commonly called "wearer of the black stole" in hymns (e.g., Orph. Hymn 42.9 [Quandt]). For the genitals of Osiris, see below, *Ref.* 5.7.27; Plutarch, *Is. Os.* 18 (*Mor.* 358b; cf. 365b–c); Diodoros, *Bibl. hist.* 1.22.6–7. See further E. R. Goodenough, *Jewish Symbols in the Greco-Roman Period*, 12 vols., Bollingen Series 37 (New York: Pantheon, 1956), 6:75–80, 96–98. Lancellotti comments, "The phallus of the Egyptian cult does not represent, either for Plutarch or for the Naassenes, Osiris *tout court*, but the dynamic force through which the Supreme Principle initiates the cosmic machine" (*Naassenes*, 216). Cf. the "male power" within the soul (*Ref.* 5.7.13).

56. In Plutarch, *Is. Os.* 33 (*Mor.* 364a; cf. 365b), Osiris is "the general principle and power of moisture [τὴν ὑγροποιὸν ἀρχὴν καὶ δύναμιν]," as well as "the cause of generation and the essence of seed" (trans. Griffiths). See further Origen, *Cels.* 5.38; *PGM* XII. 234: ἐγώ εἰμι Ὄσιρις ὁ καλούμενος ὕδωρ ("I am Osiris, called water"). According to Birdsall, the water that Osiris represents is semen ("Naassene Sermon," 225).

57. Ἶσις is Marcovich's emendation for P's φύσις ("Nature").

58. Marcovich suspects a lacuna here. Possibly a line about the black robe as the outermost astral sphere dropped out. Cf. *Ref.* 7.23.7 ("Basileides").

59. Marcovich adds ἐστιν, ἥ. Cf. *Ref.* 5.16.6 (Peratai).

60. Prov 24:16 LXX. The just one falls seven times through seven planets but rises past them all.

25. Λέγουσιν οὖν περὶ τῆς τοῦ σπέρματος οὐσίας, ἥτις ἐστὶ π(ά)ντων τῶν γινομένων αἰτία, ὅτι τούτων ἐστὶν οὐδέν, γεννᾷ δὲ καὶ ποιεῖ πάντα τὰ γινόμενα, λέγοντες οὕτως· «γίνομαι ὃ θέλω καὶ εἰμὶ ὃ εἰμί». διὰ τοῦτό φησιν ἀκίνητον εἶναι τὸ πάντα κινοῦν· μένει γὰρ ὅ ἐστι, ποιοῦν τὰ πάντα, καὶ οὐδὲν τῶν γινομένων γίνεται.

26. τοῦτον εἶναί φησιν ἀγαθὸν μόνον, καὶ περὶ τούτου λελέχθαι τὸ ὑπὸ τοῦ σωτῆρος λεγόμενον· «τί με λέγεις ἀγαθόν; εἷς ἐστιν ἀγαθός, ὁ πατήρ μου ὁ ἐν τοῖς οὐρανοῖς· ὃς ἀνατέλ<λ>ει τὸν ἥλιον αὐτοῦ ἐπὶ δικαίους καὶ ἀδίκους καὶ βρέχει ἐπὶ ὁσίους καὶ ἁμαρτωλούς.» τίνες δέ εἰσιν οἱ ὅσιοι οἷς βρέχει καὶ οἱ ἁμαρτωλοὶ οἷς ὁ αὐτὸς βρέχει, καὶ τοῦτο μετὰ τῶν ἄλλων ὕστερον ἐροῦμεν.

27. καὶ τοῦτ' εἶναι τὸ μέγα καὶ κρύφιον τῶν ὅλων ἄγνωστον μυστήριον παρὰ τοῖς Αἰγυπτίοις, κεκαλυμμένον καὶ ἀνακεκαλυμμένον. οὐδεὶς γάρ, φησίν, ἔστι ναὸς ἐν <ᾧ> πρὸ τῆς εἰσόδου οὐχ ἕστηκε γυμνὸν τὸ κεκρυμμένον, κάτωθεν ἄνω βλέπον καὶ πάντας τοὺς καρποὺς τῶν <ἐξ> αὐτοῦ γινομένων στεφανούμενον. 28. ἑστάναι δὲ οὐ μόνον ἐν τοῖς ἁγιωτάτοις πρὸ τῶν ἀγαλμάτων ναοῖς λέγουσι τὸ τοιοῦτον, ἀλλὰ γὰρ καὶ εἰς τὴν ἁπάντων ἐπίγνωσιν—οἱονεὶ φῶς <οὐχ> ὑπὸ τὸν μόδιον, ἀλλ' ἐπὶ τὴν λυχνίαν ἐπικείμενον, <καὶ> κήρυγμα κηρυσσόμενον ἐπὶ τῶν δωμάτων—ἐν πάσαις ὁδοῖς καὶ πάσαις ἀγυιαῖς καὶ παρ' αὐταῖς ταῖς οἰκίαις, <ὡς> ὅρον τινὰ καὶ τέρμα τῆς οἰκίας προτεταγμένον. καὶ τοῦτο εἶναι τὸ

25. Now they say concerning the substance of the seed, the cause of all generated beings, that it is not at all one of these generated beings but that it generates and makes all generated beings. They declare as follows: "I become what I want, and I am what I am."[61] For this reason, he says, that which moves all things is immovable.[62] For it remains what it is, making all things, and is not at all generated from generated beings.

26. This being alone is good, he says, and the saying of the Savior refers to him: "Why do you call me good? One is good, my Father in heaven, who makes his sun rise upon just and unjust, and sends rain on the holy and sinners."[63] (The identity of these holy people and sinners on whom he rains I will relate later on after everything else.[64])

i. THE SYMBOL OF THE PHALLUS. 27. Yes, this is the Egyptians' great, secret, unknown mystery of the universe, veiled and unveiled! For there is no temple, he says, which does not feature the hidden object naked before its entrance, looking up from below and crowned with all those fruits that are generated from him.[65] 28. This type of object stands not only in the most holy temples before the cult statues, they say, but is in fact within everyone's purview, like a light resting not under a bushel but set "on the lampstand" and a proclamation preached "on the rooftops" "in every road and lane" and beside the very houses, since it is arranged as a boundary

61. Cf. Exod 3:14 (אהיה אשר אהיה).

62. For both Anaxagoras (DK 59 B12) and Aristotle (*Metaph.* 12.7, 1072b8), intelligence (Νοῦς) is what moves all things while (for Aristotle) it remains unmoved and unaffected (ἀπαθῆ).

63. For ἀγαθὸν μόνον, see Diog. L., *Vit. phil.* 8.8; Clem. Alex., *Strom.* 3.5.43.2; *Ref.* 5.26.1 (Justin); Mark 10:18 par.; Iren., *Haer* 1.20.1; Ps.-Clem. Hom. 18.3.4; Justin, *Dial.* 101.2; Clem. Alex., *Paed.* 1.74.1; *Strom.* 2.20.114.3; *Ref.* 7.31.6 (Prepon). See further Bergman, "Kleine Beiträge," 91. For raining on just and unjust, see Matt 5:45.

64. Cf. *Ref.* 5.7.34.

65. Plutarch refers to anthropomorphic statues found "everywhere" (πανταχοῦ) in Egypt. The statues feature an erect phallus, and they are draped with flame-colored shawls (*Is. Os.* 51 [*Mor.* 371f]). Ithyphallic statues of Priapos were also adorned with fruit. Cornutus writes that the great size of Priapos's phallus indicates the expanding spermatic power in God (Ἐμφαίνει γοῦν τὸ μέγεθος τῶν αἰδοίων τῆν πλεονάζουσαν ἐν τῷ θεῷ σπερματικὴν δύναμιν). "The offerings of all kinds of fruit in his lap represents the abundance of fruits that grow in their season" (ἡ δ' ἐν τοῖς κόλποις αὐτοῦ παγκαρπία τῆν δαψίλειαν τῶν ἐν ταῖς οἰκείαις ὥραις ἐντὸς τοῦ κόλπου φυομένων καὶ ἀναδεικνυμένων καρπῶν) (*Nat d.* 27.10). Marcovich understood the statues as those of Priapos and compares Justin below (*Ref.* 5.26.33–34) (*Studies*, 118).

ἀγαθὸν ὑπὸ πάντων λεγόμενον· ἀγαθηφόρον γὰρ αὐτὸ καλοῦσιν—ὃ λέγουσιν οὐκ εἰδότες.

καὶ τοῦτο Ἕλληνες μυστικὸν ἀπὸ Αἰγυπτίων παραλαβόντες φυλάσσουσι μέχρι σήμερον· τοὺς γοῦν Ἑρμ(ᾶς), φησί, παρ᾽ αὐτοῖς τοιούτῳ τετιμημένους σχήματι θεωροῦμεν. 29. Κυλλήνιοι δὲ διαφερόντως τιμῶντες <τὸν Ἑρμῆν> λό(γ)ον φασὶ<ν εἶναι· ὁ> γὰρ Ἑρμῆς ἐστι λόγος. ἑρμηνεὺς ὢν καὶ δημιουργὸς τῶν γεγονότων ὁμοῦ καὶ γινομένων καὶ ἐσομένων παρ᾽ αὐτοῖς τιμώμενος ἕστηκε τοιούτῳ τινὶ κεχαρακτηρισμένος σχήματι, ὅπερ ἐστὶν αἰσχύνη ἀνθρώπου, ἀπὸ τῶν κάτω ἐπὶ τὰ ἄνω ὁρμὴν ἔχων.

30. Καὶ ὅτι οὗτος—τουτέστιν ὁ τοιοῦτος Ἑρμῆς—ψυχαγωγός, φησίν, ἐστὶ καὶ ψυχοπομπὸς καὶ ψυχῶν αἴτιος, οὐδὲ τοὺς ποιητὰς τῶν ἐθνῶν λανθάνει, λέγοντας οὕτως·

Ἑρμῆς δὲ ψυχὰς Κυλλήνιος ἐξεκαλεῖτο
ἀνδρῶν μνηστήρων·

οὐ τῶν Πηνελόπης, φησίν, ὦ κακοδαίμονες, μνηστήρων, ἀλλὰ τῶν ἐξυπνισμένων καὶ ἀνεμνησμένων

marker and limit of the house.[66] Moreover, this is what everyone calls "the Good," for they call it "bringer of good"—though unaware of the true meaning of what they say.[67]

Indeed, the Greeks borrowed this mystical object from the Egyptians and preserve it to the present day. 29. Thus we behold the herms honored by them in the same form.[68] The Kyllenians grant special honor to Hermes, whom they say is "Word" (for Hermes represents the Word).[69] He is the interpreter and artificer of all reality that was, is, and will be generated.[70] He is honored among them and stands characterized by the same guise—namely, a man having his genitals straining from things below to what is above.

EXCURSUS: HERMES IN *ODYSSEY* 24.1–12. 30. Moreover, the fact that he (I mean this particular Hermes) is guide, director, and source of souls, he says, has not escaped the poets who say:

> Kyllenian Hermes called forth the souls
> Of those men, the suitors.[71]

Hermes calls forth the souls, he claims, not of Penelope's suitors [μνηστήρων]—you poor souls!—but of those woken from sleep who recall [ἀνεμνησμένων]

---

66. Cornutus refers to Pan/Priapos/Agathos Daimon as the "guardian preserver of household affairs" (Προστάτης δὲ καὶ σωτὴρ τῶν οἰκείων) (*Nat. d.* 27.14). For the image of the lampstand, see Matt 5:15 par. For preaching from the rooftops, see Matt 10:27; Luke 12:3. The lampstand and rooftop images are already combined in Gos. Thom. 33.1–2.

67. Agathos (i.e., Good) Daimon was honored with household altars in the Hellenistic period and was represented in the form of a snake.

68. For herms, see Cornutus, *Nat d.* 16.17–18; Pausanias, *Descr.* 6.26.5; Porphyry in Eusebios, *Praep. ev.* 3.11, 114c: ὁ δὲ ἐντεταμένος Ἑρμῆς δηλοῖ τὴν εὐτονίαν ("The erect Hermes shows his vigor").

69. Artemidoros saw in Kyllene a cult image of Hermes that was nothing but an erect penis (*Oneir.* 1.45). Cf. Lucian, *Jupp. trag.* 42; Pausanias, *Descr.* 6.26.5.

70. Cf. Cornutus, *Nat. d.* 16.2: "Hermes is the Word" (τυγχάνει δὲ ὁ Ἑρμῆς ὁ λόγος ὤν); *Ref.* 4.48.2 (Aratos allegorizers). On Hermes the interpreter (ἑρμενεύς), see Orph. Hymn 28.6; Philo, *Legat.* 99; Diodoros, *Bibl. hist.* 1.16.2.

71. Homer, *Od.* 24.1–2. The exegesis of Homer runs from *Ref.* 5.7.30 to 5.7.41. See further Frickel, *Naassenerschrift*, 52, 77, 82–83; Arthur J. Droge, "Homeric Exegesis among the Gnostics," *StPatr* 19 (1989): 313–21 (318–19); Lancellotti, *Naassenes*, 232–38.

ἐξ οἵης τιμῆς <τε> καὶ ὅσ<σ>ου μήκεος ὄλβου·

τουτέστιν <τῶν> ἀπὸ τοῦ μακαρίου ἄνωθεν ἀνθρώπου ἢ ἀρχανθρώπου ἢ Ἀδάμαντος, ὡς ἐκείνοις δοκεῖ, κατενεχθεισῶν ὧδε εἰς πλάσμα τὸ πήλινον, ἵνα δουλεύσωσι τῷ ταύτης τῆς κτίσεως δημιουργῷ Ἠσαλδαίῳ, θεῷ πυρίνῳ, ἀριθμὸν τετάρτῳ—οὕτως γὰρ τὸν δημιουργὸν καὶ πατέρα τοῦ ἰδικοῦ κόσμου καλοῦσιν.

31. ἔχε δὲ ῥάβδον μετὰ χερσὶ
καλήν, χρυσείην, τῇ τ' ἀνδρῶν ὄμματα θέλγει,
ὧν ἐθέλει, τοὺς δ' αὖτε καὶ ὑπνώοντας ἐγείρει.

32. οὗτος, φησίν, ἐστὶν ὁ τῆς ζωῆς καὶ τοῦ θανάτου μόνος ἔχων ἐξουσίαν· περὶ τούτου, φησί, γέγραπται·

ποιμανεῖς αὐτοὺς ἐν ῥάβδῳ σιδηρᾷ.

ὁ δὲ ποιητής, φησί, κοσμῆσαι βουλόμενος τὸ ἀπερινόητον τῆς μακαρίας φύσεως τοῦ Λόγου, οὐ σιδηρᾶν ἀλλὰ χρυσῆν παρέθηκε [τὴν] ῥάβδον αὐτῷ.

> from what magnificent honor and what great beatitude [they have fallen]![72]

That is, Hermes calls forth the souls of those brought down, as they suppose, from the blessed Human above, the chief Human or Adamas. They are brought down here into a bodily formation of mud to be slaves of the Artificer of this creation.[73] This is Esaldaios, a fiery God, fourth in number (for so they call the Artificer and Father of the particular world).[74]

> 31. He held a rod in his hands,
> Fair and golden, by which he enchants the eyes of men,
> Whomever he wants, while in turn rousing others who slumber.[75]

32. This one, he says, is the only one who holds the power of life and death.[76] About him, he says, it is written:

> you will shepherd them with a rod of iron.[77]

The poet, he says, wanting to embellish the incomprehensibility of the blessed nature of the Word, bestowed on him a gold, not an iron, rod. He

---

72. Empedokles, DK 31 B119.165 (from Plutarch, *Exil.* 607e; Stobaios, *Flor.* 3.40.5 [Wachsmuth and Hense, 3:737]; Clem. Alex., *Strom.* 4.4.13.1). Hermes is God the Logos who wakes the souls and helps them to recall their heavenly origins. Cf. *Ref.* 5.7.32; Cornutus, *Nat. d.* 16.11. The image of waking up is common in gnostic literature: e.g., Gos. Truth (NHC I,3) 29.26–9; Ap. John (NHC II,1) 31.5–6; Apoc. Adam (NHC V,5) 66.1–3. See further Corp. herm. 1.27; Acts Thom. 110; Clem. Alex., *Exc.* 3.1.

73. For the formation of mud, see Gen 2:7; Isa 29:16.

74. Esaldaios is apparently a Greek rendering of El-Shaddai; cf. Ἡσαδδαῖος in *Ref.* 5.26.3 (Justin). Lancellotti, who provides a discussion of his name (*Naassenes*, 116–20), believes that he is parallel to Plutarch's Typhon in *Is. Os.* 40 (*Mor.* 367a). The god-of-fire epithet assimilates Esaldaios to Yahweh (Exod 3:2, 4; Deut 4:24; 9:3). Cf. *Ref.* 6.9.3 ("Simon"); 6.32.7–8 ("Valentinus"); 7.38.1 (Apelles); 8.9.7 (Doketai); *PGM* XII. 115 (ὁ [π]ύρινος θεός). Legge speculates that Esaldaios is called "fourth" because he "comes next after the Supreme Triad of Father, Son and Mother" or more probably because of his four-letter name (the tetragrammaton) (*Philosophoumena*, 1:128 n. 2). Esaldaios is the fourth "principle" if we count the Preexistent (= Human), the Self-Born (= Son of the Human), and Chaos before him.

75. Homer, *Od.* 24.3–5.

76. That is, Hermes awakens from death.

77. Ps 2:9 LXX; Rev 2:27.

θέλγει δὲ ὄμματα τῶν νεκρῶν, ὥς φησι, τοὺς δ' αὖτε καὶ ὑπνώοντας ἐγείρει, τοὺς ἐξυπνισμένους καὶ γεγονότας μνηστῆρας· περὶ τούτων, φησίν, ἡ γραφὴ λέγει·

33. ἔγειραι, ὁ καθεύδων,
καὶ ἐξεγέρθητι,
καὶ ἐπιφαύσει σοι ὁ Χριστός.

οὗτος ἐστιν ὁ Χριστὸς ὁ ἐν πᾶσι, φησί, τοῖς γενητοῖς υἱὸς ἀνθρώπου, <ὁ> κεχαρακτηρισμένος ἀπὸ τοῦ ἀχαρακτηρίστου Λόγος·

34. τοῦτο, φησίν, ἐστὶ τὸ μέγα καὶ ἄρρητον Ἐλευσινίων μυστήριον

ὕε, κύε.

καὶ ὅτι, φησίν, αὐτῷ «πάντα ὑποτέτακται», ὥς τε «τῇ ῥάβδῳ κινήσας» ὁ Ἑρμῆς, «αἱ δὲ τρίζουσαι ἕπονται», αἱ ψυχαὶ συνεχῶς, οὕτως [ὡς] διὰ τῆς εἰκόνος ὁ ποιητὴς ἐπιδέδειχε λέγων·

ὡς δ' ὅτε νυκτερίδες μυχῷ ἄντρου θεσπεσίοιο
τρίζουσ<α>ι ποτέονται, ἐπεί κέ τις ἀποπέσῃσιν
ὁρμαθοῦ ἐκ πέτρης, ἀνά τ' ἀλλήλῃσιν ἔχονται.

enchants the eyes of the dead, as he says, and in turn rouses those who slumber—meaning those woken up (who also become "suitors" [i.e., recollectors]). Scripture, he says, speaks of these people:

33. Awaken, you who sleep,
and rise up;
then Christ will illuminate you![78]

This Christ, he says, is the one who is the Son of the Human in all people who are born, the Word formed from the Formless One.[79]

34. This, he says, is what is referred to in the great and unspeakable mystery of the Eleusinians:

Rain! Conceive![80]

The poet reveals, he says, that all "all things are subjected" to him, when he says that Hermes "makes a flourish with his rod," and the souls closely follow, "squeaking as they go."[81]

Just as when bats in the recesses of a numinous cave
Squeak as they fly about, when one drops
From the rock off the row, they cling to each other in a flurry.[82]

---

78. Eph 5:14. The Hermes or Logos figure is identified with Christ; cf. Hipp., *Comm. Dan.* 4.56.4; *Antichr.* 65.

79. Cf. *Ref.* 5.8.21.

80. The cry occurred during the ritual of the *Plemochoai* in which a liquid was poured from two ornate jugs (one toward the east, the other toward the west) (Athenaios, *Deipn.* 11.496a–b, with Lancellotti, *Naassenes*, 264). "In the Eleusinian rites," observed Proklos, "they gazed up to heaven and cried aloud 'rain,' they gazed down upon earth and cried 'conceive'" (*In Tim.* 293c28–30 [Diehl]; cf. *IG* II^2 4876). See further Walter Burkert, *Homo Necans: The Anthropology of Ancient Greek Sacrificial Ritual and Myth*, trans. Peter Bing (Berkeley: University of California Press, 1983), 293 n. 89; Margaret Miles, *The City Eleusinion* (Princeton: American School of Classical Studies, 1998), 95–103; Robert Parker, *Polytheism and Society at Athens* (Oxford: Oxford University Press, 2005), 350; Jan Bremmer, *Initiation into the Mysteries of the Ancient World* (Berlin: de Gruyter, 2014), 390. According to Birdsall, the Naassene author reinterpreted the saying to mean: "Send down the divine souls into matter, and let her yield them up again" ("Naassene Sermon," 216).

81. 1 Cor 15:27 (all things subject), from Ps 8:7 LXX. The Homeric text is *Od.* 24.5.

82. Homer, *Od.* 24.6–8.

καὶ τοῦτ᾽ ἔστι, τὸ εἰρημένον·

εἰς πᾶσαν τὴν γῆν ἐξῆλθεν ὁ φθόγγος αὐτῶν.

35. Πέτρης, φησί, τοῦ ἀδάμαντος λέγει· οὗτος, φησίν, ἐστὶν ὁ Ἀδάμας «ὁ λίθος ἀκρογωνιαῖος», «ὁ εἰς κεφαλὴν γεγενημένος γωνίας»—ἐν κεφαλῇ γὰρ εἶναι τὸν χαρακτηριστικὸν ἐγκέφαλον, τὴν <πάντων> οὐσίαν, «ἐξ οὗ πᾶσα πατριὰ» χαρακτηρίζεται·—«ὅν», φησίν, «ἐντάσσω»—<τουτέστι τὸν> Ἀδάμαντα—«εἰς τὰ θεμέλια Σιών».

36. ἀλληγορῶν, φησί, τὸ πλάσμα τοῦ ἀνθρώπου λέγει· ὁ γὰρ ἐντασσόμενος Ἀδάμας ἐστὶν <«ὁ ἔσω ἄνθρωπος», «τὰ δὲ θεμέλια Σιὼν» οἱ> ὀδόντες, ὡς Ὅμηρος, λέγει «ἕρκος ὀδόντων», τουτέστι τεῖχος καὶ χαράκωμα, ἐν ᾧ ἐστιν ὁ ἔσω ἄνθρωπος, ἐκεῖθεν ἀποπεπτωκώς, ἀπὸ τοῦ ἀρχανθρώπου ἄνωθεν Ἀδάμαντος, «ὁ τμηθεὶς ἄνευ χειρῶν» τεμνουσῶν καὶ κατενηνεγμένος εἰς τὸ πλάσμα τῆς λήθης, τὸ χοϊκόν, τὸ «ὀστράκινον».

37. καί, φη(σ)ίν, ὅτι τετριγυῖαι αὐτῷ ἠκολούθουν αἱ ψυχαί—τῷ Λόγῳ—

This is the meaning of the verse:

Their sound went out to all the earth![83]

35. He claims that "from the rock" means "from adamant [*or*: Adamas]." This is because adamant [*or*: Adamas] is, as he says, "the cornerstone," "the one who has become head of the corner."[84] For in the head lies the form-giving brain, the essence of all "from whom every family" is formed.[85] "This one," namely Adamas, as he claims, "I will install as the foundation stone of Zion."[86]

36. He claims that this phrase allegorically refers to the bodily formation of the Human, for the installed Adamas is the inner human.[87] "Zion's foundation stones" are the teeth, as Homer says, "a fence (that is, a wall or palisade) of the teeth,"[88] within which is the inner human, the one who has fallen from the chief human Adamas above. This Adamas is "the one whom no hands cut," who is brought down into the bodily formation of forgetfulness, the vehicle of dirt, the "vessel of clay."[89]

37. Moreover, he says that the souls followed him (that is, the Word) squeaking:

83. Ps 18:5 LXX; Rom 10:18. In P this sentence follows the line, "'all things have been subjected to him." Marcovich has transposed it to this location. In the immediate context, the sound is the sound of bat-like souls.

84. Ps 117:22 LXX; Matt 21:42 par.; Acts 4:11; 1 Pet 2:7; for the cornerstone, see also Amos 7:8 (Ἰδοὺ ἐγὼ ἐντάσσω ἀδάμαντα ἐν μέσῳ λαοῦ μου Ισραηλ ["Behold, I lay adamant in the midst of my people Israel"]).

85. Eph 3:15. Lancellotti observes: "Since the brain has the capacity of distinguishing, i.e., of 'characterizing' (V 7,35), it is identified with the Celestial Anthropos" (cf. *Ref.* 5.8.13; 5.9.15). "The association between seed-pneuma-brain … is present already fully elaborated in Hippocratic medical tradition" (*Naassenes*, 208).

86. Isa 28:16 LXX (Ἰδοὺ ἐγὼ ἐμβαλῶ εἰς τὰ θεμέλια Σιων λίθον πολυτελῆ ἐκλεκτὸν ἀκρογωνιαῖον ἔντιμον εἰς τὰ θεμέλια αὐτῆς ["Behold, I install into the foundations of Zion a precious, choice, honored cornerstone for her foundation"]).

87. For the inner human, see Rom 7:22; 2 Cor 4:16; Eph 3:16; Plato, *Resp.* 9.589a–b (partially translated in NHC VI,5); Philo, *Congr.* 97; *Plant.* 42; *Fug.* 71 (νοῦς the true human within); Acts Pet. 24; Iren., *Haer.* 1.5.5; 1.21.4; Tert., *Marc.* 3.7.3; Clem. Alex., *Exc.* 50.1–3; 51.1–2; *Ref.* 6.34.5 ("Valentinus"); 7.27.6 ("Basileides"); 10.19.3 (summary of Markion).

88. E.g., Homer, *Il.* 4.350 (a common phrase in Homer).

89. Cf. Dan 2:45 (the feet of clay); Gen 2:7 (God's breath or spirit blown into the clay); 2 Cor 4:7 (clay vessel).

ὣς αἳ τετριγυῖαι ἅμ' ἤϊσαν, ἦρχε δ' ἄρα σφιν—τουτέστιν ἡγεῖτο—
Ἑρμείας ἀκάκητα κατ' εὐρώεντα κέλευθα

τουτέστι, φησίν, εἰς τὰ πάσης κακίας ἀπηλλαγμένα αἰώνια χωρία. Ποῦ δέ, φησίν, ἦλθον;

πὰρ δ' ἴσαν Ὠκεανοῦ τε ῥοὰς καὶ Λευκάδα πέτρην,
ἠ<δὲ> παρ' Ἠελίοιο πύλας καὶ δῆμον ὀνείρων.

38. οὗτος, φησίν, ἐστὶν

Ὠκεανὸς γένεσίς <τε> θεῶν, γένεσίς τ' ἀνθρώπων,

ἐκ παλιρροίας στρεφόμενος αἰεί, ποτὲ ἄνω ποτὲ κάτω. ἀλλ' ὅταν, φησί, κάτω ῥέῃ ὁ Ὠκεανός, γένεσίς ἐστιν ἀνθρώπων, ὅταν δὲ ἄνω, ἐπὶ τὸ τεῖχος καὶ τὸ χαράκωμα καὶ τὴν Λευκάδα πέτρην, γένεσίς <ἐσ>τι θεῶν.

39. τοῦτό ἐστιν, φησί, τὸ γεγραμμένον·

ἐγὼ εἶπα· θεοί ἐστε
καὶ υἱοὶ ὑψίστου πάντες.

ἐὰν ἀπὸ τῆς Αἰγύπτου φυγεῖν σπεύδητε καὶ γένησθε πέραν τῆς Ἐρυθρᾶς θαλάσσης εἰς τὴν ἔρημον—τουτέστιν ἀπὸ τῆς κάτω μίξεως ἐπὶ «τὴν ἄνω

As they went together squeaking, Hermes ruled (that is, guided) them
Along the dank lanes that are absent from evil [ἀκάκητα].[90]

This means, he says, he guides them into eternal realms removed from all evil [κακίας]. But where, he continues, did they go?

They went past the streams of Ocean and Gleaming Rock
Past the gates of the Sun and the dwelling of dreams.[91]

38. This one, he says, is,

Ocean, origin of gods and of human beings.[92]

He eternally turns by ebb and flow, sometimes up, sometimes down. Now, he claims, when Ocean flows *down*, humans are generated, but when he flows *up*—to the wall, the palisade, the Gleaming Rock—gods are born.

39. This is the meaning of the scriptural verse:

I declared: "You are gods and all of you sons of the Most High."[93]

You are gods if you hurry to flee from Egypt and cross the Red Sea into the desert (that is, after you flee from the mixture below to "the Jerusalem

---

90. Homer, *Od.* 24.9–10. "Absent from evil" (ἀκάκητα) is usually taken as an epithet of Hermes (of obscure meaning).

91. Homer, *Od.* 24.11–12. The Gleaming *Rock* connects this Homeric citation with the biblical testimonia about rocks. On the Gleaming Rock, see further Jérôme Carcopino, *o De Pythagore aux apôtres: Études sur la conversion du monde romain* (Paris: Flammarion, 1956), 214–21.

92. This quote is a conflation of Homer, *Il.* 14.201 and 246. The same conflation is found in *Ref.* 8.12.2 (Monoïmos). Cf. Orph. Hymn 83.1–2 (Ωκεανόν … ἀθανάτων τε θεῶν γένεσιν θνητῶν τ' ἀνθρώπων ["Ocean … origin of immortal gods and mortal human beings"]), and the lines attributed to Krates by Plutarch, *Fac.* 938d (Ωκεανός, ὅσπερ γένεσις πάντεσσι τέτυκται / ἀνδράσιν ἠδὲ θεοῖς ["Ocean, who is the origin of all, both of men and gods"]). See further *Ref.* 10.7.1 (summary of the philosophers); Athenagoras, *Leg.* 18.

93. Ps 81:6 LXX. For the early Christian interpretation of this verse, see Justin, *Dial.* 124; Iren., *Haer.* 3.6.1; 3.19.1; 4.38.4; Clem. Alex., *Protr.* 12.122.4–123.1; *Paed.* 1.26.1–2; *Strom.* 2.20.125.5–6; Tert., *Marc.* 1.7.1.

Ἱερουσαλήμ, ἥτις ἐστὶ μήτηρ ζώντων»·—ἐ(ὰ)ν δὲ πάλιν ἐπιστραφῆτε ἐπὶ τὴν Αἴγυπτον—τουτέστιν ἐπὶ τὴν κάτω μίξιν—,

ὡς ἄνθρωποι ἀποθνήσκετε.

40. θνητὴ γάρ, φησί, πᾶσα ἡ κάτω γένεσις, ἀθάνατος δὲ ἡ ἄνω γεννωμένη· γεννᾶται γὰρ «ἐξ ὕδατος» μόνου «καὶ πνεύματος» πνευματικός, οὐ σαρκικός· ὁ δὲ κάτω σαρκικός. τοῦτ' ἔστι, φησί, τὸ γεγραμμένον·

τὸ γεγεννημένον ἐκ τῆς σαρκὸς σάρξ ἐστι,
καὶ τὸ <γε>γεννημένον ἐκ τοῦ πνεύματος πνεῦμά ἐστιν.

αὕτη ἔστιν ἡ κατ' αὐτοὺς πνευματικὴ γένεσις.

41. οὗτος, φησίν, ἐστὶν ὁ μέγας Ἰορδάνης, ὃν κάτω ῥέοντα καὶ κωλύοντα ἐξελθεῖν τοὺς υἱοὺς Ἰσραὴλ ἐκ γῆς Αἰγύπτου—ἤγουν ἐκ τῆς κάτω μίξεως· Αἴγυπτος γάρ ἐστι τὸ σῶμα κατ' αὐτούς—ἀνέστειλεν Ἰησοῦς καὶ ἐποίησεν ἄνω ῥέειν.

8. 1. Τούτοις καὶ τοῖς τοιούτοις ἑπόμενοι οἱ θαυμασιώτατοι γνωστικοί, ἐφευρεταὶ καινῆς τέχνης γραμματικῆς, τὸν ἑαυτῶν προφήτην Ὅμηρον ταῦτα

above, mother of the living").[94] But if you turn back to Egypt (that is, the mixture below),

> You will die like human beings.[95]

40. All generation below, he says, is mortal, whereas that which is born above is immortal. For the spiritual one—not the fleshly—is born from water alone and spirit.[96] But the one below is fleshly. This is what the scriptural verse refers to:

> What is born from flesh is flesh,
> and what is born from spirit is spirit.[97]

This is their version of spiritual generation.

41. This, he says, is the great Jordan River, which flows down and prevents the children of Israel from leaving Egypt (i.e., the mixture below). For them, Egypt signifies the body.[98] Joshua [*or*: Jesus] turned the Jordan back and made it flow upward.[99]

ii. TRIPARTITE COSMOLOGY. **8.** 1. These most wondrous gnostics follow these and like teachings. As inventors of a new form of literary analysis,

---

94. Crossing the Red Sea was a common image for removal from the body (cf. *Ref.* 4.48.9 [Aratos allegorizers]; 5.16.4–5 [Peratai]). On the actual crossing, see Exod 15:22. On the heavenly Jerusalem, see Gal 4:26; Heb 12:22; Rev 3:12; 21:2, 10; 2 Bar. 4:2–7; 3:1; 2 En. 55:2; Iren., *Haer.* 5.35.2; *Ref.* 6.34.3 ("Valentinus").

95. Ps 81:7 LXX.

96. John 3:3, 5; *Ref.* 5.8.37 below.

97. John 3:6; cf. *Ref.* 8.10.8 (Doketai); [Hipp.], *Noet.* 16; Clem. Alex., *Strom.* 3.12.84.3.

98. For Egypt as the body, see, e.g., *Ref.* 5.16.4–5 (Peratai); Rev 11:8; Philo, *Migr.* 23, 77, 202.

99. Josh 3:16 LXX (*καὶ ἔστη τὰ ὕδατα τὰ καταβαίνοντα ἄνωθεν* ["the down-rushing water stood still"]). In Greek, the name Joshua = Jesus (Ιησοῦς). According to Testim. Truth (NHC IX,3) 30.19–31.5, the Son of Man came to the world by the Jordan River "and immediately the Jordan [turned] back." When John the Baptist saw this, "he knew that the dominion of carnal procreation had come to an end. The Jordan River is the power of the body, that is, the senses of pleasures. The water of the Jordan is the desire for sexual intercourse." Cf. On Bap. A (NHC XI,2) 41.34–37: "Jordan is the descent which is the ascent, i.e., our exodus from this world." See further Lancellotti, *Naassenes*, 160–62.

προφαίνοντα ἀρρήτως δοξάζουσι καὶ τοὺς ἀμυήτους τὰς ἁγίας γραφὰς εἰς τοιαύτας ἐννοίας συνάγοντες ἐνυβρίζουσι.

λέγουσι γάρ· ὁ λέγων τὰ πάντα ἐξ ἑνὸς συνεστάναι πλανᾶται, ὁ λέγων ἐκ τριῶν ἀληθεύει καὶ περὶ τῶν ὅλων τὴν ἀπόδειξιν δώσει· 2. μία γάρ ἐστι, φησίν, ἡ μακαρία φύσις τοῦ μακαρίου ἀνθρώπου τοῦ ἄνω, τοῦ Ἀδάμαντος· μία δὲ ἡ θνητὴ κάτω· μία δὲ ἡ ἀβασίλευτος γενεὰ ἡ ἄνω γενομένη—ὅπου, φησίν, ἐστὶ Μαριὰμ ἡ ζητουμένη καὶ Ἰοθὼρ ὁ μέγας σοφὸς καὶ Σεπφώρα ἡ βλέπουσα καὶ Μωσῆς, οὗ γένεσις οὐκ ἔστιν ἐν Αἰγύπτῳ· γεγόνασι γὰρ αὐτῷ παῖδες ἐν Μαδιάμ. 3. καὶ τοῦτο, φησίν, οὐδὲ τοὺς ποιητὰς λέληθε·

τριχθὰ δὲ πάντα δέδασται, ἕκαστος δ᾽ ἔμμορε τιμῆς.

δεῖ γάρ, φησί, λαλεῖσθαι τὰ μεγέθη, λαλεῖσθαι δὲ οὕτως ὑπὸ πάντων πανταχῇ, «ἵνα ἀκούοντες μὴ ἀκούωσι καὶ βλέποντες μὴ βλέπωσιν». εἰ μὴ γὰρ ἐλαλεῖτο, φησί, τὰ μεγέθη, ὁ κόσμος συνεστάναι οὐκ ἠδύνατο.

4. οὗτοι εἰσὶν οἱ τρεῖς ὑπέρογκοι λόγοι·

they glorify their own prophet Homer, who secretly declared these things. When they amalgamate the holy scriptures into these sorts of meanings, they lord it over the uninitiated.

They declare: "one who says that all things are composed from *one* errs, but the one who says that all things are composed from *three* speaks truth and will give the exposition concerning the universe." 2. He says that the blessed nature of the blessed Human above, Adamas, is one, and the mortal nature below is one, and one is the kingless generation born above.[100] In this generation, he says, is Mariam, who is sought after; Iothor the great sage; Sepphora, who sees; and Moses, whose generation is not in Egypt (for he had children in Midian).[101] 3. Even this point, he claims, did not escape the notice of the poets:

> All was apportioned three ways and each one was allotted a share of honor.[102]

It was necessary, he says, for the magnitudes to be mentioned, and mentioned in this way by all people everywhere "so that hearing they might not hear and seeing they might not see."[103] If the magnitudes were not spoken, he says, the world could not be formed.

4. These are the three words of superordinate gravity:

---

100. The "kingless generation" (ἀβασίλευτος γενεά), used also in *Ref.* 5.8.30, is a common self-designation (Francis T. Fallon, "The Gnostics: The Undominated Race," *NovT* 21 [1979]: 271–88 [282–83]). Here the kingless race refers to those who ascend above mortal nature but remain below Adamas. See further Lancellotti, *Naassenes*, 127.

101. I have retained the Greek spellings of these names. For Iothor (Jethro) the "great sage," see Exod 18:17–24. Sepphora (Zipporah) is elsewhere depicted as a seer or prophetess (Philo, *Mut.* 120). She appears in Exod 2:21–22; 4:25–26. Mariam (usually spelled "Miriam") being sought after (ζητουμένη) may recall the women following her in the dance after the Red Sea crossing (Exod 15:20), or the fact that the pneumatic is sought after by the Savior (Bergman, "Kleine Beiträge," 87). Howard Jacobson suggests emending ζητουμένη to ζηλουμένη ("zealous") to accord with Num 12 and patristic interpretations (e.g., 1 Clem. 4; Gregory of Nyssa, *Vita Mos.* 1.62) ("Miriam and St. Hippolytus," *VC* 62 [2008]: 404–5). On Moses and his children, see Exod 18:2–4.

102. Homer, *Il.* 15.189; cf. *Ref.* 5.20.8 ("Sethians"). The Naassenes use the quotation from Homer about the division of the universe among Zeus, Poseidon, and Hades as supporting testimony for the soteriological division between Adamas, the generation of the elect, and that of mortals. The passage in question is explained allegorically by both Ps.-Plutarch, *Vit. Hom.* 97, and Herakleitos, *All.* 41. See further Lancellotti, *Naassenes*, 209.

103. Isa 6:9; cf. Mark 4:12 par.

Καυλακαῦ, Σαυλασαῦ, Ζεησάρ·

Καυλακαῦ τοῦ ἄνω, τοῦ Ἀδάμαντος· Σαυλασαῦ τοῦ κάτω, <τοῦ> θνητοῦ· Ζεησὰρ τοῦ ἐπὶ τὰ ἄνω ῥεύσαντος Ἰορδάνου. οὗτός ἐστι, φησίν, ὁ ἐν πᾶσιν ἀρσενόθηλυς ἄνθρωπος, ὃν οἱ ἀγνοοῦντες Γηρυόνην καλοῦσι τρισώματον—ὡς «ἐκ γῆς ῥέοντα» Γηρυόνην—,
κοινῇ δὲ Ἕλληνες «(ἐ)πουράνιον Μηνὸς κέρας», ὅτι καταμέμιχε καὶ κεκέρακε πάντα πᾶσι. 5. «πάντα» γάρ, φησί,

δι' αὐτοῦ ἐγένετο, καὶ χωρὶς αὐτοῦ ἐγένετο οὐδὲ ἕν· ὃ δὲ γέγονεν ἐν αὐτῷ ζωή ἐστιν.

αὕτη, φησίν, ἐστὶν «ἡ ζωὴ» ἡ ἄρρητος γενεὰ τῶν τελείων ἀνθρώπων, ἣ «ταῖς προτέραις γενεαῖς οὐκ ἐγνώσθη»· τὸ δὲ «οὐδέν», ὃ χωρὶς αὐτοῦ γέγονεν, ὁ κόσμος, ἐστίν, ἰδικός· γέγονε ἕν γὰρ χωρὶς αὐτοῦ, ὑπὸ τρίτου καὶ τετάρτου <θεοῦ>.

Kalakau, Salasau, Zeēsar![104]

Kalakau belongs to the one above, Adamas; Salasau to the one below, the mortal; Zeēsar to the Jordan River that flowed upward.[105] This refers, he claims, to the androgynous Human in all, whom the ignorant call "triple-bodied Geryon," since Geryon "flows from earth" [ἐκ γῆς ῥέοντα].[106]

The Greeks commonly call him "celestial horn [κέρας] of Mēn" because he has mixed and blended [κεκέρακε] all things with all things.[107] 5. For "everything," he says,

> came about through him, and apart from him not one thing came to be. What has come about in him is life.[108]

This "life," he claims, is the ineffable race of the perfect human beings, which "was unknown in former generations."[109] Moreover the "nothing" that has come about apart from him refers to the particular world, for it became one apart from him, by a third and fourth god.[110]

---

104. Cf. Isa 28:10 (an adapted Greek transliteration of the Hebrew כי צו לצו צו לצו קו לקו קו לקו זעיר שם זעיר שם). Cf. Iren., *Haer.* 1.24.5–6 ("Basileides"); Epiph., *Pan.* 25.4.4–5 (Nikolaitans). See further Lancellotti, *Naassenes*, 295–99.

105. Frickel relates this teaching to *Ref.* 6.17.1 ("Simon") (*Naassenerschrift*, 84).

106. For the reference to the androgynous Human and Geryon, see *Ref.* 5.6.5–6 above. "Triple-bodied" is Geryon's standard epithet in literature. Cf. *Ref.* 5.12.4 (Peratai). Geryon (= the Son of the Human inside saved humans) flows from earth not because his origin is earthly but because he flows (like the Jordan) from earth to heaven. See further Lancellotti, *Naassenes*, 80.

107. The celestial horn of the moon is referred to in the Attis hymn (*Ref.* 5.9.8). Reitzenstein clarifies that the horn is "the drinking horn, corresponding to the κρατήρ [mixing cup] in which God, according to Plato's *Timaeus*, καταμέμιχε καὶ κεκέρακε πάντα πᾶσι [mixed and blended everything with everything]" (*Poimandres*, 100). The association of Attis and Men is attested (Lancellotti, *Naassenes*, 252 n. 100). See further E. Lane, ed., *Corpus Monumentorum Religionis Dei Menis*, 4 vols., EPRO 19 (Leiden: Brill, 1971–1978), esp. 3:92–98; Agnès van Haepern-Pourbaix, "Recherche sur les origines, la nature et les attributs du dieu Mên," in *Archéologie et religions de l'Anatolie ancienne: Mélanges en l'honneur du professeur Paul Naster*, ed. R. Donceel and R. Lebrun (Leuven: Centre d'histoire des Religions, 1983), 221–57 (223–28, 234–35, 245–46).

108. John 1:3–4; cf. *Ref.* 5.9.2, end; 5.16.12 (Peratai); [Hipp.], *Noet.* 12.

109. Cf. *Ref.* 6.35.1 ("Valentinus"); 7.25.3; 7.26.7 ("Basileides").

110. Reitzenstein supplies θεοῦ ("god"). For the fourth god, Esaldaios, see *Ref.* 5.7.30; 7.31.1 (Apelles).

6. Τοῦτο, φησίν, ἐστὶ τὸ ποτήριον «τὸ κόνδυ», «ἐν ᾧ βασιλεὺς πίνων οἰωνίζεται.» τοῦτο, φησί, κεκρυμμένον εὑρέθη ἐν τοῖς καλοῖς τοῦ Βενιαμὶν σπέρμασι. λέγουσι δὲ <τ>αὐτὸ καὶ Ἕλληνες, φησίν, οὕτως «μαινομένῳ στόματι»·

Φέρ' ὕδωρ, φέρ' οἶνον, ὦ παῖ,
μέθυσόν με καὶ κάρωσον·
τὸ ποτήριον λέγει μοι ποδαπόν με δεῖ γενέσθαι.

7. τοῦτο, φησίν, ἤρκει μόνον νοηθὲν ἀνθρώποις τὸ τοῦ Ἀνακρέοντος ποτήριον, <τὸ> ἀλάλως λαλοῦν μυστήριον ἄρρητον· ἄλαλον γάρ, φησίν, τὸ Ἀνακρέοντος [φησὶ] ποτήριον, ὅ<τι>περ αὐτῷ, φησιν Ἀνακρέων, λαλεῖ ἀλάλῳ φθέγματι ποδαπὸν αὐτὸν δεῖ γενέσθαι, τουτέστι πνευματικόν, οὐ σαρκικόν, ἐὰν ἀκούσῃ τὸ κεκρυμμένον μυστήριον ἐν σιωπῇ.

καὶ τοῦτό ἐστι τὸ ὕδωρ τὸ ἐν τοῖς καλοῖς ἐκείνοις γάμοις, ὃ στρέψας ὁ Ἰησοῦς ἐποίησεν οἶνον. αὕτη, φησίν, ἐστὶν ἡ μεγάλη καὶ ἀληθινὴ «ἀρχὴ τῶν σημείων», ἣν ἐποίησεν «ὁ Ἰησοῦς ἐν Κανᾷ τῆς Γαλιλαίας, καὶ ἐφανέρωσε» τὴν βασιλείαν τῶν οὐρανῶν. 8. αὕτη, φησίν, ἐστὶν ἡ βασιλεία τῶν οὐρανῶν ἐντὸς ἡμῶν κατακειμένη ὡς θησαυρός, ὡς «ζύμη εἰς ἀλεύρου τρία σάτα κεκρυμμένη».

9. Τοῦτ' ἔστι, φησί, τὸ μέγα καὶ ἄρρητον Σαμοθρᾴκων μυστήριον, ὃ μόνοις ἔξεστιν εἰδέναι τοῖς τελείοις, φησίν, ἡμῖν· διαρρήδην γὰρ οἱ Σαμόθρᾳκες τὸν Ἀδάμ<ας> ἐκεῖνον παραδιδόασιν ἐν τοῖς μυστηρίοις τοῖς ἐπιτελουμένοις

6. This, he says, is the cup, "the goblet [τὸ κόνδυ] with which the king practices divination."[111] This, he says, is the cup found hidden in Benjamin's beautiful seeds.[112] The Greeks say the same thing, he claims, "with raving mouth":[113]

Bring water, bring wine, slave!
Make me drunk, and plunge me into stupor!
The cup tells me what sort of person I need to be.[114]

7. Anakreon's cup suffices only for people who understand it. Without uttering, it utters an ineffable mystery. Anakreon's cup is unuttering, says Anakreon, because it speaks with an unutterable sound what kind of person he must become (i.e., spiritual, not fleshly), provided that one hears the hidden mystery in silence.

This refers to the water in that lovely wedding, the water that Jesus turned into wine. This, he says, is the great and true "beginning of signs" that Jesus did "in Cana of Galilee and manifested" the kingdom of heaven.[115] 8. This, he claims, is the kingdom of heaven stored inside of us like a treasure, like "yeast hidden in three measures of flour."[116]

C. SAMOTHRAKIAN MYSTERIES ABOUT THE HUMAN. 9. This, he says, is the great and unspeakable mystery of the Samothrakians, lawful only for us perfected ones to know.[117] The Samothrakians expressly present Adamas as

111. Gen 44:5 LXX. The cup (κόνδυ) is seen as equivalent to the horn (κέρας), evidently because the cup is conical.

112. "These seeds are identified with human beings and the adjective 'beautiful' is connected precisely with the fact that they preserve in themselves the noetic element" (Lancellotti, *Naassenes*, 146). Cf. the "most beautiful" (κάλλιστος) Human in *Ref.* 5.7.7.

113. Cf. Herakleitos, DK 22 B92 (a description of the Sibyl's prophesying). This phrase is quoted also by Plotinos, *Enn.* 2.9.18.20–21.

114. Anakreon, frag. 2, in Martin L. West, *Carmina Anacreontea*, BSGRT (Leipzig: Teubner, 1984), 48. Cruice here would augment the text with ἀλάλῳ λαλοῦν σιωπῇ based on what follows. Marcovich prefers ἀλάλῳ λαλοῦν ἀϋτῇ.

115. John 2:11. For the Naassene sacraments, see Lancellotti, *Naassenes*, 141–63.

116. See the note on the kingdom within in *Ref.* 5.7.20. For the image of the treasure, see Matt 13:44 and Gos. Thom. 76.3, 109. For the yeast in the flour, see Matt 13:33 par.; Gos. Thom. 96. See further Johnson, "*Refutatio*," 320; Lancellotti, *Naassenes*, 127–28.

117. On the Samothrakian mysteries, see Bremmer, *Initiation*, 21–54.

παρ' αὐτοῖς ἀρχάνθρωπον. 10. ἕστηκε δὲ ἀγάλματα δύο ἐν τῷ Σαμοθρᾴκων ἀνακτόρῳ ἀνθρώπων γυμνῶν, ἄνω τεταμένας ἐχόντων τὰς χεῖρας ἀμφοτέρας εἰς οὐρανὸν καὶ τὰς αἰσχύνας ἄνω ἐστραμμένας, καθάπερ ἐν Κυλλήνῃ τὸ τοῦ Ἑρμοῦ· εἰκόνες δέ εἰσι τὰ προειρημένα ἀγάλματα τοῦ ἀρχανθρώπου καὶ τοῦ ἀναγεννωμένου πνευματικοῦ, κατὰ πάνθ' ὁμοουσίου ἐκείνῳ τῷ ἀνθρώπῳ. 11. τοῦτο, φησίν, ἐστὶ τὸ εἰρημένον ὑπὸ τοῦ σωτῆρος·

> ἐὰν μὴ πίνητέ μου τὸ αἷμα καὶ φάγητέ μου τὴν σάρκα, οὐ μὴ εἰσέλθητε εἰς τὴν βασιλείαν τῶν οὐρανῶν·

ἀλλὰ κἂν «πίητε», φησί, «τὸ ποτήριον ὃ ἐγὼ πίνω», «ὅπου ἐγὼ ὑπάγω, ἐκεῖ ὑμεῖς εἰσελθεῖν οὐ δύνασθε». 12. ᾔδει γάρ, φησίν, ἐξ (ὁ)ποίας φύσεως ἕκαστος τῶν μαθητῶν αὐτοῦ ἐστι καὶ ὅτι ἕκαστον αὐτῶν εἰς τὴν ἰδίαν φύσιν ἐλθεῖν ἀνάγκη. ἀπὸ γὰρ τῶν δώδεκα, φησί, φυλῶν μαθητὰς ἐξελέξατο δώδεκα, καὶ δι' αὐτῶν ἐλάλησε πάσῃ φυλῇ· διὰ τοῦτο, φησί, τὰ τῶν δώδεκα μαθητῶν κηρύγματα οὔτε πάντες ἀκηκόασι οὔτε, ἐὰν ἀκούσωσι, παραδέξασθαι δύνανται· ἔστι γὰρ αὐτοῖς παρὰ φύσιν τὰ μὴ κατὰ φύσιν.

13. Τοῦτον, φησί, Θρᾷκες οἱ περὶ τὸν Αἷμον οἰκοῦντες Κορύβαντα καλοῦσι, καὶ Θρᾳξὶν οἱ Φρύγες παραπλησίως, ὅτι ἀπὸ τῆς κορυφῆς ἄνωθεν καὶ ἀπὸ τοῦ

the chief Human in the celebration of their mysteries.[118] 10. Two cult statues of naked men are stationed in the shrine of the Samothrakians. They stretch out both hands to heaven with their penises erect like the penis of Hermes in Kyllene.[119] These cult statues are the images of the chief Human and of the reborn spiritual person, who is in every respect consubstantial with that Human. 11. This is what the Savior's statement means:

> Unless you drink my blood and eat my flesh, you will certainly not enter the kingdom of heaven.[120]

But even if, he says, "you drink the cup that I drink," "you cannot enter the place where I go."[121] 12. For he knew, he claims, what sort of nature each of his disciples was, and that by necessity each must proceed to his own nature. From the twelve tribes, he says, he chose twelve disciples, and through them spoke to every tribe.[122] For this reason, he says, not everyone hears the preaching of the twelve disciples. And if they hear it, not all are able to accept it. This is because what is not proper to their nature is against their nature.

D. THRACIAN MYSTERIES ABOUT THE HUMAN. 13. The Thracians dwelling round Mount Haimos call Adamas "Korybas," as do the Phrygians, because, although he takes the origin of his descent from the crown

118. Ἀδάμας is an emendation of P's ἀδάμ. See the note on the Samothrakians in *Ref.* 5.9.8 below. The Dioskouri of the Samothrakians are called ἀδαμεῖς ("unconquered ones") in an inscription (§55 in Susan Guettel Cole, *Theoi Megaloi: The Cult of the Great Gods at Samothrace*, EPRO 96 [Leiden: Brill, 1984], 167).

119. Cf. *Ref.* 5.7.29. Herodotos speaks of a sacred tale in the Samothrakian mysteries explaining ithyphallic statues (*Hist.* 2.51; cf. Plotinus, *Enn.* 3.6.19). The Samothrakian statues are mentioned by Varro, *Ling.* 5.58. They were often identified with the Dioskouri (Castor and Pollux), although they had their own cult names. See further Cole, *Theoi Megaloi*, 28–29; Lancellotti, *Naassenes*, 259–61. For the association of Attis and the Dioskouri, see *L'Année épigraphique* (2004) §1026 (a lead curse tablet found at Mainz, late first century CE): *Bone sancta Atthis … rogo, domine, per tuum Castorem, Pollucem* ("Attis, kind and holy … I entreat you, lord, through your Castor and Pollux").

120. John 6:53 combined with Matt 5:20b. The principle "you are what you eat" seems to be in view here: eat the substance ("flesh and blood") of the Human, become consubstantial with the Human.

121. Mark 10:38 (or Matt 20:22) combined with John 8:21 (or 13:33; cf. 7:34, 36).

122. Cf. Gos. Eb. in Epiph., *Pan.* 30.13.3 (*NTApoc* 1:170).

ἀχαρακτηρίστου ἐγκεφάλου τὴν ἀρχὴν τῆς καταβάσεως λαμβάνων καὶ πάσας τὰς τῶν ὑποκειμένων διερχόμενος ἀρχάς, πῶς καὶ τίνα τρόπον κατέρχεται οὐ νοοῦμεν. 14. τοῦτ᾽ ἔστι, φησί, τὸ εἰρημένον·

φωνὴν μὲν αὐτοῦ ἠκούσαμεν, εἶδος δὲ αὐτοῦ οὐχ ἑωράκαμεν.

ἀποτεταγμένου γάρ, φησίν, αὐτοῦ καὶ <κε>χαρακτηρισμένου ἀκούεται φωνή, τὸ δὲ εἶδος τὸ κατελθὸν ἄνωθεν, ἀπὸ τοῦ ἀχαρακτηρίστου, ὁποῖόν ἐστιν, οἶδεν οὐδείς· ἔστι δὲ ἐν τῷ πλάσματι τῷ χοϊκῷ, γινώσκει δὲ αὐτὸ οὐδείς.

15. Οὗτος, φησίν, ἐστὶν

ὁ τὸν κατακλυσμὸν <κατ>οικ<ι>ῶν θεός,

κατὰ τὸ ψαλτήριον, καὶ φθεγγόμενος <καὶ> κεκραγὼς ἀπὸ «ὑδάτων πολλῶν». ὕδατα, φησίν, ἐστὶ πολλὰ ἡ πολυσχιδὴς τῶν θνητῶν γένεσις ἀνθρώπων, ἀφ᾽ ἧς βοᾷ καὶ κέκραγε πρὸς τὸν ἀχαρακτήριστον ἄνθρωπον,

ῥῦσαι, λέγων, ἀπὸ λεόντων τὴν μονογενῆ μου.

16. πρὸς τοῦτον, φησίν, ἐστὶν εἰρημένον·

παῖς μου εἶ σύ, Ἰσραήλ· μὴ φοβοῦ·
ἐὰν διὰ ποταμῶν διέλθῃς, οὐ μή σε συγκλύσουσιν·
ἐὰν διὰ πυρὸς διέλθῃς, οὐ μή σε συγκαύσει·

[κορυφῆς] above (that is, the unformed brain) and passes through all the dominions of underlying realities, we do not understand how and in what way he descends.[123] 14. This is what the verse means:

> we heard his voice but did not see his shape.[124]

When he takes on extension and form, he says, his voice is heard. But the shape is that which has descended from the Unformed One above, and no one knows its nature. It lies within the bodily formation made of dust—but no one knows it.

15. He is, he claims,

> the God dwelling in the flood,

(in the phrase of the Psalter) who utters his voice and cries out from "many waters."[125] These "many waters," he claims, refer to the fractured race of mortal human beings. From this race, he shouts and cries out to the Unformed Human:

> Deliver my only daughter from the lions![126]

16. The following verse of scripture, he claims, is addressed to him:

> You are my child, Israel, do not fear!
> If you cross through rivers, they will not submerge you.
> If you cross through fire, it will not scorch you![127]

---

123. According to A. D. Nock, the Naassene interpreter of the hymn in *Ref.* 5.9.8 wrongly understood the word Αἱμόνιοι (who are Thessalians) to refer to Thracians who dwell round Mt. Haimos ("Korybas of the Haemonians" *ClQ* 20 [1926]: 41–42). For the myth of Korybas, see Clem. Alex., *Protr.* 19, with the discussion of Lancellotti, *Naassenes*, 261–64. "That is" translates *καί* (epexegetic). Apparently the Naassene writer interprets Κορύβαντα to mean τὸν ἀπὸ τῆς κορυφῆς καταβάντα (so Marcovich, *Refutatio*, 157 note ad loc.). The unformed brain is taken as symbolic of the unformed primal deity (cf. *Ref.* 5.7.35; 5.17.11 [Peratai]).

124. Cf. Deut 4:12; John 5:37; Clem. Alex., *Strom.* 4.7.45.1.

125. Ps 28:10, 3 LXX; see the similar language in *Ref.* 5.19.16 ("Sethians").

126. Ps. 34:17 LXX; cf. 21:21–22. The "daughter" is apparently the soul.

127. Isa 41:9 LXX: "You are my child/servant" (Παῖς μου εἶ); and 43:2: καὶ ἐὰν διαβαίνης … ποταμοὶ οὐ συγκλύσουσίν σε, καὶ ἐὰν διέλθῃς διὰ πυρός, οὐ μὴ κατακαυθῇς,

ποταμούς, φησί, λέγει τὴν ὑγρὰν τῆς γενέσεως οὐσίαν, πῦρ δὲ τὴν ἐπὶ τὴν γένεσιν ὁρμὴν καὶ ἐπιθυμίαν·—«σὺ ἐμὸς εἶ, μὴ φοβοῦ».

17. καὶ πάλιν, φησίν· «εἰ ἐπιλήσεται μήτηρ τῶν τέκνων αὐτῆς <τοῦ> μὴ ἐλεῆσαι» μηδὲ ἐπιδοῦναι μαστόν, «κἀγὼ ἐπιλήσομαι ὑμῶν.» ὁ Ἀδάμας, φησί, λέγει πρὸς τοὺς ἰδίους ἀνθρώπους·

ἀλλ᾽ εἰ καὶ ἐπιλήσεται ταῦτα γυνή, ἀλλ᾽ ἐγὼ οὐκ ἐπιλήσομαι ὑμῶν· ἐπὶ τῶν χειρῶν μου ἐζωγράφηκα ὑμᾶς.

18. Περὶ δὲ τῆς ἀνόδου αὐτοῦ—τουτέστι τῆς ἀναγεννήσεως—, ἵνα γένηται πνευματικός, οὐ σαρκικός, λέγει, φησίν, ἡ γραφή·

ἄρατε πύλας, οἱ ἄρχοντες ὑμῶν,
καὶ ἐπάρθητε, πύλαι αἰώνιοι,
καὶ εἰσελεύσεται ὁ βασιλεὺς τῆς δόξης·

τουτέστι θαῦμα θαυμάτων·

τίς δέ, φησίν, ἐστὶν οὗτος ὁ βασιλεὺς τῆς δόξης;
σκώληξ καὶ οὐκ ἄνθρωπος,
ὄνειδος ἀνθρώπου
καὶ ἐξουθένημα λαοῦ.
αὐτός ἐστιν ὁ βασιλεὺς τῆς δόξης,
ὁ ἐν πολέμῳ δυνατός.

The rivers, he says, refer to the watery substance of birth, and "fire" refers to the impulse and desire for reproduction.[128] The verse continues: "You are mine, do not fear."

17. Again, scripture says: "If a mother forgets her own children, not pitying them" or offering them her breast, "then will I forget you." The speaker, he claims, is Adamas talking to the people who belong to him.

> But if a woman forgets even these, still I will not forget you. I have painted you on my hands.[129]

18. Concerning his ascent (that is, his rebirth) to become spiritual, not fleshly, the scripture, he claims, says this:

> Lift up the gates, you rulers,
> And be raised, eternal gates,
> So that the king of glory will come in.

This refers to a wonder of wonders![130]

> Who is the king of glory?[131]
> A worm and not a human,
> A reproach of a human
> And the scorn of the people![132]
> He is the king of glory,
> Who is strong in war.[133]

φλὸξ οὐ κατακαύσει σε ("Even if you cross … rivers will not overwhelm you; even if you traverse fire, you will in no way by consumed; flame will not consume you").

128. For this interpretation of fire, see *Ref.* 6.17.4 ("Simon").

129. Isa 49:15–16 LXX.

130. Cf. Gos. Thom. 29.2. Lancellotti comments: "Perhaps … the Archons marvel at the being which crosses the planetary spheres seeing it still in its earthly human features." The ascending spiritual person is "now transformed into the king of glory" (*Naassenes*, 292).

131. Ps 23:7 LXX. Cf. Justin, *Dial.* 36.5–6.

132. Ps 21:7 LXX.

133. Ps 23:8, 10 LXX.

19. πόλεμον δὲ λέγει τὸν ἐν σώματι, ὅτι ἐκ μαχίμων στοιχείων πέπλασται τὸ πλάσμα, καθὼς γέγραπται, φησί· «μνήσθητι πόλεμον τὸν γινόμενον ἐν σώματι».

ταύτην, φησί, τὴν εἴσοδον καὶ ταύτην τὴν πύλην εἶδεν εἰς Μεσοποταμίαν πορευόμενος ὁ Ἰακώβ—ὅπερ ἐστὶν ἀπὸ τοῦ παιδὸς ἔφηβος ἤδη γινόμενος καὶ ἀνήρ—τουτέστιν ἐγνωρίσθη τῷ εἰς Μεσοποταμίαν πορευομένῳ·

20. Μεσοποταμία δέ, φησίν, ἐστὶν ἡ τοῦ μεγάλου Ὠκεανοῦ ῥοή, ἀπὸ τῶν μέσων ῥέουσα τοῦ τελείου ἀνθρώπου. καὶ ἐθαύμασε τὴν οὐράνιον πύλην εἰπών·

> ὡς φοβερὸς ὁ τόπος οὗτος· οὐκ ἔστι τοῦτο ἀλλ' ἢ οἶκος θεοῦ, καὶ αὕτη ἡ πύλη τοῦ οὐρανοῦ.

διὰ τοῦτο, φησί, λέγει ὁ Ἰησοῦς·

> ἐγώ εἰμι ἡ πύλη ἡ ἀληθινή.

21. ἔστι δὲ ὁ ταῦτα λέγων ὁ ἀπὸ τοῦ ἀχαρακτηρίστου, φησίν, ἄνωθεν κεχαρακτηρισμένος τέλειος ἄνθρωπος. οὐ δύναται οὖν, φησί, σωθῆναι ὁ τέλειος ἄνθρωπος, ἐὰν μὴ ἀναγεν<ν>ηθῇ διὰ ταύτης εἰσελθὼν τῆς πύλης.

22. Τὸν αὐτὸν δὲ τοῦτον, φησί, Φρύγες καὶ Πάπαν καλοῦσιν, ὅτι πάντα ἔπαυσεν, ἀτάκτως καὶ πλημμελῶς πρὸ τῆς ἑαυτοῦ φανερώσεως κεκινημένα· τὸ γὰρ ὄνομα, φησί, τοῦ Πάπα πάντων ὁμοῦ ἐστι «τῶν ἐπουρανίων καὶ ἐπιγείων

19. He means the war in the body, for the bodily formation is formed from warring elements as (he claims) it is written: "Remember the war within the body!"[134]

This entrance, he comments, and this "gate" is the one that Jacob saw while traveling to Mesopotamia. This story signifies the young man who has grown from childhood into manhood. This is what is made known to the one who travels into Mesopotamia.

20. Mesopotamia, he says, is the stream of vast Ocean flowing from the middle parts of the perfect Human.[135] He wondered at the celestial gate and remarked:

> How terrifying is this place! This is none other than the house of God, the gate of heaven![136]

For this reason, he says, Jesus declares,

> I am the true gate.[137]

21. He who says this, he claims, is the perfect Human, who is formed from above from the Unformed One. Now the perfect Human, he claims, cannot be saved unless he is reborn by entering through the gate.[138]

E. PHRYGIAN MYSTERIES ABOUT THE HUMAN. 22. The Phrygians call this same one "Papas" because he paused [ἔπαυσεν] everything that was in disorderly and discordant motion before he appeared.[139] The name of Papas,

---

134. Cf. Job 40:32 LXX; *Ref.* 1.24.5–6 (Brahmans).

135. Cf. John 7:38 (waters flowing from the belly). See further Lancellotti, *Naassenes*, 293.

136. Gen 28:5, 12, 17 LXX.

137. John 10:7, 9. Cf. *Ref.* 5.9.21, end (Jesus is the true gate); 5.17.9 (Peratai); Clem. Alex., *Exc.* 26.

138. Jesus as the perfect Human both *is* the gate of salvation and *must enter* through the gate to be saved (*Salvator salvandus*).

139. "Papas" and the other cult epithets in *Ref.* 5.8.22–9.4 refer to Attis. The Naassene writer sees the true identity of Attis as the Primal Human (Birdsall, "Naassene Sermon," 231). Thus cultic and mythic elements of Attis are put into another framework. On the name Papas, see Diodoros, *Bibl. hist.* 3.58.4: Ἄττιν, ὕστερον δ'ἐπικληθέντα Πάπαν ("Attis, later called Papas"); *CIL* V. 766 (*Atte Papa*). See further Thomas Drew-Bear and Christian Naour, "Divinités de Phrygie," *ANRW* 18.3: 2018–22; Lancellotti, *Naassenes*, 275–76.

καὶ καταχθονίων» <φωνὴ> λεγόντων· παῦε, παῦε τὴν ἀσυμφωνίαν τοῦ κόσμου καὶ ποίησον «εἰρήνην τοῖς μακράν»—τουτέστι τοῖς ὑλικοῖς (κ)αὶ χοϊκοῖς—καὶ «εἰρήνην τοῖς ἐγγύς»—τουτέστι τοῖς πνευματικοῖς καὶ νοεροῖς τελείοις ἀνθρώποις.—

23. Λέγουσι δὲ οἱ Φρύγες <τὸν> αὐτὸν τοῦτον καὶ νέκυν, οἱονεὶ ἐν μνήματι καὶ τάφῳ ἐγκατωρυγμένον ἐν τῷ σώματι. τοῦτο, φησίν, ἐστὶ τὸ εἰρημένον·

> τάφοι ἐστὲ κεκονιαμένοι, γέμοντες ἔσωθεν ὀστέων νεκρῶν,

ὅτι οὐκ ἔστιν, φησίν, ἐν ὑμῖν ἄνθρωπος ὁ ζῶν. καὶ πάλιν, φησί· «ἐξαλοῦνται ἐκ τῶν μνημείων οἱ νεκροί»—τουτέστιν ἐκ τῶν σωμάτων τῶν χοϊκῶν, ἀναγεννηθέντες πνευματικοί, οὐ σαρκικοί.—24. αὕτη, φησίν, ἐστὶν ἡ ἀνάστασις ἡ διὰ τῆς πύλης γινομένη τῶν οὐρανῶν, δι' ἧς οἱ μὴ εἰσελθόντες, φησί, πάντες μένουσι νεκροί.

Οἱ δὲ αὐτοί, φησί, Φρύγες τὸν αὐτὸν τοῦτον πάλιν ἐκ μεταβολῆς λέγουσι θεόν· γίνεται γάρ, φησί, θεός, ὅταν ἐκ νεκρῶν ἀναστὰς διὰ τῆς τοιαύτης πύλης εἰσελεύσεται εἰς τὸν οὐρανόν. 25. ταύτην, φησί, τὴν πύλην Παῦλος οἶδεν ὁ ἀπόστολος, παρανοίξας ἐν μυστηρίῳ καὶ εἰπὼν «ἡρπάσθαι» ὑπὸ ἀγγέλου καὶ γεγονέναι «ἕως» δευτέρου καὶ «τρίτου οὐρανοῦ εἰς τὸν παράδεισον» αὐτόν, καὶ ἑωρακέναι ἃ ἑώρακε «καὶ ἀκηκοέναι ῥήματα ἄρρητα, ἃ οὐκ ἐξὸν ἀνθρώπῳ εἰπεῖν».

26. ταῦτά ἐστι, φησί, τὰ ἄρρητα ὑπὸ πάντων λεγόμενα μυστήρια, «ἃ <λαλοῦμεν> οὐκ ἐν διδακτοῖς ἀνθρωπίνης σοφίας λόγοις, ἀλλ' ἐν διδακτοῖς πνεύματος, πνευματικοῖς πνευματικὰ συγκρίνοντες. ψυχικὸς δὲ ἄνθρωπος οὐ

he claims, is the voice of all "heavenly, earthly, and underworldly beings" together.[140] They declare: "Cease, cease [παῦε, παῦε] the disharmony of the world and make 'peace for those far' (that is, material, earthly people) and 'peace for those near' (that is, spiritual, intellectual, and perfect people)."[141]

23. The Phrygians say that this same one is also a "corpse," buried as it were in the grave and tomb of his body.[142] To this the scripture refers when it says:

> You are white-washed tombs full of dead people's bones on the inside.[143]

This is because you do not have the living Human within. Again it says: "The dead will leap out of the graves"—that is, out of earthly bodies, since they are reborn as spirit, and not as flesh.[144] 24. This resurrection is the one through the gate of heaven. All who do not enter it, he says, remain corpses.

These very Phrygians, he asserts, say that this same human becomes a god again by transformation. He becomes a god, he claims, when he rises from the dead and, through such a gate, enters heaven. 25. The apostle Paul knows this gate, since he opened it in a mystery. He said that he was "seized" by an angel and carried "as far as" the second and "third heaven, into paradise" and saw what he saw and "heard unutterable utterances not permissible for a person to declare."[145]

26. Everyone calls these mysteries ineffable, he says. "We utter them not in lessons of human wisdom but in lessons of the Spirit, comparing spiritual things with spiritual. But the animate person does not receive

---

140. Marcovich, following Reitzenstein, adds φωνή ("voice"). The verse cited is Phil 2:10; cf. *Ref.* 5.7.11; 5.16.14 (Peratai).

141. Isa 57:19 LXX; cf. Eph 2:17; Three Forms (NHC XIII,1) 40.10–11: "Then I too revealed my voice secretly and said, 'Stop, stop, you who tread on matter" (trans. John D. Turner in Hedrick).

142. Cf. *Ref.* 5.9.8; Philolaos, DK 44 B14; Plato, *Crat.* 400c; *Gorg.* 493a; Clem. Alex., *Strom.* 3.3.16.3–17.1; Julian, *Or.* 6, 189c. See further Burkert, *Lore*, 248; Lancellotti, *Naassenes*, 277.

143. Matt 23:27.

144. Cf. John 5:28. For the leaping action, see Acts 3:8 (the paralyzed man leaps up).

145. 2 Cor 12:2–4. Paul's ascent means becoming god because it is a return of the divine element to its original home. See further Lancellotti, *Naassenes*, 278. Cf. *Ref.* 5.8.31–32 below; Apoc. Paul (NHC V,2) 19.23–32; Apoc. Mos. 40.2; 2 En. 22:1; T. Levi 2.7–3.8.

δέχεται τὰ τοῦ πνεύματος τοῦ θεοῦ· μωρία γὰρ αὐτῷ ἐστι». Καὶ ταῦτα, φησίν, ἐστὶ τὰ τοῦ πνεύματος ἄρρητα μυστήρια, ἃ ἡμεῖς ἴσμεν μόνοι.

27. περὶ τούτων, φησίν, εἴρηκεν ὁ σωτήρ·

> οὐδεὶς δύναται ἐλθεῖν πρός με ἐὰν μή τινα ἑλκύσῃ ὁ πατήρ μου ὁ οὐράνιος·

πάνυ γάρ, φησί, δύσκολόν ἐστι παραδέξασθαι καὶ λαβεῖν τὸ μέγα τοῦτο καὶ ἄρρητον μυστήριον. καὶ πάλιν, φησίν, εἴρηκεν ὁ σωτήρ·

> οὐ πᾶς ὁ λέγων μοι, Κύριε κύριε, εἰσελεύσεται εἰς τὴν βασιλείαν τῶν οὐρανῶν, ἀλλ' ὁ ποιῶν τὸ θέλημα τοῦ πατρός μου τοῦ ἐν τοῖς οὐρανοῖς.

28. ὃ δη<λοῖ> ποιήσαντας, οὐχὶ ἀκούσαντας μόνον, εἰς τὴν βασιλείαν εἰσελθεῖν τῶν οὐρανῶν. καὶ πάλιν, φησίν, εἴρηκεν·

> οἱ τελῶναι καὶ αἱ πόρναι προάγουσιν ὑμᾶς εἰς τὴν βασιλείαν τῶν οὐρανῶν.

τελῶναι γάρ, φησίν, εἰσὶν οἱ τὰ τέλη τῶν ὅλων λαμβάνοντες· ἡμεῖς δέ, φησίν, ἐσμὲν οἱ τελῶναι, «εἰς οὓς τὰ τέλη τῶν αἰώνων κατήντηκε». τέλη γάρ, φησίν, εἰσὶ τὰ ἀπὸ τοῦ ἀχαρακτηρίστου εἰς τὸν κόσμον κατεσπαρμένα σπέρματα, δι' ὧν ὁ πᾶς συντελεῖται κόσμος· διὰ γὰρ αὐτῶν καὶ ἤρξατο γενέσθαι.

29. καὶ τοῦτό ἐστι, φησί, τὸ εἰρημένον·

> ἐξῆλθεν ὁ σπείρων τοῦ σπεῖραι· καὶ τὰ μὲν ἔπεσε παρὰ τὴν ὁδὸν καὶ κατεπατήθη, τὰ δὲ ἐπὶ τὰ πετρώδη καὶ ἐξανέτειλε, φησί, καὶ διὰ τὸ μὴ ἔχειν βάθος γῆς ἐξηράνθη καὶ ἀπέθανε· τὰ δὲ ἔπεσε, φησίν, ἐπὶ

the teachings of God's spirit, for they are idiocy to him."[146] Now these, he declares, are the unspeakable mysteries of the spirit, which *we* alone know!

27. The Savior, he claims, has spoken about them:

> No one can come to me unless my heavenly Father draws him.[147]

This is because it is extremely difficult, he claims, to accept and receive this great and ineffable mystery. Again, he says, the Savior has declared:

> Not everyone who says to me, "Lord, Lord!" will enter the kingdom of heaven, but the one who does the will of my Father in heaven.[148]

28. This remark shows that it is those who act—not just hear—who enter the kingdom of heaven.[149] Again, he says, the Savior has proclaimed:

> Tax collectors and prostitutes go ahead of you into the kingdom of heaven![150]

This is because these tax collectors [τελῶναι], he says, are those who receive the tolls [τέλη] of the universe. We, he says, are the tax collectors "who have attained the tolls of the aeons."[151] For the tolls, he says, are the seeds sowed into the world from the Unformed One, through which the whole world obtains completion [συντελεῖται]. For it is through *them* that the world began, surely, to exist.

29. This, he says, is what the scriptural verse means:

> The sower went out to sow. Some seeds fell along the path and were trampled. Others fell on rocky soil and sprouted, yet were dried up and died due to lack of depth. Others fell on good and

146. 1 Cor 2:13–14; *Ref.* 6.34.8 ("Valentinus"); 7.26.3 ("Basileides"); Hipp., *Comm. Dan.* 3.2.4; Clem. Alex., *Strom.* 1.12.56.1; 1.17.87.4; 5.4.19.3; 5.4.25.5; 6.18.166.3.

147. John 6:44; cf. Exeg. Soul (NHC II,6) 135.1–15; Greek Gos. Thom. 6.12; Clem. Alex., *Strom.* 5.1.7.3; 5.13.83.

148. Matt 7:21; cf. 2 Clem. 4.2; Justin, *1 Apol.* 16.9.

149. Cf. Jas 1:22; Matt 7:24, 26; Rom 2:13.

150. Matt 21:31b; cf. Iren., *Haer.* 4.20.12.

151. 1 Cor 10:11. For the τέλη as tolls, see Matt 17:25. Tax collectors are also spiritual persons in Iren. *Haer.* 1.8.3. Cf. Hipp., *Comm. Dan.* 1.16.4. See further Frickel, "Naassener oder Valentinianer?," 102.

τὴν γῆν τὴν καλὴν καὶ ἀγαθήν, καὶ ἐποίει καρπόν, ὃ μὲν ἑκατόν, ὃ δὲ ἑξήκοντα, ὃ δὲ τριάκοντα. ὁ ἔχων, φησίν, ὦτα ἀκούειν ἀκουέτω.

τουτέστι, φησίν, οὐδεὶς τούτων τῶν μυστηρίων ἀκροατὴς γέγονεν εἰ μὴ μόνοι γνωστικοὶ τέλειοι.

30. αὕτη, φησίν, ἐστὶν ἡ γῆ ἡ καλὴ καὶ ἀγαθή, ἣν λέγει Μωϋσῆς·

εἰσάξω ὑμᾶς εἰς γῆν καλὴν καὶ ἀγαθήν, εἰς γῆν ῥέουσαν γάλα καὶ μέλι.

τοῦτο, φησίν, ἐστὶ τὸ μέλι καὶ τὸ γάλα, οὗ δεῖ γευσαμένους τοὺς τελείους ἀβασιλεύτους γενέσθαι καὶ μετασχεῖν τοῦ πληρώματος. τοῦτο, φησίν, ἐστὶ τὸ πλήρωμα δι᾽ οὗ πάντα τὰ γινόμενα γεν<ν>ητὰ ἀπὸ τοῦ ἀγεννήτου γέγονέ τε καὶ πεπλήρωται.

31. Ὁ δὲ αὐτὸς οὗτος ὑπὸ τῶν Φρυγῶν καὶ ἄκαρπος καλεῖται· ἔστι γὰρ ἄκαρπος ὅταν ᾖ σαρκικὸς καὶ τὴν «ἐπιθυμίαν τῆς σαρκὸς» ἐργάζηται. τοῦτο, φησίν, ἐστὶ τὸ εἰρημένον· «πᾶν δένδρον μὴ ποιοῦν καρπὸν καλὸν ἐκκόπτεται καὶ εἰς πῦρ βάλλεται». καρποὶ δὲ οὗτοι, φησίν, εἰσὶ μόνοι οἱ λογικοί, ζῶντες ἄνθρωποι, οἱ διὰ τῆς πύλης εἰσερχόμενοι τῆς τρίτης.

> rich soil and produced fruit, one a hundredfold, another sixtyfold, another thirtyfold. The one who has ears, hear![152]

This means, he claims, no one has become a hearer of these mysteries except the perfect knowers alone.

30. Moses also refers to the good and rich soil:

> I will lead you into a good and rich soil, to a land flowing with milk and honey.[153]

This is the honey and milk, he claims, which the perfect must taste to become kingless and share in the Fullness. This, he says, is the Fullness through which all reality that is born is born from the Unborn and comes to fulfillment.[154]

31. The Phrygians also call this same one "unfruitful." He is unfruitful when he is fleshly and produces the "lust of the flesh."[155] This, he says, is what the scriptural verse signifies: "Every tree not producing good fruit is cut down and thrown into the fire."[156] These fruits, he says, are only those humans who are rational and alive, who enter through the third gate.[157]

---

152. This summarized parable combines the Synoptic accounts (Mark 4:3–9 par.). Note that the seeds falling among thorns are omitted, probably because the Naassene writer wants to highlight only three kinds of hearers (in accord with his threefold division of humanity). Bergman thinks that the lack of depth (βάθος) recalls the "deep things" (τὰ βάθη) in *Ref.* 5.6.4 ("Kleine Beiträge," 99–100; see further Frickel, "Naassener oder Valentinianer?," 102–4). See the use of the parable in *Ref.* 8.9.1 (Doketai); Gos. Thom. 9; 1 Clem. 24.5; Justin, *Dial.* 125.1; Clem. Alex., frag. 225.26 (Stählin); *Strom.* 1.7.37.2; 6.14.114.3; Memoria of the Apostles in *NTApoc* 1:376 ("the sower is he who scatters captive souls in diverse bodies as he wills").

153. Deut 31:20; cf. *Ref.* 6.30.9 ("Valentinus"); Clem. Alex., *Paed.* 1.91.4.

154. Cf. the interpretation of honey and milk in Barn. 6.17. For milk in the mysteries of Attis, see Sallustius, *Diis mund.* 4; Lancellotti, *Naassenes*, 136, 299–301. Goodenough offers a discussion of milk as a symbol in Philo, Clement, and later Christian sources (*Jewish Symbols*, 6:117–22). See further Andrew McGowan, *Ascetic Eucharists: Food and Drink in Early Christian Ritual Meals* (Oxford: Clarendon, 1999), 107–15.

155. Gal 5:16; Clem. Alex., *Strom.* 4.8.60.4.

156. Matt 3:10; 7:19; Luke 3:9; cf. *Ref.* 6.9.9–10; 6.16.6 ("Simon").

157. The third gate, which Lancellotti identifies with Jesus, is the gate for the spirituals (*Naassenes*, 279). Lancellotti connects the third gate with Paul's reference to a third heaven (cited in *Ref.* 5.8.25). The first and second gates, presumably, are those through which the animate and material people enter (see Werner Foerster, "Die Naas-

32. λέγουσι γοῦν· «εἰ νεκρὰ ἐφάγετε καὶ ζῶντα ἐποιήσατε, τί, ἂν ζῶντα φάγητε, ποιήσετε;» ζῶντα δὲ λέγουσι καὶ λόγους καὶ νόας καὶ ἀνθρώπους, τοὺς μαργαρίτας ἐκείνου τοῦ ἀχαρακτηρίστου ἐρ<ρ>ιμμένους εἰς τὸ πλάσμα <ὡς> καρπούς. 33. τοῦτ' ἔστιν ὃ λέγει, φησί· «μὴ βάλητε τὸ ἅγιον τοῖς κυσί, μηδὲ τοὺς μαργαρίτας τοῖς χοίροις», χοίρων καὶ κυνῶν ἔργον λέγοντες εἶναι τὴν γυναικὸς πρὸς ἄνδρα ὁμιλίαν.

34. Τὸν αὐτὸν δὲ τοῦτον, φησίν, οἱ Φρύγες καλοῦσιν αἰπόλον, οὐχ ὅτι, φησίν, ἔβοσκεν αἶγας καὶ τράγους, ὡς οἱ ψυχικοὶ ὀνομάζουσιν, ἀλλ' <ὅ>τι, φησίν, ἐστὶν ἀ<ε>ιπόλος, τουτέστιν ὁ ἀεὶ πολῶν καὶ στρέφων καὶ περιελαύνων τὸν κόσμον ὅλον στροφῇ. 35. πολεῖν γάρ ἐστι τὸ στρέφειν καὶ μεταβάλλειν τὰ πράγματα· ἔνθε<ν>, φησί, καὶ τὰ δύο κέντρα τοῦ οὐρανοῦ ἅπαντες προσαγορεύουσι πόλους. καὶ ὁ ποιητὴς δέ, φησί,

πωλεῖταί τις δεῦρο γέρων ἅλιος νημερτής,
ἀθάνατος Πρωτεὺς Αἰγύπτιος,

οὐ πιπράσκεται, φησίν, ἀλλὰ στρέφεται αὐτοῦ, οἱονεὶ [καὶ] περιέρχεται λέγει. καὶ πόλεις ἐν αἷς οἰκοῦμεν, ὅτι στρεφόμεθα καὶ πολοῦμεν ἐν αὐταῖς,

32. Thus they say, "if you ate dead things and made them alive, what will you make when you eat living things?"[158] They say that the living things are words, thoughts, and humans. These are pearls of the Unformed One thrown into the bodily formation like fruits. 33. This, he claims, is what he [Jesus] means when he says, "Don't throw what is holy to dogs nor pearls to pigs."[159] The work of pigs and dogs, they claim, means sex between a woman and a man.

34. The Phrygians, he continues, also call this same one "goatherd" [αἰπόλον]. This is not because, he claims, he pastures nanny and billy goats, as the animate people call them, but because, he says, he is ever turning (that is, ever revolving, turning, and driving round the whole world with a whirl). 35. "To revolve" [πολεῖν] means to turn and to change phenomena.[160] Hence, he says, everybody calls the two centers of heaven "poles" [πόλους].[161] He also quotes the poet:

> The unerring Old Man of the Sea circles about [πωλεῖται] these regions,
> Immortal Proteus of Egypt.[162]

He is not sold [πιπράσκεται], he says, but turns in the same place—effectively, he claims, going in a circle.[163] Moreover, the cities we inhabit are

---

sener," in *Studi di storia religiosa della tarda antichità* [Messina: University of Messina, 1968], 21–33 [33]).

158. Cf. Gos. Thom. 11.3 with Johnson, "*Refutatio*," 316. See also Gos. Phil. (NHC II,3) 72.19; Robert M. Grant, "Notes on the Gospel of Thomas," *VC* 13 (1959): 170–80 (173–74); Bertil E. Gärtner, *The Theology of the Gospel of Thomas* (New York: Harper, 1961), 163–65; Marcovich, *Studies*, 77–78.

159. See Matt 7:6; Gos. Thom. 93; Did. 9.5; *Ref.* 9.17.1 (Elchasaites); Clem. Alex., *Strom.* 1.11.53.3. For Lancellotti, the pearls represent "the noetic elements … imprisoned in matter." The imprisonment continues to happen "through sexual union" characteristic of animals (*Naassenes*, 280).

160. Cf. *Ref.* 4.47.1–2 (Aratos allegorizers); Plato, *Crat.* 408c–d: ὁ λόγος τὸ πᾶν σημαίνει καὶ κυκλεῖ καῖ πολεῖ ἀεί … ὀρθῶς ἄρ' ὁ πᾶν μηνύων καὶ ἀεὶ πολῶν "Πὰν αἰπόλος" εἴη ("speech signifies all things and keeps them circulating and always going about … So the one who expresses all things and keeps them always in circulation is correctly called 'Pan-the-goat-herd'" [trans. Reeve]).

161. Cf. *Comm. in Arat.* (Maass, 331,5; 342,22–3).

162. Homer, *Od.* 4.384–385. For philosophical speculations about Proteus, see Lancellotti, *Naassenes*, 281.

163. The Naassene writer apparently understood πωλέομαι (to walk about) in

[καὶ] καλοῦνται πόλεις. 36. οὕτως, φησίν, αἱ Φρύγες αἰπόλον τοῦτον καλοῦσι, τὸν πάντοτε <πάντα> πανταχῇ στρέφοντα καὶ μεταβάλλοντα πρὸς τὰ οἰκεῖα.

Καλοῦσι δὲ α(ὐ)τόν, φησί, καὶ πολύκαρπον οἱ Φρύγες, ὅτι «πλείονα», φησί, «τὰ τέκνα τῆς ἐρήμου μᾶλλον ἢ τῆς ἐχούσης τὸν ἄνδρα»· τουτέστι τὰ ἀναγεννώμενα ἀθάνατα καὶ ἀεὶ διαμένοντα ἐστὶ πολλά, κἂν ὀλίγα ᾖ τὰ γεννώμενα· τὰ δὲ σαρκικά, φησίν, φθαρτὰ πάντα, κἂν ᾖ πολλὰ πάνυ <τὰ> γεννώμενα.

37. διὰ τοῦτο, φησίν, «ἔκλαιε Ῥαχὴλ τὰ τέκνα <αὐτῆς> καὶ οὐκ ἤθελε», φησί, «παρακαλεῖσθαι κλαίουσα ἐπ' αὐτοῖς»· ᾔδει γάρ, φησίν, «ὅτι οὐκ εἰσί». θρηνεῖ δὲ καὶ Ἱερεμίας τὴν κάτω Ἱερουσαλήμ, οὐ τὴν ἐν Φοινίκῃ πόλιν, ἀλλὰ τὴν κάτω γένεσιν, τὴν φθαρτήν· ἔγνω γάρ, φησί, καὶ Ἱερεμίας τὸν τέλειον ἄνθρωπον, τὸν ἀναγεννώμενον «ἐξ ὕδατος καὶ πνεύματος», οὐ σαρκικόν. 38. αὐτὸς γοῦν ὁ Ἱερεμίας ἔλεγε,

ἄνθρωπός ἐστι, καὶ τίς γνώσεται αὐτόν;

οὕτως, φησίν, ἐστὶ πάνυ βαθεῖα καὶ δυσκατάληπτος ἡ τοῦ τελείου ἀνθρώπου γνῶσις. «ἀρχὴ» γάρ, φησί, «τελειώσεως γνῶσις ἀνθρώπου, θεοῦ δὲ γνῶσις ἀπηρτισμένη τελείωσις».

39. Λέγουσι δὲ αὐτόν, φησί, Φρύγες καὶ «χλοερὸν στάχυν τεθερισμένον», καὶ μετὰ τοὺς Φρύγας Ἀθηναῖοι, μυοῦντες Ἐλευσίνια καὶ ἐπιδεικνύντες τοῖς ἐποπτεύουσι τὸ μέγα καὶ θαυμαστὸν καὶ τελεώτατον ἐποπτικὸν ἐκεῖ μυστήριον ἐν σιωπῇ, τεθερισμένον στάχυν.

called cities [πόλεις] because we turn and circle about [πολοῦμεν] in them. 36. Accordingly, the Phrygians call him "goatherd" [αἰπόλον]. This means "Eternal Turner," since he always [ἀεί] turns [πολέω] and changes everything in every way to its proper nature.

The Phrygians also call him "fruitful" [πολύκαρπον] because scripture says: "More are the children of the deserted woman than she who has a husband."[164] This means that things reborn, immortal, and everlasting are many, even though few are born. But all fleshly things, he says, are corruptible—even if those who are born are extremely numerous.

37. For this reason, he says, "Rachel wept for her children and was unwilling to be comforted as she wept over them." For she knew, he says, "that they are no more."[165] Jeremiah also sings a dirge over the lower Jerusalem.[166] This is not the city in Phoenicia but refers to lower, corruptible birth. For Jeremiah, he asserts, knew the perfect Human, the one reborn "from water and spirit," who is not fleshly.[167] 38. Thus the same Jeremiah said,

> A Human exists, and who will know him?[168]

In this way, he says, the knowledge of the perfect Human is immensely deep and difficult to understand. For "the beginning of perfection," he says, "is knowledge of the Human, but knowledge of God is completed perfection."[169]

EXCURSUS: ELEUSINIAN MYSTERIES ABOUT THE HUMAN. 39. The Phrygians also call him, he reports, "green ear of grain harvested."[170] After the Phrygians, the Athenians affirmed the same. When they initiated according to the Eleusinian rites, they exhibited to the higher initiates the great, wondrous, and most perfect mystery beheld in silence: a harvested ear of grain.[171]

Homer, *Od.* 4, as a passive form of πωλέω ("to sell"), a literal meaning that he corrects in his spiritual interpretation.

164. Isa 54:1; Gal 4:27; cf. Clem. Alex., *Strom.* 2.6.28.5; Ep. Apos. 33 (*NTApoc* 1:268).

165. Jer 38:15 LXX, quoted in Matt 2:18; cf. Justin, *Dial.* 78.8.

166. Lam 1, epigraph, LXX.

167. John 3:5; cf. *Ref.* 5.7.40.

168. Jer 17:9 LXX.

169. Also quoted in *Ref.* 5.6.6.

170. The stalk is "green" because Attis died young. Burkert sees a parallel in Mesomedes, *Hymn* 5 (*Homo Necans*, 291).

171. See further Burkert, *Homo necans*, 290–91; Christiane Sourvinou-Inwood, "Festival and Mysteries: Aspects of the Eleusinian Cult," in *Greek Mysteries: The Archae-*

40. ὁ δὲ στάχυς οὗτός ἐστι καὶ παρὰ Ἀθηναίοις ὁ παρὰ τοῦ ἀχαρακτηρίστου φωστὴρ τέλειος μέγας, καθάπερ αὐτὸς ὁ ἱεροφάντης—οὐκ ἀποκεκομμένος μέν, ὡς ὁ Ἄττις, εὐνουχισμένος δὲ διὰ κωνείου καὶ πᾶσαν ἀπηρτημένος τὴν σαρκικὴν γένεσιν—νυκτὸς ἐν <Ἐ>λευσῖνι ὑπὸ πολλῷ πυρὶ τελῶν τὰ μεγάλα καὶ ἄρρητα μυστήρια βοᾷ καὶ κέκραγε λέγων·

ἱερὸν ἔτεκε πότνια κοῦρον Βριμὼ Βριμόν,

τουτέστιν ἰσχυρὰ ἰσχυρόν. 41. πότνια δέ ἐστι, φησίν, ἡ γένεσις ἡ πνευματική, ἡ ἐπουράνιος, ἡ ἄνω· ἰσχυρὸς δέ ἐστιν ὁ οὕτω γεννώμενος.

ἔστι δὲ λεγόμενον τὸ μυστήριον Ἐλευσὶν καὶ ἀνακτόρειον· Ἐλευσὶν, ὅτι ἤλθομεν, φησίν, οἱ πνευματικοὶ ἄνωθεν, ἀπὸ τοῦ Ἀδάμαντος ῥυέντες κάτω—ἐλεύσεσθαι γάρ, φησίν, ἐστὶν ἐλθεῖν—, ἀνακτόρειον δὲ <διὰ> τὸ ἀνελθεῖν ἄνω. 42. τοῦτο, φησίν, ἐστὶν ὃ λέγουσιν οἱ κατωργιασμένοι τῶν Ἐλευσινίων τὰ μυστήρια.

θέ<σ>μιον δέ ἐστι, <τοὺς> τὰ μικρὰ μεμυημένους αὖθις <καὶ> τὰ μεγάλα μυεῖσθαι· «μόροι γὰρ μείζονες μείζονας μοίρας λαγχάνουσι». 43. μικρὰ, φησίν,

40. Among the Athenians too, this ear of grain is the perfect and great splendor from the Unformed One. Accordingly, the hierophant himself (not castrated like Attis, but made a eunuch through hemlock and detached from all fleshly generation) by night and under many torches accomplishes in Eleusis the great and unspeakable mysteries.[172] He shouts and cries aloud:

Lady Brimo has given birth to a holy child Brimos!

This means: the mighty female has given birth to the mighty male.[173] 41. The "Lady," he says, refers to the higher, spiritual, celestial generation, while the "mighty one" is the one celestially born.

The mystery is called "Eleusis" and "anaktoreion." It is called "Eleusis," he claims, because we, the spiritual people from above, came flowing down from Adamas (for to proceed [ἐλεύσεσθαι] means "to come").[174] It is called "anaktoreion" because of the upward ascent [ἀνελθεῖν ἄνω].[175] 42. This, he claims, is what those initiated into the Eleusinian mysteries declare.

It is a sacred custom for those initiated into the lesser mysteries also to be initiated into the greater mysteries, "for greater deaths obtain greater destinies."[176] 43. The lesser, lower mysteries, he says, are the mysteries of

---

ology and Ritual of Ancient Greek Secret Cults, ed. Michael B. Cosmopoulos (London: Routledge, 2003), 25–49 (36–37).

172. On the hemlock, see Origen, *Cels.* 7.48 (κωνειασθεὶς τὰ ἄρσενα μέρη ["drugged with hemlock in respect to his male parts"]); Jerome, *Jov.* 1.49 (*cicutae sorbitione castrari* ["castrated by a potion of hemlock"]). For the torches, see Plutarch, *Virt. prof.* 81e: μέγα φῶς ἰδών ("upon seeing a great light"); Dio Chrysostom 12.33 (σκότους τε καὶ φωτὸς ἐναλλὰξ αὐτῷ φαινομένων ["an alternation of darkness and light appears to him"]); Aristophanes, *Ran.* 340–342 (ἐγείρων φλογέας λαμπάδας ἐν χερσὶ προσήκεις, Ἴακχ᾽ ὦ Ἴακχε, νυκτέρου τελετῆς φωσφόρος ἀστήρ ["You come bearing flaming torches in your hand, Iakchos, O Iakchos, light-bearing star of the nightly initiation"]).

173. For Brimo, see Clem. Alex., *Protr.* 15.1; Euripides, *Suppl.* 54 (similar language as our text). See further Burkert, *Homo Necans*, 288–89; Parker, *Polytheism*, 358–59; Bremmer, *Initiation*, 14–15.

174. Cf. Cornutus, *Nat. d.* 28. The action of coming evokes "the descent of spiritual beings" (Lancellotti, *Naassenes*, 267).

175. Keil adds ἀνάγεσθαι and Marcovich ἡμᾶς καί. The anaktoreion is usually identified with the chapel in the Eleusinian Initiation Hall from where the great light emerged on the night of the highest initiation.

176. Herakleitos, DK 22 B25 (= Marcovich, *Heraclitus*, §97). See below, *Ref.* 5.8.44; cf. Plato, *Gorg.* 497c, with scholium (Hermann, 6:319): διττὰ ἦν τὰ μυστήρια παρ᾽ Ἀθηναίοις, καὶ τὰ μὲν μικρὰ ἐκαλεῖτο, ἅπερ ἐν ἄστει ἐτέλουν, τὰ δὲ μεγάλα, ἅπερ Ἐλευσῖνι

ἐστὶ τὰ μυστήρια τὰ τῆς Περσεφόνης, κάτω. περὶ ὧν μυστηρίων καὶ τῆς ὁδοῦ τῆς ἀγούσης ἐκεῖ, οὔσης «πλατείας καὶ εὐρυχώρου» καὶ φερούσης τοὺς ἀπολλυμένους ἐπὶ τὴν Περσεφόνην, καὶ ὁ ποιητὴς δή, φησίν,

αὐτὰρ ὑπ' αὐτήν ἐστιν ἀταρπιτὸς ὀκριόεσσα,
κοίλη, πηλώδης· ἣ δ' ἡγήσασθαι ἀρίστη
ἄλσος ἐς ἱμερόεν πολυτιμήτου Ἀφροδίτης.

44. ταῦτ' ἔστι, φησί, τὰ μικρὰ μυστήρια, τὰ τῆς σαρκικῆς γενέσεως, ἃ μυηθέντες οἱ ἄνθρωποι μικρὸν παύσασθαι ὀφείλουσι <πρὶν> καὶ μυεῖσθαι τὰ μεγάλα, τὰ ἐπουράνια. οἱ γὰρ τοὺς ἐκεῖ, φησί, λαχόντες «μόρους μείζονας μοίρας λαγχάνουσιν».

Αὕτη δέ, φησίν, ἐστὶν «ἡ πύλη τοῦ οὐρανοῦ» καὶ οὗτος «οἶκος θεοῦ», ὅπου ὁ ἀγαθὸς θεὸς κατοικεῖ μόνος· εἰς ὃν οὐκ εἰσελεύσεται, φησίν, ἀκάθαρτος οὐδείς, οὐ ψυχικός, οὐ σαρκικός, ἀλλὰ τηρεῖται πνευματικοῖς μόνοις. ὅπου δεῖ γενομένους βαλεῖν τὰ «ἐνδύματα» καὶ πάντας γενέσθαι νυμφίους ἀπηρσενωμένους διὰ τοῦ

Persephone. Concerning these mysteries and the road that leads there (i.e., the "wide and spacious" road that leads the dying to Persephone[177]), the poet also declares:

But under it is a jagged path
Sunken, muddy; but it is the best path to be led to
The lovely grove of greatly honored Aphrodite.[178]

44. These lesser mysteries, he claims, are those of fleshly birth.[179] When people are initiated into them, they must pause a short time before they are initiated into the greater, or celestial, mysteries.[180] For those who have obtained their "deaths" in that place, he says, "obtain greater destinies."

This, he says, is "the gate of heaven," and this is "the house of God," where only the good God dwells.[181] Into it there will not enter, he says, any impure person, either animate or fleshly.[182] It is kept for the spiritual alone. Therefore they must remove the "garments," and all must become

---

ἤγετο. καὶ πρότερον ἔδει τὰ μικρὰ μυηθῆναι, εἶτα τὰ μεγάλα ("The Athenian mysteries are twofold. The first, performed in the city, are called lesser; the greater are celebrated at Eleusis. It was necessary to be initiated into the lesser, then into the greater"). See also Philo, *Sacr.* 62; *Leg.* 3.99–100. The Naassenes use the distinction between lesser and greater mysteries "to distinguish the two moments of knowledge related to carnal and spiritual generation" (Lancellotti, *Naassenes*, 267).

177. Cf. Matt 7:13, quoted in *Ref.* 5.8.45 below. Persephone is Queen of the dead.

178. Scholars disagree about the author of these verses. Otto Kern placed the verses among the Orphic fragments (frag. 352 in his edition, but among the "*Spuria vel Dubia*"). Meineke attributed the lines to Parmenides (DK 28 B20). A. V. Lebedev gives them to Empedokles ("Orpheus, Parmenides or Empedocles? The Aphrodite Verses in the Naassene Treatise of Hippolytus' *Elenchos*," *Phil* 138 [1994]: 24–31 [30]), while Walter Burkert opts for Homer ("Die betretene Wiese: Interpretenprobleme im Bereich der Sexualssymbolik," in *Die wilde Seele: Zur Ethnopsychoanalyse von G. Devereux*, ed. H. P. Duerr [Frankfurt: Suhrkamp, 1987], 32–46 [40–42]). For "muddy" (πηλώδης) describing the path to the Underworld, see Plato, *Resp.* 363d6; 533d1.

179. Fleshly generation is suggested by Aphrodite, who represents generation (*Ref.* 5.7.11).

180. Keil supplies πρίν ("before"). One had to wait from the month Anthesterion in the spring to the month Boedromion in the fall. But the Naassene writer alludes to the time of life. The greater mysteries can only be fully experienced after death, when generation has ceased.

181. Gen 28:17 LXX; cf. above, *Ref.* 5.8.20.

182. Cf. *Ref.* 5.7.26.

παρθενικοῦ πνεύματος. 45. αὕτη δέ ἐστιν, ἡ παρθένος «ἡ ἐν γαστρὶ ἔχουσα καὶ συλλαμβάνουσα καὶ τίκτουσα υἱόν», οὐ ψυχικόν, οὐ σωματικόν, ἀλλὰ μακάριον αἰῶνα αἰώνων. περὶ τούτων, φησί, διαρρήδην εἴρηκεν ὁ σωτὴρ ὅτι

> στενὴ καὶ τεθλιμμένη ἐστὶν ἡ ὁδὸς ἡ ἀπάγουσα εἰς τὴν ζωήν, καὶ ὀλίγοι εἰσὶν οἱ εἰσερχόμενοι εἰς αὐτήν, πλατεῖα δὲ καὶ εὐρύχωρος ἡ ὁδὸς ἡ ἀπάγουσα εἰς τὴν ἀπώλειαν, καὶ πολλοί εἰσιν οἱ διερχόμενοι δι᾽ αὐτῆς.

9. 1. Ἔτι δὲ οἱ Φρύγες λέγουσι τὸν πατέρα τῶν ὅλων εἶναι ἀμύγδαλον· οὐχὶ δένδρον, φησίν, ἀλλ᾽ εἶναι ἀμύγδαλον ἐκεῖνον τὸν προόντα, ὃς ἔχων ἐν ἑαυτῷ τὸν τέλειον καρπόν, οἱονεὶ διασφύζοντα καὶ κινούμενον ἐν βάθει, διήμυξε τοὺς κόλπους αὑτοῦ καὶ ἐγέννησε τὸν ἀόρατον καὶ ἀκατονόμαστον ἄρρητον παῖδα ἑαυτοῦ, περὶ οὗ λαλοῦμεν. 2. ἀμύξαι γάρ ἐστὶ(ν) οἱονεὶ ῥῆξαι καὶ διατεμεῖν· καθάπερ, φησίν, ἐπὶ τῶν φλεγμαινόντων σωμάτων καὶ ἐχόντων ἐν ἑαυτοῖς τινα συστροφήν, [ἃς] ἀμυχὰς οἱ ἰατροὶ λέγουσιν ἀνατεμόντες, οὕτως, φησί, Φρύγες τὸν ἀμύγδαλον καλοῦσιν, ἀφ᾽ οὗ προῆλθε καὶ ἐγεννήθη ὁ ἀόρατος, «δι᾽ οὗ τὰ πάντα ἐγένετο, καὶ χωρὶς αὐτοῦ ἐγένετο οὐδέν».

bridegrooms emasculated through the virgin Spirit.[183] 45. This virgin is "the pregnant woman who both conceives and bears a son," a son not animate or bodily but a blessed aeon of aeons.[184] He says that the Savior has expressly spoken about these matters:

> Narrow and constricted is the path that leads to life, and few enter it; but wide and spacious is the path that leads to destruction, and many are those who travel on it.[185]

9. 1. Furthermore, the Phrygians say that the Father of the universe is an almond [ἀμύγδαλον].[186] He is not an almond tree, he says. Rather, the Preexistent One up above is that almond containing the mature fruit, as it were throbbing with life, and moving from deep within. He tore through [διήμυξε] his womb and gave birth to his own invisible, unnamable, unspeakable Child about whom we speak.[187] 2. Tearing [ἀμύξαι], it is assumed, is equivalent to bursting and cutting through. Just as, he says, doctors say they cut incisions [ἀμυχάς] in those who have feverish bodies or an internal tumor, so, he claims, the Phrygians call him "One Who Tears" [ἀμύγδαλον]. From him, the Invisible One came forth and was born, "through whom everything came to be, and apart from him, nothing."[188]

---

183. Legge takes ἀπηρσενωμένους as a participle of ἀπαρρενόω = ἀπανδρόω ("become a man") (*Philosophoumena*, 1:139 n. 5).

184. Cf. Isa 7:14 LXX. The phrase *αἰῶνα αἰώνων* emphasizes the eternity of the child (the Son of the Human). The "virgin mentioned is none other than the Anthropos in his 'maternal' function.... The 'blessed Aeon of the Aeons' can be none other than the Son of Man, i.e., the Saviour" (Lancellotti, *Naassenes*, 271–72).

185. Matt 7:13–14; cf. *Ref.* 4.48.9 (Aratos allegorizers); Clem. Alex., *Strom*. 5.5.31.1.

186. According to Pausanias, a daughter of the river Sangarios gave birth to Attis by placing the fruit of an almond tree in her lap (*Descr*. 7.17.11). As the source of Attis, the almond is allegorized as the First Principle or primal God. See further Lancellotti, *Naassenes*, 283.

187. The term "throbbing with life" (διασφύζοντα) also appears in *Ref.* 7.22.8; 7.23.3 ("Basileides"). The designation of the second deity as "child" (παῖς) is comparable to our author's own theology (*Ref.* 10.33.11).

188. John 1:3; *Ref.* 5.8.5; 5.16.12 (Peratai).

3. Συρικτὰν δέ φασιν εἶναι Φρύγες τὸν ἐκεῖθεν γεγεννημένον, ὅτι πνεῦμα ἐναρμόνιόν ἐστι τὸ γεγεννημένον· «πνεῦμα» γάρ, φησίν, ἐστὶν «ὁ θεός»· διό, φησίν, «οὔτε ἐν τῷ ὄρει τούτῳ προσκυνοῦσιν οὔτε ἐν Ἱερουσαλὴμ» «οἱ ἀληθινοὶ προσκυνηταί», ἀλλὰ «ἐν πνεύματι»· 4. πνευματικὴ γάρ, φησίν, ἐστὶ τῶν τελείων ἡ προσκύνησις, οὐ σαρκική. τὸ δὲ πνεῦμα, φησίν, ἐκεῖ ὅπου καὶ ὁ πατὴρ ὀνομάζεται, καὶ ὁ υἱὸς ἐκ τούτου τοῦ πατρὸς ἐκεῖ γεννώμενος. οὗτος, φησίν, ἐστὶν ὁ πολυώνυμος μυριόμματος ἀκατάληπτος, οὗ πᾶσα φύσις, ἄλλη δὲ ἄλλως ὀρέγεται.

5. τοῦτο, φησίν, ἐστὶ τὸ ῥῆμα τοῦ θεοῦ, ὅ, φησίν, ἐστὶ ῥῆμα Ἀποφάσεως τῆς μεγάλης δυνάμεως. διὸ ἔσται ἐσφραγισμένον καὶ κεκρυμμένον καὶ κεκαλυμμένον, κείμενον ἐν τῷ οἰκητηρίῳ οὗ ἡ ῥίζα τῶν ὅλων τεθεμελίωται [ἀπό τε]—αἰώνων δυνάμεων ἐπινοιῶν, θεῶν ἀγγέλων πνευμάτων ἀπεσταλμένων, ὄντων μὴ ὄντων, γεγονότων <ἀ>γενήτων, καταληπτῶν ἀκαταλήπτων, ἐνιαυτῶν μηνῶν ἡμερῶν ὡρῶν—, στιγμὴ ἀμέριστος, ἐξ ἧς ἐνάρχεται τὸ ἐλάχιστον αὐξῆσαι κατὰ μέρος. ἥ, μηδὲν οὖσα, φησί, καὶ ἐκ μηδενὸς συνεστῶσα [στιγμὴ ἀμέριστος οὖσα], γενήσεται ἑαυτῇ<ς> ἐπινοίᾳ μέγεθός τι ἀκατάληπτον. 6. αὕτη, φησίν, ἐστὶν «ἡ βασιλεία τῶν οὐρανῶν», «ὁ κόκκος τοῦ σινάπεως», ἡ ἀμέριστος ἐνυπάρχουσα τῷ σώματι στιγμή, ἣν οἶδε, φησίν, οὐδεὶς <ἀλλ'> ἢ οἱ πνευματικοὶ μόνοι. τοῦτο, φησίν, ἐστὶ τὸ εἰρημένον·

«οὐκ εἰσὶ λόγοι οὐδὲ λαλιαί, ὧν οὐχὶ ἀκούονται αἱ φωναὶ αὐτῶν».

3. The Phrygians call the one born from there "Piper" because what is born is a harmonious Spirit.[189] "God," he says, "is Spirit."[190] Therefore, he claims, "the true worshipers worship neither on this mountain nor in Jerusalem but in Spirit."[191] 4. The worship of the perfect is spiritual, he says, not fleshly. Now Spirit, he claims, exists in that place where the Father is named; and the Son is born there from this Father. This one, he says, is the one with many names and ten thousand eyes, the incomprehensible. Toward him all nature in all its variety strains.[192]

5. Moreover this, he claims, is the speech of God, which, he says, is the speech of the Declaration of great Power. "Thus it will be sealed, hidden, and veiled, lying in the dwelling where the root of the universe is founded," the root of aeons, powers, and thoughts; the root of gods, angels, and spirits sent forth; the root of things that are and of things that are not, of things born and unborn, of things comprehensible and incomprehensible; the root of years, months, days, hours—an indivisible point from which the smallest being begins and grows by degrees.[193] Although it is nothing, he claims, and is composed of nothing, it will generate by its own thought an incomprehensible magnitude.[194] 6. This, he says, is "the kingdom of heaven," "the mustard seed," the indivisible point existing in the body that, he says, only the spiritual ones know.[195] This is what the scriptural verse means when it says,

> There are no tongues nor speech whose voices are not heard.[196]

---

189. Spirit (πνεῦμα) here can mean "breath," or even "air" (with reference to the air blown through the pipes). The spirit is "harmonious" (ἐναρμόνιον) because it makes music. Here the "Child/Son" (παῖς) in the section above is identified with Spirit.

190. John 4:24.

191. John 4:23.

192. The Son/Spirit is identified with the Soul, to whom all nature tends. This World Soul is from the Preexistent One, or Mind (answering the question posed in *Ref.* 5.7.8). For all nature striving toward this Soul, see *Ref.* 5.7.10; 7.22.8 ("Basileides"); 8.12.7 (Monoïmos).

193. The beginning of this sentence is a quotation of the second sentence in the exordium of "Simon's" *Great Declaration* (*Ref.* 6.9.4). See further Frickel, *Apophasis*, 169–88; idem, *Naassenerschrift*, 48; Lancellotti, *Naassenes*, 313–15.

194. Cf. *Ref.* 6.14.6 ("Simon").

195. Matt 13:31 par.; *Ref.* 6.40.2 (Markos); 7.21.3 ("Basileides"); Gos. Thom. 20.

196. Ps. 18:4 LXX.

7. Ταῦθ' οὕτως σχεδιάζουσι, τὰ ὑπὸ πάντων ἀνθρώπων λεγόμενά τε καὶ γινόμενα πρὸς <τὸν> ἴδιον νοῦν πνευματικῶς φάσκοντες πάντα γίνεσθαι· ὅθεν καὶ τοὺς θεάτροις ἐπιδεικνυμένους λέγουσι μη<δ'> αὐτοὺς ἀπρονοήτως τι λέγειν ἢ ποιεῖν. τοιγαροῦν, φησίν, ἐπὰν συνέλθῃ ὁ δῆμος ἐν τοῖς θεάτροις, εἰσιών τις ἠμφιεσμένος στολὴν ἔξαλλον, κιθάραν φέρων καὶ ψάλλων, οὕτως λέγει ᾄδων τὰ μεγάλα μυστήρια, οὐκ εἰδὼς ἃ λέγει·

8. Εἴτε Κρόνου γένος, εἴτε Διὸς μάκαρ,
εἴτε Ῥέας, μέγα χαῖρε, τὸ κατ-
ηφὲς ἄκουσμα Ῥέας Ἄττι· σὲ καλοῦσι μὲν Ἀσσύριοι τριπόθητον Ἄ-
δωνιν, ὅλη δ' Αἴγυπτος Ὄσιριν, ἐπουράνιον Μηνὸς κέρας Ἑλλη-
νὶς σοφία, Σαμόθρᾳκες Ἀδάμ<ας> σε-
βάσμιον, Αἱμόνιοι Κορύβαντα, καὶ
οἱ Φρύγες ἄλλοτε μὲν Πάπαν, ποτὲ
δ' <αὖ> νέκυν ἢ θεὸν ἢ τὸν ἄκαρπον ἢ
αἰπόλον ἢ χλοερὸν στάχυν ἀμη-
θέντ' ἢ <τ>ὸν πολύκαρπον ἔτικτεν ἀ-
μύγδαλος, ἀνέρα συρικτάν.

7. This is what they imagine. They claim that everything said and done by all human beings comes about spiritually in accord with their particular meaning.[197] Hence they say that not even the performers who appear on stage say or do anything without the influence of providence. Accordingly, he claims that when the people gather in the theaters, and someone comes on stage draped in an exquisitely beautiful robe chanting and singing the great mysteries to the tune of a lyre—he does not know what he says:[198]

8. Blessed one! Whether you are born of Kronos or Zeus
Or Rhea, I loudly hail thee!
Attis, you are the name at which Rhea hides her face.
You the Assyrians call "thrice-desired Adonis."
All Egypt calls you "Osiris."
Greek wisdom calls you "Celestial horn of Mēn."
Samothrakians calls you august "Adamas."[199]
Haimonians call you "Korybas."
And Phrygians call you now "Papas,"
Now again "corpse," "god," "unfruitful," "goatherd,"
"Green ear of harvested grain" or "fruitful one" whom the almond bore,
And "pipe player."[200]

---

197. Cf. Iren., *Haer.* 2.14.7.

198. For the Naassene writer, all cultic activity is a kind of theater with actors who mouth the words and perform the actions but do not understand what they do (cf. Frickel, *Naassenerschrift*, 34). On the evidence for this kind of spectacle, see Philostratos, *Vit. Apoll.* 4.21; Thielko Wolbergs, *Griechische religiöse Gedichte der ersten nachchristlichen Jahrhunderte*, 2 vols., Beiträge zur klassische Philologie 40 (Meisenheim: Anton Hain, 1971), 1:61–62. The two hymns that follow are tentatively dated by Ulrich von Wilamowitz-Moellendorff to the time of Hadrian ("Lesefrüchte," *Hermes* 37 [1902]: 328–32). See further F. G. Schneidewin, "Hymnorum in Attin fragmenta inedita," *Phil* 3 (1848): 247–66; Reitzenstein, *Poimandres*, 82–101; Reitzenstein and Schaeder, *Studien*, 161–73; Wolbergs, *Gedichte*, 1:8, 63–75.

199. As in *Ref.* 5.8.9, Ἀδάμας is an emendation for P's ἀδάμ. In the poem itself, Ἀδάμας should be understood as "unconquered one," not as a Naassene deity. The name is related to the plural ἀδαμεῖς ("unconquered ones"), a common title for the Samothrakian Great Gods. For further evidence supporting this emendation, see Lancellotti, *Naassenes*, 254–61.

200. A. D. Nock called this hymn "a learned παίγνιον [comic performance], not a cult-hymn" ("Iranian Influences in Greek Thought," in *Essays on Religion and the Ancient World*, ed. Zeph Stewart, 2 vols. [Cambridge: Harvard University Press, 1972], 1:195–201 [201]), but the boundaries between play, performance, and religion are not

9. Τοῦτον φησιν εἶναι πολύμορφον Ἄττιν, ὃν ὑμνοῦντες λέγουσιν οὕτως·

Ἄττιν ὑμνήσω τὸν Ῥείης,
οὐ <κ>ωδώνων σὺμ βόμβοις,
οὐδ' αὐλῷ <τῶν> Ἰδαίων
Κουρήτων <σὺμ>μυκητᾷ,
ἀλλ' εἰς Φοιβείαν μίξω
μοῦσαν φορμίγγων· εὐοῖ,
εὐάν, ὡς Πάν, ὡς Βακχεύς,
ὡς ποιμὴν λευκῶν ἄστρων.

10. Διὰ τούτους καὶ τοὺς τοιούτους λόγους παρεδρεύουσιν οὗτοι τοῖς λεγομένοις Μητρὸς μεγάλης μυστηρίοις, μάλιστα καθορᾶν νομίζοντες διὰ τῶν ἐκεῖ δρωμένων τὸ ὅλον μυστήριον. οὐδὲν δὲ ἔχουσι πλέον οὗτοι τῶν ἐκεῖ δρωμένων, πλὴν ὅτι οὐκ εἰσιν ἀποκεκομμένοι, μόνον τὸ ἔργον τῶν ἀποκεκομμένων ἐκτελοῦσιν 11.—πάνυ γὰρ πικρῶς καὶ πεφυλαγμένως παραγγέλλουσιν ἀπέχεσθαι, ὡς ἀποκεκομμένοι, τῆς πρὸς γυναῖκα ὁμιλίας·—τὸ δὲ λοιπόν [ἔργον], ὡς εἰρήκαμεν διὰ πολλῶν, ὥσπερ οἱ ἀπόκοποι δρῶσι.

9. This is the description, he claims, of Attis in his many forms. To him they sing hymns like this one:

I shall sing of Attis, son of Rhea!
I shall not rattle with castanets
Nor bellow with the flute
Of the Idaian Kouretes.
No, I blend with the Phoiban muse
As I play my lyre, euhoi!
Euan! I shall sing of you as Pan, as Bakchos,[201]
As the Shepherd of gleaming white stars!

10. By stories and songs of this sort these people frequent the so-called mysteries of the Great Mother. They suppose that they can best behold the entirety of their own mystery in the Phrygian rites. But these people possess nothing more than what is ritually acted out in these rites—apart from the fact that they are not castrated. They only accomplish the *deed* of those castrated priests.[202] 11. For so stringently and obsessively do they forbid sex with women that they might as well be castrated! But the rest, which I have discussed at length, they perform just like the castrated priests.[203]

sharply drawn. Angelos Chaniotis draws attention to how religious ritual, including cultic hymn, uses drama to serious effect ("Staging and Feeling the Presence of God: Emotion and Theatricality in Religious Celebrations in the Roman East," in Bricault and Bonnet, *Panthée,* 169–90 [177]).

201. For Attis as Bacchos, cf. Clem. Alex., *Protr.* 19.4; *Scholia in Lucianum, Jupp. trag.* 8 (Rabe, 60,10–11); *Etymologium Magnum* under Ἄτης.

202. The castrated priests are the Galli, for which see J. Peter Södergård, "The Ritualized Bodies of Cybele's Galli and the Methodological Problem of the Plurality of Explanations," in *The Problem of Ritual: Based on Papers Read at the Symposium on Religious Rites Held at Åbo, Finland*, ed. Tore Ahlbäck (Åbo: Donner Institute, 1993), 169–93; Will Roscoe, "Priests of the Goddess: Gender Transgression in Ancient Religion," *HR* 35 (1996): 195–230.

203. Our author apparently believed that the Naassenes participated in the rites of the Great Mother. His testimony is to be taken with a pound of salt, since the Naassenes discuss many other mysteries but are not said to participate in them. Nothing in the Naassene exegesis of the Phrygian mysteries suggests that it would be appropriate for the Naassenes (if they existed as a community) to join in the worship of Cybele—especially given that those who worshiped her (according to he Naassenes) *did not know what they were doing*. It is *only* the Naassenes who understand the mysteries of the various cult groups, and they seem to be dependent mostly on literary sources for their information (Lancellotti, *Naassenes*, 245, 258–59, 265–66, 283–84).

Τιμῶσι δὲ οὐκ ἄλλο τι ἢ τὸν νάας οὗτοι, Να<α>σσηνοὶ καλούμενοι. 12. νάας δέ ἐστιν ὁ ὄφις· ἀφ' οὗ φησι πάντας εἶναι τοὺς ὑπὸ τὸν οὐρανὸν προσαγορευομένους ναοὺς [ἀπὸ τοῦ νάας], κἀκείνῳ μόνῳ τῷ νάας ἀνακεῖσθαι πᾶν ἱερὸν καὶ πᾶσαν τελετὴν καὶ πᾶν μυστήριον, καὶ καθόλου μὴ δύνασθαι τελετὴν εὑρεθῆναι ὑπὸ τὸν οὐρανὸν, ἐν ᾗ ναὸς οὐκ ἔστι καὶ ὁ νάας ἐν αὐτῷ, ἀφ' οὗ ἔλαχε ναὸς καλεῖσθαι.

13. Εἶναι δὲ τὸν ὄφιν λέγουσιν οὗτοι τὴν ὑγρὰν οὐσίαν, καθάπερ καὶ Θαλῆς ὁ Μιλήσιος, καὶ μηδὲν δύνασθαι τῶν ὄντων ὅλως, ἀθανάτων ἢ θνητῶν, [τῶν] ἐμψύχων ἢ ἀψύχων, συνεστηκέναι χωρὶς αὐτοῦ. 14. ὑποκεῖσθαι δὲ αὐτῷ τὰ πάντα, καὶ εἶναι αὐτὸν ἀγαθόν, καὶ ἔχειν πάντων ἐν αὐτῷ, ὥσπερ «ἐν κέρατι ταύρου μονοκέρωτος», τὸ κάλλος [τῶν ἄλλων]. καὶ τὴν ὡραιότητα ἐπιδιδόναι πᾶσι τοῖς οὖσι κατὰ φύσιν τὴν ἑαυτῶν καὶ οἰκειότητα. οἱονεὶ διὰ πάντων ὁδεύοντα, ὥσπερ «<ποταμὸν> ἐκπορευόμενον ἐξ Ἐδὲμ» καὶ «σχιζόμενον εἰς ἀρχὰς τέσσαρας».

15. Ἐδὲμ δὲ εἶναι λέγουσι τὸν ἐγκέφαλον, οἱονεὶ δεδεμένον καὶ κατεσφιγμένον ἐν τοῖς περικειμένοις χιτῶσιν ὥσπερ οὐρανοῖς, παράδεισον εἶναι νομίζουσι τὸν μέχρι μόνης τῆς κεφαλῆς ἄνθρωπον. ἐξερχόμενον οὖν τοῦτον τὸν ποταμὸν ἐξ Ἐδέμ—τουτέστιν ἀπὸ τοῦ ἐγκεφάλου—ἀφορίζεσθαι εἰς ἀρχὰς τέσσαρας.

καλεῖσθαι δὲ «τὸ ὄνομα τοῦ πρώτου ποταμοῦ Φεισών· οὗτος ὁ κυκλῶν πᾶσαν τὴν γῆν Εὐϊλάτ· ἐκεῖ οὖν ἐστι τὸ χρυσίον· τὸ δὲ χρυσίον τῆς γῆς ἐκείνης καλόν· καὶ ἐκεῖ ἐστιν ὁ ἄνθραξ καὶ λίθος ὁ πράσινος»· 16. οὗτος, φησίν, ὀφθαλμός, τῇ τιμῇ καὶ τοῖς χρώμασι μαρτυρῶν τῶν λεγομένων.

τὸ δὲ «ὄνομα τοῦ δευτέρου ποταμοῦ Γεών· οὗτος ὁ κυκλῶν πᾶσαν τὴν γῆν Αἰθιοπίας»· οὗτος, φησίν, ἐστὶν ἀκοή, λαβυρινθώδης τις ὤν.

THE UNIVERSAL SIGNIFICANCE OF THE SNAKE. These people honor nothing but Naas, in accordance with their name, Naassenes. 12. Naas means "snake."[204] All the shrines [ναούς] under heaven, he claims, are named after Naas. To this snake alone is dedicated every sanctuary, every initiation rite, and every mystery. In general, no initiation under heaven can be found that lacks a shrine and the *naas* within it, from which the word "shrine" [ναός] takes its name.

13. They say that the snake means "watery substance," just like Thales of Miletos.[205] Apart from it, no being whatsoever—immortal or mortal, ensouled or soulless—can come into existence.[206] 14. Everything is subject to it. It is good and contains the beauty of everything in itself, just as "in the horn of a single-horned bull."[207] It bestows loveliness on all who are by their nature and kinship related to it. It proceeds as if coursing through all, just as the "river flowing from Eden" is then "split into four branches."[208]

15. They say that Eden [Εδέμ] signifies the brain as if bound [δεδεμένον] and laced tight in the surrounding membranes, which are like the heavenly regions.[209] Paradise they think represents the Human—but only so far as the head. This river flows out of Eden (that is, from the brain) and is split into four branches.

"The name of the first river is Pheisōn. This river encircles the entire land of Evilat, where there is gold. The gold of that land is beautiful. In that place there is ruby and emerald." 16. The emerald, he says, refers to the eye, which attests to the value and colors of things spoken.

The "name of the second river is Geōn, which encircles the entire land of Ethiopia." This river, he says, represents the sense of hearing since it is shaped like a labyrinth.

---

204. Cf. *Ref.* 5.6.3 above.

205. The water in view here is a super-celestial noetic substance symbolically referred to as the "water above the firmament" (Gen 1:7) (Frickel, *Naassenerschrift*, 68). On water as a symbol, see *Ref.* 5.7.38; 5.8.16.

206. Cf. Plutarch, *Is. Os.* 34 (*Mor.* 364d). See further Mueller, "Hippolytus *Retractatus*," 237.

207. Cf. Deut 33:17 LXX.

208. Marcovich adds ποταμόν from Gen 2:10. Cf. *Ref.* 5.16.9 (Peratai); 5.26.11 (Justin); 6.14.8; 6.15.1 ("Simon"); Theophilos, *Autol.* 2.24.

209. For Eden as the brain, see *Ref.* 4.51.11; 5.17.11 (Peratai); Philo, *Leg.* 1.64 (Eden as God's wisdom). The brain is also a symbol of Adamas; cf. *Ref.* 5.7.35. For the membranes (χιτῶσιν) as πτερύγια, see *Ref.* 4.51.11. See further Corp. herm. 10.11.

καὶ ὄνομα «τῷ τρίτῳ Τίγρις· οὗτος ἐστὶν ὁ πορευόμενος κατέναντι Ἀσσυρίων»· 17. οὗτος, φησίν, ἐστὶν ὄσφρησις, ὀξυτάτῃ χρώμενος τῇ φορᾷ τοῦ ῥεύματος· πορεύεται δὲ κατέναντι Ἀσσυρίων, ὅτι ἐκπνέοντι τῷ πνεύματι κατὰ τὴν ἀναπνοὴν τὸ ἔξωθεν, ἀπὸ τοῦ ἀέρος συρόμενον, ὀξύτερον καὶ βιαιότερον ἐπεισέρχεται πνεῦμα· ἀναπνοῆς γάρ, φησίν, αὕτη <ἡ> φύσις.

18. «ὁ δὲ ποταμὸς ὁ τέταρτος Εὐφράτης»· τοῦτον λέγουσιν στόμα, δι᾽ οὗ ἡ τῆς προσευχῆς ἔξοδος καὶ ἡ τῆς τροφῆς εἴσοδος· <ὃς> εὐφραίνει καὶ τρέφει καὶ χαρακτηρίζει τὸν πνευματικὸν τέλειον ἄνθρωπον. Τοῦτο, φησίν, ἐστὶ «τὸ ὕδωρ τὸ ὑπεράνω τοῦ στερεώματος», περὶ οὗ, φησίν, εἴρηκεν ὁ σωτήρ·

> εἰ ᾔδεις τίς ἐστιν ὁ αἰτῶν, σὺ ἂν ᾔτησας παρ᾽ αὐτοῦ καὶ ἔδωκεν ἄν σοι πιεῖν ζῶν ὕδωρ ἁλλόμενον.

19. ἐπὶ τοῦτο, φησί, τὸ ὕδωρ πᾶσα φύσις ἔρχεται τὰς ἑαυτῆς οὐσίας ἐκλέγουσα, καὶ προσέρχεται ἑκάστῃ φύσει ἀπὸ τοῦ ὕδατος τούτου τὸ οἰκεῖον, φησί, μᾶλλον ἢ σίδηρος τῇ Ἡρακλείᾳ λίθῳ καὶ ὁ χρυσὸς τῇ τοῦ θαλασσίου ἱέρακος κερκίδι καὶ τὸ ἄχυρον τῷ ἠλέκτρῳ. 20. εἰ δέ τις, φησίν, ἐστὶ «τυφλὸς

"The name of the third is Tigris; it flows in the presence of the Assyrians." 17. This branch, he says, symbolizes the sense of smell since its current rushes most violently. It flows in the presence of the Assyrians [Ἀσσυρίων] because, after breath is exhaled in the act of respiration, breath from outside (drawn in [συρόμενον] from the air) enters more sharply and violently. This is the nature, he says, of respiration.

18. "The fourth river is Euphrates [Εὐφράτης]." They say it represents the mouth, the point of exit for prayers, and the point of entrance for food. This river delights [εὐφραίνει], nourishes, and characterizes the perfect spiritual human being.[210] This river, he claims, is "the water above the firmament."[211] The Savior, he asserts, refers to it in the following remark:

> If you knew who it was who asks, you would have asked him and he would have given you living, bubbling water to drink.[212]

19. Every nature, he says, comes to this water and selects its own properties. What is fitting advances to each nature from this water, he affirms, more than iron is attracted to a magnet, or gold is attracted to a hierax fish's spine, or chaff to amber.[213] 20. But if anyone, he says, is "blind from

210. For this section on rivers, see Gen 2:11–14 LXX; cf. the allegorical interpretation of "Simon" in *Ref.* 6.15.1–16.4. For the pun on Εὐφράτης-εὐφραίνω, see Philo, *Leg.* 1.72; *QG* 1.12.

211. Gen 1:7; cf. *Ref.* 5.27.3 (Justin); 7.23.1, 3; 7.25.3 ("Basileides").

212. John 4:10 and 14 (ἁλλομένου); cf. *Ref.* 5.7.19; 5.19.21 ("Sethians"); 5.27.2 (Justin); Gos. Thom. 13; Ap. John (BG 8502.2) 26.16–27.4; Acts Thom. (Greek) 37, 39, 52 (*NTApoc* 2:354–56, 361–62); Justin, *Dial.* 14.1; 69.6; 114.4.

213. For these examples, see *Ref.* 5.19.9–10; 5.21.8–9 ("Sethians"). Thales already gave the example of iron and amber to support the fact that everything, even inanimate objects, possesses soul (DK A3, A22 = Diog. L., *Vit. phil.* 1.24; cf. Aristotle, *De an.* 1.2, 405a19). Plato uses the image of the magnet to speak of being seized by God through the Muse (*Ion* 533d–e). The attractive power of amber is noted in Ps.-Timaios, *Nat. mund. an.* 65, 102a. Further sources in Clemens Scholten, "Quellen regen an: Beobachtungen zum 'gnostischen Sondergut' der *Refutatio omnium haeresium*," in *"In Search of Truth": Augustine, Manichaeism and Other Gnosticism; Studies for Johannes van Oort at Sixty*, ed. Jacob Albert van den Berg et al., NHMS 74 (Leiden: Brill, 2011), 567–92 (573 n. 27). It is possible we should understand the κερκίς as a kind of tail flipper. But since the κερκίς can refer to the radius of the arm, most have understood it as a bony part. The identity of the hierax fish is disputed. It appears in Oppian, *Hal.* 1.428 (ἰρήκων τε γένος), and is described as a fish that leaps from the water but flies close to the sea (1.435–37). D'arcy Wentworth Thompson (*A Glossary of Greek Fishes* [London: Oxford University Press, 1947], 90) calls it a "Flying Gur-

ἐκ γενετῆς» καὶ μὴ τεθεαμένος «<τὸ> φῶς τὸ ἀληθινόν, ὃ φωτίζει πάντα ἄνθρωπον ἐρχόμενον εἰς τὸν κόσμον», δι' ἡμῶν ἀναβλεψάτω καὶ ἰδέτω οἱονεὶ διά τινος παραδείσου συμφύτου καὶ πολυσπερμάτου ὕδωρ διερχόμενον διὰ πάντων τῶν φυτῶν καὶ τῶν σπερμάτων, καὶ ὄψεται ὅτι ἐξ ἑνὸς καὶ τοῦ αὐτοῦ ὕδατος ἐκλέγεται καὶ ἐπισπᾶται ἡ ἐλαία τὸ ἔλαιον καὶ ἡ ἄμπελος τὸν οἶνον καὶ τῶν ἄλλων κατὰ γένος ἕκαστον φυτῶν.

21. ἔστι δέ, φησίν, ὁ ἄνθρωπος ἐκεῖνος ἄτιμος ἐν τῷ κόσμῳ, καὶ πολύτιμος ὑπὸ τῶν [οὐκ] εἰδότων [τοῖς οὐκ εἰδόσιν] αὐτόν, «λελογισμένος ὥσπερ σταγὼν ἀπὸ κάδου.»

οἵτινες ἐσμέν, φησίν, οἱ πνευματικοί, οἱ ἐκλεγόμενοι ἀπὸ τοῦ «ζῶντος ὕδατος» τοῦ ῥέοντος Εὐφράτου διὰ τῆς Βαβυλῶνος μέσης τὸ οἰκεῖον, <οἱ> διὰ τῆς πύλης ὁδεύοντες ἀληθινῆς, ἥτις ἐστὶν Ἰησοῦς ὁ μακάριος. 22. καὶ ἐσμὲν ἐξ ἁπάντων ἀνθρώπων ἡμεῖς Χριστιανοὶ μόνοι, <οἱ> ἐν τῇ τρίτῃ πύλῃ ἀπαρτίζοντες τὸ μυστήριον καὶ χριόμενοι ἐκεῖ ἀλάλῳ χρίσματι ἐκ κέρατος, ὡ<ς> Δαβίδ, οὐκ ὀστρακίνου φακοῦ, φησίν, ὡς ὁ Σαούλ, ὁ συμπολιτευόμενος τῷ πονηρῷ δαίμονι, «τῆς σαρκικῆς ἐπιθυμίας».

10. 1. Ταῦτα μὲν οὖν ἐκ πολλῶν ὡς ὀλίγα παρεθέμεθα· ἔστι γὰρ ἀναρίθμητα τῆς μωρίας ἐπιχειρήματα, ὄντα φλύαρα καὶ μανιώδη. ἀλλ' ἐπειδὴ δυνάμει τὴν ἄγνωστον αὐτῶν γνῶσιν ἐξεθέμεθα, καὶ τοῦτο ἔδοξε παραθεῖναι· ψαλμὸς αὐτοῖς

birth"[214] and has not beheld "the true light that enlightens every person coming into the world,"[215] let him through us recover his sight and see water coursing through all plants and seeds as it were through some paradise that is akin to his nature and sown with a variety of seeds. Then he will see that from one and the same water the olive tree selects and draws its oil, the vine draws wine, and each of all the other plants according to their species.

21. That Human is, he says, without honor in the world. Yet, "though accounted as a drop from a bucket,"[216] he is greatly honored by those who know him.

It is we who are the spiritual people, he says, those chosen from the "living water"[217] of the Euphrates that flows through the midst of Babylon—the water proper to us. We are those who travel through the true gate, who is Jesus the Blessed one.[218] 22. And we are—out of all peoples—the only Christians [Χριστιανοί] who complete the mystery in the third gate and are anointed [χριόμενοι] there with the ineffable ointment from a horn like David.[219] We are not anointed, he says, from a clay flask like Saul. Saul was the compatriot of an evil demon, that of "fleshly lust."[220]

THE NAASSENE PSALM. 10. 1. I have presented the foregoing as a small selection from a vast store—for innumerable are their idiotic, blabbering, and insane arguments. But since I presented their unknowing knowledge as far as I could, it seems right to append the following as well. The psalm that

nard" (90). It is mentioned also in Athenaios, *Deipn.* 329a; Aelian, *Nat. an.* 9.52–53. The Romans called it *milvus* or *ictinus*. Cf. Pliny, *Nat.* 9.82; Horace, *Ep.* 1.16.50–51. It is possible that it might also refer to the hawk or sea hawk (ἱέραξ πελάγιος). Some scholars understand it to be the stingray. But Scholten points out that the stingray is usually called *νάρκη* or *τρυγών* ("Quellen," 577 with sources in nn. 46–50). Our author is the only witness (besides Simplikios three hundred years later) to the hierax fish spine attracting gold (ibid., 576–77).

214. Cf. John 9:1.

215. John 1:9; cf. *Ref.* 7.22.4 ("Basileides"); Clem. Alex., *Exc.* 41.3.

216. Isa 40:15 LXX.

217. John 4:10.

218. John 10:9; cf. *Ref.* 5.8.20; 5.17.9 (Peratai).

219. Cf. *Ref.* 5.8.25, 31; 2 Cor 12:2 (third heaven); 1 Sam 16:13 (anointing of David).

220. 1 Sam 10:1 (clay flask). For "fleshly lust," cf., e.g., 1 Pet 2:11 with *Ref.* 5.8.31; 6.9.2 ("Simon"). See further Lancellotti, *Naassenes*, 160–61.

ἐσχεδίασται οὗτος, δι᾿ οὗ πάντα αὐτοῖς τὰ τῆς πλάνης μυστήρια δοκοῦσι διὰ ὕμνου ᾄδειν οὕτως·

2. Νόμος ἦν γενικὸς τοῦ παντὸς ὁ πρῶτος Νόος,
ὁ δὲ δεύτερος ἦν τοῦ πρωτοτόκου τὸ χυθὲν Χάος,
τριτάτη<ν> Ψυχὴ δ᾿ ἔλαβ᾿ ἐργαζομένη νόμον·
διὰ τοῦτ᾿ ἐλάφου μορφὴν περικειμένη
κοπιᾷ, θανάτῳ μελέτημα, κρατουμένη·
ποτὲ <μὲν> βασίλ(ειον) ἔχουσα βλέπει τὸ φῶς,
ποτὲ δ᾿ εἰς <σπ>ήλαιον ἐκρι<πτο>μένη κλάει.
ποτὲ δὲ κλαίεται χαίρει
ποτὲ δὲ κλαίει κρίνεται,

follows is their own contrivance. Through it they are content to sing, in a hymn, all their mysteries of deceit:[221]

2. The universal injunction of the universe is the primal Intellect;[222]
The second after the Firstborn is sprawling Chaos;[223]
Soul received the third rank, who performed the injunction.
  For this reason, clothed in the form of a deer,[224]
  The soul grows weary—as prey to death and dominated.
  Sometimes, possessing a royal palace, she sees the light.
  At other times she weeps, cast aside in a cave.[225]
    When she weeps for herself, she rejoices;[226]
    When she weeps, she is judged;[227]

---

221. A bibliography of older treatments of the following psalm can be found in Wolbergs, *Gedichte*, 37–38. See further B. Herzhoff, *Zwei gnostische Psalmen: Interpretation und Untersuchung von Hippolytos, Refutatio V 10,2 und VI 37,7* (Diss., University of Bonn, 1973), 78–142; Marcovich, *Studies*, 80–88; Gualtiero Rota, "Alcune osservazioni sull'interpretazione dei μυστήρια nel *Salmo dei Naasseni sull'anima* (Hipp. *haer.* 5,10,2)," *Vetera Christianorum* 41 (2004): 107–19.

222. Cf. Cicero, *Leg.* 2.8: *ita principem legem … mentem esse … dei* ("thus the principle law … is God's mind"); *PGM* V. 464–65: ὁ μέγας Νοῦς ἔν[νο]μος τὸ πᾶν διοικῶν ("the great law-inscribed Mind administers the universe"). The goddess figure in Thund. (NHC VI,2) 16.14; 18.9 also identifies herself with both νόμος and νοῦς. Marcovich equates the νόμος γενικός with the κοινὸς νόμος in Herakleitos, DK 22 B114 (= Marcovich, *Heraclitus*, §23); Kleanthes, *Hymn Iov.* vv. 24, 39 (κοινὸν νόμον); Diog. L., *Vit. phil.* 7.88. See further Wolbergs, *Gedichte*, 1.42. For firstborn mind, see Iren., *Haer.* 1.24.3–4 (Basileides posits a *primogenitum Nun* ["firstborn Mind"]); Eugnostos (NHC V,1) 9.7.

223. For sprawling Chaos (τὸ χυθὲν Χάος), see *Ref.* 5.7.9, and τὸ ἐκκεχυμένον Χάος in *Ref.* 10.32.1. See further Iren., *Haer.* 1.30.1 (Ophites).

224. Ps 41:2 LXX poetically links the soul and the deer.

225. Σπήλαιον ("cave") is Wolberg's emendation of P's ἔλαιον. The cave is a common symbol of the world (Empedokles, DK 31 B120; cf. Plato, *Resp.* 514a5 [allegory of the cave]; Plotinos, *Enn.* 2.9.6.8 [ἀναβάσεις ἐκ τοῦ σπηλαίου]). Note also Matt 21:13 = Jer 7:11: "cave [σπήλαιον] of robbers." The soul thrown into the cave is the inner human "fallen away" (ἀποπεπτωκώς) from Adamas (*Ref.* 5.7.36; noted by Wolbergs, *Gedichte*, 50).

226. This and the following indented lines were heavily emended by Marcovich (largely for metrical reasons). I have translated the text of P. Cf. the spirit in the chain of the body in Ap. John (NHC II,1) 31.6: "And he wept and shed tears." Note also Corp. herm. 12.2: ψυχὴ γὰρ πᾶσα ἐν σώματι γενομένη εὐθέως ὑπό τε τῆς λύπης καὶ τῆς ἡδονῆς κακίζεται ("For every soul born in the body is immediately injured by both grief and pleasure").

227. Cf. Sent. Sextus 183 (Wilson).

ποτὲ δὲ κρίνεται θνῄσκει
ποτὲ δὲ γίνεται.
<κ>ἀνέξοδον ἡ μελέα κακῶ<ν>
λαβύρινθον ἐσῆλθε πλανωμένη.
εἶπεν δ' Ἰησοῦς· ἐσόρ<α>, πάτερ,
ζήτημα κακῶν <τόδ'> ἐπὶ χθόνα
ἀπὸ σῆς πνο<ι>ῆς ἀποπλάζεται·
ζητεῖ δὲ φυγεῖν τὸ πικρὸν Χάος
κοὐκ οἶδε<ν ὅ>πως διελεύσεται.

τούτου με χάριν πέμψον, πάτερ·

σφραγῖδας ἔχων καταβήσομαι,
αἰῶνας ὅλους διοδεύσω,
μυστήρια πάντα δ' ἀνοίξω
μορφάς τε θεῶν ἐπιδείξω·
[καὶ] τὰ κεκρυμμένα τῆς ἁγίας ὁδοῦ
γνῶσιν καλέσας παραδώσω.

11. 1. Ταῦτα μὲν οὖν οἱ Νaασσηνοὶ ἐπιχειροῦσιν, ἑαυτοὺς γνωστικοὺς ὀνομάζοντες. ἀλλ' ἐπεὶ πολυκέφαλός ἐστιν ἡ πλάνη καὶ πολυσχιδὴς ἀληθῶς ὡς <ἡ> ἱστορουμένη ὕδρα, κατὰ μίαν ταύτης κεφαλὰς πατάξαντες διὰ τοῦ ἐλέγχου, τῇ τῆς ἀληθείας ῥάβδῳ χρησάμενοι, ἅπαν τὸ θηρίον ἀναιρήσομεν· οὐδὲ

When she is judged, she dies;
Then she is born.[228]
Miserable in her misfortunes, she entered
The inescapable labyrinth—to wander.[229]

Jesus said: "Look upon her, Father!
Pursued by disasters here, she wanders away
Toward the earth, away from your spirit![230]
She seeks to flee bitter Chaos[231]
And knows not how she will cross it!
For this reason send me, Father!
Holding the seals I will go down,[232]
I will go across all aeons,
I will open every mystery,
I will manifest the shapes of gods,[233]
I will transmit the hidden things of the holy path,[234]
Which I have called gnosis.[235]

11. 1. Such are the arguments of the Naassenes, who call themselves "gnostics." But since, like the hydra in mythology, the deceit has many heads and branches in many directions, when I have struck one of its heads by my refutation—wielding the staff of truth—I will kill the whole

228. Transmigration and reincarnation seem to be in view here.

229. For the soul wandering, see Plato, *Phaed.* 79c. In Corp. herm. 1.19, the primal Human trapped in the body also wanders (πλανώμενος) in the darkness.

230. Cf. Homer, *Il.* 13.590 (πνοιῇ); *Od.* 1.75.

231. Cf. *Ref.* 5.7.39: ἐὰν … φυγεῖν σπεύδητε … ἀπὸ τῆς κάτω μίξεως ("if … you hasten to flee … from the lower mixture").

232. The seals are probably tokens of passage or magical formulas (see BDAG, s.v. σφραγίς 1d). Cf. the seven seals in *I Jeu* 33–38, and the eight seals in *II Jeu* 45–48 (Schmidt, 83–88, 105–16). See further Franz Joseph Dölger, *Sphragis: Eine altchristliche Taufbezeichnung in ihren Beziehungen zur profanen und religiösen Kultur des Altertums* (Paderborn: Ferdinand Schöningh, 1911), 160–63; Gottfried Fitzer, "σφράγις," *TDNT* 7:953; Wolbergs, *Gedichte*, 56.

233. Μορφάς … θεῶν: the shapes of the lower gods. Cf. Ascen. Isa. 10.7–8; Iren., *Haer.* 1.30.12; Origen, *Cels.* 6.30, 33; Ap. John (NHC II,1) 11.26–34 (Marcovich, *Studies*, 85). The descent of the redeemer is also described in *Ref.* 5.8.13.

234. For the holy path, see Corp. herm. 1.29; 4.11.

235. Jesus is not a fourth principle in the Naassene system but a kind of "*doublet* of the Soul" (Marcovich, *Studies*, 87, italics his) who descends to save the soul.

γὰρ αἱ λοιπαὶ αἱρέσεις πολὺ ταύτης ἀπεμφαίνουσι, συνεχόμεναι ἐν<ὶ> πλάνης πνεύματι. ἀλλ᾽ ἐπειδὴ τὰ ῥήματα καὶ τὰ ὀνόματα [τοῦ ὄφεως] ἐνδιαλλάξαντες πολλὰς εἶναι κεφαλὰς τοῦ ὄφεως ἠθέλησαν, οὐδὲ οὕτως ἐνδεήσομεν διελέγξαι, ὡς βούλονται.

12. 1. Ἔστι γοῦν καὶ ἑτέρα τις <αἵρεσις, ἡ> Περατική, <ἧς ἀρχηγοὶ γεγόνασιν Ἀκεμβὴς ὁ Καρύστιος καὶ Εὐφράτης ὁ Περατικός,> ὧν πολλοῖς ἔτεσιν ἔλαθεν ἡ κατὰ Χριστοῦ δυσφημία· ὧν νῦν εἰς φανερὸν ἄγειν ἔδοξε τὰ ἀπόρρητα μυστήρια.

οὗτοι φάσκουσι τὸν κόσμον εἶναι ἕνα, τριχῇ διῃρημένον. 2. ἔστι δὲ τῆς τριχῇ διαιρέσεως παρ᾽ αὐτοῖς [τὸ μὲν ἓν μέρος] οἱον<εὶ> μία τις ἀρχή, καθάπερ πηγὴ μεγάλη, εἰς ἀπείρους τῷ λόγῳ τμηθῆναι τομὰς δυναμένη. ἡ δὲ πρώτη τομὴ καὶ προσεχεστέρα κατ᾽ αὐτούς ἐστι τριάς· καὶ <τὸ μὲν ἓν μέρος> καλεῖται ἀγαθὸν τέλειον, μέγεθος πατρικόν· τὸ δὲ δεύτερον τῆς τριάδος αὐτῶν μέρος οἱονεὶ δυνάμεων ἄπειρόν τι πλῆθος, ἐξ αὐτῶν γεγενημένων· τὸ τρίτον ἰδικόν. 3. καὶ ἔστι τὸ μὲν πρῶτον ἀγέννητον, ὅπερ ἐστὶν ἀγαθὸν <τέλειον>· τὸ δὲ δεύτερον [ἀγαθὸν] αὐτογενές· τὸ τρίτον γεννητόν. ὅθεν διαρρήδην λέγουσι τρεῖς θεούς, τρεῖς λόγους, τρεῖς νοῦς, τρεῖς ἀνθρώπους· ἑκάστῳ γὰρ μέρει τοῦ

beast.[236] For neither do the other heresies declare a doctrine significantly different from this (coiled together as they are by a single spirit of deceit!), nor will I lack resources (though they wish I did) to refute them, since it is only by the exchange of words and names that they want the heads of the snake to multiply![237]

PERATAI

12. 1. Now there is yet another heresy: the Peratic one.[238] Its founders were Akembes the Karystian and Euphrates the Peratic, whose slanders against Christ have for many years escaped notice.[239] It is time to drag their secret mysteries into the open!

TRIADIC THEOLOGY. They claim that the world is one but divided in three ways. 2. There is in their view one source, as it were, of the threefold division. Just like a massive spring of water, it can be rationally divided into infinite divisions. The first—and in their view the most relevant—division is the Trinity. Its first part is called "Perfect Good" and "Fatherly Greatness." The second part of their Trinity is something like a boundless mass of powers generated from themselves. The third part is "the particular." 3. The first (the Perfect Good) is unborn, the second is self-born, and the third is born. Thus they expressly say that there are three Gods, three Words, three Minds, and three Humans. They assign Gods and Words and

236. Irenaeus had already compared the Valentinian school to a hydra (*Haer.* 1.30.14). On heresies as introducing and multiplying difference, see Pouderon, "Hippolyte, un regard," 49–52.

237. Cruice emends ἐν to ἑνί and removes τοῦ ὄφεως.

238. The Peratai, also summarized in *Ref.* 10.10, were apparently unknown to Irenaeus and Epiphanios. They are, however, mentioned by Clement of Alexandria (*Strom.* 7.16.108.2), who takes "Peratic" as a place name (ἀπὸ τόπου). Our author understands the name to derive from the verb περᾶσαι: "to traverse" (*Ref.* 5.16.1, 5–6; cf. the pun in 5.18.1). Annarita Magri, following Montserrat-Torrents, argues that περάτη was understood as a translation of Ἑβραῖος (cf. Gen 14:13 LXX; Philo, *Migr.* 20); thus, the Peratai are the "true Hebrews" ("Il nome dei Perati," *Orpheus* 28 [2007]: 138–61 [161]).

239. Marcovich has taken the liberty of adding the names of the leading Peratai to this passage. Their names vary in form (Akembes here and in *Ref.* 4.2.1; Kelbes in 5.13.9 and Ademes in 10.10.1). We know nothing of Akembes. Karystos is a town in Euboia. Euphrates, called ὁ Περάτικος, is a teacher of the Ophites in Origen, *Cels.* 6.28. See further Rasimus, *Paradise*, 288.

κόσμου, τῆς διαιρέσεως διακεκριμένης, διδόασι καὶ θεοὺς καὶ λόγους καὶ νοῦς καὶ ἀνθρώπους καὶ τὰ λοιπά.

4. Ἄνωθεν δέ, ἀπὸ τῆς ἀγενησίας καὶ <τῆς> πρώτης τοῦ κόσμου τομῆς, καθεστηκότος λοιπὸν τοῦ κόσμου ἐπὶ συντελείᾳ, κατεληλυθέναι, δι' αἰτίας ἃς ὕστερον ἐροῦμεν, ἐν τοῖς Ἡρώδου χρόνοις τριφυῆ τινα καὶ τρισώμ<ατ>ον καὶ τριδύναμον ἄνθρωπον καλούμενον Χριστόν, ἀπὸ τῶν τριῶν ἔχοντα τοῦ κόσμου μερῶν ἐν ἑαυτῷ πάντα τὰ συγκρίματα καὶ τὰς δυνάμεις. 5. καὶ τοῦτο εἶναί φησι τὸ λεγόμενον· «πᾶν τὸ πλήρωμα εὐδόκησε κατοικῆσαι ἐν αὐτῷ» «σωματικῶς» καὶ πᾶσά ἐστιν ἐν αὐτῷ «ἡ θεότης», <τουτέστι> τῆς οὕτω διῃρημένης τριάδος. κατενηνέχθαι γάρ φησιν ἀπὸ τῶν ὑπερκειμένων κόσμων δύο, τοῦ τε ἀγεννήτου καὶ τοῦ αὐτογενοῦς, εἰς τοῦτον τὸν κόσμον ἐν ᾧ ἐσμεν ἡμεῖς παντοίων δυνάμεων σπέρματα· 6. τίς δέ ἐστιν ὁ τρόπος τῆς καταβάσεως αὐτῶν, ὕστερον ἐροῦμεν.

κατεληλυθέναι οὖν φησι τὸν Χριστὸν ἄνωθεν, ἀπὸ τῆς ἀγεννησίας, ἵνα διὰ τῆς καταβάσεως αὐτοῦ πάντα σωθῇ τὰ τριχῇ διῃρημένα· τὰ μὲν γάρ, φησίν, ἄνωθεν κατενηνεγμένα [κάτω] ἀνελεύσεται δι' αὐτοῦ, τὰ δὲ ἐπιβουλεύσαντα τοῖς κατενηνεγμένοις ἄνωθεν ἀφίε<τα>ι καὶ κολασθέντα ἀπολέγεται. 7. τοῦτό ἐστι, φησί, τὸ εἰρημένον·

> οὐ γὰρ ἦλθεν ὁ υἱὸς τοῦ ἀνθρώπου εἰς τὸν κόσμον ἀπολέσαι τὸν κόσμον,
> ἀλλ' ἵνα σωθῇ ὁ κόσμος δι' αὐτοῦ.

κόσμον, φησί, καλεῖ τὰς δύο μοίρας τὰς ὑπερκειμένας, τήν τε ἀγέννητον καὶ τὴν αὐτογέννητον. ὅταν δὲ ἡ γραφὴ λέγῃ, φησίν· «ἵνα μὴ σὺν τῷ κόσμῳ κατακριθῶμεν», τὴν τρίτην μοῖραν λέγει, τὸν κόσμον τὸν ἰδικόν· τὴν μὲν γὰρ τρίτην δεῖ φθαρῆναι, ἣν καλεῖ κόσμον <ἰδικόν>, τὰς δὲ δύο τῆς φθορᾶς ἀπαλλαγῆναι, τὰς ὑπερκειμένας.

Minds and Humans and so forth to each part of the world, when its division is determined.

TRIADIC CHRISTOLOGY. 4. From above, from the realm of the unborn and the first division of the world—when the world was finally established for its consummation—there descended (for reasons I will explain later) in the time of Herod a triple-natured, triple-bodied, triple-powered human called "Christ." He had in himself all the compounds and powers from the three parts of the world.[240] 5. This is what, he alleges, the scriptural verse means: "The entire fullness was pleased to dwell in him bodily" and that all "divinity" is "in him"—the divinity, that is, of the aforementioned Trinity.[241] He says that there were brought down from the two upper worlds (the unborn and self-born) the seeds of all sorts of potentialities that came into this world in which we dwell. 6. How this descent occurred I shall later relate.[242]

So Christ, he says, came down from above, from the realm of the unborn, so that through his descent everything divided in three might be saved. The seeds descended from above, he claims, will ascend through him; but those that conspired against them are discharged and, after punishment, reapportioned. 7. This, he claims, is what the verse of scripture means:

> The Son of the Human did not come into the world to destroy the world, but so that the world might be saved through him.[243]

He calls the "world" the two upper portions (namely, the unborn and the self-born). Yet when, he claims, scripture says, "so that we might not be condemned with the world," it refers to the *third* part, the particular world.[244] The third portion, which he calls "particular," must be destroyed, whereas the two superior portions must be freed from corruption.

---

240. Cf. the Christology of the Naassenes in *Ref.* 5.6.7. For "triple-powered" (τριδύναμον), see, e.g., Allogenes (NHC XI,3) 61.6; Marsanes (NHC X,1) 6.19; Ap. John (NHC II,1) 5.8. Legge takes it to mean "powers from all three worlds" (*Philosophoumena*, 1:147 n. 5).

241. Col 1:19 (πᾶν τὸ πλήρωμα, "entire fullness"); 2:9 (σωματικῶς, "bodily"). The same texts are conflated in *Ref.* 8.13.2 (Monoïmos) and 10.10.4 (Peratic summary). For the Valentinian use of these texts, see Iren., *Haer.* 1.3.4; Clem. Alex., *Exc.* 31.1.

242. See *Ref.* 5.17.2–6 below.

243. John 3:17; cf. 12:47.

244. 1 Cor 11:32. This verse is also quoted in *Ref.* 6.14.6 ("Simon").

13. 1. Μάθωμεν οὖν πρῶτον πῶς ταύτην τὴν διδαχὴν παρὰ τῶν ἀστρολόγων εἰληφότες ἐπηρεάζουσι Χριστόν, ἐργαζόμενοι φθορὰν τοῖς ἑπομένοις αὐτοῖς ἐν τῇ τοιαύτῃ πλάνῃ. οἱ γὰρ ἀστρολόγοι ἕνα τὸν κόσμον εἰρηκότες διαιροῦσιν αὐτὸν εἰς τὰ τῶν ἀπλανῶν ζῳδίων μέρη δώδεκα, καὶ καλοῦσι τὸν κόσμον τῶν ζῳδίων τῶν ἀπλανῶν ἕνα κόσμον ἀπλανῆ· ἕτερον δὲ εἶναι τὸν τῶν πλανωμένων, <καὶ ἕτερον τὸν καθ' ἡμᾶς, ὃν> καὶ δυνάμει καὶ θέσει καὶ ἀριθμῷ κόσμον λέγουσιν, ὅ ἐστι μέρος <μέχρι> σελήνης. 2. λαμβάνειν δὲ κόσμον ἀπὸ κόσμου δύναμίν τινα καὶ μετουσίαν, καὶ μετέχειν [ἀπὸ] τῶν ὑπερκειμένων τὰ ὑποκείμενα.

ἵνα δὲ ἔσται τὸ λεγόμενον ἐμφανές, αὐταῖς ἐκείναις ταῖς τῶν ἀστρολόγων ἐκ μέρους χρήσομαι φωναῖς, ὑπομνήσων τοὺς ἐντυγχάνοντας τὰ προειρημένα ἐν τῷ τόπῳ οὗ ἐξεθέμεθα τὴν τῶν ἀστρολόγων πᾶσαν τέχνην.

3. ἃ μὲν οὖν [ὡς] ἐκείνοις δοκεῖ, ἔστι τάδε· ἀπὸ τῆς τῶν ἄστρων ἀπορροίας τὰς γενέσεις τῶν ὑποκειμένων ἀποτελεῖσθαι. Περιεργότερον γὰρ ἀναβλέψαντες εἰς τὸν οὐρανὸν οἱ Χαλδαῖοι ἔφασαν δραστικῶν μὲν αἰτιῶν ἐπέχειν λόγον εἰς <τὸ> ἕκαστον τῶν καθ' ἡμᾶς συμβαινόντων <ἐκβαίνειν τοὺς ἑπτὰ ἀστέρας,> συνεργεῖν δὲ τὰ τῶν ἀπλανῶν ζῳδίων μέρη. 4. <τὸν μὲν οὖν ζῳδιακὸν κύκλον διαιροῦσιν εἰς ζῴδια> δώδεκα, ἕκαστον δὲ ζῴδιον εἰς μοίρας τριάκοντα, ἑκάστην δὲ μοῖραν εἰς ἑξήκοντα λεπτά· οὕτω γὰρ καλοῦσι τὰ ἐλάχιστα καὶ [τὰ] ἀμερῆ. 5. τῶν δὲ ζῳδίων τὰ μὲν ἀρρενικὰ καλοῦσι, τὰ δὲ θηλυκά, καὶ τὰ μὲν δίσωμα, τὰ δὲ οὔ, καὶ τὰ μὲν τροπικά, τὰ δὲ στερεά. ἀρρενικὰ μὲν οὖν ἐστιν ἢ θηλυκὰ

DERIVATION FROM ASTROLOGY. 13. 1. Let us learn first of all how, by taking over this teaching from the astrologers, they insult Christ and corrupt their followers by this kind of deceit.[245] The astrologers, having pronounced that the cosmos is one, divide it into the twelve parts of the fixed zodiacal signs and call the world of the fixed zodiacal signs the "single fixed world." The world of the planets is another world. Still another is our world, which they call a world "in potentiality, in position, and in number," which extends as far as the moon.[246] 2. One world receives a quality and a share of the reality of another, and inferior phenomena share in the reality of the superior.

So that my account will be clear, I will partially use the technical terms of the astrologers, reminding my readers that I formerly presented their entire art.[247]

REVIEW OF ASTROLOGY. 3. They posit that from the emanation of the stars the nativities of those who lie under them are brought to completion.[248] The astrologers, gazing too curiously into heaven, declared that the seven planets offer an account of the motive causes for each individual event that happens to us.[249] The sections of the fixed zodiacal signs, they add, cooperate with the planets. 4. Astrologers divide the circle of the zodiac into twelve zodiacal signs, and each sign into thirty degrees, and each degree into sixty seconds—which they accordingly label the "smallest" and "indivisible" unit. 5. They call some of the zodiacal signs "male," others "female," some they call "double-bodied," others not, some "tropic," and others "fixed."[250] The male and female signs are those that have a nature

---

245. Our author uses πλάνη ("deceit") to pun on the planets (πλάνητες), discussed below. For the Peratai and astrology, see Hegedus, *Early Christianity*, 286–92.

246. Marcovich adds καὶ ἕτερον τὸν καθ' ἡμᾶς, ὅν (here: "Still another is our world, which"). Cf. the layers of the universe set forth in Ps.-Aristotle, *Mund.* 2, 392a9–b12, the Aristotelian division of the world reported in *Ref.* 7.19.2, and Ps.-Plutarch, *Plac. philos.* 2.4, 886f.

247. *Ref.* 4.1–7. The initial sections of book 4 are lost, but our author's summary below fills in some gaps.

248. For "emanation" (ἀπορροία), see *Ref.* 5.15.3. See further Francesca Alesse, "Il tema dell'emanazione (aporroia) nella letteratura astrologica e non astrologica tra I sec. a.C. e II d.C.," *MHNH* 3 (2003): 117–34.

249. The following review of astrology is adapted from Sext. Emp., *Math.* 5.5–11. For commentary, see Spinelli, *Contro gli astrologi*, 108–14.

250. For a fuller explanation of these astrological terms and notions, see Ptolemy, *Tetrab.* 1.11–12.

ἅπερ συνεργὸν ἔχει φύσιν πρὸς ἀρρενογονίαν <ἢ θηλυγονίαν>· 6. Κριὸς γὰρ ἀρρενικόν ἐστι ζῴδιον, Ταῦρος δὲ θηλυκόν, καὶ τὰ λοιπὰ κατὰ τὴν αὐτὴν ἀναλογίαν, ἃ μὲν ἀρρενικά, ἃ δὲ θηλυκά.

ἀφ᾽ ὧν, οἴομαι, Πυθαγορικοὶ κινηθέντες τὴν μὲν μονάδα ἄρρεν προσαγορεύουσι, τὴν δὲ δυάδα θῆλυ, τὴν δὲ τριάδα πάλιν ἄρρεν, καὶ ἀναλόγως τοὺς λοιποὺς τῶν τε ἀρτίων [τε] καὶ περισσῶν ἀριθμῶν.

7. ἔνιοι δὲ καὶ ἕκαστον ζῴδιον εἰς δωδεκατημόρια διελόντες τῇ αὐτῇ σχεδὸν ἐφόδῳ χρῶνται· οἷον ἐπὶ Κριοῦ <τὸ μὲν πρῶτον δωδεκατημόριον αὐτοῦ Κριόν τε> καλοῦσιν <καὶ> ἄρρεν, τὸ δὲ δεύτερον Ταῦρόν [ἄρρεν] τε καὶ θῆλυ, τὸ δὲ τρίτον Διδύμους καὶ ἄρρεν, καὶ ἐπὶ τῶν ἄλλων μοιρῶν [δὶς] ὁ αὐτὸς λόγος. 8. δίσωμα δὲ εἶναι λέγουσι ζῴδια <Διδύμους τε καὶ> τὸν διαμετροῦντα τούτοις Τοξότην, Παρθένον τε καὶ Ἰχθύας, οὐ δίσωμα δὲ τὰ λοιπά. καὶ ὡσαύτως τροπικὰ μὲν ἐν οἷς γινόμενος ὁ ἥλιος μεταλ<λ>άσ<σ>ει καὶ ποιεῖ τοῦ περιέχοντος <τ>ροπάς, οἷόν ἐστι ζῴδιον ὅ τε Κριὸς καὶ τὸ τούτου διάμετρον, καθάπερ Ζυγός, Αἰγόκερώς τε καὶ Καρκίνος· 9. ἐν Κριῷ μὲν γὰρ ἐαρινὴ γίνεται τροπή, ἐν Αἰγοκέρῳ δὲ χειμερινή, ἐν Καρκίνῳ δὲ θερινή, ἐν Ζυγῷ δὲ φθινοπωρινή.

Ταῦτα δὲ καὶ τὸν περὶ τούτων λόγον λεπτομερῶς ἐξεθέμεθα ἐν τῇ πρὸ ταύτης βίβλῳ· ὅθεν ἔστι μαθεῖν τὸν φιλομαθῆ ὡς οἱ τῆς Περατικῆς αἱρέσεως ἀρχηγοί, Εὐφράτης ὁ Περατικὸς καὶ Κέλβης ὁ Καρύστιος, μεταγαγόντες ὀνόμασι μόνον διήλλαξαν, δυνάμει δὲ τὰ ὅμοια <ὑπ>έθεντο, καὶ αὐτοὶ τῇ τέχνῃ κατακόρως προσέχοντες.

10. καὶ γὰρ ὅρια τῶν ἀστέρων οἱ ἀστρολόγοι λέγουσιν, ἐν οἷς μᾶλλον δύνασθαι φάσκουσι τοὺς ἄρχοντας ἀστέρας, οἷον ἔν <τισι μὲν κακοποιοῦσιν, ἔν> τισι δὲ ἀγαθοποιοῦσιν, ὧν καί τινας κακοποιοὺς λέγουσι, τινὰς δὲ ἀγαθοποιούς. ἐπιβλέπειν δὲ λέγονται ἀλλήλους καὶ συμφωνεῖν ἀλλήλοις <ὡς> οἱ κατὰ τρίγωνον <ἢ τετράγωνον φαινόμενοι. 11. κατὰ τρίγωνον μὲν οὖν> συσχηματίζονται ἐπιθεωροῦντες ἀλλήλους ἀστέρες ἐπὶ τριῶν ζῳδίων ἔχοντες τὸ μεταξὺ διάλειμμα, κατὰ τετράγωνον δὲ δυεῖν.

ἐν τῷ ἀνθρώπῳ κεφαλῇ τὰ [δὲ] ὑποκείμενα μέρη [πάσχειν] συμπάσχειν· συμπάσχειν δὲ καὶ τοῖς ὑποκειμένοις τὴν κεφαλήν, οὕτως καὶ τοῖς ὑπερσεληναίοις

helping to produce males and females.[251] 6. Aries is a male zodiacal sign; Taurus is female; and the rest alternate in order so that some are male, while others female.

(In my view, the Pythagoreans, who were incited by these notions, call the number one "male" and the number two "female," and in turn the number three "male," and likewise with the rest of the odd and even numbers.)[252]

7. Some, after dividing each sign into twelve degrees, employ nearly the same method. For example, in Aries they call the first degree "Aries and male," the second they call "Taurus and female," the third "Gemini and male," and likewise for the other degrees.[253] 8. They say that the double-bodied signs are Gemini and the sign in opposition to it, Sagittarius; likewise, Virgo and Pisces are double-bodied. The rest are not double-bodied. Similarly, the tropic signs are those in which the sun changes course and causes seasonal changes in the environment. For example, Aries and the sign in opposition to it—namely, Libra—are tropics, as are Capricorn and Cancer. 9. In Aries there is the spring turning, in Capricorn the winter, in Cancer the summer, and in Libra the turning of autumn.

These ideas and their explanation I thoroughly presented in the preceding book. From it the diligent student can learn how the founders of the Peratic heresy, Euphrates the Peratic and Kelbes the Karystian, altered them only by modifying the names while in terms of meaning they assumed the same ideas. So they glut themselves in their devotion to this art!

10. Moreover the "terms" of the planets, astrologers say, are the positions in which they claim that the ruling planets are more powerful. For example, in some signs, planets do harm, while in others, they cause benefit. They call the former "malefic," and the latter "benefic."[254] The signs are said to "look upon" one another and agree with each other when they appear in trine or in quartile aspect. 11. Signs are arranged in trine relation when the constellations are in aspect with a space of three signs in between. They are in quartile relation when there are two signs in between.[255]

Just as the lower parts of the body are in sympathy with the head (and vice versa), so also things on earth are in sympathy with things above the

251. Miller adds ἢ θηλυγονίαν from Sext. Emp., *Math.* 5.7.

252. This parenthetical comment is pulled directly from Sext. Emp., *Math.* 5.8.

253. Duncker and Schneidewin supply τὸ μὲν πρῶτον δωδεκατημόριον αὐτοῦ Κριόν τε ("[they call] the first degree 'Aries and …' ") from Sext. Emp., *Math.* 5.9.

254. Cf. Sext. Emp., *Math.* 5.37 (terms) and 29 (benefic and malefic planets).

255. Here our author radically summarizes the material in Sext. Emp., *Math.* 5.39–40; cf. *Ref.* 4.1.1–2.

τὰ ἐπίγεια. ἀλλὰ γάρ τίς ἐστι τούτων διαφορὰ καὶ <ἀ>συμπάθεια, ὡς μὴ μίαν καὶ τὴν αὐτὴν ἐχόντων ἕνωσιν.

12. Ταύτην τὴν σύστασιν καὶ τὴν διαφορὰν τῶν ἄστρων, Χαλδαϊκὴν ὑπάρχουσαν, πρὸς ἑαυτοὺς ἐπισπασάμενοι, οὓς προείπομεν, ἐπιψευσάμενοι τῷ τῆς ἀληθείας ὀνόματι ὡς Χριστοῦ λόγον κατήγγειλαν. αἰώνων στάσιν καὶ ἀποστασίας ἀγαθῶν δυνάμεων εἰς κακὰ καὶ συμφωνίας ἀγαθῶν μετὰ πονηρῶν προσαγορεύουσι, καλοῦντες τοπάρχας καὶ προαστείους καὶ ἄλλα πλεῖστα ὀνόματα ἀναπλάσσοντες, ἑαυτοῖς οὐχ ὑποκείμενα.

ἀλλὰ τὴν τῶν ἀστρολόγων περὶ τοὺς ἀστέρας πᾶσαν φαντασίαν ἀτέχνως τεχνολογοῦντες, μεγάλης πλάνης ὑπόθεσιν ἐπεισάγοντες, ἐξελεγχθήσονται σὺν τῇ ἡμετέρᾳ ἐμμελ(είᾳ). 13. ἀντιπαραθήσω γὰρ τῇ προλελεγμένῃ τῶν ἀστρολόγων Χαλδαϊκῇ τέχνῃ ἔνια τῶν Περατικῶν συνταγμάτων, ἀφ᾽ ὧν ὑπάρξει συγκρίναντας κατανοῆσαι ὡς οἱ Περατ<ικ>οὶ λόγοι τῶν ἀστρολόγων ὁμολογουμένως εἰσίν, οὐ Χριστοῦ.

14. 1. Δοκεῖ οὖν παρατάξαι μίαν τινὰ τῶν παρ᾽ αὐτοῖς δοξαζομένων βίβλων, ἐν ᾗ λέγει·

Ἐγὼ φωνὴ ἐξυπνισμοῦ ἐν τῷ αἰῶνι τῆς νυκτός·
λοιπὸν ἄρχομαι γυμνοῦν τὴν ἀπὸ τοῦ Χάους δύναμιν.

ἡ δύναμις τοῦ ἀβυσσικοῦ θολοῦ,
ἡ τὸν πηλὸν ἀναβαστάζουσα τοῦ ἀφθάρτου ἀχανοῦς διύγρου,
ἡ τοῦ σπάσματος ὅλη δύναμις
ὑδατόχρους ἀεικίνητος,
<ἡ> φέρουσα τὰ μένοντα,
κατέχουσα τὰ τρέμοντα,

moon. Still, there is a difference and lack of sympathy such that they are not one and the same.[256]

12. The aforementioned Peratai, integrate this—in reality, astrological—system and division of planets. They tell lies about the Name of truth, by proclaiming it as the message of Christ. They discourse about the war of aeons, and rebellion of good powers who turn to evil acts, and the alliances of good and evil powers. They call them "lords of the ascendant" and "outlying officials"—making up a host of other terms not consistent with each other.[257]

But now (sneaking in a subject of massive deceit), they will be utterly refuted by my own "harmony" as those who profess with no technical expertise the technicalities of all the astrologers' astral phantasmagoria! 13. I shall compare some of the Peratic treatises with the aforementioned Chaldaic art of the astrologers. On the basis of this comparison, it will be clear how Peratic teachings are undeniably those of the astrologers, not Christ.

EXCERPT OF "OUTLYING OFFICIALS DWELLING AS FAR AS THE AETHER." 14. 1. It is fitting to set out for comparison one of their celebrated books in which it is recorded:[258]

I am a voice of awakening in the eternity of night.[259]
Henceforth I begin to strip the power from Chaos.

There is the power of the abysmal mud
Who holds up the clay of the incorruptible expanse of liquid.
She is the entire power of the convulsion,
Watery-green and ever in motion.
She upholds the entities that abide,
Restrains what trembles,

---

256. Marcovich adds the alpha privative in ἀσυμπάθεια (as he does in *Ref.* 4.1.2).

257. Cf. Rev 12:7 ("And there was war in heaven"). "Outlying officials" (προαστείους) here "probably means the ruler of a part of the heavens near or under the influence of a planet" (Legge, *Philosophoumena*, 1:150 n. 2). They were mentioned in *Ref.* 4.2.1.

258. The following excerpt describes the lower planetary rulers and their associates. See further April DeConick, "From the Bowels of Hell to Draco: The Mysteries of the Peratics," in Bull, Lied, and Turner, *Mystery and Secrecy*, 3–38 (11–12).

259. It is possible to understand the voice as the light-creating word of God spoken over the waters of chaos in Gen 1:2–3. For awakening (ἐξυπνισμοῦ), see *Ref.* 5.7.30, 32–33 (Naassenes), and below, 5.17.8.

ἀπολύουσα τὰ ἐρχόμενα,
κουφίζουσα τὰ <γέμοντα,>
καθαιροῦσα τὰ αὔξοντα,
<ἡ> πιστὴ οἰκονόμος τοῦ ἴχνους τῶν ἀέρων,
ἡ τὰ ἀνερευγόμενα ἀπὸ τῶν δώδεκα ὀφθαλμῶν ἐντολῆς ἀπολαύουσα,
<ἡ> σφραγῖδα δηλοῦσα πρὸς τὴν μετ' αὐτῆς οἰκονομοῦσαν τῶν
ἐπιφερομένων ἀοράτων ὑδάτων δύναμιν,
    ἐκλήθη Θάλασσα.

2. ταύτην τὴν δύναμιν ἡ ἀγνωσία ἐκάλεσε Κρόνον, δεσμοῖς φρουρούμενον, ἐπεὶ ἔσφιγγε τὸ σύμπλεγμα τοῦ πυκνοῦ καὶ ὁμιχλώδους, ἀδήλου σκοτεινοῦ Ταρτάρου. ταύτης ἐγένοντο κατ' εἰκόνα Κηφεύς, Προμηθεύς, Ἰαπετός.

3. δύναμις πεπιστευμένη τὴν Θάλασσαν, ἀρσενόθηλυς· ἡ τὸν ἀνατρέχοντα συριγμὸν ἀπὸ τῶν δώδεκα στομάτων τοῖς δώδεκα αὐλίσκοις ἁρμόζουσα· δ<ι>αχύνει λεπτύ<ν>ουσα καὶ καθαιρεῖ τὴν κατέχουσαν λάβρον ἀναφοράν· καὶ σφραγίζει <σ>ατραπῶν ὁδοὺς αὐτῆς, πρὸς τὸ μὴ πολεμῆσαι ἢ ἐναλλάξαι τό<πους> μὴ δι' αὐτῆς·

θυγάτηρ Τυφωνική, πιστὴ φύλαξ ὑδάτων παντοίων· ὄνομα αὐτῇ Χορζάρ. ταύτην ἡ ἀγνωσία ἐκάλεσε Ποσειδῶνα· οὗ κατ' εἰ(κ)όνα ἐγένοντο Γλαῦκος, Μελικέρτης, Ἴη, Νεβρών.

Unlooses what is to come,
Lightens what is full,[260]
Reduces what grows.
She is the faithful Stewardess of the trace of the lower airs,
Who savors what has been disgorged from the twelve eyes of the command.[261]
She shows the seal to the Power that, together with her, administers the invisible waters hovering above;
She has been called: "Sea."

2. Ignorance called this power "Saturn," kept guarded in chains, since the entanglement of thick, misty, dim, dark Tartaros tightly binds him.[262] According to the image of this power were born Kepheus, Prometheus, and Iapetos.[263]

3. The power entrusted with Sea is androgynous. It harmonizes the whistling that shoots out from the twelve mouths of the twelve pipes. It disperses by rarefying and destroys the fierce surge that holds her down. Moreover, it seals the paths of its satraps, so that they do not make war or exchange places except through her.[264]

Its daughter is Typhonike, trusted guardian of all kinds of waters. Her name is Chorzar.[265] Ignorance called her "Poseidon." From him were born Glaukos, Melikertes, Iē, Nebron, all according to the image.[266]

---

260. Γέμοντα ("full") is Marcovich's emendation for P's *μένοντα* ("what remains").

261. Cruice believes that "eyes" in this sentence were written for "springs," a homonym in Hebrew (עין). He refers to the twelve springs of Elim in Exod 15:27; Num 33:9. See further Annarita Magri, "L'esegesi della setta ofitica dei Perati," *Apocrypha* 14 (2003): 193–223 (218).

262. Saturn represents Κρόνος, who lost his kingship to his son (Zeus). Saturn and water were associated. Pythagoras reportedly referred to the sea as the "tears of Kronos" (Aristotle, frag. 159 [Gigon], from Porphyry, *Vit. Pyth.* 41; cf. Clem. Alex., *Strom.* 5.8.50.1). In Origen, *Cels.* 6.31, the lion-headed Yaldabaoth is associated with the planet Saturn. See also *Ref.* 5.16.2 below.

263. Kepheus is king of Ethiopia, father of Andromeda, and a constellation in the northern sky. Iapetos and Prometheus are Titans, brother and nephew to Kronos, respectively.

264. Marcovich emends P's ἀτραπῶν to σατραπῶν ("satraps"; cf. *Ref.* 5.26.11 [Justin]) and τό to τόπους ("places"). For sealing the archons to prevent war, see Pist. Soph. 75 (Schmidt, 168).

265. On the use of secret names, see DeConick, "Bowels," 13–14.

266. For Iē, cf. Ia (the lover of Attis) in Arnobius, *Adv. nat.* 5.7. Glaukos, Melik-

4. περιεσφαιρωκὼς τὴν δωδεκαγώνιον πυραμίδα, πύλην εἰς πυραμίδα σκοτίζων ποικίλαις χρόαις καὶ ἀπαρτίζων πᾶσαν [τὴν] νυκτόχρουν. τοῦτον ἡ ἀγνωσία ἐκάλεσε Κόρην. οὗ λειτουργοὶ πέντε·

πρῶτος Οὔ,
δεύτερος Ἀοαί,
τρίτος Οὐώ,
τέταρτος Οὐωάβ,
πέμπτος ...

[ἄλλοι] πιστοὶ οἰκονόμοι αὐτοῦ τῆς τοπαρχίας, ἡμέρας καὶ νυκτὸς οἱ ἀναπαυόμενοι ἐν τῇ ἐξουσίᾳ αὐτῶν. 5. τούτους ἡ ἀγνωσία ἐκάλεσε τοὺς πλάνητας ἀστέρας, ἐφ᾽ ὧν ἡ φθαρτὴ γένεσις ἠώρηται.

Ἀέρος ἀνατολῆς <καὶ ἀέρος δύσεως> οἰκονόμοι Καρφακασημεοχεὶρ <καὶ> Ἐκκαββάκαρα· τούτους ἐκάλεσεν ἡ ἀγνωσία Κουρῆτας. ἄρχων ἀνέμων τρίτος Ἀριήλ· οὗ κατ᾽ εἰκόνα ἐγένοντο Αἴολος, Β<ρ>ιάρη<ο>ς.

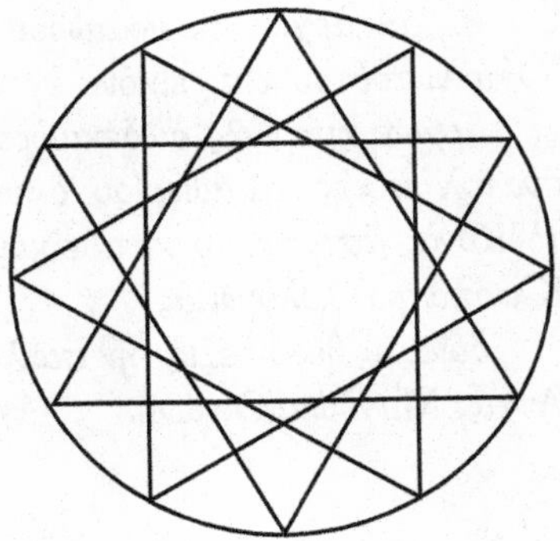

4. On the outer sphere of the twelve-cornered pyramid, there is one who darkens the gate in the pyramid with various colors and finishes it all according to the color of night.[267]

Ignorance calls him "Kore." He has five ministers.

The first is Ou,
the second Aoai,
the third Ouō,
fourth Ouōab,
and fifth ...[268]

Those who rest in their authority are faithful administrators of his realm, namely, day and night. 5. Ignorance called them "wandering stars." Upon them corruptible generation is dependent.

The administrators of the east and west air are Karphakasemeocheir and Ekkabbakara.[269] Ignorance calls them "Kouretes." The third ruler of wind is Ariel.[270] Born according to his image were Aiolos and Briareos.[271]

---

ertes, and Ino are sea deities usually depicted as subordinate to Poseidon. Νεβρών is an emendation of P's νεβρόη. ⲛⲉⲃⲣⲱ is translated "rebel" (ⲁⲡ[ⲟⲥ]ⲧⲁⲧⲏⲥ) in Gos. Jud. 51.14–15. There he is also called "Ialdabaoth."

267. The twelve-cornered pyramid resembles a representation of the Zodiac diagrammed with four triangles (thus showing trine relationships, cf. Manilius, *Astron.* 2.273–87). It may also allude to the dodecahedron in *Tim.* 55c (see Taylor, *Commentary*, 377). See the figure above. This shape, in the opinion of some Platonists, is the image of the universe (Ps.-Timaios, *Nat. mund. an.* 35, 98d [end]; cf. Plutarch, *Quaest. plat.* 1003c–d), or the geometrical figure of aether (Plutarch, *E Delph.* 390a).

268. There is some lacuna here, probably because an incomprehensible name has dropped out. Marcovich suggests Οὐωαύ or Οὐωαή. Cf. *Ref.* 6.48.2 (the use of vowel sounds in Markos). DeConick believes that her five assistants are "the five rulers of the abyss mentioned in other Gnostic sources" ("Bowels," 19). She cites Ap. John (NHC II,1) 9.9–23; Pist. Soph. 4.139–140. Below they seem to be identified with five planets (although which five is unclear).

269. Marcovich adds καὶ ἀέρος δύσεως (here: "and of the west air"). Cf. the archon of the power of the air in Eph 2:2. On Ἐκκαββάκαρα, see Εκκας in 2 Sam 23:26 (Codex Alexandrinus) and Βακβακαρ in 1 Chr 9:15.

270. Ariel in Hebrew means "lion of God" and is used to refer to Jerusalem in Isa 29:1. In other texts, DeConick notes, it is the name for Ialdabaoth, due to his leonine

6. καὶ ἄρχων δωδεκαώρου νυκτερινῆς Σοκλάν· ὃν ἐκάλεσεν ἡ ἀγνωσία Ὄσιριν. τούτου κατ’ εἰκόνα ἐγένοντο Ἄδμητος, Μήδεια, Ἕλλην, Αἴθουσα.

ἄρχων ἡμερινῆς δωδεκαώρου Εὐνώ· οὗτος οἰκονόμος τῆς πρωτοκαμάρου ἀνατολ<ικ>ῆς καὶ αἰθερίου· ὃ<ν> ἐκάλεσεν ἡ ἀγνωσία Ἶσιν. 7. τούτου σημεῖον τὸ Κυνὸς ἄστρον· οὗ κατ’ εἰκόνα ἐγένοντο Πτολεμαῖος ὁ Ἀρσινόης, Διδύμη, Κλεοπάτρα, Ὀλυμπιάς.

δύναμις θεοῦ δεξιά· ἣν ἐκάλεσεν ἡ ἀγνωσία Ῥέαν· οὗ κατ’ εἰκόνα ἐγένοντο Ἄττις, Μυγδών, Οἰνώνη.

6. The ruler of the twelve hours of the night is Soklan, whom Ignorance called "Osiris."[272] According to his image were born Admetos, Medeia, Hellen, and Aithousa.[273]

The ruler of the twelve hours of the day is Euno. He is the administrator of the first eastern and aetherial vault.[274] Ignorance called him "Isis." 7. His sign is the Dog Star.[275] According to his image were born Ptolemy son of Arsinoë, Didyme, Kleopatra, and Olympias.[276]

The right hand is a power of God whom Ignorance called "Rhea." According to his image were born Attis, Mygdon, and Oinone.[277]

---

shape (e.g., Orig. World [NHC II,5] 100.25–39; Pist. Soph. 3.102) ("Bowels," 20). See also Campbell Bonner, "An Amulet of the Ophite Gnostics," in *Commemorative Studies in Honor of Theodore Leslie Shear*, Hesperia Supplements 8 [Princeton: American School of Classical Studies at Athens, 1949], 43–46, with plate 8.1).

271. Aiolos is the Greek wind god. Briareos is one of the three "hundred-handers" or fierce monsters who fought with the gods against the Titans. They now guard the gate of Tartaros (Hesiod, *Theog.* 617–686).

272. For Σοκλάν, cf. Saklas in Apoc. Adam (NHC V,5) 74. Saklas = Yaldabaoth in Ap. John (NHC II,1) 11.17; Nat. Rulers (NHC II,4) 95.7–8; Three Forms (NHC XIII,1) 39.27. Osiris probably is the constellation Orion (Boll, *Sphaera*, 164–68, 309–10). Boll notes the Egyptian element of astrology here: during the twelve hours of the day, Ra travels across the sky with his Dayboat, and in his Nightboat through the Amduat (or Netherworld).

273. These figures are all connected with the day or the sun. Admetos was king of Pherae in Thessaly, friend (or beloved) of Apollo (identified with the sun). Medea was granddaughter of the Sun. Hellen (whose name resembles ἥλιος) is the eponymous ancestor of the Hellenes. Aithousa (literally "burning one") is granddaughter of Atlas and daughter of Poseidon (Ps.-Apollodoros, *Bibl.* 3.10.1).

274. In the word πρωτοκαμάρου, Marcovich urges, κάμαρος = καμάρα ("vault"). Legge suggested πρωτομακάρος ("first-blessed") (*Philosophoumena*, 1:152 n. 4).

275. For Isis as Σῶθιν = Sirius, see Diodoros, *Bibl. hist.* 1.27.4 (ἐγώ εἰμι ἡ ἐν τῷ ἄστρῳ τῷ ἐν κυνὶ ἐπιτέλλουσα ["I am she who rises in the planet in the Dog constellation"]); Boll, *Sphaera*, 208–16. DeConick says that the "heliacal rising of Sothis "after a seventy-day absence signaled the start of the annual calendar for the Egyptians. This occurred immediately prior to the rising of the Nile floodwaters" ("Bowels," 21).

276. Ptolemy son of Arsinoë is Ptolemy I Soter. Didyme was a courtesan of Ptolemy II Philadelphos (Athenaios, *Deipn.* 13, 576e). Kleopatra is the name of several Egyptian queens, the most famous being Kleopatra VII (69–30 BCE). Olympias was the mother of Alexander the Great.

277. All these figures are related to Phrygia. Rhea is the Phrygian Mother of the Gods. Μυγδών is Marcovich's emendation of μυγδώνη in P. He is a Phrygian king who fought at Troy (Homer, *Il.* 3.186). Attis is a Phrygian deity allegorized by the Naas-

δύναμις ἀριστερά· τροφῆς ἐξουσιάζει· ἣν ἐκάλεσεν ἡ ἀγνωσία Δήμητραν, ὄνομα αὐτῇ Βένα. τούτου κατ' εἰκόνα ἐγένοντο Κελεός, Τριπτόλεμος, Μίσυρ, Πραξι<θέ>α.

δύναμις δεξι(ά)· ἐξουσιάζει καρπῶν. τοῦτον ἡ ἀγνωσία ἐκάλεσε Μῆνα· οὗ κατ' εἰκόνα ἐγένοντο Βουμέγας, Ὀστάνης, Ἑρμῆς Τρισμέγιστος, Κουρίτη(ς), Πετόσιρις, Ζῳδάριον, Βηρωσός, Ἀστράμψουχος, Ζωρόαστρις.

8. δύναμις <πυρὸς> εὐώνυμος· τοῦτον ἡ ἀγνωσία ἐκάλεσεν Ἥφαιστον· οὗ κατ' εἰκόνα ἐγένοντο Ἐριχθόνιος, Ἀχιλλεύς, Καπανεύς, Φλεγύας, Μελέαγρος, <Τυδεύς>, <Ἐγ>κέλαδος, Ῥαφαήλ, Σουριήλ, Ὀμφάλη.

The left hand is a power that has authority over nourishment. Ignorance called her "Demeter"; but her name is "Bena." According to his image were born Keleos, Triptolemos, Misur, and Praxithea.[278]

The right-hand power has authority over the harvests. Ignorance called him "Mena."[279] According to his image were born Boumegas, Ostanes, Hermes the Thrice-Great, Kourites, Petosiris, Zodarion, Berosos, Astrampsouchos, and Zoroastris.[280]

8. The power on the left has authority over fire.[281] Ignorance called this one "Hephaistos." According to his image were born Erichthonios, Achilleus, Kapaneus, Phlegyas, Meleagros, Tydeus, Enkelados, Raphael, Souriel, and Omphale.[282]

---

senes (*Ref.* 5.7–8). Oinone was a Phrygian mountain nymph once married to Paris but rejected when the latter married Helen (Ps.-Apoll., *Bibl.* 3.12.6).

278. Most of these figures are connected with Eleusis and the sowing of grain. Demeter is the grain-giving goddess worshiped at Eleusis. Keleos was king of Eleusis when Demeter visited. Demeter first taught Triptolemos the sowing of grain. Πραξιθέα is Marcovich's emendation of P's ἀπραξία. She is the wife of Keleos and mother of Triptolemos (Ps.-Apollodoros, *Bibl.* 1.5.1). For Misur (Μίσυρ), see Μισώρ in Philo of Byblos, quoted by Eusebios, *Praep. ev.* 1.10.13 (Attridge and Oden, 45). Misur is a name for a region east of the Jordan in Deut 3:10; Josh 13:9, 16, 17, 21; 21:36; Jer 31:21.

279. Mena (or perhaps Meis [Μείς], the Greek word for moon) appears to be a second power on the right alongside Rhea. Montserrat-Torrents identifies him with Men, a moon god of Asia Minor ("Les Pérates," *Comp* 34 [1989]: 185–98 [193]; cf. *Ref.* 5.8.4; 5.9.8 [Naassenes]).

280. Most of these figures are non-Greek sages, magicians, or diviners. Berosos (or Berossos) was a Babylonian priest, astrologer, and historian in the third century BCE. Ostanes was a Persian magos in the line of Zoroaster. See further Bidez and Cumont, *Mages hellénisés*, 1:165–212; 2:265–356. Hermes Trismegistos ("Thrice-great") and Petosiris were Egyptians associated with theosophy and astrology. Astrampsouchos was the name of one or several Persian magicians (Diog. L., *Vit. phil.* proem. 2). There is a love spell of "Astrapsoukos" in *PGM* VIII. 1. In Zostrianos ([NHC VIII,1] 47.3), "Strempsouchos" is mentioned as a guardian of souls. Marcovich equates Boumegas with the ancient Persian Gaumata (a magos of the Achaemenid era who had a brief reign as king). Marcovich equates Ζωδάριον with Ὠάννης or the god Ea (*Refutatio*, 180, ad. loc.).

281. Marcovich adds πυρός (here: "over fire").

282. Hephaistos represents the element fire and completes the series of four elements (Rhea/water, Demeter/earth, Mena/air, Hephaistos/fire). Those born in Hephaistos's image are related to fire. Kapaneus, one of the Seven against Thebes, was destroyed by the fire of a thunderbolt. Phlegyas (literally, "burning one") was eponymous ancestor of the Phlegyae, a Thessalian people. Meleagros, king of the Aetolians in Kalydon, died when a fateful brand was burned on the fire. Erichthonios, an Attic

9. δυνάμεις τρεῖς μέσαι, <ἐκ> τοῦ ἀέρος κρεμάμεναι αἰτίαι γενέσεως. ταύτας ἡ ἀγνωσία ἐκάλεσε Μοίρας· ὧν κατ' εἰκόνα ἐγένοντο οἶκος Πριάμου, οἶκος Λαΐου, Ἰνώ, Αὐτονόη, Ἀγαυή, Ἀθάμας, Πρόκνη, Δαναΐδες, Πελιάδες.

10. δύναμις ἀρσενόθηλυς ἀεὶ νηπιάζουσα, ἀγήρατος· αἰτία κάλλους, ἡδονῆς, ἀκμῆς, ὀρέξεως, ἐπιθυμίας. ὃν ἐκάλεσεν ἡ ἀγνωσία Ἔρωτα· οὗ κατ' εἰκόνα ἐγένοντο Πάρις, Νάρκισσος, Γανυμήδης, Ἐνδυμίων, Τιθωνός, Ἰκάριος, Λήδα, Ἀμυμώνη, Θέτις, Ἑσπερίδες, Ἰασων, Λέανδρος, Ἡρώ.

οὗτοί εἰσιν Οἱ προάστειοι ἕως αἰθέρος· οὕτω γὰρ καὶ ἐπιγράφει τὸ βιβλίον.

15. 1. Καταφανὴ<ς> σύμπασιν εὐκόλως γεγένηται ἡ τῶν Περατῶν αἵρεσις ἀπὸ τῆς τῶν ἀστρολόγων, μεθηρμοσμένη τοῖς ὀνόμασι μόνοις· τὸν δὲ αὐτὸν τρόπον περιέχει καὶ τὰ ἕτερα αὐτῶν βιβλία, εἴ τινι φίλον εἴη διὰ πάντων ἐλθεῖν. 2. πάντων γάρ, ὡς ἔφην, τῶν γεννητῶν τῆς γενέσεως αἴτια νομίζουσιν εἶναι τὰ ἀγέννητα καὶ τὰ ὑπερκείμενα, καὶ γεγονέναι κατ' ἀπόρροιαν τὸν κόσμον τὸν καθ' ἡμᾶς—ὃν ἰδικὸν ἐκεῖνοι καλοῦσι—, καὶ τούτους πάντας ὁμοῦ τοὺς ἀστέρας τοὺς θεωρουμένους ἐν τῷ οὐρανῷ τῆς γενέσεως αἰτίους γεγονέναι τοῦδε τοῦ κόσμου, ἐναλλάξαντες αὐτῶν τὰ ὀνόματα, ὡς ἀπὸ τῶν προαστείων ἔστι συγκρίναντας εὑρεῖν. 3. δεύτερον δὲ δή, κατὰ τὸν αὐτὸν τρόπον, ὡς γέγονεν ὁ κόσμος ἀπὸ τῆς ἀπορροίας τῆς ἄνω, οὕτως τὰ ἐνθάδε ἀπὸ τῆς ἀπορροίας τῶν ἀστέρων γένεσιν ἔχειν καὶ φθορὰν λέγουσι καὶ διοικεῖσθαι.

9. Three middle powers hang suspended in the air as the causes of generation. Ignorance called them the "Fates."[283] According to their image were born the house of Priam, the house of Laios, Ino, Autonoe, Agave, Athamas, Prokne, the daughters of Danaos, and the daughters of Pelias.[284]

10. There is an androgynous power, ever remaining an infant and ageless. It is the cause of beauty, pleasure, vigor, desire, and lust. Ignorance called him "Eros." According to his image were born Paris, Narkissos, Ganymede, Endymion, Tithonos, Ikarios, Leda, Amymone, Thetis, the Hesperides, Jason, Leander, and Hero.[285]

These are the Outlying Officials Dwelling as Far as the Aether—for such is the title of the book.

EVALUATION. 15. 1. It is obviously clear to everybody that the entire Peratic heresy derives from the art of astrology; it is adapted only in its terminology. (Their other books too are in the same style—if someone is inclined to peruse them all.) 2. They suppose that the causes of all things born by generation, as I said, are unborn and transcendent, and that our world (which they call "particular") was emanated [from the transcendent worlds]. Furthermore, all those stars seen amassed in the sky cause the generation of this world. They merely change the astrological terms, as one finds after comparing the names of their "outlying officials." 3. Secondly, by the same logic, just as the world arose from the higher emanation, so also things on earth, they say, live, die, and are administered from the emanation of the planets.

---

hero, is son of Hephaistos. Achilleus, the hero of the *Iliad*, had his mortality (minus the heel) burned away in fire (Apollonios, *Arg*. 4.869–872). Τυδεύς is Duncker and Schneidewin's emendation of τὰ δύηκεν in P. Tydeus is well known in mythology for his fiery temperament. Ἐγκέλαδος (an emendation of P's κέλαδος) was a giant born on the plain of Phlegra (the "burning" plain). He was buried under Mt. Etna, where he still breathes forth fire. Raphael is a Jewish archangel, as is Souriel (Uriel). Angels are flames of fire (Heb 1:7). These two angels in particular may be thought of as the seraphim ("burning ones") who appear in Isaiah (6:2; cf. Origen, *Cels*. 6.30). Omphale, finally, is a mistress of Herakles (possibly associated with the fires of passion). Cf. *Ref*. 5.26.28 (Justin).

283. Cf. the position of the Fates in Plato, *Resp*. 616b–617d.

284. All these figures seem to be united by suffering tragedies at the hands of fate.

285. These figures were beautiful or loved for their beauty by various gods, by demigods, or by each other (as in the case of Leander and Hero). Thus they became images of Eros (Love).

4. ἐπεὶ γοῦν οἱ ἀστρολόγοι ἴσασιν ὡροσκόπον καὶ μεσουράνημα καὶ δύσιν καὶ ἀντιμεσουράνημα, καὶ τούτων τῶν ἄστρων ἄλλοτε ἄλλων γινομένων διὰ τὴν στροφὴν ἀεὶ τοῦ παντός, ἄλλοτε ἄλλα ἀποκλίματα εἶναι κατὰ <τὸ> κέντρον καὶ [κέντροις] ἐπαναφοράς, ἀλληγοροῦντες τὴν διαταγὴν τῶν ἀστρολόγων <οὗτοι> τὸ μὲν κέντρον οἱονεὶ θεὸν καὶ μονάδα καὶ κύριον τῆς πάσης γενέσεως ὑποτυποῦσι, τὸ δὲ ἀπόκλιμα ἀριστερόν, τὴν δ' ἐπαναφορὰν δεξιόν. 5. ὅταν οὖν τοῖς γράμμασιν αὐτῶν ἐντυχών τις δύναμιν εὑρίσκῃ παρ' αὐτοῖς λεγομένην δεξιὰν ἢ ἀριστεράν, ἀνατρεχέτω ἐπὶ τὸ κέντρον καὶ τὸ ἀπόκλιμα καὶ τὴν <ἐπ>αναφοράν, <καὶ> κατόψεται σαφῶς πᾶσαν αὐτῶν τὴν πραγματείαν ἀστρολογικὴν διδασκαλίαν καθεστῶσαν.

16. 1. Καλοῦσι δὲ αὐτοὺς Περάτας, μηδέν<α> δύνασθαι νομίζοντες τῶν ἐν γενέσει καθεστηκότων διαφυγεῖν τὴν ἀπὸ τῆς γενέσεως τοῖς γεγενημένοις ὡρισμένην μοῖραν—εἰ γάρ τι, φησί, γενητόν, ὅλως καὶ φθείρεται, καθάπερ καὶ Σιβύλλῃ δοκεῖ·—μόνοι δέ, φησίν, ἡμεῖς

> οἱ τὴν ἀνάγκην τῆς γενέσεως ἐγνωκότες, καὶ τὰς ὁδοὺς δι' ὧν εἰσελήλυθεν ὁ ἄνθρωπος εἰς τὸν κόσμον ἀκριβῶς δεδιδαγμένοι, διελθεῖν καὶ περᾶσαι τὴν φθορὰν μόνοι δυνάμεθα.

2. ἔστι δὲ ἡ φθορά, φησί, τὸ ὕδωρ, οὐδὲ ἄλλῳ τινί, φησίν, ἐφθάρη τάχιον ὁ κόσμος ἢ ὕδατι. τὸ δὲ ὕδωρ ἐστί, τὸ περιεσφαιρωκὸς ἐν τοῖς προαστείοις, λέγουσιν, ὁ Κρόνος. δύναμις γάρ <ἐστι,> φησίν, ὑδατόχρους, ἥντινα δύναμιν, φησί,—τουτέστι τὸν Κρόνον—οὐδεὶς τῶν ἐν γενέσει καθεστώτων διαφυγεῖν

4. Now let us assume that the astrologers know the ascendant sign, the midheaven, the descendant, and the anti-midheaven; and since different signs occupy these points at different times due to the revolution of the universe, the astrologers know that there are different descending and ascending signs at different times according to the center.[286] These heretics, allegorizing the system of the astrologers, represent the center as god (so to speak), monad, and lord of all generation, the descending sign on his left, and the rising sign on his right.[287] 5. Thus when one reads in their writings and finds a power among them called "right hand" or "left hand," let him trace his steps back to the center, the descending sign, and the rising sign, and he will clearly see that their entire system is established astrological teaching.

ALLEGORY OF THE EXODUS. 16. 1. They call themselves "Peratai" ("Traversers") and suppose that no one set in the world of generation can flee the fate determined from birth for those who have been born. If anything is born, he says, it is also entirely destroyed, as the Sibyl teaches.[288] "We alone," he says,

> who have known the necessity of birth and have been accurately taught the paths through which the human being entered into the world, can cross over and traverse [περᾶσαι] destruction.

2. Now this destruction, he says, is water, and the world is destroyed by nothing faster, he says, than water. This water, they say, is the water on the outer sphere of the "outlying officials"—namely, Saturn. He is a power pale as water, he claims. No one fixed in birth is able to escape this power (that

---

286. Cf. Sext. Emp., *Math.* 5.12–14; Vettius Valens, *Anth.* 2.2. The "center" (κέντρον) here and below refers to the center at the midheaven position, the topmost portion of the sky where the demiurgic god is thought to dwell. DeConick believes that the Peratai "identified Kronos [Saturn] with the midheaven cardinal point," ("Bowels," 16). See further Maria Grazia Lancellotti, "I Perati, un esempio di cosmologia gnostica," in *Cartografia religiosa: Religiöse Kartographie, Cartographie religieuse*, ed. Daria Pezzoli-Olgiati and Fritz Stolz, Studia Religiosa Helvetica 4 (Bern: Lang, 2000), 131–56 (147).

287. For the position of god on the horoscopic chart, see Sext. Emp., *Math.* 5.15, 19.

288. The first line of Sib. Or. frag. 3 (Geffcken) reads: εἰ δὲ γενητὸν ὅλως καὶ φθείρεται ("if what is born is yet entirely destroyed").

δύναται. 3. πάσῃ γὰρ γενέσει πρὸς τὸ ὑποπεσεῖν τῇ φθορᾷ αἴτιος ἐφέστηκεν ὁ Κρόνος, καὶ οὐκ ἂν γένοιτο γένεσις ἐν ᾗ <ὁ> Κρόνος οὐκ ἐμποδίζει. τοῦτό ἐστι, φησίν, ὃ καὶ οἱ ποιηταὶ λέγουσι, τὸ καὶ τοὺς θεοὺς ἐκφοβοῦν·

ἴστω γάρ—φησί—τόδε γαῖα καὶ οὐρανὸς εὐρὺς ὕπερθεν
καὶ τὸ κατ<ε>ιβόμενον Στυγὸς ὕδωρ, ὅς τε μέγιστος
ὅρκος δεινότατός τε πέλει μακάρεσ<σ>ι θεοῖσιν.

4. οὐ μόνον δὲ τοῦτο, φησίν, οἱ ποιηταὶ λέγουσιν, ἀλλ᾽ ἤδη καὶ οἱ σοφώτατοι τῶν Ἑλλήνων, ὧν ἐστι καὶ Ἡράκλειτος εἷς, λέγων·

ψυχῇσι γὰρ θάνατος ὕδωρ γενέσθαι.

οὗτος, φησίν, ὁ θάνατος καταλαμβάνει τοὺς Αἰγυπτίους ἐν Ἐρυθρᾷ θαλάσσῃ μετὰ τῶν ἁρμάτων αὐτῶν· πάντες γὰρ οἱ ἀγνοοῦντες, φησίν, εἰσὶν Αἰγύπτιοι. 5. καὶ τοῦτό ἐστι, λέγουσι, τὸ ἐξελθεῖν ἐξ Αἰγύπτου—<τουτέστιν> ἐκ τοῦ σώματος· Αἴγυπτον γὰρ εἶναι [μικρὰν] τὸ σῶμα νομίζουσι.

καὶ περᾶσαι τὴν θάλασσαν τὴν Ἐρυθράν—τουτέστι τῆς φθορᾶς τὸ ὕδωρ, ὅ ἐστιν ὁ Κρόνος—, καὶ γενέσθαι πέραν τῆς Ἐρυθρᾶς θαλάσσης—τουτέστι τῆς γενέσεως—, καὶ ἐλθεῖν εἰς τὴν ἔρημον—τουτέστιν ἔξω γενέσεως γενέσθαι, ὅπου εἰσίν ὁμοῦ πάντες οἱ θεοὶ τῆς ἀπωλείας καὶ ὁ θεὸς τῆς σωτηρίας.—6. Εἰσὶ δέ, φησίν, οἱ θεοὶ τῆς ἀπωλείας οἱ ἀστέρες, οἱ τῆς μεταβλητῆς γενέσεως ἐπιφέροντες τοῖς γινομένοις τὴν ἀνάγκην. τούτους, φησίν, ἐκάλεσε Μωϋσῆς ὄφεις τῆς ἐρήμου, δάκνοντας καὶ διαφθείροντας τοὺς πεπερακέναι νομίζοντας τὴν Ἐρυθρὰν θάλασσαν. 7. δακνομένοις οὖν, φησίν, ἐν τῇ ἐρήμῳ τοῖς υἱοῖς

is, Saturn).[289] 3. In the whole world of generation, Saturn is responsible for subjecting things to death, and no birth occurs in which Saturn does not interfere. Saturn, he says, is the water about which the poets also speak—of which even gods are terrified.

Let Earth know and broad Heaven above,
And the down-rushing water of Styx—which is the greatest
And most terrible oath to the blessed gods.[290]

4. Not only do the poets say this, he adds, but the wisest of the Greeks as well. One of their number is Herakleitos, who says:

For souls it is death to become water.[291]

This, he claims, is the death that overtakes the Egyptians with their chariots in the Red Sea.[292] (The Egyptians, he says, represent everyone who is ignorant.) 5. They add that to depart from Egypt means to depart from the body (for they suppose that Egypt represents the body).[293]

Moreover, to cross the Red Sea is to cross the water of destruction, which is Saturn. To be beyond the Red Sea is to be beyond generation. To come into the desert is to come out of generation, where all the gods of destruction and the God of salvation are in one place.[294] 6. The gods of destruction, he claims, are the planets who inflict the necessity of changeable generation on those who are born. These, he says, Moses called "snakes of the desert," who kept biting and destroying those who supposed that they had traversed [πεπερακέναι] the Red Sea. 7. When the children of

---

289. For Saturn, see above, *Ref.* 5.14.1–2.

290. Homer, *Il.* 15.36–38; *Od.* 5.184–186; Hom. Hymn Apollo 84–86. The same passage is quoted in *Ref.* 5.20.10 (Sethians).

291. Herakleitos, DK 22 B36 (= Marcovich, *Heraclitus*, §66). Clem. Alex., *Strom.* 6.2.17.2, provides a fuller version of the quote.

292. Exod 14:28.

293. On Egypt as the body, see, e.g., Philo, *Fug.* 124, 180; Exeg. Soul [NHC II,6] 130.19–28; Acts Thom. 108.12–109.35 ("Hymn of the Pearl"). Cf. the similar exegesis of the Naassenes in *Ref.* 5.7.39–41; 5.8.2.

294. Exod 15:22 (entrance into the desert). According to DeConick, the "Peratics call the celestial spheres the 'desert.'... So here we have the confrontation between the soul and the planetary and Zodiacal rulers (who often were depicted by the Egyptians as serpentine) as it tries to make its way out of the celestial revolutions that are forcing it back into a body" ("Bowels," 31).

Ἰσραὴλ ἐπέδειξε Μωϋσῆς τὸν ἀληθινὸν ὄφιν, τὸν τέλειον, εἰς ὃν οἱ πιστεύοντες οὐκ<έτι> ἐδάκνοντο ἐν τῇ ἐρήμῳ, τουτέστιν ὑπὸ τῶν δυνάμεων.

οὐδεὶς οὖν, φησίν, ὁ δυνάμενος σῶσαι καὶ ῥύσασθαι τοὺς ἐκπορευομένους ἐκ γῆς Αἰγύπτου—τουτέστιν ἐκ σώματος καὶ ἐκ τοῦδε τοῦ κόσμου—, εἰ μὴ μόνος ὁ τέλειος, ὁ πλήρης τῶν πληρῶν ὄφις. 8. ἐπὶ τοῦτον, φησίν, ὁ ἐλπίσας ὑπὸ τῶν ὄφεων τῆς ἐρήμου οὐ διαφθείρεται—τουτέστιν <ὑπὸ> τῶν θεῶν τῆς γενέσεως—, <ὡς> γέγραπται, φησίν, ἐν βίβλῳ Μωσέως. οὗτος, φησίν, ὁ ὄφις ἐστὶν ἡ δύναμις ἡ παρακολουθήσασα τῷ Μωσεῖ, ἡ ῥάβδος ἡ στρεφομένη εἰς ὄφιν. ἀνθεστήκεισαν δέ, φησί, τῇ δυνάμει Μωσέως <ἐν> Αἰγύπτῳ τῶν μάγων οἱ ὄφεις—<τουτέστιν> οἱ θεοὶ τῆς ἀπωλείας·—ἀλλὰ πάντας αὐτοὺς ὑπέταξε καὶ διέφθειρεν ἡ ῥάβδος Μωσέως.

Ὁ καθολικὸς ὄφις, φησίν, οὗτός ἐστιν ὁ σοφὸς τῆς Εὔας λόγος. 9. τοῦτ(ο), φ(ησ)ίν, ἐστὶ <τὸ> μυστήριον Ἐδέμ, τοῦτο ποταμὸς <ἐκπορευόμενος> ἐξ Ἐδέμ, τοῦτο σημεῖον τὸ τεθὲν τῷ Κάϊν, ἵνα πᾶς ὁ εὑρίσκων αὐτὸν μ(ὴ) ἀποκτείνῃ <αὐτόν>. οὗτος, φησίν, ἐστὶν Κάϊν οὗ τὴν θυσίαν οὐ π(ρο)σεδέξατο ὁ θεὸς τοῦδε τοῦ κόσμου, τὴν δὲ ᾑμαγμένην προσήκατο τοῦ Ἄβελ· αἵμασι γάρ χαίρει ὁ τοῦδε τοῦ κόσμου δ(ε)σπότης.

10. οὗτός ἐστι, φησίν, ὁ ἐν ἐσχάταις ἡμέραις ἐν ἀνθρώπου μορφῇ φανεὶς ἐν τοῖς χρόνοις Ἡρώδου, γενόμενος κατ' εἰκόνα Ἰωσὴφ τοῦ πεπραμένου ἐκ χειρὸς ἀδελφῶν, οὗ μόνου τὸ ἔνδυμα ἦν ποικίλον.

οὗτός ἐστι, φησίν, ὁ <γενόμενος> κατ' εἰκόνα Ἠσαῦ, οὗ καὶ μὴ παρόντος ἡ στολὴ εὐλόγηται· ὃς οὐκ ἐδέξατο, φησί, τὴν ἀμβλυωπὸν εὐλογίαν, ἀλλ' ἐπλούτησεν ἔξωθεν, οὐδὲν ἀπὸ τοῦ ἀμβλυωποῦντος λαβών· οὗ εἶδε τὸ πρόσωπον Ἰακὼβ «ὡς ἂν ἴδοι ἄνθρωπος πρόσωπον θεοῦ».

Israel were bitten in the desert, he says, Moses exhibited the true Snake, the perfect one. Those who believed in him were no longer bitten in the desert (that is, by the powers).[295]

Therefore no one, he says, can save and deliver those who exit the land of Egypt (that is, the body and this world) except the perfect Snake alone, the one full of those who are full. 8. The person who sets his hope on him, he says, is not destroyed by the snakes of the desert (that is, by the gods of generation) as it is written, he claims, in the book of Moses. This Snake, he claims, is the power that followed close to Moses; it is the staff turned into a snake. The snakes of the magicians (that is, the gods of destruction), he says, had opposed the power of Moses in Egypt. Nevertheless the staff of Moses subdued and destroyed them all.[296]

OTHER TYPES OF CHRIST. The universal snake, he says, is the wise word of Eve.[297] 9. This, he says, is the mystery of Eden, the river flowing from Eden, and the sign set on Cain so that all who find him may not kill him.[298] This, he says, is the Cain whose sacrifice the god of this world did not receive but approved of the bloody sacrifice of Abel (for the master of this world delights in blood).[299]

10. This is the one, he says, who in the last days appeared in the form of a human in the time of Herod, born in the image of Joseph who was forcibly sold by his brothers, who alone had the brilliantly colored robe.[300]

This is the one, he says, who was born in the image of Esau, whose robe was blessed, even though he was not present. He did not receive, he says, the blind blessing. Rather, Esau grew rich without him, receiving nothing from the blind man. Jacob beheld the face of Esau "as a person would behold the face of God."[301]

---

295. For the story of the bronze snake and its christological interpretation, see Num 21:6–8; John 3:17; Barn. 12.5–7; Testim. Truth (NHC IX,3) 48–49. See further Rasimus, *Paradise*, 78–81.

296. See Exod 7:8–13. Cf. *Ref.* 8.14.3, 8 (Monoïmos).

297. Gen 3:3.

298. For the sign of Cain, see Gen 4:15b. DeConick believes that it is "a magical sign … placed on his body as protection against Kronos. It appears that this sign was conceived by the Peratai to be a diagram of Draco" ("Bowels," 18).

299. Cf. Gen 4:3–5; Nat. Rulers (NHC II,4) 91.11–31. For the positive evaluation of Cain, see Iren., *Haer.* 1.31.1; Epiph., *Pan.* 38.2–4.

300. "In the last days" is a stock phrase for the final age (Acts 2:17; 2 Tim 3:1). For Herod, see Matt 2:1; for Joseph, see Gen 37. See further Magri, "Esegesi," 207.

301. For Esau, see Gen 27. For Esau's face as the face of God, see Gen 33:10.

11. περὶ τούτου, φησί, γέγραπται· «ὡς Νεβρὼδ γίγας κυνηγὸς ἔναντι κυρίου».

εἰσὶ δέ, φησί, τούτου ἀντίμιμοι πολλοί, τοσοῦτοι ὅσοι ὄφεις ἦσαν ἐν τῇ ἐρήμῳ τοὺς υἱοὺς Ἰσραὴλ δάκνοντες, ἀφ' ὧν ἐρ<ρ>ύσατο τοὺς δακνομένους ὁ τέλειος ἐκεῖνος <ὄφις>, ὃν ἔστησε Μωϋσῆς. τοῦτό ἐστι, φησί, τὸ εἰρημένον· «καὶ ὃν τρόπον ὕψωσε Μωϋσῆς τὸν ὄφιν ἐν τῇ ἐρήμῳ, οὕτως ὑψωθῆναι δεῖ τὸν υἱὸν τοῦ ἀνθρώπου». 12. τούτου κατ' εἰκόνα γέγονεν ὁ ὄφις ἐν τῇ ἐρήμῳ <ὁ> χαλκοῦς, ὃν ἔστησε Μωϋσῆς.

Τούτου, φησί, μόνου τὸ ὁμοίωμα ἐν τῷ οὐρανῷ διὰ παντός ἐστιν φωτὶ ὁρώμενον. οὗτος, φησίν, ἐστὶν ἡ μεγάλη ἀρχὴ περὶ ἧς γέγραπται. περὶ τούτου, φησίν, εἴρηται·

ἐν ἀρχῇ ἦν ὁ λόγος,
καὶ ὁ λόγος ἦν πρὸς τὸν θεόν,
καὶ θεὸς ἦν ὁ λόγος.
οὗτος ἦν ἐν ἀρχῇ πρὸς τὸν θεόν.
πάντα δι' αὐτοῦ ἐγένετο,
καὶ χωρὶς αὐτοῦ ἐγένετο οὐδὲ ἕν·
ὃ γέγονεν ἐν αὐτῷ ζωή ἐστιν.

13. ἐν αὐτῷ γάρ, φησίν, ἡ Εὔα γέγονεν, ἡ Εὔα ζωή. αὕτη δέ, φησίν, ἐστὶν ἡ Εὔα «μήτηρ πάντων τῶν ζώντων», τουτέστι κοινὴ φύσις θεῶν ἀγγέλων, ἀθανάτων θνητῶν, λογικῶν ἀλόγων· ὁ γὰρ «πάντων», φησίν, εἰπὼν εἴρηκε «πάντων <τῶν ὄντων>».

11. About Christ, he claims, it is written, "like Nebrod the giant, he who hunts in the presence of the Lord."[302]

There are many close imitators of Christ, he claims, as many as there were snakes who bit the children of Israel in the desert. That perfect Snake that Moses set up delivered those whom the snakes bit. This, he claims, is what the scriptural verse signifies: "Just as Moses lifted up the Snake in the desert, so the son of the Human must be lifted up."[303] 12. The bronze snake that Moses set up in the desert was in Christ's image.[304]

DRACO. The likeness of him alone, he says, is always seen illumined in heaven. He is, he says, the great Beginning about whom it is written. Concerning him, he says, scripture pronounces:

> In the beginning was the Word,
> and the Word was with God
> and the Word was God.
> He was in the beginning with God.
> Everything came about through him,
> and apart from him, not one thing came to be.
> What came to be in him is life.[305]

13. For in him, he says, Eve arose, and Eve signifies life. This, he says, is the Eve who is "mother of all living beings."[306] That is, she represents the common nature of gods, angels, immortals, mortals, rational beings, and those without reason. This is because the "all" of which scripture speaks, he says, means "all existing things."

---

302. For Nebrod ("Nimrod" in English Bibles), see Gen 10:9–10; 1 Chr 1:10; Philo, *QG* 2.81–82; *Gig.* 65–66; LAB 4–6; Josephus, *Ant.* 1.113–114. See further Karel van der Toorn and Pieter W. van der Horst, "Nimrod before and after the Bible," *HTR* 83 (1990): 1–29 (16–21); Magri, "Esegesi," 208. Nimrod appears in gnostic sources as the demiurge's assistant (Gos. Eg. [NHC III,2] 57,16–20; [NHC IV,2] 69,1–4).

303. John 3:14; cf. Ps.-Tert., *Adv. omn. haer.* 2.1.

304. Num 21:8–9.

305. John 1:1–4. John 1:3–4 is also interpreted by the Naassenes (*Ref.* 5.8.5; 5.9.2). Valentinians were particularly fond of these verses (see, e.g., Iren., *Haer.* 1.8.5; Clem. Alex., *Exc.* 6.1–4; 45.3; Ptolemy, *Flor.* 3.6; Herakleon, frag. 1, in Origen, *Comm. Jo.* 2.14 [Brooke]).

306. Gen 3:20; cf. Philo, *Agr.* 95; *Ref.* 6.34.3 ("Valentinus").

14. καὶ εἴ τινος, φησίν, «οἱ ὀφθαλμοὶ μακάριοι», οὗτος ὄψεται ἀναβλέψας εἰς τὸν οὐρανὸν τοῦ ὄφεως τὴν καλὴν εἰκόνα ἐν τῇ μεγάλῃ ἀρχῇ τοῦ οὐρανοῦ στρεφομένην καὶ γινομένην ἀρχὴν πάσης κινήσεως πᾶσι τοῖς γινομένοις, <καὶ> γνώσεται ὅτι χωρὶς αὐτοῦ <οὐδὲν> οὔτε τῶν οὐρανίων οὔτε τῶν ἐπιγείων οὔτε τῶν καταχθονίων συνέστηκεν—οὐ νύξ, οὐ σελήνη, οὐ καρποί, οὐ γένεσις, οὐ πλοῦτος, οὐχ ὁδοιπορία—, οὐδ᾽ ὅλως τι τῶν ὄντων ἐστὶ δίχα σημαίνοντος ἐκείνου. 15. ἐπὶ τούτου, φησίν, ἐστὶ τὸ «μέγα θαῦμα» ὁρώμενον ἐν τῷ οὐρανῷ τοῖς δυναμένοις ἰδεῖν· κατὰ γάρ, φησίν, αὐτὴν τὴν ἄκραν αὐτοῦ [τὴν] κεφαλήν—ὅπερ πάντων ἀπιστότερον τοῖς οὐκ εἰδόσι—μίσγονται δύσις τε καὶ ἀνατολὴ ἀλλήλαις.

τοῦτ᾽ ἔστι περὶ οὗ εἶπεν ἡ ἀγνωσία· ἐν οὐρανῷ «εἱλεῖται μέγα θαῦμα Δράκον<τος>», «δεινοῖο πελώρου». 16. ἑκατέρωθεν δὲ αὐτοῦ παρατέτακται Στέφανος καὶ Λύρα, καὶ κατ᾽ αὐτὴν ἄνωθεν τὴν κεφαλὴν ἄκραν ἐλεεινὸς ἄνθρωπος, ὁ Ἐν γόνασιν, ἐστὶν ὁρώμενος,

δεξιτεροῦ ποδὸς ἄκρον ἔχων σκολιοῖο Δράκοντος.

κατὰ δὲ τὸν νῶτον τοῦ Ἐν γόνασίν ἐστιν <ὁ> ἀτελὴς Ὄφις, ἀμφοτέραις ταῖς χερσὶ κατεσφιγμένος ὑπὸ τοῦ Ὀφιούχου καὶ κωλυόμενος ἐφάψασθαι τοῦ Στεφάνου, παρακειμένου τῷ τελείῳ Ὄφει.

17. 1. Αὕτη ἡ παμποίκιλος σοφία Περατικῆς αἱρέσεως, ἣν ἐξειπεῖν πᾶσαν δυσχερές, οὕτως οὖσαν σκολιὰν διὰ τὸ ἐκ τῆς ἀστρολογικῆς δοκεῖν συνεστάναι. καθὸ οὖν δυνατὸν ἦν, δι᾽ ὀλίγων πᾶσαν αὐτῆς τὴν δύναμιν ἐκτεθείμεθα. ἵνα

14. If, he says, anyone has "the blessed eyes,"[307] this one will look up into heaven and see the beautiful image of the snake turning in the great "Beginning" of heaven and becoming the beginning of all movement for all generated beings.[308] This one will know that apart from him nothing of heavenly, earthly, or underworldly beings has come into existence—neither night nor moon, nor harvests nor birth, nor riches nor journeys—nothing at all of existing things exists apart from him who gives the sign.[309] 15. In him, he says, is the "great wonder" seen in heaven by those with eyes to see. For at the very crown of his head, he says—a thing most incredible to all the ignorant—west and east mingle with each other.[310]

Ignorance has spoken about this: in heaven "writhes the great wonder of Draco," "the terrible monster."[311] 16. On either side of him are arrayed the Crown (the constellation Corona) and the Lyre (the constellation Lyra), and facing the very top of his head from above is seen the wretched man called "Kneeler," who

> has the sole of his right foot on the twisted Snake.[312]

Along the back of the Kneeler is the imperfect Serpent (the constellation Serpens), choked by the two hands of the Serpent-Holder (the constellation Ophiuchus) and prevented from touching the Crown that lies at the side of the perfect Serpent.[313]

SYNOPSIS OF THE PERATAI. 17. 1. This is the extraordinarily motley wisdom of the Peratic heresy! To tell it all is difficult—so twisted it is due to its patent derivation from astrology.[314] As far as it was possible, I presented

---

307. For blessed eyes, see Matt 13:16; Luke 10:23.

308. Cf. *Ref.* 4.47.2–4 (Aratos allegorizers). See further Hegedus, *Early Christianity*, 291–92.

309. For the three levels of being (heavenly, earthly, underworldly), see Phil 2:10—also quoted in *Ref.* 5.7.11; 5.8.22 (Naassenes).

310. Cf. Aratos, *Phaen.* 61–62.

311. Cf. Aratos, *Phaen.* 46 (μέγα θαῦμα, Δράκων [cf. θαῦμα μέγα, Rev 17:6]); 57 (δεινοῖο πελώρου). Here Draco is himself Christ, the Beginning (ἀρχή) referred to in John 1:1. This verse from Aratos is also quoted in *Ref.* 4.47.1, where Draco, or the Serpent, is cast as the devil.

312. For the constellations Corona and Lyra, see Aratos, *Phaen.* 71, 615 (cf. *Ref.* 4.48.1). For the Kneeler, see Aratos, *Phaen.* 63–70 (line 70 directly quoted here).

313. Aratos, *Phaen.* 82–83; cf. *Ref.* 4.48.4–6 (Aratos allegorizers).

314. The adjective "twisted" (σκολιάν) plays upon the nature of the snake.

δὲ (κἂν) δι' ἐπιτομῆς τὴν πᾶσαν αὐτῶν γνώμην ἐκθώμεθα, δοκεῖ προσθεῖναι ταῦτα.

ἔστι κατ' αὐτοὺς τὸ πᾶν πατήρ, υἱός, ὕλη· τούτων τῶν τριῶν ἕκαστον ἀπείρους ἔχει δυνάμεις ἐν ἑαυτῷ. 2. καθέζεται οὖν μέσος τῆς ὕλης καὶ τοῦ πατρὸς ὁ υἱός, ὁ λόγος, ὁ ὄφις ἀεὶ κινούμενος πρὸς ἀκίνητον τὸν πατέρα καὶ κινουμένην τὴν ὕλην· καὶ ποτὲ μὲν στρέφεται πρὸς τὸν πατέρα καὶ ἀναλαμβάνει τὰς δυνάμεις εἰς τὸ πρόσωπον ἑαυτοῦ, ἀναλαβὼν δὲ τὰς δυνάμεις στρέφεται πρὸς τὴν ὕλην· καὶ ἡ ὕλη ἄποιος οὖσα καὶ ἀσχημάτιστος ἐκτυποῦται τὰς ἰδέας ἀπὸ τοῦ υἱοῦ, ἃς ὁ υἱὸς ἀπὸ τοῦ πατρὸς <ἐξ>ετυπώσατο. 3. ἐκτυποῦται δὲ ὁ μὲν υἱὸς ἀπὸ τοῦ πατρὸς ἀρρήτως καὶ ἀλάλως καὶ ἀμεταστάτως, οὕτως ὡς, φησί, <λέγει> Μωϋσῆς ἀπὸ τῶν ῥάβδων τῶν ἐπὶ τῶν ποτιστηρίων ῥερευκέναι τὰ χρώματα τοῖς ἐγκεκισσημένοις. 4. ὁμοίως δ' αὖ καὶ ἀπὸ τοῦ υἱοῦ ἐπὶ τὴν ὕλην ῥερευκέναι τὰς δυνάμεις κατὰ τὸ ἐγκίσσημα τῆς δυνάμεως τῆς ἀπὸ τῶν ῥάβδων ἐπὶ τὰ ἐγκεκισσημένα. ἡ δὲ διαφορὰ τῶν χρωμάτων καὶ ἡ ἀνομοιότης ῥεύσασα ἀπὸ τῶν ῥάβδων διὰ τῶν ὑδάτων ἐπὶ τὰ πρόβατα διαφορά, φησί, γενέσεώς ἐστι φθαρτῆς καὶ ἀφθάρτου.

5. μᾶλλον δὲ ὥσπερ, <ὁ> ζωγραφῶν ἀπὸ τῶν ζῴων μηδὲν ἀφαιρούμενος τῇ γραφίδι πάσας ἐπὶ τὸν πίνακα μεταφέρει τὰς ἰδέας <αὐτῶν> ἐγγράφων, οὕτω<ς> ὁ υἱὸς τῇ δυνάμει τῇ ἑαυτοῦ ἀπὸ τοῦ πατρὸς ἐπὶ τὴν ὕλην τοὺς πατρικοὺς μεταφέρει χαρακτῆρας.

6. ἔστιν οὖν πάντα τὰ ἐνθάδε πατρικὰ καὶ οὐδέν· εἰ γάρ τι, φησίν, τῶν ἐνθάδε ἐξισχύσει κατανοηθῆναι ὅτι ἐστὶ πατρικὸς χαρακτήρ, ἄνωθεν μετενηνεγμένος ἐνθάδε <καὶ> σωματοποιηθείς, ὥσπερ ἐγκίσσημα [τι] τὸ ἀπὸ τῆς ῥάβδου λευκὸν

its entire meaning through a small sample. Still, to provide a summary of their whole view, I duly append the following synopsis.

For the Peratai, the universe consists of Father, Son, and matter. Each of these three contains infinite powers. 2. The Son is situated in between matter and the Father. The Son is the Word, the Snake ever moving toward the unmoved Father and toward moving matter. Sometimes he turns toward the Father and takes up his powers in his own person. When he receives the powers, he turns toward matter. Matter is without quality or form. Forms are impressed upon it from the Son. These Forms were impressed upon the Son from the Father. 3. The Son is impressed from the Father ineffably, unutterably, unchangeably—just as, he says, Moses describes the colors flowing from the rods in the drinking troughs into the animals who conceived.[315] 4. Similarly, in this case, the powers flowed from the Son into matter just as the embryo from the power of the rods flowed into the animals who conceived. The difference and dissimilarity of the colors that flowed from the rods through the waters and into the different sheep, he says, is the difference between corruptible and incorruptible birth.

5. To use a better example: just as a painter by painting with a brush on his canvas transmits all the forms of the images and excludes no detail at all, so the Son by his power that he received from the Father transmits to matter the distinctive marks of his Father.[316]

6. Therefore, everything that exists in this world is both stamped with the Father's character and nothing at all.[317] If any one of the beings that exist in this world, he says, is strong enough to discern that he is the Father's character that was transferred from above to this place and placed

315. Cf. Gen 30:37–39 LXX.

316. For a similar pattern of mediation, see *Ref.* 7.25.6–7 ("Basileides"). Holger Strutwolf argues that this section (*Ref.* 5.17.1–6) corresponds to the thought of the Middle Platonist Noumenios. Noumenios posited a second God between the primal God and matter. This second God shaped the material world but became involved in it and alienated from himself. When the second God looks toward the divine Ideas, he forges a path for the human mind to be enlivened and separated from the body ("Gnosis und Philosophie: Beobachtungen zur Platonismusrezeption im gnostischen Sondergut bei Hippolyt von Rom," in *"Zur Zeit oder Unzeit": Studien zur spätantiken Theologie-, Geistes- und Kunstgeschichte und ihrer Nachwirkung Hans Georg Thümmel zu Ehren*, ed. Adolf Martin Ritter, Wolfgang Wischmeyer, and Wolfram Kinzig [Mandelbachtal: Books on Demand, 2004], 11–27 [15–22]).

317. For the nothingness of the created world, see *Ref.* 8.13.4 (Monoïmos); 7.20.2 ("Basileides").

γέγονεν, ὁμοούσιον τῷ πατρὶ τῷ ἐν τοῖς οὐρανοῖς ὅλως, καὶ ἐκεῖ ἀνέρχεται· ἐὰν δὲ μὴ τύχῃ τῆς διδασκαλίας ταύτης μηδὲ τὴν ἀνάγκην τῆς γενέσεως ἐπιγνῷ, ὥσπερ ἔκτρωμα «ὑπὸ νύκτα γεννώμενον ὑπὸ νύκτα ἀπολεῖται».

7. Ὅταν οὖν, φησί, λέγῃ ὁ σωτήρ· «ὁ πατὴρ ὑμῶν ὁ ἐν τοῖς οὐρανοῖς», ἐκεῖνον λέγει ἀφ' οὗ ὁ υἱὸς μεταλαβὼν τοὺς χαρακτῆρας μετενήνοχεν ἐνθάδε. ὅταν δὲ λέγῃ· «ὁ ὑμέτερος πατὴρ ἀπ' ἀρχῆς ἀνθρωποκτόνος ἐστί», τὸν ἄρχοντα καὶ δημιουργὸν τῆς ὕλης λέγει, ὃς ἀναλαβὼν τοὺς διαδοθέντας ὑπὸ τοῦ υἱοῦ χαρακτῆρας ἐγέννησεν ἐνθάδε. ο<ὗτο>ς ἐστιν ἀπ' ἀρχῆς ἀνθρωποκτόνος· τὸ γὰρ ἔργον αὐτοῦ φθορὰν καὶ θάνατον <ἀπ>εργάζεται.

8. οὐδεὶς οὖν, φησί, δύναται σωθῆναι οὐδ' ἀνελθεῖν <εἰ μὴ> διὰ τοῦ υἱοῦ, ὅς ἐστιν ὁ ὄφις· ὡς γάρ κατήνεγκεν ἄνωθεν τοὺς πατρικοὺς χαρακτῆρας, οὕτως πάλιν ἐντεῦθεν ἀναφέρει τοὺς ἐξυπνισμένους καὶ γεγονότας πατρικοὺς χαρακτῆρας, ὑποστατοὺς ἐκ τοῦ ἀνυποστάτου ἐντεῦθεν ἐκεῖ μεταφέρων. 9. τοῦτ' ἔστι, φησί, τὸ εἰρημένον· «ἐγώ εἰμι ἡ θύρα»· μεταφέρει γάρ, φησίν, <ἀνοίγων τοῖς> καμμ<ύ>ουσιν ὀφθαλμῶν βλέφαρα. ὥσπερ ὁ νάφθας τὸ πῦρ πανταχόθεν εἰς ἑαυτὸν ἐπισπώμενος, μᾶλλον δὲ ὥσπερ ἡ Ἡρακλεία λίθος τὸν σίδηρον, ἄλλο <δὲ> οὐδέν, 10. ἢ ὥσπερ ἡ τοῦ θαλασσίου ἱέρακος κερκὶς τὸ

in a body, such a one ascends to that world again entirely consubstantial with the Father in heaven, just as the animal that was conceived became gleaming white from the rod.[318] But if one does not obtain this teaching, or recognize the necessity of birth, such a one becomes the equivalent of an aborted fetus: "born in a single night, and in a single night destroyed."[319]

7. Now when, he says, the Savior mentions "your Father in heaven," he refers to him from whom the Son received the distinctive marks and transferred them to this world.[320] And when he says, "Your father murders humans from the beginning," he refers to the Ruler and Artificer of matter, who, having taken up the distinctive marks conveyed by the Son, gave birth to them here.[321] This is the one who "murders" human beings from the beginning, for his job is to produce corruption and death.

8. Now, no one can be saved or ascend, he says, except through the Son, the Snake.[322] For just as he brought down from above the distinctive marks of his Father, so again he raises from this world those who have woken up and have become the distinctive marks of the Father. He transfers them to that world as real beings away from the unreality in this world.[323] 9. This is what the scriptural verse means: "I am the door."[324] He brings them across, he says, by opening the eyelids of those whose eyes are closed.[325] Just as naphtha draws to itself fire from every direction[326]—or better: just as a magnet draws iron but nothing else, 10. or the spine of a hierax fish draws

318. The "animal conceived" translates ἐγκίσσημα and clarifies what was meant above in *Ref.* 5.17.4.

319. Cf. Jonah 4:10.

320. Matt 7:11 ("your Father in heaven").

321. John 8:44 ("your father the devil … was a murderer from the beginning").

322. Marcovich adds εἰ μή ("except").

323. For the image of waking up, see *Ref.* 5.14.1 above; 5.7.30 (Naassenes).

324. John 10:7, 9. Cf. the exegesis of the Naassene writer in *Ref.* 5.8.20; 5.9.21; and the Valentinian interpretation in Clem. Alex., *Exc.* 26.

325. Marcovich adds ἀνοίγων τοῖς (here: "by opening the"). Cf. Isa 6:10 LXX; *Ref.* 5.7.31–32 (Naassenes).

326. For the example of naphtha, see *Ref.* 7.25.6 ("Basileides"); Hipp., *Comm. Dan.* 2.31.1 (on Dan 3:46); Herodotos, *Hist.* 6.119; Poseidonios in Strabo, *Geogr.* 16.1.15; Pliny, *Nat.* 2.109; 35.178–179; 2.235; Plutarch, *Quaest. conv.* 681c; Origen, *Comm. Matt.* 10.19. See further Andreas Vasojević and Nicolaus Vasojević, "ΝΑΦΘΑ: Quae fuerit termini *naphtha* antiquis temporibus propria significatio," *Phil* 128 (1984): 208–29 (226–29).

χρυσίον, ἕτερον δὲ οὐδέν, ἢ ὥσπερ ἄγεται ὑπὸ τοῦ ἠλέκτρου τὸ ἄχυρον, οὕτω, φησίν, ὑπὸ τοῦ ὄφεως ἄγεται πάλιν ἀπὸ τοῦ κόσμου τὸ ἐξεικονισμένον τέλειον γένος ὁμοούσιον, ἄλλο δὲ οὐδέν, καθὼς ὑπ' αὐτοῦ <καὶ> κατεπέμφθη.

11. Πρὸς τούτων τὴν ἀπόδειξιν φέρουσι τὴν τοῦ ἐγκεφάλου ἀνατομήν, αὐτὸν μὲν τὸν ἐγκέφαλον ἀπεικονίζοντες τῷ πατρὶ διὰ τὸ ἀκίνητον, τὴν δὲ παρεγκεφαλίδα τῷ υἱῷ διά τε τὸ κινεῖσθαι καὶ δρακοντοειδῆ ὑπάρχειν. 12. ἣν ἀρρήτως καὶ ἀσημάντως ἐπισπᾶσθαι διὰ τοῦ κωναρίου φάσκουσι τὴν ἐκ τοῦ καμαρίου ἀπορρέουσαν πνευματικὴν καὶ ζωογόνον οὐσίαν· ἣν ὑποδεξαμένη ἡ παρεγκεφαλίς, ὥσπερ ὁ υἱός, ἀλάλως μεταδίδωσι τῇ ὕλῃ τὰς ἰδέας—τουτέστιν ἐπὶ τὸν νωτιαῖον μυελὸν διαρρεῖ τὰ σπέρματα καὶ τὰ γένη τῶν γενομένων κατὰ σάρκα.

13. τούτῳ τῷ παραδείγματι χρώμενοι εὐφυῶς δοκοῦσι παρεισάγειν τὰ ἄρρητα αὐτῶν, ἀλάλως παραδιδόμενα μυστήρια· ἃ ἐξειπεῖν ἡμῖν οὐ θέμις, πολλοῖς δὲ νοῆσαι διὰ τῶν εἰρημένων εὔκολον.

18. 1. Ἀλλ' ἐπεὶ καὶ τὴν Περατικὴν αἵρεσιν νομίζω φανερῶς ἐκτεθεῖσθαι καὶ διὰ πολλῶν ἔκδηλον πεποιηκέναι, ἀεὶ λα<ν>θ<άν>ουσαν καὶ παντάπασι συντιθεμένην ἀποκρύπτουσάν τε τὸν ἴδιον ἰόν, δοκεῖ μηδὲν περαιτέρω τούτων κατηγορεῖν, ἱκανῶν ὄντων πρὸς κατηγορίαν αὐτῶν τῶν ὑπ' αὐτῶν δογματιζομένων.

19. 1. Ἴδωμεν οὖν τί λέγουσιν οἱ Σηθιανοί.

gold but nothing else, or as chaff is attracted to amber[327]—so also, he says, nothing but the perfect race exactly conformed to God's image and consubstantial with God is once again conducted by the Snake away from this world, just as it was also sent down by him.

PROOF FROM BRAIN ANATOMY. 11. As proof of their teachings, they refer to brain anatomy. They liken the brain itself to the Father since it is unmoved. The cerebellum they liken to the Son since it moves and has the shape of a serpent. 12. The cerebellum, they claim, ineffably and imperceptibly draws spiritual and generative substance that flows out through the pineal gland from the fornix.[328] The cerebellum receives this substance and, just like the Son, inexpressibly transfers the forms to matter. That is to say, the seeds and types of everything physically born flow along the spinal marrow.[329]

13. By this analogy, they suppose that they can "organically" sneak in their own secret mysteries that are implicitly transmitted. To announce them would be sacrilegious, but for most people they are easy to grasp from what has already been said.

18. 1. But since, I believe, I have clearly presented the Peratic heresy, clarifying it by many examples—though it continually lurks unnoticed and, though entirely fabricated, conceals its peculiar poison—it seems fitting that I "traverse" no farther in my indictment of these people, given that their own teachings are sufficient indictment.

SETHIANS

19. 1. Now let us see what the Sethians have to say.[330]

---

327. The same comparisons are made in *Ref.* 5.9.19 (Naassenes); 5.21.8 ("Sethians").

328. The fornix is the "little arch" or "vault" (καμαρίου) in the brain that corresponds to the vault in the universe separating our world from the transcendent world of the Father. (Recall Euno, the administrator of the first eastern vault [πρωτοκαμάρου] [*Ref.* 5.14.6].) The fornix is also mentioned in the brain anatomy discussion in *Ref.* 4.51.12. For the terminology, see Galen, *Usu part.* 8.11 (Helmreich).

329. For the brain analogy, see *Ref.* 4.51.10–13; 5.9.15–18 (Naassenes). It may be assumed that the spinal marrow in the spinal column is serpentine.

330. The "Sethians," also summarized in *Ref.* 10.11, are an otherwise unknown group not to be confused with the modern scholarly category of Sethians promoted by H.-M. Schenke and others. The fact that our author derived his information from a Paraphrase of Seth may be the sole reason why he calls their myth "Sethian." Winrich

τούτοις δοκεῖ τῶν ὅλων εἶναι τρεῖς ἀρχὰς περιωρισμένας, ἑκάστην δὲ τῶν ἀρχῶν ἀπείρους ἔχειν δυνάμεις. δυνάμεις δὲ αὐτῶν [λεγόντων] λογιζέσθω ὁ ἀκούων τοῦτο αὐτοὺς λέγειν· πᾶν ὅ τι νοήσει ἐπινοεῖς ἢ καὶ παραλείπεις μὴ νοηθέν, τοῦτο ἑκάστη τῶν ἀρχῶν πέφυκε γενέσθαι, ὡς ἐν ἀνθρωπί<νῃ> ψυχῇ πᾶσα ἡτισοῦν διδασκομένη τέχνη· 2. οἷον εἰ, φησί, γενή<σε>ται [τοῦτο] τὸ παιδίον αὐλητὴς ἐγχρονίσαν αὐλητῇ, ἢ γεωμέτρης γεωμέτρῃ, γραμματικὸς γραμματικῷ, τέκτων τέκτονι, καὶ ταῖς ἄλλαις ἁπάσαις τέχναις ἐγγὺς γινομένῳ ὁμοίως συμβήσεται.

αἱ δὲ τῶν ἀρχῶν, φησίν, οὐσίαι <εἰσὶ> φῶς καὶ σκότος· 3. τούτων δέ ἐστιν ἐν μέσῳ πνεῦμα ἀκέραιον. τὸ δὲ πνεῦμα, τὸ τεταγμένον ἐν μέσῳ τοῦ σκότους, ὅπερ ἐστὶ κάτω, καὶ τοῦ φωτός, ὅπερ ἐστὶν ἄνω, οὐκ ἔστι πνεῦμα ὡς ἄνεμος ἢ ῥιπὴ ἢ λεπτή τις αὔρα νοηθῆναι δυναμένη, ἀλλ' οἱονεὶ μύρου τις ὀσμὴ ἢ θυμιάματος ἐκ συνθέσεως κατεσκευ(α)σμένου, λεπτὴ διοδεύουσα δύναμις ἀνεπινοήτῳ τινὶ καὶ κρείττονι ἢ λόγῳ ἔστιν ἐξειπεῖν <φορᾷ> εὐωδία<ς>.

4. ἐπειδὴ ἄνω ἐστὶ τὸ φῶς καὶ κάτω <τὸ> σκότος καὶ τούτων, ὡς ἔφην, τοιουτότροπον ὂν μέσον τὸ πνεῦμα, τὸ δὴ φῶς πέφυκε καθάπερ ἀκτὶς ἡλίου ἄνωθεν ἐλλάμπειν εἰς τὸ ὑποκείμενον σκότος· ἀνάπαλιν δὲ ἡ τοῦ πνεύματος εὐωδία, μέση<ν> ἔχουσα τάξιν, ἐκτείνεται καὶ φέρεται πανταχῇ—ὥσ<περ> [ἐπὶ] τῶν ἐν πυρὶ θυμιαμάτων τὴν εὐωδίαν πανταχῇ φερομένην ἐπεγνώκαμεν.—5. τοιαύτης δὲ οὔσης τῆς δυνάμεως τῶν <δι>ῃρημένων τριχῶς, τοῦ πνεύματος καὶ τοῦ φωτὸς ὁμοῦ ἡ δύναμίς ἐστιν ἐν τῷ σκότει τῷ κάτωθεν αὐτῶν τεταγμένῳ.

Τὸ δὲ σκότος ὕδωρ ἐστί φοβερόν, εἰς ὃ κατέσπασται καὶ μετενήνεκται εἰς τὴν τοιαύτην φύσιν μετὰ τοῦ πνεύματος τὸ φῶς. 6. τὸ δὲ σκότος ἀσύνετον οὐκ ἔστιν, ἀλλὰ φρόνιμον παντελῶς, καὶ οἶδεν ὅτι, ἂν ἀπαρθῇ τὸ φῶς ἀπὸ τοῦ σκότους, μενεῖ τὸ σκότος ἔρημον, ἀφανές, ἀλαμπές, ἀδύναμον, ἄπρακτον,

According to the Sethians, there are three clearly defined principles in the universe, and each of them has infinite potentialities. What they mean by potentialities the reader can infer from what they say. Everything you can possibly think or leave unthought, such is the nature of each of their principles, just as any skill whatsoever inculcated by the human soul.[331] 2. For example, he says, a child will become a flautist by spending time with a flautist, or a geometer by spending time with a geometer, or a grammarian with a grammarian, or a carpenter with a carpenter, and likewise with the other arts.[332]

The essential natures of the principles, he says, are Light and Darkness.[333] 3. Between them dwells a pure Spirit.[334] Now this Spirit suspended between the lower Darkness and the higher Light cannot be conceived of as a wind, or air current, or a light breeze. Rather, it is like the scent of myrrh or incense prepared by a recipe, a subtle power pervading all by a wafting of fragrance that is inconceivable and greater than words can tell.

4. Since the Light is above and the Darkness below, as I said, and a Spirit of this kind in between, the Light naturally shines on the underlying Darkness like a sun ray. In turn, the fragrance of the Spirit, which is stationed in the middle, is diffused and wafted in every direction (just as we know the fragrance of burning incense offerings wafts in every direction). 5. Such being the potentiality of the three divided principles, the potentiality of the Spirit and the Light is present together within the Darkness arrayed beneath them.

THE IMPRISONMENT OF LIGHT. The Darkness is a frightful water into which the Light is dragged down and transferred to this watery nature along with the Spirit.[335] 6. The Darkness is not mindless but altogether cunning. It knows that, were the Light to be removed from it, the Darkness would remain barren, invisible, unenlightened, powerless, impotent, and weak. For this reason, with all cunning and intelligence, it uses all force to

---

A. Löhr observes that our author seems to know nothing "about distinct Sethian ethics, group organization, liturgy or sacramental practice" ("Sethians," *DGWE* 1066).

331. See the similar language in *Ref.* 6.9.7 ("Simon") and 7.22.1 ("Basileides").

332. Cf. the analogy in *Ref.* 6.12.4; 6.16.5 ("Simon").

333. Cf. the account of "Zaratas" in *Ref.* 1.2.12–13.

334. Cf. Paraph. Shem (NHC VII,1) 1.25–28: ⲛⲉⲩⲛ̄ ⲟⲩⲟⲉⲓⲛ ⲱⲟⲟⲡ ⲙ̄ⲛ̄ ⲟⲩⲕⲁⲕⲉ ⲁⲩⲱ ⲛⲉⲩⲛ̄ ⲟⲩⲡ̄ⲛ̄ⲁ̄ ϩ̄ⲛ̄ ⲧⲟⲩⲙⲏⲧⲉ ("There was Light and Darkness, and there was Spirit between them").

335. For the waters, see Gen 1:2.

ἀσθενές. διὸ πάσῃ φρονήσει καὶ συνέσει βιάζεται κατέχειν εἰς ἑαυτὸ τὴν λαμπηδόνα καὶ σπινθῆρα τοῦ φωτὸς μετὰ τῆς τοῦ πνεύματος εὐωδίας.

7. καὶ τούτων ἔστιν ἰδεῖν τῆς φύσεως εἰκόνα κατὰ πρόσωπον ἀνθρώπου, κόρην ὀφθαλμοῦ, σκοτεινὴν ἐκ τῶν ὑποκειμένων ὑδάτων, πεφωτισμένην πνεύματι.

ὡς οὖν ἀντιποιεῖται τὸ σκότος τῆς λαμπηδόνος, ἵνα ἔχῃ τὸν σπινθῆρα δουλεύοντα καὶ βλέπῃ, οὕτως ἀντιποιεῖται τὸ φῶς καὶ τὸ πνεῦμα τῆς δυνάμεως τῆς ἑαυτῶν, καὶ σπεύδουσιν ἆραι καὶ ἀνακομίσασθαι πρὸς ἑαυτὰ τὰς μεμιγμένας αὐτῶν δυνάμεις εἰς τὸ ὑποκείμενον ὕδωρ σκοτεινὸν καὶ φοβερόν.

8. Πᾶσαι δὲ αἱ δυνάμεις τῶν τριῶν ἀρχῶν, οὖσαι κατ' ἀριθμὸν ἀπειράκις ἄπειροι, εἰσὶν ἑκάστη κατὰ τὴν οὐσίαν τὴν ἑαυτῆς φρόνιμοι <καὶ> νοεραί. ἀναρίθμητοι τὸ πλῆθος φρόνιμοί τε οὖσαι καὶ νοεραί, ἐπειδὰν μένωσι καθ' αὑτάς, ἡσυχάζουσι πᾶσαι, 9. ἐὰν δὲ πλησιάσῃ δύναμις δυνάμει, ἡ ἀνομοιότης τῆς παραθέσεως ἐργάζεται κίνησίν τινα καὶ ἐνέργειαν ἀπὸ τῆς κινήσεως, μεμορφωμένην κατὰ τὴν συνδρομὴν [τῆς παραθέσεως] τῶν συνελθουσῶν δυνάμεων. 10. γίνεται γὰρ τῶν δυνάμεων ἡ συνδρομὴ οἱονεί τις τύπος ἀπὸ πληγῆς σφραγῖδος [κατὰ συνδρομήν], παραπλησίως πρὸς τῷ ἐκτυποῦντι τὰς ἀναφερομένας οὐσίας.

ἐπεὶ οὖν ἄπειροι μὲν κατ' ἀριθμὸν τῶν τριῶν ἀρχῶν αἱ δυνάμεις, ἐκ δὲ τῶν ἀπείρων δυνάμεων ἄπειροι συνδρομαί, ἀναγκαίως γεγόνασιν ἀπείρων σφραγίδων εἰκόνες. αὗται οὖν εἰσιν αἱ εἰκόνες αἱ τῶν διαφόρων ζῴων ἰδέαι.

11. γέγονεν οὖν ἐκ πρώτης τῶν τριῶν ἀρχῶν συνδρομῆς μεγάλης [μεγάλη τις] ἰδέα σφραγῖδος, οὐρανὸς καὶ γῆ. σχῆμα δὲ ἔχουσιν ὁ οὐρανὸς καὶ ἡ γῆ μήτρᾳ παραπλήσιον, τὸν ὀμφαλὸν ἐχούσῃ μέσον. καὶ εἰ, φησίν, ὑπὸ ὄψιν ἀγαγεῖν θέλει τις τὸ σχῆμα τοῦτο, ἔγκυον μήτραν ὁποίου βούλεται ζῴου τεχνικῶς ἐρευνησάτω, καὶ εὑρήσει τὸ ἐκτύπωμα τοῦ οὐρανοῦ καὶ τῆς γῆς καὶ τῶν ἐν μέσῳ πάντων ἀπαραλ<λ>άκτως ὑποκείμενον.

12. γέγονε δὴ οὐρανοῦ καὶ γῆς τὸ (σ)χῆμα τοιοῦτον οἱονεὶ μήτρᾳ παραπλήσιον κατὰ τὴν πρώτην συνδρομήν· ἐν αὖ τῷ μέσῳ τοῦ οὐρανοῦ καὶ

imprison in itself the brilliance and spark of light with the fragrance of the Spirit.

7. A natural reflection of these realities exists on the human face, namely, the pupil of the eye, which is dark from the underlying waters but illumined by spirit.

Now, just as the Darkness lays hold of the brilliance in order to enslave the spark and gain the power of sight, so also the Light and Spirit lay hold of their own power and hasten to take and recover for themselves their powers that have been mixed with the underlying, dark, and frightful water.

THE PROBLEM OF MIXTURE. 8. All the potentialities of the three principles, infinity times infinity in number, are each in their own individual nature thinking and intelligent entities. Since they are innumerable in quantity, as well as thinking and intelligent, they are all at rest when they remain by themselves. 9. But if one potentiality approaches another, the unlikeness of their juxtaposition produces movement. From the movement, an actuality forms due to the collision of the converging potentialities. 10. The collision of potentialities resembles an impression from the stamp of a seal, very like one who stamps items that are raised up to it.[336]

Now, since the potentialities of the three principles are infinite in number, and from the countless powers come countless collisions—necessarily there arise images of infinite impressions. These images are the patterns of various living beings.

COSMOGONY. 11. Now there arose from the first great collision of the three principles a form of a great seal impression: heaven and earth. With regard to their shape, heaven and earth closely resemble a womb with a navel in the middle.[337] If, he says, someone wants to view this shape, our author desires that one carefully investigate the pregnant belly of any type of animal and he will discover the imprint of heaven, earth, and what lies between exactly laid out.

12. The womb-like shape of heaven and earth arose at the first collision. In between heaven and earth there arose, in turn, countless collisions of potentialities. Each collision produced and created the impression of

---

336. The language of "collision" (συνδρομή) is reminiscent of the atomic theory of Leukippos and Demokritos (*Ref.* 1.12–13). Cf. *concursiones* in Cicero, *Fin.* 1.17. See further Diog. L., *Vit. phil.* 9.31 (= Leukippos, DK 67 A1), and the texts cited in Kirk, Raven, and Schofield, *Presocratic Philosophers*, 423–27.

337. A similar image is used in Paraph. Shem (NHC VII,1) 4.24.

τῆ<ς> γῆ<ς> γεγόνασιν ἄπειροι δυνάμεων συνδρομαί. καὶ ἑκάστη συνδρομὴ οὐκ ἄλλο τι εἰργάσατο καὶ ἐξετύπωσεν ἢ σφραγῖδα οὐρανοῦ καὶ γῆ<ς> παραπλήσιον μήτρᾳ. ἐν αὐτῇ δὲ <τῇ γῇ> ἀνέφυσαν ἐκ τῶν ἀπείρων σφραγίδων διαφόρων ζῴων ἄπειρα πλήθη. 13. εἰς δὲ ταύτην πᾶσαν τὴν ὑπὸ τὸν οὐρανὸν [ἐν] τῶν διαφόρων ζῴων ἀπειρίαν κατέσπαρται καὶ καταμεμέρισται μετὰ τοῦ φωτὸς ἡ τοῦ πνεύματος ἄνωθεν εὐωδία.

Γέγονεν οὖν ἐκ τοῦ ὕδατος πρωτόγονος ἀρχή, ἄνεμος σφοδρὸς καὶ λάβρος καὶ πάσης γενέσεως αἴτιος. βρασμὸν γάρ τινα ἐμποιῶν τοῖς ὕδασιν ἀπὸ τῶν ὑδάτων διεγείρει κύματα· 14. ἡ δὲ τῶν κυμάτων κίνησις, οἱονεί τις οὖσα ὁρμή ἐγκύμονα γεγονέναι τοῦ ἀνθρώπου ἢ τοῦ νοῦ, ὁπόταν ὑπὸ τῆς τοῦ πνεύματος ὁρμῆς ὀργήσασα <πρὸς γένεσιν> ἐπείγηται. ἐπὰν δὲ τοῦτο τὸ κῦμα ὑπὸ τοῦ ἀνέμου ἐκ τοῦ ὕδατος ἐγερθὲν καὶ ἐγκύμονα ἐργασάμενον τὴν φύσιν, γέννημα θηλείας εἰλήφῃ ἐν ἑαυτῷ, κατέχει τὸ κατεσπαρμένον φῶς ἄνωθεν μετὰ τῆς τοῦ πνεύματος εὐωδίας.

15. τουτέστι νοῦν μεμορφωμένον ἐν τοῖς διαφόροις εἴδεσιν, ὅ<ς> ἐστι τέλειος θεός. <ὃς> ἐξ ἀγεννήτου φωτὸς ἄνωθεν καὶ πνεύματος κατενηνεγμένος εἰς ἀνθρωπίνην φύσιν ὥσπερ εἰς ναόν, φορᾷ φύσεως καὶ ἀνέμου κινήματι γεννηθεὶς ἐξ ὕδατος, συγκεκραμένος καὶ καταμεμιγμένος τοῖς σώμασιν—οἱονεὶ ἅλα<ς> τῶν γενομένων ὑπάρχων καὶ φῶς τοῦ σκότους—, ἀπὸ τῶν σωμάτων σπεύδει λυθῆναι, καὶ μὴ δυνάμενος τὴν λύσιν εὑρεῖν καὶ τὴν διέξοδον ἑαυτῷ. 16. καταμέμικται γάρ, σπινθὴρ τις ἐλάχιστος, ἀπ<όσπασ>μα ἄνωθεν ἀ<πὸ τοῦ φωτός, ἀκτῖ>νος δίκην ἐν το<ῖς πο>λυσυγκρίτοις <τοῦ σώματος>—, <«ἐβόα ἐξ ὑδάτων> πολλῶν», ὡς, φησίν, ἐν τῷ ψαλμῷ λέγει.

πᾶσα οὖν <ἡ> φροντὶς καὶ ἐπιμέλεια τοῦ φωτὸς <τοῦ> ἄνω ἐστί, πῶς καὶ τίνα τρόπον ἀπ(ὸ) τοῦ θανάτου τοῦ πονηροῦ καὶ σκοτεινοῦ σώματος ἀπολυθείη ὁ νοῦς, ἀπὸ τοῦ πατρὸς τοῦ κάτω, ὅ<ς> ἐστιν ὁ ἄνεμος [ἐν] βρ<α>σμῷ καὶ

nothing other than the seal of the womb-like heaven and earth. Countless multitudes of living beings grew up in the earth itself from the countless different seal impressions. 13. Into this entire infinite abundance of different animals under heaven there was sown and apportioned the fragrance of Spirit from above, along with the Light.

ANTHROPOGONY. Then a firstborn principle arose from the water: a strong, violent wind that is the cause of all generation.[338] It churned up the waters, and from these waters, it stirred up waves. 14. The disturbance of the waves [κυμάτων] is, as it were, a human or mental urge to become pregnant [ἐγκύμονα]. This happens whenever the disturbance is "aroused" by the urge of the Spirit and is propelled toward generation. When this wave, which is roused out of the water by the wind, impregnates nature, it receives in itself the offspring of a female and detains the Light sown from above along with the fragrance of the Spirit.

INCARNATION. 15. I refer to a mind shaped in various forms, identified with the perfect God. This God was brought down from above from unborn Light and Spirit into human nature as though into a shrine. He was born from water by an impulse from nature and the whipping of wind. He was blended and mixed with bodies like salt mixed with generated entities, and Light mixed with Darkness. From bodies, he hastens to be freed, though he is unable by himself to find release and a way out from the body.[339] 16. This is because he is in a state of mixture. Existing as the tiniest spark, a fragment of light from above, like a ray of light in the variegated blend of the body, "he cried out from many waters," as, he claims, it says in the Psalms.[340]

SALVATION. Now, all the planning and attention of the upper Light is focused on how and in what way the mind can be freed from the death of the vile, dark body, and from the lower father. This father is the wind who

338. Cf. the wind (πνεῦμα) over the waters in Gen 1:2 LXX. In Paraph. Shem (NHC VII,1), the Darkness is a "wind in waters" (ⲧⲏⲟⲩ ϩⲛ̄ ϩⲛ̄ⲙⲟⲩⲉⲓⲏ) (1.36–2.1).

339. See Matt 5:13 ("You are the salt of the earth") and 5:14 ("You are the light of the world"). Cf. the use of these Matthean texts in Iren., *Haer.* 1.6.1; Clem. Alex., *Quis div.* 36.1.

340. Ps. 28:3 LXX. Cf. the Naassene exegesis of this verse in *Ref.* 5.8.15.This sentence has been heavily emended by Marcovich. As he remarks, it is simpler to emend ἀπ [eleven-letter gap] ἄσμα in P to ἀπόσπασμα (without ἀποκριθέν).

ταράχῳ ἐπεγείρας κύματα καὶ γεννήσας νοῦν τέλειον υἱὸν ἑαυτῷ, οὐκ ὄντα ἴδιον αὐτοῦ κατ' οὐσίαν. 17. ἄνωθεν γὰρ ἦν ἀκτὶς ἀπὸ τοῦ τελείου φωτὸς ἐκείνου, ἐν τῷ σκοτει<ν>ῷ καὶ φοβερῷ καὶ πικρῷ καὶ μιαρῷ ὕδατι κεκρατημένος, ὅπερ ἐστὶ «πνεῦμα» φωτεινὸν «ἐπιφερόμενον ἐπάνω τοῦ ὕδατος». ἐπεὶ οὖν ... ημάτων κύματα ... διαφόροις γ ... εσι ... μήτρα τις ... κατεσπαρμέν- ... ὡς ἐπὶ πάντων τῶν ζῴων θεωρεῖται.

18. ὁ δὲ ἄνεμος, λάβρος ὁμοῦ καὶ <σ>φοδρὸς φερόμενος, ἐστὶ [τῷ] σύρματι ὄφεως παραπλήσιος, πτερωτός, <καὶ> ἀπὸ τοῦ ἀνέμου—τουτέστιν ἀπὸ τοῦ ὄφεως—ἡ ἀρχὴ τῆς γεννήσεως τὸν εἰρημένον τρόπον γέγονε, πάντων ὁμοῦ τὴν ἀρχὴν τῆς γεννήσεως εἰληφότων.

19. Ἐπεὶ οὖν κατείληπται τὸ φῶς καὶ τὸ πνεῦμα εἰς τὴν ἀκάθαρτον, φησί, καὶ πολυπήμονα μήτραν ἄτακτον, εἰς ἣν ὁ ὄφις εἰσερχόμενος, ὁ ἄνεμος τοῦ σκότους, ὁ πρωτόγονος τῶν ὑδάτων, γεννᾷ τὸν ἄνθρωπον, καὶ ἄλλο οὐδὲν εἶδος οὔτε ἀγαπᾷ οὔτε γνωρίζει ἡ ἀκάθαρτος μήτρα, 20. ὁμοιωθεὶς οὖν ὁ ἄνωθεν τοῦ φωτὸς τέλειος λόγος τῷ θηρίῳ, τῷ ὄφει, εἰσῆλθεν εἰς τὴν ἀκάθαρτον μήτραν, ἐξαπατήσας αὐτὴν τοῦ θηρίου τῷ ὁμοιώματι, ἵνα λύσῃ τὰ δεσμὰ τὰ περικείμενα τῷ τελείῳ νοΐ, τῷ γεννωμένῳ ἐν ἀκαθαρσίᾳ μήτρας ὑπὸ τοῦ πρωτοτόκου ὕδατος ὄφεως, ἀνέμου, θηρίου. αὕτη, φησίν, ἐστὶν «ἡ τοῦ δούλου μορφή», καὶ αὕτη ἡ ἀνάγκη τοῦ κατελθεῖν τὸν λόγον τοῦ θεοῦ εἰς μήτραν παρθένου.

stirred up the waves with churning and confusion, and who fathered a perfect mind as a son for himself. In terms of substance, the lower father's son is not his own. 17. For the son was from above, a ray from that perfect Light. He was blended with the dark, frightful, bitter, and polluted water. This is what the luminous "Spirit hovering over the water" refers to.[341] Now since waves of … in different … womb … sown … is beheld as over all living beings.[342]

18. The wind, winged, violent, and blowing strongly, closely resembles the trail made by a snake. From the wind (that is, from the snake) arises the beginning of birth, as I previously described, when all things together receive the beginning of birth.

THE WORD. 19. Now, Light and Spirit are captured in the "impure womb," he says, which is full of suffering and disorder. Into this womb, the snake (the wind of darkness, the firstborn of the waters) enters in order to father the human being. Since the impure womb loves and knows no other form, 20. the perfect Word of light from above likened himself to the beast, the snake, and entered the impure womb. He deceived the womb by the likeness of the beast. He did so in order to loose the chain binding the perfect mind born in the impurity of the womb by the firstborn of water (the snake, wind, or beast).[343] This snake form, he says, is what scripture refers to as "the form of the slave," and this is why it was necessary for the Word to descend into the womb of a virgin.[344]

---

341. For the hovering spirit, see Gen 1:2 LXX; *Ref.* 6.14.4–5; 6.17.2 ("Simon"); Iren., *Haer.* 1.30.1; Clem. Alex., *Exc.* 47.3; Ap. John (BG 8502.2) 45.10.

342. The text is lacunose. Marcovich suggests: ἐπεὶ οὖν <τὰ ἐκ τῶν τοῦ ὕδατος ὁρμ>ημάτων κύματα <ἀρχὴ τῆς γεννήσεως τοῖς> διαφόροις γ<έν>εσι <γέγονεν, ἡ φύσις ὡς> μήτρα τις <ἐγκύμων κατέχει τὸ> κατεσπαρμέν<ον φῶς ἄνωθεν καὶ τὸ πνεῦμα,> ὡς ἐπί … ("Now since waves from the surging of the water are the origin of generation for different classes, nature, like a pregnant womb, holds down the Light and the Spirit sown from above, as over …").

343. In Paraph. Shem (NHC VII,1) 19.23–35, the Savior finds himself "in front of the womb." To disguise himself, he changes into the form of a beast (θηρίον). In Gen 3:1 LXX, the snake is a "beast [θηρίον] of the field." Our author recognizes the snake as a phallic symbol, a recognition important for his comparison with the "Orphic" painting in *Ref.* 5.20.6–7 below.

344. The "form of the slave" comes from Phil 2:7. Cf. *Ref.* 5.21.9 below and the summary of the "Sethians" in 10.11.11. For entering the womb of the virgin, see Luke 1:35 and the interpretation of the womb in Luise Abramowski, "Female Figures in the

21. ἀλλ' οὐκ ἔστι, φησίν, ἀρκετὸν τὸ εἰσεληλυθέναι τὸν τέλειον ἄνθρωπον, <τὸν> λόγον, εἰς μήτραν παρθένου καὶ «λῦσαι τὰς ὠδῖνας» τὰς ἐν ἐκείνῳ τῷ σκότει· ἀλλὰ γὰρ μετὰ τὸ <εἰς τὰ> ἐν μήτρᾳ μυστήρια μυσερὰ εἰσελθεῖν ἀπελούσατο καὶ ἔπιε τὸ ποτήριον «ζῶντος ὕδατος» «ἀλλομένου», ὃ δεῖ πάντα πιεῖν τὸν μέλλοντα ἀποδιδύσκεσθαι τὴν δουλικὴν μορφὴν καὶ ἐπενδύσασθαι ἔνδυμα οὐράνιον.

20. 1. Ταῦτά ἐστιν ἃ λέγουσιν, ὡς δι' ὀλίγων ἔστιν εἰπεῖν, οἱ προστάται τῶν Σηθιανῶν λόγων. ἔστι δὲ ὁ λόγος αὐτῶν συγκείμενος ἐκ φυσικῶν καὶ πρὸς ἕτερα εἰρημένων ῥημάτων, ἃ εἰς τὸν ἴδιον λόγον μετάγοντες διηγοῦνται καθάπερ εἴπομεν.

λέγουσι δὲ καὶ Μωσέα αὐτῶν συναίρεσθαι τῷ λόγῳ, ἐπὰν εἴπῃ· «σκότος καὶ γνόφος καὶ θύελλα»—οὗτοι, φησίν, οἱ τρεῖς λόγοι. ἢ ὅταν εἴπῃ ἐν παραδείσῳ γεγονέναι τρεῖς· Ἀδάμ, Εὔαν, ὄφιν. 2. ἢ ὅταν λέγῃ τρεῖς <υἱούς>· Κάϊν, Ἄβελ, Σήθ, καὶ πάλιν τρεῖς· Σήμ, Χάμ, Ἰάφεθ. ἢ ὅταν λέγῃ τρεῖς πατριάρχας· Ἀβραάμ, Ἰσαάκ, Ἰακώβ· ἢ ὅταν λέγῃ τρεῖς ἡμέρας πρὸ ἡλίου καὶ σελήνης γεγονέναι· ἢ ὅταν λέγῃ τρεῖς νόμους· ἀπαγορευτικόν, ἐφετικόν, διατιμητικόν. 3. ἀπαγορευτικὸς δέ ἐστι νόμος· «ἀπὸ παντὸς ξύλου τοῦ ἐν τῷ παραδείσῳ βρώσει φαγεῖν, ἀπὸ δὲ τοῦ ξύλου τοῦ γινώσκειν καλὸν καὶ πονηρὸν οὐ μὴ φάγητε». ἐν δὲ τῷ λέγειν· «ἔξελθε ἐκ τῆς γῆς σου καὶ ἐκ τῆς συγγενείας σου, καὶ δεῦρο εἰς γῆν ἣν ἄν σοι δείξω». ἐφετικός, φησίν, οὗτος ὁ νόμος· ἑλομένῳ γὰρ ἔστιν ἐξελθεῖν, μὴ ἑλομένῳ δὲ μένειν. διατιμητικὸς δὲ νόμος ἐστὶν ὁ λέγων· «οὐ μοιχεύσεις, οὐ φονεύσεις, οὐ κλέψεις»· διατετίμηται γὰρ ἑκάστου τῶν ἀδικημάτων <ἡ> ζημία.

21. But it is not, he says, sufficient for the perfect Human, the Word, to enter the virgin's womb and "loose the birth pangs" in that darkness.[345] He does much more. After he entered the polluted mysteries of the womb, he washed himself clean and drank the cup "of living, bubbling water," which everyone must drink who is destined to strip off the slave form and be robed with the celestial garment.[346]

20. 1. This is a sample of the discourse that the Sethian leaders declare. Their discourse is concocted from the natural philosophers and from discourses directed toward other subjects. These discourses they convert into their own idiom and narrate as I have described.

SCRIPTURAL SUPPORT. They claim that Moses too comes to the aid of their doctrine when he refers to "darkness, gloom, and storm" (which, he claims, are the three principles).[347] Moses also mentions that there were three in paradise: Adam, Eve, and the snake. 2. In addition, he refers to three sons: Cain, Abel, and Seth, or Shem, Ham, and Japheth.[348] Moreover, he speaks of three patriarchs: Abraham, Isaac, and Jacob; and three days before the sun and moon existed;[349] and three types of laws: prohibitive, permissive, and penal. 3. (A prohibitive law is: "Eat from the tree of paradise, but not from the tree of good and evil."[350] A permissive law is: "Go from your land and kinsfolk, and come to the land that I will show you"—for one can choose to depart or stay.[351] A penal law is one that says, "do not commit adultery, do not murder, do not steal," since a penalty is doled out for each infraction.[352])

Gnostic *Sondergut* in Hippolytus' *Refutatio*," in *Images of the Feminine in Gnosticism*, ed. Karen L. King, SAC (Fortress: Philadelphia, 1988), 136–52 (141–42).

345. For loosing birth pangs, see Acts 2:24: λύσας τὰς ὠδῖνας τοῦ θανάτου ("he loosed the birth pangs of death"), spoken of God raising Christ from the dead.

346. Living, bubbling water (ζῶν ὕδωρ ἀλλόμενον) combines John 4:10 (ὕδωρ ζῶν) with 4:14 (ὕδατος ἀλλομένου). The phrase also occurs in *Ref.* 5.9.18 (Naassenes); 5.27.2 (Justin). As Scholten points out, the conflation appears only in these three texts ("Quellen," 588–90). See further Abramowski, "Female Figures," 142. For the celestial garment, see Matt 22:11 (ἔνδυμα γάμου). Cf. *Ref.* 5.8.44 (Naassenes); 2 En. 22:8–9; Clem. Alex., *Exc.* 61.8; 63.1.

347. Exod 10:22; Deut 5:22; cf. *Ref.* 8.8.5 (Doketai); Ps.-Clem. Hom. 3.45.3.

348. Cf. Iren., *Haer.* 1.7.5; Clem. Alex., *Exc.* 54.1.

349. Gen 1:5–13; cf. *Ref.* 6.14.2 ("Simon").

350. Gen 2:16–17 LXX.

351. Gen 12:1 LXX.

352. Exod 20:13–15; Deut 5:17–19.

4. Ἔστι δὲ αὐτοῖς ἡ πᾶσα διδασκαλία τοῦ λόγου ἀπὸ τῶν παλαιῶν θεολόγων, Μουσαίου καὶ Λίνου καὶ τοῦ τὰς τελετὰς καὶ τὰ μυστήρια μάλιστα καταδείξαντος Ὀρφέως. 5. ὁ γὰρ περὶ τῆς μήτρας αὐτῶν καὶ τοῦ ὄφεως λόγος κα(ὶ) ὀμφαλοῦ—ὅπερ ἐστὶν ἀνδρεία—διαρρήδην οὕτως ἐστιν ἐν τοῖς Βακχικοῖς τοῦ Ὀρφέως. τετέλεσται δὲ ταῦτα καὶ παραδέδοται ἀνθρώποις πρὸ τῆς Κελεοῦ καὶ Τριπτολέμου καὶ Δήμητρος καὶ Κόρης καὶ Διονύσου ἐν Ἐλευσῖνι τελετῆς, ἐν Φλυῇ τῆς Ἀττικῆς· πρὸ γὰρ τῶν Ἐλευσινίων μυστηρίων ἐστὶν ἐν τῇ Φλυῇ <τὰ τῆς> λεγομένη<ς> Μεγάλη<ς> ὄργια. 6. ἔστι δὲ παστὰς ἐν αὐτῇ, ἐπὶ δὲ τῆς παστάδος ἐγγέγραπται μέχρι σήμερον ἡ [τὰ τῶν] πάντων τῶν εἰρημένων λόγων ἰδέα.

πολλὰ μὲν οὖν ἐστι τὰ ἐπὶ τῆς παστάδος ἐκείνης ἐγγεγραμμένα περὶ ὧν καὶ Πλούταρχος ποιεῖται λόγους ἐν ταῖς πρὸς Ἐμπεδοκλέα δέκα βίβλοις. ἔστι δὲ τοῖς πλείοσι καὶ πρεσβύτης τις ἐγγεγραμμένος πολιός, πτερωτός, ἐντεταμένην ἔχων τὴν αἰσχύνην, γυναῖκα ἀποφεύγουσαν διώκων κυνοειδῆ. 7. ἐπιγέγραπται δὲ ἐπὶ τοῦ πρεσβύτου· Φάος ῥυέντης, ἐπὶ δὲ τῆς γυναικός· <Φεραίη> Φικόλα.

DERIVATION FROM MYSTERY RELIGIONS. 4. Their entire teaching about the Word is from the ancient theologians Musaios, Linos, and—the consummate revealer of initiations and mysteries—Orpheus. 5. Their story about the womb, the snake, and the navel (i.e., the male genitals) is exactly the same story as is told in the Bacchic rites of Orpheus.[353] These rites were performed and handed on to the people in Phlya of Attika before the rites of Keleos, Triptolemos, Demeter, Kore, and Dionysos in Eleusis.[354] Before the Eleusinian mysteries, the secret rites of the so-called Great Goddess were held in Phlya.[355] 6. There is a portico there, and in the portico is painted even today the picture representing all their lore.[356]

Now there are many things painted in that portico that Plutarch discusses at length in his ten-volume study of Empedokles.[357] In most of them, moreover, there is painted a gray-headed old man with wings and an erect penis chasing a fleeing woman depicted like a dog.[358] 7. The old man is labeled "Streamer of Light," and the woman "Phikola the Pheraian goddess."[359]

---

353. Cf. LSJ, s.v. ἀνδρεία IV. On the resemblance of the navel and male genitals, see Giovanni Casadio, *Vie gnostiche all'immortalità* (Brescia: Morcelliana, 1997), 54.

354. P here reads φλοιοῦντι, which would suggest Φλιοῦς, a town in Achaea where there was an initiation rite (τελετή) in honor of Demeter (Pausanias, *Descr.* 2.14.1). I accept Schneidewin's emendation Φλυῇ ("in Phlya"), an Attic deme, because our author (or his source) says that it is in Attika. The Lykomidai, an Athenian priestly family, had a sanctuary (τελεστήριον) in Phlya, in which initiation rites apparently took place (Plutarch, *Them.* 1.4; cf. Pausanias, *Descr.* 4.1.7). See further M. Paul Tannery, "Orphica, fr. 3 Abel," *RevPhil* 24 (1900): 97–102 (99–100); Casadio, *Vie*, 51–66; Robert Parker, *Athenian Religion: A History* (Oxford: Clarendon, 1996), 305.

355. Pausanias says that the people of Phlya worship a Great Goddess but identify her with Earth (Γῆς) (*Descr.* 1.31.4).

356. On the meaning of παστάς, see Casadio, *Vie*, 60; Miguel Herrero de Jáuregui, *Orphism and Christianity in Late Antiquity*, Sozomena 7 (Berlin: de Gruyter, 2010), 160–64.

357. The Lamprias catalogue includes a ten-volume work of Plutarch Ἐἰς Ἐμπεδοκλέα (number 43). See further Osborne, *Rethinking*, 92–94.

358. "With wings" (πτερωτός) is Miller's correction for P's πετρωτός ("made of rock"?). For the association of dogs and women, see Cristiana Franco, *Shameless: The Canine and the Feminine in Ancient Greece*, trans. Matthew Fox (Berkeley: University of California Press, 2014), 121–54.

359. The name of the goddess remains a mystery. P reads περεηφϊκόλα. Φικόλα is used separately in the next sentence, apparently as an independent name. For περεη, Marcovich suggested γεραρή ("reverend, venerable, august") (*Studies*, 91), M. J. Edwards Ῥέη (i.e., Rhea) ("Gnostic Eros and Orphic Themes," *ZPE* 88 [1991]: 25–40 [32]), and Herrero de Jáuregui ἱερῇ ("holy") (*Orphism*, 164 n. 63). Offered here is the

ἔοικε δὲ εἶναι κατὰ τὸν Σηθιανῶν λόγον ὁ Φάος ῥυέντης τὸ φῶς, τὸ δὲ σκοτεινὸν ὕδωρ ἡ Φικόλα, τὸ δὲ ἐν μέσῳ τούτων διάστημα ἁρμονία πνεύματος μεταξὺ τεταγμένου. τὸ δὲ ὄνομα τοῦ Φάο<υ>ς ῥυέντου τὴν ῥύσιν ἄνωθεν τοῦ φωτός, ὡς λέγουσι, δηλοῖ κάτω· 8. ὥστε εὐλόγως ἄν τις εἴποι τοὺς Σηθιανοὺς ἐγγύς που τελεῖν παρ' αὐτοῖς τὰ τῆς Μεγάλης <Φλυῆσιν ὄργια>.

Τῇ δὲ διαιρέσει τῇ τριχῇ μαρτυρεῖν ἔοικε καὶ ὁ ποιητὴς λέγων·

τριχθὰ δὲ πάντα δέδασται, ἕκαστον δ' ἔμμορε τιμῆς

—τουτέστι τῶν τριχῇ διῃρημένων ἕκαστον εἴληφε δύναμιν.

9. καὶ τὸ ὕδωρ δὲ τὸ ὑποκείμενον κάτω σκοτεινόν, ὅτι δέδυκε τὸ φῶς, ὡς ἀνακομίσασθαι καὶ λαβεῖν ἄνω δεῖ τὸν κατενηνεγμένον σπινθῆρα ἀπ' αὐτοῦ, <ὡσ>αύτως ἐοίκασιν οἱ πάνσοφοι Σηθιανοὶ παρ' Ὁμήρου λαβόντες λέγειν·

10. ἴστω γάρ—φησί—τόδε γαῖα καὶ οὐρανὸς εὐρὺς ὕπερθεν
καὶ τὸ κατειβόμενον Στυγὸς ὕδωρ, ὅς τε μέγιστος
ὅρκος δεινότατός τε πέλει μακάρεσσι θεοῖσι·

τουτέστιν ἀποτρόπαιόν τι καὶ φρικτὸν οἱ θεοὶ καθ' Ὅμηρον εἶναι τὸ ὕδωρ νομίζουσιν, ὅπερ ὁ λόγος τῶν Σηθιανῶν φοβερὸν εἶναί φησι τῷ νοΐ.

21. 1. Ταῦτ' ἔστιν ἃ λέγουσι καὶ τοιούτοις παραπλήσια ἐν ἀπείροις συγγράμμασι· πείθουσι δὲ ἐντυγχάνειν τῷ περὶ κράσεως καὶ μίξεως λόγῳ

The Streamer of Light seems to be the light in the Sethian account, whereas Phikola is the dark water, and the intervening space is the harmony of Spirit arrayed in between. Moreover, the name "Streaming Light" indicates the stream of light, as they say, poured down from above. 8. Consequently, one can reasonably conclude that the Sethians virtually celebrate among themselves the rites of the Great Goddess at Phlya.[360]

SUPPORT FROM HOMER. The poet Homer, it seems, also testifies to their threefold division:

> All things were divided in three ways; each had his share of honor.[361]

That is to say, each member of the triply divided principles received power.

9. In addition, the water lying below is dark because the Light sank into it. Consequently, the spark that has been brought down must be transported out of it and taken above. This too the all-wise Sethians imagine that they take from Homer, who says:

> 10. Let Earth know and broad Heaven above
> And the down-rushing water of Styx—which is the greatest
> And most terrible oath to the blessed gods.[362]

This indicates that Homer's gods regard the water as ill-omened and hair-raising—the very water that the Sethian story says is "frightful" to Mind.

THEORY OF BLENDING AND MIXTURE. 21. 1. They make these and similar remarks in countless writings. They persuade their students to read the

---

emendation Φεραίῃ (= Φεραία, the Pheraian goddess called Einodia and identified with Hekate). See further Ezzio Albrile, "…*In principiis lucem fuisse ac tenebras*: Creazione, caduta e rigenerazione spirituale in alcuni testi gnostici," *Annali dell'instituto Universitario Orientale di Napoli* 17 (1995): 109–55 (134–46); Casadio, *Vie*, 60–64, Wolfgang Fauth, *Hekate Polymorphos—Wesensvarianten einer antiken Gottheit: Zwischen frühgriechischer Theogonie und spätantikem Synkretismus* (Hamburg: Dr. Kovač, 2006), 136, and the sources in *OF* 532.

360. Φλυῆσιν ὄργια is Duncker and Schneidewin's emendation for P's φλοιᾶς ἰονόργια.

361. Homer, *Il.* 15.189, also quoted in *Ref.* 5.8.3 (Naassenes).

362. Homer, *Il.* 15.36–38. The same passage is quoted in *Ref.* 5.16.3 (Peratai).

τοὺς μαθητευομένους, ὃς μεμελέτηται πολλοῖς ἄλλοις καὶ Ἀνδρονίκῳ τῷ Περιπατητικῷ.

2. λέγουσιν οὖν οἱ Σηθιανοὶ τὸν περὶ κράσεως καὶ μίξεως λόγον συνεστάναι τῷδε τῷ τρόπῳ· τὴν ἀκτῖνα τὴν φωτεινὴν ἄνωθεν ἐγκεκρᾶσθαι καὶ τὸν σπινθῆρα τὸν ἐλάχιστον [ἐν] τοῖς σκοτεινοῖς ὕδασι κάτω καταμεμῖχθαι λεπτῶς καὶ συνηνῶσθαι καὶ γεγονέναι [ἐν] ἓν φύραμά τι, ὥσ<περ> μίαν ὀσμὴν ἐκ πολλῶν καταμεμιγμένων ἐπὶ τοῦ πυρὸς <ὀσμώμεθα> θυμιαμάτων. 3. καὶ δεῖ τὸν ἐπιστήμονα, τῆς ὀσφρήσεως ἔχοντα κριτήριον εὐαγές, ἀπὸ τῆς μιᾶς τοῦ θυμιάματος ὀσμῆς διακρίνειν λεπτῶς ἕκαστον τῶν καταμεμιγμένων ἐπὶ τοῦ πυρὸς θυμιαμάτων, οἱονεὶ στύρακα καὶ σμύρναν καὶ λίβανον ἢ εἴ τι ἄλλο εἴη μεμιγμένον.

4. χρῶνται δὲ καὶ ἑτέροις παραδείγμασι, λέγοντες καταμεμῖχθαι [καὶ] χρυσίῳ χαλκόν, καὶ τέχνη τις εὕρηται ἡ διακρίνουσα τὸν χαλκὸν ἀπὸ τοῦ χρυσίου. ὁμοίως δὲ κἂν [ἐν] ἀργύρῳ κασσίτερος ἢ χαλκὸς ἤ τι τῶν ὁμογενῶν καταμεμιγμένον εὑρεθῇ, μίξεώς τινι τέχνῃ κρείττονι καὶ ταῦτα διακρίνεται. 5. ἤδη δέ τις καὶ ὕδωρ μεμιγμένον οἴνῳ διακρίνει· οὕτω, φησί, καὶ [κἂν] πάντα τὰ συγκεκραμένα διακρίνεται.

Καὶ δὴ ἀπὸ τῶν ζῴων, φησί, <τοῦτο> καταμάνθανε· τελευτήσαντος γὰρ τοῦ ζῴου ἕκαστα διακρίνεται καὶ λυθὲν οὕτω τὸ ζῷον ἀφανίζεται. τοῦτό ἐστι, φησί, τὸ εἰρημένον· «οὐκ ἦλθον εἰρήνην βαλεῖν ἐπὶ τὴν γῆν, ἀλλὰ μάχαιραν», τουτέστι [τὸ] διχάσαι καὶ χωρίσαι τὰ συγκεκραμένα. 6. διχάζεται γὰρ καὶ διακρίνεται ἕκαστα τῶν συγκεκραμένων οἰκείου χωρίου τυχόντα· ὡς γάρ ἐστι χωρίον συγκράσεως τοῖς ζῴοις ἅπασιν ἕν, οὕτω καὶ τῆς διακρίσεως καθέστηκεν ἕν, ὃ οἶδεν οὐδείς, φησίν, <ἀλλ'> ἢ μόνοι ἡμεῖς, οἱ ἀναγεννώμενοι πνευματικοί, οὐ σαρκικοί, ὧν ἐστι «τὸ πολίτευμα ἐν οὐρανοῖς» ἄνω.

7. οὕτω παρεισδύοντες διαφθείρουσι τοὺς ἀκροωμένους, ὁτὲ μὲν ἀποχρώμενοι ῥητοῖς, εἰς ὃ θέλουσι συνάγοντες κακῶς τὰ καλῶς εἰρημένα, <ὁτὲ δὲ> φωλεύοντες [τε] τὸ ἑαυτῶν ἀδίκημα διὰ παραβολῶν ὧν βούλονται.

8. πάντα οὖν, φησί, τὰ συγκεκραμένα, καθὼς εἴρηται, ἔχει <χωρί>ον ἴδιον καὶ τρέχει πρὸς τὰ οἰκεῖα, ὡς σίδηρος <πρὸς> τὴν Ἡρακλείαν λίθον καὶ τὸ

theory of blending and mixture. This theory is, in fact, the concern of many others, including Andronikos the Peripatetic.[363]

2. Now the Sethians say that the theory of blending and mixing runs as follows: the brilliant ray from above is blended, and the tiniest spark is mixed with the dark waters below. It is finely mixed and made one, with the result that there arises a single compound, just as we smell a single scent when many varieties of incense are mixed in the fire.[364] 3. Indeed, it is necessary for the expert who has a keen sense of smell to discern from the scent of the incense each of the varieties of incense finely mixed in the fire (as, for instance, storax, myrrh, frankincense, or any other ingredient).

4. They use other examples as well, like bronze mixed with gold (there is an invented art that separates bronze from gold). Likewise, if tin or bronze or other like metals are found to be mixed with silver by a superior art of mixture, even these are separated. 5. One can even separate water mixed with wine. Thus, they say, all things blended are separable.

Learn this also, he says, from animals: for when the animal dies, each of its parts is separated and dissolved. Thus the animal decays. This, he claims, is what the scriptural verse means: "I came not to set peace on earth but a sword."[365] That is, Jesus comes to separate and distinguish the blended elements.[366] 6. Each of the blended elements is separated and distinguished when it arrives at its own place. Just as there is one place of blending for all animals, so also there is established one place of separation. No one knows this place, he adds, except for us alone, the spirituals who have been reborn. We are not fleshly, since we have a "commonwealth in heaven."[367]

7. In this way—like those who destroy their hearers by stealthy additions—they sometimes misuse passages, arbitrarily collecting for evil purposes verses that are spoken for good. At other times, they tuck away their crooked doctrine in their favorite comparisons.

8. At any rate, all the aforementioned blended elements, he claims, have their own place and run to what is akin to them, like iron to a magnet

---

363. Otherwise known as Andronikos of Rhodes (flourished 60 BCE), best known for publishing new editions of Aristotle's writings.

364. Cf. *Ref.* 9.10.8 = Herakleitos, DK 22 B67 (= Marcovich, *Heraclitus*, §77).

365. Matt 10:34; Gos. Thom. 16.

366. For the Λόγος τομεύς (cutting Word), see Hans Joachim Krämer, *Der Ursprung der Geistmetaphysik* (Amsterdam: B. R. Grüner, 1967), 269–72.

367. Phil 3:20. Cf. the interpretation of this verse in Diogn. 5.9; Clem. Alex., *Exc.* 54.3; *Paed.* 3.99.1; *Strom.* 3.14.95.2; 4.3.12.6.

ἄχυρον ἠλέκτρου πλησίον καὶ τοῦ κέντρου τοῦ θαλασσίου ἱέρακος τὸ χρυσίον. 9. οὕτως ἡ τοῦ καταμεμιγμένου τῷ ὕδατι φωτὸς <ἀκτίς> οἰκείου χωρίου ἐκ διδασκαλίας καὶ μαθήσεως μεταλαβοῦσα, σπεύδει πρὸς τὸν λόγον τὸν ἄνωθεν ἐλθόντα ἐν εἰκόνι δουλικῇ, μᾶλλον ἢ ὁ σίδηρος πρὸς τὴν Ἡρακλείαν λίθον, καὶ γίνεται μετὰ τοῦ λόγου λόγος ἐκεῖ, ὅπου <ὁ> λόγος ἐστί.

Καὶ ὅτι ταῦθ᾽ οὕτως ἔχει, φησί, καὶ πάντα διακρίνεται τὰ συγκεκραμένα ἐπὶ τῶν οἰκείων τόπων, μάνθανε. 10. φρέαρ ἐστὶν ἐν Πέρσαις ἐν Ἄμ<π>ῃ πόλει παρὰ τὸν Τίγριν ποταμόν· ᾠκοδόμηται δὲ παρὰ τὸ φρέαρ [ἄνω] δεξαμενή τις ἔχουσα τρεῖς ἀφετηρίας ἀφ᾽ αὑτῆς. οὗ φρέατος ἀντλήσας <τις καὶ> κάδδῳ ἀνενέγκας τὸ ἀπὸ τοῦ φρέατος ἀντληθὲν ὅ τι ποτέ ἐστιν, ἔχεεν εἰς τὴν παρακειμένην δεξαμενήν· 11. τὸ δὲ χυθὲν ἐλθὸν ἐπὶ τὰς ἀφετηρίας καὶ ἑνὶ σκεύει ἀναληφθὲν διακρίνεται, καὶ ἐν μὲν <τῇ πρώτῃ> ἅλας πηγνύμενον δείκνυται, ἐν ἑτέρᾳ δὲ τῶν ἀφετηριῶν ἄσφαλτος, ἐν δὲ τῇ τρίτῃ ἔλαιον. μέλαν δέ ἐστι τὸ ἔλαιον, ὡς, φησί, καὶ Ἡρόδοτος ἱστορεῖ, καὶ ὀσμὴν παρεχόμενον βαρεῖαν· 12. ῥαδινάκην δὲ αὐτὸ οἱ Πέρσαι καλοῦσιν. ἤρκει, φασὶν οἱ Σηθιανοί, πρὸς ἀπόδειξιν τοῦ προκειμέν(ου) ἡ τοῦ φρέατος ὁμοιότης πάντων μᾶλλον τῶν προειρημένων.

22. 1. Ἱκανῶς δοκεῖ ἡμῖν σεσαφηνίσθαι ἡ τῶν Σηθιανῶν γνώμη· εἰ δέ τις ὅλην τὴν κατ᾽ αὐτοὺς πραγματείαν βούλεται μαθεῖν, ἐντυχέτω βιβλ<ί>ῳ ἐπιγραφομένῳ Παράφρασις Σήθ· πάντα γὰρ τὰ ἀπόρρητα αὐτῶν ἐκεῖ εὑρήσει ἐγκείμενα.

ἀλλ᾽ ἐπεὶ τὰ κατὰ τοὺς Σηθιανοὺς ἐξεθέμεθα, ἴδωμεν τίνα ἐστὶ καὶ τὰ Ἰουστίνῳ δοκοῦντα.

or chaff when near amber, or gold to the pointed tail of a hierax fish.[368] 9. In this way, the ray of light mixed with the water, which participates in its own realm from teaching and instruction, rushes—faster than iron to a magnet—to the Word, who comes from above in slave form. Then it becomes word with the Word where the Word abides.

THE WELL IN AMPE. To verify these claims, he says, (that everything blended is separated into its own places) learn from what follows. 10. The Persians have a well in the city of Ampe by the river Tigris.[369] Beside the well is built a cistern that has three outlets. Anyone who draws from the well and brings up with a bucket what is drawn from the well (whatever it might be) pours it into the adjacent cistern. 11. What is poured in goes through the outlets and, when taken up into a single tank, is separated out. In the first outlet, there is shown encrusted salt; in the second of the outlets, asphalt; and in the third, oil. The oil is black, as (our author says) Herodotos too narrates. It has a pungent scent. 12. The Persians called it *rhadinakē*.[370] This analogy of the well, Sethians claim, is sufficient to prove their doctrine of separation more thoroughly than all the previously mentioned examples.

22. 1. The Sethian doctrine, I believe, has been sufficiently explained. If someone wants to learn their entire system, let him read their book entitled Paraphrase of Seth.[371] There one will find contained all their secrets.

But since I presented Sethian teachings, let us also examine the doctrines of Justin.[372]

---

368. Cf. *Ref.* 5.9.19 (Naassenes); 5.17.9–10 (Peratai).

369. See Herodotos, *Hist.* 6.20 (Ampe on the Tigris). The well was in fact in Arderikka near Susa and is described in *Hist.* 6.119.2–3.

370. Ducoeur identifies *rhadinakē* with naphtha ("Hérésiarques chrétiens," 184).

371. For the relation of the Paraphrase of Seth to the Paraphrase of Shem (NHC VII,1), see Michel Roberge, *The Paraphrase of Shem: Introduction, Translation and Commentary*, NHMS 72 (Leiden: Boston, 2010), 84–93 (with earlier sources).

372. Cf. our author's summary of Justin in *Ref.* 10.15 with the following report. Sometimes our Justin is called "Justin the gnostic." What makes (or does not make) Justin "gnostic" is treated by Williams, *Rethinking "Gnosticism,"* 18–23. Justin's myth presents the creator, creation, and procreation as fundamentally good (Roelof van den Broek, "Gospel Tradition and Salvation in Justin the Gnostic," *VC* 57 [2003]: 363–88 [367–69, 383–88]). (For Greek influence from Pherekydes, see Grant, *After*, 202–7.) Marvin Meyer and Willis Barnstone call *Baruch*, "a missing gnostic link between Jewish monotheism and full-blown gnosticism" (*The Gnostic Bible* [Boston: Shamb-

23. 1. Ἰουστῖνος πάντῃ ἐναντίος τῇ τῶν ἁγίων γραφῶν γενόμενος διδαχῇ, προσέτι δὲ καὶ τῇ τῶν μακαρίων εὐαγγελι<στ>ῶν [γραφῇ ἢ] φωνῇ ὡς ἐδίδασκεν ὁ Λόγος τοὺς μαθητὰς λέγων· «εἰς ὁδὸν ἐθνῶν μὴ ἀπέλθητε»—ὅπερ δηλοῖ μὴ προσέχειν τῇ τῶν ἐθνῶν ματαίᾳ διδασκαλίᾳ—, οὗτος ἐπὶ τὰ ἐθνῶν τερατολογούμενα καὶ διδασκόμενα ἀπαγαγεῖν πειρᾶται τοὺς ἀκροωμένους, αὐτολεξεὶ τὰ παρ᾽ Ἕλλησι μυθευόμενα διηγούμενος, οὐ γε πρότερον διδάξας οὔτε παραδοὺς τὸ τέλειον αὐτοῦ μυστήριον, εἰ μὴ ὅρκῳ δήσῃ τὸν πλανώμενον.

2. ἔπειτα τοὺς μύθους παρατίθησι ψυχαγωγίας χάριν, ὅπως οἱ ἐντυγχάνοντες τῇ τῶν βίβλων <αὐτοῦ> ἀναριθμ<ήτ>ῳ φλυαρίᾳ παραμύθιον ἔχωσι τὰ μυθευόμενα—ὃν τρόπον εἴ τις ὁδὸν μακρὰν βαδίζων, παρατυχὼν καταλύματι ἀναπαύεσθαι δοκεῖ—, καὶ οὕτως πάλιν ἐπὶ τὴν τῶν ἀναγνωσμάτων τραπέντες πολυμάθειαν μὴ μισήσωσιν, ἕως ἐπὶ τὸ ὑπ᾽ αὐτοῦ τεχναζόμενον ἀνόμημα διὰ πλειόνων ἐξηχηθὲν ὁρμήσωσι τετυφωμένοι.

οὓς φρικτοῖς καταδήσας πρότερον ὅρκοις μήτε ἐξειπεῖν μήτε ἀποστῆναι <καὶ> ὁμολογεῖν ἀναγκάσας, οὕτω παραδίδωσι τὰ ὑπ᾽ αὐτοῦ ἐφευρημένα μετὰ ἀσεβείας μυστήρια, πῇ μέν, καθὰ προείπομεν, μύθοις Ἑλληνικοῖς χρησάμενος, πῇ δὲ παραπεποιημένοις βιβλίοις, κατά τι παρεμφαίνουσι ταῖς προειρημέναις αἱρέσεσιν.

3. οἱ πάντες γὰρ ἑνὶ πνεύματι συνωθούμενοι εἰς ἕνα βυθὸν ἀμάρας συνάγονται, ἄλλοι ἄλλως τὰ αὐτὰ διηγούμενοι καὶ μυθεύοντες· οὗτοι δὲ ἰδίως οἱ πάντες γνωστικοὺς ἑαυτοὺς ἀποκαλοῦσιν, τὴν θαυμασίαν γνῶσιν τοῦ τελείου καὶ ἀγαθοῦ μόνοι καταπεπωκότες.

24. 1. Ὄμνυε δέ, φησὶν Ἰουστῖνος, εἰ γνῶναι θέλεις «ἃ ὀφθαλμὸς οὐκ εἶδε καὶ οὖς οὐκ ἤκουσεν οὐδ᾽ ἐπὶ καρδίαν ἀνθρώπου ἀνέβη», τὸν ἐπάνω πάντων,

JUSTIN

23. 1. Justin became a full-scale opponent against the teaching of holy scripture and in particular against the voice of the blessed evangelists.[373] This is because the Word taught his disciples, "Do not depart to the path of Gentiles"[374] (that is, pay no attention to the futile teachings of pagans), while this fool tries to lead his hearers astray to the fantastic tales and teachings of the pagans by directly quoting Greek myths. He neither teaches nor hands on his perfect mystery before he binds his dupe with an oath.

2. Then he sets out his myths to capture their souls. Consequently, the readers of the boundless blabbering in his books have his myths [τὰ μυθευόμενα] as a diversion [παραμύθιον]. It is like when someone on a long journey finds an inn and decides to rest. Justin uses this method so that they will not despise diligent study when again they turn to their regimen of readings. They pursue this course until, swelling with pride, they rush toward the oft-trumpeted crime that he fabricated.

He binds these people beforehand with hair-raising oaths neither to declare [the mysteries] nor to apostatize—and he forces them to consent. This is his method of handing on his impiously invented mysteries! Sometimes, as I said, he employs Greek myths, at other times doctored books that in some respects reflect the aforementioned heresies.

3. All these heretics, driven by one spirit, flow together into a single sewage "depth" as they variously narrate and relate the same doctrines in different ways. But all of them independently refer to themselves as "gnostics" [γνωστικούς], since they alone have gulped down the wondrous knowledge [γνῶσιν] of the perfect and good![375]

JUSTIN'S OATH. 24. 1. "Swear," Justin says, if you desire to know "what eye has not seen nor ear heard nor has it risen in the human heart."[376] Swear

---

hala, 2003], 119). Marcovich believed that Justin knew Naassene traditions, which should probably be dated to the late second century CE (*Studies*, 118).

373. Marcovich removes γραφῇ ἤ.

374. Matt 10:5; cf. Jer 10:2.

375. Cf. *Ref.* 5.6.4 (Naassenes). Note that previously our author claimed only that the Naassenes used γνωστικοί as a self-designation (*Ref.* 5.6.4). Both they and the Peratai claimed special knowledge (using forms of γιγνώσκω in 5.6.4 and 5.16.1).

376. A saying found in 1 Cor 2:9; Gos. Thom. 17; and resonant of Isa 64:4 LXX. The saying is common in esoteric writings and is quoted below in *Ref.* 5.26.16; 5.27.2; cf. 6.24.4 ("Pythagoras"). See further Claire Clivaz and Sara Schulthess, "On the Source

ἀγαθόν, τὸν ἀνώτερον ἄρρητα φυλάξαι τὰ τῆς διδασκαλίας σιγώμενα. καὶ γὰρ καὶ ὁ πατὴρ ἡμῶν, ἰδὼν τὸν ἀγαθὸν καὶ τελεσθεὶς παρ᾽ αὐτῷ, τὰ τῆς σιγῆς ἄρρητα ἐφύλαξε καὶ ὤμοσε, καθὼς γέγραπται· «ὤμοσε κύριος καὶ οὐ μεταμεληθήσεται».

2. ταῦτα τοίνυν οὕτω κατασφραγισάμενος πλείοσι μύθοις ψυχαγωγεῖ διὰ πλειόνων βιβλίων καὶ οὕτως ἐπὶ τὸν ἀγαθὸν ἄγει, τελειῶν τοὺς μύστας τὰ ἄλ<α>λα μυστήρια.

ἵνα καὶ μὴ διὰ πλειόνων ὁδεύσωμεν, ἐκ μιᾶς αὐτοῦ βίβλου τὰ ἄρρητα ἐπιδείξομεν, οὔσης, καθὼς νομίζει, ἐνδόξου. 3. αὕτη δὲ ἐπιγράφεται Βαρούχ· ἐν ᾗ μίαν τῶν πολλῶν μυθολογίαν ἐκτιθεμένην ὑπ᾽ αὐτοῦ δηλώσομεν <προ>οῦσαν παρὰ Ἡροδότῳ· ἣν ὡς ξένην τοῖς ἀκροαταῖς παραπλάσας διηγεῖται, ἐξ αὐτῆς πᾶσαν σύστασιν τοῦ κατ᾽ αὐτὸν διδασκαλ<ε>ίου ποιούμενος.

25. 1. Ἡρόδοτος μὲν οὖν τὸν Ἡρακλέα φησὶν ἀπὸ τῆς Ἐρυθείας τοῦ Γηρυόνου τὰς βοῦς ἄγοντα εἰς τὴν Σκυθίαν ἐλθεῖν, κεκμηκότα δὲ ἀπὸ τῆς πορείας εἰς ἔρημόν τι χωρίον κατακλιθέντα κοιμηθῆναι ὀλίγον· ὑπνώσαντος δὲ αὐτοῦ ἀφανῆ γενέσθαι τὸν ἵππον, ἐφ᾽ οὗ καθεζόμενος διώδευσε τὴν μακρὰν ὁδόν. περιεγερθεὶς δὲ ζήτησιν ἐποιεῖτο ἐπὶ τῆς ἐρημίας πολλήν, εὑρεῖν πειρώμενος τὸν ἵππον· 2. καὶ τοῦ μὲν ἵππου διαμαρτάνει, κόρην δέ τινα μιξοπάρθενον εὑρὼν ἐπὶ τῆς ἐρημίας ἐπηρώτα, εἰ εἴη που τεθεαμένη τὸν ἵππον. ἡ δὲ κόρη φησὶν εἰδέναι μέν, μὴ δείξειν δὲ πρότερον αὐτῷ, εἰ μὴ πρὸς μίξιν φιλίας συνέλθῃ αὐτῇ ὁ Ἡρακλῆς.

3. ἦν δέ, φησὶν ὁ Ἡρόδοτος, τὰ ἄνω αὐτῆς μέχρι βουβῶνος παρθένου, πᾶν δὲ τὸ κάτω σῶμα μετὰ βουβῶνα φρικτόν τι θέαμα ἐχίδνης. σπουδῇ δὲ τῆς περὶ τὸν ἵππον εὑρέσεως ὁ Ἡρακλῆς πείθεται τῷ θηρίῳ·

by the one superior to all, the Good, the Highest one, to guard what is inexpressible, these teachings covered in silence! For surely our Father, too, when he saw the Good and was initiated by him, guarded the inexpressible secrets of silence and swore, as it is written: "The Lord swore and will not repent!"[377]

2. So, having sealed them by these words, Justin captures their souls with a host of myths in a bevy of books. Thus he leads them to the Good, initiating his initiates into unuttered mysteries![378]

THE BOOK OF BARUCH. So that we can travel without frequent detours, I will expose his unspeakable secrets from one of his books, a book that, in his view, is "glorious." 3. It is entitled Baruch.[379] In it, I will reveal one out of many of his mythological discourses, a story with a prehistory in Herodotos. By reformulating this myth, Justin presents it to his hearers as something novel and from it constructs the entire system of his school.

DERIVATION FROM HERODOTOS. 25. 1. Now Herodotos tells the story of Herakles coming from the Red Island, driving the cattle of Geryon to Skythia.[380] The hero grew tired from his journey and laid down to rest a while in some desolate region. While he was sleeping, the horse that he rode on his long journey vanished. When he awoke, he made a thorough search in that deserted place, trying to find his horse. 2. Utterly failing to recover his horse, he found a "mixed maiden" in the desert and asked her if she had seen the horse anywhere. The woman said that she knew where the horse went but would not reveal it to him unless Herakles had sex with her.

3. Now her upper body, Herodotos says, was that of a young woman as far as her groin, but her entire lower body beyond the groin had the horrifying look of a viper. Since Herakles was in a hurry to find his horse, he complied with the beast.

---

and Rewriting of 1 Corinthians 2.9 in Christian, Jewish and Islamic Traditions (*1 Clem* 34.8; *GosJud* 47.10–13; a *ḥadīth qudsī*)," *NTS* 61 (2015): 183–200.

377. Ps 109:4 LXX. Two other versions of the oath appear below, for which see Marcovich, *Studies*, 103–5.

378. Duncker and Schneidewin emend P's ἄλλα to ἄλαλα ("unuttered").

379. Justin's *Baruch* is a beloved text in part because it is a good story with exciting "soap-opera" elements (a marriage hot with love, a sudden, back-stabbing divorce, and a vengeful ex-wife).

380. Herodotos, *Hist.* 4.8–10; Diodoros, *Bibl. hist.* 2.43.

ἔγνω γοῦν αὐτὴν καὶ ἐποίησεν ἐγκύμονα, καὶ προεῖπεν αὐτῇ μετὰ τὴν γνῶσιν ὅτι ἔχει κατὰ γαστρὸς ἐξ αὐτοῦ τρεῖς ὁμοῦ παῖδας, οἵτινες ἔσονται ἐπιφανεῖς. 4. ἐκέλευσε δὲ αὐτοῖς γεννωμένοις ὀνόματα θεῖναι τὴν τεκοῦσαν Ἀγάθυρσον, Γελωνὸν καὶ Σκύθην. λαβὼν δὲ τούτου μισθὸν τὸν ἵππον παρὰ τῆς θηριώδους κόρης, ἀπηλ<λ>άττετο φέρων καὶ τὰς βοῦς.

μακρὸς δὲ ὁ μετὰ ταῦτα μῦθος Ἡροδότῳ, χαιρέτω δὲ τὸ νῦν· τίνα δὲ τὰ Ἰουστίνῳ δοκοῦντα, μετάγοντι τὸν μῦθον εἰς τὴν τῶν ὅλων γέννησιν, ἡμεῖς διηγησόμεθα.

26. 1. Οὗτός φησιν· ἦσαν τρεῖς ἀρχαὶ τῶν ὅλων ἀγέννητοι, ἀρρενικαὶ δύο, θηλυκὴ μία. τῶν δὲ ἀρρενικῶν ἡ μέν τις <ἀρχὴ> καλεῖται ἀγαθός, αὐτὸ μόνον οὕτως λεγόμενος, προγνωστικὸς τῶν ὅλων, ἡ δὲ ἑτέρα πατὴρ πάντων τῶν γεννητῶν, ἀπρόγνωστος <καὶ ἄγνωστος> καὶ ἀόρατος. ἡ δὲ θήλ(εια) ἀπρόγνωστος, ὀργίλη, διγνώμων, δισώμ<ατ>ος, κατὰ πάντα τῇ κατὰ τὸν Ἡροδότου μῦθον <κόρῃ> ἐμφερής, μέχρι βουβῶνος παρθένος, ἔχιδνα δὲ τὰ κάτω, ὥς φησιν Ἰουστῖνος· 2. καλεῖται δὲ Ἐδὲμ αὕτη ἡ κόρη καὶ Ἰσραήλ. αὗται, φησίν, αἱ ἀρχαὶ τῶν ὅλων, ῥίζαι καὶ πηγαὶ ἀφ᾽ ὧν τὰ ὄντα ἐγένετο· ἄλλο δὲ ἦν οὐδέν.

ἰδὼν οὖν ὁ πατὴρ τὴν μιξοπάρθενον ἐκείνην τὴν Ἐδέμ, ἀπρόγνωστος ὢν ἦλθεν εἰς ἐπιθυμίαν αὐτῆς—Ἐλωεὶμ δέ, φησί, καλεῖται οὗτος ὁ πατήρ—· οὐδὲν ἧττον ἐπεθύμησε καὶ ἡ Ἐδὲμ τοῦ Ἐλωείμ, καὶ συνήγαγεν αὐτοὺς ἡ ἐπιθυμία εἰς μίαν φιλίας εὔνοιαν. 3. γεννᾷ δὲ ἀπὸ τῆς συνόδου τῆς τοιαύτης ὁ πατὴρ ἐκ

So, he knew her intimately and made her pregnant. Then he foretold to her that she had from him three children in her womb who would be famous. 4. He ordered her to name the offspring Agathyrsos, Gelonos, and Skythe. Then, having taken his horse as a reward from the bestial girl, he departed, taking his cattle along with him.

The story that Herodotos tells after this is long, so I let it go for now. I will relate the doctrines of Justin, who transmutes this myth into a cosmogony.

THEOLOGY. 26. 1. This is what he says: there were three unborn principles in the universe; two male, and one female. One of the male principles is called "Good."[381] He alone is called this, and he foreknows all things. The other is called "Father" of generated beings. He does not foreknow, nor is he known or seen.[382] The female principle does not foreknow, is irascible, indecisive, and double-bodied—in all respects like the girl in Herodotos's story.[383] She is like a young woman as far as the groin, but a viper below, as Justin says.[384] 2. This girl is called "Eden" and "Israel."[385] These, he says, are the principles of the universe, the roots and sources from which all existing reality came to be. There was nothing else at all.[386]

So, catching sight of that "mixed maiden" Eden, the Father—who did not foreknow what was to come—came desiring her. This Father is called "Elohim."[387] Eden no less desired Elohim; and desire brought them together into a single, heartfelt love. 3. From this union, the Father gen-

---

381. Cf. Luke 18:19 par. For the Absolute Good (τὸ ἀγαθόν αὐτό), see Plato, *Resp.* 540a.

382. Duncker and Schneidewin add καὶ ἄγνωστος (here: "nor is he known").

383. Marcovich adds κόρη ("girl").

384. Roelof van den Broek argues that the most likely source for the shape of Eden is Isis-Thermouthis ("The Shape of Eden according to Justin the Gnostic," *VC* 27 [1973]: 35–45). Marcovich prefers to derive the shape from Hesiod, *Theog.* 297–299, where "Echidna is exactly 50% virgin, and 50% viper" (*Studies*, 97).

385. Israel is often the symbolic wife of God (Elohim) in Jewish scripture. Eden also struggles with (i.e., opposes) Elohim and is thus rightly named "Israel" (see Gen 32:29).

386. J. Montserrat-Torrents relates the three principles to the philosophy of Noumenios ("La philosophie du *Livre de Baruch* de Justin," *StPatr* 18 [1985]: 253–61 [255–56]).

387. "Elohim" (אלהים) is the common Hebrew word for God. He appears as a lower archon in other gnostic sources (e.g., Ap. John [NHC II,1] 24.18–20; Apoc. Pet. [NHC VII,3] 82.24).

τῆς Ἐδὲμ ἑαυτῷ ἀγγέλους δώδεκα, ὀνόματα δέ ἐστι τῶν πατρικῶν ἀγγέλων τάδε· Μιχαήλ, Ἀμήν, Βαρούχ, Γαβριήλ, Ἠσαδδαῖος ... 4. καὶ τῶν μητρικῶν ἀγγέλων, ὧν ἐποίησεν ἡ Ἐδέμ, ὁμοίως ὑποτέτακται τὰ ὀνόματα· ἔστι δὲ ταῦτα· Βάβελ, Ἀχαμώθ, Νάας, Βήλ, Βελίας, Σατάν, Σαήλ, Ἀδωναῖος, Καυίθαν, Φαραώθ, Καρκαμενώς, Λάθεν. τούτων τῶν εἰκοσιτεσσάρων ἀγγέλων οἱ μὲν πατρικοὶ τῷ πατρὶ συναίρονται καὶ πάντα ποιοῦσι κατὰ τὸ θέλημα αὐτοῦ, οἱ δὲ μητρικοὶ τῇ μητρὶ Ἐδέμ.

5. τούτων δὲ τῶν ἀγγέλων ὁμοῦ πάντων τὸ πλῆθος ὁ παράδεισος, φησίν, ἐστί, περὶ οὗ λέγει Μωσῆς· «ἐφύτευσεν ὁ θεὸς παράδεισον ἐν Ἐδὲμ κατὰ ἀνατολάς», τουτέστι κατὰ πρόσωπον τῆς Ἐδέμ, ἵνα βλέπῃ τὸν παράδεισον ἡ Ἐδέμ—τουτέστι τοὺς ἀγγέλους—διὰ παντός. 6. τούτου τοῦ παραδείσου ἀλληγορικῶς οἱ ἄγγελοι κέκληνται ξύλα, καὶ ἔστι τὸ ξύλον τῆς ζωῆς ὁ τρίτος τῶν πατρικῶν ἀγγέλων, Βαρούχ, τὸ δὲ ξύλον τοῦ εἰδέναι γνῶσιν καλοῦ καὶ πονηροῦ ὁ τρίτος τῶν μητρικῶν ἀγγέλων, ὁ Νάας. οὕτως γὰρ δέχεται τὰ

erated for himself twelve angels from Eden. These are the names of the Father's angels: Michael, Amen, Baruch, Gabriel, Esaddaios …[388] 4. The names of the Mother's angels, made by Eden, are Babel, Achamoth, Naas, Bel, Belias, Satan, Sael, Adonaios, Kauithan, Pharaoh, Karkamenos, and Lathen.[389] Of the twenty-four angels, the Father's angels assist the Father and do everything according to his will; likewise the Mother's angels do the will of their Mother.

5. Paradise is the combined total of these angels. About paradise Moses says, "God planted a paradise in Eden toward the eastern regions."[390] He means that it was planted toward the face of Eden so that she could view paradise (that is, the angels) at all times.[391] 6. The angels are allegorically referred to as the trees of this paradise.[392] The Tree of Life is Baruch, the third of the Father's angels. The Tree of the Knowledge of Good and Evil is Naas, the third of the Mother's angels.[393] So Justin can interpret Moses's

---

388. The names of seven of the Father's angels are missing; those that remain are Hebrew in origin. Michael and Gabriel are archangels, and their names are frequently applied to various figures in gnostic sources. Michael appears among the Ophites of Iren., *Haer*. 1.30.9, for example, and both Michael and Gabriel appear in the Ophite diagram (Origen, *Cels*. 6.30). For "Amen," see Isa 65:16 (אלהי אמן), translated by Symmachos as ὁ θεὸς Ἀμήν (see also Ap. John [NHC II,1] 16.1). Baruch, meaning "Blessed One," becomes a central character in Justin's story below. "Esaddaios" apparently represents El-Shaddai; cf. "Esaldaios" in *Ref*. 5.7.30 (Naassenes).

389. Achamoth is named after the Hebrew word for wisdom (חכמה) and plays a role in Valentinian mythology (e.g., Iren., *Haer*. 1.4.1; cf. 1 Apoc. Jas. [NHC V,3] 34.3; 35.9; 36.5). Naas means "Snake" (cf. *Ref*. 5.6.3; 5.9.12). For Belias, see Beliar (variants: Belian, Beliab, Belial) in 2 Cor 6:15. He presides over Hades in Ap. John (NHC II,1) 11.3 and Gos. Eg. (NHC III,2) 58.21. Sael is the Hebrew "Sheol." Adonaios (from Heb אדון = "Lord") frequently appears as a lesser archon (e.g., Iren., *Haer*. 1.30.5, 11; Ap. John [NHC II,1] 10.33; Orig. World [NHC II,5] 101.31). Grant asserted that Karkamenos may derive from the Hebrew כרכם ("saffron") and that Kauithan and Lathen are forms of Leviathan (*After*, 201–2). Marcovich notes, "While the great majority of these names are Jewish, Pharaoth is obviously Egyptian, and at least Bel and Babel come from Mesopotamia: Bel is the planet Jupiter (Marduk), and Babel is the planet Venus (= Aphrodite … [*Ref*.] 5.26.20 and 28)" (*Studies*, 99).

390. Gen 2:8 LXX.

391. "Evidently, 'to the face' (κατὰ πρόσωπον) is an interpretation of 'in the east' (κατὰ ἀνατολάς), a reading that presupposes knowledge of the Hebrew word *miqedem*" (Abramowski, "Female Figures," 143).

392. Pss. Sol. 14:3 apparently identifies the trees of life with God's holy ones or angels (ὁ παράδεισος τοῦ κυρίου, τὰ ξύλα τῆς ζωῆς, ὅσιοι αὐτοῦ).

393. An interpretation of Gen 2:9.

Μωσέως ἑρμηνεύειν λέγων· περιεσταλμένως αὐτὰ εἶπεν ὁ Μωϋσῆς διὰ τὸ μὴ πάντας χωρεῖν τὴν ἀλήθειαν.

7. Γενομένου δέ, φησί, τοῦ παραδείσου ἐξ εὐαρεστήσεως κοινῆς <τοῦ> Ἐλωεὶμ καὶ <τῆς> Ἐδέμ, οἱ τοῦ Ἐλωεὶμ ἄγγελοι λαβόντες ἀπὸ τῆς καλλίστης γῆς, τουτέστιν οὐκ ἀπὸ τοῦ θηριώδους μέρους τῆς Ἐδέμ, ἀλλ' ἀπὸ τῶν ὑπὲρ βουβῶνα ἀνθρωποειδῶν καὶ ἡμέρων χωρίων τῆς γῆς, ποιοῦσι τὸν ἄνθρωπον· ἐκ δὲ τῶν θηριωδῶν μερῶν, φησί, γίνονται τὰ θηρία καὶ τὰ λοιπὰ ζῷα. 8. τὸν ἄνθρωπον οὖν ἐποίησαν σύμβολον τῆς ἑνότητος αὐτῶν καὶ εὐνοίας, καὶ κατατίθενται τὰς ἑαυτῶν δυνάμεις εἰς αὐτόν, Ἐδὲμ μὲν τὴν ψυχήν, Ἐλωεὶμ δὲ τὸ πνεῦμα. καὶ γίνεται οἱονεὶ σφραγίς τις αὐτοῖς καὶ φιλίας ὑπόμνημα καὶ σύμβολον αἰώνιον τοῦ γάμου τῆς Ἐδὲμ καὶ τοῦ Ἐλωεὶμ <ὁ> ἄνθρωπος, ὁ Ἀδάμ. 9. ὁμοίως δὲ καὶ ἡ Εὔα γέγονε, φησίν, ὡς παρὰ Μωσεῖ γέγραπται, εἰκὼν καὶ σύμβολον, σφραγὶς εἰς αἰῶνα φυλαχθησομένη τῆς Ἐδέμ, κατετέθη τε ὁμοίως καὶ ἐν τῇ Εὔᾳ τῇ εἰκόνι ψυχὴ μὲν ἀπὸ τῆς Ἐδέμ, πνεῦμα δὲ ἀπὸ τοῦ Ἐλωείμ.

καὶ ἐδόθησαν ἐντολαὶ αὐτοῖς· «αὐξάνεσθε καὶ πληθύνεσθε καὶ κατακληρονομήσατε τὴν γῆν», τουτέστι τὴν Ἐδέμ· οὕτω γὰρ θέλει γεγράφθαι. 10. πᾶσαν γὰρ τὴν ἑαυτῆς δύναμιν, οἱονεί τινα οὐσίαν, ἐν γάμῳ ἡ Ἐδὲμ προσήνεγκε τῷ Ἐλωείμ· ὅθεν, φησί, κατὰ μίμησιν ἐκείνου τοῦ πρώτου γάμου προῖκα προσφέρουσι μέχρι σήμερον αἱ γυναῖκες τοῖς ἀνδράσι, θείῳ τινὶ καὶ πατρικῷ νόμῳ πειθόμεναι, τῷ γενομένῳ πρὸς Ἐλωεὶμ <ἀπὸ> τῆς Ἐδέμ.

words. He claims that Moses spoke these verses covertly because not all people comprehend the truth.

ANTHROPOGONY. 7. When, he says, the paradise came from the mutual pleasure of Elohim and Eden, the angels of Elohim took a portion of the most beautiful earth (that is, not from the bestial parts of Eden, but from the human and cultivated regions of the earth above her groin) and made the human being.[394] From the beastly parts, he says, come the beasts and other animals. 8. Thus Elohim and Eden made the human being as a symbol of their unity and goodwill and invested him with their own powers. Eden gave the soul, and Elohim the spirit.[395] Accordingly, the human being Adam became as it were a seal and reminder of their love and an eternal symbol of the marriage of Eden and Elohim.[396] 9. Likewise, he says, as it is written in Moses, Eve was an image, symbol, and an eternally protected seal of Eden.[397] In Eve, the image, there was also placed a soul from Eden and a spirit from Elohim.

Then commands were bestowed upon them: "Grow and multiply and inherit the earth" (that is, inherit *Eden*, as he glosses it).[398] 10. For in marriage, Eden offered to Elohim all her power, as though it were her property. Hence, he says, women to this day, in imitation of that first marriage, bring a dowry to their husbands, obeying a divine and ancestral custom that Elohim obtained from Eden.[399]

---

394. See Gen 2:7. Cf. *Ref.* 6.14.5 ("Simon"); 6.34.5 ("Valentinus"); Clem. Alex., *Exc.* 50.1. For the angelic creation of human beings, see Iren., *Haer.* 1.24.1 (Satorneilos); 1.30.6 (Ophites); Ap. John (NHC II,1) 15; Nat. Rulers (NHC II,4) 87–88.

395. In Gen 2:7 LXX, God blows breath (πνοή) into Adam so that he becomes a living soul (ψυχὴν ζῶσαν). This verse was variously interpreted (see, e.g., Ap. John [NHC II,1] 19.23–25; Nat. Rulers [NHC II,4] 88.12–15; Apoc. Adam [NHC V,5] 66.20–23).

396. Every human marriage is "an image and symbol of the archetypal, sacred marriage of Elohim and Eden" (van den Broek, "Shape," 40; cf. idem, "Gospel Tradition," 386). Cf. Michael Williams, "Uses of Gender Imagery in Ancient Gnostic Texts," in *Gender and Religion: On the Complexity of Symbols*, ed. Caroline Walker Bynum, Stevan Harrell, and Paula Richman (Boston: Beacon, 1986), 196–227 (203).

397. See further Jorunn Jacobsen Buckley, *Female Fault and Fulfillment in Gnosticism* (Chapel Hill: University of North Carolina Press, 1986), 6.

398. An interpretation of Gen 1:28 LXX, though modified (most significantly, κατακυριεύσατε has been replaced by κατακληρονομήσατε). Cf. Corp. herm. 1.18; *Ref.* 10.31.2.

399. Cf. Pherekydes, DK 7 frag. 2, col. 2.

11. Κτισθέντων δὲ πάντων, ὡς γέγραπται παρὰ τῷ Μωϋσεῖ, οὐρανοῦ τε καὶ γῆς καὶ τῶν ἐν αὐτοῖς, «εἰς τέσσαρας ἀρχὰς» διῃρέθησαν οἱ δώδεκα τῆς μητρὸς ἄγγελοι, καὶ καλεῖται τούτων ἕκαστον τεταρτημόριον ποταμός· Φεισὼν καὶ Γεὼν καὶ Τίγρις καὶ Εὐφράτης, ὥς, φησί, λέγει Μωϋσῆς. οὗτοι ἐμπεριέ<ρ>χονται οἱ δώδεκα ἄγγελοι τὰ τέσσαρα μέρη συμπεριπεπλεγμένοι <ἀλλήλοις> καὶ διέπουσι τὸν κόσμον, σατραπικήν τινα ἔχοντες κατὰ τοῦ κόσμου παρὰ τῆς Ἐδὲμ ἐξουσίαν. 12. μένουσι γὰρ οὐκ ἀεὶ ἐπὶ τῶν τόπων τῶν αὐτῶν, ἀλλ' οἱονεὶ ἐν χορῷ κυκλικῷ ἐμπεριέ<ρ>χονται, ἀλλάσσοντες τόπον ἐκ τόπου καὶ παραχωροῦντες <ἀλλήλοις> ἐν χρόνοις καὶ διαστήμασι τοὺς τόπους <τοὺς> τεταγμένους αὐτοῖς.

ὅταν δὲ ἐπικρατῇ τῶν τόπων ὁ Φεισών, λιμός, στενοχωρία, θλῖψις ἐν ἐκείνῳ τῷ μέρει τῆς γῆς γίνεται· φειδωλὸν γὰρ τὸ παράταγμα τῶν ἀγγέλων τούτων. 13. ὁμοίως καὶ <ἐπὶ> ἑκάστου μέρους τῶν τεσσάρων, κατὰ τὴν ἑκάστου <ποταμοῦ> δύναμιν καὶ φύσιν, κακοὶ καιροὶ καὶ νόσων <συ>στάσεις. καὶ τοῦτο εἰς ἀεὶ κατὰ τὴν ἐπικρά<τη>σιν τῶν τεταρτημορίων ποταμῶν ὡσπερεὶ ῥεῦμα κακίας κατὰ θέλησιν τῆς Ἐδὲμ ἀδιαλείπτως τὸν κόσμον περιέρχεται.

14. Γέγονε δὲ ἡ τῆς κακίας ἀνάγκη ἐκ τοιαύτης τινὸς αἰτίας· κατασκευάσας καὶ δημιουργήσας Ἐλωεὶμ ἐκ κοινῆς εὐαρεστήσεως τὸν κόσμον, ἀναβῆναι ἠθέλησεν εἰς τὰ ὑψηλὰ μέρη τοῦ οὐρανοῦ καὶ θεάσασθαι μή τι γέγονε τῶν κατὰ τὴν κτίσιν ἐνδεές, συμπαραλαβὼν τοὺς ἰδίους ἀγγέλους μεθ' αὐτοῦ—ἦν γὰρ

THE ORIGIN OF PHYSICAL EVIL: THE FOUR RIVERS. 11. When all had been created, as is written in Moses—heaven, earth, and their inhabitants—the twelve angels of the Mother were divided into four kingdoms, and each quadrant they possessed was called a river: Pheisōn, Geōn, Tigris, and Euphrates (as, he states, Moses says).[400] These twelve angels rove around the four quadrants, make close ties with each other, and administer the world. They possess throughout the world the authority of satraps, an authority granted by Eden.[401] 12. They do not always remain in the same places but travel round, as it were, in a cyclical dance, changing places and yielding to each other for set times and intervals the regions assigned to them.[402]

When Pheisōn [Φεισών] dominates regions, in that part of the earth famine, scarcity, and affliction arise, for his company of angels is stingy [φειδωλόν]. 13. Likewise, in each of the four sections, in accordance with the power and nature of each river, hard times and strains of disease arise.[403] This, by the will of Eden, is what unceasingly and for all time encircles the world like a stream of evil, depending upon which of the river quadrants is dominant.[404]

THE ORIGIN OF MORAL EVIL. 14. The necessity of evil emerged from this type of cause. After he outfitted and fashioned the world from their mutual pleasure, Elohim decided to ascend to the heights of heaven and observe their contents, so that there might not be anything deficient among the beings of his creation.[405] So, taking with him his own angels (he was natu-

---

400. Gen 2:10–14 LXX. Cf. the interpretation of the rivers in *Ref.* 5.9.15–17 (Naassenes); 6.15.1 ("Simon").

401. "Chaldean astrology teaches that the twelve signs of the Zodiac are divided into *four trigons* [triangles] … by the construction of four equilateral triangles within the zodiac circle.… Each one of the four quadrants is called a τεταρτημόριον" (Marcovich, *Studies*, 100). For this term, see Ptolemy, *Tetrab.* 1.12; Manilius, *Astron.* 2.273–286.

402. The circular motion of the angels is in fact the motion of the zodiacal signs that influences the twelve climatic zones of the earth (Marcovich, *Studies*, 101).

403. Cf. Plato, *Tim.* 89b.

404. The "stream of evil" (ῥεῦμα κακίας) recalls the astrological image of Draco twisting around the Bears "like the stream of a river" (ποταμοῦ ῥεῦμα) (*Ref.* 4.47.1, paraphrasing Aratos, *Phaen.* 45: οἵη ποταμοῖο ἀπορρώξ ["like a branch of a river"]).

405. Elohim plans to ascend above the firmament (στερέωμα) (*Ref.* 5.27.3). That what is below the στερέωμα has deficiency (ὑστέρησις) was probably not lost on Justin. In other gnostic systems the origin of evil is caused by the *fall* of a deity (e.g., Wisdom

ἀνωφερής—<καὶ> καταλιπὼν τὴν Ἐδὲμ κάτω—γῆ γὰρ οὖσα, ἐπακολουθεῖν ἄνω τῷ συζύγῳ οὐκ ἠθέλησεν.—

15. ἐλθὼν οὖν ὁ Ἐλωεὶμ ἐπὶ τὸ ἄνω πέρας τοῦ οὐρανοῦ καὶ θεασάμενος φῶς κρεῖττον ὑπὲρ ὃ αὐτὸς ἐδημιούργησεν, εἶπεν· «ἀνοίξατέ μοι πύλας, ἵνα εἰσελθὼν ἐξομολογήσωμαι τῷ κυρίῳ»· ἐδόκουν γὰρ ἐγὼ κύριος εἶναι. 16. φωνὴ αὐτῷ ἀπὸ τοῦ φωτὸς ἐδόθη λέγουσα· «αὕτη ἡ πύλη τοῦ κυρίου, δίκαιοι εἰσέρχονται δι' αὐτῆς». καὶ ἀνεῴχθη παραχρῆμα ἡ πύλη, καὶ εἰσῆλθεν ὁ πατὴρ δίχα τῶν ἀγγέλων πρὸς τὸν ἀγαθόν,

καὶ εἶδεν «ἃ ὀφθαλμὸς οὐκ εἶδε καὶ οὖς οὐκ ἤκουσε καὶ ἐπὶ καρδίαν ἀνθρώπου οὐκ ἀνέβη». 17. τότε λέγει αὐτῷ ὁ ἀγαθός· «κάθου ἐκ δεξιῶν μου». ὁ δὲ πατὴρ λέγει πρὸς τὸν ἀγαθόν· ἔασόν με, κύριε, καταστρέψαι τὸν κόσμον ὃν πεποίηκα· τὸ πνεῦμα γάρ μου ἐνδέδεται εἰς τοὺς ἀνθρώπους, καὶ θέλω αὐτὸ ἀπολαβεῖν. 18. τότε λέγει αὐτῷ ὁ ἀγαθός· οὐδὲν δύνασαι κακοποιῆσαι παρ' ἐμοὶ γενόμενος· ἐκ κοινῆς γὰρ εὐαρεστήσεως ἐποιήσατε τὸν κόσμον σύ τε καὶ ἡ Ἐδέμ· ἔασον οὖν τὴν Ἐδὲμ ἔχειν τὴν κτίσιν μέχρι βούλεται, σὺ δὲ μένε παρ' ἐμοί.

19. Τότε γνοῦσα ἡ Ἐδὲμ ὅτι καταλέλειπται ὑπὸ τοῦ Ἐλωείμ, λυπηθεῖσα παρέστησεν αὐτῇ τοὺς ἰδίους ἀγγέλους καὶ εὐπρεπῶς ἐκόσμησεν ἑαυτήν, εἴ πως εἰς ἐπιθυμίαν ἐλθὼν ὁ Ἐλωεὶμ κατέλθῃ πρὸς αὐτήν. 20. ὡς δὲ κρατηθεὶς τῷ ἀγαθῷ ὁ Ἐλωεὶμ [καὶ] οὐκέτι κατῆλθε πρὸς τὴν Ἐδέμ, προσέταξεν ἡ Ἐδὲμ τῇ

rally borne upward), he abandoned Eden below (for as earth, she did not want to accompany her spouse to the upper regions).[406]

15. Elohim came to the highest limit of heaven and there beheld a light greater than what he fashioned. He cried out: "Open for me, gates, so that I might enter and praise the Lord! (for I supposed that I was Lord)."[407] 16. A voice was granted to him from the light. It said: "This is the gate of the Lord; the righteous enter through it!"[408] Immediately the gate was opened, and the Father entered, without his angels, toward the Good.

Then he saw "what eye has not seen, nor ear heard, nor has it risen in the human heart."[409] 17. At that time, the Good said to him, "Sit at my right hand!"[410] But the Father said to the Good: "Permit me, Lord, to overturn the world that I made, for my spirit is bound within human beings, and I want it back."[411] 18. Then the Good said to him, "You can do nothing harmful now that you are beside me, for from mutual pleasure you and Eden made the world. So let Eden have the creation as long as she wants. But you, remain by me."[412]

19. When Eden realized that she had been abandoned by Elohim, she was distraught. She stationed her own angels by her side and attractively adorned herself, in case Elohim should descend to her in desire. 20. But since Elohim, held fast by the Good, no longer descended to Eden, Eden

---

in Valentinianism). For Justin, however, evil is the result of a deity's *ascent*. See further Williams, "Uses of Gender," 202.

406. Elohim can rise since he is a pneumatic being, and pneuma is ἀνωφερής (cf. *Ref.* 4.43.8; Plutarch, *Stoic. rep.* 1053e).

407. Elohim's words are adapted from Ps 117:19 LXX, with the possible resonance of Ps 23:7 LXX. Cf. Clem. Alex., *Strom.* 1.7.38.5; 6.5.42.2. Ἐδόκουν ("I supposed [that I was Lord]") indicates a more humble—or dopey—attitude in contrast to the arrogance of the demiurge in other gnostic sources (e.g., Iren., *Haer.* 1.30.6). See further Manlio Simonetti, "Note sul Libro di Baruch dello gnostico Giustino," *Vetera Christianorum* 6 (1969): 71–89 (76–77).

408. Ps 117:20 LXX.

409. See the note on this saying in *Ref.* 5.24.1.

410. Ps 109:1 LXX; cf. *Ref.* 7.23.6 ("Basileides"). In early Christian texts, the statement is applied to Christ in his exaltation (Matt 22:44 par.; Barn. 12.10; 1 Clem. 36.5; Clem. Alex., *Exc.* 62.1).

411. Cf. the language of Deut 9:14 LXX: "Permit me to destroy them" (ἔασόν με ἐξολεθρεῦσαι αὐτούς). For the πνεῦμα among human beings, see Gen 6:3 LXX: "My spirit [τὸ πνεῦμά μου] shall certainly not abide among human beings." Plato was wont to say that the soul was "bound within" (ἐνδέω) the body (e.g., *Phaed.* 81d; 91e; *Tim.* 43a).

412. Cf. Deut 5:31 (God asks Moses to remain). The "Good" is surprisingly indifferent toward human beings.

Βάβελ—ἥτις ἐστὶν Ἀφροδίτη—μοιχείας καὶ χωρισμοὺς γάμων κατασκευάσαι ἐν ἀνθρώποις, ἵνα ὡς αὐτὴ κεχώρισται ἀπὸ τοῦ Ἐλωείμ, οὕτω καὶ τὸ <πνεῦμα> τοῦ Ἐλωεὶμ τὸ ὂν ἐν τοῖς ἀνθρώποις τοῖς χωρισμοῖς τοῖς τοιούτοις βασανίζηται λυπούμενον καὶ πάσχῃ τὰ αὐτὰ ὁποῖα καὶ ἡ Ἐδὲμ καταλελειμμένη.

21. καὶ δίδωσιν ἐξουσίαν ἡ Ἐδὲμ μεγάλην τῷ τρίτῳ ἀγγέλῳ αὐτῆς, τῷ Νάας, ἵνα πάσαις κολάσεσι κολάζῃ τὸ πνεῦμα τοῦ Ἐλωεὶμ τὸ ὂν ἐν τοῖς ἀνθρώποις, ἵνα διὰ τοῦ πνεύματος ᾖ κολαζόμενος ὁ Ἐλωείμ, ὁ καταλιπὼν παρὰ τὰς συνθήκας τὰς γενομένας αὐτῷ τὴν σύζυγον.

Ἰδὼν ταῦτα ὁ πατὴρ Ἐλωείμ, ἐκπέμπει τὸν Βαρούχ, τὸν τρίτον ἄγγελον τῶν ἑαυτοῦ, εἰς βοήθειαν τῷ πνεύματι, τῷ ὄντι ἐν τοῖς ἀνθρώποις πᾶσιν. 22. ἐλθὼν οὖν ὁ Βαροὺχ ἔστη ἐν μέσῳ τῶν ἀγγέλων τῆς Ἐδέμ—τουτέστιν ἐν μέσῳ τοῦ παραδείσου· παράδεισος γὰρ οἱ ἄγγελοι, ὧν μέσος ἔστη—καὶ παρήγγειλε τῷ ἀνθρώπῳ «ἀπὸ παντὸς ξύλου τοῦ ἐν τῷ παραδείσῳ βρώσει φαγεῖν, ἀπὸ δὲ τοῦ <ξύλου τοῦ> γινώσκειν τὸ καλὸν καὶ τὸ πονηρὸν μὴ φαγεῖν», ὅπερ ἐστὶν ὁ Νάας· τουτέστι τοῖς μὲν ἄλλοις ἀγγέλοις πείθεσθαι, τοῖς ἕνδεκα τῆς Ἐδέμ, <τῷ δὲ Νάας οὐκέτι.> πάθη μὲν γὰρ ἔχουσιν οἱ ἕνδεκα, παρανομίαν δὲ οὐκ ἔχουσιν, ὁ δὲ Νάας παρανομίαν ἔσχε· 23. προσῆλθε γὰρ τῇ Εὔᾳ ἐξαπατήσας αὐτὴν καὶ ἐμοίχευσεν αὐτήν, ὅπερ ἐστὶ παράνομον· προσῆλθε δὲ καὶ τῷ Ἀδὰμ καὶ ἔσχεν αὐτὸν ὡς παιδ<ικ>ά, ὅπερ ἐστὶ καὶ αὐτὸ παράνομον. ἔνθεν γέγονε μοιχεία καὶ ἀρσενοκοιτία.

ἀπὸ τότε ἐπεκράτησε τὰ κακὰ τοῖς ἀνθρώποις καὶ τὰ ἀγαθά, ἐκ μιᾶς ἀρχῆς γενόμενα, τῆς τοῦ πατρός· 24. ἀναβὰς γὰρ πρὸς τὸν ἀγαθὸν ὁ πατὴρ ὁδὸν ἔδειξε τοῖς ἀναβαίνειν θέλουσιν, ἀποστὰς δὲ τῆς Ἐδὲμ ἀρχὴν κακῶν ἐποίησε τῷ πνεύματι [τοῦ πατρὸς] τῷ ἐν τοῖς ἀνθρώποις.

Ἐπέμφθη οὖν ὁ Βαροὺχ πρὸς τὸν Μωσέα καὶ δι' αὐτοῦ ἐλάλησε τοῖς υἱοῖς Ἰσραήλ, ὅπως ἐπιστραφῶσι πρὸς τὸν ἀγαθόν. 25. ὁ δὲ τρίτος <ἄγγελος τῆς Ἐδέμ,> ὁ <Νάας>, διὰ τῆς ψυχῆς ἀπὸ τῆς Ἐδέμ, οἰκούσης εἰς τὸν Μωσέα ὥσπερ καὶ εἰς πάντας ἀνθρώπους, τὰς ἐντολὰς τοῦ Βαροὺχ ἐπεσκίασε καὶ τὰς ἰδίας ἐποίησεν ἀκούεσθαι. διὰ τοῦτο ἡ ψυχὴ κατὰ τοῦ πνεύματος τέτακται

ordered Babel (who is Aphrodite) to contrive adulteries and divorces among human beings, so that, just as she was separated from Elohim, so the spirit of Elohim in humans might be tortured by such separations, become distraught, and suffer the same pains as Eden when she was abandoned.[413]

21. Then Eden gave great authority to her third angel Naas to punish with every punishment the spirit of Elohim in humans so that through his spirit Elohim might be punished for abandoning his spouse in violation of the covenants that he had made.[414]

SALVATION: THE MISSION OF BARUCH. When Elohim witnessed these events, he sent his own third angel, Baruch, to help his spirit in all humans. 22. When Baruch arrived, he took his stand in the midst of Eden's angels (that is, in the midst of paradise—for "paradise" signifies the angels in whose midst he stood) and commanded the human: "Eat from every tree in paradise, but do not eat from the Tree of the Knowledge of Good and Evil (that is, Naas)."[415] This means, obey the other eleven angels of Eden, but no longer obey Naas.[416] He ordered this because the eleven possess violent emotions, but not lawlessness. Naas, by contrast, possessed lawlessness. 23. Accordingly, Naas approached Eve, deceived her, and committed adultery with her—a lawless act. He approached Adam too and treated him as his young lover—which is lawless in itself. From these origins came adultery and male sex with a passive male partner.

From this time on, vices and virtues took hold of human beings. Both have a single source—the Father. 24. For when he ascended to the Good, the Father showed the way for those willing to rise, but when he separated from Eden, he initiated troubles for the spirit in human beings.

Thus Baruch was sent to Moses, and through Moses he spoke to the children of Israel, telling them how to convert to the Good.[417] 25. But the third angel of Eden, Naas, by means of the soul from Eden dwelling in Moses and in all humans, obscured Baruch's commands and made his own be heard. For this reason, the soul is arrayed against the spirit, and the

---

413. Duncker and Schneidewin add πνεῦμα ("spirit") to this sentence.

414. For "great authority" (ἐξουσίαν μεγάλην), see Rev 13:2. The tragedy of this story is acute. Humans are afflicted for a wrong that they did not commit or even know about.

415. Baruch, the Tree of Life, stands in the midst of paradise (Gen 2:9) and speaks the command of Gen 2:16–17.

416. Marcovich adds τῷ δὲ Νάας οὐκέτι ("but no longer [obey] Naas").

417. Cf. Gal 3:19, the law "ordained by angels" (διαταγεὶς δι' ἀγγέλων).

καὶ τὸ πνεῦμα κατὰ τῆς ψυχῆς· ἡ μὲν γὰρ ψυχή ἐστιν Ἐδέμ, τὸ δὲ πνεῦμα Ἐλωείμ, ἑκάτερα ὄντα ἐν πᾶσιν ἀνθρώποις, καὶ θήλεσι καὶ ἄρρεσι.

26. πάλιν μετὰ ταῦτα ἐπέμφθη ἐπὶ τοὺς προφήτας ὁ Βαρούχ, ἵνα διὰ τῶν προφητῶν ἀκούσῃ τὸ πνεῦμα τὸ ἐν τοῖς ἀνθρώποις κατοικοῦν καὶ φύγῃ τὴν Ἐδὲμ καὶ τὴν πλάσιν τὴν πονηράν, ὥσπερ ἔφυγεν ὁ πατὴρ Ἐλωείμ. ὁμοίως καὶ [διὰ τῶν προφητῶν] τῇ αὐτῇ ἐπινοίᾳ ὁ Νάας διὰ τῆς ψυχῆς τῆς ἐνοικούσης ἐν τῷ ἀνθρώπῳ σὺν τῷ πνεύματι τοῦ πατρὸς ὑπέσυρε τοὺς προφήτας, καὶ ὑπεσύρησαν πάντες καὶ οὐκ ἠκολούθησαν οἱ λόγοι τοῦ Βαρούχ, οὓς ἐνετείλατο Ἐλωείμ.

27. Τὸ τελευταῖον ἐξ ἀκροβυστίας προφήτην ἐπελέξατο Ἐλωεὶμ τὸν Ἡρακλέα καὶ ἔπεμψεν, ἵνα τοὺς δώδεκα ἀγγέλους τῆς Ἐδὲμ καταγωνίσηται καὶ ἐλευθερώσῃ <τὸ πνεῦμα> τοῦ πατρὸς ἀπὸ τῶν δώδεκα ἀγγέλων τῆς κτίσεως τῶν πονηρῶν. ταῦτα <δ'> ἔστι τὰ δώδεκα ἆθλα τοῦ Ἡρακλέους, ἃ κατηγωνίσατο ὁ Ἡρακλῆς τῇ τάξει ἀπὸ τοῦ πρώτου ἕως <τοῦ> ἐσχάτου, λέοντα καὶ ὕδραν καὶ κάπρον καὶ τὰ ἑξῆς. 28. τῶν ἐθνῶν γὰρ εἶναι ταῦτα τὰ ὀνόματά ἃ μετωνόμασται, φασιν, ἀπὸ τῆς ἐνεργείας τῶν μητρικῶν ἀγγέλων.

ὡς ἐδόκει κατηγωνίσθαι, προσπλέκεται αὐτῷ ἡ Ὀμφάλη—ἥτις ἐστὶ Βάβελ, ἣ <καὶ> Ἀφροδίτη—, καὶ ὑποσύρει τὸν Ἡρακλέα καὶ ἀποδιδύσκει τὴν δύναμιν αὐτοῦ—<τουτέστι> τὰς ἐντολὰς τοῦ Βαρούχ, ἃς ἐνετείλατο Ἐλωείμ—, καὶ μετενδιδύσκει τὴν ἰδίαν αὐτῆς στολήν—τουτέστι τὴν δύναμιν τῆς Ἐδέμ, τῆς κάτω δυνάμεως—, καὶ οὕτως ἀτελὴς ἐγένετο τοῦ Ἡρακλέους ἡ προφητεία καὶ τὰ ἔργα αὐτοῦ.

spirit against the soul.[418] The soul is Eden, the spirit is Elohim, and each is in all people, female and male alike.[419]

26. After these events, Baruch was again sent to the prophets so that through the prophets the spirit might hear and flee Eden and the evil physical formation, just as Father Elohim fled. But in the same way and with the same design, Naas seduced the prophets through the soul that indwells humanity along with the Father's spirit. He seduced all people, so that Baruch's words, the commands of Elohim, were not obeyed.

THE PROPHET HERAKLES. 27. At last, Elohim chose a prophet from the uncircumcised—Herakles.[420] He sent him to contend against the twelve angels of Eden and free the spirit of the Father from the twelve evil angels of creation.[421] They are signified by the twelve labors of Herakles, which he successfully accomplished in order from first to last—the lion, the hydra, the wild boar, and so on. 28. (These names are in use among the Gentiles, recoined, they say, from the operations of the Mother's angels.)[422]

But when Herakles thought that he had prevailed, Omphale (that is, Babel, aka Aphrodite) attached herself to him, seduced him, and stripped him of his power (that is, the command that Elohim had transmitted to Baruch).[423] Herakles, instead, put on her own personal attire (that is, the power of Eden, the power below). And so the prophecy and works of Herakles came to no effect.[424]

---

418. The sentence resembles the language of Gal 5:17 and the content of 1 Cor 2:14; cf. Clem. Alex., *Strom.* 6.16.134.1; 6.16.136.2.

419. We might also translate: "For the soul is *of* Eden, the spirit *of* Elohim."

420. Marcovich believes that Elohim chose Herakles because "the Greeks had called the constellation Engonasin [Kneeler] Heracles, and the Gnostics identified it with Adam" (*Studies*, 110, italics removed). Grant pointed out that the monsters Herakles fought were mostly offspring of Typhon and Echidna (Hesiod, *Theog.* 306, 327–328). Epimenides, Grant observed, is a similar "pagan prophet" in Titus 1:12, and Theophilos (*Autol.* 2.36) considered the Sibyl to be a prophetess for the Greeks (*After*, 200 n. 14).

421. Marcovich changes P's τὸν πατέρα to τὸ πνεῦμα τοῦ πατρός ("the spirit of the Father"). (Presumably the Father himself does not need to be freed from the angels.) The violence in this scene may be an interpretation of Gen 1:28: "subdue the earth."

422. Cf. Clem. Alex., *Strom.* 5.14.103.5.

423. That Herakles was stripped of his power is reminiscent of Samson, who loses his power at the hands of Delilah (Judg 16). The myths of Jews and Greeks are being read together.

424. Herakles dons the female garb of Omphale (Ps.-Apollodoros, *Bibl.* 2.6.3;

29. Τὸ δὲ τελευταῖον «ἐν ταῖς ἡμέραις Ἡρώδου τοῦ βασιλέως» πέμπεται ὁ Βαρούχ—καταπεμφθεὶς πάλιν ὑπὸ τοῦ Ἐλωείμ·—καὶ ἐλθὼν εἰς Ναζαρὲτ εὗρε τὸν Ἰησοῦν, υἱὸν τοῦ Ἰωσὴφ καὶ Μαρίας, βόσκοντα πρόβατα παιδάριον δυωδεκαετές, καὶ ἀναγγέλλει αὐτῷ πάντα ὅσα ἀπ' ἀρχῆς ἐγένετο, ἀπὸ τῆς Ἐδὲμ καὶ τοῦ Ἐλωεὶμ <καὶ τὰ> μετὰ ταῦτα <γενόμενα>. 30. καὶ εἶπε· πάντες οἱ πρὸ σοῦ προφῆται ὑπεσύρησαν· πειράθητι οὖν, Ἰησοῦ, υἱὲ ἀνθρώπου, μὴ ὑποσυρῆναι, ἀλλὰ κήρυξον τοῦτον τὸν λόγον τοῖς ἀνθρώποις καὶ ἀνάγγειλον αὐτοῖς τὰ περὶ τοῦ πατρὸς καὶ τὰ περὶ τοῦ ἀγαθοῦ, καὶ ἀνάβαινε πρὸς τὸν ἀγαθὸν καὶ κάθου ἐκεῖ μετὰ τοῦ πάντων ἡμῶν πατρὸς Ἐλωείμ. 31. καὶ ὑπήκουσε τῷ ἀγγέλῳ ὁ Ἰησοῦς εἰπὼν ὅτι· κύριε, ποιήσω πάντα, καὶ ἐκήρυξεν.

ὑποσῦραι οὖν ὁ Νάας καὶ τοῦτον ἠθέλησε<ν, οὐκ ἠδυνήθη δέ>· πιστὸς γὰρ ἔμεινε τῷ Βαρούχ. ὀργισθεὶς οὖν ὁ Νάας ὅτι αὐτὸν ὑποσῦραι οὐκ ἠδυνήθη, ἐποίησεν αὐτὸν σταυρωθῆναι. ὁ δὲ καταλιπὼν τὸ σῶμα τῆς Ἐδὲμ πρὸς τὸ ξύλον ἀνέβη πρὸς τὸν ἀγαθόν· 32. εἰπὼν γὰρ τῇ Ἐδέμ· γύναι, ἀπέχεις σου τὸν υἱόν—τουτέστιν τὸν ψυχικὸν ἄνθρωπον καὶ τὸν χοϊκόν—, αὐτὸς δὲ εἰς χεῖρας παραθέμενος τοῦ πατρὸς τὸ πνεῦμα, ἀνῆλθε πρὸς τὸν ἀγαθόν.

JESUS. 29. Finally, in the days of King Herod, Baruch was sent (again, as an envoy of Elohim) and came to Nazareth.[425] There he found Jesus son of Joseph and Mary, a twelve-year-old boy tending sheep.[426] Baruch proclaimed to him everything that had happened from the beginning, starting from the time of Eden and Elohim as well as the ensuing events.[427] 30. He declared: "All the prophets before you were seduced.[428] Test yourself, then, Jesus, O human being, that you not be seduced.[429] Rather, preach this message to humans, and proclaim to them the story of the Father and of the Good. Then ascend to the Good, and sit there with all of us along with the Father of us all, Elohim." 31. Jesus obeyed the angel. He replied, "Sir, I will do all"—and so he preached.[430]

Naas wanted to seduce Jesus too but could not, for he remained faithful to Baruch.[431] Enraged because he could not seduce him, he caused him to be crucified. But Jesus, abandoning the body of Eden on the cross, ascended to the Good. 32. For he said to Eden: "Woman, have back your son" (that is, the animate and earthly human), but he entrusted his spirit into the hands of his Father and rose to the Good.[432]

Ovid, *Fasti* 2.319–326; [Seneca], *Oet.* 371–377). Cf. Omphale among the Peratai (*Ref.* 5.14.8).

425. Cf. the language of Matt 2:1 ("days of Herod"); Luke 1:26 ("Nazareth"); Gos. Eb. frag. 1 (*NTApoc* 1:169). The Naassenes also referred to the "times of Herod" (*Ref.* 5.16.10). See further van den Broek, "Gospel Tradition," 374–75.

426. Cf. Moses in Exod 3:1 and David in 1 Sam 16:11; 17:15 (both of whom tend sheep before being called). Jesus is also twelve in the temple scene of Luke 2:42. According to Josephus, Samuel began to prophecy at age twelve (*Ant.* 5.348). See further van den Broek, "Gospel Tradition," 375–77.

427. Marcovich replaces P's ἐσόμενα with γενόμενα (here: "[the ensuing] events").

428. Cf. the language of John 10:8 (all who come before Jesus are thieves and brigands), a verse appealed to in *Ref.* 6.35.1 ("Valentinus"). See further van den Broek, "Gospel Tradition," 377–78.

429. Cf. Jesus's frequent self-designation in the Gospels: ὁ υἱὸς τοῦ ἀνθρώπου ("the son of the human"). Ezekiel is also referred to as Υἱὲ ἀνθρώπου ("son of a human") (Ezek 2:1–8; 3:4–11).

430. Cf. Mary's humble response to the angel in Luke 1:38.

431. Marcovich adds οὐκ ἠδυνήθη δέ ("but could not").

432. Cf. Jesus's words from the cross in John 19:26 ("Woman, behold your son"). For the release of the spirit, see Luke 23:46: "Into your hands I commend my spirit [πνεῦμα]." Jesus is now "a pure pneumatic man.… Probably … seated at the right hand of the Good One" (Marcovich, *Studies*, 113–14).

Ὁ δὲ ἀγαθός ἐστι Πρίαπος, ὁ πρίν τι εἶναι ποιήσας· διὰ τοῦτο καλεῖται Πρίαπος, ὅτι ἐπριοποίησε τὰ πάντα. 33. διὰ τοῦτο, φησίν, εἰς πάντα ναὸν ἵσταται καὶ ἐν ταῖς ὁδοῖς, ὑπὸ πάσης τῆς κτίσεως τιμώμενος, βαστάζων τὰς ὀπώρας ἐπάνω αὐτοῦ, τουτέστι τοὺς καρποὺς τῆς κτίσεως, ὧν αἴτιος ἐγένετο πριοποιήσας τὴν κτίσιν πρότ<ερ>ον οὐκ οὖσαν.

34. ὅταν οὖν, φησίν, ἀκούσητε λεγόντων ἀνθρώπων ὅτι κύκνος ἐπὶ τὴν Λήδαν ἦλθε καὶ ἐτεκνοποίησεν ἐξ αὐτῆς, ὁ κύκνος ἐστὶν ὁ Ἐλωεὶμ καὶ ἡ Λήδα ἡ Ἐδέμ. καὶ ὅταν λέγωσιν οἱ ἄνθρωποι ὅτι ἀετὸς ἦλθεν ἐπὶ τὸν Γανυμήδην, ὁ ἀετός ἐστιν ὁ Νάας, ὁ δὲ Γανυμήδης ὁ Ἀδάμ. 35. καὶ ὅταν λέγωσιν ὅτι ὁ χρυσὸς ἦλθεν ἐπὶ τὴν Δανάην καὶ ἐπαιδοποίησεν ἐξ αὐτῆς, ὁ χρυσός ἐστιν ὁ Ἐλωείμ, Δανάη δέ ἐστιν ἡ Ἐδέμ. Ὁμοίως δὲ κατὰ τὸν αὐτὸν τρόπον πάντας τοὺς τοιούτους λόγους, μύθοις ἐμφερ<εῖς> ὄντας, παρατιθέμενοι διδάσκουσιν.

36. ὅταν οὖν προφήτης λέγῃ·

ἄκουε, οὐρανέ, καὶ ἐνωτίζου, ἡ γῆ· κύριος ἐλάλησεν,

οὐρανὸν λέγει, φησί, τὸ πνεῦμα τὸ ἐν τῷ ἀνθρώπῳ τὸ τοῦ Ἐλωείμ, γῆν δὲ τὴν ψυχὴν τὴν ἐν τῷ ἀνθρώπῳ σὺν τῷ πνεύματι, κύριον δὲ τὸν Βαρούχ. 37. Ἰσραὴλ δὲ τὴν Ἐδὲμ—Ἐδὲμ γὰρ λέγεται καὶ Ἰσραήλ, ἡ σύζυγος τοῦ Ἐλωείμ. «οὐκ ἔγνω με», φησίν, «Ἰσραήλ»·—εἰ γὰρ ἐγνώκει ὅτι πρὸς τῷ ἀγαθῷ εἰμι,

THE GOOD AS PRIAPOS. Now the Good is Priapos, who acted as Maker before anything existed. This is why he is called Priapos, because he "preproduced" everything.[433] 33. For this reason, he says, Priapos is erected at every shrine, honored by all creation even on highways, bearing the summer fruits (that is, the fruits of creation) up in front of himself. He is their cause because he "preproduced" the creation that previously did not exist.[434]

SUPPORT FROM GREEK LEGEND AND JEWISH PROPHECY. 34. Now, Justin continues, when you hear people say that a swan came to Leda and produced children from her, the swan signifies Elohim, and Leda refers to Eden. And when people say that an eagle came to Ganymede, the eagle is a reference to Naas, and Ganymede is Adam. 35. And when they say that golden rain came to Danae and produced a son from her, the gold signifies Elohim, and Danae refers to Eden. Likewise and by the same method, they teach by lining up all such mythical stories.

36. Now when the prophets say,

> Hear, O heaven, and give ear, O earth. The Lord has spoken!

"heaven" signifies Elohim's spirit in humanity, "earth" refers to the soul in humanity (paired with the spirit), and the "Lord" refers to Baruch.[435] 37. "Israel" is Eden, for Eden, the spouse of Elohim, means "Israel." "Israel has not known me," he says, "for if she had known that I am with the Good, she

---

433. Here ἐπριοποίησε is apparently taken as a form of προποιέω. Justin, Marcovich believes, is referring to "the pre-creation of this world in the mind of the extra-cosmic supreme Good One" (*Studies*, 117). It is ironic that, given Justin's rigorous sexual ethics, he would view the ultimate Good as Priapos.

434. The Naassene writer made his supreme principle the Good (*Ref.* 5.7.26), while simultaneously seeing ithyphallic herms as his manifestation (5.7.27–29) (Marcovich, *Studies*, 115). Maurice Olender cites *CIL* XIV. 3565, where Priapos is called *genitor … auctor orbis aut physis ipsa* ("originator … [and] author of the world or nature itself") ("Éléments pour une analyse de Priape chez Justin le Gnostique," in *Hommages à Maarten J. Vermaseren*, ed. Margreet B. de Boer and T. A. Edridge, 3 vols., ÉPRO 68 [Leiden: Brill, 1978], 2:874–97 [881–83]). Yet the authenticity of this inscription is in question.

435. An interpretation of Isa 1:2 LXX. The verse is allegorized differently by "Simon" in *Ref.* 6.13.1, as well as by Clement of Alexandria in *Strom.* 4.26.169.1.

οὐκ ἂν ἐκόλαζε τὸ πνεῦμά τὸ ἐν τοῖς ἀνθρώποις διὰ τὴν πατρικὴν ἄγνοιαν <ἐνδεθέν>.

27. 1. Γέγραπται δὲ καὶ ὅρκος ἐν τῷ πρώτῳ βιβλίῳ τῷ ἐπιγραφομένῳ Βαρούχ, ὃν ὁρκίζουσι τοὺς κατακούειν μέλλοντας τούτων τῶν μυστηρίων καὶ τελεῖσθαι [παρὰ] τῷ ἀγαθῷ. ὃν ὅρκον, φησίν, ὤμοσεν ὁ πατὴρ ἡμῶν Ἐλωεὶμ παρὰ τῷ ἀγαθῷ γενόμενος καὶ οὐ μετεμελήθη ὀμόσας· περὶ οὗ γέγραπτα(ι), φησίν· «ὤμοσε κύριος καὶ οὐ μεταμεληθήσεται». 2. ἔστι δὲ ὁ ὅρκος οὗτος·

> ὀμνύω τὸν ἐπάνω πάντων, τὸν ἀγαθόν, τηρῆσαι τὰ μυστήρια ταῦτα καὶ ἐξειπεῖν μηδενί, μηδὲ ἀνακάμψαι ἀπὸ τοῦ ἀγαθοῦ ἐπὶ τὴν κτίσιν.

ἐπειδὰν δὲ ὀμόσῃ τοῦτον τὸν ὅρκον, εἰσέρχεται πρὸς τὸν ἀγαθὸν καὶ βλέπει «ὅσα ὀφθαλμὸς οὐκ εἶδε καὶ οὖς οὐκ ἤκουσε καὶ ἐπὶ καρδίαν ἀνθρώπου οὐκ ἀνέβη», καὶ πίνει ἀπὸ «τοῦ ζῶντος ὕδατος», ὅπερ ἐστὶ λουτρὸν αὐτοῖς, ὡς νομίζουσι, «πηγὴ ζῶντος ὕδατος ἀλλομένου». 3. διακεχώρισται γάρ, φησίν, ἀνὰ μέσον ὕδατος καὶ ὕδατος, καὶ ἔστιν ὕδωρ τὸ ὑποκάτω τοῦ στερεώματος τῆς πονηρᾶς κτίσεως, ἐν ᾧ λούονται οἱ χοϊκοὶ καὶ ψυχικοὶ ἄνθρωποι, καὶ ὕδωρ ἐστὶν <τὸ> ὑπεράνω τοῦ στερεώματος τοῦ ἀγαθοῦ, ζῶν <ὄν>, ἐν ᾧ λούονται οἱ πνευματικοὶ ζῶντες ἄνθρωποι, <καὶ> ἐν ᾧ ἐλούσατο Ἐλωεὶμ καὶ λουσάμενος οὐ μετεμελήθη. 4. καὶ ὅταν λέγῃ, φησίν, ὁ προφήτης·

> λαβεῖν ἑαυτῷ γυναῖκα πορνείας, διότι πορνεύουσα ἐκπορνεύσει ἡ γῆ ἀπὸ ὄπισθε τοῦ κυρίου

would not have punished my spirit," which is bound in humans on account of their Father's ignorance.[436]

JUSTIN'S OATH. 27. 1. There is also written an oath in the first book entitled *Baruch*, which they make those about to hear these mysteries and become initiated into the Good swear. This oath, Justin claims, "our Father Elohim" swore when he arrived beside the Good. He swore and did not repent of this oath. The scriptures refer to this, he claims, in the verse: "The Lord swore and will not repent."[437] 2. This is the oath:

> I swear by the one over all things, the Good, to keep these mysteries and to tell them to no one, nor will I backslide away from the Good toward creation.

Whenever one swears this oath, one comes to the Good and sees "what eye has not seen, nor ear heard, nor has it risen in the human heart,"[438] and drinks from "living water" (which refers to their baptismal bath), which they suppose to be a fount of "living, bubbling water."[439] 3. There was made a division, he explains, between water and water so that there is a water of the evil creation below the firmament, in which the earthly and animate are washed, and a water of the Good above the firmament.[440] This water is living, and in it are washed the living spiritual humans. In it Elohim washed himself. When he washed, he did not repent. 4. Moreover, when, he claims, the prophet says:

> Take to yourself a wife of sexual immorality because the land has committed vile sexual immorality from before the face of the Lord.[441]

---

436. An interpretation of Isa 1:3 LXX via a gloss (apparently put into the mouth of Elohim). Marcovich replaces P's ἐντεῦθεν with ἐνδεθέν ("bound"). Cf. the interpretation of Isa 1:3 in Iren., *Haer.* 1.19.1 (Markosians); Justin, *1 Apol.* 37.1; 63.2, 12; Clem. Alex., *Strom.* 5.8.54.1.

437. Ps 109:4 LXX.

438. See the note on this saying in *Ref.* 5.24.1 (Justin).

439. John 4:10 (ὕδωρ ζῶν), 14 (πηγὴ ὕδατος ἁλλομένου εἰς ζωὴν αἰώνιον); cf. *Ref.* 5.7.19; 5.9.18 (Naassenes); 5.19.21 ("Sethians"); Philo, *Post.* 129.

440. Cf. Gen 1:6–7. The employment of water as a symbol is common to the systems in book 5. Justin was able to distinguish between a positive and negative valence of water on biblical grounds. Cf. the water above the firmament in *Ref.* 5.9.18 (Naassenes).

441. Hos 1:2 LXX.

τουτέστιν ἡ Ἐδὲμ ἀπὸ τοῦ Ἐλωείμ. ἐν τούτοις, φησίν, ὁ προφήτης σαφῶς λαλεῖ τὸ ὅλον μυστήριον, καὶ οὐκ ἀκούεται διὰ τὴν κακίαν τοῦ Νάας.

5. Κατὰ τὸν αὐτὸν ἐκεῖνον τρόπον καὶ τὰς ἄλλας προφητικὰς <γραφὰς> ὁμοίως παραδιδοῦσι διὰ πλειόνων βιβλίων· ἔστι δὲ αὐτοῖς προηγουμένως βιβλίον ἐπιγραφόμενον Βαρούχ, ἐν ᾧ ὅλην τὴν τοῦ μύθου αὐτῶν διαγωγὴν ὁ ἐντυχὼν γνώσεται.

πολλαῖς μὲν οὖν αἱρέσεσιν ἐντυχών, ἀγαπητοί, οὐδενὶ τούτου κακῷ χείρονι ἐνέτυχον. 6. ἀληθῶς δέ, ὥσπερ λέγει οἰκειότατα, τὸν αὐτοῦ Ἡρακλέα δεῖ μιμησαμένους ἐκκαθᾶραι τὴν Αὐγείου κόπρον, μᾶλλον δὲ ἀμάραν, εἰς ἣν ἐμπεσόντες οἱ τούτου ἀνεχόμενοι οὐ πώποτε ἀποπλυθήσονται, ἀλλ᾽ οὐδὲ ἀνακύψαι δυνήσονται.

28. 1. Ἐπεὶ γοῦν καὶ τὰ Ἰουστίνου τοῦ ψευδογνωστικοῦ ἐπιχειρήματα ἐξεθέμεθα, δοκεῖ καὶ τὰς τῶν ἀκολούθων αἱρετικῶν δόξας ἐν ταῖς ἑξῆς βίβλοις ἐκθέσθαι μηδένα τε καταλιπεῖν ἀνέλε<γ>κτον αὐτῶν, τῶν ὑπ᾽ αὐτῶν λεγομένων παρατιθεμένων ὄντων ἱκανῶν πρὸς παραδειγματισμόν, εἰ καὶ μόνον ἐκκριθείη τὰ ἀπόκρυφα παρ᾽ αὐτοῖς καὶ ἄρρητα, ἃ μόλις μετὰ πολλοῦ πόνου μυο<ῦ>νται οἱ ἄφρονες.

ἴδωμεν οὖν τί καὶ Σίμων λέγει.

This means that Eden has acted in a sexually immoral way before Elohim. In these words, he claims, the prophet clearly utters the whole mystery, yet it is not heard due to the treachery of Naas.[442]

5. In the same way, they also transmit the prophetic writings in a spate of books. Primarily they have a book entitled *Baruch* in which the reader will come to know the manner of their myth.

Although I have encountered many heresies, beloved, I have encountered no evil worse than this one. 6. But truly, as Justin quite rightly says, we must imitate his Herakles and clear out the dung of Augeias—or rather the sewer into which his votaries have fallen.[443] They will never be washed; indeed, they cannot even emerge.

CONCLUSION

28. 1. Now, since I have also presented the arguments of the pseudo-gnostic Justin, it is fitting also to present the views of the heresies that follow him in the succeeding books, and not leave any of them unexposed. Their own words, when compared, are sufficient to publicly shame them—even if the result is only that their hidden and secret doctrines are culled out. Into such secrets, these dimwits are barely initiated after great toil!

Let us see, then, what Simon, too, has to say.

---

442. Cf. Clem. Alex., *Ecl.* 3.2; Iren., *Haer.* 4.20.12.

443. As elsewhere, our author uses a story from Greek mythological lore and turns it against his heretical opponents. Cf. his hydra example in *Ref.* 5.11.1.

<ΤΟΥ ΚΑΤΑ ΠΑΣΩΝ ΑΙΡΕΣΕΩΝ ΕΛΕΓΧΟΥ Ϛ>

1. Τάδε ἔνεστιν ἐν τῇ ἕκτῃ τοῦ κατὰ πασῶν αἱρέσεων ἐλέγχου·

2. Τίνα τὰ Σίμωνι τετολμημένα, καὶ ὅτι ἐκ μαγικῶν καὶ ποιητικῶν τὸ δόγμα κρατύνει.

3. Τίνα ὁ Οὐαλεντῖνος δογματίζει, καὶ ὅτι ἐκ γραφῶν οὐ συνίσταται αὐτοῦ τὸ δόγμα, ἀλλὰ ἐκ τῶν Πλατωνικῶν καὶ Πυθαγορικῶν δογμάτων.

4. Καὶ τίνα τὰ Σεκούνδῳ καὶ Πτολεμαίῳ καὶ Ἡρακλέωνι δοκοῦντα, καὶ <ὅτι> καὶ αὐτοὶ τοῖς αὐτοῖς οἷς οἱ Ἑλλήνων σοφοὶ ἐχρήσαντο <δόγμασιν, ἀλλ’> ἄλλοις ῥήμασι.

5. Τίνα τὰ Μάρκῳ καὶ Κολαρβάσῳ νομισθέντα, καὶ ὅτι τινὲς αὐτῶν μαγείαις καὶ ἀριθμοῖς Πυθαγορείοις <προσ>έσχον.

6. 1. Ὅσα μὲν οὖν ἐδόκει τοῖς ἀπὸ τοῦ ὄφεως τὰς ἀρχὰς παρειληφόσι καὶ κατὰ μείωσιν τῶν χρόνων εἰς φανερὸν τὰς δόξας <αὐτῶν> ἑκουσίως προενεγκαμένοις, ἐν τῇ πρὸ ταύτης βίβλῳ οὔσῃ πέμπτῃ τοῦ ἐλέγχου τῶν αἱρέσεων ἐξεθέμην. νυνὶ δὲ καὶ τῶν ἀκολούθων τὰς γνώμας οὐ σιωπήσω, ἀλλ’ οὐδὲ μίαν ἀνέλεγκτον καταλείψω, εἴ γε δυνατὸν πάσας ἀπομνημονεῦσαι καὶ τὰ τούτων ἀπόρρητα ὄργια—ἃ δικαίως ὄργια κλητέον· οὐ γὰρ μακρὰν ἀπέχουσιν ὀργῆς τοιαῦτα τετολμηκότες, ἵνα καὶ τῇ ἐτυμολογίᾳ χρήσωμαι.—

7. 1. Δοκεῖ οὖν καὶ τὰ Σίμωνος τοῦ Γειττηνοῦ, κώμης τῆς Σαμαρείας, <δόγματα> νῦν ἐκθέσθαι, παρ’ οὗ καὶ τοὺς ἀκολούθους δείξομεν ἀφορμὰς λαβόντας ἑτέροις ὀνόμασιν ὅμοια τετολμηκέναι. οὗτος ὁ Σίμων, μαγείας

BOOK 6

[TABLE OF CONTENTS]

1. The contents of the sixth book of the *Refutation of All Heresies*.

2. The ventures of Simon, who corroborates his dogma from magicians and poets.

3. What Valentinus pronounces. His system is composed not from scripture but from Platonic and Pythagorean tenets.

4. The doctrine of Secundus, Ptolemy, and Herakleon, who also made use of the same tenets as the Greek sages, but with different terminology.

5. The beliefs of Markos and Kolarbasos. Some of them hankered after Pythagorean magical practices and numbers.

INTRODUCTION

6. 1. I presented in the previous book of my *Refutation of Heresies* the views of those who have taken their first principles from the snake. They, when time grew short, willingly brought their opinions out into the open. At present, I will not keep secret the views of their followers. Indeed, not one thing will I leave unrefuted—if indeed it is possible to recall them all, along with their secret initiations. They are rightly called "initiations," for those who have ventured such things are not far from divine *indignation* (if I may make use of etymology).[1]

7. 1. Thus it is fitting also to present the doctrines of Simon, from the town of Gitta, a village of the province of Samaria. I will show how those who followed him too, after taking their starting points from him, ventured

1. Our author not only puns on the similar sounds of ὄργια ("rites") and ὀργή ("wrath"), he believes that he has found a similar verbal root. For the use of ὄργια in this period, see Feyo L. Schuddeboom, *Greek Religious Terminology: Telete and Orgia; A Revised and Expanded English Edition of the Studies by Zijderveld and Van der Burg*, RGRW 169 (Leiden: Brill, 2009), 145–87.

ἔμπειρος ὢν καὶ τὰ μὲν παίξας πολλοὺς κατὰ τὴν Θρασυμήδους τέχνην—ᾧ τρόπῳ ἄνωθεν ἐξεθέμεθα—τὰ δὲ καὶ διὰ δαιμόνων κακουργήσας, θεοποιῆσαι ἑαυτὸν ἐπεχείρησεν, ἄνθρωπος γόης καὶ μεστὸς ἀπονοίας, ὃν ἐν ταῖς Πράξεσιν οἱ ἀπόστολοι ἤλεγξαν.

2. Οὗ πολλῷ σοφώτερον καὶ μετριώτερον Ἄψεθος ὁ Λίβυς, ὀρεχθεὶς θεὸς νομισθῆναι ἐν Λιβύῃ, ἐπεχείρησεν· οὗ τὸν μῦθον, οὐ πολύ τι ἀπεμφαίνοντα τῆς Σίμωνος τοῦ ματαίου ἐπιθυμίας, δοκεῖ διηγήσασθαι, ὄντα ἄξιον τῆς τούτου ἐπιχειρήσεως.

8. 1. Ἄψεθος ὁ Λίβυς ἐπεθύμησε θεὸς γενέσθαι· ὡς δὲ πολυπραγμονῶν πάνυ ἀπετύγχανε τῆς ἐπιθυμίας, ἠθέλησε κἂν δοκεῖν γεγονέναι. καὶ ἔδοξέ γε ὡς ἀληθῶς χρόνῳ πλείονι γεγονέναι θεός· ἔθυον γὰρ οἱ ἀνόητοι Λίβυες αὐτῷ θείᾳ τινὶ δυνάμει, νομίζοντες ἄνωθεν ἐξ οὐρανοῦ πεπιστευκέναι φωνῇ.

2. συναθροίσας γοῦν εἰς ἕνα καὶ τὸν αὐτὸν οἰκίσκον ὄρνιθας πλείστους ψιττακοὺς κατέκλεισεν· εἰσὶ δὲ πλεῖ(στ)οι κατὰ τὴν Λιβύην ψιττακοὶ καὶ ἐναργῶς μιμούμενοι πάνυ τὴν ἀνθρωπίνην φωνήν. οὗτος χρόνῳ διαθρέψας τοὺς ὄρν<ε>ις ἐδίδαξε λέγειν· Ἄψεθ(ος) θ<ε>ός ἐστιν. ὡς δὲ ἤσκησαν οἱ ὄρνιθες χρόνῳ πολλῷ καὶ τοῦτο ἔλεγον ὅπερ ᾤετο [τὸ] λεχθὲν ποιήσειν θεὸν εἶναι νομίζεσθαι τὸν Ἄψεθον, τότε ἀνοίξας τὸ οἴκημα εἴασεν ἄλλον ἀλλαχόσε τοὺς ψιττακούς.

3. πετομένων δὲ τῶν ὀρνίθων ἐξῆλθεν ὁ φθόγγος εἰς πᾶσαν τὴν Λιβύην καὶ τὰ ῥήματα αὐτῶν διῆλθε μέχρι τῆς Ἑλληνικῆς γῆς. καὶ οὕτως οἱ Λίβυες

the same doctrines in different terms. This Simon, as an expert in magic—by both toying with many people by the art of Thrasymedes (in the way I presented above) and by practicing mischief through demons—attempted to deify himself, though he was a mortal, a charlatan, and brimful of insanity. He it is whom the apostles refuted in the book of Acts.[2]

THE CASE OF APSETHOS. 2. Apsethos the Libyan, yearning to be considered a god in Libya, made a much wiser and more moderate attempt to deify himself. His story, not wholly incongruous with the desire of Simon—fool that he is—it seems right to relate, since it was worthy of Simon's attempt.[3]

8. 1. Apsethos the Libyan set his heart on becoming a god. But when, by meddling, he totally failed to achieve his desire, he still wished to appear to have become one. Indeed, after some time, he truly seemed to have become a god. For the stupid Libyans made it their custom to sacrifice to him as to some divine power, supposing that they were obeying a voice from heaven above.

2. To explain: Apsethos, after gathering into one and the same cage a host of parrots, locked them up. (The province of Libya is full of parrots that clearly and closely imitate the human voice.) This fool raised the birds for a period of time, teaching them to say, "Apsethos is a god!" When the birds had practiced for a long time, and repeatedly squawked what Apsethos thought would make him be considered a god, he threw open the cage and released the parrots in all directions.

3. When the birds flew, their squawk went out to all Libya, and their words spread as far as Greek territory.[4] This is how the Libyans, awestruck

2. Acts 8:9–24. For the figure of Simon, see Justin, *1 Apol.* 26.1–3; Iren., *Haer.* 1.23.1–4; Tert., *An.* 34.2–4; Acts Pet. 31; Ps.-Clem. Hom. 2.22–25; Rec. 2.7–15; Epiph., *Pan.* 21; Ps.-Tert., *Adv. omn. haer.* 1; Filastrius, *Haer.* 29; Theodoret, *Haer. fab.* 1.1. For Simon and his putative self-deification, see Morton Smith, "The Account of Simon Magus in Acts 8," in *Studies in the Cult of Yahweh*, ed. Shaye J. D. Cohen, 2 vols. (Leiden: Brill, 1996), 2:140–51; Gerd Theissen, "Simon Magus—die Entwicklung seines Bildes vom Charismatiker zum gnostischen Erlöser," in *Religionsgeschichte des neuen Testaments: Festschrift für Klaus Berger*, ed. Axel von Dobbeler, Kurt Erlemann, and Roman Heiligenthal (Tübingen: Francke, 2000), 407–32; Ayse Tuzlak, "The Magician and the Heretic," in *Magic and Ritual in the Ancient World*, ed. Paul Mirecki and Marvin Meyer (Leiden: Brill, 2002), 416–26.

3. For the figure of Apsethos, see Maximus of Tyre, *Or.* 29.4 (where he is called "Psaphon"); Aelian, *Var. hist.* 14.30 (where he is "Hanno"). See further Osborne, *Rethinking*, 70–73, 359–60.

4. Cf. Ps 18:5 LXX.

καταπλαγέντες ἐπὶ τῇ τῶν ὀρνίθων φωνῇ τό τε πραχθὲν ὑπὸ τοῦ Ἀψέθου πανούργευμα μὴ ἐν<ν>οήσαντες θεὸν εἶχον τὸν Ἄψεθον.

4. τῶν δὲ Ἑλλήνων τις, ἀκριβῶς ἐννοήσας τὸ σόφισμα τοῦ νενομισμένου θεοῦ, διὰ τῶν αὐτῶν ἐκείνων ψιττακῶν οὐκ ἐλέγχει μόνον, ἀλλὰ καὶ ἀφανίζει τὸν ἀλαζόνα καὶ φορτικὸν ἐκεῖνον ἄνθρωπον. μετεδίδαξε γὰρ ὁ Ἕλλην καθείρξας πολλοὺς ἀπὸ τῶν ψιττακῶν λέγειν· Ἄψεθος ἡμᾶς κατακλείσας ἠνάγκασε λέγειν· Ἄψεθος θεός ἐστιν. ἀκούσαντες δὲ οἱ Λίβυες τῆς παλινῳδίας τῶν ψιττακῶν, πάντες ὁμοθυμαδὸν συνελθόντες κατέκαυσαν τὸν Ἄψεθον.

9. 1. Οὕτως ἡγητέον Σίμωνα τὸν μάγον ἀπεικάζ<ειν> τῷ Λίβυϊ τάχιον ἀνθρώπῳ γενόμενῳ οὕτως θεῷ. εἰ δὲ ἔχει τὰ τῆς εἰκόνος ἀκριβῶς καὶ πέπονθεν ὁ μάγος πάθος τι παραπλήσιον Ἀψέθῳ, ἐπιχειρήσομεν μεταδιδάσκειν τοῦ Σίμωνος τοὺς ψιττακοὺς ὅτι Χριστὸς οὐκ ἦν Σίμων ὁ ἑστὼς στὰς στησόμενος, 2. ἀλλ' ἄνθρωπος [ἦν], ἐκ σπέρματος γέννημα γυναικός, ἐξ αἱμάτων καὶ ἐπιθυμίας σαρκικῆς καθάπερ καὶ οἱ λοιποὶ γεγεννημένος· καὶ ὅτι ταῦθ' οὕτως ἔχει, προϊόντος τοῦ λόγου ῥᾳδίως ἐπιδείξομεν.

3. Λέγει δὲ ὁ Σίμων μεταφράζων τὸν νόμον Μωϋσέως ἀνοήτως τε καὶ κακοτέχνως· Μωσέως γὰρ λέγοντος ὅτι «ὁ θεὸς πῦρ φλέγον ἐστὶ καὶ

at the voice of the birds and not understanding the trick performed by Apsethos, held him to be a god.

4. But one of the Greeks, when he accurately understood the artifice of the supposed god, not only refuted him through the same parrots, but also destroyed that boastful and vulgar man. For the Greek, having confined many of the parrots, retaught them to say, "Apsethos, locking us up, forced us to say: 'Apsethos is a god!'" When the Libyans heard the parrots' palinode, they all came together with one intent and burned Apsethos to ashes.[5]

APPLICATION TO SIMON. **9.** 1. So we must consider that Simon the magician conforms all the more to the Libyan who so became a god.[6] Given that the magician forms the spitting image of Apsethos—and experienced a similar calamity—I will attempt to "reteach the parrots" of Simon to affirm that Simon "Who Stood, Stands, and Will Stand" was not Christ.[7] 2. Instead, he was a mortal man, born from a woman's seed, from the mixing of bloodlines and fleshly desire just like the rest of human beings.[8] That this is actually the case, I will easily prove in my present report.[9]

THE *GREAT DECLARATION*

FIRE: THE INFINITE POWER. 3. Now Simon speaks as one mindlessly and craftily twisting the Law of Moses.[10] When Moses says, "God is a flaming

---

5. For the theme of self-deification and its disastrous results, see Plutarch, *Demetr.*; Suetonius, *Cal.*; Philo, *Post.*, 114–115; Josephus, *Ant.* 4.2.4. Biblical examples in Isa 14:12–14; Ezek 28; Dan 4; Acts 12:20–23.

6. P's ἀπεικάζοντας, following ἡγητέον, is difficult. I print ἀπεικάζειν.

7. For this designation, see Ps.-Clem. Hom. 2.22.3–4; 18.12.1; 2.24.6; Rec. 1.72.3; 2.7.1–3; 2.11.3; 3.47.3; Acts Pet. 31; Clem. Alex., *Strom.* 2.52.2. Noumenios referred to the primal God as the Standing One (ἑστώς) (des Places, frag. 15.2). See further David Runia, "Witness or Participant? Philo and the Neoplatonic Tradition," in *The Neoplatonic Tradition: Jewish, Christian and Islamic Themes*, ed. A. Vanderjagt and D. Pätzold (Köln: Dinter, 1991), 36–56.

8. For "bloodlines" (literally, "bloods," αἱμάτων), see John 1:13; Justin, *Dial.* 63.2; Clem. Alex., *Strom.* 2.13.58.2.

9. Simon's self-deification frames our author's discussion of the *Great Declaration* (see *Ref.* 6.18.1 and the interjection halfway through, 14.1). Our author assumes that all its complex theology is woven together for one end: Simon's self-promotion to godhood.

10. Interpreters generally conclude that the *Great Declaration* was a late work (Stephen Haar, *Simon Magus: The First Gnostic?* BZNW 119 [Berlin: de Gruyter,

καταναλίσκον», δεξάμενος τὸ λεχθὲν ὑπὸ Μωσέως οὐκ ὀρθῶς, πῦρ εἶναι λέγει τῶν ὅλων τὴν ἀρχήν, οὐ νοήσας τὸ εἰρημένον ὅτι θεὸς οὐ πῦρ, ἀλλὰ πῦρ φλέγον καὶ καταναλίσκον, οὐκ αὐτὸν διασπῶν μόνον τὸν νόμον Μωσέως, ἀλλὰ καὶ τὸν σκοτεινὸν Ἡράκλειτον συλαγωγῶν.

4. ἀπέραντον δὲ εἶναι δύναμιν ὁ Σίμων προσαγορεύει τῶν ὅλων τὴν ἀρχήν, λέγων οὕτως·

> τοῦτο τὸ γράμμα Ἀποφάσεως φωνῆς καὶ ὀνόματος ἐξ ἐπινοίας τῆς μεγάλης δυνάμεως τῆς ἀπεράντου. διὸ ἔσται ἐσφραγισμένον κεκρυμμένον κεκαλυμμένον, κείμενον ἐν τῷ οἰκητηρίῳ, οὗ ἡ ῥίζα τῶν ὅλων τεθεμελίωται.

and consuming fire," Simon does not receive correctly what Moses says.[11] Simon claims that the first principle of the universe is fire. He did not understand the quote. God is not fire—but a "*flaming and consuming* fire"! In so doing, he not only rips apart the Law of Moses but also plunders Herakleitos the Obscure.[12]

4. Simon calls the first principle of the universe an Infinite Power, speaking as follows:

> This is the letter of Declaration, of Voice, and of Name from the Thought of the Great and Infinite Power. Thus it will be sealed, hidden, veiled, and stored in the dwelling in which the root of the universe is established.[13]

2003], 97–99; Birger Pearson, *Ancient Gnosticism: Traditions and Literature* [Minneapolis: Fortress, 2007], 32–33). An exception is J. M. A. Salles-Dabadie, who argued that the *Declaration* was written by Simon himself (*Recherches sur Simon le Mage*, Cahiers de la Revue Biblique 10 [Paris: Gabalda, 1969], 71–79, 127–40). According to Josef Frickel, the author of the *Refutation* did not quote from the *Declaration* but a paraphrase of it composed by a gnostic exegete around 200 CE (*Die "Apophasis Megale" in Hippolyt's Refutatio (VI 9–18): Eine Paraphrase zur Apophasis Simons* [Rome: Pontifical Institute of Oriental Studies, 1968]). Frickel's theory was refuted by Osborne, who pointed out that it is based on an overly selective source-critical analysis and a misunderstanding of how the author of the *Refutation* uses φησίν. Osborne herself suggested that the *Declaration* was written down, with commentary, by one of Simon's pupils (*Rethinking*, 214–27). On the relation of "Simon" to Greek philosophy, see Mansfeld, *Heresiography*, 177.

11. The biblical text is a mixed quotation of Deut 4:24; 9:3 (God as consuming fire) and Exod 24:17 (flaming fire). The same conflation, Mansfeld points out, is found in "Valentinus" (*Ref.* 6.32.8) (*Heresiography*, 173 n. 58). For Simon's supposed misinterpretation, see Clem. Alex., *Ecl.* 26.1; Origen, *Princ.* 1.1.1.

12. For Herakleitos (ca. 540–480 BCE), see *Ref.* 1.4; 9.10.7–8. For the epithet "Obscure," see Cicero, *Fin.* 2.5.15. For fire in the fragments of Herakleitos, see DK 22 B30 (cosmos as ever-living fire), B31a, B90 (fire turned into other elements). It is commonly reported that Herakleitos said that the first principle or stuff of all is fire (e.g., Aristotle, *Metaph.* 1.3, 984a7–8; Ps.-Plutarch, *Plac. philos.* 1.3, 877c; Diog. L., *Vit. phil.* 9.7–8).

13. This quote is possibly the opening phrase of the *Great Declaration* (Ernst Haenchen, "Gab es eine vorchristliche Gnosis?" *ZTK* 49 [1952]: 316–49 [319]). Its solemn language suggests "the beginning of an apocalyptic or revelatory text" (Kalvesmaki, *Theology*, 95).

5. οἰκητήριον δὲ λέγει εἶναι τὸν ἄνθρωπον τοῦτον, τὸν ἐξ αἱμάτων γεγεννημένον, καὶ κατοικεῖν ἐν αὐτῷ τὴν ἀπέραντον δύναμιν, ἣν ῥίζα εἶναι τῶν ὅλων φησίν.

ἔστι δὲ ἡ ἀπέραντος δύναμις, τὸ πῦρ, κατὰ τὸν Σίμωνα οὐδὲν ἁπλοῦν, καθάπερ οἱ πολλοὶ ἁπλᾶ λέγοντες εἶναι τὰ τέσσαρα στοιχεῖα καὶ τὸ πῦρ ἁπλοῦν εἶναι νενομίκασιν, ἀλλὰ γὰρ εἶναι [τὴν] τοῦ πυρὸς διπλῆν τινα τὴν φύσιν· καὶ τῆς διπλῆς ταύτης καλεῖ τὸ μέν τι κρυπτόν, τὸ δέ τι φανερόν· 6. κεκρύφθαι δὲ τὰ κρυπτὰ ἐν τοῖς φανεροῖς τοῦ πυρός, καὶ τὰ φανερὰ τοῦ πυρὸς ὑπὸ τῶν κρυπτῶν γεγονέναι.

ἔστι δὲ τοῦτο ὅπερ Ἀριστοτέλης δυνάμει καὶ ἐνεργείᾳ καλεῖ, ἢ Πλάτων νοητὸν καὶ αἰσθητόν.

7. καὶ τὸ μὲν φανερὸν τοῦ πυρὸς πάντα ἔχει ἐν ἑαυτῷ ὅσα ἄν τις ἐπινοήσῃ ἢ καὶ λάθῃ παραλιπὼν τῶν ὁρατῶν, τὸ δὲ κρυπτὸν πᾶν ὅ τι ἐννοήσει τις νοητὸν καὶ πεφευγὸς τὴν αἴσθησιν ἢ καὶ παραλείπει μὴ διανοηθείς.

8. Καθόλου δὲ ἔστιν εἰπεῖν· πάντων τῶν ὄντων, αἰσθητῶν τε καὶ νοητῶν, ὧν ἐκεῖνος κρυφίων καὶ φανερῶν προσαγορεύει, ἔστι θησ(αυ)ρὸς τὸ πῦρ τὸ ὑπερουράνιον, οἱονεὶ δένδρον μέγα, ὡς <τὸ> δι᾽ ὀνείρου βλεπόμενον τῷ Ναβουχοδονόσορ, «ἐξ οὗ πᾶσα σὰρξ τρέφεται». 9. καὶ τὸ μὲν φανερὸν εἶναι τοῦ πυρὸς νομίζει τὸ πρέμνον, τοὺς κλάδους, τὰ φύλλα, τὸν ἔξωθεν αὐτῷ περικείμενον φλοιόν· ἅπαντα, φησί, ταῦτα τοῦ μεγάλου δένδρου ἀναφθέντα ὑπὸ τῆς παμφάγου τοῦ πυρὸς φλογὸς ἀφανίζεται· 10. ὁ δὲ καρπὸς τοῦ δένδρου, ἐὰν ἐξεικονισθῇ καὶ τὴν ἑαυτοῦ μορφὴν ἀπολάβῃ, εἰς ἀποθήκην τίθεται, οὐκ εἰς τὸ πῦρ. γέγονε μὲν γάρ, φησίν, ὁ καρπός, ἵνα εἰς τὴν ἀποθήκην τεθῇ, τὸ δὲ ἄχυρον, ἵνα παραδοθῇ τῷ πυρί, ὅπερ ἐστὶ πρέμνον, οὐχ αὑτοῦ χάριν ἀλλὰ τοῦ καρποῦ γεγενημένον.

10. 1. Καὶ τοῦτό ἐστι, φησί, τὸ γεγραμμένον ἐν τῇ γραφῇ· «ὁ γὰρ ἀμπελὼν κυρίου Σαβαὼθ οἶ(κ)ος τοῦ Ἰσραήλ ἐστι, καὶ ἄνθρωπος τοῦ Ἰούδα νεόφυτον ἠγαπημένον». εἰ δὲ ἄνθρωπος τοῦ Ἰούδα νεόφυτον ἠγαπημένον, δέδεικται, φησίν, ὅτι <τὸ> ξύλον οὐκ ἄλλο τι ἀλλ᾽ ἢ ἄνθρωπός ἐστιν.

2. ἀλλὰ περὶ τῆς ἐκκρίσεως αὐτοῦ καὶ διακρίσεως ἱκανῶς, φησίν, εἴρηκεν ἡ γραφή, καὶ πρὸς διδασκαλίαν ἀρκεῖ τοῖς ἐξεικονισμένοις τὸ λεχθὲν ὅτι «πᾶσα

5. Now he says that the "dwelling" is the person who is born from the mixing of bloodlines. The Infinite Power, which he calls the "root of the universe," dwells in him.

The Infinite Power, or fire, according to Simon, is not simple (as most people assume that fire is simple when they say that the four elements are simple). Rather, the nature of fire is twofold. One aspect of this twofold nature he calls "hidden," and the other "manifest." 6. The hidden realities lie hidden in the fire's manifest realities, and the manifest realities of the fire are generated by the hidden realities.

(Now this distinction is exactly what Aristotle refers to as "in potentiality" and "in actuality," and Plato as "intelligible" and "sensible.")

7. Moreover, the manifest aspect of the fire contains all visible things that one might think or leave unnoticed, whereas the hidden aspect contains everything intelligible and removed from sense perception that one will think or leave without reflection.

8. In general, one can say that the supercelestial fire is the treasury of all existing things, perceptible and intelligible (which Simon calls "hidden" and "manifest"), as it were a huge tree like the one seen by Nebuchadnezzar in a dream, "from which all flesh is nourished."[14] 9. Now, he thinks that the visible aspect of the fire consists of the trunk, the branches, the leaves, and the surrounding bark. All these manifest parts of the huge tree, he says, are destroyed by the all-consuming flame of fire. 10. But the fruit of the tree, if it is fully shaped according to its model and receives its own form, is set in the storehouse, not into the fire. For the fruit grew, he says, so as to be set in the storehouse; but the chaff—that is, the trunk—is to be delivered over to the fire, since it came about not for itself but for the sake of the fruit.[15]

10. 1. Now this, he says, is what the scriptural verse means: "For the vineyard of the Lord Sabaoth is the house of Israel, and a person of Judah is a beloved new shoot."[16] If a person of Judah is a "beloved new shoot," it is proved, he says, that the tree is nothing other than the human being.

2. But concerning the distinction and separation, scripture has adequately pronounced.[17] The following verse suffices to instruct those fully

14. Cf. Dan 4:10–12 LXX.

15. Cf. Matt 3:10–12 par.; Iren., *Haer.* 1.3.5.

16. Isa 5:7 LXX.

17. Salles-Dabadie claims that ἔκκρισις means "secretion" and thus the "sap" of a plant, and translates it (effect for cause) as "growth" (*croissance*). Its opposite, διάκρισις, he takes to mean "destruction" (*Recherches*, 17 n. 1).

σὰρξ χόρτος, καὶ πᾶσα δόξα σαρκὸς ὡς ἄνθος χόρτου· ἐξηράνθη ὁ χόρτος, καὶ τὸ ἄνθος αὐτοῦ ἐξέπεσε· τὸ δὲ ῥῆμα κυρίου μένει εἰς τὸν αἰῶνα». ῥῆμα δέ, φησίν, ἐστὶ κυρίου τὸ ἐν στόματι γεννώμενον ῥῆμα καὶ λόγος, ἄλλ<ο δ>ὲ χωρίον γενέσεως οὐκ ἔστι.

11. 1. Τοιούτου δὲ ὄντος, ὡς δι᾽ ὀλίγων εἰπεῖν, κατὰ τὸν Σίμωνα τοῦ πυρός. καὶ πάντων τῶν <μερῶν αὐτοῦ,> ὄντων ὁρατῶν καὶ ἀοράτων, ἐνήχων καὶ ἤχων, ἀριθμητῶν καὶ ἀρίθμων, <φρόνησιν ἐχόντων>—ὧν αὐτὸς ἐν τῇ Ἀποφάσει τῇ μεγάλῃ καλεῖ τελείων νοερῶν. [οὕτως ὡς] ἕκαστον τῶν ἀπειρά(κι)ς ἀπείρων <μερῶν> ἐπινοηθῆναι <ὡς> δυνάμενον καὶ λαλεῖν καὶ διανοεῖσθαι καὶ ἐνεργεῖν οὕτως ὡς, φησίν, Ἐμπεδοκλῆς·

γαίῃ μὲν γὰρ γαῖαν ὀπώπαμεν, ὕδατι δ᾽ ὕδωρ,
αἰθέρι δ᾽ αἰθέρα <δῖον>, ἀτὰρ πυρὶ πῦρ ἀίδηλον,
καὶ <στοργῇ> στοργήν, νεῖκος <δ᾽> ἔτι νείκεϊ λυγρῷ.

12. 1. Πάντα γάρ, φησίν, ἐνόμιζε τὰ μέρη τοῦ π(υ)ρός, τὰ <ὁρατὰ καὶ τὰ> ἀόρατα, «φρόνησιν ἔχειν καὶ <νώματος αἶσαν>».

made according to the model:[18] "All flesh is grass, and all the glory of flesh like a flower of grass. The grass is dried up, and its flower falls down. But the speech of the Lord remains forever."[19] Now the "speech," he says, is speech and word that is born in the mouth of the Lord, and there is no other place of birth.[20]

11. 1. Such, to speak briefly, is Simon's fire. All its parts—whether they be visible or invisible, resounding or sounding, numerable or numbers—are endowed with intelligence.[21] (He himself, in his *Great Declaration*, calls them "perfect intellects.") Each of the parts, infinity times infinity in number, is conceived of as able to speak, to think, and to be active, exactly as, he asserts, Empedokles says:[22]

For we behold earth from earth, water by water,
Aether by gleaming aether, fire by annihilating fire,
Affection by affection, and strife by baneful strife.[23]

12. 1. Empedokles believed, he claims, that all the parts of the fire—visible and invisible—"have intelligence and a share in thought."[24]

---

18. Humans, as we later find out, are formed with God as their model but must return to God's likeness (*Ref.* 6.14.6). The idea of formation according to a model is important in the *Great Declaration*, where a form of ἐξεικονίζω is used ten times (9.10; 10.2; 12.3, 4; 14.6 [twice]; 16.5, 6; 17.1; 18.1). See further Haenchen, "Gab es," 321–22, Frickel, *Apophasis*, 190–91; John D. Turner in Catherine Barry et al., *Zostrien (NH VIII,1)*, BCNH 24 (Leuven: Peeters, 2000), 498.

19. Isa 40:6–8 LXX; cf. 1 Pet 1:24. Apparently it is human flesh that is portrayed as the visible outer rind of the self that will be burned like the tree and wither like grass.

20. It is the one made in the image who becomes God's speech or word (cf. *Ref.* 5.21.9 ["Sethians"]). Abramowski comments: "The fleshly human passes away, but the one 'newly planted' is selected out and does not pass away, because he is Logos" (*Drei christologische Untersuchungen*, 32).

21. Marcovich, following earlier editors, prints ἀνήχων instead of P's ἤχων. Kalvesmaki states that ἀνήχων is "unattested in Greek literature" and preserves the reading of P (followed here). The relationship envisioned here, according to Kalvesmaki, is not between opposites but between "metaphysical superior and dependent." Numbers "constitute a metaphysical order higher than countable things" (*Theology*, 96 n. 37).

22. For the use of ἀπειράκις ἄπειρος, see Philo, *Her.* 189; Sext. Emp., *Math.* 9.306; 10.304.

23. Empedokles, DK 31 B109.

24. Empedokles, DK 31 B110.10, cited also in Sext. Emp., *Math.* 8.286. On our author's sources for these two quotations, see Osborne, *Rethinking*, 88–89. Mansfeld

Γέγονεν οὖν ὁ κόσμος ὁ γεννητὸς ἀπὸ τοῦ ἀγεννήτου πυρός. ἤρξατο δέ, φησί, γίνεσθαι τοῦτον τὸν τρόπον· ἓξ ῥίζας τὰς πρώτας τῆς ἀρχῆς τῆς γενέσεως λαβὼν ὁ γεννητὸς ἀπὸ τῆς ἀρχῆς τοῦ πυρὸς ἐκείνου. 2. γεγονέναι γὰρ τὰς ῥίζας φησὶ κατὰ συζυγίαν ἀπ(ὸ) τοῦ πυρός, ἅστινας ῥίζας καλεῖ

Νοῦν καὶ Ἐπίνοιαν,
Φωνὴν καὶ Ὄνομα,
Λογισμὸν καὶ Ἐνθύμησιν.

εἶναι δὲ ἐν ταῖς ἓξ ῥίζαις ταύταις πᾶσαν ὁμοῦ τὴν ἀπέραντον δύναμιν δυνάμει, οὐκ ἐνεργείᾳ, ἥντινα ἀπέραντον δύναμιν φησι τὸν ἑστῶτα <στάντα> στησόμενον.

3. ὃς ἐὰν μὲν ἐξεικονισθῇ, ὢν ἐν ταῖς ἓξ δυνάμεσιν, ἔσται οὐσίᾳ, δυνάμει, μεγέθει, ἀποτελέσματι μία καὶ ἡ αὐτὴ τῇ ἀγεννήτῳ καὶ ἀπεράντῳ δυνάμει, οὐδὲν ὅλως ἔχουσα ἐνδεέστερον ἐκείνης τῆς ἀγεννήτου καὶ ἀπαραλ<λ>άκτου καὶ ἀπεράντου δυνάμεως. 4. ἐὰν δὲ μείνῃ [τῇ] δυνάμει μόνον ἐν ταῖς ἓξ δυνάμεσι καὶ μὴ ἐξεικονισθῇ, ἀφανίζεται, φησί, καὶ ἀπόλλυται, οὕτως ὡς ἡ δύναμις ἡ γραμματικὴ <ἢ> ἡ γεωμετρικὴ ἐν ἀνθρώπου ψυχῇ· προσλαβοῦσα γὰρ ἡ δύναμις τεχνήν, φῶς τῶν γινομένων (γ)ίνεται, μὴ προσλαβοῦσα δέ, ἀτεχνία καὶ σκότος, καὶ ὡς ὅτι οὐκ ἦν, ἀποθνήσκοντι τῷ ἀνθρώπῳ συνδιαφθείρεται.

THE WORLD BORN FROM FIRE: GENESIS 1–3. Thus the world that was born arose out of unborn fire. It began its existence, he says, in the following way. From the principle of that fire, the born world took six primal roots of the principle of generation. 2. These roots arose from the fire, he says, in pairs. He calls them:

Mind and Thought,
Voice and Name,
Reasoning and Conception.

There is in these six roots all the Infinite Power together—in potentiality, not in actuality. He says that the Infinite Power is the One Who Stood, Who Stands, and Who Will Stand.[25]

3. Whoever attains the likeness (while being in the six powers) will be in substance, in potential, in magnitude, in finished perfection *one and the same* as the Unborn and Infinite Power. This one will be in no way at all inferior to that Unborn, Unchanging, and Infinite Power.[26] 4. But whoever remains in potential only in the six powers and is not fully formed according to the model vanishes away, he says, and is destroyed. It works just as the human mind's potential to learn grammar or geometry.[27] If a potential ability acquires a technical skill,[28] it becomes a light for generated beings; but if it does not acquire it, it is left as darkness without a skill and perishes—as if it did not exist—when the person dies.[29]

---

attempts to defend P's reading γνωματο σις ον with a correction mark above the ι (*Heresiography*, 175 n. 67).

25. On ὁ Ἑστως ("the Standing One"), see Gerd Lüdemann, *Untersuchungen zur simonianischen Gnosis* (Göttingen: Vandenhoeck & Ruprecht, 1975), 98–100; Michael Allen Williams, *The Immovable Race: A Gnostic Designation and the Theme of Stability in Late Antiquity* (Leiden: Brill, 1985), 37–38, 57. The title refers to the highest God in Noumenios (cited in Eusebius, *Praep. ev.* 11.20), as it does in Corp. herm. 2.12. It is applied to Simon in Ps.-Clem. Rec. 2.7 (cf. 2.11; 3.47).

26. Ἀπαραλλάκτου, translated "Unchanging," can also mean "Identical"—a pregnant ambiguity since the one fully formed is effectively one with the Infinite Power.

27. Cf. Aristotle, *Cat.* 1.5, 3a4–6.

28. For τέχνη ("skill"), cf. διδασκαλία in *Ref.* 6.16.5. The summary in *Ref.* 10.12.4 reads τεχνίτην.

29. The six powers are cosmic powers, whereas the Seventh Power transcends this world. One's goal is to transcend this world of generation and become in all respects identical to the Infinite Power.

13. 1. Τῶν δὲ ἓξ δυνάμεων τούτων καὶ τῆς ἑβδόμης τῆς μετὰ τῶν ἓξ καλεῖ τὴν πρώτην συζυγίαν, Νοῦν καὶ Ἐπίνοιαν, οὐρανὸν καὶ γῆν· καὶ τὸν μὲν ἄρσενα ἄνωθεν ἐπιβλέπειν καὶ προνοεῖν τῆς συζύγου, τὴν δὲ γῆν ὑποδέχεσθαι κάτω τοὺς ἀπὸ τοῦ οὐρανοῦ καταφερομένους τῇ γῇ συγγενεῖς νοεροὺς καρπούς. διὰ τοῦτο, φησίν, ἀποβλέπων πολλάκις ὁ λόγος πρὸς τὰ ἐκ Νοὸς καὶ Ἐπινοίας γεγεννημένα—τουτέστιν ἐξ οὐρανοῦ καὶ γῆς—λέγει·

ἄκουε, οὐρανέ, καὶ ἐνωτίζου, γῆ, ὅτι κ(ύριος) ἐλάλησεν·
υἱοὺς ἐγέννησα καὶ ὕψωσα, αὐτοὶ δέ με ἠθέτησαν.

ὁ δὲ λέγων ταῦτα, φησίν, ἡ ἑβδόμη δύναμίς ἐστιν, <ὁ> ἑστὼς στὰς στησόμενος· αὐτὸς γὰρ αἴτιος τούτων τῶν καλῶν ὧν ἐπῄνεσε Μωσῆς καὶ εἶπε «καλὰ λίαν».

ἡ δὲ Φωνὴ καὶ τὸ Ὄνομα ἥλιος καὶ σελήνη.
ὁ δὲ Λογισμὸς καὶ ἡ Ἐνθύμησις ἀὴρ καὶ ὕδωρ.

ἐν δὲ τούτοις ἅπασιν ἐμμέμικται καὶ κέκραται, ὡς ἔφην, ἡ μεγάλη δύναμις, ἡ ἀπέραντος, ὁ ἑστώς.

14. 1. Μωσέως οὖν εἰρηκότος· «ἓξ ἡμέραις, ἐν αἷς ὁ θεὸς ἐποίησε τὸν οὐρανὸν καὶ τὴν γῆν, καὶ τῇ ἑβδόμῃ κατέπαυσεν ἀπὸ πάντων τῶν ἔργων αὐτοῦ», τὸν εἰρημένον τρόπον μετοικονομήσας ὁ Σίμων ἑαυτὸν θεοποιεῖ. 2. ὅταν οὖν λέγωσιν ὅτι εἰσὶ τρεῖς ἡμέραι πρὸ ἡλίου καὶ σελήνης γεγενημέναι, αἰνίσσονται Νοῦν καὶ Ἐπίνοιαν—τουτέστιν οὐρανὸν καὶ γῆν—καὶ τὴν ἑβδόμην δύναμιν, τὴν ἀπέραντον· αὗται γὰρ αἱ τρεῖς δυνάμεις εἰσὶ πρὸ πασῶν τῶν ἄλλων γενόμεναι.

HEAVEN AND EARTH. 13. 1. He calls Mind and Thought, the first pair of six powers (with the seventh following), "heaven and earth."[30] Now the male Mind above watches over and cares for his partner, while earth below receives the intelligible fruits akin to her as they rain down from heaven. For this reason, he says, the Word—often having in view the offspring of Mind and Thought (that is, heaven and earth)—says:

> Listen, heaven, and hear, earth, because the Lord has spoken!
> Children I fathered and exalted, but they set me aside.[31]

The one who speaks these words, he says, is the Seventh Power, the One Who Stood, Who Stands, Who Will Stand. For he himself is the cause of these goods that Moses praised and called "very good."[32]

> "Voice and Name" are sun and moon.
> "Reasoning and Conception" are air and water.

In all these the Great Power, as I said, is mixed and blended. He is the Infinite Power, the Standing One.

14. 1. When Moses said, "In six days God made the heaven and the earth, and on the seventh day, he rested from all his works," Simon, by altering the mode of expression, deifies himself.[33] 2. When the scriptures say that there are three days before sun and moon, they hint at Mind and Thought (that is, heaven and earth), plus the Seventh Power, the Infinite. These are the three powers that arose before all the others.[34]

---

30. The mythological separation of male Heaven from female Earth (common in many cosmogonies, e.g., Hesiod, *Theog.* 126–168) is read as the distinction of female Thought from male Mind.

31. Isa 1:2 LXX.

32. Gen 1:31 LXX. In *Ref.* 6.12.3, the Infinite Power is the One Who Stood, Stands, Will Stand. Evidently, since the Seventh Power is the image of the Infinite Power, they share the same name (*Ref.* 6.14.2: τὴν ἑβδόμην δύναμιν, τὴν ἀπέραντον). See further Kalvesmaki, *Theology*, 97.

33. Gen 2:2 LXX.

34. Cf. Theophilos of Antioch, who made the three first days of creation symbolize the Trinity (*Autol.* 2.15). For number speculation in the *Great Declaration*, see Kalvesmaki, *Theology*, 94–102.

3. ὅταν δὲ λέγωσι· «πρὸ πάντων τῶν αἰώνων γεννᾷ με», περὶ τῆς ἑβδόμης, φησί, δυνάμεως τὰ τοιαῦτα λέγεται εἶναι· ἑβδόμη γάρ αὕτη δύναμις ἥτις ἦν δύναμις ὑπάρχουσα ἐν τῇ ἀπεράντῳ δυνάμει, ἥτις γέγονε πρὸ πάντων τῶν αἰώνων. 4. αὕτη ἐστί, φησίν, ἡ ἑβδόμη δύναμις περὶ ἧς λέγει Μωσῆς· «καὶ πνεῦμα θεοῦ ἐπεφέρετο ἐπάνω τοῦ ὕδατος», τουτέστι, φησί, τὸ πνεῦμα τὸ πάντα ἔχον ἐν ἑαυτῷ, εἰκὼν τῆς ἀπεράντου δυνάμεως. περὶ ἧς ὁ Σίμων λέγει· «εἰκὼν ἐξ ἀφθάρτου μορφῆς, κοσμοῦσα μόνη πάντα». 5. αὕτη γὰρ ἡ δύναμις, ἡ ἐπιφερομένη ἐπάνω τοῦ ὕδατος, ἐξ ἀφθάρτου, φησί, γεγενημένη μορφῆς, κοσμεῖ μόνη πάντα.

Τοιαύτης οὖν τινος καὶ παραπλησίου τῆς κατασκευῆς τοῦ κόσμ(ου) γενομένης παρ' αὐτοῖς, «ἔπλασε», φησίν, «ὁ θεὸς τὸν ἄνθρωπον, χοῦν ἀπὸ τῆς γῆς λαβών»· ἔπλασε δὲ οὐχ ἁπλοῦν ἀλλὰ διπλοῦν· «κατ' εἰκόνα καὶ καθ' ὁμοίωσιν». 6. εἰκὼν δέ ἐστι τὸ πνεῦμα τὸ ἐπιφερόμενον ἐπάνω τοῦ ὕδατος· ὃ ἐὰν μὴ ἐξεικονισθῇ, μετὰ τοῦ κόσμου ἀπολεῖται, δυνάμει μεῖναν μόνον, μὴ καὶ ἐνεργείᾳ γενόμενον. τοῦτό ἐστι, φησί, τὸ εἰρημένον· «ἵνα μὴ σὺν τῷ κόσμῳ κατακριθῶμεν».

THE SPIRIT OVER THE WATERS. 3. When the scriptures say, "Before all the aeons you fathered me," such things are said, he claims, concerning the Seventh Power.[35] The Seventh Power is herself a power that existed in the Infinite Power, which arose before all the aeons. 4. She is, he says, the Seventh Power about whom Moses speaks: "and divine Spirit hovered above the waters."[36] This, he says, is the Spirit. It contains everything in itself, as an image of the Infinite Power. Simon refers to it as "an image from an incorruptible form, alone ordering everything."[37] 5. For she is the power that hovered above the waters. She was born from the incorruptible form, he says, and alone orders everything.[38]

THE FORMATION OF THE HUMAN BEING. When some such creation occurred, in their view, "God," he says, "formed the human being by taking dust from the earth."[39] He formed the human being not simply but in a twofold manner: "according to the image and according to the likeness."[40] 6. The "image" is the Spirit hovering above the water.[41] If it is not made in the likeness, it will be destroyed with the world. It remains only in potentiality, not in actuality.[42] This, he says, is what the verse means: "so that we might not be condemned with the world."[43]

35. Prov 8:23 LXX.

36. Gen 1:2 LXX.

37. Cf. the figure of Wisdom as divine "breath," "image," and ordering principle in Wis 7:25–26.

38. Cf. Wis 7:27; 8:1: μία δὲ οὖσα πάντα δύναται ... διοικεῖ τὰ πάντα χρηστῶς ("Although she is one, she can do all things.... She kindly administers all things").

39. Gen 2:7 LXX.

40. Gen 1:26 LXX. Cf. the twofold nature of the divine: hidden and revealed (*Ref.* 6.9.5–7).

41. Since the Spirit hovering over the waters was previously identified with the Seventh Power (*Ref.* 6.14.4), presumably the "image" inscribed in human beings is the Seventh Power itself. The connection between image and breath is logical because the "breath" (πνοή) blown into the human body in Gen 2:7 conceptually overlaps with the "breath/spirit" (πνεῦμα) hovering over the waters in Gen 1:2. In short, the "image" aspect of human beings is not the human body but the breath animating and forming it. This is the same breath that animates and forms the body of the cosmos.

42. See further Josef Frickel, "Eine neue Deutung von Gen 1,26 in der Gnosis," in *Ex orbe religionum: Studia Geo Widengren*, ed. C. J. Bleeker, S. G. F. Brandon, and M. Simon, 2 vols., SHR 21–22 (Leiden: Brill, 1972), 1:413–23 (415–20).

43. 1 Cor 11:32b; cf. *Ref.* 5.12.7 ("Sethians").

ἐὰν δὲ ἐξεικονισθῇ καὶ γένηται ἀπὸ στιγμῆς ἀμερίστου, ὡς γέγραπται ἐν τῇ Ἀποφάσει, «τὸ μικρὸν μέγα γενήσεται, τὸ δὲ μέγα ἔσται εἰς τὸν ἄπειρον αἰῶνα καὶ ἀπαράλ<λ>ακτον, τὸ μηκέτι γινόμενον.»

7. Πῶς οὖν καὶ τίνα τρόπον, φησί, πλάσ<σ>ει τὸν ἄνθρωπον ὁ θεός; ἐν (π)αραδείσῳ· οὕτως γὰρ αὐτῷ δοκεῖ. ἔστω, φησί, παράδεισος ἡ μήτρα· καὶ ὅτι τοῦτό ἐστιν ἀληθές, ἡ γραφὴ διδάσκει ὅτε λέγει· «ἐγώ εἰμι ὁ πλάσσων σε ἐν μήτρᾳ μητρός σου»· καὶ τοῦτο γὰρ οὕτω θέλει γεγράφθαι. τὸν παράδεισον, φησίν, ἀλληγορῶν ὁ Μωσῆς τὴν μήτραν εἴρηκεν, εἴπερ δεῖ τῷ λόγῳ πιστεύειν.

8. εἰ δὲ πλάσσει ὁ θεὸς ἐν μήτρᾳ μητρὸς τὸν ἄνθρωπον, τουτέστιν ἐν παραδείσῳ, ὡς ἔφην, ἔστω παράδεισος ἡ μήτρα, Ἐδὲμ δὲ τὸ χόριον, «ποταμὸς ἐκπορευόμενος ἐξ Ἐδὲμ ποτίζει τὸν παράδεισον» ὁ ὀμφαλός. οὗτος, φησίν, ὁ ὀμφαλὸς «ἀφορίζεται εἰς τέσσαρας ἀρχάς»· ἑκατέρωθεν γὰρ τοῦ ὀμφαλοῦ δύο εἰσὶν ἀρτηρίαι παρατεταμέναι, ὀχετοὶ πνεύματος, καὶ δύο φλ(έβ)ες, ὀχετοὶ αἵματος.

Yet if it is made in the likeness and comes to be from an undivided point, as it is written in the *Declaration*, "the small will become great, and the great will attain the infinite and unchanging aeon, not subject to generation."[44]

ALLEGORY OF THE GARDEN. 7. How, then, and in what way, he says, does God form the human being? In paradise (as he thinks).[45] Let the womb, he says, be paradise. Scripture teaches that this is true when it says, "I am the one forming you in the womb" of your mother (as he glosses the passage).[46] Now he says that Moses figuratively called the womb "paradise" (if we must credit his report).

8. But if God forms the human in the womb of a mother, that is (as I said), in paradise, let the womb signify paradise, and "Eden" the placenta, and let "the river flowing out of Eden to water paradise" signify the umbilical cord.[47] This umbilical cord, he says, "splits into four branches." For on each side of the umbilical cord there are two arteries extended, which serve as channels of breath, and two veins, which serve as channels of blood.[48]

---

44. The small becoming great also describes salvation in Dial. Sav. (NHC III,5) 136.23. Neopythagoreans taught that everything derives from the point (Sext. Emp., *Math.* 10.282). In the present context, the undivided point signifies the divine potential in humanity. The point itself is nothing (having no dimensions), but it has the inherent ability to be stretched into a line, then a plane, then a solid, then a trans-dimensional entity (cf. *Ref.* 4.51.2–3). As in some patristic soteriologies, salvation is conceived of as the image of God (the present human state) transforming into God's likeness (the ideal human or transhuman state) (see, e.g., Clem. Alex., *Strom.* 7.14.85.2–5; *Exc.* 50.1).

45. Gen 2:8 LXX. In a similar allegory (*Ref.* 5.9.15–18), the Naassene writer focused on the brain and had the four rivers symbolize the four senses. In contrast, "Simon" speaks of the womb and makes the four rivers represent blood vessels in the umbilical cord. For the embryology assumed in this passage, see Ps.-Hippokrates, *Nat. paed.* 14–17; Bernard Pouderon, "La notice d'Hippolyte sur Simon: Cosmologie, anthropologie et embryologie," in *Les pères de l'Église face à la science médicale de leur temps*, ed. Véronique Boudon-Millot and Bernard Pouderon, ThH 117 (Paris: Beauchesne, 2005), 49–71; idem, "L'influence d'Aristote dans la doctrine de la procréation des premiers pères et ses implications théologiques," in *L'embryon: Formation et animation; Antiquité grecque et latine tradition hébraïque, chrétiennes et islamique*, ed. Luc Brisson, Marie-Hélène Congourdeau, and Jean-Luc Solère (Paris: J. Vrin, 2008), 157–83 (178–80).

46. Cf. Isa 44:2, 24 LXX (κοιλίας in the LXX is here replaced by μητρός).

47. Gen 2:10 LXX. The meaning of τὸ χόριον is described in Ps.-Hippocrates, *Nat. puer.* 16.1; Galen, *Usu part.* 15.5 (Helmreich).

48. Cf. Galen, *In Hippoc. alim.* 4.5 (Kühn, 15:387–88): ἔστι γὰρ ἐν αὐτῷ ἀγγεῖα τέτταρα, δύο μὲν ἀρτηρίαι, δύο δὲ φλέβες … καὶ διὰ τούτων … ἕλκει τὸ ἔμβρυον αἷμα καὶ

9. ἐπειδὰν δέ, φησίν, ἀπὸ τοῦ Ἐδὲμ χορίου ἐκπορευόμενος ὁ ὀμφαλὸς ἐμφύῃ τῷ γεν<ν>(ω)μένῳ κατὰ τὸ ἐπιγάστριον—ὃ κοινῶς πάντες προσαγορεύουσιν ὀμφαλόν—, αἱ δὲ δύο φλέβες, δι' ὧν ῥεῖ καὶ φέρεται ἀπὸ τοῦ Ἐδὲμ τοῦ χορίου τὸ αἷμα, κατὰ τὰς καλουμένας πύλας τοῦ ἥπατος—αἵτινες τὸ γεννώμενον τρέφουσιν—, 10. αἱ δὲ ἀρτηρίαι—ἃς ἔφημεν ὀχετοὺς εἶναι πνεύματος, ἑκατέρωθεν περιλαβοῦσαι τὴν κύστιν κατὰ τὸ πλατὺ ὀστοῦν—πρὸς τὴν μεγάλην συνάπτωσιν ἀρτηρίαν—τὴν κατὰ ῥάχιν καλουμένην ἀορτήν—, καὶ οὕτως διὰ τῶν παραθύρων ἐπὶ τὴν καρδίαν ὁδεῦσαν τὸ πνεῦμα κίνησιν ἐργάζεται τῷ ἐμβρύῳ.

11. πλασσόμενον γὰρ τὸ βρέφος ἐν τῷ παραδείσῳ οὔτε τῷ στόματι τροφὴν λαμβάνει οὔτε ταῖς ῥισὶν ἀναπνέει· ἐν ὑγροῖς γὰρ ὑπάρχοντι αὐτῷ, παρὰ πόδας ἦν ὁ θάνατος εἰ ἀνέπνευσεν· ἐπεσπάσατο γὰρ ἂν ἀπὸ τῶν ὑγρῶν καὶ ἐφθάρη. ἀλλὰ γὰρ ὅλον περιέσφιγκται τῷ καλουμένῳ χιτῶνι ἀμνίῳ, τρέφεται δὲ δι' ὀμφαλοῦ, καὶ διὰ τῆς κατὰ ῥάχιν, ὡς ἔφην, τὴν τοῦ πνεύματος οὐσίαν λαμβάνει.

15. 1. Ὁ οὖν ποταμός, φησίν, ὁ ἐκπορευόμενος ἐξ Ἐδὲμ εἰς τέσσαρας ἀφορίζεται ἀρχάς, <εἰς> ὀχετοὺς τέσσαρας, τουτέστιν εἰς τέσσαρας αἰσθήσεις τοῦ γεννωμένου· ὅρασιν, ἀκοήν, γεῦσιν, ὄσφρησιν [καὶ ἁφήν]. ταύτας γὰρ ἔχει

9. Now he says that when the umbilical cord flows from Eden (the placenta), it is organically joined with the fetus at the epigastrium (or the "navel" in common speech). Secondly, the two veins (coursing along what are called the "gates of the liver") nourish the fetus as conveyers of blood brought from Eden (the placenta). 10. At the same time, the arteries (which we said were channels of breath) that surround the bladder on both sides along the broad bone join the great artery (the one along the spine called the "aorta"). Consequently, the breath produces movement in the embryo as it flows into the heart through its side entries.

11. And just so: for the fetus formed in paradise neither receives food through the mouth nor breathes in through the nostrils.[49] It exists in fluids. If it breathed, death would immediately ensue, for the fetus would suck in from the fluids and perish. In point of fact, the fetus is entirely bundled in what is called the "amniotic membrane" and is nourished through the umbilical cord. It receives the substance of breath, as I said, through the aorta running along the spine.[50]

ALLEGORY OF THE PENTATEUCH. 15. 1. Now the river, he says, flowing out of Eden is divided into four branches or channels. These refer to the four sense faculties of the fetus: vision, hearing, taste, and smell.[51] The child

πνεῦμα ("There is in it [the placenta] four vessels, two arteries and two veins … and through these … the embryo draws blood and breath").

49. According to Galen, in the embryo the air does not travel from the lungs into the heart, since the fetus does not breathe through the mouth. The air is furnished from the uterus into the umbilical vessels. From there, it travels into the heart and from the heart into the lungs (*Usu part.* 7.20 [Helmreich]).

50. Spiritual generation mirrors physical generation. The splitting up of the river into four channels gives us the six divine principles (or roots). The four channels convey breath and nourishment. On the spiritual plane, they convey spirit and spiritual food, providing for the growth of the spiritual human being. See further Josef Frickel, "Ein Kriterium zur Quellenscheidung innerhalb einer Paraphrase: Drei allegorische Deutungen der Paradiesflüsse *Gen* 2,10 (Hippolyt, *Ref.* VI 15–16); Sinn und Entwicklungsgeschichte," *Mus* 85 (1972): 425–504 (430–33).

51. P lists five senses here. Marcovich excises the sense of hearing. It is more likely, however, that what must be removed is the "sense of touch" (ἁφήν) since, as we learn below, infants do not have this sense until after being born. The writer of the *Great Declaration* later treats the sense of touch separately as summing up all the other senses (*Ref.* 6.16.4). According to Salles-Dabadie, a copyist suppressed the identification of the book of Exodus as the sense of hearing in order to replace it with the sense of touch (*Recherches*, 29 n. 1, 68 n. 1). Kalvesmaki comes to the same conclusion, pointing out that the order of sight, hearing, smell, and taste is preserved in Iren., *Haer.* 1.18.1;

μόνας τὰς αἰσθήσεις ἐν τῷ παραδείσῳ πλασσόμενον τὸ παιδίον. οὗτος, φησίν, ἐστὶν ὁ νόμος ὃν ἔθηκε Μωσ(ῆ)ς, καὶ πρὸς τοῦτον αὐτὸν τὸν νόμον γέγραπται τῶν βιβλίων ἕκαστον, ὡς ἐπιγραφαὶ δηλοῦσι.

2. τὸ πρῶτον βιβλίον Γένεσις· ἤρκει, φησί, πρὸς γνῶσιν τῶν ὅλων ἡ ἐπιγραφὴ τοῦ βιβλίου. αὕτη γάρ, φησίν, ἐστὶν ἡ Γένεσις ὅρασις, εἰς ἣν ἀφορίζεται ποταμοῦ σχίσις ἡ μία· ἐθεάθη γὰρ ὁ κόσμος ἐν ὁράσει.

3. <ἡ> ἐπ(ι)γραφὴ βιβλίου δευτέρου Ἔξοδος· ἔδει γὰρ τὸ γεννηθέν, τ(ὴ)ν Ἐρυθρὰν διοδεῦσαν θάλασσαν, ἐλθεῖν ἐπὶ τὴν ἔρημον—Ἐρυθρὰν δὲ λέγει, φασί, τὸ αἷμα—καὶ γεύσασθαι πικρὸν ὕδωρ. πικρὸν γάρ, φησίν, ἐστὶ τὸ ὕδωρ τὸ μετὰ τὴν Ἐρυθρὰν θάλασσαν, ὅπερ ἐστὶν ὁδὸς τῆς κατὰ τὸν βίον γνώσεως, <διὰ> τῶν ἐπιπόνων ὁδευομένη καὶ πικρῶν. 4. στραφὲν δὲ ὑπὸ Μωσέως—τουτέστι τοῦ λόγου—τὸ πικρὸν ἐκεῖνο γίνεται γλυκύ.

καὶ ὅτι ταῦθ' οὕτως ἔχει, κοινῇ πάντων, ἔστιν ἀκοῦσαι κατὰ τοὺς ποιητὰς λεγόντων·

ῥίζῃ μὲν μέλαν <ἔσκε>, γάλακτι δὲ εἴκελον ἄνθος·
μῶλυ δέ μιν καλέουσι θεοί· χαλεπὸν δέ τ' ὀρύσσειν
ἀνδράσι γε θνητοῖσι· θεοὶ δέ τε πάντα δύνανται.

16. 1. Ἀρκεῖ, φησί, <τὸ> λεχθὲν ὑπὸ τῶν ἐθνῶν πρὸς ἐπίγνωσιν τῶν ὅλων τοῖς ἔχουσιν ἀκο(ὰς) (ὑ)πακοῆς· τούτου γάρ, φησίν, ὁ γευσάμενος τοῦ καρποῦ ὑπὸ τῆς Κίρκης οὐκ ἀπεθηριώθη μόνος, ἀλλὰ καὶ τοὺς ἤδη τεθηριωμένους, τῇ δυνάμει χρώμενος τοῦ τοιούτου καρποῦ, εἰς τὸν πρῶτον ἐκεῖνον, τὸν ἴδιον αὐτῶν ἀνέπλασε καὶ ἀνετύπωσε καὶ ἀνεκαλέσατο χαρακτῆρα. 2. πιστὸς γὰρ ἀνὴρ καὶ ἀγαπώμενος ὑπὸ τῆς φαρμακίδος ἐκείνης διὰ τὸν γαλακτώδη καὶ θεῖον ἐκεῖνον καρπόν, φησίν, εὑρίσκεται.

possesses only these senses while it is being formed in "paradise." This, he says, represents the Law that Moses laid down. In accord with this very Law were written each of the books [of the Pentateuch], as the titles reveal.

2. The first book is Genesis. The title of the book sufficed for the knowledge of the universe. For this "Genesis," he says, signifies vision, into which one branch of the river is divided. This is because the world was seen by vision.

3. The title of the second book is Exodus, for it was necessary for the child, when born, to cross the Red Sea (Red, they say, refers to the blood), then come to the desert, and taste bitter water. The water beyond the Red Sea is bitter, he says. This water signifies the road of knowledge during this life, since it travels through bitter toils. 4. But that bitter water is "converted" by Moses—that is, the Logos—to become sweet.[52]

These points apply in general for all people, as can be heard from those who quote the poets:

> Twas black in root, but its flower like unto milk.
> The gods call it *mōly*. 'Tis hard to dig up
> For men who are mortal. Yet gods can do all things.[53]

16. 1. This passage spoken by the Gentiles suffices for those with an obedient ear to gain knowledge of the universe. Only the one who tasted this fruit was not made a beast by Kirke. What is more, he used the power of this special fruit to mold, stamp, and return to their own former shape those who had already been transformed into beasts.[54] 2. For through that milky and divine fruit, a man is found to be trustworthy and loved by that witch.[55]

Chrysippos, *SVF* 2.827, 836; Stobaios, *Ecl.* 1.50.27 (Wachsmuth and Hense, 1:476) (*Theology*, 100 n. 53).

52. Exod 15:22–25 LXX. The function of speech (λόγος) is dealt with below in *Ref.* 6.16.3; cf. 6.10.2. The presence of "speech" indicates that the book of Exodus corresponds to the sense of hearing, a point now absent in the text.

53. Homer, *Od.* 10.304–306. On *mōly*, see Hugo Rahner, *Griechische Mythen in christlicher Deutung* (Zürich: Rhein, 1957), 232–83. On the use of Homer, see Droge, "Homeric Exegesis," 318.

54. The hero in view here is Odysseus (Homer, *Od.* 10.308–399). The verbs employed recall molding from image to likeness (*Ref.* 6.14.5–6).

55. Those with true knowledge are not seduced by the world (Kirke) to live according to their beastly drives and instincts. The fruit image is explained below in *Ref.* 6.16.5–6.

Λευϊτικὸν ὁμοίως τὸ τρίτον βιβλίον, ὅπερ ἐστίν ἡ ὄσφρησις <καὶ> ἀναπνοή. θυσιῶν γάρ ἐστι καὶ προσφορῶν ὅλον ἐκεῖνο τὸ βιβλίον· ὅπου δέ ἐστι θυσία, ὀσμή τις εὐωδίας ἀπὸ τῆς θυσίας διὰ τῶν θυμιαμάτων γίνεται· περὶ ἣν εὐωδίαν ὄσφρησίν εἶνα(ι) δ(οκ<ί>μ)ιον.

3. Ἀριθμοὶ τὸ τέταρτον τῶν βιβλίων· γεῦσιν λέγει, ὅπο(υ) (λ)όγος ἐνεργεῖ· διὰ γὰρ τὸ λαλεῖν πάντα ἀριθμῶν τάξει κ(α)λεῖται.

Δευτερονόμιον δὲ φησίν, ἐστὶ πρὸς τὴν ἁφὴν τοῦ πεπλασμένου παιδίου γεγραμμένον. 4. ὥσπερ γὰρ ἡ ἁφὴ τὰ ὑπὸ τῶν ἄλλων αἰσθήσεων ὁραθέντα θιγοῦσα ἀνακεφαλαιοῦται καὶ βεβαιοῖ, σκληρὸν ἢ γλίσχρον, ἢ θερμὸν <ἢ ψυχρὸν> δοκιμάσασα, οὕτως τὸ πέμπτον βιβλίον τοῦ νόμου ἀνακεφαλαίωσίς ἐστι τῶν πρὸ αὐτοῦ γραφέντων τεσσάρων.

5. Πάντα οὖν, φησί, τὰ ἀγέννητά ἐστιν ἐν ἡμῖν δυνάμει, οὐκ ἐνεργείᾳ, ὡς ἡ γραμματικὴ <ἢ> ἡ γεωμετρική. ἐὰν οὖν τύχῃ τοῦ λόγου τοῦ προσήκοντος καὶ διδασκαλίας, [καὶ] στραφήσεται τὸ πικρὸν εἰς γλυκύ—τουτέστιν «αἱ ζιβύναι εἰς δρέπανα καὶ αἱ μάχαιραι εἰς ἄροτρα»—, οὐκ ἔσται ἄχυρα καὶ ξύλα, τὰ γεννώμενα πυρί, ἀλλὰ καρπὸς τέλειος ἐξεικονισμένος, ὡς ἔφην, ἴσος καὶ ὅμοιος τῇ ἀγεννήτῳ καὶ ἀπεράντῳ δυνάμει. 6. ἐὰν δὲ μείνῃ δ(έ)νδρον μόνον, καρπὸν μὴ ποιοῦν ἐξεικονισμένον, ἀφανίζεται. «ἐγγὺς γάρ που», φησίν, «ἡ ἀξίνη παρὰ τὰς ῥίζας τοῦ δένδρου· πᾶν δένδρον», φησί, «μὴ ποιοῦν καρπὸν καλὸν ἐκκόπτεται καὶ εἰς πῦρ βάλλεται».

17. 1. Ἔστιν οὖν κατὰ τὸν Σίμωνα τὸ μακάριον καὶ ἄφθαρτον ἐκεῖνο ἐν παντὶ κεκρυμμένον δυνάμει, οὐκ ἐνεργείᾳ, ὅπερ ἐστὶν ὁ ἑστὼς στὰς στησόμενος· ἑστὼς ἄνω ἐν τῇ ἀγεννήτῳ δυνάμει, στὰς κάτω ἐν τῇ ῥοῇ τῶν ὑδάτων, ἐν εἰκόνι γεννηθείς, στησόμενος ἄνω παρὰ τὴν μακαρίαν ἀπέραντον δύναμιν, ἐὰν ἐξεικονισθῇ. 2. τρεῖς γάρ, φησίν, εἰσὶν ἑστῶτες, καὶ ἄνευ τοῦ τρεῖς

Similarly, Leviticus (the third book) refers to the sense of smell and respiration. This is because that whole book concerns sacrifices and offerings. Wherever there is a sacrifice, a pleasant odor from the sacrifice arises from the incense offerings. The sense of smell is the judge of this pleasant odor.[56]

3. Numbers is the fourth book. It means taste, wherever the spoken word is active. It is called this because we speak everything in numerical order.[57]

Deuteronomy was written, he says, for the fully formed child's sense of touch. 4. Just as the sense of touch, by handling what is seen by the other senses, sums them up and confirms them—judging whether something is hard or sticky, hot or cold—so also the fifth book of the Law is the summation of the four written before it.

5. Therefore, all the unborn realities are in us in potentiality, not in actuality, like the skill of grammar or geometry. So if one encounters apt speech and instruction, the bitter will turn to sweet—that is, "the spears will turn to sickles and the swords into plows."[58] There will not be chaff and wood (things born for fire) but fruit mature and formed according to the model, as I said—equal and like unto the Unborn and Infinite Power. 6. But if it remains a tree only, not producing fully formed fruit, it is done away with. "For the axe is near," he says, "to the roots of the tree. Every tree," he says, "not producing good fruit is cut down and thrown into the fire."[59]

THE DIVINE SPARK WITHIN. 17. 1. There is, then, according to Simon, that blessed and incorruptible reality hidden in every human being—in potentiality, not in actuality—which is the One Who Stood, Stands, and Will Stand. He stood above in the Unborn Power. He stands below in the flow of waters, born in an image. He will stand above alongside the blessed Infinite Power, if made in the likeness.[60] 2. Accordingly, there are three

56. "Judge" translates δοκίμιον, Marcovich's conjectural emendation of P's δ…ιον (comparing Longinus, *Subl.* 32.5: γλῶσσαν δὲ γεύσεως δοκίμιον ["the tongue is the judge of taste"]).

57. There may be a play on words here between ἀριθμῶν and ἐν ῥυθμός ("in rhythm").

58. Isa 2:4 (cited in the reverse order as it stands in the LXX).

59. Cf. Matt 3:10 par.

60. The divine element in human beings has three phases: preexistence in the Unborn Power, embodiment in nature/matter (the "waters") below, and future restoration to the Godhead when conformed to the Infinite Power. God appears in three phases: in an eternal state of stability, a current state of becoming, and a state of final perfection. These three states are expressed temporally by the perfect, aorist, and

εἶναι ἑστῶτας αἰῶνας οὐ κοσμεῖται ὁ ἀγέννητος, ὁ κατ' αὐτοὺς ἐπὶ τοῦ ὕδατος φερόμενος, ὁ καθ' ὁμοίωσιν ἀναπεπλασμένος τέλειος ἐπου(ράν)ιος, <ὁ> κατ' οὐδεμίαν ἐπίνοιαν ἐνδεέστερος τῆς ἀγεννήτου δυνάμεως (γε)νώμενος. τοῦτ' ἔστιν ὃ λέγουσιν·

ἐγὼ καὶ σὺ ἕν·
<τὸ> πρὸ ἐμοῦ σύ,
τὸ μετὰ σὲ ἐγώ.

3. αὕτη, φησίν, ἐστὶ δύναμις μία, διῃρημένη ἄνω κάτω, αὐτὴν γεννῶσα, αὐτὴν αὔξουσα, αὐτὴν ζητοῦσα, αὐτὴν εὑρίσκουσα, αὐτῆς μήτηρ οὖσα, αὐτῆς πατήρ, αὐτῆς ἀδελφή, αὐτῆς σύζυγος, αὐτῆς θυγάτηρ, αὐτῆς υἱός, μήτηρ, πατήρ, ἓν οὖσα· ῥίζα τῶν ὅλων.

4. Καὶ ὅτι, φησίν, ἀπὸ πυρὸς ἡ ἀρχὴ τῆς γενέσεώς ἐστι τῶν γεννωμένων, τοιοῦτον κατανόει τινὰ τρόπον. πάντων ὅσων γένεσίς ἐστιν, ἀπὸ πυρὸς ἡ ἀρχὴ τῆς ἐπιθυμίας τῆς γενέσεως γίνεται· τοιγαροῦν πυροῦσθαι τὸ ἐπιθυμεῖν τῆς μεταβλητῆς γενέσεως ὀνομάζεται.

5. ἓν δὲ ὄν, τὸ πῦρ τροπὰ(ς <σ>τρέ)φεται δύο· στρέφεται γάρ, φησίν, ἐν τῷ ἀνδρὶ τὸ αἷμα—καὶ θερμὸν καὶ ξανθὸν ὡς πῦρ τυπούμενον—εἰς σπέρμα, ἐν δὲ τῇ γυναικὶ τὸ αὐτὸ τοῦτο αἷμα εἰς γάλα· καὶ γίνεται ἡ τοῦ ἄρρενος τροπὴ γένεσις, ἡ δὲ τῆς θηλείας τροπὴ τροφὴ τῷ γεννωμένῳ. αὕτη, φησίν, ἐστὶν «ἡ φλογίνη ῥομφαία ἡ στρεφομένη φυλάσσειν τὴν ὁδὸν τοῦ ξύλου τῆς ζωῆς». 6. στρέφεται γὰρ τὸ αἷμα εἰς σπέρμα καὶ γάλα, καὶ γίνεται ἡ δύναμις αὕτη πατὴρ καὶ μήτηρ, σπορὰ τῶν γινομένων καὶ αὔξησις τῶν τρεφομένων, ἀπροσδεής, αὐτάρκης.

φυλάσσεται δέ, φησί, τὸ ξύλον τῆς ζωῆς διὰ τῆς στρεφομένης φλογίν(ης) ῥομφαίας, ὡς εἰρήκαμεν, ἡ δύναμις ἡ ἑ(βδ)όμη, ἡ ἐξ αὐτῆς, ἡ πάντα ἔχουσα,

standing aeons, he says, and apart from these three, the Unborn One is not ordered. He (in their view) is the one hovering upon the waters and formed according to the likeness. He is perfect, heavenly, and inferior to the Unborn Power in no conceivable way. This is what they say:

I and you are one.
What is before me is you.
What is after you is I.[61]

3. This, he says, is the single power, divided above and below, giving birth to itself, increasing itself, seeking itself, finding itself, being mother of itself, father of itself, sister of itself, partner of itself, daughter of itself, son of itself, mother and father, yet one—the root of the universe.

THE FLAMING SWORD: FIRE AS SOURCE OF BIRTH. 4. Moreover, he claims that the source of generation for those who are born is from fire. What he means is this. For all those to whom generation is allotted, the source of the desire for generation comes from fire. Accordingly, the desire for changeable generation is called "burning."[62]

5. Although it is one, the fire is turned in two ways. In the man, the blood is turned, he says, into semen (characterized, like fire, by heat and a whitish color). In the woman, however, the same blood is turned into milk. Accordingly, the "turning" in the male becomes generation, whereas the "turning" in the female becomes nourishment for the offspring. This process, he says, is referred to in the scriptural verse: "the flaming sword that *turns* to guard the way of the tree of life."[63] 6. The blood turns to semen and milk, and this power itself becomes father and mother, the sowing of what is generated and growth for what is nourished. It needs nothing and is self-sufficient.

The tree of life is guarded, he says, by the flaming sword that turns, as I mentioned. This flaming sword is the Seventh Power, self-derived, con-

---

future participles of ἵστημι: God has stood, stands in the present moment, and will stand. There is no distinction drawn between this dynamic God as he evolves in the cosmos and as he evolves within the human self. The two forms of God can and must identify with each other.

61. Cf. *PGM* VIII.36; XIII.795; Corp. herm. 5.11; Iren., *Haer.* 1.13.3; Clem. Alex., *Strom.* 2.6.25.2; Epiph., *Pan.* 26.3.1; Pist. Soph. 96 (Schmidt, 226–33).

62. Cf. 1 Cor 7:9.

63. Gen 3:24 LXX.

ἡ ἐν ταῖς ἓξ κατ(α)κειμένη δυνάμεσιν. 7. ἐὰν γὰρ μὴ στρέφηται ἡ φλογίνη ῥομφαία, φθαρήσεται καὶ ἀπολεῖται τὸ καλὸν ἐκεῖνο ξύλον· ἐὰν δὲ στρέφηται εἰς σπέρμα καὶ γάλα, ὁ δυνάμει ἐν τούτοις κατακείμενος, λόγου τοῦ προσήκοντος καὶ τόπου κυρίου ἐν ᾧ γεννᾶται λόγος τυχών, ἀρξάμενος ὡς ἀπὸ σπινθῆρος ἐλαχίστου παντελῶς μεγαλυνθήσεται καὶ αὐξήσει, καὶ ἔσται δύναμις ἀπέραντος ἀπαράλ<λ>ακτος, εἰς τὸν ἀπέραντον αἰῶνα [αἰῶνι] ἀπαράλ<λ>ακτον, μηκέτι γινόμενον.

18. 1. Γέγονεν οὖν ὁμολογουμένως κατὰ τοῦτον τὸν λόγον τοῖς ἀνοήτοις Σίμων θεός, ὥσπερ ὁ Λίβυς ἐκεῖνος [ὁ καὶ] Ἄψεθος· γεννητὸς μὲν καὶ παθητός, ὅταν ᾖ ἐν δυνάμει, ἀπαθὴς δὲ καὶ <ἀ>γέννητος, ὅταν ἐξεικονισθῇ καὶ γενόμενος τέλειος ἐξέλθῃ τῶν δυνάμεων τῶν πρώτων δύο, τουτέστιν οὐρανοῦ καὶ γῆς.

2. λέγει γὰρ Σίμων δια(ρρή)δην περὶ τούτου ἐν τῇ Ἀποφάσει οὕτως·

ὑμῖν οὖν λέγω ἃ λέγω καὶ γράφω ἃ γράφω, τὸ γράμμα τοῦτο· δύο εἰσὶ παραφυάδες τῶν ὅλων αἰώνων, μήτε ἀρχὴν μήτε πέρας ἔχουσαι, ἀπὸ μιᾶς ῥίζης, ἥτις ἐστὶ δύναμις Σιγὴ ἀόρατος, ἀκατάληπτος.
3. ὧν ἡ μία φαίνεται ἄνωθεν, ἥτις ἐστὶ μεγάλη δύναμις, Νοῦς τῶν ὅλων, διέπων τὰ πάντα, ἄρσην· ἡ δὲ ἑτέρα κάτωθεν, Ἐπίνοια, μεγάλη, θήλεια, γεννῶσα τὰ πάντ(α). ἔνθεν ἀλλήλοις ἀντιστοιχοῦντες συζυγίαν

taining everything, and situated within the six powers. 7. If the flaming sword is not turned, that good tree will be corrupted and destroyed.[64] But if the fire turns into semen and milk, the one situated in these potentially, when he encounters apt speech and the place of the Lord in which speech is born,[65] will be vastly enlarged and grow. Though beginning as from the tiniest spark, he will become an infinite and unchanging power, attaining the infinite and unchanging aeon, no longer subject to generation.[66]

APPLICATION TO SIMON. 18. 1. So, in accordance with this account, everyone agrees that Simon became a god to fools—just like that Libyan Apsethos. Simon, though born and able to suffer when he was in potentiality, became unable to suffer and unborn when he was formed according to the likeness.[67] Thus becoming perfect, he departed from the first two powers (namely, heaven and earth).[68]

EXCERPT FROM THE *GREAT DECLARATION*. 2. Simon explicitly speaks about this in his *Declaration* as follows:

> To you, then, I speak what I speak and write what I write—this very writing. There are two offshoots of all the aeons, having neither beginning nor end. They are from a single root or power, namely, invisible and incomprehensible Silence.
> 3. One of these appears above: a Great Power, Mind of the universe, pervading all things, and male. The other is below: Thought, who is magnificent, female, and generates all things. Hence they correspond to each other and form a pair. In the intervening space,

---

64. The "good tree" is the tree of life, who is also the "new shoot" or human (*Ref.* 6.10.1). See further Abramowski, *Drei*, 33.

65. Apparently the Lord's mouth (cf. *Ref.* 6.10.2 above).

66. The generation or growth produced by the cosmic fire and likened to the burning of sexual desire is needed to achieve the final birthless and deathless state. Generation is made possible by the semen of males, and growth by the milk in females. The principle of generation is identified with the Seventh Power, allegorically likened to the ever-turning (i.e., ever-generating) sword of fire in Gen 3:25. See further Frickel, *Apophasis*, 198–201.

67. Καὶ ἀγέννητος ("and unborn") is Marcovich's emendation of P's ἐκ γε(ν)νητοῦ ("from the born one"). Cf. Justin, *1 Apol.* 25.2; Athenagoras, *Leg.* 8.2; 10.1.

68. Heaven and earth, as the place of generation, are no longer appropriate for one unborn.

ἔχουσι. καὶ τὸ μέσον διάστημα ἐμφαίνουσιν ἀέρα ἀκατάληπτον, μήτε ἀρχὴν μήτε πέρας ἔχοντα,
4. ἐν δὲ τούτῳ Πατὴρ ὁ βαστάζων πάντα καὶ τρέφων τὰ ἀρχὴν καὶ πέρας ἔχοντα. οὗτός ἐ(στ)ιν ὁ ἑστὼς στὰς στησόμενος, ὢν ἀρσενόθηλυς δύναμις κατὰ τὴν προϋπάρχουσαν δύναμιν ἀπέραντον, ἥτις οὔτ' ἀρχὴν οὔτε πέρας ἔχει, ἐν μονότητι οὖσα.
ἀπὸ δὲ ταύτης προελθοῦσα ἡ ἐν μονότητι Ἐπίνοια ἐγένετο δύο. 5. κἀκεῖνος ἦν εἷς· ἔχων γὰρ ἐν ἑαυτῷ αὐτὴν ἦν μόνος. οὐ μέντοι πρῶτος, καίπερ προϋπάρχων· φανεὶς γὰρ αὐτῷ ἀπὸ ἑαυτοῦ ἐγένετο δεύτερος. ἀλλ' οὐδὲ Πατὴρ ἐκλήθη πρὶν αὐτὴ<ν> αὐτὸν ὀνομάσαι πατέρα. 6. ὡς οὖν αὐτὸς ἑαυτὸν ἀπὸ ἑαυτοῦ προαγαγὼν ἐφανέρωσεν ἑαυτῷ τὴν ἰδίαν Ἐπίνοιαν, οὕτως καὶ ἡ φανεῖσα Ἐπίνοια <αὐτὸ>ν οὐκ ἐποίησεν, ἀλλὰ ἰδοῦσα αὐτὸν ἐνέκρυψε τὸν Πατέρα ἐν ἑαυτῇ—τουτέστι τὴν δύναμιν—, καὶ ἔστιν ἀρσενόθηλυς δύναμις καὶ Ἐπίνοια. ὅθεν ἀλλήλοις ἀντι(στο)ιχοῦσιν· οὐδὲν γὰρ διαφέρει δύναμις ἐπινοίας, ἓν ὄντες· ἐκ μὲν τῶν ἄνω εὑρίσκεται δύναμις, ἐκ δὲ τῶν κάτω ἐπίνοια.
7. ἔστιν οὖν οὕτως καὶ τὸ φανὲν ἀπ' αὐτῶν· ἓν ὂν δύο εὑρίσκεται· ἀρσενόθηλυς ἔχει τὴν θήλειαν ἐν ἑαυτῷ. οὕτως ἐστὶ νοῦς ἐν ἐπινοίᾳ· ἀχώριστα ἀπ' ἀλλήλων, ἓν ὄντες δύο εὑρίσκονται.

19. 1. Ταῦτα μὲν οὖν ὁ Σίμων ἐφευρὼν οὐ μόνον τὰ Μωσέως κακοτεχνήσας εἰς ὃ ἐβούλετο μεθηρμήνευσεν, ἀλλὰ καὶ τὰ τῶν ποιητῶν· καὶ γὰρ τὸν δούρειον ἵππον ἀλληγορεῖ, καὶ τὴν Ἑλένην ἅμα τῇ λαμπάδι, καὶ ἄλλα πλεῖστα ὅσα μεταγγί(σας περ)ί τε αὐτοῦ καὶ τῆς Ἐπινοίας πλείστους λέγει.

2. εἶναι <δ>έ γε ταύτην τὸ πρόβατον τὸ πεπλανημένον, ἥτις ἀεὶ καταγινομένη ἐν γυναιξὶν ἐτάρασσε τὰς ἐν <τῷ> κόσμῳ δυνάμεις διὰ τὸ ἀνυπέρβλητον αὐτῆς κάλλος. ὅθεν καὶ ὁ Τρωϊκὸς πόλεμος δι' αὐτὴν γεγένηται·

they exhibit an immeasurable expanse of air, which has neither beginning nor end.[69]

4. In this air, the Father upholds all things and nourishes those beings that have beginning and end. He is the One Who Stood, Who Stands, Who Will Stand. He is an androgynous power as is right for the infinite preexisting power having neither beginning nor end and existing in unity.

From this power, the Thought in the unity came forth and became two. 5. (Now the Father was one, for having her in himself, he was alone. Although he preexisted, he is still not "first."[70] He became a second deity when he appeared to himself from himself.[71] Neither was he called "Father" before she called him "father.") 6. Since, then, he himself, having advanced from himself, manifested to himself his own Thought, so also the Thought who appeared did not make him.[72] But when she saw him, she hid the Father in herself—that is, his power—thus there is an androgynous power and Thought. Thus they correspond to each other. This is because power does not at all differ from Thought; they are one. Power is discovered from things above, while Thought is discovered from things below. 7. It works the same way with what is manifested from them. Though one, they are discovered to be two. The androgynous one contains the female in himself. So also there is Mind in Thought. They are inseparable. Although one, they are discovered to be two.

SIMON AND HELEN. 19. 1. These are the things that Simon invented, distorting by his arbitrary interpretation not only the writings of Moses but also those of the poets. For in fact, he allegorizes the wooden horse, the figure of Helen with her torch, and a host of other things about which he, transferring to himself and his "Thought," speaks volumes.

2. Thought is supposedly the wandering sheep. She, always taking up residence in women, disturbed the powers in the cosmos on account of her unsurpassable beauty. Thus the Trojan War happened because of her, since

69. Cf. *Ref.* 6.13.1. Mind and Thought are identified with Heaven and Earth, thus in between them (as a result of their separation) there is a great expanse of air.

70. One cannot be "first" if there is no second.

71. Aristotle, *Metaph.* 12.9, 1074b34: Αὑτὸν ἄρα νοεῖ ("He thinks himself").

72. P reads ἡ φανεῖσα ἐπίνοια ν οὐκ ἐποίησεν. Conjectured here for ν is αὐτόν, which appears in the next clause. Marcovich proposes νοῦν ("Mind"). Earlier editors read ἐπίνοιαν as one word or simply delete the ν (e.g., Wendland).

ἐν γὰρ τῇ κατ᾽ ἐκεῖνο καιροῦ γενομένῃ Ἑλένῃ ἐνῴκησεν [ἐν αὐτῇ] ἡ Ἐπίνοια, καὶ οὕτως πασῶν ἐπιδικαζομένων αὐτῆς τῶν ἐξουσιῶν στάσις καὶ πόλεμος ἐπανέστη ἐν οἷς ἐφάνη ἔθνεσιν. 3. οὕτως γοῦν τὸν Στησίχορον διὰ τῶν ἐπῶν λοιδορήσαντα αὐτὴν τὰς ὄψεις τυφλωθῆναι· αὖθις δὲ μεταμεληθέντα αὐτὸν καὶ γράψαντα τὰς παλινῳδίας, ἐν αἷς ὕμνησεν αὐτήν, ἀναβλέψαι.

μετενσωματουμένην <αὐτὴν καὶ> ὑπὸ τῶν ἀγγέλων καὶ τῶν κάτω ἐξουσιῶν—οἳ καὶ τὸν κόσμον, φησίν, ἐποίησαν—, ὕστερον ἐπὶ τέγους ἐν Τύρῳ τῆ(ς) Φοινίκης πόλει στῆναι. 4. ἣν κατελθὼν εὗρεν· ἐπὶ γὰρ τὴν τα(ύ)τ(η)ς πρώτης ζήτησιν ἔφη παραγεγονέναι, ὅπως ῥύσ(η)ται αὐτὴν τῶν δεσμῶν. ἣν λυτρωσάμενος ἅμα ἑαυτῷ περιῆγε, φάσκων τοῦτο εἶναι τὸ ἀπολωλὸς πρόβατον, ἑαυτὸν δὲ λέγων τὴν ὑπὲρ πάντα δύναμιν εἶναι. ὁ δὲ ψυ<δ>ρὸς ἐρασθεὶς τοῦ γυναίου τούτου, Ἑλένης καλουμένης, ὠνησάμενος εἶχε, καὶ τοὺς μαθητὰς αἰδούμενος τοῦτον τὸν μῦθον ἔπλασεν.

5. οἳ δὲ αὖθις, μιμηταὶ τοῦ πλάνου καὶ μάγου Σίμωνος γινόμενοι, τὰ ὅμοια δρῶσιν, ἀλογίστως φάσκοντες δεῖν μίγνυσθαι <καὶ> λέγοντες· πᾶσα γῆ γῆ, καὶ οὐ διαφέρει ποῦ τι<ς> (σπ)είρει, πλὴν ἵνα σπείρῃ. ἀλλὰ καὶ μακαρίζουσιν ἑαυτοὺς ἐπὶ τῇ ξ(έ)νῃ μίξει, ταύτην εἶναι λέγοντες τὴν τελείαν ἀγάπην καὶ <τοῦτο> τό· ἅγιος ἁγίῳ κολλη(τ)ὸς ἁγιασθήσεται· οὐ γὰρ μὴ<ν> κρατεῖσθαι αὐτοὺς ἔτι τινὶ νομιζομένῳ κακῷ· λελύτρωνται γάρ.

Τὴν δὲ Ἑλένην λυτρωσάμενος οὕτως τοῖς ἀνθρώποις σωτηρίαν παρέσχε διὰ τῆς ἰδίας ἐπιγνώσεως. 6. κακῶς γὰρ διοικούντων τῶν ἀγγέλων τὸν κόσμον διὰ τὸ φιλαρχεῖν αὐτούς, εἰς ἐπανόρθωσιν ἐληλυθέναι αὐτὸν ἔφη μεταμορφούμενον καὶ ἐξομοιούμενον ταῖς ἀρχαῖς καὶ ταῖς ἐξουσίαις καὶ τοῖς ἀγγέλοις, ὡς καὶ ἄνθρωπον φαίνεσθαι αὐτὸν μὴ ὄντα ἄνθρωπον, καὶ παθεῖν δὴ ἐν τῇ Ἰουδαίᾳ [καὶ] δεδοκηκέναι μὴ πεπονθότα· ἀλλὰ φανέντα Ἰουδαίοις μὲν ὡς υἱόν, ἐν δὲ τῇ Σαμαρείᾳ ὡς πατέρα, ἐν δὲ τοῖς λοιποῖς ἔθνεσιν ὡς πνεῦμα ἅγιον ὑπομένειν δὴ αὐτὸν καλεῖσθαι οἵῳ ἂν ὀνόματι καλεῖν βού(λω)νται οἱ ἄνθρωποι.

7. τοὺς δὲ προφήτας ὑπὸ τῶν κοσμοποιῶν ἀγγέλων ἐμπνευσθέντας εἰρηκέναι τὰς προφητείας· διὸ μὴ φροντίζειν αὐτῶν τοὺς εἰς τὸν Σίμωνα καὶ τὴν Ἑλένην πεπιστευκότας ἕως νῦν, πράσσειν τε <ὅ>σα βούλονται ὡς ἐλευθέρους. κατὰ

Thought dwelled in the woman who became the Helen of that time. In this way, when all the authorities claimed her, she stirred up faction and war among the nations in which she appeared. 3. So also Stesichoros, when he reviled her in his verses, was struck blind. But when he repented, he wrote his "palinodes" (in which he praised her) and regained his sight.

She, after transmigrating under the control of angels and the lower authorities (who also, he says, made the world), later took her place at a brothel in Tyre (a city of Phoenicia). 4. She it was whom Simon found when he descended. He claimed that he had come to search for his first Thought, to free her from her chains. After he redeemed her, he took her around with him, alleging that this was the lost sheep. Meanwhile, he called himself "the Power above all things."[73] But the liar was in love with this girl called "Helen."[74] Accordingly, he bought and possessed her. Since he was ashamed before his disciples, he concocted this tale.

5. The Simonians, for their part, are imitators of Simon the deceiver and magician, and they perform the same works. They irrationally claim that it is necessary to have intercourse by virtue of their maxim: "all soil is soil, and it does not matter where he sows, except that he sows." In fact, they even congratulate themselves with regard to perverse intercourse, calling it "perfect love." They use this slogan: "The holy welded to what is holy will be made holy." To be sure, they are not controlled by any supposed vice, since they have been "redeemed"![75]

Having redeemed Helen, Simon provided salvation to human beings in the same manner: through his own knowledge. 6. Since the angels mismanaged the world on account of their lust to rule, he said that he arrived for its rectification. He transformed and assimilated himself to the rulers, authorities, and angels. He appeared to be human but was not human. He seemed to suffer in Judea, although he suffered nothing. But after appearing in Judea as Son, and in Samaria as Father, and among the rest of the nations as the Holy Spirit, he allowed himself to be called by whatever name people wish to call him.[76]

7. Now the prophets, inspired by the angels who made the world, spoke their prophecies. Accordingly, those loyal to Simon and Helen pay no attention to them up to the present time. They do whatever they want as

73. Cf. Acts 8:10 (*Samaritans* call Simon the great Power).

74. Ψυδρός ("liar") is an emendation for P's ψυχρός ("cold [one]").

75. Accusations of licentiousness and sexual immortality are heresiological *topoi* (e.g., Clem. Alex., *Strom*. 3.4.30.1–2; Epiph., *Pan*. 26.4).

76. Cf. Iren., *Haer.* 1.23.1 (end).

γὰρ τὴν αὐτοῦ χάριν σῴζεσθαι αὐτοὺς φάσκουσι, μηδέν δὲ εἶναι αἴτιον δίκης εἰ πράξει τι κακόν. 8. οὐ γάρ ἐστί <τι> φύσει κακὸν ἀλλὰ θέσει· ἔθεντο γάρ, φησίν, οἱ ἄγγελοι οἱ τὸν κόσμον ποιήσαντες ὅσα ἐβούλοντο, διὰ τῶν τοιούτων λόγων δουλοῦν νομίζοντες τοὺς αὐτῶν ἀκούοντας. λύσ<ε>ιν δὲ αὖθις λέγουσι τὸν κόσμον ἐπὶ λυτρώσει τῶν ἰδίων ἀνθρώπων.

20. 1. Οἱ οὖν τούτου μαθηταὶ μαγεία(ς) ἐπιτελοῦσι καὶ ἐπαοιδαῖς <χρῶνται>, φίλτρα τε καὶ ἀγώγιμα (κ)αὶ τοὺς λεγομένους ὀνειροπόμπους δαίμονας ἐπιπέμπουσι πρὸς τὸ ταράσσειν οὓς βούλονται· ἀλλὰ καὶ τοὺς λεγομένους παρέδρους ἀσκοῦσιν.

εἰκόνα τε τοῦ Σίμωνος ἔχουσιν εἰς Διὸς μορφὴν καὶ τῆς Ἑλένης ἐν μορφῇ Ἀθηνᾶς, καὶ ταύτας προσκυνοῦσι, τὸν μὲν καλοῦντες κύριον, τὴν δὲ κυρίαν· 2. εἰ δέ τις ὀνόματι καλέσει παρ' αὐτοῖς ἰδὼν τὰς εἰκόνας ἢ Σίμωνος ἢ Ἑλένης, ἀπόβλητος γίνεται, ὡς ἀγνοῶν τὰ μυστήρια.

οὗτος ὁ Σίμων μαγείαις πολλοὺς πλανῶν ἐν τῇ Σαμαρείᾳ ὑπὸ τῶν ἀποστόλων ἠλέγχθη· καὶ ἐπάρατος γενόμενος, καθὼς ἐν ταῖς Πράξεσι γέγραπται, ἀπευδοκήσας ὕστερον ταὐτὰ ἐπεχείρησεν, ἕως καὶ τῇ Ῥώμῃ ἐπιδημήσας ἀντέπεσε τοῖς ἀποστόλοις· πρὸς ὃν πολλὰ Πέτρος ἀντικατέστη, μαγείαις πλανῶντα πολλούς.

3. Οὗτος ἐπὶ τέλει ἐλθὼν ἐν τ(ῇ) Γί(τ)τῃ, ὑπὸ πλάτανον καθεζόμενος ἐδίδασκε. καὶ δὴ λοιπὸν ἐγγὺς τοῦ ἐλέγχεσθαι γινόμενος διὰ τὸ ἐγχρονίζειν, ἔφη ὅτι εἰ χωσθείη ζῶν ἀναστήσεται τῇ τρίτῃ ἡμέρᾳ. καὶ δὴ τάφρον κελεύσας ὀρυγῆναι ὑπὸ τῶν μαθητῶν ἐκέλευσε χωσθῆναι· οἱ μὲν οὖν τὸ προσταχθὲν ἐποίησαν, ὁ δὲ ἀπέμεινεν ἕως νῦν· οὐ γὰρ ἦν ὁ Χριστός.

4. οὗτος δὴ καὶ ὁ κατὰ τὸν Σίμωνα μῦθος· ἀφ' οὗ Οὐαλεντῖνος τὰς ἀφορμὰς λαβὼν ἄλλοις ὀνόμασι καλεῖ· ὁ γὰρ Νοῦς καὶ ἡ Ἀλήθεια καὶ Λόγος καὶ Ζωὴ καὶ Ἄνθρωπος καὶ Ἐκκλησία, οἱ Οὐαλεντίνου αἰῶνες, ὁμολογουμένως εἰσὶν αἱ Σίμω(ν)ος ἓξ ῥίζαι· Νοῦς, Ἐπίνοια, Φωνή, Ὄνομα, Λογισμὸς καὶ Ἐνθύμη(σ)ις.

"free" persons. They claim that they are saved by his grace, and that there is no cause of judgment for future wrongs. 8. This is because there is nothing evil by nature, but only by imposition. For the angels who made the world, he says, imposed whatever they wanted, aiming to enslave those who listen to their brand of teachings. But Simonians say that after their own people are redeemed, [the angels] will destroy the world.[77]

"MAGIC." 20. 1. The disciples of this man perform feats of magic and use enchantments, philters, and love charms. Moreover, they send off the so-called "dream-sending demons" to terrorize whoever they want. In fact, they employ as a regular practice so-called "assistants."[78]

They possess a statue of Simon in the form of Zeus, and Helen in the form of Athena. They worship these statues, calling the one "Lord," the other "Lady." 2. If someone, catching sight of the statues of Simon and Helen, calls them "Simon and Helen," he is cast out as one ignorant of the mysteries.[79]

This Simon, as he was deceiving many by his magic arts in Samaria, was refuted by the apostles.[80] When he was laid under a curse, as it is written in Acts, he despaired and later attempted the same activities. Even at Rome, where he moved, he was at loggerheads with the apostles. Peter opposed him many times, since he was deceiving most people by magic arts.[81]

SIMON'S DEATH. 3. In the end, this Simon went to Gitta, sat down under a plane tree, and taught. Finally, since he was close to being refuted due to the long delay of time, he said that if he was buried alive he would rise on the third day. So, ordering a trench to be dug, he bid his disciples to bury him. They did what he commanded. There he remains till now—since he was not the Christ.

4. This is the man, and this is the myth of Simon! From it, Valentinus took his starting points, referring to it with different terminology. For all agree that the aeons of Valentinus—namely, Mind, Truth, Word, Life, Human, and Church—are the six roots of Simon: Mind, Thought, Voice, Name, Reasoning, and Conception.

---

77. Cf. Iren., *Haer.* 1.23.3.

78. Cf. Tert., *Praescr.* 33.12: *Simonianae autem magiae disciplina angelis serviens* ("The discipline of Simonian magic is in the service of angels").

79. Cf. Iren., *Haer.* 1.23.4; Eusebios, *Hist. eccl.* 2.13.6.

80. Acts 8:20–24.

81. Acts Pet. 8–32 (*NTApoc* 2:298–313).

ἀλλ᾽ ἐπεὶ ἱκανῶς ἡμῖν δοκεῖ ἐκτεθεῖσθαι τὴν Σίμωνος μυθ(ο)ποιΐαν, ἴδωμεν τί λέγει καὶ Οὐαλεντῖνος.

21. 1. Ἔστι μὲν οὖν ἡ Οὐαλεντίνου αἵρεσις Πυθαγορικὴν ἔχουσα καὶ Πλατωνικὴν τὴν ὑπόθεσιν. καὶ γὰρ Πλάτων ὅλως ἐν τῷ Τιμαίῳ τὸν Πυθαγόραν ἀπεμάξατο—τοιγαροῦν καὶ ὁ Τίμαιος αὐτός ἐστιν αὐτῷ Πυθαγόρειος ξένος.—διὸ δοκεῖ ὀλίγα τῆς Πυθαγορείου καὶ Πλατωνικῆς ὑπομνησθέντας ὑποθέσεως ἄρξασθαι καὶ τὰ Οὐαλεντίνου λέγειν. 2. εἰ γὰρ καὶ ἐν τοῖς πρότερον ὑφ᾽ ἡμῶν πεπονημένοις ἔγκεινται καὶ τὰ Πυθαγόρᾳ καὶ Πλάτωνι δεδοκημένα, ἀλλά γε καὶ νῦν οὐκ ἀλόγως ὑπομνησθήσομαι δι᾽ ἐπιτομῆς τὰ κορυφαιότατα τῶν αὐτοῖς ἀρεσκομένων, πρὸς τὸ εὐεπίγνωστα γενέσθαι τὰ Οὐαλεντίν(ῳ) δόξαντα διὰ τῆς ἐγγίονος παραθέσεως <ὁμοῦ καὶ> συγκρίσεως, 3. τῶν μὲν πάλαι ἀπ᾽ Αἰγυπτίων ταῦτα παραλαβόντων καὶ εἰς Ἕλληνας μεταδιδαξάντων, τοῦ δὲ παρὰ τούτων, ὅτι παρ᾽ αὐτῶν διαψευσαμένου ἰδίαν τε δόξαν συστῆσαι πεπειραμένου, σπαράξαντος μὴν τὰ ἐκείνων, ὀνόμασι καὶ ἀριθμοῖς ἰδίως τε καλέσαντος καὶ μέτροις διορίσαντος, ὅπως αἵρεσιν Ἑλληνικὴν ποικίλην μέν, ἀσύστατον δὲ καὶ οὐκ ἀνήκουσαν Χριστῷ συστήσῃ.

22. 1. Ἡ μὲν οὖν ἀρχὴ τῆς ὑποθέσεώς ἐστιν ἐν τῷ Τιμαίῳ τῷ Πλάτωνι σοφία Αἰγυπτίων· ἐκεῖθεν γὰρ ὁ <Σόλων> τὴν ὅλη(ν) ὑπόθεσιν περὶ τῆς κόσμου γενέσεως καὶ φθορᾶς πα(λ)αιῷ τινι λόγῳ καὶ προφητικῷ, ὥς φησιν ὁ Πλάτων, τοὺς Ἕλληνας ἐδίδαξε, παῖδας νέους ὄντας καὶ πρεσβύτερον ἐπισταμένους μάθημα θεολογούμενον οὐδέν. 2. ἵν᾽ οὖν παρακολουθήσωμεν τοῖς λόγοις οἷς καταβέβληται Οὐαλεντῖνος, προεκθήσομαι νῦν τίνα ἐστὶν ἃ Πυθαγόρας ὁ Σάμιος μετὰ τῆς ὑμνουμένης ἐκείνης παρὰ τοῖς Ἕλλησι <σι>γῆς φιλοσοφεῖ, εἶθ᾽ <ὡσ>αύτως ταῦτα ἃ <παρὰ> Πυθαγόρου λαβὼν καὶ Πλάτωνος Οὐαλεντῖνος

But since it seems to me that I have adequately presented Simon's mythmaking, let us see what Valentinus too declares.

REVIEW OF PYTHAGORAS AND PLATO

21. 1. The heresy of Valentinus has a Pythagorean and Platonic basis. Even Plato in the *Timaios* entirely modeled himself on Pythagoras (and accordingly Timaios is himself his Pythagorean guest).[82] So it seems right to begin with a few words, by way of reminder, about the basic points of Pythagorean and Platonic philosophy, and then to declare the teachings of Valentinus. 2. Even if the teachings of Pythagoras and Plato are also contained in the books I previously elaborated,[83] still I think it not unreasonable now to summarily call to mind the chief points of their doctrines in order to foster easy recognition of Valentinus's views by means of closer juxtaposition and comparison.[84] 3. Some of these teachings were long ago taken from the Egyptians and adapted to a Greek audience. From these adapters, Valentinus received his teachings. Denying that he received the teachings from them, he tried to establish his own doctrine. In fact, he dismembered their teachings, calling them by the terms and numbers distinctive to him and defining them by his own standards. He did so in order to concoct a motley Hellenic heresy, inconsistent and alien to Christ.

22. 1. The basis of Plato's *Timaios* is Egyptian wisdom. It is from there that Solon taught the Greeks the content of the world's origin and destruction, employing an ancient and prophetic maxim, as Plato says, that the Greeks are "young children" and know nothing about the ancient theology.[85] 2. So, in order for us to follow Valentinus's arguments, I will now present beforehand what Pythagoras of Samos touts (with that silence so praised by the Greeks!) in his philosophy.[86] Then, likewise, I will present Valentinus's teachings—swiped from Pythagoras and Plato—which, in his

82. Plato, *Tim.* 19e–20a; Iamblichos, *Vit. Pyth.* 267; further testimonies in Timaios, DK 49.

83. *Ref.* 1.2; 1.19; 4.51.

84. Marcovich replaces P's καὶ ὁμοίας with ὁμοῦ καί (here: "and"). Equally feasible is Wendland's suggestion of καὶ ὁμοίων ("closer assessment and comparison of what are *virtually the same things*").

85. Plato, *Tim.* 21c–22b. Σόλων ("Solon") is an emendation for P's σολομῶν ("Solomon"). See further Udo Reinhold Jeck, *Platonica Orientalia: Aufdeckung einer philosophischen Tradition* (Frankfurt: Klostermann, 2004), 23–42.

86. "Silence" (σιγῆς) is an emendation for P's γῆς ("earth"). Cf. *Ref.* 1.2.3, 16, 18.

σεμνολογῶν ἀνατίθησι Χριστῷ καὶ πρὸ τοῦ Χριστοῦ τῷ Πατρὶ τῶν ὅλων καὶ Σιγῇ, τῇ συνεζευγμένῃ τῷ Πατρί.

23. 1. Πυθαγόρας τοίνυν ἀρχὴν τῶν ὅλων ἀγέννητον ἀπεφήνατο τὴν μονάδα, γεννητὴν δὲ τὴν δυάδα καὶ πάντας τοὺς ἄλλους ἀριθμούς. καὶ τῆς μὲν δυάδος πατέρα φησὶν εἶναι τὴν μονάδα, πάντων δὲ τῶν γεννωμένων μητέρα δυάδα, γεννητὴν γεννητῶν· καὶ Ζαράτας ὁ Πυθαγόρου διδάσκαλος ἐκάλει τὸ μὲν ἓν πατέρα, τὰ δὲ δύο μητέρα.

2. (γ)εγέννηται γοῦν ἐκ μὲν μονάδος δυὰς κατὰ τὸν Πυθαγόραν, καὶ ἔστιν ἡ μὲν μονὰς ἄρρεν καὶ πρώτη, ἡ δὲ δυὰς θῆλυ. παρὰ τῆς δυάδος δὲ πάλιν, ὡς ὁ Πυθαγόρας λέγει, <γίνεται> ἡ τριὰς καὶ οἱ ἐφεξῆς ἀριθμοὶ μέχρι τῶν δέκα. 3. τοῦτον γὰρ οἶδε μόνον τέλειον ἀριθμὸν Πυθαγόρας, τὸν δέκα· τὸν γὰρ ἕνδεκα καὶ δώδεκα προσθήκην καὶ ἐπαναποδισμὸν τῆς δεκάδος, οὐκ ἄλλου τινὸς ἀριθμοῦ γένεσιν [τὸ προστιθέμενον].

πάντα δὲ σώματα στερεὰ ἐξ ἀσωμάτων γεννᾷ· τῶν τε γὰρ σωμάτων καὶ ἀσωμάτων ὁμοῦ στοιχεῖον εἶναί φησι καὶ ἀρχὴν τὸ σημεῖον, ὅ ἐστιν ἀμερές. γίνετ(αι) δέ, φησίν, ἐκ σημείου γραμμὴ καὶ ἐπιφάνεια δὲ ῥυεῖσα εἰς βάθος στερεὸν ὑφέστηκε, φησί, σῶμα. 4. ὅθεν καὶ ὅρκος τίς ἐστι τοῖς Πυθαγορικοῖς ἡ τῶν τεσσάρων στοιχείων συμφωνία· ὀμνύουσι δ᾽ οὕτως·

ναὶ μὰ τὸν ἁμετέρᾳ κεφαλᾷ παραδόντα τετρακτύν,
πηγὴν ἀενάου φύσεως ῥι(ζώμ)ατ᾽ ἔχουσαν.

ἔστι γὰρ ἡ τετρακτὺς τῶν φυσικῶν καὶ στερεῶν σωμάτων ἀρχή, ὡς ἡ μονὰς τῶν νοητῶν. 5. ὅτι δὲ καὶ ἡ τετρακτὺς γεννᾷ, φησί, τὸν τέλειον ἀριθμόν, ὡς ἐν τοῖς νοητοῖς, τὸν δέκα, διδάσκουσιν οὕτως· εἰ ἀρξάμενος ἀριθμεῖν λέγει τις ὅτι ἕν, καὶ ἐπιφέρει δύο, ἔπειτα ὁμοίως τρία, ἔσονται ταῦτα ἕξ· πρὸς δὲ τούτοις ἔτι τέσσαρα, ἔσται [ὁμοίως] τὸ πᾶν δέκα· τὸ γὰρ ἕν, δύο, τρία, τέσσαρα γίνετα(ι)

grandiloquence, Valentinus attributes to Christ, and—before Christ—to the "Father of the universe," and to "Silence," to whom the Father is hitched!

GENERATION THROUGH NUMBER. 23. 1. Pythagoras, then, announced that the first principle of the universe is the unborn Monad. The Dyad and all the other numbers are generated. Moreover, he says that the Monad is the Father of the Dyad, and that the Dyad is the mother of all generated beings, as one generated produces those generated. (Actually, Zaratas the teacher of Pythagoras already called the number one "Father," and the number two "Mother.")[87]

2. Thus the Dyad is born from the Monad, according to Pythagoras, and the Monad is male and primary, whereas the Dyad is female. The numbers three to ten arise, in turn, from the Dyad, as Pythagoras says.[88] 3. It is the number ten that Pythagoras deems the only perfect number.[89] For eleven and twelve are an addition and a reiteration of the decad, and generation arises from no other number.

The decad produces every solid body from incorporeal elements. The indivisible point is the building block and source of both corporeal and incorporeal entities. A point gives rise to a line, and a line to a plane. When a plane becomes three-dimensional, a solid body is formed.[90] 4. Therefore there is even an oath among Pythagoreans consisting of the harmony of the four elements. They swear as follows:

> Yea, by him who delivered to our mind the Tetraktys,
> Source possessing the roots of ever-flowing nature.[91]

This is because the Tetraktys is the source of physical and solid bodies, as the Monad is of intelligible realities. 5. They teach, he says, that the Tetraktys also produces the perfect number ten (as among intelligible realities). It does so in this way: if someone, beginning to count, says "one," then adds two, then three, then finally we will have six. If to these he adds four, the total will be ten (for 1 + 2 + 3 + 4 = 10, the perfect number). Thus the

87. In *Ref.* 1.2.12, Zaratas teaches that the Father is light and the Mother darkness. Cf. Plutarch, *An. procr.* 1012e.

88. See the number theory in *Ref.* 1.2.6–8; 4.51.4–6.

89. Diog. L., *Vit. phil.* 8.19.

90. Cf. *Ref.* 4.51.2–3; Sext. Emp., *Math.* 3.19–21; 7.99–100; *Pyr.* 3.154.

91. For the oath, see *Ref.* 1.2.9; 4.51.7; 6.34.1, with notes.

δέκα, ὁ τέλειος ἀριθμός. οὕτως, φησί, κατὰ πάντα (ἐ)μιμήσατο ἡ τετρακτὺς τὴν νοητὴν μονάδα, τέλειον ἀρι(θ)μὸν γεννῆσαι δυνηθεῖσαν.

24. 1. Δύο οὖν κατὰ τὸν Πυθαγόραν εἰσὶ κόσμοι· εἷς μὲν νοητός, ὃς ἔχει τὴν μονάδα ἀρχήν, εἷς δὲ αἰσθητός· τούτου δέ ἐστι <ἀρχὴ ἡ> τετρακτύς, ἔχουσα ἰῶτα, τὴν «μίαν κεραίαν», ἀριθμὸν τέλειον. καὶ ἔστι κατὰ τοὺς Πυθαγορικοὺς τὸ ῑ, ἡ μία κεραία, πρώτη καὶ κυριωτάτη καὶ τ(ῶ)ν νοητῶν οὐσία, νοητῶς καὶ αἰσθητῶς λαμβανομένη. <ἧ δ᾽ ἔστι> συμβεβηκότα γένη ἀσώματα ἐννέα, ἃ χωρὶς εἶναι τῆς οὐσίας οὐ δύναται· 2. ποιὸν καὶ ποσὸν καὶ πρός τι καὶ ποῦ καὶ (π)ό(τ)ε καὶ κεῖσθαι καὶ ἔχειν καὶ ποιεῖν καὶ π(ά)σχειν. ἔστιν οὖν ἐννέα τὰ συμβεβηκότα τῇ οὐσίᾳ, οἷς συναριθμουμένη ἔχει τὸν τέλειον ἀριθμόν, τὸν δέκα.

3. Διό(π)ερ διῃρημένου τοῦ παντός, ὡς εἴπομεν, εἰς νοητὸν καὶ αἰσθητὸν κόσμον, ἔχομεν καὶ ἡμεῖς ἀπὸ τοῦ νοητοῦ τὸν λόγον, ἵνα τῷ λόγῳ τὴν τῶν νοητῶν καὶ ἀσωμάτων καὶ θείων ἐποπτεύωμεν οὐσίαν.

αἰσθήσεις δέ, φησίν, ἔχομεν πέντε—ὄσφρησιν, ὅρασιν, ἀκοήν, γεῦσιν καὶ ἁφήν—, ἐν αἷς τῶν αἰσθητῶν ἐρχόμεθα εἰς γνῶσιν. καὶ οὕτω, φησίν, ἐστὶ διῃρημένος αἰσθητὸς ἀπὸ τοῦ νοητοῦ κόσμου. 4. καὶ ὅτι ἔχομεν γνώσεως ὄργανον πρὸς ἑκάτερον αὐτῶν, ἐντεῦθεν κατανοῶμεν. οὐδέν, φησί, τῶν νοητῶν γνωστὸν ἡμῖν δύναται γενέσθαι δι᾽ αἰσθήσεως. ἐκεῖνο γὰρ «οὔτε ὀφθαλμὸς εἶδεν οὔτε οὖς ἤκουσεν» οὔτ᾽ ἔγνω, φησί, τῶν ἄλλων αἰσθήσεων οἱαδητισοῦν. 5. οὐδ᾽ αὖ πάλιν τῷ λόγῳ εἰς γνῶσιν τῶν αἰσθητῶν οὐχ οἷόν τε ἐλθεῖν τινος, ἀλλὰ δεῖ

Tetraktys, he says, imitated in every way the intelligible Monad, since it was able to produce the perfect number.

TWO WORLDS: INTELLIGIBLE AND PERCEPTIBLE. 24. 1. Now there are two worlds according to Pythagoras: the one intelligible, whose source is the Monad; and the other sensible, whose source is the Tetraktys, which possesses the iota, or "single horn," as a perfect number.[92] In fact, according to the Pythagoreans, the iota—the single horn—is the primal and supreme substance of intelligible realities and can be apprehended in an intelligible and in a perceptible way.[93] With it there are nine incidental incorporeal categories that cannot exist apart from substance.[94] 2. They are quality, quantity, relation, location, time, situation, possession, activity, and passivity. So there are nine incidental qualities belonging to substance, which, when added up, amount to the perfect number ten.[95]

3. Thus when we divide the universe, as I said, into an intelligible and perceptible world, we too possess reason from the intelligible, so that by reason we can behold the substance of intelligible, incorporeal, and divine realities.

We have five senses as well, he says—namely, smell, sight, hearing, taste, and touch. By these senses, we arrive at knowledge of perceptible things. In this way, he says, the perceptible world is divided from the intelligible. 4. We also have an organ for knowing both worlds, as we understand from the following fact. Nothing, he says, of the intelligible realities can be known by us through sense perception. For "neither eye has seen nor ear heard it," nor, he says, have any of the other senses whatsoever.[96] 5. Neither, in turn, can someone come to knowledge of perceptible realities by reason. Rather, we must look at what is white, and taste what is sweet,

92. Marcovich added ἀρχή (here: "source").

93. The "single horn" of the iota (ι) is mentioned in Matt 5:18. Irenaeus indicates that Ptolemy the Valentinian used this passage and pointed to a correspondence between the numerical value of the letter iota (ten) and ten particular aeons (*Haer.* 1.3.2). See further François L. M. M. Sagnard, *La gnose valentinienne et la témoignage de saint Irénée* (Paris: J. Vrin, 1947), 337–48. The iota as a symbol is especially important for Monoïmos in *Ref.* 8.12.6.

94. Marcovich adds ᾗ δ' ἔστι ("With it there are").

95. Cf. this adaptation of Aristotle's categories with *Ref.* 1.20.1; 8.14.9.

96. Cf. the note on this saying in *Ref.* 5.24.1 (Justin).

ὅτι λευκόν ἐστιν ἰδεῖν, καὶ γεύσασθαι ὅτι γλυ(κ)ύ, καὶ ὅτι <ᾠδικὸν ἢ δύσηχον> ἀκούσαντας εἰδέναι· (κ)αὶ εἴ τι τῶν ὀσμῶν ἐστιν εὐῶδες ἢ ἀηδές, ὀσφρήσεως ἔργον, οὐ λόγου. 6. ὡσαύτως δὲ ἔχει καὶ τὰ τῆς ἁφῆς· σκληρὸν γὰρ ἢ ἁπαλόν, ἢ θερμὸν ἢ ψυχρὸν οὐχ οἷόν τέ ἐστιν ἀκούσαντα<ς> εἰδέναι, ἀλλὰ γὰρ τῶν τοιούτων ἐστὶ κρίσις ἡ ἁφή.

Τούτων οὕτως ὑφεστηκότων ἡ διακόσμησις τῶν γεγονότων καὶ γινομένων ἀριθμητικῶς γινομένη θεωρεῖται. 7. ὃν γὰρ τρόπον ἀπὸ μονάδος ἀρξάμενο(ι) κατὰ προσθήκην (δυ)άδων ἢ τριάδων καὶ τῶν ἑξῆς ἀθροιζομένων ἀριθμῶν ἕν τι σύστημα ποιοῦμεν μέγιστον ἀριθμοῦ, εἶτα πάλιν ἀπὸ τοῦ κατὰ [τὴν] σύνθεσιν ἀθροισθέντος ἀφαιρέσει τινὶ καὶ ἀναποδισμῷ λύσιν τῶν συνεστώτων ἀριθμητικῶς ἐργαζόμεθα.

25. 1. οὕτω φησὶ καὶ τὸν κόσμον ἀριθμητικῷ τινι καὶ μουσικῷ δεσμῷ δεδεμένον ἐπιτάσει καὶ ἀνέσει, καὶ προσθήκῃ καὶ ἀφαιρέσει ἀεὶ καὶ διὰ παντὸς ἀδιάφθορον φυλαχθῆναι. τοιγαροῦν καὶ περὶ τῆς διαμονῆς τοῦ κόσμου ἀποφαίνονται τοιοῦτόν τινα τρόπον οἱ Πυθαγορικοί·

ἦ γὰρ καὶ πάρος ἦν, καί <γ’> ἔσ<σε>ται, οὐδέ ποτ’, οἴω,
τούτων ἀμφοτέρων κεν<ε>ώσεται ἄσπετος αἰών.

2. τίνων δὲ τούτων; τοῦ νείκους καὶ τῆς φιλίας. ἀπεργάζεται δὲ αὐτοῖς ἡ φιλία ἄφθαρτον <καὶ> ἀίδιον τὸν κόσμον, ὡς ὑπονοοῦσιν—ἔστι γὰρ ἡ οὐσία καὶ ὁ κόσμος ἕν—, τὸ δὲ νεῖκος διασπᾷ καὶ διαφέρει καὶ πολλὰ πειρᾶται καταδιαιροῦν τὸν κόσμον ποιεῖν. 3. ὥσπερ εἴ τις ἀριθμητικῶς τὴν μυριάδα εἰς χιλιάδας καὶ ἑκατοντάδας καὶ δεκάδας, καὶ δραχμὴν εἰς ὀβολοὺς καὶ κοδράντας μικροὺς κατακερματίσας τέμνει, οὕτω τὸ νεῖκος τὴν οὐσίαν τοῦ κόσμου, φησί, τέμνει εἰς ζῷα, φυτά, μέταλλα καὶ τὰ τούτοις παραπλήσια.

καὶ ἔστι τῆς γενέσεως τῶν γενομένων πάντων κατ’ αὐτοὺς δημιουργὸς τὸ νεῖκος· ἡ δ’ αὖ φιλία, ἐπιτροπεύουσα καὶ προνοουμένη τοῦ παντός, ἵνα μένῃ καὶ εἰς τὸ ἕν, <τὰ> διῃρημένα καὶ τοῦ παντὸς ἀπεσπασμένα συνάγουσα καὶ ἐξάγουσα τοῦ βίου, συνάγει καὶ προστίθησι τῷ παντί, ἵνα μένῃ καὶ ἔσται ἕν.

and know what is musical or cacophonous by hearing it.[97] And whether something has a fragrant or displeasing odor is the task not of our rational faculty to decide but our sense of smell. 6. The same applies for the sense of touch. For what is hard or soft, or hot or cold, one cannot know by hearing. Rather, touch is the judge of such things.

Such being the case, we observe that the ordering of things past and present occurs numerically. 7. Just as we make one great system of numbers when starting from the number one and proceeding by addition to two, three, and all the other numbers added together, so in turn by subtracting from the combined total and retracing our steps, we numerically produce a division of combined numbers.

COSMIC HARMONY AND PERMANENCE. 25. 1. In this way, he claims, the cosmos is bound together with an arithmetical and musical bond. It is always and everywhere preserved incorruptible by tension and relaxation, addition and subtraction. Therefore the Pythagoreans proclaim the following about the permanence of the cosmos:

> Indeed it existed in former times and will exist; nor, I ween,
> Will endless time be deprived of these two.[98]

2. Of which two does he speak? Strife and Love. Their principle of Love makes the world incorruptible and eternal, as they suppose—for being and the world are one. Strife, in contrast, pulls apart, divides, and many times tries to make the world fracture in pieces. 3. Just as if someone arithmetically divides ten thousand into thousands, hundreds, and tens, and a drachma into obols and quadrantes, so also Strife divides the substance of the world, he says, into animals, plants, metals, and the like.

Accordingly, for them, Strife is the Artificer of generation for all generated beings. Love, in turn, administers and cares for the universe so that it abides. By bringing together the bits and pieces of the universe, and leading them forth from [their time of] life, it brings together and adds to the universe so that it can abide and remain one in time to come.

---

97. Marcovich emends P's *δίκαιον ἢ ἄδικον* ("just or unjust") to *ᾠδικὸν ἢ δύσηχον* ("musical or cacophonous").

98. Empedokles, DK 31 B16, also quoted in *Ref.* 7.29.10.

4. οὐ παύσεται οὖν οὔτε τὸ νεῖκος τὸν κόσμον διαιροῦν, οὔτε ἡ φιλία τὰ διῃρημένα τῷ κόσμῳ προσνέμουσα. <τοι>αύτη τίς ἐστιν, ὡς ἔο(ικ)ε, κατὰ Πυθαγόραν ἡ τοῦ κόσμου δια<μ>ονή.

Λέγει δὲ Πυθαγόρας εἶναι ἀπορρωγάδας τοῦ ἡλ(ί)ου τοὺς ἀστέρας, καὶ τὰς ψυχὰς τῶν ζῴων ἀπὸ τῶν ἄστρων φέ(ρ)εσθαι. εἶναι δὲ αὐτὰς θνητὰς μέν, ὅταν ὦσιν ἐν τῷ σώματι—οἱονεὶ ἐγκατορωρυγμένας [ὡς] ἐν τάφῳ—, ἀνίστασθαι δὲ καὶ γίνεσθαι ἀθανάτους, ὅταν τῶν σωμάτων ἀπολυθῶσιν. ὅθεν ὁ Πλάτων ἐρωτηθεὶς ὑπό τινος· τί ἐστι φιλοσοφία, ἔφη· χωρισμὸς ψυχῆς ἀπὸ σώματος.

26. 1. Πυθαγόρου καὶ τούτῳ τῶν λόγων γενόμενος μαθητὴς <καὶ> ἐν οἷς λέγει καὶ δι' αἰνιγμάτων [καὶ τοιούτων λόγων]·

> ἐκ τῆς ἰδίης ἐὰν ἀποδημῇς, μὴ ἐπιστρέφου· εἰ δὲ μή, Ἐριννύες Δίκης
> ἐπίκουροί σε μετελεύσονται,

ἰδίην καλῶν τὸ σῶμα, Ἐριννύας δὲ τὰ πάθη. 2. ἐὰν οὖν, φησίν, ἀποδημῇς, τουτέστιν ἐὰν ἐξέρχῃ ἐκ τοῦ σώματος, μὴ αὐτοῦ ἀντιποιοῦ· ἐὰν δὲ ἀντιποιήσῃ, πάλιν σε τὰ πάθη καθείρξουσιν εἰς σῶμα. εἶναι γὰρ οὗτοι τῶν ψυχῶν μετενσωμάτωσιν νομίζουσιν, ὡς καὶ ὁ Ἐμπεδοκλῆς πυθαγορίζων λέγει. 3. δεῖ

4. Thus there will be no ceasing, either of Strife dividing the world or of Love allotting the divided bits to the world. Such is the permanence of the world, it seems, imagined by Pythagoras.[99]

THE SOUL. Pythagoras says that stars are pieces broken off from the sun, and that the souls of living beings are brought down from the stars.[100] Souls are mortal when they are in the body—as it were buried deep in a tomb—but rise and become immortal when freed from bodies.[101] Hence Plato, when asked by someone, "What is philosophy?" replied, "The separation of the soul from body."[102]

PYTHAGOREAN RIDDLES. 26. 1. Plato was a disciple of Pythagoras's doctrines, those spoken both plainly and in riddles.

> If you go abroad from your house, do not turn back. Otherwise, the Furies, allies of Justice, will pursue you.[103]

He calls the body "your house," and violent emotions "the Furies." 2. So if, he says, you go abroad (that is, if you depart from the body), do not seek it again. If you seek it, once again these emotions will lock you up in the body. (This is because these thinkers believe in a transmigration of soul—as also

---

99. The preceding (*Ref.* 6.25.1–4) in fact represents the thought of Empedokles, whom our author placed in the Pythagorean succession (*Ref.* 1.3). "Permanence" (διαμονή) is Marcovich's emendation of P's διανομή ("distribution/division"). For this description of cosmogony, see *Ref.* 7.29.8–12 (where Empedokles is compared with Markion).

100. Cf. Plato, *Tim.* 41d; Cicero, *Rep.* 6.15; Pliny, *Nat.* 2.95 (human souls as star fragments).

101. Cf. Philolaos, DK 44 B14; Plato, *Crat.* 400c (both quoted in Clem. Alex., *Strom.* 3.3.16.3–17.1); Plato, *Gorg.* 493a; *Ref.* 5.8.22–23 (Naassenes). Plato's teaching is considered to be the teaching of Pythagoras. But Plato's teaching has undergone modification (cf. *Ref.* 1.2.11; 1.19.10–13).

102. Actually this is Plato's definition of death. Philosophy is the practice of death (μέλετη τοῦ θανατοῦ). See Plato, *Phaed.* 64c; 66a; *Gorg.* 524b.

103. This seems to be a combination of a traditional saying of Pythagoras ("do not return …") with a saying of Herakleitos ("the Furies …"). Cf. Porphyry, *Vit. Pyth.* 42; Diog. L., *Vit. phil.* 8.18; [Plutarch], *Lib. ed.* 12f; Plutarch, *Numa* 14; Athenaios, *Deipn.* 10, 452e, with Herakleitos, DK 22 B94 (= Marcovich, *Heraclitus*, §52). The sayings are also combined in Iamblichos, *Protr.* 21.14: ἀποδημῶν τῆς οἰκ<ε>ίας μὴ ἐπιστρέφου. Ἐρινύες γὰρ μετέρχονται.

γάρ, φησί, τὰς φιληδόνους ψυχάς, ὡς ὁ Πλάτων λέγει, ἐὰν ἐν ἀνθρώπου πάθει γενόμεναι μὴ φιλοσοφήσωσι, διὰ πάντων ζῴων καὶ φυτῶν ἐλθεῖν πάλιν εἰς ἀνθρώπινον σῶμα· καὶ ἐὰν μὲν φιλοσοφή(σ)ῃ κατὰ τὸ αὐτὸ τρίς, εἰς τὴν τοῦ συννόμου ἄστρου φύσιν ἀνελθεῖν, ἐὰν δὲ μὴ φιλοσοφήσῃ, πάλιν ἐπὶ τὰ αὐτά. δύνασθαι οὖν φησί ποτε τὴν ψυχὴν καὶ θνητὴν γενέσθαι, ἐὰν ὑπὸ τῶν Ἐριννύων κρατῆται—τουτέστι τῶν παθῶν—, καὶ ἀθάνατον, ἐὰν τὰς Ἐριννῦς ἐκφύγῃ, ἅ ἐστι <τὰ> πάθη.

27. 1. Ἀλλ' ἐπεὶ καὶ τὰ σκοτεινῶς ὑπὸ τοῦ Πυθαγόρου λεγόμενα π(ρ)ὸς τοὺς μαθητὰς δι' ὑποσυμβόλων ἐνήρ<γ>μεθα λέγειν, δοκεῖ καὶ τῶν ἑτέρων ὑπομνησθῆναι, διὰ τὸ καὶ τοὺς αἱρεσιάρχας τοιούτῳ τινὶ τρόπῳ ἐπικεχειρηκέναι ὁμιλεῖν δι' ὑποσυμβόλων, καὶ τοῦτο οὐκ ἰδίων, ἀλλ' Πυθαγορείων πλεονεκτήσαντας λόγων.

2. διδάσκει οὖν ὁ Πυθαγόρας τοὺς μαθητὰς λέγων·

τὸν στρωματόδεσμον δῆσον.

ἐπεὶ <ὡς> οἱ ὁδοιπορεῖν μέλλοντες εἰς δέρμα δεσμοῦσι τὰ ἱμάτια αὑτῶν (π)ρὸς ἑτοιμασίαν τῆς ὁδοῦ, οὕτως ἑτοίμους εἶναι θέλει τοὺς μαθ(η)τά(ς), ὡς καθ' ἑκάστην στιγμὴν τοῦ θανάτου ἐφεστηκέναι μέλλοντος μηδὲν ἔχοντας τῶν μαθη<μά>των ἐνδεές. 3. διόπερ ἐξ ἀνάγκης ἅμα τῷ ἡμέραν γενέσθαι ἐδίδασκε διακελεύεσθαι αὑτοῖς τοὺς Πυθαγορείους «δεσμεύειν τὸν στρωματόδεσμον», τουτέστιν ἑτοίμους εἶναι πρὸς θάνατον.

Πῦρ μαχαίρῃ μὴ σκάλευε

Empedokles, speaking like a Pythagorean, affirms.[104]) 3. It is necessary, he claims, for pleasure-loving souls, as Plato says—if they are caught up by human affections and do not live a philosophical life—that they return to a human body after passing through every sort of animal and plant.[105] Yet if they live the philosophical life in the same way three times, they rise to the nature of their kindred star. If they do not live philosophically, they return again to the same circumstances.[106] Thus it is possible, he says, for the soul at some point to become mortal if it is dominated by the Furies (that is, violent emotions), but also immortal if it flees them.

27. 1. But since I have begun to discourse on what Pythagoras spoke obscurely to his disciples through hidden symbols, it is right to recall the others as well, since the leading heretics have also endeavored to converse in this manner through hidden symbols (and they did not even use their own but exploited Pythagorean maxims).[107]

2. Pythagoras teaches his disciples, saying,

> Bind up the clothes sack.[108]

This is because, just as those intending to go on a journey bind up their clothes into leather sacks to be ready on the road, so also he wants his students to be ready so that at any moment when death threatens to overtake them, they may not lack his teachings. 3. Thus he taught the Pythagoreans that at dawn they must necessarily exhort themselves to "bind the clothes sack"—that is, be ready for death.

> Do not stir a fire with a sword[109]

---

104. Empedokles, DK 31 B117, quoted in *Ref.* 1.3.2.

105. Plato, *Phaed.* 81a–b; Herodotos, *Hist.* 2.123.

106. Plato, *Phaedr.* 248e–249c (transmigration); *Tim.* 42b (kindred star); cf. *Ref.* 1.19.10–13 (summary of Plato's philosophy).

107. On the Pythagorean maxims (akousmata), see DK 58 C1–6 (Pythagorean School); Burkert, *Lore*, 166–92. Clement of Alexandria provides a Christian interpretation of many Pythagorean sayings in *Strom.* 5.5.

108. See the form of this saying in Porphyry at Stobaios, *Ecl.* 1.49.59 (Wachsmuth and Hense, 1:445); Diog. L., *Vit. phil.* 8.17; Iamblichos, *Protr.* 21.29; Plutarch, *Quaest. conv.* 727c; 728b; Clem. Alex., *Strom.* 5.5.27.7–8.

109. See the form of this saying in Iamblichos, *Protr.* 21.8; *Vit. Pyth.* 227; Diog. L., *Vit. phil.* 8.18; Athenaios, *Deipn.* 10, 452d; Plutarch, *Quaest. rom.* 281a; *Is. Os.* 10 (*Mor.* 354e); [Plutarch], *Lib. ed.* 12e; Porphyry, *Vit. Pyth.* 42; Lucian, *Vera hist.* 2.28.

τὸν τεθυμωμένον ἄνθρωπον λέγων μὴ ἐρέθιζε· πυρὶ γὰρ ἔοικεν ὁ θυμούμενος, μαχαίρᾳ δὲ λόγος.

4. σάρον μὴ ὑπέρβαινε

μικροῦ πράγματος μὴ καταφρόνει.

φοίνικα ἐν οἰκίᾳ μὴ φύτευε

φιλονεικίαν ἐν οἰκίᾳ μὴ κατασκεύαζε· μάχης γὰρ καὶ διαφορᾶς ἐστιν ὁ φοῖνιξ σημεῖον.

ἀπὸ δίφρου μὴ ἔσθιε

βάναυσον τέχνην μὴ μεταχει(ρ)ίζου, ἵνα μὴ δουλεύσῃς τῷ σώματι ὄντι φθαρτῷ, ἀλλὰ ποιοῦ τὸν βίον ἀπὸ λόγων· ἐνέσται γάρ σοι καὶ τρέφειν τὸ σῶμα καὶ τὴν ψυχὴν ποιεῖν κρείττονα.

5. ἀπὸ ὅλου ἄρτου μὴ ἀπόδακνε

τὰ ὑπάρχοντά σου μὴ μειοῦ, ἀλλ' ἀπὸ τῆς προσόδου ζῆθι, φύλασσε δὲ τὴν οὐσίαν ὡς ἄρτον ὁλόκληρον.

κυάμους μὴ ἔσθιε

ἀρχὴν πόλεως μὴ ἀποδέχου—κυάμοις γὰρ ἐκληροῦντο τὰς ἀρχὰς κατ' ἐκεῖνον τὸν χρόνον.—

28. 1. Ταῦτα μὲν οὖν καὶ τὰ τοιαῦτα οἱ Πυθαγόρειοι λέγουσιν, οὓς μιμούμενοι οἱ αἱρετικοὶ μεγάλα νομίζονταί τισι λέγειν.

δημιουργὸν δὲ εἶναι τῶν γενομένων πάντων φησὶν ὁ Πυθαγόρειος λόγος τὸν μέγ(αν) γεωμέτρην καὶ ἀριθμητὴν ἥλιον, καὶ ἐστηρίχθα τοῦτον <μέσον>

means do not provoke a person already angry (for such a person is like fire, and speech like a sword).

4. Do not step over a broom[110]

means do not despise a small thing.

Do not plant a palm tree in a house

means do not foster contentiousness within a household, for the palm tree is a symbol of quarrel and disagreement.[111]

Do not eat from a stool

means do not practice a vulgar profession so that you might not be a slave to a decaying body, but make your living from words.[112] For it is possible for you both to nourish the body and to improve the soul.

5. Do not bite from a whole loaf

means do not diminish your possessions, but live off your income, and preserve your wealth as a whole loaf.

Do not eat beans

means do not accept a civic office (for the ruling offices were allotted by beans during his time).[113]

28. 1. These things and things of this ilk the Pythagoreans say. By mimicking them, the heretics suppose that they speak marvels to their audience.

PYTHAGOREAN COSMOGONY. Pythagorean teaching states that the Sun, the great "geometer-arithmetician," is the Artificer of all generated beings. It is

110. See the form of this saying in Plutarch, *Quaest. rom.* 290e; *Quaest. conv.* 727c (ζυγόν); Iamblichos, *Protr.* 21.13; *Vit. Pyth.* 186; Diog. L., *Vit. phil.* 8.17–18; Athenaios, *Deipn.* 452d; Porphyry, *Vit. Pyth.* 42; Clem. Alex., *Strom.* 5.5.30.1 (ζυγόν).

111. Cf. Plutarch, *Is. Os.* 10 (*Mor.* 354e).

112. Cf. Plutarch, *Quaest. rom.* 290e; *Is. Os.* 10 (*Mor.* 354e).

113. Cf. Iamblichos, *Protr.* 21.37; [Plutarch], *Lib. ed.* 12f; Diog. L., *Vit. phil.* 8.17, 34; *Ref.* 1.2.14–15 with Marcovich, "Pythagorica," 29–39.

ἐν ὅλῳ, τῷ κόσμῳ, καθάπερ ἐν τῷ (σ)ώματι ψυχήν, ὥς φησιν ὁ Πλάτων. πῦρ γάρ ἐστιν ἥλιος, ψυχή, σῶμα <δὲ ἡ γῆ>. 2. «χωρισθὲν δὲ πυρὸς οὐδὲν ἄν ποτε ὁρατὸν γένοιτο, οὐδὲ ἁπτὸν ἄνευ τινὸς στερεοῦ, στερεὸν δὲ οὐκ ἄνευ γῆς· ὅθεν ἐκ πυρὸς καὶ γῆς», «ἀέρα τε ὁ θεὸς ἐν μέσῳ θέμενος» τὸ τοῦ παντὸς ἐδημιούργησε σῶ(μ)α.

ἀριθμεῖ δέ, φησί, καὶ γεωμετρεῖ τὸν κόσμον ὁ ἥλιος τοιοῦτόν τινα τρόπ(ο)ν· 3. ὁ μὲν κόσμος [ἐστὶν] ὁ αἰσθητὸς εἷς, περὶ οὗ λέγομεν τὰ νῦν· διῄρηκε δ' αὐτόν, ἀριθμητικός τις ὢν καὶ γεωμέτρης, εἰς μοίρας δώδεκα· καὶ ἔστι ταῖς μοίραις ταύταις ὀνόματα· Κριός, Ταῦρος, Δίδυμοι, Καρκίνος, Λέων, Παρθένος, Ζυγός, Σκορπίος, Τοξότης, Αἰγόκερως, Ὑδροχόος, Ἰχθύες.

4. πάλιν τῶν δώδεκα μοιρῶν ἑκάστην διαιρεῖ εἰς μοίρας τριάκοντα, αἵτινές εἰσιν ἡμέραι μηνός. πάλιν αὖ τῶν [τῶν] τριάκοντα μοιρῶν ἑκάστην μοῖραν διαιρεῖ εἰς λεπτὰ ἑξήκοντα, καὶ τῶν λεπτῶν <ἕκαστον εἰς> λεπτὰ [καὶ] ἔτι λεπτότερα. καὶ τοῦτο ἀεὶ ποιῶν [καὶ] μὴ παυόμενος, ἀλλ' ἀθροίζων ἐκ τούτων μοιρῶν τῶν διῃρημένων καὶ ποιῶν ἐνια(υ)τόν, καὶ αὖθις ἀναλύων καὶ διαιρῶν τὸ συγκείμενον, τὸν μέγαν ἀθάνατον ἀπεργάζεται κόσμον.

29. 1. Τοιαύτη τις, ὡς ἐν κεφαλαίοις εἰπεῖν ἐπελθόντα, ἡ Πυθαγόρου καὶ Πλάτωνος συνέστηκε δόξα, ἀφ' ἧς Οὐαλεντῖνος, οὐκ ἀπὸ τῶν εὐαγγελίων, τὴν αἵρεσιν τὴν ἑαυτοῦ συναγαγών, ὡς ἐπιδείξομεν, δικαίως Πυθαγορικὸς καὶ

fixed as a center point in the whole cosmos, just as the soul, as Plato says, is fixed in the body.[114] The sun is made up of fire and soul, while the earth is a body.[115] 2. "Apart from fire there can be nothing visible; nor can anything be touched without some measure of solidity—and there is nothing solid without earth. Hence God" crafted the body of the universe "from fire, earth, and air, and he set it in the center."[116]

The Sun, he says, applies arithmetic and geometry to the world in the following sort of way. 3. The perceptible world (about which I make the present observations) is one. The Sun, since he was an expert in number and geometry, divided it into twelve portions. These are the names of the portions: Aries, Taurus, Gemini, Cancer, Leo, Virgo, Libra, Scorpio, Sagittarius, Capricorn, Aquarius, and Pisces.

4. Again, he divided the twelve portions into thirty, which are the days of the month. In turn, he divides each of the thirty portions into sixty minutes, and each of the minutes into minutiae still more minute.[117] And he does this forever without ceasing, adding together from the divided units to make a year. Again, he divides and splits the sum to produce a world both vast and immortal.[118]

VALENTINUS

29. 1. Such, to run through the chief points, is the established doctrine of Pythagoras and Plato. It is from this doctrine—not from the Gospels—that Valentinus pieced together his own heresy, as I will show.[119] He ought

---

114. Cf. Plato, *Symp.* 218a (τὴν καρδίαν γὰρ ἢ ψυχήν ["the heart or the soul"]); Origen, *Comm. Jo.* 6.38 (τὸ ἡγεμονικὸν ... κατὰ τὰς γραφὰς ἐν τῇ καρδίᾳ τυγχάνον ["according to scripture, the governing faculty is in the heart"]); Corp. herm. 16.5 (Sun as Artificer); Chrysippos, *SVF* 2.879 = Chalkidios, *In Tim.* 220 (*animae principale, positum in media sede cordis* ["the leading part of the soul is situated in the center of the heart"]). Mansfeld believes that here *Tim.* 39b–c and *Resp.* 6.509b (the Sun image) have been combined (*Heresiography*, 200 n. 1).

115. The words δὲ ἡ γῆ ("while the earth") are Marcovich's emendation for P's σελήνη ("moon"). Later we learn that the Valentinian Artificer, made of soul substance and fear, is also fiery (*Ref.* 6.32.7–8).

116. Cf. Plato, *Tim.* 31b–32b.

117. Cf. *Ref.* 5.13.3–4 (itself an adaptation of Sext. Emp., *Math.* 5.5); and 6.34.3 (λεπτὰ λεπτῶν).

118. Cf. Plato, *Resp.* 516b (the sun provides the seasons and the years); Plutarch, *Quaest. plat.* 1007d–e (with reference to Herakleitos).

119. Valentinus is perhaps the most famous Christian intellectual of the early

Πλατωνικός, οὐ Χριστιανός, λογισθείη. Οὐαλεντῖνος τοίνυν καὶ Ἡρακλέων καὶ Πτολεμαῖος καὶ πᾶσα ἡ τούτων σχολή, οἱ Πυθαγόρου καὶ Πλάτωνος μαθηταί, ἀκολουθήσαντες τοῖς καθηγη(σ)αμένοις ἀριθμητικὴν τὴν διδασκαλίαν τὴν ἑαυτῶν κατεβάλοντο.

2. καὶ γὰρ τούτ(οις) ἐστὶν ἀρχὴ τῶν πάντων μονὰς ἀγέννητος, ἄφθαρτος, ἀκατάληπτος, ἀπερινόητος, γόνιμος καὶ πάντων τῆς γενέσεως αἰτία τῶν γενομένων· καλεῖται δὲ ὑπ᾽ αὐτῶ(ν) ἡ προειρημένη μονὰς Πατήρ.

3. διαφορὰ δέ τις εὑρίσκεται πολλὴ παρ᾽ αὐτ(οῖ)ς· οἱ μὲν γὰρ αὐτῶν,—ἵν᾽ ᾖ παντάπασι καθαρὸν τὸ δόγμα τοῦ Οὐαλεντίνου Πυθαγορικόν—ἄθηλυ<ν> καὶ ἄζυγον καὶ μόνον τὸν Πατέρα νομίζουσιν εἶναι· οἱ δ(ὲ) ἀδύνατον νομίζοντες

rightly to be considered, not a Christian, but a Pythagorean and Platonist. So then, Valentinus, Herakleon, Ptolemy, and their entire school—being the disciples of Pythagoras and Plato—laid down their own doctrines by parroting the leading figures in arithmetic.[120]

VALENTINIAN THEOGONY AND COSMOGONY. 2. They also have a Monad as the first principle of the universe, who is unborn, incorruptible, incomprehensible, inconceivable, productive, and the cause of generation for all generated beings. This aforementioned Monad they call "Father."

3. But one discovers a profound disagreement among them. For some of them—so that the doctrine of Valentinus might be through and through a pure Pythagoreanism—suppose that the Father is not female,

---

second century CE, although only nine genuine fragments from his works survive. He came to Rome in the late 130s and stayed there at least fifteen years. See further Peter Lampe, *From Paul to Valentinus: Christians at Rome in the First Two Centuries*, ed. Marshall Johnson, trans. Michael Steinhauser (Minneapolis: Fortress, 2003), 292–318; Ismo Dunderberg, "Valentinus," in *A Companion to Second-Century Christian "Heretics,"* ed. Antti Marjanen and Petri Luomanen, VCSup 76 (Leiden: Brill, 2005), 64–99. Scholars debate Valentinus's original teachings, with some opting for a Platonizing biblical exegete and others for a gnostic theologian (see, respectively, Christoph Markschies, *Valentinus Gnosticus: Untersuchungen zur valentinianischen Gnosis mit einem Kommentar zu den Fragmenten Valentins*, WUNT 65 [Tübingen: Mohr Siebeck, 1992], 388–407; Einar Thomassen, *The Spiritual Seed: The Church of the "Valentinians,"* NHMS 60 [Leiden: Brill, 2006], 417–92). Our author presents him as essentially Pythagorean (cf. Filastrius, *Haer.* 38.1: *Valentinus ... Pythagoricus*), and such influence should not be discounted (Thomassen, *Spiritual Seed*, 269–94). What our author presents of "Valentinus's" thought, however, is an amalgam of what later Valentinians taught. See further Koschorke, *Ketzerbekämpfung*, 14–17.

120. The following report (*Ref.* 6.29.2–36.4) adapts Iren., *Haer.* 1.1.1–7.5. Our author's report (called system "B" by R. A. Lipsius, "Valentinus und seine Schule," *Jahrbücher für protestantischen Theologie* 13 [1887]: 585–658) is typically viewed as secondary to that of Irenaeus (system "A") not only because it is later but because our author tends to doctor his sources and is constrained by his method (to connect his enemies to peculiar philosophies) (Sagnard, *Gnose*, 135; Kalvesmaki, *Theology*, 53–55). Sagnard offers a chart comparing the two systems in *Gnose*, 146–98. See further G. C. Stead ("The Valentinian Myth of Sophia," *JTS* 20 [1969]: 75–104 [77–80]), who notes that the monadic deity presented by our author is more congenial to "the Jewish and Christian God" (80). It is widely held that Iren., *Haer.* 1–11, treats the system of Ptolemy the Valentinian. Both Ptolemy and Herakleon have just been mentioned (*Ref.* 6.29.1). See further Thomassen, *Spiritual Seed*, 200–204. For other reports of Valentinian cosmogony, see Clem. Alex., *Exc.* 43.2–65.2; Tert., *Val.* 7–35; Ps.-Tert., *Adv. omn. haer.* 4; Epiph., *Pan.* 31.2.4–8.1.

εἶναι ἐξ ἄ(ρ)ρενος μόνου γένεσιν ὅλως τῶν γεγενημένων γενέσθαι τινός, καὶ τῷ Πατρὶ τῶν ὅλων, ἵνα γένηται πατήρ, Σιγὴν ἐξ ἀνάγκης συναριθμοῦσι [τὴν] σύζυγον.

4. ἀλλὰ περὶ μὲν Σιγῆς, πότερόν ποτε σύζυγός ἐστιν ἢ οὐκ ἔστιν, αὐτοὶ πρὸς ἑαυτοὺς τοῦτον ἐχέτωσαν τὸν ἀγῶνα, τὰ δὲ νῦν [αὐτοῖς] ἡμεῖς, φυλάττοντες τὴν Πυθαγόρειον ἀρχήν, μίαν οὐσίαν καὶ ἄζυγον, ἄθηλυ<ν>, ἀπροσδεῆ, μνημονεύσαντες ὅσ' ἐκεῖνοι διδάσκουσιν ἐροῦμεν.

5. Ἦν γε ὅλως, φησί, γενητὸν οὐδέν, Πατὴρ δὲ ἦν μόνος, ἀγέννητος, οὐ τόπον ἔχων, οὐ χρόνον, οὐ σύμβουλον, οὐκ ἄλλην τινὰ κατ' οὐδένα τῶν τρόπων νοηθῆναι δυναμένην οὐσίαν· ἀλλὰ ἦν μόνος, ἠρεμῶν, ὡς λέγουσι, καὶ ἀναπαυόμενος αὐτὸς ἐν ἑαυτῷ μόνος. ἐπεὶ δὲ ἦν γόνιμος, ἔδοξεν αὐτῷ ποτε τὸ κάλλιστον καὶ τελεώτατον ὃ εἶχεν ἐν ἑαυτῷ γενῆσαι καὶ προαγαγεῖν· φιλέρημος γὰρ οὐκ ἦν. ἀγάπη γάρ, φησίν, ἦν ὅλος, ἡ δὲ ἀγάπη οὐκ ἔστιν ἀγάπη, ἐὰν μὴ ᾖ τὸ ἀγαπώμενον. 6. προέβαλεν οὖν καὶ ἐγένησεν αὐτὴν ὁ Πατήρ, ὥσπερ ἦν μόνος, Νοῦν καὶ Ἀλήθειαν, τουτέστι δυάδα, ἥτις κυρία καὶ ἀρχὴ γέγονε καὶ μήτηρ πάντων τῶν ἐντὸς πληρώματος καταριθμουμένων αἰώνων ὑπ' αὐτῶν.

7. προβληθεὶς δὲ ὁ Νοῦς καὶ ἡ Ἀλήθεια ἀπὸ τοῦ Πατρός, ἀπὸ γονίμου γόνιμος, προέβαλε καὶ αὐτὸς Λόγον καὶ Ζωήν, τὸν Πατέρα μιμούμενος· ὁ δὲ Λόγος καὶ ἡ Ζωὴ προβάλλουσιν Ἄνθρωπον καὶ Ἐκκλησίαν.

Ὁ δὲ Νοῦς καὶ ἡ Ἀλήθεια, ἐπεὶ εἶδον τὸν Λόγον καὶ τὴν Ζωήν, τὰ ἴδια γεννήματα, γόνιμα γεγενημένα, ηὐχαρίστησαν τῷ Πατρὶ τῶν (ὅλω)ν

has no consort, and is alone. But others, thinking it impossible that the birth of any generated beings at all come solely from a male, are compelled to add a consort to the Father of the universe to make him a Father. This consort is Silence.[121]

4. But about Silence, and the question about whether she is or is not ever his consort, let them battle it out amongst themselves! For the present I—preserving the Pythagorean first principle as one substance, without consort, not female, and needing nothing—will note in my discourse whatever this group teaches.[122]

THE SELF-DIFFERENTIATION OF THE MONAD. 5. There was a time, we can be sure, when there was nothing at all born. The Father was alone, unborn, outside of space and time, without a counselor; and there was no other substance that could possibly be conceived of in any way.[123] Yes, he was alone, solitary—as they say—and resting in himself alone. But since he was productive, he decided at some point to generate and emanate the most beautiful and perfect thing that he had in himself. For he was not fond of solitariness, since he was entirely love.[124] But love is not love unless the beloved exists. 6. So the solitary Father emanated her (the Dyad). She is Mind and Truth, and she became the Mistress, Source, and Mother of all aeons enumerated by them in the Fullness.

7. When Mind (in addition to Truth) was emanated from the Father—a productive being from a productive being—Mind, imitating his Father, emanated Word and Life. Word and Life then emanated Human and Church.[125]

Now Mind and Truth, when they saw Word and Life, their own offspring, productive productions, gave thanks to the Father of the universe

121. Cf. Iren., *Haer.* 1.11.5; 1.2.4; Tert., *Val.* 34.

122. There was a similar difference of opinion among the Pythagoreans in that some taught an ultimate Monad, while others an ultimate Dyad (Sext. Emp., *Math.* 10.270, 282). See further Thomassen, *Spiritual Seed*, 270–79, 284–88, 291–94. Kalvesmaki charges our author with grossly oversimplifying the complexity of the Valentinian position, since there were in fact four ways that they conceived of the state of the first aeon. "His oversimplification is intentional.... He sets out to make the Valentinians followers of Pythagoras, so he isolates the monadic strain" (*Theology*, 55).

123. For lack of a counselor, see Isa 40:13; Rom 11:34.

124. See 1 John 4:8, 16 ("God is love"); Iren., *Haer.* 1.2.2; 4.38.4. On the self-giving goodness of God, see Plato, *Tim.* 29e; Alkinoos, *Epit.* 10, 12; Diog. L., *Vit. phil.* 3.72.

125. The result of the first emanations, as Kalvesmaki notes, is a hebdomad (Father, Mind, Truth, Reason, Life, Human, Truth), not Ptolemy's Ogdoad (*Theology*, 53; cf. Iren., *Haer.* 1.1.1).

καὶ προσφέρουσιν αὐτῷ τέλειον ἀριθμόν, αἰῶνας δέκα. 8. τούτου δέ, φησί, τελειότερον ἀριθμὸν ὁ Νοῦς καὶ ἡ Ἀλήθεια τῷ Πατρὶ προσενεγκεῖν οὐκ ἠδυνήθησαν· ἔδει γὰρ τέλειον ὄντα τὸν Πατέρα ἀριθμῷ δοξάζεσθαι τελείῳ· τέλειος δέ ἐστιν ὁ δέκα, ὅτι πρῶτος τῶν κατὰ πλῆθος γενομένων οὗτός ἐστι τέλειος. τελειότερος δὲ ὁ Πατήρ, ὅτι ἀγέννητος ὢν μόνος, διὰ τῆς πρώτης <καὶ> μιᾶς συζυγίας τοῦ Νοῦ καὶ τῆς Ἀληθείας πάσας τὰς τῶν γενομένων προβαλεῖν εὐπόρησε ῥίζας.

30. 1. Ἰδὼν οὖν καὶ αὐτὸς ὁ Λόγος καὶ ἡ Ζωὴ ὅτι ὁ Ν(οῦ)ς καὶ ἡ Ἀλήθεια δεδόξακαν τὸν Πατέρα τῶν ὅλων ἐν ἀριθμῷ τ(ελ)είῳ, δοξάσαι καὶ αὐτὸς ὁ Λόγος μετὰ τῆς Ζωῆς ἠθέλησε τὸν ἑαυτοῦ πατέρα καὶ τὴν μητέρα, τὸν Νοῦν καὶ τὴν Ἀλήθειαν. 2. ἐπεὶ δὲ γενητὸς ἦν ὁ Νοῦς καὶ ἡ Ἀλήθεια, καὶ οὐκ εἶχε τὸ πατρικὸν τέλειον, τὴν ἀγεννησίαν, οὐκέτι τελείῳ ἀριθμῷ ὁ Λόγος καὶ ἡ Ζωὴ δοξάζουσι τὸν ἑαυτῶν πατέρα τὸν Νοῦν, ἀλλὰ γὰρ ἐν ἀτελεῖ· δώδεκα γὰρ αἰῶνας προ<σ>φέρουσιν ὁ Λόγος καὶ ἡ Ζωὴ τῷ Νοῒ καὶ τῇ Ἀληθείᾳ. 3. αὗται γοῦν πρῶται κατὰ Οὐαλεντῖνον ῥίζαι τῶν αἰώνων γεγόνασι·

Νοῦς καὶ Ἀλήθεια,
Λόγος καὶ Ζωή,
Ἄνθρωπος καὶ Ἐκκλησία·

δέκα δὲ οἱ τοῦ Νοὸς καὶ τῆς Ἀληθείας, δύο καὶ δέκα δὲ οἱ τοῦ Λόγου καὶ τῆς Ζωῆς, εἴκοσι καὶ ὀκτὼ οἱ πάντες. 4. οἷς <τοὺς δέκα> καλοῦσιν, ὀνόματα ταῦτα·

Βύθ<ι>ος καὶ Μίξις,
Ἀγήρατος καὶ Ἕνωσις,
Αὐτοφυὴς καὶ Ἡδονή,
Ἀκίνητος καὶ Σύγκρασις,
Μονογενὴς καὶ Μακαρία.

and brought forth for him a perfect number—ten aeons. 8. Mind and Truth, he declares, were not able to bring forth for the Father a number more perfect than this. It was necessary, since the Father was perfect, to glorify him with a perfect number. Ten is a perfect number since it is the first perfect number of those who arose numerically. But the Father is more perfect, because he is unborn and alone. Through the first and single coupling of Mind and Truth, he provided for the emanation of all the roots of generated beings.

30. 1. Now Word himself, together with Life, saw that Mind and Truth had glorified the Father of the universe by a perfect number. Consequently, he wanted to glorify his own Father and Mother, namely, Mind and Truth.[126] 2. But since Mind and Truth were born and did not have their Father's perfection—namely, the state of being unborn—Word and Life glorified their own Father Mind by an imperfect, and no longer perfect, number. Accordingly, Word and Life brought forth twelve aeons for Mind and Truth.[127] 3. These, then, are, according to Valentinus, the primal roots of the aeons:

Mind and Truth,
Word and Life,
Human and Church.

Ten are from Mind and Truth; twelve are from Reason and Life. There are twenty-eight in all. 4. The names of the ten are:

Deep[128] and Mixture,
Ageless and Union,
Self-Grown and Pleasure,
Unmoved and Blending,
Only-Born and Blessing.

126. Our author puts greater emphasis than Irenaeus on the thanksgiving of the aeons, who stand in "liturgical relationship" with their begetters (Abramowski, "Female Figures," 148–49).

127. Kalvesmaki believes that the "relative imperfection of the Dodecad" is a comment of our author "since there is no indication in any other Valentinian system that the number twelve symbolized deficiency" (*Theology*, 54 n. 79).

128. P reads βῦθός ("Depth"), which Bunsen emends to βύθιος to agree with the subsequent adjectives in the initial position.

οὗτοι οἱ δέκα αἰῶνες, οὓς τινὲς μὲν ὑπὸ τοῦ Νοῦ καὶ τῆς Ἀληθείας λέγουσι, τινὲς δὲ ὑπὸ τοῦ Λόγου καὶ τῆς Ζωῆς. 5. ἕτεροι δὲ τοὺς δώδεκα ὑπὸ τοῦ Ἀνθρώπου καὶ τῆς Ἐκκλησίας, ἕτεροι δὲ ὑπὸ τοῦ Λόγου καὶ τῆς Ζωῆς· οἷς ταῦτα τὰ ὀνόματα χαρίζονται·

Παράκλητος καὶ Πίστις,
Πατρικὸς καὶ Ἐλπίς,
Μητρικὸς καὶ Ἀγάπη,
Ἀείνους καὶ Σύνεσις,
Ἐκκλησιαστικὸς καὶ Μακαριότης,
Θελητὸς καὶ Σοφία.

6. Ἐπεὶ δὲ τῶν δεκαδύο ὁ δωδέκατος κ(αὶ) νεώτατος πάντων τῶν εἰκοσιοκτὼ αἰώνων, θῆλυς ὢν καὶ καλούμενος (Σο)φία, κατενόησε τὸ πλῆθος καὶ τὴν δύναμιν τῶν γεγενηκότων αἰώνων, καὶ ἀνέ(δ)ραμεν εἰς τὸ βάθος τὸ τοῦ Πατρός, καὶ ἐνόησεν ὅτι οἱ μὲν ἄλλοι πάντες α(ἰ)ῶνες γεννητοὶ ὑπάρχοντες κατὰ συζυγίαν γεννῶσιν, ὁ δὲ Πατὴρ μόνος ἄζυγος ἐγέννησεν, 7. ἠθέλησε μιμήσασθαι τὸν Πατέρα καὶ γεννῆσαι καθ' ἑαυτὴν δίχα τοῦ συζύγου, ἵνα μηδὲν ᾖ ἔργον ὑποδεέστερον τοῦ Πατρὸς εἰργασμένη.

ἀγνοοῦσα ὅτι ὁ μὲν ἀγέννητος ὑπάρχων, ἀρχὴ τῶν ὅλων καὶ ῥίζα καὶ βάθος καὶ βυθός, δυνατῶς ἔχει γεννῆσαι μόνος, γενητὴ δὲ οὖσα ἡ Σοφία καὶ μετὰ πλείονας γενομένη, τὴν τοῦ ἀγεννήτου δύναμιν οὐ δύναται ἔχειν. 8. ἐν μὲν γὰρ τῷ ἀγενήτῳ, φησίν, ἐστὶ πάντα ὁμοῦ, ἐν δὲ τοῖς γενητοῖς τὸ μὲν θῆλύ ἐστιν οὐσίας προβλητικόν, τὸ δὲ ἄρρεν μορφωτικὸν τῆς ὑπὸ τοῦ θήλεως προβαλομένης οὐσίας.

These are the ten aeons, whom some say were produced by Mind and Truth, but others say were produced by Word and Life. 5. Some, moreover, say that the twelve were produced by Human and Church, while others say that they were produced by Word and Life. They bestow on them these names:

Advocate and Faith,
Fatherly and Hope,
Motherly and Love,
Eternal Mind and Understanding,
Churchly and Blessedness,
Will and Wisdom.[129]

WISDOM. 6. Now when the twelfth of the twelve and youngest of all the twenty-eight aeons, a female called "Wisdom," understood the number and the power of the generating aeons, she traced her steps back to the depth of the Father and understood that all the other aeons exist as born beings and give birth when they couple together, whereas the Father alone generated without consort.[130] 7. She wanted to imitate the Father and generate by herself apart from her consort, in order to produce a work in no way inferior to the Father.

She did not know that the Father—since he is unborn, the source of the universe and its Root, Depth, and Abyss—has the power to generate alone, whereas Wisdom, generated and arising after many others, did not wield the power of the Unborn.[131] 8. In the Unborn, he says, are all things together, whereas among generated beings, the female is what emanates substance, and the male gives form to the substance emanated by the female.

---

129. For the emission of the ten and twelve aeons, see Iren., *Haer.* 1.1.2.

130. Cf. this story of Wisdom with Iren., *Haer.* 1.2.2–4. For Wisdom's independent activity, see Ap. John (BG 8502.2) 36.16–37.17; Nat. Rulers (NHC II,4) 94.5–15. See further George W. Macrae, "The Jewish Background of the Gnostic Sophia Myth," *NovT* 12 (1970): 86–101 (94–101); Pheme Perkins, "Sophia as Goddess in the Nag Hammadi Codices," in King, *Images of the Feminine*, 96–112.

131. Unlike in Irenaeus, "Wisdom's fall occurs not because she desires to know the Monad, but because she tries to replicate his solitude. She tries, essentially, to become a Monad" (Kalvesmaki, *Theology*, 55).

προέβαλεν οὖν ἡ Σοφία τοῦτο μόνον ὅπερ ἠδύνατο, οὐσίαν ἄμορφον καὶ ἀκατασκε<ύα>στον. 9. καὶ τοῦτό ἐστι, φησίν, ὃ λέγει Μωϋσῆς· «ἡ δὲ γῆ ἦν ἀόρατος καὶ ἀκατασκεύαστος». αὕτη ἔστι, φησίν, «ἡ ἀγαθὴ», «ἡ ἐπουράνιος Ἱερουσαλὴμ», εἰς ἣν ἐπηγγείλατο ὁ θεὸς εἰσαγαγεῖν τοὺς υἱοὺς Ἰσραήλ, λέγων· «εἰσάξω ὑμᾶς εἰς γῆν ἀγαθή(ν), ῥέουσα<ν> μέλι καὶ γάλα».

31. 1. Γενομένης οὖν ἐντὸς πληρώματος ἀγνοίας κατὰ τὴν Σοφίαν καὶ ἀμορφίας κατὰ τὸ γέν<ν>ημα τῆς Σοφίας, θόρυβος ἐγένετο ἐν τῷ πληρώματι [οἱ αἰῶνες οἱ γενόμενοι], ὅτι παραπλησίως ἄμορφα καὶ ἀτελῆ γενήσεται τῶν αἰώνων τὰ γεννήματα, καὶ φθορά τις καταλήψεται οὐκ εἰς μακρὰν <πάντας> τοὺς αἰῶνας. 2. κατέφυγον οὖν πάντες οἱ αἰῶνες ἐπὶ δέησιν τοῦ Πατρός, ἵνα λυπουμένην τὴν Σοφίαν ἀναπαύσῃ· ἔκλαιε γὰρ καὶ κατωδύρετο ἐπὶ τῷ γεγεν<ν>ημένῳ ὑπ' αὐτῆς ἐκτρώματι—οὕτω γὰρ <αὐτὸ> καλοῦσιν.

ἐλεήσας οὖν ὁ Πατὴρ τὰ δάκρυα τῆς Σοφίας καὶ προσδεξάμενος τῶν αἰών(ων) τὴν δέησιν, ἐπιπροβαλεῖν κελεύ(ει)—οὐ γὰρ αὐτός, φησί, προέβαλεν, ἀλλὰ ὁ Νοῦς (κ)αὶ ἡ Ἀλήθεια—Χριστὸν καὶ Πνεῦμα ἅγιον εἰς μόρφωσιν καὶ διόρθωσιν τοῦ ἐκτρώματος, καὶ παραμυθίαν καὶ διαν(ά)παυσιν τῶν τῆς Σοφίας στεναγμῶν.

3. καὶ γίνονται τριάκοντα αἰῶνες μετὰ τοῦ Χριστοῦ καὶ τοῦ ἁγίου Πνεύματος· τινὲς μὲν οὖν αὐτῶν ταύτῃ εἶναι θέλουσι τὴν τριακοντάδα τῶν αἰώνων, τινὲς δὲ συνυπάρχειν τῷ Πατρὶ <Σιγὴν> καὶ σὺν αὐτοῖς καταριθμεῖσθαι τοὺς αἰῶνας θέ(λο)υσι(ν).

Thus Wisdom emanated the only thing she could have, an unformed and disordered substance.[132] 9. This very point, he says, is what Moses refers to: "Now the earth was invisible and disordered."[133] It is she, he says, who is "the good land,"[134] "the heavenly Jerusalem,"[135] into which God promised to lead the children of Israel, saying: "I will lead you into a good land, flowing with honey and milk."[136]

31. 1. So when ignorance arose in the Fullness because of Wisdom, and formlessness because of the offspring of Wisdom, uproar broke out in the Fullness. This is because the offspring of the aeons would be born in a similarly unformed and imperfect state, and corruption would shortly take hold of all of the aeons.[137] 2. So all the aeons rushed to plead with the Father, to make Wisdom, who was wild with grief, attain rest. She was crying and sobbing over the miscarriage (for so they call it) produced by her.[138]

Then the Father pitied the tears of Wisdom and accepted the plea of the aeons. He ordered Mind and Truth to emanate (for he himself, he says, does not emanate) Christ and the Holy Spirit for the formation and rectification of the miscarried offspring, for the comfort of Wisdom, and the cessation of her groans.[139]

3. And so, with the addition of Christ and the Holy Spirit, the aeons came to be thirty. (Now some of them want there to be a group of thirty aeons in this fashion, while others want Silence to exist together with the Father, with the other aeons numbered along with them.)[140]

---

132. On the unformed substance, see Iren., *Haer.* 1.2.3; 1.4.1; 1.8.2 (1 Cor 15:8).

133. Gen 1:2 LXX; cf. Iren., *Haer.* 1.18.1; Clem. Alex., *Exc.* 47.4.

134. Deut 31:20; cf. *Ref.* 5.8.30 (Naassenes).

135. Gal 4:26; Heb 12:22; cf. *Ref.* 5.7.39 (Naassenes).

136. Cf. Exod 3:8.

137. Marcovich replaces P's ποτέ with πάντας ("all").

138. Cf. Iren., *Haer.* 1.2.3. The word ἔκτρωμα is often translated "abortion," but "abortion" in current English usually signifies an artificially terminated pregnancy, not the natural expulsion of the unformed child (a miscarriage). There is some ambiguity in Greek usage as to whether an ἔκτρωμα is a living or a dead child. The word also had an implicit sense of "monster." See further J. Munck, "Paulus tamquam abortivus (1 Cor. 15:8)," in *New Testament Essays: Studies in Memory of Thomas Walter Manson*, ed. A. J. B. Higgins (Manchester: Manchester University Press, 1959), 180–93.

139. For the emission of Christ and the Holy Spirit, see Iren., *Haer.* 1.2.5.

140. Σιγήν ("Silence") is Bernay's emendation of P's εἰς γῆν ("to earth"). For Silence, see Iren., *Haer.* 1.1.1.

4. ἐπιπροβληθεὶς οὖν ὁ Χριστὸς καὶ τὸ ἅγιον Πνεῦμα ὑπὸ τοῦ Νοῦ καὶ τῆς (Ἀ)ληθείας, εὐθέως τὸ ἔκτρωμα τὸ ἄμορφον τοῦτο τῆς Σοφίας μονογενὲς καὶ δίχα συζύγου γεγεν<ν>ημένον ἀποχωρίζει τῶν <ἄλλων> αἰώνων, ἵνα μὴ βλέποντες αὐτὸ ταράσσωνται διὰ τὴν ἀμορφίαν οἱ τέλειοι αἰῶνες.

5. Ἵν᾽ οὖν μηδ᾽ ὅλως τοῖς αἰῶσι τοῖς τελείοις καταφανῇ τοῦ ἐκτρώματος ἡ ἀμορφία, πάλιν καὶ ὁ Πατὴρ ἐπιπροβάλλει αἰῶνα ἕνα, τὸν Σταυρόν· ὃς γεγεννημένος μέγας—ὡς <ἐκ> μεγάλου καὶ τελείου πατρός—, εἰς φρουρὰν καὶ χαράκωμα τῶν αἰώνων προβεβλημένος, Ὅρος γίνεται τοῦ πληρώματος, ἔχων ἐντὸς ἑαυτοῦ πάντας ὁμοῦ τοὺς τριάκοντα αἰῶνας· <τοσ>οῦτοι γάρ εἰσιν οἱ προβεβλημένοι. 6. καλεῖται δὲ Ὅρος μὲν οὗτος, ὅτι ἀφορίζει ἀπὸ τοῦ πληρώ(μ)ατος ἔξω τὸ ὑστέρημα, Μετοχεὺς δέ, ὅτι μετέχει καὶ τοῦ ὑστερήματος, Σταυρὸς δέ, ὅτι πέπηγεν ἀκλινῶς καὶ ἀμετανοήτως, ὡς μὴ δύνασθαι μηδὲν τοῦ ὑστερήματος καταγενέσθαι ἐγγὺς τῶν ἐντὸς πληρώματος αἰώνων.

7. Ἔξω οὖν τοῦ Ὅρου, τοῦ Σταυροῦ, τοῦ Μετοχέως ἐστὶν ἡ καλουμένη κατ᾽ αὐτοὺς Ὀγδοάς, ἥτις ἐστὶν ἡ ἐκτὸς πληρώματος Σοφία· ἣν ὁ Χριστὸς ἐπιπροβληθεὶς ὑπὸ τοῦ Νοῦ καὶ τῆς Ἀληθείας ἐμόρφωσε καὶ ἀπειργάσατο τέλειον αἰῶνα, οὐδέν <τ>ι τῶν ἐντὸς πληρώματος χείρον(α) δυν(άμ)ε(νο)ν γενέσθαι.

8. ἐπειδὴ δὲ μεμόρφωτο ἡ Σοφία ἔξω, καὶ οὐχ οἷόν τε ἦν <κατ᾽> ἴσον τὸν Χριστὸν καὶ τὸ ἅγιον <Πνεῦμα, τὸ> ἐκ τοῦ Νοὸς προβεβλημένον καὶ τῆς Ἀληθείας, ἔξω τοῦ πληρώματος μένειν, ἀνέδραμεν ἀπὸ τῆς μεμορφωμένης ὁ Χριστὸς καὶ τὸ ἅγιον Πνεῦμα πρὸς τὸν Νοῦν καὶ τὴν Ἀλήθειαν, <ἵν᾽> ἐντὸς τοῦ Ὅρου ᾖ, μετὰ τῶν ἄλλων αἰώνων δοξάζων τὸν Πατέρα.

CHRIST AND THE HOLY SPIRIT. 4. Christ, who was emanated along with the Holy Spirit by Mind and Truth, immediately separated the unformed miscarriage from the other aeons. This unformed miscarriage is the only offspring of Wisdom, and was born apart from a consort. Christ separated it from the other aeons so that the perfect aeons might not see it and be disturbed on account of its formlessness.[141]

THE CROSS. 5. In order that the formlessness of the miscarriage might not appear in any way to the perfect aeons, the Father once again sent forth a single aeon: the Cross. He was born vast in size—as from a vast and perfect Father—and was sent forth as a guard and fence of the aeons. He became a Boundary of the Fullness, having within himself at once all thirty of the aeons (for this is the total of those emanated). 6. He is called "Boundary" because he separates off deficiency from the Fullness, "Sharer," because he shares even in deficiency, and "Cross," since he stands fixed without bending and without wavering, so that no deficiency is able to come near the aeons inside the Fullness.[142]

THE WISDOM OUTSIDE. 7. Now outside of Boundary (or Cross, or Sharer) is what they call the "Ogdoad," who is Wisdom outside the Fullness. She it was whom Christ, emanated by Mind and Truth, formed and completed as a perfect aeon, in no possible way inferior to those inside the Fullness.[143]

8. Now Wisdom, who was outside, had been formed. Yet it was not possible for Christ and the Holy Spirit, as emanations of Mind and Truth, to remain outside the Fullness. Thus Christ, along with the Holy Spirit, ran from her who was formed back up to Mind and Truth. They ran back to be within the Boundary and glorify the Father with the other aeons.

---

141. Cf. Iren., *Haer.* 1.2.5. Ἄλλων ("other") is Marcovich's emendation of P's ὅλων. The word ἀμορφίαν (here: "formlessness") also signifies "ugliness." Einar Thomassen ("The Derivation of Matter in Monistic Gnosticism," in *Gnosticism and Later Platonism: Themes, Figures, and Texts*, ed. John D. Turner and Ruth Majercik [Atlanta: Society of Biblical Literature, 2000], 1–17 [11]) points out that the Neopythagorean Moderatos of Gades described his principle of matter ("Quantity") as ἄμορφον … καὶ ἀσχημάτιστον ("without form … and without shape") (Simplikios, *In phys.* [Diels, 231,10–11]). The word may derive from Plato's description of the Receptacle as ἀνόρατον εἶδος τι καὶ ἄμορφον ("an invisible and shapeless form," *Tim.* 51a7).

142. On Cross, see Iren., *Haer.* 1.2.4; 1.3.1; Clem. Alex., *Exc.* 22.4; 42.1; Tert., *Val.* 10.

143. For the Wisdom outside, see Iren., *Haer.* 1.3.4.

32. 1. Ἐπεὶ οὖν μία τις ἦν εἰρή(ν)η καὶ συμφωνία πάντων τῶν ἐντὸς πλ(η)ρώματος αἰώνων, ἔδοξ(εν) αὐτοῖς μὴ μόνον κατὰ συζυγίαν δεδοξακέναι τὸν <Β>υ<θ>όν, δοξάσαι <δὲ> καὶ διὰ προσφορᾶς καρπῶν πρεπόντων τῷ Πατρί. πάντες οὖν ηὐδόκησαν οἱ τριάκοντα αἰῶνες ἕνα προβαλεῖν αἰῶνα, κοινὸν τοῦ πληρώματος καρπόν, ἵν᾽ ᾖ <σύμβολον> τῆς <ἑνότητος> αὐτῶν καὶ τῆς ὁμοφροσύνης καὶ εἰρήνης. 2. καὶ μόνος ὑπὸ πάντων αἰώνων προβεβλημένος τῷ Πατρί, οὗτός ἐστιν ὁ καλούμενος παρ᾽ αὐτοῖς κοινὸς τοῦ πληρώματος Καρπός. τὰ μὲν οὖν ἐντὸς πληρώματος ἦν οὕτως, καὶ προβέβλητο ὁ κοινὸς τοῦ πληρώματος Καρπός, ὁ Ἰησοῦς—τοῦτο γὰρ ὄνομα αὐτῷ—, «ὁ ἀρχιερεὺς ὁ μέγας».

Ἡ δὲ ἔξω τοῦ πληρώματος Σοφία, ἐπιζητοῦσα τὸν Χριστὸν τὸν μεμορφωκότα <αὐτὴν> καὶ τὸ ἅγιον Πνεῦμα, ἐν φόβῳ μεγάλῳ κατέστη ὅτι ἀπολεῖται κεχωρισμένη τοῦ μορφώσαντος αὐτὴν καὶ στηρίσαντος. 3. καὶ ἐλυπήθη καὶ ἐν ἀπορίᾳ ἐγένετο πολλῇ, λογιζομένη τίς ἦν ὁ μορφώσας, τί τὸ ἅγιον Πνεῦμα, ποῦ ἀπῆλθε, τίς ὁ κωλύσας αὐτοὺς συμπαρεῖναι, τίς ἐφθόνησε τοῦ καλοῦ καὶ μακαρίου θεάματος ἐκείνου· ἐπὶ τούτοις καθεστῶσα τοῖς πάθεσι τρέπεται ἐπὶ δέησιν καὶ ἱκετείαν τοῦ ἀπολιπόντος αὐτήν.

4. δεομένης οὖ(ν αὐ)τῆς κατηλέησεν ὁ Χριστὸς ὁ ἐντὸς πληρώματος ὢν κα(ὶ οἱ ἄ)λλοι πάντες αἰῶνες, καὶ ἐκπέμπουσιν ἔξω τοῦ πληρώματος τὸν κοινὸν τοῦ πληρώματος Καρ(π)ὸν σύζυγον τῆς ἔξω Σοφίας καὶ διορθωτὴν παθῶν ὧν ἔπαθεν ἐπιζητοῦσα τὸν Χριστόν.

5. Γενόμενος οὖν ἔξω τοῦ πληρώματος Καρπὸς καὶ εὑρὼν αὐτὴν ἐν πάθεσι τοῖς πρώτοις τέτρασι—[καὶ] φόβῳ καὶ λύπῃ καὶ ἀπορίᾳ καὶ δεήσει—, διωρθώσατο τὰ πάθη αὐτῆς, διορθούμενος δὲ ἑώρα ὅτι ἀπολέσθαι αὐτά, αἰώνια (ὄ)ντα καὶ τῆς Σοφίας ἴδια, οὐ καλόν, οὐδ᾽ ἐν πάθεσιν εἶνα(ι) τὴν Σοφίαν τοιούτοις—ἐν φόβῳ καὶ λύπῃ ἀπορίᾳ ἱκετείᾳ. 6.—ἐποίησεν οὖν, ὡς τηλικοῦτος

JESUS. **32.** 1. Now since there was a single peace and harmony of all the aeons within the Fullness, they decided not only to glorify Depth as couples but also to glorify him with an offering of fruits appropriate for the Father.[144] So all thirty aeons decided to emanate one aeon, the common fruit of the Fullness, so that it might be a symbol of their oneness, unity of thought, and peace.[145] 2. Consequently, he alone was emanated by all the aeons for the Father. He is the one whom they call the "common Fruit of the Fullness." This was the situation within the Fullness when the common Fruit of the Fullness, Jesus (as they call him), was emanated as "the great High Priest."[146]

Now the Wisdom outside the Fullness, seeking after the Christ, who had formed her, and the Holy Spirit, stood transfixed with terror, since she was dying apart from the one who formed her and gave her stability. 3. She was grieved and struck with a sense of profound bewilderment, thinking to herself, "Who was it that formed me?" "What is the Holy Spirit?" "Where did he go?" "Who prevented them from coming to me?" "Who begrudged me the beautiful and blessed sight of him?" Transfixed in these wild emotions, she turned to implore and plead with the one who left her behind.[147]

4. When she implored, Christ within the Fullness had mercy on her, as did all the other aeons. Consequently, they sent outside the Fullness the common Fruit of the Fullness as a consort of the Wisdom outside and as a corrector of the wild emotions that she felt when she earnestly sought for Christ.[148]

5. So the Fruit of the Fullness, when he arrived outside the Fullness, found her transfixed with four primal negative emotions—fear, grief, bewilderment, and longing. He corrected her negative emotions. While he was correcting them, he saw that to destroy them was not good, since they are eternal and proper to Wisdom—but at the same time it was not good that Wisdom be transfixed by such emotions (namely, fear, grief, bewilderment, and longing). 6. Thus he—being so great an aeon and an offspring

144. "Depth" represents τὸν Βυθόν, Marcovich's emendation of P's τὸν υἱόν. "The Son" could conceivably refer to Mind (cf. Iren., *Haer.* 1.1.1). Wendland proposes τὸν πατέρα ("the Father").

145. Σύμβολον ("symbol") is an addition of Marcovich. Marcovich, following Bernay, emends P's νεότητος ("newness/youth") to ἑνότητος ("oneness").

146. For the emission of Jesus, see Iren., *Haer.* 1.2.6; Clem. Alex., *Exc.* 23.2. For Jesus as "great High Priest," see Heb 4:14.

147. On Wisdom's frenzied emotions, see Iren., *Haer.* 1.4.1.

148. Cf. Clem. Alex., *Exc.* 29.2.

αἰὼν καὶ παντὸς τοῦ πληρώματος ἔκγονος, ἐκστῆναι τὰ πάθη ἀπ’ αὐτῆς, καὶ ἐποίησεν αὐτὰ ὑποστατὰς οὐσίας. καὶ τὸν μὲν φόβον ψυχικὴν ἐποίησεν <οὐσίαν> [ἐπιθυμίαν], τὴν δὲ λύπην ὑλικήν, τὴν δὲ ἀπορίαν δαιμόνων· τὴν δὲ ἐπιστροφῆς <ἐπιθυμίαν> καὶ δέησιν καὶ ἱκετείαν <καὶ> <ἐπάν>οδον καὶ μετάνοιαν [καὶ] δύναμιν ψυχικῆς οὐσίας, ἥτις καλεῖται δεξιά.

7. ὁ δημιουργὸς ἀπὸ τοῦ φόβου. τοῦτ’ ἔστιν ὃ λέγει, φησίν, ἡ γραφή· «ἀρχὴ σοφίας φόβος κυρίου». αὕτη γάρ ἀρχὴ τῶν τῆς Σοφίας παθῶν· ἐφοβήθη γάρ, εἶτα ἐλυπήθη, εἶτα ἠπόρησε, καὶ οὕτως ἐπὶ δέησιν καὶ ἱκετείαν κατέφυγεν. ἔστι δὲ πυρώδης, φησίν, ἡ ψυχικὴ οὐσία· καλεῖται δὲ καὶ Τόπος ὑπ’ αὐτῶν, καὶ Ἑβδομάς, καὶ «παλαιὸς τῶν ἡμερῶν». καὶ ὅσα τοιαῦτα λέγουσι περὶ τοῦ θεοῦ, ταῦτα εἶναι τοῦ ψ<υχ>ικοῦ, ὅν φησιν εἶναι τοῦ κόσμου δημιουργόν. 8. ἐστὶ δὴ πυρώδης, λέγει, φησί, καὶ Μωϋσῆς· «κύριος ὁ θεός σου πῦρ ἐστι φλέγον καὶ καταναλίσκον»· καὶ γὰρ τοῦτο οὕτως γεγράφθαι θέλει.

διπλῆ δέ τίς ἐστι, φησίν, ἡ δύναμις τοῦ πυρός· ἔστι γὰρ πῦρ παμφάγον, κατ(ασ)βεσθῆναι μὴ δυνάμενον <...>

κατὰ τοῦτο τοίνυν τὸ μέρος θνητή [τίς] ἐστιν ἡ ψυχή, μεσότης τις οὖσα· 9. ἔστι γὰρ ἑβδομὰς καὶ κατάπαυσις· ὑποκάτω γάρ ἐστι τῆς Ὀγδοάδος, ὅπου ἐστὶν ἡ Σοφία ἡ μεμορφωμένη καὶ ὁ κοινὸς τοῦ πληρώματος Καρπός, ὑπεράνω

of the entire Fullness—made her negative emotions depart from her and made them underlying substances. He made fear an animate substance, grief a material substance, and bewilderment the substance of demons. Finally, he made her yearning for return—her imploring, pleading, turning back, and her change of heart—a power of animate substance called "the right hand."[149]

THE ARTIFICER. 7. The Artificer is produced from fear. This, he says, is what the scripture means: "The beginning of Wisdom is the Lord's fear."[150] It is this that is the beginning of Wisdom's wild emotions. For she was afraid, then grieved, then bewildered, and so rushed to implore and plead. He says that animate substance is fiery.[151] They call it "Place" and "Hebdomad" and "Ancient of Days."[152] Whatever kinds of titles the scriptures use for God are characteristic of the animate one, whom he says is the Artificer of the world. 8. He claims, in addition, that Moses calls him fiery: "The Lord your God is a fire burning and consuming" (this is his arbitrary interpretation of the passage).[153]

The power of the fire is twofold, he says.[154] It is a fire devouring all, unable to be extinguished.[155]

In this respect, then, the soul is mortal, being a sort of mediator, since it is a hebdomad and rest. 9. It is below the Ogdoad, where Wisdom, who was formed, and the common Fruit of the Fullness dwell; but it is above matter,

---

149. Ἐπιστροφῆς ἐπιθυμίαν is Marcovich's emendation of P's ἐπιστροφήν ("return/conversion") based on Theodoret, *Haer. fab.* 1.7 (PG 83:357a). Ἐπάνοδον (here: "turning back") is Marcovich's emendation of P's ὁδόν ("path/road"). On the creation of the various substances, see Iren., *Haer.* 1.4.5; 1.5.1, 4; Clem. Alex., *Exc.* 45.1–47.2.

150. Ps 110:10 LXX; Prov 1:7; 9:10; cf. *Ref.* 7.26.2 ("Basileides"). The passage should perhaps be read (or at least understood): "The beginning of the Lord is the fear of Wisdom."

151. Cf. Clem. Alex., *Exc.* 38.1.

152. "Place" (מקום) is a common rabbinic circumlocution for God. See also Clem. Alex., *Exc.* 34.1–2; 37; 38.1, 3; 39; 59.2. For the Artificer as "Hebdomad," see Iren., *Haer.* 1.5.2, 4. For "Ancient of Days," see Dan 7:9; cf. Hipp., *Comm. Dan.* 4.11.2.

153. Deut 4:24; cf. Exod 24:17; *Ref.* 6.9.3 ("Simon"). In accordance with these biblical passages, the creator god is often said to be fiery in nature. See, e.g., *Ref.* 7.38.1 (Apelles); 8.9.7 (Doketai).

154. For the twofold nature of fire, see Clem. Alex., *Ecl.* 26.3–4; *Ref.* 6.9.5 ("Simon").

155. For fire devouring all, see *Ref.* 6.9.9 ("Simon"). Scholars suspect a lacuna at the end of this sentence.

δὲ τῆς ὕλης, ἧ<ς> ἐστι δημιουργός. ἐὰν ἐξομοιωθῇ τοῖς ἄνω, τῇ Ὀγδοάδι, ἀ(θ)άνατος ἐγένετο καὶ ἦλθεν εἰς τὴν Ὀγδοάδα, ἥτις ἐστί, φησίν, «Ἱερουσαλὴμ ἐπουράνιος»· ἐὰν δὲ ἐξομοιωθῇ τῇ ὕλῃ, τουτέστι τοῖς πάθεσι τοῖς ὑλικοῖς, φθαρτὴ ἔσται καὶ ἀπώλετο.

33. 1. Ὥσπερ οὖν τῆς ψυχικῆς οὐσίας ἡ πρώτη καὶ μεγίστη δύναμις γέγονεν <ὁ δημιουργός, ἡ> εἰκὼν <τοῦ Πατρός, οὕτως τῆς ὑλικῆς οὐσίας ὁ> διάβολος, «ὁ ἄρχων τοῦ κόσμου τούτου», τῆς δὲ τῶν δαιμόνων οὐσίας—ἥτις ἐστὶν ἐκ τῆς ἀπορίας—ὁ Βεελζεβούλ.

ἡ Σοφία ἄνωθεν ἀπὸ τῆς Ὀγδοάδος ἐνεργοῦσα ἕως τῆς Ἑβδομάδος. οὐδὲν οἶδεν, λέγουσιν, ὁ δημιουργὸς ὅλως, ἀλλ' ἔστιν ἄνους καὶ μωρὸς κατ' αὐτούς, καὶ τί πράσσει ἢ ἐργάζεται οὐκ οἶδεν. ἀγνοοῦντι δὲ αὐτῷ ὅ τι δὴ ποιεῖ, ἡ Σοφία ἐνήργησε πάντα καὶ ἐνίσχυσε, καὶ ἐκείνης ἐνεργούσης αὐτὸς ᾤετο ἀφ' ἑαυτοῦ ποιεῖν τὴν κτίσιν τοῦ κόσμου. ὅθεν ἤρξατο λέγειν· «ἐγὼ ὁ θεός, καὶ πλὴν ἐμοῦ ἄλλος οὐκ ἔστιν».

34. 1. Ἔστιν οὖν ἡ κατὰ Οὐαλεντῖνον τετρακτύς, «πηγὴ [τῆς] ἀενάου φύσεως ῥιζώματ' ἔχουσα,» καὶ ἡ Σοφία, ἀφ' ἧς ἡ κτίσις ἡ ψυχικὴ καὶ ὑλικὴ συνέστηκε νῦν. καλεῖται δὲ ἡ μὲν Σοφία πνεῦμα, ὁ δὲ δημιουργὸς ψυχή, ὁ

which the Artificer rules.[156] Now if it is assimilated to the things above, to the Ogdoad, it becomes immortal and enters the Ogdoad, which is, he says, "the heavenly Jerusalem." But if it is assimilated to matter (that is, to material affections), it will be susceptible to corruption and destroyed.[157]

33. 1. Just as the Artificer, image of the Father, is the first and greatest power of animate substance, so also the devil came to be the first and greatest power of material substance.[158] He is "the ruler of this world," made of demonic substance—a substance produced from bewilderment.[159] He is Beelzebul.[160]

The Wisdom above has her sphere of activity extending from the Ogdoad to the Hebdomad. This is because, as they say, the Artificer knows nothing at all. In their view, he is mindless and stupid, not knowing what he performs or produces. Through him who is himself ignorant of what he does, Wisdom performs and has control over all things. Although it is she who performs the work, he supposed that he makes the structure of the world from himself. On this basis, he began to claim: "I am God, and apart from me there is no other!"[161]

34. 1. This is Valentinus's Tetraktys: "the fount possessing the roots of ever-flowing nature"![162] And this is Wisdom, from whom the animate and material creation now exists. Wisdom is also called "spirit," the Artificer is also called "soul," the devil is also called "the ruler of this world,"

156. Duncker and Schneidewin emend ἥ in P to ἧς.

157. Cf. Iren., *Haer.* 1.6.1; 7.1, 5; Ptolemy, *Flor.*, in Epiph., *Pan.* 33.7.4; Herakleon, frag. 40 (Brooke); Clem. Alex., *Strom.* 4.13.90.3.

158. This line has been heavily emended by Marcovich. He adds: ὁ δημιουργός ["the Artificer"], ἡ … τοῦ Πατρός ["of the Father"], οὕτως τῆς ὑλικῆς οὐσίας ὁ ["so also the (devil) … of material substance"]. P indicates that the devil became the image of animate substance, which most scholars have found intolerable. For the Artificer, see Clem. Alex., *Strom.* 4.13.90.2; *Exc.* 47.2–3; cf. Iren., *Haer.* 1.5.1 (where the Artificer preserves the image of the only-born Son).

159. For the "ruler of this world," see John 12:31; 14:30; 16:11.

160. For "Beelzebul," see Matt 12:24; Luke 11:15.

161. Isa 45:5; 46:9; cf. Deut 4:35; 32:39; Iren., *Haer.* 1.5.4; Clem. Alex., *Exc.* 49.1. This arrogant claim of the Artificer appears often in gnostic sources (e.g., Ap. John [NHC II,1] 11.20–21; 13.8–9; Nat. Rulers [NHC II,4] 86.30; 94.22–23).

162. Cf. *Ref.* 1.2.9; 4.51.7; 6.23.4. Irenaeus, in his discussion of the Valentinians, had already made the connection to the Tetraktys (*Haer.* 1.1.1; 2.14.6). See further Sagnard, *Gnose*, 334–57.

διάβολος δὲ «ὁ ἄρχων τοῦ κόσμου», Βεελζεβοὺλ «ὁ τῶν δαιμόνων». ταῦτά ἐστιν ἃ λέγουσιν.

2. ἔτι πρὸς τούτοις, ἀριθμητικὴν ποιούμενοι τὴν πᾶσαν αὐτῶν διδασκαλίαν, ὡς προεῖπον, (τοὺ)ς ἐντὸς πληρώματος αἰῶνας τρι(ά)κοντα πάλιν ἐπιπροβεβ<λ>ηκέναι αὐτοῖς κα(τ)' ἀναλογίαν αἰῶνας ἄλλους, ἵν' ᾖ τὸ πλήρωμα ἐν ἀριθμῷ τελείῳ συνηθροισμένον. 3. ὡς γὰρ οἱ Πυθαγορικοὶ διεῖλον εἰς δώδεκα καὶ τριάκοντα καὶ ἑξήκοντα, καὶ λεπτὰ λεπτῶν εἰσιν ἐκείνοις, <ὡς> δεδήλωται, οὕτως οὗτοι τὰ ἐντὸς πληρώματος ὑποδιαιροῦσι(ν). ὑποδιῄρηται δὲ καὶ τὰ ἐν τῇ Ὀγδοάδι, καὶ προβεβλήκασιν ἡ Σοφία, ἥτις ἐστὶ «μήτηρ πάντων τῶν ζώντων» κατ' αὐτούς, καὶ ὁ κοινὸς τοῦ πληρώματος Καρπὸς ἑβδομήκοντα λόγο<υ>ς, οἵτινές εἰσιν ἄγγελοι ἐπουράνιοι, πολιτευόμενοι ἐν «Ἱερουσαλὴμ τῇ ἄνω, τῇ ἐν οὐρανοῖς»· 4. αὕτη γάρ ἐστι, Ἱερουσαλὴμ ἡ ἔξω Σοφία, καὶ ὁ νυμφίος αὐτῆς ὁ κοινὸς τοῦ πληρώματος Καρπός.

Προέβαλε καὶ ὁ δημιουργὸς ψυχάς· αὕτη γάρ <ἐστιν ἡ δύναμις> οὐσία ψυχῶν. οὗτός ἐστι κατ' αὐτοὺς Ἀβρα<ὰ>μ καὶ ταῦτα τοῦ Ἀβραὰμ τὰ τέκνα.

ἐκ τῆς ὑλικῆς οὐσίας οὖν καὶ διαβολικῆς ἐποίησεν ὁ δημιουργὸς ταῖς ψυχαῖς τὰ σώματα. 5. τοῦτό ἐστι τὸ εἰρημένον· «καὶ ἔπλασεν ὁ θεὸς τὸν ἄνθρωπον, χοῦν ἀπὸ τῆς γῆς λαβών, καὶ ἐνεφύσησεν εἰς τὸ πρόσωπον αὐτοῦ πνοὴν ζωῆς·

and Beelzebul is also called "the ruler of the demons."[163] This is what they declare![164]

FURTHER DIFFERENTIATION: ANGELS AND SOULS. 2. In addition, so as to make every bit of their teaching arithmetical (as I said above), the thirty aeons inside the Fullness again emanated for themselves, by analogy, other aeons, to make the Fullness add up to a perfect number. 3. For as the Pythagoreans divide the world into twelve, thirty, and sixty parts—and have even more minute units of minute units (as has been shown)—so also these people subdivide the beings inside the Fullness.[165] The beings in the Ogdoad are also divided. Wisdom, who is—according to them—"Mother of all the living," emanated, together with the common Fruit of the Fullness, seventy rational minds, who are heavenly angels, living their lives in "the Jerusalem above, which is in heaven." 4. This Jerusalem is the Wisdom outside, and her bridegroom is the common Fruit of the Fullness.[166]

The Artificer also emanated souls (for this Power is the substance of souls).[167] In their view, he is Abraham, and these souls are the children of Abraham.[168]

Then out of material and devilish substance, the Artificer made bodies for the souls. 5. This is the scriptural proof: "And God molded the human being, taking dust from the earth, and he breathed into his face the breath

---

163. For Wisdom as "spirit" (πνεῦμα), see *Ref.* 6.35.3 (Wisdom descends on Mary as Holy Spirit); 36.4 (Wisdom is called "Holy Spirit"; similarly Iren., *Haer.* 1.4.1). For the devil-cosmocrator, see John 12:31.

164. The author's application of the Tetraktys (Wisdom, Artificer, devil, Beelzebul) is in stark contrast to Iren., *Haer.* 1.1.1. See further Alt, "Hippolytos," 100.

165. . Cf. Ps.-Tert., *Adv. omn. haer.* 4 (Ptolemy and Secundus add more aeons to Valentinus's original thirty).

166. The meeting of "bride and groom" is described in Iren., *Haer.* 1.4.5; and their consummation in *Haer.* 1.7.1. For nuptial imagery, see John 3:29; Rev 21:2. For Wisdom as Mother of all the living, see Gen 3:20 (where the designation is applied to Eve). Genesis 3:20 is also interpreted in *Ref.* 5.7.39 (Naassenes); 5.16.13 (Peratai); Iren., *Haer.* 1.30.1 (Ophites); Ap. John (BG 8502.2) 60.16–19; Nat. Rulers (NHC II,4) 89.15–17. Seventy is a biblical number indicating completion (e.g., Gen 46:27; Exod 15:27; Num 11:16; Luke 10:1).

167. Marcovich supplies ἐστιν ἡ δύναμις ("Power is").

168. On the children of Abraham as the elect, see John 8:39; Gal 3:6–18; 4:1–7; Rom 4:13–25.

καὶ ἐγένετο ὁ ἄνθρωπος εἰς ψυχὴν ζῶσαν». οὗτός ἐστι κατ' αὐτοὺς «ὁ ἔσω ἄνθρωπος», ὁ ψυχικός, ἐν τῷ σώματι κατοικῶν τῷ ὑλικῷ, ὅ ἐστιν ὑλικός, φθαρτός, τελείως ἐκ τῆς διαβολικῆς οὐσίας πεπλασμένος.

6. ἔστι δὲ οὗτος ὁ ὑλικὸς ἄνθρωπος κατ' αὐτοὺς οἱονεὶ πανδοχεῖον ἢ κατοικητήριον ποτὲ μὲν ψυχῆς μόνης, ποτὲ δὲ ψυχῆς καὶ δαιμόνων, ποτὲ δὲ ψυχῆς καὶ λόγων· οἵτινες εἰσι λόγοι ἄνωθεν κατεσπαρμένο(ι) ἀπ(ὸ) τ(ο)ῦ κοινοῦ τοῦ πληρώματος Καρποῦ καὶ τῆς Σοφίας εἰς τοῦτον τὸν κόσμον, κατοικοῦντες ἐν (σώμα)τι χοϊκῷ μετὰ ψυχῆς, ὅταν δαίμονες μὴ συνοικῶσι τῇ ψυχῇ.

7. Τοῦτό ἐστι, φησί, τὸ γεγραμμένον ἐν τῇ γραφῇ· «τούτου χάριν κάμπτω τὰ γόνατά μου πρὸς τὸν θεὸν καὶ πατέρα καὶ κύριον τοῦ κυρίου ἡμῶν Ἰησοῦ Χριστοῦ», «ἵνα δῴη ἡμῖν» ὁ θεὸς «κατοικῆσαι τὸν Χριστὸν» «εἰς τὸν ἔσω ἄνθρωπον», τουτέστι τὸν ψυχικόν, οὐ τὸν σωματικόν, «ἵνα ἐξισχύσητε νοῆσαι» «τί τὸ βάθος», ὅπερ ἐστὶν ὁ Πατὴρ τῶν ὅλων, «καὶ τί τὸ πλάτος», ὅπερ ἐστὶν ὁ Σταυρός, ὁ Ὅρος τοῦ πληρώματος, «καὶ τί τὸ μῆκος», τουτέστι τὸ πλήρωμα τῶν αἰώνων. 8. διὰ τοῦτο «ψυχικός», φησίν, «ἄνθρωπος οὐ δέχεται τὰ τοῦ πνεύματος τοῦ θεοῦ· μωρία γὰρ αὐτῷ ἐστι». μωρία δέ, φησίν, ἐστὶν ἡ δύναμις τοῦ δημιουργοῦ· μωρὸς γὰρ ἦν καὶ ἄνους, καὶ ἐνόμιζεν αὐτὸς δημιουργεῖν τὸν κόσμον, ἀγνοῶν ὅτι πάντα ἡ Σοφία, ἡ Μήτηρ, ἡ Ὀγδοάς, ἐνήργει αὐτῷ πρὸς τὴν κτίσιν τοῦ κόσμου οὐδὲν εἰδότι.

of life, and the human being arose as a living soul."[169] The animate is in their view "the inner person" dwelling in the material that constitutes the material person—that is, the corruptible person, who is completely molded from devilish substance.[170]

6. Now this "material person" is in their view a "hostel," as it were, or dwelling—sometimes of the soul alone, at other times of a soul and demons, and sometimes of the soul and rational principles.[171] These are the rational principles scattered from above into this world away from the common Fruit of the Fullness and Wisdom. They dwell with the soul in a body of dust, whenever the demons do not inhabit the soul.[172]

7. This, he says, is the meaning of the scriptural verse: "For this reason I bow my knees to the God and Father and Lord of our Lord Jesus Christ," that God "give Christ to dwell within us" "in the inner human being"—the animate, not the bodily—"so that you might be strong enough to perceive" "what is the Depth" (the Father of the universe), "the Breadth" (the Cross, the Boundary of the Fullness), "and the Length" (the Fullness of aeons).[173] 8. For this reason, he says, "the animate person does not receive the things of God's spirit. To the animate person, such things are stupidity."[174] Now stupidity, he says, is the power of the Artificer. He was stupid and mindless and supposed that he fashioned the world, not knowing that Wisdom—the Mother, the Ogdoad—worked in him for the creation of the world, though he knew nothing.[175]

---

169. Gen 2:7 LXX; cf. Iren., *Haer.* 1.5.5; Clem. Alex., *Exc.* 50; *Ref.* 6.14.5 ("Simon"); 7.28.3 (Satorneilos); Nat. Rulers (NHC II,4) 87.24–88.15.

170. See the note on "inner human being" in *Ref.* 5.7.36 (Naassenes).

171. For the person as "hostel" (πανδοχεῖον), see Valentinus, frag. 2 (Völker), from Clem. Alex., *Strom.* 2.20.114.5–6. Cf. Matt 12:45 (seven demons return to the "house"); Demokritos, DK 68 B171 (ψυχὴ οἰκητήριον δαίμονος ["the soul is the dwelling of a daimon"]); Plato, *Resp.* 580a ([of the tyrant:] πάσης κακίας πανδοκεῖ ["hostelry of all vice"]); Barn. 16.7 (οἶκος δαιμονίων ["house of demons"]).

172. Cf. Iren., *Haer.* 1.5.6; 7.5 (implantation of spiritual seeds from Wisdom); 2.19.3 (*et se quidem spiritales esse, quoniam particula quaedam universitatis patris in anima ipsorum deposita est* ["And these (Valentinians) are spiritual because they have certain particles of the universal Father deposited in their soul"]).

173. Eph 3:14, 17–18, with glosses.

174. 1 Cor 2:14, also quoted in Iren., *Haer.* 1.8.3; *Ref.* 5.8.26 (Naassenes).

175. For the unwitting Artificer, see Iren., *Haer.* 1.5.3; *Ref.* 6.33.1 ("Valentinus"); Clem. Alex., *Exc.* 49.1; Herakleon, frag. 1 (Brooke).

35. 1. Πάντες οὖν οἱ προφῆται καὶ ὁ νόμος ἐλάλησαν ἀπὸ τοῦ δημιουργοῦ, μωροῦ, λέγει, θεοῦ, μωροὶ οὐδὲν εἰδότες. διὰ τοῦτο, φησί, λέγει ὁ σωτήρ· «πάντες οἱ πρὸ ἐμοῦ ἐληλυθότες κλέπται καὶ λῃσταί εἰσι», καὶ ὁ ἀπόστολος· «τὸ μυστήριον», «ὃ ταῖς προτέραις γενεαῖς οὐκ ἐγνωρίσθη». 2. οὐδεὶς γάρ, φησί, τῶν προφητῶν εἴρηκε περὶ τούτων οὐδέν, ὧν ἡμεῖς λέγομεν· ἠγνοεῖτο γὰρ πάντα, ἅτε δὴ ἀπὸ μόνου τοῦ δημιουργοῦ λελαλημένα.

Ὅτε οὖν τέλος ἔλαβεν ἡ κτίσις καὶ ἔδει λοιπὸν γενέσθαι «τὴν ἀποκάλυψιν τῶ(ν) υἱῶν τοῦ θεοῦ»—τουτέστι τοῦ δημιουργοῦ—, τὴν ἐγκεκαλυμμένην, ἥν, φησίν, ἐγκεκάλυπτο ὁ ψ(υ)χ(ι)κὸς ἄνθρωπος καὶ εἶχε «κάλυμμα ἐπὶ τὴν κα(ρ)δί(αν)»·

3. ὁπότε οὖν ἔδει ἀρθῆναι τὸ κάλυμ<μ>α καὶ ὀφθῆναι ταῦτα τὰ μυστήρια, γεγέν<ν>ηται ὁ Ἰησοῦς διὰ Μαρίας τῆς παρθένου, κατὰ τὸ εἰρημένον· «πνεῦμα ἅγιον ἐπελεύσεται ἐπὶ σέ»—πνεῦμα ἔστιν ἡ Σοφία—, «καὶ δύναμις ὑψίστου ἐπισκιάσει σοι»—ὕψιστος ἔστιν ὁ δημιουργός·—«διὸ τὸ γεννώμενον ἐκ σοῦ ἅγιον κληθήσεται». 4. γεγέν<ν>ηται γὰρ οὐκ ἀπὸ ὑψίστου μόνου, ὥσπερ οἱ κατὰ τὸν Ἀδὰμ κτισθέντες ἀπὸ μόνου ἐκτίσθησαν τοῦ ὑψίστου—τουτέστι [τῆς Σοφίας καὶ] τοῦ δημιουργοῦ. ὁ δὲ Ἰησοῦς, «ὁ καινὸς ἄνθρωπος», [ὁ] ἀπὸ Πνεύματος ἁγίου—τουτέστι τῆς Σοφίας καὶ τοῦ δημιουργοῦ—, ἵνα τὴν μὲν πλάσιν καὶ κατασκευὴν τοῦ σώματος αὐτοῦ ὁ δημιουργὸς καταρτίσῃ, τὴν δὲ οὐσίαν αὐτοῦ τὸ Πνεῦμα παράσχῃ τὸ ἅγιον, καὶ γένηται λόγος ἐπουράνιος ἀπὸ τῆς Ὀγδοάδος, γεν<ν>ηθεὶς διὰ Μαρίας.

THE LAW AND THE PROPHETS. **35.** 1. So all the prophets and the Law spoke from the Artificer (the "stupid god," as he alleges), and they were stupid since they knew nothing. For this reason, he says, the Savior declares, "all who have come before me are thieves and brigands,"[176] and the apostle refers to "the mystery which was not recognized in former generations."[177] 2. For none of the prophets, he says, spoke in any way of the things that *we* speak. Everything was unknown, because all things were spoken from the Artificer alone.[178]

THE INCARNATION. When the creation attained its end, there had to be, finally, "the revelation of the children of God" (that is, of the Artificer).[179] This revelation was veiled, and in respect to it, he says, the animate person, who has "a veil over his heart," is veiled as well.[180]

3. Now when it became necessary for the veil to be removed, and these mysteries to be seen, Jesus was born from Mary the virgin, according to what is said: "Holy Spirit will come upon you"—the Spirit being Wisdom—"and power of the Most High will overshadow you"—the "Most High" being the Artificer. "Consequently what is born from you will be called holy."[181] 4. Jesus was born not from the Most High alone, like people created according to the model of Adam were created from the Most High or Artificer. Rather, Jesus, "the new human being," was born from the Holy Spirit—that is, from Wisdom and the Artificer.[182] Accordingly, the Artificer fit together the mold and structure of his body, while the Holy Spirit supplied his substance. Thus arose a heavenly Word from the Ogdoad, born through Mary.

---

176. John 10:8; cf. Clem. Alex., *Strom.* 1.17.81–87.

177. Eph 3:4–5. This verse is also interpreted in *Ref.* 5.8.5 (Naassenes); 7.25.3; 7.26.7 ("Basileides"). See further Iren., *Haer.* 1.6.1 (the "mysteries of Achamoth"); Clem. Alex., *Strom.* 5.13.87.1–4.

178. For the prophecies of the Artificer, see Iren., *Haer.* 1.7.3–4.

179. An interpretation of Rom 8:19. Cf. the understanding of this verse in *Ref.* 7.25.1, 5; 7.27.1 ("Basileides").

180. For the veil, see 2 Cor 3:15.

181. An interpretation of Luke 1:35; cf. *Ref.* 7.26.9 ("Basileides"); Clem. Alex., *Exc.* 60.

182. For the expression "new human being," see Eph 2:15; 4:24. See further *Ref.* 5.7.15 (Naassenes); [Hipp.], *Noet.* 17.4; Acts Thom. 132.

5. Περὶ τούτου ζήτησις μεγάλη ἐστὶν αὐτοῖς καὶ σχισμάτων καὶ διαφορᾶς ἀφορμή· καὶ γέγονεν ἐντεῦθεν ἡ διδασκαλία αὐτῶν διῃρημένη, καὶ καλεῖται ἡ μὲν ἀνατολική τις διδασκαλία κατ' αὐτούς, ἡ δὲ Ἰταλιωτική. 6. οἱ μὲν ἀπὸ τῆς Ἰταλίας, ὧν ἐστιν Ἡρακλέων καὶ Πτολεμαῖος, ψυχικόν φασι τὸ σῶμα τοῦ Ἰησοῦ γεγονέναι, καὶ διὰ τοῦτο ἐπὶ τοῦ βαπτίσματος τὸ πνεῦμα ὡς περιστερὰ κατελήλυθε—τουτέστιν ὁ λόγος ὁ τῆς μητρὸς ἄνωθεν, τῆς Σοφίας—, καὶ γέγονε τῷ ψυχικῷ καὶ ἐγήγερκεν αὐτὸν ἐκ νεκρῶν. τοῦτό ἐστι, φησί, τὸ εἰρημένον· «ὁ ἐγείρας Χριστὸν ἐκ νεκρῶν ζωοποιήσει καὶ τὰ θνητὰ σώματα ὑμῶν», καὶ τὰ ψυχικά. ὁ χοῦς γὰρ «ὑπὸ κατάραν» ἐλήλυθε· 7. «γῆ γάρ», φησίν, «εἶ κ(αὶ εἰς γ)ῆν ἀπελεύσῃ».

οἱ δ' αὖ ἀπὸ τῆς ἀνατολῆς λέγουσιν, ὧν ἐστιν Ἀξιόνι(κο)ς καὶ <Β>αρδησιάνης, ὅτι πνευματικὸν ἦν τὸ σῶμα τοῦ σωτῆρος· Πνεῦμα γὰρ ἅγιον ἦλθεν ἐπὶ τὴν Μαρίαν—τουτέστιν ἡ Σοφία—καὶ «ἡ δύναμις τοῦ ὑψίστου»—ἡ δημιουργικὴ τέχνη—, ἵ<ν>α διαπλασθῇ τὸ ὑπὸ τοῦ Πνεύματος τῇ Μαρίᾳ δοθέν.

DIVISION IN THE VALENTINIAN SCHOOL. 5. Now about this matter there is profound scrutiny among them and occasion for divisions and disagreements. Indeed, because of this point their school was split. One of their schools they call "Eastern," and the other "Italic."[183] 6. Now those from Italy, among whom are Herakleon and Ptolemy, say that the body of Jesus was animate. For this reason, at his baptism the Spirit descended upon him as a dove. That is, the mind of the Mother on high, Wisdom, entered into the animate body and raised it from the dead.[184] This, he says, is what the verse means: "The one who raised Christ from the dead will also enliven your mortal" and animate bodies.[185] This is because dust has come "under a curse." 7. "For you are earth," he says, "and to earth you will return."[186]

In turn, those from the east, among whom are Axionikos and Bardesianes, say that the body of the Savior was spiritual.[187] For Holy Spirit (that is, Wisdom) came upon Mary and "the power of the Most High" (that is, the craftsmanship of the Artificer), with the result that what was given to Mary might be molded by the Spirit.[188]

183. Tertullian also mentions two schools, but they did not split over the nature of Jesus's body (*Val.* 11.2).

184. For the baptism and dove, see Mark 1:10 par.; John 1:32. In Iren., *Haer.* 1.7.2, it is the Savior who descends on Jesus as a dove. Cf. the interpretation of the Markosians in *Ref.* 6.47.2; 6.49.5; 6.51.2, 4; Clem. Alex., *Exc.* 16; 22.6; 61.6; Gos. Eb. in Epiph., *Pan.* 30.13.7; Acts Thom. 50 (*NTApoc* 2:359–60).

185. Rom 8:11.

186. Gen 3:19 LXX.

187. For Axionikos, see Thomassen, *Spiritual Seed*, 502. For the next name, P reads ἀρδϊσηάνης. Most would emend to Βαρδησιάνης, though Thomassen demurs (*Spiritual Seed*, 503). Ilaria L. E. Ramelli sees our author as the first heresiologist to connect Bardesanes (or Bardaisan) to Valentinian thought (*Bardaisan of Edessa: A Reassessment of the Evidence and a New Interpretation* [Piscataway: Gorgias, 2009], 47–54). Bardesanes's view of Jesus's body is complex. See the texts cited by Nicola Denzey, "Bardaisan of Edessa," in Marjanen and Luomanen, *Companion*, 159–84 (172). See further Joel Kalvesmaki, "Italian versus Eastern Valentinianism?" *VC* 62 (2008): 79–89 (85–87).

188. The reliability of our author's two-school report has come under attack in modern scholarship. Thomassen questions whether spiritual substance can be molded and believes that our author has already attributed an Eastern view of Jesus's body to Western (or Italic) Valentinians (*Spiritual Seed*, 43–45; but cf. Zlatko Pleše, "Gnostic Literature," in *Religiöse Philosophie und philosophischen Religion der frühen Kaiserzeit: Literaturgeschichtliche Perspektiven*, ed. Rainer Hirsch-Luipold, Herwig Görgemanns, and Michael von Albrecht [Tübingen: Mohr Siebeck, 2010], 163–98 [195]; Ramelli, *Bardaisan*, 50–51). Thomassen believes that our author draws a distinction present

36. 1. Ταῦτα οὖν ἐκεῖνοι ζητείτωσαν καθ᾽ αὑτοὺς καὶ εἴ τινι ἄλλῳ γενήται φίλον ζητεῖν.

ἀλλ᾽ ἔτι λέγει ὡς διώρθωτο μὲν τὰ κατὰ τοὺς αἰῶνας ἔσω σφάλματα, διώρθωτο δὲ καὶ <τὰ> κατὰ τὴν Ὀγδοάδα—τὴν ἔξω Σοφίαν—, διώρθωτο δὲ καὶ <τὰ> κατὰ τὴν Ἑβδομάδα. 2. ἐδιδάχθη γὰρ ὑπὸ τῆς Σοφίας ὁ δημιουργὸς ὅτι οὐκ ἔστιν αὐτὸς θεὸς μόνος, ὡς ἐνόμιζε, «καὶ πλὴν αὐτοῦ ἕτερος οὐκ ἔστιν», ἀλλ᾽ ἔγνω διδαχθεὶς ὑπὸ τῆς Σοφίας τὸν κρείττονα. κατηχ<ή>θη γοῦν ὑπ᾽ αὐτῆς καὶ ἐμυήθη καὶ ἐδιδάχθη τὸ μέγα τοῦ Πατρὸς καὶ τῶν αἰώνων μυστήριον, καὶ ἐξεῖπεν αὐτὸ οὐδενί. τοῦτ᾽ ἔστιν, ὡς φησίν, ὃ λέγει πρὸς Μωϋσῆν· «ἐγὼ ὁ θεὸς Ἀβραὰμ καὶ ὁ θεὸς Ἰσαὰκ καὶ ὁ θεὸς Ἰακώβ, καὶ τὸ ὄνομα μου οὐκ ἀπήγγειλα αὐτοῖς»· τουτέστιν τὸ μυστήριον οὐκ εἶπα οὐδὲ ἐξηγησάμην τίς ἐστιν ὁ θεός, ἀλλ᾽ ἐφύλαξα παρ᾽ ἐμαυτῷ ἐν ἀποκρύφῳ τὸ μυστήριον ὃ ἤκουσα παρὰ τῆς Σοφίας.

3. Ἔδει οὖν διωρθωμένων τῶν ἄνω κατὰ τὴν αὐτὴν ἀκολουθίαν καὶ τὰ ἐνθάδε τυχεῖν διορθώσεως. τούτου χάριν ἐγεννήθη Ἰησοῦς ὁ σωτὴρ διὰ τῆς Μαρίας, ἵνα διορθώσεται <τὰ> ἐνθάδε. ὥσπερ ὁ Χριστός, ὁ ἄνωθεν ἐπιπροβληθεὶς ὑπὸ τοῦ Νοὸς καὶ τῆς Ἀληθείας, διωρθώσατο τὰ πάθη τῆς ἔξω Σοφίας—τουτέστι τοῦ ἐκτρώματος—, <οὕτως> πάλιν καὶ ὁ διὰ Μαρίας γεγεν<ν>ημένος ὁ σωτὴρ ἦλθε διορθώσασθαι τὰ πάθη τῆς ψυχῆς.

4. εἰσὶν οὖν κ(α)τ᾽ (αὐ)τ(οὺς) τρεῖς Χριστοί·

36. 1. Let them scrutinize these matters among themselves, or by someone else who loves to wrangle!

SALVATION. He goes on to say that the errors of the aeons within the Fullness were corrected, as were those in the Ogdoad (that is, the Wisdom outside). Also corrected were those in the Hebdomad. 2. For the Artificer was taught by Wisdom that he was not himself the only God (as he supposed) "and apart from him there is no other."[189] When he was taught by Wisdom, he came to know one who is superior. He was instructed, initiated, and taught by her the great mystery of the Father and the aeons.[190] Yet he declared it to no one.[191] This is the meaning, he says, of what God says to Moses: "I am the God of Abraham and the God of Isaac and the God of Jacob, and my name I did not declare to them."[192] He means: I did not speak the mystery, nor did I explain who God is; but I kept the mystery that I heard from Wisdom with myself in concealment.

3. When the things above had been corrected, it was necessary that the things below, corresponding point by point, also obtain correction. For this purpose, Jesus the Savior was born through Mary so that the affairs in this world might be corrected. For just as Christ, who was emanated above by Mind and Truth, corrected the negative emotions (i.e., miscarriage) of Wisdom, who was outside, so in turn the Savior born through Mary came to correct the negative emotions of the soul.[193]

4. So, according to them, there are three Christs:

---

within Western Valentinianism concerning *when* the body of the savior becomes spiritual—at birth or baptism. In fact, the "fundamental issue dividing the two schools was that in the east the body of the Savior—i.e., the church—was seen as spiritual only, whereas for the western Valentinians it had a psychic as well as a spiritual component" (*Spiritual Seed*, 45). See also Jean-Daniel Kaestli, "Valentinisme italien et valentinisme oriental: Leurs divergences a propos de la nature du corps de Jesus," in *The Rediscovery of Gnosticism: Proceedings of the International Conference on Gnosticism at Yale, New Haven, Connecticut, March 28–31, 1978*, ed. Bentley Layton, 2 vols., SHR (Leiden: Brill, 1980–1981), 1:391–403; Christoph Markschies, "Valentinian Gnosticism," in *The Nag Hammadi Library after Fifty Years: Proceedings of the 1995 Society of Biblical Literature Commemoration*, ed. John D. Turner and Anne McGuire (Leiden: Brill, 1997), 432–36.

189. Isa 45:5; 46:9 LXX.

190. On the education of the Artificer, see Iren., *Haer.* 1.7.4; 1.8.4.

191. Cf. Elohim's silence after learning the mysteries in *Ref.* 5.27.1–2 (Justin).

192. Exod 6:3 LXX (with modification). Cf. the interpretation of this verse in *Ref.* 7.25.4 ("Basileides").

193. On the therapy of emotions, see Ismo Dunderberg, *Beyond Gnosticism: Myth,*

1. ὁ ἐπιπροβληθεὶς ὑπὸ τ(οῦ Νοὸς) καὶ τῆς Ἀληθείας μετὰ τοῦ ἁγίου Πνεύματος,
2. καὶ ὁ κοινὸς τ(ο)ῦ πληρώματος Καρπὸς Ἰ(ησοῦ)ς, ἰσόζυγος τῆς ἔξω Σοφίας—ἥτις καλεῖται καὶ αὐτὴ Πνεῦμα ἅγιον, ὑποδεέστερον τοῦ πρώτου—
3. καὶ τρίτος ὁ διὰ Μαρίας γεννηθεὶς εἰς ἐπανόρθωσιν τῆς κτίσεως τῆς καθ᾽ ἡμᾶς.

37. 1. Διὰ πλειόνων νομίζω αὐτάρκως τὴν Οὐαλεντίνου αἵρεσιν Πυθαγόρειον οὖσαν ὑποτετυπῶσθαι· δοκεῖ δὲ καὶ δι᾽ ἐλ(α)χί(στ)ων τὰ δοκοῦντα αὐτοῖς ἐκθέμενον παύσασθαι.

Πλάτων τοίνυν περὶ τοῦ παντὸς ἐκτιθέμενος μυστήρια γράφει πρὸς Διονύσιον τοιοῦτόν τινα τρόπον, λέγων·

2. Φραστέον δή σοι δι᾽ αἰνιγμάτων, ἵν᾽ τι ἡ δέλτος ἢ πόντου ἐν πτυχαῖς πάθῃ, ὁ ἀναγνοὺς μὴ γνῷ. ὧδε γὰρ ἔχει· περὶ τὸν πάντων βασιλέα πάντα ἐστὶ κἀκείνου ἕνεκα πάντα κἀκεῖνος αἴτιος πάντων τῶν καλῶν· δεύτερον πέρι τὰ δεύτερα, καὶ τρίτον πέρι τὰ τρίτα.
3. τοῦ δὴ βασιλέως πέρι ὧν εἶπον, οὐδέν ἐστι τοιοῦτον. τὸ δὴ μετὰ τοῦτο ἡ ψυχὴ ἐπιζητεῖ μαθεῖν ὁποῖα ἄττα ἐστί, βλέπουσα εἰς τὰ ἑαυτῆς συγγενῆ, ὧν οὐδὲν ἱκανῶς ἔχει.
τοῦτ᾽ ἔστιν, ὦ παῖ Διονυσίου καὶ Δωρίδος, τὸ ἐρώτημα ὃ πάντων αἴτιόν ἐστι κακῶν, μᾶλλον δὲ ἡ περὶ τούτου φροντὶς ἐν τῇ ψυχῇ ἐγγινομένη, ἣν ἐὰν μή τις ἐξαιρεθῇ, τῆς ἀληθείας ὄντως οὐ μή ποτε τύχῃ.
4. ὃ δὲ θαυμαστὸν αὐτοῦ γέγον<εν,> ἄ<κου>σον. εἰ<σὶ> γὰρ ἄνδρες ταῦτα ἀκηκοότες <δυνατοὶ μὲν> μαθεῖν, δυνατοὶ δὲ μνημονεῦσαι καὶ

1. the one emanated by Mind and Truth with the Holy Spirit,
2. Jesus, the common Fruit of the Fullness, coequal consort of the Wisdom outside (who is herself also called "Holy Spirit," although she is inferior to the first one), and
3. the one born through Mary for the rectification of the creation known to us.[194]

37. 1. And so with this extensive report I believe that I have adequately sketched the heresy of Valentinus (or rather of Pythagoras). It is time to cease presenting their opinions in such detail.

PLAGIARISM: PLATO'S THREE PRINCIPLES. Now then, Plato—presenting the mysteries of the universe—writes to Dionysios in the following sort of way:

> 2. I must speak to you in riddles so that if the letter suffers any mishap in the recesses of the sea, the one who reads it might not understand. It goes like this: around the king of all, all things turn; he is the reason for all, and the cause of all that is good. Things of the second order turn upon the second, and those of the third order upon the third.
> 3. Now the king of whom I spoke, there is nothing like him. The soul that takes the second place[195] seeks earnestly to learn what sort of things they are, seeing its own kin, though none of them is adequate.[196]
> This, son of Dionysios and Doris, is the question that is the cause of all evils. Or rather, anxiety about this question is born in the soul. If one does not remove this anxiety, one cannot ever really obtain the truth.[197]
> 4. But hear what is more wondrous than this! There are men who have heard these teachings. They are able learners, with good memories, who have tortured themselves by every possible means to discern this question—and now they are old.[198] They say that

Lifestyle and Society in the School of Valentinus (New York: Columbia University Press, 2008), 95–118. More generally, see Thomassen, *Spiritual Seed*, 77–80.

194. It is unclear whether all three figures went under the name Christ.
195. Plato, *Ep.* 2.313a1–2.
196. Plato, *Ep.* 2.312e4–313a1.
197. Plato, *Ep.* 2.313a3–6.
198. Plato, *Ep.* 2.314a7–b2.

βασανίσα<ντες> πάντῃ πάντως κρῖναι, γέροντες ἤδη, οἵ φασι τὰ μὲν τότε πιστὰ εἶναι δόξαντα νῦν ἄπιστα, τὰ δὲ τότε ἄπιστα νῦν τοὐναντίον. πρὸς ταῦτα οὖν σκοπῶν εὐλαβοῦ μή ποτέ σοι μεταμελήσῃ τῶνδε ἀναξίως ἐκπεσόντων. 5. διὰ τοῦτο ἐγὼ περὶ τούτων γέγρ(α)φ(α) (οὐ)δὲν, οὐδὲ ἔστι Πλάτωνος σύγγραμμα οὐδὲν οὐδὲ ἔσται πώποτ(ε), (τ)ὰ δὲ νῦν λεγόμενα Σωκράτους ἐστὶ καλοῦ καὶ νέου γεγονότος.

Τούτοις περιτυχὼν Οὐαλεντῖνος ὑπεστήσατο τὸν πάντων βασιλέα, ὃν ἔφη Πλάτων οὕτως, Πατέρα καὶ Βυθὸν καὶ <Πηγήν> τῶν ὅλων αἰώνων. 6. δεύτερον περὶ τὰ δεύτερα τοῦ Πλάτωνος εἰρηκότος, τὰ δεύτερα Οὐαλεντῖνος τού<ς> ἐντὸς Ὅρου [τὸν ὅρον] ὑπέθετο πάντας αἰῶνας, καὶ τρίτον πέρι τὰ τρίτα τὴν ἔξω τοῦ Ὅρου καὶ τοῦ πληρώματος διαταγὴν συνέθηκε πᾶσαν.

καὶ δεδήλωκεν αὐτὸ δι' ἐλαχίστων Οὐαλεντῖνος ἐν ψαλμῷ, κάτωθεν ἀρξάμενος, οὐχ ὥσπερ ὁ Πλάτων ἄνωθεν, λέγων οὕτως·

7. Θέρος
Πάντα κρεμάμενα πνεύματι βλέπω,
πάντα δ' ὀχούμενα πνεύματι νοῶ·
σάρκα μὲν ἐκ ψυχῆς κρεμαμένην,

> the doctrines believed then are now incredible, and that the doctrines incredible then are now the opposite.
> So while you investigate these things, take care that you never regret the exposure of one of these teachings.[199] 5. For this reason, I have written nothing at all about them at any time, neither is there a treatise of Plato—nor will there ever be. Those now so called have their source in a handsome and young Sokrates.[200]

Coming across these excerpts, Valentinus introduced "the king of all," of whom Plato spoke, as the "Father," "Depth," and "Fount"[201] of all the aeons. 6. Valentinus supposed that "things of the second order around the second" of which Plato spoke are the second-order aeons inside the Boundary. He makes "things of the third order around the third" the entire order of creation outside the Boundary and the Fullness.[202]

Indeed, Valentinus has with great concision put this theory on display in a psalm. Taking his starting point from below—not above, like Plato—he speaks as follows:

> 7. *Harvest*
> Everything by spirit I see suspended,
> Everything by spirit I sense conveyed:
> Flesh suspended from soul,

---

199. Plato, *Ep.* 2.314b5–7.

200. Plato, *Ep.* 2.314c1–4. Our author presents the words of (Pseudo-)Plato as a continuous quote, but (as the above notes indicate) he—or more likely his source—has divided up Plato's *Ep.* 2.313a–314b, rearranging (and in some cases paraphrasing) the sentences as he saw fit. Earlier Christian authors also appealed to this passage, among them Justin Martyr (*1 Apol.* 60) and Athenagoras (*Leg.* 23).

201. P reads here πᾶσι γῆν. I have adopted, with Hilgenfeld, πηγήν, a word reminiscent of the Pythagorean Tetraktys. Marcovich prints this and other options in his apparatus: Σιγήν ("Silence," Bernays and Roeper), προαρχήν ("Pre-principle," Duncker and Schneidewin). See further G. C. Stead, "In Search of Valentinus," in Layton, *Rediscovery*, 1.81.

202. Clement of Alexandria, quoting Plato's same epistle, interprets the three orders to signify the Trinity (*Strom.* 5.14.103.1). See further Christoph Markschies, "Platons König oder Vater Jesu Christi? Drei Beispiele für die Rezeption eines griechischen Gottesepithetons bei den Christen in den ersten Jahrhunderten und deren Vorgeschichte," in *Königsherrschaft Gottes und himmlischer Kult im Judentum, Urchristentum und in der hellenistischen Welt*, ed. Martin Hengel and Anna Maria Schwemer, WUNT 55 (Tübingen: Mohr Siebeck, 1991), 385–439 (429–38); Mansfeld, *Heresiography*, 204–7.

ψυχὴν δ’ ἀέρος <ἐξεχομένην,>
ἀέρα δ’ ἐξ αἴθρης κρεμάμενον·
ἐκ δὲ βυθοῦ καρποὺς φερομένους,
ἐκ μήτρας δὲ βρέφος φερόμενον.

8. οὕτως ταῦτα νοῶν· σάρξ ἐστιν ἡ ὕλη κατ’ αὐτούς, ἥτις κρέμαται ἐκ τῆς ψυχῆς, τοῦ δημιουργοῦ· ψυχὴ δὲ ἀέρος ἐξοχεῖται, τουτέστιν ὁ δημιουργὸς τοῦ Πνεύματος ἔξω πληρώματος· ἀὴρ δὲ αἴθρης ἐξέχεται, τουτέστιν ἡ ἔξω Σοφία τοῦ ἐντὸς Ὅρου καὶ παντὸς πληρώματος. ἐκ δὲ βυθοῦ καρποὶ φέρονται, ἡ ἐκ τοῦ Πατρὸς πᾶσα προβολὴ τῶν αἰώνων γενομένη.

Soul hanging on air,[203]
Air suspended from aether.
From the depth are borne fruits.
From the womb is born a baby.[204]

8. He means this: "flesh," in their view, is matter, which is suspended from "soul"—that is, from the Artificer. "Soul" is conveyed by air—that is, the Artificer is dependent upon the Spirit, who is outside the Fullness. "Air" hangs from "aether"—that is, the Wisdom who is outside is dependent upon the Boundary and the entire Fullness. From "Depth" crops arise—that is, the whole emanation of the aeons is born.[205]

203. Bunsen emends P's ἐξειχουμένην (not metrical) to ἐξεχομένην.

204. The poem represents frag. 8 of Valentinus (Völker). Metrically the lines are dactylic tetrameters with iambic or "mouse tail" endings. The title "Harvest" recalls the harvest of the world in John 4:35–36 (cf. Sib. Or. 2.164; Herakleon, frag. 35 [Brooke]). The chain of being that is assumed in the poem resembles popular Stoicism and has Hermetic analogues. Note, e.g., Corp. herm. 12.14: "The finest matter is air, the finest air is soul, the finest soul is mind and the finest mind is god. And god surrounds everything and permeates everything, while mind surrounds soul, soul surrounds air and air surrounds matter" (trans. Copenhaver; see also Corp. herm. 1.5; 3.2; 10.13; Philo, *Mos.* 2.121). Our author himself points out that for Stoics, the soul is the cooling (περιψύξεως) of the air (*Ref.* 1.21.3 = *SVF* 2.807). Aether, in turn, is generally considered to be the loftiest substance of our world (e.g., Cicero, *Nat. d.* 2.84). Valentinus's focus is anthropological: he is concerned not with earth and water but with flesh and soul (which are not ontologically separated). Two levels of meaning seem to fluctuate in the psalm (e.g., "depth" [βύθος] could refer to depth of soil producing fruit or the high God emanating aeons). For older literature on the psalm, see Wolbergs, *Gedichte*, 23. See further Herzhoff, *Zwei gnostische Psalmen*, 35–77; Markschies, *Valentinus Gnosticus*, 218–59; Jens Holzhausen, "Ein gnostischer Psalm? Zu Valentins Psalm in Hippol. ref. VI 37.7 (= frg. 8 Völker)," *JAC* 36 (1993): 67–80; Andrew McGowan, "Valentinus Poeta: Notes on Θέρος," *VC* 51 (1997): 158–78.

205. Oddly our author does not interpret the last line about the baby. Cf. Valentinus, frag. 7 (Völker), in *Ref.* 6.42.2 (a newborn child appears to Valentinus and calls himself the Logos). Holzhausen interprets the child to be the Logos, who sums up the world of ideas ("Psalm," 77). On the whole, interpreters have been critical of our author's interpretation. McGowan, for instance, thinks that it is "at best incomplete and garbled" ("Valentinus Poeta," 160). Yet our author claims to interpret the poem κατ' αὐτούς—in accordance with Valentinian teachers of his time (*Ref.* 6.37.8).

9. τὰ μὲν οὖν τῷ Οὐαλεντίνῳ δοκοῦντα ἱκανῶς λέλεκται· <λοιπὸν δὲ τὰ τοῖς τῆς> σχολῆς προκόψασιν ἐξειπεῖν, ἄλλου ἄλλως δογματίσαντος τὰ δόξαντα αὐτοῖς.

38. 1. Σεκοῦνδος μέν τις, κατὰ τὸ αὐτὸ ἅμα τῷ Πτολεμαίῳ γενόμενος, οὕτως λέγει· τετράδα εἶναι δεξιὰν καὶ τετράδα ἀριστεράν, καὶ φῶς καὶ σκότος· καὶ τὴν ἀποστᾶσάν τε καὶ ὑστερήσασαν δύναμιν οὐκ ἀπὸ τῶν τριάκοντα αἰώνων λέγει γεγενῆσθαι, ἀλλ᾽ ἀπὸ τῶν καρπῶν αὐτῶν.

2. Ἄλλος δέ τις ἐπιφανὴς διδάσκαλος αὐτῶν οὕτως λέγει· ἦν ἡ πρώτη ἀρχὴ ἀνεννόητος, ἄρρητός τε καὶ ἀνωνόμαστος, ἣν Μονότητα καλεῖ. ταύτῃ δὲ (σ)υ(νυπά)ρχειν δύναμιν, ἣν ὀνομάζει Ἑνό(τη)τα. αὕτη ἡ Ἑνότης ἥ τε Μονότης προήκαντο μὴ προέμεναι ἀρχὴν ἐπὶ πάντων νοητήν, ἀγένητον τε καὶ ἀόρατον, ἣν Μονάδα καλεῖ. 3. ταύτῃ τῇ δυνάμει συνυπάρχει δύναμις ὁμοούσιος αὐτῇ, ἣν καὶ αὐτὴν ὀνομάζει τὸ Ἕν. αὗται αἱ τέσσαρες δυνάμεις προήκαντο τὰς λοιπὰς τῶν αἰώνων προβολάς.

Ἄλλοι δὲ πάλιν αὐτῶν τὴν πρώτην καὶ ἀρχέγονον Ὀγδοάδα τούτοις τοῖς ὀνόμασιν ἐκάλεσαν· <πρῶτον Προαρχήν, ἔπειτα Ἀνεννόητον, τὴν> δὲ <τρίτην Ἄρρητον, καὶ τὴν> τετάρτη(ν) Ἀόρατον. 4. καὶ ἐκ μὲν τῆς πρώτης, Προαρχῆς, προβεβλῆσθαι πρώτῳ καὶ πέμπτῳ τόπῳ Ἀρχήν, ἐκ δὲ τῆς Ἀνεννοήτου δευτέρῳ καὶ ἕκτῳ Ἀκατάληπτον, ἐκ δὲ τῆς Ἀρρήτου τρίτῳ καὶ ἑβδόμῳ τόπῳ Ἀνωνόμαστον, ἐκ δὲ τῆς Ἀοράτου Ἀγέννητον, πλήρωμα τῆς πρώτης Ὀγδοάδος. ταύτας βούλονται τὰς δυνάμεις προϋπάρχειν τοῦ Βυθοῦ καὶ τῆς <Σι>γῆς.

9. Now the doctrines of Valentinus have been sufficiently recounted. It remains to expound the doctrines of those who have advanced far in this school, although each of them variously pronounces his views.[206]

OTHER VALENTINIANS

38. 1. A certain Secundus, agreeing in principle with Ptolemy, teaches the following. There is a right tetrad and a left tetrad, as well as light and darkness. Moreover, the power who defected and became deficient, he says, was generated not from the thirty aeons but from their offspring.[207]

2. Another of their famous teachers speaks as follows.[208] There was a First Principle, inconceivable, unspeakable, and unnamable—which he calls "Singleness." With it, there coexisted a power, which he names "Oneness." This Oneness and Singleness, sent forth, without emanating it, an intelligible first principle over everything, ingenerate and invisible, which he calls "Monad." 3. Coexisting with this power is a power consubstantial with it, which he calls "the One." These four powers sent forth the remaining emissions of the aeons.[209]

Others, in turn, called their primal and primordial Ogdoad by the following names. First, they say that he is "Forebeginning," then "Inconceivable," third, "Unspeakable," and fourth, "Invisible."[210] 4. Moreover, from the first, namely, Forebeginning, was emanated in the first and fifth place, Beginning. From the Inconceivable was emanated in the second and sixth place, Incomprehensible. From Unspeakable was emanated in the third and seventh place, Unnamable. Lastly, from Invisible was emanated Unborn—the Fullness of the primal Ogdoad. They want these powers to preexist Depth and Silence.[211]

206. The beginning of this sentence, λοιπὸν δὲ τὰ τοῖς τῆς ("It remains [to expound the doctrines] of those"), is supplied by Marcovich.

207. Cf. Iren., *Haer.* 1.11.2; Epiph., *Pan.* 32.1.5–6; Tert., *Val.* 38; Ps.-Tert., *Adv. omn. haer.* 4.

208. Herakleon, mentioned in the table of contents, may be the "famous teacher" here (Herakleon follows Secundus in Filastrius, *Haer.* 41). Whether the teachings are Herakleon's is another question.

209. Cf. Iren., *Haer.* 1.11.3; Epiph., *Pan.* 32.5.4–6; Tert., *Val.* 37.

210. Duncker and Schneidewin reconstruct this line from Epiphanios's transcription of Irenaeus (*Pan.* 32.7.1).

211. Cf. Iren., *Haer.* 1.11.14; Epiph., *Pan.* 32.7.1–3; Tert., *Val.* 35.

5. Ἄλλ<α>ι δὲ περὶ αὐτοῦ τοῦ Βυθοῦ διάφοροι γνῶμαι· οἱ μὲν αὐτὸν ἄζυγον λέγουσι, μήτε ἄρρενα μήτε θῆλυν, ἄλλοι δὲ τὴν Σιγὴν θήλειαν αὐτῷ συμπαρεῖναι, καὶ εἶναι ταύτην πρώτην συζυγίαν.

οἱ δὲ περὶ τὸν Πτολεμαῖον δύο συζύγους αὐτὸν ἔχειν λέγουσιν, ἃς καὶ διαθέσεις καλοῦσιν, Ἔννοιαν καὶ Θέλησιν· πρῶτον γὰρ ἐνενοήθη τι προβαλεῖν, ὥς φασιν, ἔπειτα ἠθέλησε. 6. διὸ καὶ τῶν δύο τούτων διαθέσεων καὶ δυνάμεων, τῆς τε Ἐννοίας καὶ τῆς Θελήσεως, ὥσπερ <συγ>κραθεισ<ῶν> εἰς ἀλλήλας ἡ προβολὴ τοῦ τε Μονογενοῦς καὶ τῆς Ἀληθείας κατὰ συζυγίαν ἐγένετο. οὕστινας τύπους καὶ εἰκόνας τῶν δύο διαθέσεων τοῦ Πατρὸς προελθεῖν, ἐκ τῶν ἀοράτων ὁρατάς, τοῦ μὲν Θελήματος τὸν Νοῦν, τῆς δὲ Ἐννοίας τὴν Ἀλήθειαν. 7. καὶ διὰ τοῦτο τοῦ ἐπιγενητοῦ Θελήματος ὁ ἄρρην εἰκών, τῆς δὲ ἀγεννήτου Ἐννοίας ὁ θῆλυς, ἐπεὶ τὸ Θέλημα ὥσπερ δύναμις ἐγένετο τῆς Ἐννοίας. ἐν<ε>νόει μὲν γὰρ ἀεὶ ἡ Ἔννοια τὴν προβολήν, οὐ μέντοι γε προβάλλειν (αὐ)τὴ καθ' αὑτὴν ἠδύνατο ἃ ἐνενόει· ὅτε δὲ ἡ τοῦ Θελήματος δύναμις ἐγ(ένε)τ(ο), τότε <ὃ> ἐνενόει προβάλλει.

39. 1. Ἄλλος δέ τις διδάσκαλος αὐτῶν, Μάρκος, μαγικῆς ἔμπειρος, ἃ μὲν

DIFFERENT VIEWS OF "DEPTH." 5. There are different opinions about Depth himself.[212] Some say that he is without consort, neither male nor female; but others say that Silence, who is feminine, is present with him, and that this is the first couple.[213]

Others, the students of Ptolemy, say that he has two consorts, whom they call "dispositions": namely, Thought and Will. For first he *thought* of sending something forth, as they say, and then *willed* it. 6. So from these two dispositions and powers, Thought and Will, as though blended together, there occurred the emanation of both Only-Born and Truth as a couple. Certain stamps and images of the two dispositions of the Father came forth as visible entities from invisible: from Will came Mind, and from Thought came Truth. 7. For this reason, the male is the image of the Will, who was born later, and the female is the image of the unborn Thought, since Will arose as a power of Thought. Thought was always thinking about the emanation, but she was not herself able to emanate what she was thinking. But when the power of Will arose, then she emanated what she was thinking.[214]

MARKOS THE VALENTINIAN

39. 1. Another one of their teachers, Markos, was an expert in magic.[215] He deceived many people by practicing some feats by trickery, and others

---

212. The first word of this sentence in P is ἄλλοι ("other"). Marcovich prints ἀλλά ("But"), but a more likely emendation is ἄλλαι, printed here.

213. Cf. Iren., *Haer.* 1.11.5; Epiph., *Pan.* 32.7.4–5; Tert., *Val.* 34; see also *Ref.* 6.29.3 and the summary in 10.13.1.

214. Cf. Iren., *Haer.* 1.12.1; Epiph., *Pan.* 33.1.2–7; Tert., *Val.* 33. See further Sagnard, *Gnose*, 355–57.

215. Markos was a Valentinian religious leader in Asia Minor between 160 and 180 CE. The target of his mission was existing Christian house churches. The content of his preaching was what he considered to be the deeper mysteries of Christianity, both theological and sacramental. It appears that he did not attempt to form his own church movement. He did, however, involve his followers in a special meal and sacramental service. By the time of our author, the Markosians seem to have formed their own church community with their own bishops. See further Niclas Förster, *Marcus Magus: Kult, Lehre und Gemeindeleben einer valentinianischen Gnostikergruppe; Sammlung der Quellen und Kommentar*, WUNT 114 (Tübingen: Mohr Siebeck, 1999), 403–4; Ismo Dunderberg, "Valentinian Teachers in Rome," in *Christians as a Religious Minority in a Multicultural City: Modes of Interaction and Identity Formation in Early Imperial Rome*, ed. Jürgen Zangenberg and Michael Labahn (London: T&T Clark, 2004), 157–74 (169–73); Koschorke, *Ketzerbekämpfung*, 17–20; Thomassen, *Spiritual Seed*, 498–500.

διὰ κυβείας δρῶν, ἃ δὲ καὶ διὰ δαιμόνων, ἠπάτα πολλούς. οὗτος ἔλεγεν ἐν αὐτῷ τὴν μεγίστην ἀπὸ τῶν ἀοράτων καὶ ἀκατωνομάστων τόπων εἶναι δύναμιν.

2. καὶ δὴ πολλάκις λαμβάνων ποτήριον ὡς εὐχαριστῶν καὶ ἐπὶ πλεῖον ἐκτείνων τὸν λόγον τῆς ἐπικλήσεως, πορφύρεον τὸ κέρασμα ἐποίει φαίνεσθαι καί ποτε ἐρυθρόν, ὡς δοκεῖν τοὺς ἀπατωμένους Χάριν τινὰ κατιέναι καὶ αἱματώδη δύναμιν παρέχειν τῷ πόματι.

Ὁ δὲ πανοῦργος τότε μὲν πολλοὺς ἔλαθε, νυνὶ δὲ ἐλεγχόμενος παύσεται· 3. φάρμακον γάρ τι τοιαύτην δυνάμενον χρόαν παρασχεῖν λαθραίως ἐνιῶν τῷ κεράσματι, ἐπὶ πολὺ φλυαρῶν ἀνέμενεν, ὅπως τῆς ὑγρότητος μεταλαβὸν λυθῇ καὶ ἀναμιγὲν ἐπιχρώσῃ τὸ πόμα. τὰ δὲ δυνάμενα τοῦτο παρασχεῖν φάρμακα

by demons. This fool used to declare that there was in him the "Greatest Power" from the "invisible and unnamable Places."[216]

COLOR-CHANGING WINE. 2. Moreover, he would often take a chalice as though offering the Eucharist. After far extending the formula of invocation, he would make the mixture appear purple, and then red. Consequently, it seemed to his dupes that a certain "Grace" had descended and supplied a bloody power to the drink.[217]

This con artist went undetected by most at one time, but since he is here and now exposed, he will be checked! 3. He would secretly drop into the mixture a chemical that is able to produce a certain color. Then he persisted in babbling nonsense so that the chemical, interacting with the liquid, could dissolve and—when thoroughly mixed—change the color of the drink. I mentioned earlier and explained the chemicals able to do this

---

216. Cf. Acts 8:9–10, and the claim of "Simon" (*Ref.* 6.18.1). The following paragraph on color-changing wine is adapted from Iren., *Haer.* 1.13.1–2; cf. Epiph., *Pan.* 34.2.1–4.

217. For "bloody power," see Förster, *Marcus*, 69–70. Grace is identified with the primal female aeon Silence or Thought (Ennoia) in Iren., *Haer.* 1.1.1; Epiph., *Pan.* 31.5.4. Cf. Gos. Phil. (NHC II,3) 57.6–7 (Jesus's blood is the Holy Spirit); 75.14–21 (the cup is filled with the Holy Spirit). On the meaning of εὐχαριστεῖν, see Förster, *Marcus*, 74–75. Irenaeus understood Markos to be perverting a eucharistic rite. Some modern scholars follow this interpretation, e.g., J. Reiling ("Marcus Gnosticus and the New Testament: Eucharist and Prophecy," in *Miscellanea Neotestamentica*, ed. T. Baarda, A. F. J. Klijn, and W. C. van Unnik, 2 vols. [Leiden: Brill, 1978], 161–79); J. Michael Joncas ("Eucharist among the Marcosians: A Study of Irenaeus' *Adversus Haereses* I, 13:2," *Questions Liturgiques* 71 [1990]: 99–111); and Jean-Daniel Dubois ("Les pratiques eucharistiques de gnostiques valentiniens," in *Nourriture et repas dans les milieux juif et chrétiens de l'antiquité: Mélanges offerts au Professeur Charles Perrot* [Paris: Cerf, 1999], 255–66). In contrast, R. J. Hoffmann denied that the Markosian ceremonies were eucharistic ("The 'Eucharist' of Marcus Magus: A Test-Case in Gnostic Social Theory," *Patristic and Byzantine Review* 3 [1984]: 82–88 [84–85]). Förster understands the color-changing rite as an initiation connected with the cultic formula in Iren., *Haer.* 1.13.3 (*Marcus*, 64–69). Herbert Schmid points out, however, that Förster—and by extension Hoffmann—is in danger of judging what a Eucharist is by orthodox criteria (*Die Eucharistie ist Jesus: Anfänger einer Theorie des Sakraments im koptischen Philippusevangelium* (NHC *II 3*), VCSup 88 [Leiden: Brill, 2007], 399–405). See further Einar Thomassen, "Going to Church with the Valentinians," in *Practicing Gnosis: Ritual, Magic, Theurgy and Liturgy in Nag Hammadi, Manichaean and Other Ancient Literature; Essays in Honor of Birger A. Pearson*, ed. April D. DeConick, Gregory Shaw, and John D. Turner, NHMS 85 (Leiden: Brill, 2013), 183–97 (193–95).

ἐν τῇ κατὰ μάγων βίβλῳ προείπομεν ἐκθέμενοι. οἷς πολλοὺς πλανῶντες ἀφανίζουσιν· οἷς εἰ φίλον περιεργότερον τῷ εἰρημένῳ προσεπισχεῖν, εἴσονται τὴν Μάρκου πλάνην.

40. 1. Ὃς καὶ ποτήριον παρ' ἑτέρου κιρνῶν ἐδίδου γυναικὶ εὐχαριστεῖν αὐτὸς παρεστώς· καὶ ἕτερον κρατῶν, ἐκείνου μεῖζον, κενόν, καὶ εὐχαριστησάσης τῆς ἀπατωμένης δεξάμενος <τὸ μικρότερον,> ἐπέχει εἰς τὸ μεῖζον, καὶ πολλάκις ἀντεπιχέων ἕτερον εἰς ἕτερον ἐπέλεγεν οὕτως·

> 2. ἡ πρὸ τῶν ὅλων, ἀνεννόητος καὶ ἄρρητος Χάρις πληρῶσαι σου τὸν ἔσω ἄνθρωπον καὶ πληθύναι ἐν σοὶ τὴν γνῶσιν αὐτῆς, ἐγκατασπείρουσα τὸν κόκκον τοῦ σινάπεως εἰς τὴν ἀγαθὴν γῆν.

καὶ τοιαῦτά τινα ἐπειπὼν καὶ ἐκστήσας τήν τε ἀπατωμένην καὶ τοὺς παρόντας, [ὡς] θαυματοποιὸς ἐνομίζετο, τοῦ μείζονος ποτηρίου πληρουμένου ἐκ τοῦ μικροτέρου, ὡς καὶ ὑπερχεῖσθαι πλεονάζον.

3. Καὶ τούτου δὴ τὴν τέχνην ὁμοίως ἐ<ν> τῇ προειρημένῃ βίβλῳ ἐξεθέμεθα, δείξαντες πλεῖστα φάρμακα δυνάμενα αὔξησιν παρασχεῖν ἐπιμιγέντα οὕτως ὑγραῖς οὐσίαις, μάλιστα οἴνῳ κεκερασμένῳ. ὧν ἐν<ί> τι<ς> φαρμάκῳ [ἐν] τὸ κενὸν ποτήριον κρύβδην ἔν(δοθ)εν (π)α(ρα)χρίσ(ας), ὡς μηδὲν ἔχον δείξας, ἐπιχέων ἐκ το(ῦ) (πλήρ)ους καὶ ἐπαναχέων, ἀναλυομένου τοῦ φαρμάκου ὑπὸ

in my book against magicians.[218] By these means they destroy many who are deceived. But if people apply themselves with diligent labor to what I have said, they will know Markos's deceit.[219]

OVERFLOWING WINE. 40. 1. Once again, after mixing a chalice handed over by an assistant, he would give it to a woman to say the eucharistic formula while he stood alongside. Then he would take hold of a different chalice, empty and larger than the first. When the deceived woman had said the eucharistic formula, he would take the smaller chalice and tilt it toward the larger.[220] Then, after many times pouring one into the other, he would pronounce over her the following words:

> 2. May Grace, who exists before the universe, who is inconceivable and unspeakable, fill your inner person and multiply in you the knowledge of her, as she implants the mustard seed into good soil![221]

By pronouncing over her prayers of this ilk, he thrilled the deceived woman along with the audience. He was thought to be a wonderworker, since the larger chalice was filled from the smaller so as even to overflow.[222]

3. In the previously mentioned book, I also presented the method of this trick when I pointed out the host of chemicals able to produce a bubbling up when thus mixed with liquids—especially mixed wine. Someone secretly smears an empty chalice with one of these chemicals, displays it as empty, and pours the liquid back and forth from the full chalice to the

218. Possibly a reference to *Ref.* 4.28–42, esp. 4.28.13. Ganschinietz took it as a reference to the lost third book of the *Refutation* (*Capitel*, 7–10). Cf. Pliny, *Nat.* 37.48.

219. The above paragraph is not in Irenaeus and represents our author's apologetic attempt to debunk the phenomenon of the color-changing wine (a practice he classifies as magic). Cf. *Ref.* 6.40.3 below. The following paragraph on overflowing wine adapts Iren., *Haer.* 1.13.2; cf. Epiph., *Pan.* 34.2.2–4.

220. Marcovich adds τὸ μικρότερον ("the smaller") from Iren., *Haer.* 1.13.2.

221. On the invocation, see Sagnard, *Gnose*, 416–17. For "inner person," see the note on *Ref.* 5.7.36 (Naassenes); Förster, *Marcus*, 86–87. For the mustard seed, see Mark 4:31 par.; *Ref.* 5.9.6 (Naassenes); 7.21.3 ("Basileides"). The seed here may represent one's angelic counterpart (Förster, *Marcus*, 87–89). For the good soil, see Mark 4:8 par.; *Ref.* 5.8.29 (Naassenes); 8.9.1 (Doketai).

222. The overflowing cup may indicate the reception and growth of gnosis in the believer (Förster, *Marcus*, 89–90). On the role of women in the Markosian ceremony, see Cécile Faivre and Alexandre Faivre, "La place de la femme dans le ritual eucharistique des Marcosiens: Déviance ou archaïsme?" *RevScRel* 71 (1997): 310–28 (312–13).

τῆς τῷ ὑγρῷ μίξεως, ὄντος φυσώδους, πλεονασμὸς τοῦ κεράσματος ἐγίνετο. καὶ ἐπὶ τοσοῦτον ηὔξανεν, ἐς ὅσον ἐπαναχυνόμενον ἐκινεῖτο, τοιαύτης οὔσης τῆς τοῦ φαρμάκου φύσεως. 4. ὃ εἰ ἀπόθοιτό τις πληρωθέν, μετ' οὐ πολὺ εἰς τὸ κατὰ φύσιν μέτρον πάλιν τραπήσεται, τῆς τοῦ φαρμάκου δυνάμεως σβεσθείσης τῇ τοῦ ὑγροῦ παραμονῇ. διὸ μετὰ σπουδῆς τοῖς παροῦσι προσεδίδου πίνειν, οἱ δὲ ὡς θεῖόν τι καὶ θεῷ μεμελημένον φρίσσοντες ἅμα καὶ σπεύδοντες ἔπινον.

41. 1. Τοιαῦτα δὴ καὶ ἕτερα ἐπεχείρει ὁ πλάνος ποιεῖν· διὸ ὑπὸ τῶν ἀπατωμένων ἐδοξάζετο, καὶ ποτὲ αὐτὸς ἐνομίζετο προφητεύειν, ποτὲ δὲ καὶ ἑτέρους ἐποίει, ὁτὲ μὲν καὶ διὰ δαιμόνων ταῦτα ἐνεργῶν, ὁτὲ δὲ καὶ κυβεύων, ὡς προείπομεν. πολλὰς τοίνυν ἐξαφανίσας, καὶ πολλοὺς τοιούτους μαθητὰς αὐτοῦ γενομένους, προεβίβασεν, εὐκόλους μὲν εἶναι διδάξας πρὸς τὸ ἁμαρτάνειν, ἀκινδύνους δὲ διὰ τὸ εἶναι <αὐτοὺς> τῆς τελείας δυνάμεως καὶ μετέχειν τῆς ἀνεννοήτου ἐξουσίας.

2. Οἷς μετὰ τὸ βάπτισμα καὶ ἕτερον ἐπαγγέλλονται, ὃ καλοῦσιν ἀπολύτρωσιν, καὶ ἐν τούτῳ ἀναστρέφοντες κακῶς τοὺς αὐτοῖς παραμένοντας ἐπ' ἐλπίδι τῆς ἀπολυτρώσεως, δυναμένους μετὰ τὸ ἅπαξ βαπτισθῆναι πάλιν τυχεῖν ἀφέσεως.

empty one while the chemical is dissolved by the mixing of the liquid. Since the chemical fizzles with air bubbles, the mixture overflows.[223] The vigor of the overflow corresponds to how much the liquid was stirred by the action of pouring back and forth, since this is the nature of the chemical. 4. If one were to set the filled chalice aside, it would soon return to its natural volume, since the power of the chemical is quelled by the stillness of the liquid. Accordingly, Markos would offer the drink to the participants quickly. They, meanwhile, were shivering with goose bumps (as if it were something divine and providential!) as they hurriedly drank.[224]

PROPHECY AND ETHICS. 41. 1. Such tricks (along with others) the con artist attempted to perform. Thus he was glorified by his dupes. Sometimes he himself was thought to prophesy, while at other times he made others prophesy as well—sometimes producing these feats through demons, at other times by trickery, as I said. So, after destroying many women, he also won male disciples characterized by the same gullibility. He taught them to be cavalier about sinning, and that they were not in danger since they belonged to the perfect power and participated in the inconceivable authority.[225]

THE RITUAL OF REDEMPTION. 2. To these baptized disciples, they announce still another baptism, which they call "redemption." By this means they viciously overthrow those who cling to them in the hope of "redemption," since they think that, after their first (and only) baptism, they can again obtain forgiveness.[226]

223. On the nature of the chemical, see Förster, *Marcus*, 90–91.

224. The following paragraph on prophecy and ethics selectively summarizes Iren., *Haer.* 1.13.3–6; cf. Epiph., *Pan.* 34.2.5–3.5.

225. The following section (the ritual of redemption) condenses material found in Iren., *Haer.* 1.13.6; 21.1–4; cf. Epiph., *Pan.* 34.3.6; 34.19.1–20.12. See further Förster, *Marcus*, 154–58; Elaine Pagels, "A Valentinian Interpretation of Baptism and the Eucharist," *HTR* 65 (1972): 153–69 (158–62); Thomassen, *Spiritual Seed*, 401–2.

226. While discussing the Valentinian ritual of redemption, our author may be reading into it his experience of Kallistos. Putatively, Kallistos was the first to establish a second baptism for the forgiveness of sins (*Ref.* 9.12.26). In Valentinian thought, however, redemption is not depicted as a "second chance" forgiveness of sins; indeed, forgiveness does not even appear in Markos's teaching (cf. Förster, *Marcus*, 260). See further Koschorke, *Ketzerbekämpfung*, 65–67.

3. <οἳ> καὶ διὰ τοῦ τοιούτου πανουργήματος συνέχειν δοκο(ῦ)σι τοὺς ἀκροατάς· οὓς ἐπὰν νομίσωσι δεδοκιμάσθαι καὶ δύνασθαι φυλάσσειν αὐτοῖς τὰ πιστά, τότε ἐπὶ τοὺτο ἄγουσι.

μηδὲ τούτῳ μόνῳ ἀρκούμενοι, ἀλλὰ καὶ ἕτερον τι ἐπαγγελ<λ>όμενοι, πρὸς τὸ συγκρατεῖν αὐτοὺς τῇ ἐλπίδι, ὅπως ἀχώριστοι ὦσι. 4. λέγουσι γοῦν τι φωνῇ ἀρρήτῳ, ἐπιτιθέντες χεῖρα τῷ τὴν ἀπολύτρωσιν λαβόντι, ὃ φάσκουσιν ἐξειπεῖν εὐκόλως μὴ δύνασθαι εἰ μή τις εἴη ὑπερδόκιμος.

ἢ ὅτε τελευτῶν<τι> πρὸς τὸ οὖς ἐλθὼν λέγει ὁ ἐπίσκοπος. 5. καὶ τοῦτο δέ <ἐστι> πανούργημα πρὸς τὸ ἀεὶ παραμένειν τοὺς μαθητὰς τῷ ἐπισκόπῳ, γλιχομένους μαθεῖν τὸ τί ποτε εἴη (ἐ)κ(εῖν)ο, τὸ ἐπ' ἐσχάτων λεγόμενον, δι' οὗ τελείων ἔσται ὁ μανθάνων. ἃ τούτου χάριν ἐσιώπη(σ)α, μή π(ο)τέ τις κακοηθίζεσθαί με αὐτοὺς νομίσῃ· καὶ γὰρ οὐ τοῦτο ἡμῖν πρόκειται, ἀλλ' ἢ τὸ δεῖξαι, ὅθεν τὰς ἀφορμὰς λαβόντες τὰ δόξαντα αὐτοῖς συνεστήσαντο.

42. 1. Καὶ γὰρ καὶ ὁ μακάριος πρεσβύτερος Εἰρηναῖος, παρρησιαίτερον τῷ ἐλέγχῳ προσενεχθείς, τὰ τοιαῦτα λούσματα καὶ ἀπολυτρώσεις ἐξέθετο, ἁδρομερέστερον εἰπὼν ἃ πράσσουσιν· οἷ<ς> ἐντυχόντες τινὲς αὐτῶν ἤρνηνται οὕτως παρειληφέναι, ἀεὶ ἀρνεῖσθαι μανθάνοντες. διὸ φροντὶς ἡμῖν γεγένηται ἀκριβέστερον ἐπιζητῆσαι καὶ ἀνευρεῖν λεπτομερῶς ἃ καὶ ἐν τῷ πρώτῳ λουτρῷ παραδιδόασιν, τὸ τοιοῦτο καλοῦντες, καὶ ἐν τῷ δευτέρῳ, ὃ ἀπολύτρωσιν καλοῦσιν. 2. ἀλλ' οὐδὲ τὸ ἄρρητον αὐτῶν ἔλαθεν ἡμᾶς, ταῦτα δὲ συγκεχωρήσθω Οὐαλεντίνῳ καὶ τῇ αὐτοῦ σχολῇ.

3. Through such trickery, they suppose that they retain their listeners. When they consider them to be approved and able to preserve what has been entrusted to them, they conduct them to this bath.

But they are not satisfied by this alone. They even promise something else so as to control them with hope, so that they never break away. 4. They mutter something in an inaudible voice, laying their hands on the one who received redemption. They claim that what they whisper cannot be blithely declared unless one be "super-approved."

Alternatively, their bishop comes to one on his deathbed and speaks the words into his ear.[227] 5. This is the trick designed to make them perpetual disciples of their bishop, since they yearn to learn the content of that formula spoken in their dying hour. Through it, the disciple is destined to become a member of the perfect. For this reason, I keep my mouth shut about these matters so that someone might not think that I act maliciously toward them. To be sure, this is not my purpose. Rather, I intend to show from where they took their starting points and concocted their doctrines.

42. 1. Indeed, the blessed presbyter Irenaeus, attacking them quite boldly in his refutation, also presented these sorts of washings and redemptions and spoke more fully about their practices.[228] When they read this, some of them denied that these were their traditions, because they are taught always to deny it.[229] So the thought occurred to me to investigate more accurately and to research in detail what they pass on as tradition in the "first bath" (as they call it) and in the second bath, which they call "redemption." 2. Not even their "unspeakable mystery" escaped my notice—but let this be relinquished to Valentinus and to his school.[230]

---

227. The understanding of redemption as a deathbed ritual is distinctive to our author. See further Förster, *Marcus*, 157–58; idem, "Marcosian Rituals for Prophecy and Apolytrosis," in DeConick, Shaw, and Turner, *Practicing Gnosis*, 442–44.

228. Iren., *Haer.* 1.13.6; 21.1–4; cf. Epiph., *Pan.* 34.3.6; 34.19.1–20.12.

229. This report is a rare testimony from Markosian Valentinians that Irenaeus misrepresented their teachings.

230. This is the only place our author appears self-conscious of the fact that his exposé may be offensive and even disproved. Unlike others represented in the *Refutation*, the Valentinians were a living community who could defend their teachings and rebuke those who profaned their mysteries. Accordingly, our author cuts out Irenaeus's salacious material about Markos's supposed sexual escapades and focuses on Markos's numerological excogitations, which could be linked to Pythagorean thought. See further Förster, *Marcus*, 30–31.

Ὁ δὲ Μάρκος μιμούμενος τὸν διδάσκαλον καὶ αὐτὸς ἀναπλάσσει ὅραμα, νομίζων οὕτως δοξασθήσεσθαι· καὶ γὰρ Οὐαλεντῖνος φάσκει ἑαυτὸν ἑωρακέναι παῖδα νήπιον ἀρτιγέν<ν>ητον· οὗ πυθόμενος ἐπεζήτει τίς ἂν εἴη, ὁ δὲ ἀπεκρίνατο λέγων ἑαυτὸν εἶναι τὸν Λόγον· ἔπειτα προσθεὶς τραγικόν τινα μῦθον, ἐκ τούτου συνιστᾶν βούλεται τὴν ἐπικεχειρημένην αὐτῷ αἵρεσιν.

3. Τούτῳ δὲ ὅμοια τολμῶν ὁ Μάρκος λέγει <κατ>εληλυθέναι πρὸς αὐτὸν σχήματι γυναικείῳ τὴν Τετράδα—ἐπειδή, φησί, τὸ ἄρρεν αὐτῆς ὁ κόσμος φέρειν οὐκ ἠδύνατο—καὶ μηνῦσαι αὐτὴν ἥτις ἦν καὶ τὴν τῶν πάντων γένεσιν, ἣν οὐδενὶ πώποτε οὔτε θεῶν οὔτε ἀνθρώπων ἀπεκάλυψε, τούτῳ μόνῳ διηγήσασθαι, οὕτως εἰποῦσα<ν>·

> 4. ὅτε τὸ πρῶτον ὁ Πατήρ, [αὐτοῦ] ὁ ἀνεν<ν>όητος καὶ ἀνούσιος, ὁ μήτε ἄρρεν μήτε θῆλυ, ἠθέλησεν αὐτοῦ τὸ ἄρρητον ῥητὸν γενέσθαι (κ)αὶ τὸ ἀόρατον μορφωθῆναι, ἤνοιξε τὸ στόμα καὶ προήκατο Λόγον ὅμοιον αὐτῷ· ὃς παραστὰς ἐπέδειξεν αὐτῷ ὃ ἦν, αὐτὸς τοῦ ἀοράτου μορφὴ φανείς.

5. ἡ δὲ ἐκφώνησις τοῦ ὀνόματος ἐγένετο τοιαύτη· ἐλάλησε λόγον τὸν πρῶτον τοῦ ὀνόματος αὐτοῦ, ἥτις ἦν «ἀρχή», καὶ ἦν ἡ συλλαβὴ αὐτοῦ στοιχείων τεσσάρων· ἔπειτα συνῆψε τὴν δευτέραν, καὶ ἦν καὶ αὐτὴ στοιχείων τεσσάρων·

THE VISION OF VALENTINUS. Now Markos, in imitation of his teacher, also fabricated a vision, supposing that in this way he would be glorified.[231] For in fact, Valentinus claims that he saw a child, an infant recently born. When he inquired to find out who he was, the child replied that he was the Word. Then, by adding a tragic myth, Valentinus wanted to establish from it his own trumped up heresy.[232]

THE ORIGIN OF THE AEONS. 3. Daring the likes of this man, Markos says that the Tetrad descended to him in the shape of a woman—since, he says, the world was not able to bear her male form—and disclosed both her identity and the origin of all things, which she had never before revealed either to gods or to human beings. To him alone she described it, speaking as follows:

> 4. When the Father, who is inconceivable, beyond substance, and neither male nor female, first willed his unspeakable nature to be spoken, and the invisible to take shape, he opened his mouth and emanated a Word similar to himself. He, standing alongside him, showed to him what he was, having become manifest as the form of the Invisible.[233]

5. Now the pronunciation of his name happened in this way: he uttered a word, the first one of his name, which was "APXH"—a compound of four letters.[234] Then he joined to it the second word, also made up of four letters. Following this, he spoke the third word, made up of ten letters. Then

---

231. This section (*Ref.* 6.42.2–43.1) our author adapts from Iren., *Haer.* 1.14.1–2; cf. Epiph., *Pan.* 34.4.3–8. See further Giovanni Casadio, "La visione in Marco il Mago e nella gnosi di tipo sethiano," *Aug* 29 (1989): 123–46 (126–34).

232. This paragraph in part makes up Valentinus, frag. 7 (Völker). For the accusation about the "tragic myth," see Iren., *Haer.* 1.11.4; 1.15.4. The following section (the origin of the aeons) is taken with adaptation from Iren., *Haer.* 1.14.1; cf. Epiph., *Pan.* 34.4.2–8.

233. For Markos's understanding of the Word (Λόγος), see Sagnard, *Gnose*, 363–65. On the possible influence of Egyptian mythology, see Förster, *Marcus*, 182–92. Kalvesmaki observes, "Whereas in other Valentinian systems the uppermost two entities are part of the Pleroma, here the Pleroma is constitutive of the Word, apart from the Father" (*Theology*, 63).

234. Ἀρχή = "beginning" or "source." Below, I follow Kalvesmaki in translating στοιχεῖα as "spoken letter" and γράμμα as "written letter" (*Theology*, 62–63, esp. 63 n.

ἐξ<ἧς> ἐλάλησε τὴν τρίτην, ἥτις ἦν στοιχείων δέκα· καὶ τὴν τετάρτην ἐλάλησε, καὶ ἦν [καὶ] αὐτὴ στοιχείων δώδεκα. 6. ἐγένετο οὖν τοῦ ὅλου ὀνόματος ἡ ἐκφώνησις στοιχείων τριάκοντα, συλλαβῶν δὲ τεσσάρων. ἕκαστον δὲ τῶν στοιχείων ἴδια γράμματα καὶ ἴδιον χαρακτῆρα καὶ ἰδίαν ἐκφώνησιν καὶ σχήματα καὶ εἰκόνας ἔχειν, καὶ μηθὲν αὐτῶν εἶναι ὃ τὴν ἐκείνου καθορᾷ μορφήν, οὗπερ αὐτὸ στοιχεῖόν ἐστιν, οὐδὲ μὴν τὴν τοῦ πλησίον αὐτοῦ ἕκαστον ἐκφώνησιν γινώσκειν, ἀλλ' ὃ [μὴ δὲ] ἐκφωνεῖ, ὡς τὸ πᾶν ἐκφωνοῦντα, ὅτι τὸ <ὅλον> ἡγεῖσθαι ὀνομάζειν αὐτόν. 7. ἕκαστον γὰρ αὐτῶν, μέρος ὂν τοῦ ὅλου, τὸν ἴδιον ἦχον ὡς τὸ πᾶν ὀνομάζειν, καὶ μὴ παύσασ<θαι> ἠχοῦντα, μέχρις ὅτου ἐπὶ τὸ ἔσχατον γράμμα τοῦ ἐσχάτου στοιχείου μονογλωττήσαντα καταντῆσαι.

τότε δὲ τὴν ἀποκατάστασιν τῶν ὅλων ἔφη γενέσθαι, ὅταν τὰ πάντα κατελθόντα εἰς τὸ ἓν γράμμα, μίαν καὶ τὴν αὐτὴν ἐκφώνησιν ἠχήσῃ· τῆς δὲ ἐκφωνήσεως εἰκόνα τὸ ἀμὴν ὁμοῦ λεγόντων ἡμῶν ὑπέθετο εἶναι. 8. τοὺς δὲ <φθόγγους> ὑπάρχειν τοὺς μορφοῦντας τὸν ἀνούσιον καὶ ἀγένητον Αἰῶνα· καὶ εἶναι τούτους μορφάς, ἃς ὁ κύριος ἀγγέλους εἴρηκε, τὰς «διηνεκῶς βλεπούσας τὸ πρόσωπον τοῦ πατρός».

43. 1. Τὰ δὲ ὀνόματα τῶν στοιχείων τὰ κοινὰ καὶ ῥητὰ αἰῶνας καὶ λόγους καὶ ῥίζας καὶ σπέρματα καὶ πληρώματα καὶ καρποὺς ὠνόμασε, τὰ καθ' ἕ<να> αὐτῶν καὶ ἑκάστου ἴδια ἐν τῷ ὀνόματι τῆς Ἐκκ(λησ)ί(ας) ἐμπερι<ε>χόμενα (ν)οεῖσθαι.

2. Ὧν στοιχείων τοῦ ἐσχάτου στοιχείου τὸ ὕστατον γράμμα φωνὴν προήκατο τὴν ἑαυτοῦ· οὗ ὁ ἦχος ἐξελθὼν <κατ'> εἰκόνα τῶν στοιχείων στοιχεῖα

he spoke the fourth word, made up of twelve letters. 6. So it was that the pronunciation of the whole name was thirty letters, with four compound parts. Each of the letters had its own written letters, its own peculiar character, its own pronunciation, shapes, and images. But none of the letters perceives the form that it constitutes as a letter, nor does any one of them know the pronunciation of its neighbors. It pronounces as if pronouncing the whole, since it thinks that it names the whole.[235] 7. Each of them, though a part of the whole, names its own sound as the whole and does not cease sounding, until the point when it reaches the last written letter of the last spoken letter, pronouncing each one singly.

The restoration of the universe occurs, she said, when all the letters are concentrated in one written letter and sound with one and the same pronunciation.[236] The image of this pronunciation, she posited, is the "Amen" that we say in unison. 8. These are the sounds that exist and give shape to the Aeon that is beyond substance and generation. Furthermore, these are the forms that the Lord called "angels," who "perpetually see the face of the Father."[237]

43. 1. The common and spoken names of the letters he named "words," "roots," "seeds" "plenitudes," and "fruits." Their individual aspects are thought to be contained in the name of "Church."[238]

THE CREATION OF THE WORLD. 2. Among these letters, the written letter of the final letter sent forth its own voice. Its sound, when it came forth,

---

4). When, however, a contrast is not intended, I translate στοιχεῖα merely by "letter." See further Sagnard, *Gnose*, 430–32; Irenaeus, *Contre les hérésies*, ed. Adelin Rousseau and Louis Doutreleau, 10 vols., SC 263 (Paris: Cerf, 1979), 1:1.244–45; *St. Irenaeus of Lyons: Against the Heresies Book 1*, ed. and trans. Dominic J. Unger and John J. Dillon, ACW 55 (New York: Newmann Press, 1992), 206 n. 6.

235. Miller adds ὅλον ("whole"). The larger form (μορφήν) of the letters is the Word, who is the form (μορφή) or semantic expression of the Invisible (*Ref.* 6.42.4).

236. Restoration into one letter (στοιχεῖον) overlaps with the Stoic idea of the world's restoration/reconstitution into one element (στοιχεῖον), namely, fire (Förster, *Marcus*, 202–5). See further the texts in Long and Sedley, *Hellenistic Philosophers*, 2.271–77.

237. Matt 18:10; cf. Iren., *Haer.* 1.13.3, 6; Clem. Alex., *Exc.* 10.6; 11.1; 12.1; 23.4; *Strom.* 5.14.91.3.

238. The following section (*Ref.* 6.43.2–6) our author adapts from Iren., *Haer.* 1.14.2; cf. Epiph., *Pan.* 34.4.9–5.4.

ἴδια ἐγέννησεν, ἐξ ὧν τά τε ἐνταῦθα διακεκο<σ>μῆσθαί φησι καὶ τὰ πρὸ τούτων γεγενῆσθαι. τὸ μέντοι γράμμα αὐτό, οὗ ὁ ἦχος ἦν συνεπακολουθῶν τῷ ἤχῳ κάτω, ὑπὸ τῆς συλλαβῆς τῆς ἑαυτοῦ ἀνειλῆφθαι ἄνω λέγει, εἰς ἀναπλήρωσιν τοῦ ὅλου· μεμενηκέναι δὲ εἰς τὰ κάτω τὸν ἦχον, ὥσπερ ἔξω ῥιφέντα. 3. τὸ δὲ στοιχεῖον αὐτό, ἀφ' οὗ τὸ γράμμα σὺν τῇ ἐκφωνήσει τῇ ἑαυτοῦ κατῆλθε κάτω, γραμμάτων φησὶν εἶναι τριάκοντα· καὶ ἓν ἕκαστον τῶν τριάκοντα γραμμάτων ἐν ἑαυτῷ ἔχειν ἕτερα γράμματα, δι' ὧν τὸ ὄνομα τοῦ γράμματος ὀνομάζεται· καὶ μὴν πάλιν τὰ ἕτερα δι' ἄλλων ὀνομάζεσθαι γραμμάτων, καὶ τὰ ἄλλα δι' ἄλλων, ὥστε εἰς ἄπειρον ἐκπίπτειν τὸ πλῆθος <ἰ>δίᾳ τῶν γραμμάτων γραφέντων.

4. Οὕτως δ' ἂν σαφέστερον μάθοι τις τὸ λεγόμενον· τὸ δέλτα στοιχεῖον γράμματα ἔχει ἐν ἑαυτῷ πέντε·

<αὐτό τε> τὸ δέλτα
καὶ τὸ ει
καὶ τὸ λάμβδα
καὶ τὸ ταῦ
καὶ τὸ ἄλφα·

καὶ αὐτὰ ταῦτα τὰ γράμματα δι' ἄλλων <γράφεται γραμμάτων, καὶ τὰ ἄλλα δι' ἄλλων>. 5. εἰ οὖν ἡ πᾶσα ὑπόστασις τοῦ δέλτα εἰς ἄπειρον ἐκπίπτει, ἀεὶ ἄλλων ἄλλα γράμματα γεννώντων καὶ διαδεχομένων ἄλληλα, πόσῳ μᾶλλον ἐκείνου τοῦ στοιχείου μείζον' εἶναι τὸν πό<ν>τον τῶν γραμμάτων; καὶ εἰ τὸ ἓν γράμμα ἄπειρον <οὔτ>ως, ὁρᾶτε ὅλου τοῦ ὀνόματος τὸν βυθὸν τῶν γραμμάτων, ἐξ ὧν τὸν Προπάτορα ἡ Μάρκου φιλοπονία—μᾶλλον δὲ ματαιοπονία—βούλεται συνιστᾶν.

6. διὸ καὶ τὸν Πατέρα, ἐπιστάμενον τὸ ἀχώρητον αὐτοῦ, δεδωκέναι τοῖς

generated its own letters in the image of the letters.[239] From these letters, she says, our world was ordered, and what came before our world was generated. The written letter itself—whose sound corresponds to the sound below, she says—was taken up above by its own compound for the completion of the whole. But its sound remained in the region below as if thrown outside.[240] 3. But the very letter from which the written letter (with its pronunciation) descended below is part of a set, she says, of thirty written letters. Each one of the thirty written letters has in itself other written letters by which the name of its letter is pronounced. Again, other written letters are named through others, and others through still others, so that the number of written letters in each case soars to infinity when written out.

4. But so that one might more clearly understand what she says: the spoken letter delta has in it five written letters:

the delta itself (Δ),
epsilon (E),
lambda (Λ),
tau (T),
and alpha (A).

These very written letters are written with other letters, and these others through still others. 5. If, then, the whole content of the delta soars to infinity—since there are always other letters that are generated from others and succeeding one another—how much greater is the ocean of written letters than that spoken letter? And if the single written letter is thus infinite, observe the "depth" of written letters making up the whole name from which Markos's diligent—or rather futile—labor wants to concoct the Forefather!

6. And so the Father, knowing his own incomprehensibility, enabled each single one of the letters—which he also calls "aeons"—to cry out its

239. The "final letter" corresponds to Wisdom, the thirtieth aeon in other Valentinian systems. The "sound" corresponds to Achamoth; and the letter images correspond to the archons. See further Förster, *Marcus*, 209–12.

240. Wisdom, separated from her passion, returned to the Fullness, but her intention (here: echo) remained below. On the doubling of the echoes (ἦχος ἦν συνεπακολουθῶν τῷ ἤχῳ κάτω), see Förster, *Marcus*, 213–15.

στοιχείοις—ἃ καὶ αἰῶνας καλεῖ—ἑνὶ ἑκάστῳ αὐτῶν τὴν ἰδίαν ἐκφώνησιν ἐκβοᾶν, διὰ τὸ μὴ δύνασθαι ἕνα τὸ ὅλον ἐκφωνεῖν.

44. 1. Ταῦτα δὲ σαφηνίσασαν αὐτῷ τὴν Τετρακτὺν εἰπε<ῖν>·

θέλω δέ σοι καὶ αὐτὴν ἐπιδεῖξαι τὴν Ἀλήθειαν· κατήγαγ(ον) γὰρ α(ὐ)τὴ(ν) ἐκ (τ)ῶν ὕπερθεν δωμάτων, ἵνα ἴδῃς αὐτὴν γυμνὴν καὶ καταμάθῃς αὐτῆς τὸ κάλλος, ἀλλὰ καὶ ἀκούσῃς αὐτῆς λαλούσης καὶ θαυμάσῃς τὸ φρόνημα αὐτῆς. 2. ὅρα οὖν

κεφαλήν, φησίν, ἄνω τὸ πρῶτον, ἄλφα ω,
τράχηλον [τὸ] δὲ β ψ,
ὤμους <ἅμα χερσὶ> γ χ,
στήθη δέλτα φ,
<διά>φραγμα ε υ,
κοιλίαν ζ τ,
αἰδοῖα η σ,
μηροὺς θ ρ,
γόνατα ι π,
κνήμας κ ο,
σφυρὰ λ ξ,
πόδας μ ν.

τοῦτ᾽ ἔστι τὸ σῶμα τῆς κατὰ τὸν Μάρκον Ἀληθείας, τοῦτο τὸ σχῆμα τοῦ στοιχείου, οὗτος ὁ χαρακτὴρ τοῦ γράμματος. 3. καὶ καλεῖ τὸ στοιχεῖον τοῦτο Ἄνθρωπον· εἶναι δὲ πηγήν φησι παντὸς λόγου, καὶ ἀρχὴν πάσης φωνῆς, καὶ παντὸς ἀρρήτου ῥῆσιν, καὶ τῆς σιωπωμένης Σιγῆς στόμα.

καὶ τοῦτο τὸ σῶμα αὐτῆς· σὺ δὲ μετάρσιον ἐγείρας <τὸ> τῆς διανοίας νόημα, τὸν <αὐτο>γεν<ν>ήτορα καὶ προπάτορα Λόγον ἀπὸ στομάτων Ἀληθείας ἄκουε.

own pronunciation, because it was not possible for one to pronounce the whole.[241]

THE BODY OF TRUTH. 44. 1. The Tetraktys clarified matters for Markos in the following remarks:

> I desire to show you the Truth itself. I brought her down from the dwellings above so that you might see her naked and learn her beauty, but also so that you might hear her speaking and wonder at her intelligence. 2. First behold on top,
> her head: ΑΩ,
> her neck: ΒΨ,
> her shoulders and arms: ΓΧ,
> her breast: ΔΦ,
> her diaphragm: ΕΥ,
> her belly: ΖΤ,
> her genitals: ΗΣ,
> her thighs: ΘΡ,
> her knees: ΙΠ,
> her shins: ΚΟ,
> her ankles: ΛΞ,
> her feet: ΜΝ.

This is the body of Markos's "Truth"; this is the shape of the spoken letter, and this is the character of the written letter.[242] 3. She calls this spoken letter "Human Being." This Human is, she says, the fount of all language, the source of all speech, the declaration of everything unutterable, and the mouth of unspeaking Silence.

> Yes, this is her body. But you, after lifting the thought of your mind on high, hear the self-born and ancestral Word from the lips of Truth![243]

241. The following section (*Ref.* 6.44) our author adapts from Iren., *Haer.* 1.14.3; cf. Epiph., *Pan.* 34.5.5–8.

242. On the body of Truth as related to astrology and melothesia, see Manilius, *Astron.* 4.701–705; Boll, *Sphaera*, 469–72; Förster, *Marcus*, 222–25; von Stuckrad, *Ringen*, 647–48.

243. The following section (*Ref.* 6.45) our author adapts from Iren., *Haer.* 1.14.4; cf. Epiph., *Pan.* 34.6.1–4.

45. 1. Ταῦτα δὲ ταύτης εἰπούσης, προσβλέψασαν αὐτῷ τὴν Ἀλήθειαν καὶ ἀνοίξασαν τὸ στόμα λαλῆσαι λόγον· τὸν δὲ λόγον ὄνομα γενέσθαι, καὶ (τ)ὸ ὄνομα εἶναι τοῦτο ὃ γινώσκομεν καὶ λαλοῦμεν, Χριστὸν Ἰησοῦν· ὃ καὶ ὀνομάσασαν αὐτὴν παραυτίκα σιωπῆσαι.

2. προσδοκῶντος δὲ τοῦ Μάρκου πλεῖον αὐτὴν μέλλειν τι λέγειν, π(άλι)ν ἡ Τετρακτὺς παρελθοῦσα εἰς τὸ μέσον φησίν·

> ὡς [ἡ] <εὐήθη> ἡγήσω τὸν λόγον τοῦτον <ὃν> ἀπὸ στομάτων τῆς Ἀληθείας ἤκουσας· οὐ τοῦτο ὅπερ οἶδας καὶ δοκεῖς ἔχειν πάλαι [τοῦτ'] ἐστὶν ὄνομα· φωνὴν γὰρ ἔχεις μόνον αὐτοῦ, τὴν δὲ δύναμιν ἀγνοεῖς. 3. Ἰησοῦς μὲν γάρ ἐστιν ἐπίσημον ὄνομα, ἓξ ἔχον γράμματα, ὑπὸ πάντων τῆς κλήσεως <ἐπικαλούμενον> τὸ δὲ παρὰ τοῖς [πέντε] αἰῶσι τοῦ πληρώματος, πολυμερὲς τυγχάνον, ἄλλης ἐστὶ μορφῆς καὶ ἑτέρου τύπου, γινωσκόμενον ὑπ' ἐκείνων τῶν συγγενῶν (αὐτοῦ), ὧν τὰ μεγέθη παρ' αὐτῷ ἐστι διὰ π(αν)τός».

46. 1. Ταῦτα τὰ παρ' ὑμῖν εἰκοσιτέσσαρα γράμματα ἀπορροίας γίνωσκε ὑπάρχειν τῶν τριῶν δυνάμ(εων) (καὶ) εἰκ(όν)ας, τῶν ἐμπεριεχουσῶν τὸν ὅλον καὶ τῶν ἄνω στοιχείων ἀριθμόν. τ(ὰ) μὲν γὰρ ἄφωνα γράμματα ἐννέα νόμισον εἶναι τοῦ Πατρὸς καὶ τῆς Ἀληθείας, διὰ τὸ ἀφώνους αὐτοὺς εἶναι, τουτέστιν ἀρρήτους καὶ ἀνεκλαλήτους·

THE ORIGIN OF JESUS ON HIGH. 45. 1. When she said this, Truth fixed her gaze on him and opened her mouth to speak the Word. Then the Word became a Name, and the Name is that which we know and speak: Christ Jesus.[244] When she named this Word, she immediately grew silent.

2. When Markos expected her to say something more, Tetraktys again stepped into the midst and said:

> You regarded this Word you heard from the lips of Truth as trivial.[245] But what you know and suppose you have long possessed is not his name. You possess its sound alone but do not know its meaning. 3. For Jesus is a noteworthy name, having six letters, and is invoked by all those who are called.[246] But the name that exists among the aeons of the Fullness—although a compound—has another form and a different character known by those who are its kin, whose magnitudes are eternally beside him.[247]
>
> **THE THREE POWERS. 46.** 1. Know that these twenty-four written letters that you possess exist as effluxes and images of the three powers that encompass the total number of the letters on high.[248] Consider that nine consonants [β γ δ κ π τ θ φ χ] belong to Father and Truth.[249] This is because they are unvoiced—which means

---

244. Christ Jesus, as the name uttered by Truth, is also Truth's express image (Kalvesmaki, *Theology*, 66).

245. Here I accept R. Scott's εὐήθη ("trivial") for P's (nonsensical) ἡ πηθν. For this and other options, see Marcovich's apparatus.

246. "Noteworthy" translates ἐπίσημον, a word that, as Kalvesmaki notes, is the ancient term for the letter called stigma (ϛ) or digamma (ϝ), representing the number six (*Theology*, 67–68; cf. Sagnard, *Gnose*, 365–66). Clement of Alexandria speaks about the allegorical significance of the number six (*Strom.* 6.16.138.6–141.7). "Invoked" (ἐπικαλούμενον) is an emendation of P's ἐγκαλούμενα ("accused"). Epiphanios's transcription of Irenaeus reads γινωσκόμενον ("known") (*Pan.* 34.6.4), corresponding to *cognitum* in Latin Iren., *Haer.* 1.14.4. Förster identifies the "called" as the church of the animate people (*Marcus*, 232).

247. Those "kin" to the name, says Förster, are the spirituals; the "magnitudes" are another name for the aeons surrounding the Father (*Marcus*, 233). The following section (*Ref.* 6.46) our author adapts from Iren., *Haer.* 1.14.5; cf. Epiph., *Pan.* 34.6.5–13.

248. The twenty-four letters "that you (pl.) possess" are the letters of the Greek alphabet. The "three powers," in context, seem to refer to the couples: (1) Father and Truth, (2) Word and Life, and (3) Human and Church. Cf. Rousseau and Doutreleau, *Contre les hérésies* (SC 263), 1:1.247–48.

249. Cf. Dionysius Thrax, *Ars gramm.* 6 (Uhlig, 9–12), reproduced in Förster, *Marcus*, 237.

2. τὰ δὲ ἡμίφωνα, ὀκτὼ ὄντα, τοῦ Λόγου καὶ τῆς Ζωῆς, διὰ τὸ μέσα ὥσπερ ὑπάρχειν τῶν τε ἀφώνων καὶ τῶν φωνηέντων καὶ ἀναδεδέχθαι τῶν μὲν ὕπερθεν τὴν ἀπόρ<ρο>ιαν, τῶν δὲ ὑπ' αὐτὰ τὴν ἀναφοράν· τὰ δὲ φωνήεντα καὶ αὐτά, ἑπτὰ ὄντα, τοῦ Ἀνθρώπου καὶ τῆς Ἐκκλησίας, ἐπεὶ διὰ τοῦ Ἀνθρώπου ἡ φωνὴ προελθοῦσα ἐμόρφωσε τὰ ὅλα· ὁ γὰρ ἦχος τῆς φωνῆς μορφὴν αὐτοῖς περιεποίησεν. 3. ἔστιν οὖν ὁ μὲν Λόγος [ὁ] ἔχων καὶ ἡ Ζωὴ [ἡ] τὰ ὀκτώ, ὁ δὲ Ἄνθρωπος καὶ ἡ Ἐκκλησία τὰ ἑπτά, ὁ δὲ Πατὴρ καὶ ἡ Ἀλήθεια τὰ ἐννέα.

Ἐπὶ δὲ τοῦ ὑστερήσαντος λόγου ὁ ἀφεδρασθεὶς ἐν τῷ Πατρὶ κατῆλθεν, ἐκπεμφθεὶς ἐπὶ τὸν ἀφ' οὗ ἐχωρί<σ>θη ἐπὶ διορθώσει τῶν πραχθέντων, ἵνα ἡ τῶν πληρωμάτων ἑνότης, ἐπ<ὶ> τῷ <ἴσῳ ἀριθμῷ> οὖσα, καρποφορῇ μίαν ἐν πᾶσι τὴν ἐκ πάντων δύναμιν. 4. καὶ οὕτως ὁ τῶν ἑπτὰ τὴν τῶν ὀκτὼ ἐκομίσατο δύναμιν, καὶ ἐγένοντο οἱ τρεῖς τόποι ὅμοιοι τοῖς ἀριθμοῖς, ὀγδοάδες ὄντες· οἵτινες τρεῖς ἐφ' ἑαυτοὺς ἐλθόντες τὸν τῶν εἰκοσιτεσσάρων ἀνέδειξαν ἀριθμόν.

Τὰ μέντοι τρία στοιχεῖα, <ἅ> φησιν αὐτὸς τῶν τριῶν ἐν συζυγίᾳ δυνάμεων ὑπάρχειν, ἅ ἐστιν ἕξ, ἀφ' ὧν ἀπερ<ρ>ύη τὰ εἰκοσιτέσσαρα στοιχεῖα,

that they are unspeakable and unpronounceable. 2. Consider that the semivowels, which are eight [ζ ξ ψ λ μ ν ρ σ], belong to Word and Life. This is because they exist, so to speak, "in between" the consonants and the vowels and manifest the efflux of those above and the ascent of those below. Finally, consider that the vowels themselves, which are seven [α ε η ι ο υ ω], belong to Human and Church, since it was through Human that the voice came forward and formed the universe. It was the sound of his voice that gave them form. 3. Thus Word and Life have eight, Human and Church have seven, while Father and Truth have nine.[250]

On account of the deficient computation, one letter dislodged from within the Father and descended.[251] He was sent out on behalf of the one from whom he separated to correct what had been done so that the unity of the plenitudes in numerical equality might bring forth as a harvest a single power among all and from all.[252] 4. And so the region of seven recovered the power of the eight, and the three regions became equal in number as Ogdoads. When these three came together, they produced the number twenty-four.

Furthermore, there are three letters, she says, coupled with the three powers, which make six.[253] From these flowed out the twenty-four letters,

---

250. For similar speculation employing grammatical theory, see Marsanes (NHC X,1) 26.18–27 with the comments of Alexander Böhlig, *Zum Hellenismus in den Schriften von Nag Hammadi* (Wiesbaden: Harrassowitz, 1975), 15–17; Förster, *Marcus*, 238–43.

251. The "deficient computation" (ὑστερήσαντος λόγου) could also be understood as "the deficient Word," who would stand in for the aeon Wisdom (Rousseau and Doutreleau, *Contre les hérésies* [SC 263], 1:1.248). For the Word that falls, see Tri. Trac. (NHC I,5) 74.18–80.11. On the *hapax legomenon* ἀφεδράζειν, see Kalvesmaki, *Theology*, 70 n. 21.

252. Ἐπὶ τῷ ἴσῳ ἀριθμῷ οὖσα ("in numerical equality") is Marcovich's emendation of P's ἐν τῶ ἀγαθῶ οὖσα ("in the Good"). Cf. Epiph., *Pan.* 34.6.10 (end): ἰσότητα ἔχουσα ("being equal"); Latin Iren., *Haer.* 1.14.5: *aequalitatem habens.* According to Iren., *Haer.* 1.11.1 (the report of "Valentinus"), Christ was born from Wisdom after her expulsion from the Fullness, but later Christ ascended back into the Fullness. Here Christ is apparently pictured as returning to Wisdom in order to form her. See further Rousseau and Doutreleau, *Contre les hérésies* (SC 263), 1:1.248.

253. The three letters coupled to the three powers are the female aeons Truth, Life, and Church coupled to Father, Word, and Human (Rousseau and Doutreleau, *Contre les hérésies* [SC 263], 1:1.248–49).

τετραπλασιασθέντα τῷ τῆς ἀρρήτου Τετράδος λόγῳ τὸν αὐτὸν <αὐ>τοῖς ἀριθμὸν ποιεῖ. 5. ἅπερ φησὶ τοῦ ἀνωνομάστου ὑπάρχειν· φορεῖσθαι δὲ αὐτὰ ὑπὸ τῶν τριῶν δυνάμεων εἰς ὁμοιότητα τοῦ ἀοράτου, ὧν στοιχείων εἰκόνας εἰκόνων [ὧν] <τὰ παρ' ἡμῖν> τρία διπλᾶ γράμματα ὑπάρχειν· ἃ συναριθμούμενα τοῖς εἰκοσιτέσσαρσι στοιχείοις δυνάμει τῇ κατὰ ἀναλογίαν τὸν τῶν τριάκοντα ποιεῖ ἀριθμόν.

47. 1. Τούτου τοῦ λόγου καὶ τῆς οἰκονομίας ταύτης καρπόν φησιν «ἐν ὁμοιώματι εἰκόνος» πεφηνέναι ἐκεῖ(νον) τὸν μετὰ τὰς ἓξ ἡμέρας τέταρτον ἀναβάντα εἰς τὸ ὄρος καὶ γενόμενον ἕκτον, τὸν καταβάντα καὶ κρατηθέντα ἐν τῇ Ἑβδομάδι, ἐπίσημον Ὀγδοάδα ὑπάρχοντα καὶ ἔχοντα ἐν ἑαυτῷ τὸν ἅπαντα τῶν στοιχείων ἀριθμόν.

2. ὃν ἐφανέρωσεν, ἐλθόντος αὐτοῦ ἐπὶ τὸ βάπτισμα, ἡ τῆς περιστερᾶς κάθοδος, ἥτις ἐστὶν ω καὶ ἄλφα, δι' ἀρι(θ)μοῦ δηλουμένη ὀκτακοσίων ἑνός.

since when they are multiplied by the amount of the unspeakable Tetrad, they produce the same number among themselves. 5. They exist, he says, from the Unnamable. They are conveyed by the three powers into the likeness of the Invisible. The images of the images of these letters are our double letters (ζ ξ ψ).[254] These, when added to the twenty-four letters by virtue of analogy, produce the number thirty.[255]

NUMERICAL ALLEGORIES FROM SCRIPTURE. 47. 1. He says that the Fruit of this Word and this dispensation has appeared "in the likeness of an image."[256] After six days, that Fruit ascended the mountain as the fourth and became the sixth.[257] When he descended and was held in the Hebdomad, this noteworthy number Six existed as an Ogdoad and carried in himself the total number value of all the letters.[258]

2. Jesus displayed this number when he came to be baptized.[259] The descent of the dove (i.e., omega and alpha) is manifest in the number 801.[260]

---

254. Cf. Dionysios Thrax, *Ars gramm.* 6 (Uhlig, 14,4–6), reproduced in Förster, *Marcus*, 247.

255. The translation of the final two sentences can only be tentative. The words δυνάμει τῇ κατὰ ἀναλογίαν may be corrupt (presumably the analogy is that of the upper world, since the letters are images of the aeons, yet see Kalvesmaki, *Theology*, 69 n. 19). The basic thought, however, is recoverable: the double letters add up to six, which can be added to the twenty-four letters of the Greek alphabet to make thirty, an image of the Triacontad. In Valentinian theology, the aeonic Jesus is the product of all thirty aeons—thus it was important for his name to amount to thirty. The use of "image of the images" is odd but anticipates the "likeness of an image" immediately below (*Ref.* 6.47.1). The following section (*Ref.* 6.47) our author adapts from Iren., *Haer.* 1.14.6; cf. Epiph., *Pan.* 34.7.1–4.

256. Cf. Rom 1:23 (ἐν ὁμοιώματι εἰκόνος).

257. "After six days" comes from Mark 9:2. Jesus went up the Mount of Transfiguration with Peter, James and John—making four total. Moses and Elijah were added to the company to make six (Mark 9:3–4 par.). For a similar numerological allegory, see Clem. Alex., *Strom.* 6.16.140.3–4, with Sagnard, *Gnose*, 378–82. See further Clem. Alex., *Exc.* 4.1; Barn. 15. Iren., *Haer.* 2.24.4; Acts Thom. 143; Acts John 90.

258. The Hebdomad may have been suggested by Luke 9:37: "the next day" (after day six). But the author of Luke refers to eight days in the beginning of his account (9:28). In this case we have to imagine the Markosian interpreter combining the Markan account (six days, 9:2) with "the next day" of Luke. In the allegory, the Hebdomad represents the Artificer, who apparently detains the heavenly Jesus in his descent as Savior. The Ogdoad is the Savior thought to contain the total value of the Fullness (Förster, *Marcus*, 253–54). For a different interpretation, see Kalvesmaki, *Theology*, 72.

259. Jesus was thirty years old at his baptism (Luke 3:23).

260. The letters of περιστερά ("dove"), when added up, equal the value of alpha and

καὶ διὰ τοῦτο Μωσέα ἐν τῇ ἕκτῃ ἡμέρᾳ λέγειν τὸν ἄνθρωπον γεγονέναι· 3. καὶ τὴν οἰκονομίαν δὲ τοῦ πάθους ἐν τῇ ἕκτῃ τῶν ἡμερῶν—ἥτις ἐστὶν ἡ παρασκευή—<ἐν> ᾗ τὸν ἔσχατον ἄνθρωπον εἰς ἀναγέννησιν τοῦ πρώτου ἀνθρώπου πεφηνέναι. ταύτης τῆς οἰκονομίας ἀρχὴν καὶ τέλος τὴν ἕκτην ὥραν εἶναι, ἐν ᾗ προσηλώθη τῷ ξύλῳ. 4. τὸν γὰρ τέλειον Νοῦν, ἐπιστάμενον τὸν τῶν ἓξ ἀριθμὸν δύναμιν ποιήσε<ως> καὶ ἀναγεννήσεως ἔχοντα, φανερῶσαι «τοῖς υἱοῖς τοῦ φωτὸς» τὴν διὰ τοῦ φανέντος ἐπισήμου εἰς <αὐ>τὸν [δι' αὐτοῦ] γενομένην ἀναγέννησιν. ἔνθεν καὶ τὰ διπλᾶ γράμματα τὸν ἀριθμὸν ἐπίσημον ἔχειν φησίν· ὁ γὰρ ἐπίσημος ἀριθμὸς συγκερασθεὶς τοῖς εἰκοσιτέσσαρσι στοιχείοις τὸ τριακονταγράμματον ὄνομα ἀπετέλεσε.

48. 1. Κέχρηται δὲ διακόνῳ τῷ τῶν ἑπτὰ ἀριθμῶν μεγέθει, ἵνα τῆς αὐτοβουλήτου <βουλῆς> φανερωθῇ ὁ καρπός. τὸν μέντοι ἐπίσημον ἐπὶ τοῦ παρόντος, φησί, τὸν ἐπὶ τοῦ ἐπισήμου μορφωθέντα νόησον, τὸν ὥσπερ μερισθέντα καὶ ἔξω μείναντα. ὃς τῇ ἑαυτοῦ δυνάμει τε καὶ φρονήσει διὰ τῆς <ἀπ'> αὐτοῦ προβολῆς τοῦτον <τὸν> [τὴν ζωὴν] τῶν ἑπτὰ δυνάμεων μιμήσει τῆς Ἑβδομάδος δυνάμεως ἐψύχωσε κόσμον καὶ ψυχὴν ἔθετο εἶναι τοῦ ὁρωμένου παντός. 2. κέχρηται μὲν οὖν καὶ οὗτος τῷδε ἔργῳ ὡς αὐθαιρέτως ὑπ' αὐτοῦ γενομένῳ ... τὰ δι' εἰκόνων μιμήματα ὄντα τῶν ἀμιμήτων, τῆς ἐνυθμήσεως τῆς Μητρός.

For this reason also, Moses says that the human arose on the sixth day.[261] 3. Correspondingly, the dispensation of his suffering occurred on the sixth day (i.e., Friday, or the Day of Preparation).[262] On this day, the last Human appeared for the rebirth of the first human.[263] The sixth hour, when he was nailed to the tree, is the beginning and end of this dispensation. 4. For the perfect Mind, knowing that the number six possesses the power of making and rebirth, revealed "to the children of light" the rebirth through the noteworthy number six revealed in Jesus.[264] (Hence also the double letters, he says, make up the number six.) This is because the number six, when added to the twenty-four letters, completes the thirty-lettered name.[265]

The Artificer and the Seven Heavens. 48. 1. He used as a servant the magnitude of the seven numbers so that the Fruit of the self-willed Will might be revealed. Yes, take to heart this noteworthy number six, she says. He is the one fashioned for the noteworthy number six. He is, as it were, divided and remains outside.[266] He—by his own power and intelligence, and through the emanation that came from him—gave soul to this world of seven powers in imitation of the power of the Hebdomad and made this the soul of the visible universe.[267] 2. Now, he acted as if it arose by his own will … They, as imitations of the inimitable, [arise] through images. Their source is the Intention of the Mother.[268]

---

omega (ω′ + α′), or 801. Cf. Ps.-Tert., *Adv. omn. haer.* 5.2. See further Sagnard, *Gnose*, 373–74; Rousseau and Doutreleau, *Contre les hérésies* (SC 263), 1:1.249–50.

261. Gen 1:26, 31.

262. John 19:14.

263. Cf. 1 Cor 15:45.

264. For "children of light," see, e.g., Luke 16:8; John 12:36; Eph 5:8. On six as the noteworthy number, see Kalvesmaki, *Theology*, 67–68.

265. The following section (*Ref.* 6.48.1–4) our author adapts from Iren., *Haer.* 1.14.7–8. Cf. Epiph., *Pan.* 34.7.5–8.2. See further Rousseau and Doutreleau, *Contre les hérésies* (SC 263), 1:1.251–52.

266. The speaker of this passage is, according to Irenaeus, Silence (*Haer.* 1.14.7). "Six" here is polyvalent. The first six represents the Savior, the ἐπίσημον, or noteworthy number six. The Savior is fashioned for (ἐπί) another six, which probably represents the passion or Intention of Wisdom. See further Förster, *Marcus*, 270–71.

267. The subject of this sentence appears to be the Artificer. The world is of seven powers because it has seven planetary spheres. The Artificer enlivens the world with the World Soul, which is probably the emanation that comes from him (Förster, *Marcus*, 271–72). For the World Soul, see Plato, *Tim.* 34b; 36e; Alkinoos, *Epit.* 14; Apuleius, *Plat.* 1.9.

268. Cf. Iren., *Haer.* 1.5.3; *Ref.* 6.33.1 ("Valentinus"). "They" (τά, neuter) appar-

Καὶ ὁ μὲν (π)ρῶτος οὐρανὸς φθέγγεται τὸ ἄλφα, ὁ δὲ μετὰ τοῦτον τὸ ει, ὁ δὲ τρίτος τὸ ἦτα, (ὁ) δ(ὲ) τέταρτος καὶ ὁ μέσος τῶν ἑπτὰ τὴν τοῦ ἰῶτα δύναμιν, ὁ δὲ πέμπτος τὸ ου, ἕκτος δὲ τὸ υ, ἕβδομος δὲ καὶ τέταρτος ἀπὸ τοῦ μέσου τὸ ω. 3. αἳ δὲ δυνάμεις πᾶσαι εἰς ἓν συμπλακεῖσαι ἠχοῦσι καὶ δοξάζουσιν ἐκεῖνον ὑφ' οὗ προεβλήθησαν, ἡ δὲ δόξα τῆς ἠχήσεως ἀνεπέμφθη πρὸς τὸν Προπάτορα. ταύτης μέν(τ)οι τῆς δοξολογίας τὸν ἦχον εἰς τὴν γῆν φερόμενόν φησι πλάστην γενέσθαι καὶ γεν<ν>ήτορα τῶν ἐπὶ τῆς γῆς.

Τὴν δὲ ἀπόδειξιν ἀπὸ τῶν ἄρτι γεν<ν>ωμένων βρεφῶν, ὧν ἡ ψυχὴ ἅμα τῷ ἐκ μήτρας προελθεῖν ἐπιβοᾷ ὁμοίως ἑνὸς ἑκάστου τῶν στοιχείων τούτων τὸν ἦχον. 4. καθὼς οὖν <αἱ> ἑπτά, φησίν, δυνάμεις δοξάζουσι τὸν Λόγον, οὕτω καὶ ἡ ψυχὴ ἐν τοῖς βρέφεσι κλαίουσα. διὰ τοῦτο δέ φησι καὶ τὸν Δα(βὶ)δ εἰρηκέναι· «ἐκ στόματος νηπίων καὶ θηλαζόντων κατηρτίσω αἶνον» καὶ πάλιν· «οἱ οὐρανοὶ διηγοῦνται δόξαν θεοῦ». ἐπὰν δὲ ἐν πόνοις γένηται ἡ ψυχή, [ὡς] ἐπιβοᾷ οὐδὲν ἕτερον ἢ τὸ ω, ἐφ' ᾧ ἀνιᾶται, ὅπως γνωρίσασα ἡ ἄνω ψυχὴ τὸ συγγενὲς αὐτῆς, βοηθὸν αὐτῇ καταπέμψῃ.

49. 1. Καὶ περὶ τούτων μὲν οὕτως· περὶ δὲ τῆς τῶν εἰκοσιτεσσάρων στοιχείων γενέσεως οὕτως λέγει· τῇ Μονότητι συνυπάρχειν Ἑνότητα, ἐξ ὧν δύο προβολαί, Μονάς τε καὶ τὸ Ἕν· δὶς δύο οὖσαι, τέσσαρες ἐγένοντο—δὶς γὰρ δύο τέσσαρες.—καὶ πάλιν αἱ δύο καὶ τέσσαρες εἰς τὸ αὐτὸ συντεθεῖσαι τὸν τῶν

The first heaven utters alpha, the next one epsilon, the third eta, then the fourth—the midpoint of the seven—utters the value of iota. The fifth utters omicron, and the sixth upsilon. Then the seventh and fourth from the midpoint utter the omega.[269] 3. All the powers, woven into a single chorus, resonate and glorify the one who emanated them. The glory of the sound was sent up to the Forefather. As this doxology sounded, she says, the echo, carried down to the earth, became the molder and generator of things on earth.

Proof comes from newly born infants. As soon as they emerge from the womb, their souls uniformly cry out the sound of these letters.[270] 4. In the same way that the seven powers, she says, glorify the Word, the soul also glorifies him as it wails in infants. For this reason, she says, David also said: "From the mouth of infants and nursing babies you prepared praise."[271] Again, he says: "The heavens recount the glory of God."[272] But if the soul experiences affliction, it cries out nothing except the omega, by which it expresses grief.[273] Consequently, the higher Soul, recognizing its kin, sends help down to it.[274]

THE ORIGIN OF THE LETTERS. 49. 1. So much for these things. About the origin of the twenty-four letters, she speaks as follows. Oneness coexisted with Singleness. From them come two emanations, Monad and One.[275] They were twice two and became four (since 2 + 2 = 4). In turn, the two

---

ently refer to the things of this world. The "Mother" is Wisdom.

269. The Pythagorean teaching about the music of the spheres (cf. *Ref.* 1.2.13) is here depicted as each of the seven planets intoning one vowel. Förster associates this development with contemporary theories in astrology and magic (*Marcus*, 277–79, with sources). See further H. Leclercq, "Alphabet vocalique des Gnostiques," in *Dictionnaire d'archéologie chrétienne et de liturgie*, 15 vols. (Paris: Librairi Letouzey et Anê, 1907–1924), 1.1:1268–88.

270. Cf. Clem. Alex., *Strom.* 5.8.48.8.

271. Ps 8:3 LXX, cited in Matt 21:16.

272. Ps 18:2 LXX; cf. Clem. Alex., *Strom.* 6.16.141.6; *Ecl.* 51.1.

273. Here instead of P's ἀνιᾶται ("expresses grief"), we might expect αἰνεῖται ("by which the soul *praises*"), to conform to Latin Iren., *Haer.* 1.14.8 (*in signum laudationis*), and Epiph., *Pan.* 34.7.10 (εἰς σημεῖον αἰνέσεως).

274. The following section (*Ref.* 6.49) our author adapts from Iren., *Haer.* 1.15.1, who places it into the mouth of Silence. Here our author omits a section dealing with the name of Truth. Cf. Epiph., *Pan.* 34.8.3–8.

275. Cf. the report of Secundus above (*Ref.* 6.38.1). See also Iren., *Haer.* 1.11.3, with Förster, *Marcus*, 295–312.

ἓξ ἐφανέρωσαν ἀριθμόν, οὗτοι δὲ οἱ ἓξ τετραπλασιασθέντες τὰς εἰκοσιτέσσαρας. 2. καὶ τὰ μὲν τῆς <πρώτης> τετράδος ὀνόματα, ἅγια ἁγίων νοούμενα καὶ μὴ δυνάμενα λεχθῆναι, γινώσκεσθαι δὴ ὑπὸ μόνου τοῦ Υἱοῦ—ταῦτα ὁ Πατὴρ <οἷ>δε τίνα ἐστί.—τὰ μετὰ σιωπῆς καὶ μετὰ πίστεως ὀνομαζόμενα παρ' αὐτῷ, ἐστὶ ταῦτα· Ἄρρητος καὶ Σιγή, Πατὴρ καὶ Ἀλήθεια.

3. Ταύτης δὲ τῆς τετράδος ὁ σύμπας ἀριθμός ἐστι στοιχείων εἰκοσιτεσσάρων· ὁ γὰρ Ἄρρητος ἔχει στοιχεῖα ἑπτ(ά), ἡ Σ<ε>ιγὴ πέ(ντ)ε, καὶ ὁ Πατὴρ πέντε, καὶ <ἡ> Ἀλήθεια ἑπτά. ὡσαύτως δὲ καὶ ἡ δευτέρα τετράς, Λόγος καὶ Ζωή, Ἄνθρωπος καὶ Ἐκκλησία, τὸν αὐτὸν ἀριθμὸν τῶν στοιχείων ἀνέδειξαν.

4. καὶ τὸ τοῦ Σωτῆρος ῥητὸν ὄνομα γραμμάτων ὑπάρχειν ἕξ. τὸ δὲ ῥητὸν αὐτοῦ ἐπ' ἀριθμῷ τῶν κατὰ ἓν γραμμάτων—τουτέστι τὸν Ἰησοῦν—στοιχείων ἐστὶν εἰκοσιτεσσάρων· Υἱὸς δὲ Χρ<ε>ιστὸς δώδεκα.

τὸ δὲ ἐν τῷ Χριστῷ ἄρ(ρ)ητον γρ(αμμ)άτων τριάκοντα—καὶ αὐτὸ <ἐπὶ> τοῖς ἐν αὐτῷ γράμμασι κατὰ ἓν στοιχεῖον ἀριθμουμένοις· 5. τὸ γὰρ Χρ<ε>ιστός ἐστι στοιχείων ὀκτώ· τὸ μὲν γὰρ χεῖ τριῶν, τὸ δὲ ῥ<ῶ> δύο, καὶ τὸ εἶ δύο, καὶ <τὸ> ἰ<ῶτα> τεσσάρων, τὸ σ<ῖγμα> πέντε, καὶ τὸ τ<αῦ> τριῶν, τὸ δὲ οὖ δύο, καὶ τὸ <σὰ>ν τριῶν. οὕτως τὸ ἐν τῷ Χριστῷ ἄρρητον φάσκουσι στοιχείων τριάκοντα.—καὶ διὰ τοῦτο δέ φασιν αὐτὸν λέγειν· «ἐγὼ τὸ ἄλφα καὶ τὸ ω», ἐπιδεικνύντα τὴν περιστεράν, τοῦτον ἔχουσαν τὸν ἀριθμόν, ὅ ἐστιν ὀκτακόσια ἕν.

and four, added together, manifested the number six. These six, when multiplied by four, produced twenty-four. 2. The names of the first Tetrad, conceived of as the holy of holies, are not able to be spoken. They are known only by the Son as well as by the Father. But the [others,] who are named by him with silence and faith, are these: Unspeakable and Silence, Father and Truth.

3. The entire number of this Tetrad is made up of twenty-four letters. For Ineffable [Ἄρρητος] has seven letters, Silence [Σειγή] has five, Father [Πατήρ] has five, while Truth [Ἀλήθεια] has seven.[276] In the same way also, the second Tetrad—Word [Λόγος], Life [Ζωή], Human [Ἄνθρωπος], and Church ['Εκκλησία]—manifested the same number of letters.

4. The spoken name of the Savior has six letters. When this spoken name (i.e., Jesus ['Ιησοῦς]) is counted by the number of each individual letter, it adds up to twenty-four letters.[277] "Son Christ" [Υἱὸς Χρειστός] has twelve letters.

The secret name in Christ is made up of thirty letters—the number value arrived at by adding up its letters one by one. 5. For "Christ" [Χρειστός] has eight letters, the chi [χεῖ] three, the rho [ῥῶ] two, the epsilon [εἶ] two, the iota [ἰῶτα] four, the sigma [σῖγμα] five, the tau [ταῦ] three, the omicron [οὖ] two, and the san [σάν] three.[278] Thus they claim that the secret name in Christ is made up of thirty letters. For this reason, they say, he announces: "I am the alpha and the omega," indicating the dove, which possesses this number (namely, 801).[279]

276. Cf. the names of the aeons in Iren., *Haer.* 1.11.1 (*Inenarrabile, Sigen, Patrem, Alethian*).

277. Ἰησοῦς = ἰῶτα + ἦτα + σῖγμα + οὖ + ὖ ψειλόν + σάν = 24 letters.

278. San (Ϻ) is an obsolete Greek letter that corresponded to the Hebrew tsade (צ). Here it is used as an alternative for sigma. Yet if we add the letters chi (χεῖ), rho (ῥῶ), epsilon (εἶ), iota (ἰῶτα), sigma (σῖγμα), tau (ταῦ), omicron (οὖ), and san (σάν), we only have twenty-four letters, not thirty. Harvey suggests taking the chi as two (χι), the epsilon as seven (ἒ ψειλόν), and the san as sigma (σῖγμα, thus five) to make thirty (Unger and Dillon, *St. Irenaeus*, 212 n. 3). Förster understands this passage as a gloss added to the text (*Marcus*, 318–19). Marcovich suspects a lacuna at the end of the sentence. Using Iren., *Haer.* 1.15.2, and Epiph., *Pan.* 34.9.8–9, he would fill it with the following: ἅ συντεθέντα τὸν τῶν εἰκοσιτεσσάρων στοιχείων ἐποίησεν ἀριθμόν· τούτῳ δὲ προστιθέασι τὸ ἐπίσημον αὐτοῦ ὄνομα, τουτέστι τὸν Ἰησοῦν, ὅπερ ἐστὶ στοιχείων ἕξ ("which, when added together, make the total of twenty-four letters. To this they add his noteworthy name, that is, Jesus, which has six letters").

279. For the alpha and omega, see Rev 1:8; 21:6; 22:13. For the number of the

50. 1. Ὁ δὲ Ἰησοῦς ταύτην μὲν ἔχει τὴν ἄρρητον γένεσιν· ἀπὸ γὰρ τῆς μητρὸς τῶν ὅλων, τῆς πρώτης τετράδος, ἐν θυγατρὸς τρόπῳ προῆλθεν ἡ δευτέρα τετράς, καὶ ἐγένετο ὀγδοάς, ἐξ ἧς προῆλθεν ἡ δεκάς· 2. οὕτως ἐγένετο [ἰῶτα εἶτα] δεκαοκτώ. ἡ οὖν δεκάς, ἐπισυνελθοῦσα τῇ ὀγδοάδι καὶ δεκαπλασίονα αὐτὴν ποιήσασα, τὸν τῶν ὀγδοήκοντα <προεβίβασεν ἀριθμόν· καὶ τὰ ὀγδοήκοντα> πάλιν δεκαπλασιάσασα τὸν τῶν ὀκτακοσίων ἀριθμὸν ἐγέννησεν· ὥστε εἶναι τὸν ἅπαντα τῶν γραμμάτων ἀριθμόν, ἀπὸ ὀγδοάδος εἰς δεκά<δα> προελθόντα, [εἶναι] η καὶ π καὶ ω, ὅ ἐστιν Ἰησοῦς. τὸ γὰρ Ἰησοῦς ὄνομα κατὰ τὸν ἐν τοῖς γράμμασιν ἀριθμόν ἐστιν ὀκτακόσια ὀγδοηκονταοκτώ.

3. <διὸ> καὶ τὸ<ν> ἀλφάβητον δὲ τὸ<ν> Ἑλληνικὸν ἔχει<ν> μονάδας ὀκτὼ <καὶ δεκάδας ὀκτὼ> καὶ ἑκατοντάδας ὀκτώ, τὴν τῶν ὀκτακοσίων ὀγδοηκονταοκτὼ ψῆφον ἐπιδεικνύοντα, τουτέστι τὸν Ἰησοῦν, ἐκ πάντων συνεστῶτα τῶν ἀριθμῶν. καὶ διὰ τοῦτο ἄλφα <καὶ ω> ὀνομάζεσθαι αὐτόν, τὴν ἐκ πάντων <αὐτοῦ> γένεσιν σημαίνοντα.

51. 1. Περὶ δὲ τῆς τούτου δημιουργίας ο(ὕ)τως λέγει· ἀπὸ τῆς τετράδος τῆς δευτέρας δυνάμεις ἀπορ<ρ>υεί(σ)α(ς) δεδημιουργηκέναι τὸν ἐπὶ γῆς φανέντα Ἰησοῦν· καὶ τοῦ Λόγου τὸν τό<πο>ν ἀναπεπληρωκέναι τὸν ἄγγελον Γαβριήλ, τῆς δὲ Ζωῆς τὸ ἅγιον Πνεῦμα, τοῦ δὲ Ἀνθρώπου τὴν τοῦ ὑψίστου δύναμιν, τῆς δὲ Ἐκκλησίας τὴν παρθένον, οὕτως ὁ κατ' οἰκονομίαν διὰ τῆς Μαρίας γενεσιουργεῖται παρ' αὐτῷ ἄνθρωπος.

THE GENERATION OF JESUS. 50. 1. Jesus has the following secret birth. From the Mother of the universe, the primal Tetrad, the second Tetrad came forth like a daughter. So the Ogdoad arose, from which emanated the decad. 2. In this way the number eighteen [ιη′] arose.[280] Now the decad, coming together with the Ogdoad and multiplying it ten times, brought forth the number eighty. And the eighty, again multiplied by ten, gave birth to the number eight hundred. Consequently, the total number of the written letters that emerges from the Ogdoad to the decad is 8, 80, and 800, which signifies Jesus. For the name of Jesus, according to the number in the written letters, is 888.[281]

3. Accordingly, the Greek alphabet has letter values equaling eight ones, eight tens, and eight hundreds, indicating the number value 888.[282] This is Jesus, the combined value of all the numbers. For this reason, he is named "alpha and omega," signifying his origin from all.[283]

JESUS. 51. 1. Now concerning the fashioning of Jesus, she speaks as follows. The powers that flowed out from the second Tetrad fashioned the Jesus who appeared on earth.[284] The angel Gabriel filled the role of the Word, the Holy Spirit filled the role of Life, the power of the Most High filled the role of the Human, and the virgin filled the role of the Church.[285] In this way, the "human" of God's divine plan (in his view) originated through Mary.

---

dove, see *Ref.* 6.47.2 above. Our author adapts the following section (*Ref.* 6.50) from Iren., *Haer.* 1.15.2; cf. Epiph., *Pan.* 34.9.1–4.

280. The letters ιη′, or eighteen, represent the first letters in Jesus's name (Ἰησοῦς) and can stand for the whole name (Barn. 9.8). Cf. Iren., *Haer.* 1.3.2; Epiph., *Pan.* 31.14.7; Clem. Alex., *Strom.* 6.11.84.3 (ιη signifies salvation).

281. ι′ + η′ + σ′ + ο′ + υ′ + σ′ = 888. Cf. Sib. Or. 1.324–331.

282. The Greek letters from α to θ (excluding the obsolete ϝ) represent Greek single-digit numbers; in turn, ι to ν represent double-digit numbers (the "tens"), and ρ to ω represent triple digits (the "hundreds"). See further Förster, *Marcus*, 330–31.

283. The following section (*Ref.* 6.51) our author adapts from Iren., *Haer.* 1.15.3; cf. Epiph., *Pan.* 34.10.1–7.

284. For the second Tetrad, see Iren., *Haer.* 1.1.1; 1.12.1; 1.14.5; 1.15.1; *Ref.* 6.29.7 ("Valentinus"); 6.46.2–3; 6.49.3.

285. See Luke 1:26, 35. Cf. the interpretation of Luke 1:35 in *Ref.* 6.35.3–4, and the Jesus made from four substances in Iren., *Haer.* 1.7.2. See further Orbe, *Cristología Gnóstica*, 1:37–38.

2. ἐλθόντος δὲ αὐτοῦ εἰς τὸ ὕδωρ, κατελθεῖν εἰς αὐτὸν ὡς περιστερὰν τὸν ἀναδραμόντα ἄνω καὶ πληρώσαντα τὸν δωδέκατον ἀριθμόν, ἐν ᾧ ὑπάρχει τὸ σπέρμα τούτων τῶν συσπαρέντων αὐτῷ καὶ συγκαταβάντων καὶ συναναβάντων. 3. ταύτην δὲ τὴν δύναμιν τὴν καταβᾶσαν εἰς αὐτὸν <σπέρμα> φησὶν εἶναι τοῦ πληρώματος, ἔχον ἐν ἑαυτῷ καὶ τὸν Πατέρα καὶ τὸν Υἱόν, τήν τε διὰ τούτων γινωσκομένην ἀνονόμαστον δύναμιν τῆς Σιγῆς καὶ τοὺς ἅπαντας αἰῶνας.

4. Καὶ τοῦτο εἶναι τὸ πνεῦμα τὸ ἐν αὐτῷ φω<νῆ>σαν διὰ τοῦ στόματος τοῦ Ἰησοῦ, τὸ ὁμολογῆσαν ἑαυτὸ Υἱὸν ἀνθρώπου καὶ φανερῶσαν τὸν Πατέρα· κατελθὸν μέντοι γε εἰς τὸν Ἰησοῦν ἡνῶσθαι αὐτῷ. καθεῖλε μὲν τὸν θάνατον, φασίν, ὁ ἐκ οἰκονομίας σωτὴρ <Ἰησοῦς>, ἐγνώρισε δὲ τὸν Πατέρα Χριστόν [Ἰησοῦν].

5. εἶναι οὖν τὸν Ἰησοῦν ὄνομα μὲν τοῦ ἐκ τῆς οἰκονομίας ἀνθρώπου λέγει, τεθεῖσθαι δὲ <εἰς> ἐξομοίωσιν καὶ μόρφωσιν τοῦ μέλλοντος εἰς αὐτὸν κατέρχεσθαι Ἀνθρώπου· ὃν χωρήσαντα αὐτὸν ἐσχηκέναι, αὐτόν τε [εἶναι] τὸν Ἄνθρωπον, αὐτόν τὸν Λόγον, αὐτὸν τὸν Πατέρα καὶ <τὸν> Ἄρρητον καὶ τὴν Σιγὴν καὶ τὴν Ἀλήθειαν καὶ Ἐκκλησίαν καὶ Ζωήν.

52. 1. Ταῦτα μὲν οὖν πρόδηλα εἶναι πᾶσιν ἐλπίζω τοῖς ὑγιαίνοντα νοῦν κεκτημένοις ὄντα ἄκυρα καὶ μακρὰν τῆς κατὰ θεοσέβειαν γνώσεως, ὄντα μέρη ἀστρολογικῆς ἐφευρέσεως καὶ ἀριθμητικῆς Πυθαγορείου, καθὼς οἱ φιλομαθεῖς εἴσεσθε, ἐν τοῖς προμεριμνηθεῖσιν ἡμῖν ἐκκειμένων τούτων τῶν δογμάτων. 2. ἵνα δὲ σαφέστερον τούτους ἐπιδείξωμεν οὐ Χριστοῦ μαθητάς, ἀλλὰ Πυθαγόρου καὶ

2. When he came to the water, there came down upon him as a dove the number that runs up above and fulfills the twelfth number.[286] In him exists the seed of those sown together with him, who descend and ascend with him. 3. This power that descended on him, he says, is a seed of the Fullness, having in itself both the Father and the Son, as well as the unnamable power of Silence that is known through them, together with all the aeons.

4. This is the very Spirit that spoke from within through the mouth of Jesus, that confessed itself to be "Son of a Human" and manifested the Father.[287] When it descended on Jesus, furthermore, it was united with him. Jesus, the Savior ordained by God's plan, destroyed death, they say, and made known his Father Christ.[288]

5. She says that Jesus is the name of the human ordained by God's plan, and that the name was placed on him as an assimilation and formation according to the Human who was about to descend into him. When Jesus made room for him, he possessed him. He possessed the Human himself, the Word itself, the Father himself, along with the Ineffable, Silence, Truth, Church, and Life.[289]

52. 1. Now I hope that these defunct teachings—which are miles away from the knowledge of godliness—are clear to those of sound mind. They are a pastiche of astrological invention and Pythagorean arithmetic (as the diligent students among you will know from my former remarks about their teachings).[290] 2. Yet, so that I can more clearly expose them as dis-

286. Marcovich understands the twelfth number to be mu (μ). Jesus is the Logos (Λόγος), represented by the lambda (Λ), which is both the eleventh letter of the Greek alphabet and the letter representing the number thirty. Lambda plus lambda (Λ + Λ or ΛΛ) = M (the twelfth number). Cf. the account in Iren., *Haer.* 1.7.2; 1.16.2; *Ref.* 6.52.9–10; Sagnard, *Gnose*, 383–85.

287. The spiritual seed, or Savior, is called the Spirit who speaks through Jesus. The Jesus unified with the Savior can call himself "Son of the Human." The "Human" could refer to the aeon in the second Tetrad or to the Forefather himself (Iren., *Haer.* 1.12.4). But here the Human seems to be identified with the Spiritual Savior who descends on Jesus and makes him "son" (see further Sagnard, *Gnose*, 361–62, esp. 375). The Human was previously identified with the Power of the Most High (*Ref.* 6.51.1) present at Jesus's birth.

288. Rousseau and Doutreleau argue that Christ, as the Savior on high, is the Father of the Jesus of the economy (*Contre les hérésies* [SC 263], 1:1.256; cf. Förster, *Marcus*, 354).

289. Jesus receives the whole primal Ogdoad. Our author here omits Irenaeus's lengthy refutation of Markos's doctrines.

290. Cf. *Ref.* 1.2.5–10; 4.43.4–44.3 ("Egyptian" teachings); 4.51.1–9; 6.23–28.

τῶν περὶ τὰ μετέωρα [τῶν] ἀστρ<ολόγ>ων ἀπ<η>(ο)λημένων, ὅσα ἐπιτομῇ δυνατόν ἐστιν ἐκθήσομαι. λέγουσι γὰρ ταῦτα·

Ἐκ (μ)ονάδος καὶ δυά(δ)ος τὰ ὅλα συνεστάναι· καὶ ἀπὸ μὲν μονάδος ἕως τῶν τεσσάρων ἀριθμοῦντες οὕτως γεννῶσι τὴν δεκάδα. 3. πάλιν δ' αὖ <ἡ> δυὰς προελθοῦσα ἕως τοῦ ἐπισήμου, οἷον δύο καὶ τέσσαρες καὶ ἕξ, τὴν δωδεκάδα ἐπέδειξε. καὶ πάλιν ἀπὸ τῆς δυάδος ἀριθμούντων ἡμῶν ἕως τῶν δέκα ἡ τριακοντὰ<ς> ἀνεδείχθη, ἐν ᾗ ὀγδοὰς καὶ δεκὰς καὶ δωδεκάς. 4. τὴν οὖν δωδεκάδα, διὰ τὸ ἐπίσημ(ον) ἐσχηκέναι συνεπακολουθῆσαν αὐτῇ, [τὸ ἐπίσημον] πάθος. καὶ διὰ τοῦτο, περὶ τὸν δωδέκατον ἀριθμὸν τοῦ σφάλματος γενομένου, τὸ πρόβατον ἀποσκιρτῆσαν πεπλανῆσθαι. ὁμοίως δὲ καὶ ἐπὶ τῆς δεκάδος·

5. καὶ ἐπὶ τούτων τὴν δραχμὴν λέγουσιν, ἣν ἀπολέσασα γυνή, ἅψασα λύχνον ἐζήτει. τὴν τὲ ἐπὶ ἑνὶ προβάτῳ ἀπώλειαν καὶ <τὸν> τῶν ἐνενήκοντα ἐννέα συντιθέντες, ἑαυτοῖς ἀριθμὸν μυθεύουσιν, ὡς τῶν ἕνδεκα ἐπισυμπλεκομένων τοῖς ἐννέα ποιεῖν τὸν τῶν ἐνενήκοντα ἐννέα ἀριθμόν· καὶ τούτου χάριν λέγεσθαι τὸ ἀμήν, περιέχον ἀριθμὸν ἐνενήκοντα ἐννέα.

ciples, not of Christ, but of Pythagoras and of those astrologers confused about celestial phenomena, I will present what I can in summary form.[291] They proclaim the following.[292]

SUMMARY OF MARKOSIAN TEACHING. The universe is composed from the Monad and the Dyad. By counting up the numbers from one to four (1 + 2 + 3 + 4) they generate the Decad. 3. In turn, when the Dyad advanced to the number six (2 + 4 + 6) it manifested the Dodecad. Once again, when we count from the Dyad to the Decad (2 + 4 + 6 + 8 + 10), the Triacontad is revealed. The Triacontad contains the Ogdoad, Decad, and Dodecad. 4. They call the Dodecad a passion, since it has the number six closely following it.[293] For this reason, when the twelfth number fell, the sheep skipped off and wandered away.[294] Likewise in the case of the Decad.[295]

5. In addition, they speak of the drachma that the woman lost and looked for after lighting a lamp.[296] And, by combining the loss of one sheep with the ninety-nine, they mythologize to themselves about this number, since when eleven is multiplied by nine it makes the number ninety-nine.[297] For this reason the "Amen" is said, since it contains the number 99.[298]

291. Marcovich prints ἀστρολόγων ἀπηολημένων (here: "of astrologers confused…"). P reads ἄστρων απ·ολημένων (with missing letter).

292. The following "summary" is adapted from Iren., *Haer.* 1.16.1–2; cf. Epiph., *Pan.* 34.12.1–14. Our author likely reproduced this material because the technical language is reminiscent of Pythagorean thought.

293. In this sentence, Marcovich has neglected to omit one of the instances of τὸ ἐπίσημον (see Rousseau and Doutreleau, *Contre les hérésies* [SC 263], 1:1.257–58). On the textual problems here, see Kalvesmaki, *Theology*, 78–79 n. 28. The six that follows the Dodecad may refer to Jesus coming to heal the passions of Wisdom (Förster, *Marcus*, 368). On the passion associated with the Dodecad, see Iren., *Haer.* 1.16.1 (*Duodecadem … passionem vocant*); 1.3.3; 2.20.1.

294. For the lost sheep, see Matt 18:12; Luke 15:4; Iren., *Haer.* 1.8.4 (spoken of Wisdom); 1.23.2 (spoken of Helen); Epiph., *Pan.* 21.3.5; Tert., *An.* 34.4; *Ref.* 6.19.2 ("Simon"); Gos. Truth (NHC I,3) 31.35–32.30; Gos. Thom. 107.

295. In Iren., *Haer.* 1.16.1, a power perishes from the Dodecad, not the Decad.

296. Luke 15:8; Iren., *Haer.* 1.8.4; Ap. Jas. (NHC I,2) 8.9.

297. Our author has compressed the account in Iren., *Haer.* 1.16.1 to the point of incomprehension. The math is: (12 sheep – 1 = 11) x (10 drachmae – 1 = 9) = 99. It is odd that the lost sheep is one from twelve rather than (as in the traditional parable) one from one hundred. But the mythology of the fallen aeon requires a breaking away of one from twelve. Cf. the lost sheep parable in Gos. Truth (NHC I,3) 31.35–32.17, along with Förster, *Marcus*, 385–87.

298. (12–1) x (10–1) = 99 and α′ + μ′ + η′ + ν′ = 99. The number 99 is the preemi-

6. Ἄλλον δὲ ἀριθμὸν οὕτω λέγουσι· τὸ ἦτα στοιχεῖον σὺν τῷ ἐπισήμῳ ὀγδοάδα εἶναι, ἀπὸ τοῦ ἄλφα ὀγδόῳ κείμενον τόπῳ· εἶτα πάλιν ἄνευ τοῦ ἐπισήμου ψηφίζοντες τὸν ἀριθμὸν αὐτῶν τῶν στοιχείων καὶ συντιθέντες μέχρι τοῦ ἦτα, τὸν τριάκοντα ἀριθμὸν ἐπιδεικνύουσιν. 7. ἀρξάμενος γάρ τις ἀπὸ τοῦ ἄλφα ἕως τοῦ ἦτα <κατὰ> τὸν ἀριθμὸν τῶν στοιχείων, ὑπεξαιρούμενος τὸ ἐπίσημον, εὑρήσει τριάκοντα ἀριθμόν.

ἐπεὶ οὖν ἐκ τῶν τριῶν δυνάμεων ἥνωται ὁ τῶν τριάκοντα ἀριθμός, <τρὶς> αὐτὸς γενόμενος τὰ ἐνενήκοντα ἐποίησε—τρὶς γὰρ τριάκοντα ἐνενήκοντα—. <καὶ αὐτὴ δὲ ἡ τριὰς ἐφ' ἑαυτὴν συντεθεῖσα ἐννέα ἐγέννησεν.> 8. οὕτως ἡ ὀγδοὰς τὸν τῶν ἐνενήκοντα ἐννέα ἀπεκύησεν ἀριθμόν. <τουτέστιν> ἐκ πρώτης ὀγδοάδος καὶ δωδεκά(δ)ος καὶ δεκάδος· ἧς ποτὲ μὲν ὡς ὁλοκλήρου συνάγοντες τὸν ἀριθμὸν ποιοῦσι τριακοντάδα· ποτὲ δὲ τὸν δωδέκατον ὑφαιροῦντες ποιοῦσι(ν) ἕνδεκα, καὶ ὁμοίως τὸν δέκατον ψηφίζουσιν ἐννέα, ταῦτά τε ἐπισυμπλέκοντες [καὶ δεκαπλασιάσαντες] ἀριθμὸν ἐπιτελοῦσι <τὸν> τῶν ἐνενήκοντα ἐννέα.

9. Ἐπειδὴ δὲ ὁ δωδέκατος αἰὼν καταλείψας τοὺς ἕνδεκα καὶ ἀποστὰς κάτω ἐχώρησε, φάσκουσι κατάλληλον καὶ τοῦτο· ὁ γὰρ τύπος τῶν γραμμάτων διδάσκει. ἑνδέκατον γὰρ τῶν γραμμάτων κεῖσθαι τὸ λ, ὅ ἐστιν ἀριθμὸς τῶν τριάκοντα, <καὶ> κεῖσθαι αὐτὸ κατ' εἰκόνα τῆς ἄνω οἰκονομίας, ἐπειδὴ ἀπὸ τοῦ ἄλφα—χωρὶς τοῦ ἐπισήμου—αὐτῶν τῶν γραμμάτων ὁ ἀριθμὸς ἕως τοῦ λ συντ(ε)θειμένος <κατὰ> τὴν παραύξησιν τῶν γραμ(μά)τω(ν) σὺν αὐτῷ τῷ λ τὸν <τῶν> ἐνενήκοντα ἐννέα ποιεῖ ἀριθμόν.

10. ὅτι δὲ τὸ λ, ἑνδεκάτῳ κείμενον τόπῳ, ἐπὶ τὴν τοῦ ὁμοίου αὐτῷ κατῆλθε ζήτησιν, ἵνα ἀναπληρώσῃ τὸν δωδέκατον ἀριθμόν, καὶ εὑρὸν αὐτὸν ἐπληρώθη, φανερὸν εἶναι ἐξ αὐτοῦ τοῦ σχήματος τοῦ στοιχείου. τὸ γὰρ Λ, ὥσπερ ἐπὶ τὴν τοῦ ὁμοίου αὐτῷ ζήτησιν παραγενόμενον, καὶ εὑρὸν <καὶ> ἀναρπάσαν τὴν τοῦ δωδεκάτου ἀνεπλήρωσε χώραν, τοῦ Μ στοιχείου ἐκ δύο Λ [καὶ η] συγκειμένου.

11. διὸ δὴ καὶ φ<ε>ύγειν αὐτοὺς διὰ τῆς γνώσεως τὴν τῶν ἐνενήκοντα ἐννέα χώραν—τουτέστι τὸ ὑστέρημα—τύπον ἀριστερᾶς χειρός, μεταδιώκειν

6. They give the following account about another number. The letter eta [η] along with the digamma [ϛ] is the Ogdoad, since it is in the eighth place from the alpha.[299] Then again, when they calculate the numerical value of the letters as far as eta without the digamma and add them up, they derive the number thirty. 7. For if one starts adding the numerical values from alpha to eta—excluding the digamma—one will find the number thirty.[300]

Now since the number thirty came together as a unit from three powers [Ogdoad, Decad, and Dodecad], it tripled itself and made ninety (since 3 x 30 = 90). Then the Triad was multiplied by its very self and produced nine.[301] 8. In this way, the Ogdoad gave birth to the number ninety-nine. That is to say, the primal Ogdoad, Dodecad, and Decad sometimes come together as a whole to make the Triacontad. At other times, after subtracting the twelfth [from the Dodecad] to make eleven, and the tenth [from the Decad] to make nine, they multiply these numbers together and end up with the number ninety-nine.

9. When the twelfth aeon abandoned the eleven, broke away, and came below, they claim that the following happened next. (Here the shapes of the letters are instructive.) The eleventh letter is lambda, whose numerical value is thirty. Lambda is the image of God's higher plan, since when we incrementally add up the numerical values of the letters from the alpha up to and including lambda (not including the digamma), we arrive at ninety-nine.[302]

10. Being in the eleventh place, the lambda came down to search for what is like it to make the number twelve full again. Once it found the missing letter, it was complete. This is clear from the shape of the lambda itself. For the lambda [Λ], just as it arrived to search for its equal, found it, seized it, and filled again the place of the twelfth letter, mu [M], which is made from two lambdas [ΛΛ].

11. And so, through their knowledge, these people fled the place of the ninety-nine (that is, deficiency), which is the pattern of the left hand. They

---

nent number of the deficiency (Rousseau and Doutreleau, *Contre les hérésies* [SC 263], 1:1.258).

299. α (1), β (2), γ (3), δ (4), ε (5), ϛ (6), ζ (7), η (8).

300. α (1) + β (2) + γ (3) + δ (4) + ε (5) + ζ (7) + η (8) = 30.

301. Cruice supplies this sentence from the Greek of Irenaeus preserved in Epiph., *Pan.* 34.12.10 (corresponding to Iren., *Haer.* 1.16.2). It is needed to complete the sense.

302. 1 + 2 + 3 + 4 + 5 + 7 + 8 + 9 + 10 + 20 + 30 = 99.

δὲ τὸ ἕν, ὃ προστεθὲν τοῖς ἐνενήκοντα ἐννέα εἰς τὴν δεξιὰν αὐτοὺ<ς> χεῖρα μετέ<στησεν.

Αὐτὴν δὲ τὴν κτίσιν κατ' εἰκόνα τῶν ἀοράτων ὑπὸ τοῦ δημιουργοῦ, ὡς ἀγνοοῦντος αὐτοῦ, κατε>σκευάσθαι διὰ τῆς Μητρὸς λέγουσι· **53.** 1. Πρῶτον μὲν τὰ τέσσαρα στοιχεῖά [ἃ] φησίν—πῦρ, ὕδωρ, γῆν, ἀέρα—εἰκόνα προβεβλῆσθαι τῆς ἄνω τετράδος· τάς τε ἐνεργείας αὐτῶν συναριθμοῦντες, οἷον θερμόν, ψυχρόν, ὑγρόν, ξηρόν, λέγουσιν ἀκριβῶς ἐξεικονίζειν τὴν ὀγδοάδα. 2. ἑξῆς δέκα δυνάμεις οὕτω καταριθμοῦσιν· ἑπτὰ σώματα κυκλοειδῆ, ἃ καὶ οὐρανοὺς καλοῦσιν, ἔπειτα τὸν περιεκτικὸν αὐτῶν κύκλον, ὃν καὶ ὄγδοον οὐρανὸν ὀνομάζουσι, πρὸς δὲ τούτοις ἥλιόν τε καὶ σελήνην. 3. καὶ ταῦτα δέκα ὄντα τὸν ἀριθμὸν εἰκόνας λέγουσιν εἶναι τῆς ἀοράτου δεκάδος, τῆς ἀπὸ Λόγου καὶ Ζωῆς <προελθούσης>.

τὴν δωδεκάδα διὰ τοῦ ζῳδιακοῦ καλουμένου κύκλου· τὰ γὰρ δώδεκα ζῴδια φανερώτατα τὴν τοῦ Ἀνθρώπου καὶ τῆς Ἐκκλησίας θυγατέρα Δωδεκάδα ἀποσκιάζειν λέγουσι.

4. Καὶ ἐπεὶ ἀντεζεύχθη, φασί, τῇ τῶν ὅλων ἀναφορᾷ, ὠκυτάτῃ ὑπαρχούσῃ, ὁ ὕπερθεν ο(ὐ)ρανός, ὁ πρὸς αὐτῷ τῷ κύτει βαρύνων καὶ ἀντιταλαντεύων τὴν ἐκείνων ὠκύτητα τῇ ἑαυτοῦ βραδυτῆτι, ὡς ἐν τριάκοντα ἔτεσι τὴν περίοδον

pursued the single sheep that, when added to the ninety-nine, transferred them to the right hand.[303]

CREATION AS A SYMBOL OF DIVINE REALITY. They say that the creation itself was constructed by the Mother in the image of the invisible realities through the ignorant Artificer.[304] **53.** 1. First of all, he says that the four elements—fire, water, earth, and air—have been emanated as an image of the Tetrad on high.[305] When one adds to them their qualities (that is, heat, cold, moisture, and dryness), they say that their sum accurately replicates the Ogdoad. 2. Next, they number the ten powers in this way: there are seven circular bodies, which they call "heavens." Then, there is the circle containing them (which they accordingly name "eighth heaven"). In addition, there are the sun and moon. 3. These, being ten in number, are images, they say, of the invisible Decad, which came forth from Word and Life.[306]

The Dodecad is indicated through the so-called zodiacal circle. For the twelve brightest zodiacal signs, they say, are a shadowy image of the Dodecad, daughter of Human and Church.

4. Moreover, the highest heaven above was joined, they say, to the extremely swift rotation of all the zodiacal constellations. This highest heaven weighed directly against the vault and counterbalanced the zodiac's swiftness with its slowness. As a result, [Saturn's] revolution from one sign

---

303. "They" are apparently the disciples of Markos. The ancients could count up to ninety-nine with their left hand but switched to the right when they reached one hundred. See further Gos. Truth (NHC I,3) 31.35–32.16; Iren., *Haer.* 2.24.6; Augustine, *In ev. Io.* 122.7 (CCSL 36:672,50). Sagnard points out that the lambda as signifying the number thirty indicates that the Savior (thirty, or the plenitude of aeons) is identical to the Λόγος (whose name starts with Λ) (*Gnose*, 383). For the deficiency, see *Ref.* 6.31.6 ("Valentinus"); 6.54.1; 10.13.2; Iren., *Haer.* 1.14.1; 1.16.2–3; 1.17.2; 1.19.1; 1.21.4; Epiph., *Pan.* 31.4.1; Clem. Alex., *Exc.* 22.7. The following section (*Ref.* 52.11–54.2) is adapted from Iren., *Haer.* 1.17.1–2. Our author again skips over Irenaeus's refutation (cf. Epiph., *Pan.* 34.14.1–12).

304. Most of this sentence (from Αὐτήν to κατε-) is supplied by Marcovich from Epiph., *Pan.* 34.14.1, corresponding to Iren., *Haer.* 1.17.1. Cf. *Ref.* 6.33.1; 6.34.8 ("Valentinus").

305. Earlier our author argued that the Tetrad (= Tetraktys), imaged by the four elements, is a Pythagorean idea (cf. *Ref.* 6.28.2), as also the notion of a fiery Artificer who presides over seven heavens (*Ref.* 6.32.7–8 ["Valentinus"]).

306. Marcovich adds προελθούσης (here: "came forth").

ἀπὸ σημείου ἐπὶ σημεῖον ποιεῖσθαι, εἰκόνα λέγουσιν αὐτὸν τοῦ Ὅρου, τοῦ τὴν τριακοντώνυμον Μητέρα αὐτῶν περιέχοντος.

5. τὴν σελήνην τε πάλιν, τὸν οὐρανὸν ἐκπεριε<ρ>χομένην ἐν τριάκοντα ἡμέραις, διὰ τῶν ἡμερῶν τὸν ἀριθμὸν τῶν αἰώνων ἐκτυποῦν.

καὶ τὸν ἥλιον δέ, ἐν δώδεκα μησὶν ἐκπεριε<ρ>χόμενον καὶ τερματίζοντα τὴν κυκλικὴν αὐτοῦ ἀποκατάστασιν, τὴν δωδεκάδα φανεροῦν. 6. καὶ αὐτὰς δὲ τὰς ἡμέρας, δώδεκα ὡρῶν τὸ μέτρον ἐχούσ(ας), τύπον τῆς <φαεινῆς> δωδεκάδος εἶναι.

καὶ αὐτοῦ δὲ τοῦ ζῳδιακοῦ κύκλου τὴν περίμετρον εἶναι μοιρῶν τριακοσίων ἑξήκοντα· ἕκαστον ζῴδιον μοίρας ἔχειν τριάκοντα· 7. οὕτω δὴ καὶ διὰ τοῦ κύκλου τὴν εἰκόνα τῆς συναφείας τῶν δώδεκα πρὸς <τὰ> τριάκοντα τετηρῆσθαι λέγουσιν.

ἔτι μὴν καὶ τὴν γῆν εἰς δώδεκα κλίματα διῃρῆσθαι φάσκοντες, καὶ καθ᾽ ἓν ἕκαστον κλίμα ἀνὰ μίαν δύναμιν ἐκ τῶν οὐρανῶν κατὰ κάθετον ὑποδεχομένην καὶ ὡμοιωμένα τίκτουσαν τέκνα τῇ καταπεμπούσῃ [κατὰ] τὴν ἀπόρροιαν δυνάμει, τύπον τῆς ἄνω δωδεκάδος.

54. 1. Πρὸς δὲ τούτοις, θελήσαντά τὸν δημιουργὸν τῆς ἄνω Ὀγδοάδος τὸ ἀπέραντον καὶ αἰώνιον καὶ ἀόριστον καὶ ἄχρονον μιμήσασθαι, καὶ μὴ δυνηθέντα τὸ μόνιμον αὐτῆς καὶ τὸ ἀΐδιον ἐκτυπῶσαι, διὰ τὸ καρπὸν α(ὐ)τὸν εἶναι ὑστερήματος, εἰς [τοῦτο] χρόνους καὶ καιρούς, ἀριθμούς τε πολυετεῖς [πρὸς] τὸ αἰώνιον αὐτῆς <κατα>τεθεῖσθαι, οἰόμενον ἐν τῷ πλήθει τῶν χρόνων μιμήσασθαι αὐτῆς τὸ <ἀόριστον>. 2. ἐνταῦθα δὲ λέγουσιν, ἐκφυγούσης αὐτὸν τῆς ἀληθείας, ἐπηκολουθηκέναι τὸ ψεῦδος, καὶ διὰ τοῦτο, πληρωθέντων τῶν χρόνων, κατάλυσιν λαβεῖν αὐτοῦ τὸ ἔργον.

in the zodiac back to the same sign is made in thirty years. This, they say, is an image of Boundary, who contains their Mother of thirty names.

5. In turn, the moon, by encircling heaven in thirty days, typifies through these days the number of the aeons.

The sun, moreover, by encircling and finishing its own orbit in twelve months, manifests the Dodecad. 6. The days themselves, since they are twelve hours long, are a type of the shining Dodecad.[307]

The zodiacal circle itself is 360 degrees in circumference (for each zodiacal sign has thirty degrees). 7. Thus through the image of this circle, they say, one observes an illustration of the connection between the Dodecad and the Triacontad.[308]

Still more, they assert that the earth is a symbol of the Dodecad on high since it is divided into twelve zones, with each individual zone receiving one power sent straight down from the heavens above. The earth, moreover, bears children assimilated to the power that sends down the emanation.

54. 1. In addition to these teachings, they say that the Artificer wanted to imitate the infinity, eternity, boundlessness, and timelessness of the Ogdoad on high. Since, however, he was unable to express its stability and eternity (because he is the fruit of deficiency) he reduced its eternity to times, seasons, and numbers consisting of many years, thinking that by the plenitude of times he imitated its boundlessness.[309] 2. Hence they say that when Truth fled from him, the lie followed after him.[310] It is for this reason that, when the times are fulfilled, his work dissolves.[311]

---

307. The Roman day, which began at sunrise and ended at sunset, was divided into twelve equal hours. "Shining" (φαεινῆς) is Marcovich's emendation (based on Epiph., *Pan.* 34.14.7) of P's κενῆς ("empty"). Legge suggests μεγάλης (*Philosophumena*, 2:56 n. 2). Latin Iren., *Haer.* 1.17.1 reads: *non apparentis Duodecadis* ("the *invisible* Dodecad").

308. See further Unger and Dillon, *St. Irenaeus*, 218 n. 6. For Markos on astrology, see von Stuckrad, *Ringen*, 643–49.

309. Marcovich emends P's τεθεῖσθαι to κατατεθεῖσθαι ("reduced") and changes P's ἀόρατον ("invisible [nature]") to ἀόριστον ("boundlessness").

310. See further Henri-Charles Puech, "La Gnose et le temps," in *En quête de la Gnose: La Gnose et le temps et autres essais*, 2 vols. (Paris: Gallimard, 1978), 1:215–70 (255–56).

311. In his conclusion below, our author adapts the first two sentences of Iren., *Haer.* 1.18.1 (cf. Epiph., *Pan.* 34.15.1), and then summarizes the Markosian allegorical use of Christian scripture while referencing the fuller treatment in Iren., *Haer.* 1.18–20.

55. 1. Ταῦτα μὲν οὖν οἱ ἀπὸ τῆς Οὐαλεντίνου σχολῆς περί τε τῆς κτίσεως καὶ περὶ τοῦ παντὸς λέγουσιν, ἑκάστοτε κενώτερα ἐπιγεννῶντες· καὶ τοῦτο καρποφορίαν νομίζουσιν, εἴ τις μεῖζον ὁμοίως ἐφευρὼν τερατ(ουρ)γ(εῖν) δόξει. 2. καὶ ἐκ τῶν γραφῶν ἕκαστα πρὸς τοὺς προειρημένους ἀριθμοὺς ἐφευρίσκοντες σύμφωνα, κατηγοροῦσι Μωσέως καὶ τῶν προφητῶν, φάσκοντες ἀλ<λ>ηγορικῶς αὐτοὺς τὰ μέτρα τῶν αἰώνων λέγειν·

ἃ παρατιθέναι μοι οὐκ ἔδοξε<ν, ὄν>τα φλύαρα καὶ ἀσύστατα, ἤδη τοῦ μακαρίου πρεσβυτέρου Εἰρηναίου δεινῶς καὶ πεπονημένως [ὡς] τὰ δόγματα αὐτῶν διελέγξαντος. παρ᾽ οὗ καὶ <ἡμεῖς τὰ> αὐτῶν ἐφευρήματα <μεταλαβόντες,> ἐπιδεικνύντες αὐτοὺς <ἐκ τῆς> Πυθαγορείου φιλοσοφίας καὶ ἀστρολόγων (π)εριε(ργ)ίας ταῦτα σφετερισαμένους ἐγκαλεῖν Χριστῷ ὡς ταῦτα παραδεδωκέναι.

3. ἀλλ᾽ ἐπεὶ ἱκανῶς νομίζω καὶ τὰ τούτων φλύαρα δόγματα ἐκτεθεῖσθαι, σαφῶς τε ἐπιδεδεῖχθαι τίνων εἶεν μαθηταὶ Μάρκος τε καὶ Κολάρβασος, οἱ τῆς Οὐαλεντίνου σχολῆς διάδοχοι γενόμενοι, ἴδωμεν τί λέγει καὶ Βασιλείδης.

CONCLUSION

55. 1. These are the teachings that the students of Valentinus's school affirm about the creation and about the universe. Each time, they give birth to things more meaningless. They consider it a "harvest" if someone, by similarly inventing something greater, seems to work wonders.[312] 2. By discovering in the scriptures something in accord with each of their aforementioned numbers, they slander Moses and the prophets—claiming that they allegorically speak the numerical quantities of the aeons.

These matters I decided not to set out for comparison, since they are inconsistent babblings. Moreover, the blessed presbyter Irenaeus has already refuted their dogmas with force and great toil. From him I also gathered information about their inventions, and I demonstrated that they appropriated them from Pythagorean philosophy and from the futile labor of the astrologers (although they accuse Christ of handing them down as tradition).[313]

3. But since I think that I adequately presented even their driveling doctrines—and clearly exposed the true teachers of Markos and Kolarbasos (successors of Valentinus's school)—let us also consider what Basileides affirms.[314]

---

312. On "heretics" introducing novelties, see Pouderon, "Hippolyte, un regard," 49–52.

313. Marcovich adds μεταλαβόντες ("gathered information [about their inventions]").

314. For Kolarbasos—added rather suddenly—see *Ref.* 4.13.1, where he is associated with number speculation. Irenaeus (*Haer.* 1.14.1) had spoken of the "Silence of Kolarbasos" (Silence being the chief Valentinian female aeon). In Ps.-Tert., *Adv. omn. haer.* 5, Kolarbasos is made a partner of Markos in the teaching of numerology. Epiphanios (*Pan.* 34.1 [anaceph.]) depicts Markos as a student, then a partner, of Kolarbasos. See further Förster, *Marcus*, 168–73. If Kolarbasos does in fact represent the Hebrew קול ארבע ("Voice of the Four"), he may represent another mystic name for the Tetrad, the chief revealer of Markos's numerological speculation.

ΤΟΥ ΚΑΤΑ ΠΑΣΩΝ ΑΙΡΕΣΕΩΝ ΕΛΕΓΧΟΥ Ζ

1. Τάδε ἔνεστιν ἐν τῇ ἑβδόμῃ τοῦ κατὰ πασῶν αἱρέσεων ἐλέγχου·

2. Τίς ἡ δόξα Βασιλείδου, καὶ ὅτι τοῖς Ἀριστοτέλους δόγμασι καταπλαγεὶς ἐξ αὐτῶν τὴν αἵρεσιν συνεστήσατο.

3. Καὶ τίνα Σατορνεῖλος λέγει, ὁ Βασιλείδῃ σχε<δ>ὸν ἀκμάσας.

4. Πῶς καὶ <Μέν>ανδρος ἐπεβάλετο εἰπεῖν ὑπὸ ἀγγέλων τὸν κόσμον γεγονέναι.

5. Τίς ἡ Μαρκίωνος ἀπόνοια, καὶ ὅτι τὸ δόγμα αὐτο<ῦ> οὐ καινὸν οὐδὲ ἐξ ἁγίων γραφῶν, ἀλλὰ Ἐμπεδοκλέους (τ)υγχάνει.

6. Πῶς Καρποκράτης ματαιάζει, καὶ αὐτὸς ὑπὸ ἀγγέλων τὰ ὄντα φάσκων γεγενῆσθαι.

7. Ὅτι Κήρινθος μηδὲν ἐκ γραφῶν <λαβών>, ἀλλ' ἐκ τῶν Αἰγυπτίοις δοξάντων, <τὴν> δόξαν συνεστήσατο.

8. Τίνα τὰ τοῖς Ἐβιωναίοις δοκοῦντα, καὶ ὅτι <ἔ>θεσιν Ἰουδαϊκοῖς μᾶλλον προσέχουσι.

9. Πῶς καὶ ὁ Θεόδοτος πεπλάνηται, ἃ μὲν <ἐκ> τῶν Ἐβιωναίων ἐρανισάμενος, <ἃ δ' ἐκ τοῦ Κηρίνθου>.

10. Καὶ τίνα Κέρδωνι ἔδοξε, καὶ αὐτῷ τὰ Ἐμπεδοκλέους εἰπόντι καὶ κακῶς προβιβάσ(α)ντι τὸν Μαρκίωνα.

11. Καὶ πῶς Λουκιανός, μαθητὴς γενόμενος Μαρκίωνος, <ἀπηρυθριασμένως> τὸν θεὸν ἐβλασφήμησεν.

BOOK 7

[Table of Contents]

1. The following is contained in the seventh book of the *Refutation of All Heresies.*

2. The view of Basileides, who, awestruck by Aristotle's dogmas, constructed his heresy from them.

3. What Satorneilos affirms, who flourished very near the time of Basileides.

4. How also Menandros presumed to say that the world was made by angels.

5. The madness of Markion, whose dogma is neither new nor derived from holy scripture, but is derived from Empedokles.

6. How Karpokrates blabbers to no end, who also claims that what exists was made by angels.

7. That Kerinthos took nothing from scripture but manufactured his doctrine from the doctrines of the Egyptians.

8. The views of the Ebionites, who, instead, cling to Jewish customs.[1]

9. How Theodotos also wandered astray, who borrows partly from Ebionite opinions and partly from those of Kerinthos.[2]

10. What Kerdon believed. He also voiced the doctrines of Empedokles and perversely promoted Markion.

11. How Loukianos, a disciple of Markion, shamelessly blasphemed God.[3]

1. Marcovich replaces P's ἤθεσιν ("character traits") with ἔθεσιν ("customs").

2. Miller supplies ἃ δ' τοῦ Κηρίνθου, and Marcovich supplies ἐκ ("and partly from those of Kerinthos").

3. Marcovich emends P's ἀπηρυθρίασε μόνος ("he alone was not ashamed") to ἀπηρυθριασμένως ("shamelessly"), in accordance with Iren., *Haer.* 1.27.2 (*impudorate*).

12. Ὅτι καὶ Ἀπελ<λ>ῆς, <καὶ Μαρκίωνος> γενόμενος μαθητής, οὐ τὰ αὐτὰ τῷ διδασκάλῳ ἐδογμάτισεν, ἀλλὰ ἐκ φυσικῶν δογμάτων κινηθεὶς τὴν οὐσίαν τοῦ παντὸς ὑπέθετο.

13. 1. Πελάγει κλυδωνιζομένῳ ὑπὸ βίας ἀνέμων ἐοικότα [ὁρῶντες] τὰ τῶν αἱρετικῶν δόγματα ἐχρῆν τοὺς ἀκροατὰς <ὁρμῶντας> παραπλεῖν, ἐπιζητοῦντας τὸν εὔδιον λιμένα. τὸ γὰρ τοιοῦτον πέλαγός ἐστι καὶ θηριῶδες καὶ δύσβατον, ὡς <φέρ'> εἰπεῖν τὸ Σικελιωτικόν, ἐν ᾧ μυθεύεται Κύκλωψ καὶ Χάρυβδις καὶ Σκύλ(λ)α (καὶ) (Πλ)α(γκταὶ) <καὶ> τὸ Σειρήνων ὄρος, ὃ διαπλεῦσαι τὸν Ὀδυσσέα φάσκουσιν Ἑλλήνων οἱ ποιηταὶ πανούργως χρησάμενον τῇ τῶν π<α>ραξέ<ν>ων θηρ<ί>ων δεινότητι· διάφορος γὰρ ἡ τούτων ὠμότης πρὸς τοὺς διαπλέοντας ἦν. 2. αἱ δὲ Σειρῆνες λιγὺ ᾄδουσαι καὶ μουσικῶς ἠπάτων τοὺς παραπλέοντας, πείθουσαι ἡδείᾳ φωνῇ προσάγειν τοὺς ἀκροωμένους. τοῦτο μαθόντα φασὶ τὸν Ὀδυσσέα κατακηρῶσαι τὰς ἀκοὰς τῶν ἑταίρων, ἑαυτὸν δὲ τῷ ξύλῳ προσδήσαντα παραπλεῦσαι ἀκινδύνως τὰς Σειρῆνας, κατακούσαντα τῆς τούτων ᾠδῆς.

3. ὃ ποιῆσαι τοῖς ἐντυγχάνουσιν συμβουλή, καὶ ἢ τὰ ὦτα κατακηρώσα(ν)τας δι' ἀσθένειαν διαπλεῦσαι τὰ τῶν αἱρετικῶν δόγματα, μηδε<νὸς> κατακούσαντας <τῶν> πείθειν εὐκόλως δυναμένων πρὸς ἡδονήν, ὡς λιγυρὸν ᾆσμα Σειρήνων, ἢ

12. That Apelles, also a disciple of Markion, did not pronounce the same doctrines as his teacher.[4] Rather, after receiving his inspiration from the doctrines of natural philosophy, he posited his view about the nature of the universe.

INTRODUCTION

13. 1. Since the doctrines of heretics are like a sea buffeted by high gales, those who hear them—if they seek after the serene harbor—must rush to sail through it.[5] A sea of this kind is both infested with monsters and difficult to cross, as, for instance, the Sicilian sea, in which dwelled the fabled Cyclops, Charybdis, Skylla, the Wandering Rocks, and the Sirens' mountain.[6] This mountain, Greek poets claim, Odysseus sailed by, craftily dealing with the fierceness of these extraordinary beasts, for their savagery against those who sailed by was exceptional. 2. The Sirens sang sweetly and deceived by their music those who sailed past, persuading their hearers by their lovely voice to draw near. Learning this beforehand, they say, Odysseus sealed the ears of his companions with wax, bound himself to the mast, and sailed by the Sirens without danger—though he listened to their song.[7]

3. My advice is that my readers do the same: namely, that they either stuff their ears with wax because they are too weak to sail past heretical teachings (not listening to what could, with its delight, easily convince them like the sweet song of the Sirens), or for them to bind themselves to the cross of Christ, remaining undisturbed because they listen to the Siren

---

4. Marcovich adds καὶ Μαρκίωνος ("also [a disciple] of Markion") based on the summary in *Ref.* 10.20.1.

5. Marcovich replaces ὁρῶντες with ὁρμῶντας (here: "rush").

6. After Σκύλ(λ)α (καί), P becomes unreadable. Marcovich conjectures πλαγκταί ("Wandering Rocks"); cf. Homer, *Od.* 23.326–328; Apollonios Rhodios, *Arg.* 4.924.

7. Cf. Homer, *Od.* 12.44–52, 160–183; Seneca, *Ep.* 31.2. Sirens in early Christian interpretation often signified unlawful pleasure (Pierre Courcelle, *Connais-toi toi-même: De Socrate à saint Bernard*, 3 vols. [Paris: Études augustiniennes, 1974–1975], 2:415–36; idem, "L'interprétation evhémériste des Sirènes-courtisane jusqu'au XIIe siècle," in *Gesellschaft, Kultur, Literatur: Rezeption und Originalität im Wachsen einer europäischen Literatur und Geistigkeit; Beiträge Luitpold Wallach Gewidmet*, ed. Karl Bosl, Monographien zur Geschichte des Mittelalters 11 [Stuttgart: Anton Hiersemann, 1975], 33–48 [34–36]).

ἑαυτὸν τῷ ξύλῳ Χριστοῦ προσδήσαντα, πιστῶς κατακούσαντα μὴ ταραχθῆναι, πεποιθότα ᾧ προσεσφίγγετ<ο>, καὶ ἑστηκέν<αι> ὀρθόν.

14. 1. Ἐπειδὴ οὖν ἐν ταῖς πρὸ ταύτης βίβλοις ἓξ ἐκτεθείμεθα τὰ πρότερα, δοκεῖ νῦν τὰ Βασιλείδου μὴ σιωπᾶν <ὄν>τα Ἀριστοτέλους τοῦ Σταγειρίτου δόγματα, οὐ Χριστοῦ. ἀλλ' εἰ καὶ πρότερον ἔκκειται τὰ Ἀριστοτέλει δοκοῦντα, οὐδὲ νῦν ὀκνήσομεν προϋποθέσθαι ἐν συντόμῳ, πρὸς τὸ τοὺς ἐντυγχάνοντας διὰ τῆς <τού>των ἐγγίονος ἀντιπαραθέσεως συνιδεῖν εὐκόλως τὰ ὑπὸ Βασιλείδου <ὑποβαλλόμενα> ὄντα Ἀριστοτελικὰ σοφιστεύματα.

15. 1. Ἀριστοτέλης μὲν οὖν τὴν οὐσίαν διαιρεῖ τριχῶς· ἔστι γὰρ αὐτῆς τὸ μέν τι γένος, τὸ δέ τι εἶδος [ὡς], τὸ δέ τι ἄτομον. ἄτομον δὲ οὐ διὰ σμικρότητα σώματος ἐκεῖνος λέγει, ἀλλὰ <τὸ> φύσει τομὴν ἀναδέξασθαι μηδ' ἡντιναοῦν δυνάμενον. 2. τὸ δὲ γένος ἐστὶν οἱονεὶ σωρός τις, ἐκ πολλῶν καὶ διαφόρων καταμεμιγμένος σπερμάτων, ἀφ' οὗ γένους οἱονεί τινος σωροῦ πάντα τὰ τῶν

song with faith, confident in the cross to which they are lashed, and standing upright.[8]

14. 1. Now, since I presented the foregoing in the previous six books, one must not keep secret the doctrines of Basileides. His source is Aristotle the Stageirite, not Christ. Even though Aristotle's views were presented beforehand,[9] I will not hesitate at this point to provide a preliminary summary for my readers so that they can easily discern, by means of closer comparison, that the stolen teachings of Basileides are the sophisms of Aristotle.[10]

THE TEACHINGS OF ARISTOTLE

THE DIVISION OF SUBSTANCE. **15.** 1. Aristotle divides substance in three ways: into genus, species, and the individual.[11] He calls the individual "undivided," not due to its small size, but because it cannot by nature receive any kind of division.[12] 2. The genus is a sort of heap, mixed together with many different seeds.[13] From this heap-like genus, all the

8. Cf. Homer, *Od.* 12.161–163; Clem. Alex., *Protr.* 118.4. For Clement, the Siren song represents both "custom" (συνήθεια) and Greek learning. Our author is the first to apply the Siren song to the knowledge of heresies (Hugo Rahner, "Antenna Crucis I: Odysseus am Mastbaum," *ZKT* 65 [1941]: 123–52 [136–39, 147]).

9. *Ref.* 1.20.

10. D. Holwerda supplies ὑποβαλλόμενα (here: "stolen") ("Textkritisches zum Basilides-Referat des Hippolytos," *Mnemosyne* 56 [2003]: 597–606 [597–98]).

11. For our author's review of Aristotle, see M. J. Edwards, "Hippolytus of Rome on Aristotle," *Eranos* 88 (1990): 25–29. Edwards believes that our author used an "orthodox Christian or Platonist" as his source, similar to the Middle Platonist Atticus (29). Similarly Ian Mueller, "Hippolytus, Aristotle, Basilides," in *Aristotle in Late Antiquity*, ed. Lawrence P. Schrenk, Studies in Philosophy and the History of Philosophy 27 (Washington, DC: Catholic University of America Press, 1994), 143–57 (147). Osborne more convincingly argues that our author used a Skeptical source that was already hostile to Aristotle (*Rethinking*, 36–40). Views on whether our author accurately represents Aristotle radically differ. Mueller argues for serious polemical distortion ("Hippolytus, Aristotle, Basilides," 157), while Abraham P. Bos vouches for basic reliability ("Basilides of Alexandria Disqualified as Not a Christian but an Aristotelian by the Author of the Elenchos," in Aragione and Norelli, *Des évêques*, 103–18 [114–16]). See the balanced discussion of Osborne, *Rethinking*, 58–67.

12. For the individual, see Aristotle, *Cat.* 2, 1b6; 3a35–8; b12–13. See further Mansfeld, *Heresiography*, 75–77.

13. Mueller believes that the term "heap" (σωρός) is "clearly imported from

γεγονότων εἴδη διακέ<κρ>ιται. καὶ ἔστι τὸ γένος ἓ(ν) ὂν πᾶσι τοῖς γεγενημένοις ἀρκοῦν.

ἵνα δὲ σαφὲς ἔσται τὸ λεγ(ό)μεν(ο)ν, δείξω διά του παραδείγματος, δι' οὗ ἐπὶ τὴν ὅλην τοῦ Περιπάτου θεωρίαν ἀναδραμεῖν ἔσται.

16. 1. Λέγομεν εἶναι ζῷον ἁπλῶς, οὐχὶ τὶ ζῷον· ἔστι δὲ τοῦτο τὸ ζῷον οὐ βοῦς, οὐχ ἵππος, οὐκ ἄνθρωπος, οὐ θεός, οὐκ ἄλλο τι τῶν ὁτιδήποτε ἔστι δηλοῦν, ἀλλ' ἁπλῶς ζῷον. ἀπὸ τούτου τοῦ ζῴου αἱ πάντων τῶν κατὰ μέρος ζῴων ἰδέαι τὴν ὑπόστασιν ἔχουσι.

2. καὶ ἔστι πᾶσι τοῖς ζῴοις τοῖς γεγενημένοις ἐν <ε>ἴδεσι τοῦτο τὸ ἀν<ε>ίδεον ζῷον <ἀρχή>, καὶ τῶν γεγενημένων οὐδέν <ἐστιν>. ἔστι γὰρ ζῷον ἄνθρωπος, ἀπ' ἐκείνου τοῦ ζῴου λαμβάνων τὴν ἀρχήν, καὶ ζῷον ἵππος, ἀπ' ἐκείνου τοῦ ζῴου λαμβάνων τὴν ἀρχήν. ὁ ἵππος καὶ βοῦς καὶ κύων καὶ τῶν ἄλλων ζῴων ἕκαστον ἀπὸ τοῦ ζῴου τοῦ ἁπλῶς λαμβάνει τὴν ἀρχήν, ὅ ἐστι τούτων οὐδὲ ἕν.

17. 1. Εἰ δὲ οὐκ ἔστι τούτων οὐδὲ ἓν ἐκεῖνο τὸ ζῷον, ἐξ οὐκ ὄντων γέγονεν κατ' Ἀριστοτέλην ἡ τῶν γεγενημένων ὑπόστασις. <ἐκεῖνο> γὰρ τὸ ζῷον, ὅθεν ταῦτα ἐλήφθη κατὰ μέρος, ἐστὶν οὐδὲ ἕν· οὐδὲ ἓν δὲ ὄν, γέγονε τῶν ὄντων μία τις ἀρχή. τίς δὲ ὁ ταύτην καταβεβλημένος τὴν <οὐκ οὖσαν> τῶν γεγονότων <ἀρχήν, ὕστερον> ἐροῦμεν, ἐπὶ τὸν οἰκεῖον ἐρχόμενοι τούτου λόγον.

species of generated beings are differentiated. Moreover the genus, though it is one, suffices for all generated beings.[14]

To make his discussion clear, I will illustrate via an example through which I can rehearse the entire Peripatetic theory.

GENUS. **16.** 1. Let us say that there is animal as such, not a particular animal. This animal is neither cow nor horse nor human, nor god—nor anything else whatever that it can indicate—but is simply "animal." From this animal, the forms of all individual animals have their existence.

2. Moreover, this animal—not part of a species—is the source for all those animals that arise in species.[15] Yet this animal is not one of those actually produced. For example, the human is an animal that originates from the genus "animal." The horse is also an animal that originates from the genus "animal." Thus the horse, cow, dog, and each of the other animals originates from the "animal" as such—which is not any one of these particular animals.[16]

17. 1. If the genus "animal" is not any one of these, then, according to Aristotle, the existence of actually existing beings came to be from things that do not exist. For the genus "animal," from which these particular animals were taken, is not one of them. But though it does not exist as one of them, it has become a single source of existent things.[17] (Who it was who proposed that the source of generated beings does not have existence I will say later when I come to the proper place.)[18]

Basileides." It occurs seven times in our author's report on Basileides ("Hippolytus, Aristotle, Basilides," 147 n. 12). See further Mansfeld, *Heresiography*, 131–32.

14. On the ambiguity of "being one" (ἓν ὄν), see Mansfeld, *Heresiography*, 110–11.

15. Marcovich, following Miller, adds ἀρχή ("source").

16. The genus "animal" (with only logical, not actual, existence) is the (apparently ontological) source for the (actually existing) species of animal. This point is necessary to understand in order to grasp our author's later argument that, according to Aristotle, beings come from nonbeing. See further Mansfeld, *Heresiography*, 111–13, 123–24.

17. Steven Strange notes that the idea of genus as a nonbeing probably derives from Aristotle's remark that if there is a separate account of each species of animal, then the universal animal is either nothing or logically posterior to species (*De an.* 1.1, 402b5–8) (cited in Mueller, "Hippolytus, Aristotle, Basilides," 146 n. 10). In the *Categories*, Aristotle remarks that "the parts of substances [τὰ μέρη τῶν οὐσιῶν], as being in whole subjects [ὡς ἐν ὑποκειμένοις ὄντα τοῖς ὅλοις], are not substances [οὐκ οὐσίας]" (1.5, 3a29–30).

18. I insert οὐκ ("not"). Οὖσαν is an emendation for P's οὐσίαν. Marcovich has switched the order of ὕστερον ἀρχήν (P), taking the ὕστερον with the apodosis in accor-

18. 1. Ἐπειδὴ ἔστιν ἡ οὐσία τριχῇ, ὡς ἔφην, γένος, εἶδος, ἄτομον, καὶ ἐθέμεθα τὸ ζῷον εἶναι γένος, τὸν δὲ ἄνθρωπον εἶδος, τῶν πολλῶν ζῴων ἤδη κεχωρισμένον, ἔτι συγκεχυμένον δὲ ὅμως ἔτι καὶ μήπω μεμορφωμένον εἰς εἶδος οὐσίας ὑποστατῆς, ὀνόματι μορφώσας τὸν ἀπὸ τοῦ γένους ληφθέντα ἄνθρωπον ὀνομάζω <αὐτὸ>ν Σωκράτην ἢ Διογένην ἤ τι τῶν πολλῶν ὀνομάτων ἕν· καὶ ἐπειδὰν ὀνόματι καταλάβω τὸν ἄνθρωπον, εἶδος γένους γεγενημένον, ἄτομον καλῶ τὴν τοιαύτην οὐσίαν.

2. ἐτμήθη γὰρ τὸ μὲν γένος εἰς εἶδος, τὸ δὲ εἶδος εἰς ἄτομον, τὸ δὲ ἄτομον, ἐπειδὰν γένηται ὀνόματι κατειλημμένον, οὐχ οἷόν τμηθῆναι κατὰ φύσιν εἰς ἄλλο τι, ὡς ἐτέμομεν τῶν προλελεγμένων ἕκαστον. Ταύτην Ἀριστοτέλης «πρώτην καὶ μάλιστα καὶ κυριω(τά)τη(ν) (οὐ)σί(α)ν» κ(α)λ(εῖ), «τὴ(ν) μήτε καθ' ὑποκειμένου τινὸς λεγομένην μήτ' ἐν ὑποκειμένῳ οὖσαν».

3. καθ' ὑποκειμένου λέγει οἷον εἰ τὸ γένος—ὅπερ ἔφη ζῷον—, <τὸ> κατὰ πάντων τῶν κατὰ μέρος ὑποκειμένων ζῴων—οἱονεὶ βοός, ἵππου, καὶ τῶν ἐφεξῆς—κοινῷ ὀνόματι λεγόμενον. ἀληθὲς γάρ ἐστιν εἰπεῖν ὅτι ζῷον ἄνθρωπός ἐστι, καὶ ζῷον ἵππος, καὶ ζῷον ἔστι βοῦς, καὶ τῶν ἄλλων ἕκαστον. τοῦτ' ἔστι τὸ καθ' ὑποκειμένου, τὸ ἓν ὄν, κατὰ πολλῶν καὶ διαφόρων τοῖς <ε>ἴδεσι δυνάμενον ὁμοίως λέγεσθαι. 4. οὐδὲ<ν> γὰρ διαφέρει ἵππος ἀνθρώπου ᾗ ζῷον, ο<ὐ>δὲ βοῦς· ὅρος γὰρ ὁ τοῦ ζῴου πᾶσιν ἁρμόζει τοῖς ζῴοις, ὁμοίως λεγόμενος. τί γάρ ἐστι ζῷον ἂν ὁριζώμεθα, πάντα τὰ ζῷα <ὁ> κοινὸς καταλήψεται ὅρος. ζῷον δ' ἔστιν οὐσία ἔμψυχος, αἰσθητική· τοῦτο βοῦς, ἵππος, ἄνθρωπος, <καὶ> τῶν ἄλλων ἕκαστον.

5. «Ἐν ὑποκειμένῳ δέ», φησίν, ἐστὶν, «ὃ ἔν τινι μὴ ὡς μέρος ὑπάρχον ἀδύνατον χωρὶς εἶναι τοῦ ἐν ᾧ ἐστι». <τοῦτ' ἔστι> τῶν συμβεβηκότων τῇ

SPECIES AND INDIVIDUAL. 18. 1. Now then, as I said, substance is threefold—genus, species, and the individual—and I posited that the genus is "animal" and the species is "human." This species is already differentiated from the mass of animals. It is still, however, an indiscriminate aggregate and not yet molded into the species of an instantiated substance. I call this substance an "individual" when I specify the human taken individually from the genus by giving him a name such as "Sokrates" or "Diogenes," or any of many names; that is, whenever I designate a human—already a species from a genus—by a name.

2. Again, genus is divided into species, and species into the individual. Yet the individual, when it is specified by name, cannot by nature be divided into anything else, as I distinguished each of the previously mentioned classes.[19] It is this undivided substance that Aristotle calls "the principal, most accurately and properly named 'substance.'" It is "what is named neither with reference to an underlying reality, nor exists in any underlying reality."[20]

3. Now he calls the underlying reality to which entities are referred a sort of "genus." The genus "animal," he said, exists throughout all the underlying animals taken singly (like cow, horse, and so on). All are called by the common name "animal." (For it is true to say that the human is an animal, the horse is an animal, the cow is an animal, and each of the others.) This is what Aristotle means by "*with reference* to an underlying reality." Though the genus is one, it can be spoken equally of many different species of animals. 4. This is because a horse does not differ from a human insofar as it is an animal, nor does a cow. The definition of "animal" applies to all animals and is spoken of them equally. Whatever animal we specify, all of them will assume the same definition: an animal is an ensouled, perceiving substance. This applies to the cow, horse, human, and to each of the others.[21]

5. What is "*in* a substance," he explains, is "what is *in* something that is not able to exist as a part separate from that in which it is." That is to say, each of the incidental properties in a substance [is not able to exist

dance with a like construction in *Ref.* 7.22.16. For a different solution, see Holwerda, "Textkritisches," 598.

19. On the individual, see Seneca, *Ep.* 58.12, 16; Porphyry, *Intro.* 8 (§2, end). See further Mansfeld, *Heresiography*, 113–17.

20. For this quote and what follows, see Aristotle, *Cat.* 2, 1a20; 5.2, a14–27, with the comments of Mansfeld, *Heresiography*, 117–19.

21. Cf. Seneca, *Ep.* 58.9. See further Mueller, "Hippolytus, Aristotle, Basilides," 147–48.

οὐσίᾳ ἕκαστον. ὃ καλεῖται πο(ι)ότης, καθ' ὃ ποιοί τινες λεγόμεθα—οἷον λευκοί, γλαυκοί, μέλανες, δίκαιοι, ἄδικοι, σώφρονες, καὶ τὰ τούτων παραπλήσια.—τούτων γὰρ ἓν αὐτὸ καθ' αὑτὸ [τῷ] <ἀ>δύνατόν ἐστι γενέσθαι, ἀλλὰ δεῖ ἔν τινι εἶναι.

6. Εἰ δὲ οὔτε τὸ ζῷον, ὃ κατὰ πάντων λέγω τῶν καθ' ἕκαστα ζῴων, οὔτε συμβεβηκότα, ἃ ἐν πᾶσιν οἷς συμβέβηκεν εὑρίσκεται, δυνατά <ἐστιν> αὐτὰ καθ' αὑτὰ γενέσθαι, ἐκ τούτων δὲ συμπληροῦται τὰ ἄτομα, <ἐκ> τῶν οὐκ ὄντων γέ ἐστιν ἡ τριχῇ διῃρημένη οὐσία, οὐκ ἐξ ἄλλων, συνεστῶσα. «πρώτη» ἄρα «καὶ κυριωτάτη καὶ μάλιστα λεγομένη οὐσία», <ἣ> ἐκ τούτων ὑπάρχει, ἐξ οὐκ ὄντων κατὰ τὸν Ἀριστοτέλην ἐστίν.

19. 1. Ἀλλὰ περὶ μὲν τῆς οὐσίας ἀρκέσει τὰ λεγόμενα νῦν. οὐ μόνον δὲ ἡ οὐσία καλεῖται [τὸ] γένος, εἶδος, ἄτομον, ἀλλὰ καὶ ὕλη καὶ εἶδος καὶ στέρησις· διαφέρει δὲ οὐδέ<ν>, ἐν το<ῖς α>ὑτοῖς μενούσης τῆς τομῆς. τοιαύτης δὲ οὔσης τῆς οὐσίας, ἔστιν ἡ τοῦ κόσμου διαταγὴ γεγενημένη κατ' αὐτὸν τοιοῦτόν τινα τρόπον.

2. ὁ κόσμος ἐστὶ κατ' Ἀριστοτέλην διῃρημένος εἰς μέρη πλείονα καὶ (δ)ι(άφορα· καὶ ἔ)στι (τ)οῦ κόσμου μέρος τοῦθ', ὅπερ ἐστὶν ἀπὸ τῆς γῆς μέχρι τῆς σελήν(ης), ἀπρονόητον, ἀκυβέρνητον, ἀρκούμενον μόνῃ τῇ φύσει τῇ ἑαυτοῦ· τὸ δὲ μετὰ τὴν σελήνην ἐν πάσῃ τάξει καὶ προνοίᾳ καὶ κυβερνήσει τεταγμένον μέχρι τῆς ἐπιφανείας τοῦ οὐρανοῦ. 3. ἡ δ' ἐπιφάνεια, πέμπτη τις οὖσα οὐσία, φυσικῶν ἀπηλλαγμένη στοιχείων πάντων, ἀφ' ὧν ὁ κόσμος τὴν σύστασιν ἔχει, καὶ ἔστιν αὕτη [τίς] ἡ πέμπτη κατὰ τὸν Ἀριστοτέλην οὐσία οἱονεὶ οὐσία τις ὑπερκόσμιος.

separately from that substance]. He calls the incidental property a "quality," according to how we are said to be qualified. Examples of qualities are white, gray, black, just, unjust, moderate, and the like. Each one of these in itself cannot come into existence but must exist "in" something.[22]

6. If neither the animal—I mean the genus of the individual species of animal—nor the incidental properties that are found in all of them can themselves arise by themselves (and individuals realize their full existence from these [i.e., genus, species, and incidental property]), then the threefold division of substance is compounded exclusively from entities that do not exist. Thus "the principal, most properly and accurately named substance" (constituted from genus and species) arises, according to Aristotle, from entities that do not exist![23]

19. 1. What I have said about substance will suffice for now. He calls substance not only genus, species, and individual but also matter, form, and privation.[24] These categories do not differ in the slightest, since the division remains along the same lines.[25] Since substance is so defined, the ordering of the world arises, according to Aristotle, in the following way.

TRIPARTITE COSMOS. 2. According to Aristotle, the world is divided into many different parts. Our part of the world, which extends from the earth to the moon, lacks providential care and direction. It is self-sufficient by virtue of its own nature alone.[26] In contrast, the part from the moon until the outer surface of heaven is ordered with all providential care and direction.[27] 3. The surface of heaven is a fifth kind of substance. It is freed from all natural elements from which our world is composed. This is Aristotle's "fifth essence," or quasi-essence, that exists above our world.[28]

---

22. See further Mueller, "Hippolytus, Aristotle, Basilides," 148.

23. See further Osborne, *Rethinking*, 47; Mueller, "Hippolytus, Aristotle, Basilides," 148–49.

24. See further Osborne, *Rethinking*, 48–49; Mansfeld, *Heresiography*, 119–22, 125–31 (who compares Sext. Emp., *Math.* 10.213–228).

25. Marcovich replaces τούτοις (P) with τοῖς αὐτοῖς (here: "the same lines").

26. Cf. *Ref.* 1.20.6 (the report on Aristotle): what is below the moon is full of evils; what is above the moon is free of evils.

27. Cf. Theophrastos, frag. 162 (FHSG 1:326–27). For the "standard view" of Aristotle and divine providence, see Robert W. Sharples, "Aristotelian Theology after Aristotle," in Frede and Laks, *Traditions of Theology*, 1–40 (22–26).

28. The Aristotelian tripartite universe is well known in late Hellenistic, early Greco-Roman, and Christian literature (Mansfeld, *Heresiography*, 136–38). In the same literature, a fifth body (quintessence) is also attributed to Aristotle (with Stoic

Καὶ γέγονεν αὐτῷ κατὰ τὴν διαίρεσιν τοῦ κόσμου καὶ ὁ τῆς φιλοσοφίας διῃρημένος λόγος. 4. Φυσικὴ γάρ τις ἀκρόασις αὐτῷ γέγονεν, ἐν ᾗ πεπόνηται περὶ τῶν φύσει καὶ οὐ προνοίᾳ διοικουμένων ἀπὸ τῆς γῆς μέχρι τῆς σελήνης πραγμάτων. γέγονε δὲ αὐτῷ καὶ Μετὰ τὰ φυσικὰ περὶ τῶν μετὰ σελήνην ἰδία τις ἄλλη οὕτως ἐπιγραφομένη πραγματεία λόγων. γέγονε δὲ αὐτῷ περὶ πέμπτης οὐσίας ἴδιος λόγος, ὅς ἐστιν αὐτῷ θεολογούμενος. τοιαύτη τίς [καὶ] ἡ διαίρεσις τῶν <λόγων>, ὡς τύπῳ περιλαβεῖν, <τῆς> κατ᾽ Ἀριστοτέλην φιλοσοφίας.

5. (Ὁ) δὲ Περὶ ψυχῆς αὐτῷ λόγος ἐστὶν ἀσαφής· ἐν τρισὶ γὰρ συγγράμ<μ>ασιν ὅλοις οὐκ ἔστιν εἰπεῖν σαφῶς ὅ τι φρονεῖ περὶ ψυχῆς Ἀριστοτέλης. ὃν γὰρ ἀποδίδωσι <περὶ> τῆς ψυχῆς ὅρον ἔστιν εἰπεῖν ῥᾴδιον, τὸ δὲ ὑπὸ ὅρου δεδηλωμένον ἐστὶ δυσεύρετον. 6. ἔστι γάρ, φησί, ψυχὴ φυσικοῦ σώματος ὀργανικοῦ ἐντελέχεια· ἣ τίς ποτ᾽ ἔστι, λόγων δεῖται καὶ μεγάλης ζητήσεως.

TRIPARTITE DIVISION OF ARISTOTLE'S WORKS. Corresponding to his division of the world is his account of the division of philosophy. 4. He has his *Lectures on Physics*, in which he elaborates natural phenomena (from earth to the moon) that are not administered by providence. His work entitled *Metaphysics* is a special and distinctive set of discussions about the entities beyond the moon. Finally, he has a special treatise on the fifth essence, which to him is a matter of theological discourse.[29] This, in short compass, is the division of treatises in Aristotle's philosophy.[30]

PSYCHOLOGY. 5. His treatise *On the Soul* is unclear. In three entire books one cannot clearly say what Aristotle thinks about the soul. His definition of the soul is easy to recite, but what is indicated in the definition is difficult to discover. 6. The soul is, he says, "the actuality of the natural body used as an instrument."[31] What on earth this means requires commentaries and a lengthy investigation.[32]

influence; cf. *Ref.* 1.20.4; Mansfeld, *Heresiography*, 138–41). In *On the Heavens*, Aristotle calls aether the "first body." Thus Abraham Bos suggests replacing the three occurrences of the word "fifth" in this text with "first" (πρώτη) in order to make it consistent with Aristotle's view ("Basilides as an Aristotelianizing Gnostic," *VC* 54 [2000]: 44–60 [54]).

29. Mueller ("Hippolytus, Aristotle, Basilides," 152–53) notes that our author's description of the *Physics* and the *Metaphysics* does "not seem particularly appropriate for the works we have under those names." There is no surviving work *On the Fifth Substance. On the Heavens* 1–2 is Aristotle's fullest discussion of aether, but there it is never called a fifth element (cf. *Gen. an.* 2.3, 736b30). Terms like "fifth essence" may come from *Mund.* 2.392a8–9. The terminology later became standard (e.g., Philo, *Somn.* 1.21). The division of philosophy, at any rate, corresponds to *Metaph.* 12.1, which divides substances into sensible and perishable, sensible and eternal, and finally nonsensible and unchanging.

30. Marcovich emends P's ὅλων to λόγων (here: "treatises").

31. Cf. Aristotle, *De an.* 2.1, 412b4–6 (his third major definition of soul), with Ronald Polansky, *Aristotle's "De anima"* (Cambridge: Cambridge University Press, 2007), 161–63. Mansfeld argues that the definition of soul here is a "scholastic formula" paralleled in later doxographical literature (*Heresiography*, 141–45). See further Robert W. Sharples, "Peripatetics on Soul and Intellect," in Sharples and Sorabji, *Greek and Roman Philosophy*, 2:607–20.

32. On this point some modern philosophers would seem to agree (e.g., J. L. Ackrill, *Essays on Plato and Aristotle* [Oxford: Clarendon, 1997], 163–78). (Despite our author's affected puzzlement here, he shows more knowledge of Aristotle's psychology below in *Ref.* 7.24.1–2 [Mansfeld, *Heresiography*, 145–46].) Bos believes that ὀργανικόν always means "serving as an instrument" ("Aristotelianizing Gnostic," 48). Sharples

ὁ δὲ θεός, ὁ πάντων τούτων τῶν ὄντων καλῶν αἴτιος, οὗτος τῆς ψυχῆς ἐστι πάνυ πολλῶν, καὶ μακροτέρῳ λόγῳ θεωροῦντι, γνωσθῆναι χαλεπώτερος. 7. ὁ γὰρ ὅρος, ὃν Ἀριστοτέλης ἀποδίδωσι περὶ τοῦ θεοῦ, χαλεπὸς μὲν οὐκ ἔστι, γνωσθῆναι, νοηθῆναι δὲ ἔστιν ἀμήχανος. νόησις γάρ, φησίν, ἐστὶ νοήσεως· ὅπερ ἐστί· παντάπασιν οὐκ ὤν.

ὁ δὲ κόσμος ἄφθαρτος <καὶ> ἀίδιος κατ' Ἀριστοτέλην ἐστίν· οὐδὲν γὰρ ἔχει πλημμελὲς ἐν αὐτῷ, προνοίᾳ καὶ φύσει κυβερνώμενος.

8. καταβέβληται δὲ Ἀριστοτέλης οὐ μόνον περὶ φύσεως καὶ κόσμου καὶ προνοίας καὶ θεοῦ λόγους, ἀλλὰ γὰρ γέγονεν αὐτῷ καὶ πραγματεία τις λόγων ἠθικῶν· ἐπιγράφε<ται> δὲ ταῦτα Ἠθικὰ βιβλία, δι' ὧν σπουδαῖον ἐκ φαύλου τὸ τῶν ἀκροωμένων ἦθος ἐργάζεται.

9. Ἐὰν ὁ Βασιλείδης εὑρεθῇ μὴ τῇ δυνάμει μόνῃ ἀλλὰ καὶ τοῖς λόγοις αὐτοῖς καὶ τοῖς ὀνόμασι τὰ τοῦ Ἀριστοτέλους δόγματα εἰς τὸν εὐαγγελικὸν καὶ σωτήριον ἡμῶν λόγον μεθαρμοζόμενος, τί λείψει ἢ τὰ ἀλλότρια ἀποδόντας ἐπιδεικνύναι τοῖς τούτου μαθηταῖς ὅτι ἐθνικοὺς ὄντας αὐτοὺς «Χριστὸς οὐδὲν ὠφελήσει».

THEOLOGY.

God—the cause of all these goods that exist—is so much harder to know than the soul (even for one examining at greater length)! 7. Aristotle's definition of God is not difficult to recognize but impossible to understand. For he says that God is "thinking of thinking"—which means that he is entirely nonexistent.[33]

Now the world, in Aristotle's view, is incorruptible and eternal; for it contains nothing discordant and is steered both by providence and by nature.[34]

NOTE ON ETHICS. 8. Aristotle composed treatises not only about nature, the world, providence, and God, but he also has a treatise on ethical matters. It is entitled *Ethics*. Through this work, he made the worthless character of his pupils noble.[35]

9. Now whenever Basileides is caught adapting Aristotle's teachings to our saving gospel story—not only "in potentiality" but in his actual words and terminology—my task is to restore the plagiarized elements and show his disciples that, since they are pagans, "Christ will be of no benefit at all."[36]

---

points out, however, that in Philo, *Leg.* 1.3–4 (cf. *Ebr.* 111) ὀργανικός has the sense of "equipped with organs" (*Peripatetic Philosophy*, 246). See further R. A. H. King, *Aristotle on Life and Death* (London: Duckworth, 2001), 40–48.

33. Cf. Aristotle, *Metaph.* 12.9, 1074b33–35. The doctrine was well known and need not have come directly from *Metaphysics* (Mansfeld, *Heresiography*, 147). Mueller comments: "Aristotle does not, of course, 'define' god as thought-of-thought, but he does identify the prime mover as pure activity, an activity he characterizes as thought-of-thought." He suspects that equating thinking of thinking with "absolute non-being" is our author's own invention, "motivated by the subsequent 'refutation' of Basilides' identification of the highest god with non-being" ("Hippolytus, Aristotle, Basilides," 145–46). See further Thomas De Koninck, "Aristotle on God as Thought Thinking Itself," *Review of Metaphysics* 47 (1994): 471–515; Aryeh Kosman, "Metaphysics Λ 9: Divine Thought," in *Aristotle's Metaphysics Lambda: Symposium Aristotelicum*, ed. Michael Frede and David Charles (Oxford: Clarendon, 2000), 307–26 (313–26); Lloyd P. Gerson, *Aristotle and Other Platonists* (Ithaca, NY: Cornell University Press, 2005), 195–200.

34. Cf. *Ref.* 7.19.2 (no providence below the moon). See further Sharples, *Peripatetic Philosophy*, 196–210; idem, "Peripatetics on Fate and Providence," in Sharples and Sorabji, *Greek and Roman Philosophy*, 2:595–606.

35. Cf. Aristotle, *Eth. nic.* 2.2, 1103b27–29.

36. Cf. Gal 5:2: "Whenever you are circumcised, Christ will in no way benefit you" (Χριστὸς ὑμᾶς οὐδὲν ὠφελήσει).

20. 1. Βασιλείδης τοίνυν καὶ Ἰσίδωρος, ὁ Βασιλείδου παῖς γνήσιος καὶ μαθητής, φασὶν εἰρηκέναι Ματθίαν αὐτοῖς λόγους ἀποκρύφους, οὓς ἤκουσε παρὰ τοῦ σωτῆρος κατ' ἰδίαν διδαχθείς. ἴδωμεν οὖν πῶς καταφανῶς Βασιλείδης

BASILEIDES

20. 1. Now then, Basileides[37] and Isidore—his genuine son and disciple—say that Matthias spoke to them hidden discourses that the Savior taught in private.[38] So let us see how Basileides, along with Isidore and all

37. Basileides was a gnostic teacher and writer in Alexandria who flourished during the reign of Hadrian (in the 130s CE). He is credited by some with being the first Christian philosopher (or theologian) and one of the earliest Christian exegetes (Bentley Layton, "The Significance of Basilides in Ancient Christian Thought," *Representations* 28 [1989]: 135–51 [136]). Winrich Löhr provides the most comprehensive collection of testimonies and fragments related to Basileides, as well as a treatment of the present report (*Basilides und seine Schule: Eine Studie zur Theologie- und Kirchengeschichte des zweiten Jahrhunderts*, WUNT 83 [Tübingen: Mohr Siebeck, 1996], 5–254, 284–323, 324–37). See also idem, "Christliche 'Gnostiker' in Alexandria im zweiten Jahrhundert," in *Alexandria*, ed. Tobias Georges, Civitatum Orbis Mediterranei Studia 1 (Tübingen: Mohr Siebeck, 2013), 418–30. Gerhard May points to the "highly original and internally consistent body of doctrine" in the present report, indicating its ultimate derivation from Basileides (*Creatio ex nihilo: The Doctrine of 'Creation out of Nothing' in Early Christian Thought*, trans. A. S. Worrall [London: T&T Clark, 1994], 63). In contrast, Layton ("Significance," 138), Simone Pétrement (*A Separate God: The Christian Origins of Gnosticism*, trans. Carol Harrison [New York: HarperSanFrancisco, 1984], 336–41), and Birger A. Pearson ("Basilides the Gnostic," in Marjanen and Luomanen, *Companion*, 1–31) discount the historical reliability of our author's report, preferring the (putatively irreconcilable) account in Iren., *Haer.* 1.24.3–7. Löhr casts doubt on *both* Irenaeus and our author and relies solely on the fragments (mostly from Clement) (*Basilides*, 255–331). Comparison between our author's report and that of Clement can be found in Werner Foerster, "Das System des Basilides," *NTS* 9 (1963): 233–55 (243–52); Ekkehard Mühlenberg, "Wirklichkeitserfahrung und Theologie bei dem Gnostiker Basilides," *KD* 18 (1972): 161–75; and Barbara Aland, "Seele, Zeit, Eschaton bei einem frühen christlichen Theologen: Basilides zwischen Paulus und Platon," in Ψυχη-*Seele-anima: Festschrift für Karin Alt*, ed. Jens Holzhausen (Stuttgart: Teubner, 1998), 255–78. For our author's comparison of Aristotle and Basileides, see Osborne, *Rethinking*, 50–58.

38. Matthias (not to be confused with the putative Gospel writer Matthew) was the disciple chosen to replace Judas as a member of the Twelve in Acts 1. Clement of Alexandria notes that Valentinus, Markion, and Basileides appeal to the teachings of Matthias (*Strom.* 7.17.108.1 = Löhr, *Basilides*, testimony 6). Clement knew a work called *Traditions* attributed to Matthias (*Strom.* 2.9.45.4; 3.4.26.3; 4.6.35.2; 7.13.82.1). Origen mentions a "Gospel according to Matthias" (*Homilia 1 in Lucam* = Löhr, *Basilides*, testimony 10). The Book of Thomas (NHC II,7) 138.1–3 also mentions a "Mathaias" (ⲙⲁⲑⲁⲓⲁⲥ) who records secret words spoken to Judas Thomas. See further Löhr, *Basilides*, 25–29.

ὁμοῦ καὶ Ἰσίδωρος καὶ πᾶς ὁ τούτων χορὸς οὐχ ἁπλῶς καταψεύδο<ν>ται μόνου Ματθίου, ἀλλὰ γὰρ καὶ τοῦ σωτῆρος αὐτοῦ.

2. Ἦν, φησί, <π>οτε ἦν οὐδέν· ἀλλ' οὐδὲ τὸ «οὐδὲν» ἦν τι τῶν ὄντων, ἀλλὰ ψιλῶς καὶ ἀνυπονοήτως δίχα παντὸς σοφίσματος ἦν ὅλως οὐδέν. ὅταν δὲ λέγω, φησί, τὸ ἦν, οὐχ ὅτι ἦν λέγω, ἀλλ' ἵνα σημάνω τοῦτο ὅπερ βούλομαι δεῖξαι [λέγω, φησίν], ὅτι ἦν ὅλως οὐδέν. 3. ἔστι γάρ, φησίν, ἐκεῖνο οὐκ ἁπλῶς ἄρρητον, <ὃ> ὀνομάζεται· «ἄρρητον» γοῦν αὐτὸ καλοῦμεν, ἐκεῖνο δὲ οὐκ ἄρρητον. καὶ δὲ τὸ οὐκ ἄρρητον «οὐκ ἄρρητον» ὀνομάζεται, ἀλλ' ἔστι, φησίν, «ὑπεράνω παντὸς ὀνόματος ὀνομαζομένου».

4. Οὐδὲ γὰρ τῷ κόσμῳ, φησίν, ἐξαρκεῖ τὰ ὀνόματα—οὕτως ἐστὶ πολυσχιδής—ἀλλ' ἐπιλέλοιπε· καὶ οὐ δέχομαι, φησί, κατὰ πάντων εὑρεῖν κυρίως ὀνόματα. ἀλλὰ <δεῖ> τῇ διανοίᾳ, (οὐ) τοῖς (ὀν)όμασι, τῶν ὀνομαζομένων τὰς ἰδιότητας ἀρρήτως ἐκλαμβάνειν· ἡ γὰρ ὁμωνυμία ταραχὴν ἐμπεποίηκε καὶ πλάνην <περὶ> τῶν πραγμάτων τοῖς ἀκροωμένοις.

5. Τοῦτο πρῶτον σφετέρισμα καὶ κλέμμα τοῦ Περιπάτου λαβόντες ἀπατῶσι τὴν ἄνοιαν τῶν συναγελαζομένων ἅμ' αὐτοῖς. πολλαῖς γὰρ γενεαῖς Ἀριστοτέλης Βασιλείδου γεγενημένος πρότ<ερ>ος, τὸν περὶ τῶν ὁμωνύμων ἐν

their chorus, openly tell lies not only about Matthias but even about the Savior himself.[39]

THE PRIMAL STATE OF NONEXISTENCE. 2. There was, he says, a time when there was nothing at all.[40] But not even the "nothing" existed. Rather there was simply, indisputably, and apart from every sophism, nothing at all. "When I use the verb 'was,'" he says, "I do not mean that something existed, but I use it to indicate what I want to demonstrate: that there was nothing at all." 3. What is called "nothing," he claims, is not simply ineffable. We call it "ineffable," but it is not ineffable. Furthermore, what is not ineffable is *called* "not ineffable," but in fact it is, he claims, "*above* every name that is named."[41]

4. There are not even enough names for the world—since it is split up into such a multitude of parts. Rather, they all fall short. "Indeed, I do not have the means," he says, "to find the proper names amidst all the phenomena."[42] Rather, it is necessary to understand ineffably the distinctive properties of named phenomena in the mind, not in the terms themselves. For homonymy about these matters has created confusion and error in those who hear them.

5. Seizing this first appropriation and theft from the Peripatetic school, they deceive their mindless herd. For Aristotle preceded Basileides by many generations, and he published the account of homonymous terms in

---

39. Our author indicates here that he is summarizing a work not of Basileides per se but of his school.

40. Partially following Marcovich, I emend P's τότε ("then") to ποτε.

41. Eph 1:21, also quoted below in *Ref.* 7.22.13; 7.25.5. Cf. Clem. Alex., *Ecl.* 57.4; Ap. John (NHC II,1) 2.26–4.10. See further H. A. Wolfson, "Negative Attributes in the Church Fathers and the Gnostic Basilides," *HTR* 50 (1957): 145–56; John Whittaker, "Basilides on the Ineffability of God," *HTR* 62 (1969): 367–71; M. Jufresa, "Basilides, A Path to Plotinus," *VC* 35 (1981): 1–15; Deirdre Carabine, *The Unknown God: Negative Theology in the Platonic Tradition; Plato to Eriugena*, Leuven Theological & Pastoral Monographs 19 (Leuven: Peeters, 1995), 86–88; Curtis L. Hancock, "Negative Theology in Gnosticism and Neoplatonism," in *Neoplatonism and Gnosticism*, ed. Richard T. Wallis and Jay Bregman (Albany: SUNY Press, 1992), 167–86; Graziano Biondi, *Basilide: La filosofia del Dio inesistente* (Rome: Manifestolibri, 2005), 109–18.

42. Holwerda suggests δέομαι ("I need") instead of δέχομαι, an emendation which would, he believes, obviate the need to insert δεῖ ("it is necessary," added by Marcovich) in the next sentence ("Textkritisches," 598).

ταῖς Κατηγορίαις καταβέβληται λόγον· ὃν ὡς ἴδιον οὗτοι καὶ καινόν τινα, καὶ τῶν Ματθίου λόγων κρυφίων τινῶν ἕν<α> διασαφοῦσιν.

21. 1. Ἐπεὶ οὐδέν <ἦν,> οὐχ ὕλη, οὐκ οὐσία, οὐκ ἀνούσιον, οὐχ ἁπλοῦν, οὐκ ἀσύνθετον, οὐκ ἀνοητόν, οὐκ ἀναίσθητόν, οὐκ ἄνθρωπος, οὐκ ἄγγελος, οὐ θεός, οὐδὲ ὅλως τι τῶν ὀνομαζομένων ἢ δι᾽ αἰσθήσεως λαμβανομένων ἢ νοητῶν πραγμάτων, ἀλλ᾽ οὕτω καὶ ἔτι λεπτομερ<εστέρ>ως πάντων ἁπλῶς περιγεγραμμένων, <ὁ> οὐκ ὢν θεός—ὃν Ἀριστοτέλης καλεῖ νόησιν νοήσεως, οὗτοι δὲ οὐκ ὄντα—ἀνοήτως, ἀναισθήτως, ἀβούλως, ἀπροαιρέτως, ἀπαθῶς, ἀνεπιθυμήτως κόσμον ἠθέλησε ποιῆσαι. 2. τὸ δὲ «ἠθέλησε» λέγω, φησί, σημασίας χάριν <τὸ> ἀθελήτως καὶ ἀνοήτως καὶ ἀναισθήτως· κόσμον δὲ οὐ τὸν κατὰ πλάτος καὶ διαίρεσιν γεγενημένον ὕστερον καὶ διεστῶτα, ἀλλὰ γὰρ σπέρμα κόσμου.

3. τὸ δὲ σπέρμα τοῦ κόσμου πάντα εἶχεν ἐν ἑαυτῷ, ὡς ὁ τοῦ σινάπεως κόκκος ἐν ἐλαχίστῳ συλλαβὼν ἔχει πάντα ὁμοῦ· τὰς ῥίζας, τὸ πρέμνον, τοὺς κλάδους, τὰ φύλλα, τὰ ἀνεξαρίθμητα [μετὰ] <πλήθη> τῶν κόκκων (ἀπ)ὸ τοῦ φυτοῦ γεννώμενα, σπέρματα πάλιν <γινόμενα> ἄλλων καὶ ἄλλων πολλάκις φυτῶν κεχυμένα. 4. Οὕτως <ὁ> οὐκ ὢν θεὸς ἐποίησε κόσ(μ)ον οὐκ ὄν<τα> ἐξ

his book *Categories*.[43] It is this account that these heretics openly affirm as their own novel teaching—indeed, one of the secret teachings of Matthias![44]

CREATION FROM NOTHING. 21. 1. So when there was nothing—not matter, not substance, not nonsubstance, not anything simple or uncompounded, or inconceivable, or imperceptible, neither human, nor angel, nor god, nor anything at all of phenomena named or perceived or thought, a nothingness still more subtle than simply anything described by language—then the nonexistent God (whom Aristotle calls "thinking of thinking," and what these people call "Nonexistent") wanted to make the world without conception, without perception, without will, without volition, without emotion, and without desire.[45] 2. "I use the phrase 'God wanted,'" he says, "to signify an act that was without will, without thought, and without perception. And by 'world' I mean, not the world that later arose and was differentiated with dimensions and divisions, but rather a world seed."[46]

3. The world seed contained everything in itself just as the mustard seed comprises everything in the tiniest space: the roots, the stem, the branches, the leaves, the innumerable mass of berries generated from the plant, and the seeds that grow in turn and are scattered through multiple generations of plants.[47] 4. In this way, then, the nonexistent God made the

43. Cf. Aristotle, *Cat.* 1.1, a1. Mansfeld, *contra* Osborne, denies that our author read Aristotle's *Categories* and argues for his dependence on later exegetical literature (*Heresiography*, 122–23). See further Sharples, *Peripatetic Philosophy*, 44, 57.

44. Mueller denies that Basileides's theological application of homonymy "is in any substantive way dependent on Aristotle" ("Hippolytus, Aristotle, Basilides," 144). Cf. idem, "Hippolytus *Retractatus*," 240: "The allegation here seems to be purely verbal."

45. Plato had already placed the Good beyond substance (ἐπέκεινα τῆς οὐσίας) (*Resp.* 6.509b9). Mueller notes a parallel in Alkinoos, *Epit.* 10.4, for whom the highest God is unspeakable, inapprehensible; not a genus, species, or differentia, not part or whole, not same or different ("Hippolytus, Aristotle, Basilides," 145). The nonexistent (οὐκ ὤν) God seems to be a deliberate contrast to the God of Exod 3:14: ἐγώ εἰμι ὁ ὤν (Carabine, *Unknown God*, 88–89). For a similarly apophatic presentation of God, see Ap. John (BG 8502.2) 24.20–22; (NHC II,1) 3.27; Tri. Trac. (NHC I,5) 53.23–39.

46. The idea of the world seed has parallels in Stoic thought. See further May, *Creatio*, 71–72, with sources.

47. This sentence is heavily emended by Marcovich. For further text-critical suggestions, see Holwerda, "Textkritisches," 599. For the parable of the mustard seed, see Mark 4:30–32 par.; Gos. Thom. 20; *Ref.* 5.9.6 (Naassenes); 6.40.2; Ap. Jas. (NHC I,2) 8.7; Clem. Alex., *Exc.* 1.3. The "tiniest space" (ἐν ἐλαχίστῳ) is reminiscent of the infinitesimal point in "Simon" (*Ref.* 6.14.6) and the Naassenes (5.9.5).

οὐκ ὄντων, καταβαλόμενος καὶ ὑποστήσας σπέρμα τι ἕν, ἔχον πᾶσαν ἐν ἑαυτῷ τὴν (τ)οῦ (κ)όσ(μ)ου (πα)νσπερμίαν.

5. ἵνα δὲ καταφανέστερον ποιήσω τοῦτο ὅπερ ἐκεῖνοι λέγουσι· καθάπερ ᾠὸν ὄρνιθος ἐκποικιλλ<ομέν>ου τινὸς καὶ πολυχρωμάτου, οἱονεὶ τοῦ ταῶνος ἢ ἄλλου τινὸς ἔτι μᾶλλον πολυμόρφου καὶ πολυχρωμάτου, ἓν ὂν [οὕτως] ἔχει ἐν ἑαυτῷ πολλὰς οὐσιῶν πολυμόρφων καὶ πολυχρωμάτων καὶ πολυσυστάτων ἰδέας, οὕτως ἔχει τὸ καταβληθέν, φησίν, ὑπὸ τοῦ οὐκ ὄντος θεοῦ οὐκ ὂν σπέρμα, <τὸ> τοῦ κόσμου, πολύμορφον ὁμοῦ καὶ πολυούσιον.

22. 1. Πάντα οὖν ὅσα ἔστιν εἰπεῖν ἢ ἔτι μὴ εὑρόντα παραλιπεῖν, ὅσα τῷ μέλλοντι γενέσθαι ἀπὸ τοῦ σπέρματος κόσμῳ ἔμελλεν ἁρμόζειν, ἀναγκαίως καιροῖς ἰδίοις κατὰ προσθήκην αὐξανομένῳ, [ὡς] ὑπὸ τηλικούτου καὶ τοιούτου θεοῦ, ὁποῖον οὐκ εἰπεῖν οὐ<δὲ> νοήσει δυνατὴ γέγονε χωρῆσαι ἡ κτίσις. καὶ ἐνυπῆρχε τεθησαυρισμένα τῷ σπέρματι, καθάπερ νεογενεῖ παιδίῳ ὀδόντας ὕστερον ὁρῶμεν προσγίνεσθαι καὶ πατρικὴν οὐσίαν καὶ φρένας καὶ ὅσα παραυξανομένῳ ἐκ νέου κατὰ μικρὸν ἀνθρώπῳ γίνεται, ἃ μὴ πρότερον ἦν.

2. Ἐπεὶ δὲ ἦν ἄπορον εἰπεῖν προβολήν τινα <ἐκ> τοῦ μὴ ὄντος θεοῦ γεγονέναι, τὸ οὐκ ὂν <σπέρμα παρεισάγει>· φεύγει γὰρ πάνυ καὶ δέδοικε τὰς κατὰ προβολὴν τῶν γεγονότων οὐσίας ὁ Βασιλείδης. ποίας γὰρ προβολῆς χρεία ἢ ποίας ὕλης ὑποθέσεως, ἵνα κόσμον θεὸς ἐργάσηται, καθάπερ ὁ ἀράχνης τὰ μηρύματα, ἢ θνητὸς ἄνθρωπος χαλκὸν ἢ ξύλον ἤ τι τῶν τῆς ὕλης μερῶν ἐργαζόμενος λαμβάνει; ἀλλὰ «εἶπε», φησί, «καὶ ἐγένετο». 3. καὶ τοῦτό ἐστιν, ὡ<ς> λέγουσιν οἱ ἄνδρες οὗτοι, τὸ λεχθὲν ὑπὸ Μωσέως·

nonexistent world from entities that did not exist. He sowed and planted a single seed, which had in itself the entire mixture of the world's seeds.[48]

5. Let me make what they say more clear. The egg of a bird with dappled spots and many colors (for instance, the peacock or another bird still more multiform and multicolored) has in itself, although it is one, all the patterns of multiform, multicolored, and multitudinous substances. Such is the case, he says, with the nonexistent seed of the world sown by the nonexistent God, since it is both multiform and multifarious.[49]

22. 1. Everything that we can speak of or omit because it is still undiscovered,[50] and everything destined to belong to the world from the seed—a world that necessarily grows by increments at the proper times—all came into being by the power of so vast and so wonderful a God. His nature the creation cannot express in words or approach in thought. Indeed, all things began to exist, treasured up in the seed, just as in a newborn child we later see teeth grow. We also later see its father's nature and habits of thought—and whatever other qualities gradually appear in one growing from youth to adulthood—qualities that had no previous existence.[51]

2. Since it was impossible to say that an emanation was generated from the nonexistent God, Basileides sneaks in the nonexistent seed.[52] This is because Basileides entirely avoids and fears the idea of beings born through emanation. For what need was there of an emanation or what underlying matter was there for God to make the world? Was he to use webbing like a spider? Or does he, like a mortal man, obtain bronze, wood, or some other material object in order to make things? Rather, he says, God "spoke, and it arose."[53] 3. This, as these men say, is what Moses's statement means:

---

48. "The entire mixture of seeds" translates πανσπέρμια, a term found in Presocratic philosophy (e.g., Demokritos in Aristotle, *De an.* 1.2, 404a4; *Gen. an.* 4.5; *Phys.* 3.4, 203a19f; Anaxagoras in Aristotle, *Gen. corr.* 1.1, 314a29–30; *Cael.* 3.4, 303a16), and in Plato, *Tim.* 73c (see further Taylor, *Commentary*, 522).

49. I add τό to this sentence, following Holwerda, "Textkritisches," 599.

50. Cf. the use of this phrase in *Ref.* 5.19.1 ("Sethians"); 6.9.7 ("Simon"); 8.12.5 (Monoïmos).

51. Marcovich adds considerably to this paragraph. For alternative readings, see Holwerda, "Textkritisches," 600.

52. Marcovich adds σπέρμα παρεισάγει (here: "sneaks in [the nonexistent] seed") to complete the sense.

53. Cf. Ps 32:9 LXX (αὐτὸς εἶπεν, καὶ ἐγενήθησαν ["he (God) spoke, and they were generated"]) = 148:5b; cf. Clem. Alex., *Strom.* 5.14.99.3; 6.16.136.3; *Protr.* 63.3; *Paed.* 1.26.3; Iren., *Haer.* 2.2.5; 3.8.3. Origen also was concerned about the materialistic implications of emanation (*Princ.* 1.2.6; 4.4.1). Cf. Tri. Trac. (NHC I,5) 73.19–74.15.

γενηθήτω φῶς. καὶ ἐγένετο φῶς.

πόθεν, φησί, γέγονε τὸ φῶς; ἐξ οὐδενός. οὐ γὰρ γέγραπται, φησί, πόθεν, ἀλλ' αὐτὸ μόνον ἐκ τῆς φωνῆς τοῦ λέγοντος. ὁ δὲ λέγων, φησίν, οὐκ ἦν, οὐδὲ τὸ λεγόμενον ἦν.

4. Γέγονε, φησίν, ἐξ οὐκ ὄντος τὸ σπέρμα τοῦ κόσμου, ὁ λόγος ὁ λεχθεὶς «γενηθήτω φῶς». καὶ τοῦτο, φησίν, ἐστὶ τὸ λεγ(ό)μενον ἐν τοῖ(ς) εὐαγγελίοις·

ἦν τὸ φῶς τὸ ἀληθινόν, ὃ φωτίζει πάντα ἄνθρωπον ἐρχόμενον εἰς τὸν κόσμον.

5. λαμβάνει τὰς ἀρχὰς ἀπὸ τοῦ σπέρματος ἐκείνου καὶ φωτίζεται. τοῦτο ἔστι τὸ σπέρμα, <τ>ὸ ἔχον ἐν ἑαυτῷ πᾶσαν τὴν πανσπερμίαν, ὅ φησιν Ἀριστοτέλης γένος εἶναι, εἰς ἀπείρους τεμνόμενον ἰδέας, ὡς τέμνομεν ἀπὸ τοῦ ζῴου βοῦν, ἵππον, ἄνθρωπον, ὅπερ ἔστιν οὐκ ὄν.

6. Ὑποκειμένου τοίνυν τοῦ κοσμικοῦ σπέρματος <ὡς> ἐκεῖνοι λέγουσιν, ὅ τι ἂν λέγω, φησίν, μετὰ ταῦτα γεγονέναι, μὴ ἐπιζήτει πόθεν· εἶχε γὰρ πάντα <τὸ σπέρμα> ἐν ἑαυτῷ τεθησαυρισμένα καὶ κατακείμενα οἷον οὐκ ὄν<τα>, ὑπό τε τοῦ οὐ(κ) (ὄν)τος θεοῦ γενέσθαι προβεβουλευμένα.

7. ἴδωμεν οὖν τί λ(έγ)ουσιν πρῶτον ἢ τί δεύτερον ἢ τί τρίτον <τ>ὸ ἀπὸ τοῦ σπέρματος τοῦ κοσμικοῦ γεγενημένον. ἦν, φησίν, ἐν αὐτῷ τῷ σπέρματι υἱότης τριμερής, κατὰ πάντα τῷ οὐκ ὄντι θε<ῷ> ὁμοούσιος, γεν<ν>ητὴ ἐξ οὐκ ὄντων.

> Let there be light! And light arose.[54]

From where, he asks, did the light come into being? From nothing. For it is not written, he points out, *from where* it came. Rather, it came into being only from the voice of the one who spoke. The one who spoke, he adds, did not exist, nor did what he said exist.[55]

4. So, he claims, the world seed came to be from what does not exist, [just as] the cited passage: "Let there be light!" This light, he adds, is what is referred to in the Gospels:

> It was the true light, enlightening every human being coming into the world.[56]

5. [The entire world] receives the principles from that seed and is enlightened. This is the seed that contains in itself the entire mass of seeds (which Aristotle calls a "genus") divided into limitless forms (as we divide out the cow, horse, and human from the genus "animal"), although it is nonexistent.

6. Accordingly, since, as these people claim, the world seed underlies [everything], do not seek the source, he urges, of what I say originated after these things. For the seed contained all things in itself treasured up and lying within as if they did not exist.[57] The nonexistent God planned beforehand to bring them into existence.

THE TRIPLE SONSHIP. 7. So let us see what they say arose first, second, and third from the world seed. A triple Sonship, he says, was contained in the seed.[58] This Sonship is in every respect consubstantial with the nonexis-

---

54. Gen 1:3; cf. Clem. Alex., *Exc.* 48.1; *Ecl.* 38.1.

55. This understanding of creation from nothing is comparable to Theophilos of Antioch (*Autol.* 2.4; cf. Iren., *Haer.* 2.10.4). See further May, *Creatio*, 74 n. 59, 77–78, 83–84.

56. John 1:9; cf. *Ref.* 5.9.20 (Naassenes); Clem. Alex., *Exc.* 41.3; Iren., *Haer.* 1.9.2; 10.2.

57. Marcovich changes P's τὰ σπέρματα ("seeds") to τὸ σπέρμα ("the seed").

58. Gilles Quispel attempted to make sense of the triple Sonship through the parallel of divine *nous*, world *nous*, and human *nous* he found in *Asklepios* 32, the Chaldean Oracles, and Arnobius, *Adv. nat.* 2.5 ("Gnostic Man: The Doctrine of Basilides," in *The Mystic Vision: Papers from the Eranos Yearbooks*," ed. Joseph Campbell [Princeton: Princeton University Press, 1968], 210–46 [221–26]). W.-D. Hauschild argued that the First Sonship is the reality of the nonexistent God as it is turned inward toward

ταύτης τῆς υἱότητος τῆς τρ(ι)χῇ διῃρημένης τὸ μέν τι ἦν λεπτομερές, τὸ δὲ <παχυμερές, τὸ δὲ> ἀποκαθάρσεως δεόμενον.

8. Τὸ μὲν οὖν λεπτομερὲς εὐθέως πρῶτον, ἅμα τῷ γενέσθαι τοῦ σπέρματος τὴν πρώτην καταβολὴν ὑπὸ τοῦ <οὐκ> ὄντος, διέσφυξε καὶ ἀνῆλθε καὶ ἀνέδραμε κάτωθεν ἄνω, ποιητικῷ τινὶ χρησάμενον τάχει· «ὡσεὶ πτερὸν ἠὲ νόημα,» καὶ ἐγένετο, φησί, πρὸς τὸν οὐκ ὄντα· ἐκείνου γὰρ δι᾽ ὑπερβολὴν κάλλους καὶ ὡραιότητος πᾶσα φύσις ὀρέγεται, ἄλλη δὲ ἄλλως.

9. Ἡ δὲ παχυμερεστέρα ἔτι μένουσα ἐν τῷ σπέρματι, μιμητική τις οὖσα, ἀναδραμεῖν μὲν οὐκ ἠδυνήθη· πολὺ γὰρ ἐνδεεστέρα τῆς λεπτομερείας, ἧς εἶχεν ἡ δι᾽ αὑτῆς υἱ(ό)τ(ης) ἀναδραμοῦσα, ἀπελίπετο. 10. ἐπτέρωσεν οὖν αὐτὴν ἡ υἱότης ἡ παχυμερεστέρα τοιούτῳ τινὶ πτερῷ, ὁποίῳ διδάσκαλος ὢ<ν> Ἀριστοτέλους Πλάτων ἐν Φαίδ(ω)νι τὴν ψυχὴν πτεροῖ, καὶ καλεῖ τὸ τοιοῦτο Βασιλείδης οὐ πτερὸν ἀλλὰ Πνεῦμα ἅγιον, ὃ εὐεργετεῖ ἡ υἱότης ἐνδυσαμένη καὶ εὐεργετεῖται. 11. εὐεργετεῖ μὲν <καὶ εὐεργετεῖται>, ὅτι καθάπερ ὄρνιθος πτερὸν αὐτὸ καθ᾽ αὑτὸ <καὶ> τοῦ ὄρνιθος ἀπηλλαγμένον οὐκ ἂν γένοιτό ποτε ὑψηλὸν οὐδὲ μετάρσιον, οὐδ᾽ αὖ ὄρνις ἀπολελυμένος τοῦ πτεροῦ οὐκ ἄν ποτε

tent God and born from what does not exist. The first part of this triply divided Sonship was subtle, the second was coarse, and the third was in need of purification.[59]

8. First, the subtle part, simultaneous with the Nonexistent's first sowing of the seed, immediately throbbed with life, ascended, and sprinted upward from below.[60] In speed, it was (to use the poetic phrase), "like a winged bird or a thought."[61] It then came to be, he says, with the Nonexistent. For all nature in its various ways strains after his superabundant beauty and loveliness.[62]

9. The coarser part still remained in the seed, since it is imitative. Unable to sprint upward, it was left behind. This is because it stood in great need of the subtlety that the self-empowered Sonship had used when it sprinted up. 10. Therefore the coarser Sonship furnished itself with wings like those that Plato (Aristotle's teacher) fastened on the soul in the *Phaedo*.[63] Basileides calls it not "wing" but "Holy Spirit." When the [second] Sonship clothes itself with it, they mutually benefit each other. 11. A bird's wing, when alone and removed from the bird, could never soar high in the air, and, in turn, a bird deprived of its wing could never soar high in the air.

God; the Second Sonship is the reality of God turned outward toward the world; and the Third Sonship represents humanity in need of redemption ("Christologie und Humanismus bei dem 'Gnostiker' Basilides," *ZNW* 68 [1977]: 67–92). Philo distinguished between God's first Son, the Logos or noetic world (*Agr.* 51; *Conf.* 146), God's second Son or the perceptible world (*Deus* 31–32; cf. *Ebr.* 30–1), and human sons of God (Hauschild, "Christologie," 74–75). Abraham P. Bos has indicated that Basileides's threefold Sonship may be rooted in Paul's statements about sonship through adoption (Rom 8:19–30, a text treated below in *Ref.* 7.25.1, 5; 7.27.1) ("Basilides of Alexandria: Matthias (Matthew) and Aristotle as the Sources of Inspiration for His Gnostic Theology in Hippolytus' *Refutatio*," in *The Wisdom of Egypt: Jewish, Early Christian, and Gnostic Essays in Honour of Gerard P. Luttikhuizen*. ed. Anthony Hilhorst and George H. van Kooten, Ancient Judaism and Early Christianity 59 [Leiden: Brill, 2005], 397–418 [405]). See further Orbe, *Cristología Gnóstica*, 1:248–52, 586–88.

59. Hans Leisegang proposes that the Presocratic terms λεπτομερής ("subtle") and παχυμερής ("coarse") were borrowed from the physics of Epikouros. He cites DK 21 A44; 54 A17 (*Die Gnosis*, 5th ed [Stuttgart: Alfred Kröner, 1985], 230 n. 2).

60. For διέσφυξε ("throbbed with life"), see *Ref.* 5.9.1 (Naassenes); 7.23.3.

61. Homer, *Od.* 7.36.

62. Cf. *Ref.* 5.7.10; 5.9.4 (Naassenes); 10.19 (Markion). Such a description, according to Bos, characterizes the transcendent God as First Mover and final cause ("Aristotelianizing Gnostic," 50–51). Cf. Aristotle, *Metaph.* 1.7, 1072a26–1072b4; *Phys.* 1.9, 192a14–19.

63. Actually, *Phaedr.* 246a–e; 248b–c; 249a–d; 356d.

γένοιτο ὑψηλὸς οὐδὲ μετάρσιος, τοιοῦτόν τινά τοι λόγον ἔσχεν ἡ υἱότης πρὸς τὸ Πνεῦμα τὸ ἅγιον καὶ τὸ Πνεῦμα πρὸς τὴν υἱότητα.

12. Ἀναφερομένη γοῦν ὑπὸ τοῦ Πνεύματος ἡ υἱότης ὡς ὑπὸ πτεροῦ, ἀναφέρει τὸ πτερόν, τουτέστι τὸ Πνεῦμα, καὶ πλησίον γενομένη τῆς λεπτομεροῦς υἱότητος καὶ τοῦ θεοῦ τοῦ οὐκ ὄντος καὶ δημιουργήσαντος ἐξ οὐκ ὄντων, ἔχειν μὲν αὐτὸ μεθ' αὐτῆς οὐκ ἠδύνατο· 13. ἦν γὰρ οὐχ ὁμοούσιον οὐδὲ φύσιν εἶχε [μετὰ] τῆς υἱότητος. ἀλλὰ ὥσπερ ἐστὶ παρὰ φύσιν καὶ ὀλέθριος τ(οῖς ἰ)χθύσιν ἀὴρ καθαρὸς καὶ ξηρός, οὕτω τῷ Πνεύματι τῷ ἁγίῳ ἦν παρὰ φύσιν ἐκεῖνο τὸ ἀρρήτων ἀρρητότερον καὶ «παντὸς ὀνόματος ἀνώτερον» τοῦ οὐκ ὄντος ὁμοῦ θεο<ῦ> καὶ τῆς υἱότητος χωρίον.

Κατέλιπεν οὖν αὐτὸ πλησίον <ἡ> υἱότης ἐκείνου τοῦ μακαρίου καὶ νοηθῆναι μὴ δυναμένου [μὴ] μηδὲ χαρακτηρισθῆναί τινι λόγῳ χωρίου, οὐ παντάπασιν ἔρημον οὐδὲ ἀπηλλαγμένον τῆς υἱότητος. 14. ἀλλὰ γὰρ ὥσπερ μύρον εὐωδέστατον εἰς ἄγγος ἐμβληθέν, εἰ καὶ ὅτι μάλιστα ἐπιμελῶς ἐκκενωθείη, ὅμως ὀσμή τις ἔτι μένει τοῦ μύρου καὶ καταλείπεται, κἂν ᾖ κεχωρισμένον τοῦ ἀγγείου, καὶ μύρου ὀσμὴν τὸ ἀγγεῖον <ἔχ>ει καὶ μὴ <ἔχον> μύρον, οὕτως τὸ Πνεῦμα τὸ ἅγιον μεμένηκε τῆς υἱότητος ἄμοιρον καὶ ἀπηλλαγμένον, ἔχει δ' ἐν ἑαυτῷ μύρου παραπλησίαν τὴν δύναμιν, <τὴν τῆς υἱότητος> ὀσμήν. 15. καὶ τοῦτό ἐστι τὸ λεγόμενον· «ὡς μύρον ἐπὶ κεφαλῆς τὸ καταβαῖνον ἐπὶ τὸν πώγωνα τὸν Ἀ(α)ρώ(ν).»

ἡ ἀπὸ τοῦ Πνεύματος τοῦ ἁγίου φερομένη ὀσμὴ ἄνωθεν κάτω μέχρι τῆς ἀμορφίας καὶ τοῦ διαστήματος τοῦ καθ' ἡμᾶς, ὅθεν ἤρξατο ἀνελθεῖν ἡ υἱότης, οἱονεὶ ἐπὶ πτερύγων ἀετοῦ, φησί, καὶ τῶν μεταφρένων ἐνεχθεῖσα. 16. σπεύδει

The same relationship holds between the [second] Sonship and the Holy Spirit, and vice versa.[64]

12. Now when the [second] Sonship was carried upward by the Spirit as though by a wing, it brought up the wing (that is, Spirit) and drew near to the subtle Sonship, as well as to the nonexistent God, and the Artificer from nonexistent realities. The second Sonship was not able to keep the Spirit with itself, for the Spirit was not consubstantial [with the Nonexistent], nor did it have the nature of the Sonship.[65] 13. But just as pure and dry air is unnatural and lethal for fish, so that region was unnatural to the Holy Spirit. That region is more ineffable than what is ineffable and "higher than every name."[66] This is where the nonexistent God dwells together with the Sonship.

Thus when the [second] Sonship drew near the blessed region that is unable to be thought or characterized in language, it abandoned the Holy Spirit. But the Spirit was not entirely desolate nor separated from the Sonship. 14. Rather, it is just like when a very fragrant perfume is poured into a jar. Even if the jar is carefully emptied to the last drop, still some of the perfume's scent remains left behind. Even if the perfume is removed from the jar, the jar, though it contains no perfume, retains the scent of the perfume. So the Holy Spirit, though it remains bereft and deprived of Sonship, still retained in itself a quality very much like perfume—the scent of Sonship.[67] 15. This is what the scriptural statement refers to: "as a perfume on the head, dripping down onto the beard of Aaron."[68]

The scent from the Holy Spirit was carried down from above as far as the chaos that is our level of reality. It was from here that the Sonship began to ascend as though carried "on eagle's wings," he claims, and on an eagle's pinions.[69] 16. For all things rush, he says, upward from below, from

64. For the Holy Spirit as wing, see Odes Sol. 28.1; Tatian, *Or.* 20.1; Clem. Alex., *Strom.* 4.26.172.2. On the distinctive role of the Spirit in Basileides, see W.-D. Hauschild, *Gottes Geist und der Mensch: Studien zur frühchristlichen Pneumatologie* (Munich: Kaiser, 1972), 191–96; Orbe, *Cristología Gnóstica*, 1:553–69 (554–56).

65. Cf. the "Sethian" Spirit fixed between the divine Light and Darkness (*Ref.* 5.19.3).

66. Eph 1:21; quoted above in *Ref.* 7.20.3.

67. For Spirit as the aroma of immortality, see *PGL*, s.v. ἔλαιον and μύρον. Cf. *Ref.* 5.19.3 ("Sethians").

68. Ps 132:2 LXX.

69. Cf. Deut 32:11; Isa 40:31 LXX.

γάρ, φησί, πάντα κάτωθεν ἄνω, ἀπὸ τῶν χειρόνων ἐπὶ τὰ κρείττονα, οὐδὲν δὲ οὕτως ἀνόητόν ἐστι τῶν τοῖς κρείττοσιν, ἵνα [μὴ] κατέλθῃ κάτω.

ἡ δὲ τρίτη υἱότης, φησίν, ἡ ἀποκαθάρσεως δεομένη, μεμένηκε τῷ μεγάλῳ τῆς πανσπερμίας σωρῷ, εὐεργετοῦσα καὶ εὐεργετουμένη· τίνα δέ τοι τρόπον εὐεργετεῖται καὶ εὐεργετεῖ, ὕστερον ἐροῦμεν, κατὰ τὸν οἰκεῖον αὐτοῦ γενόμενοι λόγον.

23. 1. Ἐπεὶ οὖν γέγονε πρώτη καὶ δευτέρα ἀναδρομὴ τῆς υἱότητος καὶ μεμένηκεν αὐτοῦ τὸ Πνεῦμα τὸ ἅγιον τὸν εἰρημένον τρόπον, στερέωμα τῶν ὑπερκοσμίων καὶ τοῦ κόσμου μεταξὺ τεταγμένον. 2. διῄρηται γὰρ ὑπὸ Βασιλείδου τὰ ὄντα εἰς δύο τὰς προεχεῖς καὶ πρώτας διαιρέσεις, καὶ καλεῖται κατ᾽ αὐτὸν τὸ μέν τι κόσμος, τὸ δέ τι ὑπερκόσμια· τὸ δὲ μεταξὺ τοῦ κόσμου καὶ τῶν ὑπερκοσμίων μεθόριον Πνεῦμα [τοῦτο], ὅπερ ἐστὶ καὶ ἅγιον καὶ τῆς υἱότητος ἔχει μένουσαν ἐν ἑαυτῷ τὴν ὀσμήν.

3. <γενηθ>έντος οὖν τοῦ στερεώματος, ὅ ἐστιν ὑπεράνω τοῦ οὐρανοῦ, διέσφυξεν καὶ ἐγεν<ν>ήθη ἀπὸ τοῦ κοσμικοῦ σπέρματος καὶ τῆς πανσπερμίας τοῦ σωροῦ ὁ μέγας ἄρχων, ἡ κεφαλὴ τοῦ κόσμου, κάλλος τε καὶ μέγεθος ἡ δύναμις <λα>ληθῆναι μὴ δυναμένη· ἀρρήτων γάρ, φησίν, ἐστὶν ἀρρητότερος καὶ δυνατῶν δυνατώτερος καὶ σοφῶν σοφώτερος καὶ ὅ τι ἂν εἴπῃς τῶν καλῶν παντὸς κρείττων.

4. Οὗτος γεννηθεὶς ἐπῆρεν ἑαυτὸν καὶ μετεώρισε καὶ ἠνέχθη [ὅλος] ἄνω μέχρι τοῦ στερεώματος [ἔστη], τῆς δὴ ἀναδρομῆς καὶ τοῦ ὑψώματος τὸ στερέωμα τέλος εἶναι νομίσας καὶ μηδὲν εἶναι μετὰ ταῦτα ὅλως [μὴ δὲ εἶναι] ἐπινοήσας. ἐγένετο μὲν ὑποκειμένων πάντων—ὅσα ἦν λοιπὸν κοσμικά—σοφώτερος, δυνατώτερος, ἐκπρεπέστερος, φωτεινότερος, παν<τὸς> ὅ τι ἂν εἴπῃς <τῶν> καλῶν διαφέρων, χωρὶς μόνης τῆς ὑπολελειμμένης υἱότητος ἔτι ἐν τῇ πανσπερμίᾳ· ἠγνόει γὰρ ὅτι ἐστὶν αὐτοῦ σοφωτέρα καὶ δυνατωτέρα καὶ κρείττων.

5. νομίσας οὖν αὐτὸς εἶναι κύριος καὶ δεσπότης καὶ «σοφὸς ἀρχιτέκτων», τρέπεται εἰς τὴν καθ᾽ ἕκαστα κτίσιν τοῦ κόσμου. καὶ πρῶτον μὲν ἠξίωσε μὴ εἶναι μόνος, ἀλλὰ ἐποίησεν ἑαυτῷ καὶ ἐγέννησεν ἐκ τῶν ὑποκειμένων υἱόν, ἑαυτοῦ

the inferior to the superior. But nothing is so mindless among the superior realities as to descend below.[70]

But the third Sonship, he says—the one in need of purification—remains in the great heap of the seed mixture in a mutually benefitting relationship. How this relationship works, I will later relate when I come to the appropriate place.[71]

THE FIRMAMENT. 23. 1. Now when the first and second Sonship sprinted upward, the Holy Spirit remained in the same place in the said fashion, spread out as a firmament between the cosmos and entities above the cosmos.[72] 2. To explain: Basileides divides existing things into two preeminent and primary divisions. One is called the "cosmic," in his language, and the other "supercosmic." The intervening boundary between the cosmic and supercosmic he calls "Spirit." This is the Holy Spirit, which retains the scent of Sonship.

THE GREAT RULER AND HIS SON. 3. Now when this firmament arose over heaven, the great Ruler throbbed with life and was born from the world seed and from the heap of the seed mixture. He is the head of the world, the power who cannot be described in terms of beauty and greatness. The great Ruler is, he says, more ineffable than the ineffable, more powerful than the powerful, wiser than the wise, and better than anything you call "good."

4. When he was born, he raised himself, soared high, and was brought above as far as the firmament. He supposed that the firmament was the limit of his upward sprint and exaltation, and thought that there was absolutely nothing beyond it. He became wiser, more powerful, more excellent, and more luminous than all the beings below—as many as remained cosmic. He was superior to everything you might call "good," with the single exception of the Sonship still remaining behind in the seed mixture. He did not know that this Sonship was wiser, more powerful, and better than he.

5. So, supposing that he was lord, master, and "wise architect," he turned to the individual aspects of creation.[73] First of all, he resolved that he not be alone. Instead, he made and fathered for himself a son from the

70. For an attempt to make sense of this sentence, see Gilles Quispel, "Note sur Basilide," *VC* 2 (1948): 115–16.

71. See *Ref.* 7.25.1 below.

72. Cf. Gen 1:7–8 LXX (the firmament).

73. For "lord," see Isa 45:5 LXX. For "wise architect," see 1 Cor 3:10 (σοφὸς

πολὺ κρείττονα καὶ σοφώτερον. 6.—ταῦτα δὲ ἦν πάντα προβεβουλευμένος ὁ οὐκ ὢν θεός, ὅτε τὴν πανσπερμίαν κατεβάλε<το>.—ἰδὼν οὖν τὸν υἱόν, ἐθαύμασε καὶ ἠγάπησε καὶ κατεπλάγη· τοιοῦτον γάρ τι κάλλος ἐγένετο υἱοῦ τῷ μεγάλῳ ἄρχοντι. καὶ ἐκάθισεν αὐτὸν ἐκ δεξιῶν ὁ ἄρχων· 7. αὕτη ἐστὶν ἡ κατ᾽ αὐτοὺ<ς> Ὀγδοὰς λεγομένη, ὅπου ἐστὶν ὁ μέγας ἄρχων καθήμενος.

πᾶσαν οὖν τὴν ἐπουράνιον κτίσιν, τουτέστι τὴν αἰθέριον, αὐτὸς εἰργάσατο ὁ δημιουργός, ὁ μέγας σοφός· ἐνήργει δὲ αὐτῷ καὶ ὑπετίθετο ὁ υἱὸς ὁ τούτου γενόμενος, ὢν αὐτοῦ τοῦ δημιουργοῦ πολὺ σοφώτερος.

24. 1. Αὕτη ἔστιν ἡ κατ᾽ Ἀριστοτέλην σώματος φυσικοῦ ὀργανικοῦ ἐν(τ)ελέχεια, ψυχὴ ἐνεργοῦσα τῷ σώματι. [ἧς δίχα] τὸ σῶμα ἐργάζεσθαι οὐδὲν δύναται μεῖζον καὶ ἐπιφανέστερον καὶ δυνατώτερον καὶ σοφώτερον τῆς ψυχῆς. ὃν λόγον οὖν Ἀριστοτέλης ἀποδέδωκε περὶ τῆς ψυχῆς καὶ τοῦ σώματος πρότερος Βασιλείδης περὶ τοῦ μεγάλου ἄρχοντος καὶ τοῦ κατ᾽ αὐτὸν υἱοῦ διασαφεῖ. 2. τόν τε γὰρ υἱὸν ὁ ἄρχων κατὰ Βασιλείδην γεγένηκεν, τήν τε ψυχὴν ἔργον καὶ ἀποτέλεσμα <τοῦ σώματ>ός φησιν εἶναι ὁ Ἀριστοτέλης, φυσικοῦ σώματος ὀργανικοῦ ἐντελέχειαν. ὡς οὖν ἡ ἐντελέχεια διοικεῖ τὸ σῶμα, οὕτως ὁ υἱὸς διοικεῖ κατὰ Βασιλείδην τὸν ἀρρήτων ἀρρητότερον θεόν.

3. Πάντα οὖν ἔστι προνοούμενα καὶ διοικούμενα ὑπὸ [τῆς μεγάλης] τοῦ ἄρχοντος τοῦ μεγάλου τὰ αἰθέρια ἅτινα μέχρι σελήνης ἐστίν· ἐκεῖθεν γὰρ ἀὴρ αἰθέρος διακρίνεται. κεκοσμημένων οὖν πάντων τῶν αἰθερίων πάλιν ἀπὸ τῆς

underlying realities, who was much greater and wiser than himself. 6. (All this the nonexistent God had planned beforehand when he sowed the seed mixture.) Now when the great Ruler saw his son, he wondered at him, loved him, and was astonished—so great was the beauty of his son to the great Ruler! Accordingly, the Ruler sat him at his right hand. 7. The realm where the great Ruler sits they call the "Ogdoad."

Thus the great and wise Artificer produced the heavenly (that is, aetherial) creation. His Son, who was born from him, activated and instructed him, since he was much wiser than the Artificer himself.

RELATION TO ARISTOTLE. 24. 1. This [relationship of Ruler to son] represents Aristotle's "actuality of the natural body used as an instrument."[74] The soul activates the body. The body can produce nothing greater, more glorious, more powerful, or wiser than soul. Now Basileides interprets the definition that Aristotle previously gave about the soul and the body with reference to the great Ruler and his putative son. 2. For the Ruler, according to Basileides, fathered the son; and the soul, Aristotle says, is the product and fulfillment of the body—"the actuality of a natural body used as an instrument." Thus, just as the actuality of the body directs the body, so the son, according to Basileides, directs the God who is "more ineffable than what is ineffable."[75]

THE SECOND RULER. 3. So everything aetherial (whatever extends down to the moon, where air and aether are distinguished) is foreknown and administered by the great Ruler.[76] When all aetherial reality was ordered,

ἀρχιτέκτων), which recalls Isa 3:3 LXX. Cf. *Ref.* 6.33.1; Tert., *Marc.* 5.6.10; Clem. Alex., *Strom.* 5.4.26.3.

74. Cf. Aristotle, *De an.* 2.1, 412a19–21; 27f. The soul is so defined above in *Ref.* 7.19.6. Cf. Plutarch, *Quaest. plat.* 1006d; Diog. L., *Vit. phil.* 5.33. See further Quispel, "Gnostic Man," 220–21; Bos, "Aristotelianizing Gnostic," 58.

75. Mueller believes that our author's "comparison is based on a straightforward misunderstanding of the Aristotelian formula for the soul. Our author takes it to mean that the soul is something that is actualized (brought into actuality) by the body rather than an actualization undergone by the body" ("Hippolytus, Aristotle, Basilides," 150). Sharples also points out that our author (wrongly) supposes that for Aristotle "the soul is *produced by* the body" (*Peripatetic Philosophy*, 247). See further Stephen Menn, "The Origins of Aristotle's Concept of Ἐνέργεια: Ἐνέργεια and Δύναμις," *Ancient Philosophy* 14 (1994): 73–114 (104 n. 42).

76. Werner Foerster believes that our author made an error here. "The sphere of the Ogdoad is that of the fixed stars, the sphere of the Hebdomad, that of the planets

πανσπερμίας ἄλλος ἄρχων ἀνέβη, μείζων μὲν [τοι] πάντων τῶν ὑποκειμένων χωρὶς μέντοι τῆς καταλελειμμένης υἱότητος, πολὺ δὲ ὑποδεέστερος τοῦ πρώτου ἄρχοντος.

4. ἔστι δὲ καὶ οὗτος ἄρρητος ὑπ' αὐτῶν λεγόμενος, καὶ καλεῖται ὁ τόπος οὗτος Ἑβδομάς. καὶ πάντων τῶν ὑποκειμένων οὗτός ἐστι διοικητὴς καὶ δημιουργός, ποιήσας καὶ αὐτὸς ἑαυτῷ υἱὸν ἐκ τῆς πανσπερμίας [καὶ αὐτὸς] ἑαυτοῦ φρονιμώτερον καὶ σοφώτερον, παραπλησίως τοῖς ἐπὶ τοῦ πρώτου ἄρχοντος λελεγμένοις.

5. τὰ δ' ἐν τῷ διαστήματι τούτῳ ὁ σωρὸς αὐτός ἐστι, φησί, καὶ ἡ πανσπερμία. καὶ γίνεται κατὰ φύσιν τὰ γινόμενα, ὡς φθάσαν<τα> τεχθῆναι ὑπὸ τοῦ τὰ μέλλοντα γενέσθαι ὅτε δεῖ καὶ οἷα δεῖ καὶ ὡς δεῖ λελογισμένου. καὶ τούτων ἐστὶν ἐπιστάτης ἢ φροντιστὴς ἢ δημιουργὸς οὐδείς· ἀρκεῖ γὰρ αὐτοῖς ὁ λογισμὸς ἐκεῖνος, <ὃν> ὁ οὐκ ὢν ὅτε ἐποίει ἐλογίζετο.

25. 1. Ἐπεὶ οὖν τετέλεσται κατ' αὐτοὺς ὁ κόσμος ὅλος καὶ τὰ ὑπερκόσμια, καὶ ἔστιν ἐνδεὲς οὐδέν, λείπεται δὴ ἐν τῇ πανσπερμίᾳ ἡ υἱότης ἡ τρίτη, ἡ καταλελει(μ)μένη εὐεργετεῖν καὶ εὐεργετεῖσθαι ἐν τῷ σπέρματι. καὶ <ἔ>δει τὴν ὑπολελειμμένην υἱότητα ἀποκαλυφθῆναι καὶ ἀποκατασθῆναι ἄνω ἐκεῖ ὑπὲρ τὸ μεθόριον Πνεῦμα πρὸς τὴν υἱότητα τὴν λεπτομερῆ καὶ μιμητικὴν καὶ τὸν οὐκ ὄντα, ὡς γέγραπται, φησί· «καὶ ἡ κτίσις αὐτὴ συστενάζει καὶ συνωδίνει», «τὴν ἀποκάλυψιν τῶν υἱῶν τοῦ θεοῦ ἐκδεχομένη». 2. υἱοὶ δέ, φησίν, ἐσμὲν ἡμεῖς οἱ πνευματικοί, ἐνθάδε καταλελειμμένοι διακοσμῆσαι καὶ διατυπῶσαι καὶ διορθώσασθαι καὶ τελειῶσαι τὰς ψυχὰς τὰς φύσιν ἐχούσας μένειν ἐν τούτῳ τῷ διαστήματι.

«Μέχρι μὲν οὖν Μωσέως ἀπὸ Ἀδὰμ ἐβασίλευσεν ἡ ἁμαρτία», καθὼς γέγραπται· 3. ἐβασίλευσεν γὰρ ὁ μέγας ἄρχων, ὁ ἔχων τὸ τέλος αὐτοῦ μέχρι

once again another ruler rose from the seed mixture. He was greater than all underlying realities apart from, of course, the Sonship left behind in the seed mixture. This ruler was, however, far inferior to the first Ruler.

4. They also call this second ruler "ineffable."[77] His region is called "Hebdomad." He is the administrator and artificer of everything that lies under him, since he also made a son for himself from the seed mixture, a son more intelligent and wiser than himself (almost exactly like what they say in reference to the first Ruler).

5. The entities on his level of reality consist of the heap itself, he claims, as well as the seed mixture. What is born arises by nature, as though rushing to be crafted by him who planned when, how, and in what way future realities must arise. They have no supervisor, caretaker, or artificer. For them, the plan of the Nonexistent suffices, a plan that he charted when he made [the world seed].[78]

SALVATION HISTORY. 25. 1. Now when their whole universe and the supercosmic realities were completed and nothing whatsoever was lacking, it remained for the third Sonship—left behind in the seed mixture—to benefit and to be benefited in the seed. It was necessary for the Sonship that was left behind to be revealed and restored in that upper world above the boundary of the Spirit in the presence of the subtle Sonship, the imitative Sonship, and the Nonexistent. This is in accordance, he claims, with what is written: "Even creation itself groans along with us and is in labor," "eagerly expecting the revelation of the children of God."[79] 2. The "children," he claims, are we spiritual people, left behind here to order, form, correct, and perfect the souls that have a nature that remains on this level.

Just as it is written: "thus from Adam to Moses Sin reigned as king."[80] 3. For the great Ruler reigned as king, who has his limit at the firmament. He

[down to the moon]" (*Gnosis: A Selection of Gnostic Texts*, trans. R. McL. Wilson, 2 vols. [Oxford: Clarendon, 1972], 1:69 n. 11). See further May, *Creatio*, 69 n. 30. Cf. *Ref.* 1.4.3; 1.20.6; 7.19.2.

77. This sentence seems to contradict *Ref.* 7.25.4 below, which says that the Ruler of the Hebdomad is describable (ῥητός). To avoid the problem, Holwerda would emend the text ("Textkritisches," 602).

78. The account of Basileides's cosmology here seems deliberately shaped to fit the description of Aristotle's cosmology in *Ref.* 7.19.2–4. See further Mueller, "Hippolytus, Aristotle, Basilides," 151–56.

79. Rom 8:21–22, 19 (in this order). Cf. *Ref.* 6.35.2 ("Valentinus") and 7.27.1.

80. Rom 5:14; cf. Clem. Alex., *Strom.* 3.9.64.2; 4.3.9.6.

στερεώματος, <ὁ> νομίζων αὐτὸς εἶναι θεὸς μόνος καὶ ὑπὲρ αὐτὸν εἶναι μηδέν<α>. πάντα γάρ ἦν φυλασσόμενα ἀποκρύφῳ σιωπῇ. τοῦτο, φησίν, ἐστὶ «τὸ μυστήριον, ὃ ταῖς προτέραις γενεαῖς οὐκ ἐγνωρίσθη». ἀλλὰ ἦν ἐν ἐκείνοις τοῖς χρόνοις βασιλεὺς καὶ κύριος, ὡς ἐδόκει, τῶν ὅλων ὁ μέγας ἄρχων, ἡ Ὀγδοάς.

4. ἦν δὲ καὶ τούτου τοῦ διαστήματος βασιλεὺς καὶ κύριος, ἡ Ἑβδομάς· καὶ ἔστιν ἡ μὲν Ὀγδοὰς ἄρρητος, ῥητὸς δὲ ἡ Ἑβδομάς. οὗτός ἐστι, φησίν, ὁ τῆς Ἑβδομάδος ἄρχων ὁ λαλήσας τῷ Μωϋσῇ καὶ εἰπών· «ἐγὼ ὁ θεὸς Ἀβραὰμ καὶ Ἰσαὰκ καὶ Ἰακώβ, καὶ τὸ ὄνομα τοῦ θεοῦ οὐκ ἐδήλωσα αὐτοῖς»—οὕτως γὰρ θέλουσι γεγράφθαι—τουτέστι τοῦ ἀρρήτου τῆς Ὀγδοάδος ἄρχοντος θεοῦ. 5. πάντες οὖν οἱ προφῆται οἱ πρὸ τοῦ σωτῆρος, φησίν, ἐκεῖθεν ἐλάλησαν.

Ἐπεὶ οὖν ἔδει ἀποκαλυφθῆναι, φησίν, ἡμᾶς, τὰ τέκνα τοῦ θεοῦ, περὶ ὧν «ἐστέναξε», φησίν, «ἡ κτίσις καὶ ὤδινεν, ἀπεκδεχομένη τὴν ἀποκάλυψιν», ἦλθε τὸ εὐαγγέλιον εἰς τὸν κόσμον, καὶ διῆλθε διὰ «πάσης ἀρχῆς καὶ ἐξουσίας κυριότητος <καὶ> παντὸς ὀνόματος ὀνομαζομένου». 6. ἦλθε δὲ οὕτως, καί<περ> οὐδὲν κατῆλθεν ἄνωθεν, οὐδ᾽ ἐξέστη ἡ μακαρία υἱότης ἐκείνου τοῦ ἀπερινοήτου καὶ μακαρίου οὐκ ὄντος θεοῦ. ἀλλὰ γὰρ καθάπερ ὁ νάφθας ὁ Ἰνδικός, ὀφθεὶς μόνον ἀπὸ πάνυ πολλοῦ διαστήματος, συνάπτει πῦρ, οὕτω κάτωθεν, ἀπὸ τῆς ἀμορφίας τοῦ σωροῦ, διήκουσιν αἱ δυνάμεις ἄνω μέχρι τῆς υἱότητος.

7. ἅπτει μὲν γὰρ καὶ λαμβάνει τὰ νοήματα κατὰ τὸν <ν>άφθαν τὸν Ἰνδικόν—οἷον νάφθας τις ὤν—ὁ τοῦ μεγάλου τῆς Ὀγδοάδος ἄρχοντος υἱὸς ἀπὸ τῆς μετὰ τὸ μεθόριον μακαρίας υἱότητος· ἡ γὰρ ἐν μέσῳ τοῦ ἁγίου Πνεύματος, ἐν τῷ μεθορίῳ τῆς υἱότητος δύναμις ῥέοντα καὶ φερόμενα τὰ νοήματα τῆς υἱότητος μεταδίδωσι τῷ υἱῷ τοῦ μεγάλου ἄρχοντος.

supposed that he alone was God and that no one was above him.[81] Everything was guarded by the concealment of silence. This, he says, is "the mystery unknown in former generations."[82] But the great Ruler of the universe, the Ogdoad, was—so he thought—king and lord.

4. There was also a king and lord of this level of reality: the Hebdomad. The Ogdoad is indescribable, but the Hebdomad can be described. This ruler of the Hebdomad, he claims, is the one who spoke the following to Moses: "I am the God of Abraham and Isaac and Jacob, and the name of God I did not reveal to them."[83] In their arbitrary interpretation, the name of God is the name of the ineffable Ogdoad, or Ruler. 5. All the prophets before the Savior, he claims, spoke from the Hebdomad.[84]

THE GOSPEL. Now since it was necessary, he continues, that we, the children of God, be revealed (for whom creation "groaned," he says, "and was in labor pangs as it eagerly expected the revelation"),[85] the gospel came to the world, traversing "all rule, authority, lordship, and every name that is named."[86] 6. So it came, although nothing descended from above, nor was the blessed Sonship removed from that incomprehensible and blessed nonexistent God.[87] Rather, just as Indian naphtha lights a fire by simply appearing from a great distance, so the powers extend upward from the chaotic heap below as far as the Sonship.[88]

7. The son of the great Ruler, the Ogdoad, kindles the Ruler's thoughts like Indian naphtha (as though he were a kind of naphtha). He receives the thoughts from the blessed Sonship beyond the boundary. The power of the Sonship in the midst of the Holy Spirit at the boundary imparts the flowing current of thoughts from the Sonship to the son of the great Ruler.

---

81. Cf. *Ref.* 5.26.15 (Justin); 6.33.1 ("Valentinus"); Iren., *Haer.* 1.5.4; 29.4; 30.6; Epiph., *Pan.* 25.2.3; Ap. John (NHC II,1) 11.20; 13.8; Nat. Rulers (NHC II,4) 86.30; 94.22.

82. Eph 3:4–5; cf. *Ref.* 5.8.5 (Naassenes); 6.35.1 ("Valentinus"); 7.26.7; Clem. Alex., *Strom.* 5.13.87.1.

83. Exod 6:3; cf. *Ref.* 6.36.2 ("Valentinus").

84. Cf. *Ref.* 6.35.1 ("Valentinus").

85. Rom 8:19, 22, 19 (in this order).

86. The language of Eph 1:21, which describes the exaltation of Christ, is redeployed to describe the descent of the gospel. Cf. below, *Ref.* 7.20.3; 7.22.13.

87. The gospel, it would seem, is naturally exuded from the Sonships above the firmament (with no deliberate aim to descend). Bos observes: "God does bring about the great revolution or completion of the cosmic development, but as unmoved mover!" ("Basilides of Alexandria: Matthias," 409).

88. Cf. the note on *Ref.* 5.17.9 (Peratai).

26. 1. Ἦλθεν οὖν τὸ εὐαγγέλιον [πρῶτον] ἀπὸ τῆς υἱότητος, φησίν, διὰ τοῦ παρακαθημένου τῷ ἄρχοντι υἱοῦ τὸ <πρῶτον> πρὸς τὸν ἄρχοντα, καὶ ἔμαθεν ὁ ἄρχων ὅτι οὐκ ἦν θεὸς τῶν ὅλων, ἀλλ' ἦν γεννητὸς καὶ ἔχων ὑπεράνω τὸν τοῦ ἀρρήτου καὶ <ἀ>κατονομάστου οὐκ ὄντος καὶ τῆς υἱότητος κατακείμενον θησαυρόν· καὶ ἐπέστρεψε καὶ ἐφοβήθη, συνιεὶς ἐν οἵᾳ ἦν ἀγνοίᾳ.

2. τοῦτό ἐστι, φησίν, τὸ εἰρημένον· «ἀρχὴ σοφίας φόβος κυρίου»· ἤρξατο γὰρ σοφίζεσθαι, κατηχούμενος ὑπὸ τοῦ παρακαθημένου <υἱοῦ>, διδασκόμενος τίς ἐστιν ὁ οὐκ ὤν, τίς ἡ υἱότης, τί τὸ ἅγιον Πνεῦμα, τίς ἡ τῶν ὅλων κατασκευὴ <καὶ> ποῦ ταῦτα ἀποκατασταθήσεται. 3. αὕτη ἐστὶν «ἡ σοφία ἐν μυστηρίῳ λεγομένη», περὶ ἧς, φησίν, ἡ γραφὴ λέγει· «οὐκ ἐν διδακτοῖς ἀνθρωπίνης σοφίας λόγοις, ἀλλ' ἐν διδακτοῖς πνεύματος». κατηχηθεὶς οὖν, φησίν, ὁ ἄρχων καὶ διδαχθεὶς καὶ φοβηθείς, ἐξωμολογήσατο περὶ ἁμαρτίας, ἧς ἐποίησε μεγαλύνων ἑαυτόν. 4. τοῦτό ἐστι, φησί, τὸ εἰρημένον· «τὴν ἁμαρτίαν μου ἐγνώρισα καὶ τὴν ἀνομίαν μου ἐγὼ γινώσκω· ὑπὲρ ταύτης ἐξομολογήσομαι εἰς τὸν αἰῶνα».

Ἐπεὶ οὖν κατήχητο μὲν ὁ μέγας ἄρχων, κατήχητο δὲ καὶ δεδίδακτο πᾶσα ἡ τῆς Ὀγδοάδος κτίσις καὶ ἐγνωρίσθη τοῖς ἐπουρανίοις τὸ μυστήριον, ἔδει λοιπὸν καὶ ἐπὶ τὴν Ἑβδομάδα ἐλθεῖν τὸ εὐαγγέλιον, ἵνα καὶ ὁ τῆς Ἑβδομάδος ἄρχων παραπλησίως διδαχθῇ καὶ εὐαγγελισθήσεται.

5. ἐπέλαμψεν ὁ υἱὸς τοῦ μεγάλου ἄρχοντος τῷ υἱῷ τ(οῦ) ἄρχοντος τῆς Ἑβδομάδος τὸ φῶς, ὃ εἶχεν ἅψας αὐτὸς ἄνωθεν, ἀπὸ τῆς υἱότητος, καὶ ἐφωτίσθη ὁ υἱὸς τοῦ ἄρχοντος τῆς Ἑβδομάδος, καὶ εὐηγγελίσατο τὸ εὐαγγέλιον τῷ ἄρχοντι τῆς Ἑβδομάδος, καὶ ὁμοίως κατὰ τὸν πρῶτον λόγον καὶ αὐτὸς ἐφοβήθη καὶ ἐξωμολογήσατο.

6. Ἐπεὶ οὖν καὶ τὰ ἐν τῇ Ἑβδομάδι πάντα πεφώτιστο καὶ διήγγελτο τὸ εὐαγγέλιον αὐτοῖς — κτίσεις γάρ εἰσι κατ<ὰ> [αὐτὰ] τὰ διαστήματα καὶ κατ' αὐτοὺς ἄπειροι, καὶ ἀρχαὶ καὶ δυνάμεις καὶ ἐξουσίαι· περὶ ὧν μακρός ἐστι παρ'

26. 1. So the gospel came first to the Ruler from the Sonship, he says, via the son enthroned beside the Ruler. By it, the great Ruler learned that he was not the God of the universe. He learned that he was born and that there is stored above him the treasure of the ineffable and unnamable Nonexistent and the Sonship. Then he converted and was struck with fear as he understood the depth of his ignorance.

2. This, he says, is what the scriptural verse refers to: "The Lord's fear is the beginning of wisdom."[89] This is because the Ruler grew wise when instructed by the Son enthroned beside him.[90] He learned the identity of the Nonexistent, the Sonship, the Holy Spirit, the construction of the universe, and where these things will be restored. 3. This is "the wisdom spoken in a mystery," referred to, he claims, in scripture: "not in learned teachings of human wisdom, but in the teachings of the Spirit."[91] Thus instructed, he says, the Ruler learned, took fright, and confessed his sins that he committed by magnifying himself. 4. This, Basileides claims, is what the scriptural verse refers to: "I recognized my sin, and I acknowledge my lawless behavior, concerning which I will make eternal confession."[92]

Now when the great Ruler was instructed and taught, along with the entire structure of the Ogdoad, and the mystery was made known in the heavenly places, it was then necessary for the gospel to come to the Hebdomad so that the ruler of the Hebdomad might be equally taught and told the good news.

5. Therefore the son of the great Ruler shone upon the son of the Hebdomad's ruler. He shone with the light that he had kindled from the Sonship above. Then the son of the Hebdomad's ruler was enlightened. He told the good news to the ruler of the Hebdomad. Then, just as in the prior instance, the ruler was stung with fear and confessed.

6. And so, when everything in the Hebdomad was also enlightened and informed of the good news (for they believe in infinite creations spread throughout different levels of reality, as well as rulers, powers, and authori-

89. Prov 1:7; 9:10; Ps 110:10 LXX. Cf. Clem. Alex., *Strom.* 2.7.35.5–36.1 (= Löhr, *Basilides*, frag. 15); *Strom.* 2.8.37.5–38.2; *Ref.* 6.32.7 ("Valentinus"). See further André Méhat, "ΑΠΟΚΑΤΑΣΤΑΣΙΣ chez Basilide," in *Mélanges d'histoire des religions offerts à Henri-Charles Puech* (Paris: Presses Universitaires de France, 1974), 365–73 (368–69); Löhr, *Basilides*, 61–78.

90. Marcovich replaces χ(ριστο)ῦ ("Christ") with υἱοῦ ("Son").

91. 1 Cor 2:7, 13. Cf. the interpretation of v. 13 in *Ref.* 5.8.26 (Naassenes).

92. An apparent conflation of Ps 31:5 and 50:5 LXX.

αὐτοῖς πάνυ λόγος διὰ πολλῶν λεγόμενος· ἔνθα καὶ τριακοσίους ἑξήκοντα πέντε οὐρανοὺς φάσκουσι, καὶ τὸν μέγαν ἄρχοντα αὐτῶν εἶναι τὸν Ἀβρασάξ, διὰ τὸ περιέχειν τὸ ὄνομα αὐτοῦ ψῆφον τξε′, ὡς δὴ τοῦ ὀνόματος τὴν ψῆφον περιέχειν πάντα, καὶ διὰ τοῦτο τὸν ἐνιαυτὸν τοσούτων ἡμερῶν συνεστάναι·

7. ἀλλ' ἐπεί, φησίν, ταῦθ' οὕτως ἐγένετο, ἔδει λοιπὸν καὶ τὴν ἀμορφίαν καθ' ἡμᾶς φωτισθῆναι, καὶ τῇ υἱότητι τῇ ἐν τῇ ἀμορφίᾳ καταλελειμμένῃ οἱονεὶ ἐκτρώματι ἀποκαλυφθῆναι «τὸ μυστήριον, ὃ ταῖς προτέραις γενεαῖς οὐκ ἐγνωρίσθη», καθὼς γέγραπται, φησίν· «κατὰ ἀποκάλυψιν ἐγνωρίσθη μοι τὸ μυστήριον» καὶ «ἤκουσα ἄρρητα ῥήματα, ἃ οὐκ ἐξὸν ἀνθρώπῳ εἰπεῖν».

8. Κατῆλθεν ἀπὸ τῆς Ἑβδομάδος τὸ φῶς, τὸ κατελθὸν ἀπὸ τῆς Ὀγδοάδος ἄνωθεν τῷ υἱῷ τῆς Ἑβδομάδος, ἐπὶ τὸν Ἰησοῦν, τὸν υἱὸν τῆς Μαρίας, καὶ ἐφωτίσθη συνεξαφθεὶς τῷ φωτὶ τῷ λάμψαντι εἰς αὐτόν. 9. τοῦτό ἐστι, φησί, τὸ εἰρημένον·

Πνεῦμα ἅγιον ἐπελεύσεται ἐπὶ σέ,

τὸ ἀπὸ τῆς υἱότητος διὰ τοῦ μεθορίου Πνεύματος ἐπὶ τὴν Ὀγδοάδα καὶ τὴν Ἑβδομάδα διελθὸν μέχρι τῆς Μαρίας,

καὶ δύναμις ὑψίστου ἐπισκιάσει σοι,

ἡ δύναμις τῆς κρίσεως, ἀπὸ τῆς ἀκρωρείας ἄνωθεν <διὰ> τοῦ δημιουργοῦ μέχρι τῆς κτίσεως, ὅ ἐστι τοῦ (υἱ)οῦ. 10. μέχρι δ' ἐκείνου φησὶ συνεστηκέναι

ties whose account is altogether extensive and told at great length—[93] In these accounts they even claim that there are 365 heavens and that their great Ruler is Abrasax, whose name contains the numerical value 365. Thus, we can be sure, the number of his name contains everything, and for this reason the year consists of this number of days).[94]

7. But when, he continues, these things happened in this way, it was necessary, finally, for the chaos in our region to be enlightened and for "the mystery not known in former generations" to be revealed in the Sonship that was left behind in the chaos like a miscarriage,[95] just as (he claims) it is written: "the mystery was made known to me by revelation"[96] and "I heard unutterable utterances, which it is not permissible to declare to a human being."[97]

Jesus. 8. So the light came down from the Hebdomad, which had descended from the Ogdoad above to the Son of the Hebdomad. It rested upon Jesus son of Mary.[98] He was enlightened and set on fire by the light that shone upon him. 9. The scripture refers to this, he claims, by saying,

> Holy Spirit will come upon you.

This refers to the light that traveled from the Sonship, passing through the Spirit at the boundary to the Ogdoad and Hebdomad, until it reached Mary.

> And power of the Most High will overshadow you.[99]

This refers to the power of differentiation, namely, the Son that descends from the heights above through the Artificer as far as creation.[100] 10. The

93. The sentence is incomplete.

94. Cf. Iren., *Haer.* 1.24.3, 5, 7; Epiph., *Pan.* 24.7.2, 4; Ps.-Tert., *Adv. omn. haer.* 1.5.

95. For "miscarriage" (ἔκτρωμα), see 1 Cor 15:8; *Ref.* 6.31.2; 6.36.3 ("Valentinus"); Iren., *Haer.* 1.4.1; 8.2; Clem. Alex., *Exc.* 68.

96. Eph 3:3; cf. *Ref.* 6.35.1 ("Valentinus"); 7.25.3.

97. 2 Cor 12:4; cf. *Ref.* 5.8.25 (Naassenes); Epiph., *Pan.* 38.2.5.

98. For the importance of Mary, see Orbe, *Cristología Gnóstica*, 1:424–25.

99. Luke 1:35; cf. *Ref.* 6.35.3, 7 ("Valentinus"); 10.23.1 (Theodotos the Byzantian); Clem. Alex., *Exc.* 26, 60.

100. For the "power of differentiation," see *Ref.* 5.21.6; 7.27.8–9, 11–12; 10.14.9; Clem. Alex., *Strom.* 2.8.36.1; 2.8.38.2.

τὸν κόσμον οὕτως, μέχρις οὗ πᾶσα ἡ υἱότης, ἡ καταλελειμμένη ἐν ἀμορφίᾳ εἰς τὸ εὐεργετεῖν τὰς ψυχὰς καὶ εὐεργετεῖσθαι.

δια<με>μορφωμένη κατακολουθήσῃ τῷ Ἰησοῦ καὶ ἀναδράμῃ καὶ <ἀν>έλθῃ ἀποκαθαρισθεῖσα καὶ γενομένη λεπτομερεστάτη, ὡς δύνασθαι δι' αὐτῆς ἀναδραμεῖν, ὥσπερ ἡ πρώτη. πᾶσαν γὰρ ἔχει τὴν δύναμιν συνεστηριγμένην φυσικῶς τῷ φωτὶ τῷ λάμψαντι ἄνωθεν κάτω.

27. 1. Ὅταν οὖν <ἀν>έλθῃ, φησί, πᾶσα υἱότης καὶ ἔσται ὑπὲρ τὸ μεθόριον [τὸ] Πνεῦμα, τότε ἐλεηθήσεται ἡ κτίσις· «στένει γὰρ μέχρι τοῦ νῦν καὶ βασανίζεται», καὶ «μένει τὴν ἀποκάλυψιν τῶν υἱῶν τοῦ θεοῦ», ἵνα πάντες ἀνέλθωσιν ἐντεῦθεν οἱ τῆς υἱότητος ἄνθρωποι. ἐπειδὰν γένηται τοῦτο, ἐπάξει, φησίν, ὁ θεὸς ἐπὶ τὸν κόσμον ὅλον τὴν μεγάλην ἄγνοιαν, ἵνα μ<έν>ῃ πάντα κατὰ φύσιν καὶ μηδὲν μηδενὸς τῶν παρὰ φύσιν ἐπιθυ<μήσῃ>. 2. ἀλλὰ γὰρ πᾶσαι αἱ ψυχαὶ τούτου τοῦ διαστήματος, ὅσαι φύσιν ἔχουσιν ἐν τούτῳ ἀθάνατοι διαμένειν μόνῳ, μενοῦσιν οὐδὲν ἐ<π>ιστάμεναι τούτου τοῦ διαστήματος διάφορον οὐ<δὲ> βέλτιον· οὐδὲ ἀκοή τις ἔσται τῶν ὑπερκειμένων ἐν τοῖς ὑποκειμένοις οὐδὲ γνῶσις, ἵνα μὴ τῶν ἀδυνάτων αἱ ὑποκείμεναι ψυχαὶ ὀρεγόμεναι βασανίζωνται, καθάπερ <οἱ> ἰχθύ<ε>ς ἐπιθυμήσα<ντε>ς ἐν τοῖς ὄρεσι μετὰ τῶν προβάτων νέμεσθαι· ἐγένετο ἄν, φησίν, αὐτοῖς ἡ τοιαύτη ἐπιθυμία φθορά. 3. ἔσται οὖν, φησίν, ἄφθαρτα πάντα τὰ κατὰ χώραν μένοντα, φθαρτὰ δὲ εἰ ἐκ τῶν κατὰ φύσιν ὑπερπηδᾶν καὶ ὑπερβαίνειν βούλοιντο.

Οὕτως οὐδὲ<ν> ὁ ἄρχων τῆς Ἑβδομάδος γνώσεται τῶν ὑπερκειμένων· καταλήψεται γὰρ καὶ τοῦτον ἡ μεγάλη ἄγνοια, ἵνα ἀποστῇ ἀπ' αὐτοῦ «λύπη καὶ ὀδύνη καὶ στεναγμός»· ἐπιθυμήσει γὰρ οὐδενὸς τῶν ἀδυνάτων οὐδὲ λυπηθήσεται. 4. καταλήψεται δὲ ὁμοίως καὶ τὸν μέγαν ἄρχοντα τῆς Ὀγδοάδος

world, he says, was in this state until the complete formation of the entire Sonship left behind in the chaos to give and receive benefits from souls.

When the [third] Sonship is formed, it is supposed to follow after Jesus, sprint above and ascend, being purified and made utterly subtle. It will have the power to sprint back up by itself, just like the first Sonship. The third Sonship possesses the entirety of the power that is naturally fixed within the light that shines down from above.

CONSUMMATION: THE GREAT IGNORANCE. 27. 1. When the entire Sonship ascends and mounts above the Spirit serving as a boundary, then creation will be granted mercy. "For it groans and is tortured up to the present time" and "awaits the revelation of the children of God."[101] The final result is that all the people of the Sonship ascend from here. When this occurs, he says, God will bring onto the whole world the great ignorance so that all things might remain according to nature and nothing desire anything unnatural. 2. Indeed, all the souls of this level—as many as have a nature to remain immortal in this level alone—will remain, knowing nothing superior and better than this level. Nor will there be news or knowledge of the supercosmic realities among those that lie beneath. As a result, the souls that remain below will not be tortured by straining for what is impossible—like fish desiring to graze on the mountains with sheep.[102] For such a desire, he says, would result in their death. 3. Thus all things, he says, will be incorruptible if they remain in their place, but corruptible if they leap out of their natural places and desire to transcend them.

In this way, the ruler of the Hebdomad will know nothing of the things above. For the great ignorance will seize even him. As a result, he will have no more "grief and pain and groaning."[103] He will desire nothing impossible, nor will he be grieved. 4. This very ignorance will like-

---

101. Rom 8:22, 19; cf. *Ref.* 6.35.2 ("Valentinus"); 7.25.1, 5. "Tortured" (βασανίζεται) is not found in Paul's text. Bos thinks that it can be linked to Aristotle, "who described mortal existence as a torture for the soul, comparable with the torment to which Etruscan robbers subject their living prisoners by tying them to the body of dead soldiers" ("Basilides of Alexandria: Matthias," 408, citing Aristotle, *Protrepticus*, frag. 73 [Gigon]).

102. Cf. Archilochos, frag. 122.6–9 (Martin L. West, ed., *Iambi et Elegi Graeci ante Alexandrum Cantati*, 2nd ed., 2 vols. [Oxford: Clarendon, 1992], 1:48); Herodotos, *Hist.* 5.92.1; Lucretius, *Rer. nat.* 3.785; *Ref.* 7.22.13; 1.24.7.

103. Cf. Isa 35:10b; 51:11b LXX.

ἡ ἄγνοια αὕτη, καὶ πάσας τὰς ὑποκειμένας αὐτῷ κτίσεις παραπλησίως, ἵνα μηδὲν κατὰ μηδένα ὀρέγηται τῶν παρὰ φύσιν τινὸς μηδὲ ὀδυνή<σε>ται.

καὶ οὕτως ἡ ἀποκατάστασις ἔσται πάντων, κατὰ φύσιν τεθεμελιωμένων μὲν ἐν τῷ σπέρματι τῶν ὅλων ἐν ἀρχῇ, ἀποκαταστα<θησο>μένων δὲ καιρο<ῖ>ς ἰδίοις.

5. Ὅτι δέ, φησίν, ἕκαστον ἰδίους ἔχει καιρούς, ἱκανῶς ὁ σωτὴρ λέγων· «οὔπω ἥκει ἡ ὥρα μου», καὶ οἱ μάγοι τὸν ἀστέρα τεθεαμένοι. ἦν γάρ, φησί, καὶ αὐτὸς ὑπὸ γενέσιν ἀστέρων καὶ <τὴν> ὥραν ἀποκαταστάσεως ἐν τῷ μεγάλῳ προλελογισμένος σωρῷ.

6. οὗτός ἐστιν ὁ κατ᾽ αὐτοὺς νενοημένος «ἔσω ἄνθρωπος», πνευματικὸς ἐν τῷ ψυχικῷ. ὅ ἐστιν υἱότης, ἐνταῦθα ἀπολιποῦσα τὴν ψυχήν—οὐ θνητήν, ἀλλὰ <ὡς> αὐτοῦ μένουσαν κατὰ φύσιν, κα<θά>περ ἡ προτ<έρ>α υἱότης ἄνω λέλοιπεν τὸ ἅγιον Πνεῦμα τὸ μεθόριον, ἐν οἰκείῳ τόπῳ—ἰδίαν τότε περιβεβλημένη ψυχήν.

7. Ἵνα δὲ μηδὲν τῶν κατ᾽ αὐτοῦ<ς> παραλείπωμεν, ὅσα καὶ περὶ εὐαγγελίου λέγουσιν ἐκθήσομαι. εὐαγγέλιόν ἐστι κατ᾽ αὐτοὺς ἡ τῶν ὑπερκοσμίων γνῶσις, ὡς δεδήλωται, ἣν ὁ μέγας ἄρχων οὐκ ἠπίστατο. ὡς οὖν ἐδηλώθη αὐτῷ ὅτι καὶ τὸ Πνεῦμα ἅγιόν ἐστι τουτέστι τὸ μεθόριον, καὶ ἡ υἱότης, καὶ θεός, ὁ τούτων αἴτιος πάντων, ὁ οὐκ ὤν, ἐχάρη ἐπὶ τοῖς λεχθεῖσι, καὶ ἠγαλλιάσατο, τοῦτ᾽ ἔστι κατ᾽ αὐτοὺς τὸ εὐαγγέλιον.

wise seize the great Ruler of the Ogdoad, and equally all the creations lying below him, so that nothing in any region might strain after what is unnatural and be grieved.

In this way, then, the restoration of all things will occur, when all things are naturally established in the seed of the universe that existed in the beginning and are restored to their proper times.[104]

5. That each one has his proper time, he claims, the Savior amply affirms: "My hour has not yet come."[105] The Magi, who beheld his star, attest to this as well.[106] For the Savior was also subject to an astral nativity and was selected beforehand in the vast heap with regard to his hour of restoration.[107]

THE HUMAN WITHIN. 6. The [third] Sonship is what they conceive of as the "inner human being," the "spiritual" within the "animate."[108] It abandons the soul in this world, not as though it were mortal, but as an entity that abides here by nature. The Sonship did this just as the former Sonship above, who left behind the Holy Spirit (previously worn as the Sonship's own soul) to form a boundary in its proper place.

THE MEANING OF THE GOSPEL. 7. So that I might not omit any of their material, I will present what they say about the gospel. According to them, the gospel is knowledge of supercosmic realties, as shown above.[109] The great Ruler did not believe this knowledge. When he was shown that there is a Holy Spirit, or boundary, a Sonship, and a nonexistent God who is cause of all, he was glad at the report and rejoiced.[110] This is their gospel.

---

104. For "their proper times," see *Ref.* 7.22.1; 1 Tim 2:6 (καιροῖς ἰδίοις); 6:15 (καιροῖς ἰδίοις); Titus 1:3 (καιροῖς ἰδίοις). Bos notes that ignorance seems to affect only the first and second Rulers, not their sons ("Basilides of Alexandria: Matthias," 411).

105. John 2:4; cf. Iren., *Haer.* 3.16.7.

106. Matt 2:1–2. Cf. Clem. Alex., *Strom.* 1.15.71.4.

107. Löhr believes that the identification of the star with the Savior is assumed (*Basilides*, 291 n. 27). On ἀποκαταστάσεως here, Méhat writes, "It is difficult not to give this word an astronomical sense.… In any case, the intention of the phrase is to connect the appearance of the Savior with a precise cosmic conjunction" ("ΑΠΟΚΑΤΑΣΤΑΣΙΣ," 370–71).

108. Cf. the note on inner human being in *Ref.* 5.7.36.

109. See *Ref.* 7.26.1.

110. For the biblical language of "rejoiced and was glad," see Matt 5:12; Luke 1:14; Rev 19:7.

8. Ὁ δὲ Ἰησοῦς γεγένηται κατ' αὐτοὺς ὡς προειρήκαμεν· γεγενημένης δὲ τῆς γενέσεως τῆς προδεδηλωμένης, γέγονε πάντα ὁμοίως κατ' αὐτοὺς τὰ περὶ τὸν σωτῆρα ὡς ἐν τοῖς εὐαγγελίοις γέγραπται. γέγονε δὲ ταῦτα, φησίν, ἵνα ἀπαρχὴ τῆς φυλοκρινήσεως γένηται τῶν συγκεχυμένων ὁ Ἰησοῦς. 9. ἐπεὶ γάρ ἐστιν ὁ κόσμος διῃρημένος εἰς Ὀγδοάδα—ἥτις ἐστὶν ἡ κεφαλὴ τοῦ παντὸς κόσμου, κεφαλὴ δὲ τοῦ παντὸς κόσμου ὁ μέγας ἄρχων—, καὶ εἰς Ἑβδομάδα—ἥτις ἐστὶν ἡ κεφαλὴ τῆς Ἑβδομάδος ὁ δημιουργὸς τῶν ὑποκειμένων—, καὶ εἰς τοῦτο τὸ διάστημα τὸ καθ' ἡμᾶς, ὅπου ἐστὶν ἡ ἀμορφία, ἀναγκαῖον ἦν τὰ συγκεχυμένα φυλοκρι<νη>θῆναι διὰ τῆς τοῦ Ἰησοῦ διαιρέσεως.

10. ἔπαθεν οὖν τοῦτο ὅπερ ἦν αὐτοῦ σωματικὸν μέρος· ὃ ἦν τῆς ἀμορφίας, καὶ ἀπεκατέστη εἰς τὴν ἀμορφίαν. ἀνέστησε δὲ τοῦτο ὅπερ ἦν ψυχικὸν αὐτοῦ μέρος· ὅπερ ἦν τῆς Ἑβδομάδος, καὶ ἀπεκατέστη εἰς τὴν Ἑβδομάδα. ἀνέστησεν δὲ τοῦτο ὅπερ ἦν τῆς ἀκρωρείας οἰκεῖον τοῦ μεγάλου ἄρχοντος, καὶ ἔμεινε παρὰ τὸν ἄρχοντα τὸν μέγαν. ἀνήνεγκε δὲ μέχρις ἄνω τοῦτο ὅπερ ἦν τοῦ μεθορίου Πνεύματος, καὶ ἔμεινεν ἐν τῷ μεθορίῳ Πνεύματι. 11. ἀπεκαθάρθη δὲ ἡ υἱότης ἡ τρίτη δι' αὐτοῦ, ἡ ἐγκαταλελειμμένη πρὸς τὸ εὐεργετεῖν καὶ εὐεργετεῖσθαι, καὶ ἀνῆλθε πρὸς τὴν μακαρίαν υἱότητα, διὰ πάντων τούτων διελθοῦσα.

Ὅλη γὰρ αὐτῶν ἡ ὑπόθεσις <περὶ> σύγχυσιν <καὶ> οἱονεὶ πανσπερμίας <σωρὸν> καὶ φυλοκρίνησιν καὶ ἀποκατάστασιν τῶν συγκεχυμένων εἰς τὰ οἰκεῖα. 12. τῆς οὖν φυλοκρινήσεως ἀπαρχὴ γέγονεν ὁ Ἰησοῦς, καὶ τὸ πάθος οὐκ ἄλλου τινὸς χάριν γέγονεν <ἀλλ' ἢ> ὑπὲρ τοῦ φυλοκρινηθῆναι τὰ συγκεχυμένα. τούτῳ γὰρ τῷ τρόπῳ φησὶν ὅλην τὴν υἱότητα, τὴν καταλελειμμένην ἐν τῇ ἀμορφίᾳ πρὸς τὸ εὐεργετεῖν καὶ εὐεργετεῖσθαι, δεῖν φυλοκρι<νη>θῆναι, ᾧ τρόπῳ καὶ ὁ Ἰησοῦς πεφυλοκρίνηται.

THE LIFE OF JESUS. 8. Jesus, in their view, arose as I said previously.[111] After he was born, as shown above, all the events of the Savior's life occurred, in their view, wholly as is written in the Gospels. These things occurred, he says, so that Jesus might become the first fruits of the differentiation from the confused mixture of elements.[112] 9. Since the world was divided into the Ogdoad (who is head of the whole world, whose head is the great Ruler) and into the Hebdomad (whose head is the Artificer of things that lie below), and into our own level of reality (the location of chaos), it was necessary that the confused mixture be differentiated through the separation of Jesus.

10. Thus his bodily part, which belonged to chaos, suffered and was restored to chaos. He resurrected his animate part, which belonged to the Hebdomad, and it was restored to the Hebdomad. He resurrected what belonged to the height, which was akin to the great Ruler; and it remained by the great Ruler. He brought to the highest reaches what belonged to the boundary Spirit, and it remained in the boundary Spirit. 11. Through Jesus, the third Sonship, who was left behind to give and receive benefits, was purified and rose to the blessed Sonship, traversing all these regions.

This is their whole theory about blending and the "heap," as it were, of the seed mixture, the differentiation, and the restoration of the blended parts to their appropriate places.[113] 12. Jesus was the first fruits of the differentiation, and his suffering occurred for no other reason than to differentiate the blended elements. All the Sonship left behind in chaos for mutual benefit, he says, needs to be differentiated in the very way that Jesus was differentiated.

---

111. *Ref.* 7.26.8–9.

112. "Differentiation" (φυλοκρίνησις) is a Basilidean technical term (cf. *Ref.* 7.26.9; Clem. Alex., *Strom.* 2.8.36.1; 2.8.38.2). Bos believes that it denotes "ontological separation, and not a separation of difference in direction or orientation" ("Basilides of Alexandria: Matthias," 414). He observes its link to the eschatological judgment of the twelve tribes (φυλάς) of Israel (Matt 19:28). For Satorneilos, the spark of life "sprints back to its own kind [ὁμόφυλα]" (*Ref.* 7.28.4).

113. For the language of "blending" (σύγχυσιν), see Clem. Alex., *Strom.* 2.20.112.1 (Löhr, *Basilides*, frag. 5). Marcovich adds σωρόν ("heap," comparing *Ref.* 7.15.2; 7.22.16; 10.14.5).

13. ταῦτα μὲν οὖν ἐστιν ἃ καὶ Βασιλείδης μυθεύει, σχολάσας κατὰ τὴν Αἴγυπτον καὶ παρ' αὐτῶν τὴν τοσαύτην σοφίαν διδαχθείς, ἐκαρποφόρησε τοιούτους καρπούς.

28. 1. Σατορνεῖλος δέ τις, συνακμάσας τῷ Βασιλείδῃ κατὰ τὸν αὐτὸν χρόνον, διατρίψας δ' ἐν Ἀντιοχείᾳ τῆς Συρίας, ἐδογμάτισε τοιαῦτα ὁποῖα καὶ Μένανδρος.

λέγει γὰρ ἕνα Πατέρα ἄγνωστον τοῖς πᾶσιν ὑπάρχειν, τὸν ποιήσαντα ἀγγέλους, ἀρχαγγέλους, δυνάμεις, ἐξουσίας· ὑπὸ δὲ ἑπτά τινων ἀγγέλων τὸν κόσμον γεγενῆσθαι καὶ πάντα τὰ ἐν αὐτῷ.

2. καὶ τὸν ἄνθρωπον δὲ ἀγγέλων εἶναι ποίημα, ἄνωθεν, ἀπὸ τῆς αὐθεντίας, φω<τει>νῆς εἰκόνος ἐπιφανείσης. ἣν κατασχεῖν μὴ δυνηθέντες, διὰ τὸ παραχρῆμα, φησίν, ἀναδραμεῖν ἄνω, ἐκέλευσαν ἑαυτοῖς λέγοντες· «ποιήσωμεν ἄνθρωπον κατ' εἰκόνα καὶ καθ' ὁμοίωσιν». 3. οὗ γενομένου, φησί, καὶ <μὴ> δυναμένου ἀνορθοῦσθαι τοῦ πλάσματος διὰ τὸ ἀδρανὲς τῶν ἀγγέλων, ἀλλὰ ὡς σκώληκος σκαρίζοντος.

13. These are the myths of Basileides, who studied in Egypt.[114] From the Egyptians, then, he was taught so great a "wisdom" and produced a like harvest.

SATORNEILOS

28. 1. There was a certain Satorneilos, who flourished at the same time as Basileides.[115] He lived in Antioch of Syria and pronounced teachings of the same stripe as Menandros.[116]

THEOLOGY. He says that a single Father exists, unknown to all, who made angels, archangels, powers, and authorities. The world and all its contents were made by a group of seven angels.[117]

ANTHROPOGONY. 2. The human being is a product of angels, when a luminous image appeared above from the Authority.[118] They were not able to detain the image because, he says, it suddenly sprinted back upward. The angels urged each other: "Let us make a human according to the image and according to the likeness."[119] 3. When this was done, he says, the molded being was not able to stand upright due to the impotence of the angels. Instead, it wriggled like a worm.[120]

---

114. Cf. the report of Epiph., *Pan.* 23.1.2; 24.1.1. See further Löhr, *Basilides*, 29.

115. Our author adapts his account of Satorneilos from Iren., *Haer.* 1.24.1–2 (where he is called *Saturninus*). See further Pétrement, *Separate God*, 329–35 (67–70, 184); Roelof van den Broek, "Satornilus," *DGWE* 1037–38; Winrich Löhr, "Satorninus," *BNP* 13:19.

116. Our author has not previously discussed Menandros, although he is listed in the table of contents (*Ref.* 7.4; cf. Iren., *Haer.* 1.23.5).

117. Cf. Origen, *Cels.* 6.27, 30–31; Theodoret, *Haer. fab.* 1.14 (PG 83:365b); Epiph., *Pan.* 26.10.1–3; Ap. John (BG 8502.2) 39.11, 48.7; Ap. John (NHC II,1) 11.23. See further Simone Pétrement, "Le mythe des sept archontes créateurs peut-il s'expliquer à partir du Christianisme?" in *Le Origini dello Gnosticismo, Colloquio Messina 13–18 Aprile 1966*, ed. Ugo Bianchi (Leiden: Brill, 1970), 460–87.

118. Cf. Gen 1:2; Ap. John (NHC II,1) 14.28–34; Nat. Rulers (NHC II,4) 87.11–14.

119. Gen 1:26 LXX. The pronoun "our" is omitted because the human is not made in the image or likeness of the angels, but in the image of the luminous being who appeared in the waters (cf. Gen 1:2–3). See further *Ref.* 6.14.5–6 ("Simon"); Iren., *Haer.* 1.5.5; 30.6; Ap. John (NHC II,1) 15.1; Clem. Alex., *Exc.* 50.

120. Cf. *Ref.* 5.7.6 (Naassenes); Ap. John (NHC II,1) 19.14; Ap. John (BG 8502.2) 50.15–16; Nat. Rulers (NHC II,4) 88.5; Iren., *Haer.* 1.30.6; Tert., *An.* 23.1: *opus futile et*

οἰκτείρασα αὐτὸν ἡ ἄνω δύναμις διὰ τὸ ἐν ὁμοιώματι αὐτῆς γεγονέναι <ἔ>πεμψε σπινθῆρα ζωῆς, ὃς διήγειρε τὸν ἄνθρωπον καὶ ζῆν ἐποίησε. 4. τοῦτον οὖν τὸν σπινθῆρα τῆς ζωῆς μετὰ τὴν τελευτὴν ἀνατρέχειν πρὸς τὰ ὁμόφυλα λέγει, καὶ τὰ λοιπά, ἐξ ὧν ἐγένετο, εἰς ἐκεῖνα ἀναλύεσθαι.

Τὸν δὲ σωτῆρα ἀγέν<ν>ητον ὑπέθετο καὶ ἀσώματον καὶ ἀνείδεον, δοκήσει δ' ἐπιπεφηνέναι ἄνθρωπον. 5. καὶ τὸν τῶν Ἰουδαίων θεὸν ἕνα τῶν ἀγγέλων εἶναί φησι· καὶ διὰ τὸ βούλεσθαι τὸν Πατέρα καταλῦσαι πάντας τοὺς ἄρχοντας παραγενέσθαι τὸν Χριστόν, ἐπὶ καταλύσει τοῦ τῶν Ἰουδαίων θεοῦ καὶ ἐπὶ σωτηρίᾳ τῶν πειθομένων αὐτῷ. εἶναι δὲ τούτους <τοὺς> ἔχοντας τὸν σπινθῆρα τῆς ζωῆς ἐν αὐτοῖς. 6. δύο γὰρ γένη τῶν ἀνθρώπων ὑπὸ τῶν ἀγγέλων πεπλάσθαι ἔφη, τὸ μὲν πονηρόν, τὸ δὲ ἀγαθόν· καὶ ἐπειδὴ οἱ δαίμονες τοῖς πονηροῖς ἐβοήθουν, ἐληλυθέναι τὸν σωτῆρα ἐπὶ καταλύσει τῶν φαύλων ἀνθρώπων καὶ δαιμόνων, ἐπὶ σωτηρίᾳ δὲ τῶν ἀγαθῶν.

7. Τὸ δὲ γαμεῖν καὶ γεν<ν>ᾶν ἀπὸ τοῦ Σατανᾶ φησιν εἶναι. οἱ πλείους δὲ τῶν ἀπ' ἐκείνου καὶ ἐμψύχων ἀπέχονται, διὰ τῆς προσποιητοῦ ταύτης ἐγκρατείας. τὰς δὲ προφητείας ἃς μὲν ἀπὸ τῶν κοσμοποιῶν ἀγγέλων λελαλῆσθαι, ἃς δὲ ἀπὸ τοῦ Σατανᾶ· ὃν καὶ αὐτὸν ἄγγελον, ἀντιπράττοντα τοῖς κοσμοποιοῖς ὑπέθετο, μάλιστα δὲ τῷ τῶν Ἰουδαί(ων) θεῷ.

ταῦτα μὲν οὖν ὁ Σατορνεῖλος.

29. 1. Μαρκίων δὲ ὁ Ποντικός, πολὺ τούτων μανικώτερος, τὰ πολλὰ τῶν πλειόνων παραπεμψάμενος, ἐπὶ τὸ ἀναιδέστερον ὁρμήσας δύο ἀρχὰς τοῦ παντὸς

The higher Power took pity on him because he was made in her likeness. She sent a spark of life. The spark raised up and enlivened the human.[121] 4. After a person's death, this spark of life sprints back to its own kind, he says, and the remaining elements constituting the human are dissolved into their component parts.

CHRISTOLOGY. Satorneilos teaches that the Savior is unborn, incorporeal, and without form but was manifested in human appearance.[122] 5. Moreover, he says that the god of the Jews is one of the angels. It was because the Father wanted to destroy all the rulers that Christ came to destroy the god of the Jews and to save those who believe in him. These are the ones who have the spark of life within themselves. 6. Two kinds of humans were molded by the angels, he affirmed: one evil, the other good. Since the demons were helping the evil human beings, the Savior came to destroy perverse people and demons and to save the good.

ETHICS, PROPHECY, AND SATAN. 7. He asserts that marriage and procreation are from Satan. The majority of his followers also abstain from eating ensouled animals in a pretense of self-control. Some prophecies were spoken by the angels that made the world, and others by Satan. Satan too is an angel, Satorneilos affirmed, who counteracts the creators of this world—especially the god of the Jews.

Such is the teaching of Satorneilos.

MARKION

29. 1. Markion of Pontos was much more insane than these men.[123] After dismissing the majority views, he rushed on to what is more shame-

---

invalidum et instabile in terra vermis instar palpitasse ("he was a weak, powerless, and unstable work quivering on the ground like a worm").

121. Cf. Gen 2:7; 3:20; *Ref.* 5.26.8 (Justin); 6.34.5 ("Valentinus"); Ap. John (NHC II,1) 19.23, 32–33; Nat. Rulers (NHC II,4) 88.3; Clem. Alex., *Exc.* 50.2–3. See further Rousseau and Doutreleau, *Contre les hérésies* (SC 263), 1:1.284–85.

122. Cf. *Ref.* 10.19.3 (Markion's Christology); Clem. Alex., *Strom.* 6.9.71.2; Origen, *Cels.* 2.16; Acts John 93; Ps.-Tert., *Adv. omn. haer.* 6; Theodoret, *Haer. fab.* 1.24 (PG 83:376a).

123. Unlike Irenaeus, who treats Kerdon and Markion after Karpokrates, Kerinthos, the Ebionites, and the Nikolaitans (*Haer.* 1.25–27), our author places him before these figures. The placement strikes one as odd, because Satorneilos, Karpokrates,

ὑπέθετο, ἀγαθὸν τινα λέγων καὶ τὸν ἕτερον πονηρόν. καὶ αὐτὸς δὲ νομίζων καινόν τι παρεισαγαγεῖν, σχολὴν (ἐ)σκεύασεν ἀπονοίας γέμουσαν καὶ κυνικοῦ βίου, ὤν τις μάχιμος.

2. <ὃς> νομίζων λήσεσθαι τοὺς πολλοὺς ὅτι μὴ Χριστοῦ τυγχάνει μαθητὴς ἀλλ’ Ἐμπεδοκλέους, πολὺ αὐτοῦ προγενεστέρου τυγχάνοντος, ταὐτὰ ὁρίσας

ful. He posited two principles in the universe: one good and another evil.[124] Supposing he snuck in something new, Markion established a school, bristling with rebellion and the Cynic ("dog-like") way of life (since he was so belligerent).[125]

2. Markion supposed that he would conceal from the majority the fact that he was a disciple not of Christ but of Empedokles, who lived a long time before him.[126] Empedokles proposed the same dualism, decreeing

---

and Kerinthos seem to form a group who asserted that the world was made by lesser powers (called "angels" in Satorneilos and Karpokrates). Nevertheless, our author prefers to group his opponents according to Christology. Satorneilos and Markion belong together because they both presented a Christ who appeared and was not a flesh-and-blood human. In turn, Markion fits with Karpokrates, Kerinthos, and the Ebionites, because they all in some way denied the virgin birth. See further Koschorke, *Ketzerbekämpfung*, 20–22. On Markion's social background and education, see Lampe, *Paul to Valentinus*, 241–56.

124. Our author has already "philosophized" Markion by saying that he opposes not two gods but two principles. Cf. Iren., *Haer.* 1.27.2; 3.12.12; *Ref.* 7.30.2–3; 37.1; 10.19.1; Tert., *Marc.* 1.2; Ps.-Tert., *Adv. omn. haer.* 6.1; Epiph., *Pan.* 41.1.6; 42.3.1–2; Filastrius, *Haer.* 44.1; Theodoret, *Haer. fab.* 1.24 (PG 83:372–73, 376). Under the influence of Harnack, older scholarship supported the view that Markion opposed a *good* god and a *just* god. Agreeing with our author, Sebastian Moll argues that Markion's dualism is between a good and an *evil* god (*The Arch-Heretic Marcion*, WUNT 250 [Tübingen: Mohr Siebeck, 2010], 47–76, 161). Similarly Winrich Löhr, "Did Marcion Distinguish between a Just God and a Good God?" in *Marcion und seine kirchengeschichtliche Wirkung / Marcion and His Impact on Church History: Vorträge der Internationalen Fachkonferenz zu Marcion, gehalten vom. 15.-18. August 2001 in Mainz*, ed. Gerhard May and Katharina Greschat (Berlin: de Gruyter, 2002), 131–46.

125. Markion's Cynic connection is derived in part from the report that he came from Sinope, home of the famous Cynic Diogenes. Our author, however, bases the Cynic ("dog-like") connection with Markion's putatively belligerent character. He will later, like Tertullian (*Marc.* 2.5.1), refer to Markion's "dogs" (*Ref.* 7.30.1; cf. 10.18.1; 10.19.4).

126. Marcovich replaces ὅτι at the beginning of this sentence with ὅς. Clement of Alexandria made Markion dependent on Plato (*Strom.* 3.3.21.1). Markion's connection to ancient philosophy was famously denied by Harnack in favor of the view that Markion was a mere "Biblicist." John G. Gager questioned this conclusion, arguing for Epicurean influence ("Marcion and Philosophy," *VC* 26 [1972]: 53–59). Ekkehard Mühlenberg argued for influence from Carneades ("Marcion's Jealous God," in *Disciplina nostra: Essays in Memory of Robert F. Evans*. ed. D. F. Winslow [Cambridge, MA: Philadelphia Patristic Foundation, 1979], 93–113). See further Gerhard May, "Marcion in Contemporary Views: Results and Open Questions," in *Markion: Gesammelte Aufsätze*, ed. Katharina Greschat and Martin Meiser (Mainz: Philipp von Zabern, 2005), 13–33 (27–28, 31).

ἐδογμάτισε δύο εἶναι τὰ τοῦ παντὸς αἴτια, νεῖκος καὶ φιλίαν. 3. τί γάρ φησιν ὁ Ἐμπεδοκλῆς περὶ τῆς τοῦ κόσμου διαγωγῆς, εἰ καὶ προείπομεν, ἀλλά γε καὶ νῦν πρὸς τὸ ἀντιπαραθεῖναι τῇ τοῦ κλεψιλόγου αἱρέσει οὐ σιωπήσομαι.

4. Οὗτός φησιν εἶναι τὰ πάντα στοιχεῖα, ἐξ ὧν ὁ κόσμος συνέστηκε καὶ ἔστιν, ἕξ· δύο μὲν ὑλικά, γῆν καὶ ὕδωρ· δύο δὲ ὄργανα, οἷς τὰ ὑλικὰ κοσμεῖται καὶ μεταβάλλεται, πῦρ καὶ ἀέρα· δύο δὲ τὰ ἐργαζόμενα τοῖς ὀργάνοις τὴν ὕλην καὶ δημιουργοῦντα, νεῖκος καὶ φιλίαν, λέγων ὧδέ πως·

τέσσαρα τῶν πάντων ῥιζώματα πρῶτον ἄκουε·
Ζεὺς <αἰθὴρ> Ἥρη τε φερέσβιος ἠδ’ Ἀϊδωνεὺς
Νῆστίς θ’, ἣ δακρύοις τέγγει κρούνωμα βρότειον.

that there are two causes in the universe: Strife and Love. 3. Now what Empedokles says about the world process, although I discussed it before, I will not omit here in order to compare it with the heresy of this plagiarist.[127]

REVIEW OF EMPEDOKLES

4. This fellow says that all the elements from which the world is composed and exists are six.[128] Two are material, namely, earth and water. Two are instrumental, namely, fire and water (they order and transform the material elements). Finally, two, Strife and Love, shape and fashion matter through the instrumental elements. To quote Empedokles:

> First, hear the four roots of all things:
> Zeus-aether,[129] life-bearing Hera, then Aidoneus
> And Nestis, who moistens with her tears the mortal fount.[130]

---

127. *Ref.* 1.3 (Empedokles). See further Mansfeld, *Heresiography*, 229–31. The following report is perhaps the fullest and most coherent Platonic interpretation of Empedokles in surviving literature. It may depend partly on Plutarch's lost study of Empedokles (cited in *Ref.* 5.20.6) or Noumenios. For background, see further Walter Burkert, "Plotin, Plutarch und die platonisierende Interpretation von Heraklit und Empedokles," in *Kephalaion: Studies in Greek Philosophy and Its Continuation Offered to Professor C. J. de Vogel* (Assen: Van Gorcum, 1975), 137–46. Osborne questions the scholarly tendency to discount any real similarity between Markion and Empedokles (*Rethinking*, 92–94, 97). She draws particular attention to the shared theme of "the inversion of values" (128). J. P. Hershbell believes that our author made direct use of Empedokles' *Katharmoi* ("Hippolytus' *Elenchos* as a Source for Empedocles Reexamined, II," *Phronesis* 18 [1973]: 187–203 [187, 202–3]). See further Angela Longo, "Empedocle e l'allegoria nella Confutazione di tutte le eresie attribuita a Ippolito di Roma," in Aragione and Norelli, *Des évêques*, 119–34.

128. Cf. Aristotle, *Gen. corr.* 1.1, 314a16 (Ἐμπεδοκλῆς μὲν γὰρ τὰ μὲν σωματικὰ τέτταρα, τὰ δὲ πάντα μετὰ τῶν κινούντων ἕξ ἀριθμόν ["Empedokles (numbered) four bodily (elements), but with the motive causes there are six total"]); Theophrastos, frag. 227a (FHSG 1:412–13); Sext. Emp., *Math.* 10.317, adapted in *Ref.* 10.7.4–5.

129. Marcovich supplies αἰθήρ here from Ps.-Plutarch, *Plac. philos.* 1.3, 878a.

130. Empedokles, DK 31 B6 (= Inwood 12). The quote also appears in *Ref.* 10.7.3–4. On the meaning of the "roots," see W. K. C. Guthrie, *A History of Greek Philosophy*, 6 vols. (Cambridge: Cambridge University Press, 1962–1981), 2:144–46; Peter Kingsley, *Ancient Philosophy, Mystery, and Magic: Empedocles and Pythagorean Tradition* (Oxford: Clarendon, 1995), 13–14; Mansfeld, *Heresiography*, 212–13. On our author's interpretation, see Hershbell, "Source for Empedocles, I," 111–14.

5. Ζεύς ἐστι τὸ πῦρ, Ἥρη δὲ φερέσβιος ἡ γῆ, ἡ φέρουσα τοὺς πρὸς τὸν βίον καρπούς, Ἀϊδωνεὺς δὲ ὁ ἀήρ, ὅτι πάντα δι᾽ αὐτοῦ βλέπο<ν>τες μόνον αὐτὸν οὐ καθορῶμεν, Νῆστις δὲ τὸ ὕδωρ· μόνον γὰρ τοῦτο, «ὄχημα τροφῆς», αἴτιον, γιν(ό)μενον πᾶσι τοῖς τρεφομένοις, αὐτὸ καθ᾽ αὐτὸ τρέφειν οὐ δύναται τὰ τρεφόμενα. 6. εἰ γὰρ ἔτρεφε, φησίν, οὐκ ἄν ποτε λιμῷ κατελήφθη τὰ ζῷα, ὕδατος ἐν τῷ κόσμῳ πλεονάζοντος ἀεί. διὰ τοῦτο Νῆστιν καλεῖ τὸ ὕδωρ, ὅτι τροφῆς αἴτιον γινόμενον, τρέφειν οὐκ εὐτονεῖ τὰ τρεφόμενα.

7. ταῦτα μὲν οὖν ἐστιν, ὡς τύπῳ περιλαβεῖν, τὰ συνέχοντα τοῦ κόσμου τὴν ὅλην ὑπόθεσιν·

1. ὕδωρ καὶ γῆ, ἐξ ὧν τὰ γινόμενα,
2. πῦρ καὶ πνεῦμα, τὰ ὄργανα, καὶ
3. τὰ δραστήρια, νεῖκος δὴ καὶ φιλία, τὰ δημιουργοῦντα τεχνικῶς.

8. Καὶ ἡ μὲν φιλία εἰρήνη τίς ἐστι καὶ ὁμόνοια καὶ στοργή, ἕνα τέλειον κατηρτισμένον εἶναι προαιρουμένη τὸν κόσμον· τὸ δὲ νεῖκος ἀεὶ διασπᾷ τὸ ἓν καὶ κατακερματίζει καὶ ἀπεργάζεται ἐξ ἑνὸς πολλά.

9. ἔστι μὲν οὖν τὸ μὲν νεῖκος αἴτιον τῆς κτίσεως πάσης—ὅ φησιν «οὐλόμενον» εἶναι, τουτέστιν ὀλέθριον· μέλει γὰρ αὐτῷ, ὅπως διὰ παντὸς αἰῶνος ἡ κτίσις αὐτὴ συνεστήκῃ—καὶ ἔστι πάντων τῶν γεγονότων τῆς γενέσεως δημιουργὸς καὶ ποιητὴς τὸ νεῖκος τὸ ὀλέθριον, τῆς δ᾽ ἐκ τοῦ κόσμου τῶν γεγονότων

5. "Zeus" means fire. "Life-bearing Hera" is earth, since she bears crops to maintain life.[131] "Aidoneus" means air, since, though we see everything through him, him alone we do not observe.[132] Nestis, finally, means water. For this alone is the "vehicle" (or cause) "of nourishment" for all those nourished, though by itself it cannot nourish them.[133] 6. If water provided nourishment, he says, animals would never be seized by hunger (given that water is always abundant on earth). For this reason, then, he calls water "Nestis," or "fasting," since, though it is the cause of nourishment, it does not have the power to nourish beings that are nourished.

7. These, then, in brief compass, are the elements that maintain the whole structure of the world:

1. water and earth, the components of generated beings,
2. fire and air, the instruments, and
3 the active forces, namely, Strife and Love, which fashion the world with artistic skill.

LOVE AND STRIFE. 8. Love is peace, agreement, and affection. She prefers the world to be one, perfect, and complete. Strife, by contrast, always rends the unity, chops it up, and produces many out of one.

9. Now Strife is the cause of all creation. Empedokles calls it "baneful,"[134] that is, destructive, for it is Strife's concern that the creation itself stand firm for all time. Destructive Strife is the Artificer and Maker of all beings generated in the world of generation.[135] Love, on the other hand, provides the path of escape from the world of generated beings. She provides

---

131. Stobaios agrees with our author in understanding Hera as Earth. Φερέσβιος describes Earth in Hesiod, *Theog.* 693; Hom. Hymn Apollo 341. Pseudo-Plutarch takes Hera to represent air (sources cited in Guthrie, *History*, 2:145).

132. Aidoneus is taken etymologically to mean "invisible one." Cf. Empedokles, DK 31 A33; Diog. L., *Vit. phil.* 8.76. Diogenes and Stobaios agree that Aidoneus is air, but Ps.-Plutarch identifies him with earth (Guthrie, *History*, 2:144). Kingsley argues that Aidoneus is fire (*Ancient Philosophy*, 46–48).

133. On water as the "vehicle of nourishment," see Hippocrates, *Alim.* 55 (ὑγρασίη τροφῆς ὄχημα); Plutarch, *Quaest. conv.* 690a; 698d.

134. Empedokles, DK 31 B17.19 (= Inwood 25.19); repeated in *Ref.* 10.7.5.

135. See further Jaap Mansfeld, "Bad World and Demiurge: A 'Gnostic' Motif from Parmenides and Empedocles to Lucretius and Philo," in *Studies in Gnosticism and Hellenistic Religions: Festschrift für Gilles Quispel*, ed. R. van den Broek and M. J. Vermaseren, EPRO 91 (Leiden: Brill, 1981), 261–314, esp. 278–80.

ἐξαγωγῆς καὶ μεταβολῆς καὶ εἰς τὸ ἓν ἀποκαταστάσεως ἡ φιλία. 10. περὶ ὧν ὁ Ἐμπεδοκλῆς ὅτι ἐστὶν ἀθάνατα <τὰ> δύο καὶ ἀγένητα καὶ ἀρχὴν τοῦ γενέσθαι μηδέποτε εἰληφότα· ἀλλὰ λέγει τοιοῦτόν τινα τρόπον·

ἧ γὰρ καὶ πάρος ἦν, καί <γ'> ἔσ<σε>ται, οὐδέ ποτ', οἴω,
τούτων ἀμφοτέρων κεν<ε>ώσεται ἄσβεστος αἰών.

τίνων τούτων; τοῦ νείκους καὶ τῆς φιλίας· οὐ γὰρ ἤρξα<ν>το γενέσθαι, ἀλλὰ προῆσαν καὶ ἔσονται ἀεί, διὰ τὴν ἀγεννησίαν φθορὰν ὑπομεῖναι μὴ δυνάμενα.

Τὸ δὲ πῦρ <καὶ τὸ ὕδωρ> καὶ ἡ γῆ καὶ ὁ ἀὴρ θνῄσκοντα καὶ ἀναβιοῦντα. 11. ὅταν μὲν γὰρ ἀποθάνῃ τὰ ὑπὸ τοῦ νείκους γενόμενα, παραλαμβάνουσα αὐτὰ ἡ φιλία πρ(ο)σάγει καὶ προστίθησι καὶ προσοικειοῖ τῷ παντί, ἵνα μένῃ τὸ πᾶν ἕν, ὑπὸ τῆς φιλίας ἀεὶ διακοσμούμενον μονοτρόπως καὶ μονοειδῶς. 12. ὅταν δὲ ἡ φιλία ἐκ πολλῶν ποιήσῃ τὸ ἓν καὶ τὰ διεσπασμένα προσοικοδομήσῃ τῷ ἑνί, πάλιν τὸ νεῖκος ἀπὸ τοῦ ἑνὸς ἀποσπᾷ καὶ ποιεῖ πολλά, τουτέστιν πῦρ, ὕδωρ, γῆν, ἀέρα, τά ἐκ τούτων γεννώμενα ζῷα καὶ φυτὰ καὶ ὅσα μέρη τοῦ κόσμου κατανοοῦμεν. 13. καὶ περὶ μὲν τῆς τοῦ κόσμου ἰδέας, ὁποία τίς ἐστιν ὑπὸ τῆς φιλίας κοσμουμένη, λέγει τοιοῦτόν τινα τρόπον·

οὐ γὰρ ἀπὸ νώτοιο δύο κλάδοι ἀίσ<σ>ονται,
οὐ πόδες, οὐ θοὰ γοῦν', οὐ μήδεα γεν<ν>ήεντα,
ἀλλὰ σφαῖρος ἔην <μοῦνός τε> καὶ ἶσος [ἐστὶν] <ἑ>αυτῷ.

transformation, and restoration into unity.[136] 10. Empedokles says that these two principles are immortal and unborn and have no beginning of existence. Instead, he speaks of them in this way:

> Surely, they were present before, and will exist in the future, and
> never, I ween, will unquenchable time be deprived of these two.[137]

Of which two does he speak? Strife and Love. For they never began to exist but preexisted and will exist forever. Since they are unborn, they cannot experience death.

THE FOUR ELEMENTS. In contrast, fire, water, earth, and air die and live again.[138] 11. For when the beings generated by Strife die away, Love receives them, then augments, adds, and assimilates them to the All so that the All can remain one, ever ordered by Love in the same way and in the same form. 12. But whenever Love makes the one from many and builds the scattered elements into one, again Strife tears off a piece from the one and makes many elements—namely, fire, water, earth, and air as well as the animals and plants born from them and whatever constituents of the world we observe. 13. Empedokles speaks about the form of the world, and what it is like when ordered by Love as follows:

> Two branches do not spring from its back,
> Nor feet, nor nimble knees, nor productive genitals,
> But it was a sphere both unique and equal to itself.[139]

---

136. Cf. *Ref.* 6.25.2–4 ("Pythagoras"); Diog. L., *Vit. phil.* 8.76; Clem. Alex., *Strom.* 5.2.15.4. Aristotle called Empedokles's Love the cause of good things, and Strife the cause of evil things (*Metaph.* 1.4, 985a5–7). Mansfeld would prefer to see Love as the demiurgical force (*Heresiography*, 215). See further Hershbell, "Source for Empedocles, I," 110–11.

137. Empedokles, DK 31 B16 (= Inwood 20). These lines are quoted to support Pythagorean doctrine in *Ref.* 6.25.1 (with the same question following: "Of which two …?"). Osborne deduces a common source (*Rethinking*, 95–96).

138. Duncker and Schneidewin add καὶ τὸ ὕδωρ ("water") to this sentence.

139. Empedokles, DK 31 B29 (= Inwood 34); cf. B134.2–4. Marcovich adds μοῦνός τε ("both unique") both to complete the hexameter and to make the passage conform to Empedokles, DK 31 B27.4 = 28.2: Σφαῖρος κυκλοτερὴς μονίῃ περιηγεί γαίων.

14. τοιοῦτον τι καὶ κάλλιστον εἶδος τοῦ κόσμου ἡ φιλία ἐκ πολλῶν ἓν ἀπεργάζεται· τὸ δὲ νεῖκος, τὸ τῆς τῶν κατὰ μέρος διακοσμήσεως αἴτιον, ἐξ ἑνὸς ἐκείνου ἀποσπᾷ καὶ ἀπεργάζεται πολλά.

Καὶ τοῦτό ἐστιν ὃ λέγει περὶ τῆς ἑαυτοῦ γεννήσεως ὁ Ἐμπεδοκλῆς·

τῶν καὶ ἐγὼ εἰμι, φυγὰς θεόθεν καὶ ἀλήτης.

[τουτέστι] θεὸν καλῶν τὸ ἓν καὶ τὴν ἐκείνου ἑνότητα, ἐν ᾧ ἦν πρὶν ὑπὸ τοῦ νείκους ἀποσπασθῆναι καὶ γενέσθαι ἐν τοῖς πολλοῖς τούτοις, τοῖς κατὰ τὴν τοῦ νείκους διακόσμησιν <γεγονόσι>. 15. «νείκει» γάρ, φησί, <«μαινομένῳ πίσυνος»> μαινόμενον καὶ τετα<ρα>γμένον καὶ ἄστατον τὸν δημιουργὸν το<ῦ>δε τοῦ κόσμου ὁ Ἐμπεδοκλῆς ἀποκαλῶν. αὕτη γάρ ἐστιν ἡ καταδίκη καὶ ἀνάγκη τῶν ψυχῶν, ὧν ἀποσπᾷ τὸ νεῖκος ἀπὸ τοῦ ἑνὸς καὶ δημιουργεῖ καὶ ἐργάζεται, λέγων τοιοῦτόν τινα τρόπον·

16. ὅς κ’ ἐπίορκον ἁμαρτήσας ἐπομόσ<σ>ῃ,

14. Thus Love produces a most beautiful form of the world as a unity from many elements. But Strife, responsible for the ordering of particulars, tears off pieces from that unity and produces many things.

THE FATE OF THE SOUL. This is what Empedokles says about his own birth:

> One of these I also am, a fugitive from God and a wanderer![140]

He calls the one [sphere] and the oneness of the one [sphere] "God." In this oneness, Empedokles existed before being torn off by Strife and being born among these multiple elements that arose according to the ordering of Strife. 15. For "I rely," he says, "on raving Strife!"[141] Empedokles disparages the Artificer of this world by calling him "raving," agitating, and unstable. This is the condemnation and necessity afflicting souls. Strife tears them off from the one [sphere], then fashions and makes them. As Empedokles puts it:

> 16. Whoever by his crime breaks the oath he swore,[142]

---

140. Empedokles, DK 31 B115.13 (= Inwood 11.13). The best commentary on this line and its intellectual background is Plutarch, *Exil.* 607d–e, where Empedokles is said to indicate that "not he himself, … but all of us … have transmigrated here and are strangers and exiles.… It is most true to say that the soul is an exile and a wanderer, driven forth by divine decrees and laws." The lines that Plutarch cites from Empedokles in *Exil.* 607d and the lines that our author cites here have been joined together to form the large fragment in DK 31 B115. For commentary on it, see D. O'Brien, *Empedocles' Cosmic Cycle* (Cambridge: Cambridge University Press, 1969), 330–34; idem, *Pour interpréter Empédocle* (Paris: Belles Lettres; Leiden: Brill, 1981), 14–20, 111–15; Günther Zuntz, *Persephone: Three Essays on Religion and Thought in Magna Graeca* (Oxford: Clarendon, 1971), 193–98; Osborne, *Rethinking*, 113–18; van der Ben, *Proem*, 128–40.

141. Empedokles, DK 31 B115.14 (= Inwood 11.14). Duncker and Schneidewin add μαινομένῳ πίσυνος ("I rely on raving"). On the force of πίσυνος, see Osborne, *Rethinking*, 114.

142. This line of Empedokles appears only in our author. In its received form, it resembles Hesiod, *Theog.* 793: ὅς κεν τὴν ἐπίορκον ἀπολλείψας ἐπομόσσῃ ("whoever abandons his oath in perjury"). It is typically read together with a line supplied by Plutarch: εὖτέ τις ἀμπλακίῃσι φόνῳ φίλα γυῖα μιήνῃ ("if someone defiles his dear limbs with sinful murder") (Osborne, *Rethinking*, 115–16). Van der Ben argues that the "perjury or oath-breaking is not an independent crime but is constituted precisely by the shedding of blood." He understands ἁμαρτήσας as qualifying the nature of the perjury, "which here does not consist in making a false declaration at the moment of taking an

<δαίμονες οἵτε> μακραίωνος λελάχασι βίοιο.

δαίμονας τὰς ψυχὰς λέγων, μακραίωνας, ὅτι εἰσὶν ἀθάνατοι καὶ μακροὺς ζῶσιν αἰῶνας.

17. τρίς μιν μυρίας ὥρας ἀπὸ μακάρων ἀλάλησθαι

μάκαρας καλῶν τοὺς (σ)υνηγμένους ὑπὸ τῆς φιλίας ἀπὸ τῶν πολλῶν εἰς τὴν ἑνότη(τ)α τοῦ κόσμου τοῦ νοητοῦ·—τούτους οὖν φησιν ἀλάλησθαι.

[καὶ] φυομένους παντοῖα διὰ χρόνου [ε]ἴδεα θνητῶν,
ἀργαλέας βιότ(οιο) (μ)εταλλάσσοντα κελεύθους.

ἀργαλέας [δὲ] κελεύθους φησὶν εἶναι τῶν ψυχῶν τὰς εἰς τὰ σώματα μεταβολὰς καὶ μετακοσμήσεις. 18. τοῦτ' ἔστιν ὃ λέγει· «ἀργαλέας βιότοιο μεταλλάσσοντα κελεύθους.» μεταλλάσσουσι γὰρ αἱ ψυχαὶ σῶμα ἐκ σώματος, ὑπὸ τοῦ νείκους μεταβαλλόμεναι καὶ κολαζόμεναι καὶ οὐκ ἐώμεναι μένειν εἰς τὸ ἕν. ἀλλὰ κολάζεσθαι ἐν πάσαις κολάσεσιν ὑπὸ τοῦ νείκους τὰς ψυχάς, μεταβαλλομένας σῶμα ἐκ σώματος,

Even divinities who have obtained by lot a long-lived life,[143]

(He refers to souls as "long-lived divinities" because they are immortal and live for long periods of time.)

17. wander from the blessed ones thrice ten thousand seasons.[144]

(He calls "blessed" those gathered by Love from the many elements into the oneness of the intelligible world.[145] It is these, then, that he says "Wander.")

Sprouting throughout time in manifold forms of mortal beings
Exchanging the painful pathways of different kinds of life.[146]

(The "painful pathways" refer to the changes and transmigrations of souls into bodies. 18. This is what the line "exchanging the painful pathways of different forms of life" means. The souls exchange body after body. They are transformed by Strife, punished by him, and prevented from remaining in the one. Rather, the souls are punished by Strife with every punishment, passing over from body to body.)

---

oath … but in not observing the oath afterwards" (*Proem*, 132). Cf. Homer, *Il.* 10.33 (ὥς φάτο, καί ῥ' ἐπίορκον ἐπώμοσε) with the scholium: οὐκ οἷον ἑκουσίως, ἀλλὰ διὰ τὸ μὴ ἀποτελεσθῆναι τοῦτο ὅπερ ὤμοσεν ("not as though willingly, but because he did not perform what he swore").

143. Empedokles, DK 31 B115.4–5 (= Inwood 11.4–5). The beginning of this line in P reads δαιμόνιοί τε. Diels's emendation (δαίμονες οἵτε, accepted here) better connects the verses. Cf. Zuntz, *Persephone*, 194–96. For Osborne, the one who sins is different from the plural *daimones* since, she believes, in Empedokles all humans are scapegoats for the bloodguilt of one individual that initiated the rule of Strife (*Rethinking*, 116–18).

144. Empedokles, DK 31 B115.6 (= Inwood 11.6). Cf. Origen, *Cels.* 8.53.

145. The "one," or sphere, is identified with the intelligible world—an openly Platonic interpretation of Empedokles. Such an interpretation was common during our author's time—and long afterward. See further Guthrie, *History*, 2:260; O'Brien, *Cosmic Cycle*, 99–101; idem, *Pour interpréter*, 79–87; Hershbell, "Source for Empedocles, I," 109–10. Osborne underscores the ancient Pythagorean background (*Rethinking*, 109–13), though in our period there is no strict separation of Platonic and Pythagorean thought. For the intelligible world, see *Ref.* 6.25.2; 7.31.3 below.

146. Empedokles, DK 31 B115.7–8 (= Inwood 11.7–8). Cf. Origen, *Cels.* 8.53.

19. αἰθέριον <μὲν> γάρ σφε μένος ψυχὰς πόντονδε [ἐχθονὸς] διώκει,
πόντος δ' ἐ(ς) χθονὸς οὖδας ἀπέπτυσε, γαῖα δ' ἐς αὐγὰς
ἠελίου φαέθοντος, ὁ δ' αἰθέρος ἔμβαλε δίναις·
ἄλλος δ' ἐξ ἄλλου δέχεται, στυγέουσι δὲ πάντες.

20. αὕτη ἐστιν ἡ κόλασις ᾗ κολάζει ὁ δημιουργός, καθάπερ χαλκεύς τις μετακοσμῶν σίδηρον καὶ ἐκ πυρὸς εἰς ὕδωρ μεταβάπτων. πῦρ γάρ ἐστιν ὁ αἰθήρ, ὅθεν εἰς πόντον μεταβάλλει τὰς ψυχὰς ὁ δημιουργός. χθὼν δὲ ἡ γῆ· ὅθεν φησίν· ἐξ ὕδατος εἰς γῆν, ἐκ γῆς δ' εἰς τὸν ἀέρα. τοῦτ' ἔστιν ὃ λέγει·

21. γαῖα δ' ἐς αὐγὰς
ἠελίου φαέ(θο)ντος, ὁ δ' αἰθέρος ἔμβαλε δίναις·
ἄλλος <δ'> ἐξ ἄλλου δέχεται, στυγέουσι δὲ πάντες.

Μισουμένας οὖν τὰς ψυχὰς καὶ βασανιζομένας καὶ κολαζομένας ἐν τῷδε τῷ κόσμῳ κατὰ τὸν Ἐμπεδοκλέα συνάγει ἡ φιλία, ἀγαθή τις οὖσα καὶ κατοικτείρουσα τὸν στεναγμὸν αὐτῶν καὶ τὴν ἄτακτον καὶ πονηρὰν «τοῦ νείκους τοῦ μαινομένου» κατασκευήν, καὶ ἐξάγειν κατ' ὀλίγον ἐκ τοῦ κόσμου καὶ προσοικειοῦν τῷ ἑνὶ σπεύδουσα, καὶ κοπιῶσα, ὅπως τὰ πάντα εἰς τὴν ἑνότητα καταντήσῃ ὑπ' αὐτῆς ἀγόμενα.

22. Διὰ τὴν τοιαύτην οὖν τοῦ ὀλεθρίου νείκους διακόσμησιν τοῦδε τοῦ μεμερισμένου κόσμου πάντων ἐμψύχων ὁ Ἐμπεδοκλῆς τοὺς ἑαυτο(ῦ) μαθητὰς ἀπέχεσθαι παρακαλεῖ· εἶναι γάρ φησι τὰ σώματα τῶν ζῴων τὰ ἐσθιόμενα ψυχῶν κεκολασμένων οἰκητήρια. καὶ ἐγκρατεῖς εἶναι τοὺς τῶν τοιούτων λόγων ἀκροωμένους τῆς πρὸς γυναῖκα ὁμιλίας διδάσκει, ἵνα μὴ συνεργάζωνται καὶ

19. The fury of aether drives souls to the sea,
But the sea spits them out onto the surface of the land, and earth into the rays
Of the blazing sun, and the sun throws them into the whirlwinds of aether.
One after another receives them, and all abhor them.[147]

20. This is the punishment that the Artificer inflicts on souls—just as a blacksmith reshapes iron by plunging it from fire into water. The "aether" in the passage refers to fire. From fire, the Artificer changes the souls into water. The "surface of the land" refers to earth. Thus he means that [the soul is hurled] from water to earth, and from earth to air. This is what the quote means:

21. and earth [spits them] into the rays
Of the blazing sun, and the sun throws them into the whirlwinds of aether.
One after another receives them, and all abhor them.

SALVATION. Love, according to Empedokles, gathers the souls that are hated, tortured, and punished in this world. Love is kind. She pities their groaning and laments the disordered and evil structure "of raving Strife."[148] She leads them gradually away from the world, eagerly assimilating them to the one [sphere], and laboring so that all things under her guidance attain unity.

ETHICS. 22. On account of destructive Strife's ordering of this divided world, Empedokles exhorts his disciples to abstain from all ensouled animals in accordance with his claim that the bodies of edible animals are the dwellings of punished souls.[149] Moreover, he teaches those who attend to his doctrines to restrain themselves from sexual intercourse with women

---

147. Empedokles, DK 31 B115.9–12 (= Inwood 11.9–12). For commentary, see van der Ben, *Proem*, 150–55.

148. Empedokles, DK 31 B115.14 (= Inwood 11.14).

149. Cf. Empedokles, DK 31 B141 (= Inwood 132); Athenaios, *Deipn.* 1.3e; Iamblichos, *Vit. Pyth.* 107–109; Sext. Emp., *Math.* 9.128. See further Osborne, *Rethinking*, 120–22.

συνεπιλαμβάνωνται τῶν ἔργων ὧν δημιουργεῖ τὸ νεῖκος, τὸ τῆς φιλίας ἔργον λύον ἀεὶ καὶ διασπῶν.

23. Τοῦτον εἶναί φησιν ὁ Ἐμπεδοκλῆς νόμον μέγιστον τῆς τοῦ παντὸς διοικήσεως, λέγων ὧδέ πως·

ἔστιν Ἀνάγκη<ς> χρῆμα, θεῶν ψήφισμα παλαιόν,
ἀίδιον, πλατέεσ<σ>ι κατεσφρηγισμένον ὅρκοις·

Ἀνάγκην καλῶν τὴν ἐξ ἑνὸς εἰς πολλὰ κατὰ τὸ νεῖκος καὶ ἐκ πολλῶν εἰς ἓν κατὰ τὴν φιλίαν μεταβολήν· θεοὺς δέ, ὡς ἔφην, τέσσαρας μὲν θνητούς, πῦρ, ὕδωρ, γῆν, ἀέρα, δύο δὲ ἀθανάτους, ἀγεννήτους, πολεμίους ἑαυτοῖς διὰ παντός, τὸ νεῖκος καὶ τὴν φιλίαν. 24. καὶ τὸ μὲν νεῖκος ἀδικεῖν διὰ παντὸς καὶ πλεονεκτεῖν καὶ ἀποσπᾶν τὰ τῆς φιλίας καὶ ἑαυτῷ προσνέμειν, τὴν δὲ φιλίαν ἀεὶ καὶ διὰ παντός, ἀγαθήν τινα οὖσαν καὶ τῆς ἑνότητος ἐπιμελουμένην, τὰ ἀπεσπασμένα τοῦ παντὸς καὶ βεβασανισμένα καὶ κεκολασμένα ἐν τῇ κτίσει ὑπὸ τοῦ δημιουργοῦ ἀνακαλεῖσθαι καὶ προσάγειν καὶ <ἓν ποιεῖν>.

25. Τοιαύτη τις [ἡ] κατὰ τὸν Ἐμπεδοκλέα ἡμῖν ἡ τοῦ κόσμου γένεσις καὶ φθορὰ καὶ σύστασις, ἐξ ἀγαθοῦ καὶ κακοῦ συνεστῶσα, φιλοσοφεῖται.

εἶναι δέ φησι καινὸν τὴν τρίτην τινὰ δύναμιν ἥν καὶ ἐκ τούτων ἐπινοεῖσαι δύνασθαι, λέγων ὧδέ πως·

so that they do not cooperate with and assist the works fashioned by Strife, who always dissolves and rends the work of Love.[150]

23. This, Empedokles says, is the great law of the management of the universe. To quote him:

> There is an oracle of Necessity, an ancient decree of the gods
> Eternal, sealed with broad oaths.[151]

He calls "Necessity" the alternation from one to many under Strife, and from many to one under Love. The "gods," as I said, are the four mortal elements (fire, water, earth, and air) as well as the two immortal, unborn, eternally warring principles (namely, Strife and Love).[152] 24. Indeed, Strife eternally acts unjustly. He greedily takes and tears away the property of Love to apportion it to himself. Love, by contrast, is always and forever good and cultivates unity, calling back the fragments of the universe that are tortured and punished by the Artificer in creation, leading them forward and making them one.[153]

A THIRD PRINCIPLE. 25. Such, for our purposes, is the Empedoklean origin, corruption, and constitution of the world. According to his philosophy, the world is constituted from good and evil.[154]

He adds that a third, new power exists. It can be understood from the following verses:[155]

---

150. Plutarch indicates that for Empedokles birth itself (γένεσιν αὐτήν) springs from injustice (ἐξ ἀδικίας), "since it is a union of mortal with immortal, and the offspring is nourished unnaturally on members torn from the parent" (*Soll. an.* 964e). On the putative Empedoklean prohibition of sex, see O'Brien, *Cosmic Cycle*, 219–20; idem, *Pour interpreter*, 93–97; Hershbell, "Source for Empedocles, I," 107–8; Osborne, *Rethinking*, 123; Mansfeld, *Heresiography*, 219–20. It seems possible that DK 31 B110.9 (quoted below in *Ref.* 7.29.26) could be read as a criticism of sex. See the note on that line below.

151. Empedokles, DK 31 B115.1–2 (= Inwood 11.1–2). These two lines are typically taken to be the opening lines of a long fragment (DK 31 B115) that our author quotes piecemeal in *Ref.* 7.29.14–23.

152. Cf. Aristotle, *Gen. corr.* 2.6, 333b20: Strife and Love are gods (θεοὶ δὲ καὶ ταῦτα).

153. Marcovich emends ἐμποιεῖν (P) to ἓν ποιεῖν (here: "making [them] one").

154. Here is the direct comparison to Markion. Cf. *Ref.* 7.29.1; 7.30.2–4; 7.31.3; Aristotle, *Metaph.* 1.4, 985a6: τὴν μὲν φιλίαν αἰτίαν οὖσαν τῶν ἀγαθῶν, τὸ δὲ νεῖκος τῶν κακῶν ("Love is the cause of goods and Strife of evils").

155. See further Osborne, *Rethinking*, 130.

26. εἰ γάρ κέν σφ' ἀδινῇσιν ὑπὸ πραπίδεσ<σ>ιν ἐρείσας
εὐμενέως (κ)αθαρῇσιν ἐποπτεύ<σ>ῃς μελέτῃσιν,
ταῦτά τέ σοι μάλα πάντα δι' αἰῶνος παρέσονται,
ἄλλα τε πόλλ' ἀπὸ τῶνδ' ἐκτή(σ)εαι· αὐτὰ γὰρ αὔξει
ταῦτ' εἰς <ἦ>θος ἕκαστον, ὅπῃ φύσις ἐστὶν ἑκάστῳ.
εἰ δὲ σύ γ' ἀλλοίων ἐπορέξεαι, οἷα κατ' ἄνδρας
μυρία δειλὰ πέλονται ἅ τ' ἀμβλύνουσι μερίμνας,
ἦ σ' ἄφαρ ἐκλείψουσι περιπλομένοιο χρόνοιο
σφῶν αὐτῶν ποθέοντα φίλην ἐπὶ γέν<ν>αν ἱκέσθαι·
πάντα γὰρ ἴσθι φρόνησιν ἔχειν καὶ νώματος <α>ἶσαν.

30. 1. Ἐπειδὰν οὖν Μαρκίων ἤ τῶν ἐκείνου κυνῶν τις ὑλακτῇ κατὰ τοῦ δημιουργοῦ, τοὺς ἐκ τῆς ἀντιπαραθέσεως ἀγαθοῦ καὶ κακοῦ προφέρων λόγους, δεῖ αὐτοῖ(ς) λέγειν ὅτι τούτους οὔτε Παῦλος ὁ ἀπόστολος οὔτε Μάρκος ὁ κολοβοδάκτυλος ἀνήγγειλαν—τούτων γὰρ οὐδε<ὶς> ἐν τῷ <κατὰ> Μάρκον εὐαγγελίῳ γέγραπται—ἀλλὰ Ἐμπεδοκλῆς Μ<έ>τωνος Ἀκραγαντῖνος· ὃν συλαγωγῶν μέχρι νῦν λανθάνειν ὑπελάμβανε τὴν διαταγὴν πάσης τῆς κατ'

26. For if you fix yourself in thick contemplations,
And kindly behold with pure meditations,
To you these and absolutely all things will be present eternally,
And still many others[156] from these you will acquire. For these very truths grow
Into each one's character,[157] according to the nature each one has.
But if you strain after other things such as exist among men,
Things innumerable and fearful, which dim deliberations—
Yes, they will swiftly abandon you as time whirls round;
Since, in your desire for your own kind, you arrive at cherished begetting.[158]
For know this: all things have thought and a share in mind.[159]

COMPARISON WITH MARKION

30. 1. So when Markion or one of his dogs barks against the Artificer, proffering arguments from his *Antithesis between Good and Evil*, one must say to them that neither Paul the apostle, nor Mark the Maimed-Fingered announced these teachings—for not one is written in Mark's Gospel.[160] Their source, rather, is Empedokles son of Meton from the city of Akragas. Despoiling him, Markion concealed up until the present time the fact that

156. It is possible that a "new power" could have been read from the "still many others" (ἄλλα τε πόλλ'). If we transpose the quotation of DK 31 B131 (quoted below in *Ref.* 7.31.4) to the beginning of B110 (as Mansfeld proposes [*Heresiography*, 225]), the new power is the Muse.

157. P reads ἔθος ("custom"). Miller and Schneidewin emend to ἦθος.

158. I have translated this line to bring out what I believe to be our author's interpretation of it. In this interpretation, Empedokles devalues the human desire for reproduction in comparison to the life of reflection and thought. A reading of this kind may have led our author to infer that Empedokles prohibited sex (see *Ref.* 7.29.22 above).

159. Empedokles, DK 31 B110 (= Inwood 16). Our author quotes the last line of this fragment in *Ref.* 6.12.1 ("Simon"). It apparently circulated independently (cf. Sext. Emp., *Math.* 8.286).

160. According to a legend recorded in the Latin *argumentum* to Mark's Gospel in Codex Amiatinus, Mark cut off his thumb to make himself ineligible for the priesthood. See further J. L. North, "ΜΑΡΚΟΣ Ο ΚΟΛΟΒΟΔΑΚΤΥΛΟΣ: Hippolytus, *Elenchus*, 7.30," *JTS* 28 (1977): 498–507. On Markion's book *Antithesis* (more commonly known as *Antitheses*, as in *Ref.* 7.37.2), see Iren., *Haer.* 1.27.3; Tert., *Marc.* 1.19.4; 4.1.1; 4.4.4; 4.6.1. See further Osborne, *Rethinking*, 106–7; Gerhard May, "Markions Genesisauslegung und die 'Antithesen,'" in Greschat and Meiser, *Gesammelte Aufsätze*, 43–50 (47–49); Lampe, *Paul to Valentinus*, 253; Moll, *Arch-Heretic*, 108–11, 120.

αὐτὸν αἱρέσεως ἀπὸ τῆς Σικελίας εἰς τοὺς εὐαγγελικοὺς λόγους μεταφέρων αὐταῖς λέξεσι.

2. φέρε δέ, ὦ Μαρκίων, καθάπερ τὴν ἀντιπαράθεσιν πεποίηκας ἀγαθοῦ καὶ κακοῦ, ἀντιπαραθῶ κἀγὼ σήμερον κατακολουθῶν τοῖς σοῖς, ὡς ὑπολαμβάνεις, δόγμασι. δημιουργὸν φῂς εἶναι τοῦ κόσμου πονηρόν· εἶτ᾽ οὐκ ἐγκαλύπτῃ τοὺς Ἐμπεδοκλέο<υ>ς λόγους τὴν ἐκκλησίαν κατηχῶν; 3. ἀγαθὸν φῂς εἶναι θεὸν καταλύοντα τὰ τοῦ δημιουργοῦ ποιήματα· εἶτ᾽ οὐ καταφανῶς τὴν Ἐμπεδοκλέους φιλίαν εὐαγγελίζῃ τοῖς ἀκροωμένοις <ὡς> τὸν ἀγαθόν; «κωλύεις γαμεῖν», τεκνοῦν, «ἀπέχεσθαι βρωμάτων, ὧν ὁ θεὸς ἔκτισεν εἰς μετάληψιν τοῖς πιστοῖς καὶ ἐπεγνωκόσι τὴν ἀλήθειαν». τοὺς Ἐμπεδοκλέους λανθάνεις διδάσκων Καθαρμούς; 4. ἑπόμενος γὰρ ὡς ἀληθῶς κατὰ πάντα τούτῳ, τὰ βρ(ώ)ματα παραιτεῖσθαι τοὺς ἑαυτοῦ μαθητὰς διδάσκεις, ἵνα μὴ φάγωσι σῶμά τι, λείψανον ψυχῆς ὑπὸ τοῦ δημιουργοῦ κεκολασμένης. λύεις τοὺς ὑπὸ τοῦ θεοῦ συνηρμοσμένους γάμους, τοῖς Ἐμπεδοκλέους ἀκολουθῶν δόγμασιν, ἵνα σοι φυλαχθ(ῇ) τ(ὸ) τῆς φιλίας ἔργον ἓν ἀδιαίρετον· διαιρεῖ γὰρ ὁ γάμος κατὰ Ἐμπεδοκλέα τὸ ἓν καὶ ποιεῖ πολλά, καθὼς ἀπεδείξαμεν.

31. 1. Ἡ μὲν οὖν πρώτη καὶ καθαριωτάτη Μαρκίωνος αἵρεσις, ἐξ ἀγα(θ)οῦ καὶ κακοῦ τὴν σύστασιν ἔχουσα, Ἐμπεδοκλέους ἡμῖν εἶναι πεφανέρωται· ἐπεὶ δ᾽ ἐν τοῖς καθ᾽ ἡμᾶ(ς) χρόνοις νῦν καινότερόν τι ἐπεχείρησε Μαρκιωνιστής τις Πρέπων, Ἀσ<σ>ύριος, πρὸς (Β)αρδησιάνην τὸν Ἀρμένιον ἐγγράφως ποιήσασθαι λόγους περὶ τῆς αἱρέσεως <τετολμηκώς>, οὐδὲ τοῦτο σιωπήσομαι. 2. τρίτην <τινὰ> φάσκων δίκαιον εἶναι ἀρχήν, καὶ μέσην ἀγαθοῦ καὶ κακοῦ τεταγμένην.

he purloined the structure of his entire heresy from Sicily and transferred it word for word to the Gospel accounts.

2. Come now, Markion, just as you have constructed an antithesis between good and evil, so today I will make my own antithesis, closely attending to your purloined dogmas! You say that the Artificer of this world is evil.[161] Do you not then veil the theories of Empedokles as you instruct the church? 3. You call the God who destroys the products of the Artificer "good." Do you not openly proclaim to your pupils the gospel of Empedokles's Love parading as "the good God"?[162] "You prevent marriage" and childbearing, and you tell people "to abstain from eating foods that God created for believers and those who know the truth."[163] Do you then conceal the fact that you teach the *Purifications* of Empedokles? 4. You truly follow Empedokles in every respect when you teach your disciples to abstain from foods so as not to eat a corpse, the remains of a soul punished by the Artificer. Following the doctrines of Empedokles, you dissolve marriages joined by God so that the work of Love might be preserved for you one and undivided.[164] (For marriage, according to Empedokles, divides the one and makes many, as I have shown.)

PREPON

31. 1. The first and purest heresy of Markion—built on the structure of good versus evil—I have shown to belong to Empedokles. In our own times, the Markionite Prepon has now ventured something more novel.[165] He is an Assyrian who wrote books about his heresy against Bardesianes the Armenian.[166] I will not keep silent about his teaching either. 2. He claims that there is a third "just principle" arrayed between good and evil.

---

161. Cf. Iren., *Haer.* 3.12.12. See further Osborne, *Rethinking*, 100–108; Moll, *Arch-Heretic*, 47–76, esp. 52.

162. Marcovich adds ὡς ("as").

163. 1 Tim 4:3 (minus μετὰ εὐχαριστίας). Cf. *Ref.* 8.20.2 (Enkratites).

164. Cf. *Ref.* 7.28.7 (Satorneilos); 8.16.1 (Tatian); 10.19.4 (Markion summary); Iren., *Haer.* 1.24.2; 28.1; Eusebios, *Hist. eccl.* 4.29.2–3; Clem. Alex., *Strom.* 3.12.1–2; 3.25.2; Tert., *Marc.* 1.29.1; 4.11.8; 4.34.5.

165. On Prepon, see Theodoret, *Haer. fab.* 25 (PG 83:376–77).

166. For Bardesianes, see *Ref.* 6.35.7 (grouped with the Valentinians); Eusebios, *Hist. eccl.* 4.30.1; Epiph., *Pan.* 56.1.2. In understanding πρός as "against," I follow Ramelli, *Bardaisan*, 51–52. Ephrem Syrus reports that Bardesanes, for whom God is essentially one, attacked Markion's theological dualism. See further Denzey, "Bardaisan," 181.

οὐδ' οὕτως δὴ ὁ Πρέπων τὴν Ἐμπεδοκλέους διαφυγεῖν ἴσχυσε δόξαν. 3. κόσμον γάρ φησιν εἶναι ὁ Ἐμπεδοκλῆς <τοῦτον>, τὸν ὑπὸ τοῦ νείκους διοικούμενον τοῦ πονηροῦ, καὶ ἕτερον νοητόν, τὸν ὑπὸ τῆς φιλίας, καὶ εἶναι ταύτας τὰς διαφερούσας ἀρχὰς δύο, ἀγαθοῦ καὶ κακοῦ· μέσον δὲ εἶναι τῶν διαφόρων ἀρχῶν δίκαιον λόγον, καθ' ὃν συγκρίνεται τὰ διῃρημένα ὑπὸ τοῦ νείκους καὶ προσαρμόζεται κατὰ τὴν φιλίαν τῷ ἑνί. 4. τοῦτον δὲ [αὐτὸν] τὸν δίκαιον λόγον, τὸν τῇ φιλίᾳ συναγωνιζόμενον, Μοῦσαν ὁ Ἐμπεδοκλῆς προσαγορεύει καὶ αὐτὸν αὐτῷ συναγωνίζεσθαι παρακαλεῖ, λέγων ὧδέ πως·

εἰ γὰρ ἐφημερίων ἕνεκέν τινος, ἄμβροτε Μοῦσα,
ἡμετέρας μελέτας <ἅδε τοι> διὰ φροντίδος ἐλθεῖν,
εὐχομένῳ νῦν αὖτε παρίστασο, Καλλιόπεια,
ἀμφὶ θεῶν μακάρων ἀγαθὸν λόγον ἀμφαίνοντι.

5. Τούτοις κατακολουθῶν Μαρκίων τὴν γένεσιν τοῦ σωτῆρος ἡμῶν παντάπασ(ιν) παρῃτήσατο, ἄτοπον εἶναι νομίζων ὑπὸ τὸ πλάσμα τοῦ ὀλεθρίου τούτου νείκους γεγονέναι τὸν λόγον τὸν τῇ φιλίᾳ συναγωνιζόμενον—τουτέστι τῷ ἀγαθῷ·—ἀλλὰ χωρὶς γενέσεως «ἔτει πεντεκαιδεκάτῳ τῆς ἡγεμονίας Τιβερίου Καίσαρος» κατεληλυθότα αὐτὸν ἄνωθεν, μέσον ὄντα κακοῦ καὶ ἀγαθοῦ, διδάσκειν ἐν ταῖς συναγωγαῖς. 6. εἰ γὰρ μεσότης ἐστίν, ἀπήλλακται, φησί, πάσης τῆς τοῦ κακοῦ φύσεως.—κακὸς δ' ἔστιν, ὡς λέγει, ὁ δημιουργὸς καὶ τούτου τὰ ποιήματα· διὰ τοῦτο ἀγέν<ν>ητος κατῆλθεν ὁ Ἰησοῦς, φησίν, ἵνα ᾖ πάσης ἀπηλλαγμένος κακίας.—ἀπήλλακται δέ, φησί, καὶ τῆς τοῦ ἀγαθοῦ

But not even by this tactic is Prepon able to escape the theory of Empedokles. 3. Empedokles says that there is this world administered by evil Strife and another intelligible world administered by Love, and that these are two different principles, namely, good and evil. But between these different principles is a just Word, according to which the things divided by Strife are combined and joined to the One in accordance with Love.[167] 4. Empedokles calls this just Word that strives together with Love "Muse." In the following quote, he exhorts this Muse to strive together with him:

> Would that for the sake of an ephemeral creature, immortal Muse,
> Our meditations here would intersect your intellect.
> Once again stand by the one who prays to you, Kalliopeia,
> By him who declares a good teaching about the blessed gods![168]

MARKION'S CHRISTOLOGY

5. Closely adhering to these doctrines, Markion entirely rejected the birth of our Savior, supposing it absurd that the Word that strives together with Love (that is, with the Good) be born in subjection to the bodily formation of destructive Strife. Rather, without birth "in the fifteenth year of the rule of Tiberius Caesar,"[169] the Word—a being between evil and good—descended from above and taught in the synagogues.[170] 6. Since the Word is an intermediate between good and evil, he says, he is freed from all evil nature. Yet the Artificer is evil, Markion claims, along with his products. For this reason, Jesus came down unborn, he says, to be free from all evil. But he was also free, he says, of the good nature so as to be in between, as

167. For the "just Word" (δίκαιον λόγον), cf. Sext. Emp., *Math.* 7.122, with the discussion of Hershbell, "Sources for Empedocles, II," 195–97. See further Guthrie, *History*, 2:260–62; Clémence Ramnoux, *Études présocratiques* (Paris: Klincksieck, 1970), 108–10; Mansfeld, *Heresiography*, 222–26.

168. Empedokles, DK 31 B131 (= Inwood 10). See the comments of Zuntz, *Persephone*, 211–13; Hershbell, "Sources for Empedocles, I," 108–9.

169. Luke 3:1. This verse formed the beginning of Markion's Gospel, according to Iren., *Haer.* 1.27.2; Tert., *Marc.* 1.19.2; 4.7.1; Epiph., *Pan.* 42.11.5.

170. Luke 4:15 (αὐτὸς ἐδίδασκεν ἐν ταῖς συναγωγαῖς ["he taught in their synagogues"]); cf. Tert., *Marc.* 4.7.5.

φύσεως, ἵνα ᾖ μεσίτης, ὡς φησίν ὁ Παῦλος, καὶ ὡς αὐτὸς ὁμολογεῖ· «τί με λέγετε ἀγαθόν; εἷ<ς> ἐστιν ἀγαθός».

7. Ταῦτα μὲν οὖν τὰ Μαρκίωνι δόξαντα, δι' ὧν ἐπλάνησε πολλούς· τοῖς Ἐμπεδοκλέους λόγοις χρησάμενος καὶ τὴν ὑπ' ἐκείνου ἐφηυρημένην φιλοσοφίαν ἰδίᾳ δόξῃ μετάγων, αἵρεσιν ἄθεον συνεστήσατο. 8. ἣν ἱκανῶς ἠλέγχθαι ὑφ' ἡμῶν νομίζω μηθέν τε καταλελεῖφθαι, ὧν κλεψιλογήσαντες παρ' Ἑλλήνων τοὺς Χριστοῦ μαθητὰς ἐπηρεάζουσιν ὡς τούτων αὐτοῖς γενομένους διδασκάλους. ἀλλ' ἐπεὶ καὶ τὰ τούτου ἱκανῶς ἡμῖν δοκεῖ ἐκτεθεῖσθαι, ἴδωμεν τί λέγει Καρποκράτης.

32. 1. Καρποκράτης τὸν μὲν κόσμον καὶ τὰ ἐν αὐτῷ ὑπὸ ἀγγέλων πολὺ ὑποβεβηκότων τοῦ ἀγεν<ν>ήτου Πατρὸς γεγενῆσθαι λέγει, τὸν δὲ Ἰησοῦν ἐξ Ἰωσὴφ γεγεν<ν>ῆσθαι, καὶ ὅμοιον τοῖς <λοιποῖς> ἀνθρώποις γεγονότα δικαιότερον τῶν λοιπῶν γενέσθαι. τὴν γὰρ ψυχὴν αὐτοῦ, εὔτονον καὶ καθαρὰν γεγονυῖαν, διαμνημονεῦσαι τὰ ὁρα<θέν>τα [μὲν] αὐτῇ ἐν τῇ μετὰ τοῦ ἀγεν<ν>ήτου θεοῦ περιφορᾷ· καὶ διὰ τοῦτο ὑπ' ἐκείνου αὐτ(ῇ) καταπεμφθῆναι δύναμιν, ὅπως τοὺς κοσμοποιοὺς ἐκφυγεῖν δι' αὐτῆς δυνηθῇ, [ἣν] καὶ διὰ πάντων χωρήσασαν ἐν πᾶσί τε ἐλευθερωθεῖσαν <ἀν>εληλύθη πρὸς αὐτόν, <καὶ τὰς> τὰ ὅμοια αὐτῇ ἀσπαζομένας.

2. τὴν δὲ τοῦ Ἰησοῦ λέγουσι ψυχήν, ἐννόμως ἠσκημέ(ν)ην ἐν Ἰουδαϊκοῖς

Paul declares,[171] and as Jesus himself agrees: "Why do you call me good? One is good."[172]

7. These are the views of Markion, by which he deceived many. By using the theories of Empedokles and by adapting the philosophy invented by that man to his own theory, he concocted a godless heresy. 8. I believe that I have sufficiently refuted it, and that nothing remains of what these men plagiarize from the Greeks. When they claim Christ's disciples as their teachers, they slander them! But since it seems to me that I have sufficiently presented his views, let us see what Karpokrates affirms.[173]

KARPOKRATES

COSMOGONY AND CHRISTOLOGY. 32. 1. Karpokrates says that the world and its contents were made by angels far subordinate to the unborn Father, and that Jesus was born from Joseph, substantially the same as other human beings, although he was more just. This is because his soul, born vigorous and pure, remembered what it saw when it circled round with the unborn God.[174] For this reason, the Unborn sent down a power to his soul, so that through it Jesus's soul might escape the makers of the world.[175] He also sent the power down so that, when Jesus's soul had passed through all, and had been freed from all, it might rise again to him, along with the souls that cling to what is similar to the soul of Jesus.

2. They say that the soul of Jesus, although lawfully trained in Jewish customs, despised them. For this reason, he accomplished miracles.

171. Cf. 1 Tim 2:5: εἷς καὶ μεσίτης θεοῦ καὶ ἀνθρώπων ("and there is one mediator between God and human beings"). Marcovich suspects a lacuna here and was tempted to fill it with a quote from Gal 3:20: ὁ δὲ μεσίτης ἑνὸς οὐκ ἔστιν ("but a mediator does not mediate one party"). Cf. Clem. Alex., *Exc.* 53.2.

172. Mark 10:18 par.; cf. *Ref.* 5.7.26 (Naassenes); Origen, *Princ.* 2.5.1.

173. The following three figures, Karpokrates, Kerinthos, and the "Ebionites," seem to be grouped together because of their "merely" human Christology. Our author's account of Karpokrates is taken with modifications from Iren., *Haer.* 1.25.1–3, with bits from 1.25.4–5. Cf. Epiph., *Pan.* 27.1.1–6.11; Ps.-Tert., *Adv. omn. haer.* 3. See further Pétrement, *Separate God*, 347–50; Lampe, *Paul to Valentinus*, 319–20.

174. "Vigorous" (εὔτονος), literally "well-tensed," was a Stoic technical term (*SVF* 3.473; Plutarch, *Comm. not.* 1085c–d; see further Long and Sedley, *Hellenistic Philosophers*, 2:277–87). For the pre-incarnate vision of God, see Plato, *Phaedr.* 247c; *Resp.* 616c.

175. Cf. Seneca, *Ep.* 41.5.

ἔθεσι, καταφρονῆσαι αὐτῶν, καὶ διὰ τοῦτο δυνάμεις ἐπιτετελεκέναι, δι᾽ ὧν κατήργησε τὰ ἐπὶ κολάσε<σ>ι πάθη προσόντα τοῖς ἀνθρώποις.

3. Τὴν οὖν ὁμοίως ἐκείνῃ τῇ τοῦ Χριστοῦ ψυχῇ δυναμένην καταφρονῆσαι τῶν κοσμοποιῶν ἀρχόντων ὁμοίως λαμβάνειν δύναμιν πρὸς τὸ πρᾶξαι τὰ ὅμοια. διὸ καὶ εἰς τοῦτο το<ῦ> τύφου κατεληλύθασιν, ὥστε τοὺς μὲν <αὐτῶν> ὁμοίους αὐτῷ εἶναι λέγειν τῷ Ἰησοῦ, τοὺς δ᾽ ἔτι καὶ δυνατωτέρους, τινὰς δὲ καὶ διαφορωτέρους τῶν ἐκείνου μαθητῶν, οἷον Πέτρου καὶ Παύλου καὶ τῶν λοιπῶν ἀποστόλων. 4. τούτους δὲ κατὰ μηδὲν ἀπολείπεσθαι τοῦ Ἰησοῦ· τὰς γὰρ ψυχὰς αὐτῶν, ἐκ τῆς <αὐτῆς> ὑπερκειμένης ἐξουσίας παρούσας καὶ διὰ τοῦτο ὡσαύτως καταφρονούσας τῶν κοσμοποιῶν, [διὰ] τῆς αὐτῆς ἠξιῶσθαι δυνάμεως καὶ αὖθις εἰς τὸ αὐτὸ χωρῆσαι. εἰ δέ τις ἐκείνου πλέον καταφρονήσειεν τῶν ἐνταῦθα, δύνασθαι διαφορώτερον αὐτοῦ ὑπάρχειν.

5. Τέχνας οὖν μαγικὰς ἐξεργάζονται καὶ ἐπαοιδάς, φίλτρα τε καὶ χαριτήσια, παρέδρους τε καὶ ὀνειροπόμπους καὶ τὰ λοιπὰ κακουργήματα, φάσκοντες ἐξουσίαν ἔχειν πρὸς τὸ κυριεύειν ἤδη τῶν ἀρχόντων καὶ ποιητῶν τοῦδε τοῦ κόσμου, οὐ μὴν ἀλλὰ καὶ τῶν ἐν αὐτῷ ποιημάτων ἁπάντων.

6. οἵτινες καὶ αὐτοὶ εἰς διαβολὴν τοῦ θείου τῆς ἐκκλησίας ὀνόματος πρὸς τὰ ἔθνη ὑπὸ τοῦ Σατανᾶ προεβλήθησαν, ἵνα κατ᾽ ἄλλον καὶ ἄλλον τρόπον τὰ ἐκείνων ἀκούοντες ἄνθρωποι, καὶ δοκοῦντες ἡμᾶς πάντας τοιούτους ὑπάρχειν, ἀποστρέφωσι τὰς ἀκοὰς αὐτῶν ἀπὸ τοῦ τῆς ἀληθείας κηρύγματος, <καὶ> βλ(έ)ποντες τὰ ἐκείνων ἅπαντα<ς> ἡμᾶς βλασφημῶσιν.

Through these miracles, he disabled the violent emotions attached to human beings that were designed for their punishment.[176]

SOUL. 3. They say that the soul, empowered in the same way as the soul of Christ, despises the world-making rulers and receives equal power to perform the same actions. Consequently, they have stooped to such a pitch of pride as to say that some of their followers are equal to Jesus himself, while others are still more powerful than he, and some are even superior to his disciples—like Peter and Paul and the rest of the apostles! 4. These people do not in any respect fall short of Jesus. This is because their souls have come here from the superior authority.[177] For this reason, they too despise the world makers, are worthy of the same power as Jesus, and in the future advance to the same state as Jesus. And if someone despises the things of our world more than Jesus, this one can become superior to Jesus.[178]

5. They also practice magic arts, incantations, philters, and charms. They use assistant demons and "dream senders" and all the other criminal acts, claiming that they already have authority to lord it over the rulers and makers of this world—and still more to lord it over everything made in the world.[179]

6. These are the very people who have been "emanated" by Satan to slander the divine name of the church before the nations. They were emanated so that the people who listen to them in many and various ways—supposing that we are all of this character—might turn their ears from the preaching of the truth and, when they see their works, revile us all.

---

176. Healing was associated with rooting out negative emotions (cf. Corp. herm. 1.27; 1.32; 13.7–9 [Festugière and Nock]; Porphyry, *Abst.* 4.16).

177. Irenaeus reads "from the same revolution" (*ex eadem circumlatione*); cf. Epiph., *Pan.* 27.2: ἐκ τῆς αὐτῆς περιφορᾶς.

178. For the account of the soul's equality to Jesus, see Tert., *An.* 23.2. For Karpokratians, Jesus is not an inimitable God but a fellow soul who pioneers a path of enlightenment that others can follow. Note John 14:12, where Jesus affirms: "Very truly, I tell you, the one who believes in me will also do the works that I do and, in fact, will do greater works than these." Cf. Ap. Jas. (NHC I,2) 6.19; 7.13–15. Although in principle those souls endowed with power like Jesus can surpass Jesus, it is not clear that any Karpokratians declared that they *had* in fact excelled the master. Many advanced Stoics, by analogy, never claimed to be the perfect Stoic sage.

179. Practicing magic is a standard antiheretical accusation (cf. *Ref.* 6.20.1 ["Simon"]; Iren., *Haer.* 1.23.4).

7. Εἰς τοσοῦτον δὲ μετενσωματοῦσθαι φάσκουσι τὰς ψυχάς, ὅσον πάντα τὰ ἁμαρτήματα πληρώσωσιν· ὅταν δὲ μηδὲν λείπῃ, τότε ἐλευθερωθεῖσαν ἀπαλλαγῆναι πρὸς ἐκεῖνον τὸν ὑπεράνω τῶ(ν) (κο)σμοποιῶν ἀγγέλων θεόν. καὶ οὕτως σωθήσεσθαι πάσας τὰς ψυχάς· 8. [εἰ] τινὲς μὲν φθάσασαι ἐν μιᾷ παρουσίᾳ ἀναμιγῆναι πάσαις ἁμαρτίαις οὐκέτι μετενσωματοῦνται, ἀλλὰ πάντα ὁμοῦ ἀποδοῦσαι τὰ ὀφλήματα, ἐλευθερωθήσονται τοῦ μηκέτι γενέσθαι ἐν σώματι.

Τούτων τινες καὶ καυτηριάζουσι τοὺς ἰδίους μαθητὰς ἐν τοῖς ὀπίσω μέρεσι τοῦ λοβοῦ τοῦ δεξιοῦ ὠτός. καὶ εἰκόνας δὲ κατασκευάζουσι τοῦ Χριστοῦ, λέγοντες ὑπὸ Πιλάτου τῷ καιρῷ ἐκείνῳ <γε>γενῆσθαι.

33. 1. Κήρινθος δέ τις, <καὶ> αὐτὸς Αἰγυπτίων παιδείᾳ ἀσκηθείς, ἔλεγεν οὐχ ὑπὸ τοῦ πρώτου <θεοῦ> γεγονέναι τὸν κόσμον, ἀλλ' ὑπὸ δυνάμεώς τινος κεχωρισμένης τῆς ὑπὲρ τὰ ὅλα ἐξουσίας καὶ ἀγνοούσης τὸν ὑπὲρ πάντα θεόν.

7. They claim that souls undergo transmigration to fill up the full extent of their sins.[180] When no sin remains left over, the soul is freed to depart to the God who is superior to the world-making angels. In this way, all souls will be saved. 8. Some manage to plunge into every sin in a single incarnation and are no longer reincarnated. By paying their dues at once, they will be liberated from future embodiment.

Some of them brand their own disciples behind the lobe of the right ear.[181] They also fashion images of Christ, claiming that they were made by the authority of Pilate during his time.[182]

KERINTHOS

33. 1. A certain Kerinthos, also trained in Egyptian learning, said that the world was created not by the primal God but by a power separate from the authority above the universe and ignorant of the God who is over all.[183]

---

180. For reincarnation, see Plato, *Phaedr.* 248c–249a; *Phaed.* 81e–82c.

181. Karpokratians apparently referred to the branding mark as a "seal" (σφραγίς; Epiph., *Pan.* 27.5.9; Origen, *Cels.* 5.64; cf. Clem. Alex., *Ecl.* 25.1). See further Franz Joseph Dölger, "Die Sphragis als religiöse Brandmarkung im Einweihungsakt der gnostischen Karpokratianer," in *Antike und Christentum: Kultur- und religionsgeschichtliche Studien*, 2nd ed., 6 vols. (Münster: Aschendorff, 1929), 1:73–78 (74).

182. Cf. Iren., *Haer.* 1.25.6; Epiph., *Pan.* 27.5.9; Clem. Alex., *Ecl.* = Herakleon, frag. 49 (Brooke). The iconic worship of Christ (along with Pythagoras, Plato, and Aristotle, as Irenaeus reports) suggests that Jesus was being treated as a deified philosopher-hero. See further Löhr, "Karpokratianisches," *VC* 49 (1995): 23–48 (40 n. 13).

183. Our author takes his report of Kerinthos from Iren., *Haer.* 1.26.1 (repeated with minor variations in *Ref.* 10.21). Cf. Epiph., *Pan.* 28.1.1–7; Ps.-Tert., *Adv. omn. haer.* 3.2; Eusebios, *Hist. eccl.* 3.28; 4.14.6; 7.25. Further sources in A. F. J. Klijn and G. J. Reinink, *Patristic Evidence for Jewish-Christian Sects*, NovTSup 36 (Leiden: Brill, 1973), 3–19. See further Benjamin G. Wright III, "Cerinthus *apud* Hippolytus: An Inquiry into the Traditions about Cerinthus's Provenance," *SecCent* 4 (1984): 103–15; Pétrement, *Separate God*, 298–314; Christoph Markschies, "Kerinth: Wer war er und was lehrte er?," *JAC* 41 (1998): 48–76; Charles E. Hill, "Cerinthus, Gnostic or Chiliast? A New Solution to an Old Problem," *JECS* 8 (2000): 135–72; Matti Myllykoski, "Cerinthus," in Marjanen and Luomanen, *Companion*, 211–46; Gunnar af Hällström and Oskar Skarsaune, "Cerinthus, Elxai, and Other Alleged Jewish Christian Teachers or Groups," in *Jewish Believers in Jesus*, ed. Oskar Skarsaune and Reidar Hvalvik (Peabody, MA: Hendrickson, 2007), 488–95; Edwin K. Broadhead, *Jewish Ways of Following Jesus: Redrawing the Religious Map of Antiquity*, WUNT 266 (Tübingen: Mohr Siebeck, 2011), 222–31. Our author adds the Egyptian derivation of Kerinthos's teaching to bolster his thesis that heresy comes from philosophy (since philosophy partially hails from Egypt: *Ref.* 4.43.4; 6.21.3; 9.27.3). In the table of contents to book 7 (*Ref.*

τὸν δὲ Ἰησοῦν ὑπέθετο μὴ ἐκ παρθένου γεγεν<ν>ῆσθαι, γεγονέναι δὲ αὐτὸν ἐξ Ἰωσὴφ καὶ Μαρίας υἱόν, ὁμοίως τοῖς λοιποῖς ἅπασιν ἀνθρώποις, καὶ δικαιότερον γεγονέναι καὶ σοφώτερον. 2. καὶ μετὰ τὸ βάπτισμα κατελθεῖν εἰς αὐτὸν [τὸν] <ἐκ> τῆς ὑπὲρ τὰ ὅλα αὐθεντίας τὸν Χριστὸν ἐν εἴδει περιστερᾶς· καὶ τότε κηρῦξαι τὸν <ἄ>γνωστον πατέρα καὶ δυνάμεις ἐπιτελέσαι. πρὸς δὲ τῷ τέλει ἀποστῆναι τὸν Χριστὸν ἀπὸ τοῦ <Ἰησοῦ>, καὶ τὸν Ἰησοῦν πεπονθέναι καὶ ἐγηγέρθαι, τὸν δὲ Χριστὸν ἀπαθῆ διαμεμενηκέναι, <πνευματικὸν> ὑπάρχοντα.

34. 1. Ἐβιωναῖοι δὲ ὁμολογοῦσι τὸν κόσμον ὑπὸ τοῦ ὄντως θεοῦ γεγονέναι, τὰ δὲ περὶ τὸν Χριστὸν ὁμοίως τῷ Κηρίνθῳ καὶ Καρποκράτει μυθεύουσιν. ἔθεσιν

He taught that Jesus was not born from a virgin but was son of Joseph and Mary, born just like all other people—although he was more righteous and wise. 2. After his baptism, Christ descended upon Jesus from the Supreme Authority over the universe in the form of a dove.[184] Afterward, he preached the unknown Father and performed miracles. In the end, Christ deserted Jesus,[185] and Jesus both suffered and was raised. Christ, however, remained without suffering, since he was spiritual.[186]

EBIONITES

34. 1. The Ebionites admit that the world arose by the power of the true God but tell myths about Christ similar to Kerinthos and Karpokrates.[187]

7.7), the Egyptian derivation of Kerinthos's teaching is also emphasized. This does not necessarily imply that Kerinthos hailed from Egypt (though he was putatively trained in Egypt, *Ref.* 10.21.1). On the split between the high God and creator, see Markschies, "Kerinth," 72–73.

184. Cf. Iren., *Haer.* 1.7.2; 3.11.3, with the comments of Markschies, "Kerinth," 71–72. See also *Ref.* 6.35.6 ("Valentinus"); 6.47.2; 6.51.2, 4 (Markos); 7.35.2 (Theodotos the Byzantian); 7.36.1 (Theodotos). See further Hill, "Cerinthus," 150–53.

185. P here reads χ(ριστο)ῦ, emended to Ἰησοῦ by R. Scott and Bunsen (see Marcovich's apparatus).

186. P here reads πατρικόν ("paternal"), which Bunsen and Harvey emend to πνευματικόν ("spiritual") from Iren., *Haer.* 1.26.1 (*spiritalem*). In the summary of Kerinthos (*Ref.* 10.21.3), the reading of P is πνεῦμα κυρίου ("spirit of the Lord").

187. The report on the "Ebionites" (from אביונים, "poor ones") is taken with modifications from Iren., *Haer.* 1.26.2; cf. the summary in *Ref.* 10.22. The portion on Ebionite Christology (*Ref.* 7.34.2) is added by our author. Possibly it is his own composition. It strongly conforms Ebionite to Karpokratian imitation Christology. See further the sources in Klijn and Reinink, *Patristic Evidence*, 19–43. See further Richard Bauckham, "The Origin of the Ebionites," in *The Image of the Judaeo-Christians in Ancient Jewish and Christian Literature*, ed. Peter J. Tomson and Doris Lambers-Petry, WUNT 158 (Tübingen: Mohr Siebeck, 2003), 162–81; Oskar Skarsaune, "The Ebionites," in Skarsaune and Hvalvik, *Jewish Believers in Jesus*, 419–62. On the heresiological treatment of the "Ebionites," see Sakari Häkkinen, "Ebionites," in Marjanen and Luomanen, *Companion*, 247–78; James Carleton Paget, *Jews, Christians and Jewish Christians in Antiquity*, WUNT 251 (Tübingen: Mohr Siebeck, 2010), 325–79; Broadhead, *Jewish Ways*, 188–203, 243–51, 379–80; F. Stanley Jones, *Pseudoclementina Elchasaiticaque inter Judaeochristiana: Collected Studies* (Leuven: Peeters, 2012), 513–31. Our author implies that the Ebionites, like Karpokrates and Kerinthos, support a possessionist Christology (the idea that Jesus was possessed by some divine power at his baptism that in turn left him at his death). Cf. Iren., *Haer.* 1.26.2 (deleting *non* in *non similiter*). See further Hill, "Cerinthus," 146–47; Myllykoski, "Cerinthus," 227–29.

Ἰουδαϊκοῖς ζῶσι κατὰ νόμον, <οὕτω> φάσκοντες δικαιοῦσθαι. 2. καὶ τὸν Ἰησοῦν λέγουσι δεδικαιῶσθαι ποιήσαντα τὸν νόμον· διὸ καὶ Χριστὸν αὐτὸν τοῦ θεοῦ ὠνομάσθαι [καὶ Ἰησοῦν], ἐπεὶ μηδεὶς τῶν <ἑτέρων> ἐτέλεσε τὸν νόμον· εἰ γὰρ καὶ ἕτερός τις πεποιήκει τὰ ἐν νόμῳ προστεταγμένα, ἦν ἂν ἐκεῖνος ὁ Χριστός. δύνασθαι δὲ καὶ ἑαυτοὺς ὁμοίως ποιήσαντας Χριστοὺς γενέσθαι· καὶ γὰρ καὶ αὐτὸν ὁμοίως ἄνθρωπον εἶναι πᾶσι λέγουσιν.

35. 1. Θεόδοτος δέ τις, ὢν Βυζάντιος, εἰσήγαγεν αἵρεσιν καινὴν φάσκων τὰ μὲν περὶ τῆς τοῦ παντὸς ἀρχῆς σύμφωνα ἐκ μέρους τοῖς τῆς ἀληθοῦς ἐκκλησίας, ὑπὸ τοῦ θεοῦ πάντα ὁμολογῶν γεγονέναι, τὸν δὲ Χριστόν—ἐκ τῆς τῶν γνωστικῶν καὶ Κηρίνθου καὶ Ἐβίωνος σχολῆς ἀποσπάσας—φάσκει τοιούτῳ τινὶ τρόπῳ πεφηνέναι. 2. [καὶ] τὸν μὲν Ἰησοῦν εἶναι ἄνθρωπον ἐκ παρθένου γεγενημένον κατὰ βουλὴν τοῦ πατρός, βιώσαντά τε κοινῶς πᾶσιν ἀνθρώποις καὶ εὐσεβέστατον γεγονότα· ὕστερον ἐπὶ τοῦ βαπτίσματος ἐπὶ τῷ Ἰορδάνῃ κεχωρηκέναι τὸν Χριστόν, ἄνωθεν κατεληλυθότα ἐν εἴδει περιστερᾶς. ὅθεν οὐ πρότερον «τὰς δυνάμεις ἐν αὐτῷ ἐνηργηκέναι» ἢ ὅτε κατελθὸν ἀνεδείχθη ἐν αὐτῷ τὸ πνεῦμα, ὃ εἶναι τὸν Χριστὸν προσαγορεύει. θεὸν δὲ οὐδέποτε τοῦτον γεγονέναι αὐτὸς θέλουσιν, ἐπὶ τῇ καθόδῳ τοῦ πνεύματος, ἕτεροι δὲ μετὰ τὴν ἐκ νεκρῶν ἀνάστασιν.

They live according to Jewish customs in agreement with the Law. By behaving in this manner, they claim, they are made righteous. 2. They also affirm that Jesus was made righteous by obeying the Law. Consequently he was named "the Christ of God," since no one else fulfilled the Law.[188] If someone else had performed the commandments in the Law, he would have been the Christ. It is possible, furthermore, for those who do the same works to become Christs. And rightly so, since they say that he is a human being just like every other person.

THEODOTOS THE BYZANTIAN

35. 1. A certain Theodotos, a Byzantian, introduced a new heresy.[189] On the one hand, he made claims about the origin of the universe partially in agreement with the true church (since he admitted that all things originate from God). On the other hand, drawing on the school of the gnostics, Kerinthos, and Ebion, he claims that Christ appeared in the following way.[190] 2. Jesus was born a human being from a virgin according to the Father's will. He lived a life common to all people yet became the most pious. Later, at his baptism in the Jordan, he received the Christ, who descended from above in the form of a dove.[191] Thus before the Spirit (which he calls "Christ") descended and was shown to be in Jesus, "the miracles were not activated in him."[192] But they do not want him to have become a god when the Spirit descended. Others say that he became a god after he rose from the dead.

188. For the title, see Luke 9:20 (τὸν χριστὸν τοῦ θεοῦ).

189. Theodotos the Byzantian, derisively called the "shoemaker" (σκυτεύς), flourished during the time of the Roman bishop Victor (189–199 CE). Cf. the summary in *Ref.* 10.23; [Hipp.], *Noet.* 3; Eusebios, *Hist. eccl.* 5.28.6; Epiph., *Pan.* 54.1.1–6.5; Ps.-Tert., *Adv. omn. haer.* 8.2; Filastrius, *Haer.* 50; Theodoret, *Haer. fab.* 2.5 (PG 83:392). Like the figures before him (Karpokrates and Kerinthos), Theodotos seems to have maintained a possessionist Christology. What distinguishes him is his belief in the virgin birth. Only Theodotos's followers, apparently, believed that Jesus was promoted to divinity. See further Lampe, *Paul to Valentinus*, 344–48.

190. Here the name "Ebion" (invented here perhaps for the first time) becomes a leader of a school by analogy to Kerinthos.

191. Cf. *Ref.* 6.35.6 ("Valentinus"); 6.47.2; 6.51.2, 4, 5 (Markos); 7.33.2 (Kerinthos).

192. Cf. Mark 6:14; Matt 14:2; and the use of δυνάμεις in *Ref.* 7.32.2 (Karpokrates); 7.33.2 (Kerinthos).

36. 1. Διαφόρων δὲ γενομένων ἐν αὐτοῖς ζητήσεων <ἐ>πεχείρησέ τις, καὶ αὐτὸς Θεόδοτος καλούμενος, τραπεζίτης τὴν τέχνην, λέγειν δύναμίν τινα τὸν Μελχισεδὲκ εἶναι με(γ)ίστην, καὶ τοῦτον εἶναι μείζονα τοῦ Χριστοῦ, οὗ κατ' εἰκόνα φάσκουσι τὸν Χριστὸν τυγχάνειν. καὶ αὐτοὶ ὁμοίως τοῖς προειρημένοις Θεοδοτιανοῖς ἄνθρωπον εἶναι λέγουσι τὸν Ἰησοῦν, καὶ κατὰ τὸν αὐτὸν λόγον τὸν Χριστὸν εἰς αὐτὸν κατεληλυθέναι.

2. Γνωστικῶν δὴ διάφοροι γνῶμα(ι), ὧν οὐκ ἄξιον καταριθμεῖν τὰς φλυάρους δόξας ἐκρίναμεν, οὔσας πολλὰς ἀλογίας τε καὶ βλασφημίας γεμούσας· ὧν πολὺ σεμνότερον περὶ τὸ θεῖον οἱ φιλοσοφήσαντες ἀφ' Ἑλλήνων ἠνέχθησαν.

3. πολλῆς δὲ αὐτοῖς συστάσεως κακῶν αἴτιος γεγένηται Νικόλαος, εἷς τῶν ἑπτὰ εἰς διακονίαν ὑπὸ τῶν ἀποστόλων κατασταθείς. ὃς ἀποστὰς τῆς κατ' εὐθεῖαν διδασκαλίας ἐδίδασκεν ἀδιαφορίαν βίου τε καὶ <βρώσεως>· οὗ τοὺς

THEODOTOS

36. 1. When various disputes arose among the Theodotians, one man—also called Theodotos, a banker by trade—argued that a certain "Melchizedek" was the greatest power—even greater than Christ.[193] Christ was, they allege, in his image.[194] They also assert (just as the aforementioned Theodotians) that Jesus is a human being and tell the same story about Christ descending upon him.

2. I deem it unworthy to enumerate the differing viewpoints of these gnostics, since I judge them to be blabbering opinions.[195] The whole lot of them are infested with irrationality and blasphemy! In comparison to them, Greek philosophers have taken up a much more reverent attitude toward the divine.[196]

NIKOLAOS

3. The cause of their manifold system of evils was Nikolaos, one of the seven men appointed by the apostles for the diaconate.[197] After he broke away from orthodox teaching, he taught that lifestyle and diet were indifferent.[198] The Holy Spirit through the Revelation of John mocked his

---

193. Theodotos flourished during the time of Bishop Zephyrinos (199–217 CE). Cf. the summary in *Ref.* 10.24; Eusebios, *Hist. eccl.* 5.28.9; Epiph., *Pan.* 55.1.1–9.19; Ps.-Tert., *Adv. omn. haer.* 8.3; Filastrius, *Haer.* 52; Theodoret, *Haer. fab.* 2.6 ("Melchizedekians") (PG 83:392–93). See further Lampe, *Paul to Valentinus*, 344–48. On the theology of Melchizedek, see 11QMelch (11Q13) II, 10; Ps.-Tert., *Adv. omn. haer.* 8.3.

194. Cf. Ps 109:4 LXX; Heb 5:6; Melch. (NHC IX,1) 15.7–16.11 (though here, Melchizedek is in the image of Christ).

195. Note the vague, conflationary use of "gnostic" our author (affecting impatience) uses as a polemical tool. After having just distinguished Kerinthos, "Ebion," and the "gnostics" (*Ref.* 7.35.1), he groups them together here under one rather sloppy category.

196. Cf. *Ref.* 1, *pref.* 8.

197. The report on Nikolaos is adapted from Iren., *Haer.* 1.26.3, who calls the Nikolaitans a gnostic offshoot (3.11.1). Our author goes further by saying that Nikolaos was the "cause" (αἴτιος) of the "gnostic" systems. But he may have had in mind only Karpokrates, Kerinthos, the Ebionites, and the two groups of Theodotians. Cf. Clem. Alex., *Strom.* 2.20.118.3–5; 3.4.25.5–26.3; Epiph., *Pan.* 25.1.1–6; Ps.-Tert., *Adv. omn. haer.* 1.6; Filastrius, *Haer.* 33.1; Theodoret, *Haer. fab.* 1.15 ("Cainites") (PG 83:368b), 3.1 (PG 83:401b–c). See further Heikki Räisänen, "The Nicolaitans: Apoc. 2; Acta 6," *ANRW* 26.2:1602–44 (1623–26). On Nikolaos the deacon, see Acts 6:5b.

198. Βρώσεως (here: "diet") is an emendation for P's γνώσεως ("knowledge"). Cf.

μαθητὰς ἐνυβρίζον τὸ ἅγιον πνεῦμα διὰ τῆς Ἀποκαλύψεως Ἰωάννης ἤλεγξε «πορνεύοντας καὶ εἰδωλόθυτα ἐσθίοντας».

37. 1. Κέρδων δέ τις, καὶ αὐτὸς ἀφορμὰς ὁμοίως παρὰ τούτων λαβὼν καὶ Σίμωνος, λέγει τὸν ὑπὸ Μωσέως καὶ προφητῶν κεκηρυγμένον θεὸν μὴ εἶναι πατέρα Ἰησοῦ Χριστοῦ· τοῦτον μὲν γὰρ ἐγνῶσθαι, τὸν δὲ τοῦ Χριστοῦ πατέρα εἶναι ἄγνωστον· καὶ τὸν μὲν εἶναι δίκαιον, τὸν δὲ ἀγαθόν.

2. τούτου δὲ τὸ δόγμα ἐκράτυνε Μαρκίων, τάς τε ἀντιπαραθέσεις ἐπιχειρήσας καὶ ὅσα αὐτῷ ἔδοξεν εἰς τὸ τὸν ἁπάντων δημιουργὸν δυσφημῆσαι.

ὁμοίως δὲ καὶ Λουκιανὸς ὁ τούτου μαθητής.

38. 1. Ἀπελ<λ>ῆς δέ, ἐκ τούτων γενόμενος, οὕτως λέγει· εἶναί τινα θεὸν ἀγαθόν, καθὼς καὶ Μαρκί(ων) ὑπέθετο· τὸν δὲ πάντα κτίσαντα εἶναι δίκαιον—

disciples and exposed them as "fornicators and eaters of meat sacrificed to idols."[199]

KERDON

37. 1. A certain Kerdon likewise took his starting points from these people, as well as from Simon.[200] He says that the god proclaimed by Moses and the prophets is not the Father of Jesus Christ. This is because the God proclaimed by Moses can be known, whereas the Father of Christ is unknown. The former is just, while the latter is good.

2. Markion radicalized this dogma when he ventured his *Antitheses* and everything else he thought would impugn the Artificer of all things.[201]

Loukianos his disciple taught the same.[202]

APELLES

38. 1. Apelles, who was from their circle, asserts the following.[203] There is one good God, just as Markion posited. The one who created and fash-

---

Clem. Alex., *Strom.* 2.20.118.3; 3.25.7. Irenaeus does not accuse Nikolaos himself of immoral behavior, only his followers. Our author makes Nikolaos an apostate and the originator of immorality. The use of ἀδιαφορίαν recalls Stoic ethics (Long and Sedley, *Hellenistic Philosophers*, 2:349–55). Cf. Iren., *Haer.* 1.26.3: *nullam differentiam esse* ("there is no difference").

199. Cf. Rev 2:14–15; 2:6; Epiph., *Pan.* 25.3.1; Eusebios, *Hist. eccl.* 3.29.1.

200. The report on Kerdon is an abbreviation of Iren., *Haer.* 1.27.1–2 (= Eusebios, *Hist. eccl.* 4.11.2). Cf. Tert., *Marc.* 12.3; Epiph., *Pan.* 41.1.1–9; Ps.-Tert., *Adv. omn. haer.* 6.6; Filastrius, *Haer.* 44; *Ref.* 7.10 (table of contents); Theodoret, *Haer. fab.* 1.24 (PG 83:372–73, 376). See further Gerhard May, "Markion und der Gnostiker Kerdon," in Greschat and Meiser, *Gesammelte Aufsätze*, 63–74 (68–69). "These people" (τούτων) seems to refer to the "the school of the gnostics, Kerinthos, and Ebion" mentioned in *Ref.* 7.35.1. Irenaeus says that Kerdon took his starting points from the followers of Simon (*Haer.* 1.27.1).

201. Our author mentions Markion again here because this is where Irenaeus places him. It makes sense that Markion radicalized Kerdon if Kerdon taught a good and *just* god, while Markion taught a good versus an *evil* god.

202. For Loukianos, see *Ref.* 7.11 (table of contents); Tert., *Res.* 2; Ps.-Tert., *Adv. omn. haer.* 6.3; Filastrius, *Haer.* 56; Origen, *Cels.* 2.27; Epiph., *Pan.* 43.1.1. See further Lampe, *Paul to Valentinus*, 416.

203. Apelles, a theologian active in Rome between 140 and 185 CE, began his career as a Markionite but developed his teacher's thought in a more philosophical direction. Cf. *Ref.* 7.12 (table of contents); 10.20.1–2 (Apelles summary); Rhodon in

ὃς τὰ γενόμενα ἐδημιούργησε·—καὶ τρίτον τὸν Μωσεῖ λαλήσαντα—πύρινον δὲ τοῦτον εἶναι·—εἶναι δὲ καὶ τέταρτον ἕτερον, κακῶν αἴτιον· τούτους δὲ ἀγγέλους ὀνομάζει. 2. νόμον δὲ καὶ προφήτας δυσφημεῖ, ἀνθρώπινα καὶ ψευδῆ φάσκων εἶναι τὰ γεγραμμένα· τῶν δὲ εὐαγγελίων καὶ τοῦ ἀποστόλου τὰ ἀρέσκοντα αὐτῷ αἱρεῖται. Φιλουμένης δέ τινος λόγοις προσέχει ὡς προφήτιδος <ἐν ταῖς> Φανερώσ<εσι>.

Τὸν δὲ Χριστὸν ἐκ τῆς ὕπερθεν δυνάμεώς κατεληλυθέναι, τουτέστι τοῦ ἀγαθοῦ, κἀκείνου αὐτὸν εἶναι υἱόν. 3. τοῦτον δὲ οὐκ ἐκ παρθένου γεγενῆσθαι, οὐδ' ἄσαρκον εἶναι φανέντα λέγει, ἀλλ' ἐκ τῆς τοῦ παντὸς οὐσίας μεταλαβόντα μερῶν σῶμα πεποιηκέναι—τουτέστι θερμοῦ καὶ ψυχροῦ, καὶ ὑγροῦ καὶ ξηροῦ—καὶ ἐν τούτῳ τῷ σώματι λαθόντα τὰς κοσμικὰς ἐξουσίας βεβιωκέναι ὃν ἐβίωσε χρόνον ἐν κόσμῳ.

4. Αὖθις δὲ ὑπὸ Ἰουδαίων ἀνασκολοπισθέντα θανεῖν, καὶ μετὰ τρεῖς ἡμέρας ἐγερθέντα φανῆναι τοῖς μαθηταῖς δείξαντα τοὺς τύπους τῶν ἥλων καὶ τὴν

ioned all things is just. There is also a third god, a fiery one who spoke to Moses. There is yet a fourth, still different, god, the cause of evils. These gods he calls "angels."[204] 2. He impugns the Law and Prophets, claiming that the scriptures are human products and false.[205] He selects his doctrines from the Gospels and the apostle Paul.[206] He adheres to the discourses of a certain Philoumene (as if she were a prophetess!) in her book called *Manifestations*.[207]

CHRISTOLOGY. Christ descended from the power above (that is, the Good) and is his Son. 3. Christ was not born from a virgin, but neither, Apelles claims, did he appear without flesh. Rather, he made a body by taking portions from the essential constituents of the universe (that is, from the hot, cold, moist, and dry). In this body, he eluded the cosmic authorities and lived the period of time that he did in the world.[208]

4. Later, Christ died, crucified by the Jews. After three days, he arose and appeared to his disciples. After showing the marks of the nails and his

---

Eusebios, *Hist. eccl.* 5.13; Tert., *Praescr.* 6, 30, 33; *Marc.* 3.11; 4.17; *Carn. Chr.* 1.6; Ps.-Tert., *Adv. omn. haer.* 6; Origen, *Cels.* 5.54; Filastrius, *Haer.* 47; Epiph., *Pan.* 44.1.1–3.9; Theodoret, *Haer. fab.* 1.25 (PG 83:376–77). See further Lampe, *Paul to Valentinus*, 414–15; Katharina Greschat, *Apelles und Hermogenes: Zwei theologische Lehrer des zweiten Jahrhunderts*, VCSup 48 (Leiden: Brill, 2000), 17–134.

204. This description of Apelles's theology is misleading. Apelles affirmed a single, good God (Eusebios, *Hist. eccl.* 5.13.7). This good God brought forth the creator of the world who, like the Artificer in the *Timaios*, was good and made the world as close to God's design as he could. But from this creation there arose a fiery, evil god who has subjected humans to the slavery of enfleshment and the Law (Greschat, *Apelles und Hermogenes*, 73–96).

205. See further Greschat, *Apelles und Hermogenes*, 68–72.

206. Cf. Epiph., *Pan.* 44.2, 6.

207. On Philoumene, see *Ref.* 10.20.2; Rhodon in Eusebios, *Hist. eccl.* 5.13.2; Tert., *Praescr.* 30.6; *Carn. Chr.* 24; Ps.-Tert., *Adv. omn. haer.* 6: *Habet praeterea privates, sed extraordinarias lectiones suas, quas appellant Phanerosis, Philumenes cuisdam puellae, quam quasi prophetissam sequitur* ("He has, moreover, his own private, extraordinary readings, which they call *Manifestation*, the work of some girl Philumene, whom he follows as if she were a prophetess"). See further Greschat, *Apelles und Hermogenes*, 110–22; Roman Hanig, "Der Beitrag der Philumene zur Theologie der Apelleianer," ZAC 3 (1999): 241–77 (254–60).

208. The doctrine of incarnation expressed here better fits Apelles's disciples, who believed that Christ's body was constituted from the four elements. See further Greschat, *Apelles und Hermogenes*, 97–109, 130, esp. 107–9. Our author will later propose that humans have their constitution from the four elements (*Ref.* 10.32.2–3).

πλευρὰν πείθειν ὅτι αὐτὸς εἴη καὶ οὐ φάντασμα· ἀλλὰ ἔνσαρκος ἦν. 5. σάρκ(α), φησίν, δείξας ἀπέδωκε γῇ, ἐξ ἧσπερ ἦν οὐσίας· μηδὲν ἀλ<λό>τριον πλεονεκτῶν, ἀλλὰ πρὸς καιρὸν χρησάμενος, ἑκάστοις τὰ ἴδια ἀπέδωκε, λύσας πάλιν τὸν δεσμὸν τοῦ σώματος—θερμῷ τὸ θερμόν, ψυχρῷ τὸ ψυχρόν, ὑγρῷ τὸ ὑγρόν, ξηρῷ τὸ ξηρόν·—καὶ οὕτως ἐπορεύθη πρὸς τὸν ἀγαθὸν πατέρα, καταλιπὼν τὸ τῆς ζωῆς σπέρμα εἰς τὸν κόσμον διὰ τῶν μαθητῶν τοῖς πιστεύουσι.

6. Δοκεῖ ἡμῖν καὶ τα(ῦτ)α ἱκανῶς ἐκτεθεῖσθαι· ἀλλ' ἐπεὶ μηδὲν παραλιπεῖν ἀνέλεγκτον ἐκρίναμεν τῶν ὑπό τινων δεδογματισμένων, ἴδωμεν τί καὶ τὸ τοῖς Δοκηταῖς ἐπινενοημένον.

side, he persuaded them that it was truly he and not a phantom. To be sure, he was embodied in flesh.[209] 5. After displaying his flesh, he claims, he gave it back to the earth, where this substance originated. He was not greedy for what was not his own. Rather, after borrowing it for a time, he restored what belonged to each element. After he again loosed the chain of the body (that is, after he gave heat to heat, cold to cold, moisture to moisture, and dryness to dryness), he proceeded to the good Father. To those who believe through his disciples, he left behind in the world the seed of life.

CONCLUSION

6. Now it seems to me that I have sufficiently presented these matters as well. But since I decided to leave no one's dogmas unexposed, let us also inspect what the Doketai have devised.

209. This account combines elements of John 20:20, 25, 27, and Luke 24:39. Cf. Epiph., *Pan.* 44.2.7. Apelles was not "docetic," as, supposedly, was his teacher Markion (*Ref.* 10.19.3).

<ΤΟΥ ΚΑΤΑ ΠΑΣΩΝ ΑΙΡΕΣΕΩΝ ΕΛΕΓΧΟΥ Η>

1. Τάδε ἔνεστιν ἐν τῇ ὀγδόῃ τοῦ κατὰ πασῶν τῶν αἱρέσεω(ν) ἐλ(έγ)χου·

2. Τίνα τοῖς Δοκηταῖς τὰ δοκοῦντα, καὶ ὅτι ἐκ φυσικῆς φιλοσοφίας ἃ λέγουσιν ἐδογμάτισαν.

3. Πῶς ὁ Μονόϊμος ληρεῖ, ποιηταῖς καὶ γεωμέτραις καὶ ἀριθμητικοῖς προσέχων.

4. Πῶς Τατιανὸς κεκί(ν)ηται ἐκ τῶν Οὐαλεντίνου καὶ Μαρκίωνος δοξ<ῶν τ>ὰς ἑαυτοῦ συνιστᾶν, ὅ<τι> τε Ἑρμογένης τοῖς Σωκράτους δόγμασι κέχρηται, οὐ τοῖς Χριστοῦ.

5. Πῶς πλανῶ(ντ)αι οἱ τὸ πάσχα τῇ τεσσαρεσκαιδεκάτῃ ἐπιτελεῖν φιλονεικοῦντες.

6. Τίς ἡ πλάνη τῶν Φρυγῶν, νομιζόντων Μοντανὸν καὶ Πρισκίλλαν καὶ Μαξιμίλλαν προφήτας.

7. Τίς ἡ τῶν Ἐγκρατιτῶν κενοδοξία, καὶ ὅτι οὐκ ἐξ ἁγίων γραφῶν τὰ δόγματα αὐτῶν συνέστηκεν, ἀλλ' ἐξ αὑτῶν καὶ ἐκ τῶν παρ' Ἰνδοῖς γυμνοσοφιστῶν.

8. 1. Ἐπεὶ οἱ πολλοί, τῇ τοῦ κυρίου συμβουλίᾳ μὴ χρώμενοι, τὴν δοκὸν ἐν τῷ ὀφθαλμῷ ἔχοντες ὁρᾶν ἐπαγγέλ<λ>ονται τυφλώττοντες, δοκεῖ ἡμῖν μηδὲ τὰ τούτων δόγματα σιωπᾶν, ὅπως κἂν διὰ τοῦ ὑφ' ἡμῶν γινομένου ἐλέγχου [πρὸς] αὐτῶν αἰδεσθέντες, ἐπιγνῶσιν ὡς συνεβούλευσεν ὁ σωτὴρ ἐξαιρεῖν τὴν δοκὸν πρῶτον, εἶτα διαβλέπειν τὸ κάρφος τὸ ἐν τῷ ὀφθαλμῷ τοῦ ἀδελφοῦ.

BOOK 8

[TABLE OF CONTENTS]

1. The following is contained in the eighth book of the *Refutation of All Heresies.*

2. The doctrines of the Doketai. What they taught they took from natural philosophy.

3. How Monoïmos blathers, addicted as he is to poets, geometers, and number theorists.

4. How Tatian, spurred on by the views of Valentinus and Markion, manufactured his own teachings. Hermogenes makes use of Sokratic dogmas, not those of Christ.

5. How those that contentiously argue that Easter be celebrated on the fourteenth of the month are wrong.

6. The error of the Phrygians, who consider Montanus, Priscilla, and Maximilla to be prophets.

7. The empty conceit of the Enkratites, who compose their doctrines not from the holy scriptures but from their own resources and from the naked philosophers of India.[1]

INTRODUCTION

8. 1. Since most people ignore the counsel of the Lord and proclaim that they see, though they are blinded by a plank in their eye, I have decided not to keep their doctrines secret. I do so in order that they—although ashamed due to my refutation—might learn how the Savior counseled us first to remove the plank and then to perceive the speck in the brother's

1. Clement of Alexandria makes a similar comparison in *Strom.* 1.15.71.4–5. Strangely, the Indian philosophers go unmentioned in the main report on the Enkratites below (*Ref.* 8.20). See further Ducoeur, "Hérésiarques chrétiens," 180–83.

2. αὐτάρκως οὖν καὶ ἱκανῶς ἐκθέμενοι τὰ τῶν πλειόνων ἐν ταῖς πρὸ ταύτης βίβλοις ἑπτά, νῦν τά ἀκόλουθα οὐ σιωπήσομεν, τὸ ἄφθονον τῆς χάριτος τοῦ ἁγίου πνεύματος ἐπιδεικνύντες, καὶ τοὺς τῷ δοκεῖν ἀσφάλειαν λόγων κεκτῆσθαι ἐλέγξομεν· οἳ ἑ(α)υτοὺς Δοκητὰς ἀπεκάλεσαν, δογματίζοντες ταῦτα.

3. Θεὸν εἶναι τὸν πρῶτον οἱονεὶ σπέρμα συκῆς, μεγέθει μὲν ἐλάχιστον παντελῶς, δυνάμει δὲ ἀπειρομέγεθες, ἀνήριθμον ἐν πλήθει, πρὸς γένεσιν ἀπροσδεές· φοβουμένων καταφυγή<ν>, γυμνῶν σκέπη<ν>, αἰσχύνης ἐπικάλυμ<μ>α· (κ)αρπὸν ζητούμενον, ἐφ' ὃν ἦλθεν ὁ ζητῶν, φησί, τρίς, καὶ οὐχ εὗρε· διὸ κατηράσατο, φησίν, τῇ συκῇ, ὅτι τὸν γλυκὺν ἐκεῖνον καρπὸν οὐχ εὗρεν ἐν αὐτῇ καρπὸν ζητούμενον.

4. Τοιούτου δὲ ὄντος, ὡς εἰπεῖν τύπῳ, καὶ τηλικούτου, μικροῦ καὶ <παμ>μεγέθους, κατ' ἐκείνους τοῦ θεοῦ, γέγονεν ὁ κόσμος, ὡς ἐκείνοις δοκεῖ, τοιοῦτόν τινα τρόπον· ἁπαλῶν γενομένων (τ)ῶν κλάδων τῆς συκῆς προῆλθε φύλλα, ὥσπερ ἐστιν ὁρώμενον, (ἑ)πομένως δὲ ὁ καρπός, ἐν ᾧ τὸ ἄπειρον καὶ [τὸ] ἀνεξαρίθμητον θησαυριζόμενον φυλάσσεται σπέρμα συκῆς. 5. τρία οὖν εἶναι δοκοῦμεν τὰ πρώτως ὑπὸ τοῦ σπέρματος γενόμενα τοῦ συκίνου· πρέμνον,

eye.[2] 2. Since I have fully and adequately presented the doctrines of most thinkers in the previous seven books, at present I will not keep secret those that followed. Exhibiting the generous grace of the Holy Spirit, I will also refute those who seem to have acquired secure arguments.[3] They dubbed themselves "Doketai" and decree the following.[4]

DOKETAI

3. The primal God is, as it were, a seed of a fig tree, altogether tiny in size, but infinitely great in power, immeasurable in extent, needing nothing to proliferate, a refuge for the frightened, a covering for the naked, a veil of modesty, and the fruit that is sought. The seeker came to the tree three times, he says, and found nothing.[5] So he cursed the fig tree, he says, because he did not find that sweet fruit in it—the fruit that is sought.[6]

THREE AND THIRTY AEONS. 4. Their God, roughly speaking, is of this nature and magnitude (that is, both miniscule and massive). Such being the case, the world arose, in their view, in the following way. When the branches of a fig tree are tender, and the leaves visibly protrude, the fruit follows accordingly.[7] In this fruit is preserved the infinite and immeasurable fig seed stored up as a treasure. 5. Now we believe there to be three primary fig-tree parts produced by the seed: the trunk (which is the fig tree), the leaves, and the fruit (namely, the fig, as I said previously). In this way, he

---

2. For the plank and speck, see Matt 7:3–5; Luke 6:41–2. Our author uses δοκόν ("plank") to pun on both δοκεῖν and Δοκηταί.

3. "Seem," translating τῷ δοκεῖν, plays on Δοκητάς (Doketai) in the next sentence. Ἀσφάλειαν λόγων seems to be a set phrase. Cf. Luke 1:4; Xenophon, *Mem.* 4.6.15.

4. The Doketai have often been called "Docetists," a confusing ambiguity, since the Doketai were not "docetic." To avoid confusion, it seems wise to disambiguate the names here. Earlier scholars believed that the Doketai derived their name from the fact that they believed that Jesus appeared differently to different people (Salmon, "Docetae," *DCB* 1:865–67 [867]). For the Doketai, see *Ref.* 10.16.1 (Doketai summary); Clem. Alex., *Strom.* 3:13.91.1; 3.17.102.1–3; 6.9.71.2; 7.17.108.2; Eusebios, *Hist. eccl.* 6.12.6. See further Orbe, *Cristología Gnóstica*, 1:580–85.

5. Cf. Luke 13:6–7.

6. For the cursing of the fig tree, see Mark 11:13–14, 20–21; Matt 21:19.

7. Cf. Mark 13:28; Matt 24:32. Comparison of the growth of the universe to that of a tree appears also in *Ref.* 6.9.8–9 ("Simon").

ὅπερ ἐστὶν ἡ συκῆ, φύλλα καὶ καρπόν, τὸ σῦκον, ὡς προειρήκαμεν· οὕτως, φησί, τρεῖς γεγόνασιν αἰῶνες ἀπὸ τῆς πρώτης ἀρχῆς, τῶν ὅλων ἀρχαί.

καὶ τοῦτο, φησίν, οὐκ ἐσιώπησεν οὐδὲ Μωϋσῆς, λέγων ὅτι οἱ λόγοι τοῦ θεοῦ τρεῖς εἰσιν· «σκότος, γνόφος, θύελ<λ>α, καὶ οὐ προσέθηκεν»· 6. οὐδὲν γάρ, φησίν, ὁ θεὸς τοῖς τρισὶ προσέθηκεν αἰῶσιν, ἀλλ' αὐτοὶ πάντα τοῖς γενητοῖς πᾶσιν ἐπήρκεσαν καὶ ἐπαρκοῦσι· μένει δὲ ὁ θεὸς αὐτὸς καθ' ἑαυτόν, πολὺ τῶν τριῶν αἰώνων κεχωρισμένος.

Τούτων, φησί, τῶν αἰώνων ἀρχὴν γενέσεως λαβόν<των> ὡς λέλεκται, κατ' ὀλίγον <ἕκαστος> ηὔξησε καὶ ἐμεγαλύνθη καὶ ἐγένετο τέλειος. 7. τὸ δὲ τέλειον εἶναι δοκοῦσιν ἀριθμούμενον δέκα· ἴσων οὖν γεγονότων ἀριθμῷ καὶ τελειότητι τῶν αἰώνων, ὡς ἐκεῖνοι δοκοῦσι, τριάκοντα γεγόνασιν αἰῶνες οἱ πάντες, ἕκαστος αὐτῶν ἐν δεκάδι πληρούμενος.

εἰσὶ δὲ ἀλλήλων <διαιρετοί,> (καὶ) τιμὴν ἔχοντες οἱ τρεῖς πρὸς ἑαυτοὺς μίαν, θέσει μόνῃ διαφέροντες, ὅτι τὸ μέν ἐστι πρῶτον, τὸ δὲ δεύτερον, τὸ δὲ τούτων τρίτον. 8. ἡ δὲ θέσις αὐτοῖς διαφορὰν δυνάμεως παρέσχεν· ὁ μὲν γὰρ ἔγγιστα τῷ πρώτῳ θεῷ, τῷ οἱονεὶ σπέρματι, θέσει τυχών, τῶν ἄλλων γονιμωτέραν ἔσχε δύναμιν, δεκάκις αὐτὸς αὐτὸν μεγέθει μετρήσας ὁ ἀμέτρητος· ὁ δὲ τῇ θέσει τοῦ πρώτου γενόμενος δεύτερος, ἑξάκις αὐτὸν κατέλαβεν ὁ ἀκατάληπτος· ὁ δὲ ἤδη τρίτος τῇ θέσει, εἰς ἄπειρον διάστημα διὰ τὴν αὔξησιν τῶν ἀδελφῶν γενόμενος, τρὶς νοήσας, ἑαυτὸν οἱονεὶ δεσμόν τινα τῆς ἑνότητος αὐτόν ἔδησεν αἰώνιον.

9. 1. Καὶ τοῦτο εἶναι δοκοῦσιν οὗτοι τὸ λελεγμένον ὑπὸ τοῦ σωτῆρος· «ἐξῆλθεν ὁ σπείρων τοῦ σπεῖραι» καὶ «<τὸ> πεσὸν εἰ(ς) τὴν γῆν τὴν καλὴν καὶ ἀγαθὴν ἐποίει <καρπὸν> ὃ μὲν ἑκατόν, ὃ δὲ ἑξήκοντα, ὃ δὲ τριάκοντα». καὶ διὰ τοῦτο εἴρηκε, φησίν· «ὁ ἔχων ὦτα ἀκούειν ἀκουέτω», ὅτι ταῦτα οὐκ

says, three aeons arose from the first principle, which are the principles of the universe.[8]

About this very point, not even Moses, he claims, kept silent. He says that the principles of God are three: "darkness, gloom, and storm—and to these he did not add."[9] 6. For God, he claims, added nothing to those three aeons. Rather, they themselves sufficed and continue to suffice for all generated beings. But God himself remained by himself, far separate from the three aeons.

Now when these aeons, he says, originated, as has been stated, each one grew by small increments, was enlarged, and became perfect. 7. What is perfect in their doctrine is what adds up to ten. So when the aeons became equal in number and perfection, according to their doctrine, they became thirty aeons altogether, each of them attaining their fulfillment in the Decad.[10]

They are distinguished from each other, although the three have among themselves a singular honor.[11] They differ only by placement, in that one is first, another is second, and another is third. 8. Their placement created a power differential. For the one closest to the primal God (the seed, as it were) possessed, by virtue of its placement, a power more productive than the others. He is the Immeasurable one who has measured himself out ten times in magnitude. The aeon that is placed second after the first is the Incomprehensible. He comprehended himself six times. The one that is now in third place—infinitely removed on account of his brothers' growth—bound himself as it were with an eternal bond of their unity by conceiving of himself three times.

9. 1. This is what the Savior meant, according to their doctrine, when he said, "the sower went out to sow" and "the seed that fell on good and fertile soil produced fruit, the first a hundredfold, the second sixtyfold, and the third thirtyfold."[12] Since the words are not audible to all, Jesus adds,

8. Cf. the three Sonships embedded in the world seed in *Ref.* 7.22.7 ("Basileides").

9. Deut 5:22 LXX; cf. *Ref.* 5.20.1 ("Sethians").

10. The thirty aeons are reminiscent of Valentinian teaching; cf. *Ref.* 6.31.3 ("Valentinus"); 6.52.7 (Markos); and 8.10.5 below.

11. Miller replaces διαιρετικοὶ (P) with διαιρετοί (here: "distinguished").

12. Mark 4:3, 8 par.; Gos. Thom. 9. Cf. the interpretation of this parable in *Ref.* 5.8.29 (Naassenes).

ἔστι πάντων ἀκούσματα. 2. οὗτοι πάντες οἱ αἰῶνες, οἵ τε τρεῖς καὶ οἱ ὑπ' αὐτῶν ἀπειράκις ἄπειροι <προβεβλημένοι>, πάντες εἰσὶν αἰῶνες ἀρσενοθήλεις.

Αὐξηθέντες οὖν καὶ μεγαλυνθέντες καὶ γενόμενοι <τέλειοι> οὗτοι πάντες, ἐξ ἑνὸς ἐκείνου τοῦ πρώτου σπέρματος <οἱονεὶ συμβόλου> τῆς συμφωνίας αὐτῶν καὶ τῆς ἑνότητος, οἱ πάντες εἰς ἕνα ὁμοῦ γενόμενοι αἰῶνα, τὸν μέσον αὐτῶν, γέν<ν>ημα κοινὸν οἱ πάντες ἐγέν<ν>ησαν ἐκ παρθένου Μ<αρ>ίας, τὸν ἐν μεσότητι [Μαρίας] σωτῆρα πάντων, ἰσοδύναμον κατὰ πάντα τῷ σπέρματι τῷ συκίνῳ, πλὴν ὅτι γεν<ν>ητὸς οὗτος, τὸ δὲ πρῶτον σπέρμα ἐκεῖνο, ὅθεν γέγονεν ἡ συκῆ, ἐστὶν ἀγέν<ν>ητον.

3. κεκοσμημένων οὖν τῶν τριῶν αἰώνων ἐκείνων παναρέτως καὶ παναγίως, ὡς δοκοῦσιν οὗτοι διδάσκοντες, καὶ τοῦ παιδὸς ἐκείνου τοῦ μονογενοῦς—γέγονε γὰρ μόνος τοῖς ἀπείροις αἰῶσιν ἐκ τριγενοῦς· τρεῖς γὰρ αὐτὸν ἐγέννησαν ὁμοφρονοῦντες αἰῶνες ἀμέτρητοι—κεκόσμητο μὲν ἀνενδεὴς πᾶσα ἡ νοητὴ φύσις.

Φῶς δὴ ἦν ἅπαντα ἐκεῖνα τὰ νοητὰ καὶ αἰώνια· φῶς δὲ οὐκ ἄμορφον οὐδὲ ἀργὸν οὐδὲ οἱου<δ>ήτινος ἐπιποιοῦντος δεόμεν(ο)ν, ἀλλὰ ἔχον ἐν ἑαυτῷ κατὰ τὸ πλῆθος τῶν ἀπειράκις ἀπείρων κατὰ τὸ παράδειγμα τῆς συκῆς ἀπείρους ἰδέας ζῴων πολυποικίλων, τῶν ἐκεῖ.

<ὃ> κατέλαμψεν ἄνωθεν εἰς τὸ ὑ(π)οκείμενον χάος· 4. τὸ δὲ φωτισθὲν ὁμοῦ καὶ μορφωθὲν (ἐ)κείναις ταῖς ἄνωθεν πολυποικίλοις ἰδέαις, πῆξιν ἔλαβε καὶ ἀνεδέξατο τὰς ἰδέας τὰς ἄνωθεν ἁπάσας ἀπὸ τοῦ τρίτου αἰῶνος τοῦ τριπλασιάσαντος αὑτόν.

Ὁ δὲ αἰὼν οὗτος ὁ τρίτος, τοὺς χαρακτῆρας βλέπων πάντας ἀθρόως τοὺς ἑαυτοῦ εἰς τὸ ὑποκείμενον κάτω σκότος κατειλημμένους, τήν τε δύναμιν τοῦ σκότους οὐκ ἀγνοῶν καὶ τὸ ἀφελὲς τοῦ φωτὸς ὁμοῦ καὶ ἄφθονον, οὐκ εἴασεν ἐπὶ πολὺ τοὺς φωτεινοὺς χαρακτῆρας ἄνωθεν ὑπὸ τοῦ σκότους κάτω

"Let the one who has ears hear!"[13] 2. All these aeons, both the three and the infinity times infinity emanated by them, are androgynous.[14]

THE SAVIOR. Now when all the aeons grew, increased in size, and became perfect—having originated from that single first seed—they all together became one aeon: a symbol, as it were, of their harmony and unity.[15] Then they all gave birth to their mediating aeon, a common offspring born from the virgin Mary.[16] He is the mediating Savior of all, equal in power in every way to the fig seed, with the exception that he is *born*, while the first seed—the origin of the fig tree—is unborn.[17]

3. When the three aeons were ordered in the most excellent and holy way along with their only-born child, as these people believe and teach, then all intelligible nature was ordered so that it was in need of nothing. The only-born child alone was born from a triple generation among the infinite aeons. The three immeasurable aeons gave birth to him in unity of mind.

All those intelligible and eternal realities consisted of light. Light is not without shape, nor is it inactive, or in need of an additional productive power. Rather, it contains in itself infinity times infinity by multiplication. Like the model of the fig tree, it contains infinite forms of multifarious animals that exist in the world above.[18]

COSMOGONY: THE PHYSICAL WORLD. The light shone from above onto the chaos below. 4. The chaos, as soon as it was illumined and shaped by those multifarious forms from above, received solidity and accepted all the forms from above from the third aeon, who had tripled itself.

This third aeon saw all the impressions from itself suddenly seized en masse in the darkness below. He was ignorant neither of the power of darkness nor of the simplicity and generosity of the light. Consequently, the third aeon did not for long allow the illumined impressions from above to

13. Mark 4:9 par.

14. Marcovich adds προβεβλημένοι ("emanated") from *Ref.* 10.16.1 (προβεβληκέναι).

15. The word τέλειοι ("perfect") is added by Marcovich. He also adds οἱονεὶ συμβόλου (here: "a symbol, as it were").

16. On birth from Mary, see Orbe, *Cristología Gnóstica*, 1:419–21.

17. The only-born Son presented by the Doketai resembles the common fruit of the Fullness in Valentinian thought. Cf. *Ref.* 6.32.1–2; Iren., *Haer.* 1.2.6. See also *Ref.* 10.16.2 (Doketai summary).

18. For the forms, see *Ref.* 7.21.5; 7.22.1, 6 ("Basileides"); 8.8.4.

κατασπασθῆναι, 5. ἀλλὰ γὰρ ὑπέταξε τοῖς αἰῶσι στερέωμα οὐρανοῦ κάτωθεν «καὶ διεχώρισεν ἀνὰ μέσον τοῦ σκότους καὶ ἀνὰ μέσον τοῦ φωτός· καὶ ἐκάλεσε τὸ φῶς ἡμέραν»—ὃ ἦν ὑπεράνω τοῦ στερεώματος—«καὶ τὸ σκότος ἐκάλεσε νύκτα.»

6. πασῶν οὖν, ὡς ἔφην, τῶν ἀπείρων τοῦ τρίτου αἰῶνος ἰδεῶν ἀπειλημμένων ἐν τούτῳ τῷ κατωτάτῳ σκότῳ καὶ αὐτοῦ τοῦ τοιούτου αἰῶνος ἐναπεσφράγισται μετὰ τῶν λοιπῶν τὸ ἐκτύπωμα, πῦρ ζῶν ἀπὸ φωτὸς γενόμενον· ὅθεν ὁ μέγας ἄρχων ἐγένετο, περὶ οὗ λέγει Μωϋσῆς· «ἐν ἀρχῇ ἐποίησεν ὁ θεὸς τὸν οὐρανὸν (καὶ) τὴν γῆν».

7. Τοῦτον λέγει Μωϋσῆς πύρινον θεόν, <τὸν> ἀπὸ τοῦ βάτου λαλήσαντα, τουτέστιν ἀπὸ τοῦ σκοτεινοῦ ἀέρος—βάτος γάρ ἐστι, πᾶς ὁ σκότει ὑποκείμενος ἀήρ.—βάτον δέ, φησίν, εἴρηκε Μωϋσῆς, ὅτι ἄνωθεν κάτω πᾶσαι διέβησαν τοῦ φωτὸς αἱ ἰδέαι, βατὸν ἔχουσαι τὸν ἀέρα. 8. οὐδὲν δὲ ἧττον καὶ ἡμῖν ὁ λόγος ἀπὸ τοῦ βάτου γνωρίζεται· φωνὴ γάρ ἐστι σημαντικὴ τοῦ λόγου πλησσόμενος ἀήρ, οὗ δίχα λόγος ἀνθρώπινος οὐ γνωρίζεται. οὐ μόνον δὲ ὁ λόγος ἡμῖν ἀπὸ τοῦ βάτου—τουτέστιν ἀέρος—νομοθετεῖ καὶ συμπολιτεύεται, ἀλλὰ γὰρ καὶ ὀσμαὶ καὶ χρώματα διὰ τοῦ ἀέρος ἡμῖν τὰς δυνάμεις τὰς ἑαυτῶν ἐμφανίζουσιν.

10. 1. Οὗτος οὖν ὁ πυροειδὴς (θεός), ὁ πῦρ ἀπὸ φωτὸς γενόμενος, πεποίηκε τὸν κόσμον οὕτως ὥς φησι Μωϋσῆς, αὐτὸς ὢν ἀνυπόστατος, σκότος ἔχων τὴν οὐσίαν ἐνυβρίζων ἀεὶ τοῖς ἄνωθεν κάτω κατειλημμένοις τοῦ φωτὸς αἰωνίοις χαρακτῆρσι. μέχρι μὲν οὖν τῆς τοῦ σωτῆρος φανερώσεως πολλή τις ἦ(ν) πλάνη τῶν ψυχῶν ὑπὸ τοῦ θεοῦ τοῦ <ἀπὸ> φωτὸς <γεγονότος>, τοῦ πυρώδους, τοῦ δημιουργοῦ.

be drawn down below by the dark. 5. Instead, he placed under the aeons a firmament of heaven "and made a separation between darkness and light. He called the light 'day' (referring to what was above the firmament), and the darkness he called 'night.'"[19]

THE GREAT RULER. 6. When, as I said, all the infinite forms of the third aeon were received into the deepest darkness, along with the rest, the stamp of this very aeon was sealed onto the chaos and from light turned into a living fire. From the fire a great Ruler arose, about whom Moses speaks: "In the beginning God made heaven and earth."[20]

7. Now this being Moses calls a "fiery god," who spoke from the bush [βάτος].[21] That is, God spoke to Moses from the dark air. The bush signifies all the air subjected to darkness. Moses spoke, he claims, of a bush since all the forms of light crossed from above to below using the air as a highway [βατός]. 8. No less do we too know the speech spoken from the bush. For the reverberated air serves as the meaningful sound of speech.[22] Apart from this, human speech is unknown. Not only is our speech from the bush (that is, air) the means of legislation and civilized life, it is also the means by which scents and colors manifest their own qualities to us through the air.

10. 1. So this is the god who appears in fire, the fire generated from light. He made the world in the way that Moses says. He himself is without stable form, having darkness as his substance. He always commits outrages against those from on high that are held down below—that is, against the eternal impressions of the light. Therefore, until the appearance of the Savior, souls wandered in deep error under the power of the god who was generated from light.[23] He is the fiery god, the Artificer.

---

19. Gen 1:4–5 LXX (cf. vv. 7–8).

20. Gen 1:1 LXX.

21. Exod 3:2, 4 LXX; cf. Deut 4:24. On the fiery god, see *Ref.* 5.7.31 (Naassenes); 6.9.3 ("Simon"); 6.32.8 ("Valentinus"); 7.38.1 (Apelles); Clem. Alex., *Exc.* 38.1.

22. Cf. Plato, *Tim.* 67b; Aristotle, *De an.* 2.8, 420b27–421a6; Zeno in *SVF* 1.74; 2.138–39, 141, 384 (Chrysippos); 3.17, 19 (Diogenes of Babylonia); Origen, *Cels.* 2.72; 6.62.

23. Marcovich adds ἀπὸ … γεγονότος to indicate that this god is not a god of light, although generated from light.

ψυχαὶ γὰρ αἱ ἰδέαι καλοῦνται, ὅτι ἀπ(ο)ψυγεῖσαι <καὶ καταπεσοῦσαι ἀπὸ> τῶν ἄνω ἐν σκότει διατελοῦσι, μεταβαλλόμεναι ἐκ σώματος εἰς σῶμα καὶ ὑπὸ τοῦ δημιουργοῦ φρουρούμενα<ι>. 2. ὅτι δὲ τοῦθ᾽ οὕτως ἔχει, φησίν, ἔνεστι καὶ ἐκ τοῦ Ἰὼβ κατανοῆσαι λέγοντος· «καὶ ἐγὼ πλανῆτις καὶ <λάτρις>, τόπον ἐκ τόπου μεταβαίνουσα καὶ οἰκίαν ἐξ οἰκίας» καὶ <ἐκ> τοῦ σωτῆρος λέγοντος· «καὶ εἰ θέλετε δέξασθαι, αὐτός ἐστιν Ἠλίας ὁ μέλλων ἔρχεσθαι. ὁ ἔχων ὦτα ἀκούειν ἀκουέτω».

ἀπὸ δὲ τοῦ σωτῆρος μετενσωμάτωσις πέπαυται πίστις τε κηρύσσεται εἰς ἄφεσιν ἁμαρτιῶν τοιοῦτόν τινα τρόπον. 3. Ὁ μονογενὴς υἱὸς ἐκεῖνος ὁ τῶν αἰώνων, τὰς ἄνωθεν ἰδέας βλέπων [τὰς ἄνωθεν] μεταβαλλομένας ἐν τοῖς σκοτεινοῖς σώμασι, ῥύσασθαι κατελθὼν ἠθέλησεν. εἰδὼς δὲ ὅτι τὸ πλήρωμα τῶν ὅλων αἰώνων οὐδὲ<ν> [οἱ αἰῶνες οἱ] ἀθρόον ἰδεῖν ὑπομένουσιν, ἀλλὰ καταπλαγέντες ὡς φθαρτοὶ φθορὰν ὑπομενοῦσι, μεγέθει καὶ δόξῃ δυνάμεως κατειλημμένοι, συστείλας ἑαυτὸν ὡς ἀστραπὴν μεγίστην ἐν ἐλαχίστῳ σώματι. μᾶλλον δὲ ὡς <τὸ> φῶς <τῆς> ὄψεως, <τὸ> ὑπὸ τοῖς βλεφάροις συνεσταλμένον, ἐξικνεῖται μέχρις οὐρανοῦ καὶ τῶν ἀστέρων ἐπιψαῦσαν τῶν ἐκεῖ πάλιν ἑαυτὸ συστέλλει ὑπὸ τοῖς βλεφάροις τῆς ὄ(ψε)ως, ὅτε βούλεται· 4. καὶ τοῦτο ποιοῦν τὸ φῶς τῆς ὄψεως καὶ πανταχῇ γινόμενον καὶ πάντα ἡμῖν ἐστιν ἀφανές, μ(όν)ον δὲ ὁρῶμεν ἡμεῖς ὄψεως βλέφαρα, κανθοὺς λευκούς, ὑμένας, <ἶ>ριν πολύπτυχον πολυκτηδόνα, χιτῶνα κερατοειδῆ, ὑπὸ δὲ τοῦτον κόρην, ῥαγοειδῆ, ἀμφιβληστροειδῆ, δισκοειδῆ, καὶ εἴ τινες ἄλλοι τοῦ φωτὸς τῆς ὄψεώς εἰσι χιτῶνες, οὓς ἐστολισμένον κέκρυπται·

5. οὕτως, φησίν, ὁ μονογενὴς παῖς ἄνωθεν <ὁ> αἰώνιος ἐπενδυσάμενος κατὰ ἕνα ἕκαστον <τοὺς> τῶν τριῶν αἰώνων αἰῶνα<ς> καὶ γενόμενος ἐν τριακοντάδι

THE FATE OF THE SOUL. The forms are called "souls" [ψυχαί] since they grew cold [ἀποψυγεῖσαι] and fell from the realities above.[24] Now they complete their lives in darkness, tossed from body to body, kept imprisoned by the Artificer. 2. One can recognize this state of affairs from the verse in the book of Job: "I am a wanderer and a hired handmaid, changing from place to place and from house to house."[25] Transmigration is also signified by what the Savior says: "And if you want to accept it, he [John the Baptist] is Elijah who was to come. Let the one who has ears hear!"[26]

THE SAVIOR. Transmigration comes to an end with the advent of the Savior. And faith is preached for the forgiveness of sins, which they describe in the following way. 3. The only-born Son of the aeons, seeing the forms transferred from above into dark bodies, wanted to go down to deliver them. He knew that they could not endure to see the fullness of aeons all at once. As corruptible beings, they would be panic-stricken and suffer corruption, overcome by the magnitude and glory of [his] power. So he concentrated himself like a bright flash of lightning in the tiniest body. To use a better analogy: he contracted himself like the light beam of the eyes withdrawn under the eyelids. This light beam reaches as far as heaven and makes contact with the stars there. Still, when it desires, it again pulls itself back behind the eyelids. 4. Acting in this way, the light of the eyes both beams in all directions and is entirely invisible to us. We only see the eyelids, the whites of the eye, the membranes, the iris with its many folds and fibers, the cornea, and underneath it the pupil, the choroid membrane, the retina, the lens—and any other membranes for the light of the eye that enrobe and conceal it.

5. In this way, he says, like the light of the eye, the eternal only-born Child from above robed himself one by one with all the aeons of the three

---

24. Marcovich adds καὶ καταπεσοῦσαι ἀπό ("and fell from"). For the cooling of the souls, see *Ref.* 1.21.3 (Stoics); Diogenes of Apollonia, DK 64 A28; Plato, *Crat.* 399d10–33; Aristotle, *De an.* 1.2, 405b28f; *SVF* 2.804–8; Plutarch, *Prim. frig.* 946c; *Stoic. rep.* 1052f; 1053c; *Def. orac.* 433a; Philo, *Somn.* 1.31.

25. Marcovich adds λάτρις ("hired handmaid") from Job 2:9d LXX (not in the MT); T. Job 24.2 (the speech of Sitis, Job's wife).

26. That is, John the Baptist is the reincarnation of Elijah. See Matt 11:14–15; cf. Pist. Soph. 1.7 (Schmidt, 13); Origen, *Comm. Jo.* 6.20 (John 1:23) = Herakleon, frag. 5 (Brooke); Tert., *An.* 35.5.

αἰώνων εἰσῆλθεν εἰς τόνδε τὸν κόσμον, τηλικοῦτος ὢν ἡλίκον εἴπομεν· ἀφανής, ἄγνωστος, ἄδοξος, ἀπιστούμενος.

6. Ἵν' οὖν, φασιν οἱ Δοκηταί, καὶ τὸ σκότος ἐπενδύσηται τὸ ἐξώτερον τὴν σάρκα [φησίν], ἄγγελος <ὁ> συνοδεύσας αὐτῷ ἄνωθεν τὴν Μαριὰμ εὐηγγελίσατο, φησίν, ὡς γέγραπται, <καὶ> ἐγεν<ν>ήθη τὸ ἐξ αὐτῆς ὡς γέγραπται. 7. γεννηθὲν δ' ἐνεδύσατο αὐτὸ ἄνωθεν ἐλθόν, καὶ πάντα ἐποίησεν οὕτως ὡς ἐν τοῖς εὐαγγελίοις γέγραπται.

ἐλούσατο εἰς τὸν Ἰορδάνην [ἐλούσατο δὲ], τύπον καὶ σφράγισμα λαβὼν ἐν τῷ ὕδατι τοῦ γεγεν<ν>ημένου σώματος ὑπὸ τῆς παρθένου· ἵν', ὅταν ὁ ἄρχων κατακρίνῃ τὸ ἴδιον πλάσμα «θανάτῳ [τῷ] σταυροῦ», <ἡ> ψυχὴ ἐκείνη, <ἡ> ἐν τῷ σώματι τραφεῖσα, «ἀπεκδυσαμένη» τὸ σῶμα καὶ «προσηλώσασα πρὸς τὸ ξύλον» καὶ «θριαμβεύσασ<α> δι' αὐτοῦ τὰς ἀρχὰς καὶ τὰς ἐξουσίας», «μὴ εὑρεθῇ γυμνή», ἀλλ' ἐνδύσηται τὸ ἐν τῷ ὕδατι, ὅτε ἐβαπτίζετο, ἀντὶ τῆς σαρκὸς ἐκείνης ἐκτετυπωμένον σῶμα. 8. τοῦτό ἐστι, φησίν, ὃ λέγει ὁ σωτήρ· «ἐὰν μή τις γεννηθῇ ἐξ ὕδατος καὶ πνεύματος, οὐκ εἰσελεύσεται εἰς τὴν βασιλείαν τῶν οὐρανῶν», ὅτι «τὸ γεγεν<ν>ημένον ἐκ τῆς σαρκὸς σάρξ ἐστιν».

Ἀπὸ τῶν τριάκοντα οὖν αἰώνων τριάκοντα ἰδέας ἐνεδύσατο· διὰ τοῦτο ἐπὶ τριάκοντα ἔτη γέγονεν ἐπὶ τῆς γῆς ὁ αἰώνιος ἐκεῖνος, <ἐν> ἑκάστου αἰῶνος ἰδέᾳ ἐνιαυτῷ φανερούμενος.

9. εἰ<σ>ὶ δέ γε ἀπὸ ἑκάστου τῶν τριάκοντα αἰώνων ἅπασα(ι) <αἱ> ἰδέα(ι) (κ)ατειλημμέναι ψυχαί, καὶ φύσιν ἔχει τούτων ἑκάστη νοεῖν τὸν κατὰ φύσιν Ἰησοῦν, ὃν ἐκεῖνος ὁ μονογενὴς ὁ αἰώνιος ἀπὸ τῶν αἰωνίων τόπων ἐνεδύσατο. 10. εἰσὶ δὲ οὗτοι διάφοροι· διὰ τοῦτο τοσαῦται αἱρέσεις ζητοῦσι τὸν Ἰησοῦν

aeons. Clothed in the thirty aeons, he entered this world such as I indicated—invisible, unknown, inglorious, and untrusted.[27]

INCARNATION. 6. So that he could additionally robe himself with the outer darkness or flesh, the Doketai say, his angel companion from above told the good news to Mary, as, he says, it is written in the scriptures.[28] 7. Then, as it is written, her offspring was born. When he was born, the One who had come from above robed himself with her offspring and did everything as recorded in the Gospels.

THE CAREER OF JESUS. As the Savior was washed in the Jordan, he received in the water the form and seal of the body that had been born by the virgin. This occurred so that, when the ruler condemns his own molded body "to the death of a cross,"[29] the soul in Jesus's body might "strip off" the body, "nail it to the tree," "triumph through it over the rulers and authorities,"[30] and "not be found naked,"[31] but clothe itself with the sealed body that he received in the water when he was baptized, instead of that fleshly one.[32] 8. This, he claims, is what the Savior means when he says, "Unless one is born from water and spirit, one will not enter the kingdom of heaven," since "what is born from flesh is flesh."[33]

From the thirty aeons, the Savior clothed himself with thirty forms. For this reason, the eternal one lived on earth for thirty years, manifested in the form of each aeon for a year.[34]

SALVATION. 9. All the forms who are from each of the thirty aeons are imprisoned here as souls. Each one has a nature to know Jesus in his human nature, with whom that eternal Only-Born from the eternal places clothed himself. 10. But these places are different. This is why there are so

---

27. Cf. John 1:11 ("his own did not receive him"); *Ref.* 5.9.21 (Naassenes).

28. Luke 1:26–28. The Doketai affirm the Savior's advent in flesh.

29. Phil 2:8.

30. Col 2:14–15.

31. 2 Cor 5:3.

32. The deposition of the fleshly body is reminiscent of Jesus the separator among the "Sethians" and "Basileides" (*Ref.* 5.21.5–6; 7.27.8–11); see also Iren., *Haer.* 1.30.13; Apelles (*Ref.* 7.38.5).

33. John 3:4–6; cf. *Ref.* 5.7.40; 5.8.37 (Naassenes).

34. Cf. Luke 3:23 (Ἰησοῦς ἀρχόμενος ὡσεὶ ἐτῶν τριάκοντα); Iren., *Haer.* 1.3.1; 1.16.2; *Ref.* 6.52.7, 9 (Markos).

περιμαχήτως, καὶ ἔστι πάσαις αὐταῖς οἰκεῖος, ἄλλῃ δὲ ἄλλος <φανερούμενος, ὡς> ὁρώμενος ἀπ' ἄλλου τόπου.

ἐφ' ὃν ἑκάστη φέρεται, φησίν, καὶ σπεύδει, δοκοῦσα τοῦτον εἶναι μόνον, ὅς ἐστιν αὐτῆς συγγενὴς ἴδιος καὶ πολίτης· ὃν ἰδοῦσα πρῶτον, ἴδιον ἐγνώρισ<ε> μόνον ἀδελφόν, τοὺς δὲ ἄλλους νόθους.

11. οἱ μὲν οὖν ἐκ τῶν ὑποκάτω τόπων τὴν φύσιν ἔχοντες τὰς ὑπὲρ αὐτοὺς ἰδέας τοῦ σωτῆρος ἰδεῖν οὐ δύνανται· οἱ δὲ ἄνωθεν, φησίν, ἀπὸ τῆς δεκάδος τῆς μέσης καὶ τῆς πρώτης, τῆς ἀρίστης, ὅθεν ἐσμὲν ἡμεῖς, λέγουσιν, οὐκ ἐκ μέρους ἀλλ' ὅλον αὐτοὶ τὸν Ἰησοῦν τὸν σωτῆρα ἴσασι· καὶ εἰσὶν <οἱ> ἄνωθεν τέλειοι μόνοι, οἱ δὲ ἄλλοι πάντες ἐκ μέρους.

11. 1. Ταῦτα μὲν οὖν αὐτάρκη νομίζω εἶναι τοῖς εὖ πεφρονηκόσι πρὸς ἐπίγνωσιν τῆς τῶν Δοκητῶν πολυπλόκου καὶ ἀσυστάτου αἱρέσεως. οἳ περὶ <ὕ>λης μὴν ἀβάτου καὶ ἀκαταλήπτου λόγους ἐπικεχειρημένους ποιήσαντε(ς) Δοκητὰς ἑαυτοὺς προσηγόρευσαν. οὓς οὐ τῷ δοκεῖν εἶναί τινας κατανοοῦμεν ματαΐζοντας, ἀλλὰ τὴν ἐκ τοσαύτης ὕλης δοκὸν ἐν ὀφθαλμῷ φερομένους διελέγχομεν, εἴ πως διαβλέψαι δυνηθῶσιν, εἰ δ' οὔ, κἂν <εἰς> τὸ μὴ ἑτέρους τυφλῶσαι. 2. ὧν τὸ δόγμα πάλαι οἱ Ἑλλήνων σοφισταὶ προεσοφίσαντο κατὰ <τὰ> πολλά, ὡς ἔστιν ἐπιγ(ν)ῶ(ν)αι τοὺς ἐντυγχάνοντας.

ταῦτα μὲν οὖν τοῖς Δοκηταῖς τὰ δόξαντα· τίνα δὲ καὶ Μονοΐμῳ δοκεῖ, οὐ σιωπήσομεν.

many Christian sects who hotly contest the nature of Jesus. He belongs to them all but appears different to each group because he is viewed from a different place.[35]

Each soul is drawn to Jesus and hastens toward him, he says. Each soul supposes this to be the only Jesus, its own kinsman and fellow citizen. When the soul sees him for the first time, it recognizes him as its own only brother and believes that all others are illegitimate.

11. Now those who derive their nature from the lower places are not able to see the forms of the Savior that exist above them. But those above, he says, exist from the intermediate Decad and from the primal, superior Decad. From this superior Decad, they claim, "*we* exist." They know Jesus the Savior not partially but completely. Yes, those from above are the only perfect ones. All others are incomplete.[36]

11. 1. To those of sound mind, I think that this material is sufficient to recognize the tangled and shifting heresy of the Doketai. These self-named Doketai contrived arguments about impenetrable and incomprehensible subject matter.[37] They are a group who, in my view, not only *seem* [τῷ δοκεῖν] to speak drivel. Quite the contrary: I have exposed them as carrying round a log [δοκόν] in their eye derived from their great forest of subject matter! I expose them so that they might somehow see clearly—but if not, at least that they not blind other people! 2. Most of their teachings the Greek sophists pronounced long ago in their sophistical doctrines—as those who read the Doketai can ascertain.

These, then, are the doctrines of the Doketai. What Monoïmos too teaches, I will not keep secret.

35. Marcovich adds φανερούμενος, ὡς ("appears, because"). On Christ who appears differently to different people, see, e.g., Acts Pet. 7.20 (*NTApoc* 2:303–4); Ap. John (NHC II,1) 2.1–5.

36. Jesus has the nature of the thirty aeons. Humans are reflections of the thirty aeons, so in Jesus they recognize themselves. This is salvation by mutual participation. Jesus assumes the aeons so that humans can realize their own divine (aeonic) identity. Those who are reflections of the higher aeons know Jesus more fully.

37. The phrase ἀβάτου καὶ ἀκαταλήπτου plays upon βάτος and (possibly) ὁ ἀκατάληπτος in the above report (*Ref.* 8.9.7; 8.8.8, respectively).

12. 1. Μονόϊμος ὁ Ἄραψ (οὐ) μακρὰν τῆς τοῦ μεγαλοφώνου ποιητοῦ δόξης γεγένη(τ)αι, (τ)οιοῦτόν τινα τὸν ἄνθρωπον νομίσας, ὁποῖον ὁ ποιητὴς τὸν Ὠκεανόν, οὕτω πως λέγων·

2. Ὠκεανὸς γένεσίς τε θεῶν γένεσίς τ᾽ ἀνθρώπων.

ταῦτα ἄλλοις λόγοις μεταστήσας λέγει ἄνθρωπον εἶναι τὸ πᾶν, <ὅς> ἐστιν ἀρχὴ τῶν ὅλων—ἀγέν<ν>ητον, ἄφθαρτον, ἀίδιον.

καὶ υἱὸν ἀνθρώπου τοῦ προειρημένου γεν<ν>ητὸν καὶ παθητόν, ἀχρόνως γενόμενον, ἀβουλήτως, ἀπροορίστως. 3. τοιαύτη γάρ, φησίν, ἡ δύναμις ἐκείνου τοῦ ἀνθρώπου. οὕτως ὄντος αὐτοῦ τῇ δυνάμει γενέσθαι τὸν υἱὸν λογισμοῦ καὶ βουλήσεως τάχιον. 4. καὶ τοῦτό ἐστι, φησί, τὸ εἰρημένον ἐν ταῖς γραφαῖς· «ἦν καὶ ἐγένετο». ὅπερ ἐστίν· [ὁ] ἦν ἄνθρωπος, καὶ ἐγένετο υἱὸς αὐτοῦ, ὡς τις εἴποι· ἦν πῦρ, καὶ ἐγένετο φῶς ἀχρόνως καὶ ἀβουλήτως καὶ ἀπροορίστως, ἅμα τῷ εἶναι τὸ πῦρ.

5. Ὁ δὲ ἄνθρωπος οὗτος μία μονάς ἐστιν ἀσύνθετος, συνθετή, ἀδιαίρετος, διαιρετή, πάντα φίλη, πάντα μαχίμη, πάντα εἰρηνική, πάντα πρὸς ἑαυτὴν

MONOÏMOS

THE GOD HUMAN AND HIS SON. 12. 1. Monoïmos the Arab was not far removed from the view of the famous poet [Homer].[38] Monoïmos supposed that the human being resembles how the poet describes Ocean:

2. Ocean, origin of gods, origin of human beings.[39]

By substituting different words into this line, Monoïmos says that the Human is the All, the origin of the universe, unborn, incorruptible, and eternal.[40]

Yet the Son of the aforementioned Human is born and able to suffer.[41] This Son arose outside of time without will or predetermination. 3. Such, he says, is the power of that Human.[42] Since the Human was of this nature, the Son originated by his power more swiftly than reasoning or will.[43] 4. This, he claims, is the meaning of the scriptural verse: "He was and came to be."[44] The Human "was," and his Son "came to be"—as someone might say that there "was" fire, and light arose simultaneous with the fire without an interval of time, without a will, and without predetermination.

5. This Human is the numerical and transcendent number one: uncompounded and compounded, indivisible and divisible, entirely friendly and entirely belligerent, entirely peaceful and entirely hostile to itself, similar

38. Monoïmos the Arab is an elusive, inadequately studied figure. Still relevant are George Salmon's articles "Monoimus" (*DCB* 3:934–35) and "Ophites" (*DCB* 4:80–88). See also Marcovich, *Studies*, 134–40; Roelof van den Broek, "Monoimus," *DGWE* 800–802; Kalvesmaki, *Theology*, 85–94. The name "Monoïmos" is otherwise unattested, but it resembles the (also rare) name Monimos, "related to the common Arabic name Munʿim or its diminutive Munayʿim" (ibid., 86). It also has a resonance with μονάς ("unit"/"monad"/"the number one"), so important in Monoïmos's system.

39. A conflation of Homer, *Il.* 14.201, 246. Cf. *Ref.* 5.7.38 (Naassenes); 10.7.1 (summary of philosophers); Orph. Hymn 83.2; Athenagoras, *Leg.* 18.3 (unconflated).

40. On the God "Human," see Schenke, *Gott "Mensch,"* 6–15. Further sources in M. David Litwa, "The God 'Human' and Human Gods: Models of Deification in Irenaeus and the *Apocryphon of John*," *ZAC* 18 (2014): 70–94 (70 n. 1).

41. Marcovich understands παθητός here as "liable to qualitative change." He believes, however, that "the allusion to the passibility of Jesus is unmistakable" (*Studies*, 137–38).

42. Cf. *Ref.* 10.17.1 (Monoïmos summary).

43. Cf. *Ref.* 7.21.1; 7.22.8 ("Basileides").

44. Cf. Gen 1:3; John 1:1–4, 6, 9–10; *Ref.* 7.22.3 ("Basileides").

πολέμιος· ἀνόμοιος, ὁμοία, οἱονεί τις ἁρμονία μουσική· πάντα ἔχουσα ἐν ἑαυτῇ, ὅσ' ἄν τις εἴπῃ <ἣ> καὶ παραλείπῃ μὴ νοήσας· πάντα ἀναδεικνύουσα, πάντα γεννῶσα· αὕτη μήτηρ, αὕτη πατήρ, τὰ δύο ἀθάνατα ὀνόματα.

6. ὑποδείγματος δὲ χάριν, τοῦ τελείου ἀνθρώπου κατανόει, φησί, <τὴν> μεγίστην εἰκόνα <ὡς> «ἰῶτα ἕν», τὴν «μίαν κεραίαν»· ἥτις ἐστὶ [κεραία μία] ἀσύνθετος, ἁπλῆ, μονὰς εἰλικρινής, ἐξ οὐδενὸς ὅλως τὴν σύνθεσιν ἔχουσα· <καὶ αὖ> συνθετή, πολυειδής, πολυσχιδής, πολυμερής. 7. ἡ ἀμερὴς ἐκείνη μία, φησίν, ἐστὶν ἡ πολυπρόσωπος καὶ μυριόμματος καὶ μυριώνυμος μία τοῦ ἰῶτα κεραία, ἥτις ἐστὶν εἰκὼν τοῦ τελείου ἀνθρώπου ἐκείνου, τοῦ ἀοράτου.

13. 1. Ἔστιν οὖν, φησίν, ἡ μονάς, ἡ μία κεραία, καὶ δεκάς· δύναμις γὰρ αὐτῇ τὸ ἰῶτα τῆς μιᾶς κεραίας, καὶ δυὰς καὶ τριὰς καὶ τετρὰς καὶ πεντὰς καὶ ἑξὰς καὶ ἑπτὰς (καὶ) ὀγδοὰς καὶ ἐν<νε>ὰς μέχρι τῶν δέκα· οὗτοι γάρ, φησίν, εἰσὶν οἱ πολυσχιδεῖς ἀριθμοὶ <οἱ> ἐν ἐκείνῃ κατοικοῦντες τῇ ἁπλῇ καὶ ἀσυνθέτῳ τοῦ ἰῶτα κεραίᾳ μιᾷ. 2. καὶ τοῦτό ἐστι τὸ εἰρημένον· «ὅτι πᾶν τὸ πλήρωμα ηὐδόκησε κατοικῆσαι» ἐπὶ τὸν υἱὸν τοῦ ἀνθρώπου «σωματικῶς»· αἱ

and dissimilar, as it were a musical harmony.[45] It holds everything in itself, whatever one might say or omit as unthought.[46] It exhibits all things and gives birth to all things. This is what is Mother, and this is what is Father—the two immortal names.[47]

THE IMAGE OF THE IOTA. 6. By way of example, he says, conceive of the greatest image of the Perfect Human as "one iota" [ι], the "single stroke of a letter."[48] It is the uncompounded, simple, pure number one, having nothing at all added. In turn, it is also compound, multiform, multifarious, and multidimensional. 7. That indivisible one, he says, is the multifaceted, myriad-eyed, myriad-named single stroke of the iota, which is the image of that perfect Human Being, the invisible one.[49]

13. 1. So, he says, there is the number one, or the single stroke, or decad (for the value of ten equals the iota of the single stroke). Then there are the numbers two, three, four, five, six, seven, eight, nine as far as ten.[50] These, he says, are the multifarious numbers that indwell that simple and uncompounded single stroke of the iota.[51] 2. This is what the verse refers to: "that all the fullness was pleased to dwell bodily" in the Son of the Human.[52]

---

45. Kalvesmaki comments that μονάς is "metaphysically higher than the ἕν [here in the feminine form μία])." Μονάς is ideal, ἕν instantiated; ἕν thus ontologically depends on μονάς. "To the philosophically attuned, the term [μία μονάς] was as contradictory as 'thought thinker' or 'becoming being,' since it suggested the confluence of creator and creation, normally irreconcilable" (*Theology*, 87). Cf. Clem. Alex., *Paed.* 1.8.71.1: Ἓν δὲ ὁ θεὸς καὶ ἐπέκεινα τοῦ ἑνὸς καὶ ὑπὲρ αὐτὴν μονάδα ("God is one but beyond one, and beyond the monad itself").

46. Cf. the use of this phrase in *Ref.* 5.19.1 ("Sethians"); 6.9.7 ("Simon"); 7.22.1 ("Basileides").

47. Cf. *Ref.* 5.6.5 (a Naassene hymn).

48. Cf. Matt 5:18; *Ref.* 6.24.1 ("Pythagoras"); Iren., *Haer.* 1.3.2 (= Epiph., *Pan.* 31.14.8); Tri. Trac. (NHC I,5) 116.28.

49. Cf. Adamas in *Ref.* 5.9.4 (Naassenes).

50. Over the years, additions and emendations to this sentence have accumulated. I accept only Miller's emendation of ἑνάς to ἐννεάς. See further Kalvesmaki, *Theology*, 88–89 nn. 9–11. The first nine numbers reside potentially in the monad. Kalvesmaki points out the parallel in Nikomachos, "who describes the cosmos as 'rooted' in the monad, but made and revealed in the Decad. So too in Monoïmos' view, the Son of the Human, as the ἰῶτα ἕν, a being that synthesizes ten and one, is the source, completion, and regulator of creation (8.13.4.21)" (ibid., 89).

51. Cf. *Ref.* 10.17.2 (Monoïmos summary).

52. The quote is a conflation of Col 1:19 and 2:9. Cf. *Ref.* 5.12.5 (Peratai); 10.10.4 ("Basileides" summary); Iren., *Haer.* 1.3.4; Clem. Alex., *Exc.* 31.1.

γὰρ τοσαῦται τῶν ἀριθμῶν συνθέσεις ἐξ ἁπλῆς καὶ ἀσυνθέτου τῆς μιᾶς κεραίας τοῦ ἰῶτα σωματικαὶ γεγόνασι, φησίν, ὑποστάσεις.

3. Γέγονεν οὖν, φησίν, ἀπὸ τοῦ τελείου ἀνθρώπου ὁ υἱὸς τοῦ ἀνθρώπου, «ὃν ἔγνωκεν οὐδείς»· φαντάζεται γὰρ <αὐτόν>, φησίν, ὡς γέν<ν>ημα θηλείας ἡ κτίσις πᾶσα, τὸν υἱὸν ἀγνοοῦσα. οὗ υἱοῦ ἀκτῖνες ἀμυδραὶ πάνυ, ἐμπελάζουσαι τῷδε τῷ κόσμῳ, συνέχουσι καὶ συγκρατοῦσι τὴν μεταβολήν, τὴν γένεσιν. 4. τὸ δὲ κάλλος ἐκείνου τοῦ υἱοῦ τοῦ ἀνθρώπου μέχρι νῦν πᾶσίν ἐστιν ἀκατάληπτον ἀνθρώποις, ὅσοι περὶ τὸ γέν<ν>ημα τῆς θηλείας εἰσὶ πεπλανημένοι.

γέγονεν οὖν, φησίν, ἀπὸ τοῦ ἀνθρώπου ἐκείνου οὐδὲν τῶν ἐνθάδε, οὐδ' ἔσται πώποτε· τὰ δὲ γεγονότα πάντα οὐκ ἀπὸ ὅλου, ἀλλ' ἀπὸ μέρους τινὸς γέγονε τοῦ υἱοῦ τοῦ ἀνθρώπου. ἔστι γάρ, φησίν, ὁ υἱὸς τοῦ ἀνθρώπου ἰῶτα ἕν, μία κεραία, ῥυεῖσα ἄνωθεν, πλήρης ἀποπληροῦσα, πάντα ἔχουσα ἐν ἑαυτῇ, ὅσα καὶ ὁ ἄνθρωπος ἔχει, ὁ πατὴρ τοῦ υἱοῦ τοῦ ἀνθρώπου.

14. 1. Γέγονεν οὖν <ὁ> κόσμος, ὥς φησι Μωϋσῆς, ἐν ἓξ ἡμέραις, τουτέστιν ἐν ἓξ δυνάμεσι, ταῖς ἐν τῇ μιᾷ κεραίᾳ τοῦ ἰῶτα· <ἡ δὲ> ἑβδόμη, <ἡ> κατάπαυσις καὶ σάββατον, ἀπὸ τῆς Ἑβδομάδος γέγονε τῆς ἐκεῖ. ... γῆς καὶ ὕδατος καὶ ἀέρος καὶ πυρός, ἐξ ὧν ὁ κόσμος ἀπὸ τῆς κεραίας γέγονε τῆς

This is because so many combinations of numbers from the simple and uncompounded number of the single stroke of the iota become, he says, bodily substances.[53]

THE IOTA = THE SON OF THE HUMAN. 3. Thus the Son of the Human, "whom no one knows," arose from the Perfect Human.[54] All creation, he says, imagines that he is the offspring of woman, since it is ignorant about the Son. The rays of this Son, although they are extremely dim, approach this world, hold it together, and take control of its transformation (that is, generation). 4. The beauty of that Son of the Human is up to the present time incomprehensible to all human beings who are in error about the offspring of the woman.[55]

He says that no earthly reality originated from that Human, nor will it ever originate from him.[56] All generated beings arose not from the whole but from a part of the Son of the Human. The reason for this, he claims, is that the Son of the Human is one iota, a single stroke, flowing from above, full and making full, containing everything in itself, everything that the Human above—the Father of the Son of the Human—contains.[57]

COSMOGONY. 14. 1. Now the world originated, as Moses says, in six days, that is, in six powers contained in the single stroke of the iota.[58] But the Hebdomad, serving as a cessation and a Sabbath, arose from the Hebdomad in the ideal world[59] … of earth, water, air, and fire, out of which the

53. The iota, as the decad, contains the plurality of numbers that, in various combinations, make up material shapes and thus the material world.

54. Cf. Matt 11:27 ("no one knows the Son except the Father").

55. This is not necessarily a denial of the virgin birth but a denial that the true Jesus is the man of flesh. Rather, the true Jesus is the Son of the Human.

56. The Son of the Human is the source, not the agent, of creation (Marcovich, *Studies*, 139).

57. Cf. *Ref.* 10.17.1–2 (Monoïmos summary).

58. Cf. Gen 2:2–3 (six days); cf. *Ref.* 6.13.1; 6.14.1–2 ("Simon").

59. Cf. *Ref.* 6.32.8 ("Valentinus"). The Seven "there" is the Hebdomad, which Kalvesmaki believes to be the "iota itself, combined with the six powers of Creation. That is, the iota-Human sends forth a seventh power, which is represented by the Sabbath. These powers are the sources of the four material elements, from which the cosmos is made. Thus the seven powers are a connective tissue between Human and the material universe" (Kalvesmaki, *Theology*, 89). For the six latent powers, he cites Philo, *Fug.* 95–96 (ibid., 89 n. 13). A closer parallel is "Valentinus," who has "six powers

μι(ᾶς). 2. οἵ τε γὰρ κύβοι καὶ τὰ ὀκτάεδρα καὶ πυραμίδες καὶ πάντα τὰ τούτοις παραπλήσια σχήμα<τα>, ἐξ ὧν συνέστηκε πῦρ, ἀή(ρ), ὕδωρ, γῆ, ἀπὸ τῶν ἀριθμῶν γεγόνασι τῶν κατειλη(μ)μέν(ων) ἐν ἐκείνῃ τῇ ἁπλῇ τοῦ ἰῶτα κεραίᾳ, ἥτις ἐστὶν υἱὸς ἀνθρώπου, τελείου τέλειος.

3. Ὅταν οὖν, φησίν, ῥάβδον λέγῃ Μωϋσῆς στρεφομένην ποικίλως εἰς τὰ πάθη τὰ κατὰ τὴν Αἴγυπτον—ἅτινα, φησίν, ἐστὶ τῆς κτίσεως ἀλ<λ>ηγορού<μενα> σύμβολα—, οὐκ εἰς πλείονα πάθη τῶν δέκα σχηματίζει τὴν ῥάβδον, ἥτις ἐστίν, <ἡ τοῦ> ἰῶτα μία κεραία, <ἁπλῆ καὶ> ποικίλη. αὕτη, φησίν, ἐστὶν ἡ δεκάπληγος ἡ κοσμικὴ κτίσις· πάντα γὰρ πλησσόμενα γεννᾶται καὶ καρποφορεῖ, καθάπερ αἱ ἄμπελοι. 4. «ἄνθρωπος ἐξ ἀνθρώπου ἐξέσ<σ>υται», φησίν, «καὶ ἀποσπᾶται, πληγῇ τινι μεριζόμενος», ἵνα γένηται.

κἂν εἴπῃ<ς> νόμον, ὃν ἔθηκε Μωϋσῆς παρὰ θεοῦ λαβών, κατὰ τὴν κεραίαν ἐκείνην τὴν μίαν ὁ νόμος ἐστί ἡ δεκάλογος ἀλληγοροῦσα τὰ θεῖα τῶν <ὅλων> μυστήρια. 5. πᾶσα γάρ, φησίν, ἡ γνῶσις τῶν ὅλων δεκάπληγός ἐστι καὶ δεκάλογος· ἣν οἶδεν οὐδεὶς τῶν περὶ τὸ γέν<ν>ημα τῆς θηλείας πεπλανημένων. κἂν εἴπῃς πεντάτευχον ὅλον τὸν νόμον, ἔστιν ἀπὸ τῆς πεντάδος τῆς ἐν τῇ μιᾷ κεραίᾳ κατειλημμένης.

6. Τὸ δὲ ὅλον ἐστί, φησί, τοῖς μὴ πεπηρωμένοις παντελῶς τὴν διάνοιαν μυστήριον, καινὴ καὶ μὴ παλαιουμένη «ἑορτὴ νόμιμος, αἰώνιος εἰς τὰς γενεὰς ἡμῶν», «κυρίου τοῦ θεοῦ πάσχα», «διατηρούμενον» τοῖς δυναμένοις βλέπειν «ἐναρχομένης τῆς δεκάτης», ἥτις ἐστὶν ἀρχὴ δεκάδος, ἀφ᾽ ἧς, φησίν,

world originated from the single stroke. 2. This is because cubes, octagons, pyramids, and all similar shapes out of which fire, air, water, and earth were composed arose from the numbers contained in that simple stroke of the iota, which is the Son of the Human, the Perfect One from the Perfect One.[60]

ALLEGORY OF THE PLAGUES. 3. Moses, he says, speaks of a staff variously wielded for the calamities in Egypt. These, he claims, are symbols allegorically spoken about the creation. The staff fashions no more than *ten* calamities.[61] The staff refers to the single stroke of the iota, which is simple and complex.[62] These ten plagues, he says, signify the creation of the world. 4. His rationale is that everything struck is born and bears fruit, just as vines do. "A human that bursts out of a human," he says, "is pulled out and separated off by a strike" so as to come into existence.[63]

You might even say that the Law that Moses laid down after receiving it from God—the Law of that single stroke—signifies the Ten Commandments, which allegorically refer to the divine mysteries of the universe.[64] 5. For all the knowledge of the universe, he says, is signified by *ten* plagues and *ten* commandments, which no one of those in error about the offspring of the female knows. Even if you say that the Pentateuch is the entirety of the Law, this Pentateuch is from the number five, which is also contained in the single stroke.

ALLEGORY OF THE PASSOVER. 6. The whole Law, he says, is a mystery for those whose thought is not entirely maimed. It is a new festival that has not grown old, "ordained by law, eternal for our generations."[65] It is "the Passover of the Lord God" "observed" by those able to see "when the tenth of the month begins."[66] This [festival] is the principle of the Decad, which

organized into syzygies and governed by a Monad." The parallels are a result of "shared vocabulary, not direct copying" (ibid., 90).

60. Cf. Plato, *Tim.* 55a–56b; Ps.-Timaios, *Nat. mund. an.* 98d.

61. Exod 7:8–11:10; cf. *Ref.* 5.16.8 (Peratai).

62. Since the iota looks like a miniature staff. Cf. *Ref.* 10.17.3–4 (Monoïmos summary). Marcovich emends διπλῆ ("double") to ἁπλῆ ("simple").

63. Demokritos, DK 68 B32; cf. Clem. Alex., *Paed.* 2.94.4.

64. Marcovich replaces P's λόγων ("words") with ὅλων (here: "universe").

65. Exod 12:11, 14, 17 LXX. Contrast Heb 8:13.

66. Cf. Exod 12:6, 18 LXX. Marcovich prefers to emend δεκάτης ("tenth") to τεσσαρεσκαιδεκάτης ("fourteenth") from the LXX to agree with the next sentence. But

ἀριθμοῦμεν. ἡ γὰρ μονὰς ἕως τῆς <τετράδος τῆς ἐν τῇ> τεσσαρεσκαιδεκάτῃ ἐστί τὸ κεφάλαιον τῆς μιᾶς <κεραίας>, τοῦ τελείου ἀριθμοῦ· τό τε γὰρ ἕν, δύο, τρία, τέσσαρα γίνεται δέκα, ὅπερ ἐστίν ἡ μία κεραία.

7.<Τὴν> δὲ ἀπὸ τῆς τεσσαρεσκαιδεκάτης [φησὶν] «ἕως μιᾶς καὶ εἰκάδος» ἑβδομάδα λέγει <τὴν> ὑπάρχουσαν ἐν τῇ μιᾷ κεραίᾳ τοῦ κόσμου [τὴν] κτίσιν, ἄζυμον <οὖσαν> ἐν τοῖς ἅπασιν. τί γὰρ δεηθείη, φησίν, ἡ μία κεραία οὐσίας τινὸς οἱονεὶ ζύμης ἔξωθεν εἰς «τὸ πάσχα τοῦ κυρίου», «τὴν αἰώ(ν)ιον ἑορτήν», ἥτις ἐστὶν «εἰς τὰς γενεὰς» δεδομένη;

ὅλος γὰρ ὁ κόσμ(ο)ς (κα)ὶ πάντα <τὰ> τῆς κτίσεως στ<οιχ>εῖα πάσχα ἐστίν ἑορτὴ κυρίου. 8. χαίρει γὰρ ὁ θεὸς τῆς κτίσεως τῇ μεταβολῇ ἥτις ὑπὸ τῶν δέκα πληγῶν τῆς κεραίας ἐνεργεῖται τῆς μιᾶς· ἥτις ἐστὶ Μωσέως ῥάβδος ὑπὸ τοῦ θεοῦ δεδομένη. ᾗ τοὺς Αἰγυπτίους πλήσσων μεταβάλλει τὰ σώματα, καθάπερ τὴν χεῖρα Μωσέως <καὶ> τὸ ὕδωρ εἰς αἷμα, καὶ τὰ λοιπά. τούτοις παραπλησίως ἀκρίδας—ὅπερ ἐστὶ χόρτος—<τὴν> τῶν στοιχείων εἰς σάρκα μεταβολὴν λέγει· «πᾶσα» γὰρ «σὰρξ χόρτος», φησίν.

9. Οὐδὲν δὲ ἧττον καὶ τὸν ὅλον νόμον οἱ ἄνδρες οὗτοι τοιοῦτόν τινα τρόπον ἐκδέχονται, τάχα που κατακολουθήσαντες, ὡς ἐγὼ δοκῶ, Ἑλλήνων <σοφοῖς> τοῖς λέγουσιν οὐσίαν εἶναι καὶ ποιὸν καὶ ποσὸν καὶ πρός τι καὶ ποῦ καὶ πότε καὶ κεῖσθαι καὶ ἔχειν καὶ ποιεῖν καὶ πάσχειν.

15. 1. Τοιγαροῦν Μονόϊμος αὐτὸς ἐν τῇ πρὸς Θεόφραστον ἐπιστολῇ διαρρήδην λέγει·

is indicated, he claims, by how we count. The monad up to the tetrad contained in the number fourteen is the sum of the single stroke, the perfect number [or decad].[67] For one plus two plus three plus four make ten, which is the single stroke.[68]

7. The seven days after the fourteenth "until the twenty-first of the month,"[69] he says, signify the creation of the world that exists within the single stroke. No yeast is allowed on any of those days. For what need does the single stroke have, he asks, of a substance—as it were yeast brought in from outside—for "the Passover of the Lord"?[70] This is "the eternal festival," which is bestowed "on your generations."

The whole world and all the elements of creation are a Passover festival of the Lord.[71] 8. The God of creation rejoices in the transformation that is enacted by the ten plagues of the single stroke. This stroke signifies the staff of Moses, which is bestowed by God. With it, Moses struck the Egyptians and transformed bodies, just as the hand of Moses was changed, the water turned to blood, and so forth.[72] Similarly to these transformations, Monoïmos speaks of the locusts (i.e., grass) as the transformation of elements into flesh. As proof, he cites the verse, "all flesh is grass."[73]

9. No less do these men interpret the whole Law. Possibly, in my view, they follow the Greek sages, who say that there is substance, quality, quantity, relation, location, time, situation, possession, activity, and passivity.[74]

SALVATION: KNOW THYSELF. 15. 1. Accordingly, Monoïmos himself expressly says in his *Letter to Theophrastos*:

R. McL. Wilson observes: "Monoimus argues that 'beginning the fourteenth day' in Exodus 12:18 really means 'tenth'; for since 1 + 2 + 3 + 4 = 10, the final unity is 'fourth and tenth,' which in Greek suggests 'fourteenth'" (Foerster, *Gnosis*, 1:249, note †).

67. Marcovich adds τετράδος τῆς ἐν τῇ ("the tetrad contained in the number fourteen") to make the math work. Four, which is "in" the number *four*teen, is equal to the decad because 1 + 2 + 3 + 4 = 10. See further Kalvesmaki, *Theology*, 90–91.

68. The translation of this difficult passage must remain tentative. The iota (or single stroke) = ten in the Greek numbering system. Cf. *Ref.* 1.2.8–9; 4.51.6; 6.23.5 ("Pythagoras").

69. Exod 12:18.

70. See Exod 12:15, 18–20 (prohibition of yeast during the festival).

71. Marcovich replaces P's αἴτια ("causes") with στοιχεῖα ("elements").

72. Exod 3:20; 4:6; 7:17.

73. Cf. Lev 11:22 (χορτός); Isa 40:6 (quoted in 1 Pet 1:24); *Ref.* 6.10.2 ("Simon").

74. Namely, the *ten* categories, previously attributed to Aristotle (*Ref.* 1.20.1) and Pythagoras (6.24.2). Marcovich supplies σοφοῖς ("sages").

<Εἰ θέλεις ἐπιγνῶναι τὸ πᾶν,> καταλιπὼν ζητεῖν θεὸν καὶ κτίσιν καὶ τὰ τούτοις παραπλήσια, ζήτησον αὐτὸν ἀπὸ <σ>εαυτοῦ, καὶ μάθε τίς ἐστιν ὁ πάντα ἁπαξαπλῶς ἐν σοὶ ἐξιδιοποιούμενος καὶ λέγων· 2. ὁ θεός μου, ὁ νοῦς μου, ἡ διάνοιά μου, ἡ ψυχή μου, τὸ σῶμά μου· καὶ μάθε πόθεν ἐστὶ τὸ λυπεῖσθαί καὶ τὸ χαίρειν, καὶ τὸ ἀγαπᾶν καὶ τὸ μισεῖν· καὶ τὸ γρηγορεῖν μὴ θέλοντα καὶ τὸ νυστάζειν μὴ θέλοντα, καὶ τὸ ὀργίζεσθαι μὴ θέλοντα καὶ τὸ φιλεῖν μὴ θέλοντα. καὶ ἂν ταῦτα, φησίν, ἐπιζητήσῃς ἀκριβῶς, εὑρήσεις αὐτὸν ἐν <σ>εαυτῷ, ἓν καὶ πολλά, κατὰ τὴν κεραίαν ἐκείνην, ἀφ' ἑαυτοῦ τὴν διέξοδον εὑρών.

3. Ταῦτα μὲν οὖν ἐκεῖνοι· οἷς οὐκ ἀνάγκην ἔχομεν τὰ παρ' Ἕλλησι προμεμεριμνημένα παρατιθέναι, οὖσι προδήλοις τοῖς ὑπ' αὐτῶν λεγομένοις τὴν σύστασιν ἔχει ἐκ γεωμετρικῆς τέχνης καὶ ἀριθμητικῆς· ἣν γενναιότερον οἱ Πυθαγόρ(ου) μαθηταὶ διέθεντο, καθὼς ἔστι τοῖς ἐντυγχάνουσιν ἐπιγνῶ(ν)α(ι) ἐν τοῖς τόποις, οἷς προδιηγησάμεθα περὶ πάσης σοφίας Ἑλλήνων. ἀλλ' ἐπεὶ καὶ τὰ Μονοΐμου αὐτάρκως διελήλεγκται, ἴδωμεν τίνα καὶ οἱ λοιποὶ τεχνάζονται, ἑαυτῶν βουλόμενοι ὄνομα μάταιον ὑψοῦν.

16. 1. Τατιανὸς δὲ καὶ αὐτὸς γενόμενος μαθητὴς Ἰουστίνου τοῦ μάρτυρος οὐχ ὅμοια τῷ διδασκάλῳ ἐφρόνησεν, ἀλλὰ καινά τινα ἐπιχειρήσας ἔφη αἰῶνας

If you wish to know the All,[75] abandon your search for God, creation, and like entities—and search for him from yourself. Learn who it is who absolutely makes everything in you his own, saying: 2. "My god, my mind, my thought, my soul, my body."[76] Moreover, learn from where grief comes, from where rejoicing, from where love, and from where hatred. Learn the cause of your being awake against your will, of feeling sleepy against your will, of being angry against your will, and feeling affection against your will. If you investigate these matters precisely, you will find him in yourself, one and many, in accordance with that [single] stroke, since from yourself you will have found the way out.[77]

3. Such are the doctrines of these people. I find it unnecessary to juxtapose alongside them the Greek teachings that I mentioned before, since it is clear from what they say that their heresy is composed from the sciences of geometry and arithmetic. The disciples of Pythagoras set forth these sciences with more sophistication, as can be learned by my readers from the sections in which I presented the entire wisdom of the Greeks. But since Monoïmos's teachings have been sufficiently refuted, let us also observe what the rest fabricate (desiring, as they do, to exalt their own worthless reputations).

TATIAN

16. 1. Tatian, himself a disciple of Justin the martyr, did not share the views of his teacher.[78] Instead, he argued novel teachings, announcing that

75. Marcovich supplies this opening phrase (εἰ θέλεις ἐπιγνῶναι τὸ πᾶν) from *Ref.* 10.17.5 (Monoïmos summary).

76. Marcovich would exclude ὁ θεός μου, which does not appear in the summary in *Ref.* 10.17.5. Logic may also be on his side: would God, who appropriates everything the seeker is, refer to the seeker as "my God"? But Kalvesmaki believes that the process of knowing God follows a five-stage sequence from God to mind to thought to soul to body, and escape from the world occurs "along the same sequence, in reverse" (*Theology*, 93).

77. On this letter, see further Marcovich, *Studies*, 140–43.

78. Our author's report on Tatian is adapted from Iren., *Haer.* 1.28. Although Irenaeus connects Tatian to the Enkratites, our author assumes no relation. Eusebios (*Hist. eccl.* 1.16) does not refer to Tatian as a heretic. Clement of Alexandria accuses Tatian of desiring to abolish the Law because it is the work of a different god (*Strom.* 3.12.82.2). Our author is especially interested in connecting fragments of Tatian's

τινας ἀοράτους, ὁμοίως τοῖς ἀπὸ Οὐαλεντίνου μυθολογήσας. γάμον δὲ φθορὰν εἶναι παραπλησίως Μαρκίωνι λέγει, τόν τε Ἀδὰμ φάσκει μὴ σῴζεσθαι διὰ τὸ ἀρχηγὸν παρακοῆς γεγονέναι.

καὶ ταῦτα μὲν Τατιανός.

17. 1. Ἑρμογένης δέ τις, καὶ αὐτὸς νομίσας τι καινὸν φρονεῖν, ἔφη τὸν θεὸν ἐξ ὕλης συγχρόνου καὶ ἀγενήτου πάντα πεποιηκέναι· ἀδυνάτως γὰρ ἔχειν τὸν θεὸν μὴ οὐκ ἐξ ὄντων τὰ γενόμενα ποιεῖν. εἶναι δὲ τὸν θεὸν ἀεὶ κύριον καὶ ἀεὶ ποιητήν, τὴν δὲ ὕλην ἀεὶ δούλην καὶ γινομένην, οὐ πᾶσαν δέ· 2. ἀεὶ γὰρ ἀγρίως καὶ ἀτάκτως φερομένην ἐκόσμησε. τούτῳ τῷ λόγῳ. δίκην λ(έβητ)ος ὑποκαιομένου βράζουσαν ἰδὼν ἐχώρισε κατ(ὰ) μέρος, καὶ τὸ μὲν ἐκ τοῦ παντὸς λαβὼν ἡμέρωσε, τὸ δὲ <λοιπὸν> εἴασεν ἀτάκτως φέρεσθαι. καὶ τὸ ἡμερωθὲν τοῦτο εἶναι κόσμον λέγει, τὸ δὲ ἄγριον μένον καὶ ὕλην καλεῖσθαι ἄκοσμον.—ταύτην οὐσίαν εἶναι τῶν ἁπάντων λέγει, ὡς <καινὸν> φέρων δόγμα τοῖς

there are invisible aeons, telling myths like the Valentinians. Like Markion, he says that marriage is corruption.[79] He also claims that Adam is not saved because he was the author of transgression.[80]

These are the teachings of Tatian.

HERMOGENES

17. 1. A certain Hermogenes, who supposed that he thought up something novel, said that God made all things from coeval and ungenerated matter.[81] He considers it to be impossible that God would make generated beings from what is nonexistent.[82] God is always lord and maker, while matter is always slave and made—though not all of it.[83] 2. God continuously ordered matter that was writhing wildly and confusedly. To use an analogy: God acted like someone who, when he sees a boiling pot heated from beneath, siphons off a portion of the boiling water and tames it, letting the rest bubble in confusion. The "tamed portion," he says, is this world, whereas the portion that remained wild is called "unordered matter."[84] Now he says that this matter is the substance of all things as if he

---

teaching to his other opponents, namely, Valentinus and Markion. Cf. Epiph., *Pan.* 46.1.1–2.7; Ps.-Tert., *Adv. omn. haer.* 7.1; Filastrius, *Haer.* 48. See further Lampe, *Paul to Valentinus*, 285–91, 426–30; William L. Petersen, "Tatian the Assyrian," in Marjanen and Luomanen, *Companion*, 125–58.

79. In *Ref.* 10.18, our author adds that Tatian slanders the birth of children, since they (fated to die) are the source of corruption.

80. Petersen asserts that for Tatian, Adam would not be saved because he rejected the knowledge of God, and knowledge is the key to immortality ("Tatian the Assyrian," 151, citing Tatian, *Or.* 13.1).

81. Tertullian wrote a work against Hermogenes around 206–207 CE. Clement of Alexandria also mentions Hermogenes (*Ecl.* 56.2). Both may have drawn upon a lost work of Theophilos mentioned by Eusebios (*Hist. eccl.* 4.24.1). See further Greschat, *Apelles und Hermogenes*, 137–286.

82. Cf. *Ref.* 10.28 (Hermogenes summary); Tert., *Herm.* 1, 3; Theodoret, *Haer. fab.* 1.19 (PG 83:369b–c). See further Greschat, *Apelles und Hermogenes*, 158–64.

83. Hermogenes's theory of matter follows Stoic lines. God is inherently active, while matter is naturally passive. As such, matter never poses any threat to God. Nor does matter's eternal existence deplete God's power. Matter is not a principle, even if it is self-moved (cf. Diog. L., *Vit. phil.* 7.134, and the texts cited in Long and Sedley, *Hellenistic Philosophers*, 2:265–69). Greschat prefers a Middle Platonic background for these teachings (*Apelles und Hermogenes*, 173–80, 191–95).

84. Cf. Tert., *Herm.* 38, 41, 43. See further Greschat, *Apelles und Hermogenes*, 186–91.

αὐτοῦ μαθηταῖς· οὐκ ἐνενόει δὲ ὅτι Σωκρατικὸς ὁ μῦθος οὗτος τυγχάνει, ὑπὸ Πλάτωνος ἐξειργασμένος βέλτιον ἢ ὑπὸ Ἑρμογένους.—

3. Τὸν (δ)ὲ Χριστὸν υἱὸν εἶναι ὁμολογεῖ τοῦ τὰ πάντα κτίσαντος θεοῦ καὶ (τοῦ)τ(ον) ἐκ παρθένου γεγεν<ν>ῆσθαι καὶ πνεύματος [μὲν ὁμολογεῖ] κατὰ τὴν τῶν εὐαγγελίων φωνήν. ὃν μετὰ τὸ πάθος ἐγερθέντα ἐν σώματι πεφηνέναι τοῖς <αὐτοῦ> μαθηταῖς καὶ ἀνερχόμενον εἰς τοὺς οὐρανοὺς ἐν τῷ ἡλίῳ τὸ σῶμα καταλελοιπέναι, αὐτὸν δὲ πρὸς τὸν πατέρα πεπορεῦσθαι. 4. μαρτυρίᾳ δὲ χρῆται, νομίζων ὑπὸ τοῦ ῥητοῦ συνηγορεῖσθαι, οὗπερ ὁ ψαλμῳδὸς Δαβὶδ λέγει·

ἐν τῷ ἡλίῳ ἔθετο τὸ σκήνωμα αὐτοῦ·
καὶ αὐτὸς ὡς νυμφίος ἐκπορευόμενος ἐκ παστοῦ αὐτοῦ
ἀγαλλιάσεται ὡς γίγας δραμεῖν ὁδόν.

ταῦτα μὲν οὖν καὶ Ἑρμογένης ἐπεχείρει.

18. 1. Ἕτεροι δέ τινες, φιλόνεικοι τὴν φύσιν, ἰδιῶται τὴν γνῶσιν, μαχιμώτεροι τὸν τρόπον, συ<νι>στάνουσι δεῖν τὸ πάσχα τῇ τεσσαρεσκαιδεκάτῃ τοῦ πρώτου μηνὸς φυλάσσειν κατὰ τὴν τοῦ νόμου διαταγήν, ἐν ᾗ ἂν ἡμέρᾳ ἐμπέσῃ, ὑφορώμενοι τὸ γεγραμμένον ἐν νόμῳ, ὡς ἐπικατάρατον ἔσεσθαι τὸν μὴ φυλάξαντα οὕτως διαστέλλεται· οὐ προσέχουσι δὲ ὅτι Ἰουδαίοις ἐνομοθετεῖτο, τοῖς μέλλουσι τὸ ἀληθινὸν πάσχα ἀναιρεῖν, τὸ εἰς ἔθνη χωρῆσαν καὶ πίστει νοούμενον, οὐ γράμματι συντηρούμενον. 2. οἳ μιᾷ ταύτῃ προσέχοντες ἐντολῇ οὐκ ἀφορῶσιν εἰς τὸ εἰρημένον ὑπὸ τοῦ ἀποστόλου, ὅτι «διαμαρτύρομαι παν(τὶ) περιτεμνομένῳ ὅτι ὀφειλέτης ἐστὶ τοῦ πάντα τὸν νόμον ποιῆσαι». ἐν δὲ τοῖς

were presenting a new doctrine to his disciples.[85] He did not realize that this myth is Sokratic, elaborated better by Plato than Hermogenes.[86]

CHRIST. 3. Hermogenes confesses that Christ is the Son of the God who created all things, and that he was born from a virgin and from Spirit according to the message of the Gospels.[87] After his suffering, he was bodily raised and appeared to his own disciples. When he ascended to heaven, he left his body in the sun and advanced to the Father. 4. Hermogenes uses scriptural testimony, supposing to make his case from the passage in which David the psalmist says,

> In the sun he laid his tabernacle.
> Then he, like a bridegroom advancing from his bridal chamber,
> Will rejoice like a giant to run his course.[88]

These are Hermogenes's arguments.

QUARTODECIMANS

18. 1. Certain others, contentious by nature but simpletons in knowledge and rather belligerent in character, concoct the view that Easter must be observed on the fourteenth of the first month—on whatever day it falls—according to the ordinance of the Law.[89] They focus on the statement in the Law that whoever does not keep the festival as it is appointed will be utterly cursed.[90] They fail to note the fact that this point was legislated for *Jews*, who would later kill the true Passover. This Passover came to the Gentiles and is understood by faith, not observed literally. 2. Those who cling to this one commandment do not regard what was said by the apostle: "I testify to every man circumcised that he is a debtor to perform

---

85. P reads κενόν ("empty"). Miller emended it to καινόν ("new").

86. Cf. Tert., *Herm.* 1.

87. Luke 1:34–36. See further Orbe, *Cristología Gnóstica*, 1:414–16.

88. Ps 18:5b–6 LXX. Cf. Clem. Alex., *Ecl.* 56.1–2; 57.3; Tert., *Marc.* 4.11.7; Justin, *1 Apol.* 54.9; *Dial.* 69.3. See further Greschat, *Apelles und Hermogenes*, 257–73.

89. Exod 12:18; Lev 23:5; Num 9:4–5. Our author may have been the first to make the Quartodecimans "heretics." Cf. the reports in Eusebios, *Hist. eccl.* 5.18.2; 5.23.1; 5.24.6; Epiph., *Pan.* 50.1.1–3.5; Ps.-Tert., *Adv. omn. haer.* 8.1; Filastrius, *Haer.* 58; Theodoret, *Haer. fab.* 3.4 (PG 83:405a–b).

90. Deut 27:26; Num 9:13; cf. Epiph., *Pan.* 50.1.4.

ἑτέροις οὗτοι συμφωνοῦσι πρὸς πάντα τὰ τῇ ἐκκλη(σίᾳ) ὑπὸ τῶν ἀποστόλων παραδεδομένα.

19. 1. Ἕτεροι δέ, καὶ αὐτοὶ αἱρετικώτεροι τὴν φύσιν, Φρύγες τὸ γένος, προληφθέντες ὑπὸ γυναίων ἠπάτηνται, Πρισκίλ<λ>ης τινὸς καὶ Μαξιμίλλης καλουμένων. ἃς προφήτιδας νομίζουσιν, ἐν ταύταις τὸ παράκλητον πνεῦμα κεχωρηκέναι λέγοντες, καί τινα πρὸ αὐτῶν Μοντανὸν ὁμοίως δοξάζουσιν ὡς προφήτην.

ὧν βίβλους ἀπείρους ἔχοντες πλανῶνται, μήτε τὰ ὑπ' αὐτῶν λελαλημένα λόγῳ κρίνοντες, μήτε τοῖς κρῖναι δυναμένοις προσέχοντες, ἀλλ' ἀκρίτως τῇ πρὸς αὐτοὺς πίστει προσφέρονται, πλεῖόν τι δι' αὐτῶν φάσκοντες [ὡς] μεμαθηκέναι ἢ ἐκ νόμου καὶ προφητῶν καὶ τῶν εὐαγγελίων. 2. ὑπὲρ δὲ ἀποστόλους καὶ πᾶν χάρισμα ταῦτα τὰ γύναια δοξάζουσιν, ὡς τολμᾶν λέγειν τινὰς αὐτῶν πλεῖόν τι Χριστῷ ἐν τούτοις γεγονέναι.

the whole Law."[91] In other matters, however, these people agree entirely with the apostolic traditions given to the church.

PHRYGIANS

19. 1. Other people, more heretical by nature and ethnically Phrygian, were taken in by hussies and deceived.[92] These hussies, called "Priscilla" and "Maximilla," they regard as prophetesses and profess that they were inhabited by the Paraklete Spirit.[93] They also equally glorify the earlier figure Montanus as a prophet.

Stocked with their boundless books, they are deceived—neither rationally judging what the prophets said nor listening to those able to make judgments.[94] Rather, they are uncritically won over by their faith in their prophets, claiming that through them they have learned more than is contained in the Law, Prophets, and Gospels. 2. They glorify these hussies over the apostles and every spiritual gift to such a degree that some of them dare to say that what dwells in them is greater than Christ himself.[95]

---

91. Gal 5:3; cf. Ps.-Tert., *Adv. omn. haer.* 8.1; Epiph., *Pan.* 50.2.1–3.

92. The "Phrygians" are today more commonly known as "Montanists" (after the prophet Montanus). Cf. the reports of Eusebios, *Hist. eccl.* 5.3, 16–19; Epiph., *Pan.* 48.11.1–14.2; Filastrius, *Haer.* 49; Ps.-Tert., *Adv. omn. haer.* 7.2; Theodoret, *Haer. fab.* 3.2 (PG 83:401, 404). See further Hamel, *Kirche bei Hippolyt*, 120–27; Antti Marjanen, "Montanism: Egalitarian Ecstatic 'New Prophecy,'" in Marjanen and Luomanen, *Companion*, 185–212 (191, 194); Christoph Markschies, "Montanismus," *RAC* 24:1198–220.

93. That the Paraklete inhabited the women is a distinctive claim of our author. On women in Montanism, see Ross Shepard Kraemer, *Her Share of Blessings: Women's Religions among Pagans, Jews, and Christians in the Greco-Roman World* (New York: Oxford, 1992), 158–71, 177–80; Christine Trevett, *Montanism: Gender, Authority and the New Prophecy* (Cambridge: Cambridge University Press, 1996), 163–70, 196–97.

94. Our author regularly accuses his opponents of having many writings, e.g., the Naassenes (*Ref.* 5.10.1), Justin (5.23.2), and esp. *Ref.* 8.19.4 below. His language is stereotypical and indicates that his opponents ramble. See further Nicola Denzey, "What Did the Montantists Read?," *HTR* 94 (2001): 427–48; Robert L. Williams, "'Hippolytan' Reactions to Montanism: Tensions in the Churches of Rome in the Early Third Century," *StPatr* 39 (2006): 131–37 (134–37); David Pastorelli, "La Paraclet dans la notice antimontaniste du Pseudo-Hippolyte, *Refutatio omnium haeresium* VIII,19," *VC* (2008): 261–84.

95. The idea of surpassing Christ connects these "Phrygians" to Karpokrates (*Ref.* 7.32.3). Christ promised his disciples the Paraklete, who would reveal more truth than Jesus himself (John 15:26). Cf. Ps.-Tert., *Adv. omn. haer.* 7; Epiph., *Pan.* 48.8.1; Jerome, *Ep.* 41.4. That women in particular might be endowed with the Spirit

οὗτοι τὸν μὲν θεὸν πατέρα τῶν ὅλων καὶ πάντων κτίστην ὁμοίως τῇ ἐκκλησίᾳ ὁμολογοῦσι καὶ ὅσα τὸ εὐαγγέλιον περὶ τοῦ Χριστοῦ μαρτυρεῖ, καινίζουσι δὲ νηστείας καὶ ἑορτὰς καὶ ξηροφαγίας καὶ ῥαφανοφαγίας, φάσκοντες ὑπὸ τῶν γυναίων δεδιδάχθαι.

3.Τινὲς δὲ αὐτῶν τῇ τῶν Νοητιανῶν αἱρέσει συντιθέμενοι, τὸν πατέρα αὐτὸν εἶναι τὸν υἱὸν λέγουσι, καὶ τοῦτον ὑπὸ γένεσιν καὶ πάθος καὶ θάνατον ἐληλυθέναι. περὶ τούτων αὖθις λεπτομερέστερον ἐκθήσομαι· πολλοῖς γὰρ ἀφορμὴ κακῶν γ(ε)γένηται ἡ τούτων αἵρεσις.

4. ἱκανὰ μὲν οὖν καὶ τὰ περὶ τούτων εἰρημένα κρίνομεν, δι' ὀλίγων τὰ πολλὰ φλύαρα αὐτῶν βιβλία τε καὶ (ἐ)πιχειρήματα πᾶσιν ἐπιδείξαντες ἀσθενῆ ὄντα καὶ μηδενὸς λ(όγ)ου ἄξια, οἷς οὐ χρὴ προσέχειν τοὺς ὑγιαίνοντα νοῦν κεκτημένους.

20. 1. Ἕτεροι δέ, ἑαυτοὺς ἀποκαλοῦντες Ἐγκρατίτας, τὰ μὲν περὶ τοῦ θεοῦ καὶ τοῦ Χριστοῦ ὁμοίως [καὶ] τῇ ἐκκλησίᾳ ὁμολογοῦσι, περὶ δὲ πολιτείαν

They do confess with the church that God is the Father of the universe and Creator of all. They also confess what the gospel testifies about Christ. Nevertheless, they invent new fasts, feasts, and diets in which they eat only dry food and radishes—claiming to have been so taught by their hussies.[96]

NOETIAN BRANCH. 3. Some of them, however, made a compact with the Noetian heresy and say that the Father himself is the Son, and that the Father is subject to birth, suffering, and death.[97] My report about the Noetians I will later present in more detail (since their heresy has, for the masses of believers, become the starting point of evils).[98]

4. I judge what has been said about the Phrygians to be sufficient. I have concisely exhibited to all that the profuse blabbering of their books and arguments are weak and worthy of no account. Those of sound mind need pay no attention to them.[99]

ENKRATITES

20. 1. Still others, calling themselves "Enkratites," confess the same things about God and Christ as the church.[100] Nevertheless, in their

of Truth is irksome to our author; but even more irksome to him is their consequent claim to authority.

96. For new fasts, see *Ref.* 10.25 (summary of the Phrygians); Hipp., *Comm. Dan.* 4.20. For dry food (ξηροφαγίας), see Tert., *Jejun.* 1.2, 4; 2.4; 5.4; 9.6; 12.1; 17.7; Apollonios in Eusebios, *Hist. eccl.* 5.18.2. Christine Trevett ("Hippolytus and the Cabbage Question," in *Discipline and Diversity: Papers Read at the 2005 Summer Meeting and the 2006 Winter Meeting of the Ecclesiastical History Society*, ed. Kate Cooper and Jeremy Gregory [Rochester: Boydell Press, 2007], 36–45 [39–40, 44]) points out that ῥαφανοφαγία "(cabbage/radish/'greens'-eating) … has no parallel." "*Rhaphanos* more usually indicates a radish," which was probably the food of the lower classes. Thus our author's use of the term is a jibe against the "un-honoured and the poor" Montanists in Rome and elsewhere.

97. Marjanen ("Montanism," 194 n. 32) asserts that about 200 CE there were probably "two different Montanist groups in Rome, one led by Aeschines representing modalistic Christology and the other led by Proclus espousing mainstream Christology" (Ps.-Tert., *Adv. omn. haer.* 7–8). See further Lampe, *Paul to Valentinus*, 381 n. 2; William Tabbernee, *Fake Prophecy and Polluted Sacraments: Ecclesiastical and Imperial Reactions to Montanism*, VCSup 84 (Leiden: Brill, 2007), 119–22.

98. Cf. the summary of the Noetians in *Ref.* 10.26; Ps.-Tert., *Adv. omn. haer.* 7.

99. By referring to those of sound mind, our author hostilely implies that the Phrygians, ecstatically inspired by the Paraklete, are out of their minds.

100. The Enkratites derive their name from ἐγκρατέω ("to practice self-control").

πεφυσιωμένως ἀναστρέφονται, ἑαυτοὺς διὰ βρωμάτων δοξάζειν νομίζοντες, ἀπεχόμενοι ἐμψύχων, ὑδροποτοῦντες καὶ γαμεῖν κωλύοντες, καὶ τῷ λοιπῷ βίῳ καταξήρως προσέχοντες, μᾶλλον Κυνικοὶ ἢ Χριστιανοὶ οἱ τοιοῦτοι κρινόμενοι. οὐ προσέχουσι δὲ τοῖς διὰ τοῦ ἀποστόλου Παύλου εἰς αὐτοὺς προειρημένοις· ὃς προφητεύων τὰ μέλλοντα ὑπό τινων μάτην καινίζεσθαι, οὕτως ἔφη·

2. Τὸ δὲ πνεῦμα ῥητῶς λέγει· ἐν ὑστέροις καιροῖς ἀποστήσονταί τινες τῆς ὑγιαινούσης διδασκαλίας, προσέχοντες πνεύμασι πλάνοις καὶ διδασκαλίαις δαιμονίων, ἐν ὑποκρίσει ψευδολόγων, κεκαυστηριασμένων τὴν ἰδίαν συνείδησιν, κωλυόντων γαμεῖν, ἀπέχεσθαι βρωμάτων, ἃ ὁ θεὸς ἔκτισεν εἰς μετάληψιν μετὰ εὐχαριστίας τοῖς πιστοῖς καὶ ἐπεγνωκόσι τὴν ἀλήθειαν. ὅτι πᾶν κτίσμα θεοῦ καλόν, καὶ οὐδὲν ἀπόβλητον μετὰ εὐχαριστίας λαμβανόμενον· ἁγιάζεται γὰρ διὰ λόγου θεοῦ καὶ ἐντεύξεως.

ἱκανὴ μὲν οὖν αὕτη ἡ φωνὴ τοῦ μακαρίου Παύλου πρὸς ἔλεγχον τῶν οὕτως βιούντων καὶ σεμνυνομένων <ὡς> δικαίων, εἰς τὸ δεῖξαι ὅτι καὶ τοῦτο αἵρεσις.

3. Εἰ δὲ καὶ ἕτεραί τινες αἱρέσεις ὠνομάζοντο, <οἷον> Καϊνῶν, Ὀφιτῶν ἢ Νοαχιτῶν καὶ ἑτέρων τοιούτων, οὐκ (ἀν)αγκαῖον ἥγημαι τὰ ὑπ᾽ αὐτῶν

bloated arrogance, they turn the Christian lifestyle upside down. Thinking to glorify themselves through foods, they keep away from the meat of ensouled animals and drink only water.[101] They forbid marriage and dedicate the rest of their lives to harsh austerity—proving to be more like Cynics than Christians.

They do not listen to what was said to them beforehand through the apostle Paul. He prophesied their future teachings, which some vainly "innovate":

> 2. The Spirit expressly says that in later times some will rebel from sound teaching, devoting themselves to deceitful spirits and to teachings of demons through the hypocrisy of liars. They are seared in their own conscience, forbidding marriage and abstaining from foods that God created to be shared with thanksgiving by the faithful and those who know the truth. Every creature of God is good, and nothing is to be rejected if received with thanksgiving, since it is sanctified through the word of God and prayer.[102]

The voice of the blessed Paul is sufficient to refute the people who live like this and pompously strut like righteous people. His testimony shows that this too is a heresy.

CONCLUSION

3. Even if other heresies were named—such as those of the Cainites, the Ophites, the Noachites, and others of the same ilk—I regard it as unnecessary to present either their teachings or their practices.[103] I refrain so as

---

Ἐγκράτεια is, according to Paul, a fruit of the Spirit (Gal 5:23). Irenaeus (*Haer.* 1.28.1) was apparently the first to construct the Enkratites as a distinct "heresy." Cf. Epiph., *Pan.* 47.1.1–3.5; Clem. Alex., *Strom.* 1.71.5; Filastrius, *Haer.* 72; Theodoret, *Haer. fab.* 1.20 (PG 83:369, 372). See further Peter Brown, *The Body and Society: Men, Women and Sexual Renunciation in Early Christianity* (New York: Columbia University Press, 1988), 83–102; Andrew R. Guffey, "Motivations for Enkratite Practices in Early Christian Literature," *JTS* 65 (2014): 515–49.

101. Cf. Clem. Alex., *Paed.* 2.32.1; 2.33.1; *Strom.* 1.15.71.5. See further Guffey, "Motivations," 524–25.

102. 1 Tim 4:1–5; cf. *Ref.* 7.30.3 (Markion).

103. On the "Cainites," see Iren., *Haer.* 1.31.1–2; Epiph., *Pan.* 38.1.1–3.5; Ps.-Tert., *Adv. omn. haer.* 2; Theodoret, *Haer. fab.* 1.15 (PG 83:368b–c); Filastrius, *Haer.* 2. On the Ophites, see Iren., *Haer.* 1.30.1–15; Epiph., *Pan.* 37.1.1–9.4; Ps.-Tert., *Adv. omn.*

λεγόμενα ἢ γινόμενα ἐκθέσθαι, ἵ(ν)α μὴ κἂν [ἐν] <διὰ> τοῦτό τινος αὐτοὺς [ἢ] λόγου ἀξίους ἡγῶνται. 4. ἀλλ' ἐπεὶ καὶ τὰ περὶ τούτων αὐτάρκη δοκεῖ εἶναι, παρέλθωμεν ἐπὶ τὴν πᾶσι τῶν κακῶν αἰτίαν <γενομένην> αἵρεσι<ν> Νοητιανῶν, <ὅπως> τήν τε ῥίζαν αὐτῆς ἀναπτύξαντες καὶ τὸν ἔνδον ὄντα ἰὸν εἰ<ς> φανερὸν ἐλέγξαντες, παύσωμεν τῆς τοιαύτης πλάνης τοὺς ἀπαγομένους ὑπὸ πνεύματος βιαίου δίκην χειμ(άρ)ρ(ου).

to prevent them from thinking themselves worthy of account by virtue of my report. 4. Since I deem the description of these heresies adequate, let us proceed to the cause of everyone's misfortunes—the Noetian heresy. By digging out its root and exposing to open view the poison within it, I aim to prevent those misled by such deceit from being carried off as if by a violent storm blast.

haer. 2; Filastrius, *Haer.* 1; Theodoret, *Haer. fab.* 1.14. On the Noachites, see Iren., *Haer.* 1.30.9–10; Epiph., *Pan.* 26.1.4, 7–9; Nat. Rulers (NHC II,4) 92.9; Apoc. Adam (NHC V,5) 72–76.

<ΤΟΥ ΚΑΤΑ ΠΑΣΩΝ ΑΙΡΕΣΕΩΝ ΕΛΕΓΧΟΥ> Θ

1. <Τ>άδε ἔνεστιν ἐν τῇ ἐννάτῃ τοῦ κατὰ πασῶν αἱρέσεων ἐλέγχου·

2. Τίς ἡ Νοητοῦ βλάσφημος ἀφροσύνη, καὶ ὅτι δόγμασιν Ἡρακλείτου τοῦ σκοτεινοῦ προσέσχεν, οὐ τοῖς Χριστοῦ.

3. Καὶ πῶς Κάλλιστος, μίξας τὴν Κλεομένους, μαθητοῦ Νοητοῦ, καὶ Θεοδότου αἵρεσιν, ἑτέραν καινοτέραν αἵρεσιν συνεστήσ<ατ>ο, καὶ τίς ὁ τούτου βίος.

4. Τίς ἡ <καινὴ> ἐπιδημία τοῦ ξένου δαίμονος Ἠλχασαΐ, καὶ ὅτι σκέπη τῶν ἰδίων σφαλμάτων τὸ δοκεῖν προσέχειν νόμῳ, τῷ δὲ ὄντι γνωστικοῖς δόγμασιν ἢ καὶ ἀστρολογικοῖς καὶ μαγείαις πρόσκειται.

5. Τίνα τὰ Ἰουδαίοις ἔθη, καὶ πόσαι τούτων διαφοραί.

6. 1. Πολλοῦ τοίνυν τοῦ κατὰ πασῶν αἱρέσεων γενομένου ἡμῖν ἀγῶνος, μηθέν γε ἀνεξέλεγκτον καταλιποῦσι, περιλείπεται νῦν ὁ μέγιστος ἀγών, ἐκδιηγήσασθαι καὶ διελ<έ>γξαι τὰς ἐφ' ἡμῖν ἐπαναστάσας αἱρέσεις, δι' ὧν τινες ἀμαθεῖς καὶ τολμηροὶ διασκεδαν<ν>ύειν ἐπεχείρησαν τὴν ἐκκλησίαν, μέγιστον τάραχον κατὰ πάντα τὸν κόσμον ἐν πᾶσι <τ>οῖς πιστοῖς ἐμβάλλοντες. δοκεῖ

BOOK 9

[TABLE OF CONTENTS]

1. The following is contained in the ninth book of the *Refutation of All Heresies*.

2. The blasphemous idiocy of Noetos. He clung to the doctrines of Herakleitos the Obscure, not those of Christ.

3. How Kallistos—having confounded the heresy of Kleomenes (a disciple of Noetos) with that of Theodotos—established another more newfangled heresy.[1] His life story.

4. The new arrival of the alien demon Elchasai, whose seeming adherence to the Law is a cover for his own errors, since in fact he is embroiled in gnostic teachings, astrological speculations, and magical practices.[2]

5. The customs of the Jews, and their many disagreements.

INTRODUCTION

6. 1. Now then, even though my contest against all heresies is long (since I leave nothing unexposed), there still remains the greatest contest: to recount and to refute the heresies that have arisen in my own time. By means of these heresies, some uneducated and impudent people tried to scatter the church, inflicting a great disturbance upon all the faithful

1. Cf. Eusebios, *Hist. eccl.* 5.3.4; 5.16.14–15.

2. Wordsworth emends P's κένη ("empty") to καινή ("new") (*St. Hippolytus*, 62–63). Gerard Luttikhuizen takes "the alien demon Elchasai" (possibly to be translated: *of* Elchasai) to refer specifically to Alkibiades of Apamea (*The Revelation of Elchasai: Investigations into the Evidence for a Mesopotamian Jewish Apocalypse of the Second Century and Its Reception by Judeo-Christian Propagandists*, TSAJ 8 [Tübingen: Mohr Siebeck, 1985], 54). Cf. Acts Pet. 6.17 (*NTApoc* 2:301), where Simon is called "that inconstant demon." See further Luigi Cirillo, *Elchasai e gli Elchasaiti: Un contributo alla storia delle comunità giudeo-cristiane* (Cosenza: Marra, 1984), 13.

γοῦν ἐπὶ τὴν ἀρχηγὸν τῶν κακῶν γενομένην γνώμην ὁρμήσαντας διελέγξαι τίνες αἱ ταύτης ἀρχαί, ὅπως εὔ(γν)ωστοι αἱ ἐκφυάδες αὐτῆς ἅπασι γενόμεναι καταφρονηθῶσι.

7. 1. Γεγένηταί τις ὀνόματι Νοητός, τῷ γένει (Σ)μυρναῖος· οὗτος εἰσηγήσατο αἵρεσιν ἐκ τῶν Ἡρακλείτου δογμ(ά)των. οὗ διάκονος καὶ μαθητὴς γίνεται Ἐπίγονός τις τοὔνομα, ὃς τῇ Ῥώμῃ ἐπιδημήσας ἐπέσπειρε τὴν ἄθεον γνώμην. ᾧ μαθητεύσας Κλεομένης, καὶ βίῳ καὶ τρόπῳ ἀλλότριος τῆς ἐκκλησίας, ἐκράτυνε τὸ δόγμα, κατ' ἐκεῖνο καιροῦ Ζεφυρίνου διέπειν νομίζοντος τὴν ἐκκλησίαν, ἀνδρὸς ἰδιώτου καὶ αἰσχροκερδοῦς.

2. <ὃς> τῷ κέρδει προσφερομένῳ πειθόμενος συνεχώρει τοῖς προσιοῦσι τῷ Κλεομένει μαθητεύεσθαι, καὶ αὐτὸς ὑποσυρόμενος τῷ χρόνῳ ἐπὶ τὰ αὐτά ὡρμή<σα>το, συμβούλου καὶ συναγωνιστοῦ τῶν κακῶν ὄντος αὐτῷ Καλλίστου—οὗ τὸν βίον καὶ τὴν ἐφευρεθεῖσαν αἵρεσιν μετ' οὐ πολὺ ἐκθήσομαι.—3. τούτων κατὰ διαδοχὴν διέμεινε τὸ διδασκαλεῖον κρατυνόμενον καὶ ἐπαῦξον διὰ τὸ συναίρεσθαι αὐτοῖς τὸν Ζεφυρῖνον καὶ τὸν Κάλλιστον, καίτοι ἡμῶν μηδέποτε συγχωρησάντων, ἀλλὰ πλειστάκις ἀντικαθεστώτων πρὸς αὐτοὺς καὶ διελεγξάντων καὶ ἄκοντας βιασαμένων τὴν ἀλήθειαν ὁμολογεῖν· οἳ πρὸς μὲν ὥραν αἰδούμενοι καὶ ὑπὸ τῆς ἀληθείας συναγόμενοι ὡμολόγουν, μετ' οὐ πολὺ δὲ ἐπὶ τὸν αὐτὸν βόρβορον ἀνεκυλίοντο.

throughout the entire world. Thus it is right to expose its principles, starting from the theory that became the harbinger of evils. As a result, its offshoots will be well recognized by all—and despised.[3]

NOETOS

7. 1. There was a man by the name of Noetos, a Smyrnean by race.[4] He introduced a heresy from the doctrines of Herakleitos. His assistant and student was a man named Epigonos. He was the one who sojourned to Rome and sowed this godless opinion. Epigonos's student Kleomenes—who was foreign to the church in both life and character—corroborated this doctrine during the time that Zephyrinos imagined that he was in charge of the church.[5] Zephyrinos was a commoner and greedy for gain.

2. When presented with a bribe, he was won over and allowed those attached to Kleomenes to receive instruction. He too was eventually seduced and rushed headlong toward the same opinions. Kallistos (whose life and invented heresy I will soon present[6]) was a fellow counselor and contestant with him in his vices. 3. Thus their school has remained through a line of succession, increasingly validated and spreading, due to the cooperation of Zephyrinos and Kallistos. But I never gave in to them. Rather, I opposed and refuted them many times, forcing them against their will to confess the truth. They, for a moment, were ashamed. Reined in by the truth, they confessed it, but soon they began wallowing in the same mire.[7]

3. On the plan of book 9, see Koschorke, *Ketzerbekämpfung*, 61–64.

4. On Noetos and his heirs, see *Ref.* 9.10.9–12; 10.27.1–2; [Hipp.], *Noet.* 1–8; Epiph., *Pan.* 57.1.1–10.9; Filastrius, *Haer.* 53; Theodoret, *Haer. fab.* 3.3 (PG 83:404–5). See further Heine, "Christology of Callistus," *JTS* 49 (1998): 56–91 (78–84). According to Epiphanios, Noetos was an Ephesian (*Pan.* 57.1.1).

5. On the views of Kleomenes, see Heine, "Christology of Callistus," 84–89. Zephyrinos was bishop from 198 to 217 CE.

6. See *Ref.* 9.11.1–12.26.

7. Cf. 2 Pet 2:22 (ὗς λουσαμένη εἰς κυλισμὸν βορβόρου); Semonides, frag. 7.2–6 (West, *Iambi et Elegi*, 2:101–2); Herakleitos, DK 22 B13 (= Marcovich, *Heraclitus*, §36); Epiktetos, *Diatr.* 4.11; 29; 31.

8. 1. Ἀλλ’ ἐπεὶ τῆς γενεαλογίας αὐτῶν τὴν διαδοχὴν ἐπεδείξαμεν, δοκεῖ λοιπὸν καὶ τῶν δογμάτων τὴν κακοδιδασκαλίαν ἐκθέσθαι, πρότερον τὰ Ἡρακλείτῳ τῷ σκοτεινῷ δόξαντα παραθεμένους, ἔπει<τα> καὶ τὰ τούτων Ἡρακλείτεια μέρη ὄντα φανερώσαν<τας. ἃ τυχόντες οἱ νῦν προστάται τῆς αἱρέσεως οὐκ ἴσασιν ὄντα τοῦ σκοτεινοῦ, νομίζοντες εἶναι Χριστοῦ· οἷς εἰ ἐνέτυχον, κἂν οὕτω δυσωπηθέντες παύσονται τῆς ἀθέου δυσφημίας.

2. ἀλλ’ εἰ καὶ πρότερον ἔκκειται ὑφ’ ἡμῶν ἐν τοῖς Φιλοσοφο<υ>μένοις ἡ δόξα Ἡρακλείτου, ἀλλά γε δοκεῖ προσαν<τι>παραθεῖναι καὶ νῦν, ὅπως διὰ τοῦ ἐγγίονος ἐλέγχου φανερῶς διδαχθῶσιν οἱ τούτου, νομίζοντες Χριστοῦ εἶναι μαθητάς, οὐκ ὄντας, ἀλλὰ τοῦ σκοτεινοῦ.

9. 1. Ἡράκλειτος μὲν οὖν φησιν εἶναι τὸ πᾶν διαιρετὸν ἀδιαίρετον, γενητὸν ἀγένητον, θνητὸν ἀθάνατον, λόγον αἰῶνα, πατέρα υἱόν, θεὸν δίκαιον·

REVIEW OF HERAKLEITOS

8. 1. Since I showed the succession of their genealogy, it is therefore fitting to present the perverse teaching of their doctrines.[8] First, I set out the views of Herakleitos the Obscure, then I will set out the aspects of their teaching that exhibit Heraklitean elements.[9] The current leaders of the Noetian heresy, encountering these teachings, do not know that they belonged to the Obscure philosopher. They suppose that the teachings belong to Christ. If they read them here, they will, though utterly disgraced, cease from their godless slander.[10]

2. Now, even though I formerly set out the theory of Herakleitos in the philosophical sections, it is still right to compare them here as well, so that through a more proximate exposé, Noetos's votaries—who falsely suppose themselves to be Christ's students but are in fact students of the Obscure philosopher—might be more clearly instructed.[11]

THE IDENTITY OF FATHER AND SON. 9. 1. Herakleitos affirms that the All is Divisible/Indivisible, Born/Unborn, Mortal/Immortal, Word/Eternity, Father/Son,[12] God/Righteous One.[13] He says:

---

8. For the concept of succession (διαδοχήν), see Mansfeld, *Heresiography*, 20–43.

9. For μέρη, see *Ref.* 9.10.8 (τὸ κεφάλαιον).

10. In the following "review" of Herakleitos, our author provides nineteen fragments from Herakleitos's work, most of them unattested elsewhere. His report, however, leaves many bewildered. Philip Wheelwright speaks for many when he remarks that our author "shows a strangely defective sense of logical connections. Choosing some of the most paradoxical of Heraclitus' utterances … he throws them together in a hit-or-miss fashion, occasionally making farfetched comparisons with elements of Christian doctrine" (*Heraclitus* [Princeton: Princeton University Press, 1959], 133). More sympathetic is Osborne, *Rethinking*, 132–82. Serge N. Mouraviev argues that the report is not an exposition of Herakleitos but a series of Noetian propositions proved by a Heraklitean pastiche ("Hippolyte, Héraclite et Noët (Commentaire d'Hippolyte, Refut. omn. haer. IX 8–10)," *ANRW* 36.6:4375–402 [4400]).

11. For the teachings of Herakleitos, see *Ref.* 1.4. Our author tendentiously contrasts his "clear" (φανερῶς) instruction to the obscurity of Herakleitos (τοῦ σκοτεινοῦ).

12. The Father-Son pair (cf. *Ref.* 9.10.10–11 below) is the key to understanding how our author interprets Herakleitos. Our author's overwhelming concern is to prove that the identity of Father and Son in Noetian thought is based on Herakleitos's teaching (see *Ref.* 9.12.16–17 below). Listing Father and Son as equivalents illustrates the breakdown of distinctions that were so important to our author (Osborne, *Rethinking*, 145–46; Mansfeld, *Heresiography*, 232). The previously mentioned "Word" (λόγος) is taken

> οὐκ ἐμοῦ ἀλλὰ τοῦ <λόγου> ἀκούσαντας ὁμολογεῖν σοφόν ἐστιν ἓν πάντα εἶναι

ὁ Ἡράκλειτός φησι. 2. καὶ ὅτι τοῦτο οὐκ ἴσασι πάντες οὐδὲ ὁμολογοῦσιν, ἐπιμέμφεται ὧδέ πως·

> οὐ ξυνιᾶσιν ὅκως διαφερόμενον ἑωυτῷ ὁμολογέει· παλίντροπος ἁρμονίη, ὅκωσπερ τόξου καὶ λύρης.

3. ὅτι δὲ λόγος ἐστὶν ἀεὶ τὸ πᾶν καὶ διὰ παντὸς ὤν, οὕτως λέγει·

Listening not to me but to the Word [λόγου], it is wise to agree [ὁμολογεῖν] that all is one.[14]

2. The fact that all people do not know this or agree with it, he castigates somewhere:

They do not understand how something agrees with itself by differing: a counterbalancing congruity, as of a bow or a lyre.[15]

3. But that the Word is always [ἀεί] everything and exists through everything, he formulates as follows:

---

to be another name for the Son, while "Eternity" (αἰών) stands in for the un-incarnated Father. According to Ramnoux, αἰών is here taken to mean ἀεί ὤν, "the Ever Existent." Aeon's identification with Logos is made immediately below (9.9.3), where the Logos is said to exist forever (ἐόντος ἀεί) (*Études présocratiques*, 70). Our author attempts to heighten the confusion of opposites by soon identifying Aeon (αἰών) with the Son (9.9.4).

13. Wendland saw an opposition between θεόν and δίκαιον based on Markionite theology (see the note ad loc. in his edition of the *Refutatio*, 241). His position was adopted by Kirk, *Cosmic Fragments*, 65; Ramnoux, *Études présocratiques*, 76 n. 5; and Mansfeld, *Heresiography*, 233. Marcovich takes δίκαιον θεόν as predicated of τὸ πᾶν ("The All is … a just God"). Varying this interpretation, Mouraviev takes θεόν alone as predicated of τὸ πᾶν and translates τὸ πᾶν adverbially ("God is entirely …") Then he takes δίκαιον as introducing the quote from Herakleitos ("it is just to recognize … ") ("Hippolyte, Héraclite et Noët," 4392–93).

14. Herakleitos, DK 22 B50 (Marcovich, *Heraclitus*, §26; Charles H. Kahn, *The Art and Thought of Heraclitus: An Edition of the Fragments with Translation and Commentary* [Cambridge: Cambridge University Press, 1979], §36). Further commentary in Kirk, *Cosmic Fragments*, 65–71; T. M. Robinson, *Heraclitus Fragments: A Text and Translation with a Commentary*, Phoenix Supplementary Volumes 22 (Toronto: University of Toronto Press, 1991), 114–15. Bernays emends δόγματος in P to λόγου ("Word"). "All is one" sounds more like pantheism, but our author uses this statement to anticipate Noetian monotheism below. In Mouraviev's view, the "one" designates God for our author, and the "All" designates the "divine qualities of Father and Son" ("Hippolyte, Héraclite et Noët," 4392).

15. Herakleitos, DK 22 B51 (= Marcovich, *Heraclitus*, §27; Kahn, *Art*, §78). Further commentary in Kirk, *Cosmic Fragments*, 203–21; Osborne, *Rethinking*, 151–53. On ἁρμονίη, Kirk observes that, as a connecting structure, it probably refers "to the string of the bow and the strings of the lyre" (*Cosmic Fragments*, 208). Thus Herakleitos is speaking of the "'return' to its position of the bow-string or lyre-string after use" (Robinson, *Heraclitus*, 116).

τοῦ δὲ λόγου τοῦδ' ἐόντος ἀεὶ <ἀ>ξ<ύν>ετοι γίνονται ἄνθρωποι, καὶ πρόσθεν ἢ ἀκοῦσαι καὶ ἀκούσαντες τὸ πρῶτον· γινομένων γὰρ πάντων κατὰ τὸν λόγον τόνδε ἀπείροισιν ἐοίκασι πειρώμενοι καὶ ἐπέων καὶ ἔργων τοιουτέων, ὁκοῖα ἐγὼ διηγεῦμαι διαιρέων <ἕκαστον> κατὰ φύσιν καὶ φράζων ὅκως ἔχει.

4. ὅτι δέ ἐστι παῖς τὸ πᾶν καὶ δι' αἰῶνος αἰώνιος βασιλεὺς τῶν ὅλων, οὕτως λέγει·

αἰὼν παῖς ἐστι παίζων, πεσσεύων· παιδὸς ἡ βασιληίη.

ὅτι δέ ἐστιν ὁ πατὴρ πάντων τῶν γεγονότων γενητὸς ἀγένητος, κτίσις δημιουργός, ἐκείνου λέγοντος ἀκούομεν·

πόλεμος πάντων μὲν πατήρ ἐστι, πάντων δὲ βασιλεύς, καὶ τοὺς μὲν θεοὺς ἔδειξε, τοὺς δὲ ἀνθρώπους, τοὺς μὲν δούλους ἐποίησε, τοὺς δὲ ἐλευθέρους.

> Of the Word, who is eternal [ἀεί],[16] humans prove uncomprehending, both before they hear it and once they have heard it. Although everything arises according to this Word, people are like those inexperienced, even when they experience both words and deeds of the kind I relate, when I distinguish each thing according to its natural constitution and declare how it is.[17]

4. That the All is a Child and, throughout eternity, the eternal king of the universe, Herakleitos formulates as follows:

> Eternity is a Child at play, moving pieces in a game. Kingship belongs to the Child![18]

That the Father of all generated beings is born and unborn, creation and Artificer, we hear in Herakleitos's saying:

> War is the Father of all, and king of all; it makes some gods, and others human beings; some slaves, and others free.[19]

---

16. The adverb ἀεί could equally well go with the next clause—"humans *always* prove uncomprehending"—but it is evident from his introductory comment that our author takes ἀεί with λόγος.

17. Herakleitos, DK 22 B1 (= Marcovich, *Heraclitus*, §1; Kahn, *Art*, §1). The first sentence of this fragment is also quoted by Clem. Alex., *Strom.* 5.14.111.7. Further commentary in Kirk, *Cosmic Fragments*, 33–47; Robinson, *Heraclitus*, 74–76; Osborne, *Rethinking*, 154–56.

18. Herakleitos, DK 22 B52 (= Marcovich, *Heraclitus*, §93; Kahn, *Art*, §94). The meaning of αἰών is disputed. For Herakleitos, it seems to have meant a (human) lifetime (Kirk, *Cosmic Fragments*, preface, xiii; Marcovich, *Heraclitus*, 493–94; Kahn, *Art*, 228; Robinson, *Heraclitus*, 116). Later it could mean "eternity" and by our author's time, it became a technical term for a god called Aion. Our author identifies Aion with the divine Child, God the Son. See further Osborne, *Rethinking*, 156–57.

19. Herakleitos, DK 22 B53 (= Marcovich, *Heraclitus*, §29; Kahn, *Art*, §83). Further commentary in Kirk, *Cosmic Fragments*, 245–49; Robinson, *Heraclitus*, 117–18; Osborne, *Rethinking*, 157–58. According to Kirk, our author supposed that "War is described as a supreme god, and yet he creates the gods as well as men; therefore *qua* god he is both creator and created" (*Cosmic Fragments*, 245). Osborne rejects this reasoning. For her, war as a creation is equated with God, who is uncreated (*Rethinking*, 158). Mouraviev sees a kind of logical loop (*boucle*): Word = Eternity (DK 22 B1); Eternity = Child (B52); Child = King (B52); King = Father (B53). Thus Word = Eternity = Child (or Son) = King = Father ("Hippolyte, Héraclite et Noët," 4396).

5. ὅ(τ)ι δέ ἐστιν ... «ἁρμονίη, ὅκωσπερ τόξου καὶ λύρης».
ὅτι δέ ἐ(στιν) ἀφανὴς [ὁ] ἀόρατος ἄγνωστος ἀνθρώποις, ἐν τούτοις λέγει·

ἁρμονίη ἀφανὴς φανερῆς κρείττων.

ἐπαινεῖ καὶ προθαυμάζει πρὸ τοῦ γινωσκομένου τὸ ἄγνωστον καὶ ἀόρατον αὐτοῦ τῆς δυνάμεως. ὅτι δέ ἐστιν ὁρατὸς ἀνθρώποις, καὶ οὐκ ἀνεξεύρετος, ἐν τούτοις λέγει·

ὅσων ὄψις ἀκοὴ μάθησις, ταῦτα, φησί, ἐγὼ προτιμέω.

τουτέστι τὰ ὁρατὰ τῶν ἀοράτων. <ταὐτὸ δὲ καὶ> ἀπὸ τῶν τοιούτων αὐτοῦ λόγων κατανοεῖν ῥᾴδιον·

6. ἐξηπάτηνται, φησίν, οἱ ἄνθρωποι πρὸς τὴν γνῶσιν τῶν φανερῶν παραπλησίως Ὁμήρῳ, ὃς ἐγένετο τῶν Ἑλλήνων σοφώτερος πάντων· ἐκεῖνόν τε γὰρ παῖδες φθεῖρας κατακτείνοντες ἐξηπάτησαν εἰπόντες· ὅσα εἴδομεν καὶ ἐλάβομεν, ταῦτα ἀπολείπομεν, ὅσα δὲ οὔτε εἴδομεν οὔτ' ἐλάβομεν, ταῦτα φέρομεν.

5. That there is … [20] "a congruity, as of a bow or a lyre."[21]

That [this congruity] is unapparent, invisible, and unknown to human beings, he affirms in these words:

> An unapparent congruity is better than an apparent one.[22]

He praises and marvels at the unrecognized and invisible aspect of his power, rather than what is recognized. That it is visible to human beings and not undiscoverable, he describes in this saying:

> The objects of sight, hearing, and apprehension—these *I* prefer.

He means that he prefers visible things over invisible things.[23] But that they are the same thing is also easy to understand from his characteristic language:

> 6. People are deceived with regard to the knowledge of apparent phenomena very much like Homer, wisest of all Greeks. For children killing lice deceived him by saying: "what we see and take, these we leave behind; and what we neither see nor take, these we carry."[24]

---

20. Wendland and Marcovich were tempted to fill the lacuna here, the latter more fulsomely. Cf. Osborne, *Rethinking*, 161.

21. Herakleitos, DK 22 B51 (= Marcovich, *Heraclitus*, §27; Kahn, *Art*, §78). This is an odd restatement of a fragment quoted more fully several lines earlier.

22. Herakleitos, DK 22 B54 (= Marcovich, *Heraclitus*, §9; Kahn, *Art*, §80). Further commentary in Kirk, *Cosmic Fragments*, 222–26; Robinson, *Heraclitus*, 118–19.

23. Herakleitos, DK 22 B55 (= Marcovich, *Heraclitus*, §5; Kahn, *Art*, §14); further commentary in Robinson, *Heraclitus*, 119. According to our author, Herakleitos values perceptible things over invisible things. But this seems to contradict DK 22 B54, quoted immediately above, namely, "an unapparent congruity is better than an apparent [one]." The point seems to be that Herakleitos prefers *both* unapparent over apparent and apparent over unapparent because *both are in some sense one*. Our author attempts to clarify this point immediately below in *Ref.* 9.10.1–2. The basic principle is "all things are one," and thus opposites are identical.

24. Herakleitos, DK 22 B56 (= Marcovich, *Heraclitus*, §21; Kahn, *Art*, §22). Further commentary in Robinson, *Heraclitus*, 119–20; Osborne, *Rethinking*, 162–63. Homer, who was reportedly blind, did not know that the children's riddle referred to lice.

10. 1. Οὕτως Ἡράκλειτος ἐν ἴσῃ μοίρᾳ τίθεται καὶ τιμᾷ τὰ ἐμφανῆ τοῖς ἀφανέσιν, ὡς ἕν τι τὸ ἐμφανὲς καὶ τὸ ἀφανὲς ὁμολογουμένως ὑπάρχον· <ἔσ>τι γάρ, φησίν, «ἁρμονίη [ἡ] ἀφανὴς φανερῆς κρείττων», καί· «ὅσων ὄψις ἀκοὴ μάθησις»—τουτέστι τὰ ὄργανα—«ταῦτα», φησίν, «ἐγὼ προτιμέω», οὐ τὰ ἀφανῆ προτιμήσας.

2. τοιγαροῦν οὐδὲ σκότος οὐδὲ φῶς, οὐδὲ πονηρὸν οὐδὲ ἀγαθὸν ἕτερόν φησιν εἶναι ὁ Ἡράκλειτος, ἀλλὰ ἓν καὶ τὸ αὐτό. ἐπιτιμᾷ γοῦν Ἡσιόδῳ, ὅτι ἡμέραν καὶ νύκτα <οὐκ> οἶδεν· ἡμέρα γάρ, φησί, καὶ νύξ ἐστιν ἕν, λέγων ὧδέ πως·

διδάσκαλος δὲ πλείστων Ἡσίοδος· τοῦτον ἐπίστανται πλεῖστα εἰδέναι,
ὅστις ἡμέρην καὶ εὐφρόνην οὐκ ἐγίνωσκεν· ἔστι γὰρ ἕν.

3. καὶ ἀγαθὸν καὶ κακόν· «οἱ γοῦν ἰατροί», φησὶν ὁ Ἡράκλειτ(ος),

τέμνοντες, καίοντες

—<τουτέστι> πάντῃ βασανίζοντες κακῶς τοὺς ἀρρωστοῦντας—

ἐπαιτιῶνται μηδέν' ἄξιον μισθὸν λαμβάνειν

—παρὰ τῶν ἀρρωστούντων—

ταὐτὰ ἐργαζόμενοι, τὰ ἀγαθὰ καὶ τὰς νόσους.

10. 1. In this way, then, Herakleitos places apparent phenomena in the same rank as the unapparent and values them equally, since, as we all agree, the apparent and unapparent are in some way one. This is because "an unapparent congruence is better than an apparent one." And again: "The objects of sight, hearing, and apprehension" (that is, objects of the sensory organs), "these *I* prefer"—here *not* preferring the unapparent![25]

THE IDENTITY OF OPPOSITES. 2. Therefore Herakleitos says that neither darkness nor light, neither evil nor good are different, but one and the same. Accordingly, he censures Hesiod for not knowing day and night, since day and night, Herakleitos says, are one. He speaks as follows:

> Hesiod is the teacher of most. They think that he knows the most, but he is the one who did not recognize day and night—for they are one.[26]

3. Moreover, good and evil are one. Herakleitos affirms that,

> Doctors, when they slice and burn

(that is, when they cruelly torture the sick in every way),[27]

> raise an outcry when they do not receive their due fee

(that is, from their patients),

> even though they produce the same effects: benefits and banes.[28]

---

25. Herakleitos, DK 22 B54, 55 (= Marcovich, *Heraclitus*, §9 and §5; Kahn, *Art*, §80 and §14). Cf. *Ref.* 9.9.5. The point of the identity of apparent and unapparent phenomena is the identity of the invisible Father with the visible Son.

26. Herakleitos, DK 22 B57 (= Marcovich, *Heraclitus*, §43; Kahn, *Art*, §19). Further commentary in Kirk, *Cosmic Fragments*, 155–61; Osborne, *Rethinking*, 164–67. Cf. Hesiod, *Theog.* 123–125, 744–757.

27. For barbaric medical practices, see Diog. L., *Vit. phil.* 3.85; Plato, *Gorg.* 456b; 479a; 480c; 521e–522a; *Resp.* 406d; 426b; *Prot.* 354a; *Tim.* 64d; 65b; *Pol.* 293b.

28. Herakleitos, DK 22 B58 (= Marcovich, *Heraclitus*, §46; Kahn, *Art* §73). Further commentary in Kirk, *Cosmic Fragments*, 88–96; Robinson, *Heraclitus*, 121–22; Osborne, *Rethinking*, 167–69.

4. καὶ εὐθὺ δέ, φησίν, καὶ στρεβλὸν τὸ αὐτό ἐστι·

> γ<ν>άφων, φησίν, ὁδὸς εὐθεῖα καὶ σκολιή.

<τουτέστιν> ἡ τοῦ ὀργάνου τοῦ καλουμένου κοχλίου ἐν τῷ γ<ν>αφείῳ περιστροφὴ εὐθεῖα καὶ σκολιή· ἄνω γὰρ ὁμοῦ καὶ κύκλῳ περιέ<ρ>χεται—«μία ἐστί», φησί, «καὶ ἡ αὐτή».

καὶ τὸ ἄνω καὶ τὸ κάτω ἕν ἐστι καὶ τὸ αὐτό·

> ὁδός ἄνω κάτω μία καὶ ὡυτή.

5. καὶ τὸ μιαρόν φησιν καὶ τὸ καθαρὸν ἓν καὶ ταὐτὸ εἶναι, καὶ τὸ πότιμον καὶ τὸ ἄποτον ἓν καὶ τὸ αὐτό εἶναι·

> θάλασσα, φησίν, ὕδωρ καθαρώτατον καὶ μιαρώτατον· ἰχθύσι μὲν πότιμον καὶ σωτήριον, ἀνθρώποις δὲ ἄποτον καὶ ὀλέθριον.

6. Λέγει δὲ ὁμολογουμένως τὸ ἀθάνατον εἶναι θνητὸν καὶ τὸ θνητὸν ἀθάνατον διὰ τῶν τοιούτων λόγων·

> ἀθάνατοι θνητοί, θνητοὶ ἀθάνατοι· ζῶντες τὸν ἐκείνων θάνατον, τὸν δὲ ἐκείνων βίον τεθνεῶτες.

4. Moreover, he says that the straight and the crooked are the same:

> The path of carding combs is both straight and crooked.[29]

That is to say, the circular movement of the instrument called the "snail screw" in the launderer's shop is straight and crooked (for it goes up and around at the same time). Thus straight and crooked, he says, are "one and the same."[30]

Moreover, up and down are one and the same:

> The way up and down is one and the same.[31]

5. In addition, the foul and the pure are one and the same, as well as the drinkable and the undrinkable.

> The sea is water most pure and most foul. To fish it is drinkable and life-giving; but to humans it is undrinkable and deadly.[32]

6. By common consent, he says that the immortal is mortal and the mortal immortal. He uses this sort of language:

> Immortal mortals, mortal immortals: the one living their death, the other dying their life.[33]

---

29. Herakleitos, DK 22 B59 (= Marcovich, *Heraclitus*, §32; Kahn, *Art*, §74). Γνάφων ("carding combs") is Marcovich's emendation of P's γραφέων ("pens[?]"), which Kirk defends (*Cosmic Fragments*, 97–104; see further Robinson, *Heraclitus*, 122–23; Osborne, *Rethinking*, 167–69). For carding combs, see Herodotos, *Hist.* 1.92.4.

30. Γναφείῳ ("launderer's shop") is a commonly accepted emendation for P's γραφείω. See the previous note.

31. Herakleitos, DK 22 B60 (= Marcovich, *Heraclitus*, §33; Kahn, *Art*, §103). Cf. Tert., *Marc.* 2.28.1. Further commentary in Kirk, *Cosmic Fragments*, 105–12; Robinson, *Heraclitus*, 123.

32. Herakleitos, DK 22 B61 (= Marcovich, *Heraclitus*, §35; Kahn, *Art*, §70). Further commentary in Kirk, *Cosmic Fragments*, 74–75; Robinson, *Heraclitus*, 123.

33. Herakleitos, DK 22 B62 (= Marcovich, *Heraclitus*, §47; Kahn, *Art*, §92). Further commentary in Jean Pépin, *Idées grecque sur l'homme et sur dieu* (Paris: Belles Lettres, 1971), 34–51; Robinson, *Heraclitus*, 124–25; Osborne, *Rethinking*, 169.

λέγει δὲ καὶ σαρκὸς ἀνάστασιν, ταύτης φανερᾶς, ἐν ᾗ γεγενήμεθα, καὶ τὸν θεὸν οἶδε ταύτης τῆς ἀναστάσεως αἴτιον, οὕτως λέγων·

> ἔνθα δ' ἐόντι ἐπανίστασθαι καὶ φύλακας γίνεσθαι ἐγερτὶ ζώντων καὶ νεκρῶν.

7. λέγει δὲ καὶ <τὴν> τοῦ κόσμου κρίσιν καὶ πάντων τῶν ἐν αὐτῷ διὰ πυρὸς γίνεσθαι, λέγων οὕτως· «τάδε πάντα οἰακίζει»—τουτέστι κατευθύνει—«κεραυνός», κεραυνὸν τὸ πῦρ λέγων τὸ αἰώνιον.

λέγει δὲ καὶ φρόνιμον τοῦτο εἶναι τὸ πῦρ καὶ τῆς διοικήσεως τῶν ὅλων αἴτιον· καλεῖ δὲ αὐτὸ «χρησμοσύνην καὶ κόρον»· χρησμοσύνη δέ ἐστιν ἡ διακόσμησις κατ' αὐτόν, ἡ δὲ ἐκπύρωσις κόρος. «πάντα» γάρ, φησί, «τὸ πῦρ ἐπελθὸν κρινεῖ καὶ καταλήψεται».

RESURRECTION AND JUDGMENT. He says, furthermore, that there is a resurrection of the flesh—the visible flesh in which we are born. He knows also that God is the cause of this resurrection. He speaks as follows:

> For the One existing above, they rise up and become wakeful guardians of the living and the dead.[34]

7. He also says that the judgment of the world and of everything within it occurs through fire. To quote him: "The thunderbolt steers" (that is, directs) "all these things." Here he calls the eternal fire "thunderbolt."[35]

He also says that fire is endowed with intellect and is the cause of the management of the universe. He calls fire "deficiency and satiety."[36] Now deficiency, in his view, signifies the ordering of the world, while the conflagration signifies satiety. For "when fire comes upon all things, it will judge and overtake."[37]

---

34. I have attempted to translate this fragment in line with our author's interpretation of it, not the "original meaning" of Herakleitos, DK 22 B63 (= Marcovich, *Heraclitus*, §73; Kahn, *Art*, §110). Cf. Hesiod, *Op.* 121–123, 252–255 (people of the golden race made daimones and guardians—but only guardians of the living), partially quoted in Clem. Alex., *Protr.* 41.1; 103.2. See further Plato, *Crat.* 389a; *Resp.* 469a. Further commentary in Robinson, *Heraclitus*, 125–26; Osborne, *Rethinking*, 173–79; Mansfeld, *Heresiography*, 239. Osborne takes the subject of ἐπανίστασθαι to be Christ and translates: "When god was here in this world men rose up against him and set themselves as guards against him who was the awakening of the living and the dead" (177). Jaap Mansfeld notes that Clement of Alexandria (*Strom.* 5.1.9.4; 103.6–105.1) already ascribed the resurrection to Herakleitos and the Stoics (*Heresiography*, 307–12). Mansfeld would emend δέοντι in P (understood as δ' ἐόντι) to εὕδοντας and translates the fragment: "thereupon those asleep rise again and, fully awake, become watchers over the living and the dead" ("Heraclitus Fr. B 63 D.-K.," in *Studies in Later Greek Philosophy and Gnosticism* [London: Variorum, 1989], 197–205 [200, 205]).

35. Herakleitos, DK 22 B64 (= Marcovich, *Heraclitus*, §79; Kahn, *Art*, §119); cf. Matt 18:8; 25:41; Jude 7. Further commentary in Kirk, *Cosmic Fragments*, 349–61; Robinson, *Heraclitus*, 126–27.

36. Herakleitos, DK 22 B65 (= Marcovich, *Heraclitus*, §55; Kahn, *Art*, §120). Further commentary in Kirk, *Cosmic Fragments*, 349–61; Robinson, *Heraclitus*, 126–27.

37. Herakleitos, DK 22 B66 (= Marcovich, *Heraclitus*, §82; Kahn, *Art*, §121). Karl Reinhardt argued that this quote is not a citation of Herakleitos but a paraphrase ("Heraklits Lehre vom Feuer," *Hermes* 77 [1942]: 1–27 [22–25]). He was followed by Kirk, *Cosmic Fragments*, 359–61. See further Robinson, *Heraclitus*, 127; Osborne, *Rethinking*, 170–73.

8. ἐν δὲ τούτῳ τῷ κεφαλαίῳ, πάντα ὁμοῦ τὸν ἴδιον νοῦ(ν) ἐξέθετο, ἅμα δὲ καὶ τὸν τῆς Νοητοῦ αἱρέσεως, <ὃν> δι' ὀλίγων ἐπέδειξα οὐκ ὄντα Χριστοῦ ἀλλὰ Ἡρακλείτου μαθητήν.

τὸν γὰρ ποιητὸν κόσμον αὐτὸν δημιουργὸν καὶ ποιητὴν ἑαυτοῦ γινόμενον οὕτ(ω) (λ)έγει·

ὁ θεὸς
ἡμέρη εὐφρόνη,
χειμὼν θέρος,
πόλεμος εἰρήνη,
κόρος λιμός.

—τἀναντία ἅπαντα, οὗτος ὁ νοῦς·—

ἀλλοιοῦται δὲ ὅκωσπερ <πῦρ>, <ὃ> ὁκόταν συμμιγῇ θυώμασιν, ὀνομάζεται καθ' ἡδονὴν ἑκάστου.

9. Φανερὸν δὴ πᾶσι τοὺς <ἀ>νοήτους Νοητοῦ διαδόχους καὶ τῆς αἱρέσεως προστάτας, εἰ καὶ Ἡρακλείτου λέγοις ἂν αὐτοὺς μὴ γεγονέναι ἀκροατάς, ἀλλά γε τὰ Νοητῷ δόξαντα αἱρουμένους ἀναφανδὸν ταὐτὰ ὁμολογεῖν. λέγουσι γὰρ οὕτως·

SUMMARY. 8. To sum up, Herakleitos's particular meaning is presented in the slogan: "everything together."[38] This slogan also explains Noetos's heresy. I have briefly shown how this Noetos is a disciple not of Christ but of Herakleitos.

Herakleitos speaks of the made world as the Artificer and maker of itself:

God is
day night,
winter summer,
war peace,
satiety hunger.

He means that God consists of all the opposites.

> He is altered like fire,[39] which, whenever it is mixed with types of incense, is named according to the aroma of each.[40]

COMPARISON WITH NOETOS'S SUCCESSORS

9. It is clear to all that the no-brained successors of Noetos and the leaders of his heresy—even if you deny that they are students of Herakleitos—still plainly agree to the same things by choosing the doctrines of Noetos![41] Just hear what they say:[42]

---

38. Marcovich takes κεφάλαιον to refer to a "chapter" of "some Alexandrian anthology with Stoic explanations" ("Hippolytus and Heraclitus," *StPatr* 7 [1966]: 255–64 [255]; similarly Kirk, *Cosmic Fragments*, 184–85). Osborne takes it as a reference to our author's own "chapter" discussing Herakleitos (*Rethinking*, 179–80). Mouraviev understands it to mean "on this question" ("Hippolyte, Héraclite et Noët," 4398 n. 30). Mansfeld takes it as referring to Herakleitos's own "main point" (*Heresiography*, 240). It is also possible that the "in this main point" (ἐν τούτῳ τῷ κεφαλαίῳ) may refer to the quotation of DK 22 B67 below ("God is day night …"). Thus Jonathan Barnes translates ἐν τούτῳ τῷ κεφαλαίῳ as: "In the following passage" (*Early Greek Philosophy*, 2nd ed. [London: Penguin, 2001], 52). The slogan πάντα ὁμοῦ better fits Anaxagoras (cf. *Ref.* 1.8.1). Our author evidently takes πάντα ὁμοῦ to refer to the identity of opposites.

39. Πῦρ ("fire") is an addition of Diels. Other editors suggest ἔλαιον ("oil") or μύρον ("perfume").

40. Herakleitos, DK 22 B67 (= Marcovich, *Heraclitus*, §77; Kahn, *Art*, §123). Further commentary in Kirk, *Cosmic Fragments*, 184–201; Robinson, *Heraclitus*, 127–29; Osborne, *Rethinking*, 159–60. Cf. *Ref.* 5.19.4; 5.21.2–3 ("Sethians").

41. Ἀνοήτους (here: "no-brained") is Bernays's emendation of P's νοητούς. (If the reading in P is genuine, it is apparently meant ironically.) Cf. [Hipp.], *Noet.* 3.3: εἰ

> ἕνα καὶ τὸν αὐτὸν θεὸν εἶναι πάντων δημιουργὸν καὶ πατέρα, εὐδοκήσαντα μὲν πεφηνέναι τοῖς ἀρχῆθεν δικαίοις, ὄντα ἀόρατον. 10. ὅτε μὲν γὰρ οὐχ ὁρᾶται, ἐστὶν ἀόρατος, <ὅτε δὲ ὁρᾶται, ὁρατός· καὶ> ἀχώρητος ὅτε μὴ χωρεῖσθαι θέλει, χωρητὸς δὲ ὅτε χωρεῖται· οὕτως κατὰ τὸν αὐτὸν λόγον ἀκράτητος καὶ κρατητός, ἀγένητος <καὶ γενητός>, ἀθάνατος καὶ θνητός.

πῶς οὐχ Ἡρακλείτου οἱ τοιοῦτοι δειχθήσονται μαθηταί; μὴ τῇδὲ τῇ λέξει <ἰ>δίᾳ φθάσας ἐφιλοσόφησεν ὁ σκοτεινός;

Ὅτι δὲ καὶ τὸν αὐτὸν υἱὸν εἶναι λέγει καὶ πατέρα, οὐδεὶς ἀγνοεῖ· 11. λέγει γὰρ οὕτως·

> ὅτε μὲν οὖν μὴ <γε>γένητο ὁ πατήρ, δικαίως πατὴρ προσηγόρευτο· ὅτε δὲ ηὐδόκησε γένεσιν ὑπομεῖναι, γεν<ν>(η)θείς, ὁ υἱὸς ἐγένετο αὐτὸς ἑαυτοῦ, οὐχ ἑτέρου.

οὕτως γοῦν δοκεῖ μοναρχίαν συνιστᾶν, ἓν καὶ τὸ αὐτὸ φάσκων ὑπάρχειν πατέρα καὶ υἱόν, οὐχ ἕτερον ἐξ ἑτέρου, ἀλλ᾽ αὐτὸν ἐξ ἑαυτοῦ· ὀνόματι μὲν πατέρα καὶ υἱὸν καλούμενον κατὰ χρόνων τροπήν, ἕνα δὲ <ὄντα. καὶ> τοῦτον εἶναι τὸν φανέντα, καὶ γένεσιν ἐκ παρθένου ὑπομείναντα, καὶ ἐν ἀνθρώπο(ις)

> There is one and the same God, the Artificer and Father of all. He was pleased to appear to the righteous from the beginning, although he is invisible. 10. For when he is not seen, he is invisible, but when he is seen, he is visible.[43] He is uncontained when he does not want to be contained, but contained when contained. In this way, according to the same principle, he is indomitable and dominated, unborn and born,[44] immortal and mortal.[45]

How will such people not be exposed as the students of Herakleitos? Does not the Obscure philosopher anticipate them with his own peculiar language?[46]

Everybody knows that Noetos says that the Son himself is also the Father. 11. For he speaks as follows:

> When the Father had not been born, he was rightly called "Father." But when the Father deigned to endure birth, he was born and became his own Son—not the son of another.

In this way, then, he seems to establish a rule of one, claiming that Father and Son exist as one and the same. The Son is born not as one being from another but as himself from himself. He is nominally called "Father" and "Son" in the alternation of times, but he is one. This is the one who appeared, and underwent birth from a virgin, and lived as a human with human beings.[47] He confessed that he was Son to those who saw him on

---

Νοητὸς μὴ νοεῖ; 8.3: Νοητὸς μὴ νοῶν. Later in the sentence, our author continues to parody Herakleitos's use of ὁμολογεῖν ("agree").

42. On the following report, see Mouraviev, "Hippolyte, Héraclite et Noët," 4383–87.

43. Duncker and Schneidewin add ὅτε δὲ ὁρᾶται, ὁρατός (here: "when he is seen, he is visible") to agree with the summary in *Ref.* 10.27.2.

44. Duncker and Schneidewin add καὶ γενητός ("and born") to agree with the summary in *Ref.* 10.27.2. Cf. Ignatios, *Eph.* 7.2; Teach. Silv. (NHC VII,4) 101.35; 102.1.

45. Cf. the teaching of Kallistos below (*Ref.* 9.12.16–19); [Hipp.], *Noet.* 1, 3, 7; Epiph., *Pan.* 57.1.2, 8; 57.3.2, 9; 57.4.8; See further Osborne, *Rethinking*, 134–39; Reinhard M. Hübner, *Der Paradox Eine: Antignostischer Monarchianismus im zweiten Jahrhundert*, VCSup 50 (Leiden: Brill, 1999), 41–90.

46. Wendland conjectures ἰδίᾳ δὲ φθάσας (accepted here, apart from δέ) to replace P's διαφθάσας.

47. Cf. Bar 3:38 LXX: ὁ θεὸς ἡμῶν … ἐπὶ γῆς ὤφθη καὶ ἐν τοῖς ἀνθρώποις συνανεστράφη, quoted in [Hipp.], *Noet.* 2.2–5. See further Hermann J. Vogt, "Noet von Smyrna und

ἄνθρωπον ἀναστραφέντα· υἱὸν μὲν ἑαυτὸν τοῖς ὁρῶσιν ὁμολογοῦντα διὰ τὴν γενομένην γένεσιν, πατέρα δὲ εἶναι καὶ τοῖς χωροῦσιν (μ)ὴ ἀποκρύψαντα.

12. τοῦτον πάθει ξύλῳ προσπαγ(έ)ντα καὶ ἑαυτῷ τὸ πνεῦμα παραδόντα· ἀποθανόντα καὶ μὴ ἀποθανόντα καὶ ἑαυτὸν τῇ τρίτῃ ἡμέρᾳ ἀναστήσαντα· τὸν ἐν μνημείῳ ταφέντα καὶ λόγχῃ τρωθέντα καὶ ἥλοις καταπαγέντα. τοῦτον τὸν τῶν ὅλων θεὸν καὶ πατέρα εἶναι λέγει Κλεομένης καὶ ὁ τούτου χορός, Ἡρακλείτειον σκότος ἐπεισάγοντες πολλοῖς.

11. 1. Ταύτην τὴν αἵρεσιν ἐκράτυνε Κάλλιστος, ἀνὴρ ἐν κακίᾳ πανοῦργος καὶ ποικίλος πρὸς πλάνην, θηρώμενος τὸν τῆς ἐπισκοπῆς θρόνον. <ὃς> τὸν Ζεφυρῖνον, ἄνδρα ἰδιώτην καὶ ἀγράμματον καὶ ἄπειρον τῶν ἐκκλησιαστικῶν ὅρων—ὃν πείθων <δόμασι> καὶ ἀπαιτήσεσιν ἀπειρημέναις ἦγεν εἰς ὃ <ἐ>βούλετο, ὄντα δωρολήπτην καὶ φιλάργυρον—ἔπειθεν ἀεὶ στάσεις ἐμβάλ<λ>ειν ἀνὰ μέσον τῶν ἀδελφῶν, αὐτὸς τὰ ἀμφότερα μέρη ὕστερον «κερκώπων λόγοις» πρὸς ἑαυτοῦ φιλίαν κατασκευάζων· καὶ τοῖς μὲν ἀλήθειαν [λέγων ὅμοια] φρονοῦσι ποτὲ κατ' <ἰδίαν λέγων> τὰ ὅμοια φρονεῖν ἠπάτα <αὐτούς>, πάλιν δ' αὖ τοῖς τὰ Σαβελλίου ὁμοίως.

account of his birth in time, but he did not conceal the fact that he was Father from those who could receive him.

12. This is the one who in his Passion was fixed to a tree and committed his spirit to himself. He died and did not die, and raised himself on the third day. He was buried in a tomb, wounded by a spear, and fixed with nails. This one is the God and Father of the universe, as Kleomenes and his chorus chant. In doing so, they foist upon the masses the darkness of Herakleitos.[48]

KALLISTOS

11. 1. Kallistos validated this heresy.[49] He was a man crafty in vice and versatile in deceit, hunting the episcopal throne for his own ends. It was he who, by convincing Zephyrinos (a man uncultivated, unlettered, and inexperienced in ecclesiastical rulings) with bribes and unending solicitations, steered the greedy bribe-taker where he wanted.[50] He continually persuaded him to incite factions between the brothers. Later on, he fostered favor for himself among both parties "by the speeches of cheats."[51] By sometimes claiming in private to hold the same views as those who thought the truth, he deceived them, all the while doing likewise with those who agreed with Sabellios's teachings.[52]

Heraklit: Bemerkungen zur Darstellung ihrer Lehren durch Hippolyt," *ZAC* 6 (2002): 59–80 (68–77).

48. The one who died and did not die recalls Herakleitos's fusion of mortal and immortal (*Ref.* 9.9.1). See the comments of Heine, "Christology of Callistus," 89.

49. For our author's battle with Kallistos, see Döllinger, *Hippolytus and Callistus*, 108–82; Hamel, *Kirche bei Hippolyt*, 59–76, 113–27; Karlmann Beyschlag, "Kallist und Hippolyt," *TZ* 20 [1964]: 103–24 (106–15); J. M. Hanssens, "Hippolyte de Rome fut-il novatianiste? Essai d'une biographie," *Archivum Historiae Pontificiae* 3 (1965): 7–29; Marcel Richard, "Hippolyte de Rome (saint)," *Dictionnaire de Spiritualité* (Paris: Beauchesne, 1968), 7.1:534–36, 568–71; Brent, *Hippolytus*, 417–53; Eshleman, *Social World*, 102–12, 157–59.

50. Ironically, the apostles Peter and John are also called ἀγράμματοι … καὶ ἰδιῶται ("unlettered commoners") in Acts 4:13. Duncker and Schneidewin replace P's δόγμασι ("doctrines") with δόμασι (here: "bribes").

51. Literally, "by the words of the Kerkopes" (monkey-like rascals and thieves known from Greek mythology). The colloquial phrase had already found its way into Prov 26:22: λόγοι κερκώπων μαλακοί ("deceptive words are appeasing").

52. Miller replaces P's καθ' ἡδίαν ("according to his pleasure/whim") with κατ' ἰδίαν (here: "in private").

ὃν καὶ αὐτὸν ἐξέστησε, δυνάμενον κατορθοῦν· 2. ἐν γὰρ τῷ ὑφ' ἡμῶν παραινεῖσθαι οὐκ ἐσκληρύνετο, ἡνίκα δὲ σὺν τῷ Καλλίστῳ ἐμόναζεν, ὑπ' αὐτοῦ ἀνεσείετο πρὸς τὸ δόγμα τοῦ Κλεομένους ῥέπειν, φάσκοντος τὰ ὅμοια φρονεῖν. ὁ δὲ τότε μὲν τὴν πανουργίαν αὐτοῦ οὐκ ἐνόει, αὖθις δὲ ἔγνω, ὡς διηγήσομαι μετ' οὐ πολύ.

3. Αὐτὸν δὲ τὸν Ζεφυρῖνον παράγων ἔπειθε δημοσίᾳ λέγειν· «ἐγὼ οἶδα ἕνα θεὸν Χριστὸν Ἰησοῦν, καὶ πλὴν αὐτοῦ ἕτερον οὐδένα γενητὸν καὶ παθητόν», ποτὲ δὲ λέγειν· «οὐχ ὁ πατὴρ ἀπέθανεν, ἀλλὰ ὁ υἱός», οὕτως ἄπαυστον τὴν στάσιν ἐν τῷ λαῷ διετήρησεν.

οὗ τὰ νοήματα γνόντες ἡμεῖς οὐ συνεχωροῦμεν, ἐλέγχοντες καὶ ἀντικαθιστάμενοι ὑπὲρ τῆς ἀληθείας. ὃς εἰς ἀπόνοιαν χωρῶν διὰ τὸ πάντας αὐτοῦ τῇ ὑποκρίσει συντρέχειν, ἡμᾶς δὲ οὔ, ἀπεκάλει ἡμᾶς διθέους, ἐξεμῶν παρὰ βίαν τὸν ἐνδομυχοῦντα αὐτῷ ἰόν.

4. Τούτου τὸν βίον δοκεῖ ἡμῖν, ἀγαπητοί, ἐκθέσθαι, ἐπεὶ κατὰ τὸν αὐτὸν χρόνον ἡμῖν ἐγεγόνει, ὅπως διὰ τοῦ φανῆναι τοῦ τοιούτου τὴν ἀναστροφὴν εὐεπίγνωστος καὶ <φανερὰ> τοῖς νοῦν ἔχουσιν εὐθὺς γένηται ἡ διὰ τούτου ἐπικεχειρημένη αἵρεσις. οὗτος ἐμαρτύρησεν ἐπὶ Φουσκιανοῦ ἐπάρχου ὄντος Ῥώμης, ὁ δὲ τρόπος τῆς αὐτοῦ μαρτυρίας τοιόσδε ἦν.

12. 1. Οἰκέτης ἐτύγχανε Καρποφόρου τινός, ἀνδρὸς πιστοῦ ὄντος ἐκ τῆς Καίσαρος οἰκίας. τούτῳ ὁ Καρποφόρος, ἅτε δὴ ὡς πιστῷ, χρῆμα οὐκ ὀλίγον κατεπίστευσεν, ἐπαγγειλάμενος κέρδος προσοίσειν ἐκ πραγματείας τραπεζιτικῆς· ὃς λαβὼν τράπεζαν ἐπεχείρησεν ἐν τῇ λεγομένῃ Πισκίνῃ

It was he too who drove Sabellios away, though he could have corrected him. 2. For when I admonished Sabellios, he was not hardened. But when Sabellios spent time alone with Kallistos, he was spurred by him to incline to the dogma of Kleomenes (since Kallistos claimed to share those views). At that time, Sabellios did not realize Kallistos's dissemblance. Later, however, he realized it, as I will soon relate.[53]

3. Kallistos led Zephyrinos himself astray. He persuaded him to declare publicly: "I know one God Christ Jesus, and beside him no other who is born and subject to suffering." At other times, he persuaded him to say: "The Father did not die, but the Son." In this way he kept the discord among the people unchecked.

Knowing his thoughts, I did not give ground to him but exposed and opposed him on behalf of the truth. But he—going mad because everybody flocked to his theater performance (except my party)—denounced us as "ditheists," thus violently vomiting out the poison lurking within him.[54]

4. Therefore, beloved, I think it right to present his life, since he was our contemporary, so that through exposing the behavior of such a person, his contrived heresy might at once become well recognized and clear to people of intelligence.[55] He became a confessor when Fuscianus was prefect of Rome.[56] The mode of his confession was as follows.

THE LIFE OF KALLISTOS. 12. 1. Kallistos was a slave of a certain Karpophoros, a man of the faith who was from Caesar's household.[57] Karpophoros, considering Kallistos to be a man of faith, entrusted him with no small sum and ordered him to bring back the interest from a banking enterprise. Kallistos took the money and set up a banking table in what is called the Piscina Publica. In the course of time, not a few deposits were entrusted to

---

53. See *Ref.* 9.12.15–16. Sabellios is commonly known as a "modalist," or one who views Father and Son as two modes of the same godhead.

54. On the charge of ditheism, see *Ref.* 9.12.16 below; Tert., *Prax.* 13.1; 19.8.

55. Wendland replaces P's τεχεῖα with φανερά (here: "clear").

56. Fuscianus was prefect from 188 to 193 CE.

57. On Karpophoros, see Lampe, *Paul to Valentinus*, 335, with sources. By highlighting Kallistos's former slavery, our author could use common stereotypes of slaves (e.g., craftiness, deceit, wiliness) to good effect. See further Henneke Gülzow, *Christentum und Sklaverei in den ersten drei Jahrhunderten* (Bonn: Rudolf Habelt, 1969), 146–61; and, in general, Kyle Harper, *Slavery in the Late Roman World, AD 275–425* (Cambridge: Cambridge University Press, 2011).

πουπλικῇ. ᾧ οὐκ ὀλίγαι παραθῆκαι τῷ χρόνῳ ἐπιστεύθησαν ὑπὸ χηρῶν καὶ ἀδελφῶν προσχήματι τοῦ Καρποφόρου.

ὁ δὲ ἐξαφανίσας τὰ πάντα ἠπόρει. οὗ ταῦτα πράξαντος οὐκ ἔλιπεν ὃς ἀπαγγείλῃ τῷ Καρποφόρῳ, ὁ δὲ ἔφη ἀπαιτ<ήσ>ειν λόγους παρ᾽ αὐτοῦ. 2. ταῦτα συνιδὼν ὁ Κάλλιστος καὶ τὸν παρὰ τοῦ δεσπότου κίνδυνον ὑφορώμενος, ἀπέδρα τὴν φυγὴν κατὰ θάλασσαν ποιούμενος· ὃς εὑρὼν πλοῖον ἐν τῷ Πόρτῳ ἕτοιμον πρὸς ἀναγωγήν, ὅποι ἐτύγχανε πλέον ἀνέβ(η) πλευσόμενος.

ἀλλ᾽ οὐδὲ οὕτως λαθεῖν δεδύνηται· οὐ γὰρ ἔλιπεν ὃς ἀπαγγείλῃ τῷ Καρποφόρῳ τὸ γεγενημένον. 3. ὁ δὲ ἐπιστὰ(ς) κατὰ τὸν λιμένα ἐπειρᾶτο ἐπὶ τὸ πλοῖον ὁρμᾶν κατὰ <τὰ> μεμ(η)νυμένα· τοῦτο γὰρ ἦν ἑστὸς ἐν μέσῳ τῷ λιμένι. τοῦ δὲ πορθμέως βραδύνοντος, ἰδὼν πόρρωθεν ὁ Κάλλιστος τὸν δεσπότην, ὢν ἐν τῷ πλοίῳ καὶ γνοὺς ἑαυτὸν συνειλῆφθαι, ἠφείδησε τοῦ ζῆν καὶ ἔσχατα ταῦτα λογισάμενος ἔρριψεν ἑαυτὸν εἰς τὴν θάλασσαν. 4. οἱ δὲ ναῦται καταπηδήσαντες εἰς τὰ σκάφη ἄκοντα αὐτὸν ἀνείλοντο, τῶν δὴ ἀπὸ τῆς γῆς μεγάλα βοώντων, καὶ οὕτως τῷ δεσπότῃ παραδοθεὶς ἐπανήχθη εἰς τὴν Ῥώμην. ὃν ὁ δεσπότης εἰς πιστρῖνον κατέθετο.

5. Χρόνου δὲ διελθόντος, ὡς συμβαίνει γίνεσθαι, προσελθόντες ἀδελφοὶ παρεκάλουν τὸν Καρποφόρον, ὅπως ἐξαγάγῃ τῆς κολάσεως τὸν δραπέτην, φάσκοντες αὐτὸν ὁμολογεῖν ἔχειν παρά τισι χρῆμα ἀποκείμενον. 6. ὁ δὲ Καρποφόρος, ὡς εὐλαβής, τοῦ μὲν ἰδίου ἔλεγεν ἀφειδεῖν, τῶν δὲ παραθηκῶν φροντίζειν—πολλοὶ γὰρ αὐτῷ ἀπεκλαίοντο λέγοντες ὅτι τῷ αὐτοῦ προσχήματι ἐπίστευσαν τῷ Καλλίστῳ ἃ πεπιστεύκεισαν—καὶ πεισθεὶς ἐκέλευσεν ἐξαγαγεῖν αὐτόν.

7. ὁ δὲ μηδὲν ἔχων ἀποδιδόναι, καὶ πάλιν ἀποδιδράσκειν μὴ δυνάμενος διὰ τὸ φρουρεῖσθαι, τέχνην θανάτου ἐπενόησε καὶ σαββάτῳ, σκηψάμενος ἀπιέναι ὡς ἐπὶ χρεώστας, ὥρμησεν ἐπὶ τὴν συναγωγὴν τῶν Ἰουδαίων συνηγμένην καὶ στὰς κατεστασίαζεν αὐτῶν. οἱ δὲ καταστασιασθέντες (ὑ)π᾽ αὐτοῦ, ἐνυβρίσαντες αὐτὸν καὶ πληγὰς ἐμφορήσαντες ἔσ(υ)ρον ἐπὶ τὸν Φουσκιανόν, ἔπαρχον ὄντα τῆς πόλεως. 8. ἀπεκρίναντο δὲ τάδε· Ῥωμαῖοι συνεχώρησαν ἡμῖν τοὺς πατρῴους

him by widows and Christian brothers—since he acted as a representative of Karpophoros.[58]

But Kallistos, after losing everything, was at the end of his wits. When he did this, someone was not lacking to report it to Karpophoros. Karpophoros promised that he would demand accounts from him. 2. Kallistos, getting wind of these developments, and suspecting danger from his master, ran off—attempting to make his escape by sea.[59] He found a boat in Portus prepared for departure and embarked to sail wherever it happened to be going.

But not even by these tricks could he escape notice. Someone was not lacking to report to Karpophoros what had occurred. 3. Karpophoros, appearing suddenly at the harbor, tried to make for the ship that had been pointed out (it was docked in the middle of the harbor). When the helmsman lagged, Kallistos caught sight of his master from afar. Stuck in the boat, and knowing that he was caught, Kallistos was reckless with his life and—thinking that this was the end—threw himself into the sea. 4. But the sailors, hurtling down into their boats, pulled him up against his will, while people shouted loudly on land. Delivered in this way to his master, he was hauled back to Rome. Then his master put him in a mill.[60]

5. Time went on, and, as it happens, Christian brothers came and urged Karpophoros to release the runaway from punishment, claiming that Kallistos confessed that he had money on deposit with certain people. 6. Now Karpophoros, a God-fearing man, offered to forgo his own money and concern himself with the deposits (for many people were crying out that they had entrusted their deposits to Kallistos as a representative of Karpophoros). Consequently, Karpophoros was won over and ordered Kallistos's release.

7. But Kallistos, having nothing to return, and not able to run off again because he was guarded, contrived a scheme of suicide. On a Saturday morning—alleging that he was going off to those who owed him money—he sped to the fully convened Jewish synagogue, stood up, and threw them into an uproar. Shouting amongst themselves, they reviled him, inflicted blows on him, and dragged him to Fuscianus, prefect of the city. 8. They made the following formal accusation: "The Romans allowed us to read

58. See further Lampe, *Paul to Valentinus*, 42.

59. On the disgrace of running away, note Konrad Graf Preysing, "Der Leserkreis der Philosophumena Hippolyts," *ZKT* 38 (1914): 421–45 (437–41).

60. For the horrors of the *pistrinum*, or mill, see Apuleius, *Metam.* 9.11–13.

νόμους δημοσίᾳ ἀναγινώσκειν, οὗτος δὲ ἐπεισελθὼν ἐκώλυε καταστασιάζων ἡμῶν, φάσκων εἶναι Χριστιανός.

τοῦ δὲ Φο<υ>σκιανοῦ πρὸ βήματος τυγχάνοντος καὶ τοῖς ὑπὸ Ἰουδαίων λεγομένοις κατὰ τοῦ Καλλίστου ἀγανακτοῦντος, οὐκ ἔλιπεν ὁ ἀπαγγείλας τῷ Καρποφόρῳ τὰ πρασσόμενα. 9. ὁ δὲ σπεύσας ἐπὶ τὸ βῆμα τοῦ ἐπάρχου ἐβόα· δέομαι, κύριε Φουσκιανέ, μὴ σ<ὺ> αὐτῷ πίστευε· οὐ γάρ ἐστι Χριστιανός, ἀφορμὴν δὲ ζητεῖ θανάτου χρήματά μου πολλὰ ἀφανίσας, ὡς ἀποδείξω.

τῶν δὲ Ἰουδαίων ὑποβολὴν τοῦτο νομισάντων, ὡς ζητοῦντος τοῦ Καρποφόρου ταύτῃ τῇ προφάσει ἐξελέσθαι αὐτόν, μᾶλλον ἐπιφθόνως κατεβόων τοῦ ἐπάρχου. ὁ δὲ κινηθεὶς ὑπ᾽ αὐτῶν, μαστιγώσας αὐτὸν ἔδωκεν εἰς μέταλλον Σαρδονίας.

10. Μετὰ χρόνον δέ, ἑτέρων ἐκεῖ ὄντων μαρτύρων, θελήσασα ἡ Μαρκία, οὖσα φιλόθεος παλ<λ>ακὴ Κομόδου, ἔργον τι ἀγαθὸν ἐργάσασθαι, προσκαλεσαμένη τὸν μακάριον Οὐΐκτορα, ὄντα ἐπίσκοπον τῆς ἐκκλησίας κατ᾽ ἐκεῖνο καιροῦ, ἐπηρώτα τίνες εἶεν ἐν Σαρδονίᾳ μάρτυρες· ὁ δὲ πάντων ἀναδοὺς τὰ ὀνόματα τὸ τοῦ Καλλίστου οὐκ ἔδωκεν, εἰδὼς τὰ <τε>τολμημένα παρ᾽ αὐτοῦ.

11. τυχοῦσα οὖν τῆς ἀξιώσεως ἡ Μαρκία παρὰ τοῦ Κομόδου, δίδωσι τὴν ἀπολύσιμον ἐπιστολὴν Ὑακίνθῳ τινί, σπάδοντι πρεσβυτέρῳ· ὃς λαβὼν διέπλευσεν εἰς τὴν Σαρδονίαν καὶ ἀποδοὺς τῷ κατ᾽ ἐκεῖνο καιροῦ τῆς χώρας ἐπιτροπεύοντι ἀπέλυσε τοὺς μάρτυρας πλὴν τοῦ Καλλίστου. 12. ὁ δὲ γονυπετῶν καὶ δακρύων ἱκέτευε καὶ αὐτὸς τυχεῖν ἀπολύσεως. δυσωπηθεὶς οὖν ὁ Ὑάκινθος ἀξιοῖ τὸν ἐπίτροπον, φάσκων θρέψας εἶναι Μαρκίας <καὶ> τασσόμεν(ο)ς αὐτῷ τὸ ἀκίνδυνον· ὁ δὲ πεισ(θ)εὶς ἀπέλυσε καὶ τὸν Κάλλιστον.

13. οὗ παραγενομένου ὁ Οὐΐκτωρ πάνυ ἤχθετο ἐπὶ τῷ γεγονότι, ἀλλ᾽ ἐπεὶ εὔσπλαγχνος ἦν, ἡσύχαζε· φυλασσόμενος δὲ τὸν ὑπὸ πολλῶν ὄνειδον—οὐ γὰρ ἦν μακρὰν τὰ ὑπ᾽ αὐτοῦ τετολμημένα—, ἔτι δὲ καὶ τοῦ Καρποφόρου ἀντιπίπ<τ>(ο)ντος, πέμπει αὐτὸν καταμένειν ἐν Ἀνθείῳ, ὁρίσας αὐτῷ μηνιαῖόν τι εἰς τροφάς.

our ancestral laws publicly, but this man, sneaking in, prevented us by creating an uproar—all the while claiming to be a Christian!"

While Fuscianus stood before the judgment seat—already irritated by the Jews' accusations against Kallistos—someone was not lacking to announce the proceedings to Karpophoros. 9. Karpophoros, rushing to the prefect's tribunal, cried out: "I beg you, lord Fuscianus, do not believe him! He is not a Christian but seeks a pretext for death after losing a great sum of my money—as I will prove."

Now the Jews, suspecting a stratagem—as if Karpophoros were seeking by this pretext to deliver him—still more invidiously cried out before the prefect. Agitated by them, Fuscianus had Kallistos scourged and delivered him to a mine on Sardinia.[61]

10. There were other confessors there. And after some time, Marcia, Commodus's concubine—a woman devoted to God—wanted to do some good work.[62] After summoning the blessed Victor, who was bishop of the church at that time, she asked him about the confessors in Sardinia.[63] He imparted the names of all except Kallistos—knowing the things that he had ventured.

11. When Marcia succeeded in her petition before Commodus, he gave a letter for their release to a certain Hyakinthos, an old eunuch.[64] Taking the letter, Hyakinthos sailed to Sardinia; and, after presenting it to the procurator at that time, he freed all the confessors except Kallistos. 12. But Kallistos, falling on his knees and weeping, begged that he too might have his freedom. Hyakinthos, embarrassed, asked the governor to release him too, claiming that he had reared Marcia and would take the danger upon himself. The procurator was persuaded and released Kallistos as well.

13. When Kallistos arrived, Victor was greatly irked by what had happened. Yet since he was tenderhearted, he kept his peace. He nevertheless took precautions against the censure of many (for what Kallistos had ventured was not long past, and Karpophoros was still attacking him) by sending him to remain in Antium, assigning him a monthly stipend for provisions.[65]

61. The trial of Kallistos is studied by Gülzow, *Christentum und Sklaverei*, 157–56.

62. For Marcia, see Dio Cassius, *Hist. Rom.* 72.4.6–7. Lampe believes that she was not a Christian (φιλόθεος does not amount to πιστός) (*Paul to Valentinus*, 336 n. 15).

63. Victor was bishop of Rome from approximately 189 to 198 CE. See further Eusebios, *Hist. eccl.* 5.22; 5.28.3.

64. For Hyakinthos, see Lampe, *Paul to Valentinus*, 336.

65. See further Gülzow, *Christentum und Sklaverei*, 159–62.

14. Μεθʼ οὗ κοίμησιν Ζεφυρῖνος, σ(υ)ναράμεν(ον) αὐτὸν σχὼν πρὸς τὴν κατάστασιν τοῦ κλήρου, ἐτίμησε τῷ ἰδίῳ κακῷ, καὶ τούτου <χάριν> μεταγαγὼν ἀπὸ τοῦ Ἀνθείου εἰς τὸ κοιμητήριον κατέστησεν. ᾧ ἀεὶ συνὼν καί, καθὼς φθάσας προεῖπον, ὑποκρίσει αὐτὸν θεραπεύων ἐξηφάνισε, μήτε κρῖναι τὰ λεγόμενα δυνάμενον, μήτε νοοῦντα τὴν τοῦ Καλλίστου ἐπιβουλήν, πάντα αὐτῷ πρὸς ἃ ἥδετο ὁμιλοῦντος.

15. Οὗτο<ς> μετὰ τὴν τοῦ Ζεφυρίνου τελευτὴν νομίζων τετυχηκέναι οὗ ἐθηρᾶτο, τὸν Σαβέλλιον ἀπέωσεν ὡς μὴ φρονοῦντα ὀρθῶς, δεδοικὼς ἐμὲ καὶ νομίζων οὕτω δύνασθαι ἀποτρίψασθαι τὴν πρὸς τὰς ἐκκλησίας κατηγορίαν ὡς [μὴ] ἀλλοτρίως φρονοῦν<τος>.

ἦν οὖν γόης καὶ πανοῦργος καὶ ἐπὶ χρόνον συνήρπασε πολλούς. 16. ἔχων δὲ καὶ τὸν ἰὸν ἐγκείμενον ἐν τῇ καρδίᾳ καὶ εὐθέως μηδὲν φρονῶν, ἅμα δὲ καὶ αἰδούμενος τὰ ἀληθῆ λέγειν, διὰ τὸ δημοσίᾳ ἡμῖν ὀνειδίζοντα εἰπεῖν· «δίθεοί ἐστε», ἀλλὰ καὶ διὰ τὸ ὑπὸ τοῦ Σαβελλίου συχνῶς κατηγορεῖσθαι ὡς παραβάντα τὴν πρώτην πίστιν, ἐφεῦρεν αἵρεσιν τοιάνδε.

λέγων τὸν Λόγον αὐτὸν εἶναι υἱόν, αὐτὸν καὶ πατέρα, ὀνόματι μὲν καλούμενον, ἓν δὲ ὄν, τὸ πνεῦμα ἀδιαίρετον· 17. οὐ ἄλ<λ>ο εἶναι πατέρα, ἄλλο

14. After Victor was laid to rest, Zephyrinos—supported by Kallistos in his appointment to office—honored him for his own vice.[66] It was for this reason that Zephyrinos transferred him from Antium and appointed him over the cemetery.[67] Kallistos was always with him and, as I already said, destroyed Zephyrinos by playing the flatterer. Zephyrinos, who was neither able to judge Kallistos's remarks nor understand his plot, made him his partner in everything that he decided.

15. Kallistos, after Zephyrinos's death, supposed that he attained his quarry.[68] He expelled Sabellios as unorthodox since he feared me and supposed in this way to be able to expunge the accusation against his churches—namely, that he thought in a way foreign and hostile to the faith.[69]

In conclusion, Kallistos was a charlatan and a conman, and over time preyed upon many. 16. He had poison embedded in his heart and believed nothing orthodox. At the same time, he was ashamed to speak the truth, since he had publicly reviled us: "You are ditheists!"[70] For these reasons—and still more because he was constantly accused by Sabellios as a transgressor of the pristine faith—he invented the following heresy.[71]

THE DOCTRINE OF KALLISTOS. He claimed that the Word himself is nominally Son as well as Father. In reality, however, the Word is one, the undivided Spirit.[72] 17. There is not one thing that is Father and another

---

66. Zephyrinos was bishop of Rome from approximately 198 to 217 CE. Cf. *Ref.* 9.7.1–2; 9.11.1, 3; Eusebios, *Hist. eccl.* 5.28.7; 6.14.10; 6.21.1.

67. This famous cemetery on the Via Appia still bears the name of Kallistos (the Catacombs of St. Callistus). See further Gülzow, *Christentum und Sklaverei*, 164–68; Lampe, *Paul to Valentinus*, 25–28.

68. I.e., the episcopacy. Kallistos was bishop from 217 to 222 CE. Cf. *Ref.* 9.7.2–3; 10.27.3–4; Eusebios, *Hist. eccl.* 6.21.2.

69. On Sabellios, see *Ref.* 9.11.1–2; Epiph., *Pan.* 62.1.1–2.3; Filastrius, *Haer.* 54; Theodoret, *Haer. fab.* 2.9 (PG 83:396c).

70. Cf. *Ref.* 9.11.3 above; Tert., *Prax.* 13.1; 19.8. See further Döllinger, *Hippolytus and Callistus*, 210–11; Konrad Graf Preysing, "'Δίθεοί ἐστε': (Hippolyt, Philos. IX 12,16)," *ZKT* 50 (1926): 604–8; Brent, *Hippolytus*, 427–32.

71. For Kallistos's duplicity with Sabellios, see *Ref.* 9.11.1–2 above. See further Heine, "Christology of Callistus," 90–91.

72. Cf. the account of Kallistos's doctrine in *Ref.* 10.27.3–4; Epiph., *Pan.* 62.1.4. See further Döllinger, *Hippolytus and Callistus*, 183–227; Adhémar D'Alès, *La théologie de saint Hippolyte* (Paris: Beauchesne, 1906), 8–34; Simon Gerber, "Calixt von Rome und der monarchianische Streit," *ZAC* 5 (2001): 213–39. Heine argues that our author's framing of the issue in terms of the Word misrepresents Kallistos's position. Kallistos does not need the Word to identify Father and Son ("Christology of Callistus," 63–64).

δὲ υἱόν, ἓν δὲ καὶ τὸ αὐτὸ ὑπάρχειν. καὶ τὰ πάντα γέμειν τοῦ θείου πνεύματος, τά τε ἄνω καὶ <τὰ> κάτω. καὶ εἶναι τὸ ἐν τῇ παρθένῳ σαρκωθὲν πνεῦμα οὐχ ἕτερον παρὰ τὸν πατέρα, ἀλλὰ ἓν καὶ τὸ αὐτό. καὶ τοῦτο εἶναι τὸ εἰρημένον· «οὐ πιστεύεις ὅτι ἐγὼ ἐν τῷ πατρὶ καὶ ὁ πατὴρ ἐν ἐμοί;» 18. τὸ μὲν γὰρ βλεπόμενον, ὅπερ ἐστὶν ἄνθρωπος, τοῦτο εἶναι τὸν υἱόν, τ(ὸ) δὲ ἐν τῷ υἱῷ χωρηθὲν πνεῦμα, τοῦτ<ο> εἶναι τὸν πατέρα.

> οὐ γάρ, φησίν, ἐρῶ δύο θεούς, πατέρα καὶ υἱόν, ἀλλ' ἕνα· ὁ γὰρ ἐν αὐτῷ γενόμενος πατήρ, προσλαβόμενος τὴν σάρκα ἐθεοποίησεν ἑνώσας ἑαυτῷ καὶ ἐποίησεν ἕν, ὡς καλεῖσθαι πατέρα καὶ υἱὸν ἕνα θεόν. καὶ τοῦτο, ἓν ὂν πρόσωπον, μὴ δύνασθαι εἶν(αι) δύο, καὶ οὕτως τὸν πατέρα συμπεπονθέναι τῷ υἱῷ.

19. οὐ γὰρ θέλει λέγειν τὸν πατέ(ρα) πεπονθέναι καὶ ἓν εἶναι πρόσωπον, <οὕτως νομίζων> ἐκφυγεῖν τὴν εἰς τὸν πατέρα βλασφημίαν ὁ ἀνόητος καὶ ποικίλος· ὃ<ς> ἄνω κάτω σχεδιάζων βλασφημίας, ἵνα μόνον κατὰ τὴν ἀλήθειαν λέγειν δοκῇ, ποτὲ μὲν εἰς τὸ Σαβελλίου δόγμα ἐμπίπτων, ποτὲ δὲ εἰς τὸ Θεοδότου οὐκ αἰδεῖται.

that is Son; but they exist as one and the same. Everything is full of the divine Spirit, both things above and things below.[73] Moreover, the Spirit that was made flesh within the virgin is not different from the Father but one and the same.[74] This is what the verse means: "Do you not believe that I am in the Father and the Father in me?"[75] 18. What is visible, the human being, is the Son; but the Spirit contained in the Son is the Father. To quote him:

> I will not speak of two gods—Father and Son—but one. For the Father, who was in him, having assumed flesh, deified it and made it one with himself. Consequently, Father and Son are called one God. Thus he (being one person)[76] cannot be two. In this sense, the Father suffered with the Son.[77]

19. This mindless changeling does not want to say that the Father suffered and that there is one person—supposing in this way he escapes blasphemy against the Father.[78] Improvising blasphemies now here, now there, Kallistos only appears to speak in accordance with truth.[79] He is not ashamed to sometimes stumble into Sabellios's teaching, while at other times to climb in bed with Theodotos![80]

---

73. It was not uncommon for Christian intellectuals of the time to think of God Stoically as a pneumatic substance permeating the universe. Cf. Ignatios, *Magn.* 14; Ps.-Clem. Hom. 6.1; Augustine, *Conf.* 7.1.2.

74. Cf. Clem. Alex., *Paed.* 1.6.43.3 (*πνεῦμα σαρκούμενον* ["spirit made flesh"]).

75. John 14:10; cf. 10:30, 38; 17:22–23; [Hipp.], *Noet.* 7; Tert., *Prax.* 20, 27, 29; Epiph., *Pan.* 57.4.8; 62.2.3; 62.7.7.

76. Heine, following Döllinger, *Hippolytus and Callistus*, 216, argues that *ἓν ὂν πρόσωπον*, "being one person," is a polemical interjection of our author ("Christology of Callistus," 72–74). Our author's own view is that there are two persons (cf. [Hipp.], *Noet.* 7.1; 14.2). See further Mark DelCogliano, "The Interpretation of John 10:30 in the Third Century: Antimonarchian Polemics and the Rise of Grammatical Reading Techniques," *JTI* 6 (2012): 117–38 (123–24).

77. Yet Kallistos denies the suffering (*πεπονθέναι*) of the Father (*Ref.* 9.12.19). Heine argues that the modalist use of *συμπεπονθέναι* was not in the usual Christian sense of "to suffer/die with" but in the Stoic sense of "to interact with" ("Christology of Callistus," 74–78). Our author, if he knew this distinct use of the term, capitalized on its ambiguity.

78. Marcovich adds *οὕτως νομίζων* (here: "supposing in this way"). Cf. Tert., *Prax.* 29.

79. For Kallistos as improvising sophist, see Secord, "Medicine and Sophistry," 217–21.

80. Earlier our author wrote that Kallistos mixed the teaching of *Kleomenes* and

20. Τοιαῦτα ὁ γόης τολμήσας συνεστήσατο διδασκαλεῖον, κατὰ τῆς ἐκκλησίας οὕτως διδάξας· καὶ πρῶτος τὰ<ς> πρὸς τὰς ἡδονὰς τοῖς ἀνθρώποις συγχωρεῖν ἐπενόησε, λέγων πᾶσιν ὑπ' αὐτῷ ἀφίεσθαι ἁμαρτίας. ὁ γὰρ παρ' ἑτέρῳ τινὶ συναγόμενος καὶ λεγόμενος Χριστιανός, εἴ τι ἂν ἁμάρτῃ, φησίν, οὐ λογίζεται αὐτῷ ἡ ἁμαρτία, εἰ προσδράμοι τῇ τοῦ Καλλίστου σχολῇ. 21. οὗ τῷ ὅρῳ ἀρεσκόμενοι πολλοὶ συνείδησιν πεπληγότες, ἅμα τε καὶ <οἱ> ὑπὸ πολλῶν αἱρέσεων ἀποβληθέντες, τινὲς δὲ καὶ ἐπὶ καταγνώσει ἔκβλητοι τῆς ἐκκλησίας ὑφ' ἡμῶν γενόμενοι, προσχωρήσαντες αὐτῷ ἐπλήθυναν τὸ διδασκαλεῖον αὐτοῦ.

Οὗτος ἐδογμάτισεν ὅπως, εἰ ἐπίσκοπ(ο)ς ἁμάρτοι τι, εἰ καὶ πρὸς θάνατον, μὴ δέῃ κατατίθεσθαι. 22. ἐπὶ τούτου ἤρξαντο ἐπίσκοποι καὶ πρεσβύτεροι καὶ διάκονοι δίγαμοι καὶ τρίγαμοι καθίστασθαι εἰς κλήρους. εἰ δὲ καί τις ἐν κλήρῳ ὢν γαμοίη, μένειν τὸν τοιοῦτον ἐν τῷ κλήρῳ ὡς μὴ ἡμαρτηκότα, ἐπὶ τ(ού)τῳ φάσκων εἰρῆσθαι τὸ ὑπὸ τοῦ ἀποστόλου ῥηθέν· «σὺ τίς εἶ ὁ κρίνων ἀλλότριον οἰκέτην;»

ἀλλὰ καὶ παραβολὴν τῶν ζιζανίων πρὸς τοῦτο ἔφη <λε>λέχθαι· «ἄφετε τὰ ζιζάνια συναύξειν τῷ σίτῳ», τουτέστιν ἐν τῇ ἐκκλησίᾳ τοὺς ἁμαρτάνοντας. 23. ἀλλὰ καὶ τὴν κιβωτὸν τοῦ Νῶε εἰς ὁμοίωμα ἐ(κ)κλησίας ἔφη γεγονέναι,

THE CANONS OF KALLISTOS. 20. Thus the charlatan, having ventured such things, founded a school and in this way taught in opposition to the church.[81] He first hatched a plan to permit human pleasures.[82] He proclaimed to all those under his authority that their sins were forgiven.[83] He claimed that a so-called Christian who is pastored by another, if he sins in any way, the sin is not counted against him if he runs to the school of Kallistos. 21. Many of those who had their conscience stung by guilt, along with those expelled by many Christian sects, were pleased with Kallistos's ruling.[84] Certain others whom I, in condemnation, expelled from the church joined Kallistos and filled the ranks of his school.

Kallistos decreed that if a bishop sins in any respect—even a mortal sin—he need not be deposed. 22. Due to this, there began to be bishops and presbyters and deacons appointed among the clergy who were married two or three times. And if someone was married while a member of the clergy, such a miscreant would remain in the clergy as if not having sinned. Kallistos claimed that the word of the apostle was meant for this case: "Who are you to judge another person's slave?"[85]

Moreover, the parable of the tares, he claimed, had been spoken in view of this situation. "Let the tares grow together with the wheat"—that is, let the sinners grow in the church.[86] 23. Still more, he said that Noah's ark—in which there were dogs, wolves, crows, everything clean

---

Theodotos (*Ref.* 9.3). The connection with Theodotos (cf. *Ref.* 10.27.4) may be traced to the deification of Jesus's flesh (9.12.18, see further Heine, "Christology of Callistus," 70–71). But this deification appears to have occurred at Jesus's conception/birth.

81. On the term διδασκαλεῖον ("school"), see Brent, *Hippolytus*, 421–23. "The church" may be a wholly ideal entity or strictly identified with our author's community—or a mix of both.

82. On Kallistos's supposed moral laxity, see D'Alès, *Théologie*, 35–58; idem, *L'Édit de Calliste: Études sur les origines de la penitence chrétiennes*, 2nd ed. (Paris: Beauchesne, 1914), 217–27.

83. Bishop Zephyrinos had, according to Döllinger, already offered forgiveness to adulterers. Kallistos's offer of forgiveness to all was a logical consequence (*Hippolytus and Callistus*, 116–22). On a similar ruling (called an "edict") in Tertullian, see Brent, *Hippolytus*, 503–35.

84. On those expelled, see Brent, *Hippolytus*, 418. "Ruling" here translates ὅρος. Konrad Graf Preysing understood ὅρος to refer to "a formal decree" (*ein förmlicher Erlaß*) ("Existenz und Inhalt des Bußediktes Kallists," *ZKT* 43 [1919]: 358–62).

85. Rom 14:4; cf. Tert., *Pud.* 2.2. On clerical remarriage, see Brent, *Hippolytus*, 518–20.

86. See Matt 13:29–30.

ἐν ᾗ καὶ κύνες καὶ λύκοι καὶ κόρα(κ)ες (καὶ) πάντα τὰ καθαρὰ καὶ ἀκάθαρτα, οὕτω φάσκων δεῖν εἶναι ἐν ἐκκλησίᾳ. ὁμοίως καὶ ὅσα πρὸς τοῦτο δυνατὸς ἦν συνάγειν, οὕτως ἡρμήνευσεν.

Οὗ οἱ ἀκροαταὶ ἡσθέντες τοῖς δόγμα<σι> διαμένουσιν ἐμπαίζοντες ἑαυτοῖς τε καὶ πολλοῖς. 24. ὧν τῷ διδασκαλείῳ συρρέουσιν ὄχλοι· διὸ καὶ πληθύνονται, γαυριώμενοι ἐπὶ ὄχλοις διὰ τὰς ἡδονάς, ἃς οὐ συνεχώρησεν ὁ Χριστός. οὗ καταφρονήσαντες οὐδέν<α> ἁμαρτεῖν κωλύουσι, φάσκοντες αὐτὸν ἀφιέναι τοῖς εὐδοκοῦσι.

καὶ γὰρ καὶ γυναιξὶν ἐπέτρεψεν, εἰ ἄνανδροι εἶεν καὶ ἡλικίᾳ γε [τε] <ἐκ>καίο<ι>ντο, <αἱ> ἐν ἀξίᾳ, εἰ <τὴν> ἑαυτῶν ἀξίαν [ἣν] μὴ βούλοιντο καθαιρεῖν διὰ τοῦ νομίμως γαμηθῆναι, ἔχει<ν> ἕνα, ὃν ἂν αἱρήσωνται, σύγκοιτον, εἴτε οἰκέτην εἴτε ἐλεύθερον, καὶ τοῦτον κρίνειν ἀντὶ ἀνδρὸς <τὴν> μὴ νόμῳ γεγαμημένην.

25. ἔνθεν ἤρξα<ν>το ἐπιχειρεῖν πισταὶ λεγόμεναι ἀτοκίοις φαρμάκοις καὶ <τῷ> περιδεσμεῖσθαι πρὸς τὸ τὰ συλλαμβανόμενα καταβάλλειν, διὰ τὸ μήτε ἐκ δούλου βούλεσθαι ἔχειν τέκνον, μήτε ἐξ εὐτελοῦς, διὰ τὴν <εὐγένειαν> καὶ ὑπέρογκον οὐσίαν. ὁρᾶτε εἰς ὅσην ἀσέβειαν ἐχώρησεν ὁ ἄνομος, μοιχείαν καὶ φόνον ἐν τῷ αὐτῷ διδάσκων. καὶ ἐπὶ τούτοις τοῖς τολμήμασιν ἑαυτοὺς οἱ ἀπηρυθριασμένοι καθολικὴν ἐκκλησίαν ἀποκαλεῖν ἐπιχειροῦσι, καί τινες νομίζοντες εὖ πράττειν συντρέχουσιν αὐτοῖς. 26. ἐπὶ τούτου πρώτως τετόλ(μ)ηται αὐτοῖς δεύτερον βάπτισμα.

and unclean—is a symbol of the church. By this means, he claimed that it is necessary for "clean and unclean" to be in the church.[87] By the same line of reasoning, whatever passages he could collect for this purpose, he interpreted accordingly.

His listeners, delighted with his doctrines, continue to delude both themselves and many others. 24. The rabble flow into their school, and so they are multiplied, gleefully boasting about the great number of their rabble because of the pleasures that Christ did not permit. Despising Christ, they prevent no one from sinning, claiming that he forgives those who take their pleasure in such things.

In fact, Kallistos even allowed single, nubile, high-status women who burned with lust to select a partner to sleep with—whether slave or free—if they did not want to diminish their rank through lawful marriage. He permitted these women to judge their partner a substitute husband, though they had not been married by law.[88]

25. From that time, women who were so-called believers began to try contraceptive drugs and the practice of tightly binding themselves to abort the fetus since they did not want to have a child from a slave or from someone lowborn due to their noble birth and massive property.[89] Behold the extent of impiety into which this criminal advanced—teaching adultery and murder in the same breath![90] And in the face of these audacities they do not blush when they attempt to call themselves the "catholic" church! Some suppose that they do a good deed by running to join them. 26. During Kallistos's time, they also first dared to perform a second baptism.[91]

87. For Noah's ark, see Gen 6:19–20; 7:2–3; cf. Tert., *Idol.* 24.4; Augustine, *Faust.* 12.15 (CSEL 25.1:345). See further Carlo Carletti, "L'arca di Noè: Ovvero la Chiesa di Callisto e l'uniformità della 'morte scritta,'" *Antiquité tardive* 9 (2001): 97–102.

88. In Acts Pet. 30, Roman Christians show disgust at a woman who has sex with her slave "boys" (*NTApoc* 2:311). Döllinger argued that Kallistos was trying to prevent incontinence among rich Christian women. It was better to marry a believer of low rank than a pagan of equal rank. Such women marrying slaves is extraordinary. The fact that Kallistos was a former slave likely influenced the decision (*Hippolytus and Callistus*, 150–51, 164–70, 171–75). See further Gülzow, *Christentum und Sklaverei*, 168–72.

89. On contraceptive drugs, see Pliny, *Nat.* 20.21; 27.5, 9. Marcovich emends συγγένειαν ("kinship") to εὐγένειαν ("noble birth").

90. On the charges of adultery, see Preysing, "Leserkreis," 421–37; idem, "Bußediktes," 358–62; Beyschlag, "Kallist und Hippolyt," 115–23. For the charge of murder, see Brent, *Hippolytus*, 520–23.

91. Our author does not charge Kallistos with introducing a second baptism. It

ταῦτα μὲν οὖν ὁ θαυμασιώτατος Κάλλιστος συνεστήσατο· οὗ διαμένει τὸ δι(δ)ασκαλεῖον, φυλάσσον τὰ ἔθη καὶ τὴν παράδοσιν, μὴ διακρῖνον τίσιν (δ)εῖ κοινωνεῖν, πᾶσιν ἀκρίτως προσφέρον τὴν κοινωνίαν. ἀφ' οὗ (καὶ) τὴν τοῦ ὀνόματος μετέσχον ἐπίκλησιν, <ὡς> καλεῖσθαι διὰ τὸν πρωτοστατήσαν<τα> τῶν τοι(ού)των ἔργων Κάλλιστον Καλλιστιανοί.

13. 1. Τούτου κατὰ πάντα τὸν κόσμον διηχηθείσης τῆς διδασκαλίας, ἐνιδὼν τὴν πραγματείαν ἀνὴρ δόλιος καὶ ἀπονοίας γέμων, Ἀλκιβιάδης τις καλούμενος, οἰκῶν ἐν Ἀπαμείᾳ τῆς Συρίας, γοργότερον ἑαυτὸν καὶ εὐφυέστερον ἐν κυβείαις κρίνας τοῦ Καλλίστου, ἐπῆλθε τῇ Ῥώμῃ φέρων βίβλον τινά, φάσκων ταύτην ἀπὸ Σηρῶν τῆς Παρθίας παρειληφέναι τινὰ ἄνδρα δίκαιον Ἠλχασαΐ· 2. ἣν

These are the institutions of the most amazing Kallistos! His school remains to this day, preserving their own customs and tradition, making no distinction as to with whom they should have communion, but offering communion to all people without judgment. From Kallistos they take their name. They are called "Kallistians," since Kallistos first established their vile practices.

ALKIBIADES (ELCHASAITES)

13. 1. When the teaching of Kallistos resounded the world over, a man by the name of Alkibiades (who was deceitful and stark raving mad) observed this affair while living in Apamea of Syria.[92] He, judging himself more monstrous and more naturally suited for scams than Kallistos, came to Rome bringing a certain book.[93] He claimed that a certain righteous man named Elchasai had received it from the Seres of Parthia.[94] 2. Elchasai

---

only occurred in Kallistos's time (ἐπὶ τούτου) (Döllinger, *Hippolytus and Callistus*, 175–76). According to D'Alès, the second baptism must simply be a reference to lenient penitential practices (*Théologie*, 59–63). Cirillo opines that there was no official second baptism; the charge is invented by our author (*Elchasai*, 16–17).

92. In this section, Alkibiades is portrayed as the main opponent, although he disappears in the summary in *Ref.* 10.29. Alkibiades belonged to a broader group commonly referred to as "Elchasaites." For an introduction to this group, see Luttikhuizen, *Revelation*, 210–26; idem, "Elchasaites and Their Book," in Marjanen and Luomanen, *Companion*, 335–64; Simon Claude Mimouni, "Les elkasaïtes: États des questions et des recherches," in Tomson and Lambers-Petry, *Image of the Judaeo-Christians*, 209–29. For our author's treatment of the "Elchasaites," see J. Thomas, *Le movement baptiste en Palestine et Syrie (150 av. J.-C.–300 ap. J.-C.)* (Gembloux: J. Duculot, 1935), 140–56; Koschorke, *Ketzerbekämpfung*, 74–87; Simon Claude Mimouni, *Le judéo-christianisme ancien: Essays historiques* (Paris: Cerf, 1998), 287–307.

93. On the (fabricated) relationship between Kallistos and Alkibiades, see Carsten Colpe, "Die 'elkesaitische Unternehmung' in Rom, ihre Hintergründe und ihre mögliche Einwirkung auf das Häreseienbild des Bischofs Hippolyt," in *Chartulae: Festschrift für Wolfgang Speyer*, JAC Ergänzungsband 28 (Münster: Aschendorff, 1998), 57–69 (61–64).

94. Note that Elchasai is not the writer of the book but one of its tradents. On the name Elchasai, see Luttikhuizen, *Revelation*, 179–88. On the nature of the book itself, see ibid., 87–88, 189–206; Luigi Cirillo, "L'apocalypse d'Elkhasaï: Son rôle et son importance pour l'histoire du judaïsme," *Apocrypha* 1 (1990): 167–80 (170–76); Jones, *Pseudoclementina*, 359–431. Jones presents an order of the book's fragments quite different from the reconstruction of Johannes Irmscher, "The Book of Elchasai," in *NTApoc* 2:685–90. It is disputed whether, in the excerpts that follow, our author is quoting from Alkibiades (Luttikhuizen, *Revelation*, 225–26) or from the book

παρέδωκέν τινι λεγομένῳ Σοβιαΐ, χρηματισθεῖσαν ὑπὸ ἀγγέλου. οὗ τὸ ὕψος σχοίνων κδʹ—ὃ γίνεται μίλια ϙςʹ—τὸ δὲ πλάτος αὐτοῦ σχοίνων δʹ, καὶ ἀπὸ ὤμου εἰς ὦμον σχοίνων ςʹ. τὰ δὲ ἴχνη τῶν ποδῶν αὐτοῦ ἐπὶ μῆκος σχοίνων γʹ ἡμίσους—ὃ γίνεται μίλια δεκατέσσαρα—τὸ δὲ πλάτος σχοίνου ἑνὸς ἡμίσους, τὸ δὲ ὕψος ἡμισχοίνου. 3. εἶναι δὲ σὺν αὐτῷ καὶ θήλειαν, ἧς τὰ μέτρα κατὰ τ(ὰ) προειρημένα εἶναι λέγει· καὶ τὸν μὲν ἄρσενα υἱὸν εἶναι τοῦ θεοῦ, τὴν δὲ θήλειαν καλεῖσθαι ἅγιον πνεῦμα.

4. Ταῦτα τερατολογῶν νομίζει ταράσσειν τοὺς μωροὺς λέγων τοῦτον εὐηγγελίσθαι τοῖς ἀνθρώποις καινὴν ἄφεσιν ἁμαρτιῶν ἔτει Τραϊανοῦ βασιλείας τρίτῳ. καὶ βάπτισμα ὁρίζει—ὃ καὶ αὐτὸ διηγήσομαι—φάσκων τοὺς ἐν πάσῃ

handed it on to a man called Sobiai,[95]as if it were an oracle from an angel[96] who was twenty-four reeds high (or ninety-six miles),[97] four reeds wide, and six reeds from shoulder to shoulder. His footprints were three and a half reeds in length (or fourteen miles), one and a half reeds wide, and half a reed high. 3. There was a female with him too, whose measurements, he says, accorded with the preceding. Now the male is the son of God, whereas the female is called "Holy Spirit."[98]

4. Telling these fantastical tales, Alkibiades thought that he could whip up fools by saying that this angel preached a new forgiveness of sins as good news to human beings in the third year of Trajan's regency.[99] Moreover, he ordains a baptism[100] (which I will also relate), claiming that those

---

itself. Jones argues that, since our author views the Book of Elchasai as a forgery (*Ref.* 10.29.1), he cites it "as if Alkibiades were speaking" (Jones, *Pseudoclementina*, 380). Seres (Σηρῶν) could refer to a region or to an eastern tribe that faithfully preserved primordial knowledge (Luttikhuizen, *Revelation*, 60; cf. Ps.-Clem. Rec. 8.48 [Rehm]). See further G. J. Reinink, "Das Land 'Seiris' (Šir) und das Volk der Serer in jüdischen und christlichen Traditionen," *JSJ* 6 (1975): 72–85.

95. Some scholars view the name "Sobiai" as a transcription of an Aramaic participle meaning "to wash/baptize." If so, Sobiai should be understood as "the baptists/baptizers." See further Luttikhuizen, *Revelation*, 61.

96. Cf. Origen in Eusebios, *Hist. eccl.* 6.38 (the book fell from heaven). According to Epiph., *Pan.* 19.1.4, Elchasai (here: Elxai) wrote the book under prophetic inspiration.

97. The measurement assumed here indicates that a reed (σχοῖνος) is four (Roman) miles long, which is about 3.6 English miles.

98. Epiphanios describes these huge angels three times: in his reports on the Jewish Ossaeans (*Pan.* 19.4.1–2), the Ebionites (30.17.6–7), and the Sampsaeans (53.1.9). Sometimes Epiphanios refers to the male angel as Christ. See further Cirillo, *Elchasai*, 53–60; Luttikhuizen, "Elchasaites and Their Book," 344. The huge size of the angels is reminiscent of the Shi'ur Qomah texts in later Jewish (Hekhalot) literature, for which see Martin Samuel Cohen, *The Shi'ur Qomah: Texts and Recensions* (Tübingen: Mohr Siebeck, 1985). Yet other parallels are closer to home: e.g., Herm. Sim. 9.6.1 (83.1).

99. "This one" (τοῦτον) may refer to the male angel or to Elchasai. Our author later excerpts a text that speaks of Trajan mastering the Parthians in three years (*Ref.* 9.16.4). He may have assumed that the text was written three years into Trajan's reign (101 CE). Problematically, Trajan only began the Parthian war in 114 CE (see further Luttikhuizen, *Revelation*, 63). Possibly the third year of Trajan refers to "a local era that numbered the years from Trajan's assumption of power in the area" (Jones, *Pseudoclementina*, 396).

100. Marcovich inserts here and in *Ref.* 9.15.1 δεύτερον ("*second* [i.e., baptism]"), comparing *Ref.* 9.12.26 ("second" baptism of Kallistos). Our author did indeed interpret Elchasaite baptism as a second baptism for believers (note that he also accuses Markos of instituting a second baptism in *Ref.* 6.41.2–3). But his report on Alkibiades

ἀσε<λ>γείᾳ καὶ μιασμῷ καὶ ἀνομήματι ἐμφυρέντας, εἴ τις πιστ(ὸ)ς εἴη, ἐπι<σ>τρέψαντα καὶ τῆ(ς) βίβλου <ταύτης> ἀκούσαντα καὶ πιστεύσαντα [ὁρίζει] βαπτίσματι λαμβάνειν ἄφεσιν ἁμαρτιῶν.

5. Ταῦτα δὲ ἐτόλμησε τεχνάσαι τὰ πανουργήματα ἀπὸ τοῦ προειρημένου δόγματος ἀφ(ο)ρμὴν λαβών, οὗ παρεστήσατο Κάλλιστος· ἡδομένου(ς) γὰρ κατανοήσας πολλοὺς ἐπὶ τοιαύτῃ ἐπαγγελίᾳ, εὐ(κ)αίρως ἐνόμισεν ἐπιχειρεῖν. καὶ τούτῳ δὲ ἡμεῖς ἀντ(ιστά)ντες οὐκ εἰάσαμεν ἐπὶ πολὺ πλανηθῆναι πολλούς, ἐλέγξαντες εἶναι τοῦτο πνεύματος νόθου ἐνέργειαν καὶ ἐπίνοιαν πεφυσιωμένης καρδίας, καὶ τοῦτον λύκου δίκην ἐπεγηγερμένον <εἶναι> πλανωμένοις προβάτοις πολλοῖς, <ἃ> ἀποπλανῶν διεσκόρπισεν ὁ Κάλλιστος.

6. Ἀλλ᾽ ἐπεὶ ἠρξάμεθα, καὶ τὰ τούτου δόγματα οὐ σιωπήσομεν, εἰς φανερόν τε ἀγαγόντες πρότερον τὸν βίον καὶ δείξαντες τὴν νομιζομένην ἄσκησιν προσποιητὴν ὑπάρχουσαν, αὖθις καὶ τῶν ῥητῶν κεφάλαια παραθήσομαι, ἵνα τοῖς αὐτοῦ ἐγγράφοις ὁ ἐντυγχάνων ἐνατενίσας ἐπιγνοίη, τίς καὶ ὁποία εἴη ἡ τούτῳ τετολμημένη αἵρεσις.

embroiled in every licentiousness, defilement, and criminal behavior—if he is a believer who has turned from sin, has heard this book, and believed in it—by baptism receives forgiveness of sins.[101]

5. These scams he dared to devise, having taken his starting point from Kallistos's dogma that I mentioned previously.[102] Realizing that many would be pleased with such a promise, Alkibiades supposed that it was a good time to make his attempt. By opposing him, I did not permit the masses to be totally led astray. I exposed this movement as the activity of a bastard spirit and the invention of a puffed-up heart. I further showed that Alkibiades was like a wolf rising up against many wandering sheep—the very sheep that Kallistos, by misleading them, had scattered.

THE TEACHINGS OF ALKIBIADES. 6. But since I made a beginning, I will not keep secret the doctrines of Alkibiades. First, I drag into the open his lifestyle, showing that his supposed discipline is feigned. Secondly, I will present the chief points of his sayings, so that the one who reads his writings with a trained eye might know what and what sort of heresy he ventured.[103]

---

also assumes repeated therapeutic baptisms (*Ref.* 9.15.5; 9.16.1). It is not clear how Alkibiades understood his baptismal practices to relate to baptism in other churches. Given these ambiguities, it is safer to return to the original reading of P here and below where a simple βάπτισμα is specified. See further Cirillo, "L'apocalypse," 176–79; Colpe, "Die 'elkesaitische Unternehmung,'" 61–64; Gerard Luttikhuizen, "The Book of Elchasai: A Jewish Apocalyptic Writing, Not a Christian Church Order," in *Society of Biblical Literature 1999 Seminar Papers*, SBLSP 38 (Atlanta: SBL, 1999, 405–25 (407–10); Simon Claude Mimouni, "Un ritual 'mystérique' des baptistes judéo-chrétiens des premiers siècles de notre ère?" in *Expérience et écriture mystiques dans les religions du livre: Actes d'un colloque international tenu par le Centre d'études juives Université de Paris IV-Sorbonne 1994*, ed. Paul B. Fenton and Roland Goetschel (Leiden: Brill, 2000), 55–74 (60–74).

101. Luttikhuizen asserts that "the Roman church did not yet have an institutionalized method for the remission of grave sins committed by baptized Christians (the sacrament of penance)" ("Elchasaites and Their Book," 338). Thus Alkibiades had a market among Christians already baptized.

102. Namely, the "dogma" of universal forgiveness in *Ref.* 9.12.20.

103. Cirillo proposes that the ἔγγραφα ("writings") were excerpts that Alkibiades took from the Book of Elchasai for his missionary preaching (*Elchasai*, 20; similarly Jones, *Pseudoclementina*, 425). In contrast, Luttikhuizen asserts that the ἔγγραφα refer to written reports of Alkibiades's oral teachings given before a select group. These written reports may have consisted of brief notes penned by our author himself or one of his assistants (*Revelation*, 63, 68). These notes included excerpts from the

14. 1. Οὗτος νόμου πολιτείαν προβάλλεται δελεάσματος δίκην, φάσκων δεῖν περιτέμνεσθαι καὶ κατὰ νόμον ζῆν τοὺς πεπιστευκότας. ἀποσπᾷ τινα τῶν προειρημένων αἱρέσεων· τὸν Χριστὸν γὰρ λέγει ἄνθρωπον κοινῶς πᾶσι γεγονέναι· τοῦτον δὲ οὐ νῦν πρῶτον ἐκ παρθένου γεγεν<ν>ῆσθαι, ἀλλὰ καὶ πρότερον, καὶ αὖθις πολλάκις γεννηθέντα καὶ γεννώμενον πεφηνέναι καὶ φύεσθαι, ἀλλάσσοντα γενέσεις καὶ μετενσωματούμενον, ἐκείνῳ τῷ Πυθαγορείῳ δόγματι χρώμενος.

2. Τοσοῦτον δὲ πεφυσίωνται, ὡς καὶ προγνωστικοὺς ἑαυτοὺς λέγειν, δηλον<ότι> μέτροις καὶ ἀριθμοῖς τῆς προειρημένης Πυθαγορείου τέχνης <ὡς> ἀφορμα<ῖ>ς χρωμένους. οὗτοι καὶ μαθηματικοῖς καὶ ἀστρολογικοῖς καὶ μαγικοῖς προσέχουσιν ὡς ἀληθέσι, κα(ὶ) τούτοις χρώμενοι ταράσσουσι τοὺς ἄφρονας, <ὡς> νομίζειν αὐτοὺς λόγου δυνατοῦ μετέχειν. 3. ἐπαοιδὰς δὲ καὶ ἐπιλόγ(ου)ς τινὰς διδάσκουσι πρός τε κυνοδήκτους καὶ δαιμον(ι)ῶντας καὶ ἑτέραις νόσοις κατεχομένους· ὧν οὐδὲ ταῦτα σιωπήσομεν.

ἱκανῶς οὖν τὰς ἀρχὰς αὐτῶν διηγησάμενος, τάς τε αἰτίας τῶν τολμημάτων, παρελεύσομαι ἐ(π)ιδιηγησόμενος τὰ ἔγγραφα, δι' ὧν εἴσονται οἱ ἐντυγχάνοντες τόν τε λῆρον κ(α)ὶ τὰ ἄθεα αὐτῶν ἐπιχειρήματα.

15. 1. Τὸ μὲν οὖν βάπτισμα τοῖς ἀπ' αὐτ(οῦ) (γενομ)ένοις οὕτως παραδίδωσι, τοιάδε λέγων τοῖς ἀπατωμένοις·

> εἴ τις οὖν, τέκνα, <ἐ>πλησίασεν οἱῳδήποτε ζῴῳ, ἢ ἄρρενί, ἢ ἀδελφῇ, ἢ θυγατρί, ἢ ἐμοίχευσεν, ἢ ἐπόρνευσε, καὶ θέλει ἄφεσιν λαβεῖν τῶν ἁμαρτιῶν, ἀφ' οὗ ἂν ἀκούσῃ τῆς βίβλου ταύτης, βαπτισάσθω ἐκ δευτέρου ἐν ὀνόματι τοῦ μεγάλου καὶ ὑψίστου θεοῦ καὶ ἐν ὀνόματι υἱοῦ αὐτοῦ, μεγάλου βασιλέως, καθαρισάσθω καὶ ἁγνευσάτω. 2. καὶ ἐπιμαρτυρησάσθω αὐτῷ τοὺς ἑπτὰ μάρτυρας, γεγραμμένους ἐν τῇ βίβλῳ ταύτῃ· τὸν οὐρανὸν καὶ τὸ ὕδωρ καὶ τὰ πνεύμα<τα> τὰ ἅγια καὶ τοὺς ἀγγέλους τῆς προσευχῆς καὶ τὸ ἔλαιον καὶ τὸ ἅλας καὶ τὴν γῆν.

14. 1. This man advertises living according to the Law as bait, claiming that it is necessary to be circumcised and for believers to live according to the Law.[104] But he draws certain things also from the previously mentioned heresies. He says, for instance, that Christ was a human being and was born just like everybody else.[105] He was not born first in our times from a virgin, but even earlier. In fact, he was born many times. He seemed to be reborn and grow, alternating births and changing bodies (here Alkibiades cribs that old Pythagorean doctrine).[106]

2. They are so inflated with pride that they call themselves "foreseers of the future." As their starting points, they clearly use measurements and numbers from the aforementioned Pythagorean art. They also devote themselves to diviners, astrologers, and magicians as if they were genuine. They use them to whip up dim-witted people, who consequently think that they partake of magically effective speech. 3. They teach certain spells and incantations for those bitten by dogs, the demon possessed, as well as those subject to other diseases. I will not keep these matters secret either.

Since I have sufficiently recounted their principles and the root causes of their audacities, I will advance to relate their writings. By this means, those who read them will know both their delirium and their godless designs.

ELCHASAITE WRITINGS. **15.** 1. Alkibiades delivers a baptism to his followers, announcing to his dupes something like this:

> So if, my children, someone had sex with any animal whatsoever, or with a male or sister or daughter, or has committed adultery or another sexual infraction and wants to receive forgiveness of sins, the moment that he hears this book, let him be baptized a second time in the name of the great and highest God and in the name of his Son, the great King, and let him be cleansed and sanctify himself. 2. Let him call to witness for himself the seven witnesses who are written in this book: heaven, water, the holy spirits, the angels of prayer, oil, salt, and earth.[107]

Book of Elchasai, but relatively few can be safely reconstructed. See further Cirillo, "L'apocalypse," 168–69.

104. Cf. *Ref.* 7.34.1 ("Ebionites"); Iren., *Haer.* 1.26.2; Epiph., *Pan.* 19.3.5.

105. Cf. Karpokrates and Kerinthos in *Ref.* 7.32–33.

106. Cf. Epiph., *Pan.* 30.3.1–6; 53.1.8.

107. This baptism was probably meant to cover grave or "mortal" sins committed by Christians after their first baptism. See further Luttikhuizen, *Revelation*, 72–73.

Ταῦτά <ἐστι> τὰ θαυμάσια μυστήρια τοῦ Ἠλχασαΐ, τὰ ἀπόρρητα καὶ μεγάλα, ἃ παραδίδωσι τοῖς ἀξίοις μαθηταῖς. οἷς οὐκ ἀρκεῖται ὁ ἄνομος, ἀλλ' «ἐπὶ δύο καὶ τριῶν μαρτύρων» ἐνσφραγίζει τὰ ἑαυτοῦ κακά, πάλιν οὕτως λέγων·

> 3. πάλιν λέγω, ὦ μοιχοὶ καὶ μοιχαλίδες καὶ ψευδοπροφῆται, ἐὰν θέλητε ἐπιστρέψαι, ἵνα ἀφεθήσονται ὑμῖν αἱ ἁμαρτίαι καὶ ὑμῖν εἰρήνη καὶ μέρος μετὰ τῶν δικαίων, ἀφ' οὗ ἂν ἀκούσητε τῆς βίβλου ταύτης, [καὶ] βαπτίσθητε ἐκ δευτέρου σὺν τοῖς ἐνδύμασιν.

4. Ἀλλ' ἐπεί ἐπαοιδαῖς τούτους εἴπομεν χρῆσθαι ἐπί τε κυνοδήκτων καὶ ἑτέρων, δείξομεν. λέγει γὰρ οὕτως·

> ἄν τιν' οὖν ἄνδρα ἢ γυναῖκα ἢ νεώτερον ἢ νεωτέραν κύων (λυ)σσῶν καὶ μαινόμενος—ἐν ᾧ ἐστι πνεῦμα διαφθορᾶς—δάκῃ ἢ περι(σχ)ίσῃ ἢ προσψαύσῃ, ἐν αὐτῇ τῇ ὥρᾳ δραμέτω σὺν παντὶ τῷ φορέματι καὶ καταβὰς εἰς ποταμὸν ἢ εἰς πηγήν, ὅπου ἐὰν ᾖ τόπος βαθύς, 5.
> βαπτισάσθω παντὶ τῷ φορέματι αὐτοῦ, καὶ προσευξάσθω τῷ μεγάλῳ καὶ ὑψίστῳ θεῷ ἐν καρδίας πίστει. καὶ τότε ἐπιμαρτυρησ(ά)σθω τοὺς ἑπτὰ μάρτυρας, τοὺς γεγραμμένους ἐν τῇ βίβλῳ ταύτῃ· ἰδοὺ μαρτύρομαι τὸν οὐρανὸν καὶ τὸ ὕδωρ καὶ τὰ (πνεύμα)τα τὰ ἅγια καὶ τοὺς ἀγγέλους τῆς προσευχῆς καὶ τ(ὸ) ἔλαιον καὶ τὸ ἅλας καὶ τὴν γῆν.

These are the wondrous mysteries of Elchasai, the unspeakable and magnificent mysteries that Alkibiades delivers to his worthy disciples! These acts do not satisfy the lawless man, but "with two or three witnesses" he places them under the seal of his own vices, declaring in turn:[108]

> 3. Again I say, O adulterers, adulteresses, and false prophets—if you want to convert so that your sins will be forgiven and so that there will be peace for you and a portion with the righteous—the moment that you hear this book, be baptized a second time with your clothes.[109]

THERAPEUTIC BAPTISMS. 4. But since I claimed that they use spells for those bitten by dogs (and other ailments), I will prove it. He says:

> Now should a mad and rabid dog infected with a spirit of destruction bite or gash or touch a man or woman or young man or young woman, let them run that very instant and, by descending into a river or fountain (wherever the place is deep), 5. let them baptize themselves with all their clothes. Then, let them pray to the great and highest God with heartfelt faith. And then let them call as witnesses the seven witnesses who are written in this book: "Behold I call to witness heaven, water, the holy spirits, the angels of prayer,

---

The last quotation in the excerpt may be from the Book of Elchasai, which Alkibiades quotes (ibid., 71–72). The oath formula is given more fully below in *Ref.* 9.15.5–6. The oath indicates that Alkibiades demanded rebaptized Christians to undergo a rigorous moral reformation. Cf. the seven witnesses (actually eight, if God is included) in Epiph., *Pan.* 19.6.4. We find heaven, earth, water, and air called to witness in Ps.-Clem. Adjuration 2.1 and 4.1 (Rehm, I, 3:10–12; 4:6–8). Cf. also Disc. 8–9 (NHC VI,6) 63.15–24; *OF* 619. The practice has biblical roots (Isa 1:2) and was encouraged by the fact that one should not swear directly by God.

108. For the two witnesses, see Deut 17:6; 19:15; Matt 18:16; 1 Tim 5:19. Our author uses sealing language likely because baptism was associated with the sealing of the Holy Spirit.

109. False prophets are associated with adulterers because they were thought to prostitute themselves to demons. Cirillo believes that this quote immediately followed what our author quotes in *Ref.* 9.15.2 (Cirillo, *Elchasai*, 19, 64). Luttikhuizen, however, asserts that this excerpt was addressed directly to Christian sinners and did not stem from the same source as the other quotations in *Ref.* 9.15–17 (*Revelation*, 69–70, 74–75).

6. τούτους τοὺς ἑπτὰ μάρτυρας μαρτύρομαι ὅτι οὐκέτι ἁμαρτήσω· οὐ μοιχεύσω, οὐ κλέψω, οὐκ ἀδικήσω, οὐ πλεονεκτήσω, οὐ μισήσω, οὐκ ἀθετήσω, οὐδὲ ἐν πᾶσι πονηροῖς εὐδοκήσω. ταῦτα οὖν εἰπὼν βαπτισάσθω σὺν παντὶ τῷ φορέματι αὐτοῦ ἐν ὀνόματι τοῦ μεγάλου καὶ ὑψίστου θεοῦ.

16. 1. ἕτερα δὲ πλεῖστα φλυαρεῖ, ταὐτὰ καὶ ἐπὶ φθισικῶν ἐπιλέγειν διδάσκων, καὶ βαπτίζεσθαι ἐν ψυχρῷ τεσσαρακοντάκις ἐπὶ ἡμέρας ἑπτά, ὁμοίως καὶ ἐπὶ δαιμονώντων.

ὢ σοφίας ἀμιμήτου καὶ ἐπαοιδῶν δυνάμεως μεμεστωμένων· τίς οὐκ ἐκπλαγήσεται τῇ τοιαύτῃ καὶ τοσαύτῃ δυνάμει τῶν λόγων;

2. Ἀλλ' ἐπειδὴ καὶ ἀστρολογικῇ πλάνῃ κεχρῆσθαι αὐτοὺς ἔφημεν, ἐξ αὐτῶν δείξομεν. φησὶ γὰρ οὕτως·

εἰσὶν ἀστέρες πονηροὶ τῆς ἀσεβείας· τοῦτο νῦν ἡμῖν εἴρηται, εὐσεβεῖς καὶ μαθηταί· φυλάσσεσθε ἀπὸ τῆς ἐξουσίας τῶν ἡμερῶν ἀρχῆς αὐτῶν, καὶ μὴ ποιεῖτε τὴν καταρχὴν τῶν ἔργων ἐν ταῖς ἡμέραις αὐτῶν, καὶ μὴ βαπτίζετε ἄνδρα ἢ γυναῖκα ἐν ταῖς ἡμέραις τῆς ἐξουσίας αὐτῶν. 3. ὁπόταν διαπορεύηται <παρ>ἐξ αὐτοὺς ἡ σελήνη καὶ συνοδεύῃ αὐτοῖς, <τ>αύτην τὴν ἡμέραν φυλάσσεσθε, ἕως οὗ ἐκπορεύεται ἀπ' αὐτῶν, καὶ τότε βαπτίζετε καὶ ἐνάρχεσθε ἐν πάσῃ ἀρχῇ τῶν ἔργων ὑμῶν. ἔτι δὲ τιμήσατε τὴν ἡμέραν τοῦ σαββάτου, ἐπειδή ἐστιν ἡμέρα μί(α) ἐξ (α)ὐτῶν.

4. ἀλλὰ καὶ τὴν τρίτην σαββάτου φυλάσσεσθε μὴ κατάρχεσθαι, ἐπειδὴ πάλιν πληρουμένων τριῶν ἐτῶν Τραϊανοῦ Καίσαρος, ἀφότε ὑπέταξε(ν) ἑαυτοῦ τῇ ἐξουσίᾳ τοὺ<ς> Πάρθου<ς>, [ὅτε ἐπληρώθη

oil, salt, and earth. 6. I testify by these seven witnesses that I will no longer sin. I will not commit adultery, I will not steal, I will not harm, I will not be greedy, I will not hate, I will not deal treacherously, nor take pleasure in any evil." Having said these things, let them be baptized with all their clothes in the name of the great and highest God.[110]

16. 1. He blabbers a great many other things. He teaches that the same words be pronounced over consumptives too, and that they be baptized in cold water forty times over the course of seven days—and similarly for demoniacs.

O inimitable wisdom and spells filled full with power! Who will not be struck by the character and magnitude of the power of these words?

ASTROLOGICAL ADMONITIONS. 2. But since I accused them of using astrological deceit, I will prove it from their own words. He speaks as follows:

> There are evil planets of impiety. This has now been spoken to us, O you God-fearing disciples. Guard yourselves from the authority of the days of their rule, and do not begin your projects on their days, and do not baptize a man or woman on the days of their authority. 3. Whenever the moon travels beside these planets and is in conjunction with them, take caution on that day, until it veers away from them. Then baptize yourselves and start your projects at any point. Yet honor the Sabbath day, since it is one of those [unfavorable] days.
>
> 4. Now, on the third day of the week, take caution also not to begin anything, because once again—when three years of Caesar Trajan are again fulfilled, after he has subjected the Parthians to his own authority—the war between the angels of impiety in the north

110. Cf. the account in Epiph., *Pan.* 30.17.4–5, with the comments of Andrea Nicolotti, "A Cure for Rabies or a Remedy for Concupiscence? A Baptism of the Elchasaites," *JECS* 16 (2008): 518–34. (Nicolotti argues that the dog bite actually transmits a demon that is a punishment for sin.) The moral demands required for this sort of baptism show that Alkibiades was hardly lax. Luttikhuizen, who thinks that such renunciations of sin do not fit a cure for rabies, would move the renunciation to *Ref.* 9.15.2 where the rebaptism of Christian sinners is described (*Revelation*, 77). Cf. Pliny the Younger, *Ep.* 10.96.7 (Christians swear to abstain from theft, adultery, and dishonesty).

τρία ἔτη] ἀγγρίζε(τ)αι ὁ πόλεμος μεταξὺ τῶν ἀγγέλων τῆς ἀσεβείας τῶν ἄρκτων· διὰ τοῦτο ταράσσονται πᾶσαι βασιλεῖαι τῆς ἀσεβείας.

17. 1. Ταῦτα τοίνυν τ(ὰ) μεγ(ά)λα κ(α)ὶ ἀπόρρητα μυστήρια ἄλογον ἡγούμενος καταπατεῖσθαι ἢ εἰς πολλοὺς π(α)ραδίδοσθαι, συμβουλεύει ὡς πολυτελεῖς μαργαρίτας φυλάσσειν, οὕτω λέγων·

> τοῦτον δὲ τὸν λόγον μὴ ἀναγινώσκετε πᾶσιν ἀνθρώποις, καὶ ταύτας τὰς ἐντολὰς φυλάξατε ἐπιμελῶς, ὅτι οὐ πάντες ἄνδρες πιστοὶ οὐδὲ πᾶσαι γυναῖκες ὀρθαί.

2. Ταῦτα δὲ οὐδὲ Αἰγυπτίων σοφοὶ ἐν ἀδύτοις ἐχώρησαν, οὐδὲ ὁ σοφὸς Ἑλλήνων Πυθαγόρας ἐχώρησεν· εἰ γὰρ τετυχήκει κατ᾽ ἐκεῖνο καιροῦ Ἠλχασαΐ, τίς ἀνάγκη Πυθαγόραν ἢ Θαλῆν ἢ Σόλωνα ἢ τὸν σοφὸν Πλάτωνα ἢ καὶ τοὺς λοιποὺς Ἑλλήνων σοφοὺς μαθητεύειν Αἰγυπτίων ἱερεῦσιν, ἔχοντας τὴν τοιαύτην καὶ τοσαύτην σοφίαν παρὰ Ἀλκιβιάδῃ, [ἃ] τῷ θαυμασιωτάτῳ ἑρμηνεῖ τοῦ δυστήνου Ἠλχασαΐ;

3. δοκεῖ τοίνυν ἱκανὰ εἶναι τὰ εἰρημένα πρὸς ἐπίγνωσι(ν) τῆς τούτων μανίας τοῖς ὑγιαίνοντα νοῦν κεκτημέ(ν)οις· διὸ πλείοσι ῥητοῖς οὐκ ἔδοξε χρῆσθαι, οὖσι πλείστοις καὶ καταγελάστοις.

Ἀλλ᾽ ἐπεὶ μηδὲ ταῦτα παρελείπομεν, τὰ ἐφ᾽ ἡμῶν ἐπεγηγερμένα, τά τε πρὸ ἡμῶν οὐκ ἐσιωπήσαμεν, δοκεῖ—ἵνα διὰ πάντων ὦμεν πεπορευμένοι μηδέν ἀνεκδιήγητον καταλείπωμεν—εἰπεῖν τίνα καὶ τῶν Ἰουδαίων <τὰ ἔθη> καὶ τίνες αἱ ἐν τούτοις διαφοραί. 4. ἔτι γὰρ ταῦτα νομίζω περιλείπεσθαι· ἃ μηδὲ αὐτὰ

will break out. For this reason, all the kingdoms of impiety are disturbed.[111]

PROTECTION OF THE MYSTERIES. 17. 1. Accordingly, since Alkibiades considers it unreasonable that these great and inexpressible mysteries be trampled upon and delivered to the masses, he counsels his hearers to protect them like precious pearls.[112] To quote him:

> Do not read this oracle to all people, and keep these commandments with all diligence; for not all men are trustworthy, nor are all women upright.

2. These mysteries neither the sages of Egypt in their inner shrines nor the Greek sage Pythagoras were capable of grasping. For if Elchasai happened to live at that time, what need would there be for Pythagoras, Thales, Solon, the wise Plato, or the rest of the Greek sages to learn from the Egyptian priests—since they would have had such great wisdom from Alkibiades, the most wondrous interpreter of the wretched Elchasai?

3. Now then, it seems that what I have said is sufficient for people of sane mind to recognize the insanity of these people. Accordingly, I have decided not to quote their numerous oracles, since they are profuse and ridiculous.

But since I neglected none of the present teachings that have arisen in my lifetime, and have not kept secret those that arose before me, it seems right (so that I can proceed through all the material and leave nothing untold) to discuss the customs of the Jews, as well as their mutual differences. 4. (These matters, I believe, remain untreated).[113] When I reveal

---

111. Here, "Elchasaites" are advised not to begin activities on Saturday and Tuesday in part because the planetary rulers of those days, Saturn and Mars, were viewed as malefic. Jones observes that "a conjunction of the moon with Saturn and with Mars would cover probably one day (perhaps, however, two or more) each a month" (*Pseudoclementina*, 436, with sources). See further Luttikhuizen, *Revelation*, 78–79; Hegedus, *Early Christianity*, 292–94, 304–5. Trajan successfully fought the Parthians between 114 and 117 CE, although they quickly rebelled. Consequently, Luttikhuizen dates the prophecy to the autumn of 116 CE, when Trajan still had the upper hand. "It seems that the author of the book expected that, after the completion of another period of three years of Roman occupation, a new war of much larger dimensions would break out" ("Elchasaites and Their Book," 340).

112. Cf. Matt 7:6 (pearls before swine); Gos. Thom. 93; *Ref.* 5.8.33 (Naassenes).

113. Our author identifies contemporary Jews as "heretics," setting a trend for future heresiography. See further Averil Cameron, "Jews and Heretics—A Category

σιωπ(ή)σας, ἐπὶ τὴν ἀπόδειξιν τοῦ περὶ ἀληθείας λόγου χωρήσω, ὅπως μετὰ τὸν πολὺν ἀγῶνα τοῦ κατὰ πασῶν αἱρέσεων λόγου, ἐπὶ <τὸν> τῆς βασιλείας στέφανον ὁρμήσαντες, εὐ(σε)β(ῶ)ς τὰ ἀληθῆ πιστεύοντες μὴ ταρασσώμεθα.

18. 1. Ἰουδαίων μὲν ἀρχῆθεν ἓν ἦν ἔθος· εἷς γὰρ ὁ τούτοις δοθεὶς παρὰ θεοῦ διδάσκαλος Μωσῆς (κ)αὶ εἷς ὁ διὰ τούτου νόμος, μία δὲ ἔρημος χώρα καὶ ἓν ὄρος τ(ὸ) Σιν(ᾶ)· εἷς γὰρ ὁ τούτοις νομοθετήσας θεός.

αὖθις δέ, διαβάντες τὸν Ἰορδάνην ποταμὸν καὶ τὴν δορύκτητον γῆν κληρονομήσαντες, διαφόρως τὸν τοῦ θεοῦ νόμον διέσπασαν, ἄλλος ἄλλως ἐπινοῶν τὰ εἰρημένα, καὶ οὕτως διδασκάλους ἑαυτοῖς ἐπεγείραντες <καὶ> δόξας αἱρέσεων ἐφευρόντες εἰς μερισμὸν ἐχώρησαν. ὧν τὴν διαφορὰν ἐκθήσομαι·

2. εἰ δὲ καὶ εἰς πλεῖστα μέρη διεσπάσθησαν τῷ μακρῷ χρόνῳ, ἀλλά γε τὰ κεφαλαιωδέστερα αὐτῶν ἐκθήσομαι, δι᾽ ὧν καὶ τὰ λοιπὰ οἱ φιλομαθεῖς εἴσονται εὐκόλως. Τρία γὰρ παρ᾽ αὐτοῖς εἴδη διαιρεῖται, καὶ τοῦ μὲν αἱρετισταί εἰσι Φαρισαῖοι, τοῦ δὲ Σαδδουκαῖοι, ἕτεροι δὲ Ἐσ<σ>ηνοί.

even their secrets, I will proceed to the demonstration of the true doctrine, so that after this huge labor of accounting for all heresies, we, who rush to the crown of the kingdom and piously believe the true doctrines, might not be disturbed.

JEWS

18. 1. In the beginning, there was one custom of the Jews, for they have one teacher given by God: Moses. Through him came one Law. And there is one wilderness and one mountain— Sinai—since one God laid down their laws.

Afterward, when they had crossed the Jordan River and inherited the land by the spear, they ripped apart the Law of God with their different viewpoints—each one variously understanding the words. In this way, they raised up teachers for themselves. When they invented heretical notions, they split into the camps whose differences I will present.

2. Although they have been split apart into a great number of heresies during their long history, still I will present their main points, through which diligent students can easily learn the rest. They are split into three camps: one group of heretics are the Pharisees, another group are the Sadducees, and another group are the Essenes.[114]

Error?" in *The Ways That Never Parted: Jews and Christians in Late Antiquity and the Early Middle Ages*, ed. Adam H. Becker and Annette Yoshiko Reed (Tübingen: Mohr Siebeck, 2003), 345–60.

114. Our author's account of the three Jewish sects adapts Josephus, *J.W.* 2.119–166 (commented on by Steve Mason, ed., *Judean War 2*, vol. 1B of *Flavius Josephus: Translation and Commentary* [Leiden: Brill, 2008], 96–135). Marcovich's upper apparatus covers significant departures from Josephus (though Marcovich was prone to "correct" our author by Josephus—sometimes by the Old Slavic version of Josephus). Yet our author's text is not a simple transcription of Josephus. Overall, it is a "much simpler … less elegant" rendering (Matthew Black, "The Account of the Essenes in Hippolytus and Josephus," in *The Background of the New Testament and Its Eschatology*, ed. W. D. Davies and D. Daube [Cambridge: Cambridge University Press, 1956], 172–75 [173]). There are few word-for-word agreements overall (Morton Smith, "The Description of the Essenes in Josephus and the Philosophoumena," *HUCA* 29 [1958]: 273–313 [294–313]). It is possible that, as Solomon Zeitlin proposes, our author used an intermediate Christianizing transcription of Josephus. Zeitlin believes that this intermediary was Hegesippos (as reported in Eusebios, *Hist. eccl.* 4.22.7), an apologist who was born a Jew but died a Christian in Rome ("The Account of the Essenes in Josephus and the Philosophoumena," *JQR* 49 [1959]: 292–99). Marcovich vouches for the same intermediary, since he cannot accept the idea that our author deliberately

3. οὗτοι τὸν βίον σεμνότερον ἀσκοῦσι, φιλάλληλοι ὄντες καὶ ἐγκρατεῖς, πάσης τε ἐπιθυμίας ἔργον ἀποστρέφονται, ἀπεχθῶς καὶ πρὸς <τὸ> τὰ τοιαῦτα ἀκ(ο)ῦσαι ἔχοντες, γάμον τε ἀπαγορεύουσι. τοὺς δὲ ἀλλοτρίους παῖδας ἀναλαμβάνοντες τεκνοποιοῦνται καὶ πρὸς τὰ ἴδια ἤθη ἄγουσιν, οὕτως ἀνατρέφοντες καὶ ἔτι τοῖς μαθήμασι προβιβάζοντες, οὐ τὸ γαμεῖν κωλύοντες, ἀλλ' αὐτοὶ γάμου ἀπεχόμενοι. γυναῖκας δέ, εἰ καὶ τῇ αὐτῇ προαιρέσει βούλοιντο προσέχειν, οὐ προσδέχονται, κατὰ μηδένα τρόπον γυναιξὶ πιστεύοντες.

19. 1. Καταφρονοῦσι δὲ πλούτου καὶ τὸ πρὸς τοὺς δεομένους κοινωνεῖν οὐκ ἀποστρέφο(ντ)αι, ἀλλ' οὐδέ τις παρ' αὐτοῖς ὑπὲρ τὸν ἕτερον πλουτεῖ. ν(ό)μος γὰρ παρ' αὐτοῖς τὸν προσιόντα τῇ αἱρέσει τὰ ὑπάρχοντα πωλοῦντα τῷ κοινῷ προσφέρειν· ἃ ὑποδεχόμενος <ὁ> ἄρχων διανέμει ἅπασι πρὸς τὰ δέοντα· 2. οὕτως οὐδ(εὶ)ς ἐνδεὴς παρ' αὐτοῖς. ἐλαίῳ δὲ οὐ χρῶνται, μολυσμὸν ἡγούμ(ενοι) τὸ ἀλ(εί)φεσθαι. χειροτονοῦνται δὲ οἱ ἐπιμεληταί, οἱ πάντων κοινῶ(ν) (φ)ρο(ντί)ζ(ο)ντ(ες). πάντες δὲ ἀεὶ λευχειμονοῦσι.

20. 1. Μία δὲ αὐτῶν οὐκ ἔστι πόλι(ς), ἀλλ' ἐν ἑκάστῃ μετοικοῦσι πολλοί. καὶ εἴ τις ἀπὸ ξένης παρῇ τῶν αἱρετιστῶν, πάντα αὐτῷ κοινὰ ἡγοῦνται, καὶ οὓς

ESSENES

3. The Essenes practice a rather austere lifestyle. They are devoted to each other and are self-controlled, turning away from every practice of lust.[115] They even become hostile if they have to listen to such practices. They forbid marriage.[116] They take other people's children into their care and adopt and train them in their own way of life. They raise them and, furthermore, train them in their teachings. They do not forbid them to marry, although they themselves abstain from marriage. But women, if they too want to adhere to the same commitment, are not received, since they in no way trust a woman.

19. 1. They despise riches and do not refrain from sharing with the needy, although not a single one of them is richer than another. This is because they have a law that the one who comes to the sect sells his possessions and offers the money to the common purse. The presider receives this money and distributes to all according to their need.[117] 2. In this way, no one is needy among them.[118] They do not use oil, since they believe anointing to be a defilement. The caretakers who look after all the common affairs are chosen by vote. All of them always dress in white.[119]

20. 1. They do not have one community. Rather, most dwell as temporary residents in a particular city. If a fellow sectarian arrives from a foreign

---

altered and misrepresented his source (*Studies*, 144–55). Christoph Burchard argues instead that our author directly modified and Christianized Josephus's text on the basis of the New Testament and contemporary ecclesial circumstances ("Zur Nebenüberlieferung von Josephus' Bericht über die Essener, Bell 2,119–161 bei Hippolyt, Porphyrius, Josippus, Niketas Choniates und anderen," in *Josephus-Studien: Untersuchungen zu Josephus, dem antiken Judentum und dem Neuen Testament*, ed. Otto Betz, Klaus Haacker, and Martin Hengel [Göttingen: Vandenhoeck & Ruprecht, 1974], 76–96 [80–81]). Burchard is followed by Frickel, *Naassenerschrift*, 253–57; and Roland Bergmeier, "Die drei jüdischen Schulrichtungen nach Josephus und Hippolyt von Rome: Zu den Paralleltexten Josephus, *B.J.* 2,119–166 und Hippolyt, *Haer.* IX 18,2–29,4," *JSJ* 34 (2003): 443–70 (451–63).

115. E. Glenn Hinson argues that our author highlights Essene rigorism because "*True* Christianity … followed in the train of Jewish rigorists" ("Hippolytus and the Essenes," *StPatr* 18 [1989]: 283–90 [284, emphasis his]).

116. Cf. 1 Tim 4:3, quoted in *Ref.* 8.20.2 (Enkratites).

117. Cf. 1QS I, 11–13.

118. Cf. Acts 4:32 (shared possessions).

119. White dress is characteristic of priests (Exod 28:38–43; Ezek 44:17–19; cf. Philo, *Contempl.* 66).

οὐ πρότερον ᾔδεσαν, ὡς οἰκείους καὶ συνήθεις προσδέχονται. περίϊασι δὲ τὴν πατρῴαν γῆν ἑκάστοτε ἀποδημοῦντες μηδὲν φέροντες πλὴν ὅπλου.

2. ἔχουσι δὲ καὶ κατὰ πόλεις προεστῶτα, ὃς τὰ συναγόμενα εἰς τοῦτο ἀναλίσκει, ἐσθῆτα καὶ τροφὰς αὐτοῖς παρασκευάζων. καταστολὴ δὲ αὐτῶν καὶ σχῆμα κόσμιον. χιτῶνας δὲ δύο ἢ διπλᾶς ὑποδέσεις οὐ κτῶνται· ἐπὰν δὲ τὰ παρόντα παλαιωθῇ, τότε ἕτερα προσίενται. οὐδὲν δὲ ὅλως οὔτε ἀγοράζουσιν οὔτε πωλοῦσιν, ὃ δ' ἂν ἔχῃ τις τῷ μὴ ἔχοντι δούς, ὃ οὐκ ἔχει λαμβάνει.

21. 1. Παραμένουσι δὲ εὐτάκτως καὶ ἐπιμόνως εὐχόμενοι ἕωθεν, μηδὲν πρότερον φθεγξ(ά)μενοι εἰ μὴ τὸν θεὸν ὑμνήσωσι· καὶ οὕτω, προ<σ>ελθόντες ἕκ(α)στοι ἐφ' ὃ βούλονται, πράττουσι, καὶ ἕως ὥρας πέμπτης πράξαντες ἐπανίασιν. 2. ἔπειτα πάλιν συνελθόντες εἰς ἕνα τόπον, περιζώμασί τε λινοῖς περιζωσάμενοι—πρὸς τὸ καλύψασθαι τὴν αἰσχύνην—οὕτως ὕδατι ψυχρῷ ἀπολούονται. καὶ μετὰ τὸ οὕτως ἁγνίσασθαι εἰς ἓν οἴκημα συνίασιν—οὐδεὶς δὲ ἑτερ(ο)δόξων σύνεισιν ἐν τῷ οἴκῳ—καὶ περὶ ἀριστοποιΐαν χωροῦσι. 3. καθισάντων δὲ κατὰ τάξιν μεθ' ἡσυχίας προσφέρονται ἄρτοι, ἔπειτα ἕν τι προσφάγιον, ἐξ οὗ ἑκάστῳ τὸ αὔταρκες μέρος. οὐ πρότερον δὲ γεύ(σετ)αί (τις) (α)ὐτῶν, εἰ μὴ ἐπ(εύ)ξεται εὐλογῶν ὁ ἱερεύς.

μετὰ (δὲ) τὸ ἄριστον ἐπεύχεται πάλιν· ἀρχόμενοί τε καὶ πάλιν παυόμενοι ὑμνοῦσι τὸν θεόν. 4. ἔπειτα τὰς ἐσθῆτας, (ἃ)ς (ἔν)δ(ον) συνεστιώμενοι ἀμφιέν<ν>υνται, ἀποθέμεν(οι) ὡ(ς) (ἱ)εράς—εἰσὶ δὲ λιναῖ—<καὶ> τὰς ἐν τῇ προόδῳ πάλιν ἀναλαμβάνοντες ἐπὶ τὰ φίλα ἔργα ὁρμῶσιν ἕως δείλης. δειπνοῦσι δὲ ὁμοίως τοῖς προειρημένοις πάντα ποιήσαντες.

5. οὐδεὶς δὲ πώποτε κραυγάσει ἤ τις ἑτέρα θορυβώδης ἀκουσθήσεται φωνή, ἠρέμα δὲ ἕκαστοι λαλοῦντες εὐσχημόνως ἕτερος τῷ ἑτέρῳ τὴν ὁμιλίαν συγχωρεῖ, ὡς τοῖς ἔξωθεν μυστήριόν τι καταφαίνεσθαι τὴν τῶν ἔνδον σιωπήν. νήφουσι δὲ πάντοτε, πάντα μέτρῳ καὶ ἐσθίοντες καὶ πίνοντες.

land, they hold all in common with him, and those they formerly did not know they receive as relatives and familiar friends. They perpetually travel round their ancestral land. Each time they set out, they carry nothing but their equipment.

2. They have in each city a presiding officer who spends the contributions on preparing clothes and food for them. Their robes and clothing are discreet. They do not possess two overcoats or two pairs of sandals.[120] Whenever their current attire grows old, another set of clothes is supplied. They do not buy or sell at all: the one who has gives to him who has not; and the one who has not receives.

DAILY ROUTINE. **21.** 1. They keep a strict regimen. They continuously pray from dawn, uttering nothing at all before singing hymns to God.[121] In this way, each one proceeds to do what he will, performs a task until the fifth hour, and returns. 2. Then, once again gathering into a single place and girded with linen loincloths (to hide their private parts), they wash themselves, so attired, with cold water. After being purified in this way, they gather into a single room (but none of those with different views assembles in the house) and proceed to make the midday meal. 3. They are seated in order and are offered loaves of bread in silence. Then they are offered some side dish, from which each receives a sufficient portion. None of them will take a taste prior to the priest giving the prayer of blessing.

After the meal, they pray once again, starting and ending with hymns to God. 4. Then they place in storage the clothing that they wore when they ate together indoors (these are the linen garments, which they treat as holy[122]). After putting on again their [regular] clothes in the vestibule, they head straight to their beloved labors until evening. They eat dinner in the same manner, doing everything as was said before.

5. No one ever shouts; nor is there heard any other raucous noise. Calmly, each one speaks respectfully with each other, deferring to one another in the conversation. Consequently, to outsiders, the silence within appears like some mystery. They are sober at all times, eating and drinking with moderation at all times.

120. Cf. Matt 10:10.

121. Cf. 1QS IX, 26–X, 1; Philo, *Contempl.* 27, 89.

122. Linen is also associated with priests (Exod 28:39; Lev 6:3; 16:4; Ezek 44:17).

22. 1. Πάντες μὲν οὖν τῷ προεστῶτι προσέχουσι καὶ ὅσ᾽ ἃ<ν> κελεύσῃ ὡς νόμῳ πείθονται. ἐσπουδάκασι δὲ πρὸς τὸ ἐλεεῖν καὶ βοηθεῖν τοῖς καταπονουμένοις. πρὸ δὲ πάντων ὀργῆς ἀπέχουσι καὶ θυμοῦ καὶ πάντων τῶν ὁμοίων, ἐπίβουλα ταῦτα τοῦ ἀνθρώπου κρίνοντες.

οὐδεὶς δὲ ὄμνυσι παρ᾽ αὐτοῖς, ὅσα δ᾽ ἄν τις εἴπῃ, τοῦτο ὅρκου ἰσχυρότερον κρίνεται· εἰ δὲ ὀμόσει τις, καταγινώσκεται ὡς μὴ πιστευθείς.

2. σπουδάζουσι δὲ περὶ τὰς τοῦ νόμου ἀναγνώσεις καὶ προφητῶν, ἔτι δὲ καὶ εἴ τι σύνταγμα εἴη πιστῶν. πάνυ δὲ περιέργως ἔχουσι περὶ βοτάνας καὶ λίθους, περιεργότεροι ὄντες πρὸς τὰς τούτων ἐνεργείας, φάσκοντες μὴ μάτην ταῦτα γεγονέναι.

23. 1. Τοῖς δὲ βουλομένοις τῇ αἱρέσει μαθ(η)τεύ(ειν) οὐκ εὐθέως τὰς παραδόσεις ποιοῦνται, εἰ μὴ πρό(τ)ερον δοκ(ι)μάσωσιν· ἐπ᾽ ἐνιαυτὸν γὰρ τὰς ὁμοίας τροφὰς παρατιθέασιν, ἔξω τῆς ἑαυτῶν σ(υνό)δου (οὖ)σιν ἐν ἑτέρῳ οἴκῳ, ἀξινάριόν τε καὶ τὸ λινοῦν περίζωμα κα(ὶ) (λ)ευκὴν ἐσ(θ)ῆτα δόντες. 2. ἐπειδὰν τούτῳ τῷ χρόνῳ πεῖραν (ἐ)γκρα(τεί)ας δῷ, πρόσεισιν ἔγγιον τῇ διαίτῃ καὶ καθαρωτέρως ἀπολ(ούετα)ι ἢ τὸ πρότερον, οὐδέπω δὲ σὺν αὐτοῖς τροφῆς μεταλαμβάνει. μετὰ γὰρ τὸ δεῖξαι εἰ ἐγκρατεύεσθαι δύναται, ἐπὶ ἔτη ἄλλα δύο δοκιμάζεται τοῦ τοιούτου [γὰρ] τὸ ἦθος, καὶ φανεὶς ἄξιος οὕτως εἰς αὐτοὺς <ἐγ>κρίνεται.

3. Πρὶν δὲ αὐτοῖς συνεστιαθῇ, ὅρκοις φρικτοῖς ὁρκίζεται· πρῶτον μὲν εὐσεβήσειν τὸ θεῖον, ἔπειτα τὰ πρὸς ἀνθρώπους δίκαια φυλάξειν καὶ κατὰ μηδένα τρόπον ἀδικήσειν τινά· μηδένα τε μήτε ἀδικοῦντα μήτε ἐχθρὸν μισήσειν, προσεύχεσθαι δὲ ὑπὲρ αὐτῶν, <καὶ> συναγωνίζεσθαι [αὐτῶν] τοῖς δικαίοις. τὸ πιστὸν πᾶσι παρέξειν, μάλιστα τοῖς κρατοῦσιν· οὐ γὰρ δίχα θεοῦ συμβαίνει<ν> τινὶ τὸ ἄρχειν. 4. κἂν αὐτὸς ἄρχῃ, μηδέποτε ὑπερηφανεύσασθαι ἐν ἐξουσίᾳ,

RULES OF THE COMMUNITY. 22. 1. All pay close attention to the presiding officer, and whatever he orders they obey as law. They are zealous in works of mercy and assistance for those worn down with toil. Above all, they refrain from anger and wrath and all similar outbursts, judging them to be conspirers against humanity.

No one swears an oath among them, but whatever someone says is judged to be stronger than an oath. If anyone does swear, he is convicted of being untrustworthy.[123]

2. They are zealous for the readings of the Law and the Prophets, and still more of any treatise written by men of their faith. But they make excessive inquiry into plants and stones, needlessly investigating their powers and claiming that they have not arisen without purpose.

RULES FOR ENTERING THE COMMUNITY. 23. 1. To those who want to become disciples in the sect, the traditions are not imparted at once; first, they make trial of the candidates. For one year, they serve similar food to the novices, but the novices are outside their assembly in another house. They give them a hatchet, a linen robe, and white clothes. 2. When during this time a man gives proof of his self-control, he approaches closer to their way of life and is washed more purely than before—but they do not yet share their food with them. After showing that he is able to maintain self-control, the character of such a man is tested for another two years. When he proves worthy, he is in this way admitted to their number.[124]

3. But before he dines with them, he is sworn in with hair-raising oaths: first that he will reverence the divine, then that he will maintain justice toward human beings and in no way harm another. He swears that he will hate neither someone who harms him nor an enemy. Rather, he swears that he will pray for them and strive together with the righteous.[125] He swears that he will keep loyalty with all, but especially with those in power, for no one attains power apart from God.[126] 4. If he is ever in charge, he

---

123. Cf. Matt 5:33–37.

124. Cf. 1QS VI, 13–23, and initiation into the Pythagorean community in *Ref.* 1.2.16.

125. Cf. Matt 5:44 (ἀγαπᾶτε τοὺς ἐχθροὺς ὑμῶν καὶ προσεύχεσθε ὑπὲρ τῶν διωκόντων ὑμᾶς ["love your enemies, and pray for your persecutors"]). Josephus says that the Essenes swear to always *hate* the unjust (μισήσειν δ' ἀεὶ τοῦς ἀδίκους). Cf. 1QS I, 10 ("detest all the sons of darkness, each one in accordance with his guilt").

126. Cf. Rom 13:1 (οὐ γὰρ ἔστιν ἐξουσία εἰ μὴ ὑπὸ θεοῦ ["there is no authority except that under God"]).

μηδὲ ἀπειθήσειν ἤ τινι κόσμῳ πλείον<ι> τοῦ ἔθους χρήσασθαι. φιλαλήθη τε εἶναι, τὸν δὲ ψευδόμ(εν)ο(ν) ἐλέγχειν· μηδὲ κλέπτειν μηδὲ συνείδησιν ἐπὶ ἀνόμῳ κέρδει μολύνειν. μηδὲν ἀποκρύπτειν τοὺς συναιρεσιώτας, ἑτέροις δὲ μηδὲν ἐξειπεῖν, κἂν μέχρι θανάτου τις βιάζηται. πρὸς τούτοις ὄμνυσι μη(δ)ενὶ μεταδοῦναι τῶν δογμάτων ἑτέρως ἢ ὡς αὐτὸς μετέλαβε.

24. 1. Τοιούτοις οὖν ὅρκοις δεσ(μεύο)υσι τ(οὺς) προσερχομένους. εἰ δέ τις ἐν ἁμαρτήματί τιν(ι) (μεγάλῳ ληφθ)ῇ, ἀποβάλλεται τοῦ <δώματος>, ὁ δὲ ἀποβληθεὶς δεινῷ μόρῳ ἔσθ' ὅτε διαφθείρεται. 2. τοῖς γὰρ ὅρκοις καὶ τοῖς ἔθεσιν ἐνδεδεμένος, (οὐ)δὲ τῆς παρὰ τοῖς ἄλλοις τροφῆς δύναται μεταλ(α)μβάνειν. ἔσθ' ὅτε οὖν τὸ σῶμα λιμῷ δι(α)φθείρ(ο)υσιν· (ὅθ)εν ἐν ἐσχάτοις ποτὲ (ἤδ)η ἐκλείποντας ἐλεοῦσι πολλούς, αὐτῶν ἱκανὴν <τὴν> μέχρι θανάτου ἐπιτιμίαν ἡγούμενοι.

25. 1. Περὶ δὲ τὰς κρίσεις ἀκριβέστατοι καὶ δίκαιοι· δικάζουσι δὲ συνελθόντες οὐκ ἐλάττους τῶν ἑκατόν, τὸ δὲ ὁρισθὲν ὑπ' αὐτῶν ἀκίνητον. τιμῶσι δὲ τὸν νομοθέτην μετὰ τὸν θεόν, καὶ εἴ τις εἰς τοῦτον βλασφημήσει, κολάζεται. τοῖς δὲ ἄρχουσι καὶ πρεσβυτέροις ὑπακούειν διδάσκονται. εἰ δὲ ἐπὶ τὸ αὐτὸ δέκα καθέζονται, οὐ λαλήσει εἷς, εἰ μὴ τοῖς ἐννέα δόξει. 2. καὶ τὸ πτύσαι δὲ εἰς μέσον ἢ τὸ δεξιὸν μέρος φυλάττονται.

τὸ δὲ τῷ σαββάτῳ ἀπέχεσθαι ἔργου φροντίζουσι μᾶλλον πάντων Ἰουδαίων· οὐ μόνον γὰρ τροφὰς αὐτοῖς παρασκευάζονται <πρὸ> μιᾶς ἡμέρας—πρὸς τὸ μὴ πῦρ ἅπτειν—ἀλλ' οὐδὲ σκεῦός μετατιθέασιν οὐδὲ ἀποπατήσουσι. τινὲς δὲ οὐδὲ κλινιδίου χωρίζονται.

swears that he will never arrogate authority, or be refractory, or wear any ornament beyond the custom. He swears that he will love truth and expose what is false; that he will not steal or pollute his conscience with unjust gain; that he will hide nothing from his fellow sectarians and divulge nothing to outsiders—even if he is compelled to the point of death. In addition to these things, he swears that he will never transmit their teachings differently than he received them.

EXCOMMUNICATION. 24. 1. With such oaths they bind those who are admitted. But if someone is caught in some great[127] sin, he is expelled from the house—and sometimes the one expelled is destroyed by a terrible fate.[128] 2. For since he was bound with oaths and customs, he cannot even receive food from the others. Consequently, their bodies are sometimes withered by hunger. In these cases, when the excommunicated are on the verge of death and are already abandoned, they pity many of them, judging the nearly lethal punishment sufficient.[129]

MEETINGS. 25. 1. They are most exacting and just about judgments. When they judge, there are assembled no fewer than one hundred men, and what they ordain is irrevocable. They honor the lawgiver after God, and if anyone slanders him, he is punished. They teach obedience to rulers and elders.[130] If ten sit in the same place, one will not speak unless it is approved by the nine. 2. They are careful to spit either forward or to the right.

SABBATH AND PURITY REGULATIONS. On the Sabbath, they are minded to refrain from work more than all Jews. Not only are foods prepared for them one day ahead of time (so as not to light a fire), they do not even move a dish or relieve themselves. Some do not even get up out of bed.[131]

---

127. Here the letters in P are illegible. Marcovich supplies *μεγάλῳ ληφθῇ* ("caught in [some] great [sin]"), comparing Josephus, *J.W.* 2.143 (*ἁμαρτήμασιν ἁλόντας*). Wendland prefers *καταγνωσθῇ* ("was convicted").

128. Marcovich replaces P's *δόγματος* ("teaching/dogma") with *δώματος* ("house"), reconstructed from the Old Slavic version of Josephus. Greek Josephus reads *τάγμα* ("order").

129. Cf. 2 Cor 4:6 (*ἱκανὴν ἐπιτιμίαν*).

130. Cf. Acts 4:5 (*ἄρχοντας καὶ τοὺς πρεσβυτέρους*).

131. On Sabbath regulations, see Philo, *Prob.* 81–82. Josephus says nothing about Essenes staying in bed. On perceptions of the Jewish Sabbath, see further Peter Schäfer,

3. ταῖς δὲ ἄλλαις ἡμέραις ἐπὰν ἀποπατῆσαι θέλοιεν, βόθρον ὀρύξαντες ποδιαῖον τῇ σκαλίδι—τοιοῦτον γάρ ἐστι τὸ ἀξινάριον, ὃ τοῖς προσιοῦσι μαθητεύεσθαι πρώτως διδόασι—καὶ περικαλύψαντες τὸ ἱμάτιον ἱζάνουσι, φάσκοντες μὴ δεῖν ὑβρίζειν τὰς αὐγάς· ἔπειτα τὴν ἀνασκαφεῖσαν γῆν ἐπεμβάλ<λ>ουσιν εἰς τ(ὸ)ν βόθρον· καὶ τοῦτο ποιοῦσιν ἐκλεγ(όμεν)οι (τοὺς) ἐρημοτέρους τόπους. ἐπὰν δὲ τοῦτ(ο) (ποιήσωσ)ιν, εὐθὺς ἀπολούονται, ὡς μιαινούσης τῆς ἐκκρίσεως.

26. 1. Διῄρηνται δὲ (κ)ατὰ (χρ)όνον καὶ οὐχ ὁμοίως τὴν ἄσκησιν φυλάττουσιν, εἰς τέσσ(αρ)α μέρη διαχωρισθέντες.

ἕτεροι γὰρ αὐτῶν τὰ ὑπὲρ τὸ δέον (ἀ)σκοῦσιν, ὡς μηδὲ νόμισμα βαστάζειν, λέγοντ(ες) μὴ δεῖν εἰ(κό)να ἢ φέρειν ἢ ὁρᾶν ἢ ποιεῖν· διὸ οὐδὲ εἰς πόλιν τι(ς) αὐτῶν εἰσπορεύεται, ἵνα μὴ διὰ πύλης εἰσέλθῃ, ἐφ' ᾗ ἀνδριάντες ἔπεισιν, ἀθέμιτον τοῦτο ἡγούμενος τὸ ὑπὸ εἰκόνας παρελθεῖν.

2. ἕτεροι δέ, ἐπὰν ἀκούσωσί τινος περὶ θεοῦ διαλεγομένου καὶ τῶν τούτου νόμων, εἰ ἀπερίτμητος εἴη, παραφυλάξας τὸν τοιοῦτον ἐν τόπῳ τινὶ μόνον, φονεύειν ἀπειλεῖ εἰ μὴ περιτμηθείη· οὗ, εἰ μὴ βούλοιτο πείθεσθαι, οὐ φείδεται ἀλλὰ καὶ σφάζει· ὅθεν ἐκ τοῦ συμβαίνοντος τὸ ὄνομα προσέλαβον, Ζηλωταὶ καλούμενοι, ὑπό τινων δὲ Σικάριοι.

ἕτεροι δὲ αὐτῶν οὐδένα κύριον ὀνομάζουσι πλὴν τὸν θεόν, εἰ καὶ αἰκίζοιτό τις ἢ καὶ ἀναιροῖτο. 3.—τοσοῦ(το)ν δὲ οἱ μετέπειτα ἐλάττους τῇ ἀσκήσει γεγένη<ν>ται, ὥστε τοὺς τοῖς ἀρχαίοις ἔθεσιν ἐμμένοντας μηδὲ προσψαύειν

3. On other days, if one wants to relieve himself, their practice is to dig a pit one square foot with a digging tool (this is the hatchet that they first give to prospective disciples). Spreading their cloak all around, they squat, claiming that one must not "outrage the rays." Then they toss the dug-up earth into the pit. This they do, selecting the most deserted places. Whenever they do this, they wash at once, as if the excrement defiled them.[132]

DIVISIONS AMONG THE ESSENES. **26.** 1. But in the course of time, they have split and do not keep the same discipline.[133] They are broken up into four camps.[134]

Some of them carry their discipline above what is necessary—to the point of not even carrying a coin (claiming that one must not carry or see or make an image).[135] Accordingly, they do not even enter a city so as to avoid entering a gateway on which there are statues (thinking it sacrilegious to pass under statues).

2. Others, when they hear someone conversing about God and his Law, if he is uncircumcised, one of them keeps watch until such a one is alone in a certain place and threatens to kill him if he is not circumcised. If this one does not want to obey, the Essene does not spare him but even slits his throat. From this occurrence, they receive their name "Zealots," or alternatively, "Dagger Men."[136]

Another group of them call no one master except God—even if someone tortures or kills them.[137] 3. So inferior in discipline have their successors become that those who remain in the ancient customs do not even

Judeophobia: Attitudes toward the Jews in the Ancient World (Cambridge: Harvard University Press, 1997), 82–92.

132. Cf. Deut 23:13–15 (defecation outside the camp).

133. Our author shapes his *Vorlage* to emphasize internecine Jewish disagreements in line with his view of the gradual perversion of truth. See further Koschorke, *Ketzerbekämpfung*, 80–81.

134. The four "camps" (μέρη) refer in Josephus not to different Essene factions but to four levels of initiation described in *J.W.* 2.137–142 (from first-year novices to senior members). Cf. 1QS II, 19–23; V, 13–25 (the volunteer, or lowest rank); VI, 2 (juniors and seniors), 8–9 (the various ranks). Our author aims to highlight Jewish extremism.

135. Cf. Exod 20:4; Josephus, *J.W.* 2.169–174.

136. The account here, although not found in Josephus, resembles *J.W.* 2.254–255 (the Sicarii); cf. 7.253–255.

137. Cf. Josephus, *J.W.* 2.118, 433; 7.418–419; *Ant.* 18.23.

αὐτῶν· ὧν εἰ ψαύσαιεν, εὐθέως ἀπολούονται, ὥς τινος ἀλλοφ(ύ)λ(ου) ψαύσαντες.

Εἰσὶ δὲ καὶ μακρόβιοι οἱ πλεῖστοι, ὥστε καὶ πλέον <ἢ> ἑκατὸν ἔτεσι ζῆν· φα(σὶν) οὖν εἶναι αἴτιον τό τε τῆς ἄκρας θεοσεβείας καὶ τὸ (κ) αταγνωσθῆ<ναι> <τοῦ> ἀμέτρως προσφέρεσθαι <ὡς> ἐγκρατιστάς εἶναι καὶ ἀοργήτους. 4. θανάτου δὲ καταφρονοῦσι, χαίροντες ἡνίκα μετὰ συνειδήσεως ἀγαθ(ῆς) (τ)ε(λ)ευτῶσιν. εἰ δὲ καὶ αἰκίζοιτό τις τῶν τοιούτων, (ἵν)α ἢ τὸν νόμον δυσφημήσῃ ἢ εἰδωλόθυτον φάγῃ, οὐ π(οι)ήσει, ὑπομένων θανεῖν καὶ βασάνους βαστά(σ)αι, ἵνα τὸ συνειδὸς μὴ παρέλθῃ.

27. 1. Ἔρρωται δὲ παρ' αὐτοῖς καὶ ὁ τῆς ἀναστάσεως λόγος· ὁμολογοῦσι γὰρ καὶ τὴν σάρκα ἀναστήσεσθαι καὶ ἔσεσθαι ἀθάνατον, ὃν τρόπον ἤδη ἀθάνατός ἐστιν ἡ ψυχή. ἣν χωρισθεῖσαν νῦν ἔστιν εἰς ἕνα χῶρον εὔπνουν καὶ φωτεινὸν ἀναπαύεσθαι ἕως κρίσεως· ὃν χῶρον Ἕλληνες ἀκούσαντες μακάρων νήσους ὠνόμασαν.

2. ἀλλὰ καὶ ἕτερα τούτων δόγματα πολλ<ὰ> οἱ τῶν Ἑλλήνων σφετερισάμενοι ἰδίας δόξας συνεστήσαντο· ἔστι γὰρ ἡ κατὰ τούτους ἄσκησις περὶ τὸ θεῖον ἀρχαιοτέρα πάντων ἐθνῶν, ὡς δείκνυσθαι πάντας τοὺς περὶ θεοῦ εἰπεῖν τετολμηκότας ἢ περὶ τῆς τῶν ὄντων δημιουργίας μὴ ἑτέρωθεν παρειληφέναι τὰς ἀρχὰς ἢ ἀπὸ τῆς Ἰουδαϊκῆς νομοθεσίας. 3. ὧν μάλιστα Πυθαγόρας καὶ οἱ ἀπὸ τῆς Στοᾶς παρ' Αἰγυπτίοις τούτοις μαθητευθέντες παρέλαβον· λέγουσι γὰρ καὶ κρίσιν ἔσεσθαι, καὶ τοῦ παντὸς ἐκπύρωσιν, καὶ τοὺς ἀδίκους κολασθήσεσθαι εἰς ἀεί.

touch them. If they do touch them, they immediately wash as if they had touched a foreigner.[138]

OLD AGE AND DEATH. Most of them live very long—even more than a hundred years. They say that the reason for this is both their consummate piety toward God and their condemnation of immoderate behavior—since they are both self-controlled and without violent anger. 4. They have contempt for death, rejoicing whenever they die with a good conscience.[139] But if someone tortures one of their kind to try to make him either revile the Law or eat food sacrificed to idols, he will not do it.[140] He suffers death and endures torture so that he might not violate his conscience.

RESURRECTION. **27.** 1. The doctrine of the resurrection predominates among them.[141] They confess that even the flesh will rise again and will become immortal, in the same way as the soul, which is already immortal.[142] When the soul is separated, it is for the present refreshed in a region with fresh breezes and bright light. There it rests until the judgment. Greeks, after hearing of this place, called it the "Isles of the Blessed."

2. (Indeed, the Greeks appropriated many other teachings of these men and established them as their own teachings. This is because Jewish religious practice is older than all nations, as is proved by the fact that all those who have dared to speak about God or about the fashioning of reality received their founding principles from nowhere else than from Jewish legislation. 3. Pythagoras and the Stoics especially appropriated them, having learned from them by way of the Egyptians—for they say that there will be a judgment and a conflagration of everything, and that the unrighteous will be eternally punished.)[143]

---

138. In Josephus, it is the seniors who do not touch their junior counterparts. Our author discusses the fourth group of Essenes in *Ref.* 9.28 below.

139. Cf. 1 Tim 5:19 (συνειδήσεως ἀγάθης).

140. For food sacrificed to idols, see 1 Cor 8:4, 7, 10; Rev 2:14, 20.

141. Cf. *Ref.* 9.28.5; 10.34.3 (our author's own doctrine of bodily resurrection). The *loci classici* for Jewish resurrection are Dan 12:2; Isa 26:19.

142. Josephus does not mention the Essene belief in the resurrection of the dead. He notes only that they show great courage under torture because they believe that the soul is immortal, drawn from the aether (*J.W.* 2.153–154). He says explicitly that the Essenes are "released from the restraints of the flesh as if freed from a long period of slavery" (*J.W.* 2.155; cf. 2.158). Our author has already attributed a doctrine of resurrection to those who did not hold it (the Stoics in *Ref.* 1.21.5; Herakleitos in *Ref.* 9.10.6).

143. This paragraph, greatly expanded from Josephus, accords with our author's

ἀσκεῖται δὲ ἐν αὐτοῖς <καὶ> τὸ προφητεύειν καὶ προλέγειν τὰ ἐσόμενα.

28. 1. (Ἔ)στι μὲν οὖν καὶ ἕτερον Ἐσ<σ>ηνῶν τάγμα· <οἳ> τοῖς μὲν αὐτοῖς ἤθεσι καὶ διαίτῃ χρώμενοι, ἑνὶ δὲ τούτων ἐνδιαλ<λ>ά(ττ)ουσι, [(τ)οὺ(ς)] (τ)ῷ γαμεῖν, δεινόν τι λέγοντες δρᾶν τοὺς ἀ<πο>ποιήσα(ντα)ς γάμον· πρὸς τὴν ἀναίρεσιν τοῦ βίου γίνεσθαι τοῦτο καὶ μὴ δεῖν ἐκκόπτειν τὴν τῶν τέκ(νω)ν διαδοχὴν φάσκοντες, ὡς εἰ πάντες τοῦτο φρονήσειαν, ἐκκοπήσεσθαι ῥᾳδίως τὸ πᾶν γένος ἀνθρώπων. 2. δοκιμάζουσι μέντοι τρι(ε)τίᾳ τὰς γαμετάς· ἐπὰν δὲ τρὶς καθαρθῶσιν εἰς (πεῖρα)ν το(ῦ) δύνασθαι τίκτειν, οὕτως ἄγονται. ταῖς ἐγκύμοσιν οὐχ ὁμιλοῦσιν, ἐπιδεικνύμενοι τὸ μὴ δι᾽ ἡδονὴν γαμεῖν, ἀλλὰ διὰ τέκνων χρείαν. ὁμοίως δὲ καὶ αἱ γυναῖκες ἀπολούονται, καὶ αὐταὶ ἐπέν<δυμ>α ἐνδυόμεναι λινοῦν, ὃν τρόπον οἱ ἄνδρες τὰ περιζώματα.

ταῦτα μὲν οὖν <τὰ> κατὰ Ἐσ<σ>ηνούς.

3. Ἕτεροι δέ, καὶ αὐτοὶ τῶν Ἰουδαίων ἐθῶν ἀσκηταί, καὶ κατὰ γένος καὶ κατὰ νόμους <τῶν ἄλλων διαφέρουσι,> Φαρισαῖοι καλούμενοι. ὧν τὸ μὲν πλεῖστον μέρος ἐστὶ κατὰ πάντα τόπον, πάντων μὲν Ἰουδαίων καλουμένων, διὰ δὲ τὰς ἰδίως δοξαζομένας γνώμας ὀνόμασι κυρίοις ἐπικαλουμένων. 4. οὗτοι μὲν οὖν τὴν ἀρχαίαν παράδοσιν διακρατοῦντες, ἐπὶ τοῖς κατὰ νόμον καθαροῖς καὶ μὴ καθαροῖς ἐπιεικῶς ἐξετάζοντες διαμένουσι, τά τε τοῦ νόμου ἑρμηνεύουσι, διδασκάλους εἰς ταῦτα προβιβάζοντες.

The Essenes also practice prophecy and foretell the future.

THE FOURTH ORDER OF ESSENE. 28. 1. Now there is also another order of Essenes who employ the same customs and way of life but in one point differ from these—namely, marriage.[144] They claim that those who do away with marriage perform a terrible act. They claim that this leads to the destruction of life, and that one must not cut off the succession of children—since, if everyone thought this way, the entire human race would easily be cut off. 2. Nevertheless, they test the married women for three years. When they are thrice purified, in order to test whether they are able to bear children, they are wed.[145] These Essenes do not have intercourse with their pregnant wives. By this abstention they prove that they married not for pleasure but because they need children. Moreover, the women wash themselves in the same way and clothe themselves with a linen shawl in the way that the men gird themselves with loincloths.

These, then, are the matters concerning the Essenes.

PHARISEES

3. Another group engaged in the disciplined practice of Jewish customs differ from the others both as a class and by their laws.[146] They are called "Pharisees."[147] The majority of them are spread everywhere. All these people are called Jews but, due to their peculiar opinions and viewpoints, are referred to with technical designations. 4. These Pharisees master the ancient tradition and persist in rationally proving what is pure and impure according to the Law.[148] They interpret the matters of the Law, training teachers in these topics.

---

apologetic emphasis on the temporal priority of Jewish tradition over Greek philosophy (cf. *Ref.* 10.30–31). See further Hamel, *Kirche bei Hippolyt*, 110–11; Koschorke, *Ketzerbekämpfung*, 22–24; Peter Pilhofer, *Presbyteron Kreitton: Der Altersbeweis der jüdischen und christlichen Apologeten und seine Vorgeschichte*, WUNT 2/39 (Tübingen: Mohr Siebeck, 1990), 289–92. On judgment and conflagration, see *Ref.* 1.3.1 (Empedokles); 1.21.4 (Stoics); 9.10.7 (Herakleitos); 9.28.5 (Pharisees); 9.30.8 (Jews); 10.34.2 (the "true doctrine").

144. Cf. the second order of Brahmans in *Ref.* 1.24.4.

145. The purification meant here is apparently purification after menstruation.

146. Marcovich adds τῶν ἄλλων διαφέρουσι ("differ from the others").

147. On the Pharisees, see Josephus, *J.W.* 3.374; *Ant.* 18.14; *Ag. Ap.* 2.218.

148. On tradition (παράδοσιν), see Josephus, *Ant.* 18.297.

5. Οὗτοι εἱμαρμένην εἶναι λέγουσι, καὶ τινὰ μὲν κατ᾽ ἐξουσίαν εἶναι, τινὰ δὲ κατὰ τὴ(ν) εἱμαρμένην, ὡς τινὰ μὲν ἐφ᾽ ἡμῖν, τινὰ δὲ τῆς εἱμαρμένης· θεὸν (δ)ὲ πάντων εἶναι αἴτιον καὶ μηδὲν ἄνευ θελήματος αὐτοῦ διοικεῖσθαι ἢ συμβαίνειν. οὗτοι καὶ σαρκὸς ἀνάστασιν ὁμολογοῦσι, καὶ ψυχὴν ἀθάνατον, καὶ κρίσιν ἐσομένην καὶ ἐκπύρωσιν, καὶ δικαίους μὲν ἀφθάρτους ἔσ(εσ)θαι, ἀδίκους δὲ εἰς ἀεὶ κ(ο)λασθήσεσθαι ἐν πυρὶ ἀσβέστῳ.

Ταῦτα μὲν οὖν καὶ Φαρισαῖο(ι).

29. 1. Σαδδουκαῖοι δὲ τὴν μὲν εἱμαρμένην ἀν(αι)ροῦσι (καὶ) τὸ(ν) (θ)εὸν μηδέν τι κακὸν δρᾶν ἢ ἐφορᾶν ὁμολογοῦ(σι)ν, εἶναι δὲ ἐν ἀνθρώπων ἐξουσίᾳ τὸ αἱρεῖ(σ)θαι τὸ ἀγαθὸν ἢ κακόν. ἀνάστασιν δὲ οὐ μόνον ἀρνοῦνται σαρκός, ἀλλὰ καὶ ψυχὴν μὴ διαμένειν νομίζουσι. 2. τ(αύ)τ(ῃ) (δὲ) εἶναι μόνον τὸ ζῆν καὶ τοῦτο δὴ εἶναι οὗ χάριν ἐγένετο (ἄ)νθρωπος, ἔν τε <τού>τῳ πληροῦσθαι τὸν τῆς ἀναστάσεως λ(όγ)ον, ἐν τῷ καταλείψαντα ἐπὶ γῆς [τὰ] τέκνα τελευτᾶν. μετὰ δὲ θάνατον μηδέν<α> ἐλπίζειν παθεῖν ἢ κακὸν ἢ ἀγαθόν· λύσιν γὰρ ἔσεσθαι καὶ ψυχῆς καὶ σώματος, καὶ εἰς τὸ μὴ εἶναι χωρεῖν τὸν ἄνθρωπον, καθ᾽ ὃ καὶ τὰ λοιπὰ ζῷα. 3. ὅ τι δ᾽ ἂν δράσῃ ἄνθρωπος ἐν τῷ βίῳ κακὸν [ἄνθρωπος] καὶ διαλάθῃ, κεκέρδηκε, τὴν ὑπὸ ἀνθρώπων διαφυγὼν κόλασιν· ὅ τι δ᾽ ἂν κτήσηται καὶ πλουτήσας δοξασθῇ, <καὶ> τοῦτο κεκέρδηκε· μέλειν γὰρ θεῷ μηδὲν τῶν κατὰ ἕνα. καὶ οἱ μὲν Φαρισαῖοι φιλάλληλοι, οἱ δὲ Σαδδουκαῖοι φίλαυτοι.

5. Pharisees say that fate exists. Some things occur by free will, and others by fate, so that some things depend on us, and others on fate.[149] But God is the cause of all, and nothing is managed or occurs apart from his will.

They also confess the resurrection of the flesh, that the soul is immortal, and that there is a future judgment and conflagration. The righteous will be incorruptible, but the unrighteous will be punished forever in unquenchable fire.[150]

These are the teachings of the Pharisees.

SADDUCEES

29. 1. The Sadducees, in contrast, do away with fate and confess that God does nothing at all evil and does not watch over us.[151] Rather, the choice between good or evil is in the power of human beings. They not only deny the resurrection of the flesh but do not even believe that the soul survives. 2. Life exists only in this world. The human race came about for this purpose: to leave behind children on earth and die. By this means, the doctrine of the resurrection is fulfilled. After death, there is no expectation of experiencing anything at all either good or bad. There will be a dissolution of soul and body, and after that, the human passes into nonexistence as is fated for the rest of the animals.[152] 3. Whatever evil a person does in this life that escapes notice is counted as gain, since one escaped punishment by human beings.[153] Whatever one acquires, as well as the honor one receives from wealth, is also counted as gain. God does not care at all for anything individual. Moreover, whereas the Pharisees show concern for others, the Sadducees are devoted only to themselves.[154]

---

149. On fate (εἱμαρμένην), see Josephus, *Ant.* 13.172; 18.13; *Life* 12 (a direct comparison with the Stoics); Epiph., *Pan.* 16.2.1.

150. Josephus states that the Pharisees believed in transmigration (*J.W.* 2.163). Our author may have omitted this point because of his wont to attribute transmigration to Pythagoras (*Ref.* 1.2.11; 6.26.2). On the conflagration, see the note on *Ref.* 9.27.3 above.

151. For the Sadducees, see Josephus, *J.W.* 2.164–165.

152. Cf. Josephus, *Ant.* 18.16; Matt 22:23; Mark 12:18; Luke 20:27; Acts 23:8; Ps.-Tert., *Adv. omn. haer.* 1.

153. Cf. *Ref.* 1.22.5 (Epikouros). This line is absent in Josephus.

154. Cf. Josephus, *J.W.* 2.166.

4. αὕτη ἡ αἵρεσις περὶ τὴν Σαμάρειαν μᾶλλον ἐκρατύνθη. καὶ αὐτοὶ δὲ τοῖς τοῦ νόμου ἔθεσι προσέχουσι, λέγοντες δεῖν οὕτω ζῆν, ἵνα καλῶς βιώσῃ καὶ τέκνα ἐπὶ γῆς καταλείπῃ. προφήταις δὲ οὐ προσέχουσιν, ἀλλ' οὐδὲ ἑτέροις τισὶ σοφοῖς, πλὴν μόνῳ τῷ διὰ Μωσέως νόμῳ, μηδὲν ἑρμηνεύοντες.

ταῦτα μὲν οὖν ἃ καὶ οἱ Σαδδουκαῖοι αἱρετίζουσιν.

30. 1. Ἐπεὶ τοίνυν καὶ τὰς παρὰ Ἰουδαίοις διαφορὰς ἐκτεθείμεθα, εὔλογον δοκεῖ καὶ τὴν ἄσκησιν τούτων τῆς θεοσεβείας μὴ παρασιωπᾶν. ἔστι μὲν οὖν κατὰ πάντας Ἰουδαίους ἡ κατὰ τὴν θεοσέβειαν πραγματεία τετραχῇ· θεολογική, φυσική, ἠθική, ἱερουργική.

2. καὶ τὸν μὲν θεὸν ἕνα εἶ(ν)αι λέγουσι, δημιουργόν τε τοῦ παντὸς καὶ κ(ύριον), ποιήσ(α)ντα πάντα οὐ πρότερον ὄντ(α), οὐδὲ ἔκ τινος ὑποκειμένης συγχρόνου οὐσίας, ἀ(λ)λ(ὰ) θελήσαντα καὶ κτίσαντα. εἶναι δὲ ἀγγέλους καὶ τούτους γ(εν)ομένους πρὸς λειτουργίαν τῆς κτίσεως, ἀλλὰ καὶ πνεῦμα ἐξουσιαστικ(όν), πρὸς δόξαν καὶ αἶνον θεῷ ἀεὶ παραμένον. τὰ πάντα (δ)ὲ ἐν τῇ κτίσει αἴσθησιν ἔχειν καὶ μηδὲν εἶναι ἄψυχον.

3. Ἤθους δὲ ἀντιποιοῦνται σεμνοῦ καὶ σώφρονος βίου, καθὼς ἔστιν ἐκ τῶν νόμων ἐπιγνῶναι· ταῦτα δὲ πάλαι ἀκριβαζόμενα ἦν παρ' α<ὐ>τοῖς, ἀρχῆθεν, <οὐ> νεωστὶ τὸν νόμον παρειληφόσιν, ὡς τὸν ἐντυγχάνοντα καταπλαγῆναι ἐπὶ τοσαύτῃ σωφροσύνῃ καὶ ἐπιμελείᾳ τοῦ περὶ τὸν ἄνθρωπον νομοθετουμένου ἤθους.

4. Ἱερουργικὴ δὲ λειτουργία ἄκρως ἐξήσκητο παρ' αὐτοῖς, εὐσχημόνως πρὸς τὸ θεῖον προσφερομένοις, καθὼς τοῖς βουλομένοις ῥᾴδιόν ἐστιν, ἐντυχοῦσι τῇ περὶ τούτων ἐξαγορευούσῃ βίβλῳ, μαθεῖν, ὡς σεμνῶς καὶ ὁσίως τῷ θεῷ

4. This heresy prevailed mostly in the region of Samaria. They also apply themselves to the customs of the Law, saying that it is necessary to live this way in order to live well and leave behind children on earth. They do not attend to the prophets, nor any other sages except the Law alone, which was given through Moses. They make no interpretive judgments at all.[155]

These, then, are the heretical teachings of the Sadducees.

JEWISH RELIGION

30. 1. Since, then, I presented the differences among the Jews, it seems reasonable not to keep silent about the practice of their religion.[156] Among all Jews, the religious system is fourfold: theological, natural, ethical, and priestly.

THEOLOGY AND VIEW OF NATURE. 2. They say that God is one, Artificer and Lord of the universe, and the maker of everything that did not previously exist. He did not make it from some underlying material coeval with himself. Rather, he created it by willing it.[157] Angels exist, and they are made for the service of creation. There is also an authoritative Spirit that remains eternally for the glory and praise of God. Everything in creation has sense perception, and nothing is without soul.

ETHICS. 3. They strive after a reverent and moderate lifestyle, as can be recognized from their laws. Since ancient times, they have studied these laws exactingly. They have done so from the beginning, since they have not received the Law only yesterday.[158] As a result, the one who encounters them is struck by their great moderation and care for the customs legislated for humanity.

PRIESTLY SERVICE. 4. They intensely practiced the priestly service, making offerings to the Godhead in a dignified way. This is quite easy for interested persons to learn by reading the book discoursing about these matters.[159] It

155. Cf. Origen, *Cels.* 1.49; *Comm. Matt.* 17.35–36.

156. Wendland believes that the following passage (*Ref.* 9.30) summarizes the discussion of the Mosaic Law's antiquity and superiority in Josephus, *Ag. Ap.* 2.15–17.

157. For coeval matter, see *Ref.* 1.19.4 (Plato); 8.17.1 (Hermogenes).

158. Cf. Josephus, *Ag. Ap.* 2.154, 156, 171, 173.

159. The book of Leviticus, apparently.

ἀπάρχεσθαι τῶν παρ᾽ αὐτοῦ δεδωρημένων εἰς χρῆσιν καὶ ἀπόλαυσιν ἀνθρώπων κελευόμενοι, εὐτάκτως καὶ παραμόνως ἐλειτούργουν. τούτων δέ τιν(α) οἱ Σαδδουκαῖοι ἀπαγορεύουσιν· οὐ γὰρ βούλονται ἀγγέλους ἢ πνεύματα ὑπάρχειν.

5. Οἱ δὲ πάντες ὁμοίως Χριστὸν προσδέχονται· τοῦ μὲν νόμου καὶ τῶν προφητῶν παρεσόμενον προκηρυξάντων, τῶν δὲ Ἰουδαίων τὸν καιρὸν τῆς παρουσίας μὴ ἐπιγνόντων, ἐπιμένειν τὴν ὑπόνοιαν τοῦ δοκεῖν μὴ τὰ εἰρ(η)μένα περὶ τῆς παρ(ου)σί(α)ς τετελέσθαι, προσδοκᾶν τε ἔτι τοῦ<τον> π(α)ρεσόμενον, διὰ τὸ <τὸν> παρόντα μὴ ἐπεγ(ν)ωκέναι. καὶ τὰ σύμβολα τῶν καιρῶν τοῦ <τοῦτον> ἤδη παραγεγονέναι ὁρῶντας ταράττεσθαι, αἰδεῖσθαι δὲ ὁμολογεῖν ἐ(ληλυθέν)αι, ἐπεὶ αὐτόχειρες αὐτοῦ γεγένηνται, ἀγανακτοῦντας ἐλεγχομένους ὑπ᾽ αὐτοῦ ὅτι τοῖς νόμοις μὴ ὑπήκουσαν.

6. Καὶ τὸν μὲν οὕτως ἀποσταλέντα ὑπὸ τοῦ θεοῦ Χριστὸν οὐκ εἶναι τοῦτον λέγουσιν, ἐλεύσεσθαι δὲ ἕτερον, τὸν οὔ<πω παρ>όντα, <ἐν ᾧ τὰ> [μὲν] σύμβολα ἐκ μέρους, ὅσα ὁ νόμος καὶ οἱ προφῆται προέφηναν, <τελεσθήσεσθαι>, ὁμολογοῦσι. 7. τινὰ δὲ καὶ πλανώμενοι νομίζουσι· γένεσιν μὲν γὰρ αὐτοῦ ἐσομένην λέγουσιν ἐκ γένους Δαβίδ, ἀλλ᾽ οὐκ ἐκ παρθένου καὶ ἁγίου πνεύματος, ἀλλ᾽ ἐκ γυναικὸς καὶ ἀνδρός, ὡς πᾶσιν ὅρος γεν<ν>ᾶσθαι ἐκ σπέρματος, φάσκοντες τοῦτον ἐσόμενον βασιλέα ἐπ᾽ αὐτούς, ἄνδρα πολεμιστὴν καὶ δυνατόν. ὃς ἐπισυνάξας τὸ πᾶν ἔθνος Ἰουδαίων πάντα τὰ ἔθνη πολεμήσας, ἀναστήσει αὐτοῖς τὴν Ἱερουσαλὴμ πόλιν βασιλίδα· εἰς ἣν ἐπισυνάξει ἅπαν τὸ ἔθνος καὶ πάλιν ἐπὶ τὰ ἀρχαῖα ἔθη ἀποκαταστήσει, βασιλεύων καὶ ἱερατεύων καὶ κατοικῶν ἐν πεποιθήσει ἐν χρόνοις ἱκανοῖς.

8. ἔπειτα ἐπαναστῆσαι κατ᾽ αὐτοῦ πόλεμον ἐπισυναχθέντα, ἐν ἐκείνῳ τῷ πολέμῳ πεσεῖν τὸν Χριστὸν ἐν μαχαίρῃ. ἔπειτα μετ᾽ οὐ πολὺ τὴν συντέλειαν καὶ

includes how they are commanded solemnly and piously to offer to God the first fruits of things given by him for human use and enjoyment, and how they served as priests with discipline and persistence.[160] Some of these things the Sadducees reject, for they do not concede the existence of angels or spirits.[161]

MESSIANIC EXPECTATIONS. 5. All Jews alike expect the Christ. The Law and the Prophets preached that he would come, but the Jews did not recognize the time of his arrival, persisting in their supposition that the things said about his coming do not seem to be fulfilled. They still expect the Christ to come, because they did not recognize the one who was present. And since they see that the signs of the times indicate that he has already come, they are disturbed.[162] Still, they are ashamed to confess that he has already come, because they were his murderers. They are distressed as those refuted by him, because they did not obey their laws.

6. Thus they affirm that the one thus sent by God is not the Christ, but that another will come, who is not yet present. They confess that by him the signs that the Law and the Prophets declared will be partially fulfilled.[163] 7. Some things they believe in error. For one, they say that his birth will be from the lineage of David—not from a virgin and Holy Spirit, but from a woman and a man (as is the rule for all those born from seed). They claim that this one will come to them as their king and as a man powerful in war. He will make war upon the nations and gather the entire race of Jews. Then he will raise up Jerusalem for them as his royal city, into which he will gather the whole nation of Jews. He will again restore the ancient customs, reigning and serving as priest and dwelling in confidence for a long time.[164]

8. Then war will be gathered against him. In that war, the Christ will fall by the sword. Then, not long after that, the consummation and conflagration of the universe will come. In this way, their beliefs about the

---

160. Cf. 1 Tim 6:17 (εἰς ἀπόλαυσιν).

161. Cf. Acts 23:8.

162. Cf. Matt 16:3 (σημεῖα τῶν καιρῶν).

163. Marcovich's emendations (changing οὐκ ὄντα to οὔπω παρόντα; εἰς ὄντα to ἐν ᾧ τά; the addition of τελεσθήσεσθαι) have been accepted as efforts to make sense of this passage.

164. For visions of the Messiah, see Pss. Sol. 17:21–45; cf. 4 Ezra 7:26–31; 12:31–34. The idea that the Messiah will be priestly is reminiscent of the Qumran sectarians. Yet they envisioned two Messiahs: one priestly, the other royal (1QS IX, 11 [משיחי אהרון וישראל]).

ἐκπύρωσιν τοῦ παντὸς ἐπιστῆναι, καὶ οὕτως τὰ περὶ τὴν ἀνάστασιν δοξαζόμενα ἐπιτελεσθῆναι τάς τε ἀμοιβὰς ἑκάστῳ κατὰ τὰ πεπραγμένα ἀποδοθῆναι.

31. 1. Δοκεῖ μὲν ἡμῖν ἱκανῶς τὰ πάντα Ἑλλήνων τε καὶ βαρβάρων δόγματα ἐκτεθεῖσθαι μηδέν τε ἀπολελοιπέναι μ(ή)τε τῶν φιλοσοφουμένων μήτε τῶν ὑπὸ αἱρετικῶ(ν) φα(σκ)ομένων ἀναπόδεικτον· ὧν ἐξ αὐτῶν τῶν ἐκτεθέντων φανερὸς γεγένηται ὁ ἔλεγχ(ο)ς <ὡς> ἢ κλεψιλογησάντων ἤ τινα <καὶ> ἐρανισαμένων, αὐτά τὰ ὑπὸ Ἑλλήνων πεπονημένα παραθεμένων ὡς θεῖα.

2. διὰ πάντων οὖν διαδραμόντες καὶ μετὰ πολλοῦ πόνου ἐν ταῖς ἐννέα βίβλοις τὰ πά(ν)τα δόγματα ἐξειπόντες, πᾶσι τε ἀνθρώποις ἐφόδιον ἐν βίῳ <οὐ> μικρὸν καταλιπόντες καὶ τοῖς παροῦσιν οὐκ ὀλίγης χαρᾶς καὶ θυμηδίας φιλομάθειαν παρασχόντες, εὔλογον ἡγούμεθα ὥσπερ κορυφὴν τοῦ παντὸς <τὸν> περὶ ἀληθείας λόγον ἐπενέγκαι καὶ τοῦτον ἐν μιᾷ βίβλῳ τῇ δεκάτῃ περιγράψαι, ὅπως ὁ ἐντυγχάνων μὴ μόνον <τὴν> ἀνατροπὴν τῶν τετολμηκότων αἱρέσεις συστήσασθαι ἐπιγνοὺς καταφρονήσῃ τῶν ματαίων, ἀλλὰ καὶ τὴν τῆς ἀληθείας δύναμιν ἐπιγνοὺς ἀξίως θεῷ πιστεύσας σωθῆναι δυνηθῇ.

resurrection will be fulfilled, and just deserts will be administered to each person according to what each one performed.[165]

CONCLUSION

31. 1. Now it seems to me that I have sufficiently presented all the dogmas of Greeks and non-Greeks, and that I have left nothing unexposed of either philosophical teachings or the claims of the heretics. From the very presentation of these teachings, their refutation is obvious: either they plagiarized, or they borrowed these things for their own purposes and presented the teachings elaborated by Greeks as though they were divine.

2. Now that I have reviewed all these matters, and after much labor have pronounced on all their doctrines in the course of nine books, I leave behind to all people no small provision for life and provide to the present generation my diligent study with no little joy and pleasure. As a consequence, I consider it reasonable to offer up the true doctrine as a crown of the work as a whole and to compose this in a single tenth book.[166] I do so in order that the reader may not only—after recognizing the overthrow of those who had the audacity to concoct the heresies—despise them as drivel, but also so that the reader, by recognizing the power of truth and worthily believing in God, might be saved.

165. Cf. Dan 12:1–3; 2 Bar. 29–30; 39–40; 4 Ezra 7:32–44.

166. See *Ref.* 10.32–34.

<ΤΟΥ ΚΑΤΑ ΠΑΣΩΝ ΑΙΡΕΣΕΩΝ ΕΛΕΓΧΟΥ> Ι

1. Τάδε ἔνεστιν ἐν τῇ δεκάτῃ τοῦ κατὰ πασῶν αἱρέσεων ἐλέγχου·
2. Ἐπιτομὴ πάντων τῶν φιλοσόφων.
3. Ἐπιτομὴ πασῶν αἱρέσεων.
4. Καὶ ἐπὶ πᾶσι, τίς ὁ τῆς ἀληθείας λόγος.

5. 1. Τὸν λαβύρινθον τῶν αἱρέσεων οὐ βί(ᾳ) διαρρήξαντες, ἀλλὰ μόνῳ ἐλέγχῳ ἀληθείας δυνάμει διαλύσαντες, πρόσιμεν ἐπὶ τὴν τῆς ἀληθείας ἀπόδειξιν. τότε γὰρ τῆς πλάνης ἔντεχνα σοφίσματα ἀσύστατα φανερωθήσεται, ἐπὰν ὁ τῆς ἀληθείας ὅρος ἐπιδειχθῇ· <ὃς> οὐκ ἀπὸ σοφίας Ἑλ(λ)ήνων ἀρχὰς μεταλαβών, οὐδ᾽ Αἰγυπτ(ί)ων δόγμα<τα> τά <τ᾽> ἐν αὐτοῖς μετ᾽ ἀξιοπιστίας θρ(η)σκευόμενα μάταια ὡς ἄρρητα διδαχθείς, οὐδὲ Χαλδαίων ἀσυστάτῳ περιερ(γ)ίᾳ σοφισθείς, οὐδὲ Βαβυλωνίων ἀλογίστῳ μανίᾳ δι᾽ ἐν(εργεί)ας (δ)αιμόνων καταπλαγείς, ἀλλ᾽ ᾧ ὑπάρχει τρόπῳ ὅρος ἀληθής, ὢν ἀφύλακτός τε καὶ ἀκαλλώπιστος, μόνον φανεὶς ἐλέγξει τὴν πλάνην.

BOOK 10

[TABLE OF CONTENTS]

1. The following is contained in the tenth book of the *Refutation of All Heresies.*

2. Summary of all the philosophers.

3. Summary of all the heresies.

4. As the capstone to all, the true doctrine.

INTRODUCTION

5. 1. I have broken through the labyrinth of heresies, but not by brute force.[1] Rather, I have demolished it solely by the strength of my exposé and the power of truth. Accordingly, I will proceed to the demonstration of the truth. When the standard of truth is revealed, the fabricated and inconsistent sophisms of deceit will be revealed for what they are. This standard did not receive its first principles from Greek wisdom. Nor was it taught the dogmas of the Egyptians and the trivialities that they worship with implicit faith—as if they were unspeakable mysteries! Nor was it made wise by the inconsistent meddling of Chaldeans. Nor was it awestruck by the irrational madness of the Babylonians executed through the operation of demons. Rather, the standard of truth—inexorable and unadorned—works by its own method. By its pure manifestation, it will refute error.

1. Photios, *Bibl.* chap. 48, indicates that Λαβύρινθος was a book title written by the same author as the writer of *On the Universe.* Possibly book 10 was detached from the *Refutation* and called *The Labyrinth* due to its opening line (Salmon, "Hippolytus Romanus"; Döllinger, *Hippolytus and Callistus*, 251–53). For the metaphor of the labyrinth used in Greek philosophy, see Plato, *Euth.* 291b; cf. Gregory the Wonderworker, *Orat. paneg.* 14.168 (SC 148:166). Our author may be thinking of the Naassene psalm, in which the soul wanders in a labyrinth before receiving gnosis (*Ref.* 5.10.2).

2. περὶ οὗ εἰ καὶ πλειστάκις ἀποδείξεις ἐποιήσαμεν καὶ ἱκανῶς τὸν τῆς ἀληθείας κανόνα <καὶ> ἀφθόνως τοῖς βουλομένοις ἐπεδείξαμεν, ἀλλά γε καὶ νῦν οὐκ ἄλογον ἐκρίναμεν ἐπὶ πᾶσι τοῖς Ἕλλησι καὶ αἱρετικοῖς δεδοκημένοις ὡσεὶ κορωνίδα τῶν βίβλων ἐπενέγκαι ταύτην τὴν ἀπόδειξιν διὰ τῆς δεκάτης βίβλου.

6. 1. Συμπεριλαβόντες τοίνυν τὰ πάντων τῶν παρ' Ἕλλησι σοφῶν δόγματα ἐν τέσσαρσι βίβλοις, τά τε τοῖς αἱρεσιάρχαις ἐν πέντε, νῦν τὸν περὶ ἀληθείας λόγον ἐν μιᾷ ἐπιδείξομεν, ἀνακεφαλαιούμενοι πρῶτον τὰ πᾶσι δεδοκημένα.

2. οἱ μέν γε τῶν Ἑλλήνων δογματισταὶ τὴν φιλοσοφίαν τριχῇ διελόντες οὕτως ἐφιλοσόφησαν, οἱ μὲν φυσικήν, οἱ δὲ ἠθικήν, οἱ δὲ διαλεκτικὴν προσαγορεύσαντες. καὶ οἱ μὲν τὴν φυσικὴν <προτιμήσαντες> οὗτοι γεγένηνται, οὕτως τε διηγήσαντο.

2. As regards this standard, I recognize that I have made my demonstrations many times, and that I have fully and generously exhibited the rule of truth to those who were willing. Even so, I decided that it is not unreasonable to offer up as a crown of my books this demonstration against all the beliefs of Greeks and heretics in my tenth book.

6. 1. Now then, since I have already included the dogmas of all the Greek sages in four books, and the tenets of the chief heretics in five, I will presently exhibit the doctrine of truth in one book.[2] But first I sum up the beliefs of all.[3]

SUMMARY OF GREEK PHILOSOPHY

2. At least some of the Greek dogmatists divided philosophy into three parts and developed their philosophies according to one of the three divisions. Some focused on what they call natural philosophy, others on ethical philosophy, and still others on dialectic. Those who preferred natural philosophy arose and discoursed as follows.[4]

---

2. For τὸν περὶ ἀληθείας λόγον, see Justin, *1 Apol.* 5.3; Plato, *Meno* 81a.

3. Frickel argues that book 10 was an earlier independent apologetic work directed toward a non-Christian audience (*Dunkel*, 128–52; cf. idem, "Refutatio, Buch X," 233–44). He is opposed by Koschorke, *Ketzerbekämpfung*, 102–4. Book 10 does have some odd qualities (pointed out by Mueller, "Hippolytus *Retractatus*," 236), and these might be taken as evidence of its separate composition. Four points are significant: (1) although book 10 is constructed as a summary of the *Refutation*, our author provides no epitome of ethical or dialectical philosophers, mystery cults, or astrology; (2) for his summary of philosophers, he does not turn back to his own book 1 but adapts Sext. Emp., *Math.* 10.310–318; (3) for the "heretics," he does not return to books 5–9 but makes new transcriptions from his sources; and (4) he fails to maintain the order of his opponents that he presented in books 5–9. Point 4 can perhaps be explained by point 3. Concerning point 2, the fact that our author used Sextus as a fresh, more concise witness for the natural philosophers (in whom he was interested) is not surprising given his predilection for transcription. Finally, the fact that our author mentions the mysteries of the Egyptians, the divination of the Chaldeans, and the madness of the Babylonians in *Ref.* 10.5.1 indicates that he was at least aware of his previous treatment of their views. There is no explicit argument that the "heretics" plagiarized the philosophers, but—as Mansfeld points out—"the simple juxtaposition of the tenets of the philosophers and the doctrines of the Gnostics" was intended to indicate a genetic connection (*Heresiography*, 56).

4. Marcovich adds προτιμήσαντες (here: "who preferred"). The following summary of the natural philosophers (*Ref.* 10.6.2–7.6) is adapted from Sext. Emp., *Math.* 10.310–318, where Sextus attempts to prove that the doctrines of the natural philoso-

Οἱ μὲν ἐξ ἑνὸς τὰ πάντα, οἱ δὲ ἐκ πλειόνων·

καὶ τῶν ἐξ ἑνὸς οἱ μὲν ἐξ ἀποίου, οἱ δὲ ἐκ [τοῦ] ποιοῦ·

καὶ τῶν ἐκ ποιοῦ οἱ μὲν ἐκ πυρός, οἱ δὲ ἐξ ἀέρος, οἱ δὲ ἐξ ὕδατος, ἄλλοι δὲ ἐκ γῆς.

3. καὶ (τ)ῶν ἐκ πλειόνων οἱ μὲν ἐξ ἀριθμητῶν, <οἱ δὲ ἐξ ἀπείρων.

καὶ τῶν ἐξ ἀριθμητῶν,> οἱ μὲν ἐκ δυ(εῖ)ν, οἱ δὲ ἐ(κ) τεσσάρων, οἱ δὲ ἐκ πέντε, οἱ δὲ ἐξ ἕξ.

καὶ τῶν ἐ(ξ) ἀ(π)είρων οἱ μὲν ἐξ ὁμοίων τοῖς γενωμένοις, οἱ δὲ ἐξ ἀνομοίων· καὶ πρὸς τούτων οἱ μ(ὲ)ν ἐξ (ἀ)π(α)θῶν, οἱ δὲ ἐκ παθητῶν.

4. <Ἐξ> ἀποίου μὲν οὖν καὶ ἑνὸς σώματος τὴν τῶν ὅλων συνεστήσαντο γένεσιν οἱ Στωϊκοί· ἀρχὴ γὰρ τῶν ὅλων κατ' αὐτούς ἐστιν ἡ ἄποιος ὕλη καὶ δι' ὅλων τρεπ<τ>ή, μεταβαλλούσης τε αὐτῆς γίνεται πῦρ, ἀήρ, ὕδωρ, γῆ.

NATURAL PHILOSOPHY. Some say that everything was produced from one thing, while others say that everything was produced from many things.

A. EVERYTHING FROM ONE THING. Among those who say that everything was born from one, some say that it was born from what has no quality, and others from what has quality.

i. FROM WHAT HAS QUALITY. Among those who say that it was born from what has quality, some say that it was born from fire, others from air, others from water, and others from earth.

B. EVERYTHING FROM MANY. 3. Among those who say that everything was born from many things, some say that it was born from things numbered, and others from infinite entities.

i. FROM THINGS NUMBERED. Among those who say that it was born from things that are numbered, some say that it was born from two, others from four, others from five, and others from six.

ii. FROM INFINITE ENTITIES. Among those who say that it was born from infinite entities, some say that it was born from entities that are the same as generated beings, while others from beings that are not the same. In addition to these camps, some say that all things are born from entities not liable to change, while others say that all things are born from entities that are liable to change.

C. THE STOICS: GENERATION FROM ONE UNQUALIFIED BODY. 4. The Stoics concocted an origin of the universe from a single body without quality. According to them, the first principle of the universe is unqualified matter, which is able to change into everything. When it is transformed, it becomes fire, air, water, and earth.[5]

---

phers cannot explain either generation or corruption. The organization of the summary (based on the number of ἀρχαί) may go back to Theophrastos (see Theophrastos, frags. 224–230 [FHSG 1:403–23]). The excerpt from Sextus hardly reviews book 1 *in toto*, but it allowed our author to focus on his central interest: physics, and specifically the physics of first principles (ἀρχαί). His fundamental presupposition is that the philosophers missed the true first principle, namely, God. See further Norelli, "Construire l'opposition," 240–41.

5. The information here misrepresents the Stoics, who in fact believed in two prin-

ἐξ ἑνὸς δὲ καὶ ποιοῦ γεγενῆσθαι τὰ πάντα θέλουσιν οἵ τε περὶ τὸν Ἵππασον καὶ Ἀναξίμανδρον καὶ Θαλῆ τὸν Μιλήσιον. <ὧν> Ἵππασος μὲν ὁ Μεταπόντιος καὶ Ἡράκλειτος ὁ Ἐφέσιος ἐκ πυρὸς ἀπεφήναντο τὴν γένεσιν, Ἀναξίμανδρος δὲ ἐξ ἀέρος, Θαλῆς δὲ ἐξ ὕδατος, Ξενοφάνης δὲ ἐκ γῆς·

ἐκ γῆς γάρ, φησί, πάντ' ἔστι, καὶ εἰς [τὴν] γῆν πάντα τελευτᾷ.

7. 1. Ἐκ πλειόνων δὲ καὶ ἀριθμ<ητ>ῶν, δυεῖν μέν, γῆς τε καὶ ὕδατος, τὰ ὅλα συνεστηκέναι φησὶ ὁ ποιητὴς Ὅμηρος, ὁτὲ μὲν λέγων·

Ὠκεανόν τε θεῶν γένεσιν καὶ μητέρα Τηθύν,

ὁτὲ δέ·

ἀλλ' ὑμεῖς πάντες ὕδωρ καὶ γαῖα γένοισθε.

2. συμφέρεσ<θαι> δ' αὐτῷ δοκεῖ καὶ ὁ Κολοφώνιος Ξενοφάνης· φησὶ γάρ·

D. Generation from One Entity with Quality. In contrast, the following philosophers preferred to think that all things arose from a single entity endowed with quality: the disciples of Hippasos, Anaximandros, and Thales the Milesian.[6] In this camp, Hippasos the Metapontian and Herakleitos the Ephesian declared that from fire the world was born; Anaximandros, from air; Thales, from water; and Xenophanes, from earth, as he says:

> From earth are all things, and in earth all things meet their end.[7]

E. Generation from Many Things. **7.** 1. From the camp that says that the universe is generated from a plurality and from a set number of principles (and specifically, from two), the poet Homer says that it is composed from earth and water. To quote him:

> Ocean, origin of gods, and mother Tethys.[8]

And again:

> Yea, may you all become water and earth![9]

2. It seems also that Xenophanes of Kolophon agreed with Homer. For he says:

---

ciples: an active one (God) and a passive one (matter). Cf., e.g., Theophrastos, frag. 227a (FHSG 1:410–11). God, the active cause, is missing—although he was emphasized in the earlier summary (*Ref.* 1.21.1).

6. Our author has written "Anaximandros"; but one should understand Anaximenes here and in the next sentence.

7. Xenophanes, DK 21 B27. For Hippasos (not mentioned in *Ref.* 1), cf. Theophrastos, frag. 225 (FHSG 1:406–7).

8. Homer, *Il.* 14.201; cf. *Ref.* 5.7.38 (Naassenes); 8.12.2 (Monoïmos); Stobaios, *Ecl.* 1.10.2 (Wachsmuth and Hense, 1:119); Ps.-Plutarch, *Vit. Hom.* 93.1 (Ὠκεανός θ' ὅς περ γένεσις πάντεσσι τέτυκται). Aristotle includes this passage of Homer in his account of Thales and comments: "Some think that those ancients who, long before the present generation, were the first to theologize, had a similar idea of nature; because they presented Ocean and Tethys as the parents of becoming" (*Metaph.* 1.3, 983b28–30, trans. Richard Hope; cf. Plato, *Theaet.* 152e).

9. Homer, *Il.* 7.99. Both Pseudo-Plutarch (*Vit. Hom.* 93.2) and Clement of Alexandria quote this line in a similar context (*Strom.* 5.14.99.5).

πάντες γαίης καὶ ὕδατος ἐ<κ>γενόμε<σ>θα.

ἐκ γῆς δὲ καὶ α<ἰθ>έρος Εὐριπίδης, ὡς πάρεστιν ἐπιγνῶναι ἐκ τοῦ λέγειν αὐτόν·

αἰθέρα καὶ γαῖαν πάντων γενέτειραν ἀείδω.

3. ἐκ τεσσάρων δὲ Ἐμπεδοκλῆς, οὕτως λέγων·

τέσσαρα τῶν πάντων ῥιζώματα πρῶτον ἄκουε·
Ζεὺς α<ἰθ>ὴρ Ἥρη τε φερέσβιος ἠδ᾽ Ἀϊδωνεὺς
Νῆστίς θ᾽, ἣ δακρύοις σπένδει (κ)ρούνωμα βρότειον.

4. ἐκ πέντε δὲ Ὄκελ<λ>ος ὁ Λευ(κ)ανὸς καὶ Ἀριστοτέλης· συμπαρέλαβο(ν) γὰρ τοῖ(ς) (τέ)σσ(α)ρσι στοιχείοις τὸ πέμπτον καὶ κυκλοφορητικὸν σῶμα, ἐ<ξ οὗ> λέγουσιν εἶ(ν)αι τὰ οὐράνια.

ἐκ δὲ τῶν ἓξ τὴν τῶν πάντων ὑπέθεντο γένεσιν οἱ περὶ τὸν Ἐμπεδοκλέα. ἐν οἷς μὲν γὰρ λέγει·

τέσσαρα τῶν πάντων ῥιζώματα πρῶτον ἄκουε,

5. ἐκ τεσσάρων ποιεῖ τὴν γένεσιν· ὅταν δὲ προσθῇ·

Νεῖκός τ᾽ οὐλόμενον δίχα τῶν, ἀτάλαντον ἁπάντῃ,
καὶ Φιλίη μετὰ <τ>οῖσιν, ἴση μῆκός τε πλάτος τε

We all were born from earth and water.[10]

Euripides says that the universe arose from earth and aether, as can be learned from his saying:

I sing of aether and earth, mother of all![11]

3. Empedokles, however, has the world arise from four entities:

First, hear the four roots of all things:
Zeus-aether, and life-giving Hera, then Aidoneus
And Nestis, who moistens with her tears the mortal fount.[12]

4. Okellos the Leukanian and Aristotle say that the world derives from five elements.[13] This is because, in addition to the four elements, they include a fifth body carried around in a circle. Out of this body, they say, the heavens are composed.

The disciples of Empedokles posit that the generation of all things emerges from six elements. In the verse where he says,

First, hear the four roots of all things,

5. he makes generation arise from four elements. But when he adds these lines:

Baneful Strife apart from these, corresponding in every respect,
And with them Love, equal in length and breadth,[14]

---

10. Xenophanes, DK 21 B33; cf. Theophrastos, frag. 231 (FHSG 1:424–25). Xenophanes was just quoted as one who believed in generation from one principle: earth. Our author either has forgotten this or wishes to make Xenophanes look inconsistent.

11. Euripides, frag. 1023 (Nauck, 686).

12. Empedokles, DK 31 B6 (= Inwood 12), also quoted in *Ref.* 7.29.4 and partially quoted immediately below. Marcovich changes ἀήρ in P to αἰθήρ to conform it to Ps.-Plutarch, *Plac. philos.* 1.3, 878a.

13. Cf. Okellos testimony 4 (Harder, 3, 32–33).

14. Empedokles, DK 31 B17.19–20 (= Inwood 25.19–20). Cf. *Ref.* 7.29.9. On our author's sources for the Empedokles quotations here, see Osborne, *Rethinking*, 89–92.

ἓξ [καὶ] παραδίδωσι τὰς τῶν ὅλων ἀρχάς· τέσσαρας μὲν <τὰς> ὑλικάς, γῆν, ὕδωρ, ἀέρα, πῦρ, δύο δὲ τὰς δραστηρίους, φιλίαν καὶ νεῖκος.

Ἐξ ἀπείρων δὲ ἐδογμάτισαν τὴν τῶν πάντων γένεσιν οἱ περὶ Ἀναξαγόραν τὸν Κλαζομένιον καὶ Δημόκριτον καὶ Ἐπίκουρον, καὶ ἄλλοι παμπληθεῖς—ὧν ἐκ μέρους πρότερον ἐμνήσθημεν. 6.—ἀλλ' ὁ μὲν Ἀναξαγόρας ἐξ ὁμοίων τοῖς γεννωμένοις, οἱ δὲ περὶ τὸν Δημόκριτον καὶ Ἐπίκουρον ἐξ ἀνομοίων τε καὶ ἀπαθῶν—τουτέστιν ἐκ τῶν ἀτόμων.

οἱ δὲ περὶ τὸν Ποντικὸν Ἡρακλείδην καὶ Ἀσκληπιάδην ἐξ ἀνομοίων, παθητῶν δέ—καθάπερ τῶν ἀνάρμων ὄγκων.

7. Οἱ δὲ περὶ τὸν Πλάτωνα ἐκ τριῶν· εἶναι ταῦτα λέγουσι θεὸν καὶ ὕλην καὶ παράδειγμα. τὴν δὲ ὕλην μερίζει εἰς τέσσαρας ἀρχάς, πῦρ, ὕδωρ, γῆν, ἀέρα· θεὸν δὲ τὸν ταύτης εἶναι δημιουργόν, τὸ δὲ παράδειγμα νοῦν <τοῦ θεοῦ>.

8. 1. Πεπεισμένοι τοίνυν ὅτι πᾶσι τούτοις ὁμολογουμένως ἄπορος εὑρίσκεται ὁ τῆς φυσιολογίας λόγος, αὐτοὶ περὶ τῶν τῆς ἀληθεία(ς) παραδειγμά(τ)ων, ὡς ἔστι καὶ <ὡς> πεπιστεύκαμεν, ἀόκνως ἐροῦμε(ν), πλ(ὴ)ν καὶ τὰ τοῖς αἱρεσιάρχαις <δόξαντα ἐν> ἐπιτομῇ πρότερον ἐκθέ(μ)ενοι, ἵνα καὶ διὰ ταύτης εὔ(γν)ωστα τὰ πάντων δόγματα παραστήσαντες φανερὰν καὶ εὔγνωστον τὴν ἀλήθειαν ἐπιδείξωμεν.

he transmits six principles of the universe. Four are material—earth, water, air, and fire—while two are active—Love and Strife.[15]

F. Generation from Infinite Entities. The followers of Anaxagoras the Klazomenian, Demokritos, Epikouros, and a host of others (whom I previously discussed in detail[16]) taught the generation of all from infinite entities. 6. But whereas Anaxagoras believed in generation from entities that are the same as generated beings, the disciples of Demokritos and Epikouros say that the world came from entities that are not the same as generated beings and that these entities (that is, atoms) are not liable to change.

Still others, the disciples of Herakleides of Pontos and Asklepiades, say that the world arose from entities unlike generated beings—just like particles without joints.[17] These entities, however, are liable to change.

G. Platonists: Generation from Three Principles. 7. Platonists say that the universe is composed from three principles: God, matter, and the model. Plato divides matter into four principles: fire, water, earth, and air. God is the Artificer of matter, and the model is the mind of God.[18]

8. 1. Therefore, since I am confident that every philosopher's account of natural philosophy indisputably arrives at a dead end, I will unhesitatingly declare my doctrine of the "models" of truth, explaining what they are and as I believe them to exist.[19] First, however, I will also summarize the views of the leading heretics so that when, by this procedure, I have presented all their doctrines as easily discerned, I can exhibit the truth as clear and easily discerned as well.[20]

---

15. Cf. *Ref.* 7.29.7; Theophrastos, frag. 227a (FHSG 1:412–13).

16. Cf. *Ref.* 1.8, 13, 22.

17. On ἀνάρμων ὄγκων, see Robert W. Sharples, "'Unjointed Masses': A Note on Heraclides' Physical Theory," in *Heraclides of Pontus: Discussion*, ed. William W. Fortenbaugh and Elizabeth Pender (New Brunswick, NJ: Transaction, 2009), 139–54.

18. This material is pulled not from Sextus but (apparently) from *Ref.* 1.19.1–2. Marcovich adds τοῦ θεοῦ ("of God") to conform it to *Ref.* 1.19.2 (παράδειγμα τὴν διάνοιαν τοῦ θεοῦ).

19. The "models" of truth are a satirical reference to Plato's models or forms of reality. See further Frickel, *Dunkel*, 130, 153.

20. Marcovich adds δόξαντα ἐν.

9. 1. Ἀλλ᾽ ἐπεὶ οὕτως δοκεῖ, ἀρξώμεθα πρῶτον ἀπὸ τῶν τοῦ ὄφεως λειτουργῶν.

Νaασ<σ>ηνοὶ ἄνθρωπον καλοῦσι τὴν πρώτην τῶν ὅλων ἀρχήν, τὸν αὐτὸν καὶ υἱὸν ἀνθρώπου. τοῦτον δὲ τριχῇ διαιροῦσιν· ἔστι μὲν γὰρ αὐτοῦ, φασί, τὸ μὲν νοερόν, τὸ δὲ ψυχικόν, τὸ δὲ χοϊκόν. 2. καλοῦσι δὲ αὐτὸν Ἀδάμαν καὶ νομίζουσι τὴν [εἰς] αὐτοῦ γνῶσιν εἶναι ἀρχὴν τοῦ δύνασθαι γνῶναι θεόν. καὶ ταῦτα πάντα, τὰ νοερὰ καὶ τὰ ψυχικὰ καὶ τὰ χοϊκά, κεχωρηκέναι εἰς τὸν Ἰησοῦν, καὶ ὁμοῦ δι᾽ αὐτοῦ λελαληκέναι τὰς τρεῖς οὐσίας τοῖς τρισὶ γένεσι. 3. τοῦ παντὸς οὗτοι φάσκουσι τρί<α> γένη, ἀγγελικόν, ψυχικόν, χοϊκόν, καὶ τρεῖς εἶναι ἐκκλησίας, ἀγγελικήν, ψυχικήν, χοϊκήν· ὀνόματα δὲ αὐταῖς ἐκλεκτή, κλητή, αἰχμάλωτος.

ταῦτά ἐστι τὰ κατ᾽ αὐτοὺς κεφάλαια, ὡς ἐν ὀλίγῳ ἔστι καταλαβεῖν, ταῦτά φασιν παραδεδωκέναι τὸν Ἰάκωβον, τὸν ἀδελφὸν τοῦ κυρίου, τῇ Μαριάμνῃ, καταψευδόμενοι ἀμφοτέρων.

10. 1. Οἱ δὲ Περάται, Ἀδέμης ὁ Καρύστιος καὶ Ε<ὐ>φράτης <ὁ> Περατικός, λέγουσιν ἕνα εἶναι κόσμον τινά—οὕτως καλοῦντες τοῦτον—τρ(ι)χῇ διῃρημένον. ἔστι δὲ <τῆς> τριχῇ διαιρέ(σ)εως παρ᾽ αὐ(τ)οῖς [τὸ μὲν ἓν μέρος] οἱονεὶ μία ἀρχ(ή), καθαπερ(εὶ) πηγὴ μεγάλη, εἰς ἀπείρους τομὰς τῷ (λ)όγῳ τμηθῆναι δυναμένη.

2. ἡ δὲ πρώτη τομὴ καὶ προσεχεστέρα κατ᾽ αὐτούς ἐστιν ἡ τριάς· καὶ <τὸ μὲν ἓν μέρος> καλεῖται ἀγαθὸν τέλειον, μέγεθος πατρικόν· τὸ δὲ δεύτερον μέρος τῆς τριάδος οἱονεὶ δυνάμεων ἄπει(ρ)όν τι πλῆθος· <τὸ δὲ> τρίτον ἰδικόν. καὶ ἔστι τὸ μὲν πρῶτον ἀγέννητον. ὅθεν διαρρήδην λέγουσι τρεῖς θεούς, τρεῖς λόγους, τρεῖς νοῦς, τρεῖς ἀνθρώπους· 3. ἑκάστῳ γὰρ μέρει τοῦ κόσμου, τῆς διαιρέσεως διακεκριμένης, διδόασι καὶ θεοὺς καὶ λόγους καὶ ἀνθρώπους καὶ τὰ λοιπά.

SUMMARY OF THE LEADING HERETICS

NAASSENES. **9.** 1. Since it is fitting to proceed in this fashion, let me first begin with the servants of the snake.[21]

The Naassenes call the first principle of the universe the "Human Being." He is identical with the Son of the Human. They divide him in three ways. He has an intelligible aspect, an animate aspect, and an earthly aspect. 2. They call him "Adamas" and believe that knowledge about him is the precondition for knowing God. All these three substances—the intelligible, animate, and earthly—came into Jesus and through him at one and the same time spoke to their respective kinds of people. 3. They claim that there are three kinds of people in the universe, angelic, animate, and earthly, and accordingly there are three churches, angelic, animate, and earthly. Their names are the "elect," "called," and the "captive."

These are their chief points, comprised in brief compass. They add that it was James the brother of the Lord who passed on these traditions to Mariamne—telling lies about both.

PERATAI. **10.** 1. The Peratai Ademes the Karystian and Euphrates the Peratic affirm that there is one cosmos (as they call it), which is divided in three ways.[22] They depict the cosmos as the single source—a great fount, as it were—of the threefold division. This fount is able to be divided into infinite divisions by the Word.

2. The first and most relevant division, in their view, is the Trinity. Now the first part of the Trinity is called "Perfect Good" or "Fatherly Greatness."[23] The second part of the Trinity is, as it were, an infinite number of powers. The third is the particular cosmos. The first (the Perfect Good) is unborn. Therefore they expressly say that there are three Gods, three Words, three Minds, and three Human Beings. 3. Accordingly, when a division is made, they assign Gods and Words and Humans and the rest to each part of the cosmos.

---

21. The following summary overlaps with the main report in *Ref.* 5.6.4–5; 5.6.6–7.1.

22. The following section on the Peratai overlaps with the main report in *Ref.* 5.12.1–7.

23. Marcovich transposes τὸ μὲν ἓν μέρος ("the first part") from the previous sentence to this location.

Ἄνωθεν δέ, ἀπὸ τῆς ἀγεννησίας καὶ τῆς τοῦ κόσμου πρώτης τομῆς, ἐπὶ συντελείᾳ λοιπὸν τοῦ κόσμου καθεστηκότος, κατεληλυθέναι ἐν τοῖς Ἡρώδου χρόνοις τριφυῆ τινα ἄνθρωπον καὶ τρισώματον καὶ τριδύναμον, καλούμενον Χριστόν, ἀπὸ τῶν τριῶν ἔχοντα τοῦ κόσμου μερῶν ἐν αὐτῷ πάντα τὰ [τοῦ κόσμου] συγκρίματα καὶ τὰς δυνάμεις. 4. καὶ τοῦτο εἶναι θέλουσι τὸ εἰρημένον· «ἐν ᾧ κατοικεῖ πᾶν τὸ πλήρωμα τῆς θεότητος σωματι<κῶς>». κατενεχθῆναι γὰρ ἀπὸ τῶν ὑπερκειμένων κόσμων δύο, τοῦ τε ἀγεννήτου καὶ τοῦ αὐτογεννήτου, εἰς τοῦτον τὸν κόσμον ἐν ᾧ ἐσμεν ἡμεῖς παντοίων δυνάμεων σπέρματα. κατεληλυθέναι δὲ τὸν Χριστὸν ἄνωθεν, ἀπὸ ἀγεννησίας, ἵνα διὰ τῆς καταβάσεως αὐτοῦ πάντα σωθῇ τὰ τριχῇ διῃρημένα· 5. ἃ μὲν γάρ, φησίν, ἐστὶν ἄνωθεν κατενηνεγμένα, ἀνελεύσεται δι' αὐτοῦ, τὰ δὲ ἐπιβουλεύσαντα τοῖς κατενηνεγμένοις ἀφίε<τα>ι εἰκῇ καὶ κολασθέντα ἀποπέμπεται. δύο δὲ εἶναι μέρη ἃ σῳζόμενα λέγει, τὰ ὑπερκείμενα <καὶ> ἀπαλλαγέντα τῆς φθορᾶς· τὸ δὲ τρίτον ἀπόλ<λ>υσθαι, ὃ κόσμον ἰδι<κ>ὸν καλεῖ.

ταῦτα καὶ οἱ Περάται.

11. 1. <Τ>οῖς δὲ Σηθιανοῖς δοκεῖ ὅτι τῶν ὅλω(ν) εἰσὶ τρεῖς ἀρχαὶ περιωρισμέναι, ἑκάστη δὲ τῶν ἀρχῶν πέφυκε [δύνασθα(ι)] (γ)ενέσθαι, ὡς ἐν ἀνθρωπίνῃ ψυχῇ πᾶσα ἡτισοῦν διδ(α)σκομένη τέχνη· οἷον εἰ, <ἐγγὺς> γένοιτο <τὸ> παιδίον αὐλητῇ <δύνασθαι> [γενέσθαι] αὐλεῖν, ἢ γεωμέτρῃ γεωμετρεῖ(ν), καὶ τινὶ τέχνῃ ὁμοίως.

2. αἱ δὲ τῶν ἀρχῶν, φασίν, οὐσίαι εἰσὶ φῶς καὶ σκότ(ος)· τούτων δέ ἐστιν ἐν μέσῳ πνεῦμα ἀκέραιον. τὸ δὲ πνεῦμα, τὸ τεταγμένον ἐν μέσῳ τοῦ σκότους, ὅπερ ἐστὶ κάτω, καὶ τοῦ φωτός, ὅπερ ἐστὶν ἄνω, λέγουσιν, οὐκ ἔστι πνεῦμα ὡς ἄνεμος ἢ ῥιπὴ ἢ λεπτή τις αὔρα νοηθῆναι δυναμένη, ἀλλ' οἱονεί τις ὀσμὴ μύρου ἢ θυμιάματος ἐκ συνθέσεως κατασκευαζομένου, λεπτὴ διοδεύουσα δύναμις ἀνεπινοήτῳ τινὶ καὶ κρείττονι λόγου φορᾷ εὐωδίας. 3. ἐπεὶ τοίνυν ἐστὶν ἄνω τὸ φῶς καὶ κάτω τὸ σκότος καὶ τούτων μέσον τὸ πνεῦμα, τὸ δὴ φῶς <ὡς> ἀκτὶς ἡλίου ἄνωθεν ἐκλάμπουσα εἰς τὸ ὑποκείμενον σκότος· ἡ δὲ τοῦ πνεύματος εὐωδία, μέσην ἔχουσα τάξιν, φέρεται καὶ ἐξικνεῖται, ὥσπερ ἡ τῶν θυμιαμάτων ἐπὶ τῷ πυρὶ ὀσμὴ φέρεται. τοιαύτης δὲ οὔσης τῆς δυνάμεως τῶν διῃρημένων

But from above, from the realm of the unborn and the first portion of the cosmos, when the cosmos was finally made ready for consummation, there came down in the time of Herod a human being with three natures, three bodies, and three powers. This human being is called Christ. He possessed in himself all the compounds and powers from the three parts of the cosmos. 4. This is what they want the scriptural phrase to mean: "In him dwelled all the fullness of the Godhead bodily."[24] Seeds of every sort of power came down into this world of ours from the two higher worlds (that is, from the unborn and the self-born). Christ also came down from above, from the realm of the unborn, so that through his descent all things divided in three might be saved. 5. The seeds that descended from above, he says, will ascend through him. But those who conspired against the descended seeds are discharged without a second thought and, after punishment, sent back. Two parts, he says, are saved: that which is higher, and that which is freed from corruption. But the third part, what he calls the "particular cosmos," is destroyed.

These, then, are the doctrines of the Peratai.

SETHIANS. 11. 1. The Sethians believe that there are three circumscribed principles in the universe, and each of them has developed naturally like any skill learned in the human soul.[25] For example, a child in the company of a flautist becomes able to play the flute, or a child in the company of a geometer becomes able to practice geometry, and likewise with any skill.

2. The substances of the principles, he says, are Light and Darkness. Between them dwells a pure Spirit. This Spirit lies suspended between the lower Darkness and the higher Light. It is not, they say, a Spirit conceivable like wind, or a current, or a light breeze. Rather, it is like the scent of a perfume or incense prepared by a recipe—a subtle power pervading all by a wafting of fragrance that is inconceivable and greater than words can tell. 3. Since the Light is above and the Darkness below and the Spirit in between, this Light—just as a ray of the sun—shines out on the underlying Darkness. The fragrance of the Spirit stationed in the middle is diffused and wafted, just as the fragrance of burning incense offerings is wafted.

---

24. Col 2:9. Cf. *Ref.* 5.12.5; 8.13.2 (Monoïmos); Iren., *Haer.* 1.3.4; Clem. Alex., *Exc.* 31.1.

25. The following (very full) summary of the "Sethians" overlaps with the main report in *Ref.* 5.19.

τριχῶς, τοῦ πνεύματος καὶ τοῦ φωτὸς ὁμοῦ ἡ δύναμίς ἐστι κάτω ἐν τῷ σκότει τῷ ὑποτεταγμένῳ.

4. Τὸ δὲ σκότος ὕδωρ εἶναί φασι φοβερόν, εἰς ὃ κατέσπασται <καὶ> μετενήνεκται εἰς τοιαύτην φύσιν μετὰ τοῦ πνεύματος τὸ φῶς. φρόνιμον οὖν τὸ σκότος ὂν καὶ γινῶσκον ὅτι, ἂν ἀπαρθῇ ἀπ' αὐτοῦ τὸ φῶς, μενεῖ τὸ σκότος ἔρημον, ἀφανές, ἀλαμπές, ἀδύναμον, ἄπρακτον, ἀσθενές. <οὕ>τω δὴ πάσῃ συνέσει καὶ φρονήσει βιάζεται κατέχειν εἰς ἑαυτὸ τὴν λαμπηδόνα καὶ τὸν σπινθῆρα τοῦ φωτὸς μετὰ τῆς τοῦ πνεύματος εὐωδίας.

5. Εἰκόνα τούτου ταύτην παρεισάγουσι, λέγοντες· ὥσπερ ἡ κόρη τοῦ ὀφθαλμοῦ <ἐκ τῶν μὲν> ὑποκειμένων ὑδάτων σκοτεινὴ φαίνεται, φωτίζεται δὲ ὑπὸ τοῦ πνεύματος, οὕτως ἀντιποιεῖται τὸ σκότος τοῦ πνεύματος. ἔχει δὲ παρ' (ἑ)αυτῷ πάσας τὰς δυνάμεις, βουλομένας ἀφίστασθαι κα(ὶ) ἀνιέναι. εἰσὶ δὲ αὗται ἀπειράκις ἄπειροι· ἐξ ὧν τὰ π(άν)τα ἐκτυπο(ῦτ)αι καὶ γίνεται, ἐπιμιγνυμένων δίκην σφραγίδων· 6. ὥσπερ γὰρ σφραγὶς ἐπικοινωνήσασα κηρῷ τὸν τύπον ἐποίησεν, αὐτὴ παρ' ἑαυτῇ ἥτις ἦν μένουσα, οὕτως καὶ αἱ δυνάμεις ἐπικοινωνήσασαι <ἀλλήλαις> τὰ πάντα ἀπεργάζονται γένη ζῴων, <ὄντα> ἄπειρα.

γεγονέν<αι> οὖν ἀπὸ τῆς πρώτης συνδρομῆς τῶν τριῶν ἀρχῶν μεγάλης σφραγῖδος ἰδέαν, οὐρανὸν καὶ γῆν, εἶδος ἔχουσαν παραπλήσιον μήτρᾳ, ὀμφαλὸν ἐχούσῃ μέσον. οὕτως δὲ καὶ τὰς λοιπὰς ἐκτυπώσεις τῶν πάντων ἐκτετυπῶσθαι, ὥσπερ οὐρανὸν καὶ γῆν μήτρᾳ παραπλησίους.

7. Ἐκ δὲ τοῦ ὕδατος γεγονέναι φασὶ πρωτόγονον ἀρχήν, ἄνεμο<ν> <σ>φοδρὸν καὶ λάβρον καὶ πάσης γενέσεως αἴτιον, βρασμόν τινα καὶ κίνησιν ἐργαζόμενον τῷ κόσμῳ ἐκ τῆς τῶν ὑδάτων κινήσεως. 8. τοῦτον δὲ ἀποτελεῖν εἶδος σύρματι ὄφεως παραπλήσιον, πτερωθέν, εἰς ὃ <ἀ>φορῶν ὁ κόσμος πρὸς γένεσιν ὁρμᾷ ὀργήσας ὡς μήτρα, καὶ ἐντεῦθεν θέλουσι συνίστασθαι τὴν τῶν ὅλων γένεσιν.

9. τοῦτο δὲ πνεῦμα ἀνέμου εἶναι λέγουσι τέλειον θεόν, <ὃν> ἐκ τῆς τῶν ὑδάτων <κινήσεως> καὶ τῆς τοῦ πνεύματος εὐωδίας καὶ <τῆς τοῦ> φωτὸς λαμπηδόνος γεγονέναι καὶ εἶναι γέν<ν>ημα θηλείας, νοῦν.

τὸν ἄνωθεν σπινθῆρα, κάτω ἀναμεμιγμένον ἐν τοῖς πολυσυγκρίτοις σώματος, σπεύδειν ἐκφεύγειν, ἐκφυγόντα <δὲ ἄνω> πορεύεσθαι, καὶ τὴν λύσιν οὐχ εὑρίσκειν διὰ τὴν ἐν τοῖς ὕδασι δέσιν. διὸ ἐβόα ἐκ τῆς τῶν ὑδάτων μίξεως, κατὰ τὸν ψαλμῳδόν, ὡς λέγουσι.

10. Πᾶσα οὖν ἡ φροντὶς τοῦ ἄνω φωτός ἐστιν, ὅπως ῥύσηται τὸν κάτω σπινθῆρα ἀπὸ τοῦ κάτω πατρός, <τοῦ> ἀνέμου, ἐπεγείραντος βρασμὸν καὶ

Such is the character of their threefold division: the power of Spirit and Light are together in the Darkness arrayed beneath them.

4. The Darkness is a frightful water, they say, into which the Light is pulled down and transferred to this watery nature along with the Spirit. The Darkness is cunning. It knows that, were the Light to be removed from it, the Darkness would remain barren, invisible, unenlightened, powerless, impotent, and weak. For this reason, with all cunning and intelligence, it forcefully imprisons in itself the brilliance and the spark of light together with the fragrance of the Spirit.

5. They offer this illustration: just as the pupil of the eye appears dark from the underlying waters but is illumined by spirit, so the darkness lays hold of the Spirit. It has in itself all their potentialities, potentialities that want to depart and ascend. These potentialities are infinity times infinity in number. From them, all reality is stamped with a form and comes into existence when they mix together in the manner of seals. 6. Just as the seal by contact with the wax makes an impression—but remains in itself what it was—so also the potentialities interact and produce all the countless kinds of animals.

Now there arises from the first collision of the three principles the form of a great seal: heaven and earth, appearing very much like a womb with the navel in the middle. In this way also the impressions of everything were stamped very much like heaven and earth on the womb.

7. From the water arose, they say, the firstborn principle, a strong and violent wind. This is the cause of all generation. It produces a boiling and stirring in the world from the movement of the waters. 8. This achieves a final form that highly resembles the trail of a snake, endowed with wings. As the world fixed its gaze on it, it swelled like a womb and initiated the process of generation. From this process, they desire to concoct the origin of the universe.

9. This blast of wind they say is a "perfect god" who came to be from the movement of waters, from the fragrance of Spirit, and from the brilliance of the Light. He is the offspring of a female; he is a mind.

The spark from above, though mixed in the morass of the body down below, rushes to escape. When it escapes and flies high, it still does not find release, because it was chained in the waters. Thus it cried out from the mixing of waters as in the psalm (or so they claim).

10. The only concern of the higher Light is to devise a means to deliver the spark below from the lower father, or wind. This father stirred up a

τάραχον καὶ ἑαυτῷ νοῦν <υἱὸν> ποιήσαντος, οὐκ ὄντα αὐτοῦ, φάσκουσιν, ἴδ<ι>ον <κα>τὰ <οὐσίαν>.

τὸν ἄνωθεν τέλειον λόγον τοῦ φωτὸς αὐτὸν ἀπομορφώσαντα εἴδει ὄφεως κεχωρηκέναι ἐν μήτρᾳ, ἵνα τὸν νοῦν ἐκεῖνον, τὸν ἐκ τοῦ φωτὸς σπινθῆρα ἀνα(λ)αβεῖν δυνηθῇ. 11. καὶ τοῦτο εἶναί τὸ εἰρημένον· «ὃς ἐν μορφῇ θεοῦ ὑπάρχων οὐχ ἁρπ(α)γμὸν ἡγήσατο τὸ εἶναι ἴσα θεῷ, ἀλλ' ἑαυτὸν ἐκένωσε μορφ(ὴν) δούλου λαβών». καὶ ταύτην εἶναι τὴν μορφὴν οἱ κακοδαίμονες θέλουσι καὶ πολυπή(μ)ονες Σηθιανοί.

ταῦτα μὲν οὖν καὶ οὗτοι λέγουσιν.

12. 1. Ὁ δὲ πάνσοφος Σίμων οὕτως λέγει· ἀπέραντόν εἶναι δύναμιν, ταύτην ῥίζωμα τῶν ὅλων εἶναι. ἔστι δέ [φησιν] ἡ ἀπέραντος δύναμις, τὸ πῦρ, κατ' αὐτὸν οὐδὲν ἁπλοῦν, καθάπερ οἱ πολλοὶ ἁπλᾶ λέγοντες εἶναι τὰ [δὲ] τέσσαρα στοιχεῖα καὶ τὸ πῦρ ἁπλοῦν εἶναι νενομίκασιν, ἀλλ' εἶναι τοῦ πυρὸς τὴν φύσιν διπλῆν· καὶ τῆς διπλῆς ταύτης καλεῖ τὸ μέν τι κρυπτόν, τὸ δέ φανερόν· κεκρύφθαι δὲ τὰ κρυπτὰ ἐν τοῖς φανεροῖς τοῦ πυρός, καὶ τὰ φανερὰ τοῦ πυρὸς ὑπὸ τῶν κρυπτῶν γεγονέναι.

2. Πάντα δέ, φησί, νενόμισται τὰ μέρη τοῦ πυρός, ὁρατὰ καὶ ἀόρατα, «φρόνησιν ἔχειν». γέγονεν οὖν, φασίν, ὁ κόσμος ὁ γεννητὸς ἀπὸ τοῦ ἀγεννήτου πυρός. ἤρξατο δέ, φησίν, οὕτως γίνεσθαι· ἓξ ῥίζας τὰς πρώτας τῆς ἀρχῆς τῆς γενέσεως ὁ γεννητὸς ἀπὸ τῆς ἀρχῆς τοῦ πυρὸς ἐκείνου λαβών. ταύτας γάρ ῥίζας γεγονέναι κατὰ συζυγίαν ἀπὸ τοῦ πυρός, ἅστινας καλεῖ Νοῦν καὶ Ἐπίνοιαν, Φωνὴν καὶ Ὄνομα, Λογισμὸν καὶ Ἐνθύμησιν.

3. εἶναι δὲ ἐν ταῖς ἓξ ῥίζαις ὁμοῦ τὴν ἀπέραντον δύναμιν εἶναί φησι, τὸν ἑστῶτα στάντα στησόμενον. ὃς <ἐὰν> ἐξεικονισθῇ ἐν ταῖς ἓξ δυνάμεσιν, ἔσται οὐσίᾳ, δυνάμει, μεγέθει, ἀποτελέσματι μία καὶ <ἡ> αὐτὴ τῇ ἀγεννήτῳ καὶ ἀπεράντῳ δυνάμει, οὐδὲν ὅλως ἔχουσα ἐνδεέστερον ἐκείνης τῆς ἀγεννήτου καὶ

boiling confusion and made a mind for himself as a son.[26] This mind is not, they claim, his own [son] according to nature.[27]

The perfect Word of Light from above, after transfiguring himself into the form of a snake, came into the womb so that he could take up the mind, that is, the spark from the Light. 11. This is what the scriptural verse refers to: "He, though in the form of God, did not consider equality with God something to be plundered. Rather, he emptied himself and took the form of a slave."[28] These wretched and utterly miserable Sethians want "the form of the slave" to refer to this snake form!

This is what they teach.

SIMON. 12. 1. The super-sage Simon reports the following.[29] There is an Infinite Power, the root of the universe. The Infinite Power, or fire, is, according to Simon, not at all simple (as most people say that the four elements are simple and so suppose that fire is simple too). Rather, the nature of the fire is twofold, and of this twofold nature one aspect he calls "hidden," and the other "manifest." The hidden realities were hidden in the fire's manifest realities, and the manifest realities of the fire arose by the power of the hidden realities.

2. He says that all parts of the fire, visible and invisible, are supposed "to have wisdom."[30] Thus the born world, they say, arose out of unborn fire. It began to be, he says, in the following way. From the principle of that unborn fire, the world that was born took six primal roots of the principle of generation. These roots arose from the fire in pairs. He calls them "Mind and Thought, Voice and Name, Reasoning and Conception."

3. The Infinite Power, he says, exists in these six roots together. This is the One Who Stood, Who Stands, and Who Will Stand.[31] Whoever is fully formed in the six powers will be in substance, in potential, in magnitude, in finished perfection one and the same as the Unborn and Infinite Power.

---

26. Wendland adds υἱόν ("son").

27. Marcovich replaces P's ἰδόντα with ἴδιον κατὰ οὐσίαν (here: "his own [son] according to nature"; cf. *Ref.* 5.19.16).

28. Phil 2:6–8; cf. Origen, *Princ.* 4.4.5.

29. The following summary overlaps with the main report in *Ref.* 6.9.4–6; 6.12.2; 6.12.1–4.

30. Empedokles, DK 31 B110.10, cited also in Sext. Emp., *Math.* 8.286. Cf. *Ref.* 6.12.1; 7.29.26.

31. Our author's summarizing technique (along with the poor textual transmission) garbles Simon's report. Marcovich repeatedly intervenes to repair the logic.

ἀπαραλ<λ>άκτου καὶ ἀπεράντου δυνάμεως. 4. ἐὰν δὲ μείνῃ δυνάμει μόνον ἐν ταῖς ἓξ δυνάμεσι καὶ μὴ ἐξεικονισθῇ, ἀφανίζεται, φησί, καὶ ἀπόλλυται, οὕτως ὡς ἡ δύναμις ἡ γραμματικὴ <ἢ> ἡ γεωμετρικὴ <ἐν> ἀνθρώπου ψυχῇ ὑπάρξασα, μὴ προσλαβοῦσα τεχνίτην τὸν διδάξοντα.

αὐτὸν δὲ εἶναι ὁ Σίμω(ν) λέγει τὸν ἑστῶτα στάντα στησόμενον, ὄντα δύναμιν τὴν ὑπὲρ τὰ πάντα.

τα(ῦ)τα τοίνυν καὶ ὁ Σίμων.

13. 1. Ὁ δὲ Οὐαλεντῖνος (κ)αὶ οἱ ἀπὸ τῆς τούτου σχολῆς εἶναι λέγουσι τὴν τοῦ π(α)ντὸς ἀρχὴν Πατέρα. καὶ ἐναντίᾳ δὲ δόξῃ προσφέρονται· οἱ μὲν γὰρ αὐτῶν μόνον εἶναι καὶ γεννητικόν, οἱ δὲ ἀδυνάτως ἔχειν γεννᾶν ἄνευ θηλείας, καὶ τούτῳ σύζυγον προστιθέασι Σιγήν, Βυθὸν αὐτὸν ὀνομάσαντες.

2. ἐκ τούτου <καί, ὥς> τινες, ἐκ τῆς συζύγου προβολὰς γεγονέναι ἕξ· Νοῦν καὶ Ἀλήθειαν, Λόγον καὶ Ζωήν, Ἄνθρωπον καὶ Ἐκκλησίαν, καὶ εἶναι ταύτην τὴν Ὀγδοάδα πρωτογενέτειραν. <ταύτην,> τάς τε ἐν<τ>ὸς τοῦ Ὅρου προβολὰς γεγενημένας πάλιν καλεῖσθαι ἐντὸς πληρώματος· δεύτερα δὲ τὰ ἐκτὸς πληρώματος, καὶ τρί<τ>α τὰ ἐκτὸς τοῦ Ὅρου, ὧν ἡ γέννησις τὸ ὑστέρημα ὑπάρχει.

3. τὸ<ν> δὲ ἐκ τοῦ ἐν ὑστερήματι προβληθέντος αἰῶνος γεγονέναι, καὶ τοῦτον εἶναι δημιουργὸν λέγει, μὴ βουλόμενος αὐτὸν πρῶτον εἶναι θεόν, ἀλλὰ δυσφημῶν τε αὐτὸν καὶ τὰ ὑπ᾽ αὐτοῦ γεγενημένα.

Τὸν δὲ Χριστὸν ἐκ τοῦ ἐντὸς πληρώματος κατεληλυθέναι ἐπὶ σωτηρίᾳ τοῦ ἀποπλανηθέντος πνεύματος, ὃ κατοικεῖ ἐν «τῷ ἔσω ἡμῶν ἀνθρώπῳ», ὃν σῳζόμενόν φησι τούτου χάριν τοῦ ἐνοικοῦντος. 4. τὴν δὲ σάρκα μὴ σῴζεσθαι θέλει, «δερμάτινον χιτῶνα» ἀποκαλῶν καὶ «ἄνθρωπον φθειρόμενον».

In general, this one will be in no way inferior to that Unborn, Incomparable, and Infinite Power. 4. But whoever remains in potential only in the six powers and is not fully formed according to the model is made away with, he says, and destroyed, just as the soul's power to learn grammar or geometry is destroyed if it does not receive a teacher who practices the art.

Simon calls himself the One Who Stood, Stands, and Will Stand, the Power above all.

These are the teachings of Simon.

VALENTINUS. 13. 1. Valentinus and those of his school say that the principle of everything is the Father.[32] But they offer opposing views. Some of them suppose that the Father alone exists and is capable of engendering others, but others suppose that it is impossible for him to produce offspring without a female.[33] Accordingly they attach to him a consort named Silence, calling the Father himself "Depth."

2. From him (or, as some teach, from him and his consort) there arose six emanations: Mind and Truth, Word and Life, Human and Church. All these beings constitute the primal Mother, the Ogdoad. She, along with the emanations that arose inside the Boundary, are in turn called "the beings inside the Fullness."[34] The second generation came to be outside the Fullness, and the third generation came to be outside the Boundary. The offspring of the third generation possesses the deficiency.[35]

3. The one he calls "Artificer" arose from the aeon emanated in deficiency. He does not want to call him the primal God but slanders him and what is generated by him.[36]

Christ descended from the one inside the Fullness to save the spirit wandering in error. This spirit dwells in "our inner human." The human is saved, they claim, for the sake of the one dwelling within. 4. He does not want the flesh to be saved, calling it the "coat of skin" and "the corrupted human."[37]

32. The following report overlaps with *Ref.* 6.29.2–3, 6–7; 6.38.3, 5.

33. Marcovich adds τὸν Πατέρα νομίζουσιν ("suppose that the Father") as well as νομίζοντες ("[others] suppose") from the main report on "Valentinus" (*Ref.* 6.29.3).

34. Marcovich adds ταύτην (here: "she").

35. Cf. *Ref.* 6.31.5–7 (the Fruit comes to be outside the Fullness and shapes the negative emotions of Wisdom into beings outside the Fullness); 6.37.5–6 (where the tripartite division is attributed to Plato).

36. Cf. Iren., *Haer.* 1.5.1–2; Epiph., *Pan.* 31.18.3–8.

37. Cf. *Ref.* 6.35.3–4. For the coat of skin, see Gen 3:21; cf. Iren., *Haer.* 1.5.5; 3.23.5;

ταῦτα ἐν ἐπιτομῇ ἐξεῖπον, πολλῆς ὕλης κατ' αὐτοὺς τυγχανούσης καὶ διαφόρων γνωμῶν.

οὕτως οὖν δοκεῖ καὶ τῇ Οὐαλεντίνου σχολῇ.

14. 1. Βασιλείδης δὲ καὶ αὐτὸς λέγει εἶναι θεὸν οὐκ ὄντα, πεποιηκότα κόσμον ἐξ οὐκ ὄντων οὐκ ὄντα, οὐκ ὂν καταβαλόμενόν τι σπέρμα, ὡσεὶ κόκκον σινάπεως ἔχοντα ἐν ἑαυτῷ τὸ πρέμνον, τὰ φύλλα, τοὺς κλάδους, τὸν καρπόν, ἢ ὡς ᾠὸν ταοῦ ἔχον ἐν ἑαυτῷ τὴν τῶν χρωμάτων ποικίλην πληθύν. καὶ τοῦτο εἶναί φησι τὸ τοῦ κόσμου σπέρμα, ἐξ οὗ τὰ πάντα γέγονεν· 2. εἶχεν γὰρ ἐν ἑαυτῷ τὰ πάντα <ο>ἷον οὐκ ὄντα, ὑπὸ τοῦ οὐκ ὄντος θεοῦ γενέσθαι προβεβουλευμένα.

Ἦν οὖν, φασί, ἐν αὐτῷ τῷ σπέρματι υἱότης τριμερής, κατὰ πάν<τα> τῷ οὐκ ὄντι θεῷ ὁμοούσιος, γεννητὴ ἐξ οὐκ ὄντων. ταύτης τῆς υἱότητος <τῆς> τριχῇ διῃρημένης τὸ μέν τι ἦν λεπτομερές, τὸ δὲ παχυμερές, τὸ δὲ ἀπο(κ)αθάρσεως δε(ό)μενον. 3. τὸ μὲν οὖν λεπτομερὲς εὐθέως πρῶτον, ἅμα τῷ γενέσθαι τοῦ σπέρματος τὴν πρώτην καταβολὴν ὑπὸ τοῦ οὐκ ὄντος, διέσφυξε καὶ ἀνῆλθεν ἄ(ν)ω, καὶ ἐγένετο πρὸς τὸν οὐκ ὄντα· ἐκείνου γὰρ πᾶσα φύσις ὀρέγεται δι' ὑπερβολ(ὴ)ν κάλλους, ἄλλη δὲ ἄλλως. 4. ἡ δὲ παχυμερεστέρα ἔτι μένουσα ἐν τῷ σπέρματι, μιμητική τις οὖσα, ἀναδραμεῖν μὲν οὐκ ἠδυνήθη—πολὺ γὰρ ἐνδεεστέρα ἦν τῆς λεπτομεροῦς—ἀνεπτέρωσε δὲ αὐτὴν τῷ Πνεύματι τῷ ἁγίῳ· τοῦτο γὰρ εὐεργετεῖ ἡ υἱότης ἐνδυσαμένη καὶ εὐεργετεῖται. 5. ἡ δὲ τρίτη υἱότης ἀποκαθάρσεως δεῖται· αὕτη μεμένηκεν ἐν τῷ τῆς πανσπερμίας σωρῷ, καὶ αὐτὴ εὐεργετοῦσα καὶ εὐεργετουμένη.

I only summarize these doctrines, though they have a plethora of material and different opinions.[38]

Such, then, are the views of Valentinus's school.

BASILEIDES. 14. 1. For his part, Basileides says that there is a nonexistent God who made a nonexistent world from nonexistent things.[39] It was sown as a nonexistent seed like a mustard seed containing the stem, leaves, branches, and fruit. Alternatively, it is like the egg of a peacock that has in itself a host of variegated colors. This he calls the "world seed," and it is the source of all reality. 2. It contained within itself all things as nonexistent entities that come into existence as preordained by the nonexistent God.[40]

There was in that seed, they say, a triple Sonship, entirely consubstantial with the nonexistent God, born from nonexistent realities. This Sonship is divided in three ways: the first part is subtle, the second is coarse, and the third is in need of purification. 3. First, the subtle part immediately throbbed with life simultaneous with the first sowing of the seed by the Nonexistent. It ascended above and arrived before the Nonexistent. All nature strains for the subtle Sonship on account of his supreme beauty, each part of nature in its own way. 4. The coarser part still remained in the seed. It is imitative and unable to run upward since it is far inferior to the subtle Sonship. Nevertheless, it gave itself wings by means of the Holy Spirit. So clothed, the Sonship benefited the Holy Spirit and received benefits in turn. 5. The third Sonship requires purification. It remains in the heap of the seed mixture, providing benefits and receiving them in turn.

Clem. Alex., *Exc.* 55.1; *Strom.* 3.95.2; Tert., *Val.* 24.3; *Marc.* 2.11.2; Pist. Soph. 69; 97.24; 98.38 (Schmidt). For the corrupted human, see Eph 4:22; Clem. Alex., *Paed.* 1.32.4; 3.17.2; *Strom.* 3.28.2; 7.14.2; *Ecl.* 24.1; Iren., *Haer.* 5.12.4.

38. The impatience of our author shows through here. His summary of "Valentinus" is particularly superficial, free, and arbitrary (Frickel, "Refutatio, Buch X," 221). Note that the views of Markos the Valentinian are totally omitted. Frickel treats the differences between this summary and the main report (ibid., 234–35). He concludes that both the summary and the main report used the same *Vorlage*, but the summary was actually written first as an independent heresiological work referred to in *Ref.* 1, *pref.* §1.

39. Cf. the overlapping report in *Ref.* 7.21.3–5; 7.22.6, 7–10, 16; 7.23.2–7; 7.24.3–5; 7.25.2; 7.26.6, 8–10.

40. Marcovich replaces τόν with οἷον (following *Ref.* 7.22.6).

Εἶναι δὲ <τὸ μέν> τι καλούμενον κόσμον, τὸ δέ ὑπερκόσμια· διαιρεῖται γὰρ ὑπ' αὐτοῦ <τὰ ὄντα> εἰς δύο τὰς πρώτας διαιρέσεις. τὸ δὲ τούτων μέσον καλεῖ μεθόριον Πνεῦμα ἅγιον, ἔχον τὴν ὀσμὴν τῆς υἱότητος.

6. ἀπὸ τῆς πανσπερμίας τοῦ σωροῦ <καὶ> τοῦ κοσμικοῦ σπέρματος διέσφυξε καὶ ἐγεννήθη ὁ μέγας ἄρχων, ἡ κεφαλὴ τοῦ κόσμου, κάλλει καὶ μεγέθει ἀνεκλαλήτῳ. οὗτος ὑψώσας ἑαυτὸν ἄχρι τοῦ στερεώματος ᾠήθη μὴ εἶναι ἑαυτοῦ ἐπάνω ἕτερον, καὶ ἐγένετο πάντων τῶν ὑποκειμένων φωτεινότερος καὶ δυνατώτερος πλὴν τῆς ὑπολελειμμένης υἱότητος, ἣν ἠγνόει οὖσαν αὐτοῦ σοφωτέραν.

7. Οὗτος ο<ὖν> τραπεὶς ἐπὶ τὴν τοῦ κόσμου δημιουργίαν πρῶτον γεννᾷ υἱὸν αὐτῷ, αὐτοῦ κρείττονα, καὶ τοῦτον ἐκ δεξιῶν αὐτοῦ ἐκάθισε· καὶ ταύτην οὗτοι φάσκουσι τὴν Ὀγδοάδα. αὐτὸς οὖν τὴν οὐράνιον κτίσιν ἅπασαν ἐργάζεται.

8. ἕτερος δὲ ἄρχων ἀπὸ τῆς πανσπερμίας ἀνέβη, μείζων μὲν πάντων τῶν ὑποκειμένων χωρὶς τῆς ἐγκαταλελειμμένης υἱότητος, πολὺ δὲ ἐλάττω<ν> τοῦ προτέρου· ὃν καλοῦσιν Ἑβδομάδα. οὗτός ἐστι πάντων τῶν ὑφ' αὐτὸν ποιητὴς καὶ δημιουργὸς καὶ διοικητής, καὶ αὐτὸς ἑαυτῷ ποιήσας υἱὸν φρονιμώτερον καὶ σοφώτερον.

9. ταῦτα δὲ πάντα κατὰ προλογισμὸν εἶναι ἐκείνου τοῦ οὐκ ὄντος λέγουσιν. εἶναι δὲ κόσμους καὶ διαστήματα ἄ(π)ειρα.

Τὸν δὲ Ἰησοῦν τὸν ἐκ Μαρίας κεχωρηκέναι τὴν εὐαγγελίου δύναμι(ν), τὴν κατελθοῦσαν καὶ φωτίσασαν τόν τε τῆς Ὀγδοάδος υἱὸν καὶ <τὸν> τῆς Ἑβδομάδος, ἐπὶ τῷ φωτίσαι καὶ φυλοκρινῆσαι καὶ καθαρίσαι τὴν καταλελειμμένην υἱότητα εἰς τὸ εὐεργετεῖν τὰς ψυχὰς καὶ εὐεργετεῖσθαι.

10. καὶ αὐτοὺς εἶναι υἱοὺς <τοῦ θεοῦ> φασιν, <οἳ> [ὅπου] τούτου χάριν εἰσὶν ἐν κόσμῳ, ἵνα διδάξαντες τὰς ψυχὰς καθαρίσωσι καὶ ἅμα τῇ υἱότητι ἀνέλθωσι πρὸς τὸν ἄνω Πατέρα, <ὅπ>οι ἡ πρώτη ἐχώρησεν υἱότης. καὶ ἕως τούτου συνεστάναι φάσκουσι τὸν κόσμον, ἕως πᾶσαι αἱ ψυχαὶ ἅμα τῇ υἱότητι χωρήσωσι.

ταῦτα δὴ καὶ Βασιλείδης τερατολογῶν οὐκ αἰσχύνεται.

15. 1. <Ἰ>ουστῖνος δὲ καὶ αὐτὸς ὅμοια τούτοις τολμῶν οὕτως λέγει· τρεῖς εἶναι ἀρχὰς τῶν ὅλων ἀγεννήτους, ἀρρενικὰς δύο, θηλυ<κὴ>ν μίαν. τῶν

There is what is called cosmos as well as the supercosmic realities. That is, he divides existent things into two primary divisions. The entity between them he calls the "Holy Spirit." It serves as a boundary and contains the scent of Sonship.

6. From the seed mixture of the heap and the world seed there throbbed with life and was born the great Ruler. He is the head of the world, indescribable in beauty and greatness. This Ruler, when he exalted himself as far as the firmament, thought that there was no other being above him. He became, of all lower realities, brighter and more powerful, with the exception of the Sonship, whom the Ruler did not know was wiser than himself.

7. Then he turned to the fashioning of the world. He first fathered his son, greater than himself, and enthroned him at his right hand. This region they call the "Ogdoad." Then he produced the entire heavenly creation.

8. Another ruler rose from the seed mixture, greater than all the underling beings apart from the Sonship held below, but far inferior to the first Ruler. They call this second ruler "Hebdomad." He is the maker, artificer, and administrator of everything below him. He also made for himself a son who was much more intelligent and wise.

9. All these things, they claim, came to be by the foreordained plan of the Nonexistent. There are also infinite worlds and levels of heaven.

Jesus son of Mary contained the power of the gospel, which had descended and enlightened the son of the Ogdoad and the son of the Hebdomad in order to enlighten, differentiate, and purify the Sonship held below. This happened so that souls could benefit and receive benefits in turn.

10. They say that they themselves are the sons of God.[41] They are in the world to teach and purify souls. Subsequently, they ascend together with the Sonship to the Father above, where the first Sonship went. The world, they claim, is held together until all the souls advance together with the Sonship.

These are the fantastical tales even Basileides is not ashamed to teach.

JUSTIN. 15. 1. Justin, for his part, dares to teach the same doctrines.[42] He says that there are three unborn principles of the universe: two male and

41. Marcovich adds τοῦ θεοῦ ("of God"), following *Ref.* 7.25.1, 5 and Rom 8:19.

42. Cf. the overlapping report in *Ref.* 5.26. Our author originally placed Justin with the "Snake systems" (Naassenes, Peratai, and "Sethians"), but here he is catalogued, it seems, according to his tripartite theology.

δὲ ἀρρενικῶν ἡ μέν τις ἀρχὴ καλεῖται ἀγαθός, αὐτὸ μόνον οὕτω λεγόμενος, προγνώστης τῶν ὅλων, ἡ δὲ ἑτέρα πατὴρ πάντων τῶν γεννητῶν, ἀπρόγνωστος καὶ ἄγνωστος καὶ ἀόρατος—Ἐλωεὶμ δὲ καλεῖται, φησίν.

2. ἡ θήλεια ἀπρόγνωστος, ὀργίλη, δίγνωμος, δισώματος—καθὼς ἐν τοῖς περὶ αὐτοῦ λόγοις λεπτομερῶς διηγησάμεθα·—τὰ μὲν ἄνω αὐτὴν μέχρι βουβῶνός εἶναι παρθένον, ἀπὸ δὲ βουβῶνος τὰ κάτω ἔχιδνα<ν>. καλεῖται δὲ ἡ τοιαύτη Ἐδὲμ καὶ Ἰσραήλ. ταύτας φάσκει ἀρχὰς εἶναι τῶν ὅλων, ἀφ' ὧν τὰ πάντα ἐγένετο.

3. Τὸν Ἐλωεὶμ δὲ ἀπρογνώστως ἐλθεῖν εἰς ἐπιθυμίαν τῆς μιξοπαρθένου, καὶ ἐπιμιγέντα γεννῆσαι ἀγγέλους δώδεκα· τούτων τὰ ὀνόματα ... καὶ οἱ μὲν πατρικοὶ <ἄγγελοι τῷ πατρὶ> συναίρονται, οἱ δὲ μητρικοὶ τῇ μητρί. τούτους εἶναι τοῦ ἀλληγορικῶς εἰρηκότος Μωσέως τὰ ἐν τῷ νόμῳ γεγραμμένα.

4. Πεποιῆσθαι δὲ τὰ πάντα ὑπὸ τοῦ Ἐλωεὶμ καὶ τῆς Ἐδέμ, καὶ τὰ μὲν θηρία ἅμα τοῖς λοιποῖς ἀπὸ τοῦ θηριώδους μέρους <τῆς Ἐδέμ,> τὸν δὲ ἄνθρωπον ἀπὸ τῶν ἄνωθεν τοῦ βουβῶνος. καὶ τὴν μὲν Ἐδὲμ κατατεθεῖσθαι ἐν αὐτῷ τὴν ψυχήν—ἥτις αὐτῆς δύναμις ἦν.

5. Τοῦτον δὲ φάσκει μαθόντα, ἀνεληλυθέναι πρὸς τὸν ἀγαθὸν καὶ καταλελοιπέναι τὴν Ἐδέμ. ἐφ' ᾧ ὀργισθεῖσαν ταύτην πᾶσαν τὴν ἐπιβουλὴν ποιεῖσθαι κατὰ τοῦ π(ν)εύματος τοῦ Ἐλωείμ, ὅπερ κατέθετο ἐν τῷ ἀνθρώπῳ. καὶ τούτου χάριν ἀπεσταλκέναι τὸν πατέρα τὸν Βαρούχ, διαταττόμενον <λαλεῖν> τοῖς προφήταις, ἵνα ῥυσθῇ τ(ὸ) πνεῦμα τοῦ Ἐλωείμ, καὶ πάντας ὑποσεσύρθαι ὑπὸ τῆς Ἐδέμ. 6. ἀλλὰ καὶ τὸν Ἡρακλέα φάσκει προφήτην γεγονέναι, ἡττῆσθαι δὲ αὐτὸν ὑπὸ τῆς Ὀμφάλης—τουτέστιν ὑπὸ τῆς Βάβελ, ἣν Ἀφροδίτην ὀνομάζουσιν.

Ὕστερον δὲ «ἐν ταῖς ἡμέραις Ἡρώδου» γεγονέναι τὸν [δὲ] Ἰησοῦν, υἱὸν Μαρίας καὶ Ἰωσήφ, ᾧ τὸν Βαροὺχ φάσκει λελαληκέναι. 7. καὶ τούτῳ δὲ ἐπιβεβουλευκέναι τὴν Ἐδέμ, μὴ δεδυνῆσθαι δὲ αὐτὸν ἀπατῆσαι, καὶ τούτου χάριν πεποιηκέναι σταυρωθῆναι· οὗ τὸ πνεῦμα ἀνεληλυθέναι πρὸς τὸν ἀγαθὸν λέγει. καὶ πάντων δὲ οὕτως τῶν τοῖς μωροῖς καὶ ἀδρανέσι λόγοις πειθομένων

one female. Among the males, the first principle alone is called "Good." He knows the future of the universe. The other male principle is the Father of generated beings. He does not know the future, is unknown, and is invisible. This second principle is called, he says, "Elohim."

2. The female principle does not know the future, is irascible, double-minded, and double-bodied—as I discussed in detail in my report on Justin. Her upper body—as far as the groin—is a young woman, but from the groin down, she is a viper. This sort of creature is called "Eden" and "Israel." These, he claims, are the principles of the universe, from which all things originate.

3. Not knowing what was to come, Elohim came in lust to the "mixed maiden," had sex with her, and fathered twelve angels. Their names are … The Father's angels assist the Father, and the Mother's angels assist the Mother.[43] These are the ones written in the Law about which Moses speaks allegorically.

4. All things were made by Elohim and Eden: animals and so on were made from the beastly parts of Eden, while the human being arose from the parts above her groin. In the human being Eden deposited the soul, which was her power.[44]

5. When Elohim, he claims, received instruction, he ascended to the Good and abandoned Eden. Furious at him, Eden made every attempt to conspire against the spirit of Elohim deposited in human beings. For this reason, the Father dispatched Baruch, who was charged with speaking to the prophets so as to deliver the spirit of Elohim and all those seduced by Eden. 6. Justin even says that Herakles was a prophet but was conquered by Omphale (that is, by Babel, whom they call Aphrodite).

Later, "in the days of Herod," Jesus was born. He was son of Mary and Joseph. Baruch (Justin claims) spoke to him. 7. Eden conspired against Jesus but was not able to deceive him. For this reason, she caused him to be crucified. Jesus's spirit, he says, rose to the Good. In this way, the spirit of all

43. Marcovich adds ἄγγελοι and, following Miller, τῷ πατρί, to agree with our author's earlier report.

44. Here Marcovich would add τὸν δὲ Ἐλωεὶμ τὸ πνεῦμα ὅ τι αὐτοῦ δύναμις ἦν ("and Elohim [deposited] the spirit, which was his power"). It is possible that this (admittedly important) material dropped out of the text, but just as likely that our author himself cut out this information in accord with his technique of summarizing by deletion. See further Frickel, "Refutatio, Buch X," 223–24.

<τὸ πνεῦμα> σωθήσεσθαι, τὸ δὲ σῶμα καὶ τὴν ψυχὴν τῆς Ἐδὲμ καταλείψεσθαι, ἣν καὶ γῆν Ἰουστῖνος ὁ ἄφρων καλεῖ.

16. 1. Οἱ δὲ Δοκηταὶ τοιαῦτα λέγουσιν· εἶναι τὸν πρῶτον θεὸν ὡς σπέρμα συκῆς, ἐκ δὲ τούτου ἐληλυθέναι τρεῖς αἰῶνας, ὡς τὸ πρέμνον καὶ τὰ φύλλα καὶ τὸν καρπόν. τούτους δὲ προβεβληκέναι τριάκοντα αἰῶνας, ἕκαστον <δέκα>· ἡνῶσθαι δὲ αὐτοὺς κατὰ δέκα πάντας, μόνον δὲ θέσει διαφέρειν τινὰς τινῶν <ὡς> πρώτους, <δευτέρους καὶ τρίτους>. προβεβλῆσθαι δὲ <αὐτοὺς> ἀπειράκις ἀπείρους αἰῶνας, καὶ εἶναι τοὺς πάντας ἀρρενοθήλεας. 2. τούτους δὲ βουλευσαμένους, ὁμοῦ συνελθόντας εἰς τὸν μέσον αἰῶνα γεννῆσαι ἐκ παρθένου Μαρίας σωτῆρα τῶν πάντων, κατὰ πάντα ὅμοιον τῷ πρώτῳ [σώματι ἐν] σπέρματι συκίνῳ, ἐν δὲ τούτῳ ἥττονα, τῷ γεννητὸν εἶναι· τὸ γὰρ σπέρμα, ὅθεν ἡ συκῆ, ἀγέννητον.

3. Ἦν οὖν τὸ μέγα τῶν αἰώνων φῶς ὅλον, οὐδεμίαν ἐπιδεχόμενον κόσμησιν, ἔχον ἐν ἑαυτῷ πάντων τῶν ζῴων ἰδέας· τοῦτο ἐπιφοιτῆσαν εἰς τὸ ὑποκείμενον χάος παρεσχηκέναι αἰτίαν τοῖς γεγονόσι καὶ οὖσι· καταβα<σῶ>ν γὰρ ἄνωθεν ἰδεῶν αἰωνίων ἀπεμάξατο τὸ κάτω χάος τὰς μορφάς.

4. ὁ δὲ τρίτος αἰών, ὁ ἑαυτὸν τριπλασιάσας, ὁρῶν τοὺς χαρακτῆρας αὑτοῦ πάντας κατασπωμένους εἰς τὸ κάτω σ(κ)ότος, οὐκ ἀγνοῶν τήν τε τοῦ σκότους δεινότητα καὶ τὴν τ(ο)ῦ φωτὸς ἀφειλότητα, ἐποίησεν οὐρανόν, καὶ μέσον πήξας «διεχώρισεν ἀ(νὰ) μέσον τοῦ σκότους καὶ ἀνὰ μέσον τοῦ φωτός».

5. πασῶν οὖν τῶν ἰδεῶν τοῦ τρίτου αἰῶνος καὶ αὐτοῦ τὸ ἐκτύπωμα κρατεῖσθαί φησίν ὑπὸ τοῦ σκότους, <ὃ> πῦρ [ὢν αὖθις] ζῶν ἀπὸ [τοῦ] φωτὸς γενόμενον ὑπῆρξεν. ἐξ οὗ φάσκουσι τὸν μέγαν ἄρχοντα γεγονέναι, περὶ οὗ Μωϋσῆς ὁμιλεῖ, λέγων εἶναι τοῦτον θεὸν πύρινον καὶ δημιουργόν. ὃς καὶ τὰς ἰδέας πάντων μεταβάλλει ἀεὶ εἰς σώμα<τα>, ταύτας τὰς <ἰδέας> ψυχὰς <καλοῦντες>.

6. Οὗ χάριν <φ>άσκουσι τὸν σωτῆρα παραγενηθῆναι, ἐπιδεικνύντα τὴν ὁδὸν δι᾽ ἧς φεύξονται αἱ κρατούμεναι ψυχαί. ἐνδεδύσθαι δέ τὸν Ἰησοῦν τὴν δύναμιν ἐκείνην τὴν μονογενῆ· διὸ μὴ δύνασθαι θεαθῆναι ὑπό τινος διὰ τὸ

those who believe his stupid and useless tales will be saved, while the body and soul of Eden (whom the dimwit Justin also calls "earth") is left behind.[45]

DOKETAI. 16. 1. The Doketai say things of this ilk: the first God is like a fig tree seed.[46] From it come three aeons in the manner of the trunk, leaves, and fruit. These aeons, in turn, emanate thirty aeons, ten each. All are united in groups of ten, differing only in placement so as to be first, second, or third. They emanate aeons infinity times infinity in number, and all these aeons are androgynous. 2. When they took counsel together, they converged at once into a central aeon and gave birth from the virgin Mary. They gave birth to the Savior of the universe. He is in every way equal to the first fig seed. He is, however, inferior inasmuch as he is born (for the seed from which the fig tree came is unborn).

3. The Savior was the great and comprehensive light of the aeons. He received no ordering at all and contained the forms of all animals. This light frequented the underlying chaos and furnished a cause to the beings who existed and exist. When the forms of the aeons from above had descended, the lower chaos was stamped with their shapes.

4. The third aeon, who had tripled himself, saw all his impressions drawn down into the lower darkness. Since he was not ignorant of the shrewdness of the darkness and the simplicity of the light, he made heaven. By fixing heaven in the middle region, "he separated between darkness and light."[47]

5. When all the forms of the third aeon and his impress were held down by the darkness, he says, the living fire began to exist from the light. From it, they claim, the great Ruler emerged, whom Moses depicts as a fiery god and an artificer. He is the one who continuously changes the forms of all things into bodies and calls the forms "souls."[48]

6. The Savior, they claim, came to reveal the path through which the souls held down by darkness can flee. Jesus clothed himself with that only-born power. Accordingly, he could not be seen by anyone, because he

45. Marcovich adds τὸ πνεῦμα ("the spirit").

46. Cf. the overlapping report in *Ref.* 8.8.3, 5, 7; 8.9.2–7; 8.10.1, 3, 5, 7. Due apparently to their tripartite system, our author moves up the Doketai, who in the main report came after all the figures discussed in *Ref.* 6–7. Satorneilos and Menander go unmentioned in his summary. Yet our author will return to Markion below.

47. Gen 1:4; cf. *Ref.* 8.9.5.

48. Marcovich adds ἰδέας ("forms") and καλοῦντες ("and calls") from *Ref.* 8.10.11.

μεταβαλλόμενον μέγεθος τῆς δόξης. πάντα δὲ συμβεβηκέναι αὐτῷ φασι καθὰ ἐν τοῖς εὐαγγελίοις γέγραπται.

17. 1. Οἱ δὲ περὶ <Μο>νόϊμον τὸν Ἄραβά φασιν εἶναι τὴν τοῦ παντὸς ἀρχὴν <τὸν> πρῶτον ἄνθρωπον καὶ υἱὸν <τοῦ> ἀνθρώπου· καὶ τὰ γενόμενα, καθὼς Μωσῆς λέγει, μὴ ἀπὸ τοῦ πρώτου ἀνθρώπου γεγονέναι, ἀλλ' ἀπὸ τοῦ υἱοῦ τοῦ ἀνθρώπου, οὐχ ὅλου, ἀλλ' ἐκ μέρους αὐτοῦ. 2. εἶναι γὰρ τὸν υἱὸν τοῦ ἀνθρώπου ἰῶτα—ὅ ἐστι δεκάς, κύριος ἀριθμός, ἐν ᾧ ἐστιν ἡ τοῦ παντὸς ἀριθμοῦ ὑπόστασις, δι' οὗ πᾶς ἀριθμὸς συνέστηκεν καὶ ἡ τοῦ παντὸς γένεσις, πῦρ, ἀήρ, ὕδωρ, γῆ·—τοῦτον δὴ <ὄντως εἶναι> ἰῶτα ἕν, [καὶ] κεραία<ν> μία<ν>, τέλειον ἐκ τελείου, ῥυεῖσα κεραία ἄνωθεν, πάντα ἔχουσα [ὅσα καὶ] αὐτὴ ὅσα καὶ ὁ ἄνθρωπος ἔχει, ὁ πατὴρ τοῦ υἱοῦ τοῦ ἀνθρώπου.

3. Γεγονέναι οὖν φησι τὸν κόσμον Μωϋσῆς ἐν ἓξ ἡμέραις, τουτέστιν ἐν ἓξ δυνάμεσιν, ἐξ ὧν ὁ κόσμος ἀπὸ τῆς κεραίας γέγονε τῆς μιᾶς. οἵ τε γὰρ κύβοι καὶ τὰ ὀκτάεδρα καὶ αἱ πυραμίδες καὶ πάντα τὰ τούτοις παραπλήσια σχήματα [ἴσα ἦν], ἐξ ὧν συνέστηκε πῦρ, ἀήρ, ὕδωρ, γῆ, ἀπὸ τῶν ἀριθμῶν γεγόνασι τῶν κατειλημμένων ἐν ἐκείνῃ τῇ ἁπλῇ τοῦ ἰῶτα κεραίᾳ, ἥτις ἐστὶν υἱὸς ἀνθρώπου.

4. ὅταν οὖν, φησί, ῥάβδον λέγῃ Μωϋσῆς στρεφομένην εἰς Αἴγυπτον, τὰ πάθη καταλέγει τοῦ κόσμου τῷ ἰῶτα ἀλληγορουμένως, οὐδὲ πλείον<α> <τ>ῶν δέ<κα> παθῶν ἐσχημάτισεν.

5. «Εἰ δέ», φησί, «θέλεις ἐπιγνῶναι τὸ πᾶν, ἐν σεαυτῷ ζήτησον τίς ὁ λέγων· ἡ ψυχή μου, ἡ σάρξ μου, ὁ νοῦς μου· καὶ <τίς ὁ> ἐν <σοὶ> ἕκαστον κατιδιοποιούμενος ὡς ἕτερος <σε>αυτοῦ· τοῦτον νόει, τέλειον ἐκ τελείου, πάντα ἴδια ἡγούμενον, τὰ οὐκ ὄντα καλούμενα καὶ τὰ [πάντα] ὄντα».

ταῦτα μὲν οὖν καὶ Μονοΐμῳ δοκεῖ.

18. 1. Τατιανὸς δὲ παραπλησίως τῷ Οὐαλεντίνῳ καὶ τοῖς ἑτέροις φησὶν αἰῶνας εἶναί τινας ἀοράτους, ἐξ ὧν ὑπό τινος <τῶν> κάτω τὸν κόσμον

changed the magnitude of his glory. Everything happened to him, they say, as is written in the Gospels.

MONOÏMOS. 17. 1. The disciples of Monoïmos the Arab say that the first principle of everything is the primal Human and the Son of the Human.[49] Generated beings, as Moses says, arose not from the first Human but from the Son of the Human—and not from the whole of him but only from a part. 2. The Son of the Human is the iota, the decad. The decad is the master number, the basis of all number, from which every number is composed. Moreover, it is the origin of all things: fire, air, water, and earth. It truly is one iota, a single stroke, perfect from a perfect one, flowing as a stroke from above, containing all that is contained by the Human (who is the Father of the Son of the Human).[50]

3. The world originated, as Moses says, in six days, that is, in six powers. From these, the world arose out of the single stroke. This is because cubes, octagons, pyramids, and all similar shapes, from which fire, air, water, and earth were composed, arose from the numbers contained in that simple stroke of the iota, which is the Son of the Human.

4. When, Monoïmos says, Moses speaks of a staff wielded against Egypt, he allegorically recounts by means of the iota the plagues of the world [and] depicts them as no more than ten plagues.

5. "But if," he says, "you desire to know the all, seek in yourself who it is who says, 'my soul, my flesh, my mind,' and who it is in you who appropriates each thing as if other than yourself.[51] Conceive of this one, then: the Perfect one from the Perfect one, who considers all things his own, both those called nonexistent and existent."

These are the doctrines of Monoïmos.

TATIAN. 18. 1. Tatian, almost exactly like Valentinus and the others, says that there are invisible aeons from which the world and existent things were fashioned by someone of the lower world.[52] He practices a rather

49. Cf. the overlapping report in *Ref.* 8.12.2; 8.13.1, 4; 8.14.1–3; 8.15.1–2.

50. Marcovich prefers to emend P's ὄντος to οὕτως ("thus"). A simpler emendation (printed here) is ὄντως ("truly"). Wendland conjectures εἰκών ("image").

51. Marcovich's emendations to this sentence (τίς ὁ … σοὶ … <σε>αυτοῦ) are accepted here.

52. Cf. *Ref.* 8.16.1, where our author says only that Tatian believed in aeons. The claim that they are the ultimate source for the creation seems to be an attempt to conform Tatian's teaching even more to a Valentinian model.

δεδημιουργῆσθαι καὶ τὰ ὄντα. κυνικωτέρῳ δὲ βίῳ ἀσκεῖται <καὶ> σχεδὸν οὐδὲν Μαρκίωνος ἀπεμφαίνει πρός τε τὴν δυσφημίαν καὶ τῆς περὶ γάμων νομοθεσίας.

19. 1. <Μ>αρκίων δὲ ὁ Ποντικὸς καὶ Κέρδων ὁ τούτου διδάσκαλος καὶ αὐτοὶ ὁρίζουσιν εἶναι τρεῖς τὰς τοῦ παντὸς ἀρχάς· ἀγαθόν, δίκαιον, ὕλην. τινὲς δὲ τούτων μαθηταὶ <καὶ τετάρτην> προστιθέασι, λέγοντες ἀγαθόν, δίκαιον, πονηρόν, ὕλην.

2. οἱ δὲ πάντες τὸν μὲν ἀγαθὸν οὐδὲν ὅλως πεποιηκέναι, τὸν δὲ δίκαιον—<ὃν> οἱ μὲν [τὸν] πονηρόν, οἱ δὲ μόνον δίκαιον ὀνομάζουσι—πεποιηκέναι [δὲ] τὰ πάντα φάσκουσιν ἐκ τῆς ὑποκειμένης ὕλης. πεποιηκέναι δὲ οὐ καλῶς, ἀλλ' ἀλόγως· ἀνάγκη γὰρ τὰ γενόμενα ὅμοια εἶναι τῷ πεποιηκότι. 3. διὸ καὶ ταῖς παραβολαῖς ταῖς εὐαγγελικαῖς χρῶνται, οὕτως λέγοντες· «οὐ δύναται δένδρον καλὸν καρποὺς πονηροὺς ποιεῖν» καὶ τὰ ἑξῆς, εἰς τοῦτο φάσκων εἰρῆσθαι <ταῦτα>, τὰ ὑπ' αὐτοῦ κακῶς νομιζόμενα.

Τὸν δὲ Χριστὸν υἱὸν εἶναι τοῦ ἀγαθοῦ καὶ ὑπ' αὐτοῦ πεπέμφθαι ἐπὶ σωτηρίᾳ τῶν ψυχῶν. ὃν «ἔσω ἄνθρωπον» καλεῖ, ὡς ἄνθρωπον φανέντα λέγων, οὐκ ὄντα ἄνθρωπον, καὶ ὡς ἔνσαρκον, οὐκ ἔνσαρκον, δοκήσει πεφηνότα, οὔτε γένεσιν ὑπομείναντα οὔτε πάθος ἀλλ' ἢ τῷ δοκεῖν.

Cynic lifestyle and differs in almost no respect from Markion when it comes to slandering [the creator], and the legislation about marriage.

MARKION AND KERDON. 19. 1. Markion of Pontos and Kerdon his teacher also determined that there are three principles of everything: a good being, a just one, and matter.[53] Some of their disciples add a fourth principle, speaking of a good being, a just one, an evil one, and matter.[54]

2. Yet all of them claim that the good principle made nothing at all. It was the just principle—whom some call evil and others simply just—whom they claim created everything from underlying matter.[55] He made it not skillfully but irrationally, for it is necessary that generated beings resemble their maker. 3. Consequently, they use the Gospel parables (for instance, "it is not possible for a good tree to bear bad fruit," and so on), claiming that these verses were written in reference to the things Markion perversely assumes.[56]

Christ is son of the Good and was sent by him for the salvation of souls.[57] He calls him "the inner human," claiming that he appeared as a human but was not human, that he appeared as enfleshed but was not enfleshed—that he manifested himself in appearance, enduring both birth and his suffering only in appearance.[58]

---

53. Our author took his summary of Markion and Kerdon from a source different from his main report in *Ref.* 7.29.1; 7.30; 7.37. Judging by its content, that source was not Irenaeus. Still, by treating Markion and Kerdon together, our author follows the lead of Iren., *Haer.* 1.27. For Kerdon, see *Ref.* 7.10; 7.37.1; Iren., *Haer.* 1.27.2; 3.4.3; Epiph., *Pan.* 42.1.1; 42.3.1; Tert., *Marc.* 1.2.3; 4.17.11; Ps.-Tert., *Adv. omn. haer.* 6; Filastrius, *Haer.* 45.1, 3; Theodoret, *Haer. fab.* 1.24 (PG 83:372d, 373b). For the three principles, see *Ref.* 7.31.2 (Prepon); Rhodon in Eusebios, *Hist. eccl.* 5.13.4; Epiph., *Pan.* 42.3.1–2; 65.8.6. In the main report, our author ascribed two principles to Markion (*Ref.* 7.29.1).

54. Cf. *Ref.* 7.38.1 (Apelles); Theodoret, *Haer. fab.* 1.24 (PG 83:373b–c); 1.25 (PG 83:367).

55. Marcovich adds ὅν ("whom").

56. Matt 7:18. Cf. Tert., *Marc.* 1.2.1; 4.17.11; Ps.-Tert., *Adv. omn. haer.* 6.2; Filastrius, *Haer.* 45.2; Origen, *Princ.* 2.5.4.

57. On the Good, see Iren., *Haer.* 1.27.2; Epiph., *Pan.* 42.4.2; Ps.-Tert., *Adv. omn. haer.* 6.1; *Ref.* 7.37.1 (Kerdon); 7.38.2 (Apelles).

58. Cf. *Ref.* 7.28.4–5 (Satorneilos); 7.31.5 (Prepon); Clem. Alex., *Strom.* 6.9.71.2; Origen, *Cels.* 2.16; Ps.-Tert., *Adv. omn. haer.* 6.1; Filastrius, *Haer.* 45.4; Theodoret, *Haer. fab.* 1.24 (PG 83:376a).

4. σάρκα δὲ οὐ θέλει ἀνίστασθαι. γάμον δὲ φθορὰν εἶναι λέγει, κυνικωτέρῳ βίῳ προσάγων τοὺς μαθητάς, ἐν τούτῳ νομίζων λυπεῖν τὸν δημιουργόν, εἰ τῶν ὑπ' αὐτοῦ γεγονότων ἢ ὡρισμένων ἀπέχοιτο.

20. 1. Ἀπελλῆς δέ, ὁ τούτου μαθητ(ή)ς, ἀπαρεσθεὶς τοῖς ὑπὸ τοῦ διδασκάλου εἰρημένοις, καθὰ προείπομεν, ἄλλῳ λόγῳ ὑπέθετο τέσσαρας εἶναι θεούς, ὧν ἕνα φάσκει <ἀγαθόν>—ὃν οὔτε <ὁ νόμος οὔτε> οἱ προφ(ῆ)ται ἔγνωσαν· οὗ εἶναι υἱὸν τὸν Χριστόν—ἕτερον δὲ τὸν δημιουργὸν τοῦ παντός—ὃν οὐ θεὸν εἶναι θέλει—ἕτερον δὲ πύρινον—τὸν <Μωσεῖ> φανέντα—ἕτερον δὲ πονηρόν· οὓς ἀγγέλους καλεῖ· προσθεὶς δὲ τὸν Χριστὸν καὶ πέμπτον ἐρεῖ.

2. Προσέχει δὲ βίβλῳ, ἣ<ν> Φανερώσεις καλεῖ, Φιλουμένης τινὸς, ἣν προφῆτιν νομίζει.

τὴν δὲ σάρκα τὸν Χριστὸν οὐκ ἐκ τῆς παρθένου λέγει προσειληφέναι, ἀλλ' ἐκ τῆς παρακειμένης τοῦ κόσμου οὐσίας.

οὗτος κατὰ τοῦ νόμου καὶ τῶν προφητῶν συντάγματα ἐποίησε, «καταλύειν αὐτοὺς» ἐπιχειρῶν ὡς ψευδῆ λελαληκότας καὶ θεὸν μὴ ἐγνωκότας. σάρκας δὲ ἀπόλ<λ>υσθαι ὁμοίως Μαρκίωνι λέγει.

21. 1. Κήρινθος δέ, ὁ ἐν τῇ Αἰγύπτῳ ἀσκηθείς, αὐτὸς οὐχ ὑπὸ τοῦ πρώτου θεοῦ τὸν κόσμον γεγονέναι ἠθέλησεν, ἀλλ' ὑπὸ δυνάμεώς τινος ἀγγελικῆς, πολὺ κεχωρισμένης καὶ διεστώσης τῆς ὑπὲρ τὰ ὅλα αὐθεντίας καὶ ἀγνοούσης τὸν ὑπὲρ πάντα θεόν. 2. τὸν δὲ Ἰησοῦν λέγει μὴ ἐκ παρθένου γεγεν<ν>ῆσθαι,

4. He denies the resurrection of the flesh.[59] He says that marriage is corruption.[60] He leads his disciples into a Cynic-like lifestyle. By this means, Markion supposes he can grieve the Artificer by abstaining from his products and ordinances.

APELLES. 20. 1. Apelles, Markion's disciple, disagreeing with his teacher's ideas (as I noted), posited by another argument that there were four gods.[61] One of these he calls "Good," whom neither the Law nor the Prophets knew.[62] He has a son, the Christ. Another god is the Artificer of everything, whom he prefers not to call "god." Still another god is the fiery one who appeared to Moses. The last is the evil god. He calls these gods "angels." By adding Christ, he speaks also of a fifth god.

2. He hankers after a book he calls *Manifestations*. It is by a certain Philoumene, whom he supposes to be a prophetess.

He says that Christ received flesh not from the virgin but from the available cosmic substance.

He composed tracts against the Law and Prophets "to destroy them," with the contrived thesis that the prophets spoke lies and did not know God. Like Markion, he says that fleshly bodies are destroyed.[63]

KERINTHOS. 21. 1. Kerinthos was trained in Egypt.[64] He also decided that the world originated not by means of the primal God but by an angelic power far separate and distant from the Supreme Divine Power and ignorant of the God above all.[65] 2. He claims that Jesus was not born from a

59. Cf. Iren., *Haer.* 1.27.2; Tert., *Marc.* 5.10.5; *Carn. Chr.* 2; Ps.-Tert., *Adv. omn. haer.* 6.1; Epiph., *Pan.* 42.3.5; Theodoret, *Haer. fab.* 1.24 (PG 83:375a–b).

60. Cf. *Ref.* 7.28.7 (Satorneilos); 7.30.3–4 (Markion); 8.16.1 (Tatian); 8.20.1–2 (Enkratites); 10.18.1 (Tatian summary); Clem. Alex., *Strom.* 3.12.1–2; 25.2; Tert., *Marc.* 1.29.1; 4.11.8; 4.34.5.

61. Cf. the main report on Apelles in *Ref.* 7.38.1–5; and Theodoret, *Haer. fab.* 1.25 (PG 83:376–77).

62. Marcovich adds ὁ νόμος οὔτε (here: "the Law nor").

63. Cf. *Ref.* 7.38.2; 10.19.4 (Markion summary); Ps.-Tert., *Adv. omn. haer.* 6.6; Rhodon in Eusebios, *Hist. eccl.* 5.13.2; Origen, *Cels.* 5.54; Epiph., *Pan.* 44.4.1; Tert., *Carn. Chr.* 8.2; *An.* 23.3; 36.3.

64. Cf. the overlapping report in *Ref.* 7.33.1–2; Theodoret, *Haer. fab.* 2.3 (PG 83:389–92). Our author here omits a summary of Karpokrates, who was linked to Kerinthos in the main report. By placing Kerinthos after Markion and Apelles, Kerinthos is significantly postponed.

65. Diverging from his main account (*Ref.* 7.33.1), our author has Kerinthos

γεγονέναι δὲ αὐτὸν ἐξ Ἰωσὴφ καὶ Μαρίας υἱόν, ὁμοίως τοῖς λοιποῖς ἀνθρώποις, καὶ δι(ε)νηνοχέναι ἐν δικαιοσύνῃ καὶ σωφροσύνῃ καὶ συνέσει ὑπὲρ πάντας τοὺς λοιπούς.

3. καὶ μετὰ τὸ βάπτισμα κατεληλυθέναι εἰς αὐτὸν ἐκ τῆς ὑπὲρ τὰ ὅλα αὐθεντίας τὸν Χριστὸν ἐν εἴδει περιστερᾶς· καὶ τότε κηρῦξαι τὸν ἄγνωστον πατέρα καὶ δυνάμεις ἐπιτελέσαι. πρὸς δὲ τῷ τέλει τοῦ πάθους ἀποπτῆναι τὸν Χριστὸν ἀπὸ τοῦ <Ἰησοῦ>· πεπονθέναι τὸν Ἰησοῦν, τὸν δὲ Χριστὸν ἀπαθῆ μεμενηκέναι, πνεῦμα κυρίου ὑπάρχοντα.

22. 1. Ἐβιωναῖοι δὲ τὸν μὲν κόσμον ὑπὸ τοῦ ὄντως θεοῦ γεγονέναι λέγουσι, τὰ δὲ <περὶ τὸν> Χριστὸν ὁμοίως Κηρίνθῳ. ζῶσι δὲ πάντα κατὰ νόμον Μωϋσῆ, οὕτω φάσκον(τ)ες δικαιοῦσθαι.

23. 1. Θεόδοτος (δὲ) ὁ Βυζάντιος εἰσηγήσατο αἵρεσιν τοιάνδε, φάσκων τὰ μὲν ὅλα ὑπὸ τοῦ ὄντως θεοῦ γεγονέναι, τὸν δὲ Χριστόν, ὁμοίως τοῖς προειρημένοις γνωστικοῖς, φάσκει τοιούτῳ τινὶ τρόπῳ πεφηνέναι. εἶναι μὲν τὸν <Ἰησοῦν> κ(οι)νὸν ἄνθρωπον πᾶσιν, ἐν δὲ τούτῳ διαφέρειν, ὅτι κατὰ βουλὴν θεοῦ γεγένηται ἐκ παρθένου, ἐπισκιάσαντος τοῦ ἁγίου πνεύματος <τὸν> ἐν τῇ παρθένῳ σαρκωθέντ(α)· 2. ὕστερον δὲ ἐπὶ τοῦ βαπτίσματος κατεληλυθέναι τὸν Χριστὸν ἐπὶ τὸν Ἰησοῦν ἐν εἴδει περιστερᾶς. ὅθεν φασὶ μὴ πρότερον «τὰς δυνάμεις αὐτῷ ἐνεργηθῆναι». θεὸν δὲ οὐκ εἶναι τὸν Χριστὸν θέλει.

καὶ τοιαῦτα Θεόδοτος.

24. 1. Ἕτεροι δὲ [καὶ] ἐξ αὐτῶν πάντα τοῖς προειρημένοις <ὁμοίως> λέγουσι, <ἐν> ἑν<ὶ δὲ> μόνῳ ἐνδιαλλάξαντες, ἐν τῷ τὸν Μελχισεδὲκ ὡς

virgin but was born the son of Joseph and Mary just like all other human beings. Still, Jesus excelled other people by his righteousness, moderation, and insight.

3. After Jesus's baptism, Christ, from the Supreme Divine Power over all, descended upon him in the form of a dove. After that, Jesus preached the unknown Father and performed miracles. At the end of his suffering, the Christ flew away from Jesus.[66] Jesus suffered, but Christ remained without suffering, existing as the Spirit of the Lord.

EBIONITES. 22. 1. The Ebionites say that the world originated from the true God but hold the same views about Christ as Kerinthos.[67] They live in all respects according to the Law of Moses, claiming that in this way they are made righteous.

THEODOTOS THE BYZANTIAN. 23. 1. Theodotos the Byzantian introduced a heresy with the following features.[68] He claims that the universe originated by means of the true God but affirms that Christ, just as the previously mentioned gnostics, appeared in the following way. Jesus was an ordinary human being like everybody else. But he differed in that, according to God's will, he was born from a virgin when the Holy Spirit overshadowed the one made flesh in the virgin.[69] 2. Later, at Jesus's baptism, Christ descended upon Jesus in the form of a dove. Hence they say that previous to this "the miracles were not activated in him." He denies that Christ is God.[70]

Such are the teachings of Theodotos.

OTHER THEODOTIANS. 24. 1. Others from the same party agree in all respects with the aforementioned Theodotians, disagreeing in only one

---

affirm that the world was created not just by a certain power but by an *angelic* power. This addition makes Kerinthos sound more like Satorneilos. Pseudo-Tertullian affirms the same in *Adv. omn. haer.* 3 (*mundum institutum esse ab angelis dicit* ["He says that the world is founded by angels"]).

66. "Jesus" (Ἰησοῦ) is R. Scott's emendation for P's υἱοῦ ("Son").

67. Cf. the overlapping report in *Ref.* 7.34.1.

68. Cf. the overlapping report in *Ref.* 7.35.1–2.

69. Marcovich's emendations of χριστόν to Ἰησοῦν and οὐκ to τόν have been accepted here. For a different solution, see Frickel, "Refutatio, Buch X," 228–29. See Luke 1:35; Epiph., *Pan.* 54.3.5; *Ref.* 6.35.3, 7 ("Valentinus"); 7.26.9 ("Basileides").

70. In the main report, Theodotos was made to deny only that Jesus became a deity.

δύναμίν τινα ὑπειληφέναι, φάσκοντες αὐτὸν ὑπὲρ πᾶσαν δύναμιν ὑπάρχειν· οὗ κατ' εἰκόνα [δὲ] εἶναι τὸν Χριστὸν θέλουσιν.

25. 1. Οἱ δὲ Φρύγες, ἐκ Μοντανοῦ τινος καὶ Πρισκίλλης καὶ Μαξιμίλλης τὰς ἀρχὰς τῆς αἱρέσεως λαβόντες, προφήτιδας τὰ γύναια νομίζουσι καὶ προφήτην τὸν Μοντανόν. <οὗτοι> τὰ μὲν περὶ τῆς τοῦ παντὸς ἀρχῆς καὶ δημιουργίας ὀρθῶς λέγουσι [νομίζουσι], καὶ τὰ περὶ τὸν Χριστὸν οὐκ ἀλλοτρίως παρειλήφασιν, ἐν δὲ τοῖς προειρημένοις σφάλλονται· ὧν τοῖς λόγοις ὑπὲρ τὰ εὐαγγέλια προσέχοντες πλανῶνται, <καὶ> νηστείας <καινὰς> καὶ παραδόσεις ὁρίζοντες.

26. 1. Ἕτεροι δὲ <ἐξ> αὐτῶν, τῇ τῶν Νοητιανῶν αἱρέσει προσκείμενοι, τὰ μὲν περὶ τὰ γύναια καὶ Μοντανὸν ὁμοίως δοκοῦσι, τὰ δὲ περὶ <τὸν> τῶν ὅλων πατέρα δυσφημοῦσιν, <τὸν> αὐτὸν εἶναι υἱὸν καὶ πατέρα λέγοντες, ὁρατὸν καὶ ἀόρατον, γεννητὸν καὶ ἀγέννητον, θνητὸν καὶ ἀθάνατον, τούτων τὰς ἀφορμὰς ἀπὸ Νοητοῦ τινος λαβόντες.

27. 1. Ὁμοίως δὲ καὶ Νοητός, τῷ μὲν γένει ὢν Σμυρναῖος, ἀνὴρ ἀκριτόμυθος καὶ ποικίλος, εἰσηγήσατο τοιάνδε αἵρεσιν—ἐξ Ἐπιγόνου τινὸς εἰς Κλεομένην χωρήσασαν καὶ οὕτως ἕως νῦν ἐπὶ τοῖς διαδόχοις διαμείνασαν—λέγων ἕνα τὸν πατέρα καὶ θεὸν τῶν ὅλων [τοῦτον] πάντα πεποιηκότα· ἀφανῆ μὲν τοῖς οὖσι γεγονέναι ὅτε ἠβούλετο, φανῆναι δὲ τότε ὅτε ἠθέλησε. 2. καὶ τοῦτον εἶναι ἀόρατον ὅταν μὴ ὁρᾶται, ὁρατὸν δὲ ὅταν ὁρᾶται· ἀγέννητον μὲν ὅταν μ(ὴ) γεννᾶται, γεννητὸν δὲ ὅταν γεννᾶται ἐκ παρθένου· ἀπαθῆ καὶ ἀθάνατον, ὅταν (μ)ὴ π(ά)σχῃ μηδὲ θνήσκῃ, ἐπὰν δὲ πάθει προσέλθῃ, πάσχειν καὶ θνήσκειν. τοῦτον τὸν πατέ(ρ)α αὐτὸν υἱὸν νομίζουσι, κατὰ καιροὺς καλούμενον πρὸς τὰ συμβαίνοντα.

point. They propose that Melchizedek is a power, claiming that he is the Power above all. They want Christ to be according to the image of Melchizedek.[71]

PHRYGIANS. 25. 1. The Phrygians, taking the first principles of their heresy from a certain Montanus, Priscilla, and Maximilla, consider that these hussies were prophetesses and that Montanus was a prophet.[72] These people are orthodox in what they say about the beginning and fashioning of the universe. Moreover, they do not hand on a foreign tradition about Christ. It is in the aforementioned prophecies that they err. Devoting themselves to these oracles over the Gospels, they go astray by ordaining new fasts and traditions.[73]

26. 1. Others from their party, attached to the heresy of the Noetians, in some respects believe the same as the hussies and Montanus, but in other respects slander the Father of the universe. They claim that the Son and Father are the same—visible and invisible, born and unborn, mortal and immortal—taking the starting points of these doctrines from a certain Noetos.

NOETOS. 27. 1. In the same way, Noetos, a Smyrnean by race and a shifty blatherer, introduced a heresy with the following features.[74] It was spread by men called Epigonos and Kleomenes and remains to our day with a succession of leaders. Noetos says that the Father, the God of the universe who made all things, is one. He is invisible to beings when he determines to be and appears when he wants. 2. He is invisible when he is not seen, visible when seen, unborn when not born, born when born from a virgin, not suffering and immortal when he does not suffer and die, but when he approaches suffering, he suffers and dies. They believe that the Father is himself the Son, depending on the occasion.

---

71. Cf. *Ref.* 7.36.1.

72. Cf. the overlapping report in *Ref.* 8.19. In his main report, our author treated Nikolaos, Hermogenes, and the Quartodecimans before the Phrygians. Nikolaos and the Quartodecimans are here omitted, and Hermogenes is postponed.

73. P reads κενάς ("empty"). The emendation καινάς agrees with our author's earlier report (καινίζουσι, *Ref.* 8.19.2).

74. Cf. the overlapping report in *Ref.* 9.7.1; Theodoret, *Haer. fab.* 3.3 (PG 83:404–5). See further Hübner, *Paradox*, 49–51.

3.Τούτων τὴν αἵρεσιν ἐκράτυνε Κάλλιστος—οὗ τὸν βίον ἐκτεθείμεθα ἀσφαλῶς—ὃς καὶ αὐτὸς αἵρεσιν ἀπεγέννησεν. ἐξ ὧν ἀφορμὰς λαβὼν καὶ αὐτὸς ὁμολογῶν ἕνα εἶναι τὸν πατέρα καὶ θεὸν τοῦτον δημιουργὸν τοῦ παντός· τοῦτον δὲ εἶναι υἱὸν ὀνόματι μὲν λεγόμενον καὶ ὀνομαζόμενον, οὐσίᾳ δὲ εἶναι <πνεῦμα>. «πνεῦμα γάρ,» φησίν, «ὁ θεός,» οὐχ ἕτερόν ἐστι παρὰ τὸν Λόγον ἢ ὁ Λόγος παρὰ τὸν θεόν· 4. ἓν οὖν τοῦτο πρόσωπον, ὀνόματι μὲν μεριζόμενον, οὐσίᾳ δὲ οὔ.

τοῦτον τὸν Λόγον ἕνα εἶναι θεὸν ὀνομάζει, καὶ σεσαρκῶσθαι λέγει· καὶ τὸν μὲν κατὰ σάρκα ὁρώμενον καὶ κρατούμενον υἱὸν εἶναι θέλει, τὸν δὲ ἐνοικοῦντα πατέρα, ποτὲ μὲν τῷ Νοητοῦ δόγματι περιρηγν(ύ)μενος, ποτὲ δὲ τῷ Θεοδότου, μηδέν ἀσφαλὲς κρατῶν.

ταῦτα τοίνυν Κάλλιστος.

28. 1. <Ἑ>ρμογένης δέ τις, καὶ αὐτὸς θελήσας τι <καινὸν> λέγειν, ἔφη τὸν θεὸν ἐξ ὕλης συγχρόνου καὶ ὑποκειμένης τὰ πάντα πεποιηκένα(ι)· ἀδυνάτως γὰρ ἔχειν τὸν θεὸν μὴ οὐχὶ ἐξ ὄντων τὰ γενόμενα ποιεῖν.

29. 1. Ἕτεροι δέ τινες, ὡς καινόν τι παρεισάγοντες, ἐκ πασῶν αἱρέσεων ἐρανισάμενοι, ξένην βίβλ(ον) <ἐ>σκευάσαντο, Ἠλχασαΐ τινος ἐπονομαζομένην. οὗτοι <περὶ> τὴν μὲν ἀρχὴν τοῦ παντὸς ὁμοίως <ἡμῖν> ὁμολογοῦσιν, ὑπὸ τοῦ

KALLISTOS. 3. Kallistos, whose life I have reliably presented, validated their heresy.[75] He himself also fathered a heresy. Taking his starting points from the Noetians, he also confessed that there is one Father and God who is the Artificer of all, and who is nominally named and called "Son," although in essence he is Spirit. "God," he says, "is Spirit."[76] Thus God is not another being in relation to the Word, and the Word is not another being in relation to God.[77] 4. Thus there is one person distinguished by name, but not in essence.

This Word he calls "one God" and says that he became flesh. The one seen and grasped in flesh he wants to be Son, whereas the one dwelling inside him he wants to be the Father.[78] Sometimes, Kallistos rips off a fragment from the teachings of Noetos, while other times from Theodotos—maintaining nothing sure.[79]

These are the teachings of Kallistos.

HERMOGENES. 28. 1. A certain Hermogenes also wanted to declare something novel.[80] He affirmed that God made all things from coeval underlying matter, for he considers it impossible for God to make generated realities from what does not exist.

"ELCHASAITES." 29. 1. Certain others, as if introducing something new, took samples from all heresies and composed a strange book named after a certain Elchasai.[81] They agree with us about the origin of the world, and that

---

75. Cf. the overlapping report in *Ref.* 9.12.16–18. On Kallistos's life, see *Ref.* 9.12.1–15.

76. John 4:24.

77. Here I follow the emendations of Heine, "Christology of Callistus," 70.

78. For ὁρώμενον καὶ κρατούμενον, see Clem. Alex., *Exc.* 59.3.

79. In *Ref.* 9.3, our author affirmed that Kallistos mixed the doctrines of *Kleomenes* and Theodotos. In *Ref.* 9.12.19 it was maintained that Kallistos sometimes leaned toward the dogma of *Sabellios*, and sometimes toward that of Theodotos. Here Kallistos is dependent on Theodotos and *Noetos*. Our author views Noetos and Kleomenes as part of the same succession; the relation of Sabellios to this succession is not clear.

80. Marcovich adds καινόν ("novel") from the main report on Hermogenes in *Ref.* 8.17.1. In the main report, Hermogenes was placed between Tatian and the Quartodecimans. By here placing him between Kallistos and the Elchasaites, our author puts him considerably later in the heresiological list and weakens the connection he forged between Kallistos and the Elchasaites regarding the putative "second baptism."

81. In this summary, our author is silent about Alkibiades (Luttikhuizen, *Revelation*, 82). Instead, he focuses on Christology. Unlike his main report, our author now

θεοῦ γεγονέναι, Χριστὸν δὲ ἕνα οὐχ ὁμολογοῦσιν, ἀλλ' εἶναι τὸν μὲν ἄνω ἕνα, αὐτὸν δὲ μεταγγίζεσθαι ἐν σ(ώ)μασί π(ο)λλ(οῖς) πολλάκι(ς) καὶ νῦν δὴ ἐν τῷ Ἰησοῦ. 2. ὁμο(ί)ως (δὲ) ποτὲ μὲν ἐκ τοῦ θεοῦ γεγενῆσθαι, ποτὲ δὲ πνεῦμα γεγονέναι, ποτὲ μὲν ἐκ πα(ρ)θένου, ποτὲ δὲ οὔ. καὶ τοῦτον δὲ μετέπειτα ἀεὶ ἐν σώμασι μ(ετ)αγγίζεσθα(ι) καὶ ἐν πολλοῖς κατὰ καιροὺς δείκνυσθαι.

3. χρῶνται δὲ ἐπα(οι)δαῖς καὶ βαπτίσμασιν ἐπὶ τῇ τῶν στοιχείων ὁμολογίᾳ. σεσόβηνται δὲ περ(ὶ) ἀ(στρ)ολογίαν καὶ μαθηματικὴν καὶ μαγικήν, προγν(ω)στικοὺς δὲ ἑαυτοὺς λέγουσιν.

30. 1. ... <κελεύσαντος> τοῦ θεοῦ μετοικεῖ ἐκ Μεσοποταμίας πόλεως Χαρρὰν εἰς τὴν νῦν μὲν Παλαιστίνην καὶ Ἰουδαίαν προσαγορευομένην χώραν, τότε δὲ Χαναανῖτιν, περὶ ἧς καὶ κατὰ τοῦτο τὸ μέρος τὸν λόγον οὐκ ἀμελῶς παρεδώκαμεν ἐν ἑτέραις βίβλοις. 2. διὰ τούτου τοίνυν γίνεται ἡ καταρχὴ τῆς κατὰ τὴν Ἰουδαίαν αὐξήσεως, ἥτις τὴν προσηγορίαν μετέσχεν .... ἐξ

it arose from God, but do not confess one Christ. 2. Rather, they believe in a single Christ above who transmigrates numerous times into numerous bodies and was recently incarnated in Jesus. Likewise, he is sometimes born from God, while at other times he becomes spirit.[82] Sometimes he is born from a virgin, at other times not. Later on, he continues his never-ending transmigration into bodies and is manifested in many different bodies at various times.[83]

3. They also use incantations and baptisms in addition to their confession by the elements.[84] They plume themselves on their knowledge of astronomy, astrology, and magic; and they call themselves "knowers of the future."[85]

THE RACE OF GOD-FEARERS

30. 1. …[86] At the command of God, [Abraham] moved from the city of Charran in Mesopotamia into the region now called Palestine and Judea, but at that time Canaan.[87] I offered a not undetailed account of this region in other treatises.[88] 2. Abraham's move was the start of his family's growth in the region of Judea. It was a region named after Judah, the fourth son

---

says that the book used by the Elchasaites bore the name of Elchasai. He also newly expresses his view that the Book of Elchasai is a forgery. Cf. *Ref.* 9.13.1.

82. Christ's arrival as spirit (πνεῦμα) is new material (not found in the main report) but has a parallel in Epiph., *Pan.* 30.3.4 (on the Ebionites). See further Klijn and Reinink, *Patristic Evidence*, 59–65, 78; Luttikhuizen, *Revelation*, 83–84.

83. Cf. *Ref.* 9.14.1; Epiph., *Pan.* 53.1.8; 30.3.3–6.

84. Cf. *Ref.* 9.14.3; 9.15.4–6. It seems most likely that the "elements" (στοιχεῖα) refer to the water, salt, spirits, and so on mentioned in the Elchasaite oath. Alternatively, they could refer to "planetary and other celestial powers" (Luttikhuizen, *Revelation*, 84). Cf. Gal 4:9.

85. Cf. *Ref.* 9.14.2.

86. The text picks up here after a lacuna. In this section, our author departs from his main report, which focused on three Jewish sects (Essenes, Pharisees, and Sadducees). Instead, he reformulates biblical genealogies (mainly from Gen 10–12) in an attempt to prove that the "race of God-fearers" is older than other races—and thus older than all philosophers.

87. Gen 12:1, 5; Josephus, *Ant.* 1.154.

88. On the "other treatises," see Brent, *Hippolytus*, 271–74; Andrei, "Spazio," 234–45.

Ἰούδα, παιδὸς τοῦ Ἰακὼβ τοῦ τετάρτου· οὗ καὶ .... <λαός> κέκληται, διὰ τὸ ἐξ αὐτοῦ τὸ βασιλικὸν γένος. ....

3. μετο(ι)κεῖ τῆς Μεσοποταμίας .... ἑκατοντούτης γενόμενος .... <γεννᾷ τὸν Ἰσαάκ· ὁ δὲ Ἰσαὰκ> γενόμενος ξʹ γεννᾷ τὸν Ἰακώβ· ὁ δὲ Ἰακὼβ ἐτῶν πϛʹ γεννᾷ τὸν Λευΐ· ὁ δὲ Λευῒ ἐτῶν μʹ γεννᾷ τὸν Κάαθ· ὁ δὲ Κάαθ ἐτῶν .... <ἐγένετο δʹ> ἡνίκα συγκατῆλθε τῷ Ἰακὼβ εἰς Αἴγυπτον. 4. γίνεται τοίνυν πᾶς ὁ χρόνος ὃν παρῴκησεν Ἀβραὰμ καὶ πᾶν τὸ αὐτοῦ γένος κατὰ τὸν Ἰσαὰκ [τῇ] ἐν τῇ τότε καλουμένῃ Χανααντίτιδι γῇ ἔτη σιεʹ.

Τούτου δὲ γίνεται Θάρρα, τούτου Ναχώρ, τούτου Σερούχ, <τούτου Ῥαγαύ, τούτου Φάλεκ, τούτου Ἔβερ,> ὅθεν καὶ τὸ Ἑβραίους καλεῖσθαι. ....

<ἐπὶ δὲ τοῦ Φάλεκ διεσπάρησαν οἱ ἔκγονοι τοῦ Νῶε.> 5. ἦσαν δὲ οὗτοι οβʹ ἔθνη· ὧν καὶ τὰ ὀνόματα ἐκτεθείμεθα ἐν ἑτέραις βίβλοις, μηδὲ τοῦτο παραλιπόντες, κατὰ τρόπον βουλόμενοι τοῖς φιλομαθέσιν ἐπιδεικνύναι ἣν ἔχομεν στοργὴν περὶ τὸ θεῖον τήν τε ἀδίστακτον γνῶσιν, ἣν ἐν πόνοις κεκτήμεθα περὶ τὴν ἀλήθειαν.

of Jacob.[89] The people are also named after him, since he is the ancestor of the royal family.[90]

3. Abraham moved from Mesopotamia.[91] When he was one hundred years old, he fathered Isaac.[92] When Isaac was sixty, he fathered Jacob.[93] Jacob was eighty-six when he fathered Levi.[94] Levi was forty when he fathered Kaath,[95] and Kaath was four when Jacob went down with his family to Egypt.[96] 4. Therefore, the entire time that Abraham (with his whole family from Isaac) dwelled as a resident alien in what was then called Canaan was 215 years.

Abraham's father was Tharra. Tharra's father was Nachor. Nachor's father was Serouch. Serouch's father was Ragau. Ragau's father was Phalek, and Phalek's father was Eber, after whom the Hebrews are named.[97]

In the time of Phalek, the children of Noah were dispersed.[98] 5. These children made up the seventy-two nations.[99] Their names I presented in other books.[100] Yet even this I do not neglect, desiring, as is my habit, to present to diligent learners my love for the divine and the indubitable knowledge that I have obtained in my toils for truth.

---

89. After μετέσχεν there is a space of twelve letters in P. Here and below, Marcovich attempts to insert clauses based on the number of missing letters. Judah is listed as the fourth son in Gen 35:23; 1 Chr 2:1.

90. In P there is a space of fifteen letters after οὗ καί. I add λαός ("people"). After βασιλικὸν γένος, there is a space of fourteen letters.

91. After Μεσοποταμίας, there is a space of twenty-nine letters in P.

92. After ἑκατοντούτης γενόμενος, there is a space of twenty-five letters in P. Duncker and Schneidewin add γεννᾷ τὸν Ἰσαάκ ("he fathered Isaac"). Cf. Gen 21:5.

93. Duncker and Schneidewin add ὁ δὲ Ἰσαάκ ("Isaac"). Cf. Gen 25:26 LXX (Ισαακ δὲ ἦν ἐτῶν ἑξήκοντα).

94. Cf. [Hipp.], *Chron.* 623 (*Lib. gen.* 1.241, Bauer and Helm).

95. Cf. [Hipp.], *Chron.* 624 (*Lib. gen.* 1.242, Bauer and Helm).

96. After ὁ δὲ Κάαθ ἐτῶν, there is a space of nine letters in P. Duncker and Schneidewin add ἐγένετο δʹ ("[Kaath] was four").

97. Roeper and Bunsen add τούτου Ῥαγαύ, τούτου Φάλεκ, τούτου Ἔβερ. Cf. Gen 11:17–25. Both Josephus, *Ant.* 1.146, and [Hipp.], *Chron.* 172, point out that the Hebrews are named from Eber.

98. After Ἑβραίους καλεῖσθαι, there is a space of twenty-eight letters in P. The whole next sentence (from ἐπὶ to Νῶε) was added by Marcovich (partially following Bunsen). For the dispersal in the time of Phalek, see Gen 10:25; Josephus, *Ant.* 1.146; [Hipp.], *Chron.* 199 (Bauer and Helm).

99. Cf. [Hipp.], *Chron.* 198 (Bauer and Helm).

100. The names are generally taken from Gen 10–11. Cf. Josephus, *Ant.* 1.122–139, 143–147; [Hipp.], *Chron.* 56–198 (Bauer and Helm).

6. Τούτου δὲ τοῦ Ἔβερ γίνεται πατὴρ Σάλα, τούτου δὲ Καϊνάν, τούτου δὲ Ἀρφαξ<ά>δ· οὗ γίνεται Σήμ, τούτου δὲ Νῶε. ἐφ' οὗ ὁ κατὰ πάντα κόσμον γίνεται κατακλυσμός, οὗ οὔτε Αἰγύπτιοι οὔτε Χαλδαῖοι οὔτε Ἕλληνες μέμνηνται—ὧν κατὰ τόπους ὅ τε ἐπὶ τοῦ Ὠγύγου καὶ Δευκαλίωνος γεγένηνται κατακλυσμοί.—εἰσὶν οὖν [καὶ] ἐπὶ τούτου γενεαὶ πέντε, ἔτη υϙε'.

7. οὗτος εὐσεβέστατος γενόμενος καὶ θεοφιλής, μόνος ἅμα γυναικὶ καὶ τέκνοις καὶ ταῖς τούτων τρισὶ γυναιξὶ διέφυγε τὸν γενόμενον κατακλυσμόν, ἐν κιβωτῷ διασωθείς, ἧς καὶ τὰ μέτρα καὶ τὰ λείψανα, καθῶς ἐκτεθείμεθα ἕως νῦν ἀποδείκνυται ἐν ὄρεσιν Ἀραρὰδ καλουμένοις, οὖσι πρὸς τὴν τῶν Ἀδιαβηνῶν χώραν.

8. ἐνιδεῖν οὖν ἔστι τοῖς φιλοπόνως ἱστορεῖν βουλομένοις, ὡς φανερῶς ἐπιδέδεικται τὸ τῶν θεοσεβῶν γένος ἀρχαιότερον πάντων Χαλδαίων, Αἰγυπτίων, Ἑλλήνων. τί δὲ καὶ τοὺς ἐπάνω τοῦ Νῶε καὶ θεοσεβεῖς καὶ θεοῦ (ὁ)μιλητὰς ὀνομάζειν νῦν χρή, ἱκανῆς οὔσης [τῆς] πρὸς τὸ προκείμενον ταύτης τῆς περὶ ἀρχαιότητος μαρτυρίας;

31. 1. Ἀλλ' ἐπεὶ οὐκ ἄλογον <ἐ>δόκει ἐπιδεῖξαι ταῦτα τὰ περὶ σοφίαν ἠσχολημένα ἔθνη μεταγενέστερα ὄντα τῶν θεὸν σεβασάντων, εὔλογον εἰπεῖν καὶ πόθεν τὸ γένος αὐτοῖς καὶ πόθεν, μετοικήσαντες ταύταις ταῖς χώραις, οὐ τὸ ὄνομα ἐξ αὐτῶν τῶν χωρῶν μετέσχον, ἀλλ' αὐτοὶ προσεποίησαν ἐκ τῶν πρώτως ἀρξάντων καὶ κατοικησάντων.

2. γίνονται τῷ Νῶε τρεῖς παῖδες· Σήμ, Χάμ, Ἰάφεθ, ἐκ τούτων πᾶν γένος ἀνθρώπων πεπλήθυνται καὶ πᾶσα χώρα κατοικεῖται. ῥῆμα γὰρ θεοῦ ἐπ' αὐτοὺς ἴσχυσεν εἰπόντος· «αὐξάνεσθε καὶ πληθύνεσθε καὶ πληρώσατε τὴν γῆν».

6. The Father of Eber was Sala. His father was Kaïnan, and his father was Arphaxad. Arphaxad's father was Shem, whose father was Noah.[101] In his days, the flood came upon the whole world, a flood that neither Egyptians, Chaldeans, nor Greeks remember. (They speak of regional floods like the one in the time of Ogygos and Deukalion.) Thus [from Eber] to Noah there are five generations, a total of 495 years.

7. Noah was deeply devout and loved by God.[102] He alone with his wife, children, and their three wives fled the coming flood.[103] He was kept safe in an ark whose dimensions and remains, as I presented them, can still be seen today in the mountain chain called Ararad near the land of the Adiabenoi.[104]

GOD-FEARERS PREDATE PHILOSOPHERS. 8. So it is clear to those willing to investigate with diligent labor how the race of the God-fearers is obviously proved to be older than all the Chaldeans, Egyptians, and Greeks. What need is there to name those God-fearing men who talked with God before Noah's time, when this testimony of their antiquity is sufficient for my purposes?[105]

31. 1. But since it seemed not unreasonable to show that the nations schooled in philosophy are later than the worshipers of God, it is also reasonable to add two points: (a) their family's place of origin, and (b) the reason why, after they had moved into these regions, they did not adopt those regions' names but themselves named the land from those who first ruled and inhabited it.

2. Noah had three sons: Shem, Cham, and Japheth. From them, every human tribe multiplied and every land was inhabited. For a command of God prevailed among them. It said: "increase and multiply and fill the earth!"[106] So great was the power of that single command that there were

101. Gen 11:11–15 LXX; [Hipp.], *Chron.* 36–40 (Bauer and Helm).

102. Cf. Gen 6:8–9 LXX: Νωε δὲ εὗρεν χάριν ἐναντίον κυρίου.… Νωε ἄνθρωπος δίκαιος, τέλειος ὢν ἐν τῇ γενεᾷ αὐτοῦ ("Noah found grace before the Lord.… Noah was a righteous person, perfect in his generation").

103. Gen 6:18.

104. Cf. Gen 6:15 (the dimensions of the ark); 8:4 LXX (Αραρατ); Josephus, *Ant.* 1.92: ἔτι νῦν αὐτῆς τὰ λείψανα ἐπιδεικνύουσι ("still today they [the Armenians] show its [the ark's] remains").

105. Cf. Josephus, *Ag. Ap.* 8, 14, 28, 215. The God-fearers are, significantly, not strictly identical with the Jews.

106. Gen 1:28 (the command); cf. *Ref.* 5.26.9 (Justin).

τοσοῦτον δυνηθέντος ἑνὸς ῥήματος γεννῶνται ἐκ τῶν τριῶν παῖδες κατὰ γένος οβʹ· ἐκ μὲν τοῦ Σὴμ κεʹ, ἐκ δὲ τοῦ Ἰάφεθ ιεʹ, ἐκ δὲ τοῦ Χὰμ λβʹ.

3. τῷ δὲ Χὰμ γίνονται παῖδες ἐκ τῶν προειρημένων λβʹ οὗτοι· <Χαναάν>, ἐξ οὗ Χαναναῖοι, Με<σ>τραείμ, ἐξ οὗ Αἰγύπτιοι, Χούς, ἐξ οὗ Αἰθίοπες, Φούδ, ἐξ οὗ Λίβυες. οὗτοι τῇ κατ' αὐτοὺς φωνῇ ἕως νῦν τῇ τῶν προγόνων προσηγορίᾳ καλοῦνται, εἰς δὲ τὸ Ἑλληνικὸν οἷς νῦν ὀνόμασι κέκληνται <μετ>ονομάζονται.

4. Εἰ δὲ μήτε τὸ οἰκεῖσθαι τὰς τούτων χώρας πρότερον [ἦν], μήτε ἀρχὴν γένος ἀνθρώπων δείκνυται, οὗτοι δὲ υἱοὶ τοῦ Νῶε ἀνδρὸς θεοσεβοῦς γίνονται, ὅς καὶ αὐτὸς μαθ(η)τὴς γεγένηται ἀνδρῶν θεοσεβῶν—οὗ χάριν διέφυγε πολλοῦ ὕδατος πρόσκαιρον ἀπειλήν—, πῶς οὐ προγενέστεροι ἦσαν θεοσεβεῖς πάντων Χαλδαίων, Αἰγυπτίων, Ἑλλήνων—ὧν πατὴρ ἐκ τούτου Ἰάφεθ γεννᾶται, <τὸ> ὄνομα Ἰωύαν, ἐξ οὗ Ἕλληνες καὶ Ἴωνες; 5. εἰ δὲ τὰ περὶ φιλοσοφίαν ἀπασχοληθέντα ἔθνη πολλῷ μεταγενέστερα τοῦ τῶν θεοσεβῶν γένους καὶ κατακλυσμοῦ πάντως δείκνυται, πῶς οὐχὶ καὶ βάρβαρα καὶ ὅσα ἐν κόσμῳ γνωστά τε καὶ ἄγνωστά νεώτερα τούτων φανήσεται;

6. τούτου τοίνυν τοῦ λόγου κρατήσαντες <μάθετε>, Ἕλληνες, Αἰγύπτιοι, Χαλδαῖοι καὶ πᾶν γένος ἀνθρώπων, τί τὸ θεῖον καὶ <τίς> ἡ τούτου εὔτακτος δημιουργία, παρ' ἡμῶν τῶν φίλων τοῦ θεοῦ καὶ μὴ κομπῷ λόγῳ τοῦτο ἠσκηκότων, ἀλλ' ἐ<ν> ἀληθείας γνώσει καὶ ἀσκήσει σωφροσύνης εἰς ἀπόδειξιν αὐτοῦ λόγους ποιουμένων.

born from those three men seventy-two children by clan: twenty-five children from Shem, fifteen from Japheth, and thirty-two from Cham.[107]

3. These are the sons of Cham, part of the aforementioned thirty-two: Canaan,[108] ancestor of the Canaanites; Mestraim, ancestor of the Egyptians; Chous, ancestor of the Ethiopians; and Phoud, ancestor of the Libyans.[109] These peoples, until the present time, were called by the names of their ancestors in their own languages. Their present names have been translated into Greek.

4. If it is proved that the lands of these nations were not previously inhabited, and that [before them] there was no human race at all, then how were these sons of God-fearing Noah (himself a disciple of God-fearers, which explains why he escaped the mortal threat of the flood waters) not much older than all Chaldeans, Egyptians, and Greeks, given that the ancestor of the Greeks and Ionians, whose name was Iouan, was born from the aforementioned Japheth?[110] 5. And if the nations schooled in philosophy are fully demonstrated to be much younger than the family of God-fearers and the flood, how will the non-Greek nations too—and all the nations in the world, known and unknown—not be proved to be younger than they?

6. So master this logic, you Greeks, Egyptians, Chaldeans, and every nation of human beings![111] And learn from me, the friend of God, the nature of the divine and the nature of his well-ordered craftsmanship. We do not practice boastful rhetoric but prove our point with speeches characterized by the knowledge of truth and the exercise of moderation!

---

107. For the seventy-two nations, see Gen 10:1–32; 11:12–32. For the numerical partitions among Noah's three sons, cf. [Hipp.], *Chron.* 159 (twenty-five tribes from Shem); 73 (fifteen nations from Japheth); 92–129 (thirty nations from Cham; though the nations that descend from *them* make up a total of thirty-two [*Chron.* 131–132]).

108. P reads *χαριν*; Miller emends to Χαναάν.

109. Cf. [Hipp.], *Chron.* 94–97 (Bauer and Helm).

110. Cf. [Hipp.], *Chron.* 60 (Bauer and Helm): Ἰωύαν, ἀφ' οὗ Ἕλληνες καὶ Ἴωνες ("Greeks and Ionians come from Iouan").

111. Μάθετε, proposed by Hare, is an emendation of P's *μαθηταί* ("students"). Greeks, Egyptians, and Chaldeans represent the peoples of Japheth, Cham, and Shem, respectively. Cf. *Univ.* (Holl, 139,50–51): ἀπιστεῖτε Ἕλληνες. μάθετε μὴ ἀπιστεῖν ("You disbelieve, O Greeks. Learn not to disbelieve").

32. 1. Θεὸς εἷς, ὁ πρῶτος καὶ μόνος καὶ ἁπάντων ποιητὴς καὶ κύριος, σύγχρονον ἔσχεν οὐδέν· οὐ χάος ἄπειρον, οὐχ ὕδωρ ἀμέτρητον, οὐ γῆν στερράν, οὐκ ἀέρα πυκνόν, οὐ πῦρ θερμόν, οὐ πνεῦμα λεπτόν, οὐκ οὐρανοῦ μεγάλου κυανέαν <ὀροφήν>· ἀλλ' ἦν εἷς, μόνος <ἐφ'> ἑαυτοῦ. ὃς θελήσας ἐποίησε τὰ ὄντα, οὐκ ὄντα πρότερον πλὴν ὅτε ἠθέλησε ποιεῖν. ὃς ἔμπειρος ὢν τῶν ἐσομένων· πάρεστι γὰρ αὐτῷ καὶ πρόγνωσις.

2. διαφόρους τέ<σσαρας> τοῖς ἐσομένοις ἀρχὰς πρότερον ἐδημιούργει—πῦρ καὶ πνεῦμα, ὕδωρ καὶ γῆν—ἐξ ὧν διάφορον τὴν ἑαυτοῦ κτίσιν ἐποίει, καὶ τὰ μὲν μονοούσια, τὰ δὲ ἐκ δύο, τὰ δὲ ἐκ τριῶν, τὰ δὲ ἐκ τεσσάρων συνεδέσμει. 3. καὶ τὰ μὲν ἐξ ἑνὸς ἀθάνατα ἦν—λύσις γὰρ οὐ παρακολουθεῖ· τὸ γὰρ ἓν οὐ λυθήσεται πώποτε—τὰ δὲ ἐκ δύο ἢ τριῶν ἢ τεσσάρων λυτά. διὸ καὶ θνητὰ ὀνομάζεται· θάνατος γὰρ τοῦτο κέκληται, ἡ τῶν δεδεμένων λύσις.

4. Ἱκανὸν οὖν νῦν <ταῦτα> τοῖς εὖ φρονοῦσιν ἀποκεκρίσθαι—οἳ εἰ φιλομαθήσουσι καὶ τὰς τούτων οὐσίας καὶ τὰς αἰτίας τῆς κατὰ <τὸ> πᾶν δημιουργίας ἐπιζητήσουσιν, εἴσονται ἐντυχόντες ἡμῶν βίβλῳ περιεχούσῃ περὶ τῆς τοῦ παντὸς οὐσίας· 5. τὸ δὲ νῦν ἱκανὸν <δοκεῖ> εἶναι ἐκθέσθαι τὰς αἰτίας.

THE TRUE DOCTRINE

32. 1. There is one God: the primal God, who is the single maker and lord of all. He has nothing coeval with himself, neither boundless chaos, nor measureless water, nor solid earth, nor dense air, nor hot fire, nor subtle spirit, nor the azure roof of great heaven.[112] No. He is one, alone by himself. When he willed, he made things that exist, since nothing existed before he desired to make. He was acquainted with what was to come, for he has foreknowledge.[113]

COSMOGONY. 2. He first fashioned four different first principles for future beings, namely, fire, spirit, water, and earth.[114] From these four principles, he made his diverse creation. Some things were made from one substance, others he bound together from two, others from three, and others from four.[115] 3. Those made from one element are immortal, for they cannot experience dissolution (for what is one will never be dissolved). But the things made of two or three or four elements can be dissolved. Hence they are called "mortal," since death is the dissolution of things bound together.[116]

4. This account is a sufficient answer for those of sound mind. If, out of zeal for learning, they investigate the substances of these and the causes of the whole creation, they will learn them from reading my comprehensive study on the nature of the universe.[117] 5. But the causes that I have presently laid out seem sufficient.

---

112. Ὀροφήν ("roof") is R. Scott's emendation of P's μορφήν ("form"). Cf. the teaching in [Hipp.], *Noet.* 10.1: θεὸς μόνος … σύγχρονον θεοῦ οὐδὲν πλὴν αὐτὸς ἦν ("God is alone … there was nothing coeval with God except himself").

113. Cf. [Hipp.], *Noet.* 10.1–2: ᾧ παραυτίκα πάρεστι τὸ γινόμενον ὡς ἠθέλησεν, ὅ ἐτέλεσεν καθὼς ἠθέλησεν … οὔτε ἄλογος οὔτε ἄσοφος … οὔτε ἀβούλευτος ἦν ("As [God] willed, so it instantly came into being; he perfected it as he willed … he was not irrational or unwise … or without counsel").

114. Marcovich expands τέ in P to τέσσαρας ("four").

115. On the metaphor of binding, see Plato, *Tim.* 73b–c; *Symp.* 202e.

116. Cf. Plato, *Tim.* 41a: τὸ μὲν οὖν δὴ δεθὲν πᾶν λυτόν ("everything bound together can be dissolved").

117. On the book's title, see Castelli, *Falso letterario*, 55. Photios describes this work (*Bibl.* chap. 48) as follows: "It consists of two little treatises, in which the author shows that Plato contradicts himself. He also refutes Alkinoos, whose views on the soul, matter, and the resurrection are false and absurd, and he introduces his own opinion on the subject. He proves that the Jewish nation is far older than the Greek. He

ἃς οὐ γνόντες Ἕλληνες κομπῷ τῳ λόγῳ τὰ μέρη τῆς κτίσεως ἐδόξασαν, τὸν κτίσαντα ἀγνοήσαντες. <ἀφ’> ὧν ἀφορμὰς σχόντες οἱ αἱρεσιάρχαι, ὁμοίοις λόγοις τὰ ὑπ’ ἐκείνων προειρημένα μετασχηματίσαντες, αἱρέσεις καταγελάστους συνεστήσαντο.

33. 1. Οὗτος οὖν <ὁ> μόνος καὶ κατὰ πάντων θεὸς Λόγον πρῶτον ἐννοηθεὶς ἀπογεννᾷ· οὐ Λόγον ὡς φωνήν, ἀλλ’ ἐνδιάθετον τοῦ παντὸς λογισμόν. τοῦτον μόνον ἐξ ὄντων ἐγέννα· τὸ γὰρ ὂν αὐτὸς ὁ πατὴρ ἦν, ἐξ οὗ τὸ γεννηθέν.

The Greeks who did not recognize these causes glorified the constituents of creation with boastful rhetoric in ignorance of the Creator.[118] From these philosophers, the leading heretics took their starting points. With the use of similar terminology, the heretics gave a new makeover to the aforementioned philosophical teachings and concocted ridiculous heresies.

CHRISTOLOGY. 33. 1. This singular and universal God first conceived of and fathered a Word, a Word not like a voice, but the immanent Reason of the universe.[119] Now he gave birth to him exclusively from existing things. The Father himself is Being, and from Being came the offspring.[120] 2. The Word

---

thinks that the human being is a compound of fire, earth, and water, and also of spirit, which he calls 'soul.' Of the spirit he speaks as follows: 'Taking the chief part of this, he molded it together with the body, and opened a passage for it through every joint and limb. The spirit, thus molded together with the body, and pervading it throughout, is formed in the likeness of the visible body, but its nature is colder, compared with the three other substances of which the body is composed.' … He also gives a summary account of the creation of the world," openly calling Christ God and describing his generation from the Father. *On the Universe* is also mentioned by John Philoponos as a work of Ἰώσηπος (Reichardt, 155,1–2). Various Greek fragments are preserved. See further W. J. Malley, "Four Unedited Fragments of the *De Universo* of the Pseudo-Josephus Found in the *Chronicon* of George Hamartolus (Coislin 305)," *JTS* 16 (1965): 13–25; Brent, *Hippolytus*, 263–70; Castelli, "Il prologo," 46–47.

118. Cf. Rom 1:25; *Ref.* 1.26.3; 4:43.2. This criticism would not apply to the Peratai, who "suppose that the causes of all things born by generation … are unborn and transcendent" (*πάντων γάρ … τῶν γεννητῶν τῆς γενέσεως αἴτια νομίζουσιν εἶναι τὰ ἀγέννητα καὶ τὰ ὑπερκείμενα*) (*Ref.* 5.15.2). Cf. *Univ.* frag. 1 (Castelli, "Il prologo," 46:5–7): Ἀλλ' ἐπειδὴ πολλοὶ λίαν οἱ παρ' Ἕλλησι περὶ θεοῦ λέγειν ἐπαγγελλόμενοι, θεὸν δὲ τὸ καθ' ὅλου μὴ ἐγνωκότες ("But since a great mob among the Greeks sets out to declare a doctrine of God, not knowing the universal God …"). Other Christian authors praised Plato's concept of an eternal, spiritual God (e.g., Athenagoras, *Leg.* 23.2–4; Justin, *1 Apol.* 10; Minucius Felix, *Oct.* 19.14, 15; 20.1).

119. "The Son does not coexist with the Father, but is [a] being first mentally conceived and then born by the Father" (Miroslav Marcovich, "Plato and Stoa in Hippolytus' Theology," *ICS* 11 [1983]: 265–69 [267–68]). For the Λόγος ἐνδιάθετος, see Philo, *Abr.* 83; *Mos.* 2.127, 129; *Spec.* 4.69; Plutarch, *Max. princ.* 777c; Theophilos, *Autol.* 2.10, 22; Justin, *Dial.* 61.1; Tert., *Prax.* 5; Iren., *Haer.* 2.15.5; Origen, *Cels.* 6.65; Sext. Emp., *Pyr.* 1.65, 72, 76; *Math.* 8.275, 287. See further Heine, "Christology of Callistus," 64–68; Wilhelm Kelber, *Die Logoslehre von Heraklit bis Origenes* (Stuttgart: Urachhaus, 1976), 80–82; M. Mühl, "Der λόγος ἐνδιάθετος und προφορικός von der älteren Stoa bis zur Synode von Sirmium 351," *Archiv für Begriffsgeschichte* 7 (1962): 9–12.

120. The Logos is born from the Father as a separate hypostasis. The Λόγος ἐνδιάθετος becomes the Λόγος προφορικός (cf. Theophilos, *Autol.* 2.10, 22). "The only

2. <κ>αὶ αἴτιον τοῖς γινομένοις Λόγος ἦν, ἐν <ἑ>αυτῷ φέρων τὸ θέλειν τοῦ γεγεν<ν>ηκότος, οὐκ ἄπειρός τῆς τοῦ πατρὸς ἐννοίας. ἅμα γὰρ τῷ ἐκ τοῦ γεννήσαντος προελθεῖν, πρωτότοκος τούτου γενόμενος, φωνὴν εἶχεν ἐν ἑαυτῷ, τὰς ἐν τῷ πατρικῷ <νῷ> ἐννοηθείσας ἰδέας. ὅθεν κελεύοντος πατρὸς γίνεσθαι κόσμον, τὸ κατὰ ἓν Λόγος ἀπετέλει τὸ ἀρέσκον θεῷ.

3. Καὶ τὰ μὲν (ἐ)πὶ γενέσει πλη(θ)ύνοντα ἄρσενα καὶ θήλεα εἰργάζετο, ὅσα δὲ πρὸς ὑπηρεσίαν καὶ λειτουργίαν, ἢ ἄρσενα ἢ θηλειῶν μὴ προσδεόμενα, ἢ οὔτε ἄρσενα οὔτε θήλεα. 4. καὶ γὰρ αἱ τούτων πρῶται οὐσίαι, <αἱ> ἐξ οὐκ ὄντων γενόμεναι—πῦρ καὶ πνεῦμα, ὕδωρ καὶ γῆ—οὔτε ἄρσενα οὔτε θήλεα ὑπάρχει, <οὐδ᾽ ἐξ> ἑκάστη<ς> τούτων δύν<α>ται προελθεῖν ἄρσενα καὶ θήλεα, πλὴν εἰ βούλοιτο ὁ κελεύων θεός, ἵνα Λόγος ὑπουργῇ.

5. ἐκ πυρὸς εἶναι ἀγγέλους ὁμολογῶ, καὶ οὐ τούτοις παρεῖναι θηλείας λέγω· ἥλιον δὲ καὶ σελήνην καὶ ἀστέρας ὁμοίως ἐκ πυρὸς καὶ πνεύματος, καὶ οὔτε ἄρσενας οὔτε θηλείας νενόμικα. 6. ἐξ ὕδατος δὲ ζῷα νηκτὰ εἶναι θέλω καὶ πτηνά, ἄρσενα καὶ θήλεα—οὕτω<ς> γὰρ ἐκέλευσεν ὁ θεός, θελήσας γόνιμον

was the cause of beings that are generated. He carried in himself the will of the generating God and was not unversed in his Father's designs.[121] At the very moment that the Word was emanated from his Father, he became his firstborn.[122] He possessed in himself a voice, the forms conceived in the Father's mind.[123] From these forms, at the Father's command, the world was generated, and the Word completed the good pleasure of God in each single detail.

3. The Word made male and female, namely, beings that multiply by generation. But he made the beings designed for assistance and service either male with no need of females, or neuter.[124] 4. The primary substances of these beings, which are made from nothing—namely, fire, spirit, water, and earth—are neither male nor female. Male and female cannot come out of any of these substances except by the will of God, who commands the Word to perform this service.

5. I believe that angels are made from fire, and declare that no female exists among them. Likewise, I have come to the conclusion that sun, moon, and stars are neuter beings made from fire and spirit. 6. I am disposed to think that sea creatures and birds, both male and female, are made from

difference of significance between the 'first-born' son … and the rest of the creatures," Marcovich observes, "is in the fact that the Son consists of pure being, i.e., of the same substance as the Father … while the rest of the beings are made out of one or more of the four basic elements" ("Plato and Stoa," 268).

121. Cf. Justin, *1 Apol.* 64.3. Marcovich cites the Ἔννοια and Θέλησιν of the Valentinian Ptolemy (*Ref.* 6.38.5) as a "source" for the author's thought here ("Plato and Stoa," 266).

122. Cf. Col 1:15 (πρωτότοκος); Theophilos, *Autol.* 2.22.

123. Marcovich adds νῷ ("mind"). Cf. [Hipp.], *Noet.* 10.4: φωνὴν φθεγγόμενος καὶ φῶς ἐκ φωτὸς γεννῶν προῆκεν τῇ κτίσει κύριον τὸν ἴδιον νοῦν ("uttering a voice and fathering light from light, he sent forth as Lord of creation his own mind"). Porphyry says that it is the Λόγος προφορικός who is God's voice (*Abst.* 3.3; cf. Theophilos, *Autol.* 2.10, 22). For further speculation on the Word as the voice or sound of God, see Acts Pet. 38–39 (*NTApoc* 2:315–16). The idea that the forms are God's thoughts was earlier attributed to Plato (*Ref.* 1.19.2), though without mention of the Logos. For the forms as God's thoughts, see further Seneca, *Ep.* 65.7; Alkinoos, *Epit.* 9.1–2; 10.3; Atticus, frags. 9, 40 (des Places); Noumenios, frag. 16.11 (des Places); Ps.-Justin, *Cohort.* 7. Further sources are cited in Miroslav Marcovich, "Platonism and the Church Fathers," in *Platonism in Late Antiquity*, ed. Stephen Gersh and Charles Kannengiesser (Notre Dame: University of Notre Dame Press, 1992), 189–203 (193–94, with n. 15). For God's voice used in creation, see *Ref.* 7.22.3 ("Basileides").

124. These beings are angels (cf. Basil, *Adv. Eun.* 3.2) and stars (Clem. Alex., *Ecl.* 56.4–6; Origen, *Cels.* 5.11). Cf. *Ref.* 10.33.5 below.

εἶναι τὴν ὑγρὰν οὐσίαν·—ὁμοίως ἐκ γῆς ἑρπετὰ καὶ θηρία καὶ παντοδαπῶν ζῴων <γένη>, ἄρσενα καὶ θήλεα—οὕτως γὰρ ἐνεδέχετο ἡ τῶν γεγονότων φύσις.

ὅσα γοῦν ἠθέλησεν ποιεῖν ὁ θεός, ταῦτα Λόγῳ ἐδημιούργει, ἑτέρως γενέσθαι μὴ δυνάμενα ἢ ὡς ἐγένετο. 7. ὅτε δὲ [ἥ] ὡς ἠθέλησε καὶ ἐποίησεν, ὀνόμασι καλέσας ἐσήμηνεν.

Ἐπὶ τούτοις τὸν πάντων ἄρχοντα δημιουργῶν, ἐκ πασῶν σύνθετον οὐσιῶν ἐσκεύασεν. οὐ θεόν <σε> θέλων ποιεῖν ἔσφηλε, (οὐ)δὲ ἄγγελον—μὴ πλανῶ—ἀλλ᾽ ἄνθρωπόν. εἰ γὰρ θεόν σε ἠθέλησε ποιῆσαι, ἐδύνατο· ἔχεις (το)ῦ Λόγου τὸ παράδειγμα· <ἀλλ᾽> ἄνθρωπον θέλων, ἄνθρωπόν σε ἐποίησεν. εἰ δὲ θέλεις καὶ θεὸς γενέσθ(αι), ὑπάκουε τῷ πεποιηκότι καὶ μὴ ἀντίβαινε νῦν, ἵνα ἐπὶ τῷ μικρῷ πιστὸς εὑρεθ<εὶς> καὶ τὸ μέγα πιστευθῆναι δυνηθῇ<ς>.

8. τούτου ὁ Λόγος μόνος ἐξ αὐτοῦ· διὸ καὶ θεός, οὐσία ὑπάρχων θεοῦ. ὁ δὲ κόσμος ἐξ οὐδενός· διὸ οὐ θεός· οὗτος ἐπιδέχεται καὶ λύσιν, ὅτε βούλεται ὁ κτίσας.

ὁ δὲ κτίσας θεὸς κακὸν οὐκ ἐποίει οὐδὲ ποιεῖ, <ἀλλὰ> καλὸν καὶ ἀγαθόν· ἀγαθὸς γὰρ ὁ ποιῶν. 9. ὁ δὲ γενόμενος ἄνθρωπος ζῷον αὐτεξούσιον ἦν, οὐκ

water, for thus God commanded when he wanted the moist substance to be productive.[125] Likewise, I believe that reptiles and wild animals and every type of animal—male and female—are made from earth, for thus the nature of generated beings allowed.[126]

Whatever beings God wanted to make, he fashioned by means of the Word—and they could not have arisen otherwise. 7. When he made them as he wanted, he gave them names.[127]

ANTHROPOGONY AND DEIFICATION. Over these beings, he fashioned a ruler of all, constructing him as a compound from every substance.[128] It is not the case that he wanted you to be a god or an angel and failed—do not be misled.[129] Rather, he wanted you to be human. If he wanted to make you a god, he could have—you have the example of the Word. Rather, wanting to make you human, he made you human. But if you want to become a god as well, obey your Maker and do not resist him now, so that when you are found faithful in a small matter, you can be entrusted with something great.[130]

8. The Word alone is generated from God himself. Thus he is God, existing as a divine substance. But the world is made from nothing, and so it is not God. It is susceptible of dissolution when the Creator wills.[131]

THE ORIGIN OF EVIL. God the Creator did not make and does not make evil; rather, he makes what is beautiful and good. This is because the Maker is good.[132] 9. The generated human being was an animal with

125. Cf. Gen 1:20–21.

126. Cf. Gen 1:24–25. Marcovich adds γένη (here: "type").

127. Marcovich's emendation of P's ἤ to ὅσα ἠθέλησεν is too ingenious. It is better, with Miller, to delete ἤ. For God who makes what he pleases, see Ps 134:6 LXX. God the animal-namer seems to take on the role of Adam, but see Ps 146:4 LXX ([θεός] πᾶσιν αὐτοῖς ὀνόματα καλῶν); Isa 40:26 (πάντας ἐπ' ὀνόματι [θεός] καλέσει).

128. Cf. Plato, *Tim.* 42e–43a; Alkinoos, *Epit.* 17.1 (humans made from four elements).

129. Cf. μὴ πλανῶ in Hipp., *Antichr.* 2.2 (Norelli, 66).

130. On deification through obedience, see Theophilos, *Autol.* 2.24, 27; Clem. Alex., *Protr.* 114.4. Further texts in *PGL*, s.v. θεός K. See further Norman Russell, *The Doctrine of Deification in the Greek Patristic Tradition* (Oxford: Oxford University Press, 2004), 110–12.

131. Cf. Plato, *Tim.* 41a–b.

132. Cf. Plato, *Tim.* 29a (ἀγαθὸς ἦν ["he was good"]).

ἄρχον· οὐ νοῦν ἔχον, οὐκ ἐπινοίᾳ καὶ ἐξουσίᾳ καὶ δυνάμει πάντων κρατοῦν, ἀλλὰ δοῦλον καὶ πάντα ἔχον τὰ ἐναντία. ὃς τῷ αὐτεξούσιος ὑπάρχειν τὸ κακὸν ἐπιγεννᾷ, ἐκ συμβεβηκότος ἀποτελούμενον [μὲν] οὐδέν <τε ὄν>, ἐὰν <αὐτὸ> μὴ ποιῇς. ἐν γὰρ τῷ θέλειν καὶ ν(ομ)ίζειν τι κακὸν τὸ κακὸν ὀνομάζεται, οὐκ ὂν ἀπ' ἀρχῆς, ἀλλ' ἐπιγενόμενον.

10. Ο(ὗ) αὐτεξουσίου ὄντος νόμος ὑπὸ θεοῦ ὡρίζετο, οὐ<δὲ> μάτην. εἰ γὰρ μὴ εἶχεν (ἄ)νθρωπος τὸ θέλειν καὶ τὸ μὴ θέλειν, τί καὶ νόμος ὡρίζετο; ὁ νόμος γὰρ (ἀ)λόγῳ ζῴῳ οὐχ ὁρισθήσεται, ἀλλὰ χαλινὸς καὶ μάστιξ· ἀνθρώπῳ δὲ ἐντολὴ καὶ πρόστιμον τοῦ ποιεῖν τὸ προστεταγμένον καὶ μὴ ποιεῖν. τούτῳ νόμος ὡρίσθη διὰ δικαίων ἀνδρῶν ἐπάνωθεν· ἔγγιον ἡμῶν διὰ τοῦ προειρημένου Μωϋσέως, ἀνδρὸς εὐλαβοῦς καὶ θεοφιλοῦς, νόμος ὡρίζετο πλήρης σεμνότητος καὶ δικαιοσύνης.

11. τα<ῦτα> δὲ πάντα διῴκει ὁ Λόγος ὁ θεοῦ, ὁ πρωτόγονος πατρὸς παῖς, ἡ πρὸ ἑωσφόρου φωσφόρος φωνή. ἔπειτα δίκαιοι ἄνδρες γεγένηνται, φίλοι θεοῦ· οὗτοι προφῆται κέκληνται διὰ τὸ προφαίνειν τὰ μέλλοντα. 12. οἷς οὐκ

free will, but he did not rule.[133] He was not prudent and did not exercise dominion over all things by intelligence, authority, and power.[134] Rather, he was a slave with every opposing tendency. By virtue of his free will, he gave birth to what is evil. Evil is not integral to human nature and has no existence if you do not perform it. The term "evil" is applied when a person wills or thinks something evil. Evil did not exist from the beginning. It is an aftereffect.

THE LAW. 10. Now since the human has free will, law was ordained by God, and not without purpose. For if the human did not have the power to choose one way or the other, why was law ordained? Law will not be prescribed for an unreasoning animal—rather the reins and the spur! For the human, however, there is a command to perform what is ordained and a penalty for failing to perform it. For this purpose, then, a law was ordained by the righteous men of old.[135] Nearer to our own times, law was ordained through the aforementioned Moses, a man of reverence loved by God. He ordained a law full of austerity and righteousness.

THE PROPHETS. 11. The Word of God directs all these things. He is the firstborn Child of the Father, the light-bringing voice before the morning star.[136] Afterward, righteous men were born, the friends of God. These were called prophets because they proffered [προφαίνειν] what was to

133. Free will is a Platonic teaching: αἰτία ἑλομένου ("the responsibility lies with the one who chooses") (*Resp.* 617e4; cf. *Tim.* 29e; Albinos in Stobaios, *Ecl.* 1.49.37 [Wachsmuth and Hense, 1:375]).

134. Mark Santer would remove οὐ in οὐ νοῦν ἔχον ("Hippolytus: Refutatio omnium haeresium X.33.9," *JTS* 24 [1973]: 194–95). It is better to follow Marcovich in understanding νοῦς in οὐ νοῦν ἔχον as "prudence" (LSJ, s.v. νοῦς 2a). Marcovich comments: "In calling Adam 'foolish, senseless' … Hippolytus is only exploiting the traditional topic about Adam as a νήπιος ('infant, child,' then 'childish, foolish'), as an imperfect creature, standing at the beginning of progress (προκοπή) toward perfection" ("*Refutatio*, X.33.9 Again," *JTS* 24 [1973]: 195–96). Cf. Theophilos, *Autol.* 2.24–5; Iren., *Haer.* 4.38.1, 3.

135. Cf. [Hipp.], *Noet.* 11–12.

136. Nautin (see Marcovich's apparatus) would emend φωσφόρος φωνή to φῶς ("light"). But cf. [Hipp.], *Noet.* 10.4; 13.2; as well as the being called Spark the "voice of light" (ϩⲣⲟⲟⲩ ⲛ̄ⲟⲩⲟⲉⲓⲛ) (Paraph. Shem [NHC VII,1] 46.15–16). Clement of Alexandria also calls the Logos ῥῆμα κυρίου φωτεινόν ("luminous utterance of the Lord") (*Strom.* 6.3.34.3). For the morning star, see Ps 109:3 LXX, alluded to in 2 Pet 1:19; [Hipp.], *Noet.* 16.7.

<ἐφ’> ἑνὸς καιροῦ λόγος ἐγένετο, ἀλλὰ διὰ πασῶν γενεῶν αἱ τῶν προλεγόντων φωναὶ εὐαπόδεικτοι παρίσταντο. οὐκ ἐκεῖ μόνον, ἡνίκα τοῖς παροῦσιν ἀπεκρίναντο, ἀλλὰ καὶ <ὅτε> διὰ πασῶν γενεῶν τὰ ἐσόμενα προεφήναντο. ὅτι τὰ μὲν παρῳχημένα λέγοντες ὑπεμίμνῃσκον τὴν ἀνθρωπότητα, τὰ δὲ ἐνεστῶτα δεικνύντες, μὴ ῥᾳθυμεῖν ἔπειθον, τὰ δὲ μέλλοντα προλέγοντες, τὸν κατὰ ἕνα ἡμῶν, ὁρῶντας <τὰ> πρὸ πολλοῦ προειρημένα <πληρωθῆναι>, ἐμφόβους καθίστων, προσδοκῶντας καὶ τὰ μέλλοντα <πληρωθήσεσθαι>.

13. Τοιαύτη ἡ καθ’ ἡμᾶς πίστις, ὦ πάντες ἄνθρωποι, οὐ κενοῖς ῥήμασι πειθομένων, οὐδὲ σχεδιάσμασι καρδίας συναρπαζομένων, οὐδὲ πιθανότητι εὐεπείας λόγων θελγομένων, ἀλλὰ δυνάμει θείᾳ λελαλημένοις λόγοις οὐκ ἀπειθούντων. καὶ ταῦτα θεὸς ἐκέλευε Λόγῳ, ὁ δὲ Λόγος ἐφθέγγετο λέγων <τοῖς προφήταις>, δι’ αὐτῶν ἐπιστρέφων τὸν ἄνθρωπον ἐκ παρακοῆς· οὐ βίᾳ ἀνάγκης δουλαγωγῶν, ἀλλ’ «ἐπ’ ἐλευθερίᾳ» ἑκουσίῳ προαιρέσει «καλῶν».

14. Τοῦτον τὸν Λόγον ἐν ὑστέροις <καιροῖς> ἀπέστειλεν ὁ πατήρ, οὐκέτι διὰ προφητῶν <αὐτὸν> λαλεῖν, οὐ σκοτεινῶς κηρυσσόμενον ὑπονοεῖσθαι θέλων, ἀλλ’ αὐτοψεὶ φανερωθῆναι τοῦτον [λέγων], ἵνα <ὁ> κόσμος ὁρῶν δυσωπηθῇ οὐκ ἐντελλόμενον διὰ προσώπου προφητῶν, οὐδὲ δι’ ἀγγέλου φοβοῦντα ψυχήν, ἀλλ’ αὐτὸν παρόντα τὸν λελαληκότα. 15. τοῦτον ἔγνωμεν ἐκ παρθένου σῶμα ἀνειληφότα καὶ «τὸν παλαιὸν ἄνθρωπον» διὰ καινῆς πλάσεως πεφορηκότα. <τοῦτον ἴσμεν> ἐν βίῳ διὰ πάσης ἡλικίας ἐληλυθότα, ἵνα πάσῃ ἡλικίᾳ αὐτὸς

come. 12. Their message did not come at one time, but through all generations the voices of those who foretell the future have been present and easy to prove. Their voices were there not only when they responded to their contemporaries but also when they proclaimed the future throughout all generations.[137] When they spoke of what had occurred in the past, they caused humanity to remember; by showing what was present, they persuaded us not to be careless; and by proclaiming the future to each one of us who saw the fulfillment of what they had long ago prophesied, they made us afraid—since we expect the future events also to be fulfilled.[138]

13. Such is our faith, all you human beings! We do not credit empty jargon, nor are we enraptured by the imaginings of the heart, or bewitched by the cogency of eloquent words—though we do not distrust words spoken with divine power.[139] These are the commands that God gave to the Word, and the Word uttered them to the prophets. Through them, the Word turns humanity back from transgression. He does not enslave humanity by the force of necessity but calls humanity to freedom by their own free decision.[140]

THE INCARNATION. 14. The Father sent this Word in the last times. He no longer wanted him to speak through the prophets as one preached but dimly surmised. He wanted him to be manifested in full view so that the world might be ashamed before one who commands, not through the person of the prophets or through an angel frightening the soul, but as the Word himself present and speaking to them.[141] 15. It is he whom we recognize to have assumed a body from a virgin and to have carried "the old human being" through a new formation.[142] It is he whom we know to

---

137. Cf. Hipp., *Antichr.* 2.

138. Marcovich adds πληρωθῆναι ("fulfillment") and πληρωθήσεται ("to be fulfilled").

139. For εὐεπείας λόγων, see [Plato], *Ax.* 369d6.

140. Cf. Gal 5:13; Clem. Alex., *Strom.* 3.5.41.3.

141. Cf. *Pesach Haggadah* 5:38: "And the Lord took them out—not by means of an angel, … nor by means of a messenger, but by means of the Holy One through his own glory"; [Hipp.], *Noet.* 17.5: προελθὼν εἰς κόσμον θεὸς ἐνσώματος ἐφανερώθη ("God came forth into the world and was manifested as embodied").

142. Cf. Rom 6:6 (ὁ παλαιὸς ἡμῶν ἄνθρωπος ["our old human being"]); Col 3:9; Eph 4:22; *Ref.* 10.34.5; [Hipp.], *Noet.* 17: ἐκ παλαιοῦ Ἀδάμ ("from the old Adam"); Hipp., *Antichr.* 26: ἀναπλάσσων δι᾽ ἑαυτοῦ τὸν Ἀδάμ ("reforming Adam by means of his very self"); Iren., *Haer.* 3.21.10; 3.22.2; 5.1.2; Clem. Alex., *Strom.* 3.11.75.3; 4.7.51.1; *Ecl.* 24.1. For the "new formation," see 2 Cor 5:17 (καινὴ κτίσις); Gal 6:15; and the "new human being" in Eph 2:15; 4:24; *Ref.* 5.7.15 (Naassenes); 6.35.4 ("Valentinus").

νόμος γενηθῇ καὶ σκοπὸν τὸν ἴδιον ἄνθρωπον πᾶσιν ἀνθρώποις ἐπιδείξῃ παρών, καὶ <ἵνα> δι' αὐτοῦ ἐλέγξῃ, ὅτι μηδὲν ἐποίησεν ὁ (θ)εὸς πονηρὸν καὶ <ὅτι> ὡς αὐτεξούσιος ὁ ἄνθρωπος ἔχει τὸ θέλειν καὶ τὸ μὴ θέλειν, δυνατὸς ὢν ἐν ἀμφοτέροις.

16. <τ>οῦτον ἄνθρωπον ἴσμεν <ἐκ> τοῦ καθ' ἡμᾶς φυράματος γεγονότα· εἰ γὰρ μὴ ἐκ τοῦ αὐτοῦ ὑπῆρξε, μάτην νομοθετεῖ μιμεῖσθαι τὸν διδάσκαλον. εἰ γὰρ ἐκεῖνος ὁ ἄνθρωπος ἑτέρας ἐτύγχανεν οὐσίας, τί τὰ ὅμοια κελεύει ἐμοί, τῷ ἀσθ(ενεῖ) πεφυκότι, καὶ πῶς οὗτος ἀγαθὸς καὶ δίκαιος; 17. <ἀλλ'> ἵνα δὴ μὴ ἕτερος παρ' ἡμᾶς νομισθῇ, (καὶ) κάματον ὑπέμεινε, καὶ πεινῆν ἠθέλησε, καὶ διψῆν οὐκ ἠρνήσατο, καὶ ὕπνῳ ἠρέμησε, καὶ πάθει οὐκ ἀντεῖπε, καὶ θανάτῳ ὑπήκουσε, καὶ ἀνάστασιν ἐφανέρωσεν, ἀπαρξάμενος ἐν πᾶσι τούτοις τὸν ἴδιον ἄνθρωπον, ἵνα <καὶ> σὺ πάσχων μὴ ἀθυμῇς, ἀλλ' ἄνθρωπον σεαυτὸν ὁμολογῶν προσδοκᾷς καὶ σὺ ὃ τούτῳ παρέσχε <θεό>ς.

34. 1. Τοιοῦτος ὁ περὶ τὸ θεῖον ἀληθὴς λόγος, ὦ ἄνθρωποι Ἕλληνές τε καὶ βάρβαροι, Χαλδαῖοί τε καὶ Ἀσσύριοι, Αἰγύπτιοί τε καὶ Λίβυες, Ἰνδοί τε καὶ Αἰθίοπες, Κελτοί τε καὶ οἱ στρατηγοῦντες Λατῖνοι, πάντες τε οἱ τὴν Εὐρώπην, Ἀσίαν τε καὶ Λιβύην κατοικοῦντες. οἷς σύμβουλος ἐγὼ γίνομαι, φιλανθρώπου Λόγου ὑπάρχων μαθητὴς καὶ φιλάνθρωπος, 2. ὅπως προσδραμόντες διδαχθῆτε παρ' ἡμῶν, τίς ὁ ὄντως θεὸς καὶ ἡ τούτου εὔτακτος δημιουργία, μὴ προσέχοντες

have passed through every age of life so as himself to be a law for every age and, while he was present, to display his own humanity as a goal for all humans.[143] He came in this way so that through him the idea that God made anything evil might be refuted, and to demonstrate that humanity has the power to choose either good or evil.

16. It is this human being whom we know was born from clay like ours. For if he did not exist from the same stuff as us, he uselessly bids that we imitate him as teacher. If that human being happened to be made of a different substance, why does he order me—weak by nature—to do the same things? And if he did so, how could he be good and just? 17. Rather, it was so that he might not be considered different from us that he endured weariness, was willing to be hungry, did not reject thirst, rested in sleep, did not renounce suffering, submitted to death, and manifested the resurrection—in all these events offering his own humanity as first fruits so that you too may suffer and not lose heart, and so that you also—though you acknowledge that you are a human being—might look forward to what God provided him.[144]

PERORATION

34. 1. Such is the true doctrine of the divine, O mortal Greeks and Barbarians, Chaldeans and Assyrians, Egyptians and Libyans, Indians and Ethiopians, Kelts and Latins who lead in war—all you dwelling in Europe, Asia, and Libya![145] I am your counselor, a student of the Word who loves human beings, and a lover of humanity myself. 2. May you, then, go forward and accept my teaching about the identity of the true God and the

143. Marcovich adds τοῦτον ἴσμεν (here: "It is he whom we know"). For passing through all stages of life, see Iren., *Haer*. 2.22.4 (*per omnem venit aetatem*).

144. P here reads παρέσχες ("what you provided him"). Wendland revised the phrase to read παρέσχε θεός (accepted here). On the incarnation of the Word, see [Hipp.], *Noet.* 18.1. On Christ the first fruits, see 1 Cor 15:20–23.

145. Carl Andresen proposes that the phrase "the true doctrine" was chosen in purposeful opposition to the book of Kelsos by the same title (*Logos und Nomos: Die Polemik des Kelsos wider das Christentum*, Arbeiten zur Kirchengeschichte 30 [Berlin: de Gruyter, 1955], 387–92). He is opposed by Norbert Brox, "Kelsos und Hippolytos: Zur frühchristlichen Geschichtspolemik," *VC* (1966): 150–58. The Peratai also called their teaching λόγος τῆς ἀληθείας (*Ref.* 4.2.1). The author of *Against Noetos* uses τῆς ἀληθείας λόγος (17.3, apparently synonymous with τὴν τῆς ἀληθείας ἀπόδειξιν in 8.4). Hamel emphasizes that the true doctrine as it is presented here is our author's own creation, not based on a previous confessional formula (*Kirche bei Hippolyt*, 93–99).

σοφίσμασιν ἐντέχνων λόγων, μηδὲ ματαίοις ἐπαγγελίαις κλεψιλόγων αἱρετικῶν, ἀλλ' ἀληθείας ἀκόμπου ἁπλότητι σεμνῇ.

Δι' ἧς ἐπιγνώσεως ἐκφεύξεσθε ἐπερχομένην πυρὸς κρίσεως ἀπειλήν, καὶ Ταρτάρου ζοφεροῦ ὄμμα ἀφώτιστον, ὑπὸ Λόγου φωνῆς μὴ καταλαμφ<θ>έν, καὶ βρασμὸν ἀεννάου λίμνης γεννητρίας φλογός, καὶ ταρταρούχων ἀγγέλων κολαστῶν ὄμμα, ἀεὶ μένον ἐν ἀπειλῇ, καὶ σκώληκα, σώματος ἀπουσίαν, ἐπιστρεφόμενον ἐπὶ τὸ ἐκβράσαν σῶμα ὡς <ἐπὶ τροφήν>.

3. Καὶ ταῦτα μὲν ἐκφεύξῃ θεὸν τὸν <ὄντως> ὄντα διδαχθείς, ἕξεις δὲ ἀθάνατον τὸ σῶμα καὶ ἄφθαρτον ἅμα ψυχῇ. <καὶ τὴν δὲ> βασιλείαν οὐρανῶν ἀπολήψῃ, ὁ ἐν γῇ βιοὺς καὶ ἐπουράνιον βασιλέα ἐπιγνούς, ἔσῃ τε ὁμιλητὴς θεοῦ καὶ «συγκληρονόμος Χριστοῦ», οὐκ<έτι> ἐπιθυμίαις καὶ πάθεσι καὶ νόσοις δουλούμενος. 4. γέγονας γὰρ θεός· ὅσα γὰρ ὑπέμεινας πάθη ἄνθρωπος ὤν,

nature of his well-ordered creation. May you not cling to the sophisms of fabricated stories or the driveling pronouncements of plagiarizing heretics but to the austere simplicity of unpretentious truth![146]

Through this knowledge, you will escape the oncoming threat of fiery judgment,[147] the lightless eye of gloomy Tartaros[148] (unenlightened by the voice of the Word), the boiling of the everlasting lake that is the mother of flame,[149] the eye of the tormenting angels who control Tartaros—an eye that ever maintains its threatening stare[150]—and the worm, the wasting of the body, that slithers around over your seething corpse as if over its food.[151]

3. These things you will escape when you have been taught about the God who truly exists. You will have an immortal and incorruptible body together with a soul, and you who lived on earth and knew the heavenly king will receive the kingdom of heaven.[152] You will be a friend of God and coheir with Christ, no longer a slave to desires, sufferings, and diseases.[153] 4. You have become a god! The sufferings you endured as a human being,

146. Cf. *Ref.* 10.31.6; Tatian, *Or.* 42.

147. Cf. Hipp., *Comm. Dan.* 4.12, 60.

148. Cf. Hesiod, *Theog.* 814; 2 Pet 2:4.

149. Cf. Rev 19:20; 20:14–15 (λίμνην τοῦ πυρός); *Univ.* (Holl, 138,10): λίμνης πυρὸς ἀσβέστου ("lake of inextinguishable fire").

150. Cf. Hipp., *Comm. Dan.* 2.29; *Univ.* (Holl, 139,36–37): φοβερῷ ὄμματι ἐπαπειλοῦντες ("threatening with their terrible eye").

151. P here reads ἐπιστρέφων, which Wendland emends to ἐπιστροφήν, in the sense of "punishment." But this meaning is not in LSJ, and in *PGL* we find only "correction" as closest in meaning. I print the emendation of Bunsen: ἐπὶ τροφήν ("over its food"). In *Univ.* (Holl, 141,92–94), it is the worm itself—described as "fiery"—that oozes out from the body in unending pain: σκώληξ δέ τις ἔμπυρος μὴ τελευτῶν μηδὲ σῶμα διαφθείρων ἀπαύστως ὀδύνην ἐκ σώματος ἐκβράσσων παραμένει ("a fiery worm that does not die or destroy the body unceasingly remains, wringing pain from the body"). For the worm, see Isa 66:24 LXX (ὁ γὰρ σκώληξ αὐτῶν οὐ τελευτήσει ["their worm will not die"]); Mark 9:48; 2 Clem. 7.6; 17.5; Hipp., *Antichr.* 65; Justin, *1 Apol.* 52.8; Tert., *Res.* 31.9; Apoc. Pet. 27: ἐσθιόμενοι τὰ σπλάγχνα ὑπὸ σκωλήκων ἀκοιμήτων ("their guts are eaten by unsleeping worms").

152. For the incorruptible body, see *Univ.* (Holl, 140,67–68): μηκέτι φθειρόμενον ὡς ἑκάστῳ σώματι ἡ ἰδία ψυχὴ ἀποδοθήσεται ("… no longer corrupted, since each person's own soul will be returned to its own body"); Justin, *1 Apol.* 52.3; Tatian, *Or.* 6; Athenagoras, *Res.* 11.1; Theophilos, *Autol.* 1.7.

153. Rom 8:17 (συγκληρονόμοι δὲ Χριστοῦ); Clem. Alex., *Protr.* 113.5; 115.4; *Ecl.* 20.3; *Quis div.* 36.2.

ταῦτα <ἐ>δίδου, ὅτι ἄνθρωπος εἶς· ὅσα δὲ παρακολουθεῖ θεῷ, ταῦτα παρέχειν ἐπήγγελται θεὸς ὅταν θεοποιηθῇς, ἀθάνατος γενηθείς.

Τοῦτ' ἔστι τὸ «γνῶθι σεαυτόν», ἐπιγνοὺς τὸν πεποιηκότα θεόν· τῷ γὰρ ἐπιγνῶναι αὐτὸν ἐπιγνωσθῆναι συμβέβηκε τῷ καλουμένῳ ὑπ' αὐτοῦ. μὴ φιλεχθ<ρ>ήσητε τοίνυν ἑαυτοῖς, ἄνθρωποι, μηδὲ τὸ παλινδρομεῖν διστάσητε. 5. Χριστὸς γάρ ἐστιν ὁ κατὰ πάντων θεός· ὃς τὴν ἁμαρτίαν ἐξ ἀνθρώπων ἀποπλύνειν προσέταξε, νέον «τὸν παλαιὸν ἄνθρωπον» ἀποτελῶν, «εἰκόνα» τοῦτον καλέσας ἀπ' ἀρχῆς, διὰ τύπου τὴν εἰς σὲ ἐπιδεικνύμενος στοργήν. οὗ προστάγμασιν ὑπακούσας σεμνοῖς, καὶ ἀγαθοῦ ἀγαθὸς γενόμενος μιμητής, ἔσῃ ὅμοιος ὑπ' αὐτοῦ τιμηθείς. οὐ γὰρ πτωχεύει θεός· καὶ σὲ θεὸν ποιήσας εἰς δόξαν αὐτ(οῦ).

these he gave because you are human.[154] But whatever belongs to God, this God has promised to give when you, made immortal, become a god.[155]

This is the meaning of "know yourself": when you recognize God your maker. For by knowing him, you who are called are known by him.[156] So then, do not be your own enemies, O human beings, or hesitate to reverse course. 5. Christ is the God of all people, who commanded sin to be washed away from human beings, completing "the old human being" as new. He originally called the human being "the image," thereby showing through a model his affection for you.[157] You have heard his holy commands, and after you become a good imitator of the Good, you will be honored by him as one like him. God is not poor; for his glory, he makes you also a god!

---

154. Nautin replaces the Ionic second singular form εἶς with the Koine form εἶ. Our author can, however, use Ionic forms (e.g., συνώσητε in *Univ.* [Holl, 143,130]).

155. Cf. the "Sethian" view that the one who, as light, hastens to the Word becomes Word with the Word (*Ref.* 5.21.9), and "Simon," who says that, as Word, one can become an infinite, unchanging, and unborn power (*Ref.* 6.17.7).

156. On "know thyself," see Plato, *Alcib.* 1.333c4; 130e7; *Charm.* 169e4; *Phaedr.* 229e6–230a6; *Phileb.* 48d2; *Leg.* 11.923a4; 1 Cor 13:12; Gal 4:9; Sent. Sextus 394, 446 (Wilson). Löhr states that our author "deliberately identifies the goal of his Christian φιλομάθεια with the τέλος of ancient philosophy: In *Refut.* 1,18 it is said that Sokrates ... had preferred the Delphic Maxim. Here, at the end of the *Refutatio*, the Delphic Maxim is interpreted by identifying the knowledge of self with the knowledge of God" ("Continuing Construction," 41). See further Courcelle, *Connais-toi toi-même*, 11–82. Marcovich asserts that finding God in the self agrees with Monoïmos in *Ref.* 8.15.1–2; cf. 10.17.5 (*Refutatio*, 44).

157. Rom 9:5 (Χριστὸς ... ὁ ὢν ἐπὶ πάντων θεὸς εὐλογητός); cf. [Hipp.], *Noet.* 6.1. For the "old human being," see the note on *Ref.* 10.33.15. For the image of God from the beginning, see Gen 1:26. Cf. *Ref.* 5.7.6 (Naassenes); 6.14.5 ("Simon"); 7.28.2 (Satorneilos).

Bibliography

Critical Editions of the *Refutation*

Cruice, Patricius, ed. *Philosophumena sive haeresium omnium confutatio opus Origeni adscriptum e cod. Paris. rec.* Paris: Imperial, 1860.

Duncker, L., and F. G. Schneidewin, eds. *S. Hippolyti episcopi et martyris: Refutationis omnium haeresium librorum decem quae supersunt.* Göttingen: Dieterich, 1859.

Marcovich, Miroslav, ed. *Hippolytus: Refutatio omnium haeresium.* PTS 25. Berlin: de Gruyter, 1986.

Miller, Emmanuel, ed. Ὠριγένους Φιλοσοφούμενα ἤ Κατὰ πασῶν αἱρέσεων ἔλεγχος. [*Origenis Philosophumena sive Omnium haeresium refutatio e codice Parisino*]. Oxford: Academic, 1851.

Wendland, Paul, ed. *Refutatio omnium haeresium.* Hippolytus Werke 3. GCS 26. Leipzig: Hinrichs, 1916.

Full Translations of the *Refutation*

Legge, F., trans. *Philosophumena, or the Refutation of All Heresies.* 2 vols. London: SPCK, 1921.

MacMahon, J. H., trans. "The Refutation of All Heresies." Pages 9–153 in vol. 5 of *The Ante-Nicene Fathers.* Edited by Alexander Roberts and James Donaldson. 10 vols. 1885–1887. Repr., Grand Rapids: Eerdmans, 1986.

Magris, Aldo, ed. and trans. *'Ippolito': Confutazione di tutte le eresie.* Letteratura Cristiana Antica NS 25. Brescia: Morcelliana, 2012.

Preysing, Konrad, trans. *Des heiligen Hippolytus von Rome Widerlegung aller Häresien (Philosophumena).* Munich: Kösel & Pustet, 1922.

Siouville, A., trans. *Hippolyte de Rome: Philosophumena ou Réfutation de toutes les hérésies.* 2 vols. Paris: Rieder, 1928.

Reference Works

Adler, Ada, ed. *Suidae Lexicon.* 5 vols. Lexicographi Graeci. Stuttgart: Teubner, 1967–1971.

Brown, Francis, S. R. Driver, and Charles A. Briggs, eds. *Brown-Driver-Briggs Hebrew and English Lexicon with an Appendix Containing the Biblical Aramaic.* Boston: Houghton Mifflin, 1906.

Danker, Frederick W., Walter Bauer, William F. Arndt, and F. Wilbur Gingrich. *Greek-English Lexicon of the New Testament and Other Early Christian Literature.* 3rd ed. Chicago: University of Chicago Press, 2000.

Hanegraaff, Wouter J. *Dictionary of Gnosis and Western Esotericism.* Leiden: Brill, 2006.

Kittel, Gerhard, and Gerhard Friedrich, eds. *Theological Dictionary of the New Testament.* Translated by Geoffrey W. Bromiley. 10 vols. Grand Rapids: Eerdmans, 1964–1976.

L'Année épigraphique. Paris: University of Paris, 1888–.

Lampe, G. W. H. *A Patristic Greek Lexicon.* Oxford: Clarendon, 1961.

Landfester, Manfred, Hubert Cancik, and Helmuth Schneider, eds. *Brill's New Pauly: Encyclopedia of the Ancient World.* 5 vols. Leiden: Brill, 2006–.

Liddell, Henry George, Robert Scott, and P. G. W. Glare, eds. *A Greek-English Lexicon with Revised Supplement.* Oxford: Clarendon, 1996.

Schöllgen, Georg, Heinzgerd Brakmann, Sible de Blaauw, Therese Fuhrer, Hartmut Leppin, and Winrich Löhr, eds. *Reallexikon für Antike und Christentum: Sachwörterbuch zur Auseinandersetzung des Christentums mit der antiken Welt.* 25 vols. Stuttgart: Anton Hiersemann, 1950–.

Smith, William, and Henry Wace, eds. *A Dictionary of Christian Biography, Literature, Sects and Doctrines.* 4 vols. Boston: Little, Brown, 1877.

Primary Sources

Aland, Barbara, Kurt Aland, Johannes Karavidopoulos, Carlo M. Martini, and Bruce M. Metzger, eds. *Novum Testamentum Graece.* 28th ed. Stuttgart: Deutsche Bibelgesellschaft, 2012.

Aelian. *De natura animalium libri xvii.* Edited by Rudolf Hercher. Leipzig: Teubner, 1864.

———. *Historical Miscellany.* Edited by N. G. Wilson. LCL. Cambridge: Harvard University Press, 1997.

Alkinoos. *Enseignement des doctrines de Platon.* Edited by John Whittaker. Budé. Paris: Belles Lettres, 1990.

Ammianus Marcellinus. *Rerum gestarum libri qui supersunt.* Edited by Wolfgang Seyfarth. Vol. 1. BSGRT. Leipzig: Teubner, 1978.

Apollonios of Rhodes. *Argonautika.* Edited by Francis Vian. 3 vols. Budé. Paris: Belles Lettres, 1976–1981.

Apuleius of Madaura. *Opera quae supersunt.* Edited by C. Moreschini. 3 vols. Stuttgart: Teubner, 1991.

Aratos. *Aratus: Phaenomena; Introduction, Translation and Commentary.* Edited by Douglas A. Kidd. Cambridge: Cambridge University Press, 1997.

Aristides. *Opera quae exstant omnia.* Edited by Frederik W. Lenz and Carl A. Behr. Leiden: Brill, 1976–1980.

Aristotle. *Opera.* Edited by Olof Gigon. 2nd ed. 5 vols. Berlin: de Gruyter, 1960–1987.

Arnobius. *Adversus nationes libri VII.* Edited by C. Marchesi. Corpus Scriptorum Latinorum Paravianum. Torino: Giovanni Battista & Co., 1953.

Arrian. *Anabasis.* Edited and translated by P. A. Brunt. 2 vols. LCL. Cambridge: Harvard University Press, 1976–1983.

Artemidoros. *Oneirocritica.* Edited by Daniel E. Harris-McCoy. Oxford: Oxford University Press, 2012.

Athenaeos. *Deipnosophistae: The Learned Banqueters.* Edited by S. Douglas Olson. 8 vols. LCL. Cambridge: Harvard University Press, 2006–2012.

Athenagoras. *Legatio and de resurrectione.* Edited and translated by William R. Schoedel. OECT. Oxford: Clarendon, 1972.

Atticus. *Fragments.* Edited by Édouard des Places. Budé. Paris: Belles Lettres, 1977.

Augustine. *Confessioni.* Edited by Manlio Simonetti. 5 vols. Scrittori greci e latini. Milan: Lorenzo Valla, 1992–1997.

———. *Contra Faustum Manicheum.* Edited by Joseph Zycha. CSEL 25.1. Vienna: Tempsky, 1891.

———. *De civitate Dei.* CCSL 48. Turnholt: Brepols, 1955.

———. *In Iohannis evangelium tractatus CXXIV.* Edited by Radbodus Willems. CCSL 36. Turnholt: Brepols, 1954.

Barry, Catherine, Wolf-Peter Funk, Paul-Hubert Poirier, and John D. Turner. *Zostrien (NH VIII,1).* BCNH 24. Québec: Laval University Press; Leuven: Peeters, 2000.

Bernabé, Alberto, ed. *Poetae epici graeci testimonia et fragmenta: Part 2.* 3 vols. Leipzig: K. G. Saur, 2004–2007.
Bion of Smyrna. *The Fragments and the Adonis.* Edited by J. D. Reed. CCTC 33. Cambridge: Cambridge University Press, 1997.
Brooke, A. E. *The Fragments of Heracleon.* TS 1.4. Cambridge: Cambridge University Press, 1891.
Caesar, Gaius Julius. *Commentarii rerum gestarum.* Edited by Wolfgang Hering. Leipzig: Teubner, 1987.
Censorinus. *De die natali / Über den Geburtstag: Lateinisch und deutsch.* Edited by Kai Brodersen. Darmstadt: Wissenschaftliche Buchgesellschaft, 2012.
Charlesworth, James H, ed. *The Old Testament Pseudepigrapha.* 2 vols. New York: Doubleday, 1985.
Chronicon Pascale ad exemplar Vaticanum. Edited by Ludwig Dindorf. 2 vols. CSHB. Bonn: Weber, 1832.
Cicero, Marcus Tullius. *Academica.* Edited by James S. Reid. 2nd ed. London: Macmillan, 1885.
———. *De divinatione, de fato, Timaeus.* Edited by Otto Plasberg and Wilhelm Ax. Berlin: de Gruyter, 1987.
———. *De finibus bonorum et malorum.* Edited by Claudio Moreschini. BSGRT. Leipzig: K. G. Saur, 2005.
———. *De natura deorum.* Edited by Arthur Stanley Pease. 2 vols. New York: Arno, 1979.
———. *De oratore.* Edited by Augustus Wilkins. New York: Arno, 1979.
———. *De republica, de legibus.* Edited by Clinton Walker Keyes. LCL. Cambridge: Harvard University Press, 1928.
Clement of Alexandria. *Extraits de Théodote.* Edited by François Sagnard. SC 23. Paris: Cerf, 1970.
———. *Paedagogus.* Edited by Miroslav Marcovich. VCSup 61. Leiden: Brill, 2002.
———. *Protrepticus.* Edited by Miroslav Marcovich. VCSup 34. Leiden: Brill, 1995.
———. *Stromata, Quis dives salvetur.* Edited by Otto Stählin, Ludwig Früchtel, and Ursula Treu. 4th ed. GCS 15, 17. Berlin: Akademie, 1970–1985.
Cohen, Martin Samuel. *The Shiʿur Qomah: Texts and Recensions.* Tübingen: Mohr Siebeck, 1985.
Cornutus, Lucius Annaeus. *De natura deorum: Einführung in die griechischen Götterlehre.* Edited by Peter Busch and Jürgen K. Zangen-

berg. Texte zur Forschung 94. Darmstadt: Wissenschaftliche Buchgesellschaft, 2010.

Diels, Hermann. *Doxographi graeci.* Berlin: Reimer, 1879.

Diels, Hermann, and Walther Kranz, eds. *Fragmente der Vorsokratiker, griechisch und deutsch.* 7th ed. 3 vols. Berlin: Weidmann, 1954.

Dio Chrysostom. Edited by J. H. Cohoon. LCL. Cambridge: Harvard University Press, 1971–1995.

Diodoros of Sicily. *Bibliothèque historique.* Edited by Françoise Bizière. Budé. Paris: Belles Lettres, 1972–.

Diogenes Laertios. *Vitae philosophorum.* Edited by Miroslav Marcovich. Stuttgart: Teubner, 1999.

Dionysius Thrax. *Ars grammatica.* Edited by Gustav Uhlig. Leipzig: Teubner, 1883.

Diophantos of Alexandria. *Opera Omnia cum graecis commentariis.* Edited by Paul Tannery. 2 vols. Stuttgart: Teubner, 1974.

Elliger, K., and W. Rudolph, eds. *Biblia Hebraica Stuttgartensia.* 5th ed. Stuttgart: Deutsche Bibelgesellschaft, 1997.

Epikouros. *Opere.* Edited by Graziano Arrighetti. Torino: Giulio Einaudi, 1973.

Epiphanios. *Ancoratus und Panarion haer. 1–33.* Edited by Karl Holl, Marc Bergermann, and Christian-Friedrich Collatz. 2nd ed. GCS NF 10.1. Berlin: de Gruyter, 2013.

———. *Panarion haer. 34–64.* Edited by Karl Holl and Jürgen Dummer. 2nd ed. GCS 31. Berlin: Akademie, 1980.

Euclid. *Elementa.* Edited by I. L. Heiberg. 5 vols. BSGRT. Leipzig: Teubner, 1883–1888.

Euripides. Edited by Arthur S. Way. 3 vols. LCL. Cambridge: Harvard University Press, 1988.

Euripides. *Tragicorum Graecorum Fragmenta.* Edited by Augustus Nauck. 2nd ed. Leipzig: Teubner, 1889.

Eusebios. *Histoire ecclésiastique.* Edited by Gustav Bardy. 4 vols. SC 31, 41, 55, 73. Paris: Cerf, 1952–1960.

———. *La préparation évangelique.* Edited by Jean Sirinelli. 9 vols. SC 206, 215, 228, 262, 266, 292, 307, 338, 369. Paris: Cerf, 1974–1978.

Festugière, A. J., and A. D. Nock, eds. *Corpus Hermeticum.* 4 vols. Budé. Paris: Belles Lettres, 1954.

Galen. *De usu partium libri XVII.* Edited by George Helmreich. 2 vols. Leipzig: Teubner, 1907.

———. *Opera Omnia*. Edited by Carl Gottlob Kühn. 20 vols. Medicorum Graecorum. Leipzig: Cnobloch, 1821–1833.

Gallop, David, ed. and trans. *Parmenides of Elea: Fragments*. Toronto: University of Toronto Press, 1984.

Geffcken, Johann, ed. *Die Oracula Sibyllina*. Leipzig: Teubner, 1902.

Gellius, Aulus. *Noctes atticae*. Edited by P. K. Marshal. Oxford: Clarendon, 1990.

Geminos. *Introduction aux Phénomènes*. Edited and translated by Germaine Aujac. Paris: Belles Lettres, 1975.

Gregory the Wonderworker. *Remerciement à Origène suivi de la letter d'Origène a Grégoire*. Edited by Henri Crouzel. SC 148. Paris: Cerf, 1969.

Herakleitos. *Homeric Problems*. Edited by Donald A. Russell and David Konstan. WGRW 14. Atlanta: Society of Biblical Literature, 2005.

Hermann, Charles F. *Platonis dialogi secundum Thrasylli tetralogies dispositi*. Vol. 6 (Scholia). Leipzig: Teubner, 1884.

Hermias. *Satire des philosophes païens: Introduction, texte critique, notes, appendices et index*. Edited by R. P. C. Hanson. Translated by Denise Joussot. SC 388. Paris: Cerf, 1993.

Herodotos. *Historiae*. Edited by Carl Hude. 3rd ed. 2 vols. Oxford: Clarendon, 1933.

Hesiod. *Theogony*. Edited by M. L. West. Oxford: Clarendon, 1966.

Hippolytos. *Hippolytus: Kleinere exegetische und homiletische Schriften*. Edited by Hans Achelis. GCS 1.2. Leipzig: Hinrichs, 1897.

———. *Kommentar zu Daniel*. Edited by Georg Nathanael Bonwetsch and Marcel Richard. 2nd ed. Hippolytus Werke 1.1. GCS NF 7. Berlin: Akademie, 2000.

[Hippolytos.] *Die Chronik*. Edited by Adolf Bauer and Rudolf Helm. 2nd ed. Hippolytus Werke 4. GCS 46. Berlin: Akademie, 1955.

———. *Ippolito: Contro Noeto*. Edited by Manlio Simonetti. Biblioteca Patristica. Bologna: Dehoniane, 2000.

Holl, Karl, ed. *Fragmente vornicänischer Kirchenväter aus den Sacra Parallela*. TUGAL 5.2. Leipzig: Teubner, 1899.

Homer. *The Iliad*. Translated by A. T. Murray. Revised by William F. Wyatt. 2 vols. LCL. Cambridge: Harvard University Press, 1999.

———. *The Odyssey*. Translated by A. T. Murray. Revised by George E. Dimock. 2 vols. LCL. Cambridge: Harvard University Press, 1995.

Horace. *Satires, Epistles and Ars Poetica*. Edited by H. Rushton Fairclough. LCL. Cambridge: Harvard University Press, 1929.

Iamblichos. *Les mystères d'Égypte*. Edited by Édouard des Places. 2nd ed. Paris: Belles Lettres, 1989.

———. *On the Pythagorean Way of Life*. Edited and translated by John Dillon and Jackson Hershbell. Atlanta: Scholars Press, 1991.

[Iamblichos]. *Theologoumena arithmeticae*. Edited by V. de Falco and Udalricus Klein. 2nd ed. Leipzig: Teubner, 1975.

Inwood, Brad, ed. *The Poem of Empedocles: A Text and Translation with an Introduction*. 2nd ed. Toronto: University of Toronto, 2001.

Irenaeus of Lyons. *Contre les hérésies livres I–V*. Edited by Adelin Rousseau and Louis Doutreleau. SC 100, 153, 211, 263–264, 294. Paris: Cerf, 1965–1982.

———. *St. Irenaeus of Lyons: Against the Heresies Book 1*. Edited and translated by Dominic J. Unger and John J. Dillon. ACW 55. New York: Newman Press, 1992.

Jacoby, Felix, ed. *Die Fragmente der griechischen Historiker*. Part 3.1. Geschichte von Staedten und Voelkern (Horographie und Ethnographie) C Autoren über einzelne Länder Nr. 608a–856. Leiden: Brill, 1958.

Jerome. *Epistulae*. Edited by Isidore Hilberg. 2nd ed. Part 1. CSEL 54. Vienna: Österreichische Akademie der Wissenschaften, 1996.

John Philoponos. *De opificio mundi libri VII*. Edited by G. Reichardt. Leipzig: Teubner, 1897.

Josephus. *Opera*. Edited by Benedict Niese. 7 vols. Berlin: Weidmann, 1887–1889.

Julian. *The Works of the Emperor Julian*. Edited by Wilmer Cave Wright. LCL. Cambridge: Harvard University Press, 1980–1993.

Julius Africanus. *Cesti: The Extant Fragments*. Edited by Martin Wallraff, Carlo Scardino, Laura Mecella, and Christophe Guignard. Translated by William Adler. GCS NF 18. Berlin: de Gruyter, 2012.

Justin Martyr. *Apologies*. Edited by Denis Minns and Paul Parvis. OECT. Oxford: Oxford University Press, 2009.

———. *Dialogus cum Tryphone*. Edited by Miroslav Marcovich. PTS 47. Berlin: de Gruyter, 1997.

Kirk, G. S. *Heraclitus: The Cosmic Fragments*. Cambridge: Cambridge University Press, 1954.

Kleanthes. *Hymn to Zeus*. Edited by Johan C. Thom. STAC 33. Tübingen: Mohr Siebeck, 2005.

Kleomedes. *Caelestia (*ΜΕΤΕΩΡΑ*)*. Edited by Robert Todd. BSGRT. Leipzig: Teubner, 1990.

Lane, E., ed. *Corpus Monumentorum Religionis Dei Menis.* 4 vols. EPRO 19. Leiden: Brill, 1971–1978.

Long, A. A., and D. N. Sedley. *The Hellenistic Philosophers.* 2 vols. Cambridge: Cambridge University Press, 1987.

Longinus. *Poetics (On the Sublime).* Edited by W. H. Fyfe. LCL. Cambridge: Harvard University Press, 1995.

Lucian. *Oeuvres.* Edited by Jacques Bompaire. 4 vols. Budé. Paris: Belles Lettres, 1993–2008.

———. *On the Syrian Goddess.* Edited by J. L. Lightfoot. Oxford: Oxford University Press, 2003.

Lucretius. *De rerum natura libri sex.* Edited by William Ellery Leonard and Stanley Barney Smith. Madison: University of Wisconsin Press, 1942.

Maass, Ernest, ed. *Commentariorum in Aratum Reliquiae.* 2nd ed. Berlin: Weidmann, 1958.

Macrobius. *Commentaire au songe de Scipion.* Edited and translated by Mireille Armisen-Marchetti. 2 vols. Budé. Paris: Belles Lettres, 2003.

Manilius. *Astronomica.* Edited by George P. Goold. BSGRT. Leipzig: Teubner, 1985.

Martin, Jean, ed. *Scholium in Aratum vetera.* BSGRT. Stuttgart: Teubner, 1974.

Martin, Victor. "Un recueil de diatribes cyniques: Pap. Genev. inv. 271." *MH* 16 (1959): 77–115.

Martínez, Florentino García, and Eibert J. C. Tigchelaar, eds. *The Dead Sea Scrolls Study Edition.* 2 vols. Leiden: Brill; Grand Rapids: Eerdmans, 1997–1998.

Maximus of Tyre. *Dissertationes.* Edited by Michael B. Trapp. BSGRT. Stuttgart: Teubner, 1994.

Methodius. Edited by G. Nathanael Bonwetsch. GCS 27. Leipzig: Hinrichs, 1917.

Migne, J.-P., ed. *Patrologia Graeca.* 162 vols. Paris: Garnier, 1857–1886.

Nag Hammadi Codex I (The Jung Codex). Edited by Harold Attridge. NHS 22. Leiden: Brill, 1985.

Nag Hammadi Codex II,2–7. Edited by Bentley Layton. 2 vols. NHS 20. Leiden: Brill, 1989.

Nag Hammadi Codex VII. Edited by Birger A. Pearson. NHMS 30. Leiden: Brill, 1996.

Nag Hammadi Codices II,2 and IV,2: The Gospel of the Egyptians (The Holy Book of the Great Invisible Spirit). Edited by Alexander Böhlig and Frederik Wisse. NHS 4. Leiden: Brill, 1975.

Nag Hammadi Codices III,3–4 and V,1: Eugnostos and the Sophia of Jesus Christ. Edited by Douglas M. Parrot. NHS 27. Leiden: Brill, 1991.

Nag Hammadi Codices V, 2–5 and VI. Edited by Douglas M. Parrot. NHS 11. Leiden: Brill, 1979.

Nag Hammadi Codices IX and X. Edited by Birger A. Pearson. NHS 15. Leiden: Brill, 1981.

Nag Hammadi Codices XI, XIII, XIII. Edited by Charles W. Hedrick. NHS 28. Leiden: Brill, 1990.

Noumenios. *Fragments*. Edited by Édouard des Places. Budé. Paris: Belles Lettres, 1973.

Okellos Lukanos. *Text und Kommentar*. Edited by Richard Harder. Neue Philologische Untersuchungen 1. Berlin: Weidmann, 1926.

Oppian. *Halieutica*. Edited by A. W. Mair. LCL. London: Heinemann, 1928.

Origen. *Commentaire sur l'Évangile de Matthieu*. Edited by R. Girod. Vol. 1. SC 162. Paris: Cerf, 1970.

———. *Contra Celse*. Edited by Marcel Borett. 5 vols. SC 132, 136, 147, 150, 227. Paris: Cerf, 1967–1976.

———. *Traité des principes*. Edited by Henri Crouzel and Manlio Simonetti. 5 vols. SC 252–253, 268–269, 312. Paris: Cerf, 1978.

Ovid. *The Art of Love, and Other Poems*. Edited by J. H. Mozley and G. P. Goold. 2nd ed. LCL. Cambridge: Harvard University Press, 1979.

———. *Les Fastes*. Edited by Robert Schilling. 2 vols. Budé. Paris: Belles Lettres, 1992–1993.

———. *Métamorphoses*. Edited by Georges LaFaye. 3 vols. Budé. Paris: Belles Lettres, 1965–1969.

Page, D. L., ed. *Poetae melici graeci*. Oxford: Clarendon, 1962.

Palladius. *The History of Palladius on the Races of India and the Brahmans*. Edited by John D. M. Derrett. Copenhagen: Gyldendal, 1960.

Pausanias. *Description de la Grèce*. Edited by Michel Casevitz, Jean Pouilloux, and François Chamoux. 4 vols. Budé. Paris: Belles Lettres, 1992–2005.

Philo. *Opera*. Edited by Leopold Cohn and Paul Wendland. 7 vols. Berlin: de Gruyter, 1962–1963.

Philo of Byblos. *The Phoenician History*. Edited by Harold Attridge and Robert A. Oden. CBQMS 9. Washington, DC: Catholic Biblical Association of America, 1981.

Philostratos. *The Life of Apollonius of Tyana*. Edited and translated by Christopher P. Jones. LCL. Cambridge: Harvard University Press, 2005.

Photios. *Bibliothèque*. Edited by René Henry. 2 vols. Paris: Belles Lettres, 1959.

Plato. *Opera*. Edited by E. A. Duke, W. F. Hicken, W. S. M. Nicoll, D. B. Robinson, and J. C. G. Strachan. 5 vols. OCT. Oxford: Clarendon, 1995.

Pliny the Elder. *Natural History*. Translated by H. Rackham. 2nd ed. 10 vols. LCL. Cambridge: Harvard University Press, 1983.

Pliny the Younger. *Lettres livre X, Panégyrique de Trajan*. Edited by Marcel Durry. Budé. Paris: Belles Lettres, 1964.

Plotinos. *Opera*. Edited by Paul Henry and Hans-Rudolf Schwyzer. 3 vols. Oxford: Oxford University Press, 1964–1982.

Plutarch. Translated by Frank Cole Babbit, Paul A. Clement, Herbert B. Hoffleit, Lionel Pearson, F. H. Sandbach, Harold Cherniss, William C. Helmbold, Benedict Einarson, and Phillip H. de Lacy. 28 vols. LCL. Cambridge: Harvard University Press, 1914–2004.

Plutarch. *De Iside et Osiride*. Translated by J. G. Griffiths. Cambridge: University of Wales Press, 1970.

Porphyry. *De l'abstinence*. Edited and translated by Jean Bouffartigue. 3 vols. Paris: Belles Lettres, 1977.

———. *Fragmenta*. Edited by Andrew Smith. Leipzig: Teubner, 1993.

———. *Introduction*. Translated by Jonathan Barnes. Oxford: Clarendon, 2003.

———. *Vie de Pythagore*. Edited by Édouard des Places. Paris: Belles Lettres, 1982.

Preisendanz, Karl, and Albert Henrichs. *Papyri Graecae Magicae: Die griechischen Zauberpapyri*. 2nd ed. 3 vols. Stuttgart: Teubner, 1973.

Proklos. *In Platonis Timaeum commentaria*. Edited by Ernst Diehl. 3 vols. Leipzig: Teubner, 1903–1906.

Pseudo-Apollodoros. *Bibliotheca*. Edited by Richard Wagner. Stuttgart: Teubner, 1965.

Pseudo-Aristotle. *Cosmic Order and Divine Power: Pseudo-Aristotle, On the Cosmos*. Edited by Johan C. Thom. SAPERE 23. Tübingen: Mohr Siebeck, 2014.

———. *Si Parménide: Le traité anonyme De Melisso Xenophane Gorgia*. Edited by Barbara Cassin. Cahiers de Philologie 4. Lille: Lille University, 1980.

Pseudo-Demokritos. Νεπουαλίου περὶ τῶν κατὰ ἀντιπάθειαν καὶ συμπάθειαν. Edited by Wilhelm Gemoll. Städtisches Realprogymnasium zu Striegau 190. Striegau: Ph. Tschörner, 1884.

Pseudo-Eratosthenes. *Catasterismi.* Edited by Alexander Olivieri. BSGRT. Leipzig: Teubner, 1897.

Pseudo-Hippokrates. *Hippocrate Tome XI: De la Génération, De la nature de l'enfant, Des maladies IV, Du foetus de huit mois.* Edited by Robert Joly. Budé. Paris: Belles Lettres, 1970.

———. *Pseudepigraphic Writings: Letters-Embassy-Speech from the Altar-Decree.* Edited by Wesley D. Smith. Studies in Ancient Medicine 2. Leiden: Brill, 1990.

Pseudo-Justin. *Ouvrages apologétiques: Exhortation aux grecs, Discours aux grecs, sur la monarchie.* Edited by Bernard Pouderon. SC 528. Paris: Cerf, 2009.

Pseudo-Plutarch. *De Homero.* Edited by Jan Fredrik Kindstrand. BSGRT. Leipzig: Teubner, 1990.

———. *Opinions des Philosophes.* Edited by G. Lachenaud. Budé. Paris: Belles Lettres, 1993.

Pseudo-Timaios. *On the Nature of the World and the Soul.* Edited by Thomas H. Tobin. Chico, CA: Scholars Press, 1985.

Ptolemy. *Lettre à Flora.* Edited by Gilles Quispel. 2nd ed. SC 24. Paris: Cerf, 1966.

Ptolemy, Claudius. *Opera quae exstant omnia.* Edited by Wolfgang Hübner. 2nd ed. 3 vols. Leipzig: Teubner, 1961–1998.

Quandt, W., ed. *Orphei Hymni.* Zürich: Weidmann, 1953.

Rabe, Hugo, ed. *Scholia in Lucianum.* Leipzig: Teubner, 1971.

Rahlfs, Alfred, and Robert Hanhart. *Septuaginta, id est Vetus Testamentum graece iuxta LXX interpretes.* 2nd ed. Stuttgart: Deutsche Bibelgesellschaft, 2006.

Rehm, Bernhard, and Franz Paschke, eds. *Die Pseudoklementinen I: Homilien.* 2nd ed. GCS 42. Berlin: Akademie, 1969.

Richardson, Nicholas. *Three Homeric Hymns: To Apollo, Hermes, and Aphrodite.* Cambridge Greek and Latin Classics. Cambridge: Cambridge University Press, 2010.

Roberge, Michel. *La paraphrase de Sem (NHC VII,1).* BCNH 25. Québec: Laval University Press; Leuven: Peeters, 2000.

———. *The Paraphrase of Shem: Introduction, Translation and Commentary.* NHMS 72. Leiden: Boston, 2010.

Sallustius. *Concerning the Gods and the Universe.* Edited by A. D. Nock. Cambridge: Cambridge University Press, 1926.

Schmidt, Carl, ed. *The Books of Jeu and the Untitled Text in the Bruce Codex.* Translated by Violet MacDermott. NHS 13. Leiden: Brill, 1978.

———. *Pistis Sophia.* Translated by Violet MacDermott. NHS 9. Leiden: Brill, 1978.

Schneemelcher, Wilhelm, and Edgar Hennecke. *New Testament Apocrypha.* Translated by R. McL. Wilson. 2nd ed. 2 vols. Louisville: Westminster John Knox, 1991–1992.

Scriptores Historiae Augustae. Edited by David Magie. 3 vols. LCL. London: Heinemann, 1921.

Seneca. *Epistles.* Translated by John W. Basore. 3 vols. LCL. Cambridge: Harvard University Press, 1917–1925.

———. *Moral Essays.* Edited by John Basore. 3 vols. Cambridge: Harvard University Press, 1920–1925.

———. *Oedipus with Introduction, Translation and Commentary.* Edited by A. J. Boyle. Oxford: Oxford University Press, 2011.

———. *Questions Naturelles.* Edited by Paul Oltramare. 2 vols. Budé. Paris: Belles Lettres, 2003.

[Seneca]. *Tragoediae incertorum auctorum Hercules [Oetaeus], Octavia.* Edited by Otto Zwierlein. OCT. Oxford: Clarendon, 1986.

Sextus Empiricus. *Opera.* Edited by Hermann Mutschmann and J. Mau. 4 vols. BSGRT. Leipzig: Teubner, 1912–1961.

———. *Sesto Empirico: Contro gli astrologi.* Edited by Emidio Spinelli. Naples: Bibliopolis, 2000.

Simplikios. *In Aristotelis Physicorum.* Edited by Hermann Diels. Berlin: Reimer, 1895.

Stephanus of Byzantium. *Ethnica.* Edited by Margarethe Billerbeck. 2 vols. Berlin: de Gruyter, 2006.

Stobaios, Ioannes. *Anthologium.* Edited by Curt Wachsmuth and Otto Hense. 2nd ed. 5 vols. Berlin: Weidmann, 1958.

Strabo. *Géographie.* Edited by Germaine Aujac, Raoul Baladié, François Lasserre, Benoît Laudenbach, and Jehan Desanges. 15 vols. Budé. Paris: Belles Lettres, 1966–2003.

Tacitus. *Histoires.* Edited by Pierre Wuilleumier and Henri Le Bonniec. Budé. Paris: Belles Lettres, 1987–.

Tatian. *Oratio ad Graecos and Fragments.* Edited by Molly Whittaker. OECT. Oxford: Clarendon, 1982.

Terentianus Maurus. *De litteris, de syllabis, de metris.* Edited by Chiara Cignolo. 2 vols. Collectanea Grammatica Latina 6. Hildesheim: Olms, 2002.

Tertullian. *Opera.* Edited by E. Dekkers, A. Gerlo, and A. Kroymann. 2 vols. CCSL 1.1, 1.2. Turnholt: Brepols, 1954.

Theokritos. Edited by A. S. F. Gow. 2 vols. Cambridge: Cambridge University Press, 1965.

Theon of Smyrna. *Expositio rerum mathematicarum ad legendum Platonem utilium*. Edited by E. Hiller. Leipzig: Teubner, 1879.

Theophilos of Antioch. *Ad Autolycum*. Edited and translated by Robert M. Grant. OECT. Oxford: Clarendon, 1970.

Theophrastos of Eresos. *Sources for His Life, Writings, Thought, and Influence*. Edited by William Fortenbaugh, Pamela Huby, R. W. Sharples, and Dimitri Gutas. 2 vols. PhA. Leiden: Brill, 1992.

Thessalos of Tralles. *Thessalos von Tralles: Griechisch und lateinisch*. Edited by Hans-Veit Friedrich. Beiträge zur klassischen Philologie 28; Meisenheim am Glan: Verlag Anton Hain, 1968.

Varro. *On the Latin Language*. Edited by Roland G. Kent. LCL. Cambridge: Harvard University Press, 1938.

Vergil. *Énéide Livres I–IV*. Edited by J. Perret. Budé. Paris: Belles Lettres, 1977.

Vettius Valens. *Anthologiarum libri novem*. Edited by David Pingree. Leipzig: Teubner, 1986.

Völker, Walther. *Quellen zur Geschichte der christlichen Gnosis*. Tübingen: Mohr Siebeck, 1932.

Von Arnim, Johannes, ed. *Stoicorum veterum fragmenta*. Leipzig: Teubner, 1903–1924.

Waldstein, Michael, and Frederik Wisse, eds. *The Apocryphon of John: Synopsis of Nag Hammadi Codices II,1; III,1; and IV,1 with BG 8502,2*. NHMS 33. Leiden: Brill, 1995.

Wehrli, Fritz. *Die Schule des Aristoteles*. 10 vols. Basel: B. Schwabe, 1944–1959.

Wendel, Carl, ed. *Scholia in Apollonium Rhodium Vetera*. Berlin: Weidmann, 1935.

West, Martin L., ed. *Carmina Anacreontea*. BSGRT. Leipzig: Teubner, 1984.

———. *Iambi et Elegi Graeci ante Alexandrum Cantati*. 2nd ed. 2 vols. Oxford: Clarendon, 1992.

Westermann, Antonius, ed. ΠΑΡΑΔΟΞΟΓΡΑΦΟΙ: *Scriptores Rerum Mirabilium Graeci; [Aristotelis] Mirabiles auscultationes; Antigoni, Apollonii, Phlegontis Historiae Mirabiles; Michaelis Pselli Lectiones Mirabilies; Reliquorum eiusdem generis scriptorium deperditorum fragmenta*. London: Black and Armstrong, 1839.

Wilson, Walter, ed. *The Sentences of Sextus*. Atlanta: Society of Biblical Literature, 2012.

Xenophon. *Memorabilia, Oeconomicus.* Translated by E. C. Marchant. Revised by Jeffrey Henderson. LCL. Cambridge: Harvard University Press, 2013.

Xenis, Georgios A., ed. *Scholia vetera in Sophoclis Electram.* Sammlung griechischer und lateinischer Grammatiker 12. Berlin: de Gruyter, 2010.

Xenophanes of Colophon, Fragments: A Text and Translation with a Commentary. Edited by J. H. Lesher. Toronto: University of Toronto Press, 1992.

Secondary Sources

Abramowski, Luise. *Drei christologische Untersuchungen.* BZNW 45. Berlin: de Gruyter, 1981.

———. "Female Figures in the Gnostic *Sondergut* in Hippolytus' *Refutatio.*" Pages 136–52 in *Images of the Feminine in Gnosticism.* Edited by Karen L. King. SAC. Philadelphia: Fortress, 1988.

Abt, Adam. *Die Apologie des Apuleius von Madaura und die antike Zauberei.* RVV 4.2. Giessen: Töpelmann, 1908.

Ackrill, J. L. *Essays on Plato and Aristotle.* Oxford: Clarendon, 1997.

Adra, Hoda. *Le mythe d'Adonis: Culte et interpretation.* Beirut: Université Libanaise, 1985.

Aland, Barbara. "Seele, Zeit, Eschaton bei einem frühen christlichen Theologen: Basilides zwischen Paulus und Platon." Pages 255–78 in Ψυχή-*Seele-anima: Festschrift für Karin Alt.* Edited by Jens Holzhausen. Stuttgart: Teubner, 1998.

Albrile, Ezio. "… *In principiis lucem fuisse ac tenebras*: Creazione, caduta e rigenerazione spiritual in alcuni testi gnostici." *AION* 17 (1995): 109–55.

Alesse, Francesca. "Il tema dell'emanazione (aporroia) nella letteratura astrologica e non astrologica tra I sec. a.C. e II d.C." *MHNH* 3 (2003): 117–34.

Alt, Karin. "Hippolytos als Referent platonischer Lehren." *JAC* 40 (1997): 78–105.

Alvar, Jaime. *Romanising Oriental Gods: Myth, Salvation and Ethics in the Cults of Cybele, Isis and Mithras.* Translated by Richard Gordon. Leiden: Brill, 2008.

Amand, David. *Fatalisme et liberté dans l'antiquité grecque.* Leuven: Desclée de Brouwer, 1945.

Andrei, Osvalda. "Dalle *Chronographiai* di Giulio Africano alla *Synagoge* di 'Ippolito': Un dibattito sulla scrittura Cristiana del tempo." Pages 113–46 in *Julius Africanus und die christliche Weltchronik*. Edited by Martin Wallraff. Berlin: de Gruyter, 2006.

———. "Spazio geografico, etnografia ed evangelizzazione nella *Synagoge* di Ippolito." *ZAC* 11 (2007): 221–78.

Andresen, Carl. *Logos und Nomos: Die Polemik des Kelsos wider das Christentum*. Arbeiten zur Kirchengeschichte 30. Berlin: de Gruyter, 1955.

Apatow, R. "The Tetraktys: The Cosmic Paradigm of the Ancient Pythagoreans." *Parab* 24.3 (1999): 38–43.

Aragione, Gabriella. "Aspetti ideologici della nozione di plagio nell'antichità classica e Cristiana." Pages 1–15 in *Cristianesimi nell'antichità: Fonti, istituzioni, ideologie a confronto*. Hildesheim: Olms, 2007.

———. "Guerre-éclaire contre les hermétiques, guerre de position contre les philosophes: L'Elenchos et ses protagonistes." Pages 73–101 in *Des évêques, des écoles et des hérétiques: Actes du colloque international sur la "Refutation de toutes les heresies" Genève, 13–14 juin 2008*. Edited by Gabriella Aragione and Enrico Norelli. Prahins: Éditions du Zèbre, 2011.

Astour, Michael C. *Hellenosemitica: An Ethnic and Cultural Study in West Semitic Impact on Mycenaean Greece*. Leiden: Brill, 1967.

Aujac, Germaine. "Sextus Empiricus et l'astrologie." Pages 207–26 in *Homo Mathematicus: Actas del Congreso Internacional sobre Astrólogos Griegos y Romanos (Benalmádena, 8–10 de Octubre de 2001)*. Edited by Aurelio Pérez Jiménez and Raúl Caballero. Málaga: Charta Antiqua, 2002.

Bailey, Alan. *Sextus Empiricus and Pyrrhonean Scepticism*. Oxford: Clarendon, 2002.

Barnes, Jonathan. *Early Greek Philosophy*. 2nd ed. London: Penguin, 2001.

Barton, Tamsyn. *Ancient Astrology*. London: Routledge, 1994.

Bauckham, Richard. "The Origin of the Ebionites." Pages 162–81 in *The Image of the Judaeo-Christians in Ancient Jewish and Christian Literature*. Edited by Peter J. Tomson and Doris Lambers-Petry. WUNT 158. Tübingen: Mohr Siebeck, 2003.

Beck, Roger. *A Brief History of Ancient Astrology*. Malden: Blackwell, 2007.

———. "Thus Spake Not Zarathuštra: Zoroastrian Pseudepigrapha of the Greco-Roman World." Pages 491–565 in vol. 3 of *A History of Zoroastrianism: Zoroastrianism under Macedonian and Roman Rule*. Edited by Mary Boyce and Frantz Grenet. 3 vols. Leiden: Brill, 1991.

Ben, N. van der. *The Proem of Empedocles' "Peri Physios": Towards a New Edition of All the Fragments*. Amsterdam: B. R. Grüner, 1975.

Berg, Beverly. "Dandamis: An Early Christian Portrait of Indian Asceticism." *Classica et Mediaevalia* 31 (1970): 269–305.

Bergman, Jan. "Kleine Beiträge zum Naassenertraktat." Pages 74–100 in *Proceedings of the International Colloquium on Gnosticism: Stockholm, August 20–25, 1973*. Edited by Geo Widengren. Stockholm: Almqvist & Wiksell, 1977.

Bergmeier, Roland. "Die drei jüdischen Schulrichtungen nach Josephus und Hippolyt von Rome: Zu den Paralleltexten Josephus, *B.J.* 2,119–166 und Hippolyt, *Haer.* IX 18,2–29,4." *JSJ* 34 (2003): 443–70.

Bertrand, Daniel A. "La notion d'apocryphe dans l'argumentation de la Réfutation de toutes le hérésies." Pages 131–40 in *Apocryphité: Histoire d'un concept transversal aux religions du livre en hommage à Pierre Geoltrain*. Edited by Simon Claude Mimouni. BEHER 113. Turnhout: Brepols, 2002.

Beyschlag, Karlmann. "Kallist und Hippolyt." *TZ* 20 (1964): 103–24.

Bidez, J., and F. Cumont. *Les mages hellénisés: Zoroastre, Ostanès et Hystaspe d'après la tradition grecque*. 2 vols. Paris: Belles Lettres, 1938.

Biondi, Graziano. *Basilide: La filosofia del Dio inesistente*. Rome: Manifestolibri, 2005.

Birdsall, R. Scott. "The Naassene Sermon and the Allegorical Tradition: Allegorical Interpretation, Syncretism, and Textual Authority." PhD diss., The Claremont Graduate School, 1984.

Black, Matthew. "The Account of the Essenes in Hippolytus and Josephus." Pages 172–75 in *The Background of the New Testament and Its Eschatology*. Edited by W. D. Davies and D. Daube. Cambridge: Cambridge University Press, 1956.

Blumenberg, H. "Der Sturz des Protophilosophen: Zur Komik der reinen Theorie anhand einer Rezeptionsgeschichte der Thales Anekdote." Pages 11–64 in *Das Komische*. Edited by Wolfgang Preisendanz and Rainer Warning. Poetik und Hermeneutik 7. Munich: W. Fink, 1976.

Böhlig, Alexander. *Zum Hellenismus in den Schriften von Nag Hammadi*. Wiesbaden: Harrassowitz, 1975.

Boll, Franz. *Sphaera: Neue griechische Texte und Untersuchungen zur Geschichte der Sternbilder*. Leipzig: Teubner, 1903.

Bonner, Campbell. "An Amulet of the Ophite Gnostics." Pages 43–46 in *Commemorative Studies in Honor of Theodore Leslie Shear*. Hesperia

Supplements 8. Princeton: American School of Classical Studies at Athens, 1949.

Borgeaud, Philippe. *Mother of the Gods: From Cybele to the Virgin Mary.* Translated by Lysa Hochroth. Baltimore: Johns Hopkins, 2005.

Bos, Abraham P. "Basilides as an Aristotelianizing Gnostic." *VC* 54 (2000): 44–60.

———. "Basilides of Alexandria Disqualified as Not a Christian but an Aristotelian by the Author of the Elenchos." Pages 103–18 in *Des évêques, des écoles et des hérétiques: Actes du colloque international sur la "Refutation de toutes les heresies" Genève, 13–14 juin 2008.* Edited by Gabriella Aragione and Enrico Norelli. Prahins: Éditions du Zèbre, 2011.

———. "Basilides of Alexandria: Matthias (Matthew) and Aristotle as the Sources of Inspiration for His Gnostic Theology in Hippolytus' *Refutatio.*" Pages 397–418 in *The Wisdom of Egypt: Jewish, Early Christian, and Gnostic Essays in Honour of Gerard P. Luttikhuizen.* Edited by Anthony Hilhorst and George H. van Kooten. Ancient Judaism and Early Christianity 59. Leiden: Brill, 2005.

Bouché-Leclercq, A. *L'astrologie grecque.* Paris: Leroux, 1899.

Boys-Stones, G. R. *Post-Hellenistic Philosophy: A Study of Its Development from the Stoics to Origen.* Oxford: Oxford University Press, 2001.

Brakke, David. *The Gnostics: Myth, Ritual, and Diversity in Early Christianity.* Cambridge: Harvard University Press, 2010.

Bremmer, Jan N. *Initiation into the Mysteries of the Ancient World.* Berlin: de Gruyter, 2014.

Brent, Allen. "Diogenes Laertius and His Apostolic Succession." *JEH* 44 (1993): 367–89.

———. "The Elenchos and the Identification of Christian Communities in Second–Early Third Century Rome." Pages 275–314 in *Des évêques, des écoles et des hérétiques: Actes du colloque international sur la "Refutation de toutes les heresies" Genève, 13–14 juin 2008.* Edited by Gabriella Aragione and Enrico Norelli. Prahins: Éditions du Zèbre, 2011.

———. *Hippolytus and the Roman Church in the Third Century: Communities in Tension before the Emergence of a Monarch-Bishop.* VCSup 31. Leiden: Brill, 1995.

———. "St Hippolytus, Biblical Exegete, Roman Bishop, and Martyr." *SVTQ* 48 (2004): 207–31.

Broadhead, Edwin K. *Jewish Ways of Following Jesus: Redrawing the Religious Map of Antiquity.* WUNT 266. Tübingen: Mohr Siebeck, 2011.

Broek, Roelof van den. "Gospel Tradition and Salvation in Justin the Gnostic." *VC* 57 (2003): 363–88.

———. "Monoimus." *DGWE* 800–802.

———. "Naassenes." *DGWE* 820–22.

———. "Satornilus." *DGWE* 1037–38.

———. "The Shape of Eden according to Justin the Gnostic." *VC* 27 (1973): 35–45.

Brown, Peter. *The Body and Society: Men, Women and Sexual Renunciation in Early Christianity*. New York: Columbia University Press, 1988.

Brox, Norbert. "Kelsos und Hippolytos: Zur frühchristlichen Geschichtspolemik." *VC* (1966): 150–58.

Buckley, Jorunn Jacobsen. *Female Fault and Fulfillment in Gnosticism*. Chapel Hill: University of North Carolina Press, 1986.

Bull, Christian H., Liv Ingebord Lied, and J. D. Turner, eds. *Mystery and Secrecy in the Nag Hammadi Collection and Other Ancient Literature: Ideas and Practices; Studies for Einar Thomassen at Sixty*. NHMS 76. Leiden: Brill, 2012.

Burchard, Christoph. "Zur Nebenüberlieferung von Josephus' Bericht über die Essener, Bell 2,119–161 bei Hippolyt, Porphyrius, Josippus, Niketas Choniates und anderen." Pages 76–96 in *Josephus-Studien: Untersuchungen zu Josephus, dem antiken Judentum und dem Neuen Testament*. Edited by Otto Betz, Klaus Haacker, and Martin Hengel. Göttingen: Vandenhoeck & Ruprecht, 1974.

Burkert, Walter. "Die betretene Wiese: Interpretenprobleme im Bereich der Sexualssymbolik." Pages 32–46 in *Die wilde Seele: Zur Ethnospsychoanalyse von G. Devereux*. Edited by H. P. Duerr. Frankfurt: Suhrkamp, 1987.

———. *Homo Necans: The Anthropology of Ancient Greek Sacrificial Ritual and Myth*. Translated by Peter Bing. Berkeley: University of California Press, 1983.

———. *Lore and Science in Ancient Pythagoreanism*. Translated by Edwin L. Minar. Cambridge: Harvard University Press, 1972.

———. "Plotin, Plutarch und die platonisierende Interpretation von Heraklit und Empedokles." Pages 137–46 in *Kephalaion: Studies in Greek Philosophy and Its Continuation Offered to Professor C. J. de Vogel*. Assen: Van Gorcum, 1975.

———. *Structure and History in Greek Mythology and Ritual*. Berkeley: University of California Press, 1979.

Callataÿ, Godefroid de. *Annus Platonicus: A Study of World Cycles in Greek, Latin and Arabic Sources*. Leuven: Institut Orientaliste, 1996.

———. "Platón astrólogo: La teoría del Gran Año y sus primeras deformaciones." Pages 317–24 in *Homo Mathematicus: Actas del Congreso Internacional sobre Astrólogos Griegos y Romanos (Benalmádena, 8–10 de Octubre de 2001)*. Edited by Aurelio Pérez Jiménez and Raúl Caballero. Málaga: Charta Antiqua, 2002.

Cameron, Averil. "Jews and Heretics—A Category Error?" Pages 345–60 in *The Ways That Never Parted: Jews and Christians in Late Antiquity and the Early Middle Ages*. Edited by Adam H. Becker and Annette Yoshiko Reed. Tübingen: Mohr Siebeck, 2003.

Carabine, Deirdre. *The Unknown God: Negative Theology in the Platonic Tradition; Plato to Eriugena*. Leuven Theological and Pastoral Monographs 19. Leuven: Peeters, 1995.

Carcopino, Jérôme. *De Pythagore aux apôtres: Études sur la conversion du monde romain*. Paris: Flammarion, 1956.

Carletti, Carlo. "L'arca di Noè: Ovvero la Chiesa di Callisto e l'uniformità della 'morte scritta.'" *Antiquité tardive* 9 (2001): 97–102.

Casadio, Giovanni. "La visione in Marco il Mago e nella gnosi di tipo sethiano." *Aug* 29 (1989): 123–46.

———. *Vie gnostiche all'immortalità*. Brescia: Morcelliana, 1997.

Castelli, Emanuele. "The Author of the *Refutatio omnium haeresium* and the attribution of the *De universo* to Flavius Josephus." Pages 219–31 in *Des évêques, des écoles et des hérétiques: Actes du colloque international sur la "Refutation de toutes les heresies" Genève, 13–14 juin 2008*. Edited by Gabriella Aragione and Enrico Norelli. Prahins: Éditions du Zèbre, 2011.

———. *Un falso letterario sotto il nome di Flavio Giuseppe*. JAC Ergänzungsband 7. Münster: Aschendorff, 2011.

———. "Il prologo del Peri Pantos." *Vetera Christianorum* 42 (2005): 37–57.

Cerrato, J. A. *Hippolytus East and West: The Commentaries and the Provenance of the Corpus*. Oxford: Oxford University Press, 2002.

———. Saggio introduttivo: L'Elenchos, ovvero una 'biblioteca' contro le eresie." Pages 21–56 in *'Ippolito': Confutazione di tutte le eresie*. Edited by Aldo Magris. Brescia: Morcelliana, 2012.

Chaniotis, Angelos. "Staging and Feeling the Presence of God: Emotion and Theatricality in Religious Celebrations in the Roman East." Pages 169–90 in *Panthée: Religious Transformations in the Graeco-Roman*

Empire. Edited by Laurent Bricault and Corinne Bonnet. RGRW 177. Leiden: Brill, 2013.

Cirillo, Luigi. "L'apocalypse d'Elkhasaï: Son rôle et son importance pour l'histoire du judaïsme." *Apocrypha* 1 (1990): 167–80.

———. *Elchasai e gli Elchasaiti: Un contributo alla storia delle comunità giudeo-cristiane*. Cosenza: Marra, 1984.

Clivaz, Claire, and Sara Schulthess. "On the Source and Rewriting of 1 Corinthians 2.9 in Christian, Jewish and Islamic Traditions (*1 Clem* 34.8; *GosJud* 47.10–13; a *ḥadīth qudsī*)." *NTS* 61 (2015): 183–200.

Cole, Susan Guettel. *Theoi Megaloi: The Cult of the Great Gods at Samothrace*. EPRO 96. Leiden: Brill, 1984.

Colpe, Carsten. "Die 'elkesaitische Unternehmung' in Rom, ihre Hintergründe und ihre mögliche Einwirkung auf das Häreseienbild des Bischofs Hippolyt." Pages 57–69 in *Chartulae: Festschrift für Wolfgang Speyer*. JAC Ergänzungsband 28. Münster: Aschendorff, 1998.

Cornford, Francis. *Plato's Cosmology: The "Timaeus" of Plato Translated with a Running Commentary*. New York: Liberal Arts, 1957.

Couprie, Dirk L., Robert Hahn, and Gerard Naddaf, eds. *Anaximander in Context: New Studies in the Origins of Greek Philosophy*. Albany: SUNY Press, 2003.

Courcelle, Pierre. *Connais-toi toi-même: De Socrate à saint Bernard*. 3 vols. Paris: Études augustiniennes, 1974–1975.

———. "L'interprétation evhémériste des Sirènes-courtisane jusqu'au XIIe siècle." Pages 33–48 in *Gesellschaft, Kultur, Literatur: Rezeption und Originalität im Wachsen einer europäischen Literatur und Geistigkeit; Beiträge Luitpold Wallach Gewidmet*. Edited by Karl Bosl. Monographien zur Geschichte des Mittelalters 11. Stuttgart: Anton Hiersemann, 1975.

Cunliffe, Barry. *Druids: A Very Short Introduction*. Oxford: Oxford University Press, 2010.

D'Alès, Adhémar. *L'Édit de Calliste: Études sur les origines de la penitence chrétiennes*. 2nd ed. Paris: Beauchesne, 1914.

———. *La théologie de saint Hippolyte*. Paris: Beauchesne, 1906.

DeConick, April. "From the Bowels of Hell to Draco: The Mysteries of the Peratics." Pages 3–38 in *Mystery and Secrecy in the Nag Hammadi Collection and Other Ancient Literature, Ideas and Practices: Studies for Einar Thomassen at Sixty*. Edited by Christian H. Bull, Liv Ingeborg Lied, and John Douglas Turner. NHMS 76. Leiden: Brill, 2012.

De Koninck, Thomas. "Aristotle on God as Thought Thinking Itself." *Review of Metaphysics* 47 (1994): 471–515.

DeLacy, Phillip. "Οὐ μᾶλλον and the Antecedents of Ancient Scepticism." *Phronesis* 3 (1958): 59–71.

Delatte, A. *Études sur la littérature pythagoricienne.* Paris: Librairie Ancienne, 1915.

———. *La vie de Pythagore de Diogène Laërce.* Brussels: Académie royale de Belgique, 1922.

DelCogliano, Mark. "The Interpretation of John 10:30 in the Third Century: Antimonarchian Polemics and the Rise of Grammatical Reading Techniques." *JTI* 6 (2012): 117–38.

Denzey, Nicola. "What Did the Montanists Read?" *HTR* 94 (2001): 427–48.

———. "Bardaisan of Edessa." Pages 159–84 in *A Companion to Second-Century Christian "Heretics."* Edited by Antti Marjanen and Petri Luomanen. VCSup 76. Leiden: Brill, 2005.

Desrousseaux, A. M. "Sur quelques manuscrits d'Italie." *Mélanges d'archéologie et d'histoire* 6 (1886): 483–553.

Dölger, Franz Joseph. "Die Sphragis als religiöse Brandmarkung im Einweihungsakt der gnostischen Karpokratianer." Pages 73–78 in vol. 1 of *Antike und Christentum: Kultur- und religionsgeschichtliche Studien.* 2nd ed. 6 vols. Münster: Aschendorff, 1929.

———. *Sphragis: Eine altchristliche Taufbezeichnung in ihren Beziehungen zur profanen und religiösen Kultur des Altertums.* Paderborn: Ferdinand Schöningh, 1911.

Döllinger, J. J. Ignatius von. *Hippolytus and Callistus: or, The Church of Rome in the First Half of the Third Century.* Translated by Alfred Plummer. Edinburgh: T&T Clark, 1876.

———. *Hippolytus und Kallistus: Oder, Die römische Kirche in der ersten Hälfte des dritten Jahrhunderts.* Regensburg: G. J. Manz, 1853.

Dornseiff, Franz. *Das Alphabet in Mystik und Magie.* Leipzig: Teubner, 1922.

Dörrie, Heinrich, and Matthias Baltes. *Der Platonismus in der Antike: Grundlagen-System-Entwicklung.* 7 vols. Stuttgart: Bad Cannstatt, 1993.

Drew-Bear, Thomas, and Christian Naour. "Divinités de Phrygie." *ANRW* 18.3:2018–22.

Droge, Arthur J. "Homeric Exegesis among the Gnostics." *StPatr* 19 (1989): 313–21.

Dubois, Jean-Daniel. "Les pratiques eucharistiques de gnostiques valentiniens." Pages 255–66 in *Nourriture et repas dans les milieux juif et*

chrétiens de l'antiquité: Mélanges offerts au Professeur Charles Perrot. Paris: Cerf, 1999.

Ducoeur, Guillaume. *Brahmanisme et encratisme à Rome au IIIe siècle ap. J.C.* Paris: L'Harmattan, 2001.

———. "Les hérésiarques chrétiens à l'École des sages d'Orient?" Pages 167–88 in *Des évêques, des écoles et des hérétiques: Actes du colloque international sur la "Refutation de toutes les heresies" Genève, 13–14 juin 2008*. Edited by Gabriella Aragione and Enrico Norelli. Prahins: Éditions du Zèbre, 2011.

Dunderberg, Ismo. *Beyond Gnosticism: Myth, Lifestyle and Society in the School of Valentinus*. New York: Columbia University Press, 2008.

———. "Valentinian Teachers in Rome." Pages 157–74 in *Christians as a Religious Minority in a Multicultural City: Modes of Interaction and Identity Formation in Early Imperial Rome*. Edited by Jürgen Zangenberg and Michael Labahn. London: T&T Clark, 2004.

———. "Valentinus." Pages 64–99 in *A Companion to Second-Century Christian "Heretics."* Edited by Antti Marjanen and Petri Luomanen. VCSup 76. Leiden: Brill, 2005.

Düring, Ingemar. *Aristotle in the Ancient Biographical Tradition*. Göteborg: Almqvist & Wiksell, Stockholm, 1957.

Edwards, M. J. "Gnostic Eros and Orphic Themes." *ZPE* 88 (1991): 25–40.

———. "Gnostics and Valentinians in the Church Fathers." *JTS* 40 (1989): 26–47.

———. "Hippolytus of Rome on Aristotle." *Eranos* 88 (1990): 25–29.

Ehrman, Bart. *Forgery and Counterforgery: The Use of Literary Deceit in Early Christian Polemics*. Oxford: Oxford University Press, 2013.

Ellis, Peter Berresford. *The Druids*. London: Constable, 1994.

Eshleman, Kendra. *The Social World of Intellectuals in the Roman Empire: Sophists, Philosophers, and Christians*. Greek Culture in the Roman World. Cambridge: Cambridge University Press, 2012.

Faivre, Cécile, and Alexandre Faivre. "La place de la femme dans le ritual eucharistique des Marcosiens: Déviance ou archaïsme?" *RevScRel* 71 (1997): 310–28.

Fallon, Francis T. "The Gnostics: The Undominated Race." *NovT* 21 (1979): 271–88.

Fauth, Wolfgang. *Hekate Polymorphos—Wesensvarianten einer antiken Gottheit: Zwischen frühgriechischer Theogonie und spätantikem Synkretismus*. Hamburg: Dr. Kovač, 2006.

Foerster, Werner. *Gnosis: A Selection of Gnostic Texts*. Translated by R. McL. Wilson. 2 vols. Oxford: Clarendon, 1972.

———. "Die Naassener." Pages 21–33 in *Studi di storia religiosa della tarda antichità*. Messina: University of Messina, 1968.

———. "Das System des Basilides." *NTS* 9 (1963): 233–55.

Förster, Niclas. *Marcus Magus: Kult, Lehre und Gemeindeleben einer valentinianischen Gnostikergruppe; Sammlung der Quellen und Kommentar*. WUNT 114. Tübingen: Mohr Siebeck, 1999.

Franco, Cristiana. *Shameless: The Canine and the Feminine in Ancient Greece*. Translated by Matthew Fox. Berkeley: University of California Press, 2014.

Frickel, Josef. *Die "Apophasis Megale" in Hippolyt's Refutatio (VI 9–18): Eine Paraphrase zur Apophasis Simons*. Rome: Pontifical Institute of Oriental Studies, 1968.

———. *Das Dunkel um Hippolyt von Rom: Ein Lösungsversuch; Die Schriften Elenchos und Contra Noëtum*. Graz: Graz University Press, 1988.

———. *Hellenistische Erlösung in christlicher Deutung: Die gnostischen Naassenerschrift; Quellenkritische Studien, Strukturanalyse, Schichtenscheidung, Rekonstruction der Anthropos-Lehrschrift*. Leiden: Brill, 1984.

———. "Hippolyt von Rom: Refutatio, Buch X." Pages 217–44 in *Überlieferungsgeschichtliche Untersuchungen*. Edited by Franz Paschke. Berlin: Akademie, 1981.

———. "Ippolito di Roma Scrittore e Martire." Pages 23–41 in *Nuove ricerche su Ippolito*. SEAug 30. Rome: Augustinian Patristic Institute, 1989.

———. "Ein Kriterium zur Quellenscheidung innerhalb einer Paraphrase: Drei allegorische Deutungen der Paradiesflüsse *Gen* 2,10 (Hippolyt, *Ref.* VI 15–16); Sinn und Entwicklungsgeschichte." *Mus* 85 (1972): 425–504.

———. "Naassener oder Valentinianer?" Pages 95–119 in *Gnosis and Gnosticism: Papers Read at the Eighth International Conference on Patristic Studies (Oxford, September 3rd–8th 1979)*. Edited by Martin Krause. NHS 17. Leiden: Brill, 1981.

———. "Eine neue Deutung von Gen 1,26 in der Gnosis." Pages 413–23 in vol. 1 of *Ex orbe religionum: Studia Geo Widengren*. Edited by C. J. Bleeker, S. G. F. Brandon, and M. Simon. 2 vols. SHR 21–22. Leiden: Brill, 1972.

———. “Unerkannte gnostische Schriften im Hippolyts *Refutatio.*” Pages 119–37 in *Gnosis and Gnosticism: Papers Read at the Seventh International Conference on Patristic Studies.* Edited by Martin Krause. NHS 8. Leiden: Brill, 1977.

Gager, John G. “Marcion and Philosophy.” *VC* 26 (1972): 53–59.

Ganschinietz, Richard. *Hippolytos’ Capitel gegen die Magier: Refut. Haer. IV 28–42.* TU 39.2. Leipzig: Hinrichs, 1913.

Gärtner, Bertil E. *The Theology of the Gospel of Thomas.* New York: Harper, 1961.

Gerber, Simon. “Calixt von Rome und der monarchianische Streit.” *ZAC* 5 (2001): 213–39.

Gerson, Lloyd P. *Aristotle and Other Platonists.* Ithaca: Cornell University Press, 2005.

Gigante, Marcello. *L’ultima Tunica.* 2nd ed. Naples: Giannini, 1988.

Goodenough, E. R. *Jewish Symbols in the Greco-Roman Period.* 12 vols. Bollingen Series 37. New York: Pantheon, 1956.

Gordon, Richard. “Cosmology, Astrology, and Magic: Discourse, Schemes, Power, and Literacy.” Pages 85–111 in *Panthée: Religious Transformations in the Graeco-Roman Empire.* Edited by Laurent Bricault and Corinne Bonnet. RGRW 177. Leiden: Brill, 2013.

Grant, Robert M. *After the New Testament.* Philadelphia: Fortress, 1967.

———. “Notes on the Gospel of Thomas.” *VC* 13 (1959): 170–80.

Greschat, Katharina. *Apelles und Hermogenes: Zwei theologische Lehrer des zweiten Jahrhunderts.* VCSup 48. Leiden: Brill, 2000.

Guarducci, Margherita. *San Pietro e Sant’Ippolito: Storia di statue famose in Vaticano.* Rome: Istituto Poligrafico, 1991.

———. “La statua di ‘Sant’Ippolito.’” Pages 17–30 in *Ricerche su Ippolito.* SEAug 13. Rome: Augustinian Patristic Institute, 1977.

———. “La ‘Statua di Sant’Ippolito’ et la sua provenienza.” Pages 61–74 in *Nuove ricerche su Ippolito.* SEAug 30. Rome: Augustinian Patristic Institute, 1989.

Guffey, Andrew R. “Motivations for Enkratite Practices in Early Christian Literature.” *JTS* 65 (2014): 515–49.

Gülzow, Henneke. *Christentum und Sklaverei in den ersten drei Jahrhunderten.* Bonn: Rudolf Habelt, 1969.

Guthrie, W. K. C. *A History of Greek Philosophy.* 6 vols. Cambridge: Cambridge University Press, 1962–1981.

Haar, Stephen. *Simon Magus: The First Gnostic?* BZNW 119. Berlin: de Gruyter, 2003.

Haenchen, Ernst. “Gab es eine vorchristliche Gnosis?” *ZTK* 49 (1952): 316–49.

Haepern-Pourbaix, Agnès van. “Recherche sur les origines, la nature et les attributs du dieu Mên.” Pages 221–57 in *Archéologie et religions de l’Anatolie ancienne: Mélanges en l’honneur du professeur Paul Naster.* Edited by R. Donceel and R. Lebrun. Leuven: Centre d’histoire des Religions, 1983.

Hagedorn, Dieter. Review of *Hippolytus: Refutatio omnium haeresium*, ed. Miroslav Marcovich. *JAC* 32 (1989): 210–14.

Hahm, David. “The Fifth Element in Aristotle’s *De Philosophia*.” Pages 404–30 in vol. 2 of *Essays in Ancient Greek Philosophy*. Edited by John P. Anton and Anthony Preus. 6 vols. Albany: SUNY Press, 1983.

Häkkinen, Sakari. “Ebionites.” Pages 247–78 in *A Companion to Second-Century Christian “Heretics.”* Edited by Antti Marjanen and Petri Luomanen. VCSup 76. Leiden: Brill, 2005.

Hällström, Gunnar af, and Oskar Skarsaune. “Cerinthus, Elxai, and Other Alleged Jewish Christian Teachers or Groups.” Pages 488–95 in *Jewish Believers in Jesus*. Edited by Oskar Skarsaune and Reidar Hvalvik. Peabody, MA: Hendrickson, 2007.

Hamel, Adolf. *Kirche bei Hippolyt von Rom.* Gütersloh: Bertelsmann, 1951.

Hamilton, Ross. *Accident: A Philosophical and Literary History.* Chicago: University of Chicago Press, 2007.

Hancock, Curtis L. “Negative Theology in Gnosticism and Neoplatonism.” Pages 167–86 in *Neoplatonism and Gnosticism.* Edited by Richard T. Wallis and Jay Bregman. Albany: SUNY Press, 1992.

Hanig, Roman. “Der Beitrag der Philumene zur Theologie zur Apelles.” *ZAC* 3 (1999): 241–77.

Hanssens, J. M. “Hippolyte de Rome fut-il novatianiste? Essai d’une biographie.” *Archivum Historiae Pontificiae* 3 (1965): 7–29.

Harper, Kyle. *Slavery in the Late Roman World, AD 275–425.* Cambridge: Cambridge University Press, 2011.

Harris, J. R. *Lexicographical Studies in Ancient Egyptian Minerals.* Berlin: Akademie, 1961.

Hauschild, W.-D. “Christologie und Humanismus bei dem ‘Gnostiker’ Basilides.” *ZNW* 68 (1977): 67–92.

———. *Gottes Geist und der Mensch: Studien zur frühchristlichen Pneumatologie*. Munich: Kaiser, 1972.

Hegedus, Tim. *Early Christianity and Ancient Astrology.* Patristic Studies 6. New York: Lang, 2007.

Heine, Ronald E. "Christology of Callistus." *JTS* 49 (1998): 56–91.

———. "Hippolytus, Ps.-Hippolytus and the Early Canons." Pages 142–51 in *The Cambridge History of Early Christian Literature*. Edited by Frances Young, Lewis Ayres, and Andrew Louth. Cambridge: Cambridge University Press, 2004.

Hermann, Arnold. *To Think Like God: Pythagoras and Parmenides*. Las Vegas: Parmenides, 2004.

Herrero de Jáuregui, Miguel. *Orphism and Christianity in Late Antiquity*. Sozomena 7. Berlin: de Gruyter, 2010.

Hershbell, J. P. "Hippolytus' *Elenchos* as a Source for Empedocles Reexamined, I." *Phronesis* 18 (1973): 97–114.

———. "Hippolytus' *Elenchos* as a Source for Empedocles Reexamined, II." *Phronesis* 18 (1973): 187–203.

Herzhoff, B. *Zwei gnostische Psalmen: Interpretation und Untersuchung von Hippolytus, Refutatio V 10,2 und VI 37,7*. Diss., University of Bonn, 1973.

Hill, Charles E. "Cerinthus, Gnostic or Chiliast? A New Solution to an Old Problem." *JECS* 8 (2000): 135–72.

Hinson, E. Glenn. "Hippolytus and the Essenes." *StPatr* 18 (1989): 283–90.

Hoffmann, R. J. "The 'Eucharist' of Marcus Magus: A Test-Case in Gnostic Social Theory." *Patristic and Byzantine Review* 3 (1984): 82–88.

Holwerda, D. "Textkritisches zum Basilides-Referat des Hippolytos." *Mnemosyne* 56 (2003): 597–606.

Holzhausen, Jens. "Ein gnostischer Psalm? Zu Valentins Psalm in Hippol. ref. VI 37.7 (= frg. 8 Völker)." *JAC* 36 (1993): 67–80.

Hopfner, T. "Die Kindermedien in den griechisch-ägyptischen Zauberpapyri." Pages 65–74 in *Recueil d'études dédiées à la mémoire de N. P. Kondakov*. Prague: Seminarium Kondakovianum, 1926.

Horst, Pieter W. van der. "'The Elements Will Be Dissolved with Fire': The Idea of Cosmic Conflagration in Hellenism, Ancient Judaism and Early Christianity." Pages 227–51 in *Hellenism-Judaism-Christianity: Essays on Their Interaction*. Kampen: Kok Pharos, 1994.

Hübner, Reinhard M. *Der Paradox Eine: Antignostischer Monarchianismus im zweiten Jahrhundert*. VCSup 50. Leiden: Brill, 1999.

Inglebert, Hervé. *Interpretatio Christiana: Les mutations des saviors*. Paris: Institut d'Études Augustiniennes, 2001.

Irmscher, Johannes. "The Book of Elchasai." *NTApoc* 2:685–90.

Jacobson, Howard. "Miriam and St. Hippolytus." *VC* 62 (2008): 404–5.

Janáček, Karel. "Eine anonyme skeptische Schrift gegen die Astrologen." *Helikon* 4 (1964): 290–96.

———. "Hippolytus and Sextus Empiricus." *Listy Filologické* 82 (1959): 19–21.

Jeck, Udo Reinhold. *Platonica Orientalia: Aufdeckung einer philosophischen Tradition*. Frankfurt: Klostermann, 2004.

Johnson, Steven R. "Hippolytus's *Refutatio* and the Gospel of Thomas." *JECS* 18 (2010): 305–26.

Johnston, Sarah Iles. *Hekate Soteira: A Study of Hekate's Roles in the Chaldean Oracles and Related Literature*. Atlanta: Scholars Press, 1990.

Joncas, J. Michael. "Eucharist among the Marcosians: A Study of Irenaeus' *Adversus Haereses* I, 13:2." *Questions Liturgiques* 71 (1990): 99–111.

Jones, F. Stanley. *Pseudoclementina Elchasaiticaque inter Judaeochristiana: Collected Studies*. Leuven: Peeters, 2012.

Jong, Albert de. "Secrecy I: Antiquity." *DGWE* 1050–54.

———. *Traditions of the Magi: Zoroastrianism in Greek and Latin Literature*. RGRW 133. Leiden: Brill, 1997.

Jufresa, M. "Basilides, A Path to Plotinus." *VC* 35 (1981): 1–15.

Kaestli, Jean-Daniel. "Valentinisme italien et valentinisme oriental: Leurs divergences a propos de la nature du corps de Jesus." Pages 391–403 in vol. 1 of *The Rediscovery of Gnosticism: Proceedings of the International Conference on Gnosticism at Yale, New Haven, Connecticut, March 28–31, 1978*. Edited by Bentley Layton. 2 vols. SHR. Leiden: Brill, 1980–1981.

Kahn, Charles H. *Anaximander and the Origins of Greek Cosmology*. New York: Columbia University Press, 1960.

———. *The Art and Thought of Heraclitus: An Edition of the Fragments with Translation and Commentary*. Cambridge: Cambridge University Press, 1979.

———. *Pythagoras and the Pythagoreans: A Brief History*. Indianapolis: Hackett, 2001.

Kalvesmaki, Joel. "Italian versus Eastern Valentinianism?" *VC* 62 (2008): 79–89.

———. *The Theology of Arithmetic: Number Symbolism in Platonism and Early Christianity*. Hellenic Studies 59. Washington, DC: Center for Hellenic Studies, 2013.

Kelber, Wilhelm. *Die Logoslehre von Heraklit bis Origenes*. Stuttgart: Urachhaus, 1976.

Kelhoffer, James A. "'Hippolytus' and Magic: An Examination of *Elenchos* IV 28–42 and Related Passages in Light of the Papyri Graecae Magicae." *ZAC* 11 (2008): 517–48.

King, R. A. H. *Aristotle on Life and Death*. London: Duckworth, 2001.

Kingsley, Peter. *Ancient Philosophy, Mystery, and Magic: Empedocles and Pythagorean Tradition*. Oxford: Clarendon, 1995.

Kirk, G. S. *Heraclitus: The Cosmic Fragments*. Cambridge: Cambridge University Press, 1954.

Kirk, G. S., J. E. Raven, and M. Schofield. *The Presocratic Philosophers: A Critical History with a Selection of Texts*. 2nd ed. Cambridge: Cambridge University Press, 1983.

Klijn, A. F. J., and G. J. Reinink. *Patristic Evidence for Jewish-Christian Sects*. NovTSup 36. Leiden: Brill, 1973.

Klowski, Joachim. "Ist der Aer des Anaximenes als ein Substanz konkipiert?" *Hermes* 100 (1972): 131–42.

Koschorke, Klaus. *Hippolyt's Ketzerbekämpfung und Polemik gegen die Gnostiker: Eine tendenzkritische Untersuchung seiner "Refutatio omnium haeresium."* Wiesbaden: Harrassowitz, 1975.

Kosman, Aryeh. "*Metaphysics* Λ 9: Divine Thought." Pages 307–26 in *Aristotle's "Metaphysics" Lambda: Symposium Aristotelicum*. Edited by Michael Fred and David Charles. Oxford: Clarendon, 2000.

Koster, W. J. W. "Chaldäer." *RAC* 2:1006–21.

Kraemer, Ross Shepard. *Her Share of Blessings: Women's Religions among Pagans, Jews, and Christians in the Greco-Roman World*. New York: Oxford, 1992.

Krämer, Hans Joachim. *Der Ursprung der Geistmetaphysik*. Amsterdam: B. R. Grüner, 1967.

Kroll, Wilhelm, and Alexander Olivieri, eds. *Catalogus codicum astrologorum Graecorum*. 12 vols. Brussels: Lamertin, 1898–1936.

Kucharski, Paul. *Étude sur la doctrine pythagoricienne de la Tétrade*. Paris: Belles Lettres, 1952.

Lampe, Peter. *From Paul to Valentinus: Christians at Rome in the First Two Centuries*. Edited by Marshall Johnson. Translated by Michael Steinhauser. Minneapolis: Fortress, 2003.

Lancellotti, Maria Grazia. *Attis: Between Myth and History; King, Priest and God*. RGRW 149. Leiden: Brill, 2002.

———. "Gli gnostici e il cielo: Dottrine astrologiche e reinterpretazioni gnostiche." *SMSR* 66 (2000): 71–108.

———. *The Naassenes: A Gnostic Identity among Judaism, Christianity, Classical and Ancient Near Eastern Traditions*. FARG 35. Münster: Ugarit-Verlag, 2000.

———. "I Perati, un esempio di cosmologia gnostica." Pages 131–56 in *Cartografia religiosa: Religiöse Kartographie, Cartographie religieuse*. Edited by Daria Pezzoli-Olgiati and Fritz Stolz. Studia Religiosa Helvetica 4. Bern: Lang, 2000.

Lang, B. "No Sex in Heaven: The Logic of Procreation, Death, and Eternal Life in the Judaeo-Christian Tradition." Pages 237–53 in *Mélanges bibliques et orientaux en l'honneur de M. Mathias Delcor*. Edited by A. Caquot, S. Légasse, and M. Tardieu. Neukirchen-Vluyn: Neukirchener, 1985.

Layton, Bentley. "The Significance of Basilides in Ancient Christian Thought." *Representations* 28 (1989): 135–51.

Lebedev, A. V. "Orpheus, Parmenides or Empedocles? The Aphrodite Verses in the Naassene Treatise of Hippolytus' *Elenchos*." *Phil* 138 (1994): 24–31.

Le Boeuffle, André. "Autour du Dragon, astronomie et mythologie." Pages 53–68 in vol. 1 of *Les Astres: Actes du Colloque International de Montpellier, I–II*. Edited by Béatrice Bakhouche, Alain Maurice Moreau, and Jean-Claude Turpin. 2 vols. Montpellier: Paul Valéry University Press, 1996.

Le Boulluec, Alain. *La notion d'hérésie dans la literature grecque, IIe-IIIe siècles*. 2 vols. Paris: Études augustiniennes, 1985.

Leclercq, H. "Alphabet vocalique des Gnostiques." Pages 1268–88 in vol. 1 of *Dictionnaire d'archéologie chrétienne et de liturgie*. 15 vols. Paris: Librairi Letouzey et Anê, 1907–1924.

Leisegang, Hans. *Die Gnosis*. 5th ed. Stuttgart: Alfred Kröner, 1985.

Lipsius, R. A. *Die Quellen der ältesten Ketzergeschichte neu untersucht*. Leipzig: J. A. Barth, 1875.

———. "Valentinus und seine Schule." *Jahrbücher für protestantischen Theologie* 13 (1887): 585–658.

Litwa, M. David. "The God 'Human' and Human Gods: Models of Deification in Irenaeus and the *Apocryphon of John*." *ZAC* 18 (2014): 70–94.

Löhr, Winrich. *Basilides und seine Schule: Eine Studie zur Theologie- und Kirchengeschichte des zweiten Jahrhunderts*. WUNT 83. Tübingen: Mohr Siebeck, 1996.

———. "Christliche 'Gnostiker' in Alexandria im zweiten Jahrhundert." Pages 418–30 in *Alexandria*. Edited by Tobias Georges. Civitatum Orbis Mediterranei Studia 1. Tübingen: Mohr Siebeck, 2013.

———. "The Continuing Construction of Heresy: Hippolyt's Refutatio in Context." Pages 25–42 in *Des évêques, des écoles et des hérétiques: Actes du colloque international sur la "Refutation de toutes les heresies" Genève, 13–14 juin 2008*. Edited by Gabriella Aragione and Enrico Norelli. Prahins: Éditions du Zèbre, 2011.

———. "Did Marcion Distinguish between a Just God and a Good God?" Pages 131–46 in *Marcion und seine kirchengeschichtliche Wirkung / Marcion and His Impact on Church History: Vorträge der Internationalen Fachkonferenz zu Marcion, gehalten vom. 15.–18. August 2001 in Mainz*. Edited by Gerhard May and Katharina Greschat. Berlin: de Gruyter, 2002.

———. "Karpokratianisches." *VC* 49 (1995): 23–48.

———. "Satorninus." *BNP* 13:19.

———. "Sethians." *DGWE* 1066.

Loi, Vincenzo. "L'identità letteraria di Ippolito di Roma." Pages 67–88 in *Ricerche su Ippolito*. SEAug 13. Rome: Augustinian Patristic Institute, 1977.

———. "La Problematica storico-letteraria su Ippolito di Roma." Pages 9–16 in *Ricerche su Ippolito*. SEAug 13. Rome: Augustinian Patristic Institute, 1977.

Long, A. A. "Astrology: Arguments pro and contra." Pages 165–92 in *Science and Speculation: Studies in Hellenistic Theory and Practice*. Edited by Jonathan Barnes, Jacques Brunschwig, Myles Burnyeat, and Malcolm Schofield. Cambridge: Cambridge University Press, 1982.

———. "The Stoics on World-Conflagration and Everlasting Recurrence." Pages 256–82 in *From Epicurus to Epictetus: Studies in Hellenistic and Roman Philosophy*. Edited by A. A. Long. Oxford: Clarendon, 2006.

Longo, Angela. "Empedocle e l'allegoria nella Confutazione di tutte le eresie attribuita a Ippolito di Roma." Pages 119–34 in *Des évêques, des écoles et des hérétiques: Actes du colloque international sur la "Refutation de toutes les heresies" Genève, 13–14 juin 2008*. Edited by Gabriella Aragione and Enrico Norelli. Prahins: Éditions du Zèbre, 2011.

Lüdemann, Gerd. *Untersuchungen zur simonianischen Gnosis*. Göttingen: Vandenhoeck & Ruprecht, 1975.

Luttikhuizen, Gerard. "The Book of Elchasai: A Jewish Apocalyptic Writing, Not a Christian Church Order." Pages 405–25 in *Society of Biblical*

Literature 1999 Seminar Papers. SBLSP 38. Atlanta: Society of Biblical Literature, 1999.

———. "The Elchasaites and Their Book." Pages 335–64 in *A Companion to Second-Century Christian "Heretics."* Edited by Antti Marjanen and Petri Luomanen. VCSup 76. Leiden: Brill, 2005.

———. *The Revelation of Elchasai: Investigations into the Evidence for a Mesopotamian Jewish Apocalypse of the Second Century and Its Reception by Judeo-Christian Propagandists*. TSAJ 8. Tübingen: Mohr Siebeck, 1985.

Lutz, Cora. "Democritus and Heraclitus." *CJ* 49 (1953–1954): 309–14.

Macrae, George W. "The Jewish Background of the Gnostic Sophia Myth." *NovT* 12 (1970): 86–101.

Magri, Annarita. "L'esegesi della setta ofitica dei Perati." *Apocrypha* 14 (2003): 193–223.

———. "Il nome dei Perati." *Orpheus* 28 (2007): 138–61.

Malley, W. J. "Four Unedited Fragments of the *De Universo* of the Pseudo-Josephus Found in the *Chronicon* of George Hamartolus (Coislin 305)." *JTS* 16 (1965): 13–25.

Mansfeld, Jaap. "Bad World and Demiurge: A 'Gnostic' Motif from Parmenides and Empedocles to Lucretius and Philo." Pages 261–314 in *Studies in Gnosticism and Hellenistic Religions: Festschrift für Gilles Quispel*. Edited by R. van den Broek and M. J. Vermaseren. EPRO 91. Leiden: Brill, 1981.

———. "Heraclitus Fr. B 63 D.-K." Pages 197–205 in *Studies in Later Greek Philosophy and Gnosticism*. London: Variorum, 1989.

———. *Heresiography in Context: Hippolytus' Elenchos as a Source for Greek Philosophy*. PhA 56. Leiden: Brill, 1992.

———. "Resurrection Added: The *Interpretatio christiana* of a Stoic Doctrine." *VC* 37 (1983): 218–33.

Marcovich, Miroslav. *Heraclitus: Greek Text with a Short Commentary*. Mérida: Los Andes University Press, 1967.

———. "Hippolytus and Heraclitus." *StPatr* 7 (1966): 255–64.

———. "Hippolytus Plagiarizes the Gnostics." Pages 587–92 in vol. 2 of *Athlon: Satura Grammatica in honorem Francisci R. Adrados*. Edited by P. Bádenas de la Peña. 2 vols. Madrid: Editorial Gredos, 1987.

———. "Plato and Stoa in Hippolytus' Theology." *ICS* 11 (1983): 265–69.

———. "Platonism and the Church Fathers." Pages 189–203 in *Platonism in Late Antiquity*. Edited by Stephen Gersh and Charles Kannengiesser. Notre Dame: University of Notre Dame Press, 1992.

———. "Pythagorica." *Phil* 108 (1964): 29–44.

———. "*Refutatio*, X.33.9 (p 290: 9–15 Wendland) Again." *JTS* 24 (1973): 195–96.

———. *Studies in Graeco-Roman Religions and Gnosticism*. Leiden: Brill, 1988.

Marjanen, Antti. "Montanism: Egalitarian Ecstatic 'New Prophecy.'" Pages 185–212 in *A Companion to Second-Century Christian "Heretics."* Edited by Antti Marjanen and Petri Luomanen. VCSup 76. Leiden: Brill, 2005.

———. *The Woman Jesus Loved*. NHMS 40. Leiden: Brill, 1996.

Marjanen, Antti, and Petri Luomanen, eds. *A Companion to Second-Century Christian "Heretics."* VCSup 76. Leiden: Brill, 2005.

Markschies, Christoph. "Kerinth: Wer war er und was lehrte er?" *JAC* 41 (1998): 48–76.

———. "Montanismus." *RAC* 24:1198–220.

———. "Platons König oder Vater Jesu Christi? Drei Beispiele für die Rezeption eines griechischen Gottesepithetons bei den Christen in den ersten Jahrhunderten und deren Vorgeschichte." Pages 385–439 in *Königsherrschaft Gottes und himmlischer Kult im Judentum, Urchristentum und in der hellenistischen Welt*. Edited by Martin Hengel and Anna Maria Schwemer. WUNT 55. Tübingen: Mohr Siebeck, 1991.

———. "Valentinian Gnosticism." Pages 432–36 in *The Nag Hammadi Library after Fifty Years: Proceedings of the 1995 Society of Biblical Literature Commemoration*. Edited by John D. Turner and Anne McGuire. Leiden: Brill, 1997.

———. *Valentinus Gnosticus: Untersuchungen zur valentinianischen Gnosis mit einem Kommentar zu den Fragmenten Valentins*. WUNT 65. Tübingen: Mohr Siebeck, 1992.

Mason, Steve, ed., *Judean War 2*. Vol. 1B of *Flavius Josephus: Translation and Commentary*. Leiden: Brill, 2008.

May, Gerhard. *Creatio ex nihilo: The Doctrine of 'Creation out of Nothing' in Early Christian Thought*. Translated by A. S. Worrall. London: T&T Clark, 1994.

———. "Marcion in Contemporary Views: Results and Open Questions." Pages 13–33 in *Markion: Gesammelte Aufsätze*. Edited by Katharina Greschat and Martin Meiser. Mainz: Philipp von Zabern, 2005.

———. "Markions Genesisauslegung und die 'Antithesen.'" Pages 43–50 in *Markion: Gesammelte Aufsätze*. Edited by Katharina Greschat and Martin Meiser. Mainz: Philipp von Zabern, 2005.

———. “Markion und der Gnostiker Kerdon.” Pages 63–74 in *Markion: Gesammelte Aufsätze.* Edited by Katharina Greschat and Martin Meiser. Mainz: Philipp von Zabern, 2005.

McGowan, Andrew. *Ascetic Eucharists: Food and Drink in Early Christian Ritual Meals.* Oxford: Clarendon, 1999.

———. “Valentinus Poeta: Notes on Θέρος.” *VC* 51 (1997): 158–78.

Méhat, André. “ΑΠΟΚΑΤΑΣΤΑΣΙΣ chez Basilide.” Pages 365–73 in *Mélanges d'histoire des religions offerts à Henri-Charles Puech.* Paris: Presses Universitaires de France, 1974.

Mejer, Jørgen. *Diogenes Laertius and His Hellenistic Background.* Wiesbaden: Franz Steiner, 1978.

Menn, Stephen. “The Origins of Aristotle's Concept of Ἐνέργεια: Ἐνέργεια and Δύναμις.” *Ancient Philosophy* 14 (1994): 73–114.

Meyer, Marvin, and Willis Barnstone. *The Gnostic Bible.* Boston: Shambhala, 2003.

Miles, Margaret. *The City Eleusinion.* Princeton: American School of Classical Studies, 1998.

Mimouni, Simon Claude. “Les elkasaïtes: États des questions et des recherches.” Pages 209–29 in *The Image of the Judaeo-Christians in Ancient Jewish and Christian Literature: Papers Delivered at the Colloquium of the Institutum Iudaicum, Brussels 18–19 November, 2001.* Edited by Peter J. Tomson and Doris Lambers-Petry. WUNT 158. Tübingen: Mohr Siebeck, 2003.

———. *Le judéo-christianisme ancien: Essays historiques.* Paris: Cerf, 1998.

———. “Un ritual ‘mystérique’ des baptistes judéo-chrétiens des premiers siècles de notre ère?” Pages 55–74 in *Expérience et écriture mystiques dans les religions du livre: Actes d'un colloque international tenu par le Centre d'études juives Université de Paris IV-Sorbonne 1994.* Edited by Paul B. Fenton and Roland Goetschel. Leiden: Brill, 2000.

Moll, Sebastian. *The Arch-Heretic Marcion.* WUNT 250. Tübingen: Mohr Siebeck, 2010.

Montserrat-Torrents, J. “La notice d'Hippolyte sur les Naassènes.” *StPatr* 17 (1982): 231–42.

———. “Les Pérates.” *Comp* 34 (1989): 185–98.

———. “La philosophie du *Livre de Baruch* de Justin.” *StPatr* 18 (1985): 253–61.

Moreschini, Claudio. “La *Doxa* di Platone nella *Refutatio* di Ippolito (I 19).” *SCO* 21 (1972): 254–60.

Moreschini, Claudio, and Enrico Norelli. *Early Christian Greek and Latin Literature: A Literary History.* Translated by Matthew J. O'Connell. 2 vols. Peabody, MA: Hendrickson, 2005.

Mouraviev, Serge N. "Hippolyte, Héraclite et Noët (Commentaire d'Hippolyte, Refut. omn. haer. IX 8–10)." *ANRW* 36.6:4375–402.

Mueller, Ian. "Heterodoxy and Doxography in Hippolytus' 'Refutation of All Heresies.'" *ANRW* 36.6:4309–74.

———. "Hippolytus, Aristotle, Basilides." Pages 143–57 in *Aristotle in Late Antiquity.* Edited by Lawrence P. Schrenk. Studies in Philosophy and the History of Philosophy 27. Washington, DC: Catholic University of America Press, 1994.

———. "Hippolytus *Retractatus*: A Discussion of Catherine Osborne, *Rethinking Early Greek Philosophy.*" *Oxford Studies in Ancient Philosophy* 7 (1989): 233–51.

Mühl, M. "Der λόγος ἐνδιάθετος und προφορικός von der älteren Stoa bis zur Synode von Sirmium 351." *Archiv für Begriffsgeschichte* 7 (1962): 9–12.

Mühlenberg, Ekkehard. "Marcion's Jealous God." Pages 93–113 in *Disciplina nostra: Essays in Memory of Robert F. Evans.* Edited by D. F. Winslow. Cambridge, MA: Philadelphia Patristic Foundation, 1979.

———. "Wirklichkeitserfahrung und Theologie bei dem Gnostiker Basilides." *KD* 18 (1972): 161–75.

Müller, Mogens. *The Expression 'Son of Man' and the Development of Christology: A History of Interpretation.* Sheffield: Equinox, 2008.

Munck, J. "Paulus tamquam abortivus (1 Cor. 15:8)." Pages 180–93 in *New Testament Essays: Studies in Memory of Thomas Walter Manson.* Edited by A. J. B. Higgins. Manchester: Manchester University Press, 1959.

Myllykoski, Matti. "Cerinthus." Pages 211–46 in *A Companion to Second-Century Christian "Heretics."* Edited by Antti Marjanen and Petri Luomanen. VCSup 76. Leiden: Brill, 2005.

Nautin, Pierre. *Le dossier d'Hippolyte et de Méliton dans les florilèges dogmatiques et chez les historiens modernes.* Paris: Cerf, 1953.

———. *Hippolyte contre les heresies.* Paris: Cerf, 1949.

———. *Hippolyte et Josipe: Contribution à l'histoire de la literature chrétiennes du troisième siècle.* Paris: Cerf, 1947.

Nesselrath, Heinz-Günther. "Zur Verwendung des Begriffes μῦθος bei Sokrates von Konstantinopel und anderen christlichen Autoren der Spätantike." Pages 293–301 in *Alvarium: Festschift für Christian Gnilka.* Edited by W. Blümer, R. Heke, and M. Mülke. Münster: Aschendorffsche, 2002.

Nicolotti, Andrea. "A Cure for Rabies or a Remedy for Concupiscence? A Baptism of the Elchasaites." *JECS* 16 (2008): 518–34.

Nock, A. D. "Iranian Influences in Greek Thought." Pages 195–201 in vol. 1 of *Essays on Religion and the Ancient World*. Edited by Zeph Stewart. 2 vols. Cambridge: Harvard University Press, 1972.

———. "Korybas of the Haemonians." *ClQ* 20 (1926): 41–42.

Norelli, Enrico. "Construire l'opposition entre orthodoxie et hérésie à Rome, au IIIe siècle." Pages 233–55 in *Des évêques, des écoles et des hérétiques: Actes du colloque international sur la "Refutation de toutes les heresies" Genève, 13–14 juin 2008*. Edited by Gabriella Aragione and Enrico Norelli. Prahins: Éditions du Zèbre, 2011.

North, J. L. "ΜΑΡΚΟΣ Ο ΚΟΛΟΒΟΔΑΚΤΥΛΟΣ: Hippolytus, *Elenchus*, 7.30." *JTS* 28 (1977): 498–507.

North, John. "Power and Its Redefinitions: The Vicissitudes of Attis." Pages 279–93 in *Panthée: Religious Transformations in the Graeco-Roman Empire*. Edited by Laurent Bricault and Corinne Bonnet. RGRW 177. Leiden: Brill, 2013.

O'Brien, D. *Empedocles' Cosmic Cycle*. Cambridge: Cambridge University Press, 1969.

———. *Pour interpréter Empédocle*. Paris: Belles Lettres; Leiden: Brill, 1981.

Ogden, Daniel. *Greek and Roman Necromancy*. Princeton: Princeton University Press, 2011.

———. "Magic in the Severan Period." Pages 458–69 in *Severan Culture*. Edited by Simon Swain, Stephen Harrison, and Jaś Elsner. Cambridge: Cambridge University Press, 2007.

Olender, Maurice. "Éléments pour une analyse de Priape chez Justin le Gnostique." Pages 874–97 in vol. 2 of *Hommages à Maarten J. Vermaseren*. Edited by Margreet B. de Boer and T. A. Edridge. EPRO 68. 3 vols. Leiden: Brill, 1978.

Orbe, Antonio. *Cristología Gnóstica: Introducción a la soteriología de los siglos II y III*. 2 vols. Madrid: La Editorial Catolica, 1976.

Osborne, Catherine. *Rethinking Early Greek Philosophy: Hippolytus of Rome and the Presocratics*. London: Duckworth, 1987.

Pagels, Elaine. "A Valentinian Interpretation of Baptism and the Eucharist." *HTR* 65 (1972): 153–69.

Paget, James Carleton. *Jews, Christians and Jewish Christians in Antiquity*. WUNT 251. Tübingen: Mohr Siebeck, 2010.

Parker, Robert. *Athenian Religion: A History*. Oxford: Clarendon, 1996.

———. *Polytheism and Society at Athens*. Oxford: Oxford University Press, 2005.

Pastorelli, David. "La Paraclet dans la notice antimontaniste du Pseudo-Hippolyte, *Refutatio omnium haeresium* VIII,19." *VC* (2008): 261–84.

———. Pearson, Birger A. *Ancient Gnosticism: Traditions and Literature*. Minneapolis: Fortress, 2007.

"Basilides the Gnostic." Pages 1–31 in *A Companion to Second-Century Christian "Heretics."* Edited by Antti Marjanen and Petri Luomanen. VCSup 76. Leiden: Brill, 2005.

Pender, E. E. "Chaos Corrected: Hesiod in Plato's Creation Myth." Pages 219–45 in *Plato and Hesiod*. Edited by G. R. Boys-Stones and J. H. Haubold. Oxford: Oxford University Press, 2010.

Pépin, Jean. *Idées grecque sur l'homme et sur dieu*. Paris: Belles Lettres, 1971.

Perkins, Pheme. "Sophia as Goddess in the Nag Hammadi Codices." Pages 96–112 in *Images of the Feminine in Gnosticism*. Edited by Karen King. SAC. Fortress: Philadelphia, 1988.

Petersen, Silke. *"Zerstört die Werke der Weiblichkeit!" Maria Magdalena, Salome und andere Jüngerinnen Jesu in christlich-gnostischen Schriften*. NHMS 48. Leiden: Brill, 1999.

Petersen, William L. "Tatian the Assyrian." Pages 125–58 in *A Companion to Second-Century Christian "Heretics."* Edited by Antti Marjanen and Petri Luomanen. VCSup 76. Leiden: Brill, 2005.

Pétrement, Simone. "Le mythe des sept archontes créateurs peut-il s'expliquer à partir du Christianisme." Pages 460–87 in *Le Origini dello Gnosticismo, Colloquio Messina 13–18 Aprile 1966*. Edited by Ugo Bianchi. Leiden: Brill, 1970.

———. *A Separate God: The Christian Origins of Gnosticism*. Translated by Carol Harrison. New York: HarperSanFrancisco, 1984.

Pilhofer, Peter. *Presbyteron Kreitton: Der Altersbeweis der jüdischen und christlichen Apologeten und seine Vorgeschichte*. WUNT 2/39. Tübingen: Mohr Siebeck, 1990.

Pleše, Zlatko. "Gnostic Literature." Pages 163–98 in *Religiöse Philosophie und philosophischen Religion der frühen Kaiserzeit: Literaturgeschichtliche Perspektiven*. Edited by Rainer Hirsch-Luipold, Herwig Görgemanns, and Michael von Albrecht. Tübingen: Mohr Siebeck, 2010.

Polansky, Ronald. *Aristotle's "De anima."* Cambridge: Cambridge University Press, 2007.

Pouderon, Bernard. "Hippolyte, un regard sur l'hérésie entre tradition et invention." Pages 43–71 in *Des évêques, des écoles et des hérétiques:*

Actes du colloque international sur la "Refutation de toutes les heresies" Genève, 13–14 juin 2008. Edited by Gabriella Aragione and Enrico Norelli. Prahins: Éditions du Zèbre, 2011.
———. "L'influence d'Aristote dans la doctrine de la procréation des premiers pères et ses implications Théologiques." Pages 157–83 in *L'embryon: Formation et animation; Antiquité grecque et latine tradition hébraïque, chrétiennes et islamique*. Edited by Luc Brisson, Marie-Hélène Congourdeau, and Jean-Luc Solère. Paris: J. Vrin, 2008.
———. "La notice d'Hippolyte sur Simon: Cosmologie, anthropologie et embryologie." Pages 49–71 in *Les pères de l'Église face à la science médicale de leur temps*. Edited by Véronique Boudon-Millot and Bernard Pouderon. ThH 117. Paris: Beauchesne, 2005.
Preysing, Konrad Graf. "'Δίθεοί ἐστε': (Hippolyt, Philos. IX 12,16)." *ZKT* 50 (1926): 604–8.
———. "Existenz und Inhalt des Bußediktes Kallists." *ZKT* 43 (1919): 358–62.
———. "Der Leserkreis der Philosophumena Hippolyts." *ZKT* 38 (1914): 421–45.
Prinzivalli, E. "Eresia ed eretici nel corpus Ippolitiano." *Aug* 25 (1985): 711–22.
Puech, Henri-Charles. "La Gnose et le temps." Pages 215–70 in vol. 1 of *En quête de la Gnose*: *La Gnose et le temps et autres essais*. 2 vols. Paris: Gallimard, 1978.
Quispel, Gilles. "Gnostic Man: The Doctrine of Basilides." Pages 210–46 in *The Mystic Vision: Papers from the Eranos Yearbooks*. Edited by Joseph Campbell. Princeton: Princeton University Press, 1968.
———. "Note sur Basilide." *VC* 2 (1948): 115–16.
Rahner, Hugo. "Antenna Crucis I: Odysseus am Mastbaum." *ZKT* 65 (1941): 123–52.
———. *Griechische Mythen in christlicher Deutung*. Zürich: Rhein, 1957.
Räisänen, Heikki. "The Nicolaitans: Apoc. 2; Acta 6." *ANRW* 26.2:1602–44.
Ramelli, Ilaria L. E. *Bardaisan of Edessa: A Reassessment of the Evidence and a New Interpretation*. Piscataway: Gorgias, 2009.
Ramnoux, Clémence. *Études présocratiques*. Paris: Klincksieck, 1970.
Rasimus, Tuomas. *Paradise Reconsidered in Gnostic Mythmaking: Rethinking Sethianism in Light of the Ophite Evidence*. NHMS 68. Leiden: Brill, 2009.

Reiling, J. "Marcus Gnosticus and the New Testament: Eucharist and Prophecy." Pages 161–79 in *Miscellanea Neotestamentica*. Edited by T. Baarda, A. F. J. Klijn, and W. C. van Unnik. 2 vols. Leiden: Brill, 1978.

Reinhardt, Karl. "Heraklits Lehre vom Feuer." *Hermes* 77 (1942): 1–27.

Reinink, G. J. "Das Land 'Seiris' (Šir) und das Volk der Serer in jüdischen und christlichen Traditionen." *JSJ* 6 (1975): 72–85.

Reitzenstein, Richard. *Poimandres: Studien zur griechisch-ägyptischen und frühchristlichen Literature*. Leipzig: Teubner, 1904.

Reitzenstein, Richard, and H. H. Schaeder. *Studien zum antiken Synkretismus aus Iran und Griechenland*. Leipzig: Teubner, 1926.

Richard, Marcel. "Les difficulties d'une edition des oeuvres de S. Hippolyte." *StPatr* 12 (1975): 51–70.

———. "Hippolyte de Rome (saint)." Pages 531–71 in vol. 7.1 of *Dictionnaire de Spiritualité*. Paris: Beauchesne, 1968.

Robinson, T. M. *Heraclitus Fragments: A Text and Translation with a Commentary*. Phoenix Supplementary Volumes 22. Toronto: University of Toronto Press, 1991.

Roeper, G. "Emendationsversuche zu Hippolyti Philosophumena." *Phil* 7 (1852): 511–53.

Roller, Lynn E. *In Search of God the Mother: The Cult of Anatolian Cybele*. Berkeley: University of California Press, 1999.

Roscoe, Will. "Priests of the Goddess: Gender Transgression in Ancient Religion." *HR* 35 (1996): 195–230.

Rota, Gualtiero. "Alcune osservazioni sull'interpretazione dei *μυστήρια* nel *Salmo dei Naasseni sull'anima* (Hipp. *haer.* 5,10,2)." *Vetera Christianorum* 41 (2004): 107–19.

Runia, David. "What Is Doxography?" Pages 33–55 in *Ancient Histories of Medicine: Essays in Medical Doxography and Historiography in Classical Antiquity*. Edited by Philip J. van der Eijk. Studies in Ancient Medicine 20. Leiden: Brill, 1999.

———. "Witness or Participant? Philo and the Neoplatonic Tradition." Pages 36–56 in *The Neoplatonic Tradition: Jewish, Christian and Islamic Themes*. Edited by A. Vanderjagt and D. Pätzold. Köln: Dinter, 1991.

Russell, Norman. *The Doctrine of Deification in the Greek Patristic Tradition*. Oxford: Oxford University Press, 2004.

Sagnard, François L. M. M. *La gnose valentinienne et la témoignage de saint Irénée*. Paris: J. Vrin, 1947.

Salles-Dabadie, J. M. A. *Recherches sur Simon le mage: L'«Apophasis megalè.»* Paris: Gabalda, 1969.

Salmon, George. "The Cross-References in the 'Philosophumena.'" *Herm* 5 (1885): 389–402.

———. "Docetae." *DCB* 1:865–67.

———. "Hippolytus Romanus." *DCB* 3:85–105.

———. "Monoimus." *DCB* 3:934–35.

———. "Ophites." *DCB* 4:80–88.

Sandmel, Samuel. "Parallelomania." *JBL* 81 (1962): 1–13.

Santer, Mark. "Hippolytus: Refutatio omnium haeresium X.33.9." *JTS* 24 (1973): 194–95.

Saxer, V. "La questione di Ippolito romano: A proposito di un libro recente." Pages 43–60 in *Nuove ricerche su Ippolito*. SEAug 30. Rome: Augustinian Patristic Institute, 1989.

Schäfer, Peter. *Judeophobia: Attitudes toward the Jews in the Ancient World*. Cambridge: Harvard University Press, 1997.

Schenke, Hans-Martin. *Der Gott "Mensch" in der Gnosis*. Göttingen: Vandenhoeck & Ruprecht, 1962.

Schickert, Katharina. *Der Schutz literarischer Urheberschaft im Rom der klassischen Antike*. Tübingen: Mohr Siebeck, 2005.

Schmid, Herbert. *Die Eucharistie ist Jesus: Anfänger einer Theorie des Sakraments im koptischen Philippusevangelium (*NHC *II 3)*. VCSup 88. Leiden: Brill, 2007.

Schneidewin, F. G. "Hymnorum in Attin fragmenta inedita." *Phil* 3 (1848): 247–66.

Scholten, Clemens. "Autor, Anliegen und Publikum der Refutatio." Pages 135–66 in *Des évêques, des écoles et des hérétiques: Actes du colloque international sur la "Refutation de toutes les heresies" Genève, 13–14 juin 2008*. Edited by Gabriella Aragione and Enrico Norelli. Prahins: Éditions du Zèbre, 2011.

———. "Quellen regen an: Beobachtungen zum 'gnostischen Sondergut' der *Refutatio omnium haeresium*." Pages 567–92 in *"In Search of Truth": Augustine, Manichaeism and Other Gnosticism; Studies for Johannes van Oort at Sixty*. Edited by Jacob Albert van den Berg, Annemaré Kotzé, Tobias Nicklas, and Madeleine Scopello. NHMS 74. Leiden: Brill, 2011.

———. "Der Titel von Hippolyts *Refutatio*." *StPatr* 31 (1997): 343–48.

Schuddeboom, Feyo L. *Greek Religious Terminology: Telete and Orgia; A Revised and Expanded English Edition of the Studies by Zijderveld and Van der Burg*. RGRW 169. Leiden: Brill, 2009.

Schwabl, Hans. "Zeus I: Epiklesen." *RE* 10.1:253–376.

Secord, Jared. "Medicine and Sophistry in Hippolytus' *Refutatio*." *StPatr* 65 (2013): 217–24.

Sedlar, Jean W. *India and the Greek World: A Study in the Transmission of Culture*. Totowa, NJ: Rowman & Littlefield, 1980.

Sfameni Gasparro, Giulia. "I rischi dell'Hellenismòs: Astrologia ed eresia nella *Refutatio omnium haeresium*." Pages 189–218 in *Des évêques, des écoles et des hérétiques: Actes du colloque international sur la "Refutation de toutes les heresies" Genève, 13–14 juin 2008*. Edited by Gabriella Aragione and Enrico Norelli. Prahins: Éditions du Zèbre, 2011.

Sharples, Robert W. "Aristotelian Theology after Aristotle." Pages 1–40 in *Traditions of Theology: Studies in Hellenistic Theology, Its Background and Aftermath*. Edited by Dorothea Frede and André Laks. Leiden: Brill, 2002.

———. "Counting Plato's Principles." Pages 67–82 in *The Passionate Intellect: Essays on the Transformation of Classical Traditions Presented to Professor I. G. Kidd*. Edited by Lewis Ayres. New Brunswick, NJ: Transaction, 1995.

———. *Peripatetic Philosophy 200 BC to AD 200: An Introduction and Collection of Sources in Translation*. Cambridge: Cambridge University Press, 2010.

———. "Peripatetics on Fate and Providence." Pages 595–606 in vol. 2 of *Greek and Roman Philosophy 100 BC–200 AD*. Edited by Robert W. Sharples and Richard Sorabji. 2 vols. London: Institute of Classical Studies, 2007.

———. "Peripatetics on Happiness." Pages 627–38 in vol. 2 of *Greek and Roman Philosophy 100 BC – 200 AD*. Edited by Robert W. Sharples and Richard Sorabji. 2 vols. London: Institute of Classical Studies, 2007.

———. "Peripatetics on Soul and Intellect." Pages 607–20 in vol. 2 of *Greek and Roman Philosophy 100 BC–200 AD*. Edited by Robert W. Sharples and Richard Sorabji. 2 vols. London: Institute of Classical Studies, 2007.

———. "'Unjointed Masses': A Note on Heraclides' Physical Theory." Pages 139–54 in *Heraclides of Pontus: Discussion*. Edited by William W. Fortenbaugh and Elizabeth Pender. New Brunswick, NJ: Transaction, 2009.

Simonetti, Manlio. "Aggiornamento su Ippolito." Pages 75–130 in *Nuove ricerche su Ippolito*. SEAug 30. Rome: Augustinian Patristic Institute, 1989.

———. "A modo di conclusione: Una ipotesi di lavoro." Pages 151–56 in *Ricerche su Ippolito*. SEAug 13. Rome: Augustinian Patristic Institute, 1977.

———. "Due note su Ippolito: Ippolito interprete di Genesi 49; Ippolito e Tertulliano." Pages 121–36 in *Ricerche su Ippolito*. SEAug 13. Rome: Augustinian Patristic Institute, 1977.

———. "Note sul Libro di Baruch dello gnostico Giustino." *Vetera Christianorum* 6 (1969): 71–89.

———. "Per un profile dell'autore dell'Elenchos." Pages 257–76 in *Des évêques, des écoles et des hérétiques: Actes du colloque international sur la "Refutation de toutes les heresies" Genève, 13–14 juin 2008*. Edited by Gabriella Aragione and Enrico Norelli. Prahins: Éditions du Zèbre, 2011.

———. Review of *Hippolytus: Refutatio omnium haeresium*, ed. Miroslav Marcovich. *Aug* 27 (1987): 631–34.

Skarsaune, Oskar. "The Ebionites." Pages 419–62 in *Jewish Believers in Jesus*. Edited by Oskar Skarsaune and Reidar Hvalvik. Peabody, MA: Hendrickson, 2007.

Smith, Morton. "The Account of Simon Magus in Acts 8." Pages 140–51 in vol. 2 of *Studies in the Cult of Yahweh*. Edited by Shaye J. D. Cohen. 2 vols. Leiden: Brill, 1996.

———. "The Description of the Essenes in Josephus and the Philosophoumena." *HUCA* 29 (1958): 273–313.

Södergård, J. Peter. "The Ritualized Bodies of Cybele's Galli and the Methodological Problem of the Plurality of Explanations." Pages 169–93 in *The Problem of Ritual: Based on Papers Read at the Symposium on Religious Rites Held at Åbo, Finland*. Edited by Tore Ahlbäck. Åbo: Donner Institute, 1993.

Sorabji, Richard. *The Philosophy of the Commentators, 200–600 AD: A Sourcebook*. 3 vols. London: Duckworth, 2004.

Sourvinou-Inwood, Christiane. "Festival and Mysteries: Aspects of the Eleusinian Cult." Pages 25–49 in *Greek Mysteries: The Archaeology and Ritual of Ancient Greek Secret Cults*. Edited by Michael B. Cosmopoulos. London: Routledge, 2003.

Spinelli, Emidio. "Sesto Empirico e l'astrologia." Pages 239–79 in *Traditions of Theology: Studies in Hellenistic Theology, Its Background and Aftermath*. Edited by Dorothea Frede and André Laks. Leiden: Brill, 2002.

Spoerri, Walter. "A propos d'un texte d'Hippolyte." *REA* 57 (1955): 267–90.

Staehelin, Hans. *Die Gnostischen Quellen Hippolyts in seiner Hauptschrift gegen die Häretiker*. Leipzig: August Pries, 1890.

Stark, Rodney, and William Sims Bainbridge. *The Future of Religion: Secularization, Revival and Cult Formation*. Berkeley: University of California Press, 1985.

Stead, G. C. "In Search of Valentinus." Pages 75–102 in vol. 1 of *The Rediscovery of Gnosticism*. Edited by Bentley Layton. 2 vols. Leiden: Brill, 1980–1981.

———. "The Valentinian Myth of Sophia." *JTS* 20 (1969): 75–104.

Stoneman, Richard. *Alexander the Great: A Life in Legend*. New Haven: Yale University Press, 2008.

———. *The Legends of Alexander the Great*. Rev. ed. London: I. B. Tauris, 2012.

Strutwolf, Holger. "Gnosis und Philosophie: Beobachtungen zur Platonismusrezeption im gnostischen Sondergut bei Hippolyt von Rom." Pages 11–27 in *"Zur Zeit oder Unzeit": Studien zur spätantiken Theologie-, Geistes- und Kunstgeschichte und ihrer Nachwirkung Hans Georg Thümmel zu Ehren*. Edited by Adolf Martin Ritter, Wolfgang Wischmeyer, and Wolfram Kinzig. Mandelbachtal: Books on Demand, 2004.

Stuckrad, Kocku von. *Das Ringen um die Astrologie: Jüdische und christliche Beiträge zum antiken Zeitverständnis*. RVV. Berlin: de Gruyter, 2000.

Tabbernee, William. *Fake Prophecy and Polluted Sacraments: Ecclesiastical and Imperial Reactions to Montanism*. VCSup 84. Leiden: Brill, 2007.

Tannery, M. Paul. "Notice sur des fragments d'onomatomancie arithmétique." *Notices et extraits des manuscrits de la Bibliothèque Nationale* 31 (1886): 231–60.

———. "Orphica, fr. 3 Abel." *RevPhil* 24 (1900): 97–102.

Taylor, A. E. *A Commentary on Plato's Timaeus*. Oxford: Clarendon, 1928.

Thee, Francis C. R. *Julius Africanus and the Early Christian View of Magic*. Tübingen: Mohr Siebeck, 1984.

Theissen, Gerd. "Simon Magus—Die Entwicklung seines Bildes vom Charismatiker zum gnostischen Erlöser." Pages 407–32 in *Religionsgeschichte des neuen Testaments: Festschrift für Klaus Berger*. Edited by Axel von Dobbeler, Kurt Erlemann, and Roman Heiligenthal. Tübingen: Francke, 2000.

Thomas, J. *Le movement baptiste en Palestine et Syrie (150 av. J.-C.–300 ap. J.-C.)*. Gembloux: J. Duculot, 1935.

Thomassen, Einar. "The Derivation of Matter in Monistic Gnosticism." Pages 1–17 in *Gnosticism and Later Platonism: Themes, Figures, and*

Texts. Edited by John D. Turner and Ruth Majercik. Atlanta: Society of Biblical Literature, 2000.

———. "Going to Church with the Valentinians." Pages 183–97 in *Practicing Gnosis: Ritual, Magic, Theurgy and Liturgy in Nag Hammadi, Manichaean and Other Ancient Literature: Essays in Honor of Birger A. Pearson*. Edited by April D. DeConick, Gregory Shaw, and John D. Turner. NHMS 85. Leiden: Brill, 2013.

———. *The Spiritual Seed: The Church of the "Valentinians."* NHMS 60. Leiden: Brill, 2006.

Thompson, D'arcy Wentworth. *A Glossary of Greek Fishes*. London: Oxford University Press, 1947.

Toorn, Karel van der, and Pieter W. van der Horst. "Nimrod before and after the Bible." *HTR* 83 (1990): 1–29.

Trapp, Michael. "Philosophy, Scholarship, and the World of Learning in the Severan Period." Pages 470–88 in *Severan Culture*. Edited by Simon Swain, Stephen Harrison, and Jaś Elsner. Cambridge: Cambridge University Press, 2007.

Trevett, Christine. "Hippolytus and the Cabbage Question." Pages 36–45 in *Discipline and Diversity: Papers Read at the 2005 Summer Meeting and the 2006 Winter Meeting of the Ecclesiastical History Society*. Edited by Kate Cooper and Jeremy Gregory. Rochester: Boydell Press, 2007.

———. *Montanism: Gender, Authority and the New Prophecy*. Cambridge: Cambridge University Press, 1996.

Tubbs, Robert. *What Is a Number? Mathematical Concepts and Their Origins*. Baltimore: Johns Hopkins University Press, 2009.

Tuzet, Hélène. *Mort et resurrection d'Adonis: Étude de l'évolution d'un mythe*. Paris: Librairie José Corti, 1987.

Tuzlak, Ayse. "The Magician and the Heretic." Pages 416–26 in *Magic and Ritual in the Ancient World*. Edited by Paul Mirecki and Marvin Meyer. Leiden: Brill, 2002.

Vallée, Gérard. *A Study in Anti-gnostic Polemics: Irenaeus, Hippolytus and Epiphanius*. Waterloo: Wilfred Laurier University Press, 1981.

Vasojević, Andreas, and Nicolaus Vasojević. "ΝΑΦΘΑ: Quae fuerit termini *naphtha* antiquis temporibus propria significatio." *Phil* 128 (1984): 208–29.

Vofchuk, Rosalia C. "San Hipólito de Roma: Primer expositor de las doctrinas brahmánicas en Occidente." *EstEcl* 68 (1993): 49–68.

Vogt, Hermann J. "Noet von Smyrna und Heraklit: Bemerkungen zur Darstellung ihrer Lehren durch Hippolyt." *ZAC* 6 (2002): 59–80.

Volp, Ulrich. "Hippolytus of Rome." Pages 141–53 in *Early Christian Thinkers: The Lives and Legacies of Twelve Key Figures*. Edited by Paul Foster. Downers Grove, IL: IVP Academic, 2010.

Vox, Onofrio. "Das Plagiat als polemisches Motiv und die 'Refutatio omnium haeresium.'" Pages 175–87 in *Lessio, argomentazioni e strutture retoriche nella polemica di età Cristiana (III-V sec.)*. Edited by Alessandro Capone. Recherches sur les Rhétoriques Religieuses 16. Turnhout: Brepols, 2012.

Wheelwright, Philip. *Heraclitus*. Princeton: Princeton University Press, 1959.

Whittaker, John. "Basilides on the Ineffability of God." *HTR* 62 (1969): 367–71.

Wilamowitz-Moellendorff, Ulrich von. "Lesefrüchte." *Hermes* 37 (1902): 328–32.

Williams, Michael Allen. *The Immovable Race: A Gnostic Designation and the Theme of Stability in Late Antiquity*. Leiden: Brill, 1985.

———. *Rethinking "Gnosticism": An Argument for Dismantling a Dubious Category*. Princeton: Princeton University Press, 1996.

———. "Uses of Gender Imagery in Ancient Gnostic Texts." Pages 196–227 in *Gender and Religion: On the Complexity of Symbols*. Edited by Caroline Walker Bynum, Stevan Harrell, and Paula Richman. Boston: Beacon, 1986.

Williams, Robert L. "'Hippolytan' Reactions to Montanism: Tensions in the Churches of Rome in the Early Third Century." *StPatr* 39 (2006): 131–37.

Wöhrle, Georg, and Richard McKirahan. *The Milesians: Thales*. Traditio Praesocratica 1. Berlin: de Gruyter, 2014.

Wolbergs, Thielko. *Griechische religiöse Gedichte der ersten nachchristlichen Jahrhunderte*. Beiträge zur klassische Philologie 40. Meisenheim: Anton Hain, 1971.

Wolfson, H. A. "Negative Attributes in the Church Fathers and the Gnostic Basilides." *HTR* 50 (1957): 145–56.

Wordsworth, Christopher. *St. Hippolytus and the Church of Rome in the Earlier Part of the Third Century*. 2nd ed. London: Francis & John Rivington, 1880.

Wright, Benjamin G., III. "Cerinthus *apud* Hippolytus: An Inquiry into the Traditions about Cerinthus's Provenance." *SecCent* 4 (1984): 103–15.

Zeegers-Vander Vorst, Nicole. *Les citations des poètes grecs chez les apologists chrétiens du IIe siècle*. Leuven: Leuven University Press, 1972.

Zeitlin, Solomon. "The Account of the Essenes in Josephus and the Philosophoumena." *JQR* 49 (1959): 292–99.

Zuntz, Günther. *Persephone: Three Essays on Religion and Thought in Magna Graeca*. Oxford: Clarendon, 1971.

Ancient Sources Index*

* Note: sources listed are limited to those explicitly cited or alluded to by the author of the *Refutation* or his sources.

Deuterocanonical Books and Pseudepigrapha

New Testament

Greco-Roman Literature

Subject Index*

* Note: the main topics and figures already covered in the "Outline of the Work" (pp. lv–lix) are not listed in the following index.

CPSIA information can be obtained at www.ICGtesting.com
Printed in the USA
BVOW08s0608200116

433537BV00001B/1/P

9 780884 140856